COLLEGE READER

HOMER A. WATT

and

OSCAR CARGILL

New York University

New York

PRENTICE-HALL, INC.

1948

PREFACE

A good wine needs no bush, and perhaps a miscellany of readings the general plan and purpose of which are indicated in the title and the tables of contents needs no foreword. However, since there are many kinds of anthologies, the editors of the present collection feel justified in stating their objective and their plan so that their book may be judged for what they meant it to be and not for something different.

Perhaps it may be well to say first just what the present anthology is *not*. It was not designed for an historical survey of literature, either English or American; it does not attempt to present its grouped material in either a chronological or a logical sequence. Although the various divisions bear the familiar labels of rhetoric and literature—biography, poetry, drama, familiar essay, short story, exposition, narrative, and so forth—these terms have been employed principally for purposes of convenient and orderly classification and reference. There is no reason at all why any one using the book may not shuffle the sections to suit his own purposes, as he might shuffle a deck of cards.

Again, this collection is not a "great books" anthology and was never intended to be. It is, indeed, dubious if such materials should, or perhaps even could, be anthologized.

The *College Reader* was designed primarily to present literary expressions of various ideas, moods, and forms for college students who are learning to write. As a supplement to practice in composition, practice in reading—in the sense of intelligent comprehending—is a *sine qua non*. Indeed, one of the basic elements in a course in writing must be that expanding and liberalizing of the mind that comes from the reading and digesting of ideas. The mark of an educated man is partly in his possession of a fund of information from which he can draw at will and in his power to express his opinions readily, accurately, clearly, and logically. We all belong, wrote Robert Louis Stevenson, to that great parliament of talkers that is in continual session everywhere. It is not only in the halls of Congress, the town meeting-houses of Vermont, and the broadcasting stations of New York that men exchange opinions freely, but in homes and clubs, and on the streets. "Expression," said Emerson wisely, "is necessary to evolution," and the man who would grow is not the one who is muted by ignorance, indifference, and timidity but he who has a body of knowledge and sound opinion and the skill to express himself effectively. Such growth should be promoted by the reading and the writing of the college composition class, and the present anthology was designed to assist toward that end.

It will be noted that the *College Reader* is not a collection of "modern" readings but that it has much "old" material mixed with much that is "new." This combination was intentional and deliberate. Strictly speaking there is no such thing as "modern" thinking and feeling; a so-called "modern reader" contains only the current expressions of universal human themes. What John Livingston Lowes, in his brilliant definition of originality (p. 268) says of poetry is basically true also of all human expression: "Poetry may never with safety cut loose from the old, because the old is always new. The tide of generations flows on unceasingly, and for each the old experiences have their pristine freshness. That is why the old themes are perennial."

This truth of the "eternally familiar" in basic human experiences and interests is amply demonstrated in the present collection. To give a single example, the universal theme of the defence of a livelihood against invasion appears—strangely enough—in St. Luke's vivid account of the attack of the silversmiths of Ephesus on Paul (p. 561), written in the first century, and in Joseph Buchanan's reminiscences of the early railroad workers' strikes in America in the nineteenth century (p. 24). Nor are these expressions of human ideas and moods influenced by the literary or rhetorical form which the writer chooses to adopt. Again, a single illustration may suffice. Sidney Lanier's *The Symphony* (p. 763) and William Rose Benét's *Men on Strike* (p. 773) are poems, but they deal with the same theme of industrial dissension as does John Galsworthy's *Strife* (p. 879), which is a drama, and John Ruskin's *The Nature of Theft by Unjust Profits* (p. 85), which is in form a letter but in fact a bit of economic comment. Although the single theme of economic relations has been used here as an illustration of the universality of human ideas and moods in literature, *any* universal human concern in living or dying—social and domestic relations, education and religion, science and art—might just as well have been chosen.

It must have been noted already that the rhetorical and literary labels under which the selections in this anthology are grouped are more convenient than fundamental. Indeed, many of the selections might very well have been listed under more than one heading. St. Luke's story of Paul and the silversmiths, which has been already referred to, might very well have been listed under "Letters," inasmuch as it is a single episode from an epistle addressed by "the beloved physician" to the Roman governor, "most excellent Theophilus"; or it might have been put under "Reminiscences," if Luke was an eye-witness of the events which he narrates, as seems rather more than possible. Similarly, the label "Letters," used because the audience addressed by the writer is either an individual or at least a specified group of persons, is a term that covers a number of literary forms: scientific article (Professor Urey's *Bomb Control Not Impossible,* p. 112); political comment (Thomas Jefferson's *One Generation Hath No Right to Bind Another,* p. 73 and *Natural Aristocracy,* p. 76); educational treatise (Henry Adams's *Preparation for Teaching History,* p. 96); and political and social analysis and comment (Sir Osbert Sitwell's *A Letter to My Son,* p. 116). It would seem, then, that a "letter" need not be a "person to person call," but might be put under any one of many other headings if it were not for its form of direct address. Similarly, biography and history overlap, as Thomas Carlyle made clear a century ago. John Addington Symonds's *The Death of Sir Philip Sidney* (p. 37) might properly have been entered under "History," whereas Carl Van Doren's *The Treachery of General Charles Lee* (p. 709) and Vernon Louis Parrington's *General Grant* (p. 717) might just as naturally have been listed under "Biography." The editors of *Col-*

lege Reader are not in the least disturbed by these facts. They know that writers are impelled in their expression primarily by the theme, content, and mood, and not by the particular ticket which literary historians and rhetoricians may attach to their work later. Similarly, the reader who is more concerned with labels than with contents, ideas, and literary art is preferring the husk to the kernel.

But the announcers have stood too long before the microphone, and with a final suggestion and a *caveat* they will retire. The suggestion is that although this anthology was confessedly designed primarily for college students practicing composition, such students are adults, selected for their general intelligence and assembled in a forum for the purpose of reading, digesting ideas, and expressing themselves on many subjects. What is good for a group of adults engaged in taking a formal "course" is also good for other adults, in college or out, who would broaden their intelligence and increase their power to think and to talk and to write.

And now for the *caveat*. All themes of human interest—social, industrial, political, educational, religious, or artistic—discussed in the parliament of talkers are not just two-sided but have many facets. This polylateral quality of *all* discussion is represented in the *College Reader,* and the editors have emphatically made no effort to direct ideas and moods into a single channel. Let it be known, therefore, in the current familiar phrase, that opinions expressed in any broadcast over this station do not necessarily represent those of the sponsors or the producers.

And with that *caveat* the announcers turn the microphone hopefully over to the hundred and fifty odd speakers on the program, who have been pressing eagerly to be heard.

April, 1948

H. A. W.
O. C.

CONTENTS
By Form

PART 1

Biography and Exposition

PART 2

Narrative, Poetry, and Drama

XI. POETRY (*Continued*)

XII. DRAMA

CONTENTS

By Theme

Men and Women

The Inner World of Thought

Many Tongued Art

Power and Pelf

The Rights of Man

Stratagems and Spoils

Man's Inhumanity to Man

CONTENTS BY THEME

War and Peace

The Way to Dusty Death

Part I

Biography
and
Exposition

I...

PROFILE
AND
BIOGRAPHY

EDITORS OF TIME

Average Man

MILLIONS of Americans know Caspar Milquetoast as well as they know Tom Sawyer and Andrew Jackson, better than they know George F. Babbitt, and any amount better than they know such world figures as Mr. Micawber and Don Quixote. They know him, in fact, almost as well as they know their own weaknesses.

If the creator of *The Timid Soul* had done nothing but invent Milquetoast—the quavering quintessence of the Little Man at his least manly—he would have earned his modest place in the nation's pantheon. Harold Tucker Webster has done a great deal besides, in the 15,000-odd panels he has drawn in the past 43 years. Last week Webster's fourth collection of cartoons (*Webster Unabridged;* McBride; $2) appeared.

Caspar Milquetoast is the only character Cartoonist Webster has ever given a name to—and Caspar,* with appropriate shyness, sneaked into the strip as a space filler. The rest of Webster's bald-headed bores, thin, puzzled wives, and freckle-faced kids need no name; they are, when they hit the mark—as they often do—Everyman.

H. T. Webster has learned to slice and serve his generous chunks of U.S. life methodically. Caspar (*The Timid Soul*) appears Sundays and Mondays. The pitilessly fanatic and bad-mannered bridge players run Fridays. Boyhood's lovingly elaborated triumphs (*The Thrill That Comes Once in a Lifetime*) and defeats (*Life's Darkest Moment*) appear on Saturdays and Tuesdays. Thursdays bring *How to Torture Your Husband* (or *Wife*). On Wednesdays, in *The Unseen Audience,* he pokes a sharp-pointed stick at radio—which of all mixed blessings most needs satirizing, and gets it least. Webster, in fact, is possibly radio's most effective critic.

Webster is one of the few journalists of his troubled time who has managed consistently to remind people of the news that they are human beings, and that that news is not as bad as it is generally made out.

RIGHT TO LEFT. H. T. Webster insists that Milquetoast is a self-portrait. Short of perhaps Joseph Stalin, it would be difficult to think of any man who looks less like Milquetoast than his creator. Webster carries all of his 6 ft. 3 in. without either the cringing or the exaggerated erectness of the man who is uneasy in this world. His face is handsome, ruddy and unlined, his blue eyes are direct and uncomplicated.

He combines a still faintly rural quietude of speech and motion with a kind of suavity which can come only of many years of assured performance and comfortable living. Such troubles as he has encountered he has taken tranquilly; in 1927, when overwork permanently

* Webster once wrote to his friend Franklin P. Adams, who had misspelled it Casper in his column: "Mr. Milquetoast has spoken to me about your spelling of his name. He says that his family has always spelled it with an *a,* but that they are notoriously bad spellers and you are probably right."

ruined his drawing hand, he learned in four months to draw with his left. At 60, he suggests a prematurely grey ex-athlete who has not had to work very anxiously to keep in good shape.

A HAPPY BOYHOOD. As any reader of *The Thrill That Comes Once in a Lifetime* might guess, H. T. Webster had a happy boyhood. He spent it in Tomahawk, Wis. (pop. 3,365) where his dad ran the drugstore. Tomahawk (the way Webster remembers it) was a little town afloat in a forest where deer and small game were plentiful, the lakes and streams were stiff with fish, you could run onto the tracks of bear often enough almost to believe you had seen them and killed them, and school was no more interesting than it is in most other places. Webbie used to hide a .38 in his pocket going to school, and fire it off during recess.

From seven on, he liked to draw. He was not an artist; he was a cartoonist from the start. He liked best to draw Weary Willie tramps with baggy clothes so "you could conceal your lack of knowledge of anatomy." By the time he was 15 or so, Webster subscribed to a mail-order cartooning course, and was the only student to finish the course—the school folded shortly afterwards. That was the end of his formal training.

$7 TO $70. He dreamed of some day becoming Charles Dana Gibson's office boy, and cartooned for the Chicago *Daily News* in 1903 at little more than office boy's pay: $7 a week.

For three years he drew front-page political cartoons for the Chicago *Inter-Ocean*—a fellow toiler with another famed U.S. humorist, Ring Lardner. And for two years more, at a phenomenal $70 a week, he drew for the Cincinnati *Post*.

He had saved up enough money by 1911 ($700) to realize a childhood desire: a trip around the world. With George A. (*Why We Behave Like Human Beings*) Dorsey he made the second steamboat trip in history up the Yangtze Gorges to the then inconspicuous city of Chungking. The Chinese along the rim knocked off work and crowded the banks, in a friendly way, "to watch us drown." The Chinese also liked to line up, at a courteous distance, to watch the foreigners handle knives & forks. One suppertime a missionary's wife, annoyed at their staring, slung a glass of water in their faces. Webster, a gentle man, still colors up when he remembers it: "I had to control myself as hard as I ever did in my life, not to give her a piece of my mind."

The round-the-world trip ended in New York, and Webster ended—in time—on that Parnassus of Midwestern newspapermen, the New York *World*. Webster, along with any number of employes and readers, still remembers the death of Pulitzer's *World* in 1931 as nothing short of tragic. Since then he has worked for the *Herald Tribune,* and through the *Tribune* Syndicate his daily cartoons are published in some 60 papers, his Sunday Milquetoast strip in 20. Their combined circulation is around ten million, not counting uncountable millions who read their papers at second hand. Webster's probable income: about $80,000 a year.

MUGWUMP. Webster always wanted and meant to be a political cartoonist. He shifted to such relatively universal phenomena as a boy's fondness for a dog, or a wife's inability to be gracious when her husband wants a stag vacation, because they syndicated more easily, raised fewer quarrels (of a sort that involved furious letters-to-the-editor) and made more money than cartoons which took a strong stand on the tariff. As for taking a weak stand on the tariff, or on any other political issue, that was for Webster out of the question. Good political cartoons have to be simple, and the only sure way to be simple, without also being vapid, is to be very firm in your convictions. Webster calls himself a Mugwump, but the mug and wump usually lean over the conservative side of the fence, as is perhaps natural in a man who spent his most formative years, very happily, in much the sort of pre-industrial American background which had produced his gods, Lincoln and Mark Twain.

Now Webster dips his pen only rarely into politics. For Lincoln's Birthday 1940, Webster drew a forlorn, storm-whipped, benighted, wilderness cabin, a light in its window like the fever of birth. The caption: Ill-Fed—Ill-Clothed—Ill-Housed. During the war he drew a cartoon showing soldiers, under fire in the Pacific, listening to a radio's soapy-voiced report on the progress of a strike. But mostly he is content to give the U.S. newspaper public a much needed, and not too loaded, laugh for its three or five cents' worth.

MOLDY HOMILETICS. Comedy is about as inconspicuous an item in so-called comic strips today as drugs in drugstores. *Krazy Kat* died with its creator, the late George Herrimann. *The Gumps,* which in the days of the late Sidney Smith had a modest resemblance to middle-class U.S. life, has little now. Harold Gray's *Little Orphan Annie,* never any too real or too funny, has sunk so deep into moldy homiletics that it is now trying to make Tory a nice word by proving that only rabble revolted in 1776. Fantasy, outside of Crockett Johnson's *Barnaby* and Al Capp's *Li'l Abner,* is so fouled up in

gamma rays, cloaks of invisibility, space ships, and brutal omnipotence, that it has little time for fantasy's ancient, essential job of fusing the creatures of earth and heaven. The best of the rest, like Chester Gould's resourceful, blood-thirsty *Dick Tracy,* are like entertaining gangster movies that no one would confuse with truth or comedy, or—like Milton Caniff's extraordinarily proficient and accurate *Terry and the Pirates*—rattling good straight adventure strips.

Only a few, like Webster, still try to stick to the comic strip's old and worthy function: holding a mirror to a recognizable U.S. life. The late Clare Briggs's *Mr. and Mrs.,* as an appreciation of marriage, made books like *Cass Timberlane* look as naive as Daisy Ashford. Harry J. Tuthill's remarkable *Bungle Family,* almost alone among comics, dared to gaze steadily at the plain, awful ugliness and clumsiness to which the domesticated human animal is liable. When you have counted these —and Frank King's mild, wholesome *Gasoline Alley,* Chic Young's *Blondie,* J. R. Williams' homely cowhands and mechanics in *Out Our Way,* and Gluyas Williams' middle-aged suburbanites— you have about exhausted the field. Yet, characteristically, Webster disagrees with the critics who think today's sexed-up, thrill-happy comics are a menace to adolescent morals. Says he: "I used to hide my dime novels. Eventually I made the discovery that good books were better. I don't think it matters a hoot."

THE QUIET LIFE. During the 1920s Webster was a member in good standing of that ultra-American generation of writers and actors and cartoonists and illustrators which focused around the offices of the *World* and The Players and The Dutch Treat Clubs. He has long since receded to the blander pleasures of upper-middle-class suburbia in Stamford, Conn. and—with a mild sheepishness about the stylish address, and sincere enough murmurs about the Websters' susceptibility to colds—winters in Palm Beach. For years the Websters were enthusiastic theater-goers; now they wonder whether anything is as much worth coming into town for as the last show they saw, *Oklahoma!*

Webster used to play poker every Friday night through Sunday morning, in a room in the old Waldorf-Astoria. The concentration was such that once, when food was sent up, and he chomped a mouthful of broken glass in his lettuce, Webster spat it out without a murmur rather than interrupt the game.

After giving the matter "profound thought," he got married in 1916 (all of two weeks after meeting pretty Ethel Worts) and gave up poker for bridge. "The thought of life without poker," he remembers, seemed fantastic, "but when I gave it up it was like recovering from leprosy." He is a skillful bridge player —though it is safe to say he has taken in more money drawing cartoons about it.

He lives like a man who wants his thrills to come oftener than once in a lifetime. He feels about fly fishing a good deal the way Lucius Beebe feels about trains, always keeps well ahead in his work in order to be free to accept a banker friend's annual invitation to fish his private stream in Canada.

Next to becoming a cartoonist, he always wanted most to be a clown. When he was grown and married, he got his wish. He made several tours with Ringling Bros., one with his wife and the late cartoonist Clare Briggs. (Even now, when the circus comes to Bridgeport, the Websters dress up and ride in the parade.) Ethel Webster became a good enough bareback rider to receive, and reluctantly turn down, a professional offer. She is also pretty certainly the only non-professional woman ever to ride down Manhattan's Fifth Avenue on the nape of an elephant (on the occasion of Mrs. Hearst's Milk Fund Drive, in 1921).

Webster has always admired and often drawn circus people. He particularly liked one clown who, making him up with all the sweeping care of a Renaissance Master, swiped a smile-line down his cheek, stepped critically back and asked, anxiously, "How do you like it?" The amateur consulted the mirror and said it looked fine. The clown glowed. "That line's my own," he said.

CRITIC, WITH SIX RADIOS. Webster gets up fairly late in the morning, breakfasts lightly except when the cook irresistibly serves up hamburger & onions, gets to work around 2 p.m., is through by 6. Most of the time he works in a room at the rear of the house, its walls thick with signed originals of such old friends or idols as A. B. Frost (who illustrated *Uncle Remus*), "Zim" (Eugene Zimmerman) of the old *Judge,* John T. McCutcheon, Thomas Nast, George Bellows.

Ideas, on the whole, are the hardest part of his job. Fans mail in quite a few, for which he is grateful, but only rarely is one usable. In a sense, like Einstein, Webster is at work all the time: listening to the radio (the Websters have six in the house, though only three work) and, even more relaxedly, keeping an eye & ear open around the house and the neighborhood, and the bridge tables of his gregarious evenings. By the time he is done with each day's work, it looks pretty good to Webster. When he sees his cartoons in print, however, he suffers the reaction of most conscientious workmen: "They look filthy after they're made. I can't understand how I could do such dreadful work. The idea is all right but the execution is painful."

A TRIFLE APOLOGETIC. Even when Webster's figures are meant to be solid, rather than insecure, they often have an air of being a trifle apologetic; and this mitigative, tentative quality shows as clearly in their personalities as in their stance and overall shape. Even Webster's most crashing bores never suggest their real-life brutality; the wives are always at least trying to understand the jokes even if they never will; the bridge players are, in their own curious ways, so genuinely enjoying themselves that the fact outbalances all censure.

In all Webster's years of preoccupation with the psychology of timidity he seldom points up, even gently, the littleness, meanness and guile which timidity so often develops, and almost never touches on the propensity for bullying. You have to go back at least 15 years to find Milquetoast rampant. This might be merely the shrewdness of a man who makes his living through comedy. But in Webster's case it is the innocence of a man whose powers of observation are limited by his kindness.

NOT PRACTICING MORALIST. H. T. Webster, gently gifted, is somewhere near an average man, working, in a way never quite possible to the extraordinarily gifted, for somewhere near average people. He had done them no average service, merely in amusing them; a greater one still, very likely, as the kind of moralist who almost never moralizes.

This is sometimes said to be the Century of the Common Man. Webster was the first to recognize that it is certainly, by some cruel coincidence, the Era of the Timid One.

1945

JOHN R. TUNIS

First Gentleman of Philadelphia

YOU MAY not be especially interested in baseball, but if you are interested in human beings and human values he would interest you. By his looks he might be a retired manufacturer and former Sunday School Superintendent, one of the thousands each winter in those havens of refuge for the aged along the West Coast of Florida. The sort of man who sits on a sidewalk in the morning sunshine, enjoys his daily game of shuffleboard, and hears Dr. William Lyon Phelps at the weekly meeting of the Iowa Club. After all, at eighty-five a man has a right to take things easy.

Reprinted from the *Atlantic Monthly,* August, 1940, by permission of the author. The title in the *Atlantic* was "Cornelius McGillicuddy"; it has been altered and the text revised by Mr. Tunis for this book.

But at eighty-five Mr. Cornelius McGillicuddy is still in the thick of life —in the thick of a young man's game. Back in 1900 when the American League was founded, he managed the Milwaukee team, and the next year hustled over to Philadelphia where he interested a rich man named Benjamin F. Shibe in founding a club in the new organization, and set forth to collect a team. He's been in Philadelphia ever since.

In 1902, before the majority of modern baseball fans were born, he won his first pennant. In 1905 he lost his first World Series to the Giants. In the 1910 Series he defeated Chance and the Cubs; in the 1911 and 1913 Series, McGraw and the Giants. Unexpectedly he lost to Stallings and the Braves in 1914. (We must ask him to explain that one.) He beat Joe McCarthy and the Cubs in the 1929 Series, conquered Gabby Street and the Cards in 1930, and lost to them in the 1931 Series. Nine pennants and five Series triumphs are his record in forty years of baseball.

Most of his contemporaries are no more. Stallings is gone, McGraw is gone. Of the men he helped to found the American League, Ban Johnson, the first president, is gone; Shibe, the owner of the Athletics, is gone; Comiskey of Chicago is gone. Except for Clark Griffith, only Connie Mack remains, still sitting each afternoon in summer on the bench, and looking almost the same as that tall, gaunt figure of 1900. But he isn't merely the manager of a baseball team. The fans say, 'Let's go watch Connie this afternoon.' He's an institution. He's the first citizen of Philadelphia today.

It was as a mittless catcher that he caught for East Brookfield in the Central Massachusetts League in 1883, the year he was first able to vote. Later that summer he signed with Meriden for the astounding sum of $90 a month, payable whenever he could collect. Then to Hartford, and in 1886 he was sent with four other players to Washington in the National League for the total sum of $3500. Connie was still catching them on the first bounce, still catching them meat-handed.

In 1890 he played with Buffalo's Brotherhood Club in the Players' League one season; in 1891 he was a member of the Pittsburgh Nationals, becoming manager of the club in 1894 and through the summer of 1896. In 1897 he went as catcher-manager to Milwaukee, where he stayed until the American League was formed. Now at eighty-five he's the greatest living example of the fact that a man is as old as his arteries, or that anyone who has a consuming interest in some phase of existence stays young despite the years. Connie Mack loves baseball. An old-time player said, 'He'd like to die out on that-there bench.' He probably will.

Watch him at work in the morning behind the long glass-topped table in the Athletics' office in Shibe Park. He looks—well, sixty-five at the most. With a quick gesture he snatches a letter from the table, or jumps up with the reflexes of a young man, stalking rapidly across to the door. He's tall, six feet one, straight, with blue eyes, lots of gray hair parted in the middle, and a kind, mobile face. Unlike most catchers, he has long, strong fingers with few knobs or bumps on them. Even today his handshake is firm and warm. That's really the amazing thing about this amazing man; not his youthfulness, but his warmth. You feel it in his handshake, see it in his smile—a wonderful smile that lights up his clear blue eyes.

You can understand immediately the old-timer who said, 'If a man won't play for Connie Mack he won't play for anyone.'

By what magic has this gentle, warmhearted individual taken nine clubs to the top? How has he kept discipline for over forty years among those wildeyed individualists, professional ballplayers? Because even in his younger days he was never tough or hard-boiled. How did he do it? Speaking of several of his youngsters recently, he complained of their failure to assume responsibilities. Then hastily he caught himself: 'I wouldn't have them any different. They're young, and worries will come all too soon.'

Yes, but how has he maintained discipline? Not by force, but by commanding the respect of his players—'My boys,' as he likes to call them. Not by being hard-boiled, but by being human. All ballplayers like Connie Mack. Some managers enjoy slapping a fine on a recalcitrant star; Connie has other and possibly subtler methods. A player jumps from a taxi before the hotel, nods good-night to Mack, who is standing at the entrance, and goes up in the elevator. But Connie knows youth like the master of a boarding school. He merely walks round to the back entrance in time to catch the player scuttling out like a bad boy. Lots of managers would seize the moment to burst into a lecture, winding up with a fine. Connie doesn't need to. The man sees him, turns round, and goes back to his room and bed.

Moreover, Mack plays no favorites. On the A's, nobody 'sits in the manager's lap,' as ballplayers like to put it. Once a very fine star made so much trouble that although he played headsup baseball, and was of great value to

the team, Connie thoroughly disliked him. After the season Connie asked him into the clubhouse. The player came, expecting to be sold up the river. Instead he was met with a contract for a raise. There was no more trouble with that gentleman.

Lucky man, Mr. Mack. He likes people and people like him. How did he build up pennant winners? By giving players his confidence; they in turn gave him their respect. That's why he can handle those temperamental prima donnas. The hardest of the lot to manage? 'Oh . . . there wasn't any of 'em really hard. You could always talk with 'em and reason with 'em. Even Rube Waddell. Yes sir, though most of my gray hairs can be traced to wondering where he was when his bed was empty. And when he was right we've never had another could touch him!'

The easiest to manage in forty years? 'All my great players, every one.' He speaks with emphasis. 'Eddie Collins, especially.'

His 1910 team, with the famous $100,000 infield of Baker, Barry, Collins, and Davis, is his favorite. He doesn't say so, but you can see he thinks so. What was his greatest infield? 'That 1910 bunch. You see, they could rise to heights in critical moments of a Series. You just couldn't improve on those lads. My greatest outfield? Well, I guess that '29 bunch with Haas, Miller, and Simmons. They had power—they were hitters, those boys.'

Connie, himself a catcher, has had some great catchers: Ralphy (Cy) Perkins, Ossie Schreckengost, Wally Schang, Ira Thomas, Doc Powers, Jack Lapp, and the star of them all, Mickey Cochrane. But there's a soft spot for Ossie. 'Schreck was the Harpo Marx of his time. He was the fizz powder in the pinwheel that made Waddell great. He was colorful, unpredictable, eccentric, erratic, and filled with baseball genius.' The blue eyes twinkled. 'Why, he used his gloved hand like a shortstop. Schreck could do more with his glove than any catcher that ever stood behind the plate. I remember he roomed with Waddell. They used to sleep in one bed, to save money. One year, when I sent him his contract, Schreck wrote back: 'The contract is all right, but before I sign it you got to put in a clause that if I have to room with Waddell he can't eat animal crackers in bed.' The clause was inserted.

No manager has had more great pitchers than Connie Mack—starting with Waddell, Coakley, and Bender, Jack Coombs, Eddie Plank, Bush, George Earnshaw, Lefty Grove, and Waite Hoyt. The greatest of the lot? 'Everyone has his own "greatest." I don't like to use superlatives. But I think Chief Bender is the greatest one-game pitcher, the greatest money pitcher, that baseball ever had. He wasn't a Rube Waddell, no, but he was the best money pitcher in the game.'

Yet it was Bender, with Plank, who was the disappointment of the 1914 Series which the Boston Braves won in four straight games from the A's. According to Connie, there was a split in the club. The newly formed Federal League was out for players and naturally raided the Athletics, who had more than their share of stars. Some members of the club wanted to leave, others to stand by Mack. 'The loyalists and rebels were engaged in a bitter fight. Players to whom I'd given a scouting assignment never left Philadelphia. Our players were more bitter against each other than interested in a baseball Series. We lacked the spirit to win.

Stallings accomplished a baseball miracle by coming from last place on July Fourth to win the pennant and take the Series that fall; but I sincerely believe a team isn't great unless it repeats. The Braves didn't repeat in 1915.'

Why wasn't he able to meet the prices offered to his men by the Federal League? 'We simply couldn't afford to. As it was, we were paying the highest salaries in the circuit. We had no Sunday ball, and a large number of cheap seats in our park. When Bender and Plank signed up with the Federals, I decided to try to save something. So I sent out word my players were for sale, and the offers rolled in.'

Had he refused to sell his players, it would have hurt those who stayed. 'The boys who were left felt we'd be down in the cellar, and they wanted to go where the future was brighter.' Some managers never think about the players when they leave a club. Still others take good care to see that a star doesn't go to a serious contender. Not Connie. He thinks of the players. Mickey Cochrane, for instance, was sold to Detroit and won a pennant for them.

To Mack's annoyance, people still ask him what happened to his 1914 and 1932 teams. Why did he break them up? No mystery, for Connie never sells players unless he needs cash. The story runs round Philadelphia that he has invariably made money with tail-enders and lost with pennant winners. He almost admits the truth of this.

'Yes, I've made money coming up, and lost with world champions. When your club is fighting to the top, the fans take an interest and come to the park. Philadelphia's a right good ball town; folks now are loyal and turning out when we are in last place, but pennant winners get to be an old story. With a fifth-place club this year we're doing real good. When the club is behind, salaries are low; so are expenses. Champions cost money. In boxing, a manager has one champion; in baseball, twenty-five. We had almost the highest-priced club in history in 1932, not barring the Yanks with Babe Ruth's $80,000 salary. I had five men who together drew more than $100,000. Yet attendance fell away that year. When you win, you have a general rise in all expenses; more gatemen, ticket takers, ushers, and so on, are necessary.'

Yet the fans in Philadelphia say there's a reason he sold those men which Connie won't ever mention. They believe that when the A's were winning one man connected with the club took out large profits for other business ventures. The rumor also persists that Connie, in common with several others, got pretty well clipped in the market in 1929 and 1930. One fact is true: whenever he sold players he needed money. 'You don't make money by selling players in baseball. Half my 1932 team cost me more than I got by selling my entire 1914 team. If I hadn't sold some of my players I should have had to leave baseball.'

He won't leave baseball. Baseball is his love and his life. Save for indispositions such as the gallstone attack which benched him in the summer of 1937, he appears each day at the park. At eighty-five he still runs the team, still travels on the road, still climbs into the dugout every afternoon in his blue suit and high choker collar, a handkerchief wrapped round his neck if it's very hot. Removing his coat, he hangs it on a peg in the dugout, puts the team on the field, takes his scorecard in hand, places his outfield, and proceeds to run his show.

Does he ever make mistakes?

'Yep, I've made hundreds. Make 'em almost daily. Every manager does. The worst mistake of all? Let me see . . . well, to my way of thinking the worst mistake I ever made was back in 1907 when we were running nip and tuck with Detroit. I had a pitcher, name of Jimmy Dygert, who could beat anyone for seven innings. Then he was finished. I could have pitched him seven innings any day in the week. If I'd a found this out in time, I could have won that pennant. Instead, I didn't realize it until after the season. We finished second, and Detroit won the League.

'Another time we were playing the Yanks and Ruth came to bat. I waved my outfield round and they moved where I motioned, but still I wasn't satisfied, and finally had to climb out of the dugout to place them and direct the defense. Meanwhile the pitcher was waiting in the box and Babe was standing at the plate. After about three minutes' wigwagging, I got everyone set. You can guess what happened. Babe hit the first pitch over the fence.

'Fortunately for a manager it doesn't always work out that way. I'll never forget the first game Ty Cobb played for us after twenty-two years with Detroit. He'd been manager six years with the Tigers and knew the weak and strong points of all players in every club. One of the first batters was a man I knew would hit the ball I signaled my pitcher to feed him, to Ty's left. I stood up in the dugout and waved him over with my scorecard. Even the pitcher turned in the box to look. What'd he do? He saluted, like the good sport he was, and trotted over to the new position. Believe me, I felt relieved a few seconds later when the batter lined a drive so close he hardly had to move a step to grab it.'

Ask him how Cobb and the old-timers compare with the modern player, and watch his straight back in the stiff chair grow more erect. 'Oh, the old-timers were wonderful. Wonderful. They didn't have the advantages the player has nowadays. The equipment is so much better, the gloves and the bat. He has material to work with that Cobb and Schreck and those boys never had. Then, too, they've got another asset to-day—they have the experience of those old-timers to assist them. They're making plays a little easier because they know how to do it. But they aren't any smarter, no sirree.'

He believes the great difference be-tween baseball today and baseball forty years ago lies in two things. 'First, this improvement in all the equipment used. Second, the change in batting and pitch-ing. In the old days we used to throw in four or five balls a game. Nowadays they use a couple of dozen. The pitcher has been handicapped and the hitter has a great advantage. That's the chief change in baseball to my way of thinking.

'Yes, the most important position on a club was always the pitcher, still is. But, outside the battery, short and sec-ond have become vital in recent years. A club that has a double-play combina-tion that can pull them out of hot spots has a big advantage in a close race. By the way, the Cleveland club has a dandy pair, those boys Boudreau and Joe Gor-don. They can throw, and throw hard and straight, from any position. You watch 'em.'

Since the death of Charles J. Comis-key in Chicago, the Mack family is the last dynasty left in baseball. One son, Roy F., is vice president and secretary of the club, while Earle, another son, is due some day to succeed his father on the bench. Connie could retire right now to his Germantown home if he so de-sired. But, as one of his former stars put it, 'He'd die if you took him away from Shibe Park.'

Some major-league clubs have had twenty to twenty-five different manag-ers in their existence, and the average number in the forty years of the Amer-ican League is about fifteen per club. But Philadelphia has had only one man, Connie Mack. Today he's an institu-tion—not merely in the game, where he was one of the five men named as Build-ers of Baseball in the Baseball Museum in Cooperstown, New York, but in his home town, where he was presented the Bok Award of $10,000 in 1929. The fans talk about the A's, but they turn out to see Connie Mack. In fifteen minutes while I was sitting in the outer office at Shibe Park recently, a dozen telephone calls came reserving seats for the next day's game. The club may be in last place, but Connie is an institu-tion.

Since 1933 he hasn't finished in the first division, but it's unlikely that this worries him much. For he's been in the game a long while and has plenty of patience. He waited from 1902 until 1905 for another pennant winner, then started to climb again until he was vic-torious in 1910. From 1915 to 1921 he was in eighth place, waiting and build-ing for the future. By 1929 he had his championship club once more. In 1932 he sold them to raise cash, and at the age of seventy started the long slow road to the top for the fourth time in his life. Some day he'll win another pen-nant.

You'll hear it whispered round that he pays poor salaries. Yet he gave $45,-

000 bonus for signing young McCoy of Detroit, who was declared a free agent, and pays Johnson, his outfielder, $18,-000. Today he has a team of youngsters, a team with possibilities. Lacking first-class pitching, he has nevertheless the nucleus of a good ball club. 'I think next year we'll make trouble for any of them,' he declares.

You have to know Connie—to know his life, to see him, watch him on the bench, and talk with fans in Shibe Park —to appreciate what a character he is. There he sits before you, erect and straight, arms folded, discoursing in his slow, kindly way about baseball, life, or anything you like. 'Roosevelt?' His face lights up, the wrinkles in his forehead vanish in his smile. 'Say, did you hear him last night? He was wonderful. A wonderful American.' Yes, and so is Mr. Cornelius McGillicuddy.

1940

M. M. MUSSELMAN

Wheels in His Head

EVERYBODY, including Grandma, said A.J. would never amount to anything because he just wouldn't stick to a good job when he had one. In more or less chronological order he was a bicycle racer, hardware buyer, sporting-goods dealer, bicycle salesman, assistant manager of a mail-order house, tire salesman, manufacturer of golf clubs, real-estate subdivider, country-club promoter, research engineer, and gentleman farmer.

In my adolescent days I was always sorry A.J. had not realized his earliest ambition: he wanted to be an acrobat in a circus. He would have been a good one, too. Silk tights and bangles would have suited A.J. It started after Grandma took the boys over to Newton to a little one-ring circus. When they got home to the farm, A.J. tried walking on his hands. After one try he yelled for Grandma to come out and watch him.

"Hey, Ma! Look at me! Look at me!"

Grandma, who was ninety-five pounds of dynamic devotion, came to the screen door to watch A.J. demonstrate on the front porch. He flipped over on his hands and walked right across the porch.

"Careful!" warned Grandma. "You'll break your neck." And at that moment A.J. walked right off the railless porch and almost did break his neck.

But A.J. was not the least bit discouraged by his first acrobatic misstep. He practiced for weeks until he could stand on his hands, turn handsprings, and do back flips. Then he grew ambitious and wanted to turn somersaults in the air. Not by jumping from a beam in the hayloft; anybody could do that. He

From *Wheels in His Head* by M. M. Musselman, published by Whittlesey House, copyright 1945 by M. M. Musselman.

wanted to do it just the way the circus acrobats did it: right off the hard ground, with a leap, a cat-like flip, and back on his feet again, finishing with a graceful bow.

He broached the subject to Grandma one morning at breakfast. "Ma," he asked with a speculative gleam in his eye, "how do those circus acrobats learn to turn them somersaults in the air?"

"I don't know," Grandma replied, cutting an apple pie into four sections for her ravenous brood. "But if you dare to try any tomfoolery like that I'll tan your hide. I don't want you abed with broken bones just at haying time."

Grandma should have known better. Any time you dared A.J. to do something, it was as good as done. He went right out behind the barn to give that backward somersault a whirl, feeling somehow that because Grandma had forbidden him to try it, it would be easy as rolling off a log.

He clenched his teeth, leaped into the air, and landed flat on his back. When he regained his breath, he sat up and meditated for several minutes. He had no intention of repeating his experiment. It had been too painful. But he intended to figure out a way to turn somersaults with some degree of safety. All that day, as he took the cows out to pasture, fed the pigs, worked in the hayfield, and helped with the milking, he pondered the safety factor in a backward somersault. At last he solved the problem with a simple but ingenious "invention."

Grandma's clothesline was always stretched between the privy and an old apple tree. A.J. let out enough slack in the line so that it hung down just about waist high. With a short length of rope, he tied himself to the clothesline and tried a back somersault. To his delight it worked.

He practiced prodigiously for several weeks until he was sure that he was ready to attempt a somersault without the clothesline for a safety belt. Then he went out behind the barn to try it, but to his chagrin he discovered that he lacked the nerve. The memory of that first painful effort still haunted him, and he realized that he had become a slave to his safety belt. In later years A.J. told me this story many times and always pointed out the obvious moral.

"Some people go through life wearing a safety belt," he would say. "Never get up nerve enough to take a chance; stick to the same job all their life; live in the same little one-horse town; wear rubbers on rainy days; never eat oysters out of season; never kiss anybody but their wife; vote the straight Republican ticket; and then discover it's all over but the flowers and the funeral and they never had any fun out of life."

But A.J. was not long a slave to his safety belt. One morning, trudging back from the pasture, he determined to take just one more practice somersault, tied to the clothesline; and then, come what might, he would give it a whirl on his own.

Hurrying to the clothesline, he tied himself firmly in position and gave a confident leap into the air. For some reason he turned only halfway over. Fortunately the clothesline caught the weight of his body and saved his neck. But the weatherbeaten privy, to which the line was attached, could not take it. With a wooden groan it collapsed. Simultaneously, there was a scream from Grandma, who at that moment was occupying the second hole.

For an instant she sat frozen amid the ruins, her Scotch Presbyterian blood horrified by this intrusion on her privacy. Then, with fire in her eye, she dropped her skirts and started for A.J. This was one time when he could not escape Grandma's wrath, for he was still tied to the clothesline.

But A.J. was not to be deterred from his career as an acrobat. He kept on turning cartwheels and back flips and somersaults. He built a horizontal bar out behind the barn, on which to try new tricks. His three brothers were satisfied when they could chin themselves a few times and "skin the cat." Not A.J. He kept fooling around on that bar until he was as much at home on it as a monkey.

Some years later, A.J. became a Y.M.C.A. physical director on the strength of a couple of back flips and a giant swing, which was the closest he ever came to being a bona fide acrobat. But I used to brag to the neighbor kids that Pop was a circus performer—the man on the flying trapeze. If they doubted it, I would yell for him to come out and show them. A.J. would come out in the yard and turn somersaults and back flips till the other kids were popeyed. They thought a circus acrobat was about the greatest kind of dad any boy could have. I would not have told them the truth for a million dollars —that he was really an inventor.

Grandma had been left a widow with a farm to run and four sons to rear, the eldest twelve years old, all of whom, it was whispered among the neighbors, were slightly tetched. But Grandma thought they were just plain lazy. She'd send them out to pick the cherries in the orchard and they'd come in that evening and declare the trees were stripped. But next morning, when Grandma would go out to see for herself, she'd find the boys had lied to her; they hadn't picked half the cherries. The same thing would happen when they'd go out to pick apples.

"Never would pick 'em all," Grandma used to declare. "And then lie about it like little heathens!"

A.J. was the worst. He used to argue back at Grandma. Downright sass her. Then Grandma would get angry, grab her hickory switch, and chase them up into those trees again. But it never did any good.

It was not till thirty years later that Grandma heard about color-blindness. All four of her boys had it—couldn't tell red from green.

"Probably a good thing," Grandma philosophized when she found out why the boys never picked all the cherries. "They needed a certain amount of lickin' anyway."

Even as a boy, back on the farm, A.J. had a passion for things that went round and round. Wheels! Anything with wheels attached to it started him off on a mental tangent. An unattached wheel would leave him in a state of suspended animation, while he gawked at it with a dreamy, speculative expression.

A.J.'s first invention was inspired by a huge wheel from an old high-wheeled bicycle. He purloined it from a junk heap behind the village blacksmith shop, brought it home, and went to work on it. In the barn he found a long axle and a couple of old buggy shafts. These he attached in their proper places; then he hung a home-made seat on either side of the wheel.

This uni-sulky, as A.J. has always called it, had several remarkable features. In the first place, it could operate only if there were two occupants of about the same weight, and they had to jump into their seats at the same time in order to keep the contraption balanced. Secondly, the occupants had to crouch low in their seats to keep from bumping their heads against the axle, from which the seats were suspended. Third, it required two drivers—one to hold the left rein, the other to hold the right. Any difference of judgment between them was likely to result in trouble.

A.J. and his brother Joe chose a Sunday morning, about an hour before church time, to try out the wonderful uni-sulky. Dressed in their best, they led old Bill, the work mule, out of the barn and backed him between the shafts. Then, with youthful nimbleness and enthusiasm, they jumped into their seats and urged Bill out onto the road, in order to get out of Grandma's sight as quickly as possible.

It was probably the most amazing vehicle ever seen on a Kansas highway. And remarkably enough, everything went well for about half a mile, until they came to the main road into town. There, A.J. chose to turn right while his brother Joe preferred to go left. Both being of a stubborn nature, neither would compromise.

Now it happened that Bill was a precocious animal. A.J. has always claimed that he was smarter than most human beings and meaner than Simon Legree. Anyway, Bill became annoyed at the difference of opinion behind him, gave a jerk of his head, and craned his neck around to see what in hell was going on. One look at the contraption to which he was hitched convinced him that he was pulling the devil's own chariot. He gave a snort and set out across country at top speed.

There has always been a difference of opinion between A.J. and Uncle Joe as to exactly what happened. But it seems that as Bill dragged the uni-sulky through the ditch at the side of the road, each boy dropped his rein and grabbed his seat. After that Bill was on his own. He went through Ed Beem's cornfield like Greyhound out to break all records at Goshen. Then he turned south and leaped a barbed-wire fence into Ham Turner's watermelon patch. It was at this fence that Uncle Joe was unseated and hung up by his breeches.

Without Uncle Joe, the wonderful uni-sulky veered to starboard like a catboat in a high wind, causing Bill to run in circles. A.J. held on for dear life, bouncing over green watermelons so fast he felt he was riding the Santa Fe ties to Wichita.

Somewhere in the backstretch, the sulky seat broke from its moorings and took a hop, skip, and jump which landed A.J. amid a tangle of vines. By the time he had freed himself, caught his breath, and stood up to look around, Bill was just vaulting another fence, with what was left of the uni-sulky still dragging along behind him. He disappeared in the general direction of California.

Long-suffering Grandma, dressed in her black dress and bonnet, was rocking grimly on the front porch when the boys finally hove into view. She took one look at their tattered Sunday best and reached for her hickory switch.

It was late afternoon before they found Bill, grazing peacefully, down by the river. The uni-sulky was no longer attached to him. A.J. spent many days searching for the remains, but he never found them.

A man who invents a novel and useful device or process may apply for and be granted a patent from the United States government giving him a monopoly of his invention for seventeen years. Inventors sometimes become very wealthy, but more often they go bankrupt. For many years A.J. danced a jig between the two, but in the end, to everyone's amazement, he did all right.

The first invention on which he was granted a patent was a game, called "Parlor Golf," which he sold to Parker Brothers for one hundred dollars, spot cash. When he invented it, A.J. had never seen a game of golf. But apparently neither had Parker Brothers, for the game resembled golf about as much as Paris, Illinois, resembles that other and more famous Paris.

The idea of the game was to flick a marble, with thumb and forefinger, up a series of nine grooved and undulated inclines, into nine little holes. In all Wichita, where A.J. by this time owned a bicycle repair shop, he was the only person who had the patience or skill to accomplish this feat in less than par. Everyone else grew infuriated at the damned thing and gave up, leaving A.J. the first undisputed Western Open Golf Champion (Parlor Division).

There followed a number of remarkable inventions, all of which, for one reason or another, failed to produce quick riches. Many of them were contrived while he was operating a bicycle shop in Wichita.

The Tearless Onion Peeler was a gadget that should have been a welcome addition to every kitchen. It was an affair of wheels and knives with a crank to operate it. For large consumers of onions, such as hotels and restaurants, A.J. devised a model which had a foot treadle for motive power. With this super-gadget one man (or woman) could peel, A.J. estimated roughly, seven bushels of onions per hour, without shedding a single tear. And by a simple adjustment, the machine could be converted to a potato, apple, peach, turnip, or rutabaga peeler. In those days, however, labor was plentiful and cheap; consequently, manufacturers of kitchen implements were of the unanimous opinion that A.J.'s Tearless Onion Peeler was no substitute for a ten-cent paring knife.

"It was a good invention," A.J. once told me, "but nobody wanted to buy it. That's always been the trouble with the world. People are suspicious of new ideas. If you spend one year inventing something new, you have to spend two years cramming it down people's throats. There are lots of easier ways to get rich."

After the Tearless Onion Peeler, A.J. invented his Wind-Proof Umbrella. "It Can't Blow Inside Out," read the prospectus. A.J. was sure he had a winner. Every household needed an umbrella, more especially one that would not collapse at the first gust of wind. And certainly rain was usually accompanied by wind; at least it was in Kansas. He figured that if he could collect a royalty of five cents on each umbrella, he ought to make a million dollars in five years.

At the time he perfected the new umbrella, he was enamored of a girl in Wichita, whose name, according to Aunt Ora, was Bertha. A.J. told Bertha about his newest invention. She listened with round-eyed admiration and assured him, breathlessly, that he must be the cleverest man in Wichita. And would he, pretty please, give her one of his patent umbrellas when he became a famous millionaire?

A.J. didn't wait to become a millionaire. He rushed right down to Innes's Department Store and bought a lady's silk umbrella, priced at three dollars. Then he took it to his shop and rebuilt it, with the cross-bracing, truss arrangement which was the feature of his Wind-Proof Umbrella.

On Bertha's birthday he presented it to her. For a week or so, Bertha displayed her umbrella proudly, and A.J. was elevated to the position of chief swain in her retinue of admirers. And then the rains came.

It happened while Bertha was on her way downtown, clad in a new spring outfit. The sky was slightly overcast, so she was carrying her Patented Wind-Proof Umbrella. When the first drops fell, Bertha struggled with the mechanism of the Wind-Proof Umbrella and finally opened it. Then she slipped her hand through the umbrella's stout wrist-loop, grasped the handle, and quickened her pace, feeling completely secure beneath her Wind-Proof Umbrella.

Suddenly the rain began to slant; overhead, tree branches bent and groaned as a rush of wind struck them; and the sky turned a threatening yellowish gray. Bertha stopped in her tracks. She had lived in Kansas all her life and she knew what was coming: a Kansas tornado. The wind filled her umbrella and tried to tear it from her grasp. The loop tightened about her wrist. She and the umbrella were swept along like two chips on a torrent. By the time she piled up against the Onderdonks' picket fence, bruised, battered, and humiliated, the romance between Bertha and the inventor of the Patented Wind-Proof Umbrella was forever ended.

All A.J.'s most successful inventions seemed to stem from that huge wheel which was the inspiration for his unisulky: they were things that went round and round. The invention of which he is proudest is his method for making the tires now used on airplanes, farm tractors, and other vehicles. This invention created a new principle in tire construction, by means of which the cross-section could be nearly as great as one-half the diameter, resulting in very low air pressures. These tires make it possible for planes to land or take off on rough or muddy fields; they also reduced ground looping and eliminated crack-ups due to wheel failure. Unfortunately, he sold his patent before anyone could foresee the enormous production of planes that World War II would bring. The invention which has brought him the greatest financial return is his bicycle coaster brake.

"I got the idea for my bicycle coaster brake back in 1894," A.J. always begins one of his best stories. "It was while I was traveling about ninety miles an hour down the slopes of the Rockies on a bicycle."

As A.J. tells the story, he unlocked his bicycle shop one July morning and discovered that the window on the alley was standing wide open. Then he noticed that his pride and joy, a red and white Peerless bicycle, the latest thing in cycledom, was missing. It was the most expensive one in the store—priced at $125. The plush-lined case, for shipping via railroad, was undisturbed, so A.J. knew that the thief had ridden his loot away.

He hurried over to the police station, where inquiry revealed that a stranger, who had skipped out of the local hotel without paying his bill, had been seen the night before, by Patrolman Murphy, high-tailing toward Hutchinson on the Peerless.

A.J. was fit to be tied. "Why didn't Murphy pinch the fellow?" he demanded. "That was the only red and white Peerless bike in Wichita and everybody knew it belonged to me."

The Chief of Police shrugged. "Maybe Murphy thought the guy had bought it."

A.J. hurried over to the bank and drew out twenty dollars for expense money, then dashed back to his store, shouted to Aunt Ora that he was on the trail of a bicycle thief, and climbed on his Ariel road-racer.

As A.J. likes to point out, he was pretty sharp on a bicycle in those days—an amateur circuit racer and one of the best riders west of the Mississippi. He thought he could overtake the bike-rustler before nightfall, because the red and white Peerless was bound to attract attention.

But he soon discovered that his quarry was a fast rider himself. For when he arrived at Great Bend, about nine o'clock that night, the Peerless had been there and gone. A.J. started out next morning at daybreak, hoping to overtake the bike-snatcher before he lost the trail. He was at a disadvantage, of course, because he had to stop at every crossroad and make inquiries; but the trail stayed hot—as A.J. says, "hotter'n an iron pump handle in August."

The second afternoon, he arrived at a fly-infested lunchroom, where he ordered a sandwich and inquired about the man on the Peerless.

"Yeah," answered the proprietor. "There was a fellow come through here on a bike like that."

"How long ago?"

"Couple hours. Told me he was headin' fer Colorado Springs. Purty long ride, if you ask me."

A.J. didn't wait to finish his sandwich. He hit the road and settled down to ride his fox to earth. He claims this was the best race he ever pedaled in his life, but somehow the thief evaded him. He thinks the man may have bribed a brakeman on a freight train to give him and the Peerless a lift in an empty boxcar.

A.J. reached Colorado Springs early one morning. As soon as the stores were open he canvassed every bicycle shop in town, but nobody had seen the Peerless. As a last resort he went to the police station.

"Saw a fellow ridin' a bike toward Cripple Creek this morning," one of the cops told him.

"Was it a red and white Peerless?"

"Didn't notice."

A.J. took a chance and headed for Cripple Creek. He had never seen mountains before and hadn't the vaguest idea what he was in for. The last ten miles into the little mining town were so steep he had to get off and push. As he plugged up those weary miles, he had an uncomfortable feeling that he had been sent on a wild-goose chase. Sure enough, nobody in Cripple Creek had seen the Peerless.

A.J. was a very unhappy man—tired, defeated, six hundred miles from home, and with only six dollars left. His one consoling thought was that he would be able to coast all the way back to Colorado Springs and a bed.

So he climbed on his bicycle and started, with never a thought of more trouble ahead. But before he was half a mile out of town he realized that he was traveling too fast. For although the Cripple Creek road didn't look so steep, it was something like the first dip on a roller coaster. He tried to slow down by throwing his weight against the pedals, but he kept gaining speed and was heading down that road faster than a hound dog with a hive of bees on his tail.

In those days a cyclist used to brake his bicycle by slipping one toe under the frame and pressing on the front tire with the sole of his shoe. A.J. tried that. For a moment it worked; then friction made the sole of his shoe fiery hot. He let out a startled yell and jerked his foot from beneath the frame.

Then gravity took charge once more and away he went. It was time to think of something ingenious. But the only idea he could contrive was to fall off. He hit the dirt with a thud that knocked the wind out of him; in one bounce he·was off the road and rolling down the mountainside. He fetched up against a scrub pine fifty feet from the road.

For a minute or two he just lay there regaining his wind and wondering if he was all in one piece. Then he got up groggily and shook his head until the world came back into focus. He scrambled up to the road and looked about for the bicycle. It was not in sight.

After an extensive search, he found his bicycle with eight spokes broken and the frame bent. When it would run again, he sat down to think.

His pondering resulted in the invention of his first brake. He cut several pine branches and tied them into a bundle with a piece of rope from his tool kit. The end of the rope was then attached to his saddle post so that the pine branches dragged behind on the road.

It worked like a charm. The bundle of branches was just enough brake to keep things under control. He went down the mountain road throwing up a dust cloud big enough for thirty head of cattle.

For about six miles A.J. was mighty proud of his invention; then, to his dismay, he discovered that it was an infringement. He was informed of this fact by a deputy sheriff who halted him with a forty-four and a vocabulary of four-letter words.

Using a drag for a brake was old stuff in those parts. Wagon freighters had invented the device years before. The trouble was that it ruined good roads, so the state had passed a law against that invention. A.J. had to wire back to Wichita for money to pay his fine.

"And that's one reason," A.J. has often told me, "that I conceived the idea of putting a coaster brake on a bicycle."

The idea was a long time hatching. It was thirteen years before he applied for a patent. But since 1908 five million bicycles have been equipped with A.J.'s coaster brake. Even Grandma had to admit, before she died, that somehow "one of Alvey's fool inventions turned out purty good."

1945

JOHN DOS PASSOS

The American Plan

From THE BIG MONEY

FREDERICK WINSLOW TAYLOR (they called him Speedy Taylor in the shop) was born in Germantown, Pennsylvania, the year of Buchanan's election. His father was a lawyer, his mother came from a family of New Bedford whalers; she was a great reader of Emerson, belonged to the Unitarian Church and the Browning Society. She was a fervent abolitionist and believed in democratic manners; she was a housekeeper of the old school, kept everybody busy from dawn till dark. She laid down the rules of conduct:

selfrespect, selfreliance, selfcontrol
and a cold long head for figures.

But she wanted her children to appreciate the finer things so she took them abroad for three years on the Continent, showed them cathedrals, grand opera, Roman pediments, the old masters under their brown varnish in their great frames of tarnished gilt.

Later Fred Taylor was impatient of these wasted years, stamped out of the room when people talked about the finer things; he was a testy youngster, fond of practical jokes and a great hand at rigging up contraptions and devices.

At Exeter he was head of his class and captain of the ballteam, the first man to pitch overhand. (When umpires complained that overhand pitching wasn't in the rules of the game, he answered that it got results.)

As a boy he had nightmares, going to bed was horrible for him; he thought they came from sleeping on his back. He made himself a leather harness with wooden pegs that stuck into his flesh when he turned over. When he was grown he slept in a chair or in bed in a sitting position propped up with pillows. All his life he suffered from sleeplessness.

He was a crackerjack tennisplayer. In 1881, with his friend Clark, he won the National Doubles Championship. (He used a spoonshaped racket of his own design.)

At school he broke down from overwork, his eyes went back on him. The doctor suggested manual labor. So instead of going to Harvard he went into the machineshop of a small pumpmanufacturing concern, owned by a friend of the family's, to learn the trade of patternmaker and machinist. He learned to handle a lathe and to dress and cuss like a workingman.

Fred Taylor never smoked tobacco or drank liquor or used tea or coffee; he couldn't understand why his fellowmechanics wanted to go on sprees and get drunk and raise Cain Saturday nights. He lived at home, when he wasn't reading technical books he'd play parts in amateur theatricals or step up to the piano in the evening and sing a good tenor in *A Warrior Bold* or *A Spanish Cavalier*.

He served his first year's apprenticeship in the machineshop without pay;

From *U. S. A.*, published by Houghton Mifflin Company; reprinted by permission of John Dos Passos.

the next two years he made a dollar and a half a week, the last year two dollars.

Pennsylvania was getting rich off iron and coal. When he was twenty-two, Fred Taylor went to work at the Midvale Iron Works. At first he had to take a clerical job, but he hated that and went to work with a shovel. At last he got them to put him on a lathe. He was a good machinist, he worked ten hours a day and in the evenings followed an engineering course at Stevens. In six years he rose from machinist's helper to keeper of toolcribs to gangboss to foreman to master mechanic in charge of repairs to chief draftsman and director of research to chief engineer of the Midvale Plant.

The early years he was a machinist with the other machinists in the shop, cussed and joked and worked with the rest of them, soldiered on the job when they did. Mustn't give the boss more than his money's worth. But when he got to be foreman he was on the management's side of the fence, *gathering in on the part of those on the management's side all the great mass of traditional knowledge which in the past has been in the heads of the workmen and in the physical skill and knack of the workman.* He couldn't stand to see an idle lathe or an idle man.

Production went to his head and thrilled his sleepless nerves like liquor or women on a Saturday night. He never loafed and he'd be damned if anybody else would. Production was an itch under his skin.

He lost his friends in the shop; they called him niggerdriver. He was a stockily built man with a temper and a short tongue.

I was a young man in years but I give you my word I was a great deal older than I am now, what with the worry, meanness and contemptibleness of the whole damn thing. It's a horrid life for any man to live not being able to look any workman in the face without seeing hostility there, and a feeling that every man around you is your virtual enemy.

That was the beginning of the Taylor System of Scientific Management.

He was impatient of explanations, he didn't care whose hide he took off in enforcing the laws he believed inherent in the industrial process.

When starting an experiment in any field question everything, question the very foundations upon which the art rests, question the simplest, the most selfevident, the most universally accepted facts; prove everything, except the dominant Quaker Yankee (the New Bedford skippers were the greatest niggerdrivers on the whaling seas) rules of conduct. He boasted he'd never ask a workman to do anything he couldn't do.

He devised an improved steamhammer; he standardized tools and equipment, he filled the shop with college students with stopwatches and diagrams, tabulating, standardizing. *There's the right way of doing a thing and the wrong way of doing it; the right way means increased production, lower costs, higher wages, bigger profits:* the American plan.

He broke up the foreman's job into separate functions, speedbosses, gangbosses, timestudy men, orderofwork men.

The skilled mechanics were too stubborn for him, what he wanted was a plain handyman who'd do what he was told. If he was a firstclass man and did firstclass work Taylor was willing to let him have firstclass pay; that's where he began to get into trouble with the owners.

At thirtyfour he married and left Midvale and took a flyer for the big money in connection with a pulpmill started in Maine by some admirals and political friends of Grover Cleveland's; '

the panic of '93 made hash of that enterprise,

so Taylor invented for himself the job of Consulting Engineer in Management and began to build up a fortune by careful investments.

The first paper he read before the American Society of Mechanical Engineers was anything but a success, they said he was crazy. *I have found,* he wrote in 1909, *that any improvement is not only opposed but aggressively and bitterly opposed by the majority of men.*

He was called in by Bethlehem Steel. It was in Bethlehem he made his famous experiments with handling pigiron; he taught a Dutchman named Schmidt to handle fortyseven tons instead of twelve and a half tons of pigiron a day and got Schmidt to admit he was as good as ever at the end of the day.

He was a crank about shovels, every job had to have a shovel of the right weight and size for that job alone; every job had to have a man of the right weight and size for that job alone; but when he began to pay his men in proportion to the increased efficiency of their work,

the owners who were a lot of greedy smalleyed Dutchmen began to raise Hail Columbia; when Schwab bought Bethlehem Steel in 1901

Fred Taylor

inventor of efficiency

who had doubled the production of the stampingmill by speeding up the main lines of shafting from ninetysix to twohundred and twentyfive revolutions a minute

was unceremoniously fired.

After that Fred Taylor always said he couldn't afford to work for money.

He took to playing golf (using golfclubs of his own design), doping out methods for transplanting huge boxtrees into the garden of his home.

At Boxly in Germantown he kept open house for engineers, factory-managers, industrialists;

he wrote papers,

lectured in colleges,

appeared before a congressional committee,

everywhere preached the virtues of scientific management and the Barth slide rule, the cutting down of waste and idleness, the substitution for skilled mechanics of the plain handyman (like Schmidt the pigiron handler) who'd move as he was told

and work by the piece: '

production;

more steel rails more bicycles more spools of thread more armorplate for battleships more bedpans more barbedwire more needles more lightningrods more ballbearings more dollarbills;

(the old Quaker families of Germantown were growing rich, the Pennsylvania millionaires were breeding billionaires out of iron and coal)

production would make every firstclass American rich who was willing to work at piecework and not drink or raise Cain or think or stand mooning at his lathe.

Thrifty Schmidt the pigiron handler can invest his money and get to be an owner like Schwab and the rest of the greedy smalleyed Dutchmen and cultivate a taste for Bach and have hundred-

yearold boxtrees in his garden at Bethlehem or Germantown or Chestnut Hill,
and lay down the rules of conduct;
the American plan.

But Fred Taylor never saw the working of the American plan;
in 1915 he went to the hospital in Philadelphia suffering from a breakdown.

Pneumonia developed; the nightnurse heard him winding his watch;
on the morning of his fiftyninth birthday, when the nurse went into his room to look at him at fourthirty,
he was dead with his watch in his hand.

1936

JOSEPH R. BUCHANAN

The Trials of a Labor Editor

From The Story of a Labor Agitator

"ONE swallow maketh not summer," and one strike does not make a labor agitator. Indeed, strikes contribute but slightly to the equipment of the successful labor agitator. The agitator must be thoroughly acquainted with the history of the labor movement, and be capable of presenting its aims and aspirations in an attractive and convincing manner. He must possess the ability to think rapidly and to express his views and opinions clearly and forcibly. But, withal, he must inspire those whom he would lead with absolute faith in his honesty. The agitator isn't always an advocate of strikes. He has sometimes to exert his influence to prevent a strike which his judgment tells him would be unwise. It may sound like mixing terms to say so, but it is a truth that the most difficult tasks performed by the labor agitators are their "agitations" in the interest of peace— their efforts to prevent strikes. The man who is always in favor of a strike as soon as one is suggested, or who is constantly on the search for a *casus belli,* soon finds his influence as a leader gone, and thereafter he may go off and agitate by himself.

I make this explanation as a sort of preface to the chapter in which I am to tell something about my education in the labor movement.

When I took the field in the Leadville strike I was but an untrained neophyte, rushing in at the dictates of a sentimental, sympathetic nature. My heart, and not my head, was my guide. Had I known then what I knew later, I would have tried rather to prevent or compromise the strike than to aggravate it. I was not familiar with the iron law of wages. I didn't realize that labor was subject, like any other commodity, to the law of supply and demand, when it is deficient in organized strength sufficient to prevent the operation of that law. These and many other things I learned in the two years that followed the year of the Leadville strike. I had taken a climax without working up to it, but after one short and interesting campaign on the firing line, I fell back to the rear for a course in tactics beginning at "hayfoot, strawfoot."

In the spring of 1881 I again took up my residence in Denver, and went to work in the composing-room of "The Rocky Mountain News." "The News" was an "open office." In trade-union parlance there are three recognized kinds of employing establishments. The "fair" shop employs union men, pays the scale, and recognizes the union's rules, one of which is that no non-union man shall be employed. The "scab" or "rat" shop refuses to countenance the union in any manner, and, as a general thing, would not employ union men if they were willing themselves or were permitted by their union to take situations. The "opens" are conducted under compromises between the proprietors and the union. In such shops union men are permitted to work, but non-union men may also be employed, and there is no obligation upon the employer's part to conform to the union's rules, except in the matter of the scale of wages; in most cases, though not in all, the union scale is paid in the "open" shops. There is, or was at the time of which I write, besides this general classification, another condition under which union men worked for unfriendly employers. In the interest of succinctness and clearness, I will describe this system as it worked in my own trade. It was sometimes the custom of the union, in an effort to unionize a "rat" office, to allow members to work "under cover." Trustworthy men would be selected by the officers of the union to try for situations in a "rat" office. Sometimes the men so selected would secure the employment under assumed names, but usually the better

plan of removing their names from the roll of the union to a "secret list" was adopted. The men working "under cover" reported secretly as occasion required to the union's officers and received such instructions as were necessary in the same way. Of course the object of this whole proceeding was to get as many union men as possible into the "rat" office, and, as soon as the number was deemed sufficient to promise successful issue, to demand that the office be unionized. In most of the cases of this kind that have come under my personal observation, strikes have followed the unmasking and the demand for union recognition; but the union has generally improved its position, securing an "open" office where it has failed to thoroughly unionize the establishment. "The Rocky Mountain News" had been advanced from a "rat" to an "open" office by this process a short time before I secured employment on the paper.

In union offices the journeymen in each department are upon an equal footing as to wages and other conditions. Under the piece system, which, happily, has been almost entirely displaced by the day system, there were many opportunities for the practice of favoritism. In "rat" and "open" offices some workmen were frequently enabled, through favors shown them by foremen, to make larger bills than men greatly their superiors as compositors. In union offices it was difficult, under the watchful eye of the union chapel, for any one to secure, and impossible to long maintain, an unfair advantage, even though one were the pet of the owners, the editors, the foreman, or all of these together. An appeal to the union against a case of favoritism always brought prompt action, a sort of protection to fair dealing that has been an element of strength to unions.

When I entered "The News" office, ten members of the force of sixteen compositors were union men, three were non-unionists and three were "rats," having once been members. When I had been in the office about six months, the three non-unionists, under the influence of the union men on the force, made application to the union for membership and were received. Pardon was granted to two of the "rats" and they were reinstated. The remaining "rat" was refused a pardon, and when the office was declared a full union office, after a little argument with the proprietors, he went into other business. The discussion over that man's case was very animated. I wanted his name included in the pardoning resolution, and I believed the union's treatment of him was cruel and uncalled for; but men older than I in the union said that his offense could not be condoned, and it may have been they were right. That was my first contest with fellow-unionists over questions of principle and policy.

In June, 1882, the annual session of the International Typographical Union was held in St. Louis. I was elected the delegate from Denver Union No. 49. My principal opponent was Robert Higgins, fellow victim of the "Committee of 100." In that election I received my introduction to trade-union politics, a game in which I frequently took a hand in the years that followed; a game at which I received several severe drubbings and achieved some victories.

The union made a liberal appropriation to defray the expenses of the delegate, but it was suggested to me that I might secure railway passes through the influence of "The News." I mentioned the matter to the managing editor, Mr.

William Stapleton, and received a flat refusal. A few days later Mr. Stapleton came to me and said that he had been talking the subject over with Mr. Arkins, the senior owner of the paper, and that they had concluded to get me passes as far as Kansas City, but they wanted it understood that they did so out of consideration for me personally and not on account of the union, for which they had no love. I relate this apparently trifling incident because in later chapters I shall tell how those two men turned upon me and not only tried to drive me out of Denver, but publicly threatened to take my life.

The convention of the International Union was a revelation to me. The average ability of the delegates was greatly superior to what I had expected to find in an assemblage of workingmen. I discovered then what I have seen many times since: that the national and international unions of labor in this country conduct their meetings in a manner that the average legislature could copy with profit.

The subject of greatest importance considered at the International Union Convention was the "sub list." Substitute compositors, who are put on to work when regulars want a day or night off, are called "subs." These men are, of course, members of the union in union offices, and the regular is responsible for the "sub" he puts on his cases. In some of the offices the foremen in those days kept lists made up of the names of the "subs" they would allow to work in their respective rooms. It can be seen that this system furnished opportunities for the exercise of favoritism by foremen, and was, of course, open to suspicion. Great injustice was done in some cases to good union men who had not the "pull" necessary to get their names on the "sub list." An effort was made at the St. Louis convention to legislate the "sub lists" out of existence, and I joined the movement with enthusiasm. The zeal I displayed in that parliamentary struggle won me a pair of nicknames that clung to me in all my years of activity in the labor movement. They were "Kicker" and "Riproarer of the Rockies." While I brought down upon my head the wrath of the mossbacks in the convention because of the fight I made for the "subs" at that time, I had my reward in the thanks of the tramp printers, which have been laid at my feet in cities and on the road from one coast to the other.

The abolitionists lost that battle, but one year later, at Cincinnati, fought it over, and won. The defeat at St. Louis was due to a trick played upon us by the administration party. After the convention twenty-one delegates met and adopted a set of resolutions denouncing the methods employed to defeat the will of the majority and the known desires of a majority of the union men throughout the country. These resolutions we signed and made public. For this action we were published in the semi-official organ of the International Typographical Union as traitors. Frank K. Foster, of Boston, was one of the "traitors" with me, and out of that association grew a friendship between that eloquent and fearless champion of labor and myself that stood the test of many hard battles for the principles of trades-unions in the Knights of Labor and elsewhere in after years. The charge of "treason" was not pressed, and, as has been said, our principles triumphed one year later.

Back to my cases on "The News" I went after the St. Louis convention; but I was dissatisfied and uneasy. For two years I had been reading everything dealing with social conditions that I could get hold of. I had devoured the writings of the leading political economists and had formed opinions of a just and equitable social and industrial system. My theories of right would not harmonize with conditions as I knew them to exist. At Leadville I had witnessed the flash of lances, and at St. Louis I had seen what I believed to be a latent force in the workers which, if aroused and properly directed, would overthrow industrial wrong and elevate the toiler to a position commensurate with his services to society.

There was one assembly of the Knights of Labor in Denver. In November, 1882, another assembly was instituted. I was one of the charter members. John B. Lennon, subsequently prominent in the labor movement nationally as secretary of the Journeymen Tailors' Union and as treasurer of the American Federation of Labor, was also a charter member of the new assembly. All of the members at the beginning of the assembly, and indeed for some months thereafter, were trades-unionists, and for that reason the name "Union" was given to the assembly; its number was 2327. Two clergymen of national prominence, Gilbert De La Matyr, of the Methodist Episcopal Church, and Myron W. Reed, Congregationalist, became members of Union Assembly during the second year of its existence.

The principles of the Knights of Labor and the opportunities presented by the organization for educational work in the field of labor reform were irresistibly attractive to progressive and liberal trades-unionists. The sentiment among unionists of that kind, of which the organization of Union Assembly was a manifestation, was widespread at that time, and union men were forming assemblies or joining those already organized in all parts of the country. The phenomenal growth of the Knights of Labor, which culminated in 1886, was in great measure due to the affiliation of trained, able, and active trades-unionists, which began in 1882.

As a famished plant drinks the dew after a heated day, so I, burning with the desire to do something for the working-people, welcomed the principles of the Knights of Labor and the opportunity the organization presented. Its exhortation, "Agitate, Educate, Organize!" I adopted as my shibboleth, and I was foolish enough to think that I could blow a blast that would rouse the sleeping giant of labor. Others have made the same mistake.

Naturally I sought the printing-press as a means of carrying my message to the oppressed of earth. In conjunction with S. H. Laverty, a fellow-compositor, I started "The Labor Enquirer," of Denver, the first number of which was issued December 16, 1882. With little other capital than our knowledge of newspaper work, Laverty and I embarked upon a sea in whose fathomless depths lie the battered hulks of unnumbered barks whose cargoes were unmarketable "human rights" and whose log-books were records of foul weather and short rations.

There were in "The Labor Enquirer" eight pages of five columns each. It was issued weekly. While the paper was pronounced in its advocacy of the principles of trades-unionism and of the Knights of Labor, it was conservative —at the start. The motto was,—

"We will renew the times of truth and justice,

Condensing in a free, fair common-wealth—
Not rash equality, but equal rights."

It was soon evident that our news and correspondence didn't interest, nor did our editorials inspire a very large proportion of the workingmen of the community. Subscriptions came in slowly. Expenses were light, Laverty and myself, with the help of an apprentice boy, doing all the mechanical work upon the paper excepting the presswork. Our savings were soon exhausted. Laverty, who was unmarried, reduced his living expenses to the lowest possible notch. During the last three weeks he was with me he lodged in the office and ate most of his meals from the imposing-stone. There was a little fellow in my family now, and it was pretty hard picking for the three of us sometimes. Many times our rations would have been scantier had my partner accepted a fair share of what strayed into "The Enquirer's" till. He was a generous and self-sacrificing fellow—one of the kind of men that made the great labor movement that came in later years a possibility. He was brave, too, for it took courage to give up his interest in the paper, and to abandon the hopes that had soared so high. With the tenth issue of "The Enquirer" he surrendered his interest to me and retired, announcing that there wasn't enough in the paper for the support of two proprietors, and that he could better serve the cause by withdrawing than by remaining.

For four and a half years I published "The Denver Labor Enquirer," and during nearly all of that time I was in charge personally and edited the paper. I shall have occasion to refer frequently to the paper in relating the stirring events in the labor world in which I bore a part, but to me it seems fit that I should here tell those experiences which were mine simply through ownership of "The Enquirer." It was ups and downs during those four and a half years, with the down side of the score crowding the pages to the margins. Soon after Laverty left me, I was compelled to reduce the paper's size, which I did by just halving it. Then the time came when I wasn't able to pay the apprentice boy's wages, and he had to go. What a struggle it was to continue the poor little champion of the workers, which few of the workers themselves ever lifted a finger to assist! It is true "The Enquirer" wasn't a great paper; it was hardly as large as a patent medicine folder or a circus programme; but that was not my fault. The only limit to size and character I recognized was measured by the income. Although I labored from sixteen to twenty hours a day—Sundays included—I could set no more type than was required to fill the little paper and have time sufficient to attend to other matters which had claims upon me. If nature had varied her rule in my case and favored me with four instead of two hands, "The Enquirer" would have been a larger paper, because all I was and all I had went into it.

Yes, I was an enthusiast—fanatic, if you please.

And my wife? Ah, loyal soul; she battled and suffered with me. She never complained on her own account, even when we were reduced to one little room in the rear of the office, and to subsisting upon scant and uncertain fare. Sometimes she urged me to give up a fight which she saw would, sooner or later, undermine my health, but she never upbraided me because of my failure to provide a better living for my wife and child.

I remember one stormy night in December, 1883. I had been at work since early morning, pegging away at the case. I was weary, oh, so weary, and I was hungry too; but the day after tomorrow was press-day and there were several columns yet to set. The only light in the room where I worked was supplied by a pair of candles, set in tin holders fastened to the lower edge of the "cap" case. On the first of the month the gas company had removed my meter because two months' bills remained unpaid. Since then I had been working by candlelight at night. The insufficient light made my work harder, but I couldn't blame the candles for that, and probably gas companies know their business. The blame rested elsewhere. I never spoke of it and tried not to think of it. I was hanging to my hope by a very frail cord; the little blaze of one of those candles would have parted that cord in an instant, and so I kept them apart. It was near midnight when my wife entered the room.

"My dear, it is very late, and you must be almost worn out," she said. "Stop now and go to bed. You will kill yourself if you continue as you have been going on for the past three months. How I wish you could realize what has been clear to me for a long time. Those for whom you are battling care nothing for your sacrifices. They would allow you to starve at your post. Give it up, dear, give it up!"

"If we are going to talk, Lou, I must blow out the candles," I said. "I have only two besides these that are burning, and I need them for my work. It will take every cent of coin I have to buy the white paper and pay for the presswork on this issue."

"Well, come into the other room. We can open the stove door and get light enough for talking," she said.

We sat in our little parlor-bedroom-kitchen and in the faint glow of a dying fire talked for more than an hour. I returned no more to my cases that night, and ere I laid my head upon my pillow it had been decided that "The Labor Enquirer" would issue that week's number, and then quietly give up the ghost. Although the struggle which ended in that decision was comparatively short, it was fierce while it lasted, for it was myself battling with myself. My wife said little, and that little was a plea for my health, physical and mental. But I was thinking all the time about my wife and child and how I had neglected them.

Though my decision to quit was reversed within twenty-four hours, I have always felt better because I decided on the side of my little family when the test was clearly before me.

About midway of the following morning there was a rap upon the door of our living-room. The caller was the wife of a superannuated compositor, who was then living upon a little farm a few miles out from Denver. The good woman (God love her, I believe she is an angel now—she belongs in that goodly company) handed my wife a covered basket, and, with a few words of comfort and cheer, took her departure. The basket contained a dressed duck, nine eggs, and about a half peck of potatoes.

Charlie Semper and his wife were poor, very poor. They never built a library nor endowed a university; but they loved their fellow-creatures, and they believed "The Enquirer" was capable of doing some good for humanity if its editor and his family could only be kept from starving. Whether or not they wasted their provisions it is not for me to say, but if the duck, the eggs, and the potatoes were donated to an unworthy object that morning, so were the other good things that came to the office once a week thereafter from that little farm until there was no longer necessity for such help.

At 11 o'clock that same night, as I was making up the forms so that they would be ready to send to the press-room early the following morning, the door opened and a man entered my work-room. Though visitors were not often seen in my establishment, this man's entrance did not surprise me. He was one of the faithful few, and I should have felt almost entirely deserted and poor indeed had he not called to see me at least once in every forty-eight hours. His name was Charles Machette. He was a clerk in a notion store, at the princely salary of nine dollars a week. He had seen better days, and I always felt a lump rise in my throat when he gave me of his scanty income to help the paper, which he had done on several occasions.

When I saw who my visitor was, I remembered my decision to shut down the paper, and the thought that it would be rather a hard task to tell him about it flashed across my mind. He walked directly up to the stone where I was engaged and, without uttering a word, deposited a twenty-dollar gold-piece on the form in front of me. At first I thought it was a brass medal or an advertisement, but when I picked it up and turned it over I recognized an old familiar face. I had once (it seemed years ago) known the family of "yellow boys."

"Well, Charlie?" was all I could say.

"It's for you," he responded.

"Where did you get it?" I asked.

"Sold my old watch."

"I can't take it," and I tried to place the piece of money in his hand.

Shoving his hands into his pockets he stepped away from me. "Yes, you can take it; and you've got to take it. I can't set type nor do any of the other work on the paper, and so I've got to help pay for the things you have to buy, including the presswork."

"But," I said, "you've done that so often before."

"Yes, and I'll do it again whenever it's necessary, if I have to take the shirt off my back. You needn't think you are going to monopolize the sacrificing business. You write and preach against monopolies; I am doing a little practicing along that line."

And I kept the money.

If any of the publishers of the great papers of to-day read this they will smile at so much ado over so small a sum. They think nothing of giving as much, and more, for a short special. To me that twenty dollars meant white paper and presswork for two issues.

I hope the reader who pursues this volume to the end will turn back when he finishes the account given in a later chapter of the part another watch played in an attempt to succor a dying labor paper, and read again this simple little story of which Charlie Machette is the hero.

I had one friend during those dark days who, though he helped me with a cash donation occasionally, tried hard to persuade me to abandon the effort to establish a paper. He would come into the office every few weeks, and after giving me a lecture on the unworthiness and ingratitude of the workingman in general and the Denver workingman in particular, and after scolding me roundly, would always close each visit by taking five or ten dollars from his pocket and laying it down in front of me would say:—

"Well, you're a fool; but fools have to eat just like other people."

If any of the "Old Guard" of Denver read the foregoing, they will have no difficulty in recognizing O. L. ("Yank") Smith in the gentleman just described.

My friend Smith tried to get me to go into politics; for, singular as it may seem, I was apparently very popular with the workingmen, who seemed willing to do almost anything for me but support the paper. They would pack a hall to hear me talk, but few of them were willing to spend a dollar and a half a year to read the lectures I was delivering through "The Enquirer" once a week.

The Republican county committee offered me a place on the legislative ticket for Arapahoe County, and the chairman of the committee personally urged me to accept the offer. Such a nomination at that time was equivalent to election, but I refused it, and my friend Smith dressed me down in good style when he heard of what I had done.

"What in Heaven's name do you want?" he asked. "You are always howling about the wrongs of the workingmen. Here is a chance for you to help make laws in their interest and you refuse it. What's the matter with you?"

I recognized the pertinency of the question and admitted his right to ask it, despite the severity of his manner. My answer was:—

"About all I have left in this world is the love and confidence of some thousands of workingmen, and—"

"Yes, and you'll starve to death on a diet of love and confidence!"

"Never mind that, now. They believe in me, whatever they may do or not do. If I accepted that nomination, there are jealous and weak ones among them who would say I had played into the hands of the politicians by becoming a party to a sham recognition of labor; that I had sold myself for a seat in the legislature. After my election, I would be on the defensive with my own people all the time, because, strive as I might, it would be impossible for one labor man to accomplish anything of consequence in the legislature. At the end of my term I would have to choose between remaining in the political camp, with submission to the party machine, and a return to my work of agitation in the labor world, with diminished following and lessened influence. You know which I would choose. I am not willing to make a breach in the ranks for a little cheap glory and the salary of a legislator."

"I should call it good riddance to be freed from such friends as would desert you because you accepted an opportunity to agitate their cause in the legislature, though nothing practical came of it at once," said Smith.

Smith's argument looks stronger than mine, I know, and yet I refused to reconsider my decision. I leave the reader to decide whether I was short-sighted, selfish, egotistical, or cowardly. I had stated the truth to my friend: I was afraid to take the chance, just then, of weakening my influence with the workingmen, who were beginning to organize and to think as they had never organized and thought before.

My displeased friend had occasion at a later period to recall one of the reasons I had advanced to him for refusing the nomination for a political office, and I will digress sufficiently to tell the story:

He was nominated as a member of the city council, indorsed by the labor party, and elected. The night of election day was the regular meeting-time of Union Assembly, of which Smith was a member. Just before the close of the assembly that night, about ten o'clock, one of the brothers who had gone out to get the election results, returned with the information that our brother Smith was elected. I was on the floor at the time, making a general talk, but especially urging the members to stand together in all things which concerned the interests of labor. I didn't have to swing very far out of the line of my discourse, when the victory of Smith was announced, to say,—

"Now, here is one of our brothers who has just been elected to an honorable position. We all love and respect him. As he passes out across yon threshold to-night he will carry our esteem and good wishes, but it will be for the last time. Before our next meeting, two weeks hence, there will be Knights who, because Brother Smith will not be guided by them in the discharge of his public duties, and because he will not be able to secure appointments for those who ask him for positions, will charge him with betrayal, disloyalty, treachery, dishonesty, and everything else that is bad, short of murder."

My prediction was fulfilled to the letter. Bad feeling was engendered between some of the members of the assembly, and the trouble spread to other labor organizations in the city. Smith quickly dropped out of the labor movement. Before the next election day came around labor as an organized factor in politics was again at the ebb tide. And yet there are many intelligent friends of the workingman who are unable to understand why labor is not more of an organized political power in the land.

To return to "The Enquirer." There were others besides those I have mentioned who made sacrifices from their meager means to keep the paper going; there was a little band of them who, with no deserters and rarely a recruit, always rallied when the situation was most discouraging. That little band of fanatics held the paper back many times when it was hanging over the black chasm of failure. It is not necessary that I should tell of all these critical periods; they would appear very much alike to the reader, though to me each was a distinct and separate tragedy. And yet there was one more experience in that line that I think I should relate.

One evening, while I was at work, the door of my office opened and ten of my friends filed into the room. Their formal proceedings and serious aspect frightened me at first, but I soon learned that their mission was one of friendship. Quietly they formed a circle around me, and John Lennon stepped up to my side and placed in my hands a package containing a suit of clothes, made in his own shop, accompanying the gift with a few words of kindness and encouragement. I had use for that suit; labor editors in those days usually had room in their closets for things of that kind.

I had another partner in the paper for a while, not a printer, as my first one had been. Stephen Vinot, a man of considerable property,—too much, for he was "land poor,"—sympathized with the efforts of the workingmen to improve their condition. He was a Frenchman, and was full of the spirit of '93. How he sometimes made the little office shake with the thrilling strains of the Marseillaise hymn, which he rendered in French with a heavy baritone voice! Vinot's hobby was the Chinese question. He believed that if the Chinese were allowed unrestricted entrance to this country they would in time dominate the white people in every walk of life, and that American workingmen would be degraded to a coolie level. That was the prevailing belief in the West in those days,—and it has never changed,—but all were not so outspoken and radical as Stephen Vinot. I won his friendship by printing his anti-Chinese writings in "The Enquirer." He soon learned of the struggle I was engaged in to keep the paper alive, and to help me out he took a half interest in the paper, putting $200 in the cash-box. He advanced other sums at various times, but in about five months he had had enough of labor journalism. When he learned that he couldn't induce me to shut down the paper, he drew out, and once more I was the sole owner of "The Enquirer's" plant, subscription list and good will. There wasn't a great quantity of either of these, nor of all together, but I became round-shouldered from carrying the load.

It will not surprise the thoughtful reader, especially if he be a student of human nature, to be told that disappointment and discouragement reduced me at times to a very pessimistic frame of mind. More than once I lost hope that the wrongs of labor would ever be righted by peaceable means. The workingmen could not be made to appreciate the power the ballot gave them; they were, it seemed to me, slow to take advantage of the opportunities opened to them by the labor organizations, and I sometimes thought the majority of them were not only too stupid to raise themselves, but too weak to stand if raised by others. I became so discouraged over the failures of the peace measures of the trades-unions that, while I never ceased to do all in my power to strengthen those organizations, because they furnished the most available rallying-ground, I came very close to the line that divided reform from revolution. The apathy of the workingmen made me sick at heart, the indifference of the middle class discouraged me, and the cruel selfishness of the rich angered me. The grievances of the workingmen received scant courtesy and no support from the influential press. The daily papers were interested, as most of them have always been, in the affairs of the rich; business, and not humanity, concerned them. Vexed at the course of the big papers, I did one thing that my most charitable critics were kind enough to call a piece of foolishness. The Denver dailies each carried a line at the top of the first editorial column quoting the current price of silver bullion. My readers were not, I thought, interested in the bullion market, and so I gave the post of honor on my editorial page to dynamite, changing the price each week. For instance, this would be the line:—

"Dynamite is strong to-day at 47c."

Indiscreet? Well, probably it was; but it was more foolish than dangerous. If harm was done by the dynamite quotation I was the greatest sufferer, and as that bit of deviltry was the only fun I indulged in during eighteen months of sacrifice, hardship, and hunger, it isn't likely I will have to answer for it on the other side.

In after years my revolutionary views gave place to a belief in the doctrine of social evolution through the practical channel of opportunism. But I have never relinquished the theory of socialism, nor the hope of its complete adoption by mankind ultimately, which grew into and became a part of me during the thoughtful days of "The Labor Enquirer's" struggle for existence.

Why didn't the labor people support the paper? I know the reader is asking. There is but one answer to that question: They didn't think it was of any benefit to them. And now, here's something peculiar: During the first eighteen months of "The Enquirer's" existence there was comparative peace between labor and its employers in and around Denver. Not that labor was satisfied with its condition, but the dissatisfaction hadn't manifested itself in an open protest; there hadn't been a strike. While the men were at work and drawing their pay regularly, they were not disposed to spend a dollar and a half a year for a subscription to the paper. When a strike came, and wages stopped, there were busy times for the subscription agents. "A friend in need is a friend indeed," and there's the whole story. A temptation to the editor to "foment discontent!" as the enemies of the labor agitators express it. I can honestly answer "Not guilty." The discontent, in armor arrayed, came to my lonely little den and dragged me forth.

At ten o'clock on the morning of Thursday, May 4, 1884, I stood at the case setting the week's editorials, which, to save time, I had learned to put into type without writing. The door opened and five men entered. Four of them were unknown to me; the fifth, Mr. George Stuart, was an acquaintance, but I met him rarely. Stuart presented the gentlemen who were with him and then said:—

"The Union Pacific Railway shopmen have gone on strike, and, as they haven't any organization, we have come to see if you can't help them a little."

"Are all of you Union Pacific men?" I asked.

"We are, and we represent five departments," was Stuart's reply.

"When did you strike?"

"About two hours ago."

"Why did you strike?" was my next question.

"When we went to work this morning we found notices stuck up all over the shops and yards, announcing that wages would be reduced in accordance with a scale printed with the notice. The reduction hits every employee excepting the engineers and firemen, and the cut ranges from ten to twenty-five per cent., according to the wages received. In the shops, which we represent, the reduction is ten and fifteen per cent."

"How came you to strike without organization?" I asked.

"Well, after working a few minutes, one of the machinists put down his tools and said he would throw up his job before he would stand such a cut on such short notice. Some of the others gathered about him and said they wouldn't stand it either. Word passed through the other departments that the machinists were going to protest against the order, and, to make a long story short, in half an hour every man and boy had quit the shops, about five hundred in all."

"And now you want me to advise you?" I asked.

"I read your paper sometimes, and it occurred to me that you might be able and willing to tell us how to proceed," answered Stuart.

"Can you secure a convenient hall that will hold all of your men?" I asked.

"We have one now, and most of the men are up there."

"Where is it?"

"Washington Hall, on Larimer Street, near Twentieth."

"I know the place. I'll be there in half an hour. Meet me at the door, Mr. Stuart, please."

And I picked up my stick and rule, read over a few lines, rounded out my sentence, and in ten minutes was in a horse-car en route to assume for the first time leadership in a labor strike. When I reached the hall, Stuart informed me that every one of the strikers was there, and I wasn't inclined to question his statement when I got inside and saw the crowd.

I have been in many meetings of strikers since that day, but they have been of organized workingmen. I have seen union men in meetings of strikers laboring under a sense of injustice practiced by employers, and have heard some pretty strong speeches; but no gathering of union men can compete with a crowd of unorganized strikers when it comes to radicalism, denunciation of employers, threats, and incendiarism. Organization results in training, discipline, knowledge, and conservatism.

I listened to the spokesmen and newly fledged leaders of the various departments represented in the strike until I had satisfied myself as to the temper of the meeting; then I had my say. As a result of the discussion the following resolution, preceded by an appropriate preamble, was adopted, and every man present was required to sign it:—

"Resolved, That we, employees of said Union Pacific Railroad Company, in mass meeting assembled, do obligate ourselves, individually and collectively, to refuse to do any work under the jurisdiction or upon the premises of said Union Pacific Company until such time as the notice of a reduction in wages is withdrawn by the proper officials, and the old scale is re-instated."

Considerable time was required to se-cure the signatures of all those present; and while this was being done, some necessary committees and twenty-five pickets were selected. About the mid-dle of the afternoon two hundred men from the shops of the South Park Divi-sion filed into the room. They had not received notice of the reduction until 1 P. M. They were also unorganized, but they had walked out in a body, and learning of the meeting that was being held by the men of the main shop, had marched three miles through the prin-cipal streets of the city, for the purpose of joining in any protest that was to be made. They were soon informed as to what we had done and were given an opportunity to vote upon the resolution. They voted solidly for the resolution, and two hundred more names were ready for the document.

We were in almost constant session all that day and half of the night. The next day we met in the City Hall and there organized the "Union Pacific Employees' Protective Association." Thursday night and Friday telegrams were received announcing that the shop-men over the entire Union Pacific sys-tem had struck against the reduction.

There is no record of another such strike in the whole history of the labor movement in this country. Not a shop on the system was organized when the notice of reduction was posted, and yet, inside of thirty-six hours, every shop from Omaha to Ogden and upon all the branch lines was on strike. The pecu-liarity of this strike is further empha-sized by the knowledge that before the cut the Union Pacific was paying higher wages to its shopmen than was paid by

any other railroad west of the Missouri River. The company counted upon this latter fact to help make the reduc-tion successful, evidently not realizing that by paying the best wages it had se-cured the best mechanics and, as a con-sequence, the most independent men in the trades concerned.

There was another illustration of spontaneous unanimity in that strike. On Friday telegrams came from the offi-cials of the temporary organizations of the men at all points on the system re-questing the committee appointed at our Denver meeting to act for the whole system in dealing with the company. Ellis, Kansas, started that movement; and the others followed in quick order. The Denver committee accepted the re-sponsibility, and at once notified the general manager of the road, at Omaha, to that effect, at the same time wiring him a copy of the resolution adopted at Denver, the substance of which was ap-proved by the men at all other points.

Saturday afternoon the company re-called the order reducing wages, and an-nounced that on Monday work would be resumed at the old scale of prices,—a complete victory for the men in four days.

As soon as the order was recalled, some of the men were for abandoning further steps in the line of organization. They said they had gotten along all right without organization before the cut, and had shown that it was a simple matter to secure united action when necessary. They were told by myself and others that they were sadly mis-taken if they believed that the company had abandoned its purpose of reducing wages; that it would try again when the outlook was favorable, and that never again would a wholesale cut be under-taken; one experience of that character would be sufficient. We predicted that in future the company would select one department or one shop at a time, and would give no intimation that the intention was eventually to reduce all. Therefore the men should perfect their organizations and form a federation that would put them in a position to act all together at the first sign of danger, no matter which branch was threatened or attacked. We urged upon them the adoption of the motto of the Knights of Labor, "An injury to one is the concern of all."

When the situation was fully explained, the advice given by the union men who were taking an active interest in the matter was acted upon, and several organizers were put upon the road within a week from the close of the strike. The Knights of Labor was the organization chosen, and within thirty days we had a healthy assembly at each important point on the system. I organized assemblies in all the shop towns on the line from Omaha to Cheyenne, inclusive.

1903

J. A. SYMONDS

The Death of Sir Philip Sidney

From LIFE OF SIR PHILIP SIDNEY

SIDNEY's achievements in the Netherlands, except as forming part of his short life, claim no particular attention. He was welcomed by Count Maurice of Nassau, the eldest son of William, Prince of Orange; and gleanings from letters of the time show that folk expected much from his activity and probity. But he enjoyed narrow scope for the employment of his abilities. Rammekins, the fortress which commanded Flushing, was inadequately furnished and badly garrisoned. The troops were insufficient, and so ill-paid that mutinies were always imminent. In one of his dispatches, urgently demanding fresh supplies, he says: "I am in a garrison as much able to command Flushing as the Tower is to answer for London." The

Dutch government did not please him: he found "the people far more careful than the government in all things touching the public welfare." With the plain speech that was habitual to him he demanded more expenditure of English money. This irritated the Queen, and gave his enemies at Court occasion to condemn him in his absence as ambitious and proud. He began to show signs of impatience with Elizabeth. "If her Majesty were the fountain, I would fear, considering what I daily find, that we should wax dry." This bitter taunt he vented in a letter to Sir Francis Walsingham. Meanwhile the Earl of Leicester arrived upon the 10th of December, and made matters worse. He laid himself out for honors of all sorts,

From *Life of Sir Philip Sidney,* English Men of Letters, edited by John Morley. Harper and Brothers, 1894.

accepting the title of Governor-General over the United Provinces, and coquetting with some vague scheme of being chosen for their sovereign. Imposing but impotent, Leicester had no genius for military affairs. The winter of 1585-86 dragged through, with nothing memorable to relate.

The following season, however, was marked by several important incidents in Philip Sidney's private life. First, Lady Sidney joined her husband at Flushing. Then on the 5th of May Sir Henry Sidney died in the bishop's palace at Worcester. His body was embalmed and sent to Penshurst. His heart was buried at Ludlow; his entrails in the precincts of Worcester Cathedral. So passed from life Elizabeth's sturdy servant in Ireland and Wales—a man, as I conceive him, of somewhat limited capacity and stubborn temper, but true as steel, and honest in the discharge of very trying duties. Later in the same year, upon the 9th of August, Lady Mary Sidney yielded up her gentle spirit. Of her there is nothing to be written but the purest panegyric. Born of the noblest blood, surviving ambitious relatives who reached at royalty and perished, losing health and beauty in the service of an exacting queen, suffering poverty at Court, supporting husband and children through all trials with wise counsel and sweet hopeful temper, she emerges with pale luster from all the actors of that time to represent the perfect wife and mother in a lady of unpretending, but heroic, dignity. Sidney would have been the poorer for the loss of these parents, if his own life had been spared. As it was, he survived his mother but two months.

In July he distinguished himself by the surprise and capture of the little town of Axel. Leicester rewarded him for this service with the commission of colonel. Elizabeth resented his promotion. She wished the colonelcy for Count Hohenlohe, or Hollock, a brave but drunken soldier. Walsingham wrote upon the occasion: "She layeth the blame upon Sir Philip, as a thing by him ambitiously sought. I see her Majesty very apt upon every light occasion to find fault with him." Ambition, not of the vaulting kind, which "overleaps itself," but of a steady, persistent, intellectual stamp, was, indeed, I think, the leading quality in Sidney's nature. From the courtiers of the period, the Leicesters, Oxfords, Ormonds, Hattons, and so forth, this mark of character honorably distinguished him. And, if he had but lived, Elizabeth, who judged her servants with some accuracy, might by judicious curbing and parsimonious encouragement have tempered the fine steel of his frailty into a blade of trenchant edge. There was nothing ignoble, nothing frivolous, in his ambition. It was rather of such mettle as made the heroes of the commonwealth: pure and un-self-seeking, but somewhat acrid. And now he fretted himself too much because of evildoers, impatiently demanded men and munitions from England, vented his bile in private letters against Leicester. Sidney was justified by events. The campaign dragged negligently on, and the Commander of the Forces paid more attention to banquets and diplomatic intrigues than to the rough work of war. But the tone adopted by him in his irritation was hardly prudent for so young and so comparatively needy a gentleman.

Whatever he found to blame in Leicester's conduct of affairs, Sidney did not keep aloof, but used every effort to inspire his uncle with some of his own spirit. At the end of August they were both engaged in reducing the little fort of Doesburg on the Yssel, which had importance as the key to Zutphen. It fell upon the 2d of September; and on the 13th Zutphen was invested—Lewis William of Nassau, Sir John Norris, and Sir Philip Sidney commanding the land forces, and Leicester blockading the approach by water. The Duke of Parma, acting for Spain, did all he could to reinforce the garrison with men and provisions. News came upon the 21st to Leicester that a considerable convoy was at Deventer waiting an opportunity to enter the town. He resolved to cut off these supplies, and fixed an early hour of the 22d, which was a Thursday, for this operation. We have a letter, the last which Sidney penned before his fatal wound, dated from the camp at Zutphen upon the morning of the engagement. It recommends Richard Smyth, "her Majesty's old servant," to Sir Francis Walsingham, and is one among several writings of the kind which show how mindful Sidney was of humble friends and people in distress. The 22d of September opened gloomily. So thick a mist covered the Flemish lowlands that a man could not see farther than ten paces. Sidney, leading a troop of two hundred horsemen, pushed his way up to the walls of Zutphen. Chivalrous punctilio caused him to be ill-defended, for meeting Sir William Pelham in light armor, he threw off his cuisses, and thus exposed himself to unnecessary danger. The autumn fog, which covered every object, suddenly dispersed; and the English now found themselves confronted by a thousand horsemen of the enemy, and exposed to the guns of the town. They charged, and Sidney's horse was killed under him. He mounted another, and joined in the second charge. Reinforcements came up, and a third charge was made, during which he received a wound in the left leg. The bullet, which some supposed to have been poisoned, entered above the knee, broke the bone, and lodged itself high up in the thigh. His horse took fright and carried him at a gallop from the field. He kept his seat, however, and when the animal was brought to order, had himself carried to Leicester's station. On the way occurred the incident so well-known to everyone who is acquainted with his name. "Being thirsty with excess of bleeding, he called for drink, which was presently brought him; but as he was putting the bottle to his mouth, he saw a poor soldier carried along, who had eaten his last at the same feast, ghastly casting up his eyes at the bottle, which Sir Philip perceiving, took it from his head before he drank, and delivered it to the poor man, with these words, *Thy necessity is yet greater than mine.* And when he had pledged this poor soldier, he was presently carried to Arnheim."

At Arnheim he lay twenty-five days in the house of a lady named Gruitthueisens. At first the surgeons who attended him had good hopes of his recovery. Ten days after the event Leicester wrote to Walsingham: "All the worst days be passed, and he amends as well as possible in this time." Friends were around him—his wife, his brothers Robert and Thomas, and the excellent minister, George Gifford, whom he sent for on the 30th. The treatment of the wound exposed him to long and painful operations, which he bore with a sweet fortitude that moved the surgeons to admiration. With Gifford and other godly men he held discourses upon religion and the future of the soul. He told Gifford that "he had walked in a vague course; and these words he spake with great vehemence both of speech and gesture, and doubled it to the intent that it might be manifest how unfeignedly he meant to turn more thoughts unto God than ever." It is said that he amused some hours of tedious leisure by composing a poem on *La Cuisse Rompue,* which was afterwards sung to soothe him. He also contrived to write "a large epistle in very pure and eloquent Latin" to his friend Belarius the divine. Both of these are lost.

As time wore on it appeared that the cure was not advancing. After the sixteenth day, says Greville, "the very shoulder-bones of this delicate patient were worn through his skin." He suffered from sharp pangs which "stang him by fits," and felt internally that his case was desperate. "One morning, lifting up the clothes for change and ease of his body, he smelt some extraordinary noisome savor about him, differing from oils and salves, as he conceived." This he judged, and judged rightly, to be the sign of "inward mortification, and a welcome messenger of death." Thereupon he called the ministers into his presence, "and before them made such a confession of Christian faith as no book but the heart can truly and feelingly deliver." Death had its terrors for his soul, but he withstood them manfully, seeking peace and courage in the sacrifice of all earthly affections. "There came to my mind," he said to Gifford, "a vanity in which I delighted, whereof I had not rid myself. I rid myself of it, and presently my joy and comfort returned." Soon he was able to declare: "I would not change my joy for the empire of the world." Yet up to the very last he did not entirely despair of life. This is proved by the very touching letter he wrote to John Wier, a famous physician and a friend of his.

It runs thus in Latin: "Mi Wiere, veni, veni. De vita periclitor et te cupio. Nec vivus, nec mortuus, ero ingratus. Plura non possum, sed obnixe oro ut festines. Vale. Tuus Ph. Sidney." "My dear friend Wier, come, come. I am in peril of my life, and long for you. Neither living nor dead shall I be ungrateful. I cannot write more, but beg you urgently to hurry. Farewell. Your Ph. Sidney." In this way several days passed slowly on. He had made his will upon the 30th of September. This he now revised, adding a codicil in which he remembered many friends and servants. The document may be read in Collins' *Sidney Papers.* Much of it is occupied with provisions for the child, with which his wife was pregnant at this time, and of which she was afterwards delivered stillborn. But the thoughtful tenor of the whole justifies Greville in saying that it "will ever remain for a witness to the world that those sweet and large affections in him could no more be contracted with the narrowness of pain, grief, or sickness than any sparkle of our immortality can be privately buried in the shadow of death."

Reflecting upon the past he exclaimed: "All things in my former life have been vain, vain, vain." In this mood he bade one of his friends burn the *Arcadia;* but we know not whether he expressed the same wish about *Astrophel and Stella.* On the morning of the 17th of October it was clear that he had but a few hours to live. His brother Robert gave way to passionate grief in his presence, which Philip gently stayed, taking farewell of him in these memorable words: "Love my memory, cherish my friends; their faith to me may assure you they are honest. But above all, govern your will and affections by the will and word of your Creator, in me beholding the end of this world with all her vanities." Shortly afterwards he sank into speechlessness, and the bystanders thought that what he had greatly dreaded—namely, death without consciousness—would befall him. Yet when they prayed him for some sign of his "inward joy and consolation in God," he held his hand up and stretched it forward for a little while. About two o'clock in the afternoon he again responded to a similar appeal by setting his hands together in the attitude of prayer upon his breast, and thus he expired.

Sidney's death sent a thrill through Europe. Leicester, who truly loved him, wrote upon the 25th, in words of passionate grief, to Walsingham. Elizabeth declared that she had lost her mainstay in the struggle with Spain. Duplessis Mornay bewailed his loss "not for England only, but for all Christendom." Mendoza, the Spanish secretary, said that though he could not but rejoice at the loss to his master of such a foe, he yet lamented to see Christendom deprived of so great a light, and bewailed poor widowed England. The Netherlanders begged to be allowed to keep his body, and promised to erect a royal monument to his memory, "yea, though the same should cost half-a-ton of gold in the building." But this petition was rejected, and the corpse, after embalmment, was removed to Flushing. There it lay eight days, and on the 1st of November the English troops accompanied it with military honors to the *Black Prince,* a vessel which had belonged to Sidney. On the 5th it reached Tower Hill, and on the 16th of February it was buried with pomp in St. Paul's. This long delay between the landing in London and the interment arose from certain legal complications, which rendered the discharge of Sidney's debts difficult. Walsingham told Leicester that he would have to "pay for him about six thousand pounds, which I do assure your Lordship hath brought me into a most desperate and hard state, which I weigh nothing in respect of the loss of the gentleman who was my chief worldly comfort." Lest this should seem to reflect ill upon Sidney's character, it must be added that he had furnished Walsingham with a power of attorney to sell land, and had expressly considered all his creditors in his will. But his own death happened so close upon his father's, and the will was so imperfect touching the sale of land, that his wishes could not be carried into effect. This, added Walsingham, "doth greatly afflict me, that a gentleman that hath lived so unspotted in reputation, and had so great care to see all men satisfied, should be so exposed to the outcry of his creditors." When the obstacles had been surmounted the funeral was splendid and public. And the whole nation went into mourning. "It was accounted a sin," says the author of *The Life and Death of Sir Philip Sidney,* "for any gentleman of quality, for many months after, to appear at Court or City in any light or gaudy apparel."

I have told the story of Sidney's last days briefly, using the testimony of those who knew him best, or who were present at his deathbed. Comment would be superfluous. There is a singular beauty in the uncomplaining, thoughtful, manly sweetness of the young hero cut off in his prime. Numberless minute touches, of necessity omitted here, confirm the opinion that Sidney possessed unique charm and exercised a spell over those who came in contact with him. All the letters and reports which deal with that long agony breathe a heartfelt tenderness, which proves how amiable and how admirable he was. The character must have been well-nigh perfect which inspired persons so different as the Earl of Leicester, George Gifford, and Fulke Greville with the same devoted love. We have not to deal merely with the record of an edifying end, but with the longing retrospect of men whose best qualities had been drawn forth by sympathy with his incomparable goodness.

1886

HARVEY O'HIGGINS

Alias Walt Whitman

IN 1841, the editor of *The Daily Aurora* of New York City was a rather debonair young man from Brooklyn, a Mr. Walter Whitman, twenty-two years old, who "usually wore a frock coat and a high hat, carried a small cane" and had "the lapel of his coat almost invariably ornamented with a boutonnière." A contemporary described him as "tall and graceful in appearance, neat in attire, and possessed of a very pleasing and impressive eye and a cheerful and happy-looking countenance." It is also recorded that he was a success with the blue-stockings of the day. "I have been with him often in the society of ladies," a friend wrote, "and I never knew of any woman young or old but thought him a most agreeable gentleman of great culture."

It was a brave day for blue-stockings and gentlemen of great culture. A diarist of the time observes, "Walked down Broadway with all the fashion, and met the pretty blue-stocking, Miss Julia Ward. . . . She had on a blue satin cloak and a white muslin dress. I looked to see if she had on blue stockings, but I think not. I suspect that her stockings were pink, and she wore low slippers. They say that she dreams in Italian and quotes French verses." She was the same age as the editor of *The Daily Aurora,* having been born, like him, in May, 1819. And walking down Broadway, "with all the fashion," she may have seen him—tall and graceful, in his high hat and his frock coat, swinging his small cane—since he promenaded on Broadway, in those days, as devotedly as Thoreau roamed his woods.

He was more professional in literature than she; he was trying to make his living by writing, and she did not need to; but they both produced the same kind of verse—the kind that was fashionable in the literary journals of the moment. He was about to announce in print:

Not in a gorgeous hall of pride,
  Where tears fall thick and loved ones sigh,
Wished he, when the dark hour approach'd,
  To drop his veil of flesh and die.

In spite of his buttonhole bouquet and his high hat, he really much preferred to end

Amid the thunder-clash of strife,
  Where hovers War's ensanguined cloud,
And bright swords flash and banners fly
  Above the wounds and groans and blood.

As elegant sad verse, this would seem to compare favorably with Julia Ward's stanza from her poem "On Looking Over a Diary Kept While I Was Under Serious Impressions":

Oh! Happy days, gone, never to return,
At which fond memory will ever burn,
Oh! Joyous hours, with peace and gladness blest,
When hope and joy dwelt in this careworn breast.

which she had written, seven years before, at the careworn age of fifteen.

Although they were both made famous, twenty years later, by their poems about the Civil War—he by his "O Captain! My Captain!" and she by her "Battle Hymn of the Republic"—I do not know of any record that they ever met. Certainly not in the 1840's. They were worlds apart socially. As the daughter of Mr. Samuel Ward, the rich New York banker, she was "a frequenter of fashionable society," to quote her own subsequent description of herself, "a musical amateur, a dilettante in literature." He, in spite of his fashionable appearance, was the son of a Long Island farmer-carpenter, and he had worked his way up to the office of The Daily Aurora as a lawyer's errand boy, a doctor's office boy, a typesetter, and a country school-teacher. He had a rather meager education, and if any lady mistook him for "a gentleman of great culture" she must have been hypnotized by his pleasing and impressive eye. In the 1860's and 70's he could still write to

his mother, from Washington, "I wish you was here," and to his brother, "I was very sorry you wasn't able to come on to see the Review."

All he had of the fashionable gentleman were the clothes and the taste for idleness. The proprietor of the Aurora thought him "the laziest fellow who ever undertook to edit a city paper." It was his habit to arrive at his office "between eleven and twelve o'clock in the morning," according to one of his editorial associates, and after looking over "the daily and exchange papers," he always strolled down Broadway to the Battery, spent "an hour or two amid the trees, enjoying the water view," and returned "to the office location at about two or three o'clock in the afternoon." Apparently, these leisurely habits lost him his position on the Aurora, and he became what is called a free-lance.

As a free-lance, he wrote a quantity of verse and prose that was mostly worse than mediocre. The prose especially was falsely done, without conviction, without the faintest glint of artistic conscience, and faked in imitation chiefly of Edgar Allan Poe and James Fenimore Cooper. In November, 1842, he put out an anonymous novel, Franklin Evans; or The Inebriate, dedicated to the Temperance Societies of the day. It was published in a weekly story paper called The New World, and ballyhooed as written "expressly for The New World by one of the best novelists in this country, with a view to aid the great work of reform and rescue young men from the demon of Intemperance." It was really written, one of his friends records, "mostly in the reading room of Tammany Hall, which was a sort of Bohemian resort, and he afterwards told me that he frequently indulged in gin cocktails, while writing it, at the 'Pewter Mug,' another resort for Bohemians around the corner in Spruce Street."

Copies of *Franklin Evans* are now so extremely rare that it is not easy to confirm the adverse judgment of his biographers upon it as "chaotic," "ill-told," "rambling," and "difficult to treat seriously." But much of his other free-lance work of the period has been collected and reprinted, and most of it deserves the epithets that have been used on *Franklin Evans*. Among these fugitive pieces is an article called "Richard Parker's Widow" from a monthly magazine, *The Aristidean,* published in New York in 1845. It begins, "When I was in London some years since," and it describes how Whitman saw the widow of Richard Parker, a once famous mutineer, applying for "parish assistance" from a "magistrate" in a "police office." A friend, he says, pointed her out to him secretly and then "went on to give me the particulars of this celebrated mutiny." Whitman, of course, was never in London, and the story of the mutiny, as he tells it, is taken almost word for word from Pelham's *Chronicles of Crime* or *The New Newgate Calendar* (London, 1841). The only considerable change that he makes in Pelham's narrative is this: according to Pelham, the convicted mutineer, before he was hanged at the yard-arm, was given a glass of white wine which he drank "to the salvation of his soul and the forgiveness of all his enemies"; Whitman makes it "a glass of water."

The Aristidean printed also, in March 1845, a long story by Walter Whitman, called "The Arrow-Tip"; and Whitman subsequently reprinted it anonymously as "The Half-Breed," an "original novelette by a Brooklynite," in *The Brooklyn Daily Eagle,* June 1846, when he was editing that newspaper. In spite of his apparent pride in the story, it is as dull and pretentious an imitation of Fenimore Cooper as any high-school boy ever wrote. It may have been founded on some true anecdote which Whitman had heard, but there is scarcely an incident in it that has any near relation to reality. No character has any life. The plot is awkward and improbable. There is not an accent of sincerity in any line of it—from the "merry peals of laughter" among the "young elves" of school-children in the opening paragraph, down to the closing sentences in which one of the children (after the tragedy of the story has been concluded) becomes a "young political aspirant" for "a respectable legislative office"—quite irrelevantly and pathetically.

I doubt whether anyone can read these magazine contributions by Walter Whitman without concluding that he was not only a lazy young man but a stupid and insincere one. Here is a specimen of his writing when he is imitating Fenimore Cooper:

Just out from the village when the hunting party started that morning, they had been joined by Arrow-Tip's brother, the Deer. He, accompanied by a favorite dog, was watching the evolutions of a large bird that lazily skimmed near the surface of a cascade near by—a charming spot, that, were it in the neighborhood of our eastern cities, would be visited by thousands for its beauty. "Call the dog from me, brother," said the Deer, "he frightens the bird." Arrow-Tip did as he was desired. The party had passed on, bidding the two Indians to follow. And the chief sat himself down a moment, at the foot of a large tree, and waited till the successful aim of the Deer should bring the bird to the ground. One hand grasped his hunting-bow, and with the other he caressed the dog. The plot of the narrative makes it preferable not to detail minutely here all the events that took place during the day. One of these events—a startling and bloody one—has already been intimated to the reader, at the conclusion of the last chapter.

And here is a paragraph when he is imitating Poe:

And there is one, childlike, with helpless and unsteady movements, but a countenance of immortal bloom, whose long-lashed eyes droop downward. The name of the Shape is Dai. When he comes near, the angels are silent, and gaze upon him with pity and affection. And the fair eyes of the Shape roll, but fix upon no object; while his lips move, but in a plaintive tone only is heard the speaking of a single name. Wandering in the confines of earth, òr restlessly amid the streets of the beautiful land, goes Dai, earnestly calling on one he loves. Wherefore is there no response?

Although his more enthusiastic biographers exult that his contributions were printed in the same literary journals as the work of Hawthorne, Bryant, Longfellow, Lowell, Thoreau, Whittier, and Poe, it must be credited to the good taste of the magazine editors and readers of the period that Walter Whitman failed as a free-lance and returned to newspaper work. In 1846, he was editing the Booklyn *Eagle.* A number of his editorials are given in Emory Holloway's *Whitman,* and they deserve Bliss Perry's complaint, in his life of Whitman, that "the style is slovenly and the thought quite without distinction." In 1848, having lost his place on the *Eagle,* he was offered, as he says, "a good chance to go down to New Orleans on the staff of the *Crescent,* a daily to be started there with plenty of capital behind it, in opposition to the *Picayune.*" He went to the *Crescent* and worked for it for three months. Hollo-

way reprints several of his "easy-going, whimsical, sometimes puerile sketches" from the *Crescent* and concludes that he lost his position "possibly" because the proprietors saw "that his slovenly writing . . . would add distinction to no paper."

When he returned to Brooklyn he founded a free-soil journal, *The Brooklyn Daily Freeman,* and earned this contemporary notice: "Mr. Whitman is an ardent politician of the radical democratic school, and lately established the *Daily Freeman* in Brooklyn, to promulgate his favorite 'Free Soil' and other reformatory doctrines." He withdrew from the *Freeman* about a year later, and so ended his career as a newspaper man, for the time. In 1850, he wrote some articles anonymously for the New York *Advertiser* and the *Evening Post,* but they were chiefly critical articles on art and music. "I guess it was about those years," says his brother George, "he had an idea he could lecture. He wrote what mother calls barrels of lectures. We did not know what he was writing. He did not seem more abstracted than usual. He would lie abed late, and after getting up would write a few hours if he took the notion—perhaps would go off the rest of the day. We were all at work—all except Walt."

Only one of these lectures seems to have been delivered—a lecture before the art students of the Brooklyn Art Union, March 31, 1851. In his first paragraph, Walter Whitman turned his back on much of his past. "Among such a people as the Americans," he began, "viewing most things with an eye to pecuniary profit—more for acquiring than enjoying or well developing what they acquire—ambitious of the physical rather than the intellectual; a race to whom matter-of-fact is everything and the ideal nothing—a nation of whom the steam-engine is no bad symbol—he does a good work who, pausing in the way, calls to the feverish crowd that in the life we live upon this beautiful earth there may after all be something vaster and better than dress and the table, business and politics." To utter this call was "the glorious province of arts and of all artists worthy of the name." As an æsthete, contemptuous of dress and the table and business and politics, he reprobated the clothes of "fashionable tailordom"—the clothes which he had worn as editor of *The Aurora*—and especially "the fashionable hat, before which language has nothing to say because sight is the only thing that can begin to do it justice." And with characteristic sincerity, he included in his lecture, as Bliss Perry points out, "a description of the death-bed of Rousseau quite unwarranted by any historical evidence."

He had given up the costume of the *Aurora* editor and also the "neat frock coat" which he had worn as a schoolteacher. He had become progressively Bohemian in his attire as a free-lance writer. Now, suddenly, he began to dress in the rough clothes of a workingman, belted trousers, a shirt open at the neck to show his undershirt, high boots, and a soft felt hat. He had decided to become the Walt Whitman of the *Leaves of Grass,* and he went to work for his father, the carpenter, while he wrote his book.

If anyone doubts that this "Walt Whitman" was only a new alias for the Walter Whitman of *Franklin Evans* and the imitations of Poe and Cooper, I recommend him to read the anonymous reviews which Walter Whitman wrote of Walt Whitman's poems. One of the earliest of the series appeared in the Brooklyn *Times,* Sept. 29, 1855, some two months after the printing of the first edition of *Leaves of Grass.* He introduces himself, "Very devilish to some, and very divine to some, will appear the poet of these new poems, the *Leaves of Grass;* an attempt, as they are, of a naïve, masculine, affectionate, contemplative, sensual, imperious person, to cast into literature not only his own grit and arrogance, but his own flesh and form, undraped, regardless of models, regardless of modesty or law, and ignorant or silently scornful, as at first appears, of all except his own presence and experience, and all outside the fiercely loved land of his birth, and the birth of his parents, and their parents for several generations before him."

Can anybody imagine that the Walter Whitman who wrote that sentence was really the naïve, masculine, sensual, imperious, undraped, arrogant, and silently scornful person which Walt Whitman pretended to be? Is it possible that his advertisement of his devotion to "the fiercely loved land of his birth, and the birth of his parents, and their parents for several generations before him" arose out of a true patriotism and not out of a blurb-writer's desire to sell his volume to the hundred-per-centers of his day? Could Walter Whitman have been unaware of the sexual exhibitionism in his poems when he came out before his literary side-show to promise that if you paid the entrance fee you would see Walt Whitman, on the inside, "undraped," in "his own flesh and form," "regardless of modesty or law"?

Or consider the following sentence: "Of pure American breed, large and lusty—age thirty-six years—never once using medicine—never dressed in black, always dressed freshly and clean in strong clothes—neck open, shirt-collar flat and broad, countenance tawny transparent red, beard well-mottled with white, hair like hay after it has been mowed in the field and lies tossed and streaked—his physiology corroborating a rugged phrenology—a person singularly beloved and looked toward, especially by young men and the illiterate—one who has firm attachments here and associates there—one who does not associate with literary people—a man never called upon to make speeches at public dinners—never on platforms amid the crowds of clergymen, or professors, or aldermen, or congressmen—rather down in the bay with pilots in their pilot-boat—or off on a cruise with fishers in their fishing-smack—or riding on a Broadway omnibus, side by side with the driver—or with a band of loungers over the open grounds of the country —fond of New York and Brooklyn— fond of the life of the great ferries—one whom, if you should meet, you need not expect to meet an extraordinary person— one in whom you will see the singularity which consists in no singularity— whose contact is no dazzle or fascination, nor requires any deference, but has the easy fascination of what is homely and accustomed—as of something you knew before, and was waiting for— there you have Walt Whitman, the begetter of a new offspring out of literature, taking with easy nonchalance the chances of its present reception, and, through all misunderstandings and distrusts, the chances of its future reception—preferring always to speak for himself rather than have others speak for him."

And consider that the man who "never dressed in black" is the Walter Whitman of the frock coat, the high hat, and the boutonnière. He is the roughly clothed and rugged workingman "who does not associate with literary people." The Democratic politician of the *Freeman* and the public lecturer on art is "never on platforms amid the crowds of clergymen, or professors, or aldermen, or congressmen." This anxious barker for his own book is "taking with easy nonchalance the chances of its present reception," "preferring always to speak for himself"—in his poems, of course— "rather than have others speak for him," as his anonymous reviewer is supposed to be speaking.

He continues, in his false whiskers, to advertise his Walt: "A rude child of the people!—No imitation—No foreigner— but a growth and idiom of America. Not discontented—a careless slouch, enjoying to-day. No dilettante democrat— a man who is art-and-part with the commonalty, and with immediate life— loves the streets—loves the docks—loves the free rasping talk of men—likes to be called by his given name, and nobody at all need Mr. him—can laugh with laughers—likes the ungenteel ways of laborers—is not prejudiced one mite against the Irish—talks readily with them—talks readily with niggers—does not make a stand on being a gentleman, nor on learning nor manners"—and so on, down to the end of the paragraph: "You may feel the unconscious teaching of a fine brute, but you will never feel the artificial teaching of a fine writer or speaker."

In other words, the dilettante democrat, Walter Whitman, announces that he is now nothing of the sort; that he is a "careless slouch"; that he is no longer "a fine writer or speaker" but "a fine brute" who is "unconscious" of the teaching of which he is here so conscious. He is such an astonishing radical that he even "likes the ungenteel ways of laborers," and he feels so little prejudice against the Irish that he "talks readily with them." Most miraculous of all, he now likes to be called by his given name "and nobody at all need Mr. him." And this last is a proof of his utter democracy which he repeats with unction in his later self-advertisements.

He ballyhooed himself, anonymously, in the *American Phrenological Journal* as the "haughtiest of writers that has ever yet written and printed a book." And in the *United States and Democratic Review,* for the same month of September, 1855, he hailed himself, anonymously, as "One of the roughs, large, proud, affectionate, eating, drinking and breeding, his costume manly and free, his face sunburnt and bearded, his postures strong and erect." No longer the fashionable gentleman of great culture, he announced, rather incoherently: "self-restraint, with haughty eyes, assuming to himself all the attributes of his country, steps Walt Whitman into literature, talking like a man unaware that there was ever hitherto such a production as a book, or such a being as a writer." As if he were afraid that some contemporary Comstock might fail to advertise his poems by attempting to suppress them, he goes on: "Nature he proclaims inherently clean. Sex will not be put aside; it is the great ordination of the universe. He works the muscle of the male and the teeming fibre of the female, throughout his writings, as wholesome realities, impure only by deliberate intention and effort. . . . If health were not his distinguishing attribute, this poet would be the very harlot of persons. Right and left he flings his arms, drawing men and women with undeniable love to his close embrace, loving the clasp of their hands, the touch of their necks and breasts,

and the sound of their voices. All else seems to burn up under his fierce affection for persons." And he printed these three personal advertisements of himself as favorable press notices in the second edition of his poems.

As late as 1876, he was still writing of himself, anonymously: "This Walt Whitman—this queer one whom most of us have watched, with more or less amusement, walking by—this goer and comer, for years, about New York and Washington—good natured with everybody, like some farmer, or mate of some coasting vessel, familiarly accosted by all, hardly any one of us stopping to Mr. him—this man of many characters, among the rest that of volunteer help in the army hospitals and on the field during the whole of the late war, carefully tending all the wounded he could, southern or northern—if it should turn out that in this plain unsuspected old customer, dressed in gray & wearing no necktie, America and her republican institutions are possessing that *rara avis* a real national poet, chanting, putting in form, in her own proud spirit, in first-class style, for present and future time, her democratic shapes even as the bards of Judah put in song, for all time to come, the Hebrew spirit, and Homer the war-life of prehistoric Greece, and Shakespeare the feudal shapes of Europe's kings and lords!"

But perhaps his most extraordinary effort in establishing his alias is the one reported by Fred P. Hill, Jr., in the *American Mercury* of June 1924. Here it appears that Whitman wrote the greater part of the volume *Notes on Walt Whitman* by John Burroughs, published in 1867 as Burroughs' first book and since dropped from the list of his collected works. The style is clearly Whitman's; and Burroughs, shortly before his death, admitted in a letter to Hill that about one-half the book was written by Whitman and that the whole volume had been edited and revised by Whitman. The personal sketch of Whitman was supplied by Whitman himself. It is in the same tone as his anonymous reviews. "There probably lives not another man," he writes of himself, "so genuinely and utterly indifferent to literary abuse or to 'public opinion,' either when favorable or unfavorable. He has never used the usual means to defend his reputation." He describes himself as "seeking not the least conquest or display," but as "making the impression on any unsuspecting stranger of a good-willed, healthy character, without the least ostensible mark of the philosopher or poet; but all the while, though thus passive and receptive, yet evidently the most masculine of beings." And so forth, to the same end as always—to the end of having Burroughs, like the anonymous newspaper reviewers, certify to the truth of the pose which he had assumed in his poetry.

Obviously, Walter Whitman was no such person as he thus proclaimed himself to be. He could not be truly such a person and be aware of it. But what was he? What was the real Walter Whitman who adopted this alias of Walt Whitman, and put on this disguise of the "careless slouch," and pretended to all this rough and rugged democracy and sensuality and haughty-eyed contempt?

The answer is written plainly enough in every real biography of him that I have ever seen, as well as by implication in his poems. He was neither sensual, nor rough and rugged, nor truly healthy, nor lusty, nor even very masculine. He was what is nowadays called a Narcissan, in love with himself, introverted, and so wrapped up in his own ego that he got no free delivery of energy except in his exhibitionism. Hence his constitutional laziness. He was arrested in his sexual development very near the homosexual level, as several of his poems show; and like many another case of arrested development he was always "a man's man." He speaks of the "fiercely loved land of his birth" in one of his anonymous blurbs, and in another he assumes "to himself all the attributes of his country"; but when the Civil War broke out on April 12, 1861, he disappeared for eighteen months from the sight of his biographers; and the only entry in his notebook, for that period, is the following, dated April 16, 1861, four days after the beginning of hostilities: "I have this day, this hour, resolved to inaugurate for myself a pure, perfect, sweet, clean-blooded robust body, by ignoring all drinks but water and pure milk, and all fat meats, late suppers—a great body, a purged, cleansed, spiritualized, invigorated body."

This is not the vow of a patriot worrying about the fiercely-loved land of his birth. It is the resolve of a Narcissan thinking only of his fiercely-loved physique. Here is the impulse which dressed him up as a fashionable gentleman of great culture during one phase of his life, and as a rough and rugged workman during another period, and finally as the conspicuous "good, gray poet" in gray cape and wide-awake during his later years. This is the impulse that made him begin his *Leaves of Grass* with the line "I celebrate myself." It is the impulse that drove him to celebrate himself in his "own flesh and form, undraped, regardless of modesty or law." The same impulse moves humorously in a letter to two friends, written from Washington during the war, on March 19, 1863: "My health, strength, personal beauty, etc., are, I am happy to inform you, without diminution, but on the contrary quite the reverse. I weigh full 220 pounds avoirdupois, yet still retain my usual perfect shape—a regular model." It is an impulse to exhibitionism that is neither sensual nor healthy, but morbid, introverted, and very near perversion.

Narcissism is apparently produced by an adoring mother in a mother-fixated boy. Whitman loved his mother "with a sort of mariolatry" as Holloway says. He broke down, during her final illness, with a partial paralysis. At the age of fifty-six, he wrote of himself, "I occupy myself, arranging these pages for publication, still enveloped in thoughts of the death, two years since, of my dear Mother, the most perfect and magnetic character, the rarest combination of practical, moral and spiritual, and the least selfish of all and any I have ever known—and by me O so much the most deeply loved." He never married. As a young school-teacher he was "diffident with women." One of his pupils records, "The girls did not attract him. He did not especially go anywhere with them or show any extra fondness for their society. Before and after school, he was a boy among boys." A few years later, at the age of about twenty, as the editor of *The Long Islander,* he wrote of himself, "I would carefully avoid saying anything of women; because it behooves a modest personage like myself not to speak upon a class of beings whose nature, habits, notions and ways he has not been able to gather any knowledge, either by experience or observation." During his mature years in Washington, from the age of forty-

seven to fifty-four, his most intimate companion was a young street-car conductor named Peter Doyle; and Doyle has said of him, "I never knew a case of Walt's being bothered up by a woman. Woman in that sense never entered his head. Walt was too clean. No trace of any kind of dissipation in him. I ought to know about him those years— we were awful close together."

The appearance of sensuality in Whitman's verse—and in his ballyhoos—is good evidence to a modern psychiatrist that Whitman never experienced the dissoluteness which he celebrates. The sexuality in his poems is a compensation, in phantasy, for his lack of potency in experience. Much of this sexual expression is dangerously near the homosexual level—which is to be expected where the sexual impulse is anchored by a mother-fixation and unable to achieve a heterosexual goal.

When an English critic, J. A. Symonds, read the homosexual poems in "Calamus," he wrote to ask Whitman the truth about himself, and Whitman, at the age of seventy-two, replied: "My life, young manhood, mid-age, times South, etc., have been jolly bodily and doubtless open to criticism. Though unmarried, I have had six children—two are dead—one living Southern grandchild, fine boy, writes to me occasionally —circumstance (connected with their fortune and benefit) have separated me from intimate relations." But that statement, written to allay the suspicion of homosexuality, is no more to be trusted than Whitman's anonymous advertisement of himself as "a lusty breeder." He wrote of himself, by the hand of John Burroughs, in Burroughs' *Notes on Walt Whitman:* "Throughout this period (1840-1855) without entering into particulars, it is enough to say that he sounded all experiences of life, with all their passions, pleasures, and abandonments. He was young, in perfect bodily condition, and had the city of New York and its ample opportunities around him. I trace this period in some of the poems of 'Children of Adam' and occasionally in other parts of his book, including 'Calamus.'" But this testimony from John Burroughs has now been wiped out by Burroughs' own confession that Whitman wrote it. He and Whitman did not meet until 1861 in Washington, and Burroughs knew nothing of Whitman's life in the years 1840-1855, except what Whitman told him.

The truth in all this elaborate deception about "passions, pleasures, and abandonments" seems to be—as Holloway suggests in his *Whitman* — that Walter Whitman, in 1848, had some sort of love-affair in New Orleans "with a Creole octoroon," when he was working on the New Orleans *Crescent*. And it also seems probable that he ran away from that affair and never had another. Horace Traubel says, "During Walt's last sickness his grandson came to the house. I was not there at the time. When Whitman mentioned the occurrence to me, I expressed the regret that I had missed him. 'I wish I might see him.' 'God forbid!' said Whitman." Henry Bryan Binns in his *Life of Whitman* supposes that the lady in New Orleans "was of higher social rank than his own—a lady of the South where social rank is of the first consideration." And Binns asks, "Why did he leave her? Why did he allow the foulest of reproaches to blacken that whitest of reputations, a Southern lady's virtue?" The answer might seem to be that perhaps the lady was not so white as all that. And Whitman's "God forbid!" to

Traubel may mean that the grandson, if he really existed at all, was also somewhat colored.

No one ever saw that grandson, or any of the "six children," or any woman with whom Walt Whitman appeared to be having a love-affair. In his relations with the women who were emotionally attracted by him—like Mrs. Gilchrist, Mrs. Berenson, and his housekeeper, Mrs. Davis—he was coolly affectionate and detached. Says Perry, "A daily companion of Whitman in Washington tells me that he never heard him utter a word that could not have been used to his mother. There is overwhelming testimony that for thirty years thereafter his conversation, though often blunt enough, was scrupulously chaste. There is also abundant evidence that from 1862 onward his life was stainless so far as sexual relations were concerned." I do not see how anyone can doubt that previous to 1862 it had been equally "stainless," except for his adventure in New Orleans. I see no evidence that he ever gave way to "passions, pleasures, and abandonments." I do not believe his story that he wrote *Franklin Evans* on gin cocktails from the "Pewter Mug." Just previous to the period of 1840-1855, "he neither smoked nor drank nor swore," says Binns. And the impulse under which he wrote *Franklin Evans* was the same impulse that made him take the glass of white wine out of the hands of the dying mutineer and let him drink to the salvation of his soul in a glass of water. Any form of dissipation is a danger to the "pure, perfect, sweet, clean-blooded, robust body" of a Narcissan. And any real "abandonment" to love is impossible for the introvert who is in love with himself.

There remains to consider Whitman's pose as the true poet of democracy, "chanting, putting in form, in her own proud spirit, in first class style, for present & future time, her democratic shapes." And, in the first place, one must admit that, from his earliest days, Walter Whitman was a militant democrat in the sense that he was opposed to aristocracy, class rule, slavery, blue laws, or anything else that threatened or interfered with the freedom of the common American. As a newspaper man and a free-lance writer, he did valiant service in the paper wars that were fought for liberty and the free-soil doctrines before the firing on Fort Sumter. It is no disparagement of this service to point out that it was inspired by his own colossal egotism. He was an advocate of freedom and equality because it was necessary for him to feel himself the equal in freedom of any man. "I never yet knew," he wrote in his notes, "how it felt to think I stood in the presence of my superior." And in describing the "true, noble, expanded American character" he wrote, "It is to be illimitably proud, independent, self-possessed, generous and gentle. It is to accept nothing except what is equally free and eligible to anybody else. It is to be poor rather than rich—but to prefer death rather than any mean dependence."

But with his failure as an editor, a free-lance writer, an art critic, and a lecturer, he receded into a purer egotism than ever—and he accepted financial dependence, at least, without any apparent qualms. Encouraged by his reading of Emerson's famous address, "The American Scholar"—America's "intellectual Declaration of Independence," as Oliver Wendell Holmes has called it—he undertook to be a new sort of poet, the poet of the New World,

"with the feeling or ambition," as he wrote, "to articulate and faithfully express in literary or poetic form, and uncompromisingly, my own physical, emotional, moral, intellectual, and æsthetic Personality, in the midst of, and tallying, the momentous spirit and facts of its immediate days, and of current America—and to exploit that personality, identified with place and date, in a far more comprehensive sense than any hitherto poem or book." That is to say, instead of any longer identifying himself with his country and expressing its aspirations, he was now to identify his country with himself, "assuming to himself all its attributes," and expressing his own ego as "tallying the momentous spirit" of "current America."

He turned his back, at once, on the economic aspirations of the democracy. In the preface to the first edition of his poems, he wrote, "Beyond the independence of a little sum laid aside for burial money, and of a few clapboards around and shingles overhead on a lot of American soil owned, and the easy dollars that supply the year's plain clothing and meals, the melancholy prudence of the abandonment of such a great being as man is, to the toil and pallor of years of money-making, with all their scorching days and icy nights and all their stifling deceits and underhand dodging, or infinitesimals of parlors and shameless stuffing while others starve . . . and the issuing sickness and desperate revolt of a life without elevation of naïveté, and the ghastly chatter of a death without serenity or majesty, is the great fraud upon modern civilization." The average American, he declared, cheated by that fraud, suffered "all the loss of the bloom and odor of the earth and of the taste of women and men you pass or have to do with in youth or middle age." And Walt Whitman was to sing, rather, a sort of hobo democracy of the Open Road.

Being himself far from normal, he gave voice to few of the normal emotions of America. "The home, the fireside, the domestic allurements are not in him," says John Burroughs. "Love, as we find it in other poets, is not in him." They are not in his poetry and they were not in him. He neither felt them, appreciated them, nor understood them. What he chiefly voiced was his own egotism—swollen to the dimensions of his country—his own morbidity, his own introversion. These are not typically American nor democratic, and the democracy has never accepted him.

1929

DEEMS TAYLOR

The Monster

HE WAS an undersized little man, with a head too big for his body—a sickly little man. His nerves were bad. He had skin trouble. It was agony for him to wear anything next to his skin coarser than silk. And he had delusions of grandeur.

He was a monster of conceit. Never for one minute did he look at the world or at people, except in relation to himself. He was not only the most important person in the world, to himself; in his own eyes he was the only person who existed. He believed himself to be one of the greatest dramatists in the world, one of the greatest thinkers, and one of the greatest composers. To hear him talk, he was Shakespeare, Beethoven, and Plato, rolled into one. And you would have had no difficulty in hearing him talk. He was one of the most exhausting conversationalists who ever lived. An evening with him was an evening spent in listening to a monologue. Sometimes he was brilliant; sometimes he was maddeningly tiresome. But whether he was being brilliant or dull, he had one sole topic of conversation: *himself*. What *he* thought and what *he* did.

He had a mania for being in the right. The slightest hint of disagreement, from anyone, on the most trivial point, was enough to set him off on a harangue that might last for hours, in which he proved himself right in so many ways, and with such exhausting volubility, that in the end his hearer, stunned and deafened, would agree with him, for the sake of peace.

It never occurred to him that he and his doing were not of the most intense and fascinating interest to anyone with whom he came in contact. He had theories about almost any subject under the sun, including vegetarianism, the drama, politics, and music; and in support of these theories he wrote pamphlets, letters, books . . . thousands upon thousands of words, hundreds and hun-

Reprinted from *Of Men and Music* by permission of Simon and Schuster, Inc. Copyright, 1937, by Deems Taylor.

dreds of pages. He not only wrote these things, and published them—usually at somebody else's expense—but he would sit and read them aloud, for hours, to his friends and his family.

He wrote operas; and no sooner did he have the synopsis of a story, than he would invite—or rather summon—a crowd of his friends to his house and read it aloud to them. Not for criticism. For applause. When the complete poem was written, the friends had to come again, and hear *that* read aloud. Then he would publish the poem, sometimes years before the music that went with it was written. He played the piano like a composer, in the worst sense of what that implies, and he would sit down at the piano before parties that included some of the finest pianists of his time, and play for them, by the hour, his own music, needless to say. He had a composer's voice. And he would invite eminent vocalists to his house, and sing them his operas, taking all the parts.

He had the emotional stability of a six-year-old child. When he felt out of sorts, he would rave and stamp, or sink into suicidal gloom and talk darkly of going to the East to end his days as a Buddhist monk. Ten minutes later, when something pleased him, he would rush out of doors and run around the garden, or jump up and down on the sofa, or stand on his head. He could be grief-stricken over the death of a pet dog, and he could be callous and heartless to a degree that would have made a Roman emperor shudder.

He was almost innocent of any sense of responsibility. Not only did he seem incapable of supporting himself, but it never occurred to him that he was under any obligation to do so. He was convinced that the world owed him a living. In support of this belief, he borrowed money from everybody who was good for a loan—men, women, friends, or strangers. He wrote begging letters by the score, sometimes groveling without shame, at others loftily offering his intended benefactor the privilege of contributing to his support, and being mortally offended if the recipient declined the honor. I have found no record of his ever paying or repaying money to anyone who did not have a legal claim upon it.

What money he could lay his hands on he spent like an Indian rajah. The mere prospect of a performance of one of his operas was enough to set him to running up bills amounting to ten times the amount of his prospective royalties. On an income that would reduce a more scrupulous man to doing his own laundry, he would keep two servants. Without enough money in his pocket to pay his rent, he would have the walls and ceiling of his study lined with pink silk. No one will ever know—certainly he never knew—how much money he owed. We do know that his greatest benefactor gave him $6,000 to pay the most pressing of his debts in one city, and a year later had to give him $16,000 to enable him to live in another city without being thrown into jail for debt.

He was equally unscrupulous in other ways. An endless procession of women marches through his life. His first wife spent twenty years enduring and forgiving his infidelities. His second wife had been the wife of his most devoted friend and admirer, from whom he stole her. And even while he was trying to persuade her to leave her first husband he was writing to a friend to inquire whether he could suggest some wealthy woman—*any* wealthy woman—whom he could marry for her money.

He was completely selfish in his other personal relationships. His liking for his friends was measured solely by the completeness of their devotion to him, or by their usefulness to him whether financial or artistic. The minute they failed him—even by so much as refusing a dinner invitation—or began to lessen in usefulness, he cast them off without a second thought. At the end of his life he had exactly one friend left whom he had known even in middle age.

He had a genius for making enemies. He would insult a man who disagreed with him about the weather. He would pull endless wires in order to meet some man who admired his work, and was able and anxious to be of use to him—and would proceed to make a mortal enemy of him with some idiotic and wholly uncalled-for exhibition of arrogance and bad manners. A character in one of his operas was a caricature of one of the most powerful music critics of his day. Not content with burlesquing him, he invited the critic to his house and read him the libretto aloud in front of his friends.

The name of this monster was Richard Wagner. Everything that I have said about him you can find on record—in newspapers, in police reports, in the testimony of people who knew him, in his own letters, between the lines of his autobiography. And the curious thing about this record is that it doesn't matter in the least.

Because this undersized, sickly, disagreeable, fascinating little man was right all the time. The joke was on us. He *was* one of the world's great dramatists; he *was* a great thinker; he *was* one of the most stupendous musical geniuses that, up to now, the world has ever seen. The world did owe him a living.

People couldn't know those things at the time, I suppose; and yet to us, who know his music, it does seem as though they should have known. What if he did talk about himself all the time? If he had talked about himself for twenty-four hours every day for the span of his life, he would not have uttered half the number of words that other men have spoken and written about him since his death.

When you consider what he wrote—thirteen operas and music dramas, eleven of them still holding the stage, eight of them unquestionably worth ranking among the world's great musico-dramatic masterpieces—when you listen to what he wrote, the debts and heartaches that people had to endure from him do not seem much of a price. Eduard Hanslick, the critic whom he caricatured in *Die Meistersinger* and who hated him ever after, now lives only because he was caricatured in *Die Meistersinger*. The women whose hearts he broke are long since dead; and the man who could never love anyone but himself has made them deathless atonement, I think, with *Tristan und Isolde*. Think of the luxury with which for a time, at least, fate rewarded Napoleon, the man who ruined France and looted Europe; and then perhaps you will agree that a few thousand dollars' worth of debts were not too heavy a price to pay for the *Ring* trilogy.

What if he was faithless to his friends and to his wives? He had one mistress to whom he was faithful to the day of his death: Music. Not for a single moment did he ever compromise with what he believed, with what he dreamed. There is not a line of his music that could have been conceived by a little mind. Even when he is dull, or downright bad, he is dull in the grand manner. There is greatness about his worst mistakes. Listening to his music, one does not forgive him for what he may or may not have been. It is not a matter of forgiveness. It is a matter of being dumb with wonder that his poor brain and body didn't burst under the torment of the demon of creative energy that lived inside him, struggling, clawing, scratching to be released; tearing, shrieking at him to write the music that was in him. The miracle is that what he did in the little space of seventy years could have been done at all, even by a great genius. Is it any wonder that he had no time to be a man?

1937

―――――――――――――――

EDITORS OF TIME

In Egypt Land

Go tell it on the mountain,
Over the hills and everywheah;
Go tell it on the mountain,
That Jesus Christ is aborn.

At Salzburg, backdropped by magical mountains, where Austria's great musical festivals were held before the war, and where he first heard Marian Anderson sing, Arturo Toscanini cried: "Yours is a voice such as one hears once in a hundred years."

Toscanini was hailing a great artist, but that voice was more than a magnificent personal talent. It was the religious voice of a whole religious people —probably the most God-obsessed (and man-despised) people since the ancient Hebrews.

White Americans had withheld from Negro Americans practically everything but God. In return the Negroes had enriched American culture with an incomparable religious poetry and music, and its only truly great religious art —the spiritual.

This religious and esthetic achievement of Negro Americans has found profound expression in Marian Anderson. She is not only the world's greatest contralto and one of the very great voices of all time, she is also a dedicated character, devoutly simple, calm, religious. Manifest in the tranquil architecture of her face is her constant submission to the "Spirit, that dost prefer before all temples the upright heart and pure."

Up from Philadelphia. Thanks to the ostracism into which they are born, Negro Americans live very deeply to themselves. They look out upon, and shrewdly observe, the life around them, are rarely observed by it. They are not evasive about their lives; many are simply incapable of discussing them.

The known facts about Marian Anderson's personal life are few. She was born (in Philadelphia) some 40 years ago (she will not tell her age). Her mother had been a schoolteacher in Virginia. Her father was a coal & ice dealer. There were two younger sisters.

When she was twelve, her father died.

Reprinted from *Time*, December 30, 1946. Courtesy of *Time*, copyright, Time Inc., 1946.

To keep the home together, Mrs. Anderson went to work. Miss Anderson says that the happiest moment of her life came the day that she was able to tell her mother to stop working. Later she bought her mother a two-story brick house on Philadelphia's South Martin Street. She bought the house next door for one of her sisters.

Miss Anderson's childhood seems to have been as untroubled as is possible to Negro Americans. In part, this was due to the circumstances of her birth, family, and natural gift. In part, it was due to the calm with which she surmounts all unpleasantness. If there were shadows, she never mentions them. Perhaps the most characteristic fact about her childhood is that Marian disliked bright colors and gay dresses as much as her sisters loved them.

Shortly after her father's death, Marian Anderson was "converted." Her mother is a Methodist. But Marian was converted in her father's Union Baptist Church, largely because the late Rev. Wesley G. Parks was deeply interested in music, loved his choirs and encouraged any outstanding singer in them. At 13, Marian was singing in the church's adult choir. She took home the scores, and sang all the parts (soprano, alto, tenor, bass) over & over to her family until she had learned them. Since work is also a religion to her, Miss Anderson considers this one of the most important experiences of her life. She could then sing high C like a soprano.

At 15, she took her first formal music lesson. At 16, she gave her first important concert, at a Negro school in Atlanta. From then on, her life almost ceases to be personal. It is an individual achievement, but, as with every Negro, it is inseparable from the general achievement of her people. It was the congregation of the Union Baptist Church that gave Miss Anderson her start. Then a group of interested music lovers gave a concert at her church, collected about $500 to pay for training her voice under the late Philadelphia singing teacher, Giuseppe Boghetti.

In 1924 she won the New York Stadium contest (prize: the right to appear with the New York Symphony Orchestra). In 1930, she decided that she must study in Germany. When she had perfected her lieder, songs by Schubert, Brahms, Wolf, she gave her first concert on the Continent. It cost her $500 (the Germans explained that it was customary for Americans to pay for their own concerts). She never paid again.

Applause followed her through Norway and Sweden. In Finland, Composer Jean Sibelius offered her coffee, but after hearing her sing, cried: "Champagne!" In Paris, her first house was "papered." From her second concert, enthusiasts were turned away in droves. She swept through South America.

THE TROUBLE I'VE SEEN. In the U.S. the ovation continued. Only one notably ugly incident marred her triumph. In Washington, the management of Constitution Hall, owned by the Daughters of the American Revolution, announced that it would be unable to lease the hall on the date which Sol Hurok, Miss Anderson's manager, had asked for. The refusal resulted in Eleanor Roosevelt's resignation from the D.A.R. and an enormous ground swell of sympathy for Miss Anderson and her people. Miss Anderson, who has carefully kept herself and her art from being used for political purposes, said nothing.

But Washington heard her. She sang, first in the open air in front of the Lincoln Memorial. Later the D.A.R. leased her Constitution Hall, and she sang to a brilliant white and Negro audience. She had insisted only that there should be no segregation in the seating. Nobody knows the trouble that an incident like this one causes to a spirit like Marian Anderson's. No doubt such things are in her mind when she says, with typical understatement: "Religion, the treasure of religion helps one, I think, to face the difficulties one sometimes meets."

For this greatly gifted American, pouring out the riches of her art to houses that are sold out weeks in advance, could not for a long time travel about her country like her fellow citizens. She has given concerts in the South, where her voice is greatly admired (and where she avoids Jim Crow by traveling in drawing rooms on night trains). Even in the North, she could not until fairly recently stay at most good hotels. In the South, she must still stay with friends. In New York City, she used to leave frantically applauding audiences to sleep at the Harlem Y.W.C.A. Then Manhattan's Hotel Algonquin, longtime rendezvous of U.S. literati, received her. Now most other Northern hotels have also opened their doors.

Usually, Miss Anderson travels with six pieces of luggage, one of which contains her electric iron (she presses her own gowns before a concert), and cooking utensils (she likes to prepare snacks for herself and she has had some unpleasant experiences with hotel dining rooms).

AGRARIAN PROBLEMS. In 1943 Miss Anderson married Orpheus Fisher, an architect who works in Danbury, Conn.

Now they live, not far from Danbury, on a beautiful, 105-acre farm, "Marianna." Inside, the handsome, white frame, hillside house has been remodeled by Architect Fisher. He also designed the big, good-looking studio in which Miss Anderson practices.

When not on tour or practicing, Miss Anderson dabbles in farming. She sells grade-A vegetables to the local market, regrets that Marianna, like many farms run by hired help, costs more than it brings in. And there are other problems in the agrarian life. This year, Miss Anderson was much puzzled when the big (but unbred) daughter of her registered Guernsey cow did not give milk. "Heifers have to be freshened before you can milk them," she explains with some astonishment. "Did you know that?"

The question measures the very real distance she has traveled from the peasant roots of her people. But, as she has traveled, she has taken to new heights the best that Negro Americans are. For the Deep River of her life and theirs runs in the same religious channel. In her life, as in the spiritual, the Big Wheel moves by faith. With a naturalness impossible to most people, she says: "I do a good deal of praying."

GIFT FROM GOD. For to her, her voice is directly a gift from God, her singing a religious experience. This is true of all her singing (she is preeminently a singer of classical music). It is especially true of her singing of Negro spirituals. She does not sing many, and only those which she feels are suited to her voice or which, like *Crucifixion,* her favorite, move her deeply.

There are lovers of spirituals who do not care for the highly arranged versions that Miss Anderson sings, or the finished artistry with which she sings them. But if something has been lost in freshness and authenticity, much has been gained by the assimilation of these great religious songs to the body of great music. For they are the soul of the Negro people, and she has taken that soul as far as art can take it.

As the thousands who have heard her can testify, Miss Anderson's singing of spirituals is unforgettable. She stands simply, but with impressive presence, beside the piano. She closes her eyes (she always sings with her eyes closed). Her voice pours out, soft, vast, enveloping:

> *They crucified my Lord,*
> *An' He never said a mumblin' word;*
> *They crucified my Lord,*
> *An' He never said a mumblin' word.*
> *Not a word, not a word, not a word.*
>
> *They pierced Him in the side,*
> *An' He never said a mumblin' word;*
> *They pierced Him in the side,*
> *An' He never said a mumblin' word.*
> *Not a word, not a word, not a word.*
>
> *He bowed His head an' died,*
> *An' He never said a mumblin' word;*
> *He bowed His head an' died,*
> *An' He never said a mumblin' word.*
> *Not a word, not a word, not a word.*

Audiences who have heard Miss Anderson sing *Crucifixion* have sometimes been too awed to applaud. They have sensed that they are participants in an act of creation—the moment at which religion informs art, and makes it greater than itself.

BIRTH OF THE SOUL. The theme of the greatest music is always the birth of the soul. Words can describe, painting can suggest, but music alone enables the listener to participate, beyond conscious thought, in this act. Beethoven's *Violin Concerto* is a work secular beyond question. But when, in the first movement, the simple theme subtly changes, the mind is lifted and rent—not because the strings have zipped to another key, but by a tone of divinity conveyed through the composer's growing deafness by an inspiration inexplicable to the mind. The spirituals are perhaps the greatest single burst of such inspiration, communicated, not through deafness, but through the darkness of minds which knew nothing of formal music and very little of the language they were singing.

Professional musicians and musicologists are still locked in hot debate about the musical origins of the spirituals and the manner of their creation. One simple fact is clear—they were created in direct answer to the Psalmist's question: *How shall we sing the Lord's song in a strange land?* For the land in which the slaves found themselves was strange beyond the fact that it was foreign. It was a nocturnal land of vast, shadowy pine woods, vast fields of cotton whose endless rows converged sometimes on a solitary cabin, vast swamps reptilian and furtive—a land alive with all the elements of lonely beauty, except compassion. In this deep night of land and man, the singers saw visions; grief, like a tuning fork, gave the tone, and the Sorrow Songs were uttered.

Perhaps, in little unpainted churches or in turpentine clearings, the preacher, who soon became the pastor and social leader of his wretched people, gave the lead:

> *Way over yonder in the harvest fiel'—*

The flock caught the vision too:

> *Way up in the middle of the air,*
> *The angel shovin' at the chariot wheel,*

Way up in the middle of the air.
O, yes, Ezekiel saw the wheel,
Way up in the middle of the air,
Ezekiel saw the wheel,
Up in the middle of the air.
The Big Wheel moved by faith,
The Little Wheel moved by the grace of
  God,
A wheel in a wheel,
Up in the middle of the air.

Soughing Wind. It was a theological image splendid beyond any ever conceived on this continent. For a great wind of the spirit soughed through the night of slavery and, as in Ezekiel's vision, on the field of dead hope the dry bones stirred with life.

They kept stirring as, through the dismal years, the great hymnal testimonies moaned forth. Sometimes they were lyric visions of deliverance:

Swing low, sweet chariot,
Comin' for to carry me home;
I look'd over Jordan,

And what did I see,
Comin' for to carry me home,
A band of angels comin' after me,
Comin' for to carry me home.

Sometimes they were statements of bottomless sorrow:

Nobody knows de trouble I've seen,
Nobody knows but Jesus.

Sometimes they were rumbling adjurations:

Go down, Moses,
Way down in Egypt land,
Tell ol' Pharaoh
To let my people go.

Sometimes they were simple longings:

Deep River, my home is over Jordan,
Deep River, Lord,
I want to cross over into camp ground.
                                        1946

GAMALIEL BRADFORD

God's Vagabond: Saint Francis of Assisi

In this developing twentieth century the immediate world of space and time has become so ample, so rich, so varied, in its hurrying, crowding luxury of interest and splendor, that it seems to absorb and engross us altogether, especially as the sense of any other world has grown more and more obscure and dim. It is, then, surely curious and perhaps profitable to turn back seven hundred years to a man like Francis of Assisi, to whom the things of the other world, eternal things, were so vivid and so real that he literally cast the joy and the splendor and the glory of this world under his feet and trod them in the dust.

Francis Bernardone, born about 1182, was the son of a well-to-do traveling merchant of Assisi. He was

The selection from Gamaliel Bradford, *Saints and Sinners* is used by permission of the publishers, Houghton Mifflin Company.

brought up in ease and luxury and seemed at first disposed to dissipation and riotous companionship. But he had a tender heart and a vivid imagination. These things soon made him sensitive to human misery, and above all keenly alive to the injustice of his having the good things of the world while so many others were wholly without them. Since his mind was as logical as his heart was sympathetic, the next step was to discard his own advantages utterly, and to stride right out into the empty world with the spirit of Christ as his only possession. Rich in this, he preached Christ, he practiced Christ, he lived Christ, and with the aid of the Church and of those in authority, he established an order of followers, whom he sent out from his little chapel in Assisi to preach the gospel as he saw it, all over the world. He himself, after two unsuccessful attempts, got as far as the Orient, in 1219, in the track of the Crusaders, and preached the gospel to the heathen and even to the Sultan, though without converting him or attaining the ideal of martyrdom which seemed so desirable. When Francis returned to Italy, the aura of sainthood had already gathered about him, and his death in 1226 is enveloped in the usual cloud of unprofitable miracles, culminating in the mysterious Stigmata, or impress of Christ's wounds upon the saint's body, a cloud of myth and legend from which it is almost as difficult to disentangle the real man as in the case of Jesus himself. Yet Francis, like Jesus, was so vividly and intensely human that even the adoration of seven centuries is not enough to obscure him entirely.

The first principle of Francis's religion was that of absolute, complete, uncompromising poverty. It seemed to him that not only the possession of money, but the desire for money and what it brings, was the root of all evil. And it is difficult not to agree with him that if you could get rid of that desire, most social and economic evils would settle themselves. Modern society, all human society, is composed of a few people who have a great deal, and who incidentally always want more than they have, and a vast number who violently, passionately want what belongs to, or, at any rate, is in the possession of, the others. If you could once thoroughly eradicate the fatal wanting, all the economic problems would be settled. Get rid of it, want nothing but Christ, said Francis. Seven hundred years later Tolstoy adopted much the same attitude. But Tolstoy hardly attempted to get beyond this world, while Francis had the immense compensating possibilities of the other world to support him. Naturally the abolition of wanting involves all sorts of contradictions and inconsistencies. Life would appear to be wanting and the abolition of wanting would come perilously close to death. Furthermore, if nobody has anything, who is to give to others, and how is the world to go on? But Francis had a practical and concrete mind. He did not foresee the slightest danger that the world in general would adopt his principles, and if it did, the world must take care of itself. He saw what was right for him, and he was going to do it, if the heavens fell.

When I was twenty and was engaged to be married, my love and I came to see the world for the time something as Saint Francis saw it. We, too, felt that we should give up luxury and wanting, should discard the comforting equipment of material life, to which we were accustomed, but of which so many millions were destitute, and adopt voluntary poverty for the good of the world and our own souls. As a letter of that time expresses it: 'We should give up everything, live not only simply, but in poverty, with the poorest of clothes and the simplest of food, giving up everything material, everything tending to outward things, not because we want to be ascetic, but because we will have nothing to draw us from the life within and because we want to set an example of forgetting all the luxuries and comforts of the body. We want to build a little house somewhere, perfectly plain and poor, and live there in every way just as peasants would live.'

We were twenty, and simple, and foolish. Our parents and relatives and friends ridiculed us and scolded us and reasoned with us, and in the end forced us to let our ideals go—for better, for worse?—I wonder. The only point of importance is that Francis of Assisi did not let his ideals go; he let father and mother and home and wealth and friends all go hang, and followed God. When his father argued with him and bullied him and finally dragged him before the bishop to be rebuked for taking what did not belong to him, Francis came quietly into the assembled throng, tore off even every rag of clothing and threw it down at his father's feet, declaring that from that day on he had a father in heaven who would provide for him. There are times when I wish I had behaved as Francis did.

He had no doubts or hesitations or difficulties. Or if he had them he overcame them by the goodness of God. As for money, he spurned it, rejected it, cast it from him, from the beginning, to the end. As the *Speculum Perfectionis* has it, 'Francis, the true friend and imitator of Christ, despising all things

which are of this world, above all detested money and by word and example led his followers to flee it as if it were the Devil.' They were to subsist by God's loving support, and if they relied upon it, it would not fail them. This does not mean that Francis advocated direct beggary as the entire means of livelihood. On the contrary, he was always insistent upon honest labor. Those who followed him should work as they had been accustomed to do and should receive proper reward for it. Only the reward should not go beyond the bare means of subsistence, and, if there was any superfluity, it should be immediately passed on to those who were in greater need.

For Francis not only condemned and contemned money in its immediate form. He was still more hostile to the accumulation of it in possessions of any kind. No radical of the present day could be more bitter in his denunciations of capital, not only in its far-reaching aspects of vaster ownership, but even, perhaps still more, in the petty grasp on small visible holdings to which men cling with a madder grip than they extend to airy claims which they cannot see but only imagine. The owner of a cottage or a cow is a capitalist just as much as is a Rockefeller or a Ford, and he hates to have the cow or the cottage taken away from him, just as they would hate to lose their millions. All wrong, says Francis, and he speaks right out about the whole business: 'I don't want to be a thief, and to have what others lack is to be a sheer thief and nothing else.' Those who followed him were to count nothing as belonging to them except the clothes on their backs, and even those were often to be turned over to any who might be more greatly in need of them.

'Evidently Francis was starting the greatest fight in the world, the one that all fundamental reformers have undertaken, the fight against human nature. Even before his death he saw the huge forces of greed and avarice, the desire for gain and the desire for power, breaking in on the Rule he sought to establish. Over and over he enjoined upon his disciples that they must keep the simple principles before them—love, quiet, faithful labor, persistent self-sacrifice, above all the fundamental idea of not wanting, not wanting the things of this world, rooting them out of your spirit altogether. Poverty, living without money, and all the accursed things which money brings, which cannot be had without it and are of no real profit when you get them, that was the lesson that he tried to teach, by preaching and by example. And with the high-wrought, lyrical, imaginative touch that makes so much of his charm, he breaks out into a hymn of rapture to his spiritual bride, our Holy Lady Poverty: 'To trample under foot is to condemn, and Poverty tramples all things under foot, therefore she is queen of all things. But, oh, my holy Lord Jesus Christ, pity me and my Lady Poverty, for I am tortured with the love of her, nor without her can I find repose. . . . Oh, who would not love this Lady Poverty above all others? Of thee, dear Jesus of the Poor, I ask to be honored with this privilege, to be enriched with this treasure, that it may be the eternal distinction of me and mine in thy name to possess nothing whatever under heaven of our own, but to be sustained always by the scanty use of others' benefits, so long as this miserable flesh endures.'

Undeniably in these raptures and vehement assertions and injunctions of Francis there is the touch of extravagance and excess which sometimes repels and estranges. There is the mediaeval quaintness of expression, there is the ascetic forcing, which makes you feel the ideal to be elevated beyond human reach. What tempers and sweetens all this in Francis is the peculiar flavor and relish of sympathy and tenderness. When his demands seem most impossible, you feel that his penetrating eyes look right down into your heart and see the weakness as well as the strength. Does not the whole depth of the tenderness shine out in this lovely sentence from a letter of his later years? 'And I shall know whether you love God and me, his servant and yours, if you do this: see to it that there shall be no brother in the world, no matter how much he has sinned, who if he has once met your eyes, shall go away without your pity. And if he does not ask pity of you, do you ask it of him.' No harsh injunction about poverty could ever chill the infinite loving-kindness of that.

The second great fundamental principle of Francis's religion was the principle of obedience, and it seems hardly likely that this would be any more to the taste of the twentieth century than the principle of poverty. The vast individualism that has developed during the last hundred years does not greatly relish the notion of blind obedience to anyone for any purpose. Yet it must be admitted that the ideal of obedience is a very restful thing. When one has struggled long with doubtful courses, anxious above all things to do the right, but utterly unable to see where the right lies; when one has come to have a hopeless mistrust of one's reason for guiding one anywhere and to feel that the responsibility for action is the most terrible burden in the world, the dream of obedience to someone who will take all the responsibility and all the burden, to someone who knows, to someone who even thinks he knows, is an exceedingly alluring one. Moreover, obedience is one of the greatest agents in the world for getting things done. The supreme organizing saints, Dominic, Ignatius, understood this perfectly, and built their world-power upon it. Also, obedience is the very best training for command, and those who have formed the habit of taking orders quickly, intelligently, unquestioningly, are often the ones who end by giving the most effective orders themselves.

It may appear that what is apt to be the earliest phase of obedience, the submission to paternal authority, was not very conspicuous in the case of Saint Francis. But as he went on with his life and work, he came to feel that obedience was a most essential virtue, not only for others, but for himself. Great heretics in the religious sphere, like great radicals in the political, are apt to have the instinct of rebellion, even of destruction. They have often the blind impulse to root up and overthrow existing institutions to get rid of their defects, with a secure confidence that the dynamic creative force of mankind will provide something better in their places. The history of Francis's forerunners in that turbulent twelfth century, so effectively told by Miss Davison and Miss Richards, is a history of rebellion at many points. But Saint Francis was by no manner of means a rebel, either by instinct or by practice. Like Abraham Lincoln, he was essentially constructive rather than destructive. He wanted to make over the world, but he wanted to make it over by love, and love does not destroy.

From the beginning of his career he showed his profound respect and submission to the authority of the Church. There might be errors, there might be defects, but such a magnificent power in the world was to be used, not to be battled with. Therefore he approached Pope Innocent III, and Pope Honorius III, and his intimate friend Cardinal Hugolino, who afterwards became Pope Gregory IX, with an inimitable combination of reverent tact and straightforward simplicity, which repeatedly secured for him the permissions and the authorizations he required.

Nor was the obedience or the submission confined to the higher powers or to those whose exalted rank necessarily imposed it. Francis enjoined upon all who loved him at all times the profoundest respect for even humble representatives of the Church. They were to be honored and heeded for their office, independent of what they might be in themselves. Even when the hand that ministered at the altar was corrupt and unclean, you were to kiss it, not for what it was, but for what it did. And in the most authentic and undisputed of all his written words, his final Testament, Francis expressly records his feeling on the subject: 'If I had the wisdom of Solomon and should come into contact with the poor parish priests of today, dwelling in their parishes, I would not preach against their wishes. And I would reverence, love, and honor them, and all like them, as if they were my lords and masters.'

Never did Francis miss an opportunity to impress this duty of obedience and submission upon all who followed him. In one of his letters to the faithful he writes: 'We should never desire to be above others, but should rather be submissive and subject to every human creature for the sake of God.' It cannot be denied that here, as in other things, there are elements of the fantastic, of extravagance and excess. Such, for example, is his likening of complete and implicit obedience to death, since a dead body at least does absolutely what is required of it. And the story runs that he ordered an erring brother to be buried up to the neck, till death seemed immediately imminent, then asked him if he was dead, and on his agreeing, let him go with the injunction to obey his superiors as a dead man would: 'I want my followers to be dead, not living.' But here again it is not the extreme illustration but the principle that counts.

To Francis there were two roots of the supreme, self-resigning obedience. The first root was intellectual. You were to give up, to eschew, to rid yourself utterly of, the pride and exaltation of your intelligence. There has been endless controversy on this point. It has sometimes been urged that Francis was quite ignorant, even of the Scriptures, that he rejected human learning altogether. On the other side it is answered, with good appearance of reason, that he lived with the Bible and that no one could have so perfectly practiced it who was not intimately familiar with its precepts. As later scholarship inevitably made its way into Franciscan pulpits, as into all others, innumerable pleas and explanations have been offered for departing from the Founder's uncompromising attitude. But that attitude is really simple enough. Francis knew what the pride of the intellect is, knew also its abysmal weakness: he had probably had example in himself of both. Learning and scholarship have their place, and he appreciated that place. But learning and scholarship are always too ready to exalt themselves, and they are of no account when once they are placed in competition with the light and the power of the spirit. Francis lived by the spirit, and he wanted others to do the same.

And as the first root of obedience is the humility of the intellect, the obliteration of intellectual pride, so the second root is the abasement of the will. It is the determination to do things simply because you want to do them that kills. This is what you must root out and tear up and overcome. You are told to go and do things. Go and do them, no matter whether every impulse of poor, fragile human nature rebels or not. You are to face ridicule and scorn and discomfort and torture and death, simply because you are ordered to do so, without debate or dispute or discussion or delay.

After which, even for saints like Francis, or rather supremely for the saints, there remains the qualification that when human obedience grows too distasteful, you can fall back upon the will of God, beside which all human command is dwarfed and insignificant. Thus, when the highest authority of the Church suggested that he should make some alteration in his Rule, Francis gently but absolutely declined to comply: 'I, most Holy Father, did not place those precepts or words in the Rule, but Christ. . . . Therefore I must not and I cannot change or remove the words of Christ in any way whatever.' For there is degree in obedience as in other things.

Yet all the time I confess that what most appeals to me in Francis's gospel of obedience is the getting rid of responsibility, throwing the burden of settling life upon someone else. It seems to me that this is what I have always longed for, and yet I wonder if, after fifty years of erratic independence, I should really relish it. So, alas, of all Francis's virtues. In him they appear exquisite, but an old and weary body, saturated with this world, might find them onerous in practice. The marvel of Francis is that he practiced what he preached. But then he believed in God and in a future life, and perhaps that makes all the difference.

The third great principle of Francis's religion was that of chastity, symbolizing in its most vehement form the conflict between the baser, more animal instincts, and the obedience to the higher, spiritual self, an obedience even more difficult and even more significant than the submission to the external will and commands of others.

As with Francis's other principles, there is something about this one also strange, if not quite repellent, to the whole intellectual attitude of the present day. The growing tendency of the later nineteenth and opening twentieth century is to establish a unified human nature, to recognize all the natural instincts as not only respectable but normal and desirable, not to be fought with and repressed and restrained into unnatural fury and turbulence, but to be directed and guided and developed to their fullest satisfaction, limited only by the simple dictates of expediency and common-sense. It is needless to say that the view of Francis and of his age was totally different from this. The animal elements in our nature were the province of the Devil, at any rate the Devil was given power over us by means of them. It was our duty, our highest religious function and divine privilege, to control and subdue these elements by the power of God working through conscience to a higher, remote, future end, an end conforming to God's will and leading to our own supreme final

happiness, beside which the mere immediate gratification of the animal instincts seemed ineffably tame and poor.

At any rate, such self-conquest meant everything to Saint Francis of Assisi. And from the hour of his first conversion his effort was to subdue and overcome the weaknesses of the flesh in every possible way. As to the grosser temptations of sex, there is the strange legend, so much associated with other saints that it is difficult to give it more than a legendary character, of his rushing out naked and burying himself in snow-banks to teach the rebellious passions the indispensable lesson of frigidity. Much more valid and significant are the general comments and warnings as to the danger of association with the opposite sex: 'Dear brethren, we ought to avoid the intimacy, the conversation, even the sight of women, which are the occasion of ruin to so many, all the more zealously when we realize how such things disturb the weak and weaken the strong.'

Yet it is interesting to find that, for all these general injunctions, which no doubt were rigidly applied and acted upon, women played a considerable part in the Saint's life, as was only natural with a temperament so sensitive and so quickly and obviously responsive to all the more delicate emotions. There was the somewhat shadowy Roman lady, Madame Jacopa di Settesoli, to whom Francis seems to have turned for comfort and advice when he was in the Capital and who was opportunely present with him in almost his very last moments. Still more, there was the exquisite Saint Clara, who in her youth cast aside wealth and worldly happiness as Francis did and made it her glory to establish an order of feminine piety in intimate association and affiliation with his. And to Clara even more than to Jacopa, Francis turned for encouragement and inspiration in some of the darkest moments of his career. As Sabatier puts it, in one such moment, 'Clara, by urging him to persevere, instilled into him a new enthusiasm. One word of hers sufficed to restore to him all his energy, and from that time on we find in his life more poetry and more love than ever before.'

But Francis's subdual of the lower instincts extended far beyond any contest of sex. All immediate fleshly pleasures and indulgences were to be rooted out and got rid of, for the mere power of overcoming them, if for nothing else. There were the temptations of good living, warm housing, luxurious habitations, delicate food. Francis's scheme of holiness allowed for none of these things. Others could not have them, and why should you? If by any chance any little rag or shred of comfort came your way, what better could you do with it than dispose of it to someone who needed it more? The body, this wretched body, which must so soon be food for worms, why cater to it, why pamper it, why caress it? And in his strange, quaint fashion, he sometimes abused it familiarly, chiding it as 'Brother Body'; sometimes he spoke of it as 'the ass,' to be whipped and bullied and made to travel and bear burdens just exactly as its spirit owner might desire.

Doubtless this abuse of the body went to the usual excesses. It was not only denied, it was tormented. Doubtless there were extravagances of penance and self-humiliation which seem almost childish, as when the Saint ate a bit of chicken for the good of his health and then, in an agony of remorse, had one of his followers hale him into church with a rope around his neck to do penance for his weakness. And the abstinence and the privations were destructive to a physique which was never of the best, so that Francis's last years were a story of physical suffering which would be painful to read about if the sufferings were not borne with such complete spiritual tranquillity even to his final death on the bare ground with nothing beneath him but one poor garment.

But the acme and climax of Francis's self-struggle was undoubtedly his experience with the lepers. These unhappy creatures were at that time to be found in Italy in considerable numbers, and of course collected in the usual colonies. Francis had always regarded them with the peculiar horror of a sensitive nature, had pitied them, had been ready to aid them as he could—from a distance—but had shunned all intimate contact with them in instinctive disgust. Then one day, about the time of his conversion, he was riding in the country when a leper came in his way. His first, natural, impulse was to throw the man a gratuity, give him his blessing, and pass by on the other side. But the whole power of the new life that had come upon him said no. Here was the opportunity to show the stuff that was in him at its fullest and richest. He went right up to the leper, not only gave him what he had about him, but embraced him, and treated him in every respect as a brother and a friend. From that hour he felt that he had fought the great fight and won, and ever after the lepers were an object of peculiar tenderness and respect and of his constant injunctions to those who followed him. For the lepers merely symbolized the highest victory that a man can win in this world, the victory summed up in the exquisite phrase of the *Fioretti*, 'per-

fettaletizia . . . vincere se medesimo,'
the victory over self, which, alas, some
of us never achieve at all. . . .

But the freshest and most delightful
of all the elements of Francis's character
is unquestionably the impulse of wandering, of joyous, untiring, inexhaustible, vagrant peregrination. It is one of
the basic impulses of human nature,
perhaps the basic impulse, the desire
of new things and fresh experiences, of
turning perpetually from one phase of
life to another. It is the splendid impulse of youth. Only in most of us the
swift flight of years, the clouding conventions of civilized life, the involving
burden of social prejudice, numb and
kill the original impulse in this case
as in so many others. But the sweet,
sunny, vagrant ardor crops out at least
in the aspirations of the poets, as in the
lovely spring cry of Catullus,

Jam mens praetrepidans avet vagari,

or the wilder murmur of the rash hero
of the old dramatist,

Let rogues be staid that have no habitation;
A gentleman may wander.

And again there is the musical travel
sentence of old Burton, 'For peregrination hath such an infinite and sweet variety that some call him unhappy who
never traveled, but beholdeth from his
cradle to his old age the same, still, still
the same.' Only Burton traveled but
in spirit, like so many of us. Francis's
restless limbs wanted to waft his spirit
all over the world. When he was
young, he was fascinated by the wandering dreams of chivalry and knight er-
rantry, and again by the vagrant music
of the troubadours, and in later years he
used to call his proselyting followers the
chivalry of God and used to pour out his

religious ecstasies in the troubadour's
form.

With this instinct of sweet general
vagrancy, with the pleasure of letting
one's feet stray whither they will, there
is the further delight of varied human
contact, of seeing endless human faces,
and exploring endless human souls.
There was once a social-minded lady
who said, 'I should like to meet everybody in the world.' In the same way
we feel with the great human poets, the
Chaucers and the Shakespeares, the
wide love of human nature and human
beings, just because they are human.
Saint and sinner, doer and dreamer, all
are interesting, all are acceptable, because we find something of all of them
in our own hearts. The essential elements of this far-traveling human interest are, first, a limitless, inexhaustible
curiosity and, second, a considerable indifference to one's own personal comfort; in other words, a constant tendency to forget one's self in the lives of
others. And both these elements are
undyingly conspicuous in Saint Francis.
He had the vast curiosity, the interest in
all human souls, where they came from,
what their nature was, where they were
going to. And he had the instinct, the
formed habit of making himself comfortable wherever he might be. To be
sure, in later years, he seemed to show a
growing attachment to the home center, the Portiuncula at Assisi, and he
enjoined upon his followers that they
should never forget or desert it. But in
the vigorous and active portion of his
life, when 'for the space of eighteen
years his body never had rest, circulating through varied and far-flung regions,' his principle seems to have been
that which he loudly proclaimed, *'Nam
ubicumque sumus et ambulamus, habemus semper cellam nobiscum';* or, in

the words of the old poet Donne, holding up the snail as an example,

Be thou thine own home and in thyself
    dwell;
Inn anywhere; continuance maketh hell.

Also, besides the pure pleasure of vagrancy in itself and the interest in humanity, there is the infinite delight in out-of-doors, and this is always evident in Saint Francis. He was willing to meet the crowds in cities, he did not shrink from lepers in body or from lepers in spirit, but what he above all loved was wandering in the fields and woods, the bright air, the broad sky, the sun, the wind, the clouds, and the living creatures inhabiting all this. There is a sunny sweet old play of Richard Brome, called *The Merry Beggars,* which breathes all through it the delicious spirit of vagrancy. The central figure has the charming name Springlove. He is a steward, and a faithful servant, and spends his winter hours over his master's accounts and the tedious minutiae of daily care. But when spring comes, and the blossoms burst, and the nightingale and the cuckoo begin calling, calling, the blood in Springlove calls too, and he must up and away, leaving master and duty behind him, and follow the cuckoo and the nightingale.

Saint Francis had something of Springlove in his soul, and he too heard the cuckoo and the nightingale when they began their calling. He too felt the charm of the spring flowers and the lure of narrow, winding paths leading perhaps nowhere, or perhaps anywhere. When the call came, he was ready to arise and follow. And he loved all the living creatures and even the creatures that might appear not to have life. With his usual quaint exaggeration,

he cherished and reverenced even the stones on which he trod and the water he had to use for washing. He loved the flowers and the birds and the cicadas. In that strange, unearthly canticle in which he poured out his lyrical, poetical aspiration, he hailed all the works of God with exuberant praise: 'Praised be my Lord God with all his creatures; and specially our brother the sun, who brings us the day, and who brings us the light; fair is he, and shining with a very great splendour: O Lord, he signifies to us Thee!' And there is the delicious story of his preaching to the birds, which appears in so many different forms. When Francis was preparing to discourse one evening out-of-doors, he was interrupted by the mad twitter of the swallows, who gathered in clouds all about him. And at first he smiled and let them twitter. But finally he remonstrated: 'Sister swallows, you might let me have my turn.' And the swallows were suddenly silent, there was not one single twitter, while the Saint held forth to them on the goodness of God.

For all this out-of-doors of Francis is penetrated, permeated with God. It reminds me always of the sweet story of the two young lovers, sitting on an open hillside, watching the light grasses bent all one way in the light south wind, like a group of Fra Angelico angels. And the lady murmured, 'You know, my soul also is swayed gently, like the grasses, in the wind of your love. Only that would make me the flower and you the wind. And I had rather we should both be flowers and God the wind. What could be more exquisite than to be swayed forever hither and thither in the wind of His love?'

It is this pervading presence of God that gives Francis's spirit of vagrancy the final and crowning touch. It is perhaps delicious enough to roam and wander for the pure joy and revel of it. But how much of depth and delicacy and grandeur is added when you feel that it is your duty to wander, that you are called by God to travel over the wide earth, seeing all things, and visiting all men, so that you may enlarge the boundaries of God's kingdom. This is what Francis felt. He lived all his life in the intoxication of it. He imparted the intoxication to thousands who have followed him. Go forth, and do my bidding, and bear my message to the whole wide world. That was Saint Francis of Assisi, God's Vagabond, and prouder in that title than in the glory of kings or the resonant splendor of conquerors. And because the charm of inexhaustible itinerance, physical and spiritual, was blended with the God-impulse, inextricably, the religion of Francis and his preaching have always a singular and delightful touch of joy. There was no gloom about him, no pressure of misery or hell, no touch of asceticism in the tortured sense. As Renan puts it, admirably, 'Note well that Francis forbids us to possess, he does not forbid us to enjoy'; and the experience of humanity, even without

Francis, has long ago taught us that possession and enjoyment are by no means identical. Francis wanted his followers to find endless joy in their religion, in their God, and in all the delightful things that their God had scattered about them in such abundant profusion. He was even ready to carry joy to the point of a sweet and sacred merriment, and when Brother Juniper made his careless and trivial jests, Brother Juniper, who is stamped with the magnificent phrase, 'egregius Domini joculator,' the egregious jester of God, Francis smiled and sympathized, for, he said, 'What are the servants of God but as it were merry-makers who should stir the hearts of men and impel them to spiritual joy?'

So this illimitable roamer and dreamer went on wandering and wondering and loving. With such an inborn tendency, is it not hard to imagine that the wandering should ever stop? Rather you feel that he would go on eternally, traveling, soaring, adventuring, through the vast unplumbed depths of the spiritual universe, always, always, always, touching, enjoying, engrossing —and dominating souls.

1932

II. . .

LETTERS

THOMAS JEFFERSON

One Generation Hath No Right to Bind Another

To James Madison

Paris,

September 6, 1789.

Dear Sir,

I sit down to write to you without knowing by what occasion I shall send my letter. I do it, because a subject comes into my head, which I would wish to develop a little more than is practicable in the hurry of the moment of making up general despatches.

The question, whether one generation of men has a right to bind another, seems never to have been started either on this or our side of the water. Yet it is a question of such consequences as not only to merit decision, but place also among the fundamental principles of every government. The course of reflection in which we are immersed here, on the elementary principles of society, has presented this question to my mind; and that no such obligation can be transmitted, I think very capable of proof. I set out on this ground, which I suppose to be self-evident, that the *earth belongs in usufruct to the living;* that the dead have neither powers nor rights over it. The portion occupied by any individual ceases to be his when himself ceases to be, and reverts to the society. If the society has formed no rules for the appropriation of its lands in severalty, it will be taken by the first occupants, and these will generally be the wife and children of the decedent. If they have formed rules of appropriation, those rules may give it to the wife and children, or to some one of them, or

to the legatee of the deceased. So they may give it to its creditor. But the child, the legatee or creditor, takes it, not by natural right, but by a law of the society of which he is a member, and to which he is subject. Then, no man can, by *natural right,* oblige the lands he occupied, or the persons who succeed him in that occupation, to the payment of debts contracted by him. For if he could, he might during his own life, eat up the usufruct of the lands for several generations to come; and then the lands would belong to the dead, and not to the living, which is the reverse of our principle.

What is true of every member of the society, individually, is true of them all collectively; since the rights of the whole can be no more than the sum of the rights of the individuals. To keep our ideas clear when applying them to a multitude, let us suppose a whole generation of men to be born on the same day, to attain mature age on the same day, and to die on the same day, leaving a succeeding generation in the moment of attaining their mature age, all together. Let the ripe age be supposed of twenty-one years, and their period of life thirty-four years more, that being the average term given by the bills of mortality to persons of twenty-one years of age. Each successive generation would, in this way, come and go off the stage at a fixed moment, as individuals do now. Then I say, the earth belongs to each of these generations during its course, fully and in its own right. The second generation receives it clear of the debts and incumbrances of the first, the third of the second, and so on. For if the first could charge it with a debt, then the earth would belong to the dead and not to the living generation. Then, no generation can contract debts greater than may be paid during the course of its own existence. At twenty-one years of age, they may bind themselves and their lands for thirty-four years to come; at twenty-two, for thirty-three; at twenty-three, for thirty-two; and at fifty-four, for one year only; because these are the terms of life which remain to them at the respective epochs. But a material difference must be noted, between the succession of an individual and that of a whole generation. Individuals are parts only of a society, subject to the laws of a whole. These laws may appropriate the portion of land occupied by a decedent, to his creditor, rather than to any other, or to his child, on condition he satisfies the creditor. But when a whole generation, that is, the whole society, dies, as in the case we have supposed, and another generation or society succeeds, this forms a whole, and there is no superior who can give their territory to a third society, who may have lent money to their predecessors beyond their faculties of paying.

What is true of generations succeeding one another at fixed epochs, as has been supposed for clearer conception, is true for those renewed daily, as in the actual course of nature. As a majority of the contracting generation will continue in being thirty-four years, and a new majority will then come into possession, the former may extend their engagement to that term, and no longer. The conclusion then, is, that neither the representatives of a nation, nor the whole nation itself assembled, can validly engage debts beyond what they may pay in their own time, that is to say, within thirty-four years of the date of the engagement.

To render this conclusion palpable, suppose that Louis the XIV. and XV. had contracted debts in the name of the French nation, to the amount of ten thousand milliards, and that the whole had been contracted in Holland. The interest of this sum would be five hundred milliards, which is the whole rent-roll or net proceeds of the territory of France. Must the present generation of men have retired from the territory in which nature produces them, and ceded it to the Dutch creditors? No; they have the same rights over the soil on which they were produced, as the preceding generations had. They derive these rights not from them, but from nature. They, then, and their soil are, by nature, clear of the debts of their predecessors. To present this in another point of view, suppose Louis XV. and his contemporary generation, had said to the money lenders of Holland, give us money, that we may eat, drink, and be merry in our day; and on condition you will demand no interest till the end of thirty-four years, you shall then, forever after, receive an annual interest of fifteen per cent. The money is lent on these conditions, is divided among the people, eaten, drunk, and squandered. Would the present generation be obliged to apply the produce of the earth and of their labor, to replace their dissipations? Not at all.

I suppose that the received opinion, that the public debts of one generation devolve on the next, has been suggested by our seeing, habitually, in private life, that he who succeeds to lands is required to pay the debts of his predecessor; without considering that this requisition is municipal only, not moral, flowing from the will of the society, which has found it convenient to appropriate the lands of a decedent on the condition of a payment of his debts; but that between society and society, or generation and generation, there is no municipal obligation, no umpire but the law of nature.

The interest of the national debt of France being, in fact, but a two thousandth part of its rent-roll, the payment of it is practicable enough; and so becomes a question merely of honor or of expediency. But with respect to future debts, would it not be wise and just for that nation to declare in the constitution they are forming, that neither the legislature nor the nation itself, can validly contract more debt than they may pay within their own age, or within the term of thirty-four years? And that all future contracts shall be deemed void, as to what shall remain unpaid at the end of thirty-four years from their date? This would put the lenders, and the borrowers also, on their guard. By reducing, too, the faculty of borrowing within its natural limits, it would bridle the spirit of war, to which too free a course has been procured by the inattention of money lenders to this law of nature, that succeeding generations are not responsible for the preceding.

On similar ground it may be proved, that no society can make a perpetual constitution, or even a perpetual law. The earth belongs always to the living generation: they may manage it, then, and what proceeds from it, as they please, during their usufruct. They are masters, too, of their own persons, and consequently may govern them as they please. But persons and property make the sum of the objects of government. The constitution and the laws of their predecessors are extinguished then, in their natural course, with those whose will gave them being. This could preserve that being, till it ceased to be itself, and no longer. Every constitution, then, and every law, naturally expires at the end of thirty-four years. If it be enforced longer, it is an act of force, and not of right. It may be said, that the succeeding generation exercising, in fact, the power of repeal, this leaves them as free as if the constitution or law had been expressly limited to thirty-four years only. In the first place, this objection admits the right, in proposing any equivalent. But the power of repeal is not an equivalent. It might be, indeed, if every form of government were so perfectly contrived, that the will of the majority could always be obtained, fairly and without impediment. But this is true of no form. The people cannot assemble themselves; their representation is unequal and vicious. Various checks are opposed to every legislative proposition. Factions get possession of the public councils, bribery corrupts them, personal interests lead them astray from the general interests of their constituents; and other impediments arise, so as to prove to every practical man, that a law of limited duration is much more manageable than one which needs a repeal.

This principle, that the earth belongs to the living and not to the dead, is of very extensive application and consequences in every country, and most especially in France. It enters into the resolution of the questions, whether the nation may change the descent of lands holden in tail; whether they may change the appropriation of lands given anciently to the church, to hospitals, colleges, orders of chivalry, and otherwise in perpetuity; whether they may abolish the charges and privileges attached on lands, including the whole catalogue, ecclesiastical and feudal; it goes to hereditary offices, authorities and jurisdictions, to hereditary orders, distinctions and appellations, to perpetual monopolies in commerce, the arts or sciences, with a long train of *et ceteras;* renders the question of reimbursement, a question of generosity and not of right. In all these cases, the legislature of the day could authorize such appropriations and establishments for their own time, but no longer; and the present holders, even where they or their ancestors have purchased, are in the case of *bona fide* purchasers of what the seller had no right to convey.

Turn this subject in your mind, my dear Sir, and particularly as to the power of contracting debts, and develop it with that cogent logic which is so peculiarly yours. Your station in the councils of our country gives you an opportunity of producing it to public consideration, of forcing it into discussion. At first blush it may be laughed at, as the dream of a theorist; but examination will prove it to be solid and salutary. It would furnish matter for a fine preamble to our first law for appropriating the public revenue; and it will exclude, at the threshold of our new government, the ruinous and contagious errors of this quarter of the globe, which have armed despots with means which nature does not sanction, for binding in chains their fellow-men. We have already given, in example, one effectual check to the dog of war, by transferring the power of declaring war from the executive to the legislative body, from those who are to spend, to those who are to pay. I should be pleased to see this second obstacle held out by us also, in the first instance. No nation can make a declaration against the validity of long-contracted debts, so disinterestedly as we, since we do not owe a shilling which will not be paid, principal and interest, by the measures you have taken, within the time of our own lives. I write you no news, because when an occasion occurs, I shall write a separate letter for that.

I am always, with great and sincere esteem, dear Sir,

your affectionate friend and servant.

THOMAS JEFFERSON

Natural Aristocracy

To JOHN ADAMS

Monticello,
October 28, 1813.

Dear Sir,

According to the reservation between us, of taking up one of the subjects of our correspondence at a time, I turn to your letters of August the 16th and September the 2d.

The passage you quote from Theognis, I think has an ethical rather than a political object. The whole piece is a moral *exhortation,* παραινεσις, and this passage particularly seems to be a reproof to man, who, while with his domestic animals he is curious to improve the race, by employing always the finest male, pays no attention to the improvement of his own race, but intermarries with the vicious, the ugly, or the old, for considerations of wealth or ambition. It is in conformity with the principle adopted afterwards by the Pythagoreans, and expressed by Ocellus in another form; περι δε τῆς 'εκ τῶν αλλήλων ανθρωπων γενεσεως etc.,—ουχ ηδονης ενεκα η μιξις· which, as literally as intelligibility will admit, may be thus translated: "concerning the interprocreation of men, how, and of whom it shall be, in a perfect manner, and according to the laws of modesty and sanctity, conjointly, this is what I think right. First to lay it down that we do not commix for the sake of pleasure, but of the procreation of children. For the powers, the organs and desires for coition have not been given by God to man for the sake of pleasure, but for the procreation of the race. For as it were incongruous, for a mortal born to partake of divine life, the immortality of the race being taken away, God fulfilled the purpose by making the generations uninterrupted and continuous. This, therefore, we are especially to lay down as a principle, that coition is not for the sake of pleasure." But nature, not trusting to this moral and abstract motive, seems to have provided more securely for the perpetuation of the species, by making it the effect of the *oestrum* implanted in the constitution of both sexes. And not only has the commerce of love been indulged on this unhallowed impulse, but made subservient also to wealth and ambition by marriage, without regard to the beauty, the healthiness, the understanding, or virtue of the subject from which we are to breed. The selecting the best male for a harem of well-chosen females also, which Theognis seems to recommend from the example of our sheep and asses, would doubtless improve the human, as it does the brute animal, and produce a race of veritable αριστοι. For experience proves, that the moral and physical qualities of man, whether good or evil, are transmissible in a certain degree from father to son. But I suspect that the equal rights of men will rise up against this privileged Solomon and his harem, and oblige us to continue acquiescence under the "Αμαυρωσις γενεος αστων" which Theognis complains of, and to content ourselves with the accidental aristoi produced by the fortuitous concourse of breeders. For I agree with you that there is a natural aristocracy among men. The grounds of this are virtue and talents. Formerly, bodily powers gave place among the aristoi. But since the invention of gunpowder has armed the weak as well as the strong with missile death, bodily strength, like beauty, good humor, politeness and other accomplishments, has become but an auxiliary ground of distinction. There is also an artificial aristocracy, founded on wealth and birth, without either virtue or talents; for with these it would belong to the first class. The natural aristocracy I consider as the most precious gift of nature, for the instruction, the trusts, and government of society. And indeed, it would have been inconsistent in creation to have formed man for the social state, and not to have provided virtue and wisdom enough to manage the concerns of the society. May we not even say, that that form of government is the best, which provides the most effectually for a pure selection of these natural aristoi into the offices of government? The artificial aristocracy is a mischievous ingredient in government, and provision should be made to prevent its ascendency. On the question, what is the best provision, you and I differ; but we differ as rational friends, using the free exercise of our own reason, and mutually indulging its errors. You think it best to put the pseudo-aristoi into a separate chamber of legislation, where they may be hindered from doing mischief by their co-ordinate branches, and where, also, they may be a protection to wealth against the agrarian and plundering enterprises of the majority of the people. I think that to give them power in order to prevent them from doing mischief, is arming them for it, and increasing instead of remedying the evil. For if the co-ordinate branches can arrest their action, so may they that of the co-ordinates. Mischief may be done negatively as well as positively. Of this, a cabal in the Senate of the United States has furnished many proofs. Nor do I believe them necessary to protect the wealthy; because enough of these will find their way into every branch of the legislation, to protect themselves. From fifteen to twenty legislatures of our own, in action for thirty years past, have proved that no fears of an equalization of property are to be apprehended from them. I think the best remedy is exactly that provided by all our constitutions, to leave to the citizens the free election and separation of the aristoi from the pseudo-aristoi, of the wheat from the chaff. In general they will elect the really good and wise. In some instances, wealth may corrupt, and birth blind them; but not in sufficient degree to endanger the society.

It is probable that our difference of opinion may, in some measure, be produced by a difference of character in those among whom we live. From what I have seen of Massachusetts and Connecticut myself, and still more from what I have heard, and the character given of the former by yourself, who know them so much better, there seems to be in those two States a traditionary reverence for certain families, which has rendered the offices of the government nearly hereditary in those families. I presume that from an early period of your history, members of those families happening to possess virtue and talents, have honestly exercised them for the good of the people, and by their services have endeared their names to them. In coupling Connecticut with you, I mean it politically only, not morally. For having made the Bible the common law of their land, they seem to have modeled their morality on the story of Jacob and Laban. But although this hereditary succession to office with you, may, in some degree, be founded in real family merit, yet in a much higher degree, it has proceeded from your strict alliance of Church and State. These families are canonized in the eyes of the people on common principles, "you tickle me, and I will tickle you." In Virginia we have nothing of this. Our clergy, before the revolution, having been secured against rivalship by fixed salaries, did not give themselves the trouble of acquiring influence over the people. Of wealth, there were great accumulations in particular families, handed down from generation to generation, under the English law of entails. But the only object of ambition for the wealthy was a seat in the King's Council. All their court then was paid to the crown and its creatures; and they Philipized in all collisions between the King and the people. Hence they were unpopular; and that unpopularity continues attached to their names. A Randolph, a Carter, or a Burwell must have great personal superiority over a common competitor to be elected by the people even at this day. At the first session of our legislature after the Declaration of Independence, we passed a law abolishing entails. And this was followed by one abolishing the privilege of primogeniture, and dividing the lands of intestates equally among all their children, or other representatives. These laws, drawn by myself, laid the axe to the foot of pseudo-aristocracy. And had another which I prepared been adopted by the legislature, our work would have been complete. It was a bill for the more general diffusion of learning. This proposed to divide every county into wards of five or six miles square, like your townships; to establish in each ward a free school for reading, writing and common arithmetic; to provide for the annual selection of the best subjects from these schools, who might receive, at the public expense, a higher degree of education at a district school; and from these district schools to select a certain number of the most promising subjects, to be completed at an university, where all the useful sciences should be taught. Worth and genius would thus have been sought out from every condition of life, and completely prepared by education for defeating the competition of wealth and birth for public trusts. My proposition had, for a further object, to impart to these wards those portions of self-government for which they are best qualified, by confiding to them the care of their poor, their roads, police, elections, the nomination of jurors, administration of justice in small cases, elementary exercises of militia; in short, to have made them little republics, with a

warden at the head of each, for all those concerns which, being under their eye, they would better manage than the larger republics of the county or State. A general call of ward meetings by their wardens on the same day through the State, would at any time produce the genuine sense of the people on any required point, and would enable the State to act in mass, as your people have so often done, and with so much effect by their town meetings. The law for religious freedom, which made a part of this system, having put down the aristocracy of the clergy, and restored to the citizen the freedom of the mind, and those of entails and descents nurturing an equality of condition among them, this on education would have raised the mass of the people to the high ground of moral respectability necessary to their own safety, and to orderly government; and would have completed the great object of qualifying them to select the veritable aristoi, for the trusts of government, to the exclusion of the pseudalists; and the same Theognis who has furnished the epigraphs of your two letters, assures us that "Ουδεμιαν πω, Κυρν', αγαθοι πολιν ωλεσαν ανδρες." Although this law has not yet been acted on but in a small and inefficient degree, it is still considered as before the legislature, with other bills of the revised code, not yet taken up, and I have great hope that some patriotic spirit will, at a favorable moment, call it up, and make it the keystone of the arch of our government.

With respect to aristocracy, we should further consider, that before the establishment of the American States, nothing was known to history but the man of the old world, crowded within limits either small or overcharged, and steeped in the vices which that situation generates. A government adapted to such men would be one thing; but a very different one, that for the man of these States. Here every one may have land to labor for himself, if he chooses; or, preferring the exercise of any other industry, may exact for it such compensation as not only to afford a comfortable subsistence, but wherewith to provide for a cessation from labor in old age. Every one, by his property, or by his satisfactory situation, is interested in the support of law and order. And such men may safely and advantageously reserve to themselves a wholesome control over their public affairs, and a degree of freedom, which, in the hands of the *canaille* of the cities of Europe, would be instantly perverted to the demolition and destruction of everything public and private. The history of the last twenty-five years of France, and of the last forty years in America, nay of its last two hundred years, proves the truth of both parts of this observation.

But even in Europe a change has sensibly taken place in the mind of man. Science had liberated the ideas of those who read and reflect, and the American example had kindled feelings of right in the people. An insurrection has consequently begun, of science, talents, and courage, against rank and birth, which have fallen into contempt. It has failed in its first effort, because the mobs of the cities, the instrument used for its accomplishment, debased by ignorance, poverty, and vice, could not be restrained to rational action. But the world will recover from the panic of this first catastrophe. Science is progressive, and talents and enterprise on the alert. Resort may be had to the people of the country, a more governable power from their principles and subordination; and rank, and birth, and

tinsel-aristocracy will finally shrink into insignificance, even there. This, however, we have no right to meddle with. It suffices for us, if the moral and physical condition of our own citizens qualifies them to select the able and good for the direction of their government, with a recurrence of elections at such short periods as will enable them to displace an unfaithful servant, before the mischief he meditates may be irremediable.

I have thus stated my opinion on a point on which we differ, not with a view to controversy, for we are both too old to change opinions which are the result of a long life of inquiry and reflection; but on the suggestions of a former letter of yours, that we ought not to die before we have explained ourselves to each other. We acted in perfect harmony, through a long and perilous contest for our liberty and independence. A constitution has been acquired, which, though neither of us thinks perfect, yet both consider as competent to render our fellow citizens the happiest and the securest on whom the sun has ever shone. If we do not think exactly alike as to its imperfections, it matters little to our country, which, after devoting to it long lives of disinterested labor, we have delivered over to our successors in life, who will be able to take care of it and of themselves.

Of the pamphlet on aristocracy which has been sent to you, or who may be its author, I have heard nothing but through your letter. If the person you suspect, it may be known from the quaint, mystical, and hyperbolical ideas, involved in affected, new-fangled and pedantic terms which stamp his writings. Whatever it be, I hope your quiet is not to be affected at this day by the rudeness or intemperance of scribblers;

but that you may continue in tranquillity to live and to rejoice in the prosperity of our country, until it shall be your own wish to take your seat among the aristoi who have gone before you.

Ever and affectionately yours.

ABRAHAM LINCOLN

You Do Not Work Much

To John D. Johnston
　　　　　　　　January 2, 1851.

Dear Johnston:

Your request for eighty dollars I do not think it best to comply with now. At the various times when I have helped you a little you have said to me, "We can get along very well now"; but in a very short time I find you in the same difficulty again. Now, this can only happen by some defect in your conduct. What that defect is, I think I know. You are not lazy, and still you are an idler. I doubt whether, since I saw you, you have done a good whole day's work in any one day. You do not very much dislike to work, and still you do not work much, merely because it does not seem to you that you could get much for it. This habit of uselessly wasting time is the whole difficulty; it is vastly important to you, and still more so to your children, that you should break the habit. It is more important to them, because they have longer to live, and can keep out of an idle habit before they are in it, easier than they can get out after they are in.

You are now in need of some money; and what I propose is, that you shall go to work, "tooth and nail," for somebody who will give you money for it. Let father and your boys take charge of your things at home, prepare for a crop, and make the crop, and you go to work for the best money wages, or in discharge of any debt you owe, that you can get; and, to secure you a fair reward for your labor, I now promise you, that for every dollar you will, between this and the first of May, get for your own labor, either in money or as your own indebtedness, I will then give you one other dollar. By this, if you hire yourself at ten dollars a month, from me you will get ten more, making twenty dollars a month for your work. In this I do not mean you shall go off to St. Louis, or the lead mines, or the gold mines in California, but I mean for you to go at it for the best wages you can get close to home in Coles County. Now, if you will do this, you will be soon out of debt, and, what is better, you will have a habit that will keep you from getting in debt again. But, if I should now clear you out of debt, next year you would be just as deep in as ever. You say you would almost give your place in heaven for seventy or eighty dollars. Then you value your place in heaven very cheap, for I am sure you can, with the offer I make, get the seventy or eighty dollars for four or five months' work. You say if I will furnish you the money you will deed me the land, and, if you don't pay the money back, you will deliver possession. Nonsense! If you can't now live

with the land, how will you then live will but follow my advice, you will find without it? You have always been it worth more than eighty times eighty kind to me, and I do not mean to be un-dollars to you.
kind to you. On the contrary, if you

Affectionately your brother,

ABRAHAM LINCOLN

I Dislike Slavery

To Joshua F. Speed.

SPRINGFIELD,
August 24, 1855.

Dear Speed:

You know what a poor correspondent I am. Ever since I received your very agreeable letter of the 22d of May I have been intending to write you an an-swer to it. You suggest that in politi-cal action, now, you and I would differ. I suppose we would; not quite as much, however, as you may think. You know I dislike slavery, and you fully admit the abstract wrong of it. So far there is no cause of difference. But you say that sooner than yield your legal right to the slave, especially at the bidding of those who are not themselves interested, you would see the Union dissolved. I am not aware that any one is bidding you yield that right; very certainly I am not. I leave that matter entirely to yourself. I also acknowledge your rights and my obligations under the Constitution in regard to your slaves. I confess I hate to see the poor creatures hunted down and caught and carried back to their stripes and unrequited toil; but I bite my lips and keep quiet. In 1841 you and I had together a tedious low-water trip on a steamboat from Louisville to St. Louis. You may remember, as I well do, that from Louisville to the

mouth of the Ohio there were on board ten or a dozen slaves shackled together with irons. That sight was a continued torment to me, and I see something like it every time I touch the Ohio or any other slave border. It is not fair for you to assume that I have no interest in a thing which has, and continually exer-cises, the power of making me misera-ble. You ought rather to appreciate how much the great body of the North-ern people do crucify their feelings, in order to maintain their loyalty to the Constitution and the Union. I do op-pose the extension of slavery because my judgment and feeling so prompt me, and I am under no obligations to the contrary. If for this you and I must differ, differ we must. You say, if you were President, you would send an army and hang the leaders of the Missouri outrages upon the Kansas elections; still, if Kansas fairly votes herself a slave State she must be admitted, or the Un-ion must be dissolved. But how if she votes herself a slave State unfairly, that is, by the very means for which you say you would hang men? Must she still be admitted, or the Union dissolved? That will be the phase of the question when it first becomes a practical one. In your assumption that there may be a fair decision of the slavery question in

Kansas, I plainly see you and I would differ about the Nebraska law. I look upon that enactment not as a law, but as a violence from the beginning. It was conceived in violence, is maintained in violence, and is being executed in violence. I say it was conceived in violence, because the destruction of the Missouri Compromise, under the circumstances, was nothing less than violence. It was passed in violence, because it could not have passed at all but for the votes of many members in violence of the known will of their constituents. It is maintained in violence, because the elections since clearly demand its repeal; and the demand is openly disregarded.

You say men ought to be hung for the way they are executing the law; I say the way it is being executed is quite as good as any of its antecedents. It is being executed in the precise way which was intended from the first, else why does no Nebraska man express astonishment or condemnation? Poor Reeder is the only public man who has been silly enough to believe that anything like fairness was ever intended, and he has been bravely undeceived.

That Kansas will form a slave constitution, and with it will ask to be admitted into the Union, I take to be already a settled question, and so settled by the very means you so pointedly condemn. By every principle of law ever held by any court North or South, every Negro taken to Kansas is free; yet, in utter disregard of this,—in the spirit of violence merely,—that beautiful legislature gravely passes a law to hang any man who shall venture to inform a Negro of his legal rights. This is the subject and real object of the law. If, like Haman, they should hang upon the gallows of their own building, I shall not be among the mourners for their fate.

In my humble sphere, I shall advocate the restoration of the Missouri Compromise so long as Kansas remains a Territory, and when, by all these foul means, it seeks to come into the Union as a slave State, I shall oppose it. I am very loath in any case to withhold my assent to the enjoyment of property acquired or located in good faith; but I do not admit that good faith in taking a Negro to Kansas to be held in slavery is a probability with any man. Any man who has sense enough to be the controller of his own property has too much sense to misunderstand the outrageous character of the whole Nebraska business. But I digress. In my opposition to the admission of Kansas I shall have some company, but we may be beaten. If we are, I shall not on that account attempt to dissolve the Union. I think it probable, however, we shall be beaten. Standing as a unit among yourselves, you can, directly and indirectly, bribe enough of our men to carry the day, as you could on the open proposition to establish a monarchy. Get hold of some man in the North whose position and ability is such that he can make the support of your measure, whatever it may be, a Democratic party necessity, and the thing is done. Apropos of this, let me tell you an anecdote. Douglas introduced the Nebraska bill in January. In February afterward there was a called session of the Illinois legislature. Of the one hundred members composing the two branches of that body, about seventy were Democrats. These latter held a caucus, in which the Nebraska bill was talked of, if not formally discussed. It was thereby discovered that just three, and no more, were in favor of the measure. In a day or two Douglas's orders came on to have resolutions passed approving the bill; and they were passed by large majorities!!! The truth of this is vouched for by a bolting Democratic member. The masses, too, Democratic as well as Whig, were even nearer unanimous against it; but, as soon as the party necessity of supporting it became apparent, the way the Democrats began to see the wisdom and justice of it was perfectly astonishing.

You say that if Kansas fairly votes herself a free State, as a Christian you will rejoice at it. All decent slaveholders talk that way, and I do not doubt their candor. But they never vote that way. Although in a private letter or conversation you will express your preference that Kansas shall be free, you would vote for no man for Congress who would say the same thing publicly. No such man could be elected from any district in a slave State. You think Stringfellow and company ought to be hung; and yet at the next presidential election you will vote for the exact type and representative of Stringfellow. The slave-breeders and slave-traders are a small, odious, and detested class among you; and yet in politics they dictate the course of all of you, and are as completely your masters as you are the master of your own Negroes. You inquire where I now stand. That is a disputed point. I think I am a Whig; but others say there are no Whigs, and that I am an Abolitionist. When I was at Washington, I voted for the Wilmot proviso as good as forty times; and I never heard of any one attempting to unwhig me for that. I now do no more than oppose the extension of slavery. I am not a Know-nothing; that is certain. How could I be? How can any one who abhors the oppression of Negroes be in favor of degrading classes of white people? Our progress in degeneracy appears to me to be pretty rapid. As a nation we began by declaring that "all men are created equal." We now practically read it "all men are created equal, except Negroes." When the Know-nothings get control, it will read "all men are created equal, except Negroes and foreigners and Catholics." When it comes to this, I shall prefer emigrating to some country where they make no pretense of loving liberty,—to Russia, for instance, where despotism can be taken pure, and without the base alloy of hypocrisy.

Mary will probably pass a day or two in Louisville in October. My kindest regards to Mrs. Speed. On the leading subject of this letter, I have more of her sympathy than I have of yours; and yet let me say I am

Your friend forever,

ABRAHAM LINCOLN

I Will Risk the Dictatorship

To GENERAL J. HOOKER.
   EXECUTIVE MANSION, WASHINGTON,
   D. C., January 26, 1863.
MAJOR-GENERAL HOOKER.
   General: I have placed you at the head of the Army of the Potomac. Of course I have done this upon what appear to me to be sufficient reasons, and yet I think it best for you to know that there are some things in regard to which

I am not quite satisfied with you. I believe you to be a brave and skilful soldier, which of course I like. I also believe you do not mix politics with your profession, in which you are right. You have confidence in yourself, which is a valuable if not an indispensable quality. You are ambitious, which, within reasonable bounds, does good rather than harm; but I think that during General Burnside's command of the army you have taken counsel of your ambition and thwarted him as much as you could, in which you did a great wrong to the country and to a most meritorious and honorable brother officer. I have heard, in such a way as to believe it, of your recently saying that both the army and the government needed a dictator. Of course it was not for this, but in spite of it, that I have given you the command. Only those generals who gain successes can set up dictators. What I now ask of you is military success, and I will risk the dictatorship. The government will support you to the utmost of its ability, which is neither more nor less than it has done and will do for all commanders. I much fear that the spirit which you have aided to infuse into the army, of criticizing their commander and withholding confidence from him, will now turn upon you. I shall assist you as far as I can to put it down. Neither you nor Napoleon, if he were alive again, could get any good out of an army while such a spirit prevails in it; and now beware of rashness. Beware of rashness, but with energy and sleepless vigilance go forward and give us victories.

Yours very truly,

JOHN RUSKIN

The Nature of Theft by Unjust Profits

From Time and Tide

THE FIRST methods of polite robbery, by dishonest manufacture, and by debt, of which we have been hitherto speaking, are easily enough to be dealt with and ended, when once men have a mind to end them. But the third method of polite robbery, by dishonest acquisition, has many branches, and is involved among honest arts of acquisition, so that it is difficult to repress the one without restraining the other.

Observe, first, large fortunes cannot honestly be made by the work of *one* man's hands or head. If his work benefits multitudes, and involves position of high trust, it may be (I do not say that it *is*) expedient to reward him with great wealth or estate; but fortune of this kind is freely given in gratitude for benefit, not as repayment for labor. Also, men of peculiar genius in any art, if the public can enjoy the product of their genius, may set it at almost any price they choose; but this, I will show you when I come to speak of art, is unlawful on their part, and ruinous to their own powers. Genius must not be sold; the sale of it involves, in a transcendental, but perfectly true sense, the guilt both of simony and prostitution. Your labor only may be sold; your soul must not.

Now, by fair pay for fair labor, according to the rank of it, a man can obtain means of comfortable, or if he needs it, refined life. But he cannot obtain large fortune. Such fortunes as are now the prizes of commerce can be made only in one of three ways:—

1. By obtaining command over the labor of multitudes of other men, and taxing it for our own profit.

2. By treasure-trove,—as of mines, useful vegetable products, and the like, —in circumstances putting them under our own exclusive control.

3. By speculation (commercial gambling). The first two of these means of obtaining riches are, in some forms and within certain limits, lawful, and advantageous to the State. The third is entirely detrimental to it; for in all cases of profit derived from speculation, at best, what one man gains another loses; and the net result to the State is zero (pecuniarily), with the loss of time and ingenuity spent in the transaction; besides the disadvantage involved in the discouragement of the losing party, and the corrupted moral natures of both. This is the result of speculation at its best. At its worst, not only B. loses what A. gains (having taken his fair risk of such loss for his fair chance of gain), but C. and D., who never had any chance at all, are drawn in by B.'s fall, and the final result is that A. sets up his carriage on the collected sum which was once a means of living to a dozen families.

Nor is this all. For while real commerce is founded on real necessities or uses, and limited by these, speculation, of which the object is merely gain, seeks to excite imaginary necessities and popular desires, in order to gain its tempo-

rary profit from the supply of them. So that not only the persons who lend their money to it will be finally robbed, but the work done with their money will be for the most part useless, and thus the entire body of the public injured as well as the persons concerned in the transaction. Take, for instance, the architectural decorations of railways throughout the kingdom,—representing many millions of money for which no farthing of dividend can ever be forth-coming. The public will not be induced to pay the smallest fraction of higher fare to Rochester or Dover because the ironwork of the bridge which carries them over the Thames is covered with floral cockades, and the piers of it edged with ornamental cornices. All that work is simply put there by the builders that they may put the percentage upon it into their own pockets; and the rest of the money being thrown into that floral form, there is an end of it, as far as the shareholders are concerned. Millions upon millions have thus been spent, within the last twenty years, on ornamental arrangements of zigzag bricks, black and blue tiles, cast-iron foliage, and the like; of which millions, as I said, not a penny can ever return into the shareholders' pockets, nor contribute to public speed or safety on the line. It is all sunk forever in ornamental architecture, and (trust me for this!) *all that architecture is bad*. As such, it had incomparably better not have been built. Its only result will be to corrupt what capacity of taste or right pleasure in such work we have yet left to us! And consider a little, what other kind of result than that might have been attained if all those millions had been spent usefully: say, in buying land for the people, or building good houses for them, or (if it had been imperatively required to be spent decoratively) in laying out gardens and parks for them,—or buying noble works of art for their permanent possession,—or, best of all, establishing frequent public schools and libraries! Count what those lost millions would have so accomplished for you! But you left the affair to "supply and demand," and the British public had not brains enough to "demand" land, or lodging, or books. It "demanded" cast-iron cockades and zigzag cornices, and is "supplied" with them, to its beatitude for evermore.

Now, the theft we first spoke of, by falsity of workmanship or material, is indeed, so far worse than these thefts by dishonest acquisition, that there is no possible excuse for it on the ground of self-deception; while many speculative thefts are committed by persons who mean really to do no harm, but think the system on the whole a fair one, and do the best they can in it for themselves. But in the real fact of the crime, when consciously committed, in the numbers reached by its injury, in the degree of suffering it causes to those whom it ruins, in the baseness of its calculated betrayal of implicit trust, in the yet more perfect vileness of the obtaining such trust by misrepresentation, only that it *may* be betrayed, and in the impossibility that the crime should be at all committed, except by persons of good disposition and large knowledge of the world,—what manner of theft is so wholly unpardonable, so inhuman, so contrary to every law and instinct which binds and animates society?

And then consider farther, how many of the carriages that glitter in our streets are driven, and how many of the stately houses that gleam among our English fields are inhabited, by this kind of thief!

I happened to be reading this morning (29th March) some portions of the Lent services, and I came to a pause over the familiar words, "And with Him they crucified two thieves." Have you ever considered (I speak to you now as a professing Christian) why, in the accomplishment of the "numbering among transgressors," the transgressors chosen should have been especially thieves—not murderers, nor, as far as we know, sinners by any gross violence? Do you observe how the sin of theft is again and again indicated as the chiefly antagonistic one to the law of Christ? "This he said, not that he cared for the poor, but because he was a thief, and had the bag" (of Judas). And again, though Barabbas was a leader of sedition and a murderer besides—(that the popular election might be in all respects perfect)—yet St. John, in curt and conclusive account of him, fastens again on the theft. "Then cried they all again saying, Not this man, but Barabbas. Now Barabbas was a robber." I believe myself the reason to be that theft is indeed, in its subtle forms, the most complete and excuseless of human crimes. Sins of violence usually have passion to excuse them: they may be the madness of moments; or they may be apparently the only means of extrication from calamity. In other cases, they are the diseased habits of lower and brutified natures. But theft involving deliberative intellect, and absence of passion, is the purest type of wilful iniquity, in persons capable of doing right. Which being so, it seems to be fast becoming the practice of modern society to crucify its Christ indeed, as willingly as ever, in the persons of His poor; but by no means now to crucify its thieves beside Him! It elevates its thieves after another fashion; sets them upon an hill, that their light may shine before men, and that all may see their good works, and glorify their Father in—the Opposite of Heaven.

I think your trade parliament will have to put an end to this kind of business somehow! But it cannot be done by laws merely, where the interests and circumstances are so extended and complex. Nay, even as regards lower and more defined crimes, the assigned punishment is not to be thought of as a preventive means; but only as the seal of opinion set by society on the fact.

Crime cannot be hindered by punishment; it will always find some shape and outlet, unpunishable or unclosed. Crime can only be truly hindered by letting no man grow up a criminal—by taking away the *will* to commit sin; not by mere punishment of its commission. Crime, small and great, can only be truly stayed by education—not the education of the intellect only, which is, on some men, wasted, and for others mischievous; but education of the heart, which is alike good and necessary for all.

1867

THOMAS CARLYLE

The "Rape" of Alsace-Lorraine

To THE LONDON *Times*
Chelsea
18 November 1870.
Sir,

It is probably an amiable trait of human nature, this cheap pity and newspaper lamentation over fallen and afflicted France; but it seems to me a very idle, dangerous, and misguided feeling, as applied to the cession of Alsace and Lorraine by France to her German conquerors; and argues, on the part of England, a most profound ignorance as to the mutual history of France and Germany, and the conduct of France towards that Country, for long centuries back. The question for the Germans, in this crisis, is not one of "magnanimity," of "heroic pity and forgiveness to a fallen foe," but of solid prudence, and practical consideration what the fallen foe will, in all likelihood, do when once on his feet again. Written on her memory, in a dismally instructive manner, Germany has an experience of four hundred years on this point; of which on the English memory, if it ever was recorded there, there is now little or no trace visible. . . . No nation ever had so bad a neighbor as Germany has had in France for the last four hundred years; bad in all manner of ways; insolent, rapacious, insatiable, unappeasable, continually aggressive.

And now, furthermore, in all History there is no insolent, unjust neighbor that ever got so complete, instantaneous, and ignominious a smashing down as France has now got from Germany. Germany, after four hundred years of ill-usage, and generally of ill-fortune, from that neighbor, has had at last the great happiness to see its enemy fairly down in this manner:—and Germany, I do clearly believe, would be a foolish nation not to think of raising up some secure boundary-fence between herself and such a neighbor, now that she has the chance.

There is no law of Nature that I know of, no Heaven's Act of Parliament, whereby France, alone of terrestrial beings, shall not restore any portion of her plundered goods when the owners they were wrenched from have an opportunity upon them. To nobody, except to France herself for the moment, can it be credible that there is such a law of Nature. Alsace and Lorraine were not got, either of them, in so divine a manner as to render that a probability. The cunning of Richelieu, the grandiose longsword of Louis XIV., these are the only titles of France to those German countries. Richelieu screwed them loose (and, by happy accident, there was a Turenne, as General, got screwed along with them;—Turenne, I think, was mainly German by blood and temper, had not Francis I. egged on his ancestor, the little Duke of Bouillon, . . . and gradually *made* him French); Louis le Grand, with his Turenne as supreme of modern Generals, managed the rest of the operation,—except indeed, I should say, the burning of the Palatinate, from Heidelberg Palace steadily downwards, into black ruin; which Turenne would not do sufficiently, and which Louis had to get done by another. There was also a good deal of extortionate law-practice, what we may call violently-sharp attorneyism, put in use. The great Louis's *"Chambres de Réunion,"* Metz Chamber, Brissac Chamber, were once of high infamy, and much complained of, here in England, and everywhere else beyond the Rhine. The Grand Louis, except by sublime gesture, ironically polite, made no answer. He styled himself, on his very coins (*écu* of 1687, say the

Medallists), *Excelsus super omnes gentes Dominus,* but it is certain attorneyism of the worst sort was one of his instruments in this conquest of Alsace. Nay, as to Strasburg, it was not even attorneyism, much less a longsword, that did the feat; it was a housebreaker's *jemmy* on the part of the *Grand Monarque.* Strasburg was got in time of profound peace by bribing of the magistrates to do treason, on his part, and admit his garrison one night.

Nor as to Metz la Pucelle, nor any of these Three Bishoprics, was it force of war that brought them over to France; rather it was force of fraudulent pawn-broking. King Henry II. (year 1552) got these places—Protestants applying to him in their extreme need—as we may say, in the way of pledge. Henri entered there with banners spread and drums beating, "solely in defence of German liberty, as God shall witness"; did nothing for Protestantism or German liberty (German liberty managing rapidly to help itself in this instance); and then, like a brazen-faced, unjust pawn-broker, refused to give the places back,—"had ancient rights over them," extremely indubitable to him, and could not give them back. And never yet, by any pressure of persuasion, would. The great Charles V., Protestantism itself now supporting, endeavoured, with his utmost energy and to the very cracking of his heart, to compel him, but could not. The present Hohenzollern King, a modest and pacific man in comparison, could and has. I believe it to be perfectly just, rational and wise that Germany should take these countries home with her from her unexampled campaign; and, by well fortifying her own old *Wasgau* ("Vosges"), *Hundsrück* (Dog's-back), Three Bishoprics, and other military strengths, secure herself in time coming against French visits.

The French complain dreadfully of threatened "loss of honour"; and lamentable bystanders plead earnestly, "Don't dishonour France; leave poor France's honour bright." But will it save the *honour* of France to refuse paying for the glass she has voluntarily broken in her neighbour's windows? The attack upon the windows was her dishonour. Signally disgraceful to any nation was her late assault on Germany; equally signal has been the ignominy of its execution on the part of France. The honour of France can be saved only by the deep repentance of France; and by the serious determination never to do so again,—to do the reverse of so forever henceforth. In that way may the honour of France again gradually brighten to the height of its old splendour,—far beyond the *First* Napoleonic, much more than the *Third,* or any recent sort, —and offer again to our voluntary love and grateful estimation all the fine and graceful qualities Nature has implanted in the French. . . .

A hundred years ago there was in England the liveliest desire, and at one time an actual effort and hope, to recover Alsace and Lorraine from the French. Lord Carteret, called afterwards Lord Granville (no ancestor, in any sense of his now Honourable Synonym), thought by some to be, with the one exception of Lord Chatham, the wisest Foreign Secretary we ever had, and especially the "one Secretary that ever spoke German or understood German matters at all," had set his heart on this very object; and had fair prospects of achieving it,—had not our poor dear Duke of Newcastle suddenly peddled him out of it; and even out of office altogether, into sullen disgust (and too much of *wine* withal, says Walpole), and into total oblivion by his Nation, which, except Chatham, has none such to remember. That Bismarck, and Germany along with him, should now at this propitious juncture make a like demand is no surprise to me. After such provocation, and after such a victory, the resolution does seem rational, just and even modest. And considering all that has occurred since that memorable cataclysm at Sedan, I could reckon it creditable to the sense and moderation of Count Bismarck that he stands steadily by this; demanding nothing more, resolute to take nothing less, and advancing with slow calmness towards it by the eligiblest roads. The "Siege of Paris," which looks like the hugest and most hideous farce-tragedy ever played under this sun, Bismarck evidently hopes will never need to come to uttermost bombardment, to million-fold death by hunger, or the kindling of Paris and its carpentries and asphalt streets by shells and red-hot balls into a sea of fire. Diligent, day by day, seem those Prussians, never resting nor too much hasting; well knowing the proverb, "Slow fire makes sweet malt." I believe Bismarck will get his Alsace and what he wants of Lorraine; and likewise that it will do him, and us, and all the world, and even France itself by and by, a great deal of good. Anarchic France gets her first stern lesson there,—a terribly drastic dose of physic to sick France!—and well will it be for her if she can learn her lesson honestly. If she cannot, she will get another, and ever another; learnt the lesson must be.

Considerable misconception as to Herr von Bismarck is still prevalent in England. The English newspapers, nearly all of them, seem to me to be only getting towards a true knowledge of Bismarck, but not yet got to it. The standing likeness, circulating everywhere ten years ago, of demented Bismarck and his ditto King to Strafford and Charles I. *versus* our Long Parliament (*as* like as Macedon to Monmouth, and not liker) has now vanished from the earth, no whisper of it ever to be heard more. That pathetic Niobe of Denmark, reft violently of her children (which were stolen children, and were dreadfully ill-nursed by Niobe-Denmark), is also nearly gone; and will go altogether as soon as knowledge of the matter is had. Bismarck, as I read him, is not a person of "Napoleonic" ideas, but of ideas quite superior to Napoleonic; shows no invincible "lust of territory," nor is tormented with "vulgar ambition," etc.; but has aims very far beyond that sphere; and in fact seems to me to be striving with strong faculty, by patient, grand and successful steps, towards an object beneficial to Germans and to all other men. That noble, patient, deep, pious and solid Germany should be at length welded into a Nation, and became Queen of the Continent, instead of vapouring, vain-glorious, gesticulating, quarrelsome, restless and over-sensitive France, seems to me the hopefulest public fact that has occurred in my time.

I remain, Sir, yours truly,

GERARD MANLEY HOPKINS

The Communist Future

To Robert Bridges
Stonyhurst,
Whalley, Lancashire,
August 2, 1871.

My dear Bridges,

Our holidays have begun, so I will write again. I feel inclined to begin by asking whether you are secretary to the International as you seem to mean me to think nothing too bad for you but then I remember that you never relished 'the intelligent artisan'. I must tell you I am always thinking of the Communist future. The too intelligent artisan is master of the situation I believe. Perhaps it is what everyone believes, I do not see the papers or hear strangers often enough to know. It is what Carlyle has long threatened and foretold. But his writings are, as he might himself say, 'most inefficacious-strenuous heaven-protestations, caterwaul, and Cassandra-wailings'. He preaches obedience but I do not think he has done much except to ridicule instead of strengthening the hands of the powers that be. Some years ago when he published his *Shooting Niagara* he did make some practical suggestions but so vague that they should rather be called '*too* dubious moonstone-grindings and on the whole impracticable-practical unveracities'. However I am afraid some great revolution is not far off. Horrible to say, in a manner I am a Communist. Their ideal bating some

Reprinted from *The Letters of Gerard Manley Hopkins to Robert Bridges* (ed. C. C. Abbott) by permission of the poet's family and the Oxford University Press, publishers.

things is nobler than that professed by any secular statesman I know of (I must own I live in bat-light and shoot at a venture). Besides it is just.—I do not mean the means of getting to it are. But it is a dreadful thing for the greatest and most necessary part of a very rich nation to live a hard life without dignity, knowledge, comforts, delight, or hopes in the midst of plenty—which plenty they make. They profess that they do not care what they wreck and burn, the old civilisation and order must be destroyed. This is a dreadful look out but what has the old civilisation done for them? As it at present stands in England it is itself in great measure founded on wrecking. But they got none of the spoils, they came in for nothing but harm from it then and thereafter. England has grown hugely wealthy but this wealth has not reached the working classes; I expect it has made their condition worse. Besides this iniquitous order the old civilisation

embodies another order mostly old and what is new in direct entail from the old, the old religion, learning, law, art, etc and all the history that is preserved in standing monuments. But as the working classes have not been educated they know next to nothing of all this and cannot be expected to care if they destroy it. The more I look the more black and deservedly black the future looks, so I will write no more.

I can hardly believe that this is August and your letter dated May. True there has been here and I believe elsewhere no summer between. There seems some chance now. In a fortnight we are going, also for a fortnight, to Inellan in Argyleshire on the Clyde. After that I expect to pay my people a short visit down near Southampton, where they have taken a cottage. None of them are turned Catholics: I do not expect it.

Believe me your affectionate friend

GERARD MANLEY HOPKINS

Sprung Rhythm

To ROBERT BRIDGES
St. Beuno's, St. Asaph.
Aug. 21, 1877.

Dearest Bridges,

Your letter cannot amuse Father Provincial, for he is on the unfathering deeps outward bound to Jamaica: I shd. not think of telling you anything about his reverence's goings and comings if it were not that I know this fact has been chronicled in the Catholic papers.

Enough that it amuses me, especially the story about Wooldridge and the Wagnerite, wh. is very good.

Your parody reassures me about your understanding the metre. Only remark, as you say that there is no conceivable licence I shd. not be able to justify, that with all my licences, or rather laws, I am stricter than you and I might say than anybody I know. With the exception of the *Bremen* stanza, which

Reprinted from *The Letters of Gerard Manley Hopkins to Robert Bridges* (ed. C. C. Abbott) by permission of the poet's family and of the Oxford University Press, publishers.

was, I think, the first written after 10 years' interval of silence, and before I had fixed my principles, my rhymes are rigidly good—to the ear—and such rhymes as *love* and *prove* I scout utterly. And my quantity is not like 'Fĭftў̄twō Bĕdfŏrd Squāre', where *fĭftў̆* might pass but *Bĕdfŏrd* I should never admit. Not only so but Swinburne's dactyls and anapaests are halting to my ear: I never allow e.g. *I* or *my* (that is diphthongs, for $I = a + i$ and $my = ma + i$) in the short or weak syllables of those feet, excepting before vowels, semi-vowels, or *r*, and rarely then, or when the measure becomes (what is the word?) molossic —thus: ⌣–⌣ |⌣–⌣ |⌣–⌣, for then the first short is almost long. If you look again you will see. So that I may say my apparent licences are counterbalanced, and more, by my strictness. In fact all English verse, except Milton's, almost, offends me as 'licentious'. Remember this.

I do not of course claim to have invented *sprung rhythms* but only *sprung rhythm;* I mean that single lines and single instances of it are not uncommon in English and I have pointed them out in lecturing—e.g. 'why should this : desert be?'—which the editors have variously amended; 'There to meet : with Macbeth' or 'There to meet with Mac : beth'; Campbell has some throughout the *Battle of the Baltic*—'and their fleet along the deep: proudly shone'—and *Ye Mariners*—'as ye sweep : through the deep' etc; Moore has some which I cannot recall; there is one in *Grongar Hill;* and, not to speak of *Pom pom,* in Nursery Rhymes, Weather Saws, and Refrains they are very common—but what I do in the *Deutschland* etc is to enfranchise them as a regular and permanent principle of scansion.

There are no outriding feet in the *Deutschland*. An outriding foot is, by a sort of contradiction, a recognized extra-metrical effect; it is and it is not part of the metre; not part of it, not being counted, but part of it by producing a calculated effect which tells in the general success. But the long, e.g. sevensyllabled, feet of the *Deutschland,* are strictly metrical. Outriding feet belong to counterpointed verse, which supposes a well-known and unmistakeable or unforgettable standard rhythm: the *Deutschland* is not counterpointed; counterpoint is excluded by sprung rhythm. But in some of my sonnets I have mingled the two systems: this is the most delicate and difficult business of all.

The choruses in *Samson Agonistes* are intermediate between counterpointed and sprung rhythm. In reality they are sprung, but Milton keeps up a fiction of counterpointing the heard rhythm (which is the same as the mounted rhythm) upon a standard rhythm which is never heard but only counted and therefore really does not exist. The want of a metrical notation and the fear of being thought to write mere rhythmic or (who knows what the critics might not have said?) even unrhythmic prose drove him to this. Such rhythm as French and Welsh poetry has is sprung, counterpointed upon a counted rhythm, but it differs from Milton's in being little calculated, not more perhaps than prose consciously written rhythmically, like orations for instance; it is in fact the *native rhythm* of the words used bodily imported into verse; whereas Milton's mounted rhythm is a real poetical rhythm, having its own laws and recurrence, but further embarrassed by having to count.

Why do I employ sprung rhythm at all? Because it is the nearest to the rhythm of prose, that is the native and natural rhythm of speech, the least forced, the most rhetorical and emphatic of all possible rhythms, combining, as it seems to me, opposite and, one wd. have thought, incompatible excellences, markedness of rhythm — that is rhythm's self—and naturalness of expression—for why, if it is forcible in prose to say 'lashed : rod', am I obliged to weaken this in verse, which ought to be stronger, not weaker, into 'láshed birch-ród' or something?

My verse is less to be read than heard, as I have told you before; it is oratorical, that is the rhythm is so. I think if you will study what I have here said you will be much more pleased with it and may I say? converted to it.

You ask may you call it 'presumptious jugglery'. No, but only for this reason, that *presumptious* is not English.

I cannot think of altering anything.

Why shd. I? I do not write for the public. You are my public and I hope to convert you.

You say you wd. not for any money read my poem again. Nevertheless I beg you will. Besides money, you know, there is love. If it is obscure do not bother yourself with the meaning but pay attention to the best and most intelligible stanzas, as the two last of each part and the narrative of the wreck. If you had done this you wd. have liked it better and sent me some serviceable criticisms, but now your criticism is of no use, being only a protest memorialising me against my whole policy and proceedings.

I may add for your greater interest and edification that what refers to myself in the poem is all strictly and literally true and did all occur; nothing is added for poetical padding.

Believe me your affectionate friend

BILL NYE

My Thanks for the Same

To THE POSTMASTER GENERAL
Office of Daily Boomerang,
Laramie City, Wy.,
August 9, 1882

My Dear General:

I have received by telegraph the news of my nomination by the President and my confirmation by the Senate, as postmaster at Laramie, and wish to extend my thanks for the same.

I have ordered an entirely new set of boxes and post office outfit, including

new corrugated cuspidors for the lady clerks.

I look upon the appointment, myself, as a great triumph of eternal truth over error and wrong. It is one of the epochs, I may say, in the Nation's onward march toward political purity and perfection. I do not know when I have noticed any stride in the affairs of state which so thoroughly impressed me with its wisdom.

Now that we are co-workers in the

same department, I trust that you will not feel shy or backward in consulting me at any time relative to matters concerning post office affairs. Be perfectly frank with me, and feel perfectly free to just bring anything of that kind right to me. Do not feel reluctant because I may at times appear haughty and indifferent, cold or reserved. Perhaps you do not think I know the difference between a general delivery window and a three-m quad, but that is a mistake. My general information is far beyond my years.

With profoundest regard, and a hearty endorsement of the policy of the President and the Senate, whatever it may be, I remain, sincerely yours,

BILL NYE, P.M.

Gen. Frank Hatton, Washington, D.C.

MARK TWAIN

How to Lecture Impromptu

To W. D. HOWELLS

SANNA, SWEDEN,
Sept. 26, '99.

Dear Howells,

Get your lecture by heart—it will pay you. I learned a trick in Vienna—by accident—which I wish I had learned years ago. I meant to read from a Tauchnitz, because I knew I hadn't well memorized the pieces; and I came on with the book and read a few sentences, then remembered that the sketch needed a few words of explanatory introduction; and so, lowering the book and now and then unconsciously using it to gesture with, I talked the introduction, and it happened to carry me into the sketch *itself,* and then I went on, pretending that I was merely talking extraneous matter and would come to the sketch *presently.* It was a beautiful success. I knew the substance of the sketch and the telling phrases of it; and so, the throwing of the rest of it into informal talk as I went along limbered it up and gave it the snap and go and freshness of an impromptu. I was to read several pieces, and I played the same game with all of them, and always the audience thought I was being reminded of outside things and throwing them in, and was going to hold up the book and begin on the sketch presently —and so I always got through the sketch before they were entirely sure that it had begun. I did the same thing in Budapest and had the same good time over again. It's a new dodge, and the best one that was ever invented. Try it. You'll never lose your audience—not even for a moment. Their attention is fixed, and never wavers. And that is not the case where one reads from book or MS., or where he stands up without a note and frankly exposes the fact, by his confident manner and smooth phrasing, that he is not improvising, but reciting from memory. And in the heat of telling a thing that is memorised in substance only, one flashes out the happiest suddenly-begotten phrases every now and then! Try it. Such a phrase has a life and sparkle about it that twice as good a one could not exhibit if prepared beforehand, and it "fetches" an audience in such an enthusing and inspiring and uplifting way that that lucky phrase breeds another one, sure.

Your September instalment was delicious—every word of it. You haven't lost any of your splendid art. Callers have arrived.

With love

HENRY ADAMS

Preparation for Teaching History

To Henry Cabot Lodge
Luxor,
2 January, 1873.

I received your letter of November 3d just as I was leaving Cairo, and as I have been busily reading myself, I delayed answering till I knew what I had to say. So far as I can see, you are acting on such good advice and working in such good company that I can add very little to your means of getting ahead. Perhaps to a critical eye, the field you have entered may seem rather wide. I doubt whether a man can profitably spread his reading over a very large range unless he has some definite object clearly fixed in his head. My wish is to lead you gradually up to your definite object, but what it must be will depend on the bent of your own tastes. I can only tell you the style of thing that seems to me best.

The first step seems to me to be to familiarise one's mind with thoroughly good work, to master the scientific method, and to adopt the rigid principle of subordinating everything to perfect thoroughness of study. I have therefore advised your learning German, because I think the German method so sound. I am glad you are reading Sohm. But Sohm's work is on too large a scale to imitate. I would like to have you take up some of the smaller works, which have broken the way for him. Read as most kin to your interests, von Maurer's *Einleitung,* Thudichum's *Gau und Markverfassung,* Brunner's *Entstehung der Schwurgerichte.* Study these, not merely for their matter but as literary work. See how the men go at it, and then take an English work, Mayne if you like, or Freeman, and see how they reach their results. I do not mean to set up the Germans as exclusive models at all. But they have the great merit of a very high standard of knowledge. An ignorant, or a superficial work could hardly come from any distinguished German student. I can't say the same for other countries. Great as is Mr. Freeman's parade of knowledge, he has never written anything really solid, and Mr.—or rather Sir

The selections from *The Letters of Henry Adams,* edited by W. C. Ford, are used by permission of the publishers, Houghton Mifflin Company.

Henry—Mayne's book is precisely such a one as I like to give to students to admire and to criticise. I know of no writer who generalises more brilliantly. But everyone of his generalisations requires a lifetime of work to prove it.

I propose no more to the fellows who are kind enough to think my teaching worth their listening to—those of them I mean who take the thing in the spirit I offer it in—than to teach them how to do their work. The College chose to make me Professor of History—I don't know why, for I knew no more history than my neighbors. And it pitchforked me into mediæval history, of which I knew nothing. But it makes little difference what one teaches; the great thing is to train scholars for work, and for that purpose there is no better field than mediæval history to future historians. The mere wish to give a practical turn to my men has almost necessarily led me to give a strong legal bent to the study. Starting from this point, I found that at the outset the Family was the centre of early law. To study the Family therefore in its different relations, was the natural course to follow. From this point we must follow down the different lines of development. The organisation of the Family, the law of inheritance, of testaments, of land tenure, of evidence and legal procedure, the relations of the Family to the community, in its different forms of village, county and state, as well as many other parallel lines of study lay open before me and I have only to indicate them to true students whether of law or of history, and let them go to work and develop them. Of course I don't pretend to have mastered these subjects myself. No one has yet done so. But men like you and Ames can win a reputation by following up any

one line of investigation, and the occupation is as good as mathematics for the logical faculty, while it leads ultimately to all the nearer subjects of historical study.

Of course our own law and institutions are what we aim at, and we only take German institutions so far as they throw light on English affairs. I think you would do well to keep this in mind and to take some special line of work so soon as you have become tolerably acquainted with the general bearings of things. Of course you will choose whatever you think best suits your tastes. It does not follow that preliminary legal reading is to make you a historian of law, any more than preliminary grammar reading would result in making you a historian of philology. It matters very little what line you take provided you can catch the tail of an idea to develope with solid reasoning and thorough knowledge. America or Europe, our own century or prehistoric time, are all alike to the historian if he can only find out what men are and have been driving at, consciously or unconsciously. So much is this the case that I myself am now strongly impelled to write an Essay on Egyptian Law, for I have a sort of notion that I could draw out of that queer subject some rather surprising deductions, perhaps I could fix a legal landmark in history, but I have too much on my hands and must let the Cheopses and the Ramses alone.

The Nile is not a bad place for study, and I have run through a library of books here. I want to write to Ames, but until I have got some sort of order into my ideas I shall have nothing to say. But I would be very glad to have a line from him to know how he gets on and whether he has struck any new vein. There are many points I want to discuss with him but they will keep. Meanwhile pray continue to write to me how things are going with you and at Cambridge. Send for a copy of Schmid's *Gesetze der Angel-Sachsen;* it may be useful to you next year, as I want to go hard to early English law. I have got to learn to read Anglo-Saxon, but that is too much to expect from you or anyone not obliged to do it.

Pray give my best regards to your wife.

HENRY ADAMS

The Tendency of History

To HERBERT B. ADAMS
Guadalajara,
December 12, 1894
Dear Sir:

I regret extremely that constant absence has prevented me from attending the meetings of the Historical Association. On the date which your letter mentions as that of its first decennial I shall not be within reach. I have to ask you to offer my apology to the members, and the assurance that at that moment I am believed to be somewhere beyond the Isthmus of Panama. Perhaps this absence runs in some of the mysterious ways of nature's law, for you will not forget that when you did me the honor to make me your president I was still farther away—in Tahiti or Fiji, I believe—and never even had an opportunity to thank you. Evidently I am fitted only to be an absent president, and you will pardon a defect which is clearly not official, but a condition of the man.

I regret this fault the more because I would have liked to be of service, and perhaps there is service that might usefully be performed. Even the effort to hold together the persons interested in history is worth making. That we should ever act on public opinion with the weight of one compact and one energetic conviction is hardly to be expected, but that one day or another we shall be compelled to act individually or in groups I cannot doubt. With more anxiety than confidence, I should have liked to do something, however trifling, to hold the association together and unite it on some common ground, with a full understanding of the course which history seems destined to take and with a good-natured willingness to accept or reject the result, but in any case not to quarrel over it.

No one who has watched the course of history during the last generation can have felt doubt of its tendency. Those of us who read Buckle's first volume when it appeared in 1857 and almost immediately afterwards, in 1859, read the *Origin of the Species* and felt the violent impulse which Darwin gave to the study of natural laws, never doubted that historians would follow until they had exhausted every possible hypothesis to create a science of history. Year after year passed, and little progress has

From Henry Adams, *The Degradation of Democratic Dogma.* By permission of The Macmillan Company, publishers.

been made. Perhaps the mass of students are more skeptical now than they were thirty years ago of the possibility that such a science can be created. Yet almost every successful historian has been busy with it, adding here a new analysis, a new generalization there; a clear and definite connection where before the rupture of idea was absolute; and, above all, extending the field of study until it shall include all races, all countries, and all times. Like other branches of science, history is now encumbered and hampered by its own mass, but its tendency is always the same, and cannot be other than what it is. That the effort to make history a science may fail is possible, and perhaps probable; but that it should cease, is not within the range of experience. Historians will not, and even if they would they cannot, abandon the attempt. Science itself would admit its own failure if it admitted that man, the most important of all its subjects, could not be brought within its range.

You may be sure that four out of five serious students of history who are living today have, in the course of their work, felt that they stood on the brink of a great generalization that would reduce all history under a law as clear as the laws which govern the material world. As the great writers of our time have touched one by one the separate fragments of admitted law by which society betrays its character as a subject for science, not one of them can have failed to feel an instant's hope that he might find the secret which would transform these odds and ends of philosophy into one self-evident, harmonious, and complete system. He has seemed to have it, as the Spanish say, in his inkstand. Scores of times he must have dropped his pen to think how one short

step, one sudden inspiration, would show all human knowledge; how, in these thickset forests of history, one corner turned, one faint trail struck, would bring him on the highroad of science. Every professor who has tried to teach the doubtful facts which we now call history must have felt that sooner or later he or another would put order in chaos and bring light into darkness. Not so much genius or favor was needed as patience and good luck. The law was certainly there, and as certainly was in places actually visible, to be touched and handled, as though it were a law of chemistry or physics. No teacher with a spark of imagination or with an idea of scientific method can have helped dreaming of the immortality that would be achieved by the man who should successfully apply Darwin's method to the facts of human history.

Those of us who have had occasion to keep abreast of the rapid progress which has been made in history during the last fifty years must be convinced that the same rate of progress during another half century would necessarily raise history to the rank of a science. Our only doubt is whether the same rate can possibly be maintained. If not, our situation is simple. In that case, we shall remain more or less where we are. But we have reached a point where we ought to face the possibility of a great and perhaps a sudden change in the importance of our profession. We cannot help asking ourselves what would happen if some new Darwin were to demonstrate the laws of historical evolution.

I admit that the mere idea of such an event fills my mind with anxiety. When I remember the astonishing influence exerted by a mere theorist like Rousseau; by a reasoner like Adam

Smith; by a philosopher, beyond contact with material interests, like Darwin, I cannot imagine the limits of the shock that might follow the establishment of a fixed science of history. Hitherto our profession has been encouraged, or, at all events, tolerated by governments and by society as an amusing or instructive and, at any rate, a safe and harmless branch of inquiry. But what will be the attitude of government or of society toward any conceivable science of history? We know what followed Rousseau; what industrial and political struggles have resulted from the teachings of Adam Smith; what a revolution and what vehement opposition has been and still is caused by the ideas of Darwin. Can we imagine any science of history that would not be vastly more violent in its effects than the dissension roused by any one or by all three of these great men?

I ask myself, what shape can be given to any science of history that will not shake to its foundations some prodigious interest? The world is made up of a few immense forces, each with an organization that corresponds with its strength. The church stands first; and at the outset we must assume that the church will not and cannot accept any science of history, because science, by its definition, must exclude the idea of a personal and active providence. The state stands next; and the hostility of the state would be assured toward any system or science that might not strengthen its arm. Property is growing more and more timid and looks with extreme jealousy on any new idea that may weaken vested rights. Labor is growing more and more self-confident and looks with contempt on all theories that do not support its own. Yet we cannot conceive of a science of history that would not, directly or indirectly, affect all these vast social forces.

Any science assumes a necessary sequence of cause and effect, a force resulting in motion which cannot be other than what it is. Any science of history must be absolute, like other sciences, and must fix with mathematical certainty the path which human society has got to follow. That path can hardly lead toward the interests of all the great social organizations. We cannot conceive that it should help at the same time the church and the state, property and communism, capital and poverty, science and religion, trade and art. Whatever may be its orbit it must, at least for a time, point away from some of these forces toward others which are regarded as hostile. Conceivably, it might lead off in eccentric lines away from them all, but by no power of our imagination can we conceive that it should lead toward them all.

Although I distrust my own judgment and look earnestly for guidance to those who are younger than I and closer to the movement of the time, I cannot be wholly wrong in thinking that a change has come over the tendency of liberal thought since the middle of the century. Darwin led an intellectual revival much more hopeful than any movement that can now be seen in Europe, except among the socialists. Had history been converted into a science at that time, it would perhaps have taken the form of cheerful optimism which gave to Darwin's conclusions the charm of possible human perfectibility. Of late years the tone of European thought has been distinctly despondent among the classes which were formerly most hopeful. If a science of history were established to-day on the lines of its recent development, I greatly fear it would take its tone from the pessimism of Paris, Berlin, London, and St. Petersburg, unless it brought into sight some new and hitherto unsuspected path for civilization to pursue.

If it pointed to socialistic triumph it would place us in an attitude of hostility toward existing institutions. Even supposing that our universities would permit their professors in this country to announce the scientific certainty of communistic triumphs, could Europe be equally liberal? Would property, on which the universities depend, allow such freedom of instruction? Would the state suffer its foundation to be destroyed? Would society as now constituted tolerate the open assertion of a necessity which should affirm its approaching overthrow?

If, on the other hand, the new science required us to announce that the present evils of the world—its huge armaments, its vast accumulations of capital, its advancing materialism, and declining arts—were to be continued, exaggerated, over another thousand years, no one would listen to us with satisfaction. Society would shut its eyes and ears. If we proved the certainty of our results we should prove it without a sympathetic audience and without good effect. No one except artists and socialists would listen, and the conviction we should produce on them could lead only to despair and attempts at anarchy in art, in thought, and in society.

If, finally, the science should prove that society must at a given time revert to the church and recover its old foundation of absolute faith in a personal providence and a revealed religion, it commits suicide.

In whatever direction we look we can see no possibility of converting history into a science without bringing it into hostility toward one or more of the most powerful organizations of the era. If the world is to continue moving toward the point which it has so energetically pursued during the last fifty years, it will destroy the hopes of the vast organizations of labor. If it is to change its course and become communistic, it places us in direct hostility to the entire fabric of our social and political system. If it goes on, we must preach despair. If it goes back, it must deny and repudiate science. If it goes forward, round a circle which leads through communism, we must declare ourselves hostile to the property that pays us and the institutions we are bound in duty to support.

A science cannot be played with. If an hypothesis is advanced that obviously brings into direct sequence of cause and effect all the phenomena of human history, we must accept it, and if we accept, we must teach it. The mere fact that it overthrows social organizations cannot affect our attitude. The rest of society can reject or ignore, but we must follow the new light no matter where it leads. Only about two hundred and fifty years ago the common sense of mankind, supported by the authority of revealed religion, affirmed the undoubted and self-evident fact that the sun moved round the earth. Galileo suddenly asserted and proved that the earth moved round the sun. You know what followed, and the famous *"É pur si muove."* Even if we, like Galileo, should be obliged by the religious or secular authority to recant and repudiate our science, we should still have to say as he did in secret, if not in public, *"É pur si muove."*

Those of us who have reached or

passed middle age need not trouble ourselves very much about the future. We have seen one or two great revolutions in thought and we have had enough. We are not likely to accept any new theory that shall threaten to disturb our repose. We should reject at once, and probably by a large majority, a hypothetical science that must obviously be incapable of proof. We should take the attitude that our fathers took toward the theories and hypotheses of Darwin. We may meantime reply to such conundrums by the formula that has smoothed our path in life over many disasters and cataclysms: "Perhaps the crisis will never occur; and even if it does occur, we shall probably be dead." To us who have already gone as far as we set out to go, this answer is good and sufficient, but those who are to be the professors and historians of the future have got duties and responsibilities of a heavier kind than we older ones ever have had to carry. They cannot afford to deal with such a question in such a spirit. They would have to rejoin in Heine's word:

> Also fragen wir beständig,
> Bis man uns mit einer Handvoll
> Erde endlich stopft die Mäuler,
> Aber ist das eine Antwort?

They may at any time in the next fifty years be compelled to find an answer, "Yes" or "No," under the pressure of the most powerful organizations the world has ever known for the suppression of influences hostile to its safety. If this association should be gifted with the length of life that we all wish for it, a span of a century at least, it can hardly fail to be torn by some such dilemma. Our universities, at all events, must be prepared to meet it. If such a crisis should come, the universities throughout the world will have done the most to create it, and are under most obligation to find a solution for it. I will not deny that the shadow of this coming event has cast itself upon me, both as a teacher and a writer; or that, in the last ten years, it has often kept me silent where I should once have spoken with confidence, or has caused me to think long and anxiously before expressing in public any opinion at all. Beyond a doubt, silence is best. In these remarks, which are only casual and offered in the paradoxical spirit of private conversation, I have not ventured to express an opinion of my own; or, if I have expressed it, pray consider it as withdrawn. The situation seems to call for no opinion, unless we have some scientific theory to offer; but to me it seems so interesting that, in taking leave of the association, I feel inclined to invite them, as individuals, to consider the matter in a spirit that will enable us, should the crisis arise, to deal with it in a kindly temper, and a full understanding of its serious dangers and responsibilities.

Ever truly yours,

THOMAS WOLFE

A Writer's Creation and Vision of Life

To His Mother
  Harvard Club
  27 West 44th Street
  New York, November 6, 1929
Dear Mama:

I have been very busy grading papers and making up work at the University, where I fell behind somewhat after my book came out.

Mabel has written me a couple of letters, and I have also heard from others in Asheville, including George McCoy. I also read the reviews of the book in the Asheville papers. The one in the *Citizen* I thought splendid but it seemed to me the *Times* was unfairly personal. George McCoy in his letter said that the *Times* and some of the Asheville people "read the book from the local angle." This is no way to read a book: it was not written from any "local angle," and none of the reviewers in New York, or any where else besides Asheville, have mentioned any "local angle"! Instead, they have read the book as it should be read—as a writer's creation and vision of life—and they have found it a very honest and moving piece of work. I hope you read the reviews in the *New York Times* and the *New York Herald Tribune*.

I have not lived in Asheville for ten years, but I have always believed that if I ever wrote a book I could expect at least as much kindness and fairness in the town of my birth as I would get from strangers. I am very grateful to all those people, like the people at the *Citizen,* who have judged my work fairly and generously, but I am not grateful to people who try to make of my book a diary of family and town history. In the introduction to the book I stated very plainly that it was made from human experience—as all serious fiction is—but that the book was fiction and represented the writer's own picture of life—that he had taken experience and shaped it into a world of his own making. The *Times* reporter in his review accused me of evading the question "by clever twists of phrases"— there is no evasion there or elsewhere: only a very simple and direct statement of what fiction is.

In short, the characters and scenes in my book are of my own imagining and my own making—they have their roots in human experience, but what life and being they have, I gave to them. There is no scene in my book that is supposed to be literal, and I will not talk to damned fools who ask me if so-and-so in the book is meant to be such and such a person living in Asheville. What the book is about is stated on the very first page, in the opening paragraph: it says that we are born alone— all of us who ever lived or will live— that we live alone, and die alone, and that we are strangers to one another, and never come to know one another. That is not written about people in Asheville—it is written about people everywhere, North, South, East, and West.

Finally, I do not know what any one protests about in my book. The people are like people everywhere all over the world—and it seems to me, and to Scribners, and to the people who have read the book up here that on the whole they are pretty fine—People: they are not infallible and they make mistakes, but since I am writing about people and confess that I know very little about saints and angels, I shall let the reporter on the *Times* and any other people who want Gods, rather than men in their fiction do the job I am unable to do. There is not a single leading figure in my book who, when faced by a crisis, does not rise up and show a heroic spirit—they can go over the book page by page and find this true.

I have only two serious regrets—one, that I did not do a better piece of work, but I *will* next time; and two, that my book may have caused pain or distress to any person. But I will also say that if it has caused pain or distress, they are the result not of what is really in the book, but of a misunderstanding of the book's purpose.

I can not write more at present. I am tired from excitement and from having to do my work at N. Y. U. at the same time. I will write you more later. My book has had, I understand, the best reviews any first novel has had in several years, and we are now hopeful of success. The book is already in its second edition. I will send you some of the reviews as they come out—I think you will see what the world in general thinks of the book, and I don't think you will find anything in them that will cause you or anyone worry or confusion of the slightest sort. In my future work, as in this first one, I know you want me to do what I want to do myself: as good, as honest, and as conscientious work as I can. If I do that, most people of intelligence will see what I'm after, and none of us need worry about the opinions of unfair and unreasonable people.

I send you my best wishes for your health, happiness, and prosperity. Write me when you can.

Your son,

TOM

ALEXANDER WOOLLCOTT

The Town-Crier Begs to Differ

To PAUL HARPER

New York City
November 22, 1935

My dear Harper:

This is an answer to your official letter of November 22nd in which you announced that:

"*The Cream of Wheat Corporation is*

unwilling to continue the broadcasts after December 29th unless you will agree to refrain from including in your broadcasts material of a controversial nature which, in our opinion, would be offensive to individuals or groups in the radio audience."

This paragraph would be unintelligi-

From *The Portable Alexander Woollcott*, edited by Joseph Hennessey. Copyright 1944, 1946 by The Viking Press, Inc., N. Y.

ble to anyone who has not previously read your letter of November 14th in which you transmitted this message from Mr. Thomson and Mr. Clifford of the Cream of Wheat Corporation:

"They went on to say that they preferred that you didn't make any more caustic references to people like Hitler and Mussolini as there are large racial groups who are apt to be antagonized by these references."

Now, in these broadcasts the Town-Crier has for several years been freely reporting his likes and dislikes on the books, plays, pictures, prejudices, manners and customs of the day. In undertaking such an oral column, he could not with self-respect agree in advance never to take pot shots at such targets as Hitler or Mussolini. Or, for that matter, at any other bully, lyncher or jingo whose head happened to come within shooting distance. If he did embark upon a series thus hamstrung in advance, his own interest in the broadcasts would so dwindle that they would deteriorate in short order.

I am entirely in sympathy with the viewpoint of Mr. Bull and his Cream of Wheat associates. If they think an occasional glancing blow antagonizes old customers or drives away new ones, it would be folly for them to address their advertising to such an audience as I might assemble. It is my own guess that the allusions complained of have no such effect. It would seem to me as reasonable to expect every crack at Hitler to send all the Jews in America rushing to the grocery stores to stock up with Cream of Wheat. It would be as reasonable to assume that the [Sir John] Buchan broadcast (which Mr. Bull so highly approved) with its hands - across - the - sea, England - and - America shoulder - to - shoulder theme,

alienated from Cream of Wheat every Irish listener and all those whom Mr. Hearst and Father Coughlin have industriously filled with a distrust of the English. It would be as reasonable to fear that the November 10th broadcast, which you yourself loudly applauded, may have so infuriated the Scotch that they all reverted to oatmeal in a body. I have said enough to make clear what a blank check I would be signing if I recklessly promised to omit all controversial material. Before each broadcast, you see, there would be so much honest disagreement as to what material was controversial. The irony of this impasse lies in my own suspicion that it is these very elements which most promote interest in the series. The only reason I don't indulge in them oftener is because I believe they are more effective when infrequently used. They lend the series salt, provoke discussion, whip up attendance and enlarge the audience. The sponsor is therefore most worried by the broadcast which serves him best. At least, that is my guess, which may be as good as Mr. Bull's but need not be any better. And after all, it is his business and not mine.

I have overheard enough of the experiences of other broadcasters to suspect that it would be difficult to find anywhere among the big national advertisers a sponsor who would be as considerate, liberal and agreeable as the Cream of Wheat people have been throughout all our dealings. This would seem to indicate that the Town-Crier is unlikely to find any other sponsor willing to meet the terms he must insist on so long as he uses the now established formula which inevitably represents him as one citizen leaning over the fence and talking freely to his neighbors. And since all the good time on the great networks has been pre-empted by advertisers, that in turn would mean I must drop out of national broadcasting altogether, which, as you know, would be a solution entirely acceptable to me. I would merely be driven back to the comparative privacy of the printed page where, in my own opinion, I belong and where, at long last, I might get some writing done.

Yours sincerely,

Alexander Woollcott

P. S. By the way, in your final paragraph you say that I have "declined to accept any restrictions made by the sponsor" in my choice of material. When you wrote that sentence you must have been either absent-minded or disingenuous. I told you yesterday that I had no objection whatever to letting your representative cut out of my script any joke, anecdote or phrase which, in his opinion, was either coarse or suggestive. If you still do not recall this promise, [Leggett] Brown may be able to refresh your memory.

One other point. You yourself asked why I should ever need to introduce controversial matter into a broadcast since I could so easily let off steam in the various publications to which I can always contribute. Unfortunately, this suggestion is impractical. I find the weekly preparation of the next broadcast and the consequences of the preceding one so time-consuming that when I am broadcasting I am unable to do any other kind of work. I haven't even time left to write a post card to the folks.

A. W.

BRADLEY BURCH

Where Is the Humor?

September 21, 1944

Have the readers in the United States ever wondered why there have been no humorous articles about their men in troopships? They have read funny stories about American soldiers everywhere else, a G. I. encountering a sacred cow in India, a kid from Brooklyn being kissed by a French girl, the invasion of Yankee bluntness into England, Ernie Pyle telling about the New Yorker and the fellow from Arkansas splitting a can of Spam with him in a Normandy café. This is the spirit of fun, calming nerves, and making the most of un-bloody moments, reassuring the folks back home that they haven't forgotten how to laugh. But somehow they seem to have forgotten, when they are on a ship going to the places where the stories come from.

There is a tenseness on a ship filled with soldiers. A soldier is used to being crowded out, shoved around, squeezed into corners. But he can never really become used to waiting, because even if it is just a food line or a latrine line, it becomes more than the

Printed from unpublished letters by permission of the author.

few minutes, the half hours. It becomes the waiting out of the whole war, the whole thing, with the uncertain and distant return home only vaguely visible through the sadness and confusion of being alone with a thousand men.

And this is a troopship. Seven days, or twenty days, or forty days, of waiting. Waiting for breakfast before the blackout regulations are lifted in the morning. Waiting until noon on deck for the inspections below to end, so that you can go below and become stifling hot and run back to the sprawling mass on deck. Waiting for Charlie and Arnie and H. F. Brown to finish reading a pocket book, so you can read it and pass it on. Watching the flat sea bubble and foam away from the boat and miles out to the horizon.

"Sure they thought the darn thing was flat. Look at it. It's like a big plate of soup slopping off at the edges. The dopes thought it was flat because it *is* flat. Poor jerks. How could they know? Columbus was a great guy."

One of the crew of the ship, a scrawny greasy member of the crew of the great grey ship, climbs up a rope ladder towards the top of a great grey mast, with a pail of grey paint in his hand. He is going to paint over a rust spot in the mast. Then he will grease a bit of the snarl of cable stretching like tendons from its sides down to the deck. Everyone looks up. They watch him now, watch him intently as if this is the climax they have been waiting for, the height of their great adventure into nowhere. The member of the crew paints his rust spot and greases his cable and comes down the way he went up, with the little pail in his hand swinging like a potted geranium.

No, they think. That was not it. That was interesting, but that was not it. And they turn their necks level again, towards the sea, or towards a book, and continue waiting.

Where is the humor? Where is the laughter that the American soldier is so famous for? It's not on the deck. It's not below. Where is it? Maybe it is at that card game on the landing of the stairs at A Deck. Yes, of course. They are laughing at something now. The card game on A Deck is poker. There are dollar bills burning holes in pockets on the ship. Hour after hour they change hands and pockets, the cards come up in every combination in every player's hand, and a sudden bit of luck brings a spurt of laughter from a part time winner. Here is your laughter. Here it is, pure and simple. But you won't read of it in a magazine article by your all-seeing correspondent. What does it matter if a kid who never played before loses his whole pay? He wonders if he would have had the chance to spend it where he is going anyhow. He'll never play again, he says. Just wanted to get the feel of it, remembers how his Ma would slap his face if she knew, tells his buddy about his Ma, and they laugh.

There isn't much bitterness yet. There can't be much bitterness yet because the men haven't seen anything to make them bitter. This is just an adventure. "Don't sit home and wait for him. Be with him, sharing his greatest adventure now. Join the WAC and be a part of the things he is a part of." If the American soldier thought that he was really just entering an adventure, then maybe he would laugh his head off on a troopship.

"Who are they kidding? Adventure, hell. We know they need the women, just like they need every bit of effort to win the war. But why make such a stink about it? Let them know what is their duty, and then shut up." Robert Brown spits into the Atlantic Ocean.

They're not telling funny stories. Not now. This is a bit of the gnarled tightness of war. It's just too crowded or too hot to think or talk or do anything but wait. They haven't seen real hardship yet, but don't hold that against them. They are holding up under a new strain on the ships that will take them to the places where they will get their share of the hardships. When they get there, they will have their humor again, but not now. It's too crowded. Wait a little. Everybody wait. It's easy, once you get the place that itched all scratched, and get over the idea that there is anything amusing on a troopship.

BRADLEY BURCH

Eve of Battle

October 27, 1944

I have been assigned to an outfit, as a rifleman. I knew it would be that, though I had hoped a million things. But I am an infantryman and my outfit is in combat now; I will join the first battalion when they come back to the rest area. It's Company C again. Maybe there will be a sergeant as dear (groan) to me as Sergeant Culva was.

For quite a while I wondered whether or not I should tell you that I am in combat now. But, darling, if I didn't tell you, I should be stopped cold in writing. This way you will know that when I say the going is rough it will mean just that, and when I say I am resting and have a break and everything is okay, then you will know it is true. I thought you'd like it better that way than if I talked about French peasants until they came out of your ears.

Please do not worry. I will be all right. And by all right I mean capable of coming home and picking you up, and swinging you around and around.

"On my eve of battle" the kid writes home. This could be called that, but I am not calling it that. Because there are no names to describe this thing which is between us. It may not look it, but everything I do now has become a personal matter between us. The number of my division is secret, as well as my army and corps number. In a week or two I may be able to tell you so that you can know approximately where I am. My regiment is the 101st. They say it is a good regiment. They will say it is the best. I may think so myself, later.

There is a part of this war, a tiny part I guess, that is ours and that we understand. The rest of it is too big. I am not going to tell my parents that I am fighting, specifically. If you think they know, and they do not become too nervous about it, then tell me and I will know what to write home.

Please do not think about me when

Reprinted from unpublished letters by permission of the author.

you are studying. You will be using the things you learn from school for a long time.

I sent a money order as I was leaving the last replacement area. I saved it. Twenty dollars, and maybe you could have some fun with it, like buying books you like, or lending it to some-one who can't pay it back. I love you.

I got Jacky a pair of wooden shoes in a little village called Neufchateau, which I visited. Hope they're big enough.

Now I'm going to build a fire and heat my C ration for supper. Be good, wife.

BRADLEY BURCH

Don't Leave Me Here

November 3, 1944

When this war is over, we will read many stories about the men who fought at the German front. Some of them we will believe, but many of them will be pure tripe. Sometimes I wish that I could be able to tell a few of the stories as they really were, and then I know I will not be the one who will tell them. If only you could see some of it. There are so many things that may never be said, and should be.

On Broadway and 50th Street there is a penny arcade. In the center there is one game that Charles and I always spent our pennies on. Two dummy figures made of metal, standing in a ring. By working a handle in and out, you can make the dummies move and you can make them hit each other with their fists. When one is hit just right, he falls backwards and the other is left standing, and wins.

But a war is fought with a man's delicate flesh which is susceptible to a pin prick and infection, and a man's mind which is susceptible to thoughts of fear and pain and fury. Against these intricacies are thrown such powerful metals and explosives that the only way a human body can compete with them is to be present in reserve in even more overwhelming numbers. It is complete inequality.

So why couldn't they operate metal robots with wires and radios and sensitized metallic skins, against each other until one is knocked down and the other is left standing. There's no reason why the more ingenious brains behind the robots shouldn't be able to win through to a satisfying end.

But it couldn't be done. And the reason is only that what wins a war is the amount of suffering and torture the bodies and minds of the men who are fighting can stand.

So the men lie under the surface of the ground while the metal tears over their heads, and into the mud and rock. They lie in the earth for protection, they stink, they sweat, they shiver. They defecate in their helmets and cover it with soil, they quake with fear, they are enraged to heroism and to death, they eat and smoke and attack—fling their

Reprinted from unpublished letters by permission of the author.

fear before them up a hill and attack in the slippery wetness of earth and men. They attack, and they lie down again, and dig in . . .

And the almighty god, the man of stone behind them, fights his fight in the same way. Only with him the discomfort is all mental. He thinks "How many men did I lose? How many men are weakening? Where is my next hill? What will be my enemy's next move? How soon will I win?" It is hard for everyone.

And the thing that puts it into a story, is a boy hurt, shouting "Don't leave me here!"

You will read stories with that title. It could be used as a battlecry or as an epitaph. It is everything. Don't leave me here to wait, to die, to be alone, to be away. Don't leave me here.

*   *   *

WAR DEPARTMENT TELEGRAM

MRS CLAIRE BURCH
1048-75 ST BROOKLYN NY
REGRET TO INFORM YOU YOUR HUSBAND WAS SERIOUSLY WOUNDED IN ACTION IN FRANCE ELEVEN NOVEMBER UNTIL NEW ADDRESS IS RECEIVED ADDRESS MAIL FOR HIM QUOTE PRIVATE BRADLEY A BURCH SERIAL NUMBER (HOSPITALIZED) CENTRAL POSTAL DIRECTORY APO 640 CARE POSTMASTER NEW YORK UNQUOTE YOU WILL BE ADVISED AS REPORTS OF CONDITION ARE RECEIVED

WITSELL ACTING THE ADJUTANT GENERAL

BRADLEY BURCH

Glory Is a Word for Kings

March 13, 1945

I want to have nothing to do with significant days of our generation. I do not want to be even a small part of the things that will become history for our children to read and study. Because I know now that the recorders of history do not know how to record the truth. The truth is always too hard to understand. Glory is a word for kings, and kings have no place in the world I understand. We have lost this war, in all truth. We lost it when we lost our first soldier in our first battle and we have been struggling to redeem ourselves ever since. And if I rejoice when it is over, it will be because I have waited so long. I am no different from anyone else here in wanting what I already have. So much and so beautiful.

Bitterness is inevitable when such an over-all wrong is run with the efficiency and power that our greatest men have to give. Money becomes meaningless, the dollar too small a unit. Reward does not exist. Only what we feel exists. We are uninterested in staggering figures or in the magazine articles that tell all about how General so-and-so said, "It's impossible, but we'll do it."

Reprinted from unpublished letters by permission of the author.

Why should even language become incongruous? Does it make good reading to subtly exaggerate?

Things become so basic to a soldier in action that he strips himself completely of all hampering civilized accumulations, and goes about like an instinctive animal, to remain alive. Sometimes if he stops thinking, it is better for his ability to exist. The will for living is strong. It will do clever things for the body, necessary things. Perhaps once in a person's life he should react completely with his body, instead of with his mind. Perhaps it is a good lesson, that is if lessons will mean anything in helping him to understand why truth is truth.

I say truth, which is a word. It is too big. I only mean that it becomes more and more difficult for a person to be fooled once he has experienced basic existence.

I am neither tying myself in knots nor spouting meaningless nonsense. This is coming out of me from the base of my brain, clear and calm, so that I hardly know I am writing.

Love is a stronger instinct than life. Without something to love, there is no real life. And I not only have something, but a warm tangible beautiful thing to love. I love you, Claire. That is why I will continue, because it is stronger than the earth's hardest piece of steel.

Could it be that veterans are pretty well soured because they have become too hard to feel, and yet they are still trying to be fooled by the same old Camel ads? When a German soldier after the last war wrote *The Road Back* he was trying to bring together the people who were groping on both sides to understand each other again. And it's not

impossible to do, to understand that way.

You and I never had the problem at all, and will never have it. Maybe that is why I will not be soured. We are so much of one person that we never needed words to understand. But since we do see what there is to see, couldn't we explain it understandably to people who do not? All it needs is to make people happy by really being happy about something real.

So that we won't write a book called *The Road Back* or one called *All Quiet on the Western Front* . . .

It is strange to realize, darling, that there are periods as long as a half hour when it is as quiet as a library on the western front right now. Many times we have looked up at the quietness thinking, is the war over? How long will it take for them to get the word to us from Supreme Headquarters? And then we hear the noises again and we sigh back into the attitude that makes us go on every day; without hoping in our minds what we know is in our hearts, without ever making the type of jokes that end with "April Fool," without the too trying reactions of human beings used to shock (for shock is our breakfast and our supper and our afternoon tea), and without forgetting that it *will* end, but not tomorrow. There is no creed and there are no slogans. There are no cowards and every man is afraid. There are many heroes but only a few are recognized. There are thoughts of what is good, and this is not it. And we never argue or quibble or fight among ourselves unless we are drunk. And we are never drunk unless we drink to blot out the sight of blood that was shed to capture the winery. . . .

HAROLD UREY

Bomb Control Not Impossible

Columbia University
November 19, 1945

To the NEW YORK *Herald Tribune:*

All attempts to analyze dispassionately the situation created by the advent of the atomic bomb lead to the conclusion that without international control of nuclear explosives the world will find itself engaged in a desperate armament race, whose probable outcome will be an all-destructive atomic war. Because of the advantages which atomic bombs will bestow upon a ruthless aggressor and because of the vulnerability of the large industrial centers in the United States to an atomic bomb attack, our country has a particularly great interest in the establishment of controls which would prevent all nations from accumulating stocks of atomic bombs.

In absence of world government, is an effective international control of atomic explosives at all possible? It has been suggested that the scientists of the world band together and exercise this control independently of their governments. I do not believe this possible. Scientists are good citizens, loyal to their countries. Rather, the task lies squarely on the shoulders of the responsible political leaders of the world.

* * *

What I suggest to these political leaders as the best possible solution is the agreement between all countries that no individual nation should produce or stock atomic bombs, and the creation of an international control board—perhaps under the auspices of the United Nations Security Council—to supervise the observance of the agreement. This international control board should include scientists and employ scientifically trained inspectors representing all nations.

Is a simple method for regular supervision of the production of nuclear explosives feasible? The answer is yes. Since (at present, at least) all atomic explosives originate in uranium, international supervision of uranium mining could provide a sufficient basis for control of all such explosives. Uranium mining could be concentrated in a few mines administered or supervised by the international control board.

The uranium obtained in this manner could be allocated to individual countries for research purposes. The quantities would be so small as to make large-scale military use impossible; if larger quantities were to be allocated for peacetime power purposes, strict accounting could be required over all movements of the allocated materials.

* * *

Agents of the international board could then easily keep a complete up-to-date inventory of the nuclear explosives in every country. The preparation and checking of such an inventory, I believe, will not strongly interfere with the economic sovereignty of the individual nations, since the checks will extend only

Reprinted from The New York *Herald-Tribune,* November 19, 1945, by permission of the author and the publisher.

to a small number of laboratories or industrial plants registered as legitimate users of fissionable materials.

Obviously this system can be expected to work efficiently only if agreed upon by all nations wholeheartedly and without mental reservation. Despite the tenseness of the international situation and the deep mistrust existing at present between various nations, the presumption of universal goodwill in this particular undertaking is not unrealistic. There can be no doubt that each nation in the world, whatever its political system may be, shudders at the prospect of total destruction of its cities in a future atomic war and is genuinely interested in the elimination of this threat.

* * *

The danger to peace lies not so much in a nation making deliberate preparations for world conquest by atomic weapons, as in all nations drifting toward an atomic war which nobody wants, in the wake of an armament race. It is therefore not at all unlikely that all nations will be genuinely eager to make the controls work and that their establishment will bring considerable relief of international tension.

On the other hand, it is obviously impossible to eliminate all suspicions of evasion, even if the international mechanism of supervised mining, allocation and inventory of atomic explosives begins functioning in an atmosphere of goodwill. Therefore the international control board will have to be equipped with the power to conduct inspections at various industrial and scientific key points in any country.

Numerous such points exist, and the larger the number and variety of checks and surveys, the smaller will be the probability of successful evasion. These industrial and laboratory checks could be applied to essential production materials, to installations of certain types and to key scientific or engineering personnel. Investigation of suspicious mining activities could certainly bring to light any "illicit" uranium mining and heavy production of other materials used in atomic-bomb development, graphite, for example, would also call for an immediate investigation.

The same could be done with certain types of instruments (radiation detectors, for example) and machinery whose large-scale production is required only for atomic explosive plants—provided inspectors are guaranteed the right to travel freely and to enter any suspicious building. The same freedom should also be granted in connection with research laboratories.

* * *

Finally, checks can be made on the activities of individuals known to be experts in the field. During the war the most obvious indication of our atomic bomb development was the disappearance of key scientists in the field from their peace-time laboratories.

The impression which has been created in the public mind that our entire development was a secret to everybody in the world except a few top scientists and military leaders should be corrected. Actually, all scientists in the country and throughout the world knew that all the major belligerents were working feverishly on the release of atomic power for military purposes. Any intelligent spy could find out the magnitude of our experimental developments.

For this information he merely would have to consult an official government publication — the Metals Year Book, which stated in its 1943 edition that practically all uranium imported into or produced in the United States was being used for secret atomic power research. And by observing some of our campuses and following some of our prominent scientists, he could easily have put his finger on the exact location of our main experimental laboratories.

Let me emphasize that no scientific "secret" exists as to the production of the present atomic bombs. The fundamental discoveries have all been published in the 1939 and 1940 scientific journals all over the world. New fundamental discoveries, however, are certain to be made—uranium might well cease to be the only source of atomic power—and unless freedom of inspection and free exchange of information among scientists of the world is guaranteed there will be no certainty that the established controls will remain sufficient.

Therefore, the right of all scientists to publish freely the results of their investigations should be an essential part of the international control agreement.

* * *

Undoubtedly, no single or combined method of checks can provide complete safety against evasion. No police force has as yet succeeded in making all crime in a city impossible. However, well organized police can make crime unprofitable—by making the probability of detection and punishment too high. Similarly, a well organized system of checks can make the probability of discovery high enough to discourage any nation from attempting to evade the controls. Even with a 50 per cent probability of detection, no nation will be likely to embark on a program of clandestine production of atomic bombs because the consequences of discovery will be too dangerous. For compelling reasons of self-preservation, other nations cannot and will not tolerate such an evasion in the same way as they tolerated the manifest violations by Germany of the disarmament clauses after World War I.

NORBERT WIENER

A Scientist Rebels

(The letter which follows was addressed by one of our ranking mathematicians to a research scientist of a great aircraft corporation, who had asked him for the technical account of a certain line of research he had conducted in the war.) [Editor of the *Atlantic*.]

Sir:

I have received from you a note in which you state that you are engaged in a project concerning controlled missiles, and in which you request a copy of a paper which I wrote for the National Defense Research Committee during the war.

Reprinted from the *Atlantic Monthly*, January, 1947, by permission of the author.

As the paper is the property of a government organization, you are of course at complete liberty to turn to that government organization for such information as I could give you. If it is out of print as you say, and they desire to make it available to you, there are doubtless proper avenues of approach to them.

When, however, you turn to me for information concerning controlled missiles, there are several considerations which determine my reply. In the past, the comity of scholars has made it a custom to furnish scientific information to any person seriously seeking it. However, we must face these facts: The policy of the government itself during and after the war, say in the bombing of Hiroshima and Nagasaki, has made it clear that to provide scientific information is not a necessarily innocent act, and may entail the gravest consequences. One therefore cannot escape reconsidering the established custom of the scientist to give information to every person who may inquire of him. The interchange of ideas which is one of the great traditions of science must of course receive certain limitations when the scientist becomes an arbiter of life and death.

For the sake, however, of the scientist and the public, these limitations should be as intelligent as possible. The measures taken during the war by our military agencies, in restricting the free intercourse among scientists on related projects or even on the same project, have gone so far that it is clear that if continued in time of peace this policy will lead to the total irresponsibility of the scientist, and ultimately to the death of science. Both of these are disastrous for our civilization, and entail grave and immediate peril for the public.

I realize, of course, that I am acting as the censor of my own ideas, and it may sound arbitrary, but I will not accept a censorship in which I do not participate. The experience of the scientists who have worked on the atomic bomb has indicated that in any investigation of this kind the scientist ends by putting unlimited powers in the hands of the people whom he is least inclined to trust with their use. It is perfectly clear also that to disseminate information about a weapon in the present state of our civilization is to make it practically certain that that weapon will be used. In that respect the controlled missile represents the still imperfect supplement to the atom bomb and to bacterial warfare.

The practical use of guided missiles can only be to kill foreign civilians indiscriminately, and they furnish no protection whatsoever to civilians in this country. I cannot conceive a situation in which such weapons can produce any effect other than extending the kamikaze way of fighting to whole nations. Their possession can do nothing but endanger us by encouraging the tragic insolence of the military mind.

If therefore I do not desire to participate in the bombing or poisoning of defenseless peoples—and I most certainly do not—I must take a serious responsibility as to those to whom I disclose my scientific ideas. Since it is obvious that with sufficient effort you can obtain my material, even though it is out of print, I can only protest *pro forma* in refusing to give you any information concerning my past work. However, I rejoice at the fact that my material is not readily available, inasmuch as it gives me the opportunity to raise this serious moral issue. I do not expect to publish any future work of mine which may do damage in the hands of irresponsible militarists.

I am taking the liberty of calling this

letter to the attention of other people in scientific work. I believe it is only proper that they should know of it in order to make their own independent decisions, if similar situations should confront them.

Norbert Wiener
1947

SIR OSBERT SITWELL

A Letter to My Son

My Dear Boy:—

One thing at any rate we share in common—an uncommon laziness. We both of us, I know, hate writing letters —especially long letters. You will, therefore, when you receive this, and count its pages, at once comprehend how much energy it required for me to take the decision and make the effort to overcome in this single instance that mutual diffidence upon which, I fully realize, a sound father-and-son relationship must rest. But some apology from me is surely due to you for the condition of the world in which you find yourself—more especially because, before you were born, I foresaw the probability that the present conflict would ensue.

And, above all, I feel that you should know what I *really* think upon a number of matters, for, when we meet, the joy of discussing family affairs, and what we have each of us been seeing and doing, is likely to banish talk of more serious things, even if our relationship did not make us dubious of approaching too near to them. It is true, of course, that being a generation older I can give you little direct help in your career, but, since we are both artists— and here I may pause to congratulate myself, for I expected a butcher, a house-agent, a general, as a son, but never another writer—I can, nevertheless, tell you, out of a long, tedious, and at the same time enlivening experience, how to save yourself trouble in pursuit of your goal. Because it is vital to both of us that we should realize that the war is only the Great Interruption, and that your career *must* continue.

The last war—the First War to End Wars—broke out when I was twenty-one; the present war—the Sequel— when you were twenty. Formerly there were only the ordeals of the private and public school to be endured— concentration camps that were certainly vile enough (there I have seen bullying —and in one instance upon a Jew— which would have taxed the ingenuity of German storm-troopers). But the men of your generation have never for a moment been free; and unless you conquer in the battle for the hours, there will be no liberty left. The embryonic writer of after-the-war will have, not only the schoolmaster and the captain of the games, as you say, for his enemies, but the drill sergeant, the gym instructor, the leader of the fire squad, the civil defense expert, the inspirer of the youth movement, and afterwards, when

Reprinted from the *Atlantic Monthly,* April, 1945, by permission of the author.

he grows up, the official of the Labor Exchange and the shop steward, as well as the politician and the critic.

Such an existence is death to the artist; because, to be able to work at his best, it is necessary for him to have an endless vista of hours and days, within the space of which he can write or paint without any interruption except those which are casual or that he makes for himself. But the modern development of "healthy citizenship," as it is called, under which every man is obliged to take a hand to repel the attacks from land, sea, and air brought upon him by his incompetence as a voter, sterilizes all talent. To be able to exist, you will have to give up twenty-two hours out of every twenty-four. Men are no longer wanted, but only numbers; a man today —and if you are not careful, tomorrow as well—is only valuable to the extent that he can supply man-hours—or ant-hours—of labor to the politicians, and at the end a death with which to crown their policy.

As an inducement to this kind of life and a reward for leading it, the voter, the little man, is flattered morning and evening by the press, and fawned upon by his slave-masters. He is told he is World Champion No. 1, that no one can compare with him. In each country he believes himself to be absolute lord. Moreover the mental food fed to him renders him unduly excitable in the realm of gross ideas, while, too, the people of every nation are profoundly xenophobic. These last facts, unless they can be modified through education (of which development there is no sign), make popular government in the present sense of that term impossible; but they also enable any government, however bad and incompetent, in every country, to achieve an easy and invari-able popularity by abuse of foreign countries, or, in more rational cases, by a governessy upbraiding of them.

Hitler, for example, may not have truly represented his people in everything; but he does—and did—truly represent them when he denounced foreign nations. Alas, the feeling of innate racial superiority which inhabits the mind of the common man in every country, and is to be examined in its most blatant form in Nazi doctrines, equally must in every country be encouraged, in order to persuade him to consent willingly to the eventual loss of life and fortune. Yet "Love Thy Neighbor as Thyself" remains the only foundation stone of sound, peaceful relations with foreign countries.

Thus are men persuaded to yield money, career, freedom, health, life itself, to the boundless folly or iniquitous ambition of the demagogues, autocrats, and politicians—men who in England, during the last twenty years, have scarcely produced a leader. Churchill was the last, but by origin, as by ability, he was out of the ordinary run, half aristocrat, half American, and in no way derived from the middle classes who govern both here and in France, and who, by their lack of intuition and energy, except in the realm of finance, have proved so great a blight upon their countries.

It is only fair, however, to admit that where, as in Italy and Germany, the middle classes *have* yielded and the lower classes have taken over, the leaders who have arisen are, if less purely incompetent, far madder, more unbridled, violent with the violence of the turbulent mob from which they spring. Yet they are merely a reflection of those whose energies they sap and whose lives they ruin.

What can *our* politicians say in their own and our defense? They can say that here, as opposed to the enemy countries, all that has been done to render war probable was done by mistake, and not on purpose—but to an unprejudiced mind, does not this make their responsibility worse? The strangulation of your life, the chief calamity that involves every man and woman, befalls you because war is total. But remember, it is only total because the politicians have allowed it to be so. Indeed, whereas in former ages of barbarism the whole populations of whole countries were uprooted and enslaved *after* a war by a victorious foe, now every government uproots and enslaves its own people *during* a war. Only thus can a country survive in total war. This is total war. It is therefore the chief job of your generation to see that the kind of men who deceived themselves and us, and led us into total war, shall never again be returned to Parliament.

If, in states vowed to death and to fights without a finish, the lot of every man is, of course, hard, that of the artist is especially abominable. Here, unless some special status is allowed him, it will mean, in fact, that he becomes a helot. Had Mozart been a modern Englishman—or, for that, a modern Austrian—he would have spent the last four years training to fight, fighting, or engaged in forced labor; and since he died at thirty-six, this would have constituted a large slice of his art life. Conceive the loss to the world had conscription been in force! Imagine, too, how greatly a modern government would relish wasting several years of Shelley's brief span by making him a fireman, or enjoy sending Keats, with his weak lungs, upon a gas course.

Yet our governors are humane; they prefer muzzling an artist to his downright destruction. "Give the creature a safe job; make him write what *we* like." Can you imagine Shelley or Blake at a desk in the Ministry of Information, or Byron flitting in and out of the studios of the BBC? You are, alas, destined to live in an age in which no painter will be supplied with paints without a permit from the Director of the National Gallery, no writer with paper save by grace of the Paper Controller. For, in a democracy, the artist, first smeared with his own honey, is then staked down upon the ant heap. In the end, however, the artist and the thinker win. Even starvation cannot prevail against them: it has been tried before. Nevertheless, for your own sake, think the matter out, sum up your position.

It is wise not to underrate the difficulties, the cruel difficulties, before you. It will be harder for you than ever it was for your father. The true artist has always had to fight, but it is, and will be, a more ferocious struggle for you, and the artists of your generation, than ever before. The workingman, this time, will be better looked after—he will be flattered by the press and bribed with Beveridge schemes—because he possesses a plurality of votes. But who will care for you or your fate? Who will trouble to defend the cause of the young writer, painter, sculptor, musician? And what inspiration will you be offered when theater, ballet, concert hall lie in ruins and, owing to the break in training, there are no great executant artists for several decades?

Above all, do not underestimate the amount and intensity of the genuine ill-will that people will feel for you; not the workingman, for though not highly educated he has a mild respect for the arts and no preconceived notions; not the few remaining patricians; but the vast army between them, the fat middle classes and the little men. And here I must first make special mention of the civil servant as enemy. Throughout your career your liveliness will provoke his particular attention, and so you will suffer the continued passive obstruction that his resistant softness opposes to the will of the artist, towards whom he bears an inborn loathing. He envies the artist's liberty of disposition and path of enjoyment, although officially he rates the gummy persistence of the limpet above all other virtues, above the wind-swift speeding of the greyhound or any species of conscious thought.

At best, you will be ground down between the small but powerful authoritarian minority of art directors, museum racketeers, the chic, giggling modistes who write on art and literature, publishers, journalists, and dons (who will, to do them justice, try to help you, if you will write as they tell you), and the enormous remainder, who would not mind—who would indeed be pleased—if they saw you starve.

For we English are unique in that, albeit an art-producing nation, we are not an art-loving one. In the past the arts depended on a small number of very rich patrons. The enclave they formed has never been re-established. The very name "art lover" stinks. The small army of art lovers that still exist, trailing round the smashed and empty galleries, belongs to the Victorian Age. When it moves, the rattle of camphor balls sounds like a rain of bullets in the echoing scagliola halls of houses thrown open to members of the art-loving congregations. Decrepit it may be, but it still retains its power to injure. It cares only for old masters, and you will

be surprised at the vigor and satisfaction with which it will always trample on the new.

The privileges you hold today, then, as an artist, are those of Ishmael: the hand of every man is against you. Remember, therefore, that outcasts must never be afraid, and that to a writer courage should, before physical courage, signify moral courage—during wars a quality often at a discount, whatever the packs of journalists may bleat to the contrary. As an artist, the only crimes you can commit are to fail to support and uphold your peers, to agree in your heart with the herd, and, above all, to be *afraid* of ideas, *afraid* of beauty. You must never take heed for the morrow, never be afraid of the morning, for you have no more to lose than you brought with you.

Yet cultivate guile; be not, as I have been, too outspoken. Invent several manners and try them on those who like them. Consider everything upon its merits, for you need not give your own conclusions until tempers are cooler—and heads, I may add, clearer. When I was a boy of your age, in the Brigade of Guards before the last war, we young officers were taught never to argue with a drunken man. See him the next day, and interrogate him then. Similarly I counsel *you* never to argue; join in, and after the hysteria has vanished, remember to administer splashes of cold water over a long period against a recurrence. (For there will be a morning after.) But, in whatever fashion you may act, do not appear "cynical"; Swift and Pope and Shaw were "cynical," and it lessened their authority.

On the contrary, join in, as I say; accept the situation and rejoice. We live in an age of world-wide hysteria—and not without reason—when not to believe as many atrocity stories as your neighbor believes, puts you not only in danger of hell-fire, but, if he has his way, exposes you to the rigors of persecution. You would rank as a heretic, as one who refuses to place credence in the Thirty-nine Articles, or who, by declining to take part in a witch hunt, numbers himself openly among the witches.

No, adopt the homeopathic system, but prescribe large doses. Be inventive. Use your creative gift. Pretend to believe and then go one better. Enjoy yourself. Sicken them with the blatant nonsense you pour out. Tell them you know their stories are true, and repeat everything you have ever heard in the same line, however improbable. Pile it on, until *they* begin to argue against *you*. *Insist* on believing everything with a firmer belief than they do; go a hundred times better. Whenever the crowd mentions Italians, shout "Wops!" "Dagos!" "Ice-creamers!" It may prove difficult for you, since you lived in Italy as a child, but you must persist. Tell them that Raphael, Michelangelo and Leonardo, Titian and Veronese, were all really Englishmen with American mothers; and declare that Noel Coward is worth all Dante. (Point out that Dante never wrote the music for his "lyrics.")

But, at the end of all this, when a reaction has set in, you must let them know this much of the truth: that you abhor brutality, from wherever it comes, and whether shown to Jew or Christian, and that you know, and have long known, the Germans to be a brutal race; that you had been brought up to believe it, even at the time people were praising them, saying they preferred them to the French, and that "they are just like us."

(What a curious, recurrent, dangerous hallucination is that!) Otherwise, unless you emphasize this idea, you will leave them in the right to the point that their hysteria may have arisen from a hatred of oppression.

When you have satiated and disgusted them with your atrocity stories, agree with them that *perhaps* they *are* right not to believe everything they are told. And add, quickly, before leaving them, that perhaps the ability *not* to be taken in by superstitions, not to bow the knee to Mumbo-Jumbo, whether in West Africa or South Kensington, whether outside a kraal or a town hall decorated with flags, may be, after all, the test of a civilized man. Remember, for your own comfort, that you are only exaggerating for the sake of moderation; because you must ever pursue the golden mean, the most difficult of all ideals for the artist, with the clashes inherent in his temperament and his need for expression, to follow.

And after the war, for it will end one day,—when a silly woman once asked Chekov, apropos of some contemporary fracas, "How do *you* think the war will end?" he replied, after some thought, "In peace, I should say,"—after the war, then, when we may relapse to easy ways, it will become your duty once more to remind people of the brutality of the German race. For, no doubt, we shall revert to type. The hysteria will pass, for we are not, like the Germans, a feminine, emotional race, but a tolerant, masculine-minded people, who can only be worked up by outrageous events and the wickedness of the press.

You must do more, however, than recall the nature of the Germans, in case we forget it: for that would be a purely negative contribution. You must harness your vivid sense of fantasy to the cause of reality. Be practical—practical in the way the Chinese were when they used to recruit their prostitutes from among the blind. You realize, I know, that a certain proportion of Germans are born into the world with an especial love of fighting, and you must see that they get it, before they can inflict their will, first upon the stupid and slavish majority of their own countrymen, and then upon the world.

Ask yourself what can be done to obtain the correct solution: namely, to kill off this ruffianly minority at regular intervals, and before it attains power, and if possible to satisfy its deep urge to kill and be killed in such a manner as to enable it gradually to feel a certain self-respect. Thus, though you cannot cure snakes of their bite, you can deprive them of their venom and, by manufacturing a serum from it, use it for the good of humanity, as a cure for certain diseases.

Now the solution that I propose, and recommend to you most seriously, is derived from the instinctive and traditional treatment of the same problem in other epochs, and I believe it would prove successful and at the same time solve another and even more acute difficulty. During the eighteenth century, the British people had little trouble from the Germans, because they hired German troops to fight their battles, and so procured the death of the most naturally ferocious of the German race. (Indeed, because these were slaughtered in this fashion, the leftover German, with his beer and pipe and dirty mustache, became the very emblem of peace.) Unfortunately in the nineteenth century the idea spread that it was immoral to obtain the death in battle on your behalf of any but your own

people—and soon, in consequence, Germany was unleashing her hordes of trained killers upon France.

The League of Nations failed because it possessed no armed force to back up its authority. Well, then, restore the League and recruit the army necessary for the enforcement of its laws from among the German people. Those who love fighting will volunteer, and, by being made to serve an ideal, and at the same time a useful purpose, the tone of them will gradually be raised; they will feel that the future of civilization depends on them, and will respond. The fact of being dressed in a uniform will quiet many of them. And, of course, we must see to it that they are, in the interests of the whole world, decimated every few years in border clashes and in fracases in Thibet and Central Africa. This is the sole solution that will de-totalize war: for within a generation all the Germans who would most *like* war will have been given a taste of it, have become its victims without involving the rest of their race and the rest of the five continents.

The worst of conscription is that, unlike the system adumbrated above, it involves and kills off those who hate war as much as those who love it. For this reason, and also because I think that, in spite of the efforts of envenomed fanatics who find in these tragic years their happy hour, we shall return to the purely English methods of life that we have through the centuries evolved, I find it difficult to believe that we shall continue to enforce conscription forever after the war. Directly a war—for which we are always unprepared—descends upon us, the nation demands compulsion as a measure of sacrifice, equivalent to lethal dust and ashes; we do not examine whether it is judicious.

Yet conscription should never be more than a matter of convenience or its reverse; it should never be a question of religious principle or a measure of self-immolation.

And it is doubtful whether military conscription has ever suited this country, with its tremendous naval tradition and its industrial power; it is doubtful, indeed, how far it has helped any country, for it only enables the old, pre-the-last-war militarism to continue until the next outbreak. In France, it was in force up till 1870; after that Germany adopted it for the whole Reich, and was defeated in 1914. Then France and England forbade Germany to have a conscripted army, and the French was the largest and, by old standards, "the best in the world"—as *all* our politicians reiterated. The result was that, after the German Army had been reconstituted by Hitler, the French were defeated.

The two greatest and most successful military organizations of modern times, Russian and German, have been built up *since* the last war, and after a clean sweep. A triumphant nation should always celebrate peace by the destruction of the War Office—then, at the right time, and if our politicians *must* continue to make us these presents of wars, a suitable organization and army could take shape.

The Englishman, when of sound mind, recognizes the truth of these facts by instinct, more fully than would a Continental; he recognizes the wickedness and, above all, the folly of megalomaniac conceptions. He wants no youth movements, no Balillas and black-handed gangs of tub-thumping tots and thugs in miniature, no great organizations to cripple and pervert the minds of the young. And if, during real peace, an English government proposes to continue conscription, then the English people, unless they have altered their character, will tell it to go.

You asked me, when I last saw you, what were my politics, and I find it a question difficult, even now, to answer. I belong to the balance of the body politic, and have at one moment felt, and acted, in one mood; at another, in another. I believe in trying to achieve the fullest liberty for the individual within the bounds of human and political conscience.

With the late D. H. Lawrence, it is my opinion that, where finance and economics are concerned, it is man's chief misfortune that at present those who are most active and eager in these fields,—that is, in the pursuit of money or in planning to take it away,—and whose ideas are therefore the most likely to prevail, unless we can marshal the disinterested, are the most unpleasant, the most material-minded, of all men—either the most greedy, the most anxious to exploit their fellows, or the most dry, kill-joy doctrinaires.

In any case, money is a convenience we have ourselves created for our own use, not a god or a religion. And it should remain so—that is to say, money is made to be spent. But so long as the money world is ruled by the beaked and bloated tribes of the great capitalists, whose fortunes must be considered as a kind of elephantiasis, or threatened by the dour, sour looks of our old enemies, the Puritans, what can you expect?

I should not like to see—though no doubt I shall—hereditary wealth abolished. Today men seem afraid to defend it. American ideas of ant labor prevail. But, in all truth, the only kind of wealth worth having is the kind you do not earn: it is unassociated with the mean and slavish virtue of thrift. You have time to learn how to spend your money, and time in which to spend it. Obversely, I should like to see the possession and privileges of inherited wealth extended universally.

To abolish hereditary possessions to-day, instead of insisting on them for everyone, would be equivalent to the action of the Elizabethans, had they decreed the abolition of glass in all windows, because it was only to be found in the houses of the rich, and had thereby prevented its use from becoming general. Samuel Butler maintained, in *The Way of All Flesh* and in his *Notebooks,* that one day it would be as anomalous to be born without an annual income attached to you of three or four hundred, to come to you when you had reached the age of twenty-five or so years, as it is today to be born without arms or legs. Evolution should provide each of us with a fortune, as with a face. I think he was right.

I was told lately, by an American who had been in Paris at the time the Germans entered that city, that German officers could be seen sitting in the fashionable teashops, gnawing huge lumps of butter, or sometimes with twenty or thirty cakes piled on the plate in front of them; this was, of course, the ugly result of underfeeding. A gross fortune is, similarly, the result—and as indecent a result—of poverty, the most degrading of human afflictions. But the stupidity and financial fecklessness of successive governments in Britain have at least accomplished this much, that we can say that any man who today sets out to make a great fortune must be either a great fool or a great philanthropist—and, if he succeeds, a great knave; for he pays 19s. 6d. in the pound as income tax,

and at least two thirds of his possessions must go to the state when he dies.

For though governments in the past feared to overtax the people they ruled, or pretended to represent, they have now made what must be to them a most joyful discovery; that, so long as overtaxing arises through sheer muddle, lack of foresight, and incompetence, and not through intention, they can squander the national income up to any limit (and this is of benefit to them—at least indirectly—by increasing their importance). If, that is to say, they take your money, not because they believe in doing so, not because they are advocates of socialism, but because, on the contrary, having continually opposed it, they yet have floundered, of their own accord, into a position so tragic and untenable that socialism becomes their sole chance of rescue, nothing else remains to be done except to cling to an expedient in which they have no faith. But you and I would surely, even though we are not socialists, prefer to live in a state that was socialist by principle rather than by virtue of the amazing ineptitude of its politicians.

Yet it is not, perhaps, for a writer to complain. If an artist, it is scarcely probable that he will make a great fortune in a capitalist state, though it is true that he occupies, at any rate financially, a special place in it. For one thing, the proceeds of a book, which may have taken him five years to write, are liable to income tax and supertax—though a great portion of the money should surely be regarded as capital; for another, it has long been recognized that a writer's particular form of property, the copyright of the books he has created, is on a different footing from all other property, is not inalienable, and should, in fact, be snatched from his family or heirs as soon as this can be accomplished without an appearance of indecent haste.

So much for the writer's financial status. What the artist should do for his own sake, I think, is not to advocate that money be taken away from its present owners, but to support a policy which will undermine its attraction for the material-minded by diminishing the value they can set upon it. Rationing, for example, already accomplishes this. It soon becomes plain that there is little object in making too much money, if there is little or nothing to buy with it. Confine the rich to the pastures of a restricted Fortnum & Mason's. Advocate heavy permanent taxes on jewelry and old masters and decorative objects, and then you will be able to say to the rich, in the continual effort you make to educate those of them who need it, "Look! Modern pictures and books remain; their value *may* increase, while that of investments is bound to sink." Plug that over, every time.

Money, though, is not so important to you as liberty; I recur to that. You must carry out a continual campaign against civil servants, dons, masters of hounds, schoolmasters, professional football players, and all friends of national sclerosis everywhere. Use once again your sense of fantasy and of fun. Hit them where they least expect it.

If, for example, it should prove—which I do not believe—that the character of the English people has changed, should it develop that the young are to be enslaved, and the artists subjected to continual domination by pinheads, then charge the foe. If you find that it has been planned for the intelligent, the intellectual, above all, the creative and those who live for things of the spirit, to spend a large portion of their lives after the war in undergoing, one after another, courses in gas and bomb-throwing, then loudly, and on every occasion, you must demand in the name of Sacred English Fair Play that the Philistines who hate art and literature and love to handle and throw bombs and to fire guns and, generally, to be as noisy and destructive as possible, and to live with a continual BBC program from opening to close, should, as compensation, be obliged to suffer six-weeks-long compulsory courses in Dutch painting or Persian textiles, and to pass endurance tests in the Art Element in Chinese Caligraphy and in English Romantic Poetry.

Torn from their peacetime occupations of golf, darts, and reading the papers, they must be made, during these courses, to live under, for them, the most uncomfortable circumstances possible; they must be forced to sleep on planks, eighty in a hut (unless they show a liking for dormitory life, when they should be placed in the solitary confinement of a comfortable bedroom). No radio should be allowed in any hut or mess. At mealtimes, they must listen in silence to Beethoven quartets, and after dinner attend orchestral concerts of Mahler and Stravinsky. The examinations in Byzantine jewelry and Turkish tiles should be conducted to the appropriated music of the countries concerned. During the Netherlands School of Painting course, they should be taken by train, starting from London at midnight, to that flat part of East Anglia which somewhat resembles Holland in configuration, and there be made to lie for hours in a damp ditch, so as to observe the sun rise over the river from the correct angle. During the daytime they should be made to adopt the proper physical attitudes of Teniers boors, one foot in the air, an arm extended, and later to dance in the same jolly and abandoned style.

The unsuccessful candidates for promotion, the recalcitrant and stubborn, could be ordered to take further courses in French Symbolist Poetry, as well as English Romantic, and be examined minutely on the works of Baudelaire, Verlaine, and Rimbaud. Those who showed any symptom of being refractory could even be commanded to attend a lecture on the latest art movement by Group-Dupe Herbert Read. But you should be humane as well as stern, and first aid should be ready on all occasions for the mind as well as the body.

I implore you to take what I say seriously, even when I put it in a form to amuse you. You are a cavalier by type, and not a roundhead, and you will need all the fun you can make for yourself and others, as well as all the fighting spirit you can muster, if you are, as I hope, to carry on a long one-man campaign against stupidity and priggishness wherever you see it. Never allow yourself to be discouraged, however hopeless at any one moment the struggle may appear.

I must end now, for my letter is long, and at present you have not much time for reading; but there still remain several subjects on which I must talk to you in my next letter. Take care of yourself.

Your affectionate father,

1945

III. . .

FAMILIAR ESSAY

THOMAS DEKKER

Of Winter

WINTER, the sworne enemie to summer, the friend to none but colliers and woodmongers: the frostbitten churl that hangs his nose still over the fire: the dog that bites fruits, and the devil that cuts down trees, the unconscionable binder up of vintners' faggots, and the only consumer of burnt sack and sugar: This cousin to Death, father to sickness, and brother to old age, shall not show his hoary bald-pate in this climate of ours (according to our usual computation) upon the twelfth day of December, at the first entering of the sun into the first minute of the sign Capricorn, when the said Sun shall be at his greatest south declination from the equinoctial line, and so forth, with much more such stuff than any mere Englishman can understand—no, my countrymen, never beat the bush so long to find out Winter, where he lies, like a beggar shivering with cold, but take these from me as certain and most infallible rules, know when Winter plums are ripe and ready to be gathered.

When Charity blows her nails and is ready to starve, yet not so much as a watchman will lend her a flap of his frieze gown to keep her warm: when tradesmen shut up shops, by reason their frozen-hearted creditors go about to nip them with beggary: when the price of sea-coal riseth, and the price of men's labour falleth: when every chimney casts out smoke, but scarce any door opens to cast so much as a maribone to a dog to gnaw; when beasts die for want of fodder in the field, and men are ready to famish for want of food in the city; when the first word that a wench speaks at your coming into the room in a morning is, "Prithee send for some faggots," and the best comfort a sawyer beats you withal is to say, "What will you give me?"; when gluttons blow their pottage to cool them; and Prentices blow their nails to heat them; and lastly when the Thames is covered over with ice and men's hearts caked over and crusted with cruelty: Then mayest thou or any man be bold to swear it is winter.

1603

HAL BORLAND

February Winds

From THE *New York Times*

THE winds of February clear the way for Windy March. They may huff and puff and bluster mightily, but they still can't muster the authority of a wind of late December or January. Their fang is dulled, somewhat, and they come late in the season. Either that or we are used to being buffeted and refuse to bow to anything less than a zero gale.

For the most part, though, a late February wind is more likely to fade away into a gusty precursor of March than to rise into a freezing snowstorm. And even should it bring snow, it will, like as not, turn around the next day and thaw the bottom out from under it.

In the woods, of course, the February winds whistle and scream and tug at the persistent oak leaves and whip dead branches from the ash trees. But that has been going on all winter long, and the cold creak of frozen branch on branch is lacking now. This is simply wind whooping through the valleys and over the ridges, boisterous wind whipping across the land.

It is tempered somewhat by the sun, which no longer scoots from southeast to southwest in nine hours, horizon to horizon, but rises nearer east and sets nearer west and remains in sight nearly eleven full hours. That extra span of sunlight takes the edge off the chill and lessens the depth to which the cold can drop through the night. Give us another month and we shall have a vernal equinox and we can look for crocuses. Hope, too, tempers the wind as February nears its end. March is just outside the door.

1946

HAL BORLAND

A Day in March

From THE *New York Times*

GO FORTH on a spring day in March —more rare, by the way, than the proverbial day in June—and you can sense the cleanliness of change, a fresh integrity that stirs the human heart. Winter's drab debris may still litter the roadside and murk the valley stream, but the clean brightness of spring is close at hand. The ambering plumes of the weeping willow show it. Black

From the *New York Times*. Copyright Hal Borland, 1947. Reprinted by permission of Willis Kingsley Wing.

birch catkins are all a-tassel. Grass tufts are green in the south-sloping bogs. And here in the dooryard daffodils are thrusting up their rounded tips, and white-veined crocus lancelets clasp tissue-sheathed buds.

Day sky and night sky are bright with the frank promise of new and better days ahead. The air has a new warmth to it, a friendliness that was not there in February. The wind seems to come from the Carolina valleys rather than the frozen hills of Canada.

If there is integrity in the soul of man surely spring is the time when it will reveal itself. He may fuss and fume and delude even himself all winter long, but come spring and he must face his own truth, if there is truth within him. He must know that there is a faith which transcends creed. He must believe in eternal things, the innate dignity of man and his capacity for understanding, the love of mother and child and the cord that binds them, the instinct of all sane men for right and justice.

And he must understand anew the flow of time, which renews itself, and the inevitability of change. Unnumbered times spring has come to this earth, and unnumbered times man has watched it come and known somehow that he was a better man for its return.

1946

ANONYMOUS

Voice of Spring

From The Newark Evening News

IT is pleasant to believe that the first voice ever lifted on earth in praise of Spring was the voice of the peeper. Certainly the frogs and other amphibians, who came into existence after the silent fishes, were the first creatures to possess vocal powers. And perhaps among these ancient frogs the peepers were the first to greet the Spring, even as they are now.

Call him peeper, tree frog, hyla—his is the very voice of Spring. It rings from marshy hollows when the ice has barely gone; it vibrates in vast choruses through misty nights of March; it is as synonymous of Spring as pussy willows and red-winged blackbirds.

Every one knows the peeper's song, but few have ever seen the singer. He is so small that he can hide under a quarter-dollar, and he has the chameleon's ability to change color to match his surroundings. Normally a light brown, he can readily assume other shades of brown and gray. New Jersey's species has dark markings resembling a St. Andrew's cross on its back, hence its name, Hyla crucifer.

The resonant "pe-ep, pe-ep, pe-ep, pe-ep," sung while the throat is expanding like a large bubble, helps the frogs to find their mates. Eggs are laid in the water in April; in seven days they hatch into tadpoles, and in seven times seven

Reprinted from the Newark Evening News for March 27, 1946, by permission of the publishers.

days the tadpoles change into frogs. By June the borders of marshes are squirming with hordes of the little creatures, intent upon finding gnats, ants, mosquitoes. Usually they pass the Summer close to the ground, but can climb agilely, assisted by adhesive pads on toes and fingers. Singing ends in May, is resumed in early Fall.

The peeper is a steadfast fellow. He begins to sing of Spring when most of us can see only calendar indications of its approach. He sings until November robins are flown and even the witch hazel's flower is withered. Then he burrows into moss and leaves to sleep while snows are high, resting only until the first warm days of March tell him another Spring has come.

1946

HAL BORLAND

Lilacs

From THE *New York Times*

THE haunting fragrance of lilacs creeps across the countryside. Purple, and blue, and white, the generous blossoms are opening there in the dooryard, gleaming in the May sunlight and bowing gracefully in the cool May rain. And along the back fence they are opening, and beside the garden wall, and out along the country roads where farmhouses once stood but have long vanished, reminders of some countrywoman whose stone may be lilac-shaded in the near-by burying ground.

All across the land lilacs are perfuming the air, for we Americans took this beautiful shrub to our hearts long ago and have kept it there through the years. In this latitude it is practically symbolic of May. With the gentler fragrance of violets, the bold sweetness of the lilac might be called the breath of our springtime.

The lilac is said to have come originally from the north of Persia, and was first brought to Vienna, the story goes, late in the sixteenth century by Ferdinand I's Ambassador, Busbecq. From Vienna it spread throughout Europe and, eventually, to this side of the Atlantic. New England is full of lilacs, and when New Englanders went west they took lilac roots and cuttings with them. The lilac somehow spelled home, wherever they might stop and put down their own roots, and they would have memories of stone walls and rolling hills here beside the Atlantic each spring when lilacs came to bloom.

They bloom now, great heads of bloom nodding in the hesitant warmth of May, and long-remembered sweetness fills the air.

1946

HAL BORLAND

Green Hills

From THE *New York Times*

THE sun stands far to the south these mid-June days, and gleams on the green hills of America, hills green with the grass and the field crops and the broad-leafed green of oak and elm and maple and cottonwood and live oak. Deep green and bright green, and the lush, thin-bladed green of pasture land. Greens not yet tired or dusty with summer, still fresh with growth and eager for the sun.

The early season of bloom is past. Fruit trees have settled down to the task of growing apples and plums and cherries and peaches, and the maple keys, which hung in red and orange tufts so recently, are spiraling down to replenish their own kind. Bush berries still bloom, but in the general picture they are pretty well lost in the green shadows that lie over the land.

The fields are lined with the green of young corn and matted with the young brightness of oats and rye and wheat and barley. There is a harvest in the making, on the hills of America, and the June sun and the June rains are putting their sustenance and strength into the upshooting grain. Look out across a thousand hills and you can see new life and new hope for a hungering world.

A thousand hills lie green in the sun, and you can start from this Atlantic seaboard and follow the sun across those hills nearly three thousand miles before you see and smell salt water again. So doing, you will see this America in its magnificent strength, the strength of the fields that know no horizon. Here it lies, in the beauty of June, hill upon hill, with the waters of the land flowing between and all the towns and cities clinging to the green hills whence comes their strength.

1946

HAL BORLAND

Live Waters

From THE *New York Times*

SPRINGS are the live waters of this earth, full of cool sweetness and bubbling with the pent-up energy of elemental forces. They ooze or flow or gush from the stony hillsides, following an earth-fault to its open end and emerging to form a rivulet or a brook. They water the land, and the course of

From the *New York Times*. Copyright Hal Borland, 1947. Reprinted by permission of Willis Kingsley Wing.

their flow is marked by the greenest green that grows. Brookside grass achieves a peculiar lushness, and a brookside meadow is something to look upon, particularly when the heat of summer has begun to crisp the springless hillsides.

Springs feed the rivers of the land and keep them flowing. Follow them to their beginnings and you climb to the source of the brooks. You come at last to the springs where the reservoirs of the earth dole out their waters. The snows, the glaciers and the periodic rains fill and flood the channels, but the steady flow is from those sweet earthwaters that wash the rocks and hesitate in leisurely pools before leaping down the hillsides toward the distant seas.

A spring marked a home site, in the days when man was making the land his own. Spring waters quenched his thirst and served his flocks and turned his mill, and in the valleys where springs turned brooks to streams there was good soil for his crops. He could contend with stones and stumps, but unless he had water, live water, he faced odds too great to master.

The springs still flow, and their waters are still sweet. The grass stands lush beside their pools, and in the evening there is still the song of live waters making their beneficent way to the sea.

1946

LORUS J. MILNE

The Water's Skin

WHEN you sit by a pond or a winding stream, the city's hurry drains away, and from the corners of the mind thoughts come out and sun themselves. Before you on the water, bugs and beetles skip about. They stay afloat because the surface tension of the water acts as a skin, elastic and smooth, that prevents them from sinking.

Two kinds of air-breathing insects are the most familiar users of the water's skin. The shiny, black whirligig beetles zigzagging in groups on streams, ponds, and small lakes draw attention to themselves by their hurried movements. They fascinate the small boy standing dry-shod on the bank. He wants to catch one, but the beetles are safe from cupped hands as they dart and spin. If alarmed beyond their gyrating system of escape, the whirligigs tip their tail ends up to grasp a bubble of air as they dive to the bottom. There they swim around and later surface like a submarine, some distance off, their glossy backs shedding water. The front pair of their six legs are long and slender; the other four are short paddles which whip the insect through the water.

The whirligigs often climb out on floating logs or lily pads to bask in the sun, but are off into the surface film at the slightest movement within sight.

The beetles have a water line, below which they are really wet. This line passes through their compound eyes, which are divided actually into two, the upper half for vision into air, the other for watching the water's depths. In winter the whirligigs crawl under fallen leaves along the banks or in near-by woods, and come out on warm spring days to seek their fellows on little pools or in quiet bays along the river. The female beetle lays her eggs on plants just above the water's surface; there they hatch into aquatic larvae, which hunt for smaller animals within the pond.

The other commonly seen inhabitants of the surface film are the water-striders, known in Texas as "Jesus bugs," in Canada as "skaters." These insects are suspended in the same way that a clean needle can be made to "float" on water in a tumbler. They rest their weight on the short front pair of legs and on the outer third of the long hind pair, and use their middle legs as oars to push themselves along. Their waxy-haired feet press the water surface downward without breaking the film, and form elongate dimples which support them. Actually they ride the water as a result of a combination of surface tension forces pulling upward in the slanting sides of the dimples, and of the buoyant force of water displaced from these depressions in the surface.

It is very striking to watch one of these insects cleaning its legs a pair at a time, rubbing them together in the same way that a housefly does. First it cleans the front pair, the body being held unusually high above the water on the remaining four legs. Next it rubs a middle leg against a front one, lying down on the opposite side to elevate the appendages being cleaned. Finally it cleans the back pair; its head is almost in the water, the chin pressing into the surface, and the middle legs are brought far back to allow the abdomen to be raised up as far as possible.

Toilet completed, antennae brushed, the insect rows forth alertly to seek its fortune. This may be another strider or some floating carcass into which the bug's slender beak may be thrust and food obtained. Many of their dashes over the pond surface are rewarded with a struggling leafhopper or other small insect which has fallen onto the water and is supported by the surface film. Water-striders dive upon occasion, but only under threat of serious danger. Afterwards they crawl out, wet and obviously miserable, to dry and comb themselves into respectability. All active stages in a water-strider's life cycle are spent on the water surface, but for winter they fly or crawl (some are wingless even as adults) under leaves much as do the whirligig beetles.

Every so often a water-strider is noticed with a few bright red specks attached to it. On closer inspection, these are found to be the parasitic immature stages of the red water mite. The young mites suck nutritious juices from inside the water-strider. They weaken it a little but do not kill it. After a few weeks the mites drop off and shed their six-legged skins to become proper eight-legged relatives of the spiders. Then as adults, they run nimbly over the water surface, mate, and lay eggs on floating plants, where the young hatch and wait for water-striders or other pond insects. The mature water mites are very handsome with their bright, rich-red bodies. Their swimming is distinctive, for their eight short, hair-fringed legs move so rapidly that the globular red body glides along smoothly, in contrast to the jerky movements of the pond insects and crustaceans.

Perhaps the largest walker on the water is the Dolomedes spider, which could straddle a silver dollar without touching it. These are tan-colored, with dark stripes, and are members of the wolf-spider family. They are seen often around boathouses on small lakes and rivers. They run out on the water surface mainly when traveling across some small bay or when driven from the shore by the approach of danger. Fish often snap them up if they hesitate —retribution in kind since these same spiders creep down into the water and snatch small fish in their murderous jaws. The female Dolomedes, like others of her family, does not trust her precious eggs out of her sight. She wraps them up in a creamy white ball of silk and drags the spherical bundle after her through the woods, out on the water, everywhere she goes.

A more frequent spider on the water's skin is a smaller member of the same wolf-spider family. This is a very active, running spider, which nimbly skips and rushes from lily pad to shore and weed to weed, picking up food as it goes. Dead insects or live, it makes no difference, but the actual eating of the catch is reserved for the safety of some plant stem or the shelter of the bank. Like the Dolomedes, the small water spider drags her ball of eggs, and when the young have hatched, carries them upon her back and legs until they gain confidence to leave her.

Among the more spectacular yet seldom noticed inhabitants of the water film are the springtails, a group of minute insects which have a most unusual means of locomotion. Beneath the hinder end of the body, they have a long appendage, sometimes forked, which

reaches forward to engage a catch between their legs. In use, the body is tensed so as to strain the appendage against its catch. Letting go of the catch allows the appendage to strike violently against the water surface on which the insect stands, throwing the tiny body high in the air, to fall somewhere else. For a creature so minute, air has an excellent cushioning effect, so that it lands without damage, often on its feet.

Ever since someone first dropped a piece of camphor into a dish of water, people have been amused to see the chip of waxy white gum dash here and there over the water surface. The explanation was far less interesting—the camphor chip dissolved non-uniformly, and reduced the water surface tension as it dissolved. The side where most was dissolving at any one time was the side where the water surface tension was most reduced momentarily, and the water opposite yanked the chip away. The same experiment may be performed with two toothpicks or wooden matches floated in a dish of water. After a few moments they will cling together in the center of their pond. If a slender, pointed stick of soap is pushed down to touch the water surface between the two toothpicks, the surface tension there is reduced and the water film beyond the toothpicks jerks them apart. If you have a cube of sugar to spend on the experiment, dip it into the water between the spread picks. Back together they come, since the sugar solution has a higher surface tension than the pure water, whereas the soap solution has a lower tension.

All this is entertaining parlor magic, but there is a little rove beetle, Stenus by name, which actually uses this trick. Stenus, like its close relatives, is a hungry little fellow with short wings, and flies around a great deal trying to find food. Often it makes a mistake and falls into water. But it merely expels from its anal glands a substance which lowers the surface tension at its hinder end, so that the water ahead of it can draw it forward rapidly like a toy boat, often causing the beetle to reach a dry object from which it can fly on again.

Even vertebrate animals may cross the water surface if they are quick about it. Barbour tells of small lizards in Central America, the basilisks, which are common around streams and ponds. When disturbed they rush across the water surface on their hind legs, with the fore feet folded against their sides and the tail raised to counterbalance them.

Related lizards in Cuba do this too, but instead of hurrying to the opposite bank or some solid refuge, they run over the water merely to some quiet spot, where they stop, sink quickly to the bottom, and remain until they believe the danger has passed. Some of our native salamanders and newts can scamper across the water's skin in much the same way, although they use all four feet and must touch the water along their bellies too. In all of these, the animal is kept from sinking by its nimble action, feet pressing down on the water and away again so quickly that the water cannot flow around, its own inertia no match for the speed of the animal.

1946

STEPHEN LEACOCK

My Fishing Pond

IT LIES embowered in a little cup of the hills, my fishing pond. I made a last trip to it just as the season ended, when the autumn leaves of its great trees were turning color and rustling down to rest upon the still black water. So steep are the banks, so old and high the trees, that scarcely a puff of wind ever ruffles the surface of the pond. All around, it is as if the world were stilled into silence, and time blended into eternity.

I realized again as I looked at the pond what a beautiful, secluded spot it was, how natural its appeal to the heart of the angler. You turn off a country road, go sideways across a meadow and over a hill, and there it lies—a sheet of still water, with high, high banks, grown with great trees. Long years ago someone built a sawmill, all gone now, at the foot of the valley and threw back the water to make a pond, perhaps a quarter of a mile long. At the widest it must be nearly two hundred feet—the most skillful fisherman may make a full cast both ways. At the top end, where it runs narrow among stumps and rushes, there is no room to cast except with direction and great skill.

Let me say at once, so as to keep no

From *Here are My Lectures* by Stephen Leacock. Copyright, 1937, by Dodd, Mead & Company, Inc. Reprinted by permission of Dodd, Mead & Company.

mystery about it, that there are no fish in my pond. So far as I know there never have been. But I have never found that to make any difference. Certainly none to the men I bring there —my chance visitors from the outside world—for an afternoon of casting.

If there are no fish in the pond, at least they never know it. They never doubt it; they never ask, and I let it go at that.

It is well known hereabouts that I do not take anybody and everybody out to my fishpond. I only care to invite people who can really fish, who can cast a line—experts, and especially people from a distance to whom the whole neighborhood is new and attractive, the pond seen for the first time. If I took out ordinary men, especially men near home, they would very likely notice that they got no fish. The expert doesn't. He knows trout fishing too well. He knows that even in a really fine pond, such as he sees mine is, there are days when not a trout will rise. He'll explain it to you himself; and, having explained it, he is all the better pleased if he turns out to be right and they don't rise.

Trout, as everyone knows who is an angler, never rise after a rain, nor before one; it is impossible to get them to rise in the heat; and any chill in the air keeps them down. The absolutely right day is a still, cloudy day, but even then there are certain kinds of clouds that prevent a rising of the trout. Indeed, I have only to say to one of my expert friends, "Queer, they didn't bite!" and he's off to a good start with an explanation. There is such a tremendous lot to know about trout fishing that men who are keen on it can discuss theories of fishing by the hour.

Such theories we generally talk over— my guest of the occasion and I—as we make our preparations at the pond. You see, I keep there all the apparatus that goes with fishing—a punt, with lockers in the sides of it, a neat little dock built out of cedar (cedar attracts the trout), and, best of all, a little shelter house, a quaint little place like a pagoda, close beside the water and yet under the trees. Inside is tackle, all sorts of tackle, hanging round the walls in a mixture of carelessness and order.

"Look, old man," I say, "if you like to try a running paternoster, take this one," or, "Have you ever seen these Japanese leads? No, they're not a gut; they're a sort of floss."

"I doubt if I can land one with that," he says.

"Perhaps not," I answer. In fact, I'm sure he couldn't; there isn't any to land.

On pegs in the pagoda hangs a waterproof mackintosh or two, for you never know—you may be caught in a shower just when the trout are starting to rise. Then, of course, a sort of cellarette cupboard with decanters and bottles, and gingersnaps, and perhaps an odd pot of anchovy paste—no one wants to quit good fishing for mere hunger. Nor does any real angler care to begin fishing without taking just a drop (Just a touch—be careful! Whoa! Whoa!) of something to keep out the cold, or to wish good luck for the chances of the day.

I always find, when I bring out one of my friends, that these mere preparatives or preparations, these preliminaries of angling, are the best part of it. Often they take half an hour. There is so much to discuss—the question of weights of tackle, the color of the fly to use, and broad general questions of theory, such as whether it matters what kind of hat a man wears. It seems that trout will rise for some hats, and for others not. One of my best guests, who has written a whole book on fly fishing, is particularly strong on hats and color. "I don't think I'd wear that hat, old man," he says, "much too dark for a day like this." "I wore it all last month," I said. "So you might, but that was August. I wouldn't wear a dark hat in September; and that tie is too dark a blue, old man."

So I knew that that made it all right. I kept the hat on. We had a grand afternoon; we got no fish.

I admit that the lack of fish in my pond requires sometimes a little tact in management. The guest gets a little restless. So I say to him, "You certainly have the knack of casting!"—and he gets so absorbed in casting farther and farther that he forgets the fish. Or I take him toward the upper end and he gets his line caught on bulrush—that might be a bite. Or, if he still keeps restless, I say suddenly, "Hush! Was that a fish jumped?" That will silence any true angler instantly. "You stand in the bow," I whisper, "and I'll paddle gently in that direction." It's the *whispering* that does it. We are still a hundred yards away from any trout that could hear us even if a trout were there. But that makes no difference. Some of the men I take out begin to whisper a mile away from the pond and come home whispering.

You see, after all, what with frogs jumping, and catching the line in bulrushes, or pulling up a water-logged chip nearly to the top, they don't really know—my guests don't—whether they have hooked something or not. Indeed, after a little lapse of time, they think they did: they talk of the "big one they lost"—a thing over which any angler gets sentimental in retrospect.

"Do you remember," they say to me months later at our club in the city, "that big trout I lost up on your fishpond last summer?" "Indeed I do," I say. "Did you ever get him later on?" "No, never," I answer. (Neither him nor any other.)

Yet the illusion holds good. And besides, you never can tell: there *might* be trout in the pond. Why not? After all, why shouldn't there be a trout in the pond? You take a pond like that and there ought to be trout in it!

Whenever the sight of the pond bursts on the eyes of a new guest he stands entranced. "What a wonderful place for trout!" he exclaims. "Isn't it?" I answer. "No wonder you'd get trout in a pond like that." "No wonder at all." "You don't need to stock it at all, I suppose?" "Stock it!" I laughed at the idea. Stock a pond like that! Well, I guess not!

Perhaps one of the best and most alluring touches is fishing out of season— just a day or two after the season has closed. Any fisherman knows how keen is the regret at each expiring season—swallowed up and lost in the glory of the fading autumn. So if a guest turns up just then I say, "I know it's out of season, but I thought you might care to take a run out to the pond anyway and have a look at it." He can't resist. By the time he's in the pagoda and has a couple of small drinks (Careful, not too much! Whoa! Whoa!) he decides there can be no harm in making a cast or two. "I suppose," he says, "you never have any trouble with the inspectors?" "Oh, no," I answer; "they never think of troubling me." And with that we settle down to an afternoon of it. "I'm glad," says the guest at the end, "that they weren't rising. After all, we had just the same fun as if they were."

That's it: illusion! How much of life is like that! It's the *idea* of the thing that counts, not the reality. You don't need fish for fishing, any more than you need partridge for partridge shooting, or gold for gold mining. Just the illusion or expectation.

So I am going back now to the city and to my club, where we shall fish all winter, hooking up big ones, but losing the ones bigger still, hooking two trout at one throw,—three at a throw!—and for me, behind it all, the memory of my fishing pond darkening under the falling leaves. . . . At least it has made my friends happy.

1936

JOHN STEINBECK

and

EDWARD F. RICKETTS

The Sea-Cow

FROM SEA OF CORTEZ

WE COME now to a piece of equipment which still brings anger to our hearts and, we hope, some venom to our pen. Perhaps in self-defense against suit, we should say, "The outboard motor mentioned in this book is purely fictitious and any resemblance to outboard motors living or dead is coincidental." We shall call this contraption, for the sake of secrecy, a Hansen Sea-Cow—a dazzling little piece of machinery, all aluminum paint and touched here and there with spots of red. The Sea-Cow was built to sell, to dazzle the eyes, to splutter its way into the unwary heart. We took it along for the skiff. It was intended that it should push us ashore and back, should drive our boat into estuaries and along the borders of little coves. But we had not reckoned with one thing. Recently, industrial civilization has reached its peak of reality and has lunged forward into something that approaches mysticism. In the Sea-Cow factory where steel fingers tighten screws, bend and mold, measure and divide, some curious mathematick has occurred. And that secret so long sought has accidentally been found. Life has been created. The machine is at last stirred. A soul and a malignant mind have been born. Our Hansen Sea-Cow was not only a living thing but a mean, irritable, contemptible, vengeful, mischievous, hateful living thing. In the six weeks of our association we observed it, at first mechanically and then, as its living reactions became more and more apparent, psychologically. And we determined one thing to our satisfaction. When and if these ghoulish little motors learn to reproduce themselves the human species is doomed. For their hatred of us is so great that they will wait and plan and organize and one night, in a roar of little exhausts, they will wipe us out. We do not think that Mr. Hansen, inventor of the Sea-Cow, father of the outboard motor, knew what he was doing. We think the monster he created was as accidental and arbitrary as the beginning of any other life. Only one thing differentiates the Sea-Cow from the life that we know. Whereas the forms that are familiar to us are the results of billions of years of mutation and complication, life and intelligence emerged simultaneously in the Sea-Cow. It is more than a species. It is a whole new re-definition of life. We observed the following traits in it and we were able to check them again and again:

1. Incredibly lazy, the Sea-Cow loved to ride on the back of a boat, trailing its propeller daintily in the water while we rowed.

2. It required the same amount of gasoline whether it ran or not, apparently being able to absorb this fluid through its body walls without recourse to explosion. It had always to be filled at the beginning of every trip.

3. It had apparently some clairvoyant powers, and was able to read our minds, particularly when they were inflamed with emotion. Thus, on every occasion when we were driven to the point of destroying it, it started and ran with a great noise and excitement. This served the double purpose of saving its life and of resurrecting in our minds a false confidence in it.

4. It had many cleavage points, and when attacked with a screwdriver, fell apart in simulated death, a trait it had in common with opossums, armadillos, and several members of the sloth family, which also fall apart in simulated death when attacked with a screwdriver. .

5. It hated Tex, sensing perhaps that his knowledge of mechanics was capable of diagnosing its shortcomings.

6. It completely refused to run: (a) when the waves were high, (b) when the wind blew, (c) at night, early morning, and evening, (d) in rain, dew, or fog, (e) when the distance to be covered was more than two hundred yards. But on warm, sunny days when the weather was calm and the white beach close by—in a word, on days when it would have been a pleasure to row—the Sea-Cow started at a touch and would not stop.

7. It loved no one, trusted no one. It had no friends.

Perhaps toward the end, our observations were a little warped by emotion. Time and again as it sat on the stern with its pretty little propeller lying idly in the water, it was very close to death. And in the end, even we were infected with its malignancy and its dishonesty. We should have destroyed it, but we did not. Arriving home, we gave it a new coat of aluminum paint, spotted it at points with new red enamel, and sold it. And we might have rid the world of this mechanical cancer!

1941

EDWARD WEEKS

Notes on an Old Friend

OVERHEAD the oak leaves stir against the cloudless blue, and the shadow in which I am reading ripples like running water. At my feet on the borderline between the sunny and the cool grass lies Mickey dozing, gray muzzle pointed toward the driveway up which the family will return from their expedition. Periodically he rouses himself, shakes the catkins from his black curls, and moves closer to the sun. His movement renews the scolding of the mother robin in the bittersweet and interrupts my intake of print. I watch him, and through the forming impressions of the book in my lap, memory thrusts its feeling.

This is probably our last summer together. Mickey is sixteen and that is a great age for a cocker spaniel given to eating any old thing; indeed a great age for any dog. Implicit in every friendship is the trust that it will never break. Mick has no reason to doubt us, but we who note his fading hearing and his inability to spot us at any distance on the beach live with the warning to make these months good.

I remember William Morton Wheeler's remarking on the silent communication between dogs, and how, when he had taken one of his for a walk through the Arboretum, the others would gather about the traveler instantly on his return and by scent and emanation have all the news in a matter of seconds. On the Common with other dogs Mick is eager, quivering, and gregarious when I am along, and hair-on-end belligerent when accompanying his mistress. In canine years he is now well past the century mark, so it is small wonder that dogs in their prime have only a passing curiosity in what he has to say. They pause, there is the usual tail-wagging introduction. Then, while he is still standing on his dignity, they suddenly lope off. Mick will start after and then resign himself to his own grass, which he scratches up with a "What the hell." For ladies he has, I gather, the charm of an aging colonel. There is a honey-colored spaniel who, after the nosing, will describe mad circles about him as he stands immovable on the moonlit Common. But if she pushes him too roughly he loses his balance and shows his lip, and so they part.

At home his expressions are stressed for our benefit. His humor, as when with jaws open and tongue half a yard out he stands there grinning; his sneeze of expectation; his mutter—a kind of controlled yip—of annoyance; his jumping recognition of those most important words in a city dog's vocabulary, "going out" and "down country" (is it the special note that colors our voices as we say them?); his sharp demanding bark when his water dish is empty or when brownies, his passion, are cooking—these are a language no one could miss. So too his boredom when, after a decent interval in our friend's house, he fetches his leash and stands obdurate with it in his jaws. And his play: in his youth he would mouth a grape, Concord or Malaga, and then lie staring at us until sud-

Reprinted from the *Atlantic Monthly*, August, 1947, by permission of the author.

denly it would be popped over his shoulder and retrieved in a scramble. This he did untaught, and the mystery of how the grape emerged uncrushed again and again was his own invention. Now the car is his pleasure: head out the window and ears streaming, he challenges every passing dog with horrid words.

I remember other times when he spoke my language, once when in his puppyhood he was sick from the distemper injection. He began vomiting at midnight and at four I got the car and drove him to the vet's. He was so weak that he leaned limply against the corner of seat and door, but in answer to my hand his eyes said, "I'm sorry to be such a mess. But I *am* sick." And again, years later when he had to apologize for his hunting. It was summer and our little cottage adjoined the orchard and vegetable garden of our big neighbor. At sundown rabbits would make free with the tender lettuce and carrots, and their scent—when Mickey got it—drove him wild. One evening from our screened porch I spotted a cottontail in the green. Mick was asleep, but quietly opening the door I pointed him at the quarry and he got the idea. Rabbit and spaniel disappeared over the horizon with yips marking every second bound. Two hours went by, and then in darkness there was Mick scratching at the screen. "No luck," he said, and in his mouth was the half-eaten carrot the rabbit had dropped in his haste. "No luck."

Mickey is by his nature a hunter and a retriever. But now, with his teeth gone, his retrieving is limited to fishermen's corks as they curve ahead of him on the beach, and to apples in the orchard. As a hunter he fancied himself and for years he nourished a grudge against squirrels. I used to tease him about this. Walking close to one of our oaks I would peer up into the leaves and touch the bark significantly; whereupon Mick would leave the ground jumping and scrabbling as high as my arm.

The squirrels, for their part, enjoyed the feud: they knew he could never catch them. I remember one summer day when Mickey was lying on the open porch soaking up the sun which radiated from the warm boards. Close to the house stood an old apple tree, one of whose branches reached over the porch. Along this bridge, as Mickey slept, stole one of his bushy-tailed enemies. With mathematical precision the squirrel nipped clean a hard green apple, which hit the porch with a thump an inch from Mickey's nose. It was as nice a piece of natural comedy as I have ever witnessed; and the aftermath was noisy.

That dogs remember, we know from their habits and from their twitching dreams when they are so palpably reliving some activity. But how far back does their memory reach, and do those little half-uttered cries indicate that, like man, they are long haunted by old fears? If so, then Mick may still feel the most painful terror of domesticated animals—the fear of desertion. The autumn of his second year my wife and I had to answer a sudden call to New York. We closed the cottage, packed up the daughter, and to save time left the pup with the maid. She took him to her home in Watertown, and from it he naturally escaped in search of us. That was on Friday afternoon. They saw him for an instant at the garbage pail Saturday morning, and then he was gone for good.

By our return on Monday there wasn't a clue. We drove the unfamiliar streets and we put our appeal in the newspapers and on the air. In twenty-four hours we had heard from seventeen spaniel owners, fifteen of whom had lost their own dogs. But one of them gave us a tip. In their search they had seen a small black dog in the vast reaches of the Watertown Arsenal. So with the Governor's permission we drove through the gates—this was long before the war—to explore the cement strips which led between the huge closed buildings. A sergeant's son gave us hope. "Sure," he said, "a little black dog. He's here all right, only you can't get close to him." "Don't scare him," I said. "Find him if you can." Whistling and calling, we went to point after point, and once on the knoll above a huge oil tank I thought I heard the short familiar bark, but nothing moved. Three hours later we came back to the same spot, and there was the boy lying full-length on the cement wall aiming an imaginary gun. "The buffalo is down here," he called. Ten yards farther and I saw Mick's nest and his unmistakable head. "Mickey!" I shouted. Then up the slope he came on the dead run, his ears brown pancakes of burr.

Is it the fear of our leaving him that so troubles him when he can now no longer hear us as we move about the house? The sight of an open suitcase makes him more doleful than does a thunderstorm. When we pack for the country, there is no way to tell him that he will surely come too. In his heart of hearts Mick knows that he is dependent upon four people, and no comfort of maid or sitter can distract his vigil when we are gone for the evening. Our woods are his woods. The squirrels who used to scold him he no longer hears. But we shall hear him long after he is gone.

1947

HEYWOOD BROUN

The Fifty-First Dragon

OF ALL the pupils at the knight school Gawaine le Cœur-Hardy was among the least promising. He was tall and sturdy, but his instructors soon discovered that he lacked spirit. He would hide in the woods when the jousting class was called, although his companions and members of the faculty sought to appeal to his better nature by shouting to him to come out and break his neck like a man. Even when they told him that the lances were padded, the horses no more than ponies and the field unusually soft for late autumn, Gawaine refused to grow enthusiastic. The Headmaster and the Assistant Professor of Pleasaunce were discussing the case one spring afternoon and the Assistant Professor could see no remedy but expulsion.

"No," said the Headmaster, as he looked out at the purple hills which ringed the school, "I think I'll train him to slay dragons."

From *Collected Edition of Heywood Broun*, copyright, 1941, by Heywood Hale Broun. Reprinted by permission of Harcourt, Brace and Company, Inc.

"He might be killed," objected the Assistant Professor.

"So he might," replied the Headmaster brightly, "but," he added, more soberly, "we must consider the greater good. We are responsible for the formation of this lad's character."

"Are the dragons particularly bad this year?" interrupted the Assistant Professor. This was characteristic. He always seemed restive when the head of the school began to talk ethics and the ideals of the institution.

"I've never known them worse," replied the Headmaster. "Up in the hills to the south last week they killed a number of peasants, two cows and a prize pig. And if this dry spell holds there's no telling when they may start a forest fire simply by breathing around indiscriminately."

"Would any refund on the tuition fee be necessary in case of an accident to young Cœur-Hardy?"

"No," the principal answered, judicially, "that's all covered in the contract. But as a matter of fact he won't be killed. Before I send him up in the hills I'm going to give him a magic word."

"That's a good idea," said the Professor. "Sometimes they work wonders."

From that day on Gawaine specialized in dragons. His course included both theory and practice. In the morning there were long lectures on the history, anatomy, manners and customs of dragons. Gawaine did not distinguish himself in these studies. He had a marvelously versatile gift for forgetting things. In the afternoon he showed to better advantage, for then he would go down to the South Meadow and practice with a battle-ax. In this exercise he was truly impressive, for he had enormous strength as well as speed and grace. He

even developed a deceptive display of ferocity. Old alumni say that it was a thrilling sight to see Gawaine charging across the field toward the dummy paper dragon which had been set up for his practice. As he ran he would brandish his ax and shout "A murrain on thee!" or some other vivid bit of campus slang. It never took him more than one stroke to behead the dummy dragon.

Gradually his task was made more difficult. Paper gave way to papier-mâché and finally to wood, but even the toughest of these dummy dragons had no terrors for Gawaine. One sweep of the ax always did the business. There were those who said that when the practice was protracted until dusk and the dragons threw long, fantastic shadows across the meadow Gawaine did not charge so impetuously nor shout so loudly. It is possible there was malice in this charge. At any rate, the Headmaster decided by the end of June that it was time for the test. Only the night before a dragon had come close to the school grounds and had eaten some of the lettuce from the garden. The faculty decided that Gawaine was ready. They gave him a diploma and a new battle-ax and the Headmaster summoned him to a private conference.

"Sit down," said the Headmaster. "Have a cigarette."

Gawaine hesitated.

"Oh, I know it's against the rules," said the Headmaster. "But after all, you have received your preliminary degree. You are no longer a boy. You are a man. To-morrow you will go out into the world, the great world of achievement."

Gawaine took a cigarette. The Headmaster offered him a match, but he produced one of his own and began to puff away with a dexterity which quite amazed the principal.

"Here you have learned the theories of life," continued the Headmaster, resuming the thread of his discourse, "but after all, life is not a matter of theories. Life is a matter of facts. It calls on the young and the old alike to face these facts, even though they are hard and sometimes unpleasant. Your problem, for example, is to slay dragons."

"They say that those dragons down in the south wood are five hundred feet long," ventured Gawaine, timorously.

"Stuff and nonsense!" said the Headmaster. "The curate saw one last week from the top of Arthur's Hill. The dragon was sunning himself down in the valley. The curate didn't have an opportunity to look at him very long because he felt it was his duty to hurry back to make a report to me. He said the monster, or shall I say, the big lizard?—wasn't an inch over two hundred feet. But the size has nothing at all to do with it. You'll find the big ones even easier than the little ones. They're far slower on their feet and less aggressive, I'm told. Besides, before you go I'm going to equip you in such fashion that you need have no fear of all the dragons in the world."

"I'd like an enchanted cap," said Gawaine.

"What's that?" answered the Headmaster, testily.

"A cap to make me disappear," explained Gawaine.

The Headmaster laughed indulgently. "You mustn't believe all those old wives' stories," he said. "There isn't any such thing. A cap to make you disappear, indeed! What would you do with it? You haven't even appeared yet. Why, my boy, you could walk from here to London, and nobody would so much as look at you. You're nobody. You couldn't be more invisible than that."

Gawaine seemed dangerously close to a relapse into his old habit of whimpering. The Headmaster reassured him: "Don't worry; I'll give you something much better than an enchanted cap. I'm going to give you a magic word. All you have to do is to repeat this magic charm once and no dragon can possibly harm a hair of your head. You can cut off his head at your leisure."

He took a heavy book from the shelf behind his desk and began to run through it. "Sometimes," he said, "the charm is a whole phrase or even a sentence. I might, for instance, give you 'To make the'—No, that might not do. I think a single word would be best for dragons."

"A short word," suggested Gawaine.

"It can't be too short or it wouldn't be potent. There isn't so much hurry as all that. Here's a splendid magic word: 'Rumplesnitz.' Do you think you can learn that?"

Gawaine tried and in an hour or so he seemed to have the word well in hand. Again and again he interrupted the lesson to inquire, "And if I say 'Rumplesnitz' the dragon can't possibly hurt me?" And always the Headmaster replied, "If you only say 'Rumplesnitz,' you are perfectly safe."

Toward morning Gawaine seemed resigned to his career. At daybreak the Headmaster saw him to the edge of the forest and pointed him to the direction in which he should proceed. About a mile away to the southwest a cloud of steam hovered over an open meadow in the woods and the Headmaster assured Gawaine that under the steam he would find a dragon. Gawaine went forward slowly. He wondered whether it would be best to approach the dragon on the run as he did in his practice in the South Meadow or to walk slowly toward him, shouting "Rumplesnitz" all the way.

The problem was decided for him. No sooner had he come to the fringe of the meadow than the dragon spied him and began to charge. It was a large dragon and yet it seemed decidedly aggressive in spite of the Headmaster's statement to the contrary. As the dragon charged it released huge clouds of hissing steam through its nostrils. It was almost as if a gigantic teapot had gone mad. The dragon came forward so fast and Gawaine was so frightened that he had time to say "Rumplesnitz" only once. As he said it, he swung his battle-ax and off popped the head of the dragon. Gawaine had to admit that it was even easier to kill a real dragon than a wooden one if only you said "Rumplesnitz."

Gawaine brought the ears home and a small section of the tail. His school mates and the faculty made much of him, but the Headmaster wisely kept him from being spoiled by insisting that he go on with his work. Every clear day Gawaine rose at dawn and went out to kill dragons. The Headmaster kept him at home when it rained, because he said the woods were damp and unhealthy at such times and that he didn't want the boy to run needless risks. Few good days passed in which Gawaine failed to get a dragon. On one particularly fortunate day he killed three, a husband and wife and a visiting relative. Gradually he developed a technique. Pupils who sometimes watched him from the hill-tops a long way off said that he often allowed the dragon to come within a few feet before he said "Rumplesnitz." He came to

say it with a mocking sneer. Occasionally he did stunts. Once when an excursion party from London was watching him he went into action with his right hand tied behind his back. The dragon's head came off just as easily.

As Gawaine's record of killings mounted higher the Headmaster found it impossible to keep him completely in hand. He fell into the habit of stealing out at night and engaging in long drinking bouts at the village tavern. It was after such a debauch that he rose a little before dawn one fine August morning and started out after his fiftieth dragon. His head was heavy and his mind sluggish. He was heavy in other respects as well, for he had adopted the somewhat vulgar practice of wearing his medals, ribbons and all, when he went out dragon hunting. The decorations began on his chest and ran all the way down to his abdomen. They must have weighed at least eight pounds.

Gawaine found a dragon in the same meadow where he had killed the first one. It was a fair-sized dragon, but evidently an old one. Its face was wrinkled and Gawaine thought he had never seen so hideous a countenance. Much to the lad's disgust, the monster refused to charge and Gawaine was obliged to walk toward him. He whistled as he went. The dragon regarded him hopelessly, but craftily. Of course it had heard of Gawaine. Even when the lad raised his battle-ax the dragon made no move. It knew that there was no salvation in the quickest thrust of the head, for it had been informed that this hunter was protected by an enchantment. It merely waited, hoping something would turn up. Gawaine raised the battle-ax and suddenly lowered it again. He had grown very pale and he trembled violently. The dragon suspected a trick. "What's the matter?" it asked, with false solicitude.

"I've forgotten the magic word," stammered Gawaine.

"What a pity," said the dragon. "So that was the secret. It doesn't seem quite sporting to me, all this magic stuff, you know. Not cricket, as we used to say when I was a little dragon; but after all, that's a matter of opinion."

Gawaine was so helpless with terror that the dragon's confidence rose immeasurably and it could not resist the temptation to show off a bit.

"Could I possibly be of any assistance?" it asked. "What's the first letter of the magic word?"

"It begins with an 'r,' " said Gawaine weakly.

"Let's see," mused the dragon, "that doesn't tell us much, does it? What sort of a word is this? Is it an epithet, do you think?"

Gawaine could do no more than nod.

"Why, of course," exclaimed the dragon, "reactionary Republican."

Gawaine shook his head.

"Well, then," said the dragon, "we'd better get down to business. Will you surrender?"

With the suggestion of a compromise Gawaine mustered up enough courage to speak.

"What will you do if I surrender?" he asked.

"Why, I'll eat you," said the dragon.

"And if I don't surrender?"

"I'll eat you just the same."

"Then it doesn't make any difference, does it?" moaned Gawaine.

"It does to me," said the dragon with a smile. "I'd rather you didn't surrender. You'd taste much better if you didn't."

The dragon waited for a long time for Gawaine to ask "Why?" but the boy was too frightened to speak. At last the dragon had to give the explanation without his cue line. "You see," he said, "if you don't surrender you'll taste better because you'll die game."

This was an old and ancient trick of the dragon's. By means of some such quip he was accustomed to paralyze his victims with laughter and then to destroy them. Gawaine was sufficiently paralyzed as it was, but laughter had no part in his helplessness. With the last word of the joke the dragon drew back his head and struck. In that second there flashed into the mind of Gawaine the magic word "Rumplesnitz," but there was no time to say it. There was time only to strike and, without a word, Gawaine met the onrush of the dragon with a full swing. He put all his back and shoulders into it. The impact was terrific and the head of the dragon flew away almost a hundred yards and landed in a thicket.

Gawaine did not remain frightened very long after the death of the dragon. His mood was one of wonder. He was enormously puzzled. He cut off the ears of the monster almost in a trance. Again and again he thought to himself, "I didn't say 'Rumplesnitz'!" He was sure of that and yet there was no question that he had killed the dragon. In fact, he had never killed one so utterly. Never before had he driven a head for anything like the same distance. Twenty-five yards was perhaps his best previous record. All the way back to the knight school he kept rumbling about in his mind seeking an explanation for what had occurred. He went to the Headmaster immediately and after closing the door told him what had happened. "I didn't say 'Rumplesnitz,' " he explained with great earnestness.

The Headmaster laughed. "I'm glad you've found out," he said. "It makes you ever so much more of a hero. Don't you see that? Now you know that it was you who killed all these dragons and not that foolish little word 'Rumplesnitz.'"

Gawaine frowned. "Then it wasn't a magic word after all?" he asked.

"Of course not," said the Headmaster, "you ought to be too old for such foolishness. There isn't any such thing as a magic word."

"But you told me it was magic," protested Gawaine. "You said it was magic and now you say it isn't."

"It wasn't magic in a literal sense," answered the Headmaster, "but it was much more wonderful than that. The word gave you confidence. It took away your fears. If I hadn't told you that you might have been killed the very first time. It was your battle-ax did the trick."

Gawaine surprised the Headmaster by his attitude. He was obviously distressed by the explanation. He interrupted a long philosophic and ethical discourse by the Headmaster with, "If I hadn't of hit 'em all mighty hard and fast any one of 'em might have crushed me like a, like a—" He fumbled for a word.

"Egg shell," suggested the Headmaster.

"Like a egg shell," assented Gawaine, and he said it many times. All through the evening meal people who sat near him heard him muttering, "Like a egg shell, like a egg shell."

The next day was clear, but Gawaine did not get up at dawn. Indeed, it was almost noon when the Headmaster found him cowering in bed, with the clothes pulled over his head. The principal called the Assistant Professor of Pleasaunce, and together they dragged the boy toward the forest.

"He'll be all right as soon as he gets a couple more dragons under his belt," explained the Headmaster.

The Assistant Professor of Pleasaunce agreed. "It would be a shame to stop such a fine run," he said. "Why, counting that one yesterday, he's killed fifty dragons."

They pushed the boy into a thicket above which hung a meager cloud of steam. It was obviously quite a small dragon. But Gawaine did not come back that night or the next. In fact, he never came back. Some weeks afterward brave spirits from the school explored the thicket, but they could find nothing to remind them of Gawaine except the metal parts of his medals. Even the ribbons had been devoured.

The Headmaster and the Assistant Professor of Pleasaunce agreed that it would be just as well not to tell the school how Gawaine had achieved his record and still less how he came to die. They held that it might have a bad effect on school spirit. Accordingly, Gawaine has lived in the memory of the school as its greatest hero. No visitor succeeds in leaving the building to-day without seeing a great shield which hangs on the wall of the dining hall. Fifty pairs of dragons' ears are mounted upon the shield and underneath in gilt letters is "Gawaine le Cœur-Hardy," followed by the simple inscription, "He killed fifty dragons." The record has never been equaled.

1922

CHRISTOPHER MORLEY

On Time

THIS WAS a little ceremony dedicated to Time; and as I came into the Grand Central Station the early afternoon sun slanted in bright diagonal from those high windows, exactly transecting the clock on the Information Desk in a clear swath of light.

Not less decorously than a bride made ready for her groom is the Century inaugurated for departure. A strip of wedding carpet leads you down into the cathedral twilight of that long crypt. Like a bouquet of flowers her name shines in white bulbs on the observation platform. In the diner waiters' coats are laundered like surplices. Mr. Welch, the veteran conductor, carrying his little box of official sancta, has the serene benignant gravity of some high cleric. And as you walk by that long perspective of windows, you are aware they are not just a string of ten Pullman cars. They are fused by something even subtler than the liaison of airy pressure that holds them safe. They are merged into personality, become a creature loved, honored, and obeyed. This is a rite, you read it in every member of her crew. The blessed, the rich, the ultimate human faculty of Rising to the Occasion! And you can see them, porter just as gravely as Conductor, making obeisance to the little private deity each carries in his pocket. When railroad men compare notes on the time, they don't say (as you or I would) "twoforty," meaning forty minutes after two. They know the hour and take it for granted. It's minutes and seconds that concern them. Ask Mr. Brady, engineer of the electric that takes out the First Section, what he "makes it," he'll reply, "forty-fifteen." There was a severity on Mr. Brady's face as he sat studying his watch while Paul Hesse, the photographer, was trying to get a shot inside the engine—which was not planned for pictorial convenience. The time was close. It was 44-30, it was 44-45, it was 45. . . . No more of this nonsense. . . . Let's go!

Gently she steals out along a corridor of that dusty underground forest where colored lights gleam like tropic birds. "Green!" "Green!" you hear Brady and his helper saying aloud to each other, checking up each signal as soon as it comes in view. The electric engine has fascination and efficiency of its own, but in this ceremony one is bound to regard it as the father who takes the bride up the aisle on his arm. The father may be (I dare say usually is) more of a man than the groom; but the groom gets the romantic applause. So the electric is not a personality: just a miracle, smooth and swift it toles you past those upper reaches of the city. Looking out you see the Second Section spinning along, just abaft your stern, on the adjoining track. There's a little boy, perhaps four years old, who comes down to Spuyten Duyvil station every fair afternoon, with his nurse, to see the Century spin by. It's a part of an engineer's job to know his roadside clients and salute them. When Brady waves, the nurse-maid can set her watch. It's 3:05. The bell chimes musically overhead, and again one feels that there is some sort of religion in all this. And I suppose (come to think of it) that isn't a bad sort of religion either: Getting There when you said you were Going To.

But what a moment, when you glide into Harmon and see waiting for you . . . what you came to see: one of the 5200's. Of course all that talk about the groom is nonsense, for at once you adore her as She. There's only one phrase adequate for her: Some Baby! Sharp work here: it must have been a couple of minutes, but in memory it seems only a few seconds of golden excitement. They can grin as they like at your borrowed overalls, *you're* the one that's going to ride that roaring child for 110 miles. Have you seen the Central's 5200's? This was 5217 and I shan't forget her. She seems as big as an ocean liner when you're in the cab.

They hand up a slip of paper to George Tully, the engineer. If you're the engineer of the Twentieth Century they don't tell you to get anywhere by a certain time. They tell you *not* to get there *before* such and such. The message, signed with 2 sets of initials, was "Do not arrive Albany before 5:38." George Tully consults his watch (a nice fat old Hamilton, he's carried it 24 years). It's 3:36 and we're off.

I suppose the greatest moments in life are those when you don't believe its yourself. It *can't* be you, in that holy of holies of small-boy imagination, the cab of an engine—and such an engine. More than that, made so welcome and at home by George Tully and Tom Cavanagh that you feel you belong there. Perhaps the simple truth is that if men have something they're enormously

proud of, it's pure joy to show her off. And they are never so lovable as in their honest rivalries. "Well," Tom roared in my ear, as he explained the automatic stoking, "I wonder if Pennsy's got anything better than this?" For the first thing that puzzles you is two big canted cylinders in the cab. They revolve in spasms. These feed the coal into the firebox. A man couldn't shovel fast enough by hand to keep the pressure she needs (she eats up four tons between Harmon and Albany). The fireman sits comfortably, with his eye on the steam gauge, and regulates the coal feed by turning a handle. I could tell you a lot about the marvel of that firebox, and the "butterfly door" that opens in two wings to show you her fierce heart, full of flame and hardly anything else. The coal is practically consumed by the time it reaches the floor of the furnace. I fed her myself for quite a way. "Keep the gauge at 220," Tom said. "No black smoke, and don't let the safety valve lift. Every time she lifts that means twenty gallons of water wasted—costs 3 cents." "Keep her hot," George Tully shouted to me, grinning. "We've got five minutes to make up."

That was part of the fun of this ride: I had a chance to see how things go when the breaks are against you. For there's a lot of work doing along the line: four-trackage being put in, the new tunnel at Storm King, and unavoidable slow-downs. "We'll be knocked out 6 minutes before we reach Beacon," Tully said. "We'll get it back."

Astonishing how soon one adjusts one's judgments. Leaning from the cab window, watching the flash of her great pistons, watching the 2500-ton train come creaming along so obediently behind us, one soon began to think anything less than 60 mere loitering. All the imaginations that the cab might be uncomfortable riding were bosh. There is hardly—at any rate in those heavy 5200's—any more sway or movement than in the Pullmans themselves. The one thing a constant automobile driver finds disconcerting is the lack of steering. As you come rocketing toward a curve you wonder why the devil George doesn't turn a wheel to prevent her going clean off. And then you see her great gorgeous body meet the arc in that queer straight way—a constant shifting tangent—and—well, you wish you could lay your hand on her somehow so she'd know how you feel. When George began to let her out a bit beyond Beacon, I just had to go over and yell at him that I thought this 5217 of his was a good girl. With the grave pleasure of the expert he said, "They're right there when you need 'em." He let me blow the whistle, which makes one feel an absolute part of her. Yes, if you were listening (about 4:48) that was me.

Alive, shouting, fluttering her little flags, she divided the clear cool afternoon. Looking out into that stream of space I could have lapsed into dream. I came closer than ever before to the actual texture of Time whereof our minds are made. This was not just air or earth that we flew upon, this was the seamless reality of Now. We were abreast of the Instant. It was Time that we fed into the flaming furnace, it was Time that flickered in the giant wheels. This was the everlasting Now, we kept even pace with it and so the mind was (literally) in its own element, motionless and at ease. Terribly great, senseless, ecstatic, mad with her single destiny, yet with queer pathos in her whole great mass, so much at our command. Her cab looked like a clock-shop, so many gauges and dials. But there is no clock in an engine cab. She makes her litany to one god only—the intent man who sits leaning forward so gravely. And he verifies himself by the other little god—the tiny one in his pocket. As you watch him you understand what he said—"There's no two trips alike. They're always on your nerve."

Green! Green! they kept repeating to one another across the cab. Tom and I sat on the port side where I could see the whole panorama of the Hudson, and far down a curve of the river a white plume where the Second Section came merrily behind us, keeping her three mile distance. And, with Tom, I waved to the regular clients—the "Pig-Woman"; the two priests in cassocks and birettas, near Poughkeepsie; the Cleary Girls in Hyde Park, whose husband and father is the flagman at that crossing; and many more. And then Tom said suddenly, after a glance at his watch, "We've got the dope on 'em now —49 minutes to do 45 miles." I began to see that when chance works against him, the engineman instinctively personifies the unforgiving minutes into mysterious enemies who are trying to spoil things. These mischievous divinities had been hovering about us, making us scoop up water (you have to slow down to 45 for that) or what not; but now we had the dope on them. And the engineer has some very subtle inward correlation of the feel of things; so that even before he verifies his instinct by minutes and seconds, he knows how he's getting on. These men live with Time in a way we rarely dream of. Time is not their merry wanton, as she is to some of us. She's their wife, for better or worse. There was a truly husbandly grievance in George's eye when, just outside Albany, we had to slow almost to a standstill. Number 7—which left Grand Central 45 minutes earlier—was right ahead of us. There was the accent of King Tamburlaine in 5217's whistle as she shouted a blasphemy in steam. We came to a stop in Albany at 5:42. And as she wasn't due to leave there till 5:49, everything was jake. But I saw Tom, who is young and proud, taking a last look at his watch as he pulled his little black satchel out of the locker. There was about fifty seconds just outside Albany that "they" had put over on us.

We all, I hope and believe, have some little private feathers for our cap. I have mine: George Tully said I could ride with him again any time I wanted to. Well, George, I am going to take you up on that.

1928

H. M. TOMLINSON

Bed-Books and Night-Lights

THE RAIN flashed across the midnight window with a myriad feet. There was a groan in outer darkness, the voice of all nameless dreads. The nervous candle-flame shuddered by my bedside. The groaning rose to a shriek, and the little flame jumped in a panic, and nearly left its white column. Out of the corners of the room swarmed the released shadows. Black specters danced in ecstasy over my bed. I love fresh air, but I cannot allow it to slay the shining and delicate body of my little friend the candle-flame, the comrade who ventures with me into the solitudes beyond midnight. I shut the window.

They talk of the candle-power of an electric bulb. What do they mean? It cannot have the faintest glimmer of the real power of my candle. It would be as right to express, in the same inverted and foolish comparison, the worth of "those delicate sisters, the Pleiades."

That pinch of star dust, the Pleiades, exquisitely remote in deepest night, in the profound where light all but fails, has not the power of a sulphur match; yet, still apprehensive to the mind though tremulous on the limit of vision, and sometimes even vanishing, it brings into distinction those distant and difficult hints—hidden far behind all our verified thoughts—which we rarely properly view. I should like to know of any great arc-lamp which could do that. So the star-like candle for me. No other light follows so intimately an author's most ghostly suggestion. We sit, the candle and I, in the midst of the shades we are conquering, and sometimes look up from the lucent page to contemplate the dark hosts of the enemy with a smile before they overwhelm us; as they will, of course. Like me, the candle is mortal; it will burn out.

As the bed-book itself should be a sort

of night-light, to assist its illumination, coarse lamps are useless. They would douse the book. The light for such a book must accord with it. It must be, like the book, a limited, personal, mellow, and companionable glow; the solitary taper beside the only worshiper in a sanctuary. That is why nothing can compare with the intimacy of candlelight for a bed-book. It is a living heart, bright and warm in central night, burning for us alone, holding the gaunt and towering shadows at bay. There the monstrous specters stand in our midnight room, the advance guard of the darkness of the world, held off by our valiant little glim, but ready to flood instantly and founder us in original gloom.

The wind moans without; ancient evils are at large and wandering in torment. The rain shrieks across the window. For a moment, for just a moment, the sentinel candle is shaken, and burns blue with terror. The shadows leap out instantly. The little flame recovers, and merely looks at its foe, the darkness, and back to its own place goes the old enemy of light and man. The candle for me, tiny, mortal, warm, and brave, a golden lily on a silver stem!

"Almost any book does for a bed-book," a woman once said to me. I nearly replied in a hurry that almost any woman would do for a wife; but that is not the way to bring people to conviction of sin. Her idea was that the bed-book is soporific, and for that reason she even advocated the reading of political speeches. That would be a dissolute act. Certainly you would go to sleep; but in what a frame of mind! You would enter into sleep with your eyes shut. It would be like dying, not only unshriven, but in the act of guilt.

What book shall it shine upon?

Think of Plato, or Dante, or Tolstoy, or a Blue Book for such an occasion! I cannot. They will not do—they are no good to me. I am not writing about you. I know those men I have named are transcendent, the greater lights. But I am bound to confess at times they bore me. Though their feet are clay and on earth, just as ours, their stellar brows are sometimes dim in remote clouds. For my part, they are too big for bed-fellows. I cannot see myself, carrying my feeble and restricted glim, following (in pajamas) the statuesque figure of the Florentine where it stalks, aloof in its garb of austere pity, the sonorous deeps of Hades. Hades! Not for me; not after midnight! Let those go who like it.

As for the Russian, vast and disquieting, I refuse to leave all, including the blankets and the pillow, to follow him into the gelid tranquillity of the upper air, where even the colors are prismatic spicules of ice, to brood upon the erratic orbit of the poor mud-ball below called earth. I know it is my world also; but I cannot help that. It is too late, after a busy day, and at that hour, to begin overtime on fashioning a new and better planet out of cosmic dust. By breakfast-time, nothing useful would have been accomplished. We should all be where we were the night before. The job is far too long, once the pillow is nicely set.

For the truth is, there are times when we are too weary to remain attentive and thankful under the improving eye, kindly but severe, of the seers. There are times when we do not wish to be any better than we are. We do not wish to be elevated and improved. At midnight, away with such books! As for the literary pundits, the high priests of the Temple of Letters, it is interest-

ing and helpful occasionally for an aco-
lyte to swinge them a good hard one
with an incense-burner, and cut and
run, for a change, to something outside
the rubrics. Midnight is the time when
one can recall, with ribald delight, the
names of all the Great Works which
every gentleman ought to have read,
but which some of us have not. For
there is almost as much clotted nonsense written about literature as there is
about theology.

There are few books which go with
midnight, solitude, and a candle. It is
much easier to say what does not please
us then than what is exactly right.
The book must be, anyhow, something
benedictory by a sinning fellow-man.
Cleverness would be repellent at such
an hour. Cleverness, anyhow, is the
level of mediocrity to-day; we are all too
infernally clever. The first witty and
perverse paradox blows out the candle.
Only the sick in mind crave cleverness,
as a morbid body turns to drink. The
late candle throws its beams a great distance; and its rays make transparent
much that seemed massy and important. The mind at rest beside that
light, when the house is asleep, and
the consequential affairs of the urgent
world have diminished to their right
proportions because we see them distantly from another and a more tranquil place in the heavens where duty,
honor, witty arguments, controversial
logic on great questions, appear such as
will leave hardly a trace of fossil in the
indurated mud which presently will
cover them—the mind then certainly
smiles at cleverness.

For though at that hour the body may
be dog-tired, the mind is white and
lucid, like that of a man from whom a
fever has abated. It is bare of illusions.
It has a sharp focus, small and star-like,

as a clear and lonely flame left burning
by the altar of a shrine from which all
have gone but one. A book which approaches that light in the privacy of that
place must come, as it were, with honest
and open pages.

I like Heine then, though. His
mockery of the grave and great, in those
sentences which are as brave as pennants in a breeze, is comfortable and
sedative. One's own secret and awkward convictions, never expressed because not lawful and because it is hard
to get words to bear them lightly, seem
then to be heard aloud in the mild, easy,
and confident diction of an immortal
whose voice has the blitheness of one
who has watched, amused and irreverent, the high gods in eager and secret
debate on the best way to keep the gilt
and trappings on the body of the evil
they have created.

That first-rate explorer, Gulliver, is
also fine in the light of the intimate candle. Have you read lately again his
"Voyage to the Houyhnhnms"? Try it
alone again in quiet. Swift knew all
about our contemporary troubles. He
has got it all down. Why was he called
a misanthrope? Reading that last voyage of Gulliver in the select intimacy of
midnight I am forced to wonder, not at
Swift's hatred of mankind, not at his
satire of his fellows, not at the strange
and terrible nature of this genius who
thought that much of us, but how it is
that after such a wise and sorrowful revealing of the things we insist on doing,
and our reasons for doing them, and
what happens after we have done them,
men do not change. It does seem impossible that society could remain unaltered, after the surprise its appearance
should have caused it as it saw its face in
that ruthless mirror. We point instead
to the fact that Swift lost his mind in

the end. Well, that is not a matter for surprise.

Such books, and France's "Isle of Penguins," are not disturbing as bed-books. They resolve one's agitated and outraged soul, relieving it with some free expression for the accusing and questioning thoughts engendered by the day's affairs. But they do not rest immediately to hand in the book-shelf by the bed. They depend on the kind of day one has had. Sterne is closer. One would rather be transported as far as possible from all the disturbances of earth's envelope of clouds, and "Tristram Shandy" is sure to be found in the sun.

But best of all books for midnight are travel books. Once I was lost every night for months with Doughty in the "Arabia Deserta." He is a craggy author. A long course of the ordinary facile stuff, such as one gets in the Press every day, thinking it is English, sends one thoughtless and headlong among the bitter herbs and stark boulders of Doughty's burning and spacious expanse; only to get bewildered, and the shins broken, and a great fatigue at first, in a strange land of fierce sun, hunger, glittering spar, ancient plutonic rock, and very Adam himself. But once you are acclimatized, and know the language—it takes time—there is no more London after dark, till, a wanderer returned from a forgotten land, you emerge from the interior of Arabia on the Red Sea coast again, feeling as though you had lost touch with the world you used to know. And if that doesn't mean good writing I know of no other test.

Because once there was a father whose habit it was to read with his boys nightly some chapters of the Bible—and cordially they hated that habit of his—I have that Book too; though I fear I have it for no reason that he, the rigid old faithful, would be pleased to hear about. He thought of the future when he read the Bible; I read it for the past. The familiar names, the familiar rhythm of its words, its wonderful well-remembered stories of things long past—like that of Esther, one of the best in English—the eloquent anger of the prophets for the people then who looked as though they were alive, but were really dead at heart, all is solace and home to me. And now I think of it, it is our home and solace that we want in a bed-book.

1920

JAMES THURBER

The Macbeth Murder Mystery

"IT WAS a stupid mistake to make," said the American woman I had met at my hotel in the English lake country, "but it was on the counter with the other Penguin books—the little sixpenny ones, you know, with the paper covers—and I supposed of course it was a detective story. All the others were detective stories. I'd read all the others, so I bought this one without really looking at it carefully. You can imagine how mad I was when I found it was Shakespeare." I murmured something sympathetically. "I don't see why the Penguin-books people had to get out Shakespeare plays in the same size and everything as the detective stories," went on my companion. "I think they have different-colored jackets," I said. "Well, I didn't notice that," she said. "Anyway, I got real comfy in bed that night and all ready to read a good mystery story and here I had 'The Tragedy of Macbeth'—a book for high-school students. Like 'Ivanhoe,'" "Or 'Lorna Doone,'" I said. "Exactly," said the American lady. "And I was just crazy for a good Agatha Christie, or something. Hercule Poirot is my favorite detective." "Is he the rabbity one?" I asked. "Oh, no," said my crime-fiction expert. "He's the Belgian one. You're thinking of Mr. Pinkerton, the one that helps Inspector Bull. He's good, too."

Over her second cup of tea my companion began to tell the plot of a detective story that had fooled her completely —it seems it was the old family doctor all the time. But I cut in on her. "Tell me," I said. "Did you read 'Macbeth'?" "I *had* to read it," she said. "There wasn't a scrap of anything else to read in the whole room." "Did you like it?" I asked. "No, I did not," she said, decisively. "In the first place, I don't think for a moment that Macbeth did it." I looked at her blankly. "Did what?" I asked. "I don't think for a moment that he killed the King," she said. "I don't think the Macbeth woman was mixed up in it, either. You suspect them the most, of course, but those are the ones that are never guilty—or shouldn't be, anyway." "I'm

afraid," I began, "that I—" "But don't you see?" said the American lady. "It would spoil everything if you could figure out right away who did it. Shakespeare was too smart for that. I've read that people never *have* figured out 'Hamlet,' so it isn't likely Shakespeare would have made 'Macbeth' as simple as it seems." I thought this over while I filled my pipe. "Who do you suspect?" I asked, suddenly. "Macduff," she said, promptly. "Good God!" I whispered, softly.

"Oh Macduff did it, all right," said the murder specialist. "Hercule Poirot would have got him easily." "How did you figure it out?" I demanded. "Well," she said, "I didn't right away. At first I suspected Banquo. And then, of course, he was the second person killed. That was good right in there, that part. The person you suspect of the first murder should always be the second victim." "Is that so?" I murmured. "Oh, yes," said my informant. "They have to keep surprising you. Well, after the second murder I didn't know *who* the killer was for a while." "How about Malcolm and Donalbain, the King's sons?" I asked. "As I remember it, they fled right after the first murder. That looks suspicious." "Too suspicious," said the American lady. "Much too suspicious. When they flee, they're never guilty. You can count on that." "I believe," I said, "I'll have a brandy," and I summoned the waiter. My companion leaned toward me, her eyes bright, her teacup quivering. "Do you know who discovered Duncan's body?" she demanded. I said I was sorry, but I had forgotten. "Macduff discovers it," she said, slipping into the historical present. "Then he comes running downstairs and shouts, 'Confusion has broke open the Lord's anointed temple' and 'Sacrilegious murder has made his masterpiece' and on and on like that." The good lady tapped me on the knee. "All that stuff was rehearsed," she said. "You wouldn't say a lot of stuff like that, off-hand, would you—if you had found a body?" She fixed me with a glittering eye. "I—" I began. "You're right!" she said. "You wouldn't! Unless you had practiced it in advance. 'My God, there's a body in here!' is what an innocent man would say." She sat back with a confident glare.

I thought for a while. "But what do you make of the Third Murderer?" I asked. "You know, the Third Murderer has puzzled 'Macbeth' scholars for three hundred years." "That's because they never thought of Macduff," said the American lady. "It was Macduff, I'm certain. You couldn't have one of the victims murdered by two ordinary thugs—the murderer always has to be somebody important." "But what about the banquet scene?" I asked, after a moment. "How do you account for Macbeth's guilty actions there, when Banquo's ghost came in and sat in his chair?" The lady leaned forward and tapped me on the knee again. "There wasn't any ghost," she said. "A big, strong man like that doesn't go around seeing ghosts—especially in a brightly lighted banquet hall with dozens of people around. Macbeth was *shielding somebody!*" "Who was he shielding?" I asked. "Mrs. Macbeth, of course," she said. "He thought she did it and he was going to take the rap himself. The husband always does that when the wife is suspected." "But what," I demanded, "about the sleepwalking scene, then?" "The same thing, only the other way around," said my companion. "That time *she* was shielding *him*. She wasn't asleep at all. Do you remember where

it says, 'Enter Lady Macbeth with a taper'? "Yes," I said. "Well, people who walk in their sleep *never carry lights!*" said my fellow-traveler. "They have a second sight. Did you ever hear of a sleepwalker carrying a light?" "No," I said, "I never did." "Well, then, she wasn't asleep. She was acting guilty to shield Macbeth." "I think," I said, "I'll have another brandy," and I called the waiter. When he brought it, I drank it rapidly and rose to go. "I believe," I said, "that you have got hold of something. Would you lend me that 'Macbeth'? I'd like to look it over tonight. I don't feel, somehow, as if I'd ever really read it." "I'll get it for you," she said. "But you'll find that I am right."

I read the play over carefully that night, and the next morning, after breakfast, I sought out the American woman. She was on the putting green, and I came up behind her silently and took her arm. She gave an exclamation. "Could I see you alone?" I asked, in a low voice. She nodded cautiously and followed me to a secluded spot. "You've found out something?" she breathed. "I've found out," I said, triumphantly, "the name of the murderer!" "You mean it wasn't Macduff?" she said. "Macduff is as innocent of those murders," I said, "as Macbeth and the Macbeth woman." I opened the copy of the play, which I had with me, and turned to Act II, Scene 2. "Here," I said, "you will see where Lady Macbeth says, 'I laid their daggers ready. He could not miss 'em. Had he not resembled my father as he slept, I had done it.' Do you see?" "No," said the American woman, bluntly, "I don't." "But it's simple!" I exclaimed. "I wonder I didn't see it years ago. The reason Duncan resembled Lady Macbeth's father as he slept is that *it actually was her father!*" "Good God!" breathed my companion, softly. "Lady Macbeth's father killed the King," I said, "and, hearing someone coming, thrust the body under the bed and crawled into the bed himself." "But," said the lady, "you can't have a murderer who only appears in the story once. You can't have that." "I know that," I said, and I turned to Act II, Scene 4. "It says here, 'Enter Ross with an old Man.' Now, that old man is never identified and it is my contention he was old Mr. Macbeth, whose ambition it was to make his daughter Queen. There you have your motive." "But even then," cried the American lady, "he's still a minor character!" "Not," I said, gleefully, "when you realize that he was also *one of the weird sisters in disguise!*" "You mean one of the three witches?" "Precisely,"

I said. "Listen to this speech of the old man's. 'On Tuesday last, a falcon towering in her pride of place, was by a mousing owl hawk'd at and kill'd.' Who does that sound like?" "It sounds like the way the three witches talk," said my companion, reluctantly. "Precisely!" I said again. "Well," said the American woman, "maybe you're right, but—". "I'm sure I am," I said. "And do you know what I'm going to do now?" "No," she said. "What?" "Buy a copy of 'Hamlet,'" I said, "and solve *that!*" My companion's eye brightened. "Then," she said, "you don't think Hamlet did it?" "I am," I said, "absolutely positive he didn't." "But who," she demanded, "do you suspect?" I looked at her cryptically. "Everybody," I said, and disappeared into a small grove of trees as silently as I had come.

1945

WILLIAM SAROYAN

Love, Death, Sacrifice and So Forth

TOM GARNER, in the movie, on the screen, a big broadshouldered man, a builder of railroads, President of the Chicago & Southwestern, staggers, does not walk, into his room and closes the door.

You know he is going to commit suicide because he has staggered, and it is a movie, and already a long while has passed since the picture began, and something's got to happen real soon, something big, gigantic, as they say in Hollywood, a suicide or a kiss.

You are sitting in the theatre waiting for what you know is going to happen.

Poor Tom has just learned that the male offspring of his second wife is the product of his grown son by his first wife. Tom's first wife committed suicide when she learned that Tom had fallen in love with the young woman who finally became his second wife. This young woman was the daughter of the President of the Santa Clara Railroad. She made Tom fall in love with

her so that her father would go on being President of the Santa Clara. Tom
had bought the Santa Clara for nine
million dollars. Tom's first wife threw
herself beneath a streetcar when she
found out about Tom's infatuation.
She did it by acting, with her face, her
eyes, and lips and the way she walked.
You didn't get to see anything sickening, you saw only the motorman's frantic expression while he tried to bring the
car to a stop. You heard and saw the
steel wheel grinding, the wheel that
killed her. You heard people screaming the way they do about violent
things, and you got the idea. The
worst had happened. Tom's wife Sally
had gone to her Maker.

Sally met Tom when he was a trackwalker and she a teacher in a small
country school. Tom confessed to her
one day that he did not know how to
read, write or do arithmetic. Sally
taught Tom to read, write, add, subtract, divide and multiply. One evening after they were married she asked
him if he wanted to be a trackwalker all
his life, and he said that he did. Sally
asked him if he didn't have at least a little ambition, and Tom said he was satisfied, trackwalking was easy work, they
had their little home, and Tom got in a
lot of fishing on the side. This hurt
Sally, and she began to act. Tom saw
that it would mean a lot to Sally if he
became ambitious. Sitting at the supper table, he said that he would. A
strange look came into his eyes, his face
acquired great character. You could
almost see him forging ahead in life.

Sally sent Tom to school in Chicago,
and she did Tom's work as a trackwalker in order to have money with
which to pay for his tuition, a great
woman, an heroic wife. You saw her
one winter night walking along a rail-

road track, packing tools and oil cans,
snow and desolation all around her. It
was sad. It was meant to be sad. She
was doing it for Tom, so that he would
be able to become a great man. The
day Tom announced that he had been
made foreman of the construction of the
Missouri Bridge, Sally announced she
was with child, and Tom said now they
could never stop him. With Sally and
his baby to inspire him Tom would
reach the heights.

Sally gave birth to a son, and while
Tom was walking to her bedside you
heard symphonic music, and you knew
that this was a great moment in Tom's
life. You saw Tom enter the dimly
lighted room and kneel beside his wife
and baby son, and you heard him pray.
You heard him say, Our Father which
art in heaven, thine the glory and
the power, forever and forever. You
heard two people in the theatre blowing
their noses.

Sally made Tom. She took him from
the track and sent him to the president's
chair. Then Tom became infatuated
with this younger and lovelier woman,
and Sally threw herself beneath the
streetcar. It was because of what she
had done for Tom that the suicide was
so touching. It was because of this that
tears came to the eyes of so many people in the theatre when Sally destroyed
herself.

But Sally's suicide did not have any
effect on Tom's infatuation for the
younger woman, and after a short
while he married the girl, being a practical man part of the time, being practical as long as Hollywood wanted him
to be practical. Tom's son, a young
man just expelled from college for
drunkenness, moved into Tom's house,
and had an affair with Tom's second
wife.

The result was the baby, a good healthy baby, born of the son instead of the father. Tom's son Tommy is an irresponsible but serious and well-dressed young man, and he really didn't mean to do it. Nature did it. You know how nature is, even in the movies. Tom had been away from home so much, attending to business, and his second wife had been so lonely that she had turned to her husband's son, and he had become her dancing partner.

You saw her holding her hand out to the young irresponsible boy, and you heard her ask him significantly if he would like to dance with her. It took him so long to take her hand that you understand the frightening implication instantly. And she was so maddeningly beautiful, extending her hand to him, that you knew you yourself would never have been able to resist her challenge, even under similar circumstances. There was something irresistible about the perfection of her face and figure, lips so kissable, stance so elegant, body so lovely, soul so needful.

It simply had to happen. Man is flesh, and all that.

So the big railroad builder, the man who always had his way, the man who broke the strike and had forty of his men killed in a riot, and a fire, has staggered into his room and closed the door.

And you know the picture is about to end.

The atmosphere of the theatre is becoming electrical with the apprehension of middle-aged ladies who have spent the better parts of their lives in the movies, loving, dying, sacrificing themselves to noble ideals, etc. They've come again to the dark theatre, and a moment of great living is again upon them.

You can feel the spiritual tenseness of all of these ladies, and if you are listening carefully you can actually hear them living fully.

Poor Tom is in there with a terrific problem and a ghastly obligation.

For his honor's sake, for the sake of Hollywood ethics, for the sake of the industry (the third largest in America, I understand), for God's sake, for your sake and my sake, Tom has got to commit suicide. If he doesn't, it will simply mean we have been deceiving ourselves all these years, Shakespeare and the rest of us. We know he'll be man enough to do it, but for an instant we hope he won't, just to see what will happen, just to see if the world we have made will actually smash.

A long while back we made the rules, and now, after all these years, we wonder if they are the genuine ones, or if, maybe, we didn't make a mistake at the outset. We know it's art, and it even looks a little like life, but we know it isn't life, being much too precise.

We would like to know if our greatness must necessarily go on forever being melodramatic.

The camera rests on the bewildered face of Tom's old and faithful secretary, a man who knew Tom as a boy. This is to give you the full implication of Tom's predicament and to create a powerful suspense in your mind.

Then, at a trot, with the same object in view, time hurrying, culminations, ultimates, inevitabilities, Tom's son Tommy comes to the old and faithful secretary and exclaims that he has heard Tom, his father, is ill. He does not know that his father knows. It is a Hollywood moment. You hear appropriate music.

He rushes to the door, to go to his father, this boy who upset the natural order of the universe by having a sexual affair with his father's young wife, and then, bang, the pistol shot.

You know it is all over with the President of the Chicago & Southwestern. His honor is saved. He remains a great man. Once again the industry triumphs. The dignity of life is preserved. Everything is hotsytotsy. It will be possible for Hollywood to go on making pictures for the public for another century.

Everything is precise, for effect. Halt. Symphonic music, Tommy's hand frozen on the door-knob.

The old and faithful secretary knows what has happened, Tommy knows, you know and I know, but there is nothing like seeing. The old and faithful secretary allows the stark reality of the pistol shot to penetrate his old, faithful and orderly mind. Then, since Tommy is too frightened to do so, he forces himself to open the door.

All of us are waiting to see how it happened.

The door opens and we go in, fifty million of us in America and millions more all over the earth.

Poor Tom. He is sinking to his knees, and somehow, even though it is happening swiftly, it seems that this little action, being the last one of a great man, will go on forever, this sinking to the knees. The room is dim, the music eloquent. There is no blood, no disorder. Tom is sinking to his knees, dying nobly. I myself hear two ladies weeping. They know it's a movie, they know it must be fake, still, they are weeping. Tom is man. He is life. It makes them weep to see life sinking to

its knees. The movie will be over in a minute and they will get up and go home, and get down to the regular business of their lives, but now, in the pious darkness of the theatre, they are weeping.

All I know is this: that a suicide is not an orderly occurrence with symphonic music. There was a man once who lived in the house next door to my house when I was a boy of nine or ten. One afternoon he committed suicide, but it took him an hour to do it. He shot himself through the chest, missed his heart, then shot himself through the stomach. I heard both shots. There was an interval of about forty seconds between the shots. I thought afterwards that during the interval he was probably trying to decide if he ought to go on wanting to be dead or if he ought to try to get well.

Then he started to holler. The whole thing was a mess, materially and spiritually, this man hollering, people running, shouting, wanting to do something and not knowing what to do. He hollered so loud half the town heard him.

This is all I know about regular suicides. I haven't seen a woman throw herself under a streetcar, so I can't say about that. This is the only suicide I have any definite information about. The way this man hollered wouldn't please anyone in a movie. It wouldn't make anyone weep with joy.

I think it comes to this: we've got to stop committing suicide in the movies.
1934

IV...

ARTICLE

FRANZ BOAS

Racial Prejudices

From The Mind of Primitive Man

Proud of his wonderful achievements, civilized man looks down upon the humbler members of mankind. He has conquered the forces of nature and compelled them to serve him. He has transformed inhospitable forests into fertile fields. The mountain fastnesses are yielding their treasures to his demands. The fierce animals which are obstructing his progress are being exterminated, while others which are useful to him are made to increase a thousand-fold. The waves of the ocean carry him from land to land, and towering mountain-ranges set him no bounds. His genius has moulded inert matter into powerful machines which await a touch of his hand to serve his manifold demands.

With pity he looks down upon those members of the human race who have not succeeded in subduing nature; who labor to eke a meagre existence out of the products of the wilderness; who hear with trembling the roar of the wild animals, and see the products of their toil destroyed by them; who remain restricted by ocean, river, or mountains; who strive to obtain the necessities of life with the help of few and simple instruments.

Such is the contrast that presents itself to the observer. What wonder if civilized man considers himself a being of higher order as compared to primitive man, if he claims that the white race represents a type higher than all others!

Before accepting this conclusion which places the stamp of eternal inferiority upon whole races of man, we may well pause, and subject the basis of our opinions regarding the aptitude of different peoples and races to a searching analysis. The naïve assumption of the superiority of the European nations and their descendants is obviously based upon their wonderful achievements. We conclude that, as the civilization is higher, the aptitude for civilization is also higher; and, as the aptitude for civilization presumably depends upon the perfection of the mechanism of body and mind, the inference is drawn that the white race represents the highest type of perfection. In this conclusion, which is reached through a comparison of the social status of civilized man with that of primitive man, the tacit assumption is made that achievement depends solely, or at least primarily, upon the aptitude for an achievement.

The assertion of a higher aptitude of the European nations leads at once to a second inference relating to the significance of difference in type between the European race and the races of other continents, or even of differences between various European types. The line of thought which we unconsciously pursue is about as follows. Since the

From Franz Boas, *The Mind of Primitive Man*. By permission of The Macmillan Company, publishers.

aptitude of the European is highest, his physical and mental type is also highest, and every deviation from the white type necessarily represents a characteristic feature of a lower type.

That this unproved assumption underlies our judgments of races, appears from the fact that, other conditions being equal, a race is commonly described as the lower, the more fundamentally it differs from the white race. Its effect may also be noticed in the long-continued discussions of the occurrence of anatomical peculiarities in primitive man which would characterize him as a being of lower order in the zoölogical series, and in the emphasis laid upon the non-occurrence of such traits in primitive man and their occurrence in the European race.

The subject and form of these discussions show that the idea dwells in the minds of investigators that we should expect to find in the white race the highest type of man.

In drawing inferences from social distinctions, the same point of view is frequently held. It is assumed that, as the mental development of the white race is the highest, it also has the highest aptitude in this direction, and therefore its mind is supposed to have the most subtile organization. As the ultimate psychical causes are not so apparent as anatomical characteristics, the judgment of the mental status of a people is generally guided by the difference between its social status and our own: the greater the difference between their intellectual, emotional, and moral processes and those which are found in our civilization, the harsher the judgment on the people. It is only when a Tacitus finds the virtues of past stages of the life of his own people among foreign tribes that their example is held up to the gaze of his fellow-citizens, who probably had a pitying smile for the dreamer who clung to the ideas of a time which they had left far behind.

In order to understand clearly the relations between race and civilization, the two unproved assumptions to which I have referred must be subjected to a searching analysis. We must investigate in how far we are justified in assuming that achievement is primarily due to exceptional aptitude, and in how far we are justified in assuming that the European type—or, taking the notion in its extreme form, that the North European type—represents the highest development of mankind. It will be advantageous to clear up these points before we take up the detailed inquiry.

In regard to the former point, it might be said that, although achievement is not necessarily a measure of aptitude, it seems admissible to judge the one by the other. Have not most races had the same chances for development? Why, then, did the white race alone develop a civilization which is sweeping the whole world, and compared to which all other civilizations appear as feeble beginnings cut short in early childhood, or arrested and petrified in an early stage of development? Is it not, to say the least, probable that the race which attained the highest stage of civilization was the most gifted one, and that those races which remained at the bottom of the scale were not capable of rising to higher levels?

In order to find an answer to these questions, let us consider briefly the general outlines of the history of civilization; let our minds go back a few thousand years, until we reach the time when the civilizations of eastern and of western Asia were in their infancy. As time passed on, these civilizations were transferred from one people to another; some of those who had represented the highest type of culture sinking back into obscurity, while others took their places. During the dawn of history we see civilization cling to certain districts, in which it is taken up, now by one people, now by another. In the numerous conflicts of these times the more civilized people were often vanquished. The conqueror, however, learned the arts of life from the conquered, and carried on the work of civilization. Thus the centres of civilization were shifting to and fro over a limited area, and progress was slow and halting. At the same period the ancestors of the races that are now among the most highly civilized were in no way superior to primitive man as we find him now in regions that have not come into contact with modern civilization.

Was the civilization attained by these ancient people of such character as to allow us to claim for them a genius superior to that of any other race?

First of all, we must bear in mind that none of these civilizations was the product of the genius of a single people. Ideas and inventions were carried from one to the other; and, although intercommunication was slow, each people which participated in the ancient development contributed its share to the general progress. Proofs without number have been forthcoming which show that ideas have been disseminated as long as people have come into contact with one another, and that neither race nor language nor distance limits their diffusion. As all have worked together in the development of the ancient civilizations, we must bow to the genius of all, whatever group of mankind they may represent,—Hamitic, Semitic, Aryan, or Mongol.

We may now ask, Did no other races develop a culture of equal value? It would seem that the civilizations of ancient Peru and of Central America may well be compared with the ancient civilizations of the Old World. In both we find a high stage of political organization: we find division of labor and an elaborate ecclesiastical organization. Great architectural works were undertaken, requiring the co-operation of many individuals. Animals and plants were domesticated, and the art of writing had been invented. The inventions and knowledge of the peoples of the Old World seem to have been somewhat more numerous and extended than those of the races of the New World, but there can be no doubt that the general status of their civilization was nearly equally high. This will suffice for our consideration.

What, then, is the difference between the civilization of the Old World and that of the New World? It is essentially a difference in time. The one reached a certain stage three thousand or four thousand years sooner than the other.

Although much stress has been laid upon this greater rapidity of development in the Old World, I think that it is not by any means proof of greater ability of the races of the Old World, but that it is adequately explained by the laws of chance. When two bodies run through the same course with variable rapidity, sometimes quickly, sometimes slowly, their relative position will be more likely to show accidental differences, the longer the course which they run. Thus two infants a few months old will be much alike in their physiological and psychical development; two youths of equal age will differ much more; and two old men of equal age may, the one still be in full possession of his powers, the other on the decline, due mainly to the accidental acceleration or retardation of their development. The difference in period of development does not signify that the one is by heredity structurally inferior to the others.

Applying the same reasoning to the history of mankind, we may say that the difference of a few thousand years is insignificant as compared to the age of the human race. The time required to develop the existing races is entirely a matter of conjecture, but we may be sure that it is long. We also know that man existed in the Eastern and Western Hemispheres at a time that can be measured by geological standards only. Penck's recent investigations on the glacial age in the Alps have led him to the conclusion that the age of man must be measured by a span of time exceeding one hundred thousand years, and that the highly specialized civilization of the Magdalenian is not less than twenty thousand years old. There is no reason to believe that this stage was reached by mankind the world over at the same period, but we must assume as the initial point the remotest times in which we find traces of man. What does it mean then, if one group of mankind reached the same stage at the age of a hundred thousand years as was reached by the other at the age of a hundred and four thousand years? Would not the life-history of the people, and the vicissitudes of its history, be fully sufficient to explain a delay of this character, without necessitating us to assume a difference in their aptitude to social development? (See Waitz.) This retardation would be significant only if it could be shown that it occurs independently over and over again in the same race, while in other races greater rapidity of development was found repeatedly in independent cases.

The fact deserves attention, however, that at present practically all the members of the white race participate to a greater or less degree in the advance of civilization, while in none of the other races has the civilization that has been attained at one time or another been able to reach all the tribes or peoples of the same race. This does not necessarily mean that all the members of the white race had the power of originating and developing the germs of civilization with equal rapidity; for there is no evidence that the cognate tribes which have all developed under the influence of a civilization originated by a few members of the race, would not, without this help, have required a much longer time to reach the high level which they now occupy. It seems to show, however, a remarkable power of assimilation, which has not manifested itself to an equal degree in any other race.

Thus the problem presents itself of discovering the reason why the tribes of ancient Europe readily assimilated the civilization that was offered to them, while at present we see primitive people dwindle away and become degraded before the approach of civilization, instead of being elevated by it. Is not this a proof of a higher organization of the inhabitants of Europe?

I believe the reasons for this fact are not far to seek, and do not necessarily lie in a greater ability of the races of Europe and Asia. First of all, in appearance these people were alike to civilized man of their times. Therefore the fundamental difficulty for the rise of primitive people—namely, that an individual who has risen to the level of the higher civilization is still looked upon as belonging to an inferior race—did not prevail. Thus it was possible that in the colonies of ancient times society could grow by accretion from among the more primitive people.

Furthermore, the devastating influences of diseases which nowadays begin to ravage the inhabitants of territories newly opened to the whites were not so strong, on account of the permanent contiguity of the people of the Old World, who were always in contact with one another, and therefore subject to the same influences. The invasion of America and Polynesia, on the other hand, was accompanied by the introduction of new diseases among the natives of these countries. The suffering and devastation wrought by epidemics which followed the discovery are too well known to be described in full. In all cases in which a material reduction in numbers occurs in a thinly settled area, the economic life, as well as the social structure, is almost completely destroyed.

In addition to this, it may be said that the contrast between the culture represented by the modern white and that of primitive man is far more fundamental than that between the ancients and the people with whom they came in contact. Particularly, the methods of manufacture have developed so enormously, that the industries of the primitive people of our times are exterminated by the cheapness and large quantity of the products imported by the white trader, because primitive man is unable to compete with the power of production of the machines of the whites, while in olden times the superior hand-product rivalled the hand-product of a lower type. When a day's work suffices for obtaining efficient tools or fabrics from the trader, while the manufacture of the corresponding implement or material by the native himself would have required weeks, it is but natural that the slower and more laborious process should be given up speedily. It must also be considered that in several regions, particularly in America and in parts of Siberia, the primitive tribes are swamped by the numbers of the immigrating race, which is crowding them so rapidly out of their old haunts that no time for gradual assimilation is given. In olden times there was certainly no such immense inequality in numbers as we observe in many regions nowadays.

We conclude, therefore, that the conditions for assimilation in ancient Europe were much more favorable than in those countries where in our times primitive people come into contact with civilization. Therefore we do not need to assume that the ancient Europeans were more gifted than other races which have not become exposed to the influences of civilization until recent times (Gerland, Ratzel).

This conclusion may be corroborated by other facts. In the middle ages the civilization of the Arabs had reached a stage which was undoubtedly superior to that of many European nations of that period. Both civilizations had sprung largely from the same sources, and must be considered branches of one tree. The Arabs who were the carriers of civilization were by no means members of the same race as the Europeans, but nobody will dispute their high merits. It is of interest to see in what manner they influenced the Negro races of the Soudan. At an early time, principally between the second half of the eighth century and the eleventh century of our era, the Soudan was invaded by Hamitic tribes, and Mohammedanism was spreading rapidly through the Sahara and the western Soudan. We see that since that time large empires have been formed, and have disappeared again in struggles with neighboring states, and that a relatively high degree of culture has been attained. The invaders intermarried with the natives; and the mixed races, some of which are almost purely Negro, have risen high above the level of other African Negroes. The history of Bornu is perhaps one of the best examples of this kind. Barth and Nachtigal have made us acquainted with the history of this state, which has played a most important part in the history of North Africa.

Why, then, have the Mohammedans been able to civilize these tribes, and to raise them to nearly the same standard which they had attained, while the whites have not been capable of influencing the Negro in Africa to any considerable extent? Evidently on account of the different method of introduction of culture. While the Mohammedans influence the people in the same manner in which the ancients civilized the tribes of Europe, the whites send only the products of their manufactures and a few of their representatives into the Negro country. A real amalgamation between the more highly educated whites and the Negroes has never taken place. The amalgamation of the Negroes by the Mohammedans is facilitated particularly by the institution of polygamy, the conquerors taking native wives, and raising their children as members of their own family.

The spread of the Chinese civilization in eastern Asia may be likened to that of the ancient civilization in Europe. Colonization and amalgamation of kindred tribes, and in some cases extermination of rebellious subjects, with subsequent colonization, have led to a remarkable uniformity of culture over a large area.

When, finally, we consider the inferior position held by the Negro race of the United States, although the Negro lives in the closest contact with modern civilization, we must not forget that the old race feeling of the inferiority of the colored race is as potent as ever, and is a formidable obstacle to its advance and progress, notwithstanding that schools and universities are open to them. We might rather wonder how much has been accomplished in a short period against heavy odds. It is hardly possible to say what would become of the Negro if he were able to live with the whites on absolutely equal terms. Miss Ovington's discussion of the opportunities of the Negro in the United States is a convincing proof of the inequality of the conditions of economic advance of the Negro and of the white, even after the abolition of legal inequality.

Our conclusion drawn from the foregoing considerations is the following: Several races have developed a civilization of a type similar to the one from which our own had its origin. A number of favorable conditions facilitated the rapid spread of this civilization in Europe. Among these, common physical appearance, contiguity of habitat, and moderate difference in modes of manufacture, were the most potent. When, later on, civilization began to spread over other continents, the races with which modern civilization came into contact were not equally favorably situated. Striking differences of racial types, the preceding isolation which caused devastating epidemics in the newly discovered countries, and the greater advance in civilization, made assimilation much more difficult. The rapid dissemination of Europeans over the whole world destroyed all promising beginnings which had arisen in various regions. Thus no race except that of eastern Asia was given a chance to develop an independent civilization. The spread of the European race cut short the growth of the existing independent germs without regard to the mental aptitude of the people among whom it was developing. On the other hand, we have seen that no great weight can be attributed to the earlier rise of civilization in the Old World, which is satisfactorily explained as a chance. In short, historical events appear to have been much more potent in leading races to civilization than their faculty, and it follows that achievements of races do not warrant us in assuming that one race is more highly gifted than the other.

After having thus found an answer to our first problem, we turn to the second one: In how far are we justified in considering those anatomical traits in regard to which foreign races differ from the white race as marks of inferiority? In one respect the answer to this question is easier than that to the former. We have recognized that achievement alone does not justify us in assuming greater mental ability for the white race than for others, unless we can sustain our claim by other proofs. It follows from this, that differences between the white race and other races must not be interpreted to mean superiority of the former, inferiority of the latter, unless this relation can be proved by anatomical or physiological considerations.

It may not be amiss to illustrate by an example the logical error which is committed with great ease and great frequency. In a painstaking investigation made a few years ago, Mr. R. B. Bean demonstrated certain characteristic differences between the form of the whole and of the parts of the brain of the Baltimore Negro and of the Baltimore white, —differences which consist in the form and relative size of the frontal and occipital lobes and in the size of the *corpus callosum*. The interpretation of the difference is, that the smaller size of the anterior lobes and of the *callosum* indicates a lower mental development, a conclusion which has been refuted by Franklin P. Mall. It may suffice here, where we are interested chiefly in the logical fallacy of such conclusions, to call attention to the fact that a comparison of long-headed and short-headed individuals of the same race—or, let us say, of long-headed North French and of short-headed Central French—would result in similar differences, but that in a case of this kind the inference regarding greater or lesser ability would not be made with the same readiness.

There is, of course, no doubt that great differences exist in the physical characteristics of the races of man. The color of the skin, the form of the hair, and the configuration of lips and nose, distinguish the African clearly from the European. The question to decide is, What relations have these features to the mental aptitude of a race? Two points of view may be brought forward in relation to this question. First, we may claim that a race in which peculiarities are found that are characteristic of lower stages in the animal series will be in all respects of an inferior type. Secondly, we may direct our attention primarily to the central nervous system, and investigate whether the anatomical structure in one race is superior to that found in another race.

To illustrate the former viewpoint, I will mention a few of the formations in man which have been described as characterizing lower races, because they are found as typical developments in animals. One of these is a variation in the form of the temporal bone, which in man is ordinarily separated from the frontal bone by the sphenoid and parietal bones. It has been found that in some individuals the temporal bone encroaches upon the sphenoid and parietal, and comes into contact with the frontal bone. This formation is the prevalent one among the apes. It has been proved that this variation is found among all races, but with unequal frequency.

The peculiar formation of the tibia known as platycnemism (lateral flatness) has been observed in skeletons of the oldest remains of man in Europe, and also in the skeletons of various races. Other characteristics which remind us of lower forms are peculiarities in the formation of the articular surfaces of tibia and femur, which have been found in a number of human types; the *os Incæ,* or interparietal bone, which occurs among all races, but most frequently among the Peruvians and the inhabitants of the ancient pueblos; the smallness of the nasal bones and their synostosis with the maxilla; the so-called pre-nasal fossæ; and certain variations in the arrangement of arteries and of muscles. All these variable features are found among all races, but the degree of variability is not everywhere the same. Presumably such variations may be considered human characteristics which have not yet had time to become stable, and which in this sense may be considered as still in process of evolution. If this interpretation be correct, it might seem that we can consider those races in which the characteristic human features are more stable as those which are more highly organized.

It is also possible to arrange the races according to various typical features in such a manner that one appears farthest removed from the types of higher animals, others less so. In all these arrangements the gap between man and animal is a wide one, and the variations between the races are slight as compared to it. Thus we find that, in comparison to the skull, the face of the Negro is larger than that of the American, whose face is, in turn, larger than that of the white. The lower portion of his face has larger dimensions. The alveolar arch is pushed forward, and thus gains an appearance which reminds us of the higher apes. There is no denying that this feature is a most constant character of the black races, and that it represents a type slightly nearer the animal than the European type. The same may be said of the broadness and flatness of the noses of the Negro and the Mongol.

If we accept the general theories of Klaatsch, Stratz, and Schoetensack, who consider the Australian as the oldest and most generalized type of man, we might also call attention to the slenderness of the vertebræ, the undeveloped curvature of the vertebral column, to which Cunningham first called attention, and the traits of the foot, which recall the needs of an animal living in trees, and whose feet had to serve the purpose of climbing from branch to branch.

In relation to the interpretation of all these observations, it must be strongly emphasized that the races which we are accustomed to call "higher races" do not by any means stand in all respects at the end of the series, and are farthest removed from the animal. The European and the Mongol have the largest brains; the European has a small face and a high nose;—all features farther removed from the probable animal ancestor of man than the corresponding features of other races. On the other hand, the European shares lower characteristics with the Australian, both retaining in the strongest degree the hairiness of the animal ancestor, while the specifically human development of the red lip is developed most markedly in the Negro. The proportions of the limbs of the Negro are also more markedly distinct from the corresponding proportions in the higher apes than are those of the European.

When we interpret these data in the light of modern biological concepts, we may say that the specifically human features appear with varying intensity in various races, and that the divergence from the animal ancestor has developed in varying directions.

When all these differences between races are given, the question arises, whether they have any significance in regard to mental faculty. I may be permitted to disregard for the moment differences in the size and structural development of the nervous system, and confine myself to the mental significance of other traits. The general analogy of mental development of animals and of man prompts us to associate lower mental traits with theromorphic features. In our naïve, every-day parlance, brutish features and brutality are closely connected. We must distinguish here, however, between the anatomical characteristics of which we have been speaking and the muscular development of the face, trunk, and limbs, due to habitual activity. The hand, which is never employed in activities requiring those refined adjustments which are characteristic of psychologically complex actions, will lack the modelling brought about by the development of each muscle. The face whose muscles have not

responded to the innervations accompanying deep thought and refined sentiment will lack in individuality and refinement. The neck that has supported heavy loads, and has not responded to the varied requirements of delicate changes of position of head and body, will appear massive and clumsy. These physiognomic differences must not mislead us in our interpretations. But even without them, we are inclined to draw inferences in regard to mentality from a receding forehead, a heavy jaw, large and heavy teeth, perhaps even from an inordinate length of arms or an unusual development of hairiness.

From a strictly scientific point of view, these inferences seem to be open to the most serious doubt. Only a few investigations have been made in relation to these problems, but their results have been entirely negative. Most important among them is the elaborate attempt made by Karl Pearson to investigate the relationship of intelligence to size and shape of the head. His conclusions are so significant that I will repeat them here: "The onus of proof that other measurements and more subtle psychological observations would lead to more definite results may now, I think, be left to those who a priori regard such an association as probable. Personally, the result of the present inquiry has convinced me that there is little relationship between the external physical and the psychical character in man." I think all the investigations that have been made up to the present time compel us to assume that the characteristics of the osseous, muscular, visceral, or circulatory system, have practically no direct relation to the mental ability of man (Manouvrier).

We will now turn to the important subject of the size of the brain, which seems to be the one anatomical feature which bears directly upon the question at issue. It seems plausible that the greater the central nervous system, the higher the faculty of the race, and the greater its aptitude to mental achievements. Let us review the known facts. Two methods are open for ascertaining the size of the central nervous system,—the determination of the weight of the brain and that of the capacity of the cranial cavity. The first of these methods is the one which promises the most accurate results. Naturally, the number of Europeans whose brain-weights have been taken is much larger than that of individuals of other races. There are, however, sufficient data available to establish beyond a doubt the fact that the brain-weight of the whites is larger than that of most other races, particularly larger than that of the Negroes. That of the white male is about 1360 grams. The investigations of cranial capacities are quite in accord with these results. According to Topinard, the capacity of the skull of males of the neolithic period in Europe is about 1560 cc. (44 cases); that of modern Europeans is the same (347 cases); of the Mongoloid race, 1510 cc. (68 cases); of African Negroes, 1405 cc. (83 cases); and of Negroes of the Pacific Ocean, 1460 cc. (46 cases). Here we have, therefore, a decided difference in favor of the white race.

In interpreting these facts, we must ask, Does the increase in the size of the brain prove an increase in faculty? This would seem highly probable, and facts may be adduced which speak in favor of this assumption. First among these is the relatively large size of the brain among the higher animals, and the still larger size in man. Furthermore, Manouvrier has measured the capacity of the skulls of thirty-five eminent men. He found that they averaged 1665 cc. as compared to 1560 cc. general average, which was derived from 110 individuals. On the other hand, he found that the cranial capacity of forty-five murderers was 1580 cc., also superior to the general average. The same result has been obtained through weighings of brains of eminent men. The brains of thirty-four of these showed an average increase of 93 grams over the average brain-weight of 1357 grams. Another fact which may be adduced in favor of the theory that greater brains are accompanied by higher faculty is that the heads of the best English students are larger than those of the average class of students (Galton). The force of the arguments furnished by these observations must, however, not be overestimated.

First of all, the brains of not all eminent men are unusually large. On the contrary, a few unusually small brains have been found in the series. Furthermore, most of the brain-weights constituting the general series are obtained in anatomical institutes; and the individuals who find their way there are poorly developed, on account of malnutrition and of life under unfavorable circumstances, while the eminent men represent a much better nourished class. As poor nourishment reduces the weight and size of the whole body, it will also reduce the size and weight of the brain. It is not certain, therefore, that the observed difference is entirely due to the higher ability of the eminent men. This may also explain the larger size of the brains of the professional classes as compared to those of unskilled laborers (Ferraira). An additional number of restricting facts must be enumerated. The most important among these is the difference in brain-weight between men and women. When men and women of the same stature are compared, it is found that the brain of woman is much lighter than that of man. Nevertheless the faculty of woman while perhaps qualitatively different from that of man, cannot be deemed to be of an inferior character. This is therefore a case in which smaller brain-weight is accompanied throughout by equal faculty. We conclude from this fact that it is not impossible that the smaller brains of males of other races should do the same work as is done by the larger brain of the white race. But this comparison is not quite on equal terms, as we may assume that there is a certain structural difference between male and female, which causes the difference in size between the sexes; so that comparison between male and female is not the same as comparison between male and male.

Notwithstanding these restrictions, the increase of the size of the brain in the higher animals, and the lack of development in microcephalic individuals, are fundamental facts which make it more than probable that increased size of the brain causes increased faculty, although the relation is not quite as immediate as is often assumed.

The reason for a lack of close correlation between brain-weight and mental faculties is not far to seek. The functioning of the brain depends upon the nerve cells and fibres, which do not constitute, by any means, the whole mass of the brain. A brain with many cells and complex connections between the cells may contain less connective tissue than another one of simpler nervous structure. In other words, if there is a close relation between form and ability, it must be looked for rather in the morphological traits of the brain than in its size. A correlation exists between size of brain and number of cells and fibres, but the correlation is weak (Donaldson).

Notwithstanding the numerous attempts that have been made to find structural differences between the brains of different races of man that could be directly interpreted in psychological terms, no conclusive results of any kind have been attained. The status of our present knowledge has been well summed up by Franklin P. Mall, to whose investigation I referred before. He holds that, on account of the great variability of the individuals constituting each race, racial differences are exceedingly difficult to discover, and that up to the present time none have been found that will endure serious criticism.

We may now sum up the results of our preliminary inquiry. We have found that the unproved assumption of identity of cultural achievement and of mental ability is founded on an error of judgment; that the variations in cultural development can as well be explained by a consideration of the general course of historical events without recourse to the theory of material differences of mental faculty in different races. We have found, furthermore, that a similar error underlies the common assumption that the white race represents physically the highest type of man, but that anatomical and physiological considerations do not support these views.

1911

JAMES HARVEY ROBINSON

On Various Kinds of Thinking

From The Mind in the Making

WE DO NOT think enough about thinking, and much of our confusion is the result of current illusions in regard to it. Let us forget for the moment any impressions we may have derived from the philosophers, and see what seems to happen in ourselves. The first thing that we notice is that our thought moves with such incredible rapidity that it is almost impossible to arrest any specimen of it long enough to have a look at it. When we are offered a penny for our thoughts we always find that we have recently had so many things in mind that we can easily make a selection which will not compromise us too nakedly. On inspection we shall find that even if we are not downright ashamed of a great part of our spontaneous thinking it is far too intimate, personal, ignoble, or trivial to permit us to reveal more than a small part of it. I believe this must be true of everyone. We do not, of course, know what goes on in other people's heads. They tell us very little and we tell them very little. The spigot of speech, rarely fully opened, could never emit more than driblets of the ever renewed hogshead of thought—*noch grösser wie's Heidelberger Fass*. We find it hard to believe that other people's thoughts are as silly as our own, but they probably are.

We all appear to ourselves to be thinking all the time during our waking hours, and most of us are aware that we go on thinking while we are asleep, even more foolishly than when awake. When uninterrupted by some practical issue, we are engaged in what is now known as a *reverie*. This is our spontaneous and favorite kind of thinking. We allow our ideas to take their own course, and this course is determined by our hopes and fears, our spontaneous desires, their fulfillment or frustration; by our likes and dislikes, our loves and hates and resentments. There is nothing else anything like so interesting to ourselves as ourselves. All thought that is not more or less laboriously controlled and directed will inevitably circle about the beloved Ego. It is amusing and pathetic to observe this tendency in ourselves and in others. We learn politely and generously to overlook this truth, but if we dare to think of it, it blazes forth like the noontide sun.

The reverie or "free association of ideas" has of late become the subject of scientific research. While investigators are not yet agreed on the results, or at least on the proper interpretation to be given to them, there can be no doubt that our reveries form the chief index to our fundamental character. They are a reflection of our nature as modified by often hidden and forgotten experiences. We need not go into the matter further here, for it is only necessary to observe that the reverie is at all times a potent and in many cases an omnipotent rival to every other kind of thinking. It doubtless influences all our speculations in its persistent tendency to self-magnification and self-justification, which are its chief preoccupations, but it is the last thing to make directly or indirectly for honest increase of knowledge.[1] Philosophers usually talk as if such thinking did not exist or were in some way negligible. This is what makes their speculations so unreal and often worthless.

The reverie, as any of us can see for himself, is frequently broken and interrupted by the necessity of a second kind of thinking. We have to make practical decisions. Shall we write a letter or no? Shall we take the subway or a bus? Shall we have dinner at seven or half past? Shall we buy U. S. Rubber or a Liberty Bond? Decisions are easily distinguishable from the free flow of the reverie. Sometimes they demand a good deal of careful pondering and the recollection of pertinent facts; often, however, they are made impulsively. They are a more difficult and laborious thing than the reverie, and we resent having to "make up our mind" when we are tired or absorbed in a congenial reverie. Weighing a decision, it should be noted, does not necessarily add anything to our knowledge, although we may, of course, seek further information before making it.

Rationalizing

A third kind of thinking is stimulated when anyone questions our belief and opinions. We sometimes find ourselves changing our minds without any resistance or heavy emotion, but if we are told that we are wrong we resent the imputation and harden our hearts. We are incredibly heedless in the formation of our beliefs, but find ourselves filled with an illicit passion for them when anyone proposes to rob us of their companionship. It is obviously not the ideas themselves that are dear to us, but our self-esteem, which is threatened. We are by nature stubbornly pledged to defend our own from attack, whether it be our person, our family, our property, or our opinion. A United States Senator once remarked to a friend of mine that God Almighty could not make him change his mind on our Latin America policy. We may surrender, but rarely confess ourselves vanquished. In the intellectual world, at least, peace is without victory.

Few of us take the pains to study the origin of our cherished convictions; indeed, we have a natural repugnance to so doing. We like to continue to believe what we have been accustomed to accept as true, and the resentment aroused when doubt is cast upon any of our assumptions leads us to seek every manner of excuse for clinging to them. *The result is that most of our so-called reasoning consists in finding arguments for going on believing as we already do.*

I remember years ago attending a public dinner to which the Governor of the state was bidden. The chairman explained that His Excellency could not

[1] The poet-clergyman, John Donne, who lived in the time of James I, has given a beautifully honest picture of the doings of a saint's mind: "I throw myself down in my chamber and call in and invite God and His angels thither, and when they are there I neglect God and His angels for the noise of a fly, for the rattling of a coach, for the whining of a door. I talk on in the same posture of praying, eyes lifted up, knees bowed down, as though I prayed to God, and if God or His angels should ask me when I thought last of God in that prayer I cannot tell. Sometimes I find that I had forgot what I was about, but when I began to forget it I cannot tell. A memory of yesterday's pleasures, a fear of tomorrow's dangers, a straw under my knee, a noise in mine ear, a light in mine eye, an anything, a nothing, a fancy, a chimera in my brain troubles me in my prayer."—Quoted by Robert Lynd, *The Art of Letters*, pp. 46-47.

be present for certain "good" reasons; what the "real" reasons were the presiding officer said he would leave us to conjecture. This distinction between "good" and "real" reasons is one of the most clarifying and essential in the whole realm of thought. We can readily give what seem to us "good" reasons for being a Catholic or a Mason, a Republican or a Democrat, an adherent or opponent of the League of Nations. But the "real" reasons are usually on quite a different plane. Of course the importance of this distinction is popularly, if somewhat obscurely, recognized. The Baptist missionary is ready enough to see that the Buddhist is not such because his doctrines would bear careful inspection, but because he happened to be born in a Buddhist family in Tokio. But it would be treason to his faith to acknowledge that his own partiality for certain doctrines is due to the fact that his mother was a member of the First Baptist Church of Oak Ridge. A savage can give all sorts of reasons for his belief that it is dangerous to step on a man's shadow, and a newspaper editor can advance plenty of arguments against the Bolsheviki. But neither of them may realize why he happens to be defending his particular opinion.

The "real" reasons for our beliefs are concealed from ourselves as well as from others. As we grow up we simply adopt the ideas presented to us in regard to such matters as religion, family relations, property, business, our country, and the state. We unconsciously absorb them from our environment. They are persistently whispered in our ear by the group in which we happen to live. Moreover, as Mr. Trotter has pointed out, these judgments, being the product of suggestion and not of reasoning, have

the quality of perfect obviousness, so that to question them

. . . is to the believer to carry skepticism to an insane degree, and will be met by contempt, disapproval, or condemnation, according to the nature of the belief in question. When, therefore, we find ourselves entertaining an opinion about the basis of which there is a quality of feeling which tells us that to inquire into it would be absurd, obviously unnecessary, unprofitable, undesirable, bad form, or wicked, we may know that that opinion is a nonrational one, and probably, therefore, founded upon inadequate evidence.[2]

Opinions, on the other hand, which are the result of experience or of honest reasoning do not have this quality of "primary certitude." I remember when as a youth I heard a group of business men discussing the question of the immortality of the soul, I was outraged by the sentiment of doubt expressed by one of the party. As I look back now I see that I had at the time no interest in the matter, and certainly no least argument to urge in favor of the belief in which I had been reared. But neither my personal indifference to the issue, nor the fact that I had previously given it no attention, served to prevent an angry resentment when I heard *my* ideas questioned.

This spontaneous and loyal support of our preconceptions—this process of finding "good" reasons to justify our routine beliefs—is known to modern psychologists as "rationalizing"—clearly only a new name for a very ancient thing. Our "good" reasons ordinarily have no value in promoting honest enlightenment, because, no matter how solemnly they may be marshaled, they are at bottom the result of personal preference or prejudice, and not of an

[2] *Instincts of the Herd in Peace and War*, p. 44.

honest desire to seek or accept new knowledge.

In our reveries we are frequently engaged in self-justification, for we cannot bear to think ourselves wrong, and yet have constant illustrations of our weaknesses and mistakes. So we spend much time finding fault with circumstances and the conduct of others, and shifting on to them with great ingenuity the onus of our own failures and disappointments. *Rationalizing is the self-exculpation which occurs when we feel ourselves, or our group, accused of misapprehension or error.*

The little word *my* is the most important one in all human affairs, and properly to reckon with it is the beginning of wisdom. It has the same force whether it is *my* dinner, *my* dog, and *my* house, or *my* faith, *my* country, and *my* God. We not only resent the imputation that our watch is wrong, or our car shabby, but that our conceptions of the canals of Mars, of the pronunciation of "Epictetus," of the medicinal value of salicine, or the date of Sargon I, are subject to revision.

Philosophers, scholars, and men of science exhibit a common sensitiveness in all decisions in which their *amour propre* is involved. Thousands of argumentative works have been written to vent a grudge. However stately their reasoning, it may be nothing but rationalizing, stimulated by the most commonplace of all motives. A history of philosophy and theology could be written in terms of grouches, wounded pride, and aversions, and it would be far more instructive than the usual treatments of these themes. Sometimes, under Providence, the lowly impulse of resentment leads to great achievements. Milton wrote his treatise on divorce as a

result of his troubles with his seventeen-year-old wife, and when he was accused of being the leading spirit in a new sect, the Divorcers, he wrote his noble *Areopagitica* to prove his right to say what he thought fit, and incidentally to establish the advantage of a free press in the promotion of truth.

All mankind, high and low, thinks in all the ways which have been described. The reverie goes on all the time not only in the mind of the mill hand and the Broadway flapper, but equally in weighty judges and godly bishops. It has gone on in all the philosophers, scientists, poets, and theologians that have ever lived. Aristotle's most abstruse speculations were doubtless tempered by highly irrelevant reflections. He is reported to have had very thin legs and small eyes, for which he doubtless had to find excuses, and he was wont to indulge in very conspicuous dress and rings and was accustomed to arrange his hair carefully.[3] Diogenes the Cynic exhibited the impudence of a touchy soul. His tub was his distinction. Tennyson in beginning his "Maud" could not forget his chagrin over losing his patrimony years before as the result of an unhappy investment in the Patent Decorative Carving Company. These facts are not recalled here as a gratuitous disparagement of the truly great, but to insure a full realization of the tremendous competition which all really exacting thought has to face, even in the minds of the most highly endowed mortals.

And now the astonishing and perturbing suspicion emerges that perhaps almost all that had passed for social science, political economy, politics, and ethics in the past may be brushed aside by future generations as mainly rationalizing. John Dewey has already

[3] Diogenes Laertius, Book V.

reached this conclusion in regard to philosophy.[4] Veblen[5] and other writers have revealed the various unperceived presuppositions of the traditional political economy, and now comes an Italian sociologist, Vilfredo Pareto, who, in his huge treatise on general sociology, devotes hundreds of pages to substantiating a similar thesis affecting all the social sciences.[6] This conclusion may be ranked by students of a hundred years hence as one of the several great discoveries of our age. It is by no means fully worked out, and it is so opposed to nature that it will be very slowly accepted by the great mass of those who consider themselves thoughtful. As an historical student I am personally fully reconciled to this newer view. Indeed, it seems to me inevitable that just as the various sciences of nature were, before the opening of the seventeenth century, largely masses of rationalizations to suit the religious sentiments of the period, so the social sciences have continued even to our own day to be rationalizations of uncritically accepted beliefs and customs.

It will become apparent as we proceed that the fact that an idea is ancient and that it has been widely received is no argument in its favor, but should immediately suggest the necessity of carefully testing it as a probable instance of rationalization.

How Creative Thought Transforms the World

This brings us to another kind of thought which can fairly easily be distinguished from the three kinds described above. It has not the usual qualities of the reverie, for it does not hover about our personal complacencies and humiliations. It is not made up of the homely decisions forced upon us by everyday needs, when we review our little stock of existing information, consult our conventional preferences and obligations, and make a choice of action. It is not the defense of our own cherished beliefs and prejudices just because they are our own—mere plausible excuses for remaining of the same mind. On the contrary, it is that peculiar species of thought which leads us to *change* our mind.

It is this kind of thought that has raised man from his pristine, subsavage ignorance and squalor to the degree of knowledge and comfort which he now possesses. On his capacity to continue and greatly extend this kind of thinking depends his chance of groping his way out of the plight in which the most highly civilized peoples of the world now find themselves. In the past this type of thinking has been called reason. But so many misapprehensions have grown up around the word that some of us have become very suspicious of it. I suggest, therefore, that we substitute a recent name and speak of "creative thought" rather than of reason. *For this kind of meditation begets knowledge, and knowledge is really creative inasmuch as it makes things look different from what they seemed before and may indeed work for their reconstruction.*

---

[4] *Reconstruction in Philosophy.*
[5] *The Place of Science in Modern Civilization.*
[6] *Traité de Sociologie Générale, passim.* The author's term *derivations* seems to be his precise way of expressing what we have called the "good" reasons, and his *residus* correspond to the "real" reasons. He well says, *"L'homme éprouve le besoin de raisonner, et en outre d'étendre un voile sur ses instincts et sur ses sentiments"*—hence, rationalization. (P. 788.) His aim is to reduce sociology to the "real" reasons. (P. 791.)

In certain moods some of us realize that we are observing things or making reflections with a seeming disregard of our personal preoccupations. We are not preening or defending ourselves; we are not faced by the necessity of any practical decision, nor are we apologizing for believing this or that. We are just wondering and looking and mayhap seeing what we never perceived before.

Curiosity is as clear and definite as any of our urges. We wonder what is in a sealed telegram or in a letter in which someone else is absorbed, or what is being said in the telephone booth or in low conversation. This inquisitiveness is vastly stimulated by jealousy, suspicion, or any hint that we ourselves are directly or indirectly involved. But there appears to be a fair amount of personal interest in other people's affairs even when they do not concern us except as a mystery to be unraveled or a tale to be told. The reports of a divorce suit will have "news value" for many weeks. They constitute a story, like a novel or play or moving picture. This is not an example of pure curiosity, however, since we readily identify ourselves with others, and their joys and despair then become our own.

We also take note of, or "observe," as Sherlock Holmes says, things which have nothing to do with our personal interests and make no personal appeal either direct or by way of sympathy. This is what Veblen so well calls "idle curiosity." And it is usually idle enough. Some of us when we face the line of people opposite us in a subway train impulsively consider them in detail and engage in rapid inferences and form theories in regard to them. On entering a room there are those who will perceive at a glance the degree of preciousness of the rugs, the character of the pictures, and the personality revealed by the books. But there are many, it would seem, who are so absorbed in their personal reverie or in some definite purpose that they have no bright-eyed energy for idle curiosity. The tendency to miscellaneous observation we come by honestly enough, for we note it in many of our animal relatives.

Veblen, however, uses the term "idle curiosity" somewhat ironically, as is his wont. It is idle only to those who fail to realize that it may be a very rare and indispensable thing from which almost all distinguished human achievement proceeds, since it may lead to systematic examination and seeking for things hitherto undiscovered. For research is but diligent search which enjoys the high flavor of primitive hunting. Occasionally and fitfully idle curiosity thus leads to creative thought, which alters and broadens our own views and aspirations and may in turn, under highly favorable circumstances, affect the views and lives of others, even for generations to follow. An example or two will make this unique human process clear.

Galileo was a thoughtful youth and doubtless carried on a rich and varied reverie. He had artistic ability and might have turned out to be a musician or painter. When he had dwelt among the monks at Vallombrosa he had been tempted to lead the life of a religious. As a boy he busied himself with toy machines and he inherited a fondness for mathematics. All these facts are of record. We may safely assume also that, along with many other subjects of contemplation, the Pisan maidens found a vivid place in his thoughts.

One day when seventeen years old he wandered into the cathedral of his native town. In the midst of his reverie he looked up at the lamps hanging by long chains from the high ceiling of the church. Then something very difficult to explain occurred. He found himself no longer thinking of the building, worshipers, or the services; of his artistic or religious interests; of his reluctance to become a physician as his father wished. He forgot the question of a career and even the *graziosissime donne.* As he watched the swinging lamps he was suddenly wondering if mayhap their oscillations, whether long or short, did not occupy the same time. Then he tested this hypothesis by counting his pulse, for that was the only timepiece he had with him.

This observation, however remarkable in itself, was not enough to produce a really creative thought. Others may have noticed the same thing and yet nothing came of it. Most of our observations have no assignable results. Galileo may have seen that the warts on a peasant's face formed a perfect isosceles triangle, or he may have noticed with boyish glee that just as the officiating priest was uttering the solemn words, *ecce agnus Dei,* a fly lit on the end of his nose. To be really creative, ideas have to be worked up and then "put over," so that they become a part of man's social heritage. The highly accurate pendulum clock was one of the later results of Galileo's discovery. He himself was led to reconsider and successfully to refute the old notions of falling bodies. It remained for Newton to prove that the moon was falling, and presumably all the heavenly bodies. This quite upset all the consecrated views of the heavens as managed by angelic engineers. The universality of the laws of gravitation stimulated the attempt to seek other and equally im-

portant natural laws and cast grave doubts on the miracles in which mankind had hitherto believed. In short, those who dared to include in their thought the discoveries of Galileo and his successors found themselves in a new earth surrounded by new heavens.

On the 28th of October, 1831, three hundred and fifty years after Galileo had noticed the isochronous vibrations of the lamps, creative thought and its currency had so far increased that Faraday was wondering what would happen if he mounted a disk of copper between the poles of a horseshoe magnet. As the disk revolved an electric current was produced. This would doubtless have seemed the idlest kind of experiment to the staunch business men of the time, who, it happened, were just then denouncing the child labor bills in their anxiety to avail themselves to the full of the results of earlier idle curiosity. But should the dynamos and motors which have come into being as the outcome of Faraday's experiment be stopped this evening, the business man of today, agitated over labor troubles, might, as he trudged home past lines of "dead" cars, through dark streets to an unlighted house, engage in a little creative thought of his own and perceive that he and his laborers would have no modern factories and mines to quarrel about had it not been for the strange practical effects of the idle curiosity of scientists, inventors, and engineers.

The examples of creative intelligence given above belong to the realm of modern scientific achievement, which furnishes the most striking instances of the effects of scrupulous, objective thinking. But there are, of course, other great realms in which the recording and embodiment of acute observation and insight have wrought themselves into the higher life of man. The great poets and dramatists and our modern storytellers have found themselves engaged in productive reveries, noting and artistically presenting their discoveries for the delight and instruction of those who have the ability to appreciate them.

The process by which a fresh and original poem or drama comes into being is doubtless analogous to that which originates and elaborates so-called scientific discoveries; but there is clearly a temperamental difference. The genesis and advance of painting, sculpture, and music offer still other problems. We really as yet know shockingly little about these matters, and indeed very few people have the least curiosity about them.[7] Nevertheless, creative intelligence in its various forms and activities is what makes man. Were it not for its slow, painful, and constantly discouraged operations through the ages man would be no more than a species of primate living on seeds, fruit, roots, and uncooked flesh, and wandering naked through the woods and over the plains like a chimpanzee.

The origin and progress and future promotion of civilization are ill-understood and misconceived. These should be made the chief theme of education, but much hard work is necessary before we can reconstruct our ideas of man and his capacities and free ourselves from innumerable persistent misapprehensions. There have been obstructionists in all times, not merely the lethargic masses, but the moralists, the rationalizing theologians, and most of the philosophers, all busily if unconsciously engaged in ratifying existing ignorance and mistakes and discouraging creative thought. Naturally, those who reassure us seem worthy of honor and respect. Equally naturally those who puzzle us with disturbing criticisms and invite us to change our ways are objects of suspicion and readily discredited. Our personal discontent does not ordinarily extend to any critical questioning of the general situation in which we find ourselves. In every age the prevailing conditions of civilization have appeared quite natural and inevitable to those who grew up in them. The cow asks no questions as to how it happens to have a dry stall and a supply of hay. The kitten laps its warm milk from a china saucer, without knowing anything about porcelain; the dog nestles in the corner of a divan with no sense of obligation to the inventors of upholstery and the manufacturers of down pillows. So we humans accept our breakfasts, our trains and telephones and orchestras and movies, our national Constitution, or moral code and standards of manners, with the simplicity and innocence of a pet rabbit. We have absolutely inexhaustible capacities for appropriating what others do for us with no thought of a "thank you." We do not feel called upon to make any least contribution to the merry game ourselves. Indeed, we are usually quite unaware that a game is being played at all.

We have now examined the various classes of thinking which we can readily observe in ourselves and which we have plenty of reasons to believe go on, and always have been going on, in our fel-

[7] Recently a reëxamination of creative thought has begun as a result of new knowledge which discredits many of the notions formerly held about "reason." See, for example, *Creative Intelligence,* by a group of American philosophic thinkers; John Dewey, *Essays in Experimental Logic* (both pretty hard books); and Veblen, *The Place of Science in Modern Civilization.* Easier than these and very stimulating are Dewey, *Reconstruction in Philosophy,* and Woodworth, *Dynamic Psychology.*

low men. We can sometimes get quite pure and sparkling examples of all four kinds, but commonly they are so confused and intermingled in our reverie as not to be readily distinguishable. The reverie is a reflection of our longings, exultations, and complacencies, our fears, suspicions, and disappointments. We are chiefly engaged in struggling to maintain our self-respect and in asserting that supremacy which we all crave and which seems to us our natural prerogative. It is not strange, but rather quite inevitable, that our beliefs about what is true and false, good and bad, right and wrong, should be mixed up with the reverie and be influenced by the same considerations which determine its character and course. We resent criticisms of our views exactly as we do of anything else connected with ourselves. Our notions of life and its ideals seem to us to be *our own* and as such necessarily true and right, to be defended at all costs.

We very rarely consider, however, the process by which we gained our convictions. If we did so, we could hardly fail to see that there was usually little ground for our confidence in them. Here and there, in this department of knowledge or that, some one of us might make a fair claim to have taken some trouble to get correct ideas of, let us say, the situation in Russia, the sources of our food supply, the origin of the Constitution, the revision of the tariff, the policy of the Holy Roman Apostolic Church, modern business organization, trade unions, birth control, socialism, the League of Nations, the excess profits tax, preparedness, advertising in its social bearings; but only a very exceptional person would be entitled to opinions on all of even these few matters. And yet most of us have

opinions on all these, and on many other questions of equal importance, of which we may know even less. We feel compelled, as self-respecting persons, to take sides when they come up for discussion. We even surprise ourselves by our omniscience. Without taking thought we see in a flash that it is most righteous and expedient to discourage birth control by legislative enactment, or that one who decries intervention in Mexico is clearly wrong, or that big advertising is essential to big business and that big business is the pride of the land. As godlike beings why should we not rejoice in our omniscience?

It is clear, in any case, that our convictions on important matters are not the result of knowledge or critical thought, nor, it may be added, are they often dictated by supposed self-interest. Most of them are *pure prejudices* in the proper sense of that word. We do not form them ourselves. They are the whisperings of "the voice of the herd." We have in the last analysis no responsibility for them and need assume none. They are not really our own ideas, but those of others no more well-informed or inspired than ourselves, who have got them in the same careless and humiliating manner as we. It should be our pride to revise our ideas and not to adhere to what passes for respectable opinion, for such opinion can frequently be shown to be not respectable at all. We should, in view of the considerations that have been mentioned, resent our supine credulity. As an English writer has remarked:

If we feared the entertaining of an unverifiable opinion with the warmth with which we fear using the wrong implement at the dinner table, if the thought of holding a prejudice disgusted us as does a foul disease, then the dangers of man's suggestibility would be turned into advantages.[8]

The purpose of this essay is to set forth briefly the way in which the notions of the herd have been accumulated. This seems to me the best, easiest, and least invidious educational device for cultivating a proper distrust for the older notions on which we still continue to rely.

The "real" reasons, which explain how it is we happen to hold a particular belief, are chiefly historical. Our most important opinions—those, for example, having to do with traditional, religious, and moral convictions, property rights, patriotism, national honor, the state, and indeed all the assumed foundations of society—are, as I have already suggested, rarely the result of reasoned consideration, but of unthinking absorption from the social environment in which we live. Consequently, they have about them a quality of "elemental certitude," and we especially resent doubt or criticism cast upon them. So long, however, as we revere the whisperings of the herd, we are obviously unable to examine them dispassionately and to consider to what extent they are suited to the novel conditions and social exigencies in which we find ourselves today.

The "real" reasons for our beliefs, by making clear their origins and history, can do much to dissipate this emotional blockade and rid us of our prejudices and preconceptions. Once this is done and we come critically to examine our traditional beliefs, we may well find some of them sustained by experience and honest reasoning, while others must be revised to meet new conditions and our more extended knowledge. But only after we have undertaken such a critical examination in the light of experience and modern knowledge, freed from any feelings of "primary certitude," can we claim that the "good" are also the "real" reasons for our opinions.

I do not flatter myself that this general show-up of man's thought through the ages will cure myself or others of carelessness in adopting ideas, or of unseemly heat in defending them just because we have adopted them. But if the considerations which I propose to recall are really incorporated into our thinking and are permitted to establish our general outlook on human affairs, they will do much to relieve the imaginary obligation we feel in regard to traditional sentiments and ideals. Few of us are capable of engaging in creative thought, but some of us can at least come to distinguish it from other and inferior kinds of thought and accord to it the esteem that it merits as the greatest treasure of the past and the only hope of the future.

1921

[8] Trotter, *op. cit.*, p. 45. The first part of this little volume is excellent.

JOHN DEWEY

The Influence of Darwin on Philosophy

THAT the publication of the "Origin of Species" marked an epoch in the development of the natural sciences is well known to the layman. That the combination of the very words origin and species embodied an intellectual revolt and introduced a new intellectual temper is easily overlooked by the expert. The conceptions that had reigned in the philosophy of nature and knowledge for two thousand years, the conceptions that had become the familiar furniture of the mind, rested on the assumption of the superiority of the fixed and final; they rested upon treating change and origin as signs of defect and unreality. In laying hands upon the sacred ark of absolute permanency, in treating the forms that had been regarded as types of fixity and perfection as originating and passing away, the "Origin of Species" introduced a mode of thinking that in the end was bound to transform the logic of knowledge, and hence the treatment of morals, politics, and religion.

No wonder, then, that the publication of Darwin's book, a half century ago, precipitated a crisis. The true nature of the controversy is easily concealed from us, however, by the theological clamor that attended it. The vivid and popular features of the anti-Darwinian row tended to leave the impression that the issue was between science on one side and theology on the other. Such was not the case—the issue lay primarily within science itself, as Darwin himself early recognized. The theological outcry he discounted from the start, hardly noticing it save as it bore upon the "feelings of his female relatives." But for two decades before final publication he contemplated the possibility of being put down by his scientific peers as a fool or as crazy; and he set, as the measure of his success, the degree in which he should affect three men of science: Lyell in geology, Hooker in botany, and Huxley in zoology.

Religious considerations lent fervor to the controversy, but they did not provoke it. Intellectually, religious emotions are not creative but conservative. They attach themselves readily to the current view of the world and consecrate it. They steep and dye intellectual fabrics in the seething vat of emotions; they do not form their warp and woof. There is not, I think, an instance of any large idea about the world being independently generated by religion. Although the ideas that rose up like armed men against Darwinism owed their intensity to religious associations, their origin and meaning are to be sought in science and philosophy, not in religion.

Few words in our language foreshorten intellectual history as much as does the word species. The Greeks, in initiating the intellectual life of Europe, were impressed by characteristic traits of the life of plants and animals; so impressed indeed that they made these traits the key to defining nature and to explaining mind and society. And truly, life is so wonderful that a seemingly successful reading of its mystery might well lead men to believe that the key to the secrets of heaven and earth was in their hands. The Greek rendering of this mystery, the Greek formulation of the aim and standard of knowledge, was in the course of time embodied in the word species, and it controlled philosophy for two thousand years. To understand the intellectual face-about expressed in the phrase "Origin of Species," we must, then, understand the long dominant idea against which it is a protest.

Consider how men were impressed by the facts of life. Their eyes fell upon certain things slight in bulk, and frail in structure. To every appearance, these perceived things were inert and passive. Suddenly, under certain circumstances, these things — henceforth known as seeds or eggs or germs — begin to change, to change rapidly in size, form, and qualities. Rapid and extensive changes occur, however, in many things —as when wood is touched by fire. But the changes in the living thing are orderly; they are cumulative; they tend constantly in one direction; they do not, like other changes, destroy or consume, or pass fruitless into wandering flux; they realize and fulfil. Each successive stage, no matter how unlike its predecessor, preserves its net effect and also prepares the way for a fuller activity on the part of its successor. In living beings, changes do not happen as they seem to happen elsewhere, any which way; the earlier changes are regulated in view of later results. This progressive organization does not cease till there is achieved a true final term, a τελὸς, a completed, perfected end. This

final form exercises in turn a plenitude of functions, not the least noteworthy of which is production of germs like those from which it took its own origin, germs capable of the same cycle of self-fulfilling activity.

But the whole miraculous tale is not yet told. The same drama is enacted to the same destiny in countless myriads of individuals so sundered in time, so severed in space, that they have no opportunity for mutual consultation and no means of interaction. As an old writer quaintly said, "things of the same kind go through the same formalities"—celebrate, as it were, the same ceremonial rites.

This formal activity which operates throughout a series of changes and holds them to a single course; which subordinates their aimless flux to its own perfect manifestation; which, leaping the boundaries of space and time, keeps individuals distant in space and remote in time to a uniform type of structure and function: this principle seemed to give insight into the very nature of reality itself. To it Aristotle gave the name, εἶδος. This term the scholastics translated as species.

The force of this term was deepened by its application to everything in the universe that observes order in flux and manifests constancy through change. From the casual drift of daily weather, through the uneven recurrence of seasons and unequal return of seed time and harvest, up to the majestic sweep of the heavens—the image of eternity in time—and from this to the unchanging pure and contemplative intelligence beyond nature lies one unbroken fulfilment of ends. Nature as a whole is a progressive realization of purpose strictly comparable to the realization of purpose in any single plant or animal.

The conception of εἶδος, species, a fixed form and final cause, was the central principle of knowledge as well as of nature. Upon it rested the logic of science. Change as change is mere flux and lapse; it insults intelligence. Genuinely to know is to grasp a permanent end that realizes itself through changes, holding them thereby within the metes and bounds of fixed truth. Completely to know is to relate all special forms to their one single end and good: pure contemplative intelligence. Since, however, the scene of nature which directly confronts us is in change, nature as directly and practically experienced does not satisfy the conditions of knowledge. Human experience is in flux, and hence the instrumentalities of sense-perception and of inference based upon observation are condemned in advance. Science is compelled to aim at realities lying behind and beyond the processes of nature, and to carry on its search for these realities by means of rational forms transcending ordinary modes of perception and inference.

There are, indeed, but two alternative courses. We must either find the appropriate objects and organs of knowledge in the mutual interactions of changing things; or else, to escape the infection of change, we *must* seek them in some transcendent and supernal region. The human mind, deliberately as it were, exhausted the logic of the changeless, the final, and the transcendent, before it essayed adventure on the pathless wastes of generation and transformation. We dispose all too easily of the efforts of the schoolmen to interpret nature and mind in terms of real essences, hidden forms, and occult faculties, forgetful of the seriousness and dignity of the ideas that lay behind. We dispose of them by laughing at the

famous gentleman who accounted for the fact that opium put people to sleep on the ground it had a dormitive faculty. But the doctrine, held in our own day, that knowledge of the plant that yields the poppy consists in referring the peculiarities of an individual to a type, to a universal form, a doctrine so firmly established that any other method of knowing was conceived to be unphilosophical and unscientific, is a survival of precisely the same logic. This identity of conception in the scholastic and anti-Darwinian theory may well suggest greater sympathy for what has become unfamiliar as well as greater humility regarding the further unfamiliarities that history has in store.

Darwin was not, of course, the first to question the classic philosophy of nature and of knowledge. The beginnings of the revolution are in the physical science of the sixteenth and seventeenth centuries. When Galileo said: "It is my opinion that the earth is very noble and admirable by reason of so many and so different alterations and generations which are incessantly made therein," he expressed the changed temper that was coming over the world; the transfer of interest from the permanent to the changing. When Descartes said: "The nature of physical things is much more easily conceived when they are beheld coming gradually into existence, than when they are only considered as produced at once in a finished and perfect state," the modern world became self-conscious of the logic that was henceforth to control it, the logic of which Darwin's "Origin of Species" is the latest scientific achievement. Without the methods of Copernicus, Kepler, Galileo, and their successors in astronomy, physics, and chemistry, Darwin would have been helpless in the organic sciences. But prior to Darwin the impact of the new scientific method upon life, mind, and politics had been arrested, because between these ideal or moral interests and the inorganic world intervened the kingdom of plants and animals. The gates of the garden of life were barred to the new ideas; and only through this garden was there access to mind and politics. The influence of Darwin upon philosophy resides in his having conquered the phenomena of life for the principle of transition, and thereby freed the new logic for application to mind and morals and life. When he said of species what Galileo had said of the earth, *e pur se muove,* he emancipated, once for all, genetic and experimental ideas as an organon of asking questions and looking for explanations.

The exact bearings upon philosophy of the new logical outlook are, of course, as yet, uncertain and inchoate. We live in the twilight of intellectual transition. One must add the rashness of the prophet to the stubbornness of the partizan to venture a systematic exposition of the influence upon philosophy of the Darwinian method. At best, we can but inquire as to its general bearing—the effect upon mental temper and complexion, upon that body of half-conscious, half-instinctive intellectual aversions and preferences which determine, after all, our more deliberate intellectual enterprises. In this vague inquiry there happens to exist as a kind of touchstone a problem of long historic currency that has also been much discussed in Darwinian literature. I refer to the old problem of design *versus* chance, mind *versus* matter, as the causal explanation, first or final, of things.

As we have already seen, the classic notion of species carried with it the idea of purpose. In all living forms, a specific type is present directing the earlier stages of growth to the realization of its own perfection. Since this purposive regulative principle is not visible to the senses, it follows that it must be an ideal or rational force. Since, however, the perfect form is gradually approximated through the sensible changes, it also follows that in and through a sensible realm a rational ideal force is working out of its own ultimate manifestation. These inferences were extended to nature: (*a*) She does nothing in vain; but all for an ulterior purpose. (*b*) Within natural sensible events there is therefore contained a spiritual causal force, which as spiritual escapes perception, but is apprehended by an enlightened reason. (*c*) The manifestation of this principle brings about a subordination of matter and sense to its own realization, and this ultimate fulfilment is the goal of nature and of man. The design argument thus operated in two directions. Purposefulness accounted for the intelligibility of nature and the possibility of science, while the absolute or cosmic character of this purposefulness gave sanction and worth to the moral and religious endeavors of man. Science was underpinned and morals authorized by one and the same principle, and their mutual agreement was eternally guaranteed.

This philosophy remained, in spite of sceptical and polemic outbursts, the official and the regnant philosophy of Europe for over two thousand years. The expulsion of fixed first and final causes from astronomy, physics, and chemistry had indeed given the doctrine something of a shock. But, on the other hand, increased acquaintance with the details of plant and animal life operated as a counterbalance and perhaps even strengthened the argument from design. The marvelous adaptations of organisms to their environment, of organs to the organism, of unlike parts of a complex organ—like the eye—to the organ itself; the foreshadowing by lower forms of the higher; the preparation in earlier stages of growth for organs that only later had their functioning—these things were increasingly recognized with the progress of botany, zoology, paleontology, and embryology. Together, they added such prestige to the design argument that by the late eighteenth century it was, as approved by the sciences of organic life, the central point of theistic and idealistic philosophy.

The Darwinian principle of natural selection cut straight under this philosophy. If all organic adaptations are due simply to constant variation and the elimination of those variations which are harmful in the struggle for existence that is brought about by excessive reproduction, there is no call for a prior intelligent causal force to plan and preordain them. Hostile critics charged Darwin with materialism and with making chance the cause of the universe.

Some naturalists, like Asa Gray, favored the Darwinian principle and attempted to reconcile it with design. Gray held to what may be called design on the installment plan. If we conceive the "stream of variations" to be itself intended, we may suppose that each successive variation was designed from the first to be selected. In that case, variation, struggle, and selection simply

define the mechanism of "secondary causes" through which the "first cause" acts; and the doctrine of design is none the worse off because we know more of its *modus operandi*.

Darwin could not accept this mediating proposal. He admits or rather he asserts that it is "impossible to conceive this immense and wonderful universe including man with his capacity of looking far backwards and far into futurity as the result of blind chance or necessity." [1] But nevertheless he holds that since variations are in useless as well as useful directions, and since the latter are sifted out simply by the stress of the conditions of struggle for existence, the design argument as applied to living beings is unjustifiable; and its lack of support there deprives it of scientific value as applied to nature in general. If the variations of the pigeon, which under artificial selection give the pouter pigeon, are not preordained for the sake of the breeder, by what logic do we argue that variations resulting in natural species are pre-designed? [2]

So much for some of the more obvious facts of the discussion of design *versus* chance, as causal principles of nature and of life as a whole. We brought up this discussion, you recall, as a crucial instance. What does our touchstone indicate as to the bearing of Darwinian ideas upon philosophy? In the first place, the new logic outlaws, flanks, dismisses—what you will—one type of problems and substitutes for it another type. Philosophy forswears inquiry after absolute origins and absolute finalities in order to explore specific values

[1] "Life and Letters," Vol. I., p. 282; cf. 285.
[2] "Life and Letters," Vol. II., pp. 146, 170, 245; Vol. I., pp. 283-84. See also the closing portion of his "Variations of Animals and Plants under Domestication."

and the specific conditions that generate them.

Darwin concluded that the impossibility of assigning the world to chance as a whole and to design in its parts indicated the insolubility of the question. Two radically different reasons, however, may be given as to why a problem is insoluble. One reason is that the problem is too high for intelligence; the other is that the question in its very asking makes assumptions that render the question meaningless. The latter alternative is unerringly pointed to in the celebrated case of design *versus* chance. Once admit that the sole verifiable or fruitful object of knowledge is the particular set of changes that generate the object of study together with the consequences that then flow from it, and no intelligible question can be asked about what, by assumption, lies outside. To assert—as is often asserted—that specific values of particular truth, social bonds and forms of beauty, if they can be shown to be generated by concretely knowable conditions, are meaningless and in vain; to assert that they are justified only when they and their particular causes and effects have all at once been gathered up into some inclusive first cause and some exhaustive final goal, is intellectual atavism. Such argumentation is reversion to the logic that explained the extinction of fire by water through the formal essence of aqueousness and the quenching of thirst by water through the final cause of aqueousness. Whether used in the case of the special event or that of life as a whole, such logic only abstracts some aspect of the existing course of events in order to reduplicate it as a petrified eternal principle by which to explain the very changes of which it is the formalization.

When Henry Sidgwick casually remarked in a letter that as he grew older his interest in what or who made the world was altered into interest in what kind of a world it is anyway, his voicing of a common experience of our own day illustrates also the nature of that intellectual transformation effected by the Darwinian logic. Interest shifts from the wholesale essence back of special changes to the question of how special changes serve and defeat concrete purposes; shifts from an intelligence that shaped things once for all to the particular intelligences which things are even now shaping; shifts from an ultimate goal of good to the direct increments of justice and happiness that intelligent administration of existent conditions may beget and that present carelessness or stupidity will destroy or forego.

In the second place, the classic type of logic inevitably set philosophy upon proving that life *must* have certain qualities and values—no matter how experience presents the matter—because of some remote cause and eventual goal. The duty of wholesale justification inevitably accompanies all thinking that makes the meaning of special occurrences depend upon something that once and for all lies behind them. The habit of derogating from present meanings and uses prevents our looking the facts of experience in the face; it prevents serious acknowledgment of the evils they present and serious concern with the goods they promise but do not as yet fulfil. It turns thought to the business of finding a wholesale transcendent remedy for the one and guarantee for the other. One is reminded of the way many moralists and theologians greeted Herbert Spencer's recognition of an unknowable energy from which welled up the phenomenal physical processes without and the conscious operations within. Merely because Spencer labeled his unknowable energy "God," this faded piece of metaphysical goods was greeted as an important and grateful concession to the reality of the spiritual realm. Were it not for the deep hold of the habit of seeking justification for ideal values in the remote and transcendent, surely this reference of them to an unknowable absolute would be despised in comparison with the demonstrations of experience that knowable energies are daily generating about us precious values.

The displacing of this wholesale type of philosophy will doubtless not arrive by sheer logical disproof, but rather by growing recognition of its futility. Were it a thousand times true that opium produces sleep because of its dormitive energy, yet the inducing of sleep in the tired, and the recovery to waking life of the poisoned, would not be thereby one least step forwarded. And were it a thousand times dialectically demonstrated that life as a whole is regulated by a transcendent principle to a final inclusive goal, none the less truth and error, health and disease, good and evil, hope and fear in the concrete, would remain just what and where they now are. To improve our education, to ameliorate our manners, to advance our politics, we must have recourse to specific conditions of generation.

Finally, the new logic introduces responsibility into the intellectual life. To idealize and rationalize the universe at large is after all a confession of inability to master the courses of things that specifically concern us. As long as mankind suffered from this impotency, it naturally shifted a burden of responsibility that it could not carry over to the more competent shoulders of the transcendent cause. But if insight into spe-

cific conditions of value and into specific consequences of ideas is possible, philosophy must in time become a method of locating and interpreting the more serious of the conflicts that occur in life, and a method of projecting ways for dealing with them: a method of moral and political diagnosis and prognosis.

The claim to formulate *a priori* the legislative constitution of the universe is by its nature a claim that may lead to elaborate dialectic developments. But it is also one that removes these very conclusions from subjection to experimental test, for, by definition, these results make no differences in the detailed course of events. But a philosophy that humbles its pretensions to the work of projecting hypotheses for the education and conduct of mind, individual and social, is thereby subjected to test by the way in which the ideas it propounds work out in practice. In having modesty forced upon it, philosophy also acquires responsibility.

Doubtless I seem to have violated the implied promise of my earlier remarks and to have turned both prophet and partizan. But in anticipating the direction of the transformations in philosophy to be wrought by the Darwinian genetic and experimental logic, I do not profess to speak for any save those who yield themselves consciously or unconsciously to this logic. No one can fairly deny that at present there are two effects of the Darwinian mode of thinking. On the one hand, there are in the making many sincere and vital efforts to revise our traditional philosophic conceptions in accordance with its demands. On the other hand, there is as definitely a recrudescence of absolutistic philosophies; an assertion of a type of philosophic knowing distinct from that of the sciences, one which opens to us another kind of reality from that to which the sciences give access; an appeal through experience to something that essentially goes beyond experience. This reaction affects popular creeds and religious movements as well as technical philosophies. The very conquest of the biological sciences by the new ideas has led many to proclaim an explicit and rigid separation of philosophy from science.

Old ideas give way slowly; for they are more than abstract logical forms and categories. They are habits, predispositions, deeply engrained attitudes of aversion and preference. Moreover, the conviction persists—though history shows it to be a hallucination—that all the questions that the human mind has asked are questions that can be answered in terms of the alternatives that the questions themselves present. But in fact intellectual progress usually occurs through sheer abandonment of questions together with both of the alternatives they assume—an abandonment that results from their decreasing vitality and a change of urgent interest. We do not solve them: we get over them. Old questions are solved by disappearing, evaporating, while new questions corresponding to the changed attitude of endeavor and preference take their place. Doubtless the greatest dissolvent in contemporary thought of old questions, the greatest precipitant of new methods, new intentions, new problems is the one effected by the scientific revolution that found its climax in the "Origin of Species."

1909

WILLIAM BEEBE

Elephants of the Sea

From Book of Bays

THAT you and I and our children should begin to reacquire functional tails is extremely improbable but not at all impossible. If these useful appendages were only distant arboreal memories, such a thing could not occur, but tails are very real things in our individual lives. They share with Faith in being "evidence of things not seen."

When we are three weeks old (referring to the tri-hebdomades of actual existence) we are the possessors of an amazing tail, in length about a fourth of our entire being, and in substance and musculature of greater importance than any of our budding, paddle-shaped limbs. It bears no resemblance to the slender objects trailed about by mice and monkeys, but is a tail comparable rather to that of a powerful shark. Our neck at the same instant shows four pairs of most excellent gill-clefts, aligned, clearcut, unmistakable; transiently present throughout all the ages as if for possible prospect or eventuality.

Our tail does not degenerate in size as

the weeks pass, but becomes gradually embedded in our body, and when we change our first shelter for an isolated life on the planet it has usually disappeared. I say usually because occasionally a child is born with a well-developed tail, twelve inches or more of skin, muscle and bone.

Most exciting and most personal is the fact that every one of us carries about four vertebrae or backbones which are useless except to remind us of the tails of yore—very yore. Attached to these bones are sometimes as many as twelve pairs of muscles, and with these the television of past ages has left the fish far behind and advanced to reflected life within olden jungles.

These muscles are irregularly distributed, and you—for all you know—may possess all the wagging or curling muscles well developed, while your closest friend must be content with only the depressors, and your great aunt goes through life unconsciously flaunting the elevators. Science, so far, is silent concerning the possibility of correlation of these three with characteristics of friendliness, timidity or spiritedness. A bad fall may make us painfully or dangerously aware of this inner tail, but aside from this, its vital interest is a reminder or a throwback to aquatic or arboreal ancestors.

I am endeavouring with considerable sincerity to escape from the subject of human tails, for I meant it as only an introduction to the consideration of sea-elephants, but having established my premise I am led by my pencil to one or two obvious but brief elaborations. Having redeveloped a tail how should we treat it? It is difficult to understand any feeling of shame in connection with our new appendage which would represent merely the nadir of our spinal column, with our head as the zenith. Only members of the Ku Klux Klan, occasional burglars and married women of certain benighted tribes endeavour to conceal their heads. If we search far enough back in our evolutionary closet we will discover skeletons of ancestors whose heads were little more than negative tails. Even today there persists a little creature in the sands of our shores who is unbelievably close to the beginnings of fish, and consequently ourselves. Its name is Amphioxus, which significantly means sharp-ender, and it presents no evidence of swelled head as yet developed. Yet it can see, feel and swallow to its complete satisfaction. Even in our embryonic selves evidences are only too plain that our head and brain were originally fashioned from a string of vertebrae—say eight or ten. With too many of our fellow mortals the result of the toss of life—heads or tails— seems inconsequential; their cranium appears to fulfill the primary definition of Faith—"the substance of things hoped for."

The point toward which all this tail-talk is heading is the actual comparison of tail and gills. Like the brief period of totality of a solar eclipse when time itself seems halted for a moment, so for an appreciable duration of existence we seem to swim and breathe and have our minute being—an inchling shadow of ancient eons—submerged in the diminutive sea of a womb. Although tail and gills are both present at this moment, they differ radically in the possibility of persistence. Once a tail, always a tail. Our gills, however, momentarily bridging the years—say a matter of five hundred millenniums— even while we recognize them for what they are, begin to shift and bend and dissolve. We go to the trouble of developing four pairs of gills with skeletons and blood vessels ready to be nourished by a two-chambered fishy heart, all adumbrating a life beneath the water. Then swiftly, within the space of a few days we find the gills gone, transformed into a string of ear-bones, a lower jaw, larynx and tongue cartilages. In a fraction of time we have exchanged the possibility of breathing water in the silences of the sea, for a throat and tongue muscles which will not only admit the life-giving air but enable us to play upon it as it passes, to fret it into audibility—to talk, pray, curse, sing, laugh, which no fish can do. It behooves us, occasionally, to stop, listen and consider the daily worth we extract from this swap in mid-evolution. Also thanks to the idiosyncrasy of a little gill, we can or must listen to the vocal efforts of our human associates. Finally, as a life-long reminder of an auld lang syne, we retain one last gill throughout our life, the tube which extends from our ear into the throat. This is just to make good science out of the good poetry beginning:

When you were a tadpole and I was a fish
In the Paleozoic time.

Through the activity of certain hormones we might reacquire tails but we can never recapture the activity of gills; they are too evanescent and predestined. Which has brought me a step nearer to sea-elephants, which in turn stimulate thoughts of raccoons and whales.

The change from water breathing creatures into air breathing land animals is almost the greatest wonder of evolution of animal life on this whirling, lonely planet. That from a four-legged, scaly runner to a two-legged feathered flyer is less momentous; fish fly through the water in three dimen-sions, and besides, there are flyingfishes. But the marvel of marvels, utterly unexpected and inexplicable, is the deliberate regression from a fully adapted life on land back again to that in water.

Early on the morning of a November eighth I struggled through the surf, and landed on a narrow beach of the island of Guadalupe off the west coast of Mexico. There before me was a herd, or more appropriately, a snoring, of sea-elephants. They might all have been dead were it not for the snoring. Enormous grubs came to mind as an immediate simile. Then all thoughts of their shapelessness, their eternal sloth, passed and I saw them in sudden realization as Halfways, embodying all the drama and romance of evolution; I remembered those other Halfways in *Outward Bound*.

Only from occasional fossil skeletons can we imperfectly reconstruct the changes in past ages, but here in these Central American jungles we have links of living creatures which form a chain of *as ifs,* of remarkable continuity.

If we paddle along the inland creeks of the distant mainland we will be certain to see in the mud the five-toed tracks of raccoons. These familiar animals are excellent climbers and make their diurnal home in hollow trees, but they have a habit or a vice which is so pronounced that Linnaeus named them *lotor*—the washer. A coon may dig up a muddy bulb, or may capture a perfectly clean, shining beetle or a young bird. Soiled or not, every bit of food must be lugged to the nearest water's edge and thoroughly scrubbed before being eaten. In itself this has no special significance, but I like to think of it as a symbol of some creature of ages long past—a dainty dipping of fingers into the edge of a brook, which would end in complete submersion in the open sea.

A close cousin is the crab-eating raccoon which is built along more svelte lines, and possesses an uncontrollable passion for crabs in the live shell which draws it to water like a magnet, where it scoops up the crustaceans with its paws or actually dives after them. When day comes, it scurries back to land and the trees.

Unless it be a sloth, no animal would seem less a potential explorer than an opossum. Throw an ordinary opossum into the middle of a pond and after a few miserable squirms it will probably drown. But do the same with a yapock or tropical water opossum and it will dive and swim to shore with its well-webbed hind feet, probably catching some aquatic creature on the way. As a marsupial and kin to kangaroos it is far from the direct ancestral line of sea-elephants, but as an aquatic backslider it is of vital interest. Only when its pouch is filled with unweaned babies does it have to give up its search for shrimps and fish.

Equally apart from direct lineage are three vegetarians of these jungles which have deserted the traditions of their near relatives and gone waterwards. The capybara is a giant guinea-pig which seeks safety and food in the marshes and streams, and the tapir, while calling horses and rhinoceroses cousins, has shaken off the dust of their hooves and with wide-spreading splay feet, goes squelching through the mud and swimming through the nights. Our third and last deviation is the manatee or sea-cow. To find this being we must go across to the Atlantic side of middle America, and to believe it when seen, it must be touched. This is not very difficult, for when found in a shallow ditch, it can be rolled up on the bank, ex-

amined and returned, with no more opposition than would be shown by an iron-hooped barrel of excellent rum. It were better not to mention the face of the manatee, but if we must we can only say that it has the largest harelip in existence, its nostrils are often mistaken for its eyes, and it would resemble a sloth in expression had it any humour, or a pig had it any charm. Withal it has been given the name *Sirenia*. This unquestionably is due to its rounded head and its habit of holding its baby in its flipper while nursing it, which has led early myopic explorers to detect a resemblance to a mermaid or siren. It holds the extreme place in aquatic adaptations among shore or jungle animals, for its hands are flippers, its feet have disappeared and its tailflukes are useful only for swimming or for sitting upon.

Changes in habit, haunt, activity, structure are brought about more often than we realize by what might be called vacuums of opportunity. In our mid-American jungles we have plant-eating tapirs along the river banks, opossums diving after crayfish. But the more open water with its abundance of larger fish is an inviting no-man's land, to use the least apt phrase in the English language. And into this particular vacuum of opportunity otters evolved—developing into strong, swift swimmers and fishers. Crocodiles gave them healthful competition, but the field in general was theirs.

We may suppose that they increased and that young ones sought fresh fields, or rather salt waters, and found life possible and pleasant along the shore of the Pacific. As they spent more and more time in the water they developed thick, warm fur, shorter necks, with heavier bones for easier diving, and today we find the sea-otter one of the most interesting of all Halfways. Any hope of easy life in the open sea was probably rudely shattered by killer whales and sharks. So the sea-otters kept to the shallow water, where amid the kelp and offshore rocks they found ideal sanctuary. With unconscious wisdom they developed an insatiable craving for sea-urchins which no other creature could masticate or stomach. So with haunts and food all their own, sea-otters prospered and remained sea-otters.

It is most fortunate that they have not been forced ashore again, for they have burned almost all their otterian land bridges behind them. When they haul out on a rock they can no longer walk but progress by awkward hops and springs, due to their over-developed hind limbs, with long, slender, backwardly directed, webbed toes. These great feet have but one desire and function, which is eternally to seize and push backward a webful of water. The front legs are small, and the hands are made for prying off urchins from the bottom, or crabs or shellfish. Then the otter swims to the surface, turns over, and devours its fistful of food. To crush the urchins the little hands smack them together. When a baby otter demands nourishment the same paws hold it conveniently.

Neighbors but not competitors of the sea-otters are herds of sea-lions, another animal link in aquatic advance, or terrestrial retreat, whichever way we care to consider it. We are now among a very vortex of characters which pulls both ways. Sea-lions have four real flippers—hands and feet become mittened paddles. Their ears are minute, their heads pointed, their very eyes flush —every inch is stream-lined and sinuous to a degree which induces death from despair in designers of submarines and

planes. No fish is safe from them and yet they are held in thrall by the land. The young sea-lions must be born ashore and there suckled from two to five months. They still can raise their voice in loud vociferation although harmony has been lost in competition with the crash of breakers, and their efforts compare favourably with the acclaim of a peacock and the fanfare of a donkey. In spite of their dominant ocean life sea-lions can still walk, amble and gallop on dry land, although the latter gait is invariably towards the water, speed indicating prospective joy of submergence.

This node in our Pacific hegira brings us to the sea-elephants of Guadalupe which, by the way, judging by the size of their proboscises, deserve rather the name of sea-tapirs. To these we shall return when we have reached the end of the oceanic chain of life. The succeeding link is the little seal proper, whose hold upon the dry land of its forefathers is most tenuous. The young seal is born upon the shore, but sometimes even before birth it sheds its long-haired, porous coat and may be led by its mother into the water before the sun sets on the very day of its entrance into the world.

Although terrestrial ancestry is unquestionable both in the infant seal, whose primary need of land is less than a day, and any dolphin or whale, the psychological gap is significant and profound. Whether a four-foot pygmy dolphin or a hundred-foot blue whale, all have parted with their hind limbs and trust for progress to vertical sculling with the powerful tail. The hairs of these creatures are numbered and the number is exceedingly small. Never, by any chance, can they ever clamber ashore, or sun themselves on rock or sand. A Nazi, by some incredible form of self-hypnosis, endeavours to believe that the raising of the right hand indicates some cryptic proof of Aryan ancestry, but a whale, within the mittened web of his flipper, possesses indisputable proof of the five-fingered hand of his far distant, land forebear.

We lean on the rail and look out over the wonderful Pacific. A dolphin curves into view near at hand, expels a cloud of air with a long-drawn sigh, and vanishes. Farther out, the fin of a shark moves slowly along but the creature itself does not break the surface. The course of evolution has run full circle—fish, amphibian, reptile, mammal; then the reverse, the actual links wholly unknown, but illustrated well enough by raccoon, otter, sea-otter, sea-lion, sea-elephant, seal, whale and dolphin.

Even the brief glimpse we had of the latter recalls our own developmental possibilities. The dolphin has redeveloped a swimming tail, although its rhythm is now vertically north and south, not east and west; but gills are gone forever. It need never touch dry land but it must ever rise, and rise again, to breathe air.

Whales are not Halfways. They have arrived at the last station in Waterworld and have used up their round-trip ticket. As for any future evolution, any turning again back to the land (a feat which the leatherback turtle has successfully achieved) there is no chance or possibility for whales: Man has seen to that. They can hope only barely to exist for a while longer: "That's all there is; there isn't any more."

And now let us return to Guadalupe, the home and the last stand of the sea-elephants of our northern hemisphere—the most fearless and tragic, the hugest, ugliest, sleepiest, and most helpless and hopeless links in all our chain of life.

On Templeton Crocker's yacht *Zaca* on the said eighth of November, we moved slowly through the calm waters of the Pacific about two hundred miles southwest of San Diego. A rounded bit of mist disturbed the horizon in mid-ocean. Although we had a comfortable mile and a half of water beneath our keel, the mist soon changed to the definite cloud which, at a distance, is every island in the world except Barbuda—which is nothing until you hit it.

The outline of the cloud hardened into a lofty ridge whose barrenness was only partly softened by the thin mist along the top. A little nearer and the human eye cut through the cloudy grayness and distinguished colour—a great red and olive cliff shot across with enormous seams of golden-yellow, while here and there a petrified glacier of pale volcanic ash strove forever to pour itself through unclimbable gullies.

It must have been a grand sight when this volcano first broke through the ocean floor a mile and more below the surface and sizzled and roared its way upward. The fish and the squid which were boiled alive in the process were very different from those swimming today about the *Zaca*, while mankind was early in the making, still down on all fours, perhaps not yet free from scales. At any rate the crater nosed itself above the surface and on up and up into the air until it finally cooled off, a mile above the water. Whether storm-driven Melanesians ever sighted it, or strange men drifting down from cold northern regions, or if by some chance a Toltec fisherman dared the trip from the mainland, one hundred and sixty miles to the east, we shall never know.

Back on the deck of the *Zaca*, as I approached closer, the island became more and more barren to the eye. The time of volcanic activity might well have been a dozen years ago instead of millions.

So sheer fell the cliffs that there seemed to be no beaches whatever. Our engines slowed down and for minutes our fallible eyes told us nothing more, so I resorted to high-power glasses. As I focused, the blur cleared, distance dissolved. I left the *Zaca* two miles behind and a vertical hillside crystallized into perfect detail. It seemed accessible only to creatures such as flies and geckos, yet within my field of vision was a score of quadrupeds, twenty-two creamy white goats dotted about at absurdly equal distances from one another. They did not move, they stood or grazed stiffly, and I could almost smell the paint, so much did they remind me of my old Noah's Ark animals. In this case, however, they were placed in such impossible situations that even a very small child would not have arranged them thus.

Not until our launch drew close to the breakers did the beaches become visible—narrow slopes of black lava sand. The first two were vacant. On the third I made out many elongate objects, rocks perhaps which had fallen from the steep overhead cliffs. But one of them bent upward and gazed at us, which is more than rocks can do, and we turned inshore and landed close to the first sea-elephants I had ever seen.

I walked up to the nearest great beast, an elongate mound of smooth fur, a half-grown male about ten feet over all. I sat down close in front of him and waited. He lay on his side apparently sound asleep, with small, helpless flippers dangling. His profile was like some weird cartoon or mask, impossibly and yet completely Hebraic, and he was having a nightmare. He snorted and snored and his muscles quivered as, in his dream, he twisted and turned to escape from some implacable killer whale. He heaved an asthmatic sigh like escaping steam, which vibrated throughout his entire eight hundred-odd pounds of flesh and blubber. His nose badly needed wiping and tears had formed large dark patches on the fur of his cheeks. More tears now appeared. Carroll must have seen one of these lachrymose beings before he could have evolved the Mock Turtle.

Thus far, his breathing had been through the left nostril alone and now, in line with this conservation of energy, he opened a single eye, the right, and gazed at me. The orb was large, wistful, dim with tears and for a moment registered nothing. Then my sea-elephant perceived that something was amiss. It was not a killer whale which sat cross-legged so close to him, nor even a misshapen member of his own kind. His dull brain just registered an awful something.

He reared up on high, stretching up and up until his flippers hung in mid-air and he balanced on the posterior third of his body. Sphinx caterpillars draw themselves up into exactly this defense pose, but sphinx caterpillars do not open cavernous mouths lined with coral pink and expose four stubby white fangs; nor can any other creature in the world command the horrid jumble of sounds that emanated from his throat. It sounded like some noise-producing instrument which leaked at every rivet; snorts, double bellows, quivering snarls with hints of falsetto notes between. Then the beast curved himself into a crescent, elevating his tail end, spun around on the central axis and started for the water. He laboured along for perhaps twenty feet when he was over-

come by languor, exhaustion or forgetfulness and collapsed into his former
imitation of a fallen rock.

After a full minute, something of
memory stirred in his brain and he
again reared and looked back at me.
To heave eight hundred pounds about
on its pivot a second time was too much
even to consider, so he simply bent back
and back until his head almost touched
his hind flippers, and gazed with un-
comprehending wistfulness full into my
face. Whether I appeared more attractive or less fearsome wrongway up, or
whether—well, just whether—his head
slowly sank down again on the sand.
With a gargantuan sigh he cleaned out
a deep hollow and erased me from his
memory. Again my sea-elephant slept.

I glanced back along the beach whose
smooth black sand was marked by a solitary great boulder at the water's edge.
As I looked, this was rolled over by an
incoming surge and I went toward it at
once. It proved to be a gigantic male
sea-elephant and this time death, not
sleep, held it quiescent. It must have
been dead several days but as it rolled
back and forth I could see no sign of a
wound. Its flippers waved dismally
as it turned and the great proboscis
flopped gruesomely about. When a
wave left it stranded for a moment I
stepped it off hastily and estimated its
length as seventeen feet, which is not
far from the maximum. Two young
females and a male swam in as I
watched, and almost touched its hide
with their snouts before they turned
and fled at high speed in the direction of
the rookery.

At the south end of the bay near the
water, in the partial shelter of a majestic
promontory, was a closely packed
mass of fifteen immature sea-elephants.
Higher up was a gathering of twelve fe-

males and scattered about were fourteen
others, six of which, including my
first acquaintance, were males. Most of
them awoke as we came near, moving
their heads unsteadily and eternally
yawning. The high-pitched snoring
and roaring gargles almost obliterated
the calls of gulls and the cheerful songs
of rock wrens. But another sound soon
drew my attention. It was strangely
like the beat of a tom-tom, now seeming
to come from a great distance like the
voodoo drums in Haitian mountains,
and again resounding among the very
rocks around us. It was mellow and
vibrant. I climbed to the summit of the
tumbled pile and in a pool beyond I discovered the source of the reverberations
—a male quite as large as the one lying
dead in the distance.

It was partly submerged, in the favorite crescent pose, with head and dilated
trunk, and widespread hind flippers well
out of water. The deep reiterated bel-
lowing roars continued. At every utterance the proboscis rhythmically rose
above and fell almost into the open
mouth. Finally the beat died away
with a few short, abrupt grunts like the
finale of the nocturne of a howling
monkey. For minutes the giant floated
and watched me. Its hind flippers
showed the elongate first and fifth toes
which made the general webbed outline
exactly like the half-moon tail of a
swift-swimming fish.

Here, on this beach, were two and
forty living sea-elephants. November
was evidently the low tide of the year,
between births, matings, and molts.
Others would doubtless arrive in the
course of the coming months, for a
more seasonable census a few years ago
listed many more.

I put out of mind that they were "sea-
elephants" or "*Macrorhinus angustiros-*

tris" or even "members of the order *Pinnipedia."* I tried to become aware of them more directly as creatures of their environment. I thought of them again as Halfways, and suddenly realized that they were rather Four-fifths. A small group of well-grown males returned from the sea, letting wave after wave lift them through the surf like sentient stranded logs. As they came slowly up the sand they appeared more than ever veritable creatures of the deep rather than transient immigrants to ancestral haunts. On shore, in all except bust measurement and comeliness, they fulfilled the definition of a mermaid—terrestrial forward, aquatic aft. The front flippers made fairly good crutches on which to rest, while the hind limbs dragged uselessly over the sand. Progress was by inchworming or humping along, and looking down from a high rock I seemed to be viewing a galaxy of mighty maggots speeding on their normal occasions. Nostrils could be closed to a slit camelwise, or opened wide and round as a dolphin's blowhole. But no mermaid or terrestrial being would hold each breath regularly for a half a minute between exhalations. I timed two sleeping animals and got sixteen, twenty-three and thirty-five seconds.

No sooner were the sea-elephants well up on the beach than they began to show slight but distinct symptoms of discomfort. Nostrils and eyes endeavoured to alleviate the heat, dryness or light by pouring forth a copious supply of mucus and tears. As I was passing one animal I received a shower of gravel in the face, which drew my attention to the fact that all those higher up on the beach had covered themselves with protective flipperfuls of sand.

Now and then some atavistic habit would obtrude itself unexpectedly through blubber-bound inhibitions, as when a half-dozing elephant lifted its fore flipper, bent back the terminal joints and with the projecting, rather well-shaped nails delicately scratched its cheek, or with the back of the same mittened hand gracefully wiped away a stream of tears.

As I watched these great beasts I thought of myself as I was seven hundred and forty months ago—a being headed for a life on land, but fully equipped with gills, paddle limbs and tail. Could I have gone into reverse as had these sea-elephants, the gills would have dissolved into other structures, but the paddles and tail might have recouped their former usefulness. The Guadalupian giants, like myself, had passed, each of them, through a gilled stage but to no effect. Their paddles were grand paddles, hand made, but they had perforce to make shift in the water with lungs. Tails they had exchanged for sculling feet, while dolphins, their aquatic superiors, had discarded feet for consummate flukes. So are we all enmeshed in the glorious pattern woven of earthly evolution.

Sea-elephants are indeed caught in the maelstrom of Halfways. Their present home, for which they are dominantly moulded, and the squids and fish which form all their food, are beneath the surface. Yet each female must struggle ashore to give birth to her offspring, which suckles or sleeps or just lies six weeks or more on land. Mating takes place soon after the birth of the pup, and eleven months later the succeeding generation appears. Another necessary haul-out occurs at molting time when whole plaques of skin and hair peel off and are shed together.

Where the elephants go when they leave no one knows. Two things of which I am convinced are that they are more nocturnal than is usually thought, and that their speed in the water and power of deep descent are very great. On shore, sleeping sickness seems to be their chronic manifestation of abounding health; in competition for the least common denominator of activity they challenge sloths and turtles and win easily. But this phase of their life is deceiving. When the mighty webbed feet are widespread and held tightly sole to sole, they form a sculling apparatus second only to the flukes of a dolphin. Twice, as we went from shore to ship I saw shadowy forms passing with incredible swiftness beneath the launch, and I am certain they were not sharks, but sea-elephants.

The general size, shape and appearance of the females and young males are seal-like, but the huge masters of harems are three times as large as their mates, reaching, it is said, twenty feet in length and a maximum weight of perhaps four tons. They have developed a thick, tough breastplate of rough hide, a cuirass of corrugated leather which protects them in their jealous battles with rivals. The contests are seldom fatal and consist chiefly of much roaring and rearing, and hurling of themselves at each other, striking downward with their short canines. The objectives are the tender proboscis and the eyes, and I saw two half-grown welterweight amateurs each of whom had lost an eye in precocious encounters. When cornered, even the young males would rush at us for a few feet, but the sortie would invariably end in a doze of exhaustion. With sea-elephants on land the dream is mightier than the reality.

Let us leave the somnolent herd for a while and glance up and along the thousands of feet of steep cliffs. All Guada-lupe seemed barren and dry and only along the very summit was there a line of ancient trees, pines and oaks of species reported to be found only on this isolated crest. Three decades ago Edward Palmer, the botanist, visited the island and found it a paradise of birds and plants. One out of every four of the latter was peculiar to the island, while the Guadalupe caracaras, juncos, finches, flickers, petrels, towhees, rock and house wrens were also found nowhere else in the world.

In the course of years, cats, rats and mice escaped ashore from ships, and finally someone with more faith than brains turned loose a few goats. The pelts of the latter proved valueless and their numbers are now estimated at sixty to eighty thousand. Every growing thing, green or brown, leaf, sprout, seed, root or bark within reach of these acrobatic capricorns has vanished. The trees on the summit are fighting desperately in spite of shredded bark, and their lessened foliage still gleans moisture from the swirling clouds and vitalizes a few small springs. But every cone or acorn which falls to the ground is instantly devoured by mouse or goat, and the end of all plants and water cannot be far away.

The cats have blotted out one species of bird after another until only the rock wrens, as far as I could see, were left in any abundance. Some trick of nest building must have baffled the felines. Curiously enough, the mice are reported as very common, the cats evidently preferring birds at present, with eyes on the rodents for a future change of diet.

I clambered for some distance up two canyons, dry arroyos without a single living sprig, and came across two carcasses of cats and three half-eaten goats. When about a hundred feet above the water I saw at one side a patch of bright green grass and other more succulent growths. I got as near as I could, following a well-worn goat trail. At the end, by standing on tip-toe, I could just reach a few leaves. I examined the weedy refuge and saw that even a goat could not climb up nor leap down within nibbling distance. Thousands of little hooves had stamped where I stood, the face of the rock in front was worn smooth with the search for foothold, while safe in the overhung cranny the botanical tantalus flourished. In their fight for life, goats have been observed drinking salt water and at low tide feeding eagerly on exposed beds of kelp. This is the terrible struggle for existence which has been brought about by the casual impulse of one unknown man.

I saw nothing of the mice, but at the south tip of the island while I was crawling over a pile of rocks, I surprised a cat feeding on a large crab. She was a horrid creature, yellow and gray fur all awry, eyes gleaming. She snarled silently at me and fled slinking along the shadows, finally to vanish into an inaccessible crevice. The something of paradise which Edward Palmer saw has evolved into something of a hell. Only the rock wrens seemed wholly happy. They hopped and ran over the sleeping mounds of sea-elephants, snapping up a fly now and then and giving thanks in explosive bursts of song.

The two score of sleepers or near-sleepers scattered about the beach seemed to have never a worry in the world. Throughout thousands of past generations their half-and-half lives must have found natural enemies few in number. During their evolution sea-elephants seemed hardly to have had healthful competition. Newborn pups,

to be sure, had to be careful lest three or four tons of father land unexpectedly and fatally upon them, and the battling males must have won their fights and yet kept muzzles and eyes from harm. Occasional serried marks of teeth have been found on the hide of sea-elephants showing that sharks are not wholly negligible dangers, and killer whales are an ever-haunting fear, if not in nightmares on shore then at least amid the waste of waters far out at sea.

When I was watching a pair of wrens well up on the beach, a few falling bits of rock attracted my attention and I saw a diminutive landslide emanating from the hooves of a scrambling goat. On the shore we had seen evidences of recent rock slips of serious extent. A single earthquake might loose an avalanche which could conceivably wipe out the whole herd of sea-elephants.

In ages past as various land animals worked their way seaward, a most important adaptation was the counteracting of the cold of prolonged submersion. This was easy to accomplish and a dense, thick undercoat of fur in otters and fur-seals, or the development of blubber in sea-elephants and cetaceans, answered every requirement. In these north Pacific waters all was well with the world until the arrival of a race of tissue-skinned, hairless beings. They could not really swim, but had to move about in floating affairs more or less at the mercy of the winds. If sea-elephants could talk they could have applied this description equally to jellyfish and human beings. The shivering newcomers began to wrap themselves in thick fur coats and to light and warm themselves with blubber oil, and the end of an era came clearly into view.

Seals have been seals for at least fifty million years, but the slaughter hereabouts began only a short hundred and forty years ago. Today the Guadalupe fur-seal has almost gone, for the last observer who visited this island saw only three at the entrance of a cave. Two hundred thousand fur-seals were slaughtered on Guadalupe. On one beach which I visited, the stones were as smooth as if a glacier had worked upon them, but in reality they had been polished by the eternal passing and repassing of eons of generations of seal flippers. Doubtless the legions of slain seals helped to protect our grandmothers from chilblains, but today nothing remains of the Guadalupe fur-seal but a few fragments of old skulls in museums and perhaps an ancient, moth-eaten cloak in some forgotten attic chest.

All the northern sea-elephants left alive on the planet Earth are the pitiful handful which seeks sanctuary on these narrow beaches. It was a terrible thought that, were we the kind of human beings who worked havoc here in the past, we could have slain every one of the trusting, stupid creatures around and over which we stepped. Fortunately the Mexican government has been persuaded to pass a law protecting this forlorn hope, and it seems as if the creatures were, for a time, holding their own. In the southern hemisphere the

related species has been afforded protection in time, and is thriving.

The unexpected onslaught of mankind, the steel spear heads, the powder and shot all seem so manifestly unfair; the ghastly rapid invention of murderous tools appears so anti-climactic to the slow, thorough march of evolution through all the ages.

I looked about at the helpless elephants of the sea and became aware of them in a new light. Platinum and radium and certain Old Masters are not necessarily of supreme beauty, but rarity enshrines them in a false glamour of sorts. And so in the light of tragedy, the phocine pogrom of the past, the voice and the figure of these native Guadalupians assumed a dignity and a charm, as a peacock's scream is softened by distance, and mitigation of a grotesque figure comes with approaching dusk. I felt a certain responsibility and concern as a member of the race of men who had brought them to this critical pass. I would have liked to have them understand my horror and regret.

Such sentimental emotions were not lessened by the apparent pathos of wistful, limpid eyes and streaming tears, but at this point my scientific acumen intervened and banished bathos. So I turned my mind to other matters.

1942

GEORGE W. GRAY

Deeper Into the Atom

From The Advancing Front of Science

WHEN THE full story of our times is critically appraised, perhaps a century hence, many occurrences will assume an order of importance quite different from that assigned by our contemporary historians. Just as the obscure invention of gunpowder was an event more truly momentous than the Battle of Waterloo, so there are little-known happenings of to-day that the sifting of the years will bring to the fore. They will become less obscure as time advances and their fundamental nature is more generally understood and their uses become manifest. For they mark permanent gains in man's ceaseless march and countermarch. Whatever the future of governments and individuals may be, the victories of the laboratories will stand as lasting assets of the race.

Among the recent victories is a discovery made in 1936 at Washington, D. C., at the high-voltage laboratory of the Carnegie Institution's Department of Research in Terrestrial Magnetism. It brought to knowledge an unknown force of the Universe, subjected the force to tests of measurement and analysis, and defined the law by which the force operates.

For an approximate analogy, to suggest the significance of this American discovery, one must go back to the seventeenth-century contribution of Sir Isaac Newton—his discovery of the law of gravitation. As the Newtonian discovery brought a new and clarifying interpretation to certain mysterious behavior of planets that seemed to violate Galileo's rules of motion, so does this American discovery brilliantly illuminate certain perverse behavior of atoms that seemed to violate the established rules of electricity. The former discovery provided a force and a law that gave scientific meaning to celestial mechanics; the latter has provided a force and a law that give scientific meaning to atomic mechanics. Since it seems certain that in atomic mechanics are the sources and repositories of the world's energy, the consequences of this recent discovery appear to be of the highest promise to mankind.

If the world is built of atoms, as we believe, we must know atoms before we can expect to comprehend the physical reality. Nothing seems nearer, more conveniently at hand for investigation, than atoms. They are the air we breathe, the water we drink, the soil and rocks and trees and leaves; they are our physical bodies. And yet, perhaps nothing else is so hidden, so alien to our accustomed techniques, so beyond our reach. Instead of being the round hard solid particles that our fathers imagined, the atom is an abyss. Its depths are more remote in our scale of dimensions than the dim galaxies. The darkness beyond the faintest nebula is not more tantalizing to our limited organs of vision than is the blackness of the chasm within the atom.

In these atomic depths, energy breeds other energy. Here the strange eruptions of radium are initiated and controlled. There is a suspicion that here cosmic rays are born. The nature of substances, that which makes oxygen gregarious and helium a hermit, which gives iron sensitivity to magnetism and caesium a responsiveness to light, which implants in the carbon atom such capacities as a "joiner" that the huge molecules of living substances are enabled to form and to hold together—all these and other distinguishing properties of elements, although apparently "external" attributes, are determined here in the innermost depths. In the atomic nucleus—and not in some far center of galactic rotation—is the power house of the Universe, multiplied endlessly, repeated in each of the innumerable hidden microcosmic systems. Are they the "mills of the gods"? the "looms of destiny"? the "mighty workings" that somehow spin our mortality? Physicists, as scientists, cannot answer, though some in their more metaphysical moods may venture to pronounce on such questions. As scientists they believe that in the nucleus is the mechanism of matter stripped to its prime mover; hence the preoccupation of experimental physicists to-day with this field. The nucleus is the battlefront for a score of brilliant strategists in America, Europe, and Asia. Against it the artillerylike discharge tubes, the mighty cyclotrons, and other atom-smashing devices are aimed. And it was along this front that the Washington experimenters won their 1936 victory.

The story of the discovery can be simply told. And I shall make the telling very simple, beginning with familiar concepts, recalling elementary features that are common knowledge, ignoring complications such as "wave behavior" and other items of quantum theory that are so important and indeed indispensable to the technician but not necessary to the present résumé, and shall focus attention only on features primary to our picture. Admit that we are imagists. All word pictures of atoms must necessarily be in the nature of parables, of moral tales, with the whites all white, and the blacks completely black. We understand among ourselves, of course, that white shades into black along gray no-man's lands; but these defy precise picturization, and attempts to include all details in one parable result only in confusion. So let us be realistic and, therefore, imaginative. Our parable is frankly an approximation devised to illuminate one facet of truth. If it does that it will have performed its intended function, and proved itself a useful parable.

A drop of water contains about 200 million million million molecules. No one has made an actual count of course —there are not enough years in which to count that number of objects—but we know how much a drop of water weighs, we know how much a molecule of water weighs, and the rest is simple division. I mention the number to suggest the smallness of the scale of dimensions that we must accept in approaching the realm of the elementary particles. A drop of ordinary water weighs about 3,600,000,000,000,000,000,-000 atomic units. A molecule of water weighs about 18 units. The molecule is far beyond the limit of visibility even with the ultramicroscope, but we have chemical and physical ways of isolating it, measuring it, dealing with it quite objectively. Let us enter this molecular world.

Send a current of electricity through the water. The molecules begin to break up into three pieces each: one piece of oxygen and two pieces of hydrogen. These are the atoms. And by further manipulation with electricity we can break the atoms into yet more fundamental units—hydrogen into a certain number and arrangement of particles, oxygen into a different number and arrangement.

This hydrogen is highly interesting. Apparently it is the most abundant element in the Universe. Its atom is the simplest material system we know—an arrangement of two charged particles, one massive and electrically positive, the other lighter and more diffuse and electrically negative. The negative charge is the electron, and it revolves as a swiftly moving satellite round the positive charge, the proton.

And now we have reached the solid land we seek, the nucleus. For the proton is the hydrogen nucleus. If we could magnify the hydrogen atom so that its proton became just barely visible, the encircling path of the spinning electron would be about six feet from that center. Both particles barely enough to be seen, and yet the revolving system outlines a sphere twelve feet in diameter? You can see why we think of the atom as an abyss, mostly empty space, its members relatively farther apart than the Earth is from the Sun.

The proton is the simplest nucleus known. Apparently it is a single particle. Physicists find no difficulty in breaking hydrogen atoms, stripping off of each its revolving electron, and leav-

ing the proton naked. Then they subject this unprotected proton to concentrated bombardments, using projectiles even more massive than the target, and shooting them at velocities of thousands of miles a second. But somehow the proton holds together. No one yet has been able to break one—at least, we have no clear evidence of such breakage. And so we assume that the proton is an indivisible unit. It is extremely massive. If you could lay a single proton in one pan of the scales of an infinitesimal balance, you would need to pile 1835 electrons in the opposite pan to bring the weight to equilibrium. Protons represent a tremendous amount of energy concentrated in small space. And the stuff of this matter appears to be electricity.

Apparently the proton is nothing but electricity—electricity of a peculiar behavior which we label positive. Similarly, the electron is pure electricity, but negative. A curious unexplained fact of nature is that the two particles exactly balance each other in electrical characteristics. That is to say, a piece of positive electricity, which is equal to 1835 pieces of negative electricity in quantity of *mass,* is equal to only 1 negative particle in quantity of *charge.* And so we find that despite its relatively enormous weight, the proton is never attended by more than one electron. You may surround the atom with electrons, penetrate its depths with speeding electrons, but none of them will stick.

Sometimes we find a hydrogen atom of double weight. But the extra weight is entirely within the nucleus, for only a single revolving electron is found in these as in all other hydrogen atoms. Examine the double-weight nucleus and we see why this is so: the nucleus is a two-particle affair, made of one proton and one neutron. The proton is our familiar positively-charged particle. But the neutron is a curiously neutral thing; for it has no charge, and, although its mass is about the same as that of the proton, it shows no electrical characteristics, neither attracts electrons nor repels them. More recently the atomic explorers have turned up a hydrogen of triple weight; the nucleus here contains one proton and two neutrons; but even these swing only the single orbital electron. Apparently a nucleus, no matter how massive it is, can control only one electron with one proton.

With more protons, however, it can control more electrons. This we may demonstrate by examining that other partner in the water molecule, the atom of oxygen. Its nucleus is a complex of protons and neutrons. Some oxygen atoms contain eight neutrons, a few contain nine, and a still smaller proportion of the world's oxygen contains ten neutrons; but every last one of them contains eight protons, *and only eight.* And every last one of the oxygen atoms swings eight orbital electrons, *and only eight.* This arrangement of matching one orbital electron against each nuclear proton appears to be one of nature's immutable principles of architecture; for as we go up the scale of atoms the rule holds without an exception.

There is another rule of electrical behavior which we supposed held imperiously. This is the rule that if a body is positively charged and another body is negatively charged they will mutually attract each other; but contrarily, two bodies carrying the same kind of charge will be mutually repellent. Just before the upheaval of the French Revolution the Parisian scientist Charles Augustin

Coulomb made very careful measurements of these electrical forces of attraction and repulsion and discovered the law by which they operate. The nearer together the bodies are, the stronger are the forces; and the forces increase inversely with the square of the distance. This is Coulomb's law.

To illustrate its operation by a very obvious example, recall our enlarged model of the hydrogen atom, with the proton just visible at the center and the electron revolving round it at a radius of 6 feet. Suppose we measure the electrostatic force of attraction between proton and electron at that distance. Then, if we bring the electron nearer, so that it is only half as far, or 3 feet, the force of attraction will not be two times; it will be the square of two, or four times as great. If we bring the electron still nearer, so that it is only a third of the original distance, the attraction will be magnified by the square of three, or nine times. It is easy to see from this why electrons in orbits closer to the nucleus move more rapidly. Just as the velocity of the Earth in its circuit generates centrifugal force to counterbalance the gravitational influence of the Sun, so does the velocity of the electron in its curving path engender such an effect to offset the attraction of the nucleus. Hydrogen atoms would collapse were it not that the electron moves so swiftly. A velocity of 1350 miles a second has been calculated for the innermost orbit of ordinary hydrogen.

These mutual relations between the positively charged nucleus and the negatively charged satellite appear to conform strictly to Coulomb's law. This is true not only for the hydrogen atom; it has been observed also in the behavior of more complicated atoms. The eight electrons of the oxygen atom, for example, move in their orbits at velocities proportional to their distances from the eight protons in the oxygen nucleus.

Eight protons in a nucleus? The reader who has followed the parable thus far may reasonably object. How can the oxygen nucleus hold together?

This indeed is our dilemma. The nucleus of oxygen is very small, not much larger than the nucleus of hydrogen. But the primary objection is not that so many particles should exist in a space not much larger than one of them, but that the particles of positive electricity should stay together at all.

Coulomb's law insists that positive particles repel one another in the same degree that they attract negative particles. Abundant experience confirms the law. There are electric motors activated by this force of repulsion; it operates in telephone and telegraph circuits; it is used in other industrial applications. No behavior of electricity is better known among the large-scale phenomena of electrical engineering. Engineers only occasionally deal with pure charges of electricity; most of their work is with gross bodies carrying charges. But the chemist Frederick Soddy, after measuring the force of repulsion that exists between two free protons, made an interesting calculation.

A gram is a small quantity in our everyday world; it rates about the twenty-eighth part of an ounce. But Dr. Soddy's figures show that if it were possible to accumulate a gram of protons at one pole on the Earth's surface and another gram at the opposite pole on the other side of our globe, the mutually repellent force of these two small quantities of positive electricity would be equivalent to a pressure of 26 tons, even at that distance of about 8,000

miles. Try to imagine then what should be the repulsion of proton against proton within the narrow zone of the atomic nucleus, where dimensions are reckoned in tenths of million-millionths of an inch.

On the logic of Coulomb's law one could expect to find no atoms in the Universe except those of hydrogen, since it should be impossible for more than one proton to occupy a nucleus. And if by chance two or more high-speed protons collide and find themselves accidentally associated in close quarters, Coulomb's law required that they instantly fly apart at terrific speeds of repulsion. Instead of this, the searchers found that the physical world includes a complete sequence of "impossible" structures—the helium atom with 2 protons in its nucleus, the lithium with 3, beryllium with 4, boron with 5, carbon with 6, and so on up the scale to the heaviest, uranium, with its gigantic family of 92 protons housed with 146 neutrons in the diminutive confines of nuclear space.

This uranium atom, to be sure, is a wobbly structure. Every now and then one ejects a cluster of protons and neutrons from the center, to leave a less crowded residue. This residue we call radium, and its nucleus in turn also explodes with a series of ejections, breaking down to form the simpler polonium. Finally polonium, after ridding itself of a cluster of 2 protons and 2 neutrons, settles into the stable structure we call lead. But why should lead be stable? Its nucleus, even after the successive explosions, still contains 82 protons, and each of them should waste no time in getting away from the hated presence of its fellows.

Such is the anomaly that for more

than twenty years defied explanation.[1] Coulomb's law, which ruled precisely in the atomic environs and within the spaces between nucleus and orbits, did not apply to bodies in the central core. Why was it flouted there? By what supreme court, by what more powerful ordinance, was it overruled?

The Washington experiments of 1936 brought the first answer to that question. They penetrated the inner fortress to demonstrate directly the existence of a mighty force which is operative only within the small dimensions of the nuclear zone—a force more powerful than the Coulomb force of repulsion, more attractive than the Newtonian force of gravitation: a sort of central traffic control which dominates and directs the other material forces. Apparently it is responsible for the wide variety of atomic forms that matter may assume. Also we are to think of it as a unifying agency which underlies all physical reality. Without it there could be no metal, no carbon, no living cell, no Earth, no Sun, no Galaxy, no manifold Universe—there could be nothing more complex than hydrogen, and the Whole would be only a vast cloud of diffuse hydrogen gas interspersed or combined with free neutrons. At least, such is the picture we infer from the facts we know. Our new-found force is the medium that holds the world together. It is the invisible tie that binds.

Many of the great discoveries were accidental finds, but this binding force of the nucleus was not chanced upon by accident. Its detection is the culmination of ten years of experiments aimed directly at this mystery.

When the Carnegie Institution of Washington established a Department of Research in Terrestrial Magnetism in 1904, the specialists in charge realized that their studies must lead eventually to atomic physics. At that time no one dreamed of massive central nuclei surrounded by revolving electrons. But no one doubted that the secret of the earth's magnetism, of whose reality the quivering compass needle is perpetual witness, must be sought not only in the Earth and its atmosphere but also in the invisible molecules and atoms of the needle itself. Matter must be minutely explored for the magnetic mechanism within it. The early studies were directed at large-scale phenomena, magnetic surveys of the continents and seas, and mapping. But in 1926 a definite program of subatomic research was initiated.

By this time considerable data on the intimate behavior of atomic parts had been accumulated by laboratories in Europe, Canada, and the United States. Conspicuous among the anomalies thus brought to view was this curious inexplicable behavior of protons within the nucleus. The Coulomb forces are so fundamental to our idea of the response of the compass needle that any variation or suspension of their action in any region of the Universe must be a cause of concern to explorers of magnetism.

---

[1] Until the discovery of the neutron (1932) atomic nuclei were thought to contain protons and a smaller number of electrons, but the nature and binding force of such a structure were a complete puzzle, outside all conception of theory. The neutron helped the situation but little, although it conceivably could act as the intermediary for binding protons together in spite of their repulsive forces. In fact, a whole theory of nuclear structure, now abandoned, was built up on this hypothesis as soon as specific forces, assumed to be attractive, were demonstrated by neutron-scattering experiments to exist between neutrons and protons. These forces, it is now known, assist the proton-proton and neutron-neutron forces in binding the nuclear particles together.

And so, among the problems outlined for investigation by the department was that of the nature of the nuclear mechanism. A special laboratory was built to house the research. Special apparatus was designed and installed: first a high-voltage discharge tube capable of delivering momentary blows with a pressure of about 1,000,000 volts; then an electrostatic machine and tube continuously energized by 500,000 volts; and finally the present towering atom smasher of 1,200,000 volts capacity, with which the great detection was achieved.

The detectives in this search were led by Merle A. Tuve, and the group included L. R. Hafstad, O. Dahl, and N. P. Heydenberg, physicists all. At various times during the ten years other men were on the staff, and each contributed some spark of illumination to the slow plugging through the darkness. But I am naming above the fortunate four who were working with the big-atom gun that cold January day early in 1936 when the first rumors of the new result began to trickle in. Months were to pass before the discoverers made any public announcement of what they had done—for an effect so apparently exaggerated must be tested, checked and rechecked, and submitted to the penetrating eye of mathematical analysis before it could be announced as a certainty. Indeed, nearly as important as the observations themselves, which by direct inspection only showed the failure of the Coulomb law, was this mathematical analysis of the observations in terms of the "wave mechanics," a service performed by Gregory Breit and two associates. All these tests and calculations, the checkings and recheckings, were concluded successfully, and the full story of the discovery was reported to the international group of scientists assembled at Cambridge in September of 1936 for the Harvard Tercentenary Conference.

The thing sought in the experiments was a definite measurement. We may outline the logic of the campaign in three steps. Observation had shown (1) that protons dwell together within a nucleus, and (2) that protons outside a nucleus are repelled; therefore, reasoned Tuve and Breit and their associates, there must be (3) a critical distance at which the force of repulsion is overcome and within which the protons become reconciled to one another's presence. To find that critical distance became the first objective.

The means used were those of bombardment. Suppose you have a vessel full of pure hydrogen gas of a measured density. And suppose you fire a stream of protons into this atmosphere of hydrogen. Each hydrogen atom, remember, has a proton in its core; so what you are doing is a bombardment of protons with protons. Some of the bombarding protons will approach the nuclear protons head on, others may pass close by on either side, and in every case the mutual forces of repulsion will act to rebuff the particles. They will never touch; the collisions will be only approaches and the nearer the approach the more powerful will be the repulsion. Since targets and projectiles are of equal mass, the effect will be a scattering. But the scattering will not be heterogeneous; it will be quite systematic in its directions. Just as it is possible to predict the behavior of billiard balls from the angle at which the projectile ball strikes the target ball, so it is possible to predict the behavior of the protons. Some years ago the British physicist N. F. Mott made a careful mathematical study of this phenomenon, and predicted the relative number of protons that would be scattered from each angle of approach in obedience to Coulomb's law.

All these data of the ratios and numbers of particles that would be turned back at each angle were available for Dr. Tuve and his laboratory crew. They provided a sort of bench mark, a measurement of the norm of behavior to be expected of protons acting according to Coulomb's law of repulsion. Any departures from this norm might be regarded as evidence of the breakdown of the law. And what the Washington experimenters proposed was to bombard hydrogen gas with faster and still faster protons until they got a scattering different from that predicted by Mott's calculations. The greater the velocity of the protons, the greater would be their momentum, and therefore the greater would be their ability to overcome the repulsion and approach closer to the nucleus.

This game of aerial billiards with ultrascopic particles seems very simple in principle, but it proved almost infinitely difficult in execution. The measurement of the angles could mean nothing specific unless there were an equally accurate measurement of the purity of the particles, of the density of the particles in the hydrogen at the target end of the apparatus, and of the velocity of the stream of projectiles. Very precise control was required in each of these items. Without going into details of the successive steps, I can say that many expedients, many variations, many skills were tried before the actual scattering experiment was even attempted and before the present apparatus with its remarkably exact control was attained.

The atomic artillery-piece looks its part — a sort of super machine gun mounted on its sprawling tripod, towering twenty feet above the floor, with its muzzle pointing straight down and passing through the floor into the basement room below. At its top is an aluminum sphere of six feet diameter—the loading device. Descending from the sphere is a vacuum tube of sturdy glass, the aforesaid muzzle. Charges of positive electricity from a generator are fed by a traveling belt to the aluminum sphere and there are allowed to accumulate on the metal surface to build up a pressure as high as 1,200,000 volts, under conditions of accurate control and precise measurement. This pressure discharges steadily through the long vacuum tube; and by releasing protons into the tube at the top, the gunner provides projectiles for the voltage to work on. The protons may be speeded to any desired velocity, depending on the voltage applied; and, what is equally important, the installation includes clever focusing devices to concentrate the stream, and an analyzing magnet at the bottom to pull out stray particles, unwanted molecules, and stragglers along the fringes of the stream. Thus the instrument is able to deliver to the target chamber at the bottom of the tube a finely focused stream of homogeneous protons all moving in parallel lines and at the same velocity.

In effect, it is as though you had generated a continuous lightning bolt, had harnessed it within the confines of the vacuum, had sifted out all heterogeneous and diffuse elements, and concentrated its missiles into a steady beam narrowed for a measured attack on anything you choose to place as a target in its path.

The target chamber in which the scattering takes place is in the basement room, at the focus of the tube. This chamber is a small cylindrical compartment about six inches in diameter, into which highly purified hydrogen gas is released. And built into the compartment is an ion detector mounted on an axis so that it may be pointed toward the incoming stream of projectiles at any angle, ranging from zero to ninety degrees. Here is the final link in the chain of stratagems. For, by knowing precisely the original number of particles in the beam, and the number of particles (hydrogen gas) in the chamber, and then by counting the actual number of rebounding or swerving particles which strike the detector at each of its angular positions, you can tell whether or not the projectiles are being scattered according to Mott's calculations—i. e., according to Coulomb's law.

When the thing is operating there is an awesome hum, the drone of the generating mechanism. Occasionally, when affairs are not well adjusted, a spark will flash with a lively crackling from the charged belt to the ceiling above the sphere. And to stand on the floor of this room is to place oneself in the presence of invisible influences which curve through space along the mysterious lines of force which radiate from charged bodies. Indeed, one becomes a charged body. My finger put out toward another person sprayed sparks.

But the workers spend most of their time in the basement room where the targets are manipulated. Lead salts fused in the glass of the tube protects them from random X-rays and other stray radiations that might be generated by chance collisions of the proton stream passing down the tube. Very accurate is the detector device which measures the number of protons scat-

tered at each angle. Each of the bounced protons gives a signal, the signal is amplified by a powerful device, and thereby these infinitely small movements of infinitely small objects are brought within the range of man's perception.

Tuve and his associates began the bombardment with a stream energized by a pressure of 600,000 volts, which means that the protons had velocities of 6,720 miles a second. The detector registered the scattering for each angle, and found that Mott's calculations held, that Coulomb's law of repulsion was operating quite normally. Then the bombarders increased their artillery fire; the pressure was increased to 700,000 volts, speeding the particles to 7,200 miles a second—and Coulomb's law still held. They quickened the attack to 800,000 volts, producing velocities of 7,700 miles a second—and the ancient law began to show evidence of failure. Then the electrical potential was raised on up to 900,000 volts, the stream of protons moved with the momentum imparted by velocities of 8,200 miles a second, and now—something new began to happen!

Instead of recoiling or swerving as before, the projectiles moved in toward their nuclear targets. The change in the number of scatterings from certain significant angles said so—and spoke unmistakably. The inertia of the fast-moving protons carried them headlong through the zone of rapidly increasing force of repulsion until at last the critical distance had been attained by sheer brute momentum, the long, steeply ascending barrier of the nucleus had been mounted, and the invading proton was admitted to the citadel.

Hundreds of experiments of this kind were performed. There could be no doubt that the Coulomb law had failed —but why?

The records of all the observations were forwarded to Gregory Breit for further analysis. Dr. Breit is a mathematical physicist, was long on the staff of the Department of Research in Terrestrial Magnetism—indeed, he was the leader of this atom-smashing crew at the beginning of the campaign back in 1926—and is still connected with the Washington laboratory as a research associate. But he is now professor at the University of Wisconsin, and in the winter of 1936, when this body of observational data reached him, chanced to be in Princeton attending the Institute for Advanced Study. Right in the neighborhood, across the corridor in Palmer Physical Laboratory, was Edward U. Condon, whose mathematical explorations of atomic behavior have given him wide experience with these technicalities. Dr. Breit called Dr. Condon into consultation, and together they began to dissect the batch of plotted curves and numerical tabulations. Certain details of the problem made it expedient to consult another expert, and R. D. Present of Purdue University made the third member of this mathematical team. By applying the highly complex calculations of "wave mechanics" to the experimental observations, Breit and his associates showed that beyond all doubt the observed failure was not attributable to a possible added repulsion (for a sudden sharp increase of repulsion might also distort the predicted scattering), but was actually a result of encountering for the first time the long-suspected *attractive* force which binds particle to particle within the nucleus.

The results of the mathematical analysis of these experiments may be con-veniently summarized as four findings.

1. The critical distance at which the Coulomb force of repulsion between protons breaks down is about 1/12,000,-000,000,000 of an inch.

2. The sudden change which occurs in the relations between two protons separated by this critical distance can be explained if we assume the existence of a superior force of attraction which at that and lesser distances dominates the two particles.

3. The binding power of this force, as it operates between two protons at the critical distance, is approximately 10^{36} times more powerful than the Newtonian force of gravitation between the two protons.

4. Not only protons, but also neutrons are subject to this powerful force. The attractive force between a proton and a neutron or between two neutrons is the same as that between two protons, except for the absence of the Coulomb repulsion when the chargeless neutrons are involved. These conclusions regarding neutrons are derived indirectly from other data, but the evidence seems to indicate that the nuclear force of attraction is somehow intimately associated with the mass of these primary particles, and depends little, if at all, on whether or not they are electrically charged.

To grasp some concrete idea of the enormity of this force we must resort to a comparison. Remember that the proton is inconceivably small. Its weight is less than this almost infinitesimal fraction of a gram:

1/600,000,000,000,000,000,000,000

And a gram is 1/454th part of a pound.

Now the measurements show that the pull of proton for proton within the region of the nucleus is so great that the two tiny particles move toward each other as though impelled by a pressure of from 10 to 50 pounds. If the Newtonian force of gravitation operated on the same scale, a feather on the earth's surface would weigh billions of tons.

When free protons or neutrons are captured and incorporated into a nucleus, a certain proportion of the original mass of the particles is converted into energy. The nuclear force, by its bringing of the particles together, seems to take a toll out of their substance, and the whole nucleus becomes lighter than the sum of its separate parts. Thus if we weigh a single proton the scales show a mass of 1.0081; if we weigh a single neutron, 1.0091. The total weight of the two particles therefore is 2.0172. But when they unite to form the nucleus of a heavy hydrogen atom, the mass of the resulting nucleus is only 2.0147 in weight. The difference, .0025, represents the energy of the binding force which holds the two particles together. By computation we find that .0025 of mass is equivalent to 2,200,000 volts of energy. And experiment shows that to crack a heavy hydrogen nucleus and separate its neutron from its proton requires the blow of a projectile moving with an energy exceeding 2,200,000 volts.

By these means, and in other ways as well, the new-found phenomena check. There dwells within the centers of atoms —atoms of the rocks, atoms of the air, atoms of flesh and blood—this titan of forces, this indefinable dryad, if you will, which pulls masses together, expends tremendous energy to bind them into nuclear systems, and in the process makes the masses less massive.

Various names have been proposed for the new entity. One suggestion is that it be called the force of "levity," since the effect is to reduce the masses of the bound particles and, therefore, to make them lighter; but surely levity is not the most fundamental aspect of this tie that binds. Another suggestion is "supergravitation"; but the new-found force is so superlatively super that this title sounds makeshift. The thing has also been referred to as the force of "nucleation," suggesting its effect in causing elementary particles to consolidate their influences, to nucleate into atomic cores. Since the force manifests itself as the central force of all physical nature it deserves an unequivocal name.

We may surmise that gravitation, magnetism, and the electrical properties of attraction and repulsion are only special cases, or conditioned reflections, reactions, or interactions, of this mighty central Something that holds the world together.

And what shall we say of atomic power—that dream of the modern alchemists who have said that energy sufficient to propel an ocean liner across the Atlantic is locked within a teaspoon of water? Surely its secret lies here. Reckon the billions of billions of protons and neutrons contained in water, remember that each is bound to its neighbor with a force of millions of electron-volts, that proton is linked to proton as if with a pressure of many pounds, and sum up the total. If it were possible to treat a teaspoon of water expeditiously, to cause the protons of its hydrogen atoms to combine into more complex nuclear patterns and thus form atoms of heavier elements, the energy released in binding these interior particles together would total several hundred thousand kilowatt-hours — quite sufficient, if harnessed, to drive a steamship from New York to Havre. But we must admit that we know no means of harnessing the forces even if we were able to release them economically; and the plain fact is that our present methods of separating and synthesizing nuclear structures require more energy in the bombardment than we get back from the transmutations. The utilization of atomic energy is a goal for the future— as far as we can see to-day, for the very distant future—but a beginning has been made in the Washington experiments. The discovery and measurement of the forces provide a firmer basis for our dreamers and, let us hope, for our future engineers.

Dr. Tuve and his associates are planning deeper forays. In 1937 they began the construction of a new electrostatic generator and discharge tube designed to operate at potentials above 5,000,000 volts. Protons accelerated by this electrical pressure will hit the target with a velocity of 19,300 miles a second. The resulting momentum should carry the projectiles into the nuclear zones of massive atoms, such as those of the metals, whose inner cores present complexities in striking contrast with the simplicity of hydrogen. The problem is a peculiarly enticing one, and various laboratories in Europe and America are now engaged in a strong attack upon it. The frontiers have been crossed, but a vast hiddenness still awaits exploration. The nature of the internal structure, how the interior particles move and interact within their narrowly bounded zone, their degrees of freedom and compulsion—such questions beg for answers. There are inklings of news from within, fragmentary flashes of this and that, and theorists are never idle with their charming mathematical symbolism. But the ultimate battle must be won by the experimentalist. Theory must be tested and proved by experience before we can go in and possess the new land.

1937

MARGARET SCHLAUCH

Semantics: Vocabulary in Motion

From THE GIFT OF TONGUES

Extending the Use of Words

Among the words first taught to children by their doting parents are the terms for the parts of the human body. Pressing down the diminutive button-like protuberance which shows signs of one day becoming a full-blown human nose, mama asks beguilingly: "What is this?" The child, shrewd and skilled already in the enormous task of humoring grown-ups, but nevertheless somewhat confused by the rain of new terminology about him, looks up cooperatively and suggests with hope but little conviction: "Baby's ear." "Oh, no!" the mellifluous voice proceeds, while the pressure is still maintained, "Baby's nose. *Nose!*" And so the baffling epithet is learned, presumably for a lifetime.

From *The Gift of Tongues* by Margaret Schlauch. Copyright 1942 by The Viking Press, Inc., N. Y.

Now "nose" is a concrete term which will cause the child little trouble once he learns it, especially so long as he limits it to this bodily member of himself and his fellow human beings. He can even apply it to the corresponding members of familiar animals without being involved in confusion of meaning. This is also true of other members, such as eyes, ears, hands, elbows, knees, feet, and the rest. These elementary physiological identifications must give him a comfortable sense that things mean what they say. If we wish to amuse ourselves by speculating on the kinds of words which originated first in human speech, there is some reason for surmising that names for our bodily parts were among them.

But very soon in the life of a child comes the experience of metaphoric use. He is watching his mother peeling potatoes, and begins to be aware of their shape and texture. Pointing to the buds visible on the surface of the brown tuber he asks: "Mama, what are these?" She replies: "The eyes of the potato." This designation is unhesitatingly accepted. In the first place, the elliptical depressions surrounding potato buds actually resemble human eye-sockets in shape. There is enough physical similarity to make the poetic image acceptable in place of a name. Besides, the child is in no position—as yet—to observe the difference in functioning between vegetables and animals which would cause him to challenge the existence of eyes in a potato: real eyes, that is, with a potential power of vision. He can hardly ask: "But has the potato a nervous system?!" He still lives in the mysterious, animistic world of fairy-tales, in which sticks and stones, knives and forks, tables and chairs possess souls. In such a world inanimate objects may

confidently be expected to see and hear, to bless and curse, and in general to take definite attitudes of friendliness or hostility to little boys and girls. So it is not surprising if he pursues the subject of the potato-sprouts further and poses the (for him) quite logical question: "Then the Potato-man can *see* me?" This very plausible deduction is probably hailed by the mother with inner exultant glee. And aloud she may even go so far as to say: "Yes, if you're not good, the Potato-man will see you, *even in the dark* and at night he'll come for you, and *take you away.* . . ."

Thus metaphor is elevated into mythology. Fortunately for most children, these transparent lies are recognized at an early date. The slight change of tone that betrays them only complicates a bit more the day-long task of placating grown-ups. If the demonology of potatoes is taken too seriously, however, the results may be very serious. Those who have dealt with nervously maladjusted children are no doubt aware of the precise dangers involved. Considering the crude animism of the language surrounding children, it is a wonder that any of us escape undamaged!

Metaphoric Extension

When the bud of a potato is called an "eye," the designation is a metaphor. Physical similarity causes a transfer of an epithet originally clear, limited, and concrete in its application. A *semantic shift* has occurred, known as a simple transfer of meaning. It is useless to debate whether "eye" in the new context is a *new* word (in which case it should have been discussed under vocabulary and the creation of words) or not. In any event the application of the physical sound-symbol [ai] has widened. This is the extension of words to include new referents somehow resembling the original ones. Metaphor implies the perception of such resemblances. By means of this process meanings of words are constantly broadening and shifting. Here are some everyday examples:

Parts of the body are further used in references to many things which are themselves concrete and familiar. We speak of the "lip" and the "ears" of a cup, the "teeth" of a saw or a comb, the "legs" of tables and other immobile articles of furniture, the "elbows" of pipes and macaroni, the "hands" of a clock, the "tongue" of a balance or a bell, the "eye" of a needle, and the "head" of a hammer. When we travel we encounter the "foot" of a mountain, the "mouth" of a river, a "head"-land, the "shoulders" —even the "soft shoulders"—of a road, the "brow" of a hill, and the "neck" of the woods. The German speaks eloquently of a *Meeresbusen* ("bosom" of the sea or gulf). Slightly disguised from us today are the "core" (heart) of an apple—a Romance word; and "axle" (shoulder) of a wheel—cognate with German *Achsel*. In politics we hear of a "rump" session of parliament and a "head" of the state. Perhaps "ward-heeler" may be included here, though it is actually a compound.

Animal names and animal members appear in many of the least regarded units of our discourse. We have "wing" chairs and collars, clothes "horses," darning "eggs" and also "egg"-plants, the "fangs" of a machine, "goose-neck" lamps, "hare" lips, "rats" of hair. The last is, to be sure, dated; it was current only in the days when women wore pads of artificial hair to eke out what nature had given them. We refer ambiguously enough to the "cock" of a water-tap, the "beak" of a vessel, and the "crest" of a hill or wave. "Catspaw" is

more than a descriptive designation of an object similar to something else, and so presumably is "monkey wrench." Value judgments are tied up with both of these.

Plants and their parts give us the "nut" of a screw, a shoe "tree," the "stem" of a glass, and the "root" of a tooth or a cancerous growth. When we talk of the "root of the matter" we are already moving on a higher level of abstraction.

Tools and simple inventions have long supplied names for similar objects elsewhere. Carpentry and engineering use "pin" for very solid joiners; "table"-land (Spanish *mesa*) refers to plateaus; valleys have "cups"; roads and trees have "forks"; the arid section of the United States is called the "Dust Bowl." The parts of the human body are often described by simple figures taken from engineering. Thus we have the "bridge" of the nose, the "arch" of the foot, the "roof" of the mouth, the "canal" of a tooth. In addition there are vocal "cords," eye "lids," and "club" feet. Simple metaphor even furnished the names of three small bones in the middle ear: "hammer," "anvil," and "stirrup," and the ear "drum" itself. Parts of musical instruments are described in terms of simpler tools: pianos have "hammers" and "keys," violins have "bridges" and "bows" in a sense unknown to primitive warriors.

All workers in special crafts can surely augment this list. What has happened is of course that an elementary similarity in external aspect has caused a shift of the word to a new function.

Other shifts occur when words having to do with time relations are applied to space, or the reverse. Sometimes it is hard to tell which came first. We say "The tree stands *before* my house" and also "I did this *before* the spring house cleaning." Presumably one is a metaphoric application of the other. We transfer words describing impressions from one of the five senses, to make them apply to others. So it is quite usual to talk of a "sharp" tone, a "flat" taste, a "shrill" color, a "smooth" sensation of any sort. Finally, any of these physical terms can readily be applied to psychological states. "Bitter" grief is the kind that *bites* ("how sharper than a serpent's tooth . . ."); "anguish" is the kind that strangles, for the word is cognate with German *eng* and Latin *angustus* meaning "narrow, constricted." "Dreary" once meant "falling" or "dripping." Colors are taken to designate attributes of character: "He's *yellow,*" or "That's mighty *white* of you" (regional U.S.A. dialect) in English. German has an expression *einem grün sein* meaning to be favorable or devoted to someone else; and Russian uses derivatives of the word *krasnyi* (red) for adjectives to express pleasure and approbation. (This, by the way, has nothing to do with politics. It is an old semantic shift no doubt connected with that preference for bright colors evinced in peasant embroideries and woodwork.)

When these rather elemental shifts occur it is easy to trace their course and to understand their cause. Some, however, are the result of more intricate psychological readjustments.

Communication and Misunderstanding

Two human beings who talk together are accomplishing an act of "communication," as we defined it in the first chapter. Since the effort succeeds so well in most cases, we are apt to forget that the act is and must always be an approximation. To each of his friends, even to his closest *alter ego,* a man talks out of a private world of his own: the sum total of his memories and experiences. Persons strongly attracted to each other by the emotions are prone to attempt a more intimate approaching of the two worlds, so that by some kind of magic extension of personality each one may reach back into the early days of the other and build the same structure of experience. But despite the torrents of eloquence with which the miracle is sometimes attempted, the isolation remains a dreary fact.

The reason is simple. It is impossible for any two persons ever to have learned the same word under precisely the same circumstances; occupying, as it were, the same space in time, and apprehending the new term with precisely the same background. Therefore each will take it into his consciousness ringed about with a special context of associations, differing from the associations of everyone else hearing it. This is what Hermann Paul means when he says that each linguistic creation—and re-creation —is and remains the work of an individual. Yet procedures repeat themselves and approximations of understanding do occur. Our speech is a compromise between the ultimate incommunicability of one person with another and the conventional communication values attached to certain symbols.

Words and References

Let us pause a moment to analyze what happens to us in normal conversation when we employ terms for things. Suppose the subject talked about is a spider. When the word is pronounced the sounds will call up in the mind of the listener a general background of experience, not always very vivid, and not always involving a sharp photographic image of remembered spiders. The background of experience in the listener's mind is called by some writers the *reference,* as distinguished from the *referent,* or the real spider existing in the world outside ourselves. It is important to keep the three elements in the situation quite distinct:

The *word,* which is merely a symbol made up of sounds, like ['spaidə(ɹ)];
The *referent,* or concrete object (a living animal);
The *reference,* or recalled experience of past spiders evoked in the mind of the listener.

Under certain circumstances, however, an extremely vivid image is recalled in connection with a given word. The reference is sharpened. This happens especially when the referent is associated with a strong emotion like love or fear. But the same stimulus, the spoken word ['spaidə(ɹ)], may produce nothing but a vague reference in one listener while it evokes a sharp one in another. Their experiences are by no means identical.

Emotional Associations

For instance: when I first learned the word "spider," the circumstances were apparently tranquil. I had no cause for alarm, and my attention, so far as I recall, was chiefly captivated by the spinning activities of the creature. The word had no sinister connotations for me. A playmate of mine in those early days, however, must have learned the word under terrifying circumstances. She was never able to recall them or convey them to me in any way; but the mere pronunciation of the word (not to speak of the sight of an actual arachnidan creature) was enough to induce symptoms of panic amounting almost to a fit. If emotions may strongly color the reference of "spider," they may do so to some slight degree with less concrete terms such as "isosceles triangle." There is the illuminating story of a little girl who, having recently learned to read, was spelling out a political article in the newspaper. "Father," she asked, "what is Tammany Hall?" And father replied in the voice usually reserved for the taboos of social communication, "You'll understand that when you grow up, my dear." Acceding to this adult whim of evasion, she desisted from her inquiries; but something in Daddy's tone had convinced her that Tammany Hall must be connected with illicit *amour,* and for many years she could not hear this political institution mentioned without experiencing a secret non-political thrill. Another high school girl reports that the phrase "plane geometry" was first introduced to her in a context of deprecation, as applying to a science much less exciting and esoteric than something else (presumably "solid" geometry). So for a long time she understood "plane" in the sense of "plain" —a semantic confusion heightened by the homonyms of identical origin—appropriate for an unadorned Cinderella among the mathematical sisters; and it was only much later that she realized with a shock that the key word applied quite colorlessly to (imaginary) surfaces, having nothing to do with beauty or complexity.

With such varieties of individual experience in relation to words, there arise all sorts of *connotations,* as they are called, or nuances of association around the accepted factual definition. Some connotations (like the erotic aura around Tammany Hall for the little girl of our anecdote) remain strictly private and individual, the results of special accidents; others are coincidental for many persons and hence become currently attached to the word. If the sound-symbol is "spider," the situation can be thus represented:

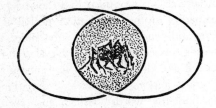

The unshaded sections in the ellipse of associations represent the special and private associations of the word due to the accidents of individual experience; the shaded portion represents a common store of connotations (tactile impressions approximately the same for anyone who has ever felt an arachnid crawl over his shin, generally current anecdotes or superstitions about spiders, etc.). In the heart of the overlapping associations is the word in its scientific sense: a designation of a biological type by (so far as possible) a colorless, unemotional scientific label. Even the label is a mere approximation of completely scientific denotation. The connotations cannot be kept away entirely, even from the abstract terms.

Changes in Meaning

The shaded matter of our diagram differs in all experiences of speaking and listening. The shifts and instabilities may be great or little, but they exist. When repeated experiences tend to push the territory of common connotations generally in the same directions, a change in meaning will occur. The semantic development is often gradual, but it may end in a great transformation of meaning eventually. The general direction of the change will be determined by the prejudices, preoccupations,

and interests prevailing over others in the community of speakers. Social tendencies appear more clearly in semantic than in phonetic change. This will be demonstrated more than once in the special types of change cited.

Pejorative change is one of the commonest and most readily observed. It means a degeneration in meaning from a comparatively noble and exalted significance to one of lower, if not downright contemptible or obscene, connotation. It has been suggested that there must be something groveling about human nature, since it has so often caused the besmirching of otherwise estimable terms. However, we must remember that here too the opposite of each tendency is perceptible concomitantly with it, and we must not despair too easily of any of the far-famed tendencies of human nature.

It is particularly words connected with sexual taboo and class snobbishness which tend to degenerate. Many words designating intimate articles of clothing have been shifted so often for this reason that it is difficult to keep abreast of them. So the homely "shirt" falls into disrepute and is replaced by "chemise." Speakers of the English language have often hidden behind an imported French word in order to spare their extremely delicate feelings. "Chemise" in its turn is either replaced by others still more vague, like "combination," or is eliminated entirely, together with the garment itself. The nether habiliments of gentlemen were at one time generally called "breeches"; later a sense of prudery caused this to be replaced by a loan word *pantaloons;* the new word was abbreviated to "pants," which quickly sank in the social scale and was superseded by "trousers." The corresponding diminutive garment of the ladies, formerly "pantalettes" or "panties" has shrunk to "step-ins," "scanties," and (adapting still another word from the masculine attire) "shorts."

In modern times many languages have witnessed a certain pejorative change in titles of class. "Sir," "lady," *monsieur, madame, Herr, Frau, señor, señora,* and the rest have lost their feudal connotations and are currently used for ordinary persons like you and me. "Bourgeois" too is by way of becoming a term of reproach after serving proudly the aspirations of a proud new class. In England, I am told, a wealthy club-*woman* speaks of her "char*lady*." The reverse was formerly true. Malodorous and sinister subjects quickly cast a pejorative pall over their vocabulary. "Slaughter-house" is avoided for *abattoir;* "undertaker" was originally adopted as a euphemism, but has itself been replaced by "funeral director." An endless source of examples is to be found in the shamefaced phrases by which civilized human beings try to gloss over "natural needs" while alluding to them obliquely. "Toilet," which at one time referred to the entire process of gowning and beautifying oneself for appearance in public, fell into disrepute because of one aspect of that preparation; it is now disappearing before various evasive expressions like "rest-room" (but who "rests" in such a place?), "powder room," "lounge," "lavatory" (a British term), and others due to the jocular originality of individual tavern keepers. Further examples of this sort of thing will be found in a later chapter. The reader may amuse himself by extending the list. Names for underlings, for inhabitants of the country (as opposed to the sophisticated city), for foreigners, for death and certain types of sickness, are particularly prone to de-generate. At certain periods of history when the dominant culture happened to be in the hands of a cynical and dissipated group, many of the most innocent words have suffered degeneration. Allardyce Nicoll reports that the society comedies of the Restoration period in England tended to vilify any and all words applied to woman, even the most sacred and dignified. To us innocents it must appear an incredible situation to find the words "sister" and even "mother" degenerated to pornographic significance as they were in the seventeenth century. In our day such pejorative modifications are more strictly confined to the underworld; they do not appear so baldly in our accepted literature.

Ameliorative change is an elevation in meaning. Here too some of the clearest examples are connected with social levels and class distinctions. A "marshal" once meant a lad who looked after mares —that is, a stable boy; a "bishop" was one who had the job of looking (Greek *skopein*) things over (*epi*)—that is, a humble "overseer." An "angel" was merely a messenger, no more exalted than one of our gray-clad postmen before the theologians took the term and exalted it by using it to designate intermediaries between divine intelligence and man's intelligence. A *cathedra* (from the Greek) was once an ordinary chair; now it is associated only with exalted dignitaries. The bishop's seat was his cathedral town. The papal "see," from Latin *sedes,* has made the original word too sacrosanct for ordinary use.

With the development of a modern mercantile culture, some adjectives not originally laudatory have assumed meliorative connotation. A "shrewd" person was once "wicked, rascally"; now he's admired because he can beat his neighbors in the game of competition.

A "smart" man, etymologically, is one to cause pain (think of German *Schmerz*); now we take our hats off to him. "Nimble" (from a verb *niman*) used to mean "good at taking things" as a pickpocket might be, but is now a synonym for general dexterity; "keen" meant "sharp," and both words have become terms of approval in the non-physical sphere; even "slick" contains overtones of admiration (albeit grudging), especially in America.

Narrowing or *restriction* of meaning occurs when a term that once applied to a general class of things is limited to special cases. This process often accompanies borrowing from one language to another. In Russian, *dog* doesn't mean the entire canine breed but only a great Dane; Russian *shtraf* (obviously taken from German) has narrowed from the sense of "punishment in general" to "money fine." Our word "corpse" is in origin identical with Latin *corpus,* meaning any sort of body, human or otherwise, alive or dead. Now it can only mean a cadaver or, as medical students would say, "a stiff." "Garage," a more recent loan word, comes from a French verbal noun originally meaning "place for storing anything," not exclusively automobiles. "Undertaker," already cited, shows narrowing as well as pejorative change. "See" as in "papal see" (quoted above) shows narrowing as well as ameliorative change.

Many words which were once abstract designations for a quality or a class have narrowed in the special direction of *concretization*. Latin *fructus* was once "the act of enjoying oneself"; now we limit "fruit" to the apples, pears, and oranges which help us to that desirable end in one definite form. Our word "city," designating a very tangible, visible, and in spots solid gathering of human beings, meant "quality of citizenship" when it was first created as Latin *civitas*. "Faculty," which for academicians evokes a group of learned gentlemen—with a few ladies sprinkled in—robed in scholastic cap and gown, once had only the vaguer sense of "the possibility of doing (*facere*) something." We still use the word in this earlier sense when we speak of a man's "faculty" of concentration, or other talent. The word "faction," too, could have been applied to any sort of "act of doing" (*facere*). Now it is restricted to political groups within a larger body. This specialized and concretized use appears quite early. On the walls of Pompeii there are inscriptions using the verb form of *facere* in a narrow, political sense which has been interpreted as "unite, get together." Thus *Caupones, facite! Pomari, facite! Lignari, facite! Unguentari, facite!* would mean: "Tradesmen, unite! Dealers in apples, wood, and perfumes, get together!" It all sounds very familiar.

Expansion is of course the opposite of restriction. A term for an individual is adopted for a class. This is exemplified, for instance, whenever a proper name or a patented trade name is extended to cover a whole group. Soon after the phonograph was invented, one particular make, the "victrola," was popularly universalized for all. "Lynch" and "dunce," as your dictionary will tell you, come from the names of individual persons now forgotten in the larger idea. A "barn" formerly meant a "barleyplace"; now it refers to a place of storage for all kinds of grain and for other things as well. "Box," once designating only receptacles made of *buxum* or boxwood, can now apply to all. "Manuscript" is often extended to cover material more accurately called "typescript."

Bréal records a curious instance from the Sanskrit. Here *go-shtha* meant "cow-place" literally, but was universalized for any kind of stable, so that it was later possible to speak of an *açva-go-shtha* or "horse-cow-place." (*Açva*, nominative *açvas*, is cognate with Latin *equus*.)

Within the general field of metaphorical change which we have already briefly discussed, it is possible to distinguish a number of special types. The shift may occur in the direction of *hyperbole*, or deliberate exaggeration, causing expressions of great strength to diminish toward feebleness. Most of our intensive words go this way. "Awfully," "enormously," "tremendously" are adverbs used for quite trivial matters now. The tendency is still more marked with the more transitory expressions of disapproval which never achieve the dignity of accepted usage. "Stinking," "lousy," "vile," "putrid" are a few of those which have been recently current on both sides of the Atlantic. Naturally one's ears become jaded by these excessive stimulants, and they are quickly discounted as hyperbolic exaggerations. On the other hand *litotes*, or understatement, occurs when a weak or colorless word assumes strength from special uses. Some recent examples are: "protective custody" (which sounds reassuring on the face of it); to "co-ordinate" (*gleichschalten*), which under certain circumstances means quite ruthless elimination of opposition; to "strafe," from German *strafen*, a simple word for "to punish," now assuming connotations of bombed cities and civilian terror.

Shift to Opposite Meanings

When words are falling into disuse they sometimes take on new meanings because of association with the few stereotyped phrases in which they survive. "Desultory reading" means "disjointed, skipping" sort of reading. It might in fact be quite feverish in tempo. But since the phrase is now felt to be primarily an opposite of "continuous, orderly, *purposeful* reading," it has assumed connotations of "lazy, relaxed," which were once foreign to it. Apparently it is natural for us to think of qualities in pairs —each one together with its opposite. When I say "bright" I am unconsciously thinking "not dark." As Jost Trier, a German scholar, expresses it concisely in a recent study: "Every word spoken evokes its own opposite meaning." We exclude the opposite while at the same time we are aware of it as a kind of negative definition. But one word may have a whole series of opposites, due to the accidents of association. It is thus that "desultory" comes to mean "lazy"— by negation of an opposite not originally associated with it. So a person who had only encountered "otiose" in the single phrase of disapproval, "otiose epithet," might assume it meant "not decent, not polite," whereas it means only "not accurate; not needed; lazy, superfluous, functionless."

By such elimination "egregious" has become petrified in a few phrases which not only limit but essentially change its earlier sense. It is a vivid compound in its origin, from Latin *ē, ex,* "out of," and *grex, gregis,* "a flock." A sheep that stood out from the rest of the flock was, literally, an "outstanding" sheep, equally so, whether for good or ill. But words in English with the sense of "outstanding, conspicuous" readily assume the sense of "immodest, blatant, ungentlemanly." (A gentleman observes a well-bred conformity with the herd.) In this particular word the pejorative tendency is strengthened by the limitation of its use to a few obsolescent phrases like "an egregious error" and "an egregious ass." Who has ever heard denizens of a conservative club (where the word is most apt to be used) speak of one with "egregious talent" or "egregious virtues"? No; a gentleman's chief virtue is to have nothing in excess. Thus the accidents of association surrounding a word rarely used have modified it so that it is now felt to describe qualities with which it originally had no concern. Another instructive example is the semantic shift in the word "meat." The archaic use, found in the phrases "bread and meat" and "meat and drink," shows that the word once had a more general scope than now. But by new associations, especially new ideas about the foods it was meant to *exclude,* it became the equivalent of "non-vegetable" as well as "non-liquid" nourishment. This in turn caused a displacement of "flesh," which had been commonly used for food in expressions like "flesh meat," but is now used alone for the muscular part of any animal body apart from (*excluding*) connotations of edibility. In Spanish *carne* means both "meat" and "flesh."

Meaning and Grammatical Use

Some of the processes here cited are sure to have an effect on syntax, as we shall see. For the moment let it suffice to point out that the key words we use to express grammatical relations have often reached their present function by some of the semantic changes here indicated. A single word with a restricted application may have its scope widened so that it does the work for a whole class. Our verb "do" substitutes for many others in allusive sentences. ("Does she play?" "No, she *doesn't.*") The English "more," once a designation for an increased amount of some physical quantity, is now widely employed as a mere device to make other adjectives comparative: "*more* beautiful," "*more* radiant," "*more* despicable." Its function has widened with its semantic widening. The same thing happened with the Romance languages, which took specific words like *magis* and *plus* and universalized them as signs of the comparative (Spanish *más,* French *plus*). Thus also do adverbs take on special functions as prepositions. In French, the grammatical form for negation has led to a curious transformation of positive terms into their opposites. There were expressions meaning "not a bit, not a step" (*ne . . . pas*), "not a thing" (*ne . . . rien*) and "not a person" (*ne . . . personne*). When part of a phrase or compound is suppressed and the remainder still has the meaning of the whole, we may call the process "shortening." But in abbreviated form, the very word meaning "not" (*ne*) might be suppressed, and the positive words for "thing" or "person" would still be felt to have negative significance. It is as if we changed "nobody" into ("body") and still felt it to be negative. That is why you say *personne* (literally "a person") in French if you wish to say "No one" in reply to a question like "Who is there?"

Semantic Archaisms

One special aspect of semantic change throws light on our earlier cultural history. When we invent new instruments we are apt to name them from something already known, thus continuing the elementary metaphors encountered by a child learning about "legs" of tables or "eyes" of potatoes. Or we name the new tool for materials long since superseded in the course of invention. This type of *substitution,* as it has been called, is a semantic change caused by changes in the outside world, not primarily by psychological factors. Yet it is impossible to separate the external and internal factors. Conservatism and inertia operate to keep our technological vocabulary archaic. We "sail" on boats which are innocent of sails. Little boys play with "marbles" which came from no quarries at all, since they are made of artificial compositions. Our "books" are so named from the "beech" tree, whose bark and branches once served for the scratching of early runes. Our "manuscripts" are no longer written by hand (*manus*) but by machine, as our "*manu*factured" products are made. Our "paper" is turned out from wood pulp, not from the papyrus reed for which it was once named. Our "pens" are no longer feathers (*pennae*). Our "pins" have little resemblance now to the primitive thorns (*spinae, spinulae;* cf. French *épingles*) once used to hold together the earliest garments of man. Yet the development from thorn to pin is clear. Some of the brooches of the early Irish, beautifully executed and elaborately designed as they were, show unmistakably the imitation of the original natural thorn.

Thus a little etymology helps us to go back quickly, by way of palpable semantic change, to the very dawn of history, to the cave dwellings of primitive man. You can try your own hand at some of this semantic paleontology by looking up a few key words in any good etymological dictionary. The German word *Wand,* for "wall," will show you that woven or wattled buildings persisted in Germanic territory into historical times. *Wand* is related to our verb "to wind" (German *winden*) by a change in the root vowel. It is still used to apply to walls of stone, brick and mortar, with steel frames as skeletons—as far removed as possible from primitive wattles!

The Study of Meanings

Fascinating as the study of semantics is, it is one of the branches of language most recently explored. Long after the details of sound change and sound correspondence had been elaborately catalogued, scholars were still comparatively indifferent to the problems of meaning. The pioneer study was made by Michel Bréal in his *Essai de Sémantique* (1897). At this late date it was actually necessary for Bréal to *create* the word he used to designate his study! His principles were almost exclusively derived from a study of the classical languages (Greek, Latin, Sanskrit), and he appeared to regard the principles as abstract characteristics of "the mind" such as "need for clearness." At first the study of semantics was in fact limited to historical etymology, and the attempts at elucidation were limited to some rather unsatisfactory phrases like Bréal's. The "tendencies" were deduced from etymologies in an abstract way at first, with little regard for social and other aspects of the human situations in which change occurred.

Since this pioneer work, increasing curiosity has been manifest about the external circumstances favoring change. There must be something in the cultural history of a people which will help us understand why *fertig,* which in German once meant "ready for a journey," now means "ready for anything"; or why Anglo-Saxon *ceorl,* which once meant a freeborn husbandman, later degenerated to "churl." Hans Sperber has recently stressed the affective or emotional aura surrounding words as used by individual speakers: the coloring which, it will be remembered, was so very strong when one child heard or used "spider," and so slight when others did. If this aura of emotional connotation happened to coincide with the general preoccupations of a group in a certain age, it tended to spread. An example would be the connotations of nobility and admiration which gathered around the figure of a man on horseback in the Middle Ages. Men elevated the Vulgar Latin word for a "nag" or "old horse," *caballus,* into a progenitor of words like *chivalry, cavalier, caballero.* The emotional aura did correspond with a dominant prejudice—at least as felt by the feudal rulers themselves. It is easy to imagine the aura of affective associations which led to the sad decline in the word "quean" (cognate with "queen"). A still more glaring example is the enormous shift from the Spanish word *negro,* referring to the color "black," to the Southern American "Nigger," with its connotations of contempt (whether good- or bad-natured), intimidation, and even terror. Here the aura of associations due to the ruling group has gathered so thickly that it has darkened the literal blackness of the original meaning still more—clearly in coincidence with the attitudes of a very definite ruling group, in a ruling age.

Other recent work has stressed the need of including the field of associations and related meanings in dealing with the history and significance of words. By discussing the semantics of groups taken together we can more readily see how the overlappings, gaps, and duplications within the field cause some words to expand in application, others to contract, and still others to vanish. Jost Trier (to whose work we have already referred) has done this for words relating to the field of intelligence

in Old and Middle High German texts. Another German scholar, W. Héraucourt, has recently made a semantic study of words for moral and ethical values in Chaucer. Such studies are more illuminating in many ways than an artificial isolation of individual words when their history is being discussed.

Popular Studies in Semantics

There has been, of late, a rather general flurry of popular interest in semantics, particularly in America. Many situations in the world about us have made people poignantly aware that they fail completely to understand each other even when they talk together volubly in the same language. The realization creates a sense of hurt loneliness, strongest in the least experienced persons. A moment's reflection shows that the counters of conversation most glibly employed, for instance in talk about politics, are the most ambiguous. The spheres of individual connotations (see the spider diagram) may overlap very slightly when terms like "dictatorship" are used. An optimist, struck by this fact, will quickly recover his good spirits and cry: "Very well, then; all we need is to get together and *define our terms.* Semantics—that's what we need!"

The solution, so expressed, sounds agreeably painless. The most obtuse observer will have guessed by now that there is something wrong with human affairs as we manage them, when they cause us to endure frequent major calamities like war, disease, and unemployment. How pleasant if it were only a matter of definitions!

For this reason, perhaps, one can understand the great popularity which has greeted a number of recent books on semantics written for the general public.

By implication at least they promise general solutions for social ills, and so their current success is quite understandable. They have created a certain interest in language problems which linguists may find gratifying; but on the other hand they leave the ordinary reader with an inaccurate impression that semantics—only a single aspect of linguistics, after all—is the *Open Sesame* of otherwise impenetrable problems in both language and sociology.

Non-Linguists on the Need for Semantic Clarity

The current interest was stimulated to a large degree by *The Meaning of Meaning,* published by C. K. Ogden and I. A. Richards in 1923. This book served the very useful function of indicating clearly the complicated nature of the general problem. Others have been impelled as a consequence to approach it from different special points of view. Professor P. W. Bridgman, for instance, has explained for the layman in his *Logic of Modern Physics* just what semantic changes are involved when a specialist in his field uses ordinary words like "time," "space," "identity," and the like. For him these terms have a significance quite different from that which we attach to them in our daily speech. The problem in meanings leads Professor Bridgman to propose a new technique in definitions, which he calls "operationalism." He draws certain sociological deductions from his method of definition in a second book, *The Intelligent Individual and Society.* His thesis is: "The concept is synonymous with the operations by which you test for it," as you test for weight in the laboratory. When he applies the method to social concepts his results are discouraging.

If you cannot test concepts like "democracy" or "duty" or "morality" by operations, he tells us, then they are "footless" (that is, meaningless) concepts, and should be abandoned. In the end nothing is left but the egocentric drives of the individuals constituting society.

The linguist and the sociologist alike may charge Bridgman with over-simplification. He has ignored the two-sided nature of a man's relation to the group, which is demonstrated afresh every time he learns and uses a new word. A speaker serves himself as well as the auditor both while he is listening and while he is speaking. The ability to talk withers and tends to die unless it is exercised in society. An equilibrium is desirable; the right degree of independence, the right degree of subordination, for linguistic fluency and presumably for health and social welfare also. It is true in particular of the creation of meanings by the collaboration of individual and group. When he talks about semantics, Bridgman overstresses the ego and understresses its necessary collaboration with others.

Thurman Arnold is another widely read non-linguist who deals with problems in semantics. Writing as a specialist in government and law, he discusses the problem of symbols, including words, and their power over us. In *The Folklore of Capitalism* he submits to sardonic and witty analysis the almost magic power of certain spell-binding references like "the founders of this country," "The Constitution," and "government interference in business." His thesis is that we are ruled by the manipulators of our symbols; and he leaves us with the uneasy sense that very little can be done about the frequent abuse of power by them, except tonic exercises in definition.

Semantic Study No Panacea

One of the most influential of non-linguists to write on semantics is Alfred Korzybski, perhaps because he has made the most extravagant promises in behalf of semantics as a panacea for human ills. Stripped of elaborate verbalization and repetition, his exhortations in *Science and Sanity* amount to a few salutary if not very original reminders: that the word—a symbol—is *not* the thing (that is, the referent); that we must distinguish sharply the levels of abstraction in the terms we use; that most of our social problems center around ambiguous "multiordinal" terms so interwoven with the emotions that our semantic reactions become tragically confused. Personal, national, and international maladjustments are reduced by Korzybski to "neuro-semantic" reactions needing re-education. "In our lives," he says, "most of our miseries do not originate in the field where the terms 'true' and 'false' apply, but in the field where they *do not apply;* namely, in the immense region of proportional function and meaninglessness, where agreement must fail." Symbols (like money, for instance) are described by Korzybski as high-power abstractions that rule our lives through the people who manipulate them. Like Arnold, Korzybski suggests that our problem is to find the right manipulators, but he throws little light on the burning question: How can we choose them, and how will they go to work on such important symbols as money?

A number of more recent writers depend directly on Korzybski and acknowledge their indebtedness to him. Stuart Chase, for instance, has undertaken to popularize the ideas of *Science and Sanity* in his *Tyranny of Words.* His enthusiasm for semantic exercise as a panacea is even more vocal than that of his predecessor. He repeatedly skirts the danger (when he does not fall headlong into it) of trying to exorcise critical practical issues by linguistic operations. His examples of the need for clarifying references and referents in law, economics, government, and sociology are most edifying, to be sure. But he also promises us too much in the way of automatic solutions to non-linguistic problems when once we have clarified the definitions and eliminated the meaningless terms.

Other disciples of Korzybski are more cautious in their promises. S. I. Hayakawa and Irving J. Lee both present useful popular texts explaining the principles of "neuro-semantics" for the layman. Their books give stimulating exercises to be worked out by the reader. The illustrations, taken from everyday life, are most instructive. The principles themselves, however, are less original than the authors appear to think. Exercises in denotative and connotative meaning have long been a part of college textbooks in rhetoric. Writers of Korzybski's school have made some contribution towards the techniques of definition by exploring some of the psychological aspects hitherto neglected. It is worth while to practice the techniques in their newer forms. Popular interest in them may be regarded as a gratifying sign of intellectual curiosity and alertness in the reading public. But readers at large may feel a corresponding disappointment, even despair, when they finally discover that semantic analysis will not solve their social problems for them after all.

Value of Semantic Studies

A student of language is apt to be more modest in his expectations and therefore less subject to disappointment than are the amateurs of popular semantics. There is no need to quit the subject on a note of complete skepticism. Even when we have discounted the exaggerated claims of the Korzybski school we may still concede the great importance and use of the study of meanings. Once the results of such study are before us, we naturally pose the question: What next? If irresponsible journalism, for instance, furnishes examples of deliberate confusion, deception by implication and connotation, and so on, what shall we do about it? Obviously it is not enough to point out the semantic malpractices.

The answer, says the linguist, lies outside my field. I do not offer solutions in my capacity as linguist. But I am glad to help my colleagues in journalism, economics, and sociology when they deal with linguistic material. And I may even act with them after the study has been made; but in that event we shall all be acting together as citizens anxious to correct an abuse. We shall

have left our studies and laboratories to participate in the affairs of the market place.

In the end, linguists will gain and give most in this field when they unite the traditional scrupulous regard for scientific method with vivid and realistic awareness of social milieu and its challenging problems. To do this they will have to receive help from, as well as give it to, other disciplines such as sociology and psychology. Teachers of language can fructify their material by availing themselves of pertinent discoveries in the adjacent territories. No part of language study, indeed, offers better occasion for scientific collaboration than the investigation of meanings against a social background. The practical effectiveness of this study will be increased rather than diminished when the popular writers limit their claims to the real advantages to be derived from it, without promising social panaceas in addition.

1942

MORTIMER J. ADLER

The Reading of "Reading"

FROM HOW TO READ A BOOK

ONE OF THE primary rules for reading anything is to spot the most important words the author uses. Spotting them is not enough, however. You have to know how they are being used. Finding an important word merely begins the more difficult search for the

meanings, one or more, common or special, which the word is used to convey as it appears here and there in the text.

You already know that "reading" is one of the most important words in this book. But, as I have already suggested, it is a word of many meanings. If you take for granted that you know what I mean by the word, we are likely to get into difficulties before we proceed much further.

This business of using language to talk about language—especially if one is campaigning against its abuse—is risky. Recently Mr. Stuart Chase wrote a book which he should have called *Words About Words*. He might then have avoided the barb of the critics who so quickly pointed out that Mr. Chase himself was subject to the tyranny of words. Mr. Chase recognized the peril when he said, "I shall frequently be caught in my own trap by using bad language in a plea for better."

Can I avoid such pitfalls? I am writing about reading, and so it would appear that I do not have to obey the rules of reading but of writing. My escape may be more apparent than real, if it turns out that a writer should keep in mind the rules which govern reading. You, however, are reading about reading. You cannot escape. If the rules of reading I am going to suggest are sound, you must follow them in reading this book.

But, you will say, how can we follow the rules until we learn and understand them? To do that we shall have to read some part of this book without knowing what the rules are. The only way I know to help you out of this dilemma is by making you reading-conscious readers as we proceed. Let us start at once by applying the rule about *finding and interpreting the important words*.

When you set out to investigate the various senses of a word, it is usually wise to begin with a dictionary and your own knowledge of common usage. If you looked up "read" in the large Oxford Dictionary, you would find, first,

that the same four letters constituted an obsolete noun referring to the fourth stomach of a ruminant, and the commonly used verb which refers to a mental activity involving words or symbols of some sort. You would know at once that we need not bother with the obsolete noun except, perhaps, to note that reading has something to do with rumination. You would discover next that the verb has twenty-one more or less closely related meanings, more or less common.

One uncommon meaning of "to read" is to think or suppose. This meaning passes into the more usual one of conjecturing or predicting, as when we speak of reading the stars, one's palm, or one's future. That leads eventually to the meaning of the word in which it refers to perusing books or other written documents. There are many other meanings, such as verbal utterance (when an actress reads her lines for the director); such as detecting what is not perceptible from what is (when we say we can read a person's character in his face); such as instruction, academic or personal (when we have someone read us a lecture).

The slight variations in usage seem endless: a singer reads music; a scientist reads nature; an engineer reads his instruments; a printer reads proof; we read between the lines; we read something into a situation, or someone out of the party.

We can simplify matters by noting what is common to many of these senses; namely, that mental activity is involved and that, in one way or another, symbols are being interpreted. That imposes a first limitation on our use of the word. We are not concerned with a part of the intestinal tract, nor are we concerned with enunciation, with speaking something out loud. A second limitation is needed, because we shall not consider—except for some points of comparison—the interpretation, clairvoyant or otherwise, of natural signs such as stars, hands, or faces. We shall limit ourselves to one kind of readable symbol, the kind which men invent for the purposes of communication—the words of human language. This eliminates the reading of other artificial signs such as the pointers on dials of physical apparatus, thermometers, gauges, speedometers, and so forth.

Henceforth, then, you must read the word "reading," as it occurs in this text, to refer to the process of interpreting or understanding what presents itself to the senses in the form of words or other sensible marks. This is not arbitrary legislation about what the word "reading" *really* means. It is simply a matter of defining our problem, which is reading in the sense of receiving communication.

Unfortunately, that is not simple to do, as you would realize at once if someone asked: "What about listening? Isn't that receiving communication, too?" I shall subsequently discuss the relation of reading and listening, for the rules of good reading are for the most part the rules of good listening, though perhaps harder to apply in the latter case. Suffice it for the present to distinguish reading from listening by restricting the communication being received to what is written or printed rather than spoken.

I shall try to use the word "reading" in the limited and special sense noted. But I know that I will not succeed without exception. It will be impossible to avoid using the word in some of its other senses. Sometimes I shall be thoughtful enough to mention explicitly that I am

shifting the meaning. Other times I may suppose that the context is sufficient warning to you. Infrequently (I hope) I may shift the meaning without being aware of it myself.

Be stout, gentle reader, for you are just beginning. What has gone before is just preliminary to finding out the even *narrower* sense in which the word "reading" will be used. We must now face the problem which the first chapter indicated. We must distinguish between the sense in which you can read this book, for instance, and are now doing so, and the sense in which you may learn from it to read better or differently than you now can.

Notice that I said "better" *or* "differently." The one word points to a difference in *degrees* of ability, the other to a distinction in *kinds*. I suspect we shall find that the better reader can also do a different *kind* of reading. The poorer can probably do only one kind—the simplest kind. Let us first examine the range of ability in reading to determine what we mean by "better" and "poorer."

One obvious fact shows the existence of a wide range of degrees in ability to read. It is that reading begins in the primary grades and runs through every level of the educational system. Reading is the first of the three R's. It is first because we have to learn to read in order to learn by reading. Since what we have to learn, as we ascend in our education, becomes more difficult or complex, we must improve our ability to read proportionately.

Literacy is everywhere the primary mark of education, but it has many degrees, from grammar-school diploma, or even less, up to a bachelor's degree or a Ph.D. But, in his recent commentary on American democracy, called *Of Human Freedom,* Jacques Barzun cautions us not to be misled by the boast that we have the most literate population in the world. "Literacy in this sense is not education; it is not even 'knowing how to read' in the sense of taking in quickly and correctly the message of the printed page, to say nothing of exercising a critical judgment upon it."

Supposedly, *gradations* in reading go along with *graduations* from one educational level to another. In the light of what we know about American education today, that supposition is not well founded. In France it is still true that the candidate for the doctor's degree must show an ability to read sufficient to admit him to that higher circle of literacy. What the French call *explication de texte* is an art which must be practiced at every educational level and in which improvement must be made before one moves up the scale. But in this country there is often little discernible difference between the *explication* which a high-school student would give and one by a college senior or even a doctoral candidate. When the task is to read a book, the high-school students and college freshmen are often better, if only because they are less thoroughly spoiled by bad habits.

The fact that there is something wrong with American education, so far as reading is concerned, means only that the gradations have become obscure for us, not that they do not exist. Our task is to remove that obscurity. To make the distinction in grades of reading sharper, we must define the criteria of better and worse.

What are the criteria? I think I have already suggested what they are, in the previous chapter. Thus, we say that one man is a better reader than another if he can read more difficult material. Anyone would agree, if Jones is able to read only such things as newspapers and magazines, whereas Brown can read the best current nonfiction books, such as Einstein and Infeld's *Evolution of Physics* or Hogben's *Mathematics for the Millions,* that Brown has more ability than Jones. Among readers at the Jones level, further discrimination may be made between those who cannot rise above the tabloids and those who can master *The New York Times.* Between the Jones group and the Brown group, there are still others measured by the better and worse magazines, better and worse current fiction, or by nonfiction books of a more popular nature than Einstein or Hogben, such as Gunther's *Inside Europe* or Heiser's *An American Doctor's Odyssey.* And better than Brown is the man who can read Euclid and Descartes as well as Hogben, or Galileo and Newton as well as Einstein and Infeld's discussion of them.

The first criterion is an obvious one. In many fields we measure a man's skill by the difficulty of the task he can perform. The accuracy of such measurement depends, of course, on the independent precision with which we can grade the tasks in difficulty. We would be moving in circles if we said, for instance, that the more difficult book is one which only the better reader can master. That is true, but not helpful. In order to understand what makes some books more difficult to read than others, we would have to know what demands they make on the skill of the reader. If we knew that, we would know what distinguishes better and worse readers. In other words, the difficulty of the reading matter is a convenient, objective sign of degrees of reading ability, but it does not tell us what the difference is in the reader, so far as his skill is concerned.

The first criterion has some use, nevertheless, to whatever extent it is true that the more difficult a book is the fewer readers it will have at any given time. There is some truth in this, because it is generally the case that, as one mounts the scale of excellence in any skill, the number of practitioners diminishes: the higher, the fewer. Counting noses, therefore, gives us some independent indication of whether one thing is more difficult to read than another. We can construct a crude scale and measure men accordingly. In a sense, that is the way all the scales, which employ reading tests made by the educational psychologists, are constructed.

The second criterion takes us further, but is harder to state. I have already suggested the distinction between active and passive reading. Strictly, all reading is active. What we call passive is simply less active. Reading is better or worse according as it is more or less active. And one reader is better than another in proportion as he is capable of a greater range of activity in reading. In order to explain this point, I must first be sure that you understand why I say that, strictly speaking, there is no absolutely passive reading. It only seems that way in contrast to more active reading.

No one doubts that writing and speaking are active undertakings, in which the writer or speaker is clearly doing something. Many people seem to think, however, that reading and listening are entirely passive. No work need be done. They think of reading and listening as *receiving* communication from someone who is actively *giving* it. So far they are right, but then they make the error of supposing that receiving communica-

tion is like receiving a blow, or a legacy, or a judgment from the court.

Let me use the example of baseball. Catching the ball is just as much an activity as pitching or hitting it. The pitcher or batter is the *giver* here in the sense that his activity initiates the motion of the ball. The catcher or fielder is the *receiver* in the sense that his activity terminates it. Both are equally active, though the activities are distinctly different. If anything is passive here, it is the ball: it is pitched and caught. It is the inert thing which is put in motion or stopped, whereas the living men are active, moving to pitch, hit, or catch. The analogy with writing and reading is almost perfect. The thing which is written and read, like the ball, is the passive object in some way common to the two activities which begin and terminate the process.

We can go a step further with this analogy. A good catcher is one who stops the ball which has been hit or pitched. The art of catching is the skill of knowing how to do this as well as possible in every situation. So the art of reading is the skill of catching every sort of communication as well as possible. But the reader as "catcher" is more like the fielder than the man behind the plate. The catcher signals for a particular pitch. He knows what to expect. In a sense, the pitcher and catcher are like two men with but a single thought before the ball is thrown. Not so, however, in the case of the batter and fielder. Fielders may wish that batters would obey signals from them, but that isn't the way the game is played. So readers may sometimes wish that writers would submit completely to their desires for reading matter, but the facts are usually otherwise. The reader has to go after what comes out into the field.

The analogy breaks down at two points, both of which are instructive. In the first place, the batter and the fielder, being on opposite sides, do not have the same end in view. Each thinks of himself as successful only if he frustrates the other. In contrast, pitcher and catcher are successful only to the extent that they co-operate. Here the relation of writer and reader is more like that between the men on the battery. The writer certainly isn't trying *not to be caught,* although the reader may often think so. Successful communication occurs in any case where what the writer wanted to have received finds its way into the reader's possession. The writer's and the reader's skill converge upon a common end.

In the second place, the ball is a simple unit. It is either *completely* caught or not. A piece of writing, however, is a complex object. It can be received more or less completely, all the way from very little of what the writer intended to the whole thing. The amount the reader gets will usually depend on the amount of activity he puts into the process, as well as upon the skill with which he executes the different mental acts that are involved.

Now we can define the second criterion for judging reading ability. Given the same thing to read, one man reads it better than another, first, by reading it more actively, and second, by performing each of the acts involved more successfully. These two things are related. Reading is a complex activity, just as writing is. It consists of a large number of separate acts, all of which must be performed in a good reading. Hence, the man who can perform more of these various acts is better able to read.

I have not really told you what good and bad reading are. I have talked about the differences only in a vague and general way. Nothing else is possible here. Until you know the rules which a good reader must follow, you will not be able to understand what is involved.

I know of no short cut by which you can be shown *now,* clearly and in detail, what I hope you will see before you have finished. You may not see it even then. Reading a book on how to play tennis may not be sufficient to make you perceive *from the side lines* the various shades of skill in playing. If you stay on the side lines, you will never know how it feels to play better or worse. Similarly, you have to put the rules of reading into practice before you are really able to understand them and competent to judge your own accomplishment or that of others.

But I can do one thing more here which may help you get the feel of what reading is. I can distinguish different types of reading for you.

I discovered this way of talking about reading under the dire necessity which a lecture platform sometimes imposes. I was lecturing about education to three thousand schoolteachers. I had reached the point where I was bemoaning the fact that college students couldn't read and that nothing was being done about it. I could see from their faces that they didn't know what I was talking about. Weren't they teaching the children how to read? In fact, that was being done in the very lowest grades. Why should I be asking that four years of college be spent primarily in learning to read and in reading great books?

Under the provocation of their general incredulity, and their growing impatience with my nonsense, I went further. I said that most people could not read.

that many university professors I knew could not, that probably my audience could not read either. The exaggeration only made matters worse. They knew they could read. They did it every day. What in the world was this idiot on the platform raving about? Then it was that I figured out how to explain. In doing so, I distinguished two *kinds* of reading.

The explanation went something like this. Here is a book, I said, and here is your mind. The book consists of language written by someone for the sake of communicating something to you. Your success in reading is determined by the extent to which you get all that the writer intended to communicate.

Now, as you go through the pages, either you understand perfectly everything the author has to say or you do not. If you do, you may have gained information, but you could not have increased your understanding. If, upon effortless inspection, a book is completely intelligible to you, then the author and you are as two minds in the same mold. The symbols on the page merely express the common understanding you had before you met.

Let us take the second alternative. You do not understand the book *perfectly at once.* Let us even assume—what unhappily is not always true—that you understand enough to know that you do not understand it all. You know there is more in the book than you understand and, hence, that the book contains something which can increase your understanding.

What do you do then? You can do a number of things. You can take the book to someone else who, you think, can read better than you, and have him explain the parts that troubled you. Or

you can get him to recommend a textbook or commentary which will make it all plain by telling you what the author meant. Or you may decide, as many students do, that what's over your head isn't worth bothering about, that you understand enough, and the rest doesn't matter. If you do any of these things, you are not doing the job of reading which the book requires.

That is done in one way only. Without external help, you take the book into your study and work on it. With nothing but the power of your own mind, you operate on the symbols before you in such a way that you gradually lift yourself from a state of understanding less to one of understanding more. Such elevation, accomplished by the mind working on a book, is reading, the kind of reading that a book which challenges your understanding deserves.

Thus I roughly defined what I meant by reading: the process whereby a mind, with nothing to operate on but the symbols of the readable matter, and with no help from outside, elevates itself by the power of its own operations. The mind passes from understanding less to understanding more. The operations which cause this to happen are the various acts which constitute the art of reading. "How many of these acts do you know?" I asked the three thousand teachers. "What things would you do by yourself if your life depended on understanding something readable which at first perusal left you somewhat in the dark?"

Now their faces frankly told a different story. They plainly confessed that they wouldn't know what to do. They signified, moreover, that they would be willing to admit there was such an art and that some people must possess it.

Clearly not all reading is of the sort

I have just described. We do a great deal of reading by which we are in no way *elevated,* though we may be informed, amused, or irritated. There would appear to be several types of reading: for information, for entertainment, for understanding. This sounds at first as if it were only a difference in the purpose with which we read. That is only partly so. In part, also, it depends on a difference in the thing to be read and the way of reading it. You cannot gain much information from the funny sheet or much intellectual elevation from an almanac. As the things to be read have different values, we must use them accordingly. We must satisfy each of our different purposes by going to the right sort of material for each. More than that, we must know how to satisfy our purposes by being able to read each sort of material appropriately.

Omitting, for the present, reading for amusement, I wish to examine here the other two main types: reading for information and reading to understand more. I think you will see the relation between these two types of reading and the degrees of reading ability. The poorer reader is usually able to do only the first sort of reading: for information. The better reader can do that, of course, and more. He can increase his understanding as well as his store of facts.

To pass from understanding less to understanding more, by your own intellectual effort in reading, is something like pulling yourself up by your bootstraps. It certainly feels that way. It is a major exertion. Obviously, it would be a more active kind of reading, entailing not only more varied activity but more skill in the performance of the various acts required. Obviously, too, the things which are usually regarded as

more difficult to read, and hence only for the better reader, are those which are most likely to deserve and demand this type of reading.

Things you can comprehend without effort, such as magazines and newspapers, require a minimum of reading. You need very little art. You can read in a relatively passive way. For everyone who can read at all, there is some material of this sort, though it may be different for different individuals. What for one man requires no or little effort may demand genuine exertion from another. How far any man may get by expending every effort will depend on how much skill he has or is able to acquire, and that is somehow relative to his native intelligence.

The point, however, is not to distinguish good and bad readers according to the favors or deprivations of birth. The point is that for each individual there exist two sorts of readable matter: on the one hand, something which he can read effortlessly to be informed, because it communicates nothing which he cannot immediately comprehend; on the other, something which is above him, in the sense of challenging him to make the effort to understand. It may, of course, be too far above him, forever beyond his grasp. But this he cannot tell until he tries, and he cannot try until he develops the art of reading—the skill to make the effort.

Most of us do not know what the limits of our comprehension are. We have never tried our powers to the full. It is my honest belief that *almost all of the great books in every field are within the grasp of all normally intelligent men,* on the condition, of course, that they acquire the skill necessary for reading them and make the effort. Of course, those more favored by birth will reach the goal more readily, but the race is not always to the swift.

There are several minor points here which you must observe. It is possible to be mistaken in your judgment of something you are reading. You may think you understand it, and be content with what you get from an effortless reading, whereas in fact much may have escaped you. The first maxim of sound practice is an old one: the beginning of wisdom is a just appraisal of one's ignorance. So the beginning of reading as a conscious effort to understand is an accurate perception of the line between what is intelligible and what is not.

I have seen many students read a difficult book just as if they were reading the sports page. Sometimes I would ask at the beginning of a class if they had any questions about the text, if there was anything they did not understand. Their silence answered in the negative. At the end of two hours, during which they could not answer the simplest questions leading to an interpretation of the book, they would admit their deficiency in a puzzled way. They were puzzled because they were quite honest in their belief that they had read the text. They had, indeed, but not in the right way.

If they had allowed themselves to be puzzled *while* reading, instead of after the class was over; if they had encouraged themselves to note the things they did not understand, instead of putting such matters immediately out of mind, almost in shame and embarrassment, they might have discovered that the book in front of them was different from their usual diet.

Let me summarize now the distinction between these two types of reading. We shall have to consider both because

the line between what is readable in one way and what must be read in the other is often hazy. To whatever extent we can keep the two kinds of reading distinct, we can use the word "reading" in two distinct senses.

The first sense is the one in which we speak of ourselves as reading newspapers, magazines, or anything else which, according to our skill and talents, is at once thoroughly intelligible to us. Such things may increase the store of information we remember, but they cannot improve our understanding, for our understanding was equal to them before we started. Otherwise, we would have felt the shock of puzzlement and perplexity which comes from getting in over our depth—that is, if we were both alert and honest.

The second sense is the one in which I would say a man has to read something that at first he does not completely understand. Here the thing to be read is initially better than the reader. The writer is communicating something which can increase the reader's understanding. Such communication between unequals must be possible, or else one man could never learn from another, either through speech or writing. Here by "learning" I mean understanding more, not remembering more information which has the same degree of intelligibility as other information you already possess.

There is clearly no difficulty about getting new information in the course of reading if, as I say, the novel facts are of the same sort as those you already know, so far as their intelligibility goes. Thus, a man who knows some of the facts of American history and understands them in a certain light can readily acquire by reading, in the first sense, more such facts and understand them in the same light. But suppose he is reading a history which seeks not merely to give him some more facts but to throw a new and, perhaps, more profound light on all the facts he knows. Suppose there is greater understanding here than he possesses before he starts to read. If he can manage to acquire that greater understanding, he is reading in the second sense. He has literally elevated himself by his own activity, though indirectly, of course, this was made possible by the writer who had something to teach him.

What are the conditions under which this kind of reading takes place? There are two. In the first place, there is initial inequality in understanding. The writer must be superior to the reader, and his book must convey in readable form the insights he possesses and his potential readers lack. In the second place, the reader must be able to overcome this inequality in some degree, seldom perhaps fully, but always approaching equality with the writer. To the extent that equality is approached, the communication is perfectly consummated.

In short, we can learn only from our betters. We must know who they are and how to learn from them. The man who has this sort of knowledge possesses the art of reading in the sense with which I am especially concerned. Everyone probably has some ability to read in this way. But all of us, without exception, can learn to read better and gradually gain more by our efforts through applying them to more rewarding materials.

1940

ARNOLD BENNETT

Why a Classic Is a Classic

FROM LITERARY TASTE: HOW TO FORM IT

THE LARGE majority of our fellow-citizens care as much about literature as they care about aeroplanes or the programme of the Legislature. They do not ignore it; they are not quite indifferent to it. But their interest in it is faint and perfunctory; or, if their interest happens to be violent, it is spasmodic. Ask the two hundred thousand persons whose enthusiasm made the vogue of a popular novel ten years ago what they think of that novel now, and you will gather that they have utterly forgotten it, and that they would no more dream of reading it again than of reading Bishop Stubbs's *Select Charters*. Probably if they did read it again they would not enjoy it—not because the said novel is a whit worse now than it was ten years ago; not because their taste has improved—but because they have not had sufficient practice to be able to rely on their taste as a means of permanent pleasure. They simply don't know

From *Literary Taste: How to Form It* by Arnold Bennett, copyright 1927, by Doubleday & Company, Inc.

from one day to the next what will please them.

In the face of this one may ask: Why does the great and universal fame of classical authors continue? The answer is that the fame of classical authors is entirely independent of the majority. Do you suppose that if the fame of Shakespeare depended on the man in the street it would survive a fortnight? The fame of classical authors is originally made, and it is maintained, by a passionate few. Even when a first-class author has enjoyed immense success during his lifetime, the majority have never appreciated him so sincerely as they have appreciated second-rate men. He has always been reinforced by the ardour of the passionate few. And in the case of an author who has emerged into glory after his death the happy sequel has been due solely to the obstinate perseverance of the few. They could not leave him alone; they would not. They kept on savouring him, and talking about him, and buying him, and they generally behaved with such eager zeal, and they were so authoritative and sure of themselves, that at last the majority grew accustomed to the sound of his name and placidly agreed to the proposition that he was a genius; the majority really did not care very much either way.

And it is by the passionate few that the renown of genius is kept alive from one generation to another. These few are always at work. They are always rediscovering genius. Their curiosity and enthusiasm are exhaustless, so that there is little chance of genius being ignored. And, moreover, they are always working either for or against the verdicts of the majority. The majority can make a reputation, but it is too careless to maintain it. If, by accident, the passionate few agree with the majority in a particular instance, they will frequently remind the majority that such and such a reputation has been made, and the majority will idly concur: "Ah, yes. By the way, we must not forget that such and such a reputation exists." Without that persistent memory-jogging the reputation would quickly fall into the oblivion which is death. The passionate few only have their way by reason of the fact that they are genuinely interested in literature, that literature matters to them. They conquer by their obstinacy alone, by their eternal repetition of the same statements. Do you suppose they could prove to the man in the street that Shakespeare was a great artist? The said man would not even understand the terms they employed. But when he is told ten thousand times, and generation after generation, that Shakespeare was a great artist, the said man believes—not by reason, but by faith. And he too repeats that Shakespeare was a great artist, and he buys the complete works of Shakespeare and puts them on his shelves, and he goes to see the marvellous stage-effects which accompany *King Lear* or *Hamlet,* and comes back religiously convinced that Shakespeare was a great artist. All because the passionate few could not keep their admiration of Shakespeare to themselves. This is not cynicism; but truth. And it is important that those who wish to form their literary taste should grasp it.

What causes the passionate few to make such a fuss about literature? There can be only one reply. They find a keen and lasting pleasure in literature. They enjoy literature as some men enjoy beer. The recurrence of this pleasure naturally keeps their interest in literature very much alive. They are for ever making new researches, for ever practising on themselves. They learn to understand themselves. They learn to know what they want. Their taste becomes surer and surer as their experience lengthens. They do not enjoy to-day what will seem tedious to them tomorrow. When they find a book tedious, no amount of popular clatter will persuade them that it is pleasurable; and when they find it pleasurable no chill silence of the street-crowds will affect their conviction that the book is good and permanent. They have faith in themselves. What are the qualities in a book which give keen and lasting pleasure to the passionate few? This is a question so difficult that it has never yet been completely answered. You may talk lightly about truth, insight, knowledge, wisdom, humour, and beauty. But these comfortable words do not really carry you very far, for each of them has to be defined, especially the first and last. It is all very well for Keats in his airy manner to assert that beauty is truth, truth beauty, and that that is all he knows or needs to know. I, for one, need to know a lot more. And I never shall know. Nobody, not even Hazlitt nor Sainte-Beuve, has ever finally explained why he thought a book beautiful. I take the first fine lines that come to hand—

The woods of Arcady are dead,
And over is their antique joy—

and I say that those lines are beautiful because they give me pleasure. But why? No answer! I only know that the passionate few will, broadly, agree with me in deriving this mysterious pleasure from those lines. I am only

convinced that the liveliness of our pleasure in those and many other lines by the same author will ultimately cause the majority to believe, by faith, that W. B. Yeats is a genius. The one reassuring aspect of the literary affair is that the passionate few are passionate about the same things. A continuance of interest does, in actual practice, lead ultimately to the same judgments. There is only the difference in width of interest. Some of the passionate few lack catholicity, or, rather, the whole of their interest is confined to one narrow channel; they have none left over. These men help specially to vitalise the reputations of the narrower geniuses: such as Crashaw. But their active predilections never contradict the general verdict of the passionate few; rather they reinforce it.

A classic is a work which gives pleasure to the minority which is intensely and permanently interested in literature. It lives on because the minority, eager to renew the sensation of pleasure, is eternally curious and is therefore engaged in an eternal process of rediscovery. A classic does not survive for any ethical reason. It does not survive because it conforms to certain canons, or because neglect would not kill it. It survives because it is a source of pleasure, and because the passionate few can no more neglect it than a bee can neglect a flower. The passionate few do not read "the right things" because they are right. That is to put the cart before the horse. "The right things" are the right things solely because the passionate few *like* reading them. Hence—and I now arrive at my point—the one primary essential to literary taste is a hot interest in literature. If you have that, all the rest will come. It matters nothing that at present you fail to find pleasure in certain classics. The driving impulse of your interest will force you to acquire experience, and experience will teach you the use of the means of pleasure. You do not know the secret ways of yourself: that is all. A continuance of interest must inevitably bring you to the keenest joys. But, of course, experience may be acquired judiciously or injudiciously, just as Putney may be reached *via* Walham Green or *via* St. Petersburg.

1909

ROBERT GRAVES AND ALAN HODGE

Recent Prose

From THE READER OVER YOUR SHOULDER

MIDDLE-CLASS family life was the subject of most early and middle-nineteenth century novels that were not Gothic tales of mystery and horror, or calmer, historical novels of the Sir Walter Scott, Harrison Ainsworth school. Though the novelists often introduced moral teaching and pleas for social reform into their stories, they were chiefly concerned with the delineation of character and the development of plot. This realism was a safeguard against over-elaborate writing, although the plain style was now regarded as 'low' even by the village constable. It was a heavily emotional realism, however, because a new emphasis upon the duty of showing mercy and charity toward the unfortunate had made pathos as highly esteemed as wit had formerly been.

There had been no sudden revolution in England as there had been in France, but successive agitations in favour of particular reforms; and these were usually prompted as much by humanitarian as by political feelings. The new industrial middle classes were enjoying a prudently guarded opulence, and at the same time, in manufacturing districts there was poverty and misery on a scale that had not been known in England since the Black Death. The middle classes felt collectively, though not individually, responsible for this state of affairs, and from their guilty humanitarianism grew numerous movements for piece-meal social reform and numerous minor philanthropic institutions. The equalitarian arguments that had brought about the French Revolution were used, in a modified form, to bring about such reforms as the abolition of slavery under the British flag; but the feelings which made them possible derived rather from the Christian charity insisted on by the Methodists, and other evangelical reformers of the period, than from equalitarianism.

The severity shown by the new religious spirit against idle and lascivious reading, especially on a Sunday, compelled popular novelists to turn humanitarian; and besides the naturally poor and oppressed, their pity had to take in

From Robert Graves and Alan Hodge, *The Reader Over Your Shoulder*. By permission of The Macmillan Company, publishers.

all those who came to moral or financial grief. The strict and sedate code of behaviour that had supervened on the lax and reckless Regency code was two-sided: public opinion first struck down all who failed to meet their social obligations, then pitied them as they lay bleeding. All personal and social problems were seen through a haze of sympathy, which was, however, not allowed to obscure the harshness of moral censure. Women, children and the poor were weaker vessels, particularly liable to sin and misfortune; when they fell, and were hurried away into charitable quarantine, the blame for their miserable fate was conscientiously laid on the defects of social circumstances.

In Thackeray's novels, pathos is usually an undertone, only occasionally rising to a loud throb, as in this passage from *Vanity Fair,* 1848:

'She was wrapped in a white morning dress, her hair falling on her shoulders and her large eyes fixed and without light. By way of helping on the preparations for the departure, and showing that she too could be useful at a moment so critical, this poor soul had taken up a sash of George's from the drawers whereon it lay and followed him to and fro, with the sash in her hand, looking on mutely while the packing proceeded. She came out and stood leaning at the wall, holding this sash against her bosom, from which the heavy net of crimson dropped like a large stain of blood.'

Several devices here raise the tone of the passage from sadness to pathos. 'Large eyes fixed and without light' is a sentimental overstatement; 'mutely' instead of 'silently' carries a further suggestion of suffering; with 'this poor soul' Thackeray enters personally on the scene to intercede for the reader's pity; and in the last sentence the simile of the bloodstain is shocking in its poignancy. Similar

devices for moving the emotions of their readers, most of whom lived dull and sheltered lives, were used by all the well-known novelists and magazine writers of this period, including George Eliot, George Borrow, Charles Kingsley, Charles Dickens, and the Americans, Edgar Allan Poe, Nathaniel Hawthorne, Herman Melville, Washington Irving. Dickens's stories are never allowed to tell themselves: he forcibly obtrudes his own emotions, often raising the pitch of the style to hysteria. He also tries to heighten the effect of his pathetic passages by a foil of robust facetiousness; as Elizabethan dramatists had heightened their tragic effects by comic relief. Here is a quotation from his *Old Curiosity Shop:*

'She was dead. Dear, patient, gentle, noble Nell was dead. Her little bird—a poor slight thing the pressure of a finger would have crushed—was stirring nimbly in its cage; and the strong heart of its child mistress was mute and motionless for ever.

Where were the traces of her early cares, her sufferings, and fatigues? All gone. Sorrow was dead indeed in her, but peace and perfect happiness were born; imaged in her tranquil beauty and profound repose.

And still her former self lay there, unaltered in this change. Yes. The old fireside had smiled upon that same sweet face; it had passed, like a dream, through haunts of misery and care; at the door of the poor schoolmaster on the summer evening, before the furnace fire on the cold wet night, at the still bedside of the dying boy, there had been the same mild lovely look. So shall we know the angels in their majesty, after death.

The old man held one languid arm in his, and had the small hand tight folded to his breast, for warmth. It was the hand she had stretched out to him with her last smile—the hand that had led him on, through all their wanderings. Ever and anon he pressed it to his lips; then hugged it to his breast again, murmuring that it was warmer now; and, as he said it, he looked, in agony, to those who stood around, as if imploring them to help her.'

And here is another passage from the same book, with death treated facetiously:

‘ "Then we have nothing for it but resignation," said Mr. Brass; "nothing but resignation, and expectation. It would be a comfort to have his body; it would be a dreary comfort."

"Oh, beyond a doubt," assented Mrs. Jiniwin hastily; "if we once had that, we should be quiet sure."

"With regard to the descriptive advertisement," said Sampson Brass, taking up his pen. "It is a melancholy pleasure to recall his traits. Respecting his legs now—?"

"Crooked, certainly," said Mrs. Jiniwin.

"Do you think they *were* crooked?" said Brass, in an insinuating tone. "I think I see them now coming up the street very wide apart, in nankeen pantaloons a little shrunk and without straps. Ah! What a vale of tears we live in. Do we say crooked?"

"I think they were a little so," observed Mrs. Quilp with a sob.

"Legs crooked," said Brass, writing as he spoke. "Large head, short body, legs crooked—"

"Very crooked," suggested Mrs. Jiniwin.

"We'll not say very crooked, ma'am," said Brass piously. "Let us not bear hard upon the weaknesses of the deceased. He is gone, ma'am, to where his legs will never come in question.—We will content ourselves with crooked, Mrs. Jiniwin."

"I thought you wanted the truth," said the old lady. "That's all." '

This is melodrama in novel-form. Versions of most of Dickens's novels were staged during his lifetime. He was a natural orator and actor. He seems to have spoken over to himself, under his breath, every sentence that he wrote; and he toured Britain and the United States, giving public readings from his works. This accounts for much of his popularity in Victorian times, when the example set by the Queen popularized domesticity—the father of the family, instead of spending his evenings drinking and singing at the club as his own father had done, was supposed to stay at home and join a family reading circle. In the *Old Curiosity Shop,* as in all Dickens's novels, each chapter begins with an obvious cue to the reader: 'This should be read by Paterfamilias, in his manly, jolly voice,' or 'This is for the gentle, womanly voice of Materfamilias,' or 'Master John may be trusted with this.'

The popular Victorian novel (which was usually published in fortnightly parts, so that no member of a family could read on to the end, ahead of the rest) cannot be judged by modern solo-reading standards: its pictorial qualities, its frequent changes in atmosphere, the crowdedness that now make it such difficult going, explain themselves if it is read aloud dramatically to a roomful of leisured people of various ages in mid-Victorian costume. The practice of home-reading gradually lapsed at the turn of the century, and virtually ended with the First World War.

Pictorial styles were also used by John Ruskin and Walter Pater, who were not novelists but literary preachers and therefore indulged in even greater complexity of language. When Ruskin confined himself to expounding moral or aesthetic theory his style was fairly straightforward, but this was rare: his elaborate word-painting usually crowded out the precepts it was supposed to illustrate. The following sentence, describing the front of St Mark's Cathedral, is taken from the *Stones of Venice,* 1851-1853:

'And well may they fall back, for beyond those troops of ordered arches there rises a vision out of the earth, and all the great square seems to have opened out of it in a kind of awe, that we may see it far away; —a multitude of pillars and white domes, clustered into a low pyramid of coloured light, a treasure-heap, it seems, partly of gold, and partly of opal and mother-of-pearl, hollowed beneath into five great vaulted porches, ceiled with fair mosaic, and beset with sculpture of alabaster, clear as amber, and delicate as ivory, sculpture fantastic and involved, of palm leaves and lilies, and grapes and pomegranates, and birds clinging and fluttering among the branches, all twined together into an endless network of buds and plumes; and, in the midst of it, the solemn forms of angels, sceptred, and robed to the feet, and leaning to each other across the gates, their figures indistinct among the gleaming of the golden ground through the leaves beside them, interrupted and dim like the morning light as it faded back among the branches of Eden, when first its gates were angel-guarded long ago.'

A luxuriant mass of details is given, but with little sense of relation between them. The majestic sweep of the rhythm carries the reader over the details before he has time to assemble them in his mind. Ruskin himself must have formed a general impression of St Mark's and then carefully studied particulars, but does not here present them in such proportion as to explain his impression. It will be noticed how frequently the word 'among' occurs in the last few lines—birds among the branches, figures among the gleaming gold, light among the branches of Eden —all entrancing items in the decoration, but with no precise or essential places in it. This is a misrepresentation of the solid design of St Mark's.

Pater was much more Classical in spirit than Ruskin, in the sense that he was clear and not luxuriant, elaborate and not profuse. But he, too, was trying to convey impressions of indescribable feelings: he wanted to catch and record in print the aesthetic *frissons,* or thrills, which he considered the highest rewards of a cultured existence. This could only be done indirectly by suggestion and parable. His novel, *Marius the Epicurean,* is one long historical parable, and his other works purely suggestive sketches.

Just as Ruskin, in a final effort to communicate his impression of St Mark's, makes use of a conceit about dawn breaking in the Garden of Eden, so Pater has recourse to fancy in trying to describe the feelings with which Leonardo da Vinci's *La Gioconda* inspired him. He imagines the mood of the painter on the day that he added the famous smile. The paragraph is taken from *Studies in the History of the Renaissance,* published in 1873; it was written at Oxford, where Pater was a college tutor, at a time when Ruskin was also lecturing there.

'On this day truly no mysterious light, no irresistibly leading hand from afar, reached him; only, the peculiarly tranquil influence of its first hour increased steadily upon him in a manner with which, as he conceived, the aspects of the place he was then visiting had something to do. The air there, air supposed to possess the singular property of restoring the whiteness of ivory, was pure and thin. An even veil of lawn-like white cloud had now drawn over the sky; and under its broad, shadowless light every hue and tone of time came out upon the yellow old temples, the elegant pillared circle of the shrine of the pastoral Sybil, the houses seemingly of a piece with the ancient fundamental rock.'

Pater calculated the pictorial suggestiveness of each word, subordinating its sense to the emotional, vocal and rhythmical context. He did this more precisely than Ruskin because his emotions had greater precision and he was better able to isolate and analyse them. Nevertheless, the repeated rhyme of 'air there, air' reads somewhat affectedly.

Among the exceptional writers who avoided both the pathetic and the pictorial styles were Anthony Trollope and Samuel Butler. Trollope escaped a formal education because of the poverty of his family; but his mother, author of *Domestic Manners of the Americans,* was a shrewd and vigorous writer and he seems to have learnt much from her. He spent most of his life as a Post Office official and hunting man. He published more than twenty long novels, all dealing with middle-class family life, plainly told and with few emotional digressions. Conversation and pure narrative make up the greater part of them, and there is far less descriptive writing than in most nineteenth-century novels from Sir Walter Scott's onwards. The following is a passage from the first chapter of *Orley Farm,* published in 1862:

'The whole stood in one line fronting on to a large lawn which fell steeply away from the house into an orchard at the bottom. The lawn was cut in terraces, and here and there upon it there stood apple trees of ancient growth; for here had been the garden of the old farmhouse. They were large, straggling trees, such as do not delight the eyes of modern gardeners; but they produced fruit by the bushel, very sweet to the palate, though probably not so perfectly round, and large, and hand-some as those which the horticultural skill of the present day requires.'

Trollope does not refrain from making general comments—for example, this comment on the modern taste in apples —but they are always short and relevant. He does not draw an elaborate 'atmosphere' out of them; the story distills its own atmosphere as it unfolds. Here he has given a brief and factual setting before breaking into the story proper.

Samuel Butler was not primarily a novelist: most of his works were treatises on art, literature, psychology and science; but he wrote a Utopian fantasy in novel form, *Erewhon,* 1872, and twenty years later a sequel, *Erewhon Revisited,* and one domestic novel, *The Way of All Flesh,* written between 1872 and 1884 but not published until after his death in 1903. He is usually described as a satirist, because these novels expose many of the shams of contemporary life, but his satire is very different from Swift's: it is more analytical and more understanding, less witty, more humorous and more original. His style is plain and unemotional, but sharper than Trollope's because his judgements are less conventionally formed. This is from *The Way of All Flesh:*

'Some people say that their schooldays were the happiest in their lives. They may be right, but I look with suspicion upon those whom I hear saying this. It is hard enough to know whether one is happy or unhappy now, and still harder to compare the relative happiness or unhappiness of different times of one's life; the utmost that can be said is that we are fairly happy so long as we are not distinctly aware of being miserable. As I was talking with Ernest one day not so long since about this, he said he was so happy now that he was sure he had never been happier, and did not wish to be so, but that Cambridge was the first place where he had ever been consciously and continuously happy.'

Butler has not let this piece of analysis get out of hand: his style is equal to it. Excesses and shortcomings in Victorian prose, and in modern prose which derives from it, are usually due to the writer's not knowing just how to reconcile the sense of what he wishes to say with the various literary devices which pride of craftsmanship has impelled him to use. Butler's style is as free from these devices as it is from fanciful emotional colouring. He lived on a small income; published all his books, except *Erewhon,* at a loss; and was generally regarded as a crank because of his refusal to conform with literary and scientific fashions.

Butler died when the twentieth century was just beginning; his own century had bequeathed it no general prose tradition. There were conventions of pathetic writing, of pictorial writing, of ornate historical and political writing, but these were suited only to certain subjects and the achievement of certain effects. Most famous writers of the late nineteenth century had worked out eccentrically individual styles. William Morris revived the mediaeval narrative manner, with a mixture of devices taken from Thomas Malory and the authors of Norse sagas. George Meredith used a complex metaphorical language, the obscure implications of which were a fascinating study for his admirers. There was also the precious and witty style of Oscar Wilde, based on Ruskin and Pater; and, based on French models, the 'sensitive' and lucid style of George Moore. Here is a painfully sensitive passage from George Moore's *Confessions of a Young Man,* 1886:

'Then there is a failure—I can do nothing, nothing; my novel I know is worthless; my life is a leaf, it will flutter out of sight. I am weary of everything and wish I were back in Paris. I am weary of reading, there is nothing to read, Flaubert bores me. What nonsense has been talked about him! Impersonal! He is the most personal writer. But his odious pessimism! How weary I am of it, it never ceases, it is lugged in *à tout propos* and the little lyrical phrase with which he winds up every paragraph, how boring it is! Happily, I have "A Rebours" to read, that prodigious book, that beautiful mosaic. Huysmans is quite right, ideas are well enough until you are twenty, afterwards only words are bearable . . . a new idea, what can be more insipid—fit for Members of Parliament. Shall I go to bed? No. I would that I had a volume of Verlaine, or something of Mallarmé's to read—Mallarmé for preference. Huysmans speaks of Mallarmé in "A Rebours," and in hours like these a page of Huysmans is as a dose of opium, a glass of something exquisite and spirituous.'

In 1878 the rugged-minded Charles Doughty, a poet and physician, went travelling in the deserts of Arabia, disguising neither his Christian distaste for Moslem superstition nor his English dislike for thievish and temperamental Arabs, and wrote a monumental account of his experiences in *Arabia Deserta,* 1888. He had not gone for adventure or for geographical or ethnological reasons, but (as he later told T. E. Lawrence) to 'redeem English from the slough into which it has fallen since the time of Spenser.' Here is an illustration of the way in which he redeemed English from neologisms:

'We journeyed in the beaten path towards Gofar; and after going a mile, "Let us wait, quoth Eyâd, and see if this Merjàn be not coming." At length we saw it was he who approached with a bundle on his head,—he brought temmn and dates, which his sister (wedded in the town) had given him. Eyâd drew out a leathern budget, in which was some victual for the way that he had received from the Mothîf, (without my knowledge): it was but a little barley meal and dates of ill kind, in all to the value of about one shilling. We sat down, Merjàn spread out his good dates, and we breakfasted; thus eating together I hoped they might yet be friendly, though only misfortunes could be before me with such unlucky rafîks. . . .

"Nay, said Eyàd, beginning to swagger, the returning shall not be as our coming; I will ride myself." I said no more; and cast thus again into the wilderness I must give them line.'

And Doughty's contemporary, the complex-minded Henry James, an American with strong English sympathies, invented a new way of teasing the sentence with carefully contrived parentheses that delayed but did not confuse the rhythm as it meandered towards a comfortable close. This is from one of his later novels, *The Golden Bowl,* 1905:

'Charlotte throned, as who should say, between her hostess and her host, the whole scene having crystallized as soon as she took her place, to the right quiet lustre; the harmony was not less sustained for being superficial, and the only approach to a break in it was while Amerigo remained standing long enough for his father-in-law, vaguely wondering, to appeal to him, invite or address him, and then, in default of any such word, selected for presentation to the other visitor a plate of *petits fours*. Maggie watched her husband—if it now could be called watching —offer this refreshment; she noted the consummate way—for "consummate" was the term she privately applied—in which Charlotte cleared her acceptance, cleared her impersonal smile, of any betrayal, of any slightest value, of consciousness; and then felt the slow surge of a vision that,

at the end of another minute or two, had floated her across the room to where her father stood, looking at a picture, an early Florentine sacred subject, that he had given her on her marriage.'

Many more styles were invented as the twentieth century advanced and since there was keen competition among writers as to who should be 'great' and since it was admitted that 'greatness' was achieved only by a highly individual style, new tricks and new devices multiplied. In this plurality of styles little writers grew confused: they imitated one Master after another—Pater, Morris, James, Moore, Wilde—in the hope of suddenly finding themselves great men in their own right. It did not occur to them that unless they had something to say there was no need to write: most of them expected the ritual of writing to produce the subject.

Robert Louis Stevenson in an essay on literary style recommended imitation. He admitted that:

'Whenever I read a book or a passage that particularly pleased me, in which a thing was said or an effect rendered with propriety, in which there was either some conspicuous force or some happy distinction in the style, I must sit down at once and set myself to ape that quality. In these vain bouts, I got some practice in rhythm, in harmony, in construction, and the co-ordination of parts. I have thus played the sedulous ape to Hazlitt, to Lamb, to Wordsworth, to Sir Thomas Browne, to Defoe, to Hawthorne, to Montaigne, to Baudelaire and to Obermann.'

The effect of this sedulous imitation was to make Stevenson's works seem rather unreal: the negative virtue of faultlessness in an artificial prose style, especially where the writer's chief object is 'to render an effect,' can be very disagreeable. A reader feels that he is being written at, not written for. Other writers were neither so industrious nor so expert as Stevenson in their imitations of 'The Masters,' and so the Edwardian pudding-stone style began. It is still used by young writers who feel that they cannot be taken seriously until they have read the chief books of ancient and advanced contemporary literature in at least six languages and mastered all the styles and devices. Naturally they do not really read these books, or know the languages; but use crammer-school methods for learning just enough to pass muster. The literary result recalls the old Scottish nonsense story of Sir Gammer Vance who had a famous collection of curiosities and 'lived in a little thumb-bottle just outside his own front door.'

Typical pudding-stone is Sir Arthur Quiller-Couch's style, though he was not a young writer when he adopted it. In his unpretentious popular novels of the 'Eighties and 'Nineties he had been at his best: with simple humorous tales of the West Country and, though avoiding any suspicion of illiteracy, with no thought of setting himself up as an authority on English. He later took up style as a simple evangelist might take up ritual; and was appointed King Edward VII Professor of English Literature at Cambridge University. The following is a quotation from his *On the Art of Writing,* 1916. It is a concoction of styles which the contemporary reader was perhaps expected to taste critically with: 'Ah! a savour of Morris! Ah! a smack of Bunyan! Ah! a touch of Henry James! Ah, oh, ah! a tang, taste, suspicion, whiff, of Burke, Hazlitt, Jeremy Taylor, Washington Irving!'

'Seeing that in human discourse, infinitely varied as it is, so much must ever depend on *who* speaks, and to *whom,* in what mood and upon what occasion; and seeing that Literature must needs take account of all manner of writers, audiences, moods, occasions; I hold it a sin against the light to put up a warning against any word that comes to us in the fair way of use and wont (as "wire," for instance, for telegram), even as surely we should warn off hybrids or deliberately pedantic impostors, such as "anti-body" and "picture-drome," and that, generally, it is better to err on the side of liberty than on the side of the censor: since by the manumitting of new words we infuse new blood into a tongue of which (or we have learnt nothing from Shakespeare's audacity) our first pride should be that it is flexible, alive, capable of responding to new demands of man's untiring quest after knowledge and experience.'

In this passage we see the first clear signs of the breakdown of prose logic that has become so evident since the end of the First World War. Even in late Victorian times, no person of Sir A. Quiller-Couch's eminence would have dared to publish a sentence so plainly grotesque as 'By the manumitting of new words we infuse new blood into a tongue which is flexible, alive, capable of responding to new demands of man's untiring quest after knowledge and experience.' When the test of translation into Latin is applied, it fails at every point. No Latin orator would have figured new words as slaves to be manumitted: he would have seen them as barbarians applying for citizenship. Nor would he have figured the act of manumission as infusing new blood into anything: he would have put in the step here left out, namely, that after manumission the former slaves would be permitted to marry into their masters' families. Nor would he have mixed metaphor and realism in the phrase 'infuse new blood into a tongue': for blood is usually infused into the veins of the arm or leg and never into a tongue. Nor would he have written of a *tongue* as 'flexible and alive': he would have known that any human tongue, unless its owner happens to be paralysed, poisoned, or frozen stiff, is flexible and alive. He would therefore have avoided the word *lingua* (which means 'tongue' in the senses both of speech and of the organ of speech) and used instead *'modus loquendi,'* a 'manner of speaking.' Nor would he have admitted that a tongue into which new blood has been infused could 'respond to man's demands' as if it were a separate person or animal. Nor would he have mixed his vocabularies—Ennius with Petronius—as is done here: the Elizabethan phrase 'I hold it a sin against the light to put up a warning against any word that comes to us in the fair way of use and wont' mixed with the late-Victorian devotional-scientific phrase 'capable of responding to new demands of man's untiring quest.'

In Victorian times there was a clean separation, in the popular mind, of journalism from literature: journalism was considered vulgar, however well the journalist worked. The favourite debating theme—'Will Kipling *live?'*—was based on a doubt whether anyone whose writing had been formed by journalistic practice could possibly be 'great,' rather than on a doubt of Kipling's integrity as an observer and a moralist. It did not occur to anyone that O. Henry, Kipling's American counterpart, could 'live'; he was a mere reporter of the language of the bar and lodging house and had a prison record. Yet it was felt that Kipling and O. Henry had some quality that Meredith and Henry James lacked; and gradually popular novelists began to

simplify their style in imitation. This made a cleavage between popular and literary writers, or, as they became known shortly after the First World War, 'Low-brows and High-brows.' If this had meant a cleavage between the writers who wrote stylistically and those who wrote plainly, it would have been excellent: but journalism then implied grammatical and verbal looseness and, as the influence of American journalism grew, a gradual weakening of logic under self-induced emotional stress. Whether to range oneself with the Low-brows or with the High-brows was a difficult choice.

As the twentieth century advanced, the competition in style became a competition in being modern rather than in being great. Writers in Britain, however, were less affected by the modernist obsession than American writers, especially those who had visited France. Throughout the Victorian era the Americans had looked to Britain to set the literary standard for all departments of writing except the humorous, in which they took the lead under Mark Twain, Artemus Ward, and Gelett Burgess. In other departments they emulated their British contemporaries, and very often surpassed them in grace and clarity of language: for example, Victorian England could not boast of two essayists so judicious and correct as Ralph W. Emerson and James Russell Lowell. But at the end of the First World War the Americans knew themselves to be the strongest and richest nation of the world, and therefore felt that this cultural dependence on Britain derogated from their national dignity. As in the War of Independence, when British political and military influence had to be shaken off, they turned for help to Paris. Paris had for long been the world-centre of literary, philosophical and artistic fashion. American writers, as would-be spokesmen of the most modern country in the world, needed the most modern of styles to express this feeling adequately; naturally, they went to Paris. For ten years Paris teemed with American literary experimentalists—the franc was low, life was free, there was no Prohibition. They returned finally to the United States in 1930, when the Great Depression deprived them of their incomes, having all served their apprenticeships in one or other of the schools of modernist writing.

The most celebrated American writer in Paris was Gertrude Stein. She had settled there several years before the tide of experimentalists flowed, and stayed for several years after it had ebbed—witnessing the defeat of France in 1940. She had been trained as a neurologist and philosopher and her experiments in writing derived from an assumption that Time and Progress, as nineteenth-century scientists and theologians had understood them, were now irrelevant concepts: in the modern world they were replaced by the simple casual relationships which arise out of mere continuous existence. This assumption was given weight by the findings of the new school of relativity-physicists, published after the First World War.

Gertrude Stein's method consisted in turning to a literary purpose the unreasoned relations of words in people's minds and the disconnection and repetition which are normal in modern conversation. She thus abandoned the tradition of orderly prose narrative—the old kind of story about the things that happened to people, arising out of some given situation and in turn giving rise to further happenings and new situations. For the most part her prose was a simple succession and repetition of words, phrases and sentences, without historical beginning or ending and without logical meaning. It was humorous and exciting, to those interested in new uses of words, but difficult to read. Solemn literary critics and newspaper comedians derided it; but in Paris in the 'Twenties she had a great following among the young American émigrés—who learnt from her how to use the simplest words and the most conversational idioms in new rhythmical movements which would give their work a characteristically American pace.

In the 'Thirties, when she had become an accepted literary figure, Gertrude Stein was invited to make important lecture-tours in the United States. She then explained what her 'nonsense' meant. Here is a paragraph from a lecture on *Narration,* delivered in 1934. If it is read over with conversational emphasis it makes plain sense, although the thought is most complicated:

'When I first began writing really just began writing, I was tremendously impressed by anything by everything having a beginning a middle and an ending. I think one naturally is impressed by anything having a beginning a middle and an ending when one is beginning writing and that is a natural thing because when one is emerging from adolescence, which is really when one first begins writing, one feels that one would not have been one emerging from adolescence if there had not been a beginning and a middle and an ending to anything. So paragraphing is a thing that anyone is enjoying and sentences are less fascinating, but then gradually well if you are an American gradually you find that it is not really necessary that anything that everything has a beginning a middle and an ending and so you struggling with anything as anything has begun and begun does not really mean that begun and thing does not really mean beginning or begun.'

Gertrude Stein solved the logical problem of Time, which she speaks about here, by frequent use of the timeless present participle.

Only one other writer in English carried his experiments in prose so far as Gertrude Stein; and he went in a totally different direction. This was James Joyce, an Irishman, whose Dublin upbringing and Jesuit education provide the constant background to his work. Like the American experimentalists, he spent the greater part of his life on the Continent, in Switzerland, France and Italy. Being out of contact with the mass of his compatriots has always helped the literary innovator. Joyce's first books, *Dubliners* and *Portrait of the Artist as a Young Man,* were straightforward stories in the realistic style of the French-influenced Anglo-Irish school. His next book, *Ulysses,* a long novel describing twenty-four hours in the lives of a group of Dublin people, is made up chiefly of their inconsequential talk and ruminations. Woven into these, by means of word-associations, are recurring Greek and Latin themes—particularly the theme of Ulysses the Wanderer which gives the book its title. *Ulysses* became famous partly because it was banned as obscene by the British and American Customs authorities, partly because it was the most ambitious attempt yet made to use 'the stream of consciousness' in writing: that is, to reveal the private thoughts of characters in all their natural confusion. This manner of writing was founded on psychological researches which had been intended to show that consciousness was a turbid stream of mixed desires and memories: it was thus a psychological assumption rather than a prose style. Many other writers made use of it, with many varying styles.

Ulysses begins in a straightforward manner but soon becomes more complicated, passing, like Harriette Wilson's *Memoirs,* through a series of imitations or parodies of all previous English styles. It is as if Joyce was testing each of them in order and finding all wanting. In his last book, *Finnegan's Wake,* published in 1940, after he had been working on it for fifteen years, he finally invented a comically composite style and language which he could call his own: a super-pudding-stone. In it, ordinary English words are portmanteau'd and deliberately misspelt, others are introduced from many foreign languages, including Hebrew and Sanskrit, and the result is an almost indecipherable system of interlacing puns and verbal associations imposed upon the familiar Irish background. Here is a comparatively easy passage:

'What wouldn't I poach—the rent in my riverside my otther shoes, my beavery honest!—for a dace feast of grannom with the finny ones, flashing down the swansway, leaps ahead of the swift mac Eels and the pursewinded carpers, rearin antis rood perches astench of me, or, when I'd like own company best, with the help of a norange and bear, to be reclined by the lasher on my logansome, my g.b.d. in my f.a.c.e., solfanelly in my shellyholders and lov'd latakia the benuvolent, for my nosethrills with jealosomines wilting away to their heart's deelight and the king of saptimber letting down his humely odours for my consternation, dapping my griffen, burning water in the spearlight, or catching trophies of the king's royal college of sturgeons for to bake pike and pie while, O twined me abower in l'Alouette's Tower, all Adelaide's naughtingerls, juckjucking benighth me, I'd tonic my twittynice Dorian blackbudds off my singasongasong-apiccolo to pipe musicall airs on numberous fairyaciodes.'

This is a fisherman's idyll spoken by an Irish priest: if it is read aloud, the Irish rhythm can be easily felt, and many familiar Irish properties recognized. If it is studied closely, more and more linguistic detail can be interpreted. This appeals to the reader's vanity of general knowledge and guessing power—'Ah,' he says, 'by the *naughtingerls* he means also *nightingales*—because the German for nightingale is *Nachtigall* and *nachte* is old English for *naughty,* and 'gal' is 'girl,' which in the Middle Ages was also spelt 'gerl'; and *nosethrills* are *nostrils*—the mediaeval spelling was *nosthrils;* and *jealosomines* are *jessamines* because of the old English term *jelsomine* from the Italian *gelsomino.* And *norange* recalls the derivation of 'orange' from the Spanish word *maranja.* And surely *'swansway,'* besides meaning the river Liffey, contains a glancing reference to Proust's long, indolent novel, Englished as *Swann's Way?* And *logansome* is a mixture of *lonesome* and *logan-stone,* or rocking stone. . . . etc., etc. In order to understand the whole book the reader would have to disentangle patiently as much more of the snarled detail as he could (a part depends on private associations of Joyce's); then he would have to put together a new book, working out the relations between the details and trying to see what Joyce intended to signify. No writer could, or need, carry stylistic or linguistic experiment further than this.

When Joyce died, shortly after the publication of this book, it was time for writers in search of literary novelty and complex styles of their own to realize that the game was played out. Joyce had caught 'all the trophies of the king's royal college of sturgeons.' Meanwhile, too, Gertrude Stein had analysed conversational speech, taking it to pieces and gradually building it up again with successive studies of the word, the phrase, the sentence, the paragraph; so there was now little more to be learned about conversation. At last writers were at liberty to use prose for simple prose purposes—and not feel behind the times in doing so.

1943

JOHN LIVINGSTON LOWES

Originality and the Moulding of Conventions

From CONVENTION AND REVOLT IN POETRY

I AM FREE as the air to-day to coin a vocabulary of my very own, and speak to you in its fresh-minted words. I should be thereby, I take it, "original" in the sense in which many of us seem to understand the term. Only one thing stands in my way: I most potently and powerfully desire to be understood by you. You exercise no compulsion whatsoever. If you don't understand, you simply cease to listen. And I, who am here to communicate, conform. Obviously, then, the individual is not the only factor to be reckoned with in what we call originality, so far as expression is concerned. We express in order to communicate; to communicate, we must be understood; in order to be understood, we must employ the language of those to whom we speak. That is a fact so obvious that we sometimes forego the desideratum of putting it on its inferences.

As a matter of fact, we are all of us original in our expression until our wings are clipped. I know a three-year-old boy who calls an automobile a "cadeúga." It is, both to him and in point of fact, an excellently descriptive term, based, like many a word in the pristine days of speech, on the sound the thing makes. But you can't go to the telephone and ask for a "cadeúga" with any valid hope of seeing it appear. And since the world with which the young adventurer must communicate prefers to call the affair a motor, or a car, or a machine (incomparably less exact and fitting terms), he will infallibly drop his own fresh and vivid coinage, and conform. The tangential energy of the individual beats its wings in vain against the centripetal force of the community, and every infant anarchist in speech yields at last to the usage of that world by which, if he is to live, he must be understood.

All this, of course, has larger implications. Expression in art can no more escape the demands of *intelligibility,* than expression in every-day speech. The poet writes in order to communicate, and to communicate he, too, must be understood. And the language of poetry in the broader sense, poetic forms and conventions of whatever sort, is established by long usage, like speech itself. It may, from the point of view of either rhyme or reason, be irrational, even absurd. So are words. But there it is. And though the poet is free as air to create a new poetic language, he takes, if he does, the chances of the youthful coiner of "cadeúga." His own immediate poetic family may understand and marvel, but the world goes on unmoved. What he *can* do is to use the common language with a new distinction, a fresh vividness, a more compelling power. And that offers to originality its richest field.

There are two deep-rooted idiosyncrasies of human nature that bear on our acceptance or rejection of what is offered us. We have, in the first place, an innate bias for the familiar. Whatever we're thoroughly unfamiliar with is apt to seem to us odd, or queer, or curious, or bizarre. For it is no mere trick of speech, but one of those appallingly veracious records of human nature and experience in which the history of words abounds, through which "outlandish" and "uncouth" attained their present meaning. For "outlandish" meant in the beginning only what does n't belong to our own land, and "uncouth" was simply "unknown." The change in meaning registers a universal trait. Whatever is alien to our own ways—the costume, manners, modes of speech of another race or of other times—is strange; and "strange" itself, which started out by meaning merely "foreign," is only another record of the same idiosyncrasy. That is one thing.

But there is still another trait that is no less broadly human. Whatever is too familiar wearies us. Incessant recurrence without variety breeds tedium;

the overiterated becomes the monotonous, and the monotonous irks and bores. And there we are. Neither that which we do not know at all, nor that which we know too well, is to our taste. We're averse to shocks, and we go to sleep under narcotics.

Now both the shock and the narcotic have, I grant, at times their fascination. But they are apt to be forward, not permanent, sweet, not lasting. The source of more or less abiding satisfaction for most normal human beings lies in a happy merging of the two—in the twofold delight in an old friend recognized as new, or a new friend recognized as old. The experience and the pleasure are universal. All the lovers who have ever lived have made experiment of it; a face that you've passed a hundred times, nor cared to see, remains the face you've always known, but becomes all at once the most beautiful and thrilling object in the world; the person you've never known before, you find all at once you've known from all eternity. Now art, like love, sends its roots deep into what we are. And our most permanent aesthetic satisfaction arises as a rule from things familiar enough to give the pleasure of recognition, yet not so trite as to rob us of the other pleasure of surprise. We are keen for the new, but we insist that it establish some connection with what is friendly and our own; we want the old, but we want it to seem somehow new. Things may recur as often as they please, so long as they surprise us—like the Ghost in "Hamlet"—each time they appear.

Let me illustrate what I mean from a single device of poetry. What is it that charms us in these stanzas from a fifteenth-century carol?

> He came al so still.
>   There his mother was,

> As dew in April
>   That falleth on the grass.

> He came al so still
>   To his mother's bour,
> As dew in April
>   That falleth on the flour.

> He came al so still
>   There his mother lay,
> As dew in April
>   That falleth on the spray.

The balance between recurrence and variation is so delicately kept that monotony itself becomes the signal for a fresh surprise. And Poe's consummate and deliberate technique, no less than the limpid simplicity of the carol, secures its almost magical effects by the same means:

> The skies they were ashen and sober;
>   The leaves they were crispèd and sere,
>   The leaves they were withering and sere;
> It was night in the lonesome October,
>   Of my most immemorial year;
> It was hard by the dim lake of Auber,
>   In the misty mid region of Weir:
> It was down by the dank tarn of Auber,
>   In the ghoul-haunted woodland of Weir.

That is but one way out of a thousand in which the familiar merges with the strange. And when a poet, through whatever secret of his art, gives to the expected the thrill of a discovery, he need have no fears for his originality.

What we call originality, then, does not so much consist in the creation of something wholly new, as in this *re-pristination* (to use Browning's word) of something old. That is not, of course, quite the whole story. But the other side may securely wait.

Let us begin with one or two conventions. And though we start out with the elder poets, we shall arrive, in the end, at the year of our Lord that we date by. We have glanced at the dreary and wire-drawn inventories of feminine charms in the poetry of courtly love. We should have to search far to find anything more nearly in the article of death, and it is worth a moment to see what could be done towards vivifying it. Here is a part of Chaucer's description of Alisoun, the racy young person who helps give zest to the "Miller's Tale." All the familiar paraphernalia of the stock catalogue are there intact. You begin with resignation (unless you happen to remember that it's Chaucer you are reading), prepared for the inevitable —whiteness of *fleur de lis,* redness of roses, smoothness of ivory, clearness of crystal, grayness of glass; and you find— the slimness of the weasel, the softness of the wool of a wether, the shrilling of the swallow's song, the blackness of the sloe, the fragrance of apples, the fairness of the pear tree in the spring. The correct and courtly formulas have gone playing truant in the fields!

Fair was this yonge wyf, and ther-with-al
As any wesele hir body gent and smal. . . .
Ful smale y-pulled were hir browes two,
And tho were bent, and blake as any sloo.
She was ful more blisful on to see
Than is the newe pere-jonette tree;
And softer than the wolle is of a wether. . . .
But of hir song, it was as loude and yerne
As any swalwe sittinge on a berne.
Ther-to she coude skippe and make game,
As any kide or calf folwinge his dame.
Hir mouth was swete as bragot or the
meeth,
Or hord of apples leyd in hey or heeth.
Winsinge she was, as is a joly colt,
Long as a mast, and upright as a bolt.

The hackneyed convention has become vivid as a branch of hawthorn leaves, and racy of good English soil. Let us see what happened to another.

One of the most notorious instances of the mediæval trick of listing things is the so-called *Ubi sunt* formula. It is a comprehensive and detailed interrogation, on the order of "Where, oh, where are the Hebrew children?" as to the whereabouts of all the ancient worthies:

Dic, ubi Salomon, olim tam nobilis,
Vel ubi Samson est, dux invincibilis—

and so on through an interminable list. That happens to be from a mediæval hymn, but the thing is everywhere. I shall give at once the most terrible example that I know. Where, asks Deschamps in one of his twelve hundred *balades*—where are David and Solomon, Methuselah, Joshua, Maccabæus, Holofernes, Alexander and Samson, Julius Cæsar and Hector and Pompey; Crœsus, King Arthur, Godfrey, Charlemagne, Darius the Great, Hercules, Ptolemy; where is Denis the felon king, Job the courteous, Tobias, Aristotle, Hippocrates and Plato, Judas, Hester, the good Penelope, Queen Dido, Pallas, Juno, Guinevere, Iseult, and Helen, fairest of all; where is Jason, Romulus, Saladin; where he who conquered Aragon, or he who built Avignon, Paris, Rheims, and Rouen? That is a list from a single *balade* only; I spare you two others in a similar strain. The old convention came to life again only the other day, in Illinois:

Where are Elmer, Herman, Bert, Tom,
and Charley . . .
Where are Ella, Kate, Mag, Lizzie, and
Edith,
The tender heart, the simple soul, the loud,
the proud, the happy one?—
All, all, are sleeping on the hill. . . .

Where are Uncle Isaac and Aunt Emily,
And old Towny Kincaid and Sevigne
Houghton,
And Major Walker who had talked
With venerable men of the revolution?—
All, all, are sleeping on the hill.

Herman and Holofernes, Elmer and Aristotle, Methuselah and Major Walker, Aunt Emily and Dido—whether it hails from Beauté-sur-Marne or from Spoon River, the *Ubi sunt* is catholic, and holds all, quietly inurned. But modern instances aside, the thing with its appalling fecundity dogs one down the Middle Ages in unrelieved monotony. All at once, in France, a supremely gifted poet took it up. He took it up and kept it; but he added one thing—the penetrating beauty of a refrain which fused the dead list into one of the most haunting symbols of human transitoriness:

Tell me now in what hidden way is
    Lady Flora the lovely Roman?
Where's Hipparchia, and where is Thaïs,
    Neither of them the fairer woman?
    Where is Echo, beheld of no man,
Only heard on river and mere,—
    She whose beauty was more than human? . . .
But where are the snows of yester-year?

Sainte-Beuve long ago pointed out that Villon's poignant refrain—his "Mais où sont les neiges d'antan!"—transformed by the alchemy of genius the hackneyed formula. It did. The one compelling phrase became a solvent, through which the hoary banalities of the convention were merged in the fleeting evanescence of all things that are.

Moreover, what Villon did with the *balade* in general is a no less illuminating case in point. He found it more dead than any modern poet has ever thought he found the chrysalids from which the spirits of Tennyson and Arnold and Swinburne have flown. It was a garment walking about with nobody in it. Deschamps in particular had used it as a catch-all for the multifarious sheddings of his mind. His

military campaigns, his maledictions on the toothache, his *Weltanschauung* in general, his dislike of tripe, his resentment against England, his observations on different ways of eating, his counsels of perfection addressed to kings and princes, his profound distaste for truffles, his lament for the misfortunes of the church, his views on the seven liberal arts, his lucubrations on the Seven Deadly Sins—all, all, are poured indiscriminately into the *balade* receptacle. It was trite, hackneyed, shop-worn, traditional, bookish, second-hand, readymade, stereotyped, artificial, rigid—a list of epithets which I have culled from a recent pronouncement of the newer poetry upon the only less new, which has already stiffened, it would seem, in death. The *balade* could cry *peccavi* to these stern indictments all and some. And so Villon found it. The thing he should have done, of course, was to discard it utterly, as fit only for the scrap-heap. He didn't, by the grace of Heaven, and everybody knows what happened. The dead awoke, and not only the "Balade des dames du temps jadis," but "La belle Heaulmière," and a dozen others stand, with vivid and imperishable freshness, among the supreme achievements of poetry.

We might dwell with no less profit upon the progressive desiccation, a little later, of the sonnet. Nobody ever put the reason for what happened better than Sidney himself, who, showing the steep and thorny way to Heaven, on occasion recked not his own rede.

You that do search for every purling spring
Which from the ribs of old Parnassus flows,
And every flower, not sweet perhaps, which
    grows
Near thereabouts, into your poesie wring;
Ye that do dictionary's method bring
Into your rimes, running in rattling rows;

You that poor Petrarch's long-deceased
woes
With new-born sighs and denizen'd wit do
sing;
You take wrong ways; these far-fet helps
be such
As do bewray a want of inward touch.

And through these far-fetched helps the
sonnet became, in the hands of innumerable practitioners, a thing of frigid
conceits worn bare by iteration; of servile borrowings; of artificial sentiment,
flat as the lees and dregs of wine. One
has only to read *seriatim* the Elizabethan
sonnet cycles (with their glorious islets
rising here and there out of the general
haze) to find every earmark of the
incorrigibly case-hardened convention.
Well, Shakespeare responded to the
vogue, and made of the sonnet, with
lapses here and there, the vehicle of
the very quintessence of poetry. "And,
when a damp Fell round the path of
Milton, in his hand The Thing became
a trumpet."

But, we are told—and not by recent
protestants alone—the sonnet's day is at
last done. Keats wrote that he was "endeavoring to discover a better sonnet
stanza than we have"—but it is worth
observing that he left as his legacy the
realms of gold in the lines: "On First
Looking into Chapman's Homer." "I
will never write another," Byron declared; "they are the most puling, petri-
fying, stupidly platonic compositions."
Fitzgerald thought sonnets were fit
only to "serve as little shapes in which
a man may mould very mechanically
any single thought which comes into
his head, which thought is not lyrical
enough in itself to exhale in a more
lyrical measure," and that its metre was
"a good excuse for the dull didactic
thoughts which naturally incline towards it." And he also expresses the

pious wish "to tie old Wordsworth's
volume about his neck and pitch him
into one of the deepest holes of his dear
Duddon." But through it all the sonnet holds its way. And Rupert Brooke,
like Villon, comes along and writes this
—of the dead, too, but not "du temps
jadis":

These hearts were woven of human joys
and cares,
Washed marvellously with sorrow, swift
to mirth.
The years had given them kindness.
Dawn was theirs,
And sunset, and the colours of the earth.
These had seen movement, and heard mu-
sic; known
Slumber and waking; loved; gone
proudly friended;
Felt the quick stir of wonder; sat alone;
Touched flowers and furs and cheeks.
All this is ended.

There are waters blown by changing winds
to laughter
And lit by the rich skies, all day. And
after,
Frost, with a gesture, stays the waves that
dance
And wandering loveliness. He leaves a
white
Unbroken glory, a gathered radiance,
A width, a shining peace, under the
night.

The new comes and takes its place beside the old, and we welcome it. But
it is not wise to give up too soon the old
for dead. The ways of genius with supposedly cast-off and lifeless forms have
to be reckoned with. For the touch of
genius is like the miracle of Spring.
Let us return, for a moment, to our
thesis. Neither familiar things grown
trite, nor things so new as still to be remote and alien, ever grip us as do those
things which are at the same time old
enough to touch the chords of memory,

and yet fresh (if I may use a poet's phrase) with some unspent beauty of surprise. And the supreme test of originality is its power to give us the sense of a footing on trodden and familiar ground, which all at once is recognized as unexplored. That is what Chaucer does times without number. That is what Villon does in the *balade*. For originality, rightly understood, seldom concerns itself with minting a new and particular medium of its own. And genius of the highest order is far more apt to disclose the unexpected resources of whatever vehicle of expression it falls heir to, than to spend itself upon the fabrication of a new.

I know that this is not the doctrine of the hour. And I know, too, that the hour, within due limits, is not without a valid case. "I holde," says that peerless natural philosopher, the Wife of Bath, "I holde a mouses herte nat worth a leek, That hath but oon hole for to sterte to." And originality undoubtedly fulfils itself in many ways. But precisely because the way of creative acceptance is just now more or less anathema, I am doubly anxious, not to defend, but to establish it. The way of constructive rejection shall have full hearing by and by. Meantime, there are certain fundamental and (I believe) still fruitful and operative principles to reckon with.

The current notion that *invention* is a mark of high originality is one of the vulgar errors that die hard. If it were true, "The House of a Thousand Candles" or the "Filigree Ball" would bear away the palm from many a masterpiece. But it is not the case. None of the great poets has ever troubled himself particularly to invent. That is especially true, of course, of narrative and dramatic poetry, and in spite of the fact that both narrative and the drama have now been largely commandeered by prose, the usage of Sophocles, and Dante, and Chaucer, and Shakespeare, and Goethe (although I am far from wishing to conjure with great names) is not without relevance still. They took, then, for the most part, materials that had come down to them—themes that had grown and developed through a selective instinct working, often, through long generations. And instead of inventing, they *discovered*. If that sounds cryptic, let us start with a modern instance that is n't poetry at all.

Dickens, as everybody knows, took over in "Pickwick Papers" a farcical series of sporting sketches, already begun, and intended to centre about a mythical Nimrod Club. In these earlier sketches Mr. Pickwick appeared (*absit omen!*) as a tall, thin man. But before he reached Dickens's hands, by one of those changes on which immortal issues turn, he had become short and fat. And so Dickens found him, and proceeded with his book. And now I quote Mr. Chesterton, lest I be suspected of building up a parallel *ad hoc*. "He made," says Chesterton of Dickens, "in the midst of this book a great discovery. . . . And that discovery constituted . . . the outstanding and arresting original feature in 'The Pickwick Papers.' . . . He had chosen (or somebody else had chosen) that corpulent old simpleton as a person peculiarly fitted to fall down trapdoors, to shoot over butter slides, to struggle with apple-pie beds, to be tipped out of carts and dipped into horse-ponds. But Dickens, and Dickens only, discovered as he went on how fitted the fat old man was to rescue ladies, to defy tyrants, to dance, to leap, to experiment with life, to be a *deus ex machinâ,* and even a knight errant. Dickens made this discovery. Dickens went into the Pickwick Club to scoff, and Dickens remained to pray." So Mr. Chesterton, and in this fashion Samuel Pickwick joined the company of the immortals. And I need not remind you, in passing, that one Sir John Falstaff, despite his own veracious rehearsal of the circumstances of his birth, had a not dissimilar pedigree.

Dickens, then, did n't invent Mr. Pickwick; he discovered him underneath his disguising habiliments. And out of his discovery grew a unique book. There is another unique performance that grew out of a similar flash of insight. Chaucer did over into English the story of Troilus and Cressida as it came to him, particularly through Boccaccio. He found it an Italianate romantic epic; he left it the first great English novel. "Nothing like it," as has been recently said, "was ever in the world before." How does he do it?

He starts out in pretty close dependence upon Boccaccio. And he reaches Cressida herself, and Pandar. Then all at once something happens, and you can see it happening before your eyes, if you read the two narratives together. Some of you will recall what Stevenson says of "Kidnapped": "In one of my books, and one only, the characters took the bit in their teeth; all at once they became detached from the flat paper; and they turned their backs on me and walked off bodily, and from that time my task was stenographic." Well, that is what happened to Chaucer. There before him was Boccaccio's Cressida, the conventionally fickle woman. "I came like water, and like wind I go," she might have said, in Omar's words. And the facility with which she went is rivalled only by the fatal ease with which she came. But something else in her seized upon Chaucer, and lifted him, and Cres-

sida with him, bodily out of Boccaccio. And as a result of that flash of vision, a conventional treatment of the hackneyed theme of a woman lightly won and quickly lost, turns into a penetrating and profoundly sympathetic portrayal of the shifting, fluctuating impulses of a woman yielding both against and with her will. And I know no character outside Shakespeare that is at once so human, and so hauntingly elusive in its complexity, or so tragically implicated in the defects of noble qualities, as the Cressida of Chaucer's discovery. What he discovered in Boccaccio's Pandaro, and the matchless figure that he made of it, time fails to tell. But through his fresh conception of what he found in the materials that came to him, he created a new and amazing literary form, and did something that was never done again until Fielding and Thackeray and Meredith appeared.

But Chaucer had the habit of discovering astounding possibilities in things that appear to have incurably gone stale. Let us take another instance. The Middle Ages had a passion for collecting. Jacobus de Voragine, in the "Golden Legend," collected saints; Boccaccio, in the "De Casibus," collected tragedies; in the "De Claris Mulieribus" he collected famous women; the mediæval preachers were indefatigable collectors of *exempla*. Story collections, then, were a stock convention. Chaucer himself had tried his hand at them more than once. He had done it in the "Legend of Good Women," and he had done it in what later came to be the "Monk's Tale." Indeed, the Monk cheerfully stated, before he launched into his string of tragedies, that he had a hundred of them in his cell! Such collections, however, were merely collections—stories strung together, or confined within some stationary framework; tales lifted from their native soil, and mounted, classified, and pressed in an herbarium. But stories *grow*. They spring from the fillip of some suggestion, and one begets another, and they smack of the qualities of their narrators. A group of men (and I am not forgetting Chaucer for a moment) are gathered in the smoking compartment of a Pullman car. The cigars burn freely, and the bars come down. The captain of industry lets himself be known by stories of big business; the soldier has tales of the trenches; the Californian sings the glories of his State in dazzling anecdote; the college professor strives to seem unacademic, but the damned spot will not out; the commercial traveller tells the story of his life, and the clergyman discreetly seeks his berth. Recall, moreover (for you find Chaucer everywhere), your transatlantic voyages, when such things were. A body of people whose paths have never crossed before are thrown together for a week or so without the possibility of respite or escape. And an act of the Human Comedy promptly takes the stage. The boat is scarcely out of sight of land till attractions and repulsions are weaving back and forth. Like gravitates to like, and propinquity has its perfect work, to make or mar; total strangers leave the boat betrothed, and friends of years no longer speak. Journeys are both fertile soil for stories, and swift reagents upon human nature.

Now Chaucer knew no Pullman cars nor transatlantic liners, but he did know something that combined the merits of them both, the pilgrimage. And pilgrims, like their modern counterparts, had their scrips chock-full of news interspersed with lies: "pilgrymes, With scrippes bret-ful of lesinges, Entremedled with tydinges." Moreover, pilgrim-

ages threw together, willy-nilly, every sort of person in the world—"a companye Of sondry folk, by aventure y-falle In felaweshipe." And they told their tales each after his kind, and as they rode they developed antipathies and disclosed affinities. And Chaucer made the great discovery. *Journeys are where stories live when they're at home.* Why leave them stranded in a collection, "lyk a fish that is waterlees"? And by a stroke of genius he turned a static into a dynamic thing, and out of a hackneyed literary type the Human Comedy itself unfolds before our eyes. For if ever the Spirit of Comedy, with its sage's brows and its slim feasting smile, was luminous and watchful overhead, it was when the "nyne and twenty in a companye" set out from Southwerk at the Tabard, on the road to Canterbury. And there, like Cressida, "I take my leve." "Who-so wol here it in a lenger wyse," says the Monk when he has told the Tale of Ugolino, "Redeth the grete poete of Itaille, That highte Dant, for he can al devyse Fro point to point; nat o word wol he faille." And what Chaucer says Dante did for Ugolino, Professor Kittredge has recently done for Chaucer himself. And the supreme originality of the "Canterbury Tales"— the matchless give-and-take along the Canterbury road, the self-revelations, the breaking into life of hackneyed narrative forms, when they fall from the racy, or stately, or ribald lips of the pilgrims— all that has been, once for all, devised from point to point, and I shall not retell what has been so luminously told.

I said I should drop the "Canterbury Tales" with that. But I must cast just one more longing, lingering look behind to those warm precincts of the cheerful day. Some of you will remember the incomparable lines in which the Wife of Bath breaks in upon her retrospect:

But, lord Crist! whan that it remembreth me
Upon my yowthe, and on my jolitee,
It tikleth me aboute myn herte rote.
Unto this day it dooth myn herte bote
That I have had my world as in my tyme.

Well, that is Chaucer's own savoring of life. And that is the secret of his originality. He was original because he could n't be anything else to save his soul. For he was alive to his finger tips, and nothing that he really touched could remain dead. And it is this invincible zest of his, this keen and intimate relish of the Human Comedy—his own rôle with the rest—through which he vitalizes everything he lays his hands on. He is everlastingly discovering that dead things are n't dead at all. He dares to begin the immortal Prologue to the "Canterbury Tales" itself with a device that had been worn to the bone in the swarming vision poems of the day. It was always Spring when the dreamer fell asleep. And the same conventional birds, trees, and breezes repeat each other, till almost one's spirit dies "for wo and wery of that companye." How deadly they were you can only know if, like Chaucer,

Thou gost hoom to thy hous anoon;
And, also domb as any stoon,
Thou sittest at [boke after] boke,
Till fully daswed is thy loke,
And livest thus as an hermyte.

But Chaucer as usual saw what others had n't seen. And he struck through the shell of the trite springtime convention to the heart of Spring itself. Spring is the time of the irrepressible *Wanderlust,* of longings for the open road, over the hills and far away: *"than* longen folk to goon on pilgrimages." And so:

Whan that Aprille with his shoures sote
The droghte of Marche hath perced to the rote,
And bathed every veyne in swich licour,
Of which vertu engendred is the flour;
Whan Zephirus eek with his swete breeth
Inspired hath in every holt and heeth
The tendre croppes, and the yonge sonne
Hath in the Ram his halfe cours y-ronne,
And smale fowles maken melodye,
That slepen al the night with open yë,
(So priketh hem nature in hir corages):
Than longen folk to goon on pilgrimages
(And palmers for to seken straunge strondes)
To ferne halwes, couthe in sondry londes;
And specially, from every shires ende
Of Engelond, to Caunterbury they wende,
The holy blisful martir for to seke.

And the pilgrimage is on. And a spirited turn to a jaded commonplace has achieved an opening that is flawlessly organic—and, incidentally, has given to English poetry the lines whose familiarity has kept its April freshness through five hundred years.

Originality, then, is independent of invention. It is rather the gift of seeing and seizing the latent possibilities of familiar things. We accept that formulation without demur when the familiar things are the appearances of earth, and air, and sea, and sky—effects of light and shade, *nuances* of color, aspects of mass and line, sound, fragrance, movement— all the bewildering, iridescent throng of old impressions that all at once flash into new, when the eye is quickened and alert. What we fail, perhaps, to realize is this: that the old and well-worn forms of art, the familiar treatments of traditional themes, stand to the poet in precisely the same relation as the world of eye and ear. And they too may flash into life under the same compelling vision that at rare moments pierces the husks of *things,* and discloses beauty.

For art is tradition, and what is handed down is itself material for the alembic. It may prove to be utterly intractable, its pristine ductility vanished forever. Well and good; that is a malady incident to art no less than to manners and costume and speech. But that is the other half of the truth—the half that is turned towards us to-day. What we are concerned with at the moment is the half that has suffered temporary eclipse: the fact that old forms and old themes have always remained, and in large measure still remain, malleable under creative energy. And what we call originality has always found rich stuff for its transmutation there.

I shall not summon Shakespeare as a witness. It is all or nothing with him. One thing only I shall say. If you wish a complete compendium of the essentials and the quintessentials of originality, in all their conceivable manifestations, go on a voyage of discovery of your own, and begin by reading Lodge's "Rosalynde," and Brooke's "Romeus and Juliet," and the old "King Leir and his Three Daughters," and North's noble translation of Plutarch's "Life of Antony," page by page, and sometimes word by word, with the plays that Shakespeare built on them. That is neither a counsel of perfection, nor an injunction to settle Hoti's business; it is a practicable and supremely illuminating enterprise. And forty thousand lectures could not, with all their quantity of lore, make up its sum. For in the first-hand comparison of what Shakespeare found and took with the astounding thing he made of it, lies the touchstone of all originality whatsoever.

There is, however, another question about originality, the answer to which is not without importance. What are the limits of originality, in its sover-eign dealing with other men's work?

The problem has been rather hopelessly muddled in our minds through a failure to remember that originality in its narrower sense, as a mere antonym for plagiarism, has always been itself a pure matter of convention. The metes and bounds between "mine" and "thine" in literary property have never remained fixed. They have been, for any given period, determined solely by the current literary usage. And the ethics of the question need concern us only so far as it is a matter of the evolution of conventions. Concern us it must, however, because we persist in judging in accordance with the conventions of to-day older practices, that were subject to a wholly different usage.

The Middle Ages, for example, had practically no sense whatever of literary property, as we conceive it. Rights of possession in other men's work were "free as the road, as large as store." Froissart's words about another matter are applicable here: "there was nothing of which one could say 'It is mine,' for everything was common as the sun and moon." Short of wholesale and servile cribbing, A was as free to incorporate what B had written, as he was to levy on the blessed sun of heaven, for his poetic needs. And it was as little incumbent upon him to state that he had done so, as it is even yet for me to announce that I lifted "the blessed sun of heaven" from Shakespeare. The works of other men, in fact, stood on practically the same footing, to a writer, as the works of God. Chaucer fuses the results of his reading into a new thing, precisely as he fuses his keen and infallible observations of life. And usually he combines the two. The Wife of Bath—who should have lived long enough hereafter to have met in Falstaff her only peer and her only match—the Wife of Bath herself is simply Chaucer's multifarious and vivid reading of books, and his alert and omnivorous reading of life, poured together *con amore* into the mould of a superbly vital imaginative conception. Now one of the Wife's chief components happens to be St. Jerome—the most amazing metamorphosis that ever a saint has undergone. St. Jerome, however, I suspect would be the first to waive acknowledgment of such a borrowing. But the Wife of Bath is no less a debtor without acknowledgment to one of Chaucer's contemporaries, Eustache Deschamps. What is to be said of that? Let Deschamps answer for himself. Long before the Wife's *apologia pro vita sua* was written, Deschamps sent across the Channel to Chaucer, by a common friend, a remarkable *balade,* the refrain of which is this: "Grand translateur, noble Geffroy Chaucier"—Geoffrey Chaucer, *the great translator.* That, to Deschamps, is Chaucer's distinction; he has, as it happens, sowed the flowers (it is the *balade* speaking, and not I) and planted the rosebush of the "Roman de la Rose" for those who are ignorant of French. But those who are ignorant of French are also deprived of Deschamps. And so, in the *envoy,* Deschamps proffers a suggestion. In Chaucer's garden, he modestly protests, he would be, to be sure, but a nettle—"En ton jardin ne seroye qu'ortie"—but he makes it unmistakably clear that he was anxious to be transplanted there, if only Chaucer would. And the sequel is this. Chaucer did find in Deschamps, as we now know, stuff for his loom, and wove it into his own tapestry. But it is only within the last dozen years that the discovery was made that he had actually done so. For, in entire accordance with the usage

of his day, which Deschamps followed with the rest, Chaucer made no acknowledgment. It would have been a work of pure supererogation if he had. For among that happy breed of men to whom all things were theirs, to take over another's "goodly words" into one's own "douce melodie" was in itself a compliment as acceptable and courtly as any that one could pay. Acknowledgment might or might not be made, precisely as one pleased. And there, indeed, lies the crux of the whole matter. Barring the single point of acknowledgment, originality meant in Chaucer's day substantially what it means now—the transmutation of what is taken over, into something that is essentially one's own. And the difference with reference to acknowledgment grew directly out of the absence of any such active sense as ours of literary property—an absence which, in turn, was the result of causes rooted deep in mediæval life. Our modern sensitiveness to any infringement of our property rights in the children of our brain is merely a stage a trifle farther on in the evolution of a convention.

I am not wholly sure, however, that our ethical gain through the development has not been offset by an æsthetic loss. At all events, our robust elders in poetry exercised the same imperial rights of eminent domain over beauty to their liking in a book, that they exerted over beauty of their finding in earth, sea, or sky. And the stipulation of their holding was in either case the same—they must improve the property. The simile in Virgil of the souls that fell from the banks of the Styx like leaves, becomes Dante's property when he enriches Virgil's lines from his own creative observation; precisely as, no more, no less, the greenness of new grass becomes inalienably his when the same penetrating observation confers on it the vividness of fresh emerald the instant it is split. Virgil and the meadow were alike priceless, and alike legitimate, treasure-trove. And all this meant, in the end, a splendid and *cumulative* bodying forth in poetry of the life of men and things. For poets like Dante, and Chaucer, and Shakespeare recognized far more clearly and surely than we the perennial vitality latent in *tradition*. And one of their glories is the interpenetration, in their work, of books and life. There they both were; and the creative energy in those more spacious days struck as straight and true for the one as for the other, to find its stuff. And this richness of assimilation of what tradition furnishes gives to the older poetry a body, a fulness of habit, of which we often feel the lack these days, when we all too seldom catch in verse that sense of a rich and varied background flashing into expression in a single poem, or pouring its profusion into the compass of one master work—the sense that sometimes in a single phrase throws windows open upon endless vistas. And qualities like those we can ill afford to miss.

For originality is more than the saying of something never said before about something now for the first time perceived. That has its own high-value, we may grant at once; but it has its limitations too. For however exciting it might well be to play a second Adam, and have the Lord God bring to each of us, all new, every beast of the field and fowl of the air to see what we would call them—however thrilling that might be to each happy individual, the universe would not thereby get far. Fresh beginnings are excellent stimulants to a jaded world, but a defective method of progression. The great constructive

element in both life and art is the dealings of genius with the continuity of tradition. And poetry becomes original by breaking with tradition at its peril. Cut the connection with the great reservoir of past achievement, and the stream runs shallow, and the substance of poetry becomes tenuous and thin.

This is not an *apologia* for bookishness in poetry. The bookish, the erudite, the academic, are worlds away from what I mean. Cut connection with the other reservoir—"the mighty world of eye and ear"—and the stream again runs shallow, and the substance of poetry becomes this time not merely tenuous and thin, but hard and dead. The vitality of tradition and the quickening impulse of immediate contact with reality—it is the fructifying influence of each of these upon the other that makes for life in poetry. Either without the other means sterility.

Originality, then, is in the main independent of derivation. Its specific quality is the individual stamp: the pervasion of thought and expression, whencesoever derived, by something that gives distinction, freshness, individuality. Take a line and a half of Wordsworth's:

> . . . that uncertain heaven received
> Into the bosom of the steady lake.

When Coleridge read that, he sat down and wrote in a letter: "had I met these lines running wild in the deserts of Arabia, I should have instantly screamed out 'Wordsworth!'" Of course he would; they are saturated through and through with him,—as

> For lo! the New-moon winter bright!
> And overspread with phantom light
> (With swimming phantom light o'erspread
> But rimmed and circled by a silver thread)—

as these lines are permeated with the very quintessence of Coleridge. But,

An ampler ether, a diviner air,

also bears Wordsworth's unequivocal image and superscription, though this time the gold is the gold of Virgil.

For although in life "the rank is but the guinea stamp, The man's the gowd for a' that," in art, where form and content are as indissolubly one as body and spirit, the distinction fails to hold. It is the cutting of the intaglio that gives its value to the gem. And "Drink to me only with thine eyes" is as inalienably Ben Jonson's, by virtue of its chiselled terseness, as if almost every phrase of it were n't buried in the letters of a Greek rhetorician; and "Still to be neat, still to be dressed" is incomparably more original than a thousand poems that are n't, like it, the transmutation of the dross of a dozen old Latin lines into a finished bit of goldsmith's work. Read some day, when your stomach is strong, the old song which Burns took over in "John Anderson my jo, John," and remember, as you read, that the soaring melody of the rondo in the Waldstein sonata is Beethoven's similar transfiguration of the air of a ribald folk-song about fleas in straw. For that matter, recall Beethoven's transformations of the conventional minuet of Haydn and Mozart into that vehicle of rollicking gaiety, and grim mystery, and tragic portent, the scherzo of the Third, Fifth, Seventh, and Ninth Symphonies. And in Miss Lowell's "Guns as Keys: and the Great Gate Swings"—to come down with a leap to the most modern of the modern—the daring constructive device is no less original because it gives a brilliant new turn to what is as old, on the one side, as the "Odyssey" (in the constant juxtaposition of its great sweep

forward and its waiting goal), and, on another, of as long date as "Aucassin and Nicolete" (in its alternation of verse and—with apologies!—prose); while from a third angle it's a superb appropriation and translation into words of the methods of the cinematograph. None of these things move us, whether in Wordsworth, or Ben Jonson, or Burns, or Beethoven, or Miss Lowell. They are stuff for the loom, clay for the potter, gold, silver, precious stones, wood, hay, stubble—it matters not what in the slightest degree. We know what they are, but we know not what they may be, when the poet is done with them. For it is n't by the materials you use that your claim to originality will stand justified or condemned; it is solely by the thing you do with them.

There is one other question that will certainly and properly be asked. Where does *inspiration* come in? Is n't it that which, after all, is the true criterion and touchstone of originality? Is it not when, as Goethe put it, "the good ideas stand suddenly before us like free children of God, and cry out: 'Here we are!' "—is n't it then that we are most authentically original? What, too, of that larger aspect of Goethe's doctrine, which comes so near expressing, once for all, what we each of us would say, if we could, of genius:

Every productivity of the highest type, every significant *aperçu,* every invention, every great idea that bears fruit and achieves results, stands in no man's power, and is exalted above all earthly might. Things that so come we must regard as unlooked-for gifts from above, as veritable children of God, to be received with reverence and with joyful gratitude. They are akin to the dæmonic, which does resistlessly with us as it will, and to which we unwittingly yield ourselves, even while we think we are acting on our own initiative.

Isn't that what we really mean by originality? you will surely ask. Let us see, in the first place, what is not involved.

The ways of genius are as manifold as the mercies of the Lord. Inspiration may spring from what Tennyson calls "unseen germination"; it may come on the spirit, as Keats once wrote, "with a fine suddenness." It may arrive through brooding over an idea and waiting patiently until it shines, as Buffon enjoined. Or it may come in the amazing way in which it came to Mozart: "When I am riding in a carriage, or in a walk after a good meal, or in a sleepless night, then the thoughts come to me in a rush, and best of all. . . . Then [the thing] goes on growing . . . and however long it be, becomes indeed almost finished in my head, so that I afterwards survey it at a glance, like a goodly picture or handsome man; and in my imagination do not hear it at all in succession . . . but as a simultaneous whole. That is indeed a feast! All the finding and making goes on in me as in a very vivid dream." Inspiration may seize on one as "Tam o' Shanter" seized on Burns, when he walked all day by the riverside, "crooning to himsel," and "in such ecstasy that the tears were happing down his cheeks," as he wrote his verses on the top of his sod-dyke along the stream. Or it may weary one, as it wearied Wordsworth: "William tired himself with seeking an epithet for the cuckoo . . . William very nervous. After he was in bed, haunted with altering 'The Rainbow.' . . . William tired himself with hammering at a passage." It may come as to Goethe, in his bare little anchorite's cell of a study, from which (he says) he scarcely stepped the whole winter through, except into the still more Spartan bedroom opening out of it; or it may come as it used to come to Scott, while he galloped on horseback over the moors. It may descend as it descended upon Gautier, working imperturbably in the midst of the clatter of printing presses; or it may respond only to cloistral isolation, as with Flaubert: "I'm like a bowl of cream: if the cream is to form, the bowl must sit immobile." One may write of pastoral scenery, as Lodge did in "Rosalynde," "in the ocean when every line was wet with a surge"; or one may write of the sea, as Tennyson made "Break, break, break," "in a Lincolnshire lane, at five o'clock in the morning, between blossoming hedges." For inspiration is like the wind, that bloweth when and where and how it listeth. And the modes of its workings are utterly irrelevant to our concern. For Wordsworth tiring himself for an epithet, or Flaubert "afflicting his soul over some dubious word," is as original as Burns gesticulating by the riverside in an ungovernable access of joy, or as Byron dashing off verses after a ball.

But what is it that *sets the winds of inspiration blowing?* That is absolutely the only question that concerns us here. For what we call inspiration, in whatever wondrous ways it may behave once started, always starts. And its starting-point is some concrete suggestion, and that suggestion may be anything. It may be a stubble-field under the autumn light, that all at once touches the springs of inspiration; it may be a visit with one's sister to the River Wye, or the bugle music of the boatmen on Lake Killarney, or the nest of a field mouse turned up by a plough. And it may equally well be a line of Virgil, or some phrase of Horace, itself "the birth of some chance morning or evening . . . among the Sabine hills," that in a flash gives wings to the imagination; or a page of "Purchas His Pilgrimes," or an old yellow book picked up in a Florentine book stall. The titanic sweep of inspiration through "King Lear," and the thoughts beyond the reaches of our souls in "Hamlet," were stirred to life by two old plays. We are back where we started. What we call inspiration is the dynamic factor in originality—that is all.

Let us end orderly as we began. Poetry may never with safety cut loose from the old, because the old is always new. The tide of generations flows on unceasingly, and for each the old experiences have their pristine freshness. That is why the old themes are perennial. Love is as dazzling a miracle to every lover who loves to-day as if unnumbered millions had n't loved since time began. Death is n't trite to you and me because it's been the common lot since life first was; nor have the moon and stars grown old because un-counted centuries ago, beside the rivers of Babylon and Egypt, or among the hills and pasture lands of Israel, or in the wide stillness of Arabia, men saw them, and brooded, and wondered, and dreamed. The oldest things in the world are the things that also have been new as many times as human beings have been born. I happened one day this summer to look across at an adjoining cottage. There on the porch was a group of urchins absorbed in constructing a fleet of whittled ships, and on the path below, two little girls, heads close together, each with an arm about the other's waist, oblivious of all but their own secrets. And there, too, was the eternal sea. And each was as old as the other—and as new.

Now that is what the greatest poetry has always built on. Its roots strike deep into the eternally familiar. But the gift of the gods to genius is the power to catch and fix that familiar in the recurrent act of becoming new. That is originality.

1919

HERBERT READ

The Politics of the Unpolitical

If certain writers feel emancipated enough from all that is human—they would say intellectual enough—to continue to fulfil, under any circumstances whatever, the strange functions of purely abstract thought, good luck to them. But those who can only conceive their rôle as writers to be a means of experiencing more deeply and of establishing more fully a mode of existence which they want to be human, those who only write in order to feel themselves living integrally— such people no longer have the right to be disinterested. The trend of events, and the evolution of ideas, if they run out their course, will lead straight to an unparalleled deforma-

Reprinted from Herbert Read's *Politics of the Unpolitical* (1943) by permission of the publishers, George Routledge & Sons Ltd.

*tion of the individual human being.
Whoever gazes into the future which
is being forged for us, and can there
perceive the monstrous and denatured
brother whom one will necessarily resemble, cannot react except by a revolt
into extreme egoism. It is this egoism which must now be rehabilitated.
To-day the problem of the person
effaces all others. The intelligence is
placed in such circumstances that for
it disinterestedness and resignation
come to the same thing.*
                    THIERRY MAULNIER,
                La Crise est dans l'homme
                        (Paris, 1932).

THE politics of the unpolitical—these
are the politics of those who desire
to be pure in heart: the politics of men
without personal ambition; of those
who have not desired wealth or an unequal share of worldly possessions; of
those who have always striven, whatever
their race or condition, for human
values and not for national or sectional
interests.

For our Western world, Christ is the
supreme example of this unselfish devotion to the good of humanity, and the
Sermon on the Mount is the source of
all the politics of the unpolitical. But
others who came before Christ and who
may have influenced him elaborated
their political ideals in pureness of heart
—Lao-Tsŭ and Zeno, for example; and
among Christ's direct disciples we must
include several philosophers and prophets nearer to our time, whose message is
still insistent, and directly applicable to
our present condition—Ruskin and Kropotkin, Morris and Tolstoy, Gandhi and
Eric Gill. These modern representatives of what we might well call an
ancient tradition form a closely inter-

related body of thought: Gandhi, for
example, has declared his debt to Ruskin
and Tolstoy; Gill is a disciple of Morris,
who was himself a disciple of Ruskin;
Kropotkin was closely associated with
Morris. Ruskin, in this succession, has
a certain pre-eminence and originality:
the vitality and transforming power[1] of
his writings seem to come straight from
his deep study of the Bible and from his
prolonged meditation on the words of
Christ; though he had in himself that
rare power which Gandhi recognized as
the specifically poetic power—his power
"to call forth the good latent in the human breast." We are still far from esti-
mating the full extent of this great
man's influence, but we can describe
it as ethical and aesthetic rather than
as religious or political. Ruskin's eloquence did not bring into being either a
new sect or a new party: his power is
emotive and not calculative, and in this
as in other respects he is nearly related
to Rousseau, having for our own revolutionary period almost exactly the same
significance as Rousseau had for the
French Revolutionary period. We may
still come to regard *Unto this Last* as the
Contrat Social of a new society—as the
Manifesto of those communists who renounce political action in their efforts to
establish a new society.

Of the six names mentioned, Morris
was the only one who compromised on
this political issue, but he never, to the
end of his life, reconciled himself to
the political methods advocated by his
friends. His lecture on "The Policy of
Abstention" (1887) is the best statement
of the case against parliamentary action
ever made in English, and it is a pity
that it is so entirely forgotten by socialists to-day, and that it is only available

[1] "The one book that brought about an instantaneous and practical transformation in my life was *Unto
This Last*."—*Mahatma Gandhi: His Own Story* (London, 1930), p. 163.

in a limited and expensive publication.[2] Towards the end of his life Gandhi also, it might be said, has made a tactical compromise of some kind with the politically minded leaders of the Congress Party. With them he has worked in close association since 1921, but always in a relationship which he himself has described as "experimental." For the whole of Gandhi's life and teaching has been directed against parliamentary action: the doctrine of *ahimsa,* or nonviolence, rejects the violence of majority government no less decisively than the violence of military oppression. But before accusing Gandhi of political compromise, it would be necessary to know in much more detail the motives which have determined his recent activities; we must wait for the outcome of his final attempt to liberate India.

It is characteristic of these six teachers that although they would be included among the most revolutionary figures of the past hundred years, we do not spontaneously associate the word "democracy" with any of them. Democracy is a very ambiguous word, and its meanings vary from a sentimental sympathy for the poor and oppressed such as we get in Christian Socialism, to a ruthless dogma of proletarian dictatorship such as we have seen established in Russia. Our Six were all democrats in the former sense; none of them was a democrat in the latter sense. But it is an important distinction, and if in the name of democracy we are more and more inevitably compelled to commit ourselves to the political machinery of the state— to the nationalization of industry, to the bureaucratic control of all spheres of life and to the doctrine of the infallibility of the People (divinely invested in a unique Party)—then it is time to renounce the democratic label and seek a less equivocal name. My use of the word "democracy" in the pages which follow is always subject to this consideration.

A complete renunciation of the word is not easy: indeed, it has been deliberately made difficult for us, not only by the common usage of many ardent seekers after the truth, but also by the deliberate propaganda of the enemies of liberty. A common form of this Machiavellian sophistry consists in presenting your opponent with an apparently inescapable alternative—an "either/or" which you accept as covering all the known facts. In our own time, in the sphere of world politics, this either/or is *either* democracy *or* fascism. Such an alternative seems to leave communism out of account, but not in reality. If you question people about the relation of communism to democracy, the communists among them will tell you that communism is the extreme form of democracy, and the anti-communists will say that communism as it exists in Russia is merely another form of totalitarianism.

Both these views are right. Communism is an extreme form of democracy, and it is totalitarian: but equally the totalitarian state in the form of fascism is an extreme form of democracy. All forms of socialism, whether state socialism of the Russian kind, or national socialism of the German kind, or democratic socialism of the British kind, are professedly democratic: that is to say, they all obtain popular assent by the manipulation of mass psychology. All are actually majority governments. It has often been pointed out that in some

[2] *William Morris: Artist, Writer, Socialist,* by May Morris (2 vols. Oxford: Basil Blackwell, 1936), vol. ii, pp. 434-53.

ways the organization of society in Nazi Germany is much more thoroughly democratic than the organization of society in Great Britain or the United States. The German army is more democratic than the British army; the German industrial system is more democratic than the capitalist industrial system; German finance is more democratically controlled than finance in a plutocracy like ours. In Germany power and responsibility are not the prerogatives of birth or wealth, but are delegated to the holders of office in a party organization; and though such a system is strongly oppressive of individual freedom and therefore not democratic in the libertarian sense of the word, it is at least as democratic as a system which delegates the symbols of authority to a parliament and leaves the real power in the hands of those who control the financial system. National Socialism relates justice to service and group loyalty, which may not be defensible from an abstract ethical point of view; but it is at least an improvement on a system which confuses justice with the competitive struggles of the jungle. It is mere hypocrisy on the part of democratic propagandists to pretend that Great Britain or the United States enjoy some mythical happiness or freedom which is denied to the Germans, the Russians, or the Italians. We "enjoy" chaos just as they "enjoy" order; we "enjoy" licence, they "discipline"; the choice is in each case equally democratic.

I am not suggesting that the democracies of Great Britain and Germany are identical. I am only pointing out that fascism in Germany is a form of democracy, even if an arbitrary one; it is only its extremism which accounts for its intolerance. It is to be observed, however, that political democracy even in Great Britain grows more intolerant day by day, and not merely under the pressure of war. The pressure of an economic system which inevitably proceeds towards monopoly—that is to say, towards a unified control designed to maintain the security of profits and wages—brings about a form of government which, however democratic in appearance, is essentially totalitarian.

The weaknesses of democracy have been exposed by every political philosopher since Plato and Aristotle. Even Rousseau, the so-called Father of Democracy, rejected it as a system practicable for any society larger than a city state. The philosophers, being men of intelligence, have never been able to suggest anything better than a dictatorship of the intelligentsia; but knowing how unlikely it is that such a dictatorship would be long tolerated by the ignorant masses, they have tried to disguise the inevitability of some alternative form of dictatorship under a picturesque formula. Historically the most effective of these is constitutional monarchy. It has always been recognized that a king might easily degenerate into a tyrant, but his natural life is limited and can at a pinch be artificially shortened; whereas the reign of an aristocracy, which is the next best possibility, has no mensurable limit: it can only be brought to an end by a civil war with all its miseries.

The plain fact about democracy is that it is a physical impossibility. In an aggregation of millions of individuals such as we always have in modern society, we may get government *of* the people and even government *for* the people, but never for a moment government *by* the people. But that is the essential test, for if a people does not govern itself, it is governed by somebody else; *ipso facto* it is no longer a democracy. This is not merely a logical quibble: democracy never has in fact existed in modern times. In our own country, for example, the monarchical system was overthrown by an oligarchy, and since the "Great" Revolution of 1688 we have been governed by a succession of oligarchies, which might be Whig or might be Tory, might represent the landed interests or the moneyed interests, but never for a moment represented the people as a whole. In our own time a new oligarchy, the oligarchy of the trade unions, as exclusive a caste as ever aspired to power, has competed, luckily in vain, for the control of the state. It is now openly merging itself with the ascendant oligarchy of monopoly capitalism, to form what James Burnham has called "the managerial class."

All this is such an obvious interpretation of the historical facts that no one but a fool can deceive himself in the belief that democracy has ever been, or is ever likely to be, a reality in a modern industrial community. A constitutional monarchy as a cloak to competing sectional interests, as a symbol of unity in a society which would otherwise disintegrate from ruthless class warfare—that is the definition of the British constitution. The French Third Republic, the United States of America, and the Third Reich are all constitutions of the same character: they only differ in nomenclature and the trimming on their uniforms.

Nevertheless this must be said (if only in justification of the lip service which so many of us have paid to democracy at various times): the political doctrine known as democracy has implied an important principle which, if it were not systematically misinterpreted and misunderstood, would still justify us in using the word. This is the *principle of equality*—an ethical doctrine, even a religious dogma. The equality of man implies many things, but never its literal meaning. No one believes that all men are equal in capacity or talent: they are in fact outrageously diverse. But nevertheless, in Christian phraseology, they are all equal in the sight of God; and to affirm our common humanity is the first article of freedom. Whatever government we establish, whatever way of life we follow, all our faith is built on error unless we respect the rights of the person —that is to say, his right to be a person, a unique entity, "human left, from human free."

This is the fundamental doctrine of a Christian community and of all other types of essential communism. It is even fundamental to the communism of Marx and Engels. But the equality acknowledged by democracy has in practice been something very different. God has been eliminated from the formula and we are left with a mere equalization or levelling of man with man. The spiritual measure has been discarded, and man is left to dangle in material scales; and for centuries the counter-weight has been a piece of silver. The only way in which democracy has been able to assess equality is in the terms of money, and it is the inability of the trade union movement, especially in Great Britain and Germany, to break away from this cash valuation of humanity which has, more than any other single factor, made the democratic working-class movement a futile diversion of revolutionary effort.[3]

---

[3] Chiefly because it has prevented the workers from concentrating on the enhancement of their human dignity by the acquisition of responsibility for the direction and control of industry. But also because,

By what values a man shall be judged absolutely we will not discuss here, but socially, as a man among his fellow-men, he should be judged by his creative ability, by his power to add to the common stock of goods. The value of a man is the value of the art he practises—whether it is the art of healing or the art of making music, the art of road-mending or the art of cooking. We might place first of all the art of making children, because on that the continuance of the human race depends. Procreation is perhaps the only art which is literally creative: the rest of the arts are merely inventive.

For this and for reasons more strictly sociological, our social philosophy must begin with the family. The Pope is right, the Archbishop of Canterbury is right, Pétain is right; the psychoanalysts and the anthropologists are right. The Stalinists are wrong, the Nazis are wrong, our own democratic socialists and public school fascists are wrong, for they all exalt the state above the family. From whatever realistic angle we approach the problems of human life, the family is seen as the integral unit, without which there is no social organization, no social progress, no social order or human happiness. But we must insist that this is a sociological problem, and we must dissociate ourselves from those who think it can be solved by moral persuasion. Families are encouraged and sustained by security of life and property, decent housing, and an environment in which nurture and education can be natural and serene. Morality and religion may give their sanction to the social unit thus established:

it is the fascist way of thinking to imagine that such sanctions are a substitute for economic action.

The next essential group is the guild—the association of men and women according to their calling or practical function. (I obstinately retain the word "guild," in spite of its medieval and sentimental associations, because it is more human, and euphonious, than such expressions as "collective," "cooperative," "soviet," etc.). The guild is a vertical and not a horizontal organization: it includes all persons associated together in the production of a particular commodity. The agricultural guild, for example, would include the drivers and mechanics who run the tractors: the engineers' guild would include the men who make the tractors. But the vertical organization will be divided into regional and district units, and the main business of the guilds will always take place in the district units; decisions will arise out of personal contacts and not from the abstract and legalistic conclaves of a central bureau.

Decentralization is thus also of the essence of this alternative to democracy. "Real politics are local politics," and power and authority should be devolved and segmented to the utmost limit of practicability. Only in such a way can the person—every person in society—be assured of an adequate sense of responsibility and human dignity. These qualities for the average person only emerge in his actual sphere of work and in his regional environment.

The trend to centralization is a disease of democracy, and not, as is so often assumed, of the machine. It arises inevi-

as Franz Borkenau has shown so effectively, it has prevented the development of international solidarity among the workers, for the wage-rate is directly dependent on the international market, not only of labour, but of commodities. For this reason the workers have been forced to realize that their interests are bound up, not only with the interests of their employers, but also with the competitive expansion of the national capital. Cf. F. Borkenau, *Socialism, National or International* (Routledge, 1942).

tably from the concentration of power in parliament, from the separation made between responsibility and creative activity, from the massing of production for greater profits and higher wages. The evolution of democracy is parallel to the growth of centralization, and centralization is in no sense an inevitable process. The present war has revealed its extraordinary inefficiency. Have not the guerillas of Jugoslavia shown more initiative than the bureaucrats of Whitehall? The centralization of control in a democratic state is clumsy, inhuman and inert. Incapable of thought, originality or enterprise, it can only act under the dictatorship of a Hitler or a Churchill—even the shrill voices of an exasperated Press have no effect on it.

The health and happiness of society depend on the labour and science of its members; but neither health nor happiness is possible unless that work and science are directed and controlled by the workers themselves. A guild is by definition autonomous and self-governing. Every man who is a master of his craft acquires thereby the right to a voice in the direction of his workshop. He also acquires security of tenure and of income. Indeed, his income and his tenure should depend on his qualifications rather than on the tally of his labours. He should begin to receive an income from the moment he has chosen a calling and been admitted as an apprentice to a trade or profession—which will be long before he has left school. His income will rise with his qualifications, and will depend entirely on his qualifications. Any rational society will naturally make use of the services of a qualified worker, because it thereby increases the general well-being. If it fails to do so, that society is restricting production; and if such restriction is in the general interest, then society should pay the worker for his qualifications until they can be used, or otherwise pay the worker to train and acquire more immediately useful qualifications. The talents and acquired skill of a person are his property: his contribution to the common wealth. Society should be organized to secure the maximum utilization of its inherent wealth, and the productive organizations themselves will then decide how this common wealth is best increased—by machinery or handicraft, by large factories or small workshops, in towns or villages. The human values involved, and not an abstract and numerical profit, will be the criterion.

Education, in such a society, is initiation. It is the revelation of innate capacities, the training of these capacities in socially useful activities, the disciplining of these activities to aesthetic and moral ends.

Such a natural organization of society leaves little activity to the state as such. The state remains merely as the arbiter, to decide in the interests of the whole the conflicts which emerge in the parts. Such a function is already exercised by an independent judiciary, which might well extend its functions to cover the rights of the citizen as consumer. An Economic Council, constituted by much the same means as the Bench, would be necessary to safeguard society as a whole against a policy of restrictionism in any particular guild, to direct the general volume of production and to maintain a balanced output among its tributary guilds. It is difficult to see the necessity for any other central authority. The Board of Education, for example, would be in fact as well as in name a board of education—an autonomous body charged with the task of educating the nation's children, governed and directed by those responsible for this task. The Bankers' Guild would carry out the functions of the Treasury and the Banks, in so far as these functions are necessary in a society whose production is organized for use and not for profit. And so for all the economic functions of society.

All this may seem to amount to a programme far more definite and dogmatic than the title of my essay promised, but to be unpolitical does not mean to be without politics: every attitude that is more than egoistic is to that extent social, and a social attitude is a political attitude. But it is one thing to have politics, and another thing to pursue them. It is one thing to have a faith, and another thing to trade on the credulity of the faithful. It is not the substance of politics we should object to, but the methods of the politician. We should refuse to invest our private interests in a public policy, for we know that what cannot be won by a change of heart, which is also a revolution of reason, is only won by cheats and impostors. Above all, we should realize by now that a new order will never be won by old pensioners, among whom are to be numbered the six hundred and fifteen pawns of our party system.

Let me summarize the essential feature of a natural society:

I. The liberty of the person.
II. The integrity of the family.
III. The reward of qualifications.
IV. The self-government of the guilds.
V. The abolition of parliament and centralized government.
VI. The institution of arbitrament.
VII. The delegation of authority.
VIII. The humanization of industry.

The social order thus envisaged is inter-national because it is essentially pacific: it is pacific because it is essentially international. It aims at the production of world-wide plenty, at the humanization of work, and at the eradication of all economic conflicts. It may be, as some philosophers hold, that an aggressive instinct is innate in man, and that no organization of society can guard against its expression. In that case the world can only be made tolerable in the degree that this instinct can be controlled by reason. Reason has no chance if men are starving, or even if they have undue cause for envy. But granted an economy which is no longer competitive, in which the highest yield of production is wisely and evenly distributed among all mankind, then reason will have a chance. Instincts are not immutable: they can be transformed, sublimated, diverted into creative channels. Energy itself is not evil: it only becomes evil by being applied to evil ends.

The world is waiting for a new faith —especially the youth of the world is waiting for a new faith. The old institutions, the old parties, are dead at the roots: they receive no refreshment. The young men and women stand apart, indifferent, inactive. But do not let us mistake their indifference for apathy, their inactivity for laziness. Intellectually, they are very wide awake. But they have rejected our abstract slogans and the hollow institutions in which old men gibber about freedom, democracy and culture. They don't want freedom if it means the freedom to exploit their fellow-men: they don't want democracy if it means the ridiculous bagmen of Westminster; they don't want culture if it means the intellectual dope of our academies and universities. They want to get rid of the profiteers and the advertising men, the petty tyrannical bureaucrats and the screaming journalists, the clubmen and the still too numerous flock of rentiers for ever cackling over their threatened nest-eggs. They want a world that is morally clean and socially just, naturally productive and aesthetically beautiful. And they know they won't get it from any of the existing parties, from any of the existing political systems. They hate fascism, they recoil from communism, and they despise democracy. They are groping towards a new faith, a new order, a new world. They are not a party and never will be a party: they have no name and will perhaps never have a name. But they will act, and onto the ruins of war they will cast the tarnished baubles and stale furnishings of those parliaments which brought death and despair to two successive generations of young men.

1943

THEODORE ROOSEVELT

The New Nationalism

WE COME here to-day to commemorate one of the epoch-making events of the long struggle for the rights of man—the long struggle for the uplift of humanity. Our country—this great Republic—means nothing unless it means the triumph of a real democracy, the triumph of popular government, and, in the long run, of an economic system under which each man shall be guaranteed the opportunity to show the best that there is in him. That is why the history of America is now the central feature of the history of the world; for the world has set its face hopefully toward our democracy; and, O my fellow citizens, each one of you carries on your shoulders not only the burden of doing well for the sake of your own country, but the burden of doing well and of seeing that this nation does well for the sake of mankind.

There have been two great crises in our country's history: first, when it was formed, and then, again, when it was perpetuated; and, in the second of these great crises—in the time of stress and strain which culminated in the Civil War, on the outcome of which depended the justification of what had been done earlier, you men of the Grand Army, you men who fought through the Civil War, not only did you justify your generation, not only did you render life worth living for our generation, but you justified the wisdom of Washington and Washington's colleagues. If this Republic had been founded by them only to be split asunder into fragments when the strain came, then the judgment of the world would have been that Washington's work was not worth doing. It was you who crowned Washington's work, as you carried to achievement the high purpose of Abraham Lincoln.

Now, with this second period of our history the name of John Brown will be

Reprinted from *Social Justice and Popular Rule*, Charles Scribner's Sons, 1927, by permission of the Roosevelt estate and the Roosevelt Memorial Association.

forever associated; and Kansas was the theatre upon which the first act of the second of our great national life dramas was played. It was the result of the struggle in Kansas which determined that our country should be in deed as well as in name devoted to both union and freedom; that the great experiment of democratic government on a national scale should succeed and not fail. In name we had the Declaration of Independence in 1776; but we gave the lie by our acts to the words of the Declaration of Independence until 1865; and words count for nothing except in so far as they represent acts. This is true everywhere; but, O my friends, it should be truest of all in political life. A broken promise is bad enough in private life. It is worse in the field of politics. No man is worth his salt in public life who makes on the stump a pledge which he does not keep after election; and, if he makes such a pledge and does not keep it, hunt him out of public life. I care for the great deeds of the past chiefly as spurs to drive us onward in the present. I speak of the men of the past partly that they may be honored by our praise of them, but more that they may serve as examples for the future.

It was a heroic struggle; and, as is inevitable with all such struggles, it had also a dark and terrible side. Very much was done of good, and much also of evil; and, as was inevitable in such a period of revolution, often the same man did both good and evil. For our great good fortune as a nation, we, the people of the United States as a whole, can now afford to forget the evil, or, at least, to remember it without bitterness, and to fix our eyes with pride only on the good that was accomplished. Even in ordinary times there are very few of us who do not see the problems of life as

through a glass, darkly; and when the glass is clouded by the murk of furious popular passion, the vision of the best and the bravest is dimmed. Looking back, we are all of us now able to do justice to the valor and the disinterestedness and the love of the right, as to each it was given to see the right, shown both by the men of the North and the men of the South in that contest which was finally decided by the attitude of the West. We can admire the heroic valor, the sincerity, the self-devotion shown alike by the men who wore the blue and the men who wore the gray; and our sadness that such men should have had to fight one another is tempered by the glad knowledge that ever hereafter their descendants shall be found fighting side by side, struggling in peace as well as in war for the uplift of their common country, all alike resolute to raise to the highest pitch of honor and usefulness the nation to which they all belong. As for the veterans of the Grand Army of the Republic, they deserve honor and recognition such as is paid to no other citizens of the Republic; for to them the republic owes its all; for to them it owes its very existence. It is because of what you and your comrades did in the dark years that we of to-day walk, each of us, head erect, and proud that we belong, not to one of a dozen little squabbling contemptible commonwealths, but to the mightiest nation upon which the sun shines.

I do not speak of this struggle of the past merely from the historic standpoint. Our interest is primarily in the application to-day of the lessons taught by the contest of half a century ago. It is of little use for us to pay lip-loyalty to the mighty men of the past unless we sincerely endeavor to apply to the problems of the present precisely the qualities which in other crises enabled the men of that day to meet those crises. It is half melancholy and half amusing to see the way in which well-meaning people gather to do honor to the men who, in company with John Brown, and under the lead of Abraham Lincoln, faced and solved the great problems of the nineteenth century, while, at the same time, these same good people nervously shrink from, or frantically denounce, those who are trying to meet the problems of the twentieth century in the spirit which was accountable for the successful solution of the problems of Lincoln's time.

Of that generation of men to whom we owe so much, the man to whom we owe most is, of course, Lincoln. Part of our debt to him is because he forecast our present struggle and saw the way out. He said:

"I hold that while man exists it is his duty to improve not only his own condition, but to assist in ameliorating mankind."

And again:

"Labor is prior to, and independent of, capital. Capital is only the fruit of labor, and could never have existed if labor had not first existed. Labor is the superior of capital, and deserves much the higher consideration."

If that remark was original with me, I should be even more strongly denounced as a Communist agitator than I shall be anyhow. It is Lincoln's. I am only quoting it; and that is one side; that is the side the capitalist should hear. Now, let the working man hear his side.

"Capital has its rights, which are as worthy of protection as any other rights. . . . Nor should this lead to a war upon the owners of property. Property is the fruit of labor; . . . property is desirable; is a positive good in the world."

And then comes a thoroughly Lincolnlike sentence:

"Let not him who is houseless pull down the house of another, but let him work diligently and build one for himself, thus by example assuring that his own shall be safe from violence when built."

It seems to me that, in these words, Lincoln took substantially the attitude that we ought to take; he showed the proper sense of proportion in his relative estimates of capital and labor, of human rights and property rights. Above all, in this speech, as in many others, he taught a lesson in wise kindliness and charity; an indispensable lesson to us of to-day. But this wise kindliness and charity never weakened his arm or numbed his heart. We cannot afford weakly to blind ourselves to the actual conflict which faces us to-day. The issue is joined, and we must fight or fail.

In every wise struggle for human betterment one of the main objects, and often the only object, has been to achieve in large measure equality of opportunity. In the struggle for this great end, nations rise from barbarism to civilization, and through it people press forward from one stage of enlightenment to the next. One of the chief factors in progress is the destruction of special privilege. The essence of any struggle for healthy liberty has always been, and must always be, to take from some one man or class of men the right to enjoy power, or wealth, or position, or immunity, which has not been earned by service to his or their fellows. That is what you fought for in the Civil War, and that is what we strive for now.

At many stages in the advance of humanity, this conflict between the men who possess more than they have earned and the men who have earned more than they possess is the central condition of progress. In our day it appears as the struggle of freemen to gain and hold the right of self-government as against the special interests, who twist the methods of free government into machinery for defeating the popular will. At every stage, and under all circumstances, the essence of the struggle is to equalize opportunity, destroy privilege, and give to the life and citizenship of every individual the highest possible value both to himself and to the commonwealth. That is nothing new. All I ask in civil life is what you fought for in the Civil War. I ask that civil life be carried on according to the spirit in which the army was carried on. You never get perfect justice, but the effort in handling the army was to bring to the front the men who could do the job. Nobody grudged promotion to Grant, or Sherman, or Thomas, or Sheridan, because they earned it. The only complaint was when a man got promotion which he did not earn.

Practical equality of opportunity for all citizens, when we achieve it, will have two great results. First, every man will have a fair chance to make of himself all that in him lies; to reach the highest point to which his capacities, unassisted by special privilege of his own and unhampered by the special privilege of others, can carry him, and to get for himself and his family substantially what he has earned. Second, equality of opportunity means that the commonwealth will get from every citizen the highest service of which he is capable. No man who carries the burden of the special privileges of another can give to the commonwealth that service to which it is fairly entitled.

I stand for the square deal. But when I say that I am for the square deal, I mean not merely that I stand for fair play under the present rules of the game, but that I stand for having those rules changed so as to work for a more substantial equality of opportunity and of reward for equally good service. One word of warning, which, I think, is hardly necessary in Kansas. When I say I want a square deal for the poor man, I do not mean that I want a square deal for the man who remains poor because he has not got the energy to work for himself. If a man who has had a chance will not make good, then he has got to quit. And you men of the Grand Army, you want justice for the brave man who fought, and punishment for the coward who shirked his work. Is not that so?

Now, this means that our government, National and State, must be freed from the sinister influence or control of special interests. Exactly as the special interests of cotton and slavery threatened our political integrity before the Civil War, so now the great special business interests too often control and corrupt the men and methods of government for their own profit. We must drive the special interests out of politics. That is one of our tasks to-day. Every special interest is entitled to justice—full, fair, and complete—and, now, mind you, if there were any attempt by mob-violence to plunder and work harm to the special interest, whatever it may be, that I most dislike, and the wealthy man, whomsoever he may be, for whom I have the greatest contempt, I would fight for him, and you would if you were worth your salt. He should have justice. For every special interest is entitled to justice, but not one is entitled to a vote in Congress, to a voice on the bench, or to representation in any public office. The Constitution guarantees protection to property, and we must make that promise good. But it does not give the right of suffrage to any corporation.

The true friend of property, the true conservative, is he who insists that property shall be the servant and not the master of the commonwealth; who insists that the creature of man's making shall be the servant and not the master of the man who made it. The citizens of the United States must effectively control the mighty commercial forces which they have themselves called into being.

There can be no effective control of corporations while their political activity remains. To put an end to it will be neither a short nor an easy task, but it can be done.

We must have complete and effective publicity of corporate affairs, so that the people may know beyond peradventure whether the corporations obey the law and whether their management entitles them to the confidence of the public. It is necessary that laws should be passed to prohibit the use of corporate funds directly or indirectly for political purposes; it is still more necessary that such laws should be thoroughly enforced. Corporate expenditures for political purposes, and especially such expenditures by public-service corporations, have supplied one of the principal sources of corruption in our political affairs.

It has become entirely clear that we must have government supervision of the capitalization, not only of public-service corporations, including, particularly, railways, but of all corporations doing an interstate business. I do not wish to see the nation forced into the ownership of the railways if it can possibly be avoided, and the only alternative is thoroughgoing and effective regulation, which shall be based on a full knowledge of all the facts, including a physical valuation of property. This physical valuation is not needed, or, at least, is very rarely needed, for fixing rates; but it is needed as the basis of honest capitalization.

We have come to recognize that franchises should never be granted except for a limited time, and never without proper provision for compensation to the public. It is my personal belief that the same kind and degree of control and supervision which should be exercised over public-service corporations should be extended also to combinations which control necessaries of life, such as meat, oil, and coal, or which deal in them on an important scale. I have no doubt that the ordinary man who has control of them is much like ourselves. I have no doubt he would like to do well, but I want to have enough supervision to help him realize that desire to do well.

I believe that the officers, and, especially, the directors, of corporations should be held personally responsible when any corporation breaks the law.

Combinations in industry are the result of an imperative economic law which cannot be repealed by political legislation. The effort at prohibiting all combination has substantially failed. The way out lies, not in attempting to prevent such combinations, but in completely controlling them in the interest of the public welfare. For that purpose the Federal Bureau of Corporations is an agency of first importance. Its powers, and, therefore, its efficiency, as well as that of the Interstate Commerce Commission, should be largely increased. We have a right to expect from the Bureau of Corporations and from the Interstate Commerce Commission a very high grade of public service. We should be as sure of the proper conduct of the interstate railways and the proper management of interstate business as we are now sure of the conduct and management of the national banks, and we should have as effective supervision in one case as in the other. The Hepburn Act, and the amendment to the act in the shape in which it finally passed Congress at the last session, represent a long step in advance, and we must go yet further.

There is a wide-spread belief among our people that, under the methods of making tariffs which have hitherto obtained, the special interests are too influential. Probably this is true of both the big special interests and the little special interests. These methods have put a premium on selfishness, and, naturally, the selfish big interests have gotten more than their smaller, though equally selfish, brothers. The duty of Congress is to provide a method by which the interest of the whole people shall be all that receives consideration. To this end there must be an expert tariff commission, wholly removed from the possibility of political pressure or of improper business influence. Such a commission can find the real difference between cost of production, which is mainly the difference of labor cost here and abroad. As fast as its recommendations are made, I believe in revising one schedule at a time. A general revision of the tariff almost inevitably leads to log-rolling and the subordination of the general public interest to local and special interests.

The absence of effective State, and, especially, National, restraint upon unfair money-getting has tended to create a small class of enormously wealthy and economically powerful men, whose chief object is to hold and increase their power. The prime need is to change the conditions which enable these men to accumulate power which it is not for the general welfare that they should hold or exercise. We grudge no man a fortune which represents his own power and sagacity, when exercised with entire regard to the welfare of his fellows. Again, comrades over there, take the lesson from your own experience. Not only did you not grudge, but you gloried in the promotion of the great generals who gained their promotion by leading the army to victory. So it is with us. We grudge no man a fortune in civil life if it is honorably obtained and well used. It is not even enough that it should have been gained without doing damage to the community. We should permit it to be gained only so long as the gaining represents benefit to the community. This, I know, implies a policy of a far more active governmental interference with social and economic conditions in this country than we have yet had, but I think we have got to face the fact that such an increase in governmental control is now necessary.

No man should receive a dollar unless that dollar has been fairly earned. Every dollar received should represent a dollar's worth of service rendered—not gambling in stocks, but service rendered. The really big fortune, the swollen fortune, by the mere fact of its size acquires qualities which differentiate it in kind as well as in degree from what is possessed by men of relatively small means. Therefore, I believe in a graduated income tax on big fortunes, and in another tax which is far more easily collected and far more effective—a graduated inheritance tax on big fortunes, properly safeguarded against evasion and increasing rapidly in amount with the size of the estate.

The people of the United States suffer from periodical financial panics to a degree substantially unknown among the other nations which approach us in financial strength. There is no reason why we should suffer what they escape. It is of profound importance that our financial system should be promptly investigated, and so thoroughly and effectively revised as to make it certain that hereafter our currency will no longer fail at critical times to meet our needs.

It is hardly necessary for me to repeat that I believe in an efficient army and a navy large enough to secure for us abroad that respect which is the surest guaranty of peace. A word of special warning to my fellow citizens who are as progressive as I hope I am. I want them to keep up their interest in our internal affairs; and I want them also continually to remember Uncle Sam's interests abroad. Justice and fair dealing among nations rest upon principles identical with those which control justice and fair dealing among the individuals of which nations are composed, with the vital exception that each nation must do its own part in international police work. If you get into trouble here, you can call for the police; but if Uncle Sam gets into trouble, he has got to be his own policeman, and I want to see him strong enough to encourage the peaceful aspirations of other peoples in connection with us. I believe in national friendships and heartiest goodwill to all nations; but national friendships, like those between men, must be founded on respect as well as on liking, on forbearance as well as upon trust. I should be heartily ashamed of any American who did not try to make the American Government act as justly toward the other nations in international relations as he himself would act toward any individual in private relations. I should be heartily ashamed to see us wrong a weaker power, and I should

hang my head forever if we tamely suffered wrong from a stronger power.

Of conservation I shall speak more at length elsewhere. Conservation means development as much as it does protection. I recognize the right and duty of this generation to develop and use the natural resources of our land; but I do not recognize the right to waste them, or to rob, by wasteful use, the generations that come after us. I ask nothing of the nation except that it so behave as each farmer here behaves with reference to his own children. That farmer is a poor creature who skins the land and leaves it worthless to his children. The farmer is a good farmer who, having enabled the land to support himself and to provide for the education of his children, leaves it to them a little better than he found it himself. I believe the same thing of a nation.

Moreover, I believe that the natural resources must be used for the benefit of all our people, and not monopolized for the benefit of the few, and here again is another case in which I am accused of taking a revolutionary attitude. People forget now that one hundred years ago there were public men of good character who advocated the nation selling its public lands in great quantities, so that the nation could get the most money out of it, and giving it to the men who could cultivate it for their own uses. We took the proper democratic ground that the land should be granted in small sections to the men who were actually to till it and live on it. Now, with the waterpower, with the forests, with the mines, we are brought face to face with the fact that there are many people who will go with us in conserving the resources only if they are to be allowed to exploit them for their benefit. That is one of the fundamental reasons why the special interests should be driven out of politics. Of all the questions which can come before this nation, short of the actual preservation of its existence in a great war, there is none which compares in importance with the great central task of leaving this land even a better land for our descendants than it is for us, and training them into a better race to inhabit the land and pass it on. Conservation is a great moral issue, for it involves the patriotic duty of insuring the safety and continuance of the nation. Let me add that the health and vitality of our people are at least as well worth conserving as their forests, waters, lands, and minerals, and in this great work the national government must bear a most important part.

I have spoken elsewhere also of the great task which lies before the farmers of the country to get for themselves and their wives and children not only the benefits of better farming, but also those of better business methods and better conditions of life on the farm. The burden of this great task will fall, as it should, mainly upon the great organizations of the farmers themselves. I am glad it will, for I believe they are all well able to handle it. In particular, there are strong reasons why the Departments of Agriculture of the various States, the United States Department of Agriculture, and the agricultural colleges and experiment stations should extend their work to cover all phases of farm life, instead of limiting themselves, as they have far too often limited themselves in the past, solely to the question of the production of crops. And now a special word to the farmer. I want to see him make the farm as fine a farm as it can be made; and let him remember to see that the improvement goes on indoors as well as out; let him remember that the farmer's wife should have her share of thought and attention just as much as the farmer himself.

Nothing is more true than that excess of every kind is followed by reaction; a fact which should be pondered by reformer and reactionary alike. We are face to face with new conceptions of the relations of property to human welfare, chiefly because certain advocates of the rights of property as against the rights of men have been pushing their claims too far. The man who wrongly holds that every human right is secondary to his profit must now give way to the advocate of human welfare, who rightly maintains that every man holds his property subject to the general right of the community to regulate its use to whatever degree the public welfare may require it.

But I think we may go still further. The right to regulate the use of wealth in the public interest is universally admitted. Let us admit also the right to regulate the terms and conditions of labor, which is the chief element of wealth, directly in the interest of the common good. The fundamental thing to do for every man is to give him a chance to reach a place in which he will make the greatest possible contribution to the public welfare. Understand what I say there. Give him a chance, not push him up if he will not be pushed. Help any man who stumbles; if he lies down, it is a poor job to try to carry him; but if he is a worthy man, try your best to see that he gets a chance to show the worth that is in him. No man can be a good citizen unless he has a wage more than sufficient to cover the bare cost of living, and hours of labor short enough so that after his day's work is done he will have time and energy to bear his share in the management of the community, to help in carrying the general load. We keep countless men from being good citizens by the conditions of life with which we surround them. We need comprehensive workmen's compensation acts, both State and National laws to regulate child labor and work for women, and, especially, we need in our common schools not merely education in book-learning, but also practical training for daily life and work. We need to enforce better sanitary conditions for our workers and to extend the use of safety appliances for our workers in industry and commerce, both within and between the States. Also, friends, in the interest of the working man himself we need to set our faces like flint against mob-violence just as against corporate greed; against violence and injustice and lawlessness by wageworkers just as much as against lawless cunning and greed and selfish arrogance of employers. If I could ask but one thing of my fellow countrymen, my request would be that, whenever they go in for reform, they remember the two sides, and that they always exact justice from one side as much as from the other. I have small use for the public servant who can always see and denounce the corruption of the capitalist, but who cannot persuade himself, especially before election, to say a word about lawless mob-violence. And I have equally small use for the man, be he a judge on the bench, or editor of a great paper, or wealthy and influential private citizen, who can see clearly enough and denounce the lawlessness of mob-violence, but whose eyes are closed so that he is blind when the question is one of corruption in business on a gigantic scale. Also remember what I said about excess in reformer and reactionary alike. If the reactionary man, who

thinks of nothing but the rights of property, could have his way, he would bring about a revolution; and one of my chief fears in connection with progress comes because I do not want to see our people, for lack of proper leadership, compelled to follow men whose intentions are excellent, but whose eyes are a little too wild to make it really safe to trust them. Here in Kansas there is one paper which habitually denounces me as the tool of Wall Street, and at the same time frantically repudiates the statement that I am a Socialist on the ground that that is an unwarranted slander of the Socialists.

National efficiency has many factors. It is a necessary result of the principle of conservation widely applied. In the end it will determine our failure or success as a nation. National efficiency has to do, not only with natural resources and with men, but it is equally concerned with institutions. The State must be made efficient for the work which concerns only the people of the State; and the nation for that which concerns all the people. There must remain no neutral ground to serve as a refuge for lawbreakers, and especially for lawbreakers of great wealth, who can hire the vulpine legal cunning which will teach them how to avoid both jurisdictions. It is a misfortune when the national legislature fails to do its duty in providing a national remedy, so that the only national activity is the purely negative activity of the judiciary in forbidding the State to exercise power in the premises.

I do not ask for overcentralization; but I do ask that we work in a spirit of broad and far-reaching nationalism when we work for what concerns our people as a whole. We are all Americans. Our common interests are as broad as the continent. I speak to you here in Kansas exactly as I would speak in New York or Georgia, for the most vital problems are those which affect us all alike. The National Government belongs to the whole American people, and where the whole American people are interested, that interest can be guarded effectively only by the National Government. The betterment which we seek must be accomplished, I believe, mainly through the National Government.

The American people are right in demanding that New Nationalism, without which we cannot hope to deal with new problems. The New Nationalism puts the national need before sectional or personal advantage. It is impatient of the utter confusion that results from local legislatures attempting to treat national issues as local issues. It is still more impatient of the impotence which springs from overdivision of governmental powers, the impotence which makes it possible for local selfishness or for legal cunning, hired by wealthy special interests, to bring national activities to a deadlock. This New Nationalism regards the executive power as the steward of the public welfare. It demands of the judiciary that it shall be interested primarily in human welfare rather than in property, just as it demands that the representative body shall represent all the people rather than any one class or section of the people.

I believe in shaping the ends of government to protect property as well as human welfare. Normally, and in the long run, the ends are the same; but whenever the alternative must be faced, I am for men and not for property, as you were in the Civil War. I am far from underestimating the importance of dividends; but I rank dividends below human character. Again, I do not have any sympathy with the reformer who says he does not care for dividends. Of course, economic welfare is necessary, for a man must pull his own weight and be able to support his family. I know well that the reformers must not bring upon the people economic ruin, or the reforms themselves will go down in the ruin. But we must be ready to face temporary disaster, whether or not brought on by those who will war against us to the knife. Those who oppose all reform will do well to remember that ruin in its worst form is inevitable if our national life brings us nothing better than swollen fortunes for the few and the triumph in both politics and business of a sordid and selfish materialism.

If our political institutions were perfect, they would absolutely prevent the political domination of money in any part of our affairs. We need to make our political representatives more quickly and sensitively responsive to the people whose servants they are. More direct action by the people in their own affairs under proper safeguards is vitally necessary. The direct primary is a step in this direction, if it is associated with a corrupt-practices act effective to prevent the advantage of the man willing recklessly and unscrupulously to spend money over his more honest competitor. It is particularly important that all moneys received or expended for campaign purposes should be publicly accounted for, not only after election, but before election as well. Political action must be made simpler, easier, and freer from confusion for every citizen. I believe that the prompt removal of unfaithful or incompetent public servants should be made easy and sure in whatever way experience shall show to be most expedient in any given class of cases.

One of the fundamental necessities in

a representative government such as ours is to make certain that the men to whom the people delegate their power shall serve the people by whom they are elected; and not the special interests. I believe that every national officer, elected or appointed, should be forbidden to perform any service or receive any compensation, directly or indirectly, from interstate corporations; and a similar provision could not fail to be useful within the States.

The object of government is the welfare of the people. The material progress and prosperity of a nation are desirable chiefly so far as they lead to the moral and material welfare of all good citizens. Just in proportion as the average man and woman are honest, capable of sound judgment and high ideals, active in public affairs—but, first of all, sound in their home life, and the father and mother of healthy children whom they bring up well—just so far, and no farther, we may count our civilization a success. We must have—I believe we have already—a genuine and permanent moral awakening, without which no wisdom of legislation or administration really means anything; and, on the other hand, we must try to secure the social and economic legislation without which any improvement due to purely moral agitation is necessarily evanescent. Let me again illustrate by a reference to the Grand Army. You could not have won simply as a disorderly and disorganized mob. You needed generals; you needed careful administration of the most advanced type; and a good commissary—the cracker line. You well remember that success was necessary in many different lines in order to bring about general success. You had to have the administration at Washington good, just as you had to have the administration in the field; and you had to have the work of the generals good. You could not have triumphed without that administration and leadership; but it would all have been worthless if the average soldier had not had the right stuff in him. He had to have the right stuff in him, or you could not get it out of him. In the last analysis, therefore, vitally necessary though it was to have the right kind of organization and the right kind of generalship, it was even more vitally necessary that the average soldier should have the fighting edge, the right character. So it is in our civil life. No matter how honest and decent we are in our private lives, if we do not have the right kind of law and the right kind of administration of the law, we cannot go forward as a nation. That is imperative; but it must be an addition to, and not a substitution for, the qualities that make us good citizens. In the last analysis, the most important elements in any man's career must be the sum of those qualities which, in the aggregate, we speak of as character. If he has not got it, then no law that the wit of man can devise, no administration of the law by the boldest and strongest executive, will avail to help him. We must have the right kind of character—character that makes a man, first of all, a good man in the home, a good father, a good husband—that makes a man a good neighbor. You must have that, and, then, in addition, you must have the kind of law and the kind of administration of the law which will give to those qualities in the private citizen the best possible chance for development. The prime problem of our nation is to get the right type of good citizenship, and, to get it, we must have progress, and our public men must be genuinely progressive.　　1910

FRANKLIN D. ROOSEVELT

First Inaugural Address

I AM CERTAIN that my fellow Americans expect that on my induction into the Presidency I will address them with a candor and a decision which the present situation of our Nation impels. This is preeminently the time to speak the truth, the whole truth, frankly and boldly. Nor need we shrink from honestly facing conditions in our country today. This great Nation will endure as it has endured, will revive and will prosper. So, first of all, let me assert my firm belief that the only thing we have to fear is fear itself—nameless, unreasoning, unjustified terror which paralyzes needed efforts to convert retreat into advance. In every dark hour of our national life a leadership of frankness and vigor has met with that understanding and support of the people themselves which is essential to victory. I am convinced that you will again give that support to leadership in these critical days.

In such a spirit on my part and on yours we face our common difficulties. They concern, thank God, only material things. Values have shrunken to fantastic levels; taxes have risen; our ability to pay has fallen; government of all kinds is faced by serious curtailment of income; the means of exchange are frozen in the currents of trade; the withered leaves of industrial enterprise lie on every side; farmers find no markets for their produce; the savings of many years in thousands of families are gone.

More important, a host of unemployed citizens face the grim problem of existence, and an equally great number toil with little return. Only a foolish optimist can deny the dark realities of the moment.

Yet our distress comes from no failure of substance. We are stricken by no plague of locusts. Compared with the perils which our forefathers conquered because they believed and were not afraid, we have still much to be thankful for. Nature still offers her bounty and human efforts have multiplied it. Plenty is at our doorstep, but a generous use of it languishes in the very sight of the supply. Primarily this is because rulers of the exchange of mankind's goods have failed through their own stubbornness and their own incompetence, have admitted their failure, and have abdicated. Practices of the unscrupulous money changers stand indicted in the court of public opinion, rejected by the hearts and minds of men.

True they have tried, but their efforts have been cast in the pattern of an outworn tradition. Faced by failure of credit they have proposed only the lending of more money. Stripped of the lure of profit by which to induce our people to follow their false leadership, they have resorted to exhortations, pleading tearfully for restored confidence. They know only the rules of a generation of self-seekers. They have no vision, and when there is no vision the people perish.

The money changers have fled from their high seats in the temple of our civilization. We may now restore that temple to the ancient truths. The meas-

From *The Public Papers and Addresses of Franklin Delano Roosevelt*, Random House, 1938.

ure of the restoration lies in the extent to which we apply social values more noble than mere monetary profit.

Happiness lies not in the mere possession of money; it lies in the joy of achievement, in the thrill of creative effort. The joy and moral stimulation of work no longer must be forgotten in the mad chase of evanescent profits. These dark days will be worth all they cost us if they teach us that our true destiny is not to be ministered unto but to minister to ourselves and to our fellow men.

Recognition of the falsity of material wealth as the standard of success goes hand in hand with the abandonment of the false belief that public office and high political position are to be valued only by the standards of pride of place and personal profit; and there must be an end to a conduct in banking and in business which too often has given to a sacred trust the likeness of callous and selfish wrongdoing. Small wonder that confidence languishes, for it thrives only on honesty, on honor, on the sacredness of obligations, on faithful protection, on unselfish performance; without them it cannot live.

Restoration calls, however, not for changes in ethics alone. This Nation asks for action, and action now.

Our greatest primary task is to put people to work. This is no unsolvable problem if we face it wisely and courageously. It can be accomplished in part by direct recruiting by the Government itself, treating the task as we would treat the emergency of a war, but at the same time, through this employment, accomplishing greatly needed projects to stimulate and reorganize the use of our natural resources.

Hand in hand with this we must frankly recognize the overbalance of population in our industrial centers and, by engaging on a national scale in a redistribution, endeavor to provide a better use of the land for those best fitted for the land. The task can be helped by definite efforts to raise the values of agricultural products and with this the power to purchase the output of our cities. It can be helped by preventing realistically the tragedy of the growing loss through foreclosure of our small homes and our farms. It can be helped by insistence that the Federal, State, and local governments act forthwith on the demand that their cost be drastically reduced. It can be helped by the unifying of relief activities which today are often scattered, uneconomical, and unequal. It can be helped by national planning for and supervision of all forms of transportation and of communications and other utilities which have a definitely public character. There are many ways in which it can be helped, but it can never be helped merely by talking about it. We must act and act quickly.

Finally, in our progress toward a resumption of work we require two safeguards against a return of the evils of the old order: there must be a strict supervision of all banking and credits and investments, so that there will be an end to speculation with other people's money; and there must be provision for an adequate but sound currency.

These are the lines of attack. I shall presently urge upon a new Congress, in special session, detailed measures for their fulfillment, and I shall seek the immediate assistance of the several States.

Through this program of action we address ourselves to putting our own national house in order and making income balance outgo. Our international trade relations, though vastly important, are in point of time and necessity secondary to the establishment of a sound national economy. I favor as a practical policy the putting of first things first. I shall spare no effort to restore world trade by international economic readjustment, but the emergency at home cannot wait on that accomplishment.

The basic thought that guides these specific means of national recovery is not narrowly nationalistic. It is the insistence, as a first consideration, upon the interdependence of the various elements in and parts of the United States —a recognition of the old and permanently important manifestation of the American spirit of the pioneer. It is the way to recovery. It is the immediate way. It is the strongest assurance that the recovery will endure.

In the field of world policy I would dedicate this Nation to the policy of the good neighbor—the neighbor who resolutely respects himself and, because he does so, respects the rights of others— the neighbor who respects his obligations and respects the sanctity of his agreements in and with a world of neighbors.

If I read the temper of our people correctly, we now realize as we have never realized before our interdependence on each other; that we cannot merely take but we must give as well; that if we are to go forward, we must move as a trained and loyal army willing to sacrifice for the good of a common discipline, because without such discipline no progress is made, no leadership becomes effective. We are, I know, ready and willing to submit our lives and property to such discipline, because it makes possible a leadership which aims at a larger good. This I propose to offer, pledging that the larger purposes will bind upon us all as a sacred obliga-

tion with a unity of duty hitherto evoked only in time of armed strife.

With this pledge taken, I assume unhesitatingly the leadership of this great army of our people dedicated to a disciplined attack upon our common problems.

Action in this image and to this end is feasible under the form of government which we have inherited from our ancestors. Our Constitution is so simple and practical that it is possible always to meet extraordinary needs by changes in emphasis and arrangement without loss of essential form. That is why our constitutional system has proved itself the most superbly enduring political mechanism the modern world has produced. It has met every stress of vast expansion of territory, of foreign wars, of bitter internal strife, of world relations.

It is to be hoped that the normal balance of Executive and legislative authority may be wholly adequate to meet the unprecedented task before us. But it may be that an unprecedented demand and need for undelayed action may call for temporary departure from that normal balance of public procedure.

I am prepared under my constitutional duty to recommend the measures that a stricken Nation in the midst of a stricken world may require. These measures, or such other measures as the Congress may build out of its experience and wisdom, I shall seek, within my constitutional authority, to bring to speedy adoption.

But in the event that the Congress shall fail to take one of these two courses, and in the event that the national emergency is still critical, I shall not evade the clear course of duty that will then confront me. I shall ask the

Congress for the one remaining instrument to meet the crisis—broad Executive power to wage a war against the emergency, as great as the power that would be given to me if we were in fact invaded by a foreign foe.

For the trust reposed in me I will return the courage and the devotion that befit the time. I can do no less.

We face the arduous days that lie before us in the warm courage of national unity; with the clear consciousness of seeking old and precious moral values; with the clean satisfaction that comes from the stern performance of duty by old and young alike. We aim at the assurance of a rounded and permanent national life.

We do not distrust the future of essential democracy. The people of the United States have not failed. In their need they have registered a mandate that they want direct, vigorous action. They have asked for discipline and direction under leadership. They have made me the present instrument of their wishes. In the spirit of the gift I take it.

In this dedication of a Nation we humbly ask the blessing of God. May He protect each and every one of us. May He guide me in the days to come.

1933

WOODROW WILSON

The Lawyer and the Community

THE WHOLE history of society has been the history of a struggle for law, for the definite establishment and continuance of such relationships as seemed to those who had the choice to be best suited to the support of their own influence and for the maintenance of the community over which they presided. Law is simply that part of the established thought and habit which has been accorded general acceptance and which is backed and sanctioned by the force and authority of the regularly constituted government of the body politic. The whole history of liberty, that history which so quickens our pulses as we look back upon it and which so sustains our confidence in the power of righteousness and of all the handsomer, nobler impulses of humanity, has been a struggle for the recognition of rights not only, but for the embodiment of rights in law, in courts and magistrates and assemblies. Such must always be the form of every high endeavour made in the interest of men and of the ideals of political life.

We do not fight to establish theses. We do not pour our blood out to vindicate a philosophy of politics. There are two great empires of human feeling, the realm of religion and the realm of political aspiration. In the one realm we work spiritually, our liberty is of the thought; in the other we work structurally, our liberty abides in institutions, is real only when it is tangible, a thing that can be put into operation,—not in our own souls merely, but in the world

Reprinted from *The Public Papers of Woodrow Wilson* (Harper and Brothers, 1925) by permission of Mrs. Woodrow Wilson.

of action outside of us as well. A right in the field of politics is a power to command the action of others in our own behoof; and that is also a right in law. Religions are mighty forces of belief, and the church, when it has its genuine and entire liberty, lies outside the state; but political liberty lives and moves and has its being in the structure and practice of society. The two fields are not, indeed, sharply separated: religious freedom must be safeguarded by institutional arrangements; but religious freedom is the right to be ungoverned, political freedom the right to be governed justly and with equity as between man and man. We fight for law as well as for faith because we fight not only for the right to think but also for the right to be and to do what we will within the limits of a just and equal order.

I remind you of these things at the beginning of my discourse because I wish to say a good deal about our present struggle for law. The old order changeth,—changeth under our very eyes, not quietly and equably, but swiftly and with the noise and heat and tumult of reconstruction. The forces of society contend openly with one another, avow their antagonisms, marshal and discipline their hosts, and are keen to win, not very willing to accommodate their differences and come to a common understanding which will be for the common advantage.

I suppose that all struggle for law has been conscious, that very little of it has been blind or merely instinctive. It is the fashion, too, to say, as if with a superior knowledge of affairs and of human weakness, that every age has been an age of transition and that no age is more full of change than another; but in very few ages of the world has the struggle for change been so widespread, so delib-

erate, or upon so great a scale as this which we are taking part in. The transition we are witnessing is no equable transition of growth and normal alteration, no silent, unconscious unfolding of one age into another, its natural heir and successor. Society is looking itself over, in our day, from top to bottom, is making fresh and critical analysis of its very elements, is questioning its oldest practices as freely as its newest, scrutinizing every arrangement and motive of its life, and stands ready to attempt nothing less than a radical reconstruction, which only frank and honest counsels and the forces of generous coöperation can hold back from becoming a revolution. We are in a temper to reconstruct economic society as we were once in a temper to reconstruct political society, and political society may itself undergo a radical modification in the process. I doubt if any age was ever more conscious of its task or more unanimously desirous of radical and extended changes in its economic and political practice.

I do not speak of these things in apprehension, because all is open and above board. This is not a day in which great forces rally in secret. The whole stupendous programme is planned and canvassed in the open, and we have learned the rules of the game of change. Good temper, the wisdom that comes of sober counsel, the energy of thoughtful, and unselfish men, the habit of coöperation and of compromise which has been bred in us by long years of free government, in which reason rather than passion has been made to prevail by the sheer virtue of candid and universal debate, will enable us to win through still another great age without revolution. I speak in plain terms of the real character of what is now patent to every man merely in order to fix your thought upon the fact that this thing that is going on about us is not a mere warfare of opinion. It has an object, a definite and concrete object, and that object is Law, the alteration of institutions upon an extended plan of change.

We are lawyers. This is the field of our knowledge. We are servants of society, officers of the courts of justice. Our duty is a much larger thing than the mere advice of private clients. In every deliberate struggle for law we ought to be the guides, not too critical and unwilling, not too tenacious of the familiar technicalities in which we have been schooled, not too much in love with precedents and the easy maxims which have saved us the trouble of thinking, but ready to give expert and disinterested advice to those who purpose progress and the readjustment of the frontiers of justice.

You cannot but have marked the recent changes in the relation of lawyers to affairs in this country; and, if you feel as I do about the great profession to which we belong, you cannot but have been made uneasy by the change. Lawyers constructed the fabric of our state governments and of the government of the United States, and throughout the earlier periods of our national development presided over all the larger processes of politics. Our political conscience as a nation was embedded in our written fundamental law. Every question of public policy seemed sooner or later to become a question of law, upon which trained lawyers must be consulted. In all our legislative halls debate thundered in the phrases of the written enactments under which our legislators and our governors exercised authority. Public life was a lawyer's forum. Laymen lent their invaluable counsel, but

lawyers guided, and lawyers framed the law.

I am not speaking of the dependence of our political movement upon the judgments of courts. That has not been altered, and cannot be. So long as we have written constitutions courts must interpret them for us, and must be the final tribunals of interpretation. I am speaking of the prominence and ascendency of lawyers in the practical political processes which precede the judgments of the courts. Until the civil war came and the more debatable portions of our fundamental law were cut away by the sword, the very platform of parties centred upon questions of legal interpretation and lawyers were our guiding statesmen. I suppose a more intensely legal polity never existed.

So long as passion was excluded it was a tonic way of life. Statesmanship necessitated precise thinking. Every policy that was proposed had to be explicitly grounded upon precedent. At every step there was a reëxamination of the fundamental principles which were alleged to justify or sustain it. Thought of the long history of English constitutional practice and of the avowed purpose with which government had been set up in America constituted the atmosphere in which everything was done. Every ancient, every recent contest for liberty threw its light forward upon the debates of Congress and of state legislatures. The newest state shared with the oldest the long tradition, and all alike were thoughtful of what had been designed and hoped for by the men whose sacrifices had given life to our freedom. No doubt it stiffened the action of government. No doubt there was a formality and a scrupulous regard for the letter in the conduct of legislation better suited to a young country just finding itself and face to face only with large problems of simple and obvious character than to an older country, whose life has grown complex and confused and whose questions of exigency square with no plain precedents of constitutional practice. Lawyers will construct for you a very definite polity, and construct it to admiration; they have not often shown themselves equally fitted to liberalize it or facilitate the processes of change. But the leadership of lawyers at least meant a repeated reëxamination of principle and precedent, and was very instructive even when it was least enlightened. It prevented fluidity. A reason had to be given for every step taken, —a reason which would commend itself to the courts after it had commended itself to statesmen. The statesman and the lawyer were clients and consorts, and the legal conscience of the people was constantly refreshed and strengthened. These are great influences. They make for character and for the solidity of institutions.

But they are gone. You have only to recall the many extraordinary interpretations of the interstate commerce clause of the Constitution upon which serious debate has been wasted in Congress in recent years to be convinced of it. Our lawyers themselves are not carefully trained as they used to be in the principles of our constitutional law. It does not stand in the foreground of their study or practice, but in the background, very vague and general, a thing to be resorted to only upon rare occasion. Our legislatures now listen to debates upon constitutional questions with ill-concealed impatience, as tedious and academic. The nation has grown keen after certain practical objects and will not willingly brook the impediments set up by constitutions. The temper of the age is very nearly summed up in a feeling which you may put into words like these: "There are certain things we must do. Our life as a nation must be rectified in certain all-important particulars. If there be no law for the change, it must be found or made. We will not be argued into impotency by lawyers. We are not interested in the structure of our governments so much as in the exigencies of our life."

There are many reasons why this change of temper and of point of view has occurred. I will venture to mention one or two of the more obvious. It is not by chance that statesmanship has grown bigger than the bounds of mere legal precedent.

In the first place, the debates and constitutional struggles of the first seventy years of our political history settled most of the fundamental questions of our constitutional law. Solid lines of decided cases carry the definite outlines of the structure and make clear the methods of its action. We seemed after the civil war to be released from the demands of formal definition. The life of the nation running upon normal lines, has grown infinitely varied. It does not centre now upon questions of governmental structure or of the distribution of governmental powers. It centres upon economic questions, questions of the very structure and operation of society itself, of which government is only the instrument. Our development has run so fast and so far along the lines sketched in the earlier day of constitutional definition, has so crossed and interlaced those lines, has piled upon them such novel structures of trust and combination, has elaborated within them a life so manifold, so full of forces which transcend the boundaries of the country itself and fill the eyes of the world, that a new nation seems to have been created which the old formulas do not fit or afford a vital interpretation of itself. The confusion has clearly come about without intention. We have been engaged in enterprises which the law as we formerly looked at it was clearly not meant to prevent or embarrass. We pushed them forward, therefore, without thinking of the effect they might have upon older conceptions of our legal processes. They seemed to spring out of the normal and necessary uses of the great continent whose riches we have been exploiting. We did not think of the legal consequences one way or the other, and therefore did not need or seek the advice of constitutional lawyers.

Constitutional lawyers have fallen into the background. We have relegated them to the Supreme Court, without asking ourselves where we are to find them when vacancies occur in that great tribunal. A new type of lawyers has been created; and that new type has come to be the prevailing type. Lawyers have been sucked into the maelstrom of the new business system of the country. That system is highly technical and highly specialized. It is divided into distinct sections and provinces, each with particular legal problems of its own. Lawyers, therefore, everywhere that business has thickened and had a large development, have become experts in some special technical field. They do not practise law. They do not handle the general, miscellaneous interests of society. They are not general counsellors of right and obligation. They do not bear the relation to the business of their neighbourhoods that the family doctor bears to the health of the community in which he lives. They do not concern themselves with the universal

aspects of society. The family doctor is himself giving place to a score of specialists; and so is also what one might call the family solicitor. Lawyers are specialists, like all other men around them. The general, broad, universal field of law grows dim and yet more dim to their apprehension as they spend year after year in minute examination and analysis of a particular part of it; not a small part, it may be, perhaps the part which the courts are for the time most concerned with, but a part which has undergone a high degree of development, which is very technical and many-sided, and which requires the study and practice of years for its mastery; and yet a province apart, whose conquest necessarily absorbs them and necessarily separates them from the dwindling body of general practitioners who used to be our statesmen.

And so society has lost something, or is losing it,—something which it is very serious to lose in an age of law, when society depends more than ever before upon the lawgiver and the courts for its structural steel, the harmony and coördination of its parts, its convenience, its permanency, and its facility. In gaining new functions, in being drawn into modern business instead of standing outside of it, in becoming identified with particular interests instead of holding aloof and impartially advising all interests, the lawyer has lost his old function, is looked askance at in politics, must disavow special engagements if he would have his counsel heeded in matters of common concern. Society has suffered a corresponding loss,—at least American society has. It has lost its one-time feeling for law as the basis of its peace, its progress, its prosperity. Lawyers are not now regarded as the mediators of progress. Society was always ready to be prejudiced against them; now it finds its prejudice confirmed.

Meanwhile, look what legal questions are to be settled, how stupendous they are, how far-reaching, and how impossible it will be to settle them without the advice of learned and experienced lawyers! The country must find lawyers of the right sort and of the old spirit to advise it, or it must stumble through a very chaos of blind experiment. It never needed lawyers who are also statesmen more than it needs them now,—needs them in its courts, in its legislatures, in its seats of executive authority,—lawyers who can think in the terms of society itself, mediate between interests, accommodate right to right, establish equity, and bring the peace that will come with genuine hearty coöperation, and will come in no other way.

The specialization of business and the extraordinary development of corporate organization and administration have led to consequences well worth the lawyer's consideration. Everyone else is considering them, and considering them with deep concern. We have witnessed in modern business the submergence of the individual within the organization, and yet the increase to an extraordinary degree of the power of the individual, of the individual who happens to control the organization. Most men are individuals no longer so far as their business, its activities or its moralities, is concerned. They are not units, but fractions; with their individuality and independence of choice in matters of business they have lost also their individual choice within the field of morals. They must do what they are told to do or lose their connection with modern affairs. They are not at liberty to ask whether what they are told to do is right or wrong. They cannot get at the men who ordered it,—have no access to them. They have no voice of counsel or of protest. They are mere cogs in a machine which has men for its parts. And yet there are men here and there with whom the whole choice lies. There are men who control the machine as a whole and the men who compose it. There are men who use it with an imperial freedom of design, whose power and whose individuality overtop whole communities. There is more individual power than ever, but those who exercise it are few and formidable, and the mass of men are mere pawns in the game.

The present task of the law is nothing less than to rehabilitate the individual, —not to make the subordinate independent of the superior, not to turn corporations into debating societies, not to disintegrate what we have been at such pains to piece together in the organization of modern industrial enterprise, but to undo enough of what we have done in the development of our law of corporations to give the law direct access again to the individual,—to every individual in all his functions.

Corporations do not do wrong. Individuals do wrong, the individuals who direct and use them for selfish and illegitimate purposes, to the injury of society and the serious curtailment of private rights. Guilt, as has been very truly said, is always personal. You cannot punish corporations. Fines fall upon the wrong persons, more heavily upon the innocent than upon the guilty, as much upon those who knew nothing whatever of the transactions for which the fine is imposed as upon those who originated and carried them through,— upon the stockholders and the customers rather than upon the men who direct the policy of the business. If you dissolve the offending corporation, you throw great undertakings out of gear. You merely drive what you are seeking to check into other forms or temporarily disorganize some important business altogether, to the infinite loss of thousands of entirely innocent persons and to the great inconvenience of society as a whole. Law can never accomplish its objects in that way. It can never bring peace or command respect by such futilities.

I regard the corporation as indispensable to modern business enterprise. I am not jealous of its size or might, if you will but abandon at the right points the fatuous, antiquated, and quite unnecessary fiction which treats it as a legal person; if you will but cease to deal with it by means of your law as if it were a single individual not only, but also,— what every child may perceive it is not, —a responsible individual. Such fictions and analogies were innocent and convenient enough so long as corporations were comparatively small and only one of many quite as important instrumentalities used in business, only a minor item in the economic order of society. But it is another matter now. They span society, and the responsibilities involved in their complex organization and action must be analyzed by the law as the responsibilities of society itself, in all its other aspects, have been.

The corporation now overshadows partnerships altogether. Still more does it overshadow all individuals engaged in business on their own capital and separate responsibility. It is an arrangement by which hundreds of thousands of men who would in days gone by have set up in business for themselves put their money into a single huge accumulation and place the entire direction of its employment in the hands of men they have never seen, with whom they never confer. These men, these quite autocratic managers, are thereby made, as it were, multiple individuals. In them are concentrated the resources, the choices, the opportunities, in brief the power, of thousands. They could never of themselves, of their own effort and sagacity, have accumulated the vast capital they employ, and employ as if it were their own; and yet they have not the full legal responsibilities of those who supplied them with it. Because they have the power of thousands they have not the responsibility common to those whose power they use! It is an extraordinary anomaly!

A modern corporation is an economic society, a little economic state,—and not always little, even as compared with states. Many modern corporations wield revenues and command resources which no ancient state possessed, and which some modern bodies politic show no approach to in their budgets. The economic power of society itself is concentrated in them for the conduct of this, that, or the other sort of business. The functions of business are differentiated and divided amongst them, but the power for each function is massed. In some instances even the functions are not separated. Railroad companies have been known to buy coal mines. Manufacturing combinations have been observed to develop a score of subsidiary industries, to spread a network of organization over related enterprises, and sometimes even over enterprises whose relation to their main undertakings it is difficult for the lay mind to perceive. Society, in short, has discovered a new way of massing its resources and its power of enterprise, is building up bodies economic outside its bodies politic which may, if we do not find the means to prevent them, the means of disclosing the responsibilities of the men who compose them, dominate bodies politic themselves.

And these huge industrial organizations we continue to treat as legal persons, as individuals, which we must not think of as consisting of persons, within which we despair of enabling the law to pick out anybody in particular to put either its restraint or its command upon! It is childish, it is futile, it is ridiculous [author's copy illegible]. As well treat society itself as a unit; insist that it impose a fine upon itself for every wrong done, no matter how notorious it may be who did it; suggest that it embarrass all its processes of action and even break itself up into its constituent parts and begin all over again when the persons whom it has trusted prove depraved or selfish. It is not even interesting to continue such an experiment. Society cannot afford to have individuals wield the power of thousands without personal responsibility. It cannot afford to let its strongest men be the only men who are inaccessible to the law. Modern democratic society, in particular, cannot afford to constitute its economic undertakings upon the monarchical or aristocratic principle and adopt the fiction that the kings and great men thus set up can do no wrong which will make them personally amenable to the law which restrains smaller men: that their kingdoms, not themselves, must suffer for their blindness, their follies, and their transgressions of right.

It does not redeem the situation that these kings and chiefs of industry are not chosen upon the hereditary principle (sometimes, alas! they are) but are men who have risen by their own capacity, sometimes from utter obscurity, with the freedom of self-assertion which should characterize a free society.

Their power is none the less arbitrary and irresponsible when obtained. That a peasant may become king does not render the kingdom democratic.

I would not have you think that I am speaking with a feeling of hostility towards the men who have in our day given the nation its extraordinary material power and prosperity by an exercise of genius such as in days gone by was used, in each great age, to build empires and alter the boundaries of states. I am drawing no indictment; no indictment that I could draw would be just. No indictment that has been drawn has been just, but only exaggerated and disquieting. The time for hostilities has gone by. The time for accommodations, for common understandings, for a surcease of economic warfare and the inauguration of the peace that will come only by common sacrifices and concessions, has come. I am simply trying to analyze the existing constitution of business in blunt words of truth, without animus or passion of any kind, and with a single, clear purpose.

That purpose is to recall you to the service of the nation as a whole, from which you have been drifting away; to remind you that, no matter what the exactions of modern legal business, no matter what or how great the necessity for specialization in your practice of the law, you are not the servants of special interests, the mere expert counsellors of this, that, or the other group of business men; but guardians of the general peace, the guides of those who seek to realize by some best accommodation the rights of men. With that purpose in view, I am asking you to look again at the corporation.

It is an indispensable convenience; but is it a necessary burden? Modern business is no doubt best conducted upon a great scale, for which the resources of the single individual are manifestly insufficient. Money and men must be massed in order to do the things that must be done for the support and facilitation of modern life. Whether energy or economy be your standard, it is plain enough that we cannot go back to the old competitive system under which individuals were the competitors. Wide organization and coöperation have made the modern world possible and must maintain it. They have developed genius as well as wealth. The nations are richer in capacity and in gifts comparable to the higher gifts of statesmanship because of them and the opportunities they have afforded exceptional men. But we have done things in pursuit of them, and have nursed notions regarding them, which are no necessary part of what we seek. We can have corporations, can retain them in unimpaired efficiency, without depriving law of its ancient searching efficiency, its inexorable mandate that men, not societies, must suffer for wrongs done. The major promise of all law is moral responsibility, the moral responsibility of individuals for their acts and conspiracies; and no other foundation can any man lay upon which a stable fabric of equitable justice can be reared.

I call your attention to the fact, therefore, that it is perfectly possible to have corporations and serve all the necessities and conveniences of modern society by means of the great combinations of wealth and energy which we have found to be so excellent, and yet dispense with a large part of the quite outworn and now in many respects deeply demoralizing fiction that a corporation is an indivisible person. Of course we must continue to regard it as an artificial person so far as is necessary to enable it to hold such property as may be proper for the execution of its charter purposes, to sue and be sued, and to conduct its business through officers who speak for it as a whole, and whose signatures and orders are, under its by-laws and resolutions, binding upon it. It must act and live as a person, and must be capable of enjoying, what individuals cannot enjoy, a certain perpetuity of power and authority, though individual men within it come and go, live, die, resign, or are translated. But there its unity should stop.

In respect of the responsibility which the law imposes in order to protect society itself, in order to protect men and communities against wrongs which are not breaches of contract but offences against the public interest, the common welfare, it is imperative that we should regard corporations as merely groups of individuals, from which it may, perhaps, be harder to pick out particular persons for punishment than it is to pick them out of the general body of unassociated men, but from which it is, nevertheless, possible to pick them out,—possible not only, but absolutely necessary if business is ever again to be moralized. Corporations must continue to be used as a convenience in the transaction of business, but they must cease to be used as a covert for wrong-doers.

The managers of corporations themselves always know the men who originated the acts charged against them as done in contravention of the law; is there no means by which their names may be disclosed to the officers of justice? Every act, every policy in the conduct of the affairs of a corporation originates with some particular officer, committee, or board. The officer, the committee, the board which orders an act or originates a policy contrary to the law of the land or intended to neutralize or contravene it is an insurgent against society: the man or men who originate any such act or policy should be punished, and they alone. It is not necessary that the corporation should be broken up. It is not fair that the stockholders should be mulcted in damages. If there are damages to be paid they should be paid out of the private means of the persons who are really guilty. An analysis of the guilt is perfectly feasible. It is the duty of lawyers, of all lawyers, to assist the makers of law and the reformers of abuses by pointing out the best and most effective way to make it.

It seems to me absurd, for example (let me say by way of parenthesis), to extend the law of libel to corporations, to suffer one publishing corporation to sue another for defamation. Somebody in particular has uttered the libel, somebody in particular has been libeled. Character cannot be incorporated; writing cannot be corporately done. Are lawyers so incapable of ascertaining the facts that they cannot find out who it is that did the thing or who it is that has been injured in his reputation?

I know that the matter is not as simple as it sounds. I know that some corporations are in fact controlled from the outside, not from the inside: that it often happens that some man or some small group of men who are not even in its directorate dictate its policy, its individual acts, its attitude towards law and society, and that the men who act within it are little better than automata. But are they really beyond discovery? On the contrary, is it not generally a matter of common knowledge who they are? Would it take extraordinary acumen and intelligence to devise laws which

would reach them also? What we are after, of course, is to obtain laws which will prevent the use of corporations to the public hurt and disadvantage. We know that the man who shoots his enemy was not in the gun, that he simply used it, and that no part of the mechanism of the gun itself is criminally liable. We can generally discover who used the gun and how he used it, whatever his cunning and secrecy. We can also find out who uses the corporations against the public interest; and we can punish him, or them, if we will, whether they belong to the actual nominal organization of the corporation or not. Our processes of evidence may have to be considerably altered, but we can alter them; our formal conception of parties in interest may have to be extended, but it is easy to extend them; our make-believe that we can see nobody in the transaction but those who are avowed and formal members of the organization may have to be discarded, but that ought to be a relief to our consciences. We have allowed ourselves to be ridiculously limited and embarrassed by the theory that a corporation is an indivisible person not only, but that nobody outside of it, no matter how intimate his use and control, may be brought into the suit by any genteel lawyer bred in the orthodox schools of law. A corporation is merely a convenient instrument of business and we may regulate its use as we please, and those who use it. Here is merely an artificial, a fictitious person, whom God did not make or endow, which we ourselves have made with our own hands and can alter as we will. I see no law of nature in our way, but only some laws of evidence and of corporate theory which we have outgrown.

You will say that in many instances it is not fair to pick out for punishment the particular officer who ordered a thing done, because he really had no freedom in the matter: that he is himself under orders, exercises no individual liberty of choice, is a dummy manipulated from without. I reply that society should permit no man to carry out orders which are against law and public policy, and that, if you will but put one or two conspicuous dummies in the penitentiary, there will be no more dummies for hire. You can stop the traffic in dummies, and then, when the idea has taken root in the corporate mind that dummies will be confiscated, pardon the one or two innocent men who may happen to have got into jail. There will not be many, and the custom of the trade will change!

There are other corporate matters worthy of your attention, but they do not intimately concern my present theme. I think you must admit, for example, that the position of the minority stockholder is, in most of our States, extremely unsatisfactory. I do not wonder that he sometimes doubts whether corporate stocks are property at all or not. He does not seem to enjoy any of the substantial rights of property in connection with them. He is merely contributing money for the conduct of a business which other men run as they please. If he does not approve of what they do, there seems nothing for it but to sell the stock (though their acts may have depreciated its value immensely). He cannot even inquire or protest without being told to mind his own business, —the very thing he was innocently trying to do! There are many things which are not satisfactory about this putting the money of many men into one pile for the use of a board of directors, and to my mind it is clearly your task as counsellors of society to make

them satisfactory. It is the duty of our profession to see to it that no man's powers exceed or lie outside of his legal and personal responsibilities,—that the corporation be made a mere convenience of business and not a means of irresponsible mastery: its interior and all men within it as accessible to the law as its exterior and the scattered individuals who have no corporate ambush from which to work their will.

I have used the corporation merely as an illustration. It stands in the foreground of all modern economic questions, so far as the United States are concerned. It is society's present means of effective life in the field of industry. Society must get complete control of its instrument or fail. But I have used it only as an illustration of a great theme, a theme greater than any single illustration could compass,—namely, the responsibility of the lawyer to the community he professes to serve.

You are not a mere body of expert business advisers in the fields of civil law or a mere body of expert advocates for those who get entangled in the meshes of the criminal law. You are servants of the public, of the state itself. You are under bonds to serve the general interest, the integrity and enlightenment of law itself, in the advice you give individuals. It is your duty also to advise those who make the laws,—to advise them in the general interest, with a view to the amelioration of every undesirable condition that the law can reach, the removal of every obstacle to progress and fair dealing that the law can remove, the lightening of every burden the law can lift and the righting of every wrong the law can rectify. The services of the lawyer are indispensable not only in the application of the accepted processes of the law, the interpretation of existing rules in the daily operations of life and business. His services are indispensable also in keeping, and in making, the law clear with regard to responsibility, to organization, to liability, and, above all, to the relation of private rights to the public interest.

The structure of modern society is a structure of law rather than of custom. The lawyer's advice is more than ever necessary to the state, therefore. Communities as well as individuals stand in constant need of his guidance. This used to be commonplace doctrine amongst us; why does it now need to be preached again? Is it mere accident that the relation of the legal profession to affairs has changed? Is it merely because the greater constitutional questions seemed for a time to be settled and legal debates gave place to industrial enterprise, a great age of material following a great age of political development? Has it been merely a change of circumstances, or has it been a change of attitude and spirit as well on the part of the profession itself? Has not the lawyer allowed himself to become part of the industrial development, has he not been sucked into the channels of business, has he not changed his connections and become part of the mercantile structure rather than part of the general social structure of our commonwealths as he used to be? Has he not turned away from his former interests and duties and become narrowed to a technical function?

Whatever may be the cause, it is evident that he now regards himself as the counsel of individuals exclusively, and not of communities. He may plead this new organization of politics, which seems to exclude all counsel except that of party success and personal control;

he may argue that public questions have changed, have drifted away from his field, and that his advice is no longer asked; but, whatever his explanation or excuse, the fact is the same. He does not play the part he used to play; he does not show the spirit in affairs he used to show. He does not do what he ought to do.

For there never was a time, in fact, when his advice, his disinterested and earnest advice, was more needed than it is now in the exigent processes of reform, in the busy processes of legislation through which we are passing, with so singular a mixture of hope and apprehension. I hear a great many lawyers join the cry of the business men, that it is time legislators left business alone, allowed it to recover from the confusion and distraction of regulative statutes, altered tariffs, and supervising commissions, find its natural methods again, and go forward upon a way of prosperity which will not be beset by fear and uncertainty. But the cry is futile, the impatience which gives rise to it is selfish and ignorant. Nothing is settled or can be let alone when it is known to be wrong until it is set right. We have settled nothing in our recent reform legislation. That is the reason it is so unsatisfactory, and why some prudent and thoughtful men grow tired of it. But that is only another reason for seeking out and finding what will be the happy and successful way of setting our economic interests in order. There has been no satisfactory settlement, but there must be one. Public opinion is wider awake about these matters than it has been within the memory of any man living, and it is not going to turn away from them until satisfactory reforms of the law are found. There will be no peace until a happy and honourable basis of peace has been hit upon. Lawyers may come into the settlement or stay out of it, as they please, but a settlement there must be. For one, I hope that they will not stay out. I fear that it would be disastrous for them to do so,—disastrous to them and to society. I covet for them their old and honourable leadership in public counsel.

Just because they have so buried themselves in modern business, just because they have been so intimate a part of it, they know better than any one else knows what legal adjustments have and have not been made,—know the practices that circumvent the law, even the existing law, and the provisions of statute and court procedure that might put a stop to them or square them with what the interests of the whole community demand, theirs is the special responsibility to advise remedies.. Theirs has been the part of intimate counsel in all that has been going on. The country holds them largely responsible for it. It distrusts every "corporation lawyer." It supposes him in league with persons whom it has learned to dread, to whom it ascribes a degree of selfishness which in effect makes them public enemies, whatever their motives or their private character may be. And the lawyer,—what does he do? He stands stoutly on the defensive. He advises his client how he may make shift, no matter how the law runs. He declares that business would go very well and every man get his due if only legislators would keep their hands off! He keeps his expert advice for private persons and criticises those who struggle without his countenance or assistance along the difficult road of reform. It is not a promising situation.

Our reforms must be legal reforms.

It is a pity they should go forward without the aid of those who have studied the law in its habit as it lives, those who know what is practicable and what is not, those who know, or should know, if anybody does, the history of liberty.

The history of liberty is a history of law. Men are not free when they have merely conceived what their rights should be. They are not set free by philosophies of right. Their theories of the rights of man may even lead them astray, may make them break their hearts in pursuit of hopes they can never realize, objects they can never grasp, ideals that will forever elude them. Nothing is more practical than the actual body of liberty. It consists of definitions based upon experience, or, rather, of practices that are the very essence of experience. A right is worth fighting for only when it can be put into operation. It can be put into operation only when its scope and limitation can be accurately defined in terms of legal procedure; and even then it may amount to nothing if the legal procedure be difficult, costly, or complicated. Liberty of speech is defined in the law of slander and of libel, and becomes mere license against which there is no protection if the law of slander or of libel be difficult or costly or uncertain to apply. Liberty of the person is defined only when the law has carefully enumerated the circumstances in which it may be violated, the circumstances in which arrests and imprisonments and army drafts, and all the other limitations upon which society may insist for its protection or convenience, will be lawful. Its reality, its solidity consists in the definiteness of the exceptions, in the practicality of the actual arrangements.

And it is part of its definiteness and reality that liberty is always personal, never aggregate; always a thing inhering in individuals taken singly, never in groups or corporations or communities. The indivisible unit of society is the individual. He is also the indigestible unit. He cannot be merged or put into combination without being lost to liberty, because lost to independence. Make of him a fraction instead of an integer, and you have broken his spirit, cut off the sources of his life. That is why I plead so earnestly for the individualization of responsibility within the corporation, for the establishment of the principle by law that a man has no more right to do a wrong as a member of a corporation than as an individual. Establish that principle, cut away the undergrowth of law that has sprung up so rankly about the corporation and made of it an ambush and covert, and it will give every man the right to say No again, to refuse to do wrong, no matter who orders him to do it. It will make a man of him. It is in his interest no less than in the interest of society, which must see to it that wrong-doing is put a stop to.

We are upon the eve, gentlemen, of a great reconstruction. It calls for creative statesmanship as no age has done since that great age in which we set up the government under which we live, that government which was the admiration of the world until it suffered wrongs to grow up under it which have made many of our own compatriots question the freedom of our institutions and preach revolution against them. I do not fear revolution. I do not fear it even if it comes. I have unshaken faith in the power of America to keep its self-possession. If revolution comes, it will come in peaceful guise, as it came when we put aside the crude government of the Confederation and created the great federal state, which governed individuals, not corporations, and which has been these hundred and thirty years our vehicle of progress. And it need not come. I do not believe for a moment that it will come. Some radical changes we must make in our law and practice. Some reconstructions we must push forward which a new age and new circumstances impose upon us. But we can do it all in calm and sober fashion, like statesmen and patriots. Let us do it also like lawyers. Let us lend a hand to make the structure symmetrical, well proportioned, solid, perfect. Let no future generation have cause to accuse us of having stood aloof, indifferent, half hostile, or of having impeded the realization of right. Let us make sure that liberty shall never repudiate us as its friends and guides. We are the servants of society, the bond-servants of justice.

1910

ROBERT R. R. BROOKS

The N.L.R.B. and Democracy

From Unions of Their Own Choosing

CONTEMPORARY European developments have compelled Americans to reëxamine their faith in democracy. Much of this reëxamination has been of the Fourth of July variety. From a pyrotechnical point of view it has been magnificent, although somewhat lacking in novelty. It has consisted chiefly of condemning all departures from the norms of our forefathers as Fascistic or Communistic.[1]

While the rockets of investigators and the indignant bombs of editors cast a red glare over the political landscape, thousands of other citizens, however, are moving toward a different conclusion. The danger to democracy does not lie in change. It lies in the failure of social institutions to adjust themselves to changes which have already taken place.[2]

The whole surge of economic development has been in the direction of centralization of power, interdependence of all parts upon each other, increasing complexity, and the inability of the individual to control his economic destiny. The individual worker cannot assure himself of employment, of freedom from industrial accident and disease, or of old-age independence.[3] The individual consumer cannot assure himself of decent quality or of a reasonable price of the goods he buys.[4] The individual investor cannot assure himself of the proper care of his funds.[5] The utmost expenditure of energy and initiative by the individual farmer or small businessman cannot assure him of a livelihood.[6] The years of training of professional specialists—engineers, doctors, lawyers, teachers—do not assure them of employment or freedom to follow their professions where their faiths may lead.[7] To just the degree that economic life becomes vast, interdependent, complex, and centrally controlled, the average

From *Unions of Their Own Choosing,* Yale University Press, 1939, by permission of the publishers.

[1] Cf. the activities of Attorney General A. Mitchell Palmer twenty years ago; the continuing policies of the Daughters of the American Revolution and large sections of the American Legion; the perennial appearance of new crops of "patriotic" organizations rallying to the defense of the much-beleaguered Constitution; and the contemporary efforts of the Dies Committee to expose "un-American" activities in the C.I.O. and the New Deal.

[2] For an able exposition of this thesis consult SOULE, GEORGE, *The Coming American Revolution* (New York, Macmillan, 1934).

[3] Cf. EPSTEIN, ABRAHAM, *Insecurity: A Challenge to America* (3d [revised] ed. New York, Random House, 1936).

[4] Cf. HARDING, T. SWAN, *The Popular Practice of Fraud* (New York, Longmans, Green, 1935). LAMB, RUTH DE F., *The American Chamber of Horrors* (New York, Farrar & Rinehart, 1936).

[5] Cf. BRANDEIS, LOUIS D., *Other People's Money* (New York, Stokes, 1932). FLYNN, JOHN T., *Security Speculation* (New York, Harcourt Brace, 1934), and *Graft in Business* (New York, Vanguard, 1931). LOWENTHAL, M., *The Investor Pays* (New York, Knopf, 1933). WINKLER, M., *Foreign Bonds, an Autopsy* (Philadelphia, Roland Swain, 1932).

[6] EZEKIAL, M., and BEAN, L. H., *Economic Bases for the Agricultural Adjustment Act,* U. S. Department of Agriculture, 1933.

[7] COREY, LOUIS, *The Crisis of the Middle Class* (New York, Covici Friede, 1935).

citizen loses his individual power to secure a livelihood.

Under these conditions, a good living can be assured only by concerted action toward such common goals as employment, health, old-age independence, opportunity, and professional freedom. If these objectives are to be reached, however, the political institutions through which individuals attempt to control their economic lives must conform to the new economic society. One change which is thus forced upon political institutions, not by conspiring politicians of any particular party but by basic economic evolution, is the growth of federal power at the expense of state and local authority.

Wages, hours, and working conditions which are determined by interstate forces not only cannot be influenced by the individual but are beyond the control of the state except in limited fields. The prices and quality of goods made and advertised by the peoples of a dozen states cannot be controlled by the people of any one state. The safety of investments and savings affected by nationwide business conditions cannot be guaranteed by individual wisdom or state authority. Unemployment and old-age dependence whose origin may lie thousands of miles from the scene of their incidence are not only beyond prevention by the state but frequently beyond its powers of adequate relief. A whole section of the national community may be so impoverished by forces beyond its control that nothing short of a helping federal hand can relieve it from its futile efforts to raise itself by its own bootstraps.[8]

Over a period of fifty years the federal government has been compelled by the force of economic developments to take over problems of railroading, the sale and advertising of goods, banking, trade practices, agriculture, unemployment, old-age dependence, investment, public-utility control, industrial relations, housing assistance, and wage and hour regulation. Each problem has usually not been taken over until the necessity for federal aid has been apparent for many years. Political adjustments have lagged behind economic change. This lag has been the result of the inertia of traditional thinking, the intense resistance of vested interests, and the honest fears of those who found greater potential danger in centralized federal power than in the present helplessness of the groups whose protection was sought.

The inertia of traditional thinking is to be expected and accepted—both as an obstacle to change and a medium through which change may be effected.[9] The resistance of vested interests is also to be expected. Sometimes these interests can be shown to be no more than apparent. Those who fight change frequently discover that they are better off after the change than before. In other cases, however, the majority is compelled to override the minority. But in the centralization of political power there lies a danger that the effort of the people to improve their economic lot through the instruments of government will itself destroy democracy. The immense weight of the federal administrative machinery may crush the people who brought it into being.[10]

[8] United States National Emergency Council, Report on *Economic Conditions of the South* (Government Printing Office, 1938).

[9] ARNOLD, THURMAN W., *The Folklore of Capitalism* (New Haven, Yale University Press, 1937).

[10] This point of view has been extensively developed by Walter Lippmann and Dorothy Thompson. Cf. LIPPMANN, WALTER, *The Good Society* (Boston, Little, Brown, 1937).

Power granted by the mass of people to federal agencies may be turned against the people either by minority interests which capture the government or by the administrators themselves. Administrators tend to become bureaucrats. That is, they become interested in their own power and perquisites. These may frequently be at variance with the interests of the mass of people. What is to prevent bureaucrats from using the means of power against the people? Or what is to prevent those whose regulation is sought—bankers, utility magnates, industrialists, financiers, stockbrokers—from taking over the means of power and turning it against the people?[11] Or what is to prevent a combination of these two groups, supported by discontented masses, from accomplishing the same end?

The more complex, technical, and remote from the ordinary citizen that government becomes, the more difficult it is for the people to compel it to aid in improving the conditions of their economic life. Every step from the town meeting to the state legislature, from the state legislature to the federal Congress, and from Congress to federal administrative agencies is a step away from direct popular control. The defenses of the people against the possible tyranny of a remote federal administrator may become as weak as the defense of a worker against a remote employer, or a consumer against the massed power of advertising,[12] or a shareholder against a corporate holding company,[13] or the farmer against a starvation price, or all of us against unemployment and old-age dependence. Is the move toward federal regulation of economic life anything more than a leap from an unbearable frying pan into a consuming flame?

There are at least three logical courses of action which present themselves in response to this question. One is to go backward. Another is to sit down and hang on tight. The third is to take courage in hand and proceed as cautiously as possible.

Going backward may be a logical possibility, but it is scarcely a social and economic possibility. To reverse more than forty years of federal regulative evolution and at the same time meet the problems that compel this evolution would require the reversal of the more than forty years of economic development which created the problems. The automatic protection of workers, consumers, investors, depositors, farmers, small businessmen, and professionals requires a very simple economic society. Free competition among small units of production, investment in local concerns, production for a local market, easy access to the land or to industrial opportunity, the possibility of self-employment with inexpensive tools or machines, simple commodities limited in quantity, the self-sufficiency of each community—these are some of the prerequisites of a society in which conscious social protection of individuals and groups is relatively unnecessary.

But this is scarcely an accurate picture of modern economic society. To recapture this older society would involve the surrender of geographical specialization, the breaking up of business combinations, and the abandonment of much of

[11] The mechanics of this process have been best observed and reported by LINCOLN STEFFENS in his *Autobiography* (New York, Harcourt Brace, 1931).

[12] RORTY, JAMES, *Our Master's Voice: Advertising* (New York, John Day, 1934).

[13] BERLE, A. A., and MEANS, G. C., *The Modern Corporation and Private Property* (New York, Macmillan, 1934).

our specialized machinery. The result would be a heavy loss in the variety, quality, and quantity of commodities as well as of the population which creates and is sustained by these commodities. Railroads, telegraph, telephone and radio, electric power transmission, automobiles, steel bridges, modern cities, and super-highways are a few of the things which cannot be made without large-scale and specialized production. Even if the surrender of these things is considered by some to be a good idea, the possibility of reversing the rise of modern industry is slight.[14]

If economic evolution cannot be turned backward, the problems which it creates cannot be solved by thinking about the good old days. Perhaps, then, we should just sit still, try not to think about anything, close our eyes and ears to the sufferings of others, and yelp a little when the frying pan becomes warm in our corner. This program has its attractions, but the comfort of the frying pan and the perils of climbing out should not be overdone.

Millions of people are unemployed. Other millions, though employed, remain chronically at the verge of destitution.[15] Millions of people face the expectation of old-age dependence. Other millions are badly housed, under-schooled, or victims of accident and disease.[16] Thousands of people have lost their savings and investments through irresponsible corporate trusteeship. Thousands of people live in communities in which economic democracy is non-existent and political democracy is a farce.[17] These are some of the characteristics of the frying pan.

How stable is a democracy whose prestige is being undermined by the suffering and discontent of millions of people? Antidemocratic totalitarian states are not merely imposed from the top by greedy economic interests and grasping bureaucrats. They require mass support. They find it among the millions whose physical suffering, loss of hope, and distortion of judgment make them willing followers of anyone with a quick tongue and a messianic urge.[18] The difference between "thirty dollars every Thursday" and "the superiority of the Aryan race" is one of degree. People asking for bread are given a slogan. In exchange, they begin or complete the surrender of their democratic power to control their real well-being. There are as great dangers to democracy in federal inaction as there are in federal expansion.

Moreover, the threat to democracy comes from below in another sense. All over this country there are diseased spots in which dominant economic interests operating through corrupt political machines have effectively destroyed the civil liberties of speech, writing, assembly, and education upon which a democratic society is dependent for its existence. The danger that democracy will be destroyed by the encroachments of the federal government is at the moment far less than that these malignant spots will break into a rash. The

---

[14] CHAMBERLAIN, JOHN, *Farewell to Reform* (New York, Liveright, 1932). STRACHEY, JOHN, *The Coming Struggle for Power* (New York, Covici Friede, 1933).

[15] United States National Resources Committee, *Consumer Incomes in the United States: Their Distribution in 1935-36* (Government Printing Office, 1938).

[16] *Ibid.* POST, LANGSON W., *The Challenge of Housing* (New York, Farrar & Rinehart, 1938). EPSTEIN, A., *op. cit.*

[17] Cf. the La Follette Committee Reports cited in full in earlier chapters.

[18] Cf. SCHUMAN, FREDERICK L., *The Nazi Dictatorship* (revised ed. New York, Knopf, 1936).

federal government offers the means whereby the democratic pressures of some communities can be exerted for the protection of democracy in others. This pressure is exerted not only through the Supreme Court and such legislative bodies as the La Follette Committee, but also by federal administrative agencies. The combined action of the Department of Justice and the N.L.R.B., for example, has recently broken through the medieval defenses of Harlan County, Kentucky, and allowed a pale light of industrial democracy, at least, to fall upon its citizens.[19]

The frying pan, then, *is* a frying pan. And the alternative may not be the fire.

How can protection be assured against the possibility that federal administrators will fall a prey to powerful minority groups or to their own delusions of grandeur? There are in general two possible answers. First, that groups of people organize around their respective economic interests to obtain control over them outside political channels. Second, that when there are conflicts of group interests or problems beyond the scope of group control, these economic organizations actively participate in political government.

The most powerful economic interests are those of producers. Consumers, it is true, are interested in the price and quality of the goods they buy. But these interests are generally overshadowed by a more intense interest in the amount of income and the conditions under which it is earned. Most people think of themselves as consumers secondarily. They think and act primarily as wage earners, professionals, farm-

ers, businessmen, and investors. People may and should organize to protect consumer interests. Much can be accomplished through consumers' coöperatives and advisory services. But within these consumers' organizations, the more powerful producer interests constantly assert themselves and conflicts of policy frequently result which are difficult to resolve within the consumer organization.[20]

Among producer groups, somewhat the same thing is true of investors. They may and do organize to protect themselves. But a very small minority of people has investments great enough to produce income equal to its wages or salaries. This small minority whose income from investments is greater than from salaries is already powerfully organized through corporate and banking devices. Their problem is not acute, to put it mildly.[21] The great majority of investors, however, is incapable of organization around investment interests and must organize, if at all, as wage or salary earners.

Farmers are an extremely important producer group which has a long tradition of collective action alongside its tradition of individualism. This collective action has been chiefly directed in the past toward general political objectives such as railroad regulation and tariff reduction. In the last ten years, however, growing farmers' organizations have directed their attention toward such particular economic ends as collective purchase of materials and sale of products. In the meantime, as a result of organized farmers' political pressure, the federal government has come

[19] *The C.I.O. News,* Sept. 3, 1938.

[20] WARBASSE, J. P., *Coöperative Democracy* (New York, Harper, 1936). WEBB, SIDNEY and BEATRICE, *The Consumers' Coöperative Movement* (New York, Longmans, Green, 1921).

[21] LUNDBERG, FERDINAND, *America's Sixty Families* (New York, Vanguard, 1937).

to the farmers' aid to an unprecedented extent. This does not mean that the farmers have become dangerously dependent upon the federal government. Because of the virility of farmers' political organizations, the federal government has become dependent, to a large degree, upon the farmers.[22]

The farmers are acting through the federal machinery of government for the protection of their economic status. They are also acting directly through their buying and selling coöperatives. In both policies the farmers are being encouraged by the federal government. This advance of federal regulatory activity at the insistence of the farmers can hardly be described as authoritarian, destructive of democracy, or even paternalistic. On the contrary, it may be said that because the farmers are organizing to protect their economic interests both directly and through political channels, they are creating a democracy which conforms to modern economic life.

Small businessmen, also, have organized to protect themselves. Their most important organizations are concerned with immediate ends such as coöperative purchase of goods, common credit resources, local taxation or civic obligations, common advertising, exchange of technical information, trade practices, and price control. These organizations, of which there are scores of different types, have given to small business many of the advantages which could otherwise be enjoyed only by big business.[23] They are far more important than the efforts of small business to organize for political objectives. Such political organizations of small business as have appeared have tended to parrot the slogans and policies of big business whose interests in many respects are dissimilar.[24] But the pressure of small businessmen's organization is already a factor to be taken into account by federal legislators and administrators. Small businessmen also are adjusting the forms of democracy to the conditions of modern economic life.

Professionals—lawyers, doctors, teachers, among others—have long since been organized in an effort to regulate their working conditions. They don't call them working conditions, but professional training requirements, ethics, and freedom are the equivalent of union apprenticeship regulations, standards of production speed, and sanitary conditions. These organizations are rapidly spreading into such fields as engineering, technical service, insurance agencies, banking, and government. All of these professional organizations, from the lawyers down or up, are becoming more and more interested in exercising some control over the amount of their income, the standards of their work, the tenure of their jobs, and the conditions under which they work. Their efforts at control over these matters are being exerted both through bargaining on the job and through political pressures.[25]

---

[22] There are at present six strong farmers' organizations whose activities are great enough to influence governmental policy. Consult Labor Research Association, *Labor Fact Book III* (New York, International, 1936), chap. 7.

[23] FRAIN, H. L., *An Introduction to Economics* (Boston, Houghton Mifflin, 1937), pp. 254-256.

[24] Cf. newspaper accounts of the convention of "small" businessmen called by President Roosevelt in February, 1938. For accounts of subsequent activities of this group see the *New York Times Index,* 1938, under "Businessmen's Ass'n., National Small, Inc."

[25] There are at present five professional unions affiliated with the C.I.O., five affiliated with the A. F. of L., and one independent which are on a strictly trade-union basis. In addition to these unions there are more than a score of professional organizations whose interests lead them increasingly toward

Many doctors are interested in federally subsidized medicine both for the sake of the people's health and for the sake of their own economic skins. Engineers are interested in federal public works for similar reasons. Teachers are concerned with not only adequate education and academic freedom, but the regularity of pay day. Government workers are interested in hours and salaries as well as efficient public service. All of these groups are new forms of democracy. They attempt both to improve the economic lot of their members directly and to compel the federal government to do what the groups cannot themselves accomplish. Not only are they propelling the federal government forward into new fields but they constitute a democratic check upon possible authoritarian tyranny.

Fully two-thirds of our population is composed of wage workers and their dependents. Among them there are twenty-five to thirty million potential union members. There are perhaps eight million already in unions.[26] In their broadest aspect, these unions also represent an adjustment of democratic forms to modern economic life. Every local union is a miniature political society just as every town meeting used to be, and in some places still is. Many of the problems facing union members can be settled right in the local meeting. Others are so broad in scope that they have to be referred upward to the regional or national officers or conventions.

Just as the local and state governments have had to refer an increasing share of their problems upward to the federal

government, so the local unions are compelled to delegate the handling of industry-wide bargaining, organizing, and strike control to national officers. The democratic control of union members over their officers is more direct, however, than is the control of the average citizen over his federal officials.

First, since unions are concerned with the most immediate and primary interests of their members, frequent and relatively well-attended meetings are possible. Town or other local political meetings, on the contrary, cover such a diversity of economic interests that it is difficult, if not impossible, to arouse interest in the issues before the meeting. Consequently people don't come. There is little direct and continuous check by the people upon their representatives. Such checks as exist are indirectly applied through letter writing and unofficial polls. Frequent and active union meetings (usually every two weeks) provide a continuous check upon the officers.

Second, since unions usually cover only one industry or occupation, the issues are relatively simple and the members are united upon general ends which the officers may serve. Failure to serve these ends is soon apparent and results in dispensing with the officers' services. Selectmen, governors, Congressmen, and Presidents, on the contrary, serve geographical units including a great variety of economic interests, many of which are in conflict. Under these conditions it is often impossible for the politician to stand for anything without incurring the wrath of some group powerful in votes or funds. To be elected

the assumption of national political functions as well as the democratic method of handling many of their own economic affairs.

[26] Exact figures of dues-paying membership are difficult to obtain. There are probably about ten million workers under strong union influence of whom somewhat less than eight million are in good standing.

from such a constituency, free cigars, political favors, and Delphic utterances must be substituted for intelligent discussion of issues and objectives. Once elected, a representative has few definite commitments. He may, therefore, either do nothing at all or succumb to the pressures of group interests which are brought directly to bear upon him through channels not provided for in the constitution. Such pressure groups may represent small minorities of power and wealth whose interests are directly opposed to those of the great majority. Unless the majority is organized well enough to prevent representatives from giving in to the pressure of minorities, there is little to prevent the politician from doing so. The next election day is far away and simply repeats the free-cigar–baby-kissing–Delphic-utterance pattern.

Unions, therefore, are democracy adapted to industrial life. They make possible both the continuous, direct scrutiny of leaders' actions and the simplification of issues in a complex society. They take their place with organizations of farmers, businessmen, and professionals as efforts to apply group power to the solution of individual problems.

But none of these organizations, including wage workers' unions, can expect to deal with problems which lie outside its jurisdiction. Organized economic groups therefore turn to local, state, and federal governments for aid. Local civil liberties, state unemployment relief, federal old-age annuities, housing assistance, health insurance, and abolition of sweatshop wages and hours are all questions in which organized labor is interested but which to varying degrees lie beyond its powers of direct con-

trol. To secure these objectives, labor turns toward the government, and particularly the federal government.

It is true that the existence of the National Labor Relations Board serves to strengthen the influence of the federal government over the economic life of the nation. But the reason for the existence of the board is to encourage the development of unionism by removing the anti-union obstacles in its path. To just the extent that unionism is encouraged, the means of democratic control over the federal government are enhanced. Although the board is a federal agency, its task is to hasten the advance of local industrial democracy and democratic political checks upon federal power. Through the N.L.R.A., the federal government is atoning for its concentration of power by assisting the progress of a check upon itself.

This policy is a flat contradiction of the policies of authoritarian governments abroad. One of the first steps of a totalitarian government is to crush the independent labor movement out of existence. The obvious reason for this is that an independent labor movement, as well as independent religious, fraternal, and political groups, challenges the dominance of the totalitarian authority. It is difficult to imagine a policy more completely at variance with despotic ambitions than the encouragement provided by the N.L.R.A. to an independent labor movement.

The existence of a strong labor movement not only acts as a check upon the bureaucratic ambitions of administrative officers but also serves to forestall the capture of governmental machinery by organized economic minorities.[27] As has been suggested, the confusion of

[27] If it be urged that the labor movement is itself a minority which "captures governmental machinery" it can only be replied that the labor movement is by far the largest organized minority group in the

economic issues which arises within territorial political units increasingly tends
to transfer the formation of governmental policy from the ballot box to the
arena of pressure politics.[28] In legislative lobbies and administrative offices
the representatives of economic groups
attempt to secure the adoption and enforcement of policies which serve the
interests of their constituencies. The
forms of territorial democracy remain.
The content, however, becomes increasingly economic. Political representatives tend to become the mouthpieces of
economic representatives who stand at
their shoulder.

This process is so nearly universal that
it cannot be dismissed or condemned as
a corruption of democracy. It is, rather,
an adjustment of democracy to modern
specialized economic life. It might be
more logical to abandon territorial representation in favor of a guild congress
composed of representatives of various
economic interests.[29] This, however, is
neither likely, necessary, nor, perhaps,
desirable. It is not likely because traditional methods of doing things have
so powerful a hold upon public thinking
and action that nothing short of revolution can bring about the great symbolic
changes involved in a reorganization of
the forms of government. It is not necessary as long as group-pressure politics
can give modern economic content to
ancient political forms. It is perhaps
not desirable since the territorial units
of town, county, district, and state continue to provide representation to citizens who do not easily or quickly

fall into organized economic groups.

The chief danger of group-pressure
politics is that the better-organized minority groups may exercise greater pressure upon government policy than the
looser organizations of majority interests. In extreme form this superior
pressure of minority groups might result in their complete domination of the
machinery of government and the suppression of the organizations of opposed
economic interests. Organized pressure groups of bankers, public-utility
managements, stock traders, and large
taxpayers, for example, although representing a small minority of the total
population, may outweigh the pressures
of workers, farmers, professionals, and
small businessmen.

Protection against this danger lies in
spreading the economic and political
organization of the groups which compose the vast majority of citizens. The
progress of such organization has already been noted. To just the extent
that the National Labor Relations Act
promotes the organization of workers,
it serves to prevent the capture of governmental machinery by minority interests.

To the original question, "What can
be done to prevent the centralization of
federal power from destroying effective
democracy?" these possible answers
were given: to reverse the trend of economic change, to stand still and do nothing, and to proceed with caution. The
first of these answers was dismissed as
impossible. The second was thrown
out as being more dangerous to the

country, that the larger the minority the more likely its interests are to coincide with those of the
community as a whole, that the labor movement is at present trying as hard as its funds, energies, and
leadership capacities will allow to become a majority, and that the election of 1936 suggests that the
labor movement is already a powerful force supporting political movements which are strongly opposed
to the influence of economic minorities upon governmental policy.

[28] Cf. THOMPSON, C. D., *Confessions of the Power Trust* (New York, Dutton, 1932).

[29] Cf. COLE, G. D. H., *Guild Socialism, a Plan for Economic Democracy* (New York, Stokes, 1921).

stability of democracy than further centralization of federal power. The third has been discussed in terms of the kind of caution which the federal government now displays in proceeding toward further centralization of administrative control.

It has been indicated that by strengthening the economic organizations of workers and farmers the federal government is broadening the path of democracy in its rear before blazing a trail farther into the wilderness. This suggests a rough definition of "caution" in the extension of federal power. In military terms, the federal government should not advance beyond the point of maintaining adequate support from the democratic reinforcements at the rear. If it does, it may be cut off by the raiding parties of minority interests on its flanks. In engineering terms, the federal government should not erect a superstructure of control upon an inadequate democratic foundation. If it does, the superstructure may fall and obliterate the foundation. In terms of industry, the federal government should not proceed further in the regulation of relations between management and labor than the progress of industrial democracy will allow.

The National Labor Relations Act is concerned almost exclusively with the progress of industrial democracy. Should the federal government now go further in the direction of centralized control by substituting compulsory regulation of wages, hours, and working conditions for the settlement of these matters through collective bargaining? Curiously enough, those who view with the greatest alarm the advance of federal power as exemplified in the N.L.R.A. are often those who are most insistent in urging that labor and (occasionally) management be shorn of their economic power to settle matters of industrial relations. To propose that labor's right to strike or use other forms of economic pressure against management be legally limited, and that management's right to close down its plants or use other forms of economic pressure against labor be similarly restricted, would solve no problems of industrial relations unless something else were substituted for these economic weapons. The obvious substitute is compulsory arbitration. Since the great bulk of modern business is interstate in character, the task of carrying out compulsory arbitration would fall chiefly to the federal government. The assumption of this task would involve an extension of federal regulatory power far greater in scope and significance than any single previous advance.

The National Labor Relations Board cannot be condemned, therefore, simply because it represents an extension of federal power if at the same time it is proposed further to extend federal control over wages, hours, and working conditions. If the National Labor Relations Act and compulsory federal arbitration are to be discussed in relation to each other, they must both be recognized as extensions of federal power, but with very different objectives. The major objective of the N.L.R.A. is to increase the democratic control by workers and management through collective bargaining over industrial life. An indirect effect is to enhance the political power of labor over matters in which it is interested but which do not fall within the scope of particular organizations. The main objective of compulsory arbitration, on the contrary, is to reduce the importance of industrial self-government by turning over to federal administrators powers which would otherwise be exercised by organized management and labor. In some respects, therefore, the two objectives are flatly opposed. The N.L.R.A. encourages the assumption of industrial problems by the organizations of labor and management. Compulsory arbitration surrenders the solution of these problems to a relatively remote federal authority.

Having recognized that limitations upon the use of the economic power of labor and management to bring about industrial settlements are a move in the direction of compulsory arbitration, and having recognized that this would involve a vast increase in federal regulatory power, it must be said that compulsory arbitration has its attractions. There is nothing particularly inviting about strikes and lockouts, however sacred the right to strike and lock out may be. There is little that is scientific about resort to economic force even though a prohibition of its use may be said to result in involuntary servitude for workers or the denial of employers' right to go out of business.

Compulsory arbitration might, indeed, become a very scientific instrument of national economic planning. By reference to living standards, prices, industrial earnings, profits, salaries, and industrial trends, government arbitrators not only might arrive at more equitable solutions of industrial conflicts, but also might be able to fit the plans of one industry into those of the nation as a whole.

Against this view of compulsory arbitration, however, objections must be urged. The first is that centralized control tends toward rigidity of policy. The dynamic quality of industry demands flexibility.[30] Such flexibility can be achieved only by encouraging initiative and responsibility on the part of representatives of management and labor who are in the field. Some uniformity of policy is, of course, essential. Uniformity is beginning to develop as a result of collective bargaining, first on a local, and then on an industry-wide basis. Wherever collective bargaining has been practiced, industrial policies tend to become uniform over larger and larger economic areas, but at the same time a balance is worked out between uniformity in general policies and flexibility in their application. Such a balance is best developed slowly by the people who are intimately concerned. The ultimate outcome of collective bargaining may be the development and acceptance of industrial policies so uniform and widespread in scope as to approach the kind of economic planning involved in compulsory arbitration.

But collective bargaining is in its infancy in this country. Management and labor are just beginning to develop methods of dealing with each other. They are far from the adoption of uniform policies leading toward industrial equity and peace. To propose to leap from the present stage of industrial relations to their probable ultimate conclusion is to impose regulations from above without adequate preparation from be-

---

[30] One aspect of the Australian experience with compulsory arbitration has been that wage rates set by arbitration awards tend to remain rigidly fixed over long periods of time during which both the general productivity of an industry and the relationship among the different classes of workers within it may undergo marked alterations. Although this is also true of wage rates fixed by custom or by trade agreements, both the degree and the duration of rigidity are likely to be less than when control is relatively remote from the scene of action. This objection does not apply with equal force against *minimum* wage fixation by federal authority since wide latitude for differentials and for variation is allowed above the relatively rigid minimum.

low. Such regulation is likely to be arbitrary, rigid, and unenforceable. Compulsory arbitration can do little more than clarify and apply the policies and decisions toward which the principals are themselves moving and which they are willing to accept. When collective bargaining on a democratic basis has developed sufficiently to render compulsory arbitration relatively unnecessary, that may be the time to invoke compulsory arbitration! Some American industries, such as the railroads, and to a less degree clothing and mining, are approaching this situation.[31] Others are years or decades removed from the logical end of present developments.

The second objection to compulsory arbitration is suggested by the first. Unless compulsory arbitration takes place against a well-developed background of democratic collective bargaining, the *source* of conflict is not likely to be removed. The conflict itself is simply transferred from the industrial to the political arena. In order to win the fight, management and labor are compelled to enter politics to select or influence the arbitrators. Industrial struggles simply become political struggles. Victory in politics is little more likely to produce economic justice and peace than victory in economic warfare. No real believer in the processes of democracy can be enthusiastic about compulsory arbitration until collective bargaining in industry and organized action by labor in politics have developed sufficiently to prevent government regulation of industrial relations from being merely an arbitrary imposition of the policies of powerful economic and political minorities.

The reverse of this is that those who are opposed to democratic methods and majority rule in industry should work for the repeal of the National Labor Relations Act, the imposition of compulsory arbitration (under the guise of shearing labor of its powers to strike and picket), and the placing of obstacles in the path of political action by labor.

Labor politics now takes the form of direct lobbying by labor representatives in the legislatures, efforts in party primaries to influence the selection of party nominees, the swinging of votes from one party to another to affect the outcome of elections, and the formation of independent labor parties or farmer-labor parties which give their support either to their own candidates or to preferred nominees of other parties. These forms of labor politics represent varying degrees of adjustment of political action to economic change. The development of independent labor politics marks a somewhat more clear-cut formulation of group economic interests than is occurring in the gradual reshuffling of the older parties into liberal and conservative alignments. It is a thoroughly democratic development in the sense that political action by wage workers covers the largest single economic group interest in the country—one which contains an overwhelming potential majority of all voters.

The advance of democratic action by workers in politics is being as bitterly opposed as has been the guarantee of industrial democracy through collective bargaining under the N.L.R.A. When, for example, John L. Lewis visited the Speaker of the House in an effort to dislodge the Wages and Hours Bill from the Rules Committee, his action was denounced as "dictatorship," "an invasion," "effrontery," and so on. This

[31] Cf. "Report of the President's Commission of Industrial Relations in Great Britain," *New York Times*, Sept. 2, 1938, p. 8.

condemnation was offered in spite of the fact that the similar and frequently more effective comings and goings of lobbyists for all sorts of minority interests[32] usually attract little attention, and in spite of the fact that a very small minority of the House occupying a strategic position in the Rules Committee was blocking action desired by the administration, by large majorities in both houses of Congress, and by millions of citizens who abhor the sweatshop conditions which the Wages and Hours Act is designed to eliminate.

More important than this disapproval of labor lobbying is the demand that the N.L.R.A. be amended to prohibit contributions by unions for political purposes.[33] Such a proposal is designed to hamstring labor parties or restrict the support given by labor to the party it favors in a particular area. Hands were raised in horror at the fact that the United Mine Workers contributed approximately $500,000 to the 1936 campaign of the Democratic party and that the American Labor party in New York state raised about $85,000 for the support of its candidates. Little attention was directed toward the fact that the average contribution of a member of the miner's union was less than a dollar, and the average contribution of American Labor party supporters was twenty-six cents. As between contributions of this size and contributions of thousands or tens of thousands of dollars by wealthy individuals or families, the greater degree of democracy would appear to rest with the former rather than with the latter, as long as union members retain democratic control over union expenditures.

This and other similar efforts to use the N.L.R.A. as a weapon against labor politics are an attack upon the adjustment of democratic forms to fit modern industrial society. In whatever guise they may be cloaked, such attacks represent the effort of minority interests to stem the rising political power of a labor movement which is moving toward a majority status. The immediate objective of the National Labor Relations Act is the encouragement of collective bargaining as a means toward industrial peace. Its more remote objectives include the improvement of the lot of American workers not only through collective bargaining in industry but also through encouragement to industrial and political democracy in local and national life.[34] In the contemporary conflict between democracy and dictatorship, whether political or industrial, the National Labor Relations Board is in the center of the struggle. Its influence and power are wholly on the side of democracy.

1939

---

[32] *Time*, Aug. 20, 1938, p. 3, col. 1.

[33] Cf. Amendments to the N.L.R.A., proposed by Senator Vandenberg, Senate Bill 2712, 75th Congress, 1st Sess., p. 3, ll. 10-12.

[34] For an excellent statement of the board's own conception of its relation to the labor movement and to political and economic democracy, see *The National Labor Relations Act: Guardian of Democracy*, a speech by Edwin S. Smith, member of the N.L.R.B., before the Carolina Political Union, Durham, N. C., March 30, 1938, N.L.R.B. Press Release No. R-755.

DOROTHY CANFIELD

Supply and Demand

From Raw Material

THE THOUGHTFUL intellectual people around the fire were talking with animation and conviction, and I hoped the one business-man present, a relative of mine, was appreciating his privileges. It was not often that you could collect before your fire so many brilliant people representing so many important varieties of human activity; and when you had collected them it was not often that the talk fell on a subject big enough to draw out of each one his most hotly held conviction.

The subject was big enough in all conscience: nothing more or less than what is the matter with the world in general and with our country in particular. They all had different ideas about what the trouble is and about the best cure for it. The head nurse of the big City Hospital had started the ball rolling by some of her usual scornful remarks about the idiocy with which most people run their physical lives, and the superidiocy, as she put it, "which makes them think that doctors and nurses can put scrambled eggs back into the shell."

"We'll never have any health as a nation till we have health as individuals," she said. "See that the babies have clean milk; give the children plenty of space and time for out-door play; keep the young folks busy with athletic sports; run down all the diphtheria carriers and make it a misdemeanor not to be both vaccinated for small-pox and inoculated against typhoid . . . and we'd be a nation such as the world never saw before."

The political reformer was sincerely shocked by the narrowness of her views, and took her down in a long description of our villainously mismanaged government. "Much good mere physical health would do against our insane tolerance of such political ineptness and corruption!" he ended. "What we need is an awakening to the importance of government as every man's personal business."

Mrs. Maynard, the tragic-faced, eloquent Scotch expert on birth-control, now said in that low, bitter voice of hers which always makes every one stop to listen, "I would be obliged if you would point out to me how either physical health or the very best of municipal governments should alleviate in the slightest, the hideous ulcers of our so-called respectable married homes. When the very foundation of every-day human life is cemented in such unthinkable cruelty and suffering to defenseless women, I don't see how human beings with hearts in their bosoms can stop for an instant to consider such puerile non-essentials as athletics and party politics!"

The two or three happily married women in the group, startled by her fierce acrimony, were silent, feeling abashed by the grossly comfortable way we had managed to escape even a knowledge of the horrors which she so urgently assured us were universal. But Mr. Sharpless, the efficiency engineer, shook his head pityingly. "No, no, my dear lady, you can't cure anything by going at it with the hammer and tongs of direct action. The economic key is the only one that fits all locks, opens all doors. The women of what we call the 'upper classes' do not suffer as you describe. You know they don't. Now why do we *call* them the 'upper classes'? Because they have money. You know it! Hence, if everybody had money . . . ! I tell you the thing to do is to reorganize our wretched old producing machinery till ever so much more is produced, ever so much more easily; and then invent distributing machinery that will ensure everybody's getting his share. You may not think home life is much affected by the chemist in his laboratory, devising a way to get nitrogen chiefly from the air, or by the engineer struggling with the problem of free power out of the tides or the sun. But it is. Just once put *all* women in the comfortable upper classes. . . ."

He was interrupted here by a number of protesting voices, all speaking at once, the loudest of which, Professor Oleny's, finally drowned out the others, ". . . money without intelligence is the most fatal combination conceivable to man! Economic prosperity would spell speedy destruction without an overhauling of education." He spun like a pinwheel for a moment, in a sparkling, devastating characterization of American schools, and of their deadening effect on the brains which passed through them, and began on a description of what schools should be.

But I had heard him lecture on that only the day before and, looking away

from him, sought out the face of my cousin, the business-man. He had sat through it all, and now continued to sit through the free-for-all debate which followed, without opening his mouth except to emit an occasional thoughtful puff of cigar-smoke. His thoughts seemed to be with the billowing smoke-rings, which he sent towards the ceiling rather than with the great sweep of the subjects being discussed. I knew well enough that his silence did not come in the least from any inability to follow the pyrotechnics about him, and I felt in his absent preoccupation something of the disdain, traditionally felt for talkers and reformers by men of action—when in the twentieth century and in the United States, you say "man of action" you mean of course, "business-man."

It nettled me a little, and after the others had gone and he was finishing the end of his cigar, I said challengingly, "I suppose you think they are all off! I suppose you think that you know what is the matter with the world and that it is something quite different."

He considered the end of his cigar meditatively and answered mildly, "I don't *think* I know, I *know* I know."

"Oh, you do, do you?" I said, amused and ironic. "Would you mind telling me what it is?"

He shucked further down in his chair, tipped his head back and looked up at the ceiling. "Well, if you really want to know, I'll tell you a story that happened just lately in one of the biggest mail-order houses in this country. Of course, I know that you don't fully appreciate the importance of mail-order houses, not being in business. And they're too through and through American a growth for people like your friends to-night to know about or talk about. But some of the best brains and real sure-enough genius in the United States have gone into creating the mail-order house idea. Maybe you might allow that to be a good enough reason for considering for a moment what goes on inside one of them . . . what?

"As a matter of fact, the story isn't just about a mail-order house, but about what is the matter with the world . . . the very same subject your friends were debating. My story won't have so many long words in it as they use, nor so many abstract ideas . . . at least on the surface; but it won't do you any harm to soak it away and think it over. I'll tell you what, *I've* been thinking it over this evening, as I listened to the talk. I only heard the story this morning, and it's stuck in my head all day . . . and especially this evening, as they were all talking about how to hit on some organization of society that would really fix things up, once and for all."

He paused for a moment, stretched his legs out straight before him and put his hands into his pockets. "If I really told you all you ought to know, to understand the background and setting of the story, I'd be sitting here to-morrow morning still talking. So I won't try, I'll just tell you the plain story as it happened. You try to imagine the background: an organization as big, as complicated, with as many chances for waste motion, or overorganization, or poor organization as society itself. And not only power and glory, but *cash,* plenty of hard cash as immediate reward for the successful use of brains.

"Well now, into that arrives a smart youngster full of enthusiasm for making things run better, just like your friends to-night; dead sure just like them that *he* has the key; with lots of pep and brains and interest in his job, pushing his way right up from the stenogra-

pher's desk, with his eye on the Manager's. Do you get him? Well, he's laid awake nights, thinking how to improve the organization, partly because he wanted to improve it, partly because he wanted to get the credit for it . . . just like your friends again. And because he is a smart young fellow as keen as a razor, he soon figured out a way to increase business, to increase it like a house afire, and to handle it once it was increased.

"He went to the big man of the concern and laid out his plans. Now, you'd better believe the big men in any organization always have a glad hand out for anybody in the concern who'll show interest and brains; and the boy got treated like a king. Sure, he could try out his plan! On a small scale at first, to see how it would work. Let him take a county out of each of six selected states, and concentrate on them. And, sure, yes, indeed, he could have anything in the organization he wanted, to make his try with.

"So the boy went away bounding like a rubber-ball and planned his campaign. I won't bother you by trying to tell you what it was. . . . It wouldn't interest you, and anyhow you couldn't understand the business details. It was a mixture of intensive publicity, special attention paid to detail, a follow-up system that meant personal care and personal acquaintance with the tastes of customers, and intimate knowledge of what past orders from customers had been. To get the right kind of assistants he went through the various departments of that big organization and hand-picked his staff; the very best of the publicity men, the smartest of the order-clerks, the brightest of the stenographers. And then they just tore in and ate up the territory they were practising on! They plowed it with publicity, and sowed it with personal service, they reaped, by George, a harvest that would put your eye out! Business increased by a twenty-five per cent, by a fifty per cent! At the end of a year, the boy, too big for his skin, paraded into the Manager-in-chief's office with statistics to prove a seventy-five per cent increase over any business ever done there before! Well, that was simply grand, wasn't it? Yes, the Manager would certainly sit up and take some notice of a system that had accomplished *that!*"

My cousin had finished his cigar, now threw the butt into the fire-place, and sat looking at the embers with a somber expression. I couldn't see anything to look somber about. Indeed I found myself stifling a yawn. What did I care how much business a mail-order house did or how they did it?

My cousin answered my thought, "Don't you see that the story is all about the same general idea you were all discussing this evening? It is about getting things done more intelligently, more efficiently, about avoiding fool mistakes, about rising to big opportunities, about learning how to scramble over the obstacles that prevent human beings from being intelligent and efficient and effective. Now, then, at the first take-off, the boy had soared right over those obstacles, hadn't he? But the Manager-in-chief knew a thing or two about them, too. In fact he had grown bald and gray trying to climb over those very same obstacles. But you can be sure the boy didn't once think that his chief might be just as anxious as he was to have things done better. Boys never do. . . ." There was a pause, while my cousin considered the embers moodily.

"So, by and by, after the boy had fizzed the place all foamy with his won-derful statistics, the bald-headed, gray-haired Manager began to come down to brass tacks, and to inquire just how the thing had been done. The boy was crazy to tell him, went into every detail; and the Manager listened hard.

"And then he shook his old bald gray head. He said: 'Young fellow, you listen to me. It takes *sense* to run that system of yours. You're counting on everybody, from you right down to the boy that works your mimeograph, paying attention to what he's doing, using his brains and using them every minute. If everybody doesn't, you won't get your results, will you? Now, consider this, how did you get hold of a staff that would have any brains to use and would use them? *You* know how! We let you run a fine tooth comb through our whole organization, thousands and thousands of employees. You took out of every department the very best they had; three or four out of hundreds, and they are the only ones out of thousands who amount to anything after years of training at our expense. And then you put your very best licks into it yourself. Now, who are you? You're the first stenographer we've had in ten years who took enough interest in the business as a whole to have a single idea about it. You tell me something. Suppose we reorganized along your lines, who would I get to run all the other departments and keep up the high-speed efficiency and red-hot ambition you've shown, which is the *only* reason your scheme works? You know as well as I do I can't find another *one,* let alone the eighty or ninety I'd have to have, if we tried to do business on your plan. And if I could—supposing for the sake of argument that an angel from Heaven served such department heads to me on a silver platter, where am I going to find staffs to work with them. You've *got* all the really efficient employees we've been able to rake in from the whole United States in the past twenty years.

" 'Did you ever have to work with a plain, ordinary six-for-a-quarter stenographer, such as the business colleges turn out, such as you mostly get? You've built your machine so that only brains and sense will run it. How long would it take a couple of hundred of such stenogs to smash your system into splinters? Did you ever have to try and get work out of the average dressy young employee who puts ninety-eight and a half per cent of what gray matter he has on his neckties and the bets he made on the horse-races, and the little flier he took on stocks; and one and a half per cent of his brains on his work when somebody higher up is looking at him? How do you suppose you can persuade a crowd of light-weights like that to care a whoop whether Mrs. Arrowsmith in Cohoes, N. Y., is satisfied with the color of the linoleum rug she bought?' "

My cousin looked at me hard, and again answered an unspoken thought of mine. "Are you wondering why hadn't the boy interrupted long before this, to hold up his end, if he was really so enthusiastic as I've said? This is the reason. Though he hadn't let on to the Manager, he really had had plenty of troubles of his own, already, keeping even his hand-picked crew up to the scratch. Many's the time he'd been ready to murder them! Drive as hard as he might, he couldn't keep them steadily up to the standard he'd set for his work. He'd noticed that. Oh, yes, of course, he'd noticed it all right, and he'd been furious about it. But until that minute, he hadn't thought of it— what it meant; and the minute the Man-

ager spoke, he knew in his bones the old man was right. And he felt things come down with a smash.

"It pretty nearly knocked him silly. He never said a word. And the old bald-head looked at him, and saw that in the last three minutes the boy had grown up . . . he'd grown up! That hurts, hurts more than any visit to the dentist. I know how he felt; probably the Manager knew how he felt. Anybody who's ever tried to get anything done has run his head into that stone wall.

"Well, he was sorry for the kid, and tried to let him down easy. He went on talking, to give the boy time to catch his breath. 'You understand, I'd like, maybe more than you, to reorganize the whole ball o' wax, on any lines that would work better. And there are lots of good points in your plan that we *can* use, plenty of 'em. This invention of yours about cross-indexing orders now, that is a splendid idea. I believe we could install that . . . it looks *almost* foolproof! And maybe we might run a special mailing-list along the lines you've worked out. Lemme look at it again. Well, I guess the mistakes the stenogs would make *might* be more than offset by the extra publicity . . . maybe!'

"But the lad was feeling too cut up to pay any attention to these little poultices. He stood there, and almost fell in pieces, he was thinking so hard. Not very cheerful thoughts, at that. When he could get his breath he leaned over the table and said in a solemn, horrified voice, 'Good God, Mr. Burton, why then . . . why then . . .' He was all but plumb annihilated by the hardness of the fact that had just hit him on the head. He broke out, 'What's the *use* of inventing a better system as long as . . . as long as . . . ?' he got it out finally. 'Why, Mr. Burton, there just aren't enough folks with sense to go around!'"

My cousin stood up, moved to the hall, secured his hat and looked in at me through the door-way. "Poor kid!" he commented pityingly. "Just think of his never having thought of that before!"

1923

FRANK LLOYD WRIGHT

Organic Architecture

THE TYPICAL American dwelling of 1893 was crowding in upon itself all over the Chicago prairies as I used to go home from my work with Adler and Sullivan in Chicago to Oak Park, a Chicago suburb. That dwelling had somehow become typical American architecture but by any faith in nature implicit or explicit it did not belong anywhere. I was in my sixth year with Adler and Sullivan then, and they had completed the Wainwright Building in St. Louis, the first expression of the sky-scraper as a *tall* building. But after building the great Auditorium the firm did not build residences because they got in the way of larger, more important work. I had taken over dwellings, Mr. Sullivan's own house among them, whenever a client came to them for a house. The Charnley house was done in this way. I longed for a chance to build a sensible house and (1893) soon free to build one, I furnished an office in the Schiller Building and began my own practice of architecture. The first real chance came by way of Herman Winslow for client. I was not the only one then sick of hypocrisy and hungry for reality. Winslow was something of an artist himself, sick of it all.

What was the matter with this typical American house? Well just for an honest beginning it lied about everything. It had no sense of unity at all nor any such sense of space as should belong to a free people. It was stuck up in thoughtless fashion. It had no more sense of earth than a "modernistic" house. And it was stuck up on wherever it happened to be. To rake any one of those so-called "homes" away would have improved the landscape and helped to clear the atmosphere. The thing was more a hive than a home just as "modernistic" houses are more boxes than houses. But these "homes" were very like the home Americans were making for themselves elsewhere, all over their new country.

Nor, where the human being was concerned, had this *typical* dwelling any appropriate sense of proportion whatever. It began somewhere way down in the wet and ended as high up as it could get in the high and narrow. All materials looked alike to it or to anything or anybody in it. Essentially, were it wood or brick or stone, this "house" was a bedeviled box with a fussy lid: a complex box that had to be cut up by all kinds of holes made in it to let in light

From *Common Sense*, April, 1941. Reprinted by special permission of *The American Mercury*, with which is combined the magazine, *Common Sense*.

and air, with an especially ugly hole to go in and out of. The holes were all "trimmed"; the doors and windows themselves trimmed; the roofs trimmed; the walls trimmed. Architecture seemed to consist in what was done to these holes. "Joinery" everywhere reigned supreme in the pattern and as the soul of it all. Floors were the only part of the house left plain after "Queen Anne" had swept past. The "joiner" recommended "parquetry" but usually the housewife and the fashionable decorator covered these surfaces down under foot with a tangled rug collection because otherwise the floors would be "bare." They were "bare" only because one could not very well walk on jig-sawing or turned spindles or plaster ornament. This last limitation must have seemed somehow unkind.

THE ESCAPISTS

It is not too much to say that as a young architect, by inheritance and training a radical, my lot was cast with an inebriate lot of criminals called builders; sinners hardened by habit against every human significance except one, vulgarity. The one touch of nature that makes the whole world kin. And I will venture to say, too, that the aggregation was at the lowest aesthetic level in all history. Steam heat, plumbing, and electric light were the only redeeming features and these new features were hard put to it to function in the circumstances. Bowels, circulation, and nerves were new in buildings. But they had come to stay and a building could no longer remain a mere shell in which life was somehow to make shift as it might. When I was 11 years old I was sent to a Wisconsin farm to learn how to really work. So all this I saw around me seemed affectation, nonsense, or profane. The first feeling was hunger for reality, for sincerity. A desire for simplicity that would yield a broader, deeper comfort was natural, too, to this first feeling. A growing idea of simplicity as organic, as I had been born into it and trained in it, was new as a quality of thought, able to strengthen and refresh the spirit in any circumstances. Organic simplicity might everywhere be seen producing significant character in the ruthless but harmonious order I was taught to call nature. I was more than familiar with it on the farm. All around me, I, or anyone for that matter, might see beauty in growing things and by a little painstaking, learn how they grew to be "beautiful." None were ever insignificant. I loved the prairie by instinct as itself a great simplicity; the trees, flowers, and sky were thrilling by contrast. And I saw that a little of height on the prairie was enough to look like much more. Notice how every detail as to height becomes intensely significant and how breadths all fall short. Here was a tremendous spaciousness needlessly sacrificed, all cut up crosswise or lengthwise into 50-foot lots, or would you have 25 feet? Reduced to a money-matter, salesmanship kept on parceling out the ground, selling it with no restrictions. Everywhere, in a great new, free country, I could see only this mean tendency to tip everything in the way of a human occupation or habitation up edgewise instead of letting it lie comfortably flatwise with the ground where spaciousness was a virtue. Nor has this changed much since automobilization has made it no genuine economic issue at all but has made it a social crime to crowd in upon one another.

By now I had committed the indiscretion that was eventually to leave me no peace and keep me from ever finding satisfaction in anything superficial. That indiscretion was a determination to search for the *qualities* in all things.

I had an idea (it still seems to be my own) that the planes parallel to the earth in buildings identify themselves with the ground, do most to make the buildings belong to the ground. (Unluckily they defy the photographer.) At any rate, independently I perceived this fact and put it to work. I had an idea that every house in that low region should begin *on* the ground, and not *in* it as they then began, with damp cellars. This feeling became an idea also; eliminate the "basement." I devised one at ground level. And the feeling that the house should *look* as though it began there *at* the ground, put a protecting base course as a visible edge to this foundation where, as a platform, it was evident preparation for the building itself and welded the structure to the ground.

An idea (probably rooted deep in racial instinct) that *shelter* should be the essential look of any dwelling, put the low spreading roof, flat or hipped, or low-gabled, with generously projecting eaves over the whole. I began to see a building primarily not as a cave but as broad shelter in the open, related to vista; vista without and vista within. You may see in these various feelings all taking the same direction that I was born an American child of the ground and of space, welcoming spaciousness as a modern human need as well as learning to see it as the natural human opportunity. The farm had no negligible share in developing this sense of things in me, I am sure.

Before this, by way of innate sense of comfort, had come the idea that the size of the human figure should fix every proportion of a dwelling or anything

in it. Human scale was true building scale. Why not, then, the scale fixing the proportion of all buildings whatsoever? What other scale could I use? This was not a canon taught me by anyone. So I accommodated heights in the new buildings to no exaggerated established order nor to impress the beholder (I hated grandomania then as much as I hate it now) but only to comfort the human being. I knew the house dweller could seldom afford enough freedom to move about in built-in or built-over space, so, perceiving the horizontal line as the earth line of human life (the line of repose), this, as an individual sense of the thing, began to bear fruit. I first extended horizontal spacing without enlarging the building by cutting out all the room partitions that did not serve the kitchen or give needed privacy for sleeping apartments or (as in the day of the parlor) serve to prevent some formal intrusion into the intimacy of the family circle. The small social office I set aside as a necessary evil to receive "callers," for instance. Even this one concession soon disappeared as a relic of the barbarism called "fashion": the "parlor."

To get the house down to the horizontal in appropriate proportion and into quiet relationship with the ground and as a more humane consideration anyway, the servants had to come down out of the complicated attic into a unit of their own.

Freedom of floor space and elimination of useless heights worked a miracle in the new dwelling place. A sense of appropriate freedom had changed its whole aspect. The dwelling became more fit for human habitation on modern terms and far more natural to its site. An entirely new sense of space values in architecture began to come home. It now appears that, self-conscious of architectural implications, they first came into the architecture of the modern world. This was about 1893. Certainly something of the kind was due.

A new sense of repose in flat planes and quiet "streamline" effects had thereby and then found its way into building, as we can now see it admirably in steamships, airplanes and motorcars. The age came into its own and the "age" did not know its own. There had been nothing at all from overseas to help in getting this new architecture planted on American soil. From 1893 to 1910 Adler and Sullivan's Wainwright Buildings, the first affirmation of the tall building as *tall*—these prairie houses beginning with the Winslow house which followed the Charnley house, the Larkin Building and Unity Temple had planted it there. No, my dear "Mrs. Gablemore," "Mrs. Platerbilt," and especially, no, "Miss Flattop," nothing from "Japan" had helped at all, except the marvel of Japanese color prints. They were a lesson in elimination of the insignificant and in the beauty of the natural use of materials.

But more important than all, rising to greater dignity as idea, the ideal plasticity was now to be developed and emphasized in the treatment of the building as a whole. Plasticity was a familiar term but something I had seen in no buildings whatsoever. I had seen it in Lieber Meister's ornament only. It had not found its way into his buildings otherwise. It might now be seen creeping into the expressive lines and surfaces of the buildings I was building. You may see the appearance of the thing in the surface of your hand as contrasted with the articulation of the bony skeleton itself. This ideal, profound in its architectural implications, soon took another conscious stride forward in the form of a new aesthetic. I called it *continuity*. (It is easy to see it in the "folded plane.") Continuity in this aesthetic sense appeared to me as the natural means to achieve truly organic architecture by machine technique or by any other natural technique.

Not much yet exists in our country— no, nor in any country outside plans and models—to exemplify steel and glass at its best in the light of the new sense of building. But a new countenance, it is the countenance of principle, has already appeared around the world. A new architectural language is being brokenly, variously, and often falsely spoken by youths, with perspicacity and some breadth of view but with too little depth of knowledge that can only come from continued experience. Unfortunately, academic training and current criticism have no penetration to this inner world. The old academic order is bulging with its own important impotence. Society is cracking under the strain of a sterility. education imposes far beyond capacity; exaggerated capitalism has left all this as academic heritage to its own youth. General cultural sterility, the cause of the unrest of this uncreative moment that now stalls the world might be saved and fructified by this ideal of an organic architecture: led from shallow troubled muddy water into deeper clearer pools of thought. Life needs these deeper fresher pools into which youth may plunge to come out refreshed with new creative energy to make the United States for humanity.

1941

EDWARD GORDON CRAIG

Proposals Old and New

A Dialogue between a Theatrical Manager and an Artist of the Theatre.

FOREWORD

In this dialogue, although the Manager says but little, he condescends to say more than most managers. He echoes those two celebrated if slightly worn phrases that "Art does not pay," and that "We give the Public what it demands." He does this, we may be sure, more from habit than from any belief in their worth.

I have purposely kept the Manager from attempting to prove that what he offers the public is either original or beautiful, for I felt that my readers were tired of hearing the old lie over again. So I have kept him as quiet as possible, unwilling that he should destroy any remaining chance of retaining esteem for his methods, or sympathy for his appalling cause. I hope in this way not to have done him any injustice.

MANAGER. That is the finest scene I ever saw. But you can't realize yon drawing upon the stage.

ARTIST. You are right: I cannot.

MANAGER. Then, if you cannot reproduce it, why do you show it to me?

ARTIST. To make an impression on you. Why ask me absurd questions?

MANAGER. Because I wish to be practical; I wish to protect my interests.

ARTIST. But you are not protecting them; you are utterly at my mercy and seem to be trying to ruin them.

MANAGER. Really you look at things in a strange way. Now come down to earth and tell me how we can realize yon design upon the stage.

ARTIST. We cannot; I have told you so repeatedly, but you were so quick with your questions you would not let me tell you something which saves the situation. That design, as I have just said, is made to give you a certain impression. When I make the same scene on the stage it is sure to be quite different in form and colour, but it will create the same impression on you as this design in front of you now.

MANAGER. Two things quite different will create the same impression? Are you joking?

ARTIST. No, I am not joking, but I will do so if you insist upon it.

MANAGER. No, tell me more; explain what you mean.

ARTIST. Well, a design for a scene on paper is one thing; a scene on the stage is another. The two have no connection with each other. Each depends on a hundred different ways and means of creating the same impression. Try to adapt the one to the other, and you get at best only a good translation. You do not understand? I know it; but what would you have? You ought to be content *not* to understand—*never* to understand; if you could comprehend you would have no need to consult me.

MANAGER. Well, it all sounds very risky.

ARTST. It is; terribly risky—for you. That is my point; that is the artist's ever-

Reprinted from Edward Gordon Craig, *The Theatre Advancing,* by permission of Little, Brown and Company, publishers.

lasting point. He thinks; you risk. If you begin thinking everything is lost. Leave that to your stage manager—to me. You shall have no other risk but me. Risk me, and you stand the chance of gaining all. Avoid that risk, and you run no chance of winning anything.

MANAGER. You terrify me. I think you must be mad.

ARTIST. And you have only one thing to be careful about; you must take care to study the difference between the different types of men the world calls "artists." Sort them out, avoid the commercial fellows and search for the "mad" artist (I think you said mad). If you can find *one* I promise you you've found a fortune. Then risk him; play him first on the Red and then on the Black; throw him where you will, he's sure to bring you luck. But, my dear sir, whatever you do pray gamble like a gentleman; risk enormously, hazard all on this *surety;* risk with decency I beg; do not incessantly alter your mind—and for heaven's sake don't apologize for your method of play!

MANAGER. Upon my word, you are an original being!

ARTIST. I am. I thought that was why you came to me. All artists are "original" to business men and all business men are "original" to artists; both can truthfully be called eccentrics. This is as it should be. The securest foundation for a successful union. The mistake is for either of them to try and understand how the other works. Each should remain ignorant of the other's methods, and they should unite to a common madness called the "concentric." This would be very productive, very economic. Sometimes we get a man who is both artist and business man; Cecil Rhodes was such a man. He used the soil of a continent as a sculptor uses a handful of clay, and from it he fashioned United South Africa—and we shall probably learn in time that he made something even vaster than that. Learn to risk, my friend; and learn also that ideas are rare things, and that most artists are packed full of ideas. Therefore the artist is the finest of all commodities in the market.

MANAGER. But what if an idea doesn't pay?

ARTIST. An idea which doesn't pay has not yet been discovered. If you don't know *how* to make it pay that is not a matter I can interfere in, for if I interfere I overstep your frontiers. If you cannot make it pay that but reveals your ignorance of how to handle it, and you fail at your own game—but, observe, the idea has not failed. It waits for some one better fitted to develop it.

MANAGER. So you put the whole blame of failure on the manager or business man, not on the artist?

ARTIST. Yes, on the handling, and more especially so in the case of a very original idea. With ordinary ideas it is somewhat different. Ordinary ideas are generally rather weak, and then the only blame which can be attached to the business man is that he wasted too much time and money on working a poor field. Then the whole blame lies with the artist. The rare fields are the valuable ones, and in the realms of art the rarest field is that where the most original idea is buried. Let a shrewd business man stake all he has on that field; with patience and determination it will yield him all he desires.

MANAGER. Yes—but to return to practical matters.

ARTIST. I had never departed from them.

MANAGER. I am speaking of this design for a scene which strikes me as

quite wonderful. How are we to realize that on the stage?

ARTIST. To answer your question I
must first ask you another. If we were
standing on the edge of a very rich gold
field and long veins of pure gold were
proved to be lying buried under your
very nose, and I were to ask you how to
"realize" that gold, would you not answer me that the ore was not of practical commercial value until extracted,
washed, removed to the mint and
coined? In fact, changed entirely from
its present entrancing condition and
transformed into another, yet equally
valuable, condition and form? Well, I
answer you in the same way about this
scene. And what is more, I advise you
to work the mine from which that design came, and it will yield you all that
you desire. But don't attempt the task
with one pick and a shovel. Put money
into it—all your money—don't be frightened. I happen to be a man with imagination, and in art that is the equivalent
of a gold mine; it only needs to be properly worked. You will say I have no
false modesty about myself. Certainly
not, Sir; the best artists since time im-
memorial have always known how
to value their powers. Fools call it
conceit, but wise men know differently.

MANAGER. Why have not business
men done as you suggest before now?

ARTIST. They have. They did so in
the fifteenth century; the Renaissance
could not have happened without them.
They did so in Athens; they did so in
Egypt; they will do so in England and
America. In fact they have always done
so except when a wave of timidity has
swept over the earth and created a panic.
We are just about to emerge from such
a wave; it is the psychological moment.

MANAGER. And now you expect to
see every one spending money upon
works of art?

ARTIST. Certainly I expect to see
shrewd business men investing their
money in ideas; and as ideas are the
property of men of imagination I expect
to see these two types of man, artist and
business man, combine and place good
things before the public instead of
worthless things. In many instances
good things are already before the public; but in the branch of public service
in which we are engaged you must agree
with me (knowing what you know),
that the public is cheated.

MANAGER. But art does n't pay in this
branch of the service.

ARTIST. Again you make the ancient
excuse. Art pays no worse, no better
than anything else *if you know how to
make it pay;* and I have just hinted to
you how to make it pay, so I fail to see
what other excuse you can make for not
serving the public honestly and letting
the band strike up at once.

MANAGER. Do you insinuate that I
cheat the public?

ARTIST. No—I say it openly.

MANAGER. I give them what they demand.

ARTIST. Another excuse—the same
one that I've heard for years. Why
can't you invent some more reliable answers than *"It does n't pay,"* and *"I give
the public what it demands?"* You
probably think that what you are saying
is true, but still that does not alter the
fact that you are saying what is false.

It is false in many ways. You should
know quite well that the Public is so
vast, is composed of so many different
classes and types, its tastes varying with
each type, that it is sheer lunacy to assert
that there is no public for works of art.
It is as much as to say that the public is
incapable of appreciation. If this were

so, you would have to explain how it is that the public knows the difference between a good loaf of bread and a bad one? or explain how it is that the public can discern a good day from a rainy day —how it knows a good song and a good horse from a bad song and horse? Realize that the public knows everything which is good from everything which is bad; in fact the public is as right as rain; let us hear no more criticisms of it. If you choose to criticize *a small section of the public,* that is another matter, especially if you choose that small section which grumbles at the nation's best soldiers, sailors, statesmen, judges, doctors, priests and artists. Yet, far from criticizing this section, *it is the very section you deliberately cater for in the theatre,* for those who form it are always tired after their day's grumbling and need amusement of the dullest kind. And you call that handful of the nation "the Public!"

MANAGER. You do not convince me. I am certain that if the public wanted works of art it would create a demand for them.

ARTIST. My dear Sir, you encourage me. You say the very thing I wanted to say. "To create a demand." You realize that a public demand is CREATED and does not create itself. You realize that the nation entrusts certain of its officers with the different tasks of creating this, that and the other, and amongst these things is the "creating a demand." The public cannot speak for itself; if the whole lot speak at once no one is heard; if one man speaks he is not listened to unless he is elected as spokesman by the whole nation. Now who has the nation elected to speak for it about this matter of art? No one. Therefore until it does elect some representative, how shall we know its wishes?

MANAGER. But two hundred thousand men and women visited the Grand Theatre to see "Julius Cæsar," and thereby—

ARTIST. Two hundred thousand people are not the Public, and the directors of the public taste in theatrical matters are self-elected. A fine state of affairs indeed!

MANAGER. What would you propose doing to discern the tastes of the nation?

ARTIST. I should propose that you should try to go to the people. Send companies round England and America for the purpose of collecting votes for and against certain types of play and certain ways of producing plays. Let these companies play three plays by Shakespeare—"Hamlet," the "Merchant of Venice," and "Henry V"; a play by Sheridan and one by Ibsen; a play by Goldsmith and one by Goldoni; a play by Molière and a modern French problem play; a play by Shaw, one by Strindberg, one by Synge and one by Yeats, and one Pantomime or Dumb-show drama. Let these plays be produced very carefully by the different stage managers keen for the competition. Let this company call at every centre in America, and afterwards at several of the smaller towns, and let the people record their votes for and against the different pieces. Of course the question at issue will have to be laid clearly before them, and their serious consideration of the pieces requested.

The journals all over England and America would take the matter up and would help to make this question clear. The best journals would point out to their readers that the question was one of those affecting the national welfare, and a difficult one to answer, and would help the people to see the difference between a healthy and an unhealthy drama; between a romantic or poetic treatment and a drab and realistic treatment. The excitement created by this tour of the States would in all probability create a new and serious interest in the theatre, and the whole country would at last be glad to take up the matter of State theatres.

Such a plan as I have sketched out roughly for you is capable of development, and is just the kind of thing that would encourage the theatre. It would cost money, but it would bring in money, and the direct advantages to be derived from such a step are as obvious as they are enormous. Here then is an opportunity for a business man of ability to make his mark. After this test you will probably be surprised to find that the public has all along been opposed to the rubbish which it is forced to accept at the theatre in place of good stuff.

MANAGER. And what do you think the public wishes?

ARTIST. All that is good. It wants good statesmen and good fighters in an emergency, and it gets them. It wants good amusements and good art. The first it sometimes gets; the second is withheld from it. The cinemas, the vaudevilles and the circuses provide admirable amusement. The Theatre should provide for its art. Popular art? Certainly popular art. When certain sections of the public wish for relaxation they find it in the music hall. Excellent! But when another section of the public wants something better than leather, it looks for it and can't find it, and is disappointed. Think how invigorating Shakespeare could be made to that enormous section of the public who work with their brains all day! Think of the doctors, priests, writers, painters, musicians, architects, city men, engineers, army and navy men, politicians, secretaries, editors, journalists and other social men and women to whom a vigorous living theatre might prove *refreshing,* and who are to-day obliged to avoid the place because it is wearisome—a bore.

It is utterly impossible to believe that the failure of the theatre to-day is due to a low standard of public taste. Public taste was never better than it is going to be to-morrow. Test the statement by the method I have suggested and you will be doing a great thing for the nation. But get up early, if you want to be in time.

1910

THORSTEIN VEBLEN

Summary and Trial Balance

From THE HIGHER LEARNING

As in earlier passages, so here in speaking of profit and loss, the point of view taken is neither that of material advantage, whether of the individuals concerned or of the community at large, nor that of expediency for the common good in respect of prosperity or of morals; nor is the appraisal

From *The Higher Learning in America* by Thorstein Veblen. Copyright 1918 by B. W. Huebsch, 1946 by Ann B. Sims. By permission of The Viking Press, Inc., New York.

here ventured upon to be taken as an expression of praise or dispraise at large, touching this incursion of business principles into the affairs of learning.

By and large, the intrusion of businesslike ideals, aims and methods into this field, with all the consequences that follow, may be commendable or the reverse. All that is matter for attention and advisement at the hands of such as aim to alter, improve, amend or conserve the run of institutional phenomena that goes to make up the current situation. The present inquiry bears on the higher learning as it comes into this current situation, and on the effect of this recourse to business principles upon the pursuit of learning.

Not that this learning is therefore to be taken as necessarily of higher and more substantial value than that traffic in competitive gain and competitive spending upon which business principles converge, and in which they find their consummate expression,—even though it is broadly to be recognized and taken account of that such is the deliberate appraisal awarded by the common sense of civilized mankind. The profit and loss here spoken for is not profit and loss, to mankind or to any given community, in respect of that inclusive complex of interests that makes up the balanced total of good and ill; it is profit and loss for the cause of learning, simply; and there is here no aspiration to pass on ulterior questions. As required by the exigencies of such an argument, it is therefore assumed, *pro forma,* that profit and loss for the pursuit of learning is profit and loss without reservation; very much as a corporation accountant will audit income and outlay within the affairs of the corporation, whereas, *qua* accountant, he will perforce have nothing to say as to the ulterior expediency of the corporation and its affairs in any other bearing.

Business principles take effect in academic affairs most simply, obviously and avowably in the way of a businesslike administration of the scholastic routine; where they lead immediately to a bureaucratic organization and a system of scholastic accountancy. In one form or another, some such administrative machinery is a necessity in any large school that is to be managed on a centralized plan; as the American schools commonly are, and as, more particularly, they aim to be. This necessity is all the more urgent in a school that takes over the discipline of a large body of pupils that have not reached years of discretion, as is also commonly the case with those American schools that claim rank as universities; and the necessity is all the more evident to men whose ideal of efficiency is the centralized control exercised through a system of accountancy in the modern large business concerns. The larger American schools are primarily undergraduate establishments,—with negligible exceptions; and under these current American conditions, of excessive numbers, such a centralized and bureaucratic administration appears to be indispensable for the adequate control of immature and reluctant students; at the same time, such an organization conduces to an excessive size. The immediate and visible effect of such a large and centralized administrative machinery is, on the whole, detrimental to scholarship, even in the undergraduate work; though it need not be so in all respects and unequivocally, so far as regards that routine training that is embodied in the undergraduate curriculum. But it is at least a necessary evil in any school that is of so considerable a size as to preclude substantially all close or cordial personal relations between the teachers and each of these immature pupils under their charge, as, again, is commonly the case with these American undergraduate establishments. Such a system of authoritative control, standardization, gradation, accountancy, classification, credits and penalties, will necessarily be drawn on stricter lines the more the school takes on the character of a house of correction or a penal settlement; in which the irresponsible inmates are to be held to a round of distasteful tasks and restrained from (conventionally) excessive irregularities of conduct. At the same time this recourse to such coercive control and standardization of tasks has unavoidably given the schools something of the character of a penal settlement.

As intimated above, the ideal of efficiency by force of which a large-scale centralized organization commends itself in these premises is that pattern of shrewd management whereby a large business concern makes money. The underlying businesslike presumption accordingly appears to be that learning is a merchantable commodity, to be produced on a piece-rate plan, rated, bought and sold by standard units, measured, counted and reduced to staple equivalence by impersonal, mechanical tests. In all its bearings the work is hereby reduced to a mechanistic statistical consistency, with numerical standards and units; which conduces to perfunctory and mediocre work throughout, and acts to deter both students and teachers from a free pursuit of knowledge, as contrasted with the pursuit of academic credits. So far as this mechanistic system goes freely into effect it leads to a substitution of salesmanlike proficiency —a balancing of bargains in staple cred-

its—in the place of scientific capacity and addiction to study.

The salesmanlike abilities and the men of affairs that so are drawn into the academic personnel, are presumably, somewhat under grade in their kind; since the pecuniary inducement offered by the schools is rather low as compared with the remuneration for office work of a similar character in the common run of business occupations, and since businesslike employés of this kind may fairly be presumed to go unreservedly to the highest bidder. Yet these more unscholarly members of the staff will necessarily be assigned the more responsible and discretionary positions in the academic organization; since under such a scheme of standardization, accountancy and control, the school becomes primarily a bureaucratic organization, and the first and unremitting duties of the staff are those of official management and accountancy. The further qualifications requisite in the members of the academic staff will be such as make for vendibility,—volubility, tactful effrontery, conspicuous conformity to the popular taste in all matters of opinion, usage and conventions.

The need of such a businesslike organization asserts itself in somewhat the same degree in which the academic policy is guided by considerations of magnitude and statistical renown; and this in turn is somewhat closely correlated with the extent of discretionary power exercised by the captain of erudition placed in control. At the same time, by provocation of the facilities which it offers for making an impressive demonstration, such bureaucratic organization will lead the university management to bend its energies with somewhat more singleness to the parade of magnitude and statistical gains. It also, and in the same connection, provokes to a persistent and detailed surveillance and direction of the work and manner of life of the academic staff, and so it acts to shut off initiative of any kind in the work done.

Intimately bound up with this bureaucratic officialism and accountancy, and working consistently to a similar outcome, is the predilection for "practical efficiency"—that is to say, for pecuniary success—prevalent in the American community. This predilection is a matter of settled habit, due, no doubt, to the fact that preoccupation with business interests characterizes this community in an exceptional degree, and that pecuniary habits of thought consequently rule popular thinking in a peculiarly uncritical and prescriptive fashion. This pecuniary animus falls in with and reinforces the movement for academic accountancy, and combines with it to further a so-called "practical" bias in all the work of the schools.

It appears, then, that the intrusion of business principles in the universities goes to weaken and retard the pursuit of learning, and therefore to defeat the ends for which a university is maintained. This result follows, primarily, from the substitution of impersonal, mechanical relations, standards and tests, in the place of personal conference, guidance and association between teachers and students; as also from the imposition of a mechanically standardized routine upon the members of the staff, whereby any disinterested preoccupation with scholarly or scientific inquiry is thrown into the background and falls into abeyance. Few if any who are competent to speak in these premises will question that such has been the outcome. To offset against this work of mutilation and retardation there are cer-

tain gains in expedition, and in the volume of traffic that can be carried by any given equipment and corps of employés. Particularly will there be a gain in the statistical showing, both as regards the volume of instruction offered, and probably also as regards the enrolment; since accountancy creates statistics and its absence does not.

Such increased enrolment as may be due to businesslike management and methods is an increase of undergraduate enrolment. The net effect as regards the graduate enrolment—apart from any vocational instruction that may euphemistically be scheduled as "graduate"— is in all probability rather a decrease than an increase. Through indoctrination with utilitarian (pecuniary) ideals of earning and spending, as well as by engendering spendthrift and sportsmanlike habits, such a businesslike management diverts the undergraduate students from going in for the disinterested pursuit of knowledge, and so from entering on what is properly university work; as witness the relatively slight proportion of graduate students—outside of the professional schools—who come up from the excessively large undergraduate departments of the more expansive universities, as contrasted with the number of those who come into university work from the smaller and less businesslike colleges.

The ulterior consequences that follow from such businesslike standardization and bureaucratic efficiency are evident in the current state of the public schools; especially as seen in the larger towns, where the principles of business management have had time and scope to work out in a fair degree of consistency. The resulting abomination of desolation is sufficiently notorious. And there appears to be no reason why a similarly stale routine of futility should not overtake the universities, and give similarly foolish results, as fast as the system of standardization, accountancy and piecework goes consistently into effect,—except only for the continued enforced employment of a modicum of impracticable scholars and scientists on the academic staff, whose unbusinesslike scholarly proclivities and inability to keep the miner's-inch of scholastic credit always in mind, must in some measure always defeat the perfect working of standardization and accountancy.

As might be expected, this régime of graduated sterility has already made fair headway in the undergraduate work, especially in the larger undergraduate schools; and this in spite of any efforts on the part of the administration to hedge against such an outcome by recourse to an intricate system of electives and a wide diversification of the standard units of erudition so offered.

In the graduate work the like effect is only less visible, because the measures leading to it have come into bearing more recently, and hitherto less unreservedly. But the like results should follow here also, just so fast and so far as the same range of business principles come to be worked into the texture of the university organization in the same efficacious manner as they have already taken effect in the public schools. And, pushed on as it is by the progressive substitution of men imbued with the tastes and habits of practical affairs, in the place of unpractical scholarly ideals, the movement towards a perfunctory routine of mediocrity should logically be expected to go forward at a progressively accelerated rate. The visible drift of things in this respect in the academic pursuit of the social sciences, so-called, is an argument as to what may be hoped for in the domain of academic science at large. It is only that the executive is actuated by a sharper solicitude to keep the academic establishment blameless of anything like innovation or iconoclasm at this point; which reinforces the drift toward a mechanistic routine and a curtailment of inquiry in this field; it is not that these sciences that deal with the phenomena of human life lend themselves more readily to mechanical description and enumeration than the material sciences do, nor is their subject matter intrinsically more inert or less provocative of questions.

1918

REINHOLD NIEBUHR

Is Religion Counter-Revolutionary?

THE MARXIAN charge that religion is an opiate and that its general influence upon society is reactionary, contains several specifications which must be taken up in turn. The specification which deserves first consideration is the one which is most unequivocally true. It is that religion creates a reverence for authority and encourages a humble obedience toward and a patient acceptance

Reprinted from *Radical Religion* for Autumn, 1935, by permission of the author.

of the exactions of power, thus aggravating the injustices of a social system and retarding their elimination. This charge is broadly true. It is true that in the history of Christianity St. Paul's admonition, recorded in Romans 13, to be obedient to government because all government is an ordinance of God has had a baneful effect upon the relation of Christianity to politics. It made every Christian state a sacerdotal state and bound the Christian religion to monarchial politics, to such a degree that the democratic movement in Europe had to be anti-religious to be effective (except insofar as Calvinism provided a religious authority for rebellion against autocracy and monarchism). The undue emphasis of orthodox Christianity upon the sanctity of government not only tended to supply a particular kind of government, monarchy, with the aura of the sacred; it also gave an undue advantage to whatever prince happened to sit upon the throne, no matter by what means he had usurped it. Once entrenched there he could count upon religion to support him and to intone prayers in the churches for his health. This kind of obedience was further buttressed by the doctrine, dating from Augustine, that evil rulers must also be obeyed because they are to be regarded as punishment sent by God for the sins of men, just as government in general is also a method of holding sinful men in check.

Some of this Christian doctrine leads to such political perversity that one cannot blame the eighteenth century for imagining that perfect justice could be established if only "priests and their hypocritical tools could be eliminated." Yet the liberal and radical rationalist is quite wrong in imagining that the religious sanctification of authority is noth-ing more than the fruit of priestly hypocrisy and can be overcome merely by destroying either the Christian religion or religion in general. While priests through all the ages have no doubt manipulated the sentiments of religion to maintain either their own power or that of some warrior class to which they were attached they could not create a religious obedience to authority out of whole cloth. They could only manipulate what actually existed in life. The fact is that from the earliest tribal life through all of the glories of great empires, religion has been the chief cement of social cohesion. The early tribe was a sacred brotherhood. The later empire was held together by a sacred ruler. The larger units of cooperation and conflict were not homogeneous. They could not be held together by a religiously colored sense of brotherhood. They could be held together only by a religiously colored obedience to authority. Hence the significance of the priest in the Egyptian and the Babylonian empires. Of course force was as necessary as reverence to hold these early societies together. Either the priest was also a warrior or the authority rested in a partnership of priests and warriors. This proves that force and reverence are the two primary forces of social cohesion. The more modern and rationalistic "consent of the governed" may be a third force; but it will never be as powerful as modern rationalists imagine, for the simple reason that the binding forces in human society are not chiefly rational but emotional.

Religious reverence for authority is therefore something which springs out of a perennially fresh spring of human emotions. It is no doubt dangerous. In it the gratitude of the common man for the principle of any social order, which sustains his social life, is easily transmuted into an undue reverence for the particular social order in which he stands and the particular authority which manipulates that society. But the dangerous nature of this element in social and religious life is not dealt with successfully by a mere emotional protest against all religion. Christianity did not create this element, even though St. Paul gave it a succinct expression. The priests of old did not fashion it out of their own malevolent souls. The fact is that it is so perennial that the very communist critics who seek to destroy religion in order to eliminate this pious respect for authority have already re-established it in Russia. What are the Russian oligarchs but priest-kings? They are not even under the necessity of bargaining with other priests and prophets to maintain the sacred aura over their power. Their power is holy of itself. It is hallowed by the religious beliefs of the multitudes over whom they hold sway. For their religion teaches the multitudes that these men of power are not subject to the temptations of other men of power, that they have a mystical identity of interest with the common man and that they are the harbingers of an ultimate society in which there will be no power and no unequal division of function or privilege. Every tenet of this religion inculcates a patient and reverent obedience of the common man toward those who have been set in authority over him. This is truly a power "ordained of God" even though God bears the secular name of "dialectic of history." There will never be an age in which critical intelligence will not be called upon to corrode the undue piety and reverence with which social power is venerated in the imagi-nation of the common man. Perhaps one way of solving the problem is to allow all this emotion to be attached to some symbol of society who does not have any real power, as in the case of British constitutional monarchy.

To a certain degree this particular reactionary tendency of religion has not been as potent and as dangerous in the period of bourgeois democracy as in the feudal period. The bourgeois state is a rationalistic state, conceived in terms of the social contract. It is so lacking in religious sanctity that the gentlemen of the Liberty League are making frantic efforts to construct the constitution into an adequate symbol of this now deficient religious loyalty. It is safe to assume that a Liberty League would emerge in our political situation even if our society were completely secular and non-Christian. On the whole it is very secular, certainly more secular than either Russia or Germany. In Germany a new national religion provides the authority of the state with a more un-qualified sanctity than Christianity ever gave any state or any ruler. Yes, we must agree with the Marxians. The religiously sacred state power, hiding its injustices behind its sanctities is a dangerous hazard to justice. But if all historic religions were wiped out tomorrow, that problem would still be with us.

What the Marxian charge against religion completely obscures is that a prophetic religion has its own antidote for the poison of a too conforming piety. It has a force of spirituality which brings all authority under criticism. It believes in a God who "bringeth the princes to nothing" and before whom "all nations are as nothing." The resolute word "we must obey God rather than man" has again and again been the battle cry of men who resisted political tyranny. Their religion made them more stubborn in their resistance than any merely skeptical attitude toward authority. The pretentious sanctities of politics can be met effectively only by higher sanctities and the too simple loyalties of political man can be challenged only by higher religious loyalties. In these latter days this higher religious loyalty may be an international proletariat. But it is not the only and not the most effective higher loyalty. An international class is something less than God and when it makes itself God we will have the same old problem over again, the problem of giving undue authority to partial historical forces.

It cannot be denied that organized religion produces more piety than spirituality and more conformity to authority than rebellion against it. But that is true of every aspect of organized culture. Organized education inculcates obedience rather than criticism. Will the radical destroy education because it is conservative in its organized expression? On the contrary he will capture it to make it conforming in his new society.

The second specific charge brought against religion in general and Christianity in particular is that it beguiles men from consideration of their mundane problems by the hope of other-worldly bliss. This charge is also broadly true. As far back as the Amon worship of Egypt, religion has offered men other-worldly hopes to assuage their sorrows in this world. Undoubtedly the ruling oligarchies of every society have made good use of this other-worldliness to dampen the spirit of rebellion and to increase the patience with which their vexatious rule was borne by the poor. Yet here too we are not dealing with a reaction to life which can be neatly

called "religious" and which can be eliminated by destroying religion. Religion for the poor, declared Karl Marx "is the spirit of their spiritless condition." Translated that means that it is a kind of a desperate hope of hopeless men. No one can deny that this hope is morally deleterious when it persuades men to accept conditions which ought to be altered and which they could alter by their own strength if they had the courage. In that sense other-worldliness is a terrible evil. But just what is this other-worldly hope? Basically it is the feeling that life as is, is not what it ought to be, that therefore when we experience the anarchy and tyranny, the cruelty and injustice in human society we are confronted with a terrible aberration of the essential reality of life. The communist asserts exactly the same faith when he hopes for a day when social conflict will be abolished and perfect brotherhood established. There is almost as much illusion in that hope incidentally as in the other-worldly hopes of religious dreamers. No historic society will ever achieve perfect peace and justice. This does not imply that the social utopianism and the social apocalypticism of social, as against individual types of religion, are not more serviceable to the cause of social justice than the dualism of individualistic religion which places its hope in some pure supernal world. The evil effects of dualistic influences upon Christian thought are apparent everywhere in its history. It is a regrettable fact that Christianity frequently lost its Hebraic heritage in which salvation is promised at the end and not above history, in which, in other words, the only redemption desired is the redemption of this world of nature-history. This Hebraic heritage, neglected in Christianity, is precisely what

Marxism has developed in a secularized and naturalistic form. Nor can it be denied that the other-worldly tendencies in Christianity have either been definitely encouraged or found to be a very convenient tool by the ruling oligarchies of the feudal and the capitalistic period.

Yet this charge against other-worldliness cannot be made against religion in general. It can be made against types of Christianity; perhaps it could even be claimed that Christianity has been prevailingly dualistic. But the charge certainly does not fit the religion of prophets, not the prophetic elements in Christianity. In both America and England some of the most effective spirits of the radical movement have come out of the religious tradition. They have been driven by the religious longing for the establishment of the ideal in history. They have been set upon their way by distinctively religious motives and forces. Only an ignorant or malevolent dogmatism can persist in the convenient evasion that such lives are merely brands that have been plucked from the burning, or exceptions that prove the rule.

A further word needs to be said in qualified defense of traditional other-worldliness. It may be counter-revolutionary and dangerous. But it is also the religious expression of a permanent factor in human life, namely the conflict between the individual and society and the feeling that human destiny and individual worth always transcend and are never completely expressed in the social situation. In this sense it is true that fully developed religions will always have an individualistic motif which purely political religions do not have. Sometimes this individualistic element will be a definite detriment to, and come in opposition with, a socio-religious passion. But the latter can eliminate the former, or dream of the possibility of eliminating it, only in such periods in which men give themselves to the illusion that they can build a society in which the individual can be inserted into a frictionless social harmony and have all his longings, dreams and aspiration fulfilled in it. In such a society all tensions and all possibilities of growth would be eliminated. It would be not the beginning but the end of history. Its realization is a utopian dream. Once it is recognized that the socialist society which we intend to build will not be a perfect society and that it will not be able to save individuals from many frustrations, unfulfilled hopes and unrealized dreams, it must also be conceded that individuals are bound to express themselves not only by setting new goals for a better society but by finding ways of bearing the injustices and frustrations of the moment in terms of a faith which sees life in its essential rather than its existential reality. That is a kind of other-worldliness, even if it dispenses with traditional hopes of immortality. Inasfar as historic religions express this dimension of individual life and do justice to this individual problem, they will be and are bound to be regarded as "counter-revolutionary" from the perspective of a too utopian and a too simply political religion. They may in fact actually be counter-revolutionary in the sense that they will encourage a more qualified devotion to socio-political ends than will seem justified in a moment when all that seems good is pitted against all that is evil in a given social struggle. The truth in the approach of historic religion cannot be proved until it becomes apparent that every political religion has tendencies to absolutize itself. These tendencies have the roots of social decay in them. It is when this decay sets in that a truly prophetic religion which is not completely committed to any political cause will prove itself to be truly revolutionary, for it will have a perspective from which it can judge, criticize and condemn the partial achievements of any historical movement. It is as important for Christian radicals to defend this ultimate basis of a continual revolution in high religion as to resist the efforts of reactionaries to reduce religion to social impotence by making false use of its individualism.

The final charge brought against religion is that it is the real root of the idealistic philosophies which interpret morals, culture and the spiritual life of man in terms which obscure the relation of economic interest and physical facts to the world of ideals and ideas. This charge is broadly justified but it must be made not only against religion but against the whole rationalistic culture of western civilization and holds more unqualifiedly against a secular culture than against the religious one. It is one of the sinful pretensions of all cultural enterprises to think of themselves as the fruits of pure mind and pure conscience and to interpret their history as the development of a kind of discarnate spirituality. This charge can be levelled not only against idealistic philosophy but even against the secular liberalism of today, with its basis of philosophical empiricism. Even there, though the dependence of mind upon the stuff of nature and history is recognized, there is a foolish confidence in the possibility of developing a rationality which will transcend the social facts which it judges and thus arrive at "objective" and "impartial" judgments. In the modern day the physical and economic basis of all

culture is more frequently obscured by empiricists than by the old fashioned philosophical idealists. Whether the metaphysical system is idealistic or empirical, the real weakness of these philosophies lies in their undue confidence in rationality. They do not understand to what degree the human mind is the instrument, the victim and the prisoner of human passions and immediate necessities. The idea, for instance, that nothing but a cultural lag prevents the social sciences from achieving the precision of the physical sciences, is a very modern idea, is derived neither from philosophical idealism nor from religion. It is the product of a completely secular, bourgeois culture. Yet it reveals the weakness, which the Marxian is trying to isolate when he speaks of the idealism of religion, more perfectly than any religious system.

The real fact is that prophetic religion is much too conscious of human finitude and sin to have the confidence in human reason and human goodness which both idealistic and empirical philosophies have betrayed. Sometimes this wholesome sense of sin has been weakened in Christian orthodoxy by the belief that the Christian faith and life lifted men completely out of and redeemed them from their enslavement to the world of nature and necessity. On this issue liberal religion is worse than orthodox religion. Its moralism, and its unwillingness to recognize the facts of nature in human history (the class struggle for instance) is at the present time a greater hazard to the understanding of the socio-moral problem of modern man than all the discredited myths of orthodoxy. But this moralism and sentimentality is not a characteristic fruit of the Christian religion at all. It is the fruit of the Age of Reason which has been carried into liberal religion.

It is impossible to deal intelligently with the social problem of man if the whole world of culture, secular and religious, liberal and conservative does not give more generous understanding of the truth which Marxism has discovered, or at least rediscovered: The truth that all human ideals and ideas are conditioned by the physical, geographic, economic and political circumstances in which they rise and that the final religious effort to escape this relativity may frequently become no more than the final rationalization and justification of the partial and relative value of class, race and nation. In that sense the ultimate dishonesty of a culture is always a religious one. Yet on the other hand it is precisely in a high religion, which sees the whole world of history as relative to the absolute and final goodness in God, that these dishonesties and deceptions of culture can be best discovered. However badly organized religion has become enmeshed in the immediate interests of class and nation, it has also always generated out of itself a minority of prophetic spirits who placed the pretensions of their culture and civilization under a divine judgment. In that capacity for judging all relative and partial values and in the humility which does not claim to reach an absolutely pure judgment itself, even while it sees what is partial and incomplete in every culture, in these lie the genius of prophetic religion. In them lie also the guarantee of perpetual revolution, protest, rebellion and criticism in human affairs.

It cannot be denied that this prophetic and revolutionary spirit in religion is frequently corrupted and destroyed. But it must also be recognized that the too simple Marxian might regard it as counter-revolutionary at the precise moment when it is functioning most perfectly. For that might be a moment when it calls attention to the fact that proletarian culture can be no more absolute and final than bourgeois culture was and that therefore the working class ought to be content to fulfill a great and fateful task in history without claiming to be a messianic class which will usher in the kingdom of God. A truly prophetic religion ought to turn against the spiritual pretensions of a proletarian culture as well as against preceding cultures. It is one of the tragedies of modern culture that the radical rebel against religious complacency and dishonesty falsifies the real facts and the total situation by condemning religion for its virtues as well as for its vices. Its virtues are of course bound to appear like vices from the perspective of a purely political religion. For those virtues are the ability to see and the courage to say that history relativizes all ideals and that human passions and interests condition all ideologies, including those of the leaders of proletarian rebellion.

It is consequently the business of radical religion to contend equally against the reactionary tendencies of organized religion and against the misunderstandings of the total human situation in the philosophy, and therefore in the strategy of radicalism.

1935

V. . . .

CRITICISM

WILLIAM HAZLITT

Mr. Cobbett

PEOPLE have about as substantial an idea of Cobbett as they have of Cribb. His blows are as hard, and he himself is as impenetrable. One has no notion of him as making use of a fine pen, but a great mutton-fist; his style stuns his readers, and he "fillips the ear of the public with a three-man beetle." He is too much for any single newspaper antagonist, "lays waste" a city orator or Member of Parliament, and bears hard upon the Government itself. He is a kind of *fourth estate* in the politics of the country. He is not only unquestionably the most powerful political writer of the present day, but one of the best writers in the language. He speaks and thinks plain, broad, downright English. He might be said to have the clearness of Swift, the naturalness of Defoe, and the picturesque satirical description of Mandeville: if all such comparisons were not impertinent. A really great and original writer is like nobody but himself. In one sense, Sterne was not a wit, nor Shakespeare a poet. It is easy to describe second-rate talents, because they fall into a class and enlist under a standard: but first-rate powers defy calculation or comparison, and can be defined only by themselves. They are *sui generis,* and make the class to which they belong. I have tried half-a-dozen times to describe Burke's style without ever succeeding: its severe extravagance, its literal boldness, its matter-of-fact hyperboles, its running away with a subject and from it at the same time; but there is no making it out, for

there is no example of the same thing any where else. We have no common measure to refer to; and his qualities contradict even themselves.

Cobbett is not so difficult. He has been compared to Paine; and so far it is true there are no two writers who come more into juxtaposition from the nature of their subjects, from the internal resources on which they draw, and from the popular effect of their writings and their adaptation (though that is a bad word in the present case) to the capacity of every reader. But still, if we turn to a volume of Paine's (his Common Sense or Rights of Man) we are struck (not to say somewhat refreshed) by the difference. Paine is a much more sententious writer than Cobbett. You cannot open a page in any of his best and earlier works without meeting with some maxim, some antithetical and memorable saying, which is a sort of starting-place for the argument, and the goal to which it returns. There is not a single *bon-mot,* a single sentence in Cobbett that has ever been quoted again. If any thing is ever quoted from him, it is an epithet of abuse or a nickname. He is an excellent hand at invention in that way, and has "damnable iteration in him." What could be better than his pestering Erskine year after year with his second title of Baron Clackmannan? He is rather too fond of such phrases as *the Sons and Daughters of Corruption.* Paine affected to reduce things to first principles, to announce self-evident truths. Cobbett troubles himself about little but the details and local circumstances. The first appeared to have made up his mind beforehand to certain opinions, and to try to find the most compendious and pointed expressions for them: his successor appears to have no clue, no fixed or leading principles, nor ever to have thought on a question till he sits down to write about it. But then there seems no end of his matters of fact and raw materials, which are brought out in all their strength and sharpness from not having been squared or frittered down or vamped up to suit a theory. He goes on with his descriptions and illustrations as if he would never come to a stop; they have all the force of novelty with all the familiarity of old acquaintance. His knowledge grows out of the subject, and his style is that of a man who has an absolute intuition of what he is talking about, and never thinks of any thing else. He deals in premises and speaks to evidence: the coming to a conclusion and summing up (which was Paine's *forte*) lies in a smaller compass. The one could not compose an elementary treatise on politics to become a manual for the popular reader; nor could the other in all probability have kept up a weekly journal for the same number of years with the same spirit, interest, and untired perseverance. Paine's writings are a sort of introduction to political arithmetic on a new plan; Cobbett keeps a day-book, and makes an entry at full of all the occurrences and troublesome questions that start up throughout the year. Cobbett, with vast industry, vast information, and the utmost power of making what he says intelligible, never seems to get at the beginning or come to the end of any question: Paine in a few short sentences seems by his peremptory manner "to clear it from all controversy, past, present, and to come." Paine takes a bird's-eye view of things; Cobbett sticks close to them, inspects the component parts, and keeps fast hold of the smallest advantages they afford him. Or if I might here be indulged in a pastoral allusion, Paine tries to enclose his ideas in a fold for security and repose; Cobbett lets *his* pour out upon the plain like a flock of sheep to feed and batten. Cobbett is a pleasanter writer for those to read who do not agree with him; for he is less dogmatical, goes more into the common grounds of fact and argument to which all appeal, is more desultory and various, and appears less to be driving at a previous conclusion than urged on by the force of present conviction. He is therefore tolerated by all parties, though he has made himself by turns obnoxious to all; and even those he abuses read him. The Reformers read him when he was a Tory, and the Tories read him now that he is a Reformer. He must, I think, however, be *caviare* to the Whigs.[1]

If he is less metaphysical and poetical than his celebrated prototype, he is more picturesque and dramatic. His episodes, which are numerous as they are pertinent, are striking, interesting, full of life and *naïveté,* minute, double measure running over, but never tedious— *nunquam sufflaminandus erat.* He is one of those writers who can never tire us, not even of himself; and the reason is, he is always "full of matter." He never runs to lees, never gives us the vapid leavings of himself, is never "weary, stale, and unprofitable," but always setting out afresh on his journey, clearing away some old nuisance, and

---

[1] The late Lord Chancellor Thurlow used to say that Cobbett was the only writer that deserved the name of a political reasoner.

turning up new mould. His egotism is delightful, for there is no affectation in it. He does not talk of himself for lack of something to write about, but because some circumstance that has happened to himself is the best possible illustration of the subject; and he is not the man to shrink from giving the best possible illustration of the subject from a squeamish delicacy. He likes both himself and his subject too well. He does not put himself before it, and say "admire me first," but places us in the same situation with himself, and makes us see all that he does. There is no blind man's buff, no conscious hints, no awkward ventriloquism, no testimonies of applause, no abstract, senseless self-complacency, no smuggled admiration of his own person by proxy; it is all plain and above-board. He writes himself plain William Cobbett, strips himself quite as naked as any body could wish: in a word, his egotism is full of individuality, and has room for very little vanity in it. We feel delighted, rub our hands, and draw our chair to the fire, when we come to a passage of this sort: we know it will be something new and good, manly and simple, not the same insipid story of self over again. We sit down at table with the writer, but it is of a course of rich viands—flesh, fish, and wild fowl—and not to a nominal entertainment, like that given by the Barmecide in the Arabian Nights, who put off his visitor with calling for a number of exquisite things that never appeared, and with the honour of his company. Mr. Cobbett is not a *make-believe* writer. His worst enemy cannot say that of him. Still less is he a vulgar one. He must be a puny common-place critic indeed, who thinks him so. How fine were the graphical descriptions he sent us from America: what a transatlantic flavour,

what a native *gusto,* what a fine *sauce piquante* of contempt they were seasoned with! If he had sat down to look at himself in the glass, instead of looking about him like Adam in Paradise, he would not have got up these articles in so capital a style. What a noble account of his first breakfast after his arrival in America! It might serve for a month. There is no scene on the stage more amusing. How well he paints the gold and scarlet plumage of the American birds, only to lament more pathetically the want of the wild wood-notes of his native land! The groves of the Ohio that had just fallen beneath the axe's stroke, "live in his description," and the turnips that he transplanted from Botley "look green" in prose! How well at another time he describes the poor sheep that had got the tick, and had tumbled down in the agonies of death! It is a portrait in the manner of Bewick, with the strength, the simplicity, and feeling of that great naturalist. What havoc he makes, when he pleases, of the curls of Dr. Parr's wig and of the Whig consistency of Mr. ——! His Grammar, too, is as entertaining as a story-book. He is too hard, however, upon the style of others, and not enough (sometimes) on his own.

As a political partisan, no one can stand against him. With his brandished club, like Giant Despair in the Pilgrim's Progress, he knocks out their brains: and not only no individual, but no corrupt system, could hold out against his powerful and repeated attacks. But with the same weapon, swung round like a flail, with which he levels his antagonists, he lays his friends low, and puts his own party *hors de combat.* This is a bad propensity, and a worse principle in political tactics, though a common one. If his blows were straightforward and steadily directed to the same object, no unpopular minister could live before him; instead of which he lays about right and left impartially and remorselessly, makes a clear stage, has all the ring to himself, and then runs out of it, just when he should stand his ground. He throws his head into his adversary's stomach, and takes away from him all inclination for the fight, hits fair or foul, strikes at everything, and as you come up to his aid or stand ready to pursue his advantage, trips up your heels or lays you sprawling, and pummels you when down as much to his heart's content as ever the Yanguesian carriers belaboured Rosinante with their pack-staves. *"He has the back-trick simply the best of any man in Illyria."* He pays off both scores of old friendship and new-acquired enmity in a breath, in one perpetual volley, one raking fire of "arrowy sleet" shot from his pen. However his own reputation or the cause may suffer in consequence, he cares not one pin about that, so that he disables all who oppose or who pretend to help him. In fact, he cannot bear success of any kind, not even of his own views or party; and if any principle were likely to become popular, would turn round against it, to show his power in shouldering it on one side. In short, wherever power is, there is he against it: he naturally butts at all obstacles, as unicorns are attracted to oak-trees, and feels his own strength only by resistance to the opinions and wishes of the rest of the world. To sail with the stream, to agree with the company, is not his humour. If he could bring about a Reform in Parliament, the odds are that he would instantly fall foul of and try to mar his own handywork; and he quarrels with his own crea-

tures as soon as he has written them into a little vogue—and a prison. I do not think this is vanity or fickleness so much as a pugnacious disposition, that must have an antagonist power to contend with, and only finds itself at ease in systematic opposition. If it were not for this, the high towers and rotten places of the world would fall before the battering-ram of his hard-headed reasoning: but if he once found them tottering, he would apply his strength to prop them up, and disappoint the expectations of his followers. He cannot agree to any thing established, nor to set up any thing else in its stead. While it is established, he presses hard against it, because it presses upon him, at least in imagination. Let it crumble under his grasp, and the motive to resistance is gone. He then requires some other grievance to set his face against. His principle is repulsion, his nature contradiction: he is made up of mere antipathies; an Ishmaelite indeed, without a fellow. He is always playing at *hunt-the-slipper* in politics. He turns round upon whoever is next to him. The way to wean him from any opinion, and make him conceive an intolerable hatred against it, would be to place somebody near him who was perpetually dinning it in his ears. When he is in England, he does nothing but abuse the Borough-mongers, and laugh at the whole system: when he is in America, he grows impatient of freedom and a republic. If he had stayed there a little longer, he would have become a loyal and a loving subject of his Majesty King George IV. He lampooned the French Revolution when it was hailed as the dawn of liberty by millions; by the time it was brought into almost universal ill-odour by some means or other (partly no doubt by himself) he had turned, with one or two or three others, staunch Bonapartist. He is always of the militant, not of the triumphant party: so far he bears a gallant show of magnanimity. But his gallantry is hardly of the right stamp: it wants principle. For though he is not servile or mercenary, he is the victim of self-will. He must pull down and pull in pieces: it is not in his disposition to do otherwise. It is a pity; for with his great talents he might do great things, if he would go right forward to any useful object, make thorough-stitch work of any question, or join hand and heart with any principle. He changes his opinions as he does his friends, and much on the same account. He has no comfort in fixed principles: as soon as any thing is settled in his own mind, he quarrels with it. He has no satisfaction but in the chase after truth, runs a question down, worries and kills it, then quits it like vermin, and starts some new game, to lead him a new dance, and give him a fresh breathing through bog and brake, with the rabble yelping at his heels and the leaders perpetually at fault. This he calls sport-royal. He thinks it as good as cudgel-playing or single-stick, or any thing else that has life in it. He likes the cut and thrust, the falls, bruises, and dry blows of an argument: as to any good or useful results that may come of the amicable settling of it, any one is welcome to them for him. The amusement is over, when the matter is once fairly decided.

There is another point of view in which this may be put. I might say that Mr. Cobbett is a very honest man, with a total want of principle; and I might explain this paradox thus. I mean that he is, I think, in downright earnest in what he says, in the part he takes at the time; but in taking that part, he is led entirely by headstrong obsti-

nacy, caprice, novelty, pique or personal motive of some sort, and not by a steadfast regard for truth or habitual anxiety for what is right uppermost in his mind. He is not a feed, time-serving, shuffling advocate (no man could write as he does who did not believe himself sincere)— but his understanding is the dupe and slave of his momentary, violent, and irritable humours. He does not adopt an opinion "deliberately or for money"; yet his conscience is at the mercy of the first provocation he receives, of the first whim he takes in his head. He sees things through the medium of heat and passion, not with reference to any general principles, and his whole system of thinking is deranged by the first object that strikes his fancy or sours his temper. One cause of this phenomenon is perhaps his want of a regular education. He is a self-taught man, and has the faults as well as excellences of that class of persons in their most striking and glaring excess. It must be acknowledged that the Editor of the Political Register (the *two-penny trash,* as it was called, till a Bill passed the House to raise the price to sixpence) is not "the gentleman and scholar," though he has qualities that, with a little better management, would be worth (to the public) both those titles. For want of knowing what has been discovered before him, he has not certain general landmarks to refer to or a general standard of thought to apply to individual cases. He relies on his own acuteness and the immediate evidence, without being acquainted with the comparative anatomy or philosophical structure of opinion. He does not view things on a large scale or at the horizon (dim and airy enough perhaps); but as they affect himself—close, palpable, tangible. Whatever he finds out is his own, and he only knows what he finds out. He is in the constant hurry and fever of gestation: his brain teems incessantly with some fresh project. Every new light is the birth of a new system, the dawn of a new world to him. He is continually outstripping and overreaching himself. The last opinion is the only true one. He is wiser to-day than he was yesterday. Why should he not be wiser to-morrow than he was to-day? Men of a learned education are not so sharp-witted as clever men without it; but they know the balance of the human intellect better. If they are more stupid, they are more steady, and are less liable to be led astray by their own sagacity and the overweening petulance of hard-earned and late-acquired wisdom. They do not fall in love with every meretricious extravagance at first sight, or mistake an old battered hypothesis for a vestal, because they are new to the ways of this old world. They do not seize upon it as a prize, but are safe from gross imposition by being as wise and no wiser than those who went before them.

Paine said on some occasion, "What I have written, I have written," as rendering any farther declaration of his principles unnecessary. Not so Mr. Cobbett. What he has written is no rule to him what he is to write. He learns something every day, and every week he takes the field to maintain the opinions of the last six days against friend or foe. I doubt whether this outrageous inconsistency, this headstrong fickleness, this understood want of all rule and method, does not enable him to go on with the spirit, vigour, and variety that he does. He is not pledged to repeat himself. Every new Register is a kind of new Prospectus. He blesses himself from all ties and shackles on his understanding; he has no mortgages on his brain; his notions are free and unincumbered. If he was put in trammels, he might become a vile hack like so many more. But he gives himself "ample scope and verge enough." He takes both sides of a question, and maintains one as sturdily as the other. If nobody else can argue against him, he is a very good match for himself. He writes better in favour of reform than any body else; he used to write better against it. Wherever he is, there is the tug of war, the weight of the argument, the strength of abuse. He is not like a man in danger of being *bed-rid* in his faculties: he tosses and tumbles about his unwieldy bulk, and when he is tired of lying on one side, relieves himself by turning on the other. His shifting his point of view from time to time not merely adds variety and greater compass to his topics (so that the Political Register is an armoury and magazine for all the materials and weapons of political warfare), but it gives a greater zest and liveliness to his manner of treating them. Mr. Cobbett takes nothing for granted, as what he has proved before; he does not write a book of reference. We see his ideas in their first concoction, fermenting and overflowing with the ebullitions of a lively conception. We look on at the actual process, and are put in immediate possession of the grounds and materials on which he forms his sanguine, unsettled conclusions. He does not give us samples of reasoning, but the whole solid mass, refuse and all.

"——He pours out all as plain
As downright Shippen or as old Montaigne."

This is one cause of the clearness and force of his writings. An argument does not stop to stagnate and muddle in his brain, but passes at once to his paper. His ideas are served up, like pancakes, hot and hot. Fresh theories give him fresh courage. He is like a young and lusty bridegroom, that divorces a favourite speculation every morning, and marries a new one every night. He is not wedded to his notions, not he. He has not one Mrs. Cobbett among all his opinions. He makes the most of the last thought that has come in his way, seizes fast hold of it, rumples it about in all directions with rough strong hands, has his wicked will of it, takes a surfeit, and throws it away. Our author's changing his opinions for new ones is not so wonderful; what is more remarkable is his felicity in forgetting his old ones. He does not pretend to consistency (like Mr. Coleridge); he frankly disavows all connection with himself. He feels no personal responsibility in this way, and cuts a friend or principle with the same decided indifference that Antiphoulis of Ephesus cuts Ægeon of Syracuse. It is a hollow thing. The only time he ever grew romantic was in bringing over the relics of Mr. Thomas Paine with him from America, to go a progress with them through the disaffected districts. Scarce had he landed in Liverpool, when he left the bones of a great man to shift for themselves; and no sooner did he arrive in London, than he made a speech to disclaim all participation in the political and theological sentiments of his late idol, and to place the whole stock of his admiration and enthusiasm towards him to the account of his financial speculations, and of his having predicted the fate of paper-money. If he had erected a little gold statue to him, it might have proved the sincerity of this assertion; but to make a martyr and a patron-saint of a man, and to dig up "his canonized

bones" in order to expose them as objects of devotion to the rabble's gaze, asks something that has more life and spirit in it, more mind and vivifying soul, than has to do with any calculation of pounds, shillings, and pence! The fact is, he *ratted* from his own project. He found the thing not so ripe as he had expected. His heart failed him; his enthusiasm fled; and he made his retraction. His admiration is short-lived: his contempt only is rooted, and his resentment lasting. The above was only one instance of his building too much on practical *data*. He has an ill habit of prophesying, and goes on, though still deceived. The art of prophesying does not suit Mr. Cobbett's style. He has a knack of fixing names and times and places. According to him, the Reformed Parliament was to meet in March, 1818; it did not, and we heard no more of the matter. When his predictions fail, he takes no farther notice of them, but applies himself to new ones, like the country-people, who turn to see what weather there is in the almanac for the next week, though it has been out in its reckoning every day of the last.

Mr. Cobbett is great in attack, not in defense: he cannot fight an up-hill battle. He will not bear the least punishing. If any one turns upon him (which few people like to do), he immediately turns tail. Like an overgrown schoolboy, he is so used to have it all his own way, that he cannot submit to any thing like competition or a struggle for the mastery: he must lay on all the blows, and take none. He is bullying and cowardly; a Big Ben in politics, who will fall upon others and crush them by his weight, but is not prepared for resistance, and is soon staggered by a few smart blows. Whenever he has been set upon, he has slunk out of the controversy. The Edinburgh Review made (what is called) a dead set at him some years ago, to which he only retorted by an eulogy on the superior neatness of an English kitchen-garden to a Scotch one. I remember going one day into a bookseller's shop in Fleet Street to ask for the Review; and on my expressing my opinion to a young Scotchman, who stood behind the counter, that Mr. Cobbett might hit as hard in his reply, the North Briton said with some alarm— "But you don't think, Sir, Mr. Cobbett will be able to injure the Scottish nation?" I said I could not speak to that point, but I thought he was very well able to defend himself. He however did not, but has borne a grudge to the Edinburgh Review ever since, which he hates worse than the Quarterly. I cannot say I do.[2]

1821

[2] Mr. Cobbett speaks almost as well as he writes. The only time I ever saw him he seemed to me a very pleasant man: easy of access, affable, clear-headed, simple and mild in his manner, deliberate and unruffled in his speech, though some of his expressions were not very qualified. His figure is tall and portly: he has a good sensible face, rather full, with little grey eyes, a hard, square forehead, a ruddy complexion, with hair grey or powdered: and had on a scarlet broadcloth waistcoat, with the flaps of the pockets hanging down, as was the custom for gentlemen-farmers in the last century, or as we see it in the pictures of Members of Parliament in the reign of George I. I certainly did not think less favourably of him for seeing him.

ELIZABETH DREW

Saki

HECTOR HUGH MUNRO, born in India in 1870, a delicate child who was not expected to live, was brought up from the age of two in a damp, dark country house in Devonshire, surrounded by high walls and hedges. Here he and his brother and sister, placed in the care of two dragonlike aunts, were virtually prisoners, mewed in behind closed windows at night and in all bad weather, and permitted to play only on the front lawn in summer —"the kitchen garden being considered too tempting a place, with its fruit trees." Both the aunts, Miss Munro tells us in her memoir of her brother, "were guilty of mental cruelty." Their methods are described in those of the aunt in "The Lumber Room."

It was her habit, whenever one of the children fell from grace, to improvise something of a festival nature from which the offender would be rigorously debarred; if all the children sinned collectively they were suddenly informed of a circus in a neighbouring town, a circus of unrivalled merit and uncounted elephants, to which, but for their depravity, they would have been taken that very day.

"We often longed for revenge with an intensity I suspect we inherited from our Highland ancestry," says Miss Munro, and Hector "sublimated" that longing in the finest of his sketches in the *macabre*—"Sredni Vashtar." In that story we share all Conradin's feelings of exultant practical triumph over the aunt who made his life a misery, and the

Reprinted from *The Atlantic Monthly*, July, 1940, by permission of the author.

story itself remains as a symbol of Saki's own spiritual triumph over the Brontosauri rather than Montessori methods of his upbringing. For in his art, as in his life, there is no trace of the repressed or neurotic temperament which might have been expected.

He spent a cosmopolitan youth traveling on the continent with his father, a year in India with the Military Police, several years in Russia, the Balkans, and Paris as a newspaper correspondent, and then settled down as a free-lance journalist in London. At the outbreak of the Great War, when he was forty-four, he at once enlisted in the ranks, and he was killed in the attack on Beaumont-Hamel on November 13, 1916.

Admirers, in their natural wish to do justice to a man they loved, have pointed to passages in Saki's works in which he reveals his personality directly, and from which it is possible to construct the man of flesh and blood behind the mask of mockery he chose to wear. But such criticism does him no service. He deliberately chose a pseudonym for his writings—Sákí, the cupbearer whose "joyous errand" was to serve the guests with wine in the *Rubáiyát* of Omar Khayyám. He never sought intimacy with his readers, or gave them his confidence. He asks nothing from them but lips that can laugh, flesh that can creep, and legs that can be pulled. Saki, in fact, agreed with the eighteenth-century essayist, Shaftesbury:—

I hold it very indecent for anyone to publish his meditations, reflections and solitary thoughts. Those are the froth and scum of writing, which should be unburdened in private and consigned to oblivion, before the writer comes before the world as good company.

Saki is the most impersonal of artists. His private emotions and enthusiasms, meditations or thoughts, have no place in the world of his art. Saki is not Hector Munro, any more than Elia is Charles Lamb. But the methods of the two writers are completely opposed. Lamb dowered Elia with all his own most lovable characteristics: his warm heart, his genius for friendship, his love of life. Hector Munro, though he was richly endowed with all these qualities, denied them to Saki. That artist, in all his short sketches and stories, is allowed but three strains in his nature: the high spirits and malicious impudence of a precocious child; the cynical wit of the light social satirist; and the Gaelic fantasy of the highlander. We meet these three in turns: the irresponsible imp who invents unlimited extravagant practical jokes to mystify and enrage and outwit the heavy-minded adult world; the ironic mocker who speaks in the quips of Clovis and Reginald and the Duchess; and the Celt who sees the kettle refuse to boil when it has been bewitched by the Evil Eye, or hears Pan's laughter as he tramples to death the doubter of his powers.

Hilaire Belloc once wrote a poem beginning,—

Matilda told such awful lies
It made you gasp and stretch your eyes.

Matilda came to a bad end, but Saki's child and adult liars never come to bad ends. Triumphantly they discomfit the forces of dullness and of feeble counter-deception opposed to them, and prove indisputably that fiction is stronger than fact. It must be owned that there are times when we tire of these *enfants terribles* of all ages, just as we can have too much of Mr. P. G. Wodehouse's dithering dukes and prize pigs; but at his best the fiendish capacity for unveracious invention with which Saki endows his children, and the amazing mendacities with which his young men and women confute the commonplace, are the fine art of lying at its finest. My own favorites are the story spun by the ingenious niece of the house to the nervous caller, with the innocent opening, "You may wonder why we keep that window open on an October afternoon," or the visit of the Bishop to organize a local massacre of the Jews, invented by Clovis to animate a family in need of an "unrest cure." This, since it involved action as well as equivocation, perhaps belongs more truly to the stories dealing with elaborate hoaxes and practical jokes— such as the tale of Leaonard Bilsiter, who liked to hint of his acquaintance with the unseen forces of "Siberian magic" but was somewhat horrified when it appeared that his powers had changed his hostess into a she-wolf; or that of the titled lady who was mistaken for the new governess and plays the part by teaching the children the history of the Sabine Women by the Schartz-Metterklume method of making them act it for themselves.

There is an element of cruelty in a practical joke, and many readers of Saki find themselves repelled by a certain heartlessness in many of his tales. The cruelty is certainly there, but it has nothing perverted or pathological about it. He is not one of those whose motto might be "Our sweetest songs are those that tell of sadist thought." It is the genial heartlessness of the normal child, whose fantasies take no account of adult standards of human behavior, and to whom the eating of a gypsy by a hyena is no more terrible than the eating of Red Ridinghood's grandmother by a wolf. The standards of these gruesome tales are those of the fairy tale; their grimness is the grimness of Grimm.

The other element in Saki's cruelty springs from a certain unsparing consistency of vision which will allow no sentiment to intrude. He speaks of one young man as "one of those people who would be enormously improved by death," and he never hesitates to supply that embellishment himself on suitable occasions. Stories such as "The Easter Egg" and "The Hounds of Fate" are tragedies entirely without pity, but their callousness is consistent with the hard cynical sanity which is behind even his lightest satire, and gives it its strength. His mockery is urbane but ruthless. His wit is in the tradition of Wilde and the lesser creations of E. F. Benson's *Dodo* and Anthony Hope's *Dolly Dialogues,* and in the modern world he has affinities with Noel Coward and the early Aldous Huxley. Like them, he creates an artificial world enclosed in an element outside of which it could no more exist than we could exist outside our envelope of ether. It is embalmed in the element of Wit. To talk about Saki's "characterization" is absurd. His characters are constructed to form a front against which his light satiric artillery can most effectively be deployed. The forces against him are the common social vices of Vanity Fair: humbug and hypocrisy, greed and grab, envy and uncharitableness, sheer dullness and fatuity. Comus Bassington, listening to scraps of conversation at an At Home, comments: "I suppose it's the Prevention of Destitution they're hammering at. What on earth would become of all these dear good people if anyone should start a crusade for the prevention of mediocrity?" The crusade would be a disaster, for it would extinguish Lucas Bassett, the young poet who had the triumphant inspiration of the couplet

Cousin Teresa takes out Cæsar,
Fido, Jock and the big borzoi,

and whom we see at the end of the story docketed for a knighthood under the letter L.

"The letter L," said the secretary, who was new to his job. "Does that stand for Liberalism or liberality?"

"Literature," explained the minister.

And the crusade would probably eliminate all those ardent slum workers and society socialists "whose naturally stagnant souls take infinite pleasure in what are called 'movements'"; those Wodehouse-like moneyed aunts and impecunious and irresponsible nephews; those drones and butterflies "to whom clear soup is a more important factor in life than a clear conscience"; and those odious children whose ghastly pranks turn us into keen supporters of the canonization of good King Herod.

But the situations and characters which, left to themselves, would develop into what Jane Austen called "the elegant stupidity of a private party" develop instead into hilarious gayety and crackling brilliance, and it is Saki's wit and not his satirical material, or any of his other literary material, which will make him live. It is his sheer good fun and good spirits and capacity to be such persistent good company. His power to comment that "so many people who are described as rough diamonds turn out to be only rough paste"; his power to describe the unsophisticated diner-out consulting the wine list "with the blank embarrassment of a schoolboy suddenly called on to locate a Minor Prophet in the tangled hinterland of the Old Testament"; or his impudent morsels of dialogue.

"Such an exquisite rural retreat, and so restful and healing to the nerves. Real country scenery; apple blossom everywhere."

"Surely only on the apple trees?"

"As a companion he was an unfailing antidote to boredom," wrote one of his friends. It is an epitaph anyone might envy.

1940

THEODORE MORRISON

Dover Beach Revisited

EARLY IN the year 1939 a certain Professor of Educational Psychology, occupying a well-paid chair at a large endowed university, conceived a plot. From his desk in the imposing Hall of the Social Sciences where the Research Institute in Education was housed he had long burned with resentment against teachers of literature, especially against English departments. It seemed to him that the professors of English stood square across the path of his major professional ambition. His great desire in life was to introduce into the study, the teaching, the critical evaluation of literature some of the systematic method,

Reprinted from *Harper's Magazine*, February, 1940, by permission of the author.

some of the "objective procedure" as he liked to call it, some of the certainty of result which he believed to be characteristic of the physical sciences. "You make such a fetish of science," a colleague once said to him, "why aren't you a chemist?"—a question that annoyed him deeply.

If such a poem as Milton's "Lycidas" has a value—and most English teachers, even to-day, would start with that as a cardinal fact—then that value must be measurable and expressible in terms that do not shift and change from moment to moment and person to person with every subjective whim. They would agree, these teachers of literature, these professors of English, that the value of the poem is in some sense objective; they would never agree to undertake any objective procedure to determine what that value is. They would not clearly define what they meant by achievement in the study of literature, and they bridled and snorted when anyone else attempted to define it. He remembered what had happened when he had once been incautious enough to suggest to a professor of English in his own college that it might be possible to establish norms for the appreciation of Milton. The fellow had simply exploded into a peal of histrionic laughter and then had tried to wither him with an equally histrionic look of incredulity and disgust.

He would like to see what would happen if the teachers of English were forced or lured, by some scheme or other, into a public exposure of their position. It would put them in the light of intellectual charlatanism, nothing less . . . and suddenly Professor Chartly (for so he was nicknamed) began to see his way.

It was a simple plan that popped into his head, simple yet bold and practical. It was a challenge that could not be refused. A strategically placed friend in one of the large educational foundations could be counted on: there would be money for clerical expenses, for travel if need be. He took his pipe from his pocket, filled it, and began to puff exultantly. To-morrow he must broach the scheme to one or two colleagues; to-night, over cheese and beer, would not be too soon. He reached for the telephone.

The plan that he unfolded to his associates that evening aroused considerable skepticism at first, but gradually they succumbed to his enthusiasm. A number of well-known professors of literature at representative colleges up and down the land would be asked to write a critical evaluation of a poem prominent enough to form part of the standard reading in all large English courses. They would be asked to state the criteria on which they based their judgment. When all the answers had been received the whole dossier would be sent to a moderator, a trusted elder statesman of education, known everywhere for his dignity, liberality of intelligence, and long experience. He would be asked to make a preliminary examination of all the documents and to determine from the point of view of a teacher of literature whether they provided any basis for a common understanding. The moderator would then forward all the documents to Professor Chartly, who would make what in his own mind he was frank to call a more scientific analysis. Then the jaws of the trap would be ready to spring.

Once the conspirators had agreed on their plot their first difficulty came in the choice of a poem. Suffice it to say that someone eventually hit on Arnold's "Dover Beach," and the suggestion withstood all attack. "Dover Beach" was universally known, almost universally praised; it was remote enough so that contemporary jealousies and cults were not seriously involved, yet near enough not to call for any special expertness, historical or linguistic, as a prerequisite for judgment; it was generally given credit for skill as a work of art, yet it contained also, in its author's own phrase, a "criticism of life."

Rapidly in the days following the first meeting the representative teachers were chosen and invited to participate in the plan. Professional courtesy seemed to require the inclusion of an Arnold expert. But the one selected excused himself from producing a value judgment of "Dover Beach" on the ground that he was busy investigating a fresh clue to the identity of "Marguerite." He had evidence that the woman in question, after the episode hinted at in the famous poems, had married her deceased sister's husband, thus perhaps affecting Arnold's views on a social question about which he had said a good deal in his prose writings. The expert pointed out that he had been given a half-year's leave of absence and a research grant to pursue the shadow of Marguerite through Europe, wherever it might lead him. If only war did not break out he hoped to complete this research and solve one of the vexing problems that had always confronted Arnold's biographers. His energies would be too much engaged in this special investigation to deal justly with the more general questions raised by Professor Chartly's invitation. But he asked to be kept informed, since the results of the experiment could not fail to be of interest to him.

After a few hitches and delays from other quarters, the scheme was ripe. The requests were mailed out, and the Professor of Educational Psychology sat back in grim confidence to await the outcome.

It chanced that the first of the representative teachers who received and answered Professor Chartly's letter was thought of on his own campus as giving off a distinct though not unpleasant odor of the ivory tower. He would have resented the imputation himself. At forty-five Bradley Dewing was handsome in a somewhat speciously virile style, graying at the temples, but still well-knit and active. He prided himself on being able to beat most of his students at tennis; once a year he would play the third or fourth man on the varsity and go down to creditable defeat with some elegiac phrases on the ravages of time. He thought of himself as a man of the world; it was well for his contentment, which was seldom visibly ruffled, that he never heard the class mimic reproducing at a fraternity house or beer parlor his manner of saying: "After all, gentlemen, it is pure poetry that lasts. We must never forget the staying power of pure art." The class mimic never represents the whole of class opinion but he can usually make everyone within earshot laugh.

Professor Dewing could remember clearly what his own teachers had said about "Dover Beach" in the days when he was a freshman in college himself, phrases rounded with distant professorial unction: faith and doubt in the Victorian era; disturbing influence of Darwin on religious belief; Browning the optimist; Tennyson coming up with firm faith after a long struggle in the waters of doubt; Matthew Arnold, prophet of skepticism. How would "Dover Beach" stack up now as a poem? Pull Arnold down from the shelf and find out.

Ah, yes, how the familiar phrases came back. The sea is calm, the tide is full, the cliffs of England stand. . . . And then the lines he particularly liked:

Come to the window, sweet is the night
    air!
Only, from the long line of spray
Where the ebb meets the moon-blanch'd
    sand,
Listen! you hear the grating roar
Of pebbles which the waves draw back,
    and fling,
At their return, up the high strand,
Begin, and cease, and then again begin,
With tremulous cadence slow . . .

Good poetry, that! No one could mistake it. Onomatopoeia was a relatively cheap effect most of the time. Poe, for instance: "And the silken sad uncertain rustling of each purple curtain." Anyone could put a string of s's together and make them rustle. But these lines in "Dover Beach" were different. The onomatopoeia was involved in the whole scene, and it in turn involved the whole rhythmical movement of the verse, not the mere noise made by the consonants or vowels as such. The pauses—only, listen, draw back, fling, begin, cease— how they infused a subdued melancholy into the moonlit panorama at the same time that they gave it the utmost physical reality by suggesting the endless iteration of the waves! And then the phrase "With tremulous cadence slow" coming as yet one more touch, one "fine excess," when it seemed that every phrase and pause the scene could bear had already been lavished on it: that was Miltonic, Virgilian.

But the rest of the poem?

The sea of Faith
Was once, too, at the full, and round
    earth's shore
Lay like the folds of a bright girdle
    furl'd . . .

Of course Arnold had evoked the whole scene only to bring before us this metaphor of faith in its ebb-tide. But that did not save the figure from triteness and from an even more fatal vagueness. Everything in second-rate poetry is compared to the sea: love is as deep, grief as salty, passion as turbulent. The sea may look like a bright girdle sometimes, though Professor Dewing did not think it particularly impressive to say so. And in what sense is *faith* a bright girdle? Is it the function of faith to embrace, to bind, to hold up a petticoat, or what? And what is the faith that Arnold has in mind? The poet evokes no precise concept of it. He throws us the simple, undifferentiated word, unites its loose emotional connotations with those of the sea, and leaves the whole matter there. And the concluding figure of "Dover Beach":

we are here as on a darkling plain
Swept with confused alarms of struggle
    and flight,
Where ignorant armies clash by night.

Splendid in itself, this memorable image. But the sea had been forgotten now; the darkling plain had displaced the figure from which the whole poem tacitly promised to evolve. It would not have been so if John Donne had been the craftsman. A single bold yet accurate analogy, with constantly developing implications, would have served him for the whole poem.

Thus mused Professor Dewing, the lines of his verdict taking shape in his head. A critic of poetry of course was not at liberty to pass judgment on a poet's thought; he could only judge whether, in treating of the thought or sensibility he had received from his age, the poet had produced a satisfactory work of art. Arnold, Professor Dewing felt, had not been able to escape from the didactic tone or from a certain commonness and vagueness of expression. With deep personal misgivings about his position in a world both socially and spiritually barbarous, he had sought an image for his emotion, and had found it in the sea—a natural phenomenon still obscured by the drapings of conventional beauty and used by all manner of poets to express all manner of feelings. "Dover Beach" would always remain notable, Professor Dewing decided, as an expression of Victorian sensibility. It contained lines of ever memorable poetic skill. But it could not, he felt, be accepted as a uniformly satisfactory example of poetic art.

It was occasionally a source of wonder to those about him just why Professor Oliver Twitchell spent so much time and eloquence urging that man's lower nature must be repressed, his animal instincts kept in bounds by the exertion of the higher will. To the casual observer, Professor Twitchell himself did not seem to possess much animal nature. It seemed incredible that a desperate struggle with powerful bestial passions might be going on at any moment within his own slight frame, behind his delicate white face in which the most prominent feature was the octagonal glasses that focused his eyes on the outside world. Professor Twitchell was a good deal given to discipleship but not much to friendship. He had himself been a disciple of the great Irving Babbitt, and he attracted a small number of disciples among his own more earnest students. But no one knew him well. Only one of his colleagues, who took a somewhat sardonic interest in the mysteries of human nature, possessed a possible clue to the origin of his efforts to repress man's

lower nature and vindicate his higher. This colleague had wormed his way sufficiently into Oliver Twitchell's confidence to learn about his family, which he did not often mention. Professor Twitchell, it turned out, had come of decidedly unacademic stock. One of his brothers was the chief salesman for a company that made domestic fire-alarm appliances. At a moment's notice he would whip out a sample from his bag or pocket, plug it into the nearest electric outlet, and while the bystanders waited in terrified suspense, would explain that in the dead of night, if the house caught fire, the thing would go off with a whoop loud enough to warn the soundest sleeper. Lined up with his whole string of brothers and sisters, all older than he, all abounding in spirits, Professor Twitchell looked like the runt of the litter. His colleague decided that he must have had a very hard childhood, and that it was not his own animal nature that he needed so constantly to repress, but his family's.

Whatever the reasons, Professor Twitchell felt no reality in the teaching of literature except as he could extract from it definitions and illustrations of man's moral struggle in the world. For him recent history had been a history of intellectual confusion and degradation, and hence of social confusion and degradation. Western thought had fallen into a heresy. It had failed to maintain the fundamental grounds of a true humanism. It had blurred the distinction between man, God, and nature. Under the influence of the sciences, it had set up a monism in which the moral as well as the physical constitution of man was included within nature and the laws of nature. It had, therefore, exalted man as naturally good, and exalted the free expression of all his impulses. What were the results of this heresy? An age, complained Professor Twitchell bitterly, in which young women talked about sexual perversions at the dinner table; an age in which everyone agreed that society was in dissolution and insisted on the privilege of being dissolute; an age without any common standards of value in morals or art; an age, in short, without discipline, without self-restraint in private life or public.

Oliver Twitchell when he received Professor Chartly's envelope sat down with a strong favorable predisposition toward his task. He accepted wholeheartedly Arnold's attitude toward literature: the demand that poetry should be serious, that it should present us with a criticism of life, that it should be measured by standards not merely personal, but in some sense *real*.

"Dover Beach" had become Arnold's best-known poem, admired as his masterpiece. It would surely contain, therefore, a distillation of his attitude. Professor Twitchell pulled down his copy of Arnold and began to read and as he read he felt himself overtaken by surprised misgiving. The poem began well enough. The allusion to Sophocles, who had heard the sound of the retreating tide by the Ægean centuries ago, admirably prepared the groundwork of high seriousness for a poem which would culminate in a real criticism of human experience. But did the poem so culminate? It was true that the world

Hath really neither joy, nor love, nor light,
Nor certitude, nor peace, nor help for pain

if one meant the world as the worldling knows it, the man who conducts his life by unreflective natural impulse. Such a man will soon enough encounter the disappointments of ambition, the instability of all bonds and ties founded on

nothing firmer than passion or self-interest. But this incertitude of the world, to a true disciple of culture, should become a means of self-discipline. It should lead him to ask how life may be purified and ennobled, how we may by wisdom and self-restraint oppose to the accidents of the world a true human culture based on the exertion of a higher will. No call to such a positive moral will, Professor Twitchell reluctantly discovered, can be heard in "Dover Beach." Man is an ignorant soldier struggling confusedly in a blind battle. Was this the culminating truth that Arnold the poet had given men in his masterpiece? Professor Twitchell sadly revised his value-judgment of the poem. He could not feel that in his most widely admired performance Arnold had seen life steadily or seen it whole; rather he had seen it only on its worldly side, and seen it under an aspect of terror. "Dover Beach" would always be justly respected for its poetic art, but the famous lines on Sophocles better exemplified the poet as a critic of life.

As a novelist still referred to in his late thirties as "young" and "promising," Rudolph Mole found himself in a curious relation toward his academic colleagues. He wrote for the public, not for the learned journals; hence he was spared the necessity of becoming a pedant. At the same time the more lucrative fruits of pedantry were denied to him by his quiet exclusion from the guild. Younger men sweating for promotion, living in shabby genteel poverty on yearly appointments, their childless wives mimicking their academic shoptalk in bluestocking phrases, would look up from the stacks of five-by-three cards on which they were constantly accumulating notes and references, and would say to him, "You don't realize how lucky you are, teaching composition. You aren't expected to know anything." Sometimes an older colleague, who had passed through several stages of the mysteries of preferment, would belittle professional scholarship to him with an elaborate show of graciousness and envy, "We are all just pedants," he would say. "You teach the students what they really want and need." Rudolph noticed that the self-confessed pedant went busily on publishing monographs and being promoted, while he himself remained, year by year, the English Department's most eminent poor relation.

He was not embittered. His dealings with students were pleasant and interesting. There was a sense of reality and purpose in trying to elicit from them a better expression of their thoughts, trying to increase their understanding of the literary crafts. He could attack their minds on any front he chose, and he could follow his intellectual hobbies as freely as he liked, without being confined to the artificial boundaries of a professional field of learning.

Freud, for example. When Professor Chartly and his accomplices decided that a teacher of creative writing should be included in their scheme and chose Rudolph Mole for the post, they happened to catch him at the height of his enthusiasm for Freud. Not that he expected to psychoanalyze authors through their works; that, he avowed, was not his purpose. You can't deduce the specific secrets of a man's life, he would cheerfully admit, by trying to fit his works into the text-book patterns of complexes and psychoses. The critic, in any case, is interested only in the man to the extent that he is involved in his work. But everyone agrees, Rudolph maintained, that the man is involved in his work. Some part of the psychic constitution of the author finds expression in every line that he writes. We can't understand the work unless we can understand the psychic traits that have gained expression in it. We may never be able to trace back these traits to their ultimate sources and causes, probably buried deep in the author's childhood. But we need to gain as much light on them as we can, since they appear in the work we are trying to apprehend, and determine its character. This is what criticism has always sought to do. Freud simply brings new light to the old task.

Rudolph was fortunate enough at the outset to pick up at the college bookstore a copy of Mr. Lionel Trilling's recent study of Matthew Arnold. In this volume he found much of his work already done for him. A footnote to Mr. Trilling's text, citing evidence from Professors Tinker and Lowry, made it clear that "Dover Beach" may well have been written in 1850, some seventeen years before it was first published. This, for Rudolph's purposes, was a priceless discovery. It meant that all the traditional talk about the poem was largely null and void. The poem was not a repercussion of the bombshell that Darwin dropped on the religious sensibilities of the Victorians. It was far more deeply personal and individual than that. Perhaps when Arnold published it his own sense of what it expressed or how it would be understood had changed. But clearly the poem came into being as an expression of what Arnold felt to be the particular kind of affection and passion he needed from a woman. It was a love poem, and took its place with utmost naturalness, once the clue had been given, in the group of similar and related poems addressed to "Marguerite."

Mr. Trilling summed up in a fine sentence one strain in these poems, and the principal strain in "Dover Beach," when he wrote that for Arnold "fidelity is a word relevant only to those lovers who see the world as a place of sorrow and in their common suffering require the comfort of constancy."

Ah, love, let us be true
To one another! for the world . . .
Hath really neither joy, nor love, nor
      light . . .

The point was unmistakable. And from the whole group of poems to which "Dover Beach" belonged, a sketch of Arnold as an erotic personality could be derived. The question whether a "real Marguerite" existed was an idle one, for the traits that found expression in the poems were at least "real" enough to produce the poems and to determine their character.

And what an odd spectacle it made, the self-expressed character of Arnold as a lover! The ordinary degree of aggressiveness, the normal joy of conquest and possession, seemed to be wholly absent from him. The love he asked for was essentially a protective love, sisterly or motherly; in its unavoidable ingredient of passion he felt a constant danger, which repelled and unsettled him. He addressed Marguerite as "My sister!" He avowed and deplored his own womanish fits of instability:

I too have wish'd, no woman more,
This starting, feverish heart, away.

He emphasized his nervous anguish and contrary impulses. He was a "teas'd o'erlabour'd heart," "an aimless unallay'd Desire." He could not break through his fundamental isolation and submerge himself in another human soul, and he believed that all men shared this plight:

Yes: in the sea of life enisl'd,
With echoing straits between us thrown,
Dotting the shoreless watery wild,
We mortal millions live *alone*.

He never "without remorse" allowed himself

To haunt the place where passions reign,

yet it was clear that whether he had ever succeeded in giving himself up wholeheartedly to a passion, he had wanted to. There could hardly be a more telltale phrase than "Once-long'd-for storms of love."

In short much more illumination fell on "Dover Beach" from certain other verses of Arnold's than from Darwin and all his commentators:

Truth—what is truth? Two bleeding
      hearts
Wounded by men, by Fortune tried,
Outwearied with their lonely parts,
Vow to beat henceforth side by side.

The world to them was stern and drear;
Their lot was but to weep and moan.
Ah, let them keep their faith sincere,
For neither could subsist alone!

Here was the nub. "Dover Beach" grew directly from and repeated the same emotion, but no doubt generalized and enlarged this emotion, sweeping into one intense and far-reaching conviction of insecurity not only Arnold's personal fortunes in love, but the social and religious faith of the world he lived in. That much could be said for the traditional interpretation.

Of course, as Mr. Trilling did not fail to mention, anguished love affairs, harassed by mysterious inner incompatibilities, formed a well-established literary convention. But the fundamental sense of insecurity in "Dover Beach" was too genuine, too often repeated in other works, to be written off altogether to that account. The same sense of insecurity, the same need for some rock of protection, cried out again and again, not merely in Arnold's love poems but in his elegies, reflective pieces, and fragments of epic as well. Whenever Arnold produced a genuine and striking burst of poetry, with the stamp of true self-expression on it, he seemed always to be in the dumps. Everywhere dejection, confusion, weakness, contention of soul. No adequate cause could be found in the events of Arnold's life for such an acute sense of incertitude; it must have been of psychic origin. Only in one line of effort this fundamental insecurity did not hamper, sadden, or depress him, and that was in the free play of his intelligence as a critic of letters and society. Even there, if it did not hamper his efforts, it directed them. Arnold valiantly tried to erect a barrier of culture against the chaos and squalor of society, against the contentiousness of men. What was this barrier but an elaborate protective device?

The origin of the psychic pattern that expressed itself in Arnold's poems could probably never be discovered. No doubt the influence that Arnold's father exercised over his emotions and his thinking, even though Arnold rebelled to the extent at least of casting off his father's religious beliefs, was of great importance. But much more would have to be known to give a definite clue —more than ever could be known. Arnold was secure from any attempt to spy out the heart of his mystery. But if criticism could not discover the cause, it could assess the result, and could do so (thought Rudolph Mole) with greater understanding by an attempt, with up-to-date psychological aid, to delve a little deeper into the essential traits that manifested themselves in that result.

In 1917 Reuben Hale, a young instructor in a Western college, had lost his job and done time in the penitentiary for speaking against conscription and for organizing pacifist demonstrations. In the twenties he had lost two more academic posts for his sympathies with Soviet Russia and his inability to forget his Marxist principles while teaching literature. His contentious, eager, lovable, exasperating temperament tried the patience of one college administration after another. As he advanced into middle age, and his growing family suffered repeated upheavals, his friends began to fear that his robust quarrels with established order would leave him a penniless outcast at fifty. Then he was invited to take a flattering post at a girls' college known for its liberality of views. The connection proved surprisingly durable; in fact it became Professor Hale's turn to be apprehensive. He began to be morally alarmed at his own security, to fear that the bourgeois system which he had attacked so valiantly had somehow outwitted him and betrayed him into allegiance. When the C.I.O. made its initial drive and seemed to be carrying everything before it, he did his best to unseat himself again by rushing joyfully to the nearest picket lines and getting himself photographed by an alert press. Even this expedient failed, and he reconciled himself, not without wonder, to apparent academic permanence.

On winter afternoons his voice could be heard booming out through the closed door of his study to girls who came to consult him on all manner of subjects, from the merits of Plekhanov as a Marxist critic to their own most personal dilemmas. They called him Ben; he called them Smith, Jones, and Robinson. He never relaxed his cheerful bombardment of the milieu into which they were born, and of the larger social structure which made bourgeois wealth, bourgeois art, morals, and religion possible. But when a sophomore found herself pregnant it was to Professor Hale that she came for advice. Should she have an' abortion or go through with it and heroically bear the social stigma? And it was Professor Hale who kept the affair from the Dean's office and the newspapers, sought out the boy, persuaded the young couple that they were desperately in love with each other, and that pending the revolution a respectable marriage would be the most prudent course, not to say the happiest.

James Joyce remarks of one of his characters that she dealt with moral problems as a cleaver deals with meat. Professor Hale's critical methods were comparably simple and direct. Literature, like the other arts, is in form and substance a product of society, and reflects the structure of society. The structure of society is a class structure: it is conditioned by the mode of production of goods, and by the legal conventions of ownership and control by which the ruling class keeps itself in power and endows itself with the necessary freedom to exploit men and materials for profit. A healthy literature, in a society so constituted, can exist only if writers perceive the essential economic problem and ally themselves firmly with the working class.

Anyone could see the trouble with Arnold. His intelligence revealed to him the chaos that disrupted the society about him; the selfishness and brutality of the ruling class; the ugliness of the world which the industrial revolution had created, and which imperialism and "liberalism" were extending. Arnold was at his best in his critical satire of

this world and of the ignorance of those who governed it. But his intelligence far outran his will, and his defect of will finally blinded his intelligence. He was too much a child of his class to disown it and fight his way to a workable remedy for social injustice. He caught a true vision of himself and of his times as standing between "two worlds, one dead, one powerless to be born." But he had not courage or stomach enough to lend his own powers to the birth struggle. Had he thrown in his sympathies unreservedly with the working class, and labored for the inescapable revolution, "Dover Beach" would not have ended in pessimism and confusion. It would have ended in a cheerful, strenuous, and hopeful call to action. But Arnold could not divorce himself from the world of polite letters, of education, of culture, into which he had been born. He did his best to purify them, to make them into an instrument for the reform of society. But instinctively he knew that "culture" as he understood the term was not a social force in the world around him. Instinctively he knew that what he loved was doomed to defeat. And so "Dover Beach" ended in a futile plea for protection against the hideousness of the darkling plain and the confused alarms of struggle and flight.

Professor Chartly's envelope brought Reuben Hale his best opportunity since the first C.I.O. picket lines to vindicate his critical and social principles. He plunged into his answer with complete zest.

When Peter Lee Prampton agreed to act as moderator in Professor Chartly's experiment he congratulated himself that this would be his last great academic chore. He had enjoyed his career of scholarship and teaching, no man ever more keenly. But now it was drawing to an end. He was loaded with honors from two continents. The universities of Germany, France, and Britain had first laid their formative hands on his learning and cultivation, then given their most coveted recognition to its fruits. But the honor and the glory seemed a little vague on the June morning when the expressman brought into his library the sizable package of papers which Professor Chartly had boxed and shipped to him. He had kept all his life a certain simplicity of heart. At seventy-four he could still tote a pack with an easy endurance that humiliated men of forty. Now he found himself giving in more and more completely to a lust for trout. Half a century of hastily snatched vacations in Cape Breton or the Scottish Highlands had never allowed him really to fill up that hollow craving to find a wild stream and fish it which would sometimes rise in his throat even in the midst of a lecture.

Well, there would be time left before he died. And meanwhile here was this business of "Dover Beach." Matthew Arnold during one of his American lecture tours had been entertained by neighbors of the Pramptons. Peter Lee Prampton's father had dined with the great man, and had repeated his conversation and imitated his accent at the family table. Peter himself, as a boy of nineteen or so, had gone to hear Arnold lecture. That, he thought with a smile, was probably a good deal more than could be said for any of these poor hacks who had taken Professor Chartly's bait.

At the thought of Arnold he could still hear the carriage wheels grate on the pebbly road as he had driven, fifty odd years ago, to the lecture in town,

the prospective Mrs. Prampton beside him. His fishing rod lay under the seat. He chuckled out loud as he remembered how a pound-and-a-half trout had jumped in the pool under the clattering planks of a bridge, and how he had pulled up the horse, jumped out, and tried a cast while Miss Osgood sat scolding in the carriage and shivering in the autumn air. They had been just a little late reaching the lecture, but the trout, wrapped in damp leaves, lay safely beside the rod.

It was queer that "Dover Beach" had not come more recently into his mind. Now that he turned his thoughts in that direction the poem was there in its entirety, waiting to be put on again like a coat that one has worn many times with pleasure and accidentally neglected for a while.

The sea of faith was once, too, at the full.

How those old Victorian battles had raged about the Prampton table when he was a boy! How the names of Arnold, Huxley, Darwin, Carlyle, Morris, Ruskin had been pelted back and forth by the excited disputants! *Literature and Dogma, God and the Bible, Culture and Anarchy.* The familiar titles brought an odd image into his mind: the tall figure of his father stretching up to turn on the gas lamps in the evening as the family sat down to dinner; the terrific pop of the pilot light as it exploded into a net of white flame, shaped like a little beehive; the buzz and whine of a jet turned up too high.

Ah, love, let us be true
To one another! for the world, which seems
To lie before us like a land of dreams,
So various, so beautiful, so new,
Hath really neither joy, nor love, nor light,
Nor certitude, nor peace, nor help for pain . . .

Peter Lee Prampton shivered in the warmth of his sunny library, shivered with that flash of perception into the past which sometimes enables a man to see how all that has happened in his life, for good or ill, turned on the narrowest edge of chance. He lived again in the world of dreams that his own youth had spread before him, a world truly various, beautiful, and new; full of promise, adventure, and liberty of choice, based on the opportunities which his father's wealth provided, and holding out the prospect of a smooth advance into a distinguished career. Then, within six months, a lavish demonstration that the world has neither certitude, nor peace, nor help for pain: his mother's death by cancer, his father's financial overthrow and suicide, the ruin of his own smooth hopes and the prospect instead of a long, hampered, and obscure fight toward his perhaps impossible ambition. He lived again through the night hours when he had tramped out with himself the youthful question whether he could hold Miss Osgood to her promise in the face of such reversals. And he did not forget how she took his long-sleepless face between her hands, kissed him, and smiled away his anxiety with unsteady lips. Surely everyone discovers at some time or other that the world is not a place of certitude; surely everyone cries out to some other human being for the fidelity which alone can make it so. What more could be asked of a poet than to take so profound and universal an experience and turn it into

lines that could still speak long after he and his age were dead?

The best of it was that no one could miss the human feeling, the cry from the heart, in "Dover Beach"; it spoke so clearly and eloquently, in a language everyone could understand, in a form classically pure and simple. Or did it? Who could tell what any job-lot of academicians might be trusted to see or fail to see? And this assortment in Chartly's package might be a queer kettle of fish! Peter Lee Prampton had lived through the *Yellow Book* days of Art for Art's sake; he had read the muckrakers, and watched the rise of the Marxists and the Freudians. Could "Dover Beach" be condemned as unsympathetic with labor? Could a neurosis or a complex be discovered in it? His heart sank at the sharp sudden conviction that indeed these and worse discoveries about the poem might be seriously advanced. Well, he had always tried to go on the principle that every school of criticism should be free to exercise any sincere claim on men's interest and attention which it could win for itself. When he actually applied himself to the contents of Professor Chartly's bale he would be as charitable as he could, as receptive to light from any quarter as he could bring himself to be.

But the task could wait. He felt the need of a period of adjustment before he could approach it with reasonable equanimity. And in the meanwhile he could indulge himself in some long-needed editorial work on his dry-fly book.

1940

VIRGINIA WOOLF

The Art of Biography

THE ART of biography, we say—but at once go on to ask, Is biography an art? The question is foolish perhaps, and ungenerous certainly, considering the keen pleasure that biographers have given us. But the question asks itself so often that there must be something behind it. There it is, whenever a new biography is opened, casting its shadow on the page; and there would seem to be something deadly in that shadow, for after all, of the multitude of lives that are written, how few survive!

But the reason for this high death rate, the biographer might argue, is that biography, compared with the arts of poetry and fiction, is a young art. Interest in our selves and in other people's selves is a late development of the human mind. Not until the eighteenth century in England did that curiosity express itself in writing the lives of private people. Only in the nineteenth century was biography fully grown and hugely prolific. If it is true that there have been only three great biographers,—Johnson, Boswell, and Lockhart,—the reason, he argues, is that the time was short; and his plea, that the art of biography has had but little time to establish itself and develop itself, is certainly borne out by the textbooks. Tempting as it is to explore the reason,—why, that is, the self that writes a book of prose came into being so many centuries after the self that writes a poem, why Chaucer preceded Henry James,—it is better to leave that insoluble question unasked, and so

pass to his next reason for the lack of masterpieces. It is that the art of biography is the most restricted of all the arts. He has his proof ready to hand. Here it is in the preface in which Smith, who has written the life of Jones, takes this opportunity of thanking old friends who have lent letters, and "last but not least" Mrs. Jones, the widow, for that help "without which," as he puts it, "this biography could not have been written." Now the novelist, he points out, simply says in his foreword, "Every character in this book is fictitious." The novelist is free; the biographer is tied.

There, perhaps, we come within hailing distance of that very difficult, again perhaps insoluble, question: What do we mean by calling a book a work of art? At any rate, here is a distinction between biography and fiction—a proof that they differ in the very stuff of which they are made. One is made with the help of friends, of facts; the other is created without any restrictions save those that the artist, for reasons that seem good to him, chooses to obey. That is a distinction; and there is good reason to think that in the past biographers have found it not only a distinction but a very cruel distinction.

The widow and the friends were hard taskmasters. Suppose, for example, that the man of genius was immoral, ill-tempered, and threw the boots at the maid's head. The widow would say, "Still I loved him—he was the father of my children; and the public, who love his books, must on no account be dis-illusioned. Cover up; omit." The bi-ographer obeyed. And thus the ma-jority of Victorian biographies are like the wax figures now preserved in West-minster Abbey that were carried in fu-neral processions through the streets—effigies that have only a smooth super-ficial likeness to the body in the coffin.

Then, towards the end of the nine-teenth century, there was a change. Again for reasons not easy to discover, widows became broader-minded, the public keener-sighted; the effigy no longer carried conviction or satisfied cu-riosity. The biographer certainly won a measure of freedom. At least he could hint that there were scars and furrows on the dead man's face. Froude's Car-lyle is by no means a wax mask painted rosy red. And following Froude there was Sir Edmund Gosse, who dared to say that his own father was a fallible human being. And following Edmund Gosse in the early years of the present century came Lytton Strachey.

The figure of Lytton Strachey is so important a figure in the history of bi-ography that it compels a pause. For his three famous books, *Eminent Vic-torians, Queen Victoria,* and *Elizabeth and Essex,* are of a stature to show both what biography can do and what biog-raphy cannot do. Thus they suggest many possible answers to the question whether biography is an art, and if not why it fails.

Lytton Strachey came to birth as an author at a lucky moment. In 1918, when he made the first attempt, biog-raphy, with its new liberties, was a form that offered great attractions. To a writer like himself, who had wished to write poetry or plays but was doubtful of his creative power, biography seemed to offer a promising alternative. For at last it was possible to tell the truth about the dead; and the Victorian age was rich in remarkable figures many of whom had been grossly deformed by the effi-gies that had been plastered over them. To recreate them, to show them as they really were, was a task that called for gifts analogous to the poet's or the novel-ist's, yet did not ask that inventive power in which he found himself lack-ing.

It was well worth trying. And the anger and the interest that his short studies of Eminent Victorians aroused showed that he was able to make Man-ning, Florence Nightingale, Gordon, and the rest live as they had not lived since they were actually in the flesh. Once more they were the centre of a buzz of discussion. Did Gordon really drink, or was that an invention? Had Florence Nightingale received the Or-der of Merit in her bedroom or in her sitting room? He stirred the public, even though a European war was rag-ing, to an astonishing interest in such minute matters. Anger and laughter mixed; and editions multiplied.

But these were short studies with something of the overemphasis and the foreshortening of caricatures. In the lives of the two great Queens, Elizabeth and Victoria, he attempted a far more ambitious task. Biography had never had a fairer chance of showing what it could do. For it was now being put to the test by a writer who was capable of making use of all the liberties that biog-raphy had won: he was fearless; he had proved his brilliance; and he had learned his job. The result throws great light upon the nature of biography. For who can doubt after reading the two books again, one after the other, that the *Vic-toria* is a triumphant success, and that the *Elizabeth* by comparison is a failure? But it seems too, as we compare them, that it was not Lytton Strachey who failed; it was the art of biography. In the *Victoria* he treated biography as a craft; he submitted to his limitations. In the *Elizabeth* he treated biography as an art; he flouted its limitations.

But we must go on to ask how we have come to this conclusion and what reasons support it. In the first place it is clear that the two Queens present very different problems to their biographer. About Queen Victoria everything was known. Everything she did, almost everything she thought, was a matter of common knowledge. No one has ever been more closely verified and exactly authenticated than Queen Victoria. The biographer could not invent her, because at every moment some document was at hand to check his invention. And, in writing of Victoria, Lytton Strachey submitted to the conditions. He used to the full the biographer's power of selection and relation, but he kept strictly within the world of fact. Every statement was verified; every fact was authenticated. And the result is a life which, very possibly, will do for the old Queen what Boswell did for the old dictionary maker. In time to come Lytton Strachey's Queen Victoria will be Queen Victoria, just as Boswell's Johnson is now Dr. Johnson. The other versions will fade and disappear. It was a prodigious feat, and no doubt, having accomplished it, the author was anxious to press further. There was Queen Victoria, solid, real, palpable. But undoubtedly she was limited. Could not biography produce something of the intensity of poetry, something of the excitement of drama, and yet keep also the peculiar virtue that belongs to fact—its suggestive reality, its own proper creativeness?

Queen Elizabeth seemed to lend herself perfectly to the experiment. Very little was known about her. The society in which she lived was so remote that the habits, the motives, and even the actions of the people of that age were full of strangeness and obscurity. "By what art are we to worm our way into those strange spirits? those even stranger bodies? The more clearly we perceive it, the more remote that singular universe becomes," Lytton Strachey remarked on one of the first pages. Yet there was evidently a "tragic history" lying dormant, half revealed, half concealed, in the story of the Queen and Essex. Everything seemed to lend itself to the making of a book that combined the advantages of both worlds, that gave the artist freedom to invent, but helped his invention with the support of facts—a book that was not only a biography but also a work of art.

Nevertheless, the combination proved unworkable; fact and fiction refused to mix. Elizabeth never became real in the sense that Queen Victoria had been real, yet she never became fictitious in the sense that Cleopatra or Falstaff is fictitious. The reason would seem to be that very little was known—he was urged to invent; yet something was known—his invention was checked. The Queen thus moves in an ambiguous world, between fact and fiction, neither embodied nor disembodied. There is a sense of vacancy and effort, of a tragedy that has no crisis, of characters that meet but do not clash.

If this diagnosis is true we are forced to say that the trouble lies with biography itself. It imposes conditions, and those conditions are that it must be based upon fact. And by fact in biography we mean facts that can be verified by other people besides the artist. If he invents facts as an artist invents them—facts that no one else can verify—and tries to combine them with facts of the other sort, they destroy each other.

Lytton Strachey himself seems in the *Queen Victoria* to have realized the necessity of this condition, and to have yielded to it instinctively. "The first forty-two years of the Queen's life," he wrote, "are illuminated by a great and varied quantity of authentic information. With Albert's death a veil descends." And when with Albert's death the veil descended and authentic information failed, he knew that the biographer must follow suit. "We must be content with a brief and summary relation," he wrote; and the last years are briefly disposed of. But the whole of Elizabeth's life was lived behind a far thicker veil than the last years of Victoria. And yet, ignoring his own admission, he went on to write, not a brief and summary relation, but a whole book about those strange spirits and even stranger bodies of whom authentic information was lacking. On his own showing, the attempt was doomed to failure.

It seems, then, that when the biographer complained that he was tied by friends, letters, and documents he was laying his finger upon a necessary element in biography; and that it is also a necessary limitation. For the invented character lives in a free world where the facts are verified by one person only—the artist himself. Their authenticity lies in the truth of his own vision. The world created by that vision is rarer, intenser, and more wholly of a piece than the world that is largely made of authentic information supplied by other people. And because of this difference the two kinds of fact will not mix; if they touch they destroy each other. No one, the conclusion seems to be, can make the best of both worlds; you must choose, and you must abide by your choice.

But though the failure of *Elizabeth and Essex* leads to this conclusion, that failure, because it was the result of a daring experiment carried out with magnificent skill, leads the way to further discoveries. Had he lived, Lytton Strachey would no doubt himself have explored the vein that he had opened. As it is, he has shown us the way in which others may advance. The biographer is bound by facts—that is so; but, if it is so, he has the right to all the facts that are available. If Jones threw boots at the maid's head, had a mistress at Islington, or was found drunk in a ditch after a night's debauch, he must be free to say so—so far at least as the law of libel and human sentiment allow.

But these facts are not like the facts of science—once they are discovered, always the same. They are subject to changes of opinion; opinions change as the times change. What was thought a sin is now known, by the light of facts won for us by the psychologists, to be perhaps a misfortune; perhaps a curiosity; perhaps neither one nor the other, but a trifling foible of no great importance one way or the other. The accent on sex has changed within living memory. This leads to the destruction of a great deal of dead matter still obscuring the true features of the human face. Many of the old chapter headings—life at college, marriage, career—are shown to be very arbitrary and artificial distinctions. The real current of the hero's existence took, very likely, a different course.

Thus the biographer must go ahead of the rest of us, like the miner's canary, testing the atmosphere, detecting falsity, unreality, and the presence of obsolete conventions. His sense of truth must be alive and on tiptoe. Then again, since we live in an age when a thousand cameras are pointed, by newspapers, letters, and diaries, at every character from every angle, he must be prepared to admit contradictory versions of the same face. Biography will enlarge its scope by hanging up looking glasses at odd corners. And yet from all this diversity it will bring out, not a riot of confusion, but a richer unity. And again, since so much is known that used to be unknown, the question now inevitably asks itself, whether the lives of great men only should be recorded. Is not anyone who has lived a life, and left a record of that life, worthy of biography —the failures as well as the successes, the humble as well as the illustrious? And what is greatness? And what smallness? He must revise our standards of merit and set up new heroes for our admiration.

Biography thus is only at the beginning of its career; it has a long and active life before it, we may be sure—a life full of difficulty, danger, and hard work. Nevertheless, we can also be sure that it is a different life from the life of poetry and fiction—a life lived at a lower degree of tension. And for that reason its creations are not destined for the immortality which the artist now and then achieves for his creations.

There would seem to be certain proof of that already. Even Dr. Johnson as created by Boswell will not live as long as Falstaff as created by Shakespeare. Micawber and Miss Bates we may be certain will survive Lockhart's Sir Walter Scott and Lytton Strachey's Queen Victoria. For they are made of more enduring matter. The artist's imagination at its most intense fires out what is perishable in fact; he builds with what is durable; but the biographer must accept the perishable, build with it, imbed it in the very fabric of his work. Much will perish; little will live. And thus we come to the conclusion that he is a craftsman, not an artist; and his work is not a work of art, but something betwixt and between.

Yet on that lower level the work of the biographer is invaluable; we cannot thank him sufficiently for what he does for us. For we are incapable of living wholly in the intense world of the imagination. The imagination is a faculty that soon tires and needs rest and refreshment. But for a tired imagination the proper food is not inferior poetry or minor fiction,—indeed they blunt and debauch it,—but sober fact, that "authentic information" from which, as Lytton Strachey has shown us, good biography is made. When and where did the real man live; how did he look; did he wear laced boots or elastic-sided; who were his aunts, and his friends; how did he blow his nose; whom did he love, and how; and when he came to die did he die in his bed like a Christian, or ⋰ . .

By telling us the true facts, by sifting the little from the big, and shaping the whole so that we perceive the outline, the biographer does more to stimulate the imagination than any poet or novelist save the very greatest. For few poets and novelists are capable of that high degree of tension which gives us reality. But almost any biographer, if he respects facts, can give us much more than another fact to add to our collection. He can give us the creative fact; the fertile fact; the fact that suggests and engenders. Of this, too, there is certain proof. For how often, when a biography is read and tossed aside, some scene remains bright, some figure lives on in the depths of the mind, and causes us, when we read a poem or a novel, to feel a start of recognition, as if we remembered something that we had known before.

1939

ALLAN NEVINS

Ideas in History

From THE GATEWAY TO HISTORY

IT HAS often been remarked that the world is ruled by ideas, or as Napoleon put it with the same meaning, by imagination. The ideas that so frequently control society may be divided into two groups, the practical and the philosophical. By the former we mean those concepts which, expressing immediate mundane aims, can actually be realized by an expression of the human will. As we scan the dark backward and abysm of time we can descry a long list of such ideas which have exercised the most powerful sway over human affairs. Among them are the idea of the ecclesiastical or papal supremacy over temporal powers; the idea of the divine right of kings; the idea of nationalism; the idea of toleration; the idea of self-determination, which ruled events so potently during and after the World War; the idea of rugged individualism; the idea of State Socialism; and the idea of collectivism or the abolition of private property. These are practical ideas because they depend primarily upon man's will; because they can usually be made to work if most men agree to promote them; and because they are tested by the question whether they are useful or useless, not true or false. Mussolini's idea of the totalitarian state depends for its validity on the readiness of most Italians to employ it, and that readiness will endure just so long as most Italians believe that its advantages offset its disadvantages.

But mankind is also powerfully swayed at times by philosophical ideas. They are theoretical rather than practical, and are judged not by pragmatic tests but by men's conviction of what is valid and invalid. Society accepts or rejects them not as beneficial or injurious, but as true or false. Such is the idea of personal immortality—and few people realize how profoundly human institutions would be altered if that concept were abandoned by mankind. Such also is the Greek idea of fate, or the Calvinist idea of predestination, with other religious ideas. Such is the idea of Progress, in modern times probably the most important of all human concepts of a philosophical nature.

All historical work which pretends to any elevation or importance is written under the influence of ideas. Much of

"Ideas in History," reprinted from *The Gateway to History* by Allan Nevins, by permission of D. C. Heath and Company, Boston.

the historical work, though by no means all of it, is important by virtue of its ideas; that is, its interpretation. Consciously or unconsciously, all significant historians are affected by their intellectual environment, whether they evince hostility to some phase of the prevalent thought of the time, or espouse and defend it. And if the historian is a man of intellectual vigor, he assuredly views his task not as the mere recital of a series of facts and events, but as their arrangement in a pattern which illustrates some underlying truth. The effect of this impulse upon the history of ideas has been very great; but we are here concerned primarily with its effect upon the course of historical writing.

While the analysis of historical evidence is an important process in the study or writing of history, it is not the most important. In the highest type of history the synthesis or interpretation is a much more vital element. The task of analysis involves the discovery of the truth about various episodes or events by a combination of industry, ingenuity, judgment, and honesty. The writer collects all the authentic and relevant facts, he assorts and classifies them, he finds the best possible explanation for them, and he rigorously tests this explanation of their significance. This is a minute process. It is essentially a bit of anatomical work. But to arrive at an interpretation, the historian takes a considerable body of problems and events, and so arranges them as to illustrate some dominant idea. That is, he synthesizes his material about some concept which governs the whole of it; he utilizes a series of analyses, which at first may have seemed chaotic and jumbled, and produces a general conclusion which throws them into perspective. This is not anatomy; it is physiology.

It breathes the spark of life into dead materials and makes them move as living bodies. Or to change the figure, it lifts the reader above the immediate thicket he is exploring, and shows him the trend of the terrain—the significance of the valley, or the mountain range, of which the thickets are a part.

Thus the *Cambridge Modern History,* or the *Histoire Générale* of Lavisse, offers a huge body of facts upon human events since 1500, caught together merely in a long series of highly factual—and rather badly related—monographs. But Oswald Spengler, in *The Decline of the West,* offers an interpretation of this long period. Discarding the old simple and optimistic view of linear evolution or endless progress, he substituted—as a number of others have done—an interpretation of history as a recurring cycle, a Foucault pendulum swing, placing our own unhappy time in the bleakest part of a spring-summer-autumn-winter succession. To take a more limited example, Channing's book on the Civil War offers a score of analyses of problems, but declines to draw them together upon any interpretive thread. But in *The Rise of American Civilization* Charles and Mary Beard synthesize the Civil War according to an economic pattern. They view it as essentially a conflict between the old rural culture and the new industrial culture of America. Discarding the old concepts of the slavery and State Rights issues as dominating the Civil War period, the Beards make their concept of a sharp collision between a business civilization and an agrarian civilization the vehicle of a fresh and stimulating interpretation of the events of 1860-69.

At the outset it is important to enforce a firm distinction between a general philosophy of history, and a specific interpretation of historical materials. The distinction is mainly one of scope. But it is also related to the distinction which we have just drawn between philosophical ideas, tested by our faith in what is true, and practical ideas, tested by our experience of their workability. General philosophical concepts of history will not bend to pragmatic tests. The dominant idea of Spengler's book is obviously of this nature. No one will ever know —at least for hundreds of centuries to come—whether history does move in regular cycles or not; to read and write history in that way is simply an act of faith. So is the philosophy of history built on the doctrine of evolutionary progress, a creed so popular in the nineteenth century. So is the philosophy, toward which Pareto leans, of history as a pendulum alternating between liberty and authority. But an interpretation like that which the Beards give the Civil War can be subjected to practical tests; the facts within a limited domain either sustain or destroy it—when we learn them. The interpretation may provoke a discussion which drags on through decades, but each student will decide upon its merits by consulting the facts. A philosophy of history springs from a writer's whole view of human destiny, and thus embodies his philosophy of life; an interpretation of historical material is merely a writer's explanation of the significance of a series of events, an epoch, or a movement. The one usually bears a close relation to the thought of the age; the other is usually more personal in origin.

All the principal philosophies of history save two have originated within the past three centuries—a fact which speaks

volumes for the close alliance between rationalism and modern history. Greek and Roman writers of history knew but one philosophy, that of Fate. To them the word held a far richer theological significance than it has to us, and from Thucydides to Appian it sufficed to cover their view of human destiny. They made varying allowances for the interposition of the gods, but they never formulated any view of a grand final goal, some far-off, divine event, toward which the gods guided mankind. But early in the Christian era there naturally arose a very different philosophy of history, stamped by the fervors of the new faith; and it held almost undisputed sway for more than thirteen centuries. First enunciated by St. Augustine in *The City of God,* it asserted that the whole record of the world turned upon the overwhelming fact of divine concern for mankind. The decisive event of history was the life of Christ, before which all mankind had been doomed, and after which all of the elect were saved. St. Augustine, donning the mantle of seer, described the birth, growth, and destiny of two cities, one of this world and one of God, culminating in the triumph of the latter. His followers continued to regard the earth simply as the footstool of history; the story of humankind as simply part of the divine comedy. That view, which often had Neo-Platonist elements and which could be given a compelling grandeur, swayed medieval chroniclers no less than Dante and Milton.[1]

This Christian philosophy of history indeed continued to possess the field down to the time of Bossuet's eloquent book, the *Histoire Universelle,* which

[1] For a much more thorough account of the philosophy of history than is here possible, see the articles by Vladimir G. Simkhovitch on "Approaches to History" in the *Political Science Quarterly,* Vols. XLIV, XLV, XLVII, and XLVIII.

largely summed it up. His volume, written from the standpoint of dogmatic theology and the official Catholic hierarchy, was imbued with a belief that the pivotal event of time was the crucifixion, and that the one all-powerful force in human affairs was God's benevolent interposition. He conceived of the changes in history as all slowly tending toward the progress and universality of the true religion—not merely Christianity, but the papal form of Christianity. The book naturally passed Moslem civilization by; it treated Greece and Rome only as part of the *Preparatio Evangelicum*. Voltaire, remarking caustically that "It seems to have been written solely to suggest that everything in the world was made for the Jews," was stung by it and similar productions into an angry reply. His *Essai sur les Moeurs* a generation later wholly rejected the miraculous interposition of Providence in history, asserting instead a rationalistic interpretation of the past. In Voltaire's opinion, the events of history were attributable not to design but to chance or fortuity. His brilliant though vague exposition helped to open the way for other rationalistic philosophies. But the Christian synthesis long persisted, and even in America had its followers. Benjamin Trumbull's *General History of the United States,* of which only one of three proposed volumes appeared (1810), attempted to point out the special interposition of Providence in behalf of the American people.

Since the time of Hegel, whose brilliant *Philosophy of History* appeared in 1830-31, metaphysical analyses of the whole range of human events have become oppressively numerous. They may now be found on every counter, for it is a poor sociologist, economist, or philosopher—not to mention historian—who does not present one. Hegel, whose doctrines have inspired a whole school, attempted to show that every epoch in history was inspired and dominated by some specific idea; for example, he regarded Napoleon, the new Caesar, as "die Weltseele" of his time. He taught that each idea, affirmed as truth, brings with it the idea that is its negation; they do battle, and a new idea emerges. Then the cycle repeats itself. Such recent historians as Kuno Fischer likewise lay emphasis on the "Einheitstendenz" of every period, which permeates all aspects of its life, and by which alone it is to be understood. A quarter century after Hegel's great book the Darwinian theory of natural selection as a key of evolution seized all history in its powerful grasp, which has not yet greatly relaxed; for most historians of the non-esoteric schools still believe in progress, and believe it is attained by evolutionary processes. Indeed, evolutionary ideas long preceded Darwin, who gave them simply a special form and force. Such writers as Lecky, Freeman, Parkman, and McMaster were unconsciously pervaded by the evolutionary philosophy, and such writers as Froude, Bagehot, John Fiske, and Rhodes were very consciously pervaded by it. Challenged by few save the Marxian group, the evolutionary writers for decades ruled history with autocratic sway, and even yet dominate the field. But an increasing band of dissenters, a vigorous group of advanced intellectuals, today assert that simple evolution is nearly as absurd as the old theological view of history.

Two of the ablest statements of the evolutionary philosophy of history are to be found in Walter Bagehot's stimulating *Physics and Politics* and John Fiske's *Outlines of Cosmic Philosophy;* both the more typical for having been written in the very heart of the Victorian era. Of Fiske's views we shall say something later. Bagehot significantly gave his work the subtitle, "Thoughts on the application of the principles of natural selection and inheritance to political science." His book did more than state a theory of history; for in its deep influence upon such future leaders as Woodrow Wilson it made history. Essentially, it was an attempt to show that in social institutions as well as in the animal kingdom the rule of the survival of the fittest applies; and that as an acquired faculty of the parent animal is sometimes distinctly transmitted to its progeny (or so Bagehot believed), so acquired characteristics of society are inherited by succeeding generations. "The continuous force which binds age to age," writes Bagehot, "enables each to begin with some improvement on the last, if the last did not itself improve." This implies a general, though of course not uninterrupted, continuity of progress in the world, under which weak and erroneous institutions are gradually eliminated. Upon this view, if it is valid, a grand systematization of history can be built, and Bagehot asserts as much. "We thus perceive that a science of history is possible—a science to teach the law of tendencies, created by the mind and transmitted by the body— which act upon and incline the mind of man from age to age."

In developing his thesis, Bagehot begins with a "Preliminary Stage" of civilization in which progress was achieved by the triumph of the strong over the weak. Powerful tribes, nations, or peoples always tend to prevail over the feeble, and while Bagehot does not believe that might makes right, he does assert that "in certain marked peculiarities, the strongest tend to be the best."

In his section on "Nation Making" he accounts by evolutionary theory for the development of national traits. It has been an innate propensity of man to imitate what is before him; thus the primitive savages imitated their leaders and copied their most striking characteristics, "preserving them as they did their favorite animals." These traits gradually tinged the whole community. "Ages are required, but at last a national character is formed." National character is but the name for a collection of habits, more or less universal, which in the course of long generations have produced vast mental and physical effects. Bagehot then continues his evolutionary exposition by showing how primitive and simple nations have given way to modern and complex nations. In the former "fixity was the invariable ingredient," and the cake of custom held peoples in a mould that was sometimes as viciously static as the old-time framework of Chinese society. But as the Middle Ages ended, various tendencies broke the cake of fixed custom and ushered in the "age of discussion," which is progressive inasmuch as it gives a premium to intelligence. Though Bagehot saw certain dangers in even the modern age of discussion, notably in a tendency toward hasty political action which he calls "a hereditary barbaric impulse," and though like Malthus he feared "a diminished reserve for race maintenance," his outlook upon the future was fundamentally hopeful. All evolutionists are meliorists if not optimists. While the conclusions which flow from his evolutionary concept appear somewhat naïve to many present-day students, even they must admit that in the course of his argument he elucidates many secondary truths with memorable eloquence and force.

The "Marxian interpretation" of history is of course really a Marxian philosophy, as imposing in scope, despite its materialistic temper, as any other philosophy. It has to be carefully distinguished from the writings of many of Marx's followers, who in his own lifetime so perverted some of his doctrines that he mordantly remarked, "Je ne suis pas Marxiste." Briefly stated, his thesis is that the mode of production in economic life primarily determines the general character of the social, political, and cultural processes of life. With every change in the economic foundation brought about by changes in relationship between man and productive forces, the entire superstructure is more or less rapidly transformed. Marx thus became the first to formulate, in explicit fashion, the economic interpretation of history. Unlike some of his disciples, he and Engels never gave this interpretation so narrow a form as to exclude all non-economic factors as contributing causes of events; they merely declared the mode of production to be the dominant factor. Indeed, Marx clearly perceived that society is moulded by spirit and thought as well as material environment, and did not believe that history could be explained by a monistic materialism. Rather, he regarded society as an interacting whole of environment and thought, of objective and subjective conditions, and of activity and its practical goals, in which mode of production was the most important single element. It should also be noted that Marx's general conception of history does not have, for students of historical writing, any connection with his belief that society would be remade by passing through a dictatorship of the proletariat into a classless world. As Dr. E. R. A. Seligman says, "there is nothing in common between the economic interpretation of history and the doctrine of Socialism, except the accidental fact that the originator of both theories happened to be the same man."

This philosophy has been under intensive fire ever since Marx very briefly presented it in his *Critique of Political Economy*—for he never gave it an elaborate statement. The attack upon those of his followers who take an extremely narrow and dogmatic view of the economic interpretation has of course been more effective than the attack upon Marx himself. German Socialists like Kautsky and Hilferding compressed the Marxian theory of history into preposterously strict limits, making human thought and action not so much derivatives as by-products of economic processes. The Russian Communists have gone to equal extremes in their treatment of history. Lenin's reductive materialism in his *Materialism and Empirio-Criticism*, Bukharin's emphasis upon a technological interpretation of history, which he falsely ascribed to Marx, and Pokrovsky's monistic materialism, which completely excluded either chance or great men as real determinants of events, were all vulnerable. But the true Marxian philosophy in no way excludes ethical or spiritual forces from history. It simply asserts that the concept of morality is a social product, varying with the state of civilization or with the social class, and as such largely determined, in the last analysis, by economic forces. It does not deny that great men have sometimes exercised a controlling influence upon history. It simply asserts that in general they would never have been great had it not been for certain social conditions which made their rise possible, and that these conditions are in turn governed chiefly by economic factors. But it must be added that Marx's own brevity and partial obscurity in stating his philosophy left some of its implications vague, and opened the way for such assaults upon it as those of Dr. M. M. Bober and F. R. Salter.

The vast convulsion of the World War and its aftermath, which convinced tens of millions of men that social progress is but an empty word, and that an "evolution" which marched whole nations to death or ruin offered no hope to mankind, could not but have a profound effect upon the philosophy of history. Certain new scientific theories of the universe formulated during the same period exercised an almost equal influence. The universe, which Newton had conceived as infinite in extent and subject to fixed physical laws, was transformed by Einstein into a finite universe governed by relative laws. It was perhaps a universe, as Jeans, Eddington, and others suggested, in which a ceaseless process of destruction and construction went on without assignable object; energy being dissipated into remote space, and there gradually reconstructing new galaxies to dissipate themselves again. The fashion in historical philosophies swung abruptly to exercise in cosmic rhythm. H. G. Wells still believed in evolution, and his *Outline of History* pointed the way to a grand perfection of society through science and education. But a dozen post-war writers, most of whom dipped their pens in earthquake and gloom, explained that history was a series of pulsations; was a swing and counterswing of the pendulum; was a cycle of summer-fall-winter-spring seasons endlessly repeating themselves; was in fact anything except the magnificent upward climb toward a higher and better life which Bossuet had believed to be directed by God, and the

Victorians to be directed by Evolution (which after all, in Tennyson's if not in Huxley's view, was little else than another name for God).

Upon the principal recent treatises offering one or another rhythm-philosophy of history—Spengler's *Decline of the West,* Pareto's *Mind and Society,* Arnold Toynbee's *A Study of History,* and most pretentious of all, Pitirim Sorokin's *Culture and Cultural Dynamics*—it is happily unnecessary to speak at any length. Their own length is not a little oppressive: Spengler's two volumes, Pareto's and Sorokin's four, and Toynbee's projected thirteen. These men all differ violently as to the precise form of the rhythmic alternation, just as they differ as to the precise position of the present-day world in the grand repetitive movement. Spengler, with his four seasonal phases of the cycle, and his certainty that Western civilization has been entering a long winter of decay, deeply appealed to the pessimism of a defeated Germany. Pareto is less willing to assume the rôle of a prophet, and more inclined to present sociological evidence for his generalizations. To him history represents past sociology just as surely as to Freeman it represented retrospective politics. He sees in history a repetitive alternation of liberty and authority—the foxes and the lions—and he believes that our own post-bellum period has clearly represented the swing toward authority. Professor Sorokin presents history as a fairly complex cycle which carries it from the Ideational at one extreme to the Sensate at the other, and then back again. These terms can be roughly translated into collectivism and individualism, and Mr. Sorokin believes that Western society is just completing a Sensate (individualist) and beginning an Ideational (collectivist) period. Mr.

Toynbee's general ideas are as yet only partially adumbrated; though they postulate a challenge-and-response rhythm, he seems still to cling to a modicum of faith in evolution.[2]

In direct application, these newer philosophies are not at all helpful to practitioners of history. The Hegelian idea of history has been fruitfully applied by students and writers. So also with the evolutionary concept of history, which stimulated many writers to arrange their data in more interesting and significant patterns. But while Spengler and Pareto offer many stimulating suggestions and present many flashes of insight into detailed historical problems (as does Toynbee), their grandiose concepts of human cycles or curves seem of no practical use. The value of these ambitious philosophies is indirect. They foster a healthy discontent with existing approaches to history, which leads to an effort to obtain a deeper understanding of it. They predispose students to utilize new formulae and new scientific apparatus in an experimental search for truth. They lead to an impatience with the shallower forms of history, a demand for more profound treatments of it. Scornful as we may be of the flatulence and vagueness of some of these philosophies, or pseudo-philosophies, we must agree with Henry Adams—who himself tentatively entered the field— that the impulse behind them is natural:

You may be sure that four out of five serious students of history who are living today have, in the course of their work, felt that they stood on the brink of a great generalization that would reduce history under a law as clear as the laws which govern the material world. As the great writers of our time have touched one by one the separate fragments of admitted law by which society betrays its character as a subject for science, not one of them can have failed to feel an instant's hope that he might find the secret which would transform these odds and ends of philosophy into one self-evident, harmonious, and complete system. He has seemed to have it, as the Spanish say, in his inkstand. Scores of times he must have dropped his pen to think how one short step, one sudden inspiration, would show all human knowledge; how, in these thickset forests of history, one corner turned, one faint trail struck would bring him on the highroad of science.[3]

Yet it should be added that general agreement upon any philosophy of history is as undesirable as it is impossible. The great unifying law of which Henry Adams speaks will never be found. If men assented to any such law, it would bind history in fetters as adamantine as the old theological formula of Bossuet, and would ultimately render historical scholarship as monotonous and sterile as the work of the monkish chroniclers.

But the ordinary reader of history needs to have little concern with the grandiose conceptions of philosophy. His interest in the application of ideas to history will be confined to the more modest, more practical, more personal form which we term the historical interpretation. One of the distinguishing hallmarks of modern historical writing is its powerful interpretive tendency. While the best ancient and medieval historians had a distinct point of view, only a few of them—among the ancients,

[2] Dr. Simkhovitch, in the fourth article of his "Approaches to History," *Political Science Quarterly,* XLVIII, 23 ff., names and describes still other exponents of a rhythmical philosophy—Scherer, Karl Joel, O. Lorenz, and others. Spengler completed the first version of his *Decline* in 1914.
[3] Henry Adams, *Degradation of the Democratic Dogma,* p. 127.

Thucydides, Polybius, and their disciples—were possessed by that intense desire to revise history ever nearer the truth by arranging it in ever subtler patterns which masters most present-day historians. The element of intellectual *originality* in historical work has become steadily larger since 1750. While the forces which brought this interpretive tendency to its modern vigor are numerous, four may be singled out as particularly important.

The growth of rationalism was of course as indispensable to the unfettered use of ideas in history as it was to their unfettered use in science. It was no accident that the Age of Enlightenment coincided with the first great flowering of modern history. Originally in France, and later in England, the eighteenth century produced a special and extraordinary activity in historical work. And it is significant that this activity was promoted by the very men who were doing most in other spheres to emancipate humanity from the trammels of authority. Montesquieu's *Spirit of the Laws,* one of the most important books ever written, perhaps the greatest book of eighteenth century France, is largely historical in content, as the subtitle indicates: "du Rapport que les Lois doivent avoir avec la Constitution du Chaque Gouvernement, les Moeurs, le Climat, la Religion, du Commerce, etc." Its third part, consisting of six books which treat at length of the dependence of manners and customs upon climatic conditions, has been especially interesting to historical students. Montesquieu was the first writer to emphasize this relationship as it deserved. But the work should be considered as a whole; so taken, it is one of the foundation-stones of comparative politics, and its

novel and brilliant generalizations in this field at once suggested a number of new ways of interpreting history. With it should be considered the work of Voltaire. He realized that when he and other rationalists loosed the grip of the old supernatural versions of history, when they proved that men really made their own world, a new significance instantly enveloped the past. Historians must make use of these thousand new *aperçus.* Casting aside the murky lanterns of the religious chroniclers and churchly recorders, they must reconstruct the past under the brilliant light of reason. The same conviction animated Hume and Gibbon, two mighty assailants of the reigning superstitions, across the Channel. It was no accident that the best secular histories of the period were written by the greatest of the rationalists.

Voltaire has left an exceptionally full record of the circumstances under which he embarked upon his own rationalist interpretations of history. His active-minded friend, Mme. du Chatelet, whose special talent was for mathematics and philosophy, disliked history.[4] "What does it matter to me," she asked, "a Frenchwoman living on my estate, that Egil succeeded Haquin in Sweden, and that Ottoman was the son of Ortogrul? I read with pleasure Greek and Roman history, which offers great pictures which attract me. But I have never yet been able to finish any long history of our modern nations. There seems nothing in them but confusion, a host of minute events without connection or sequence, a thousand battles which settled nothing. I renounced a study which overwhelmed my mind without illuminating it." Voltaire replied that what was needed was simply a

[4] Voltaire, *Essai sur les Moeurs,* pp. 1, 2.

rational interpretation of history, utilizing the ideas forbidden to previous generations. If all the tedious and untrustworthy details of wars, all the pointless negotiations of diplomacy, all the minute incidents which obscured the grand tendencies of history, were shorn away, then a general and well-arranged picture could be made of the significant factors. It would be worth Mme. du Chatelet's time to read *that*. The history of the human mind, remarked Voltaire, was the truly important part of the human record. His word mind, of course, embraced a great deal—law, arts, manners, literature, ideas—which he would make the chief concern of history. But every fact that the historian recorded should lead to something else. "Details which lead to nothing are in history what baggage is to an army, impedimenta, for we must look at things in the large, for the simple reason that the human mind is limited and sinks under the weight of minutiae." [5] Unconnected minutiae he would leave to annalists and encyclopaedia-makers. These conceptions Voltaire illustrated in his *Charles XII* and *Age of Louis XIV*.

The new scientific attitude toward history was strikingly exhibited by Voltaire in his flat refusal to accept Tacitus at face value. He did not have the evidence which later scholars have found for believing Tacitus prejudiced and inaccurate. But relying on internal evidence, he pointed out the improbability of much that Tacitus had written upon Tiberius, Nero, Caligula, and other emperors. How could we accept the word of a man born long after Tiberius's death for the sensational story of how the emperor, after living to nearly eighty with unblemished name and a reputation for austerity, thereafter passed his

time in monstrous debaucheries? Voltaire applied this same scientific incredulity to other fables of so-called history, demanding more sensible interpretations. Still another new principle which he helped bring into history was his insistence that persons and personal interests are of secondary importance; that it is the community, not the individual, which counts for most. This in itself was a basis for many new interpretations of the past. As Lord Morley says in his essay on Voltaire:

Voltaire was always conscious, though not so clearly as writers are now, of the great historical principle that besides the prominent men of a generation there is something at work underneath, a moving current on whose flood they are borne. He never fixed this current by any of the names which now fall so glibly from our lips,—tendency of the times, tenor of public opinion, spirit of the age, and the like, by which we give a collective name to groups of sentiments and forces, all making in what seems to be a single direction. But although unnamed, this singular and invisible concurrence of circumstances was yet a reality to him. The age was something besides its heroes, and something besides its noisiest and most resounding occurrences. His divisions of the great epochs of humanity are undoubtedly open to much criticism, because the principles on which he drew the dividing line have lost their force in new generations. . . . Nevertheless, we are bound to recognize that a new way of regarding human action, as well as a new way of composing history, was being introduced by a writer whose first paragraph declared that he proposed to himself a greater object than an account of the life of Louis XIV; that he designed to paint for the instruction of posterity, not the actions of a single man, but the spirit of men; and that while all periods must be alike to one who only de-

[5] Voltaire, *Ibid.*, p. 9.

sires to fill his memory with facts, discrimination among them cannot be dispensed with for one who thinks.[6]

The temper of the Enlightenment appears quite as clearly in David Hume's *Essays, Moral, Political, and Literary,* as in Voltaire's works. His famous disquisition upon miracles, a masterpiece of irony, was a blow at the very padlock of the old fetters upon history. His essay upon the population of ancient cities, highly skeptical in temper, was one of the first suggestions of the importance of statistics in interpreting history. His views on money, trade, and government, marked by intellectual impartiality and critical acuteness in points of detail, carried many historical illustrations and had a clear applicability to history. Despite his allegiance to the Tory party, they pointed a clear road forward to what in the next century was called Liberalism. They had a profound influence in England and France, and it has been said that but for the conservative reaction following the French Revolution they might even have resulted in the parliamentary adoption of free trade and electoral reform before 1800. But Hume's *History of England,* which followed the *Essays,* was his greatest work. He was the first eminent Briton, as Voltaire was the first eminent Frenchman, to see clearly that history should not be a mere record of war and political intrigue, but should concern itself primarily with the mode of life, the morals, the manners, and the mind of the people. Far more than any previous writer, he had an insight into the complex social forces of history. After his six-volume work (1754-61), no Englishman could write history as it had been written before.

[6] Lord Morley, *Collected Works,* VII, 249, 250.

In Gibbon's *Decline and Fall* the Age of Enlightenment produced its principal historical monument. That work still seems, to many acute judges, the greatest piece of interpretive history yet written. To be sure, the interpretation is simple; it is largely summed up in Gibbon's famous sentence, "I have traced the triumph of Christianity and of barbarism." He was animated by a glowing admiration for the empire of Augustus and Trajan as embodying a "solid fabric of human greatness" unmatchable elsewhere; an empire which to him came nearer giving the earth its golden age than had any other régime. Imbued with this admiration, he felt little but distaste for the Christian religion which had done so much to help overthrow the Roman civilization—which had given to him in the eighteenth century the sight of barefooted and superstitious friars chanting vespers in the temple of Jupiter beside the ruins of the Capitol. That so great a work should be written upon a theme so antagonistic to all the tenets of theological historiography was, whatever we think of the validity of his interpretation, the blow of an irresistible battering ram against the old narrow citadels. Their walls collapsed in utter ruin.

The second great constructive influence upon historical interpretation came with the rise of economic science, and was ushered in by Adam Smith's *Wealth of Nations* in the same year that witnessed the Declaration of Independence and the publication of Gibbon's first volume. Smith had taken not a few of his views from the *Political Discourses* of his close friend Hume. His classic book, usually regarded as the main foundation of economics, was also one of the foundation-stones of modern historical writing. The Rationalists had dealt a shattering blow at the theory that history revolved exclusively about the facts of Christianity; Adam Smith now dealt a shattering blow at the whole aristocratic theory of history. Up to that time nearly all chroniclers of the past had held to a hierarchal conception of history, regarding the upper ranks of society as those alone worthy of a large place in the record. The king, noble, soldier, priest, and statesman had been the personalities with whom history was concerned; battles, dynastic changes, treaties, and other elements of the contest for power had been the salient events of history. But Adam Smith's ideas let in a new blaze of light. He and other writers showed that the great central currents in the life of any modern nation were economic; that the principal forces which governed that life were those of production, markets, transportation, labor-supply, prices, and raw materials. These, like an irresistible current, bore national affairs forward while kings, priests, and soldiers—with some few exceptions—were tossed like flotsam and jetsam on the surface. Important though wars and battles were, they held their importance, in general, because they grew out of economic forces or interrupted these forces; much as treaties often counted, it was usually because they were the visible outcome of greater factors beneath the surface. It was impossible for well-read men, after *The Wealth of Nations,* to write of nations without proper attention to all that built up wealth. A great new interpretive highway had been driven into the wilderness that bordered the old-fashioned history, and colonists were soon making that wilderness rich with fruitful crops.

One of the first and most influential of these explorers was Arnold H. L. Heeren, long professor at Göttingen, who was sixteen when Adam Smith's book appeared, and who lived until 1842, becoming George Bancroft's master and inspirer in the art of history. Heeren's unforgettable service was that he first fully applied the new interpretive apparatus to the ancient field. In his *Ideen über Politik, den Verkehr und den Handel der vornehmsten Völker der alten Welt,* and in other works, he presented an altogether fresh point of view. He examined ancient agriculture, manufactures, commerce, finance, and in short, the whole economic system of the early world, together with its politics, laws, and constitutions, and was thus enabled to throw a flood of light on the development of the civilizations of antiquity. His vast and varied learning, calm impartiality, and insight helped to make his works notable. Unfortunately Bancroft, while learning much from Heeren in scholarly method and zeal, never acquired his peculiar interest in the economic aspects of history. In England the Benthamite or utilitarian school of historians, like Jeremy Bentham himself, were originally inspired by Adam Smith.

As a third vivifying influence, novel political ideas also contributed to the transformation of history by supplying a number of fresh interpretations; and it need not be said that the most striking of these ideas came with the French Revolution. That event was to half of mankind as the rising of a golden sun. "Bliss was it in that dawn to be alive"— to be a young historian, no less than poet, very heaven. Through the lurid flame and smoke of the overwhelming convulsion, the masses of the people came into view. These masses, unknown to the oldtime chroniclers of royalty, military glory, and the church, had been neglected as unimportant, but they now made history with unforgettable vigor. They lifted to power one of their own number, and Napoleon took charge of the destinies of Europe for fifteen years. Thenceforth no historian could slight them. And when the era of the Napoleonic wars ended, it was also seen that history must henceforth be interpreted not merely in terms of the common man, but in terms of a rampant nationalism. Once the monarch had been thought more important than the state—often, as Louis XIV boasted of himself, he *was* the state. But now the people were the state; and the force of national sentiment diffused throughout the people brought a new Germany, a new Spain, in one sense a new Russia, into existence. In the course of another long generation, the growth of nationalism among the masses gave birth to a new Italy and a newer Germany, while still further triumphs lay before it.

Altogether, by 1830 the age of multiform historical interpretations of the past had fully opened. The presentation of the human record had been broadened in a fashion that would have been inconceivable to pious readers of Bossuet. It no longer took account of divine providence at all—or at least not in the ablest writers. Instead, it took account of all that the rationalism of that era had to suggest, for Montesquieu's enlistment of geography had been only one of various utilizations of scientific knowledge; it took account of the cultural and moral history which Voltaire had pointed out to Mme. du Chatelet as central to all understanding of man's past; it took account of economic factors; of democratic factors; and of nationalistic and patriotic factors. A se-

ries of radically new outlooks, within seventy-five years, had come in. Every student was at liberty to use one or several of them in his synthesis, his interpretation.

Yet although much had been done, fertile fields of speculation remained to be entered. The fourth great element in the modern growth of history lay in its acquisition of the new scientific tendencies of the nineteenth century. In such writers as Macaulay, Guizot, and Prescott the interpretation is what we nowadays term, with due respect, old-fashioned. Why? Because while they reflected the ideas which had been imported into history by Montesquieu and Voltaire, Hume and Gibbon, Adam Smith and Heeren, the Industrial Revolution and the French Revolution, still other ideas arose during and after their lifetimes which have profoundly impressed all subsequent historians. History had in particular to keep up with the march of the various sciences, and some were marching fast. In addition to the development of geography, economics, and biology, wholly new sciences were born—first sociology, and later psychology, both extremely useful in historical interpretation. Professional historians are justly suspicious of sweeping sociological theories as likely to be unsound and useless. But the more exact sciences are of indubitable value.

One important book which partly revealed a shift in the trend of historical interpretation, and which partly caused it, was H. T. Buckle's unfinished *History of Civilization in England,* published in 1857. As everyone knows, this huge fragment—broken off by his untimely death—is part of an introduction in which he intended, first, to state the general laws governing human progress, and second, to exemplify these laws by the history of certain strongly individualized nations—Spain, Scotland, the United States, and Germany. It is unnecessary to list all of the ten or twelve main principles, some of them largely fallacious, which he laid down. His most important contentions are as follows: (1) Inasmuch as historians have been shortsighted and unreflective, and as the social phenomena of the modern world are extremely complex, little has yet been done to establish a science of history. (2) It is nevertheless proved by scientific inquiry, and particularly by sociological statistics, that human action is controlled by fixed and predictable rules. (3) It is a basic fact of history that the chief causes of intellectual progress are climate, soil, and food, which govern it indirectly by determining the accumulation and distribution of wealth, and the aspect of nature, which touches intellectual development directly by influencing the cast and vigor of thought—for peoples reared in sublime scenery are more imaginative than their fellows, peoples reared in harsh surroundings are tougher-minded, and so on. (4) The huge distinction between European and non-European civilization rests primarily upon the fact that in Europe man has been stronger than nature, subduing it to his objects, while outside Europe nature has been stronger than man and has largely subdued him. (5) The advance of European civilization is characterized by a steady growth in the importance of intellectual laws, and a steady diminution in the influence of physical laws.

Though some of his ideas have never convinced others, and perhaps none of them is wholly true, Buckle's work was nevertheless extremely influential everywhere from Russia to the United States.

Particularly was one central thesis of his work important. He taught that written history had been too much a record of individuals or select groups, and not enough of whole societies or nations; he believed that the action of great human masses ought to be traced, especially with the aid of statistical law. He also held that in the natural surroundings of every people—its command of necessary raw materials and luxuries, its conditions of soil and climate—lie the chief moulding influences of its career, and that parliaments have nearly as little as kings and heroes to do with that moulding. In short, Buckle was one of the forerunners of a history built upon sociology, social statistics, and economic geography. His emphasis upon the life of the whole people appears in transmuted form in John Richard Green's *Short History of the English People,* and in John Bach McMaster's *History of the People of the United States.* Both these writers attempt to trace the life of a whole nation, and to deal with the people as an organic body; the people as they lived, worked, prospered, suffered, as they developed moral codes, manners, and arts in city and country. Both writers had to fall back upon description much more heavily than Buckle would have approved, for tables of statistics and other sociological data did not exist in any volume. But both were obviously influenced by his doctrines, while he had helped to prepare a reading public for them. The deep impression made by his insistence upon laws of progress was of course heightened by the publication of Darwin's *Origin of Species* only two years after his book.

Only less important than the scientific contribution made to historical interpretation by Buckle and the great evolutionists—Darwin, Lyell, Huxley, Wallace, Hooker—was the quasi-scientific contribution made by the founders of sociology. One such founder, August Comte, preceded these men; another, Herbert Spencer, followed them. Neither wrote at any length upon history in itself, but the works of both contain much incidental material upon history. Spencer was of course one of the chief apostles of evolution, who attempted to make universal the principle of evolutionary development and to formulate its law. Comte, whose *Positive Philosophy* was completed in 1843, seventeen years before Darwin's *Origin of Species,* had no connection with evolutionary theory. Nor had he the least sympathy with the desire of Buckle and others to study history by discovering the scientific laws governing society. On the contrary, he maintained that no such laws exist; that while human knowledge has as its objects phenomena in their reciprocal relations, nothing absolute lies at the base of these phenomena. With one exception stated below, the only absolute law is, All is relative. His views represented a development of the rationalistic and skeptical doctrines of Hume and Condillac.

For the purposes of the interpretive historian, the part of Comte's encyclopaedic system which holds the richest interest is the Law of the Three States laid down at the beginning of his Positive Philosophy, and always treated by both disciples and opponents as the key to it. He declared that each branch of human knowledge passes successively through three phases, or three modes in which men explain the phenomena they observe. The first phase is the Theological, in which credulous observers refer phenomena to a supernatural principle, the immediate volition of the object itself or of some supernatural being. The second phase is the Metaphysical, the phenomena being viewed not as an act of volition, but as due to an abstract force residing in, yet apart from, the object. The third is the Positive phase, when phenomena are referred by way of succession or resemblance to some other fact, and so studied. All this has been aptly illustrated by an English follower of Comte: "Take the phenomenon of the sleep produced by opium. The Arabs are content to attribute it to the 'will of God.' Molière's medical student accounts for it by a *soporific principle* contained in the opium. The modern physiologist knows that he cannot account for it at all. He can simply observe, analyze, and experiment upon the phenomena attending the action of the drug, and classify it with other agents analogous in character." The principal object of Comte's Positivistic teachings was to carry the study of social phenomena into the third stage—to remove them from the sphere of theology and metaphysics, and to see that they be given the same scientific examination of their relations and classifications as had already been given to physical and chemical phenomena. To use John Morley's summary:

While men's minds were in the theological state, political events, for example, were explained by the will of the gods, and political authority based on divine right. In the metaphysical state of mind . . . political authority was based on the will of the people, and social facts were explained by the figment of the falling away from a state of nature. When the positive method has been fully extended to society, as it has been to chemistry and physiology, these social facts will be resolved, as their ultimate analysis, into relations with one another, and instead of seeking causes in the old sense of the word, men will only examine the conditions of social existence. When that stage has been reached . . . the whole of our knowledge will be impressed with one character, the character, namely, of positivity or scientificalness; and all our conceptions in every part of knowledge will be thoroughly homogeneous. The gains of such a change are enormous.[7]

In addition to this emphasis upon the necessity for a science of society, an emphasis which could not but affect historical work in proportion as Comte's views were accepted and diffused, the Positive Philosophy had another important object. This was to show that the sciences are all branches from a single trunk, parts of one great whole. Comte's special aim was the promotion of sociology, a science never formulated until his advent; but while promoting it he tried to assign it a clear relation to other branches of knowledge. He arranged a hierarchy of sciences, each in his view more specialized than the member just before it, and dependent upon all the preceding sciences: (1) mathematics, (2) astronomy, (3) physics, (4) chemistry, (5) biology, and (6) sociology. Of course he held sociology the greatest of all. If we remember that not a few writers now view history as retrospective sociology, it is at once plain that this doctrine also has had its effect upon historical interpretation.

We have spoken of evolution as giving the world a new philosophy of history; but it also supplied various new interpretations of it, practical and immediate in nature. Until the doctrine was fully introduced to the world by Darwin, Spencer, and others, historians had talked of development rather than evolution. During the Age of Enlightenment advanced thinkers had taken a keen interest in the origin and develop-

ment of language, of philology, of law, of pictorial art, of legendary and written literature. It was natural that this should be enlarged to include an inquiry into the origin and development of animal life. This investigation, in the hands of men like Darwin, Spencer, and Huxley, soon included an inquiry into the source and means of progress of humankind; and it soon also brought forth a revolutionary conception of development. In the eighteenth century the animal world had been looked upon as a series of species or types, but it had never been supposed that the types evolved into one another; each was thought of as independent. Now it was demonstrated by careful investigation that species or types did change into others. In short, development had become evolution. Though Darwin was by far the greatest scientist to investigate the supposed laws of evolution, Herbert Spencer made the most ambitious effort to apply evolution as a universal interpretive principle, using it to explain the development of human society as well as of the animal kingdom. His doctrine of integration followed by differentiation remains highly suggestive to the historian even today.

The old view of the factors involved in the development of organic life had been childishly naïve, falling back upon a series of cosmic cataclysms to explain what was otherwise inexplicable. Darwin declared that the true factors were increasing complexity, infinite differentiation, adaptation to environment, natural selection by the survival of the fittest, and the transmission of acquired characteristics. Previously an apparently unbridgeable gap had existed between men and dumb animals; now this chasm was filled. Previously no clear alternative

[7] *Encyclopædia Britannica*, Ninth Ed., VI, 234.

had been offered to the theological doctrine of creation; now one was formulated. Previously a huge body of historical facts had seemed trivial and without sequence or relationship; now relationships could be suggested and the significance of nearly all facts demonstrated. A large number of biological analogies suggested themselves to students of history. It is hardly too much to say that most departments of human thought reoriented themselves after the publication of *The Origin of Species,* and history was one.

Within a single generation the range of evolutionary interpretations became extremely wide. It ran from Freeman's work on the evolution of the English Constitution, and Sir Henry Maine's on the evolution of law, both highly scientific in character, to such a book as Winwood Reade's summary of world history called *The Martyrdom of Man* —a book which, first published in 1872, has gone through fully a score of British and American editions. Reade pictures the past of mankind in colors of repellent darkness, and hints at a future of dazzling brightness; finding the bridge between the two in the process of evolutionary betterment. In America the Spencerian interpretation was best applied to history by John Fiske. He interpreted the rise of democracy in this country by analogy from biological evolution, and explained it as analogous to the growth of British democracy from the ancient Teutonic folk moot. The word evolution soon crept into book-titles, and has become so firmly established there that no conceivable force could dislodge it; men write on the Evolution of Congress, the Evolution of Fashions, the Evolution of the Novel, the evolution of every force or social element that has a history. The biological analogy is seldom encountered, and even when met is seldom pushed far. But it is safe to assert that more than half the historians now writing bring insensibly to their interpretation of the facts at least a few fragmentary ideas of the mutation of species or types, of adaptation to environment, and of natural selection by survival of the fittest. Their minds have consciously or unconsciously taken much of the Darwinian mould.

It is impossible to pursue further the various interpretations brought in by new scientific knowledge or theories. Psychology has resulted in the rewriting of a vast deal of history; not merely by furnishing new concepts of great leaders, but by throwing fresh light on mass-emotion, mass-thinking, the behavior of special groups, and the growth and decay of certain states of mind. The newer medical knowledge, as everyone can see by reading Dr. Hans Zinsser's *Rats, Lice, and History* or Dr. C. Mac-Laurin's works on the pathological record of eminent men and women, has affected the treatment of the past.[8] The progress of economic geography has made possible brilliant new interpretations of history. And this scientific advance goes on along an ever-widening front. Many old views are slowly discarded; few present-day historians would think of citing Buckle or Comte to buttress an interpretation—many do not even know what they taught. But

---

[8] In *Post Mortem* Dr. MacLaurin deals with the medical history of Joan of Arc, Charles V, Anne Boleyn, Napoleon I, and Cellini; in *Mere Mortals* with the medical record of Ivan the Terrible, Henry VIII, Frederick the Great, James I, and others. He thinks that the true reason for Charles V's retirement lay in arteriosclerosis.

even the exploded and outmoded theories have helped to generate a spirit of unfettered inquiry and discussion, to stimulate men to use new tools fearlessly, and to give historical study a pervading atmosphere of alertness and energy. Believers in history realize that it must be kept in touch with other branches of knowledge, and abreast of them. As a result of the successive injections of new ideas, today we have numerous large schools of historical interpretation, and a great many minor schools or sub-schools.

The oldest of the schools is the still-surviving group of religious-minded historians. While the theological philosophy of history has decayed in the sense that few men would think of making Christianity the central pattern of world-history, nevertheless many writers believe that certain phases of history illuminate God's workings in the world. Sometimes the belief is explicit, more often sub-conscious. Thomas Carlyle wrote of the French Revolution as a gigantic object-lesson in the penalty that quackery, greed, and evil bring upon themselves, a tremendous illustration of God's determination to make crooked ways straight. With theological dogmas Carlyle had no patience whatever; he condemned them as "Hebrew old-clothes," talked of priests as apes chattering by the banks of the Dead Sea, and remarked that Newman had the brains of a moderate-sized rabbit. But he was highly religious in a deeper, more mystical sense, and his histories are the utterances of a religious prophet preaching by pictures of the past—flaming and unforgettable pictures. Often accused of holding that Might makes Right, he protested sternly that he believed the precise opposite; that Right and Might are in the long run identical because Right alone is ultimately enduring. His belief that Right is the expression of the divine will he wrought into every texture of his histories. It was of course a very different type of religious history that John Henry Newman wrote, but it had more force than Carlyle believed. And many later historians have had theological preconceptions. The shallower kind of religious history receives —and deserves—general disregard. We have little patience today with George Bancroft remarking in his eulogy of Lincoln: "That God rules in the affairs of men is as certain as any truth of physical science . . . Kings are lifted up and thrown down, nations come and go . . . but nothing is by chance, though men, in their ignorance of causes, may think so. The deeds of time are governed, as well as judged, by the decrees of eternity." We have little patience with Hilaire Belloc's twaddle about the figure of an Ultramontane and very Bellocian God in all human affairs.[9] But history that discloses a deep pervasive undercurrent of religious conviction may often merit the utmost respect. As Woodrow Wilson declared, the record of nations possesses a spiritual quality, and is fundamentally a product "not of institutions, but of the heart."

An almost equally venerable school of writers still interprets history largely

[9] A famous passage in Newman's *Apologia Pro Vita Sua* (Chapter V) shows that even he sometimes lost faith in a divine pattern. He speaks of the unhappy lot of mankind—"their aimless courses, their random achievements and acquirements, the impotent conclusions of long-standing facts, the tokens so faint and broken of a superintending design, the blind evolution of what turn out to be great powers or truths, the progress of things as if from unreasoning elements, not towards final causes . . . all this . . . inflicts upon the mind the sense of a profound mystery, which is utterly beyond human solution."

by the lamp of political science. They hold that the most significant aspect of the human past lies in the effort of men to give objective form to the principles of governmental theory. Of this school Von Ranke remains the great exemplar, for even his studies in church history were essentially studies in statecraft and state-organization. To it belong such English historians as Gardiner and Froude; such French historians as Guizot and Michelet; such American historians as Schouler and Rhodes. It remains strong despite all the inroads of the "new" history. So young a scholar as Mr. Crane Brinton can write: "Not so very long ago, most of us knew what to expect when we encountered the word history. We could count on an orderly narrative of the doings of kings and statesmen, soldiers and priests ..." [10] It will continue to persist and to show strength. In the hands of this group history is a definite and dignified entity, explaining much that is undeniably of first importance in the past, and offering a fixed and solid discipline to the mind. Its history is narrow and at times a bit arid, but it possesses form and significance. While the record of mankind has become much more than the history of states, state-history remains no mean part of it.

One of the most vigorous schools of all, the school which expounds one form or another of the economic interpretation of history, now boasts of so many departments that it has become difficult to treat it under a single rubric. It has been an extremely fertile school, producing within a century a vast sea of historical literature. For example, Labriola calls the Reformation an economic rebellion of the German nation, and R. H. Tawney has placed the whole Reformative movement on an economic basis. Émile Durkheim (a sociologist rather than historian) asserts that history is essentially the progress of the principle of division of labor. [11] Marxian or pseudo-Marxian historians have interpreted the record of many communities and nations as primarily a history of the division and antagonism of classes—the class conflict. Some historians of the economic school, like Guglielmo Ferrero, have taken a highly pessimistic view of the course of the human race. Some, like H. G. Wells, who has also been greatly influenced by evolutionary doctrine and Marxian ideas, are highly optimistic; they look forward to the rise of society from level to level until it attains a millennial state. The ablest of all the compendious histories of the American people, Charles and Mary Beard's *Rise of American Civilization,* is primarily an economic interpretation. Anyone who looks at a critical bibliography of American history must be struck by the sweeping extent of the present-day movement for rewriting the history of American colonization, American expansion, the Revolutionary and Civil Wars, and the party conflicts, in terms of their economic springs. But this tendency toward economic reinterpretation has gained equal vigor in almost all Western lands.

The school which presents a geographical interpretation of history is by no means a mere subdivision of the preceding school, but maintains a place of its own. It holds that the degree of a people's civilization is determined primarily by its physical surroundings and by climatic influences. One of the most important living exponents of this

---

[10] *Saturday Review of Literature,* August 14, 1937.

[11] Cf. Émile Durkheim's *De la Division de la Travail Social* (1893).

theory, Ellsworth Huntington, has made particularly notable studies of the influence of climate upon history. To the stimulating effect of certain climates, conjoined with the possession of rich natural resources and other factors, he attributes the rise of great civilizations in a few favored lands—the western part of the European continent, the British Isles, eastern North America. To the lack of such stimulation he attributes the cultural barrenness of other lands, and to changes in the climate he would trace much of the decay of earlier civilizations in Western Asia and the Mediterranean basin. More modest and conventional uses of geography are to be found in the writings of such Americans as Ellen C. Semple and R. H. Brigham. But the whole relation of geography and history must be reserved for fuller treatment later in this volume.

Social history, cultural history, intellectual history—these names are applied to the work of various interpretive groups between which it is hard to draw clear boundary lines; groups which all unite, however, in giving history a wide and loose significance. Cultural history can perhaps be set in a special category. In the strictest sense it is a history of cultural institutions related to underlying currents of national or community life. Leslie Stephen in his *English Literature and Society in the Eighteenth Century* (1904), an admirable example, not merely furnishes a systematic and satisfactory history of English letters from Addison to Walter Scott. He goes further and shows how the *content* of this literature arose from the social conditions of the time. Not only this, but he goes still further and demonstrates that literary form itself has a vital unity with these social conditions. That is, the lines along which this form—the

drama, the epic, the essay, the novel—will develop, depend upon the character, origin, and tastes of the literary class which uses it as a vehicle for its ideas and impulses; upon the constitution of the reading class which offers a market for these ideas; and upon the correspondence between these ideas and the most powerful intellectual tendencies of the time. W. J. Courthope's comprehensive *History of English Poetry* places the development of prosody upon a solid foundation in the developing social conditions of English history. Such a striking little masterpiece of interpretation as Taine's *Art of the Netherlands* does the same. So, also, do the learned, vivid, and beautifully written (though occasionally inaccurate) volumes of John Addington Symonds on the Renaissance, and Burckhardt's single volume on the subject; Georg Brandes's *Main Currents in Nineteenth Century Literature;* and Parrington's work. Samuel Eliot Morison's history of Harvard presents a cultural history of all early New England, while Van Wyck Brooks deals admirably with a later period in *The Flowering of New England.*

Sociological and social history of course constitute a much larger and vaguer department of scholarship and letters. At the one extreme we find a group which would base history upon the dictum of Franklin H. Giddings: "Sociology is an attempt to account for the origin, growth, structure, and activities of society by the operation of physical, vital, and psychological causes working together in the process of evolution." This group has given us books like Kidd's *Social Evolution,* which is a brilliant interpretation of the function of religion in history, and J. Donald Forrest's *Development of Western Society.* At the other extreme we find a group devoted to what the Germans long ago called *kulturgeschichte*—that is, writers who attempt to describe the life of a people during a certain period in all its phases. An early example is offered by Karl Biedermann's *Germany in the 18th Century.* Excellent recent examples are offered by the best volumes of *The History of American Life,* edited by Arthur M. Schlesinger and Dixon Ryan Fox, and inspired in part by H. D. Traill's coöperative work, *Social England.* The principal weakness of this type of history is that in undisciplined hands it easily grows into an encyclopaedia of unrelated details, a mountain of petty facts piled loosely together. These facts may be departmentalized by labelling one part of them The Changing Church, another part The Educational Revival, another Home Life, another The Deepening of Culture, another Professions and Business. But an encyclopaedia is not converted into history by departmentalizing it. Carefully pondered principles of selection—principles of high and permanent significance—are necessary before the facts of social history can be properly assayed; and even when this is done, effective presentation of the facts requires an insight that approaches genius. The best specimens of social history in English remain the third chapter of Macaulay's *History of England,* and the first six chapters of Henry Adams's *History of the United States Under Jefferson and Madison.*[12]

As from philosophy we descend to interpretation, so from the latter we descend to thesis or synthesis. Perhaps few works of history are directly touched by philosophy. Many of the best are also quite untouched by any special interpretation; Macaulay and Parkman,

for example, rather wrote history according to their individual bent than according to any school of thought, though accepting to some extent the idea of the superior significance of the state. But few histories of any distinction lack a thesis, or if that word is too strong, at least a definite principle of synthesis; the author wishing to demonstrate some view. It may be a commonplace and obvious view. It may be marked by great originality and insight, and in the most brilliant histories it is. But history which lacks a thesis is a body lacking a skeleton—it is invertebrate. It may contain exhaustive research, may be striking in detail, may throw new light into dark places, but its total effect will be limp. Channing's volumes on the colonial period contain no thesis worth mentioning, while those of George Louis Beer contain a sharpcut, novel, and emphatic thesis. The result is that while nobody ever speaks of Channing's ideas, Beer's ideas have been a staple of discussion ever since they were propounded; while we try to remember Channing's facts, we very distinctly remember Beer's views.

More than once a volume enforcing a thesis has changed the views of millions and itself made history. Thus it was with Treitschke's insistence upon the importance of national unity and a powerful central government; his histories altered the attitude of a multitude of Germans toward their national destiny. Some have traced Germany's plunge into the World War to his works, as a generation earlier some students ascribed the War of 1870 to the histories of Thiers. Frederick J. Turner's thesis of the effect of the frontier upon American life and character has colored not only all historical thought

---

[12] Two political historians!

in this country, but all literary thought, all social thought, and all political thought. Alfred T. Mahan, by the vigorous thesis of his *Influence of Seapower upon History, 1660-1783,* followed by his *Influence of Seapower upon the French Revolution, 1783-1812,* affected the governmental policy of all the great maritime powers. His interpretation threw an entirely new light upon one department of the past, and read from it arresting and convincing lessons for the future. Japan, Germany, Great Britain, and the United States applied these lessons to their naval programs and strategy.

Sometimes a historical thesis may be non-controversial. Students could hardly quarrel over the central thesis of Parkman's *Jesuits in North America,* for example; which is simply that the Jesuits failed because they built their hopes of an American empire on the Hurons and their kindred tribes, and these were ultimately conquered by the hostile Iroquois. Parkman himself spoke of this thesis as "obvious," and drew from it only an elementary inference: "Liberty may thank the Iroquois that, by their insensate fury, the plans of her adversary were brought to nought and a peril and a woe averted from her future." More commonly, however, the thesis is avowedly controversial. Take, for example, any one of the half dozen principal works upon the authorship of Homer. After Friedrich A. Wolf's epochal *Prolegomena to Homer* (an astonishing piece of work for its early date, 1795), which contended that the Iliad and Odyssey in their present-day form have been materially changed from the originals, and are made up of separate poems composed at different times by various authors, it was impossible to write on that

subject without some highly argumentative thesis. Andrew Lang in *Homer and His Age* sounded a counterblast to the disintegrationists. He held that the Iliad, far from being the work of four or five centuries, a score of bards, and a medley of old and new ideas, was the product of a single age and a single state of culture, the poet describing his own environment. It was an age which had given up burial and adopted cremation, substituted iron tools for bronze while still retaining bronze weapons, and learned the art of writing, so that it preserved Homer's work on palm leaves, papyrus, or parchment, now perished. Or as examples of controversy, take the innumerable theses applied to the French Revolution. That great event is still current politics as well as past history. Pierre Saro writes of it with a Royalist thesis, and his idealization of the Ancien Règime has gone through some seventy-five editions in France; Prince Kropotkin writes of it with an Anarchist thesis; Albert Mathiez writes with a very radical left-wing, even a Communist, thesis, idealizing the Terror.

Sometimes a thesis rests upon striking new evidence which really puts an entirely different face upon an old problem. Thus several books have now been written, based upon fresh documentary material, to show that the soul of Abolitionism in the years 1835-60 was not found in William Lloyd Garrison and his Boston group, as men long supposed, but in the Tappan brothers of New York, the Grimkés, and Theodore D. Weld, that Garrison was rather an encumbrance than an aid to the progress of Abolition, and gained his prominence partly by accident, partly by rashness, and partly by an insatiable appetite for the spotlight. Sometimes the thesis represents rather a stimulating new study of old material. Henry Osborn Taylor's *The Medieval Mind* affords an example. Most of the evidence he examined was familiar to everybody. But he took the unusual view that the true key to the medieval mind lay not in the vernacular writings, English, French, Spanish, and so on, but in the Latin writings of the period, which he held incomparably more valuable for the study of medieval thought— even Dante being in a sense but a by-road from the main highway of medieval culture. He amplified this thesis by stating that the supreme medieval achievement in thought was the "vital appropriation and emotional humanizing of patristic Christianity," represented by such thinkers as Albertus Magnus and Thomas Aquinas. Or a thesis may combine interesting new material with a novel reworking of old material; see Henri Pirenne's view, in his *Economic and Social History of Medieval Europe,* that it was not the collapse of the Roman Empire but the swift rise of the Moslem empire which in the eighth century cut off Western Europe from its Eastern economic connections.

Sometimes the thesis of a book may carry almost instant conviction. Julius W. Pratt's *Expansionists of 1812,* for example, made so clear the rôle of land-hunger in provoking the second war against Great Britain that at once every student stood ready to accord that factor much greater emphasis than before. Sometimes the thesis may be regarded dubiously. A good example is presented by Owsley's *King Cotton Diplomacy.* Its argument that the blockade of the South was totally ineffective until late in the Civil War—an argument based on figures of captures rather than comparative trade figures—seems worse than

dubious to experts on the diplomacy of the period. And sometimes the extravagance of an argument soon puts its maker out of court. Take, for example, the various forms of overstatement in Sydney George Fisher's interesting and provocative *Struggle for American Independence.* He asserts, quite correctly, that the struggle did not arise from British misrule, but from an effort by the British to reorganize their colonial system, and by using the sovereignty recognized as belonging to their government, to modernize it. He goes on to say that this assertion of sovereignty was an absolute necessity after the expulsion of the French from North America—that it was imperative that it be carried through if Great Britain were to retain her control. It was not, he further argued, a policy begun carelessly and stupidly by a corrupt government and arrogant king; it was launched after long deliberation and investigation by capable statesmen who were asserting the only principles upon which, at that time, colonies could be retained and governed. On the part of the Americans, independence was the object in view from the opening hour of the quarrel, and with many even before sharp friction began. The way for it had been paved by economic interests and political ideas which had long made an attempt at independence inevitable. These last assertions all contain some truth—but they also contain a great deal of error.

It is the special glory of history that it touches the realm of ideas at more points than almost any other study. Regarded by many as singularly arid in original thought (and with some reason in view of the multitude of mere factual compilations miscalled history), its greatest productions are actually shot through with intellectual elements. Written history is in the deepest sense the world of our epistomological construction of reality; as such it draws from and contributes to the profoundest metaphysical thought of the ages. In a more prosaic sense, it responds to every great new current of ideas that flows through the Western World; it has so responded from the time of St. Augustine to that of Darwin, Bergson, and Einstein, and it will continue to respond. In still more practical fashion, it has vital connections with every other social science —economics, sociology, public law, jurisprudence, social psychology, human geography—and relations of importance with the chief physical sciences, from biology to geophysics. As they grow and change, the content and outlook of history, the range of its ideas, grow and change also. Finally, history challenges its disciples to arrange the ever-growing mass of facts in ever-better patterns, and thus offers scope for the keenest insight and the most subtle ingenuity. All in all, success in history is proportioned as exactly to intellectual power as success in pure literature or in pure science. Behind every really great history stands a great man:

Not from a vein of shallow thought
His awful Jove young Phidias brought.

With the special glory of its many-sided relation to ideas, history has also a special responsibility. The intellectual element is but one part of history, and its ideas must never be given too loose a rein. As the bounds of history widen, as its outer territories become vague and shadowy, the importance of maintaining precise standards of factual accuracy and a high level of significance increases. History pushed too far toward sociology, like sociology pushed too far toward history, falls into a limbo in which it lacks form and value. Interpretation should be the leaven of the lump; but the result of applying a pound of interpretation to an ounce of fact is disappointing. A balance must be maintained between history as a body of facts, based solidly upon research, and history as an exercise in analysis, interpretation, and generalization.

1938

NICOLAS NABOKOV

The Case of Dmitri Shostakovitch

MY FIRST encounter with the name and music of Dmitri Shostakovitch occurred sometime in 1927 or 1928. Prokofiev had just returned to Paris from one of his seasonal trips to Soviet Russia. I remember hearing him talk of a remarkable graduate of the Leningrad Conservatory whose First Symphony had won great acclaim in Russia. He had either heard or seen the score of this symphony and had met its youthful author. Prokofiev described him as a pale, lean young man with penetrating eyes, a shy and self-centered youth with

Reprinted from *Harper's Magazine*, March, 1943, by permission of Nicolas Nabokov.

a great love for sports. He spoke of his thorough knowledge of "musical grammar" and of his equally good knowledge of the piano technique—both of them characteristic qualities of most Russian composers of this generation. Included in some new Russian music which Prokofiev had brought back from the U.S.S.R. to Paris were eight preludes for the piano by Shostakovitch and also his piano sonata, which had just then appeared in print.

At this time the art of Soviet Russia was still little known in western Europe. New Russian scores and new Russian books were difficult to obtain in France and there were very few scattered performances of Soviet Russian music abroad. Quite naturally the young musicians of France and Germany were very eager to know what was being done by composers in that unknown land, and the least bit of authentic information, not to speak of such evidence as scores and books, was highly welcome.

I remember distinctly my first impression of these early piano pieces by Shostakovitch. They seemed to me to have been written with remarkable skill and were well conceived for their instrumental medium. However, on the whole, they did not impress me as being particularly new or imaginative, nor did they seem to me to reflect a well-formed musical personality of first rank. They sounded so orthodox, so well-behaved, and so reminiscent of older Russian piano music that it was odd to realize that they had emanated from the most revolutionary land in the world. They lacked completely the audacious experimental spirit which was sweeping through the music of central and western Europe in the nineteen-twenties. I could not understand why this music should be rated so highly and why so

much was to be expected from its young author. It did not seem better or worse than most of the other music of Russian composers that Prokofiev had brought back from the Soviet Union.

Some time later, in Poland, where I missed Shostakovitch by only a few weeks (he had come there for one of those international "prize fighting" musical conventions of which there were so many at this time, and this was, as a matter of fact, his only trip abroad up to this day), I had the opportunity of seeing the score of his First Symphony. This was the famous symphony which several years later received great acclaim in the United States.

When I read this score, I felt that I had to correct to a certain extent my former superficially formed opinion of his potentialities. I recognized at once that, despite its many failings, this was a piece of music written by an extremely gifted musician, a man who was not solely interested in showing off the excellency of his training in musical techniques (particularly in orchestration), but knew how to write a long and gracefully lyrical melody and also how to handle a long development section in symphonic form. Nevertheless some of my former objections remained and became even stronger and clearer. I felt that in spite of the many attractive novelties of this symphony—such as its fashionable simplicity of melodic outline or its rhythmical liveliness—there was something old about the music, something essentially conservative and unexperimental. I could not feel any definite personality in it, nor did I see very much authentic invention, musical or technical. Every theme, every rhythmical pattern, every technical device, every harmony, however charming and well written, reminded me of another piece of music. As Diaghilev would have said, here "slept" Tchaikovsky and Wagner, here Mussorgsky or Prokofiev, and here again Stravinsky or Hindemith. There was no actual plagiarism, of course, but the whole atmosphere of the piece was synthetic and impersonal. It was like a good suit of ready-made clothes, which reminds you longingly of a good London tailor, or like one of those tidy modern cubicles in a Dutch or German workers' settlement—all perfectly built, according to the best-known techniques, very proper and neat yet infinitely impersonal and, in the long run, extremely dull.

Some of my musician friends reproached me for my harsh judgment, saying that the man was still very young, that to be impersonal and imitative was a sign of youthful timidity which Shostakovitch surely would soon outgrow. They contended that this First Symphony was in this sense a very promising work, for its musical sources (or sympathies) were of a superior order. I was ready to admit that my premonitions might be wrong, since many great composers at the beginning of their careers have imitated the masters whom they admired. Beethoven and Schubert and even Bach were guilty of that during their early years.

But I still remained worried over this music, and the reason for my worry was something outside of Shostakovitch himself. It seemed to me then that Shostakovitch might be a symptom of a new era approaching in art, and that certain internal changes in the political and social structure of the Soviet Union, rather than considerations of a purely artistic nature, had been greatly responsible for the rise of this kind of music. This synthetic and retrospective score, although foreign and unacceptable to

me, was perhaps the true expression of a new period in which the aim was to establish easily comprehensible, utilitarian, and at the same time contemporaneous art. Perhaps some of the principles which had been the cornerstones of the artistic philosophy of the past two generations would be put aside by the composers of this approaching era; perhaps our demand that music be primarily good in quality, new in spirit and technique, original in outlook would be subordinated to such principles as absolute and immediate comprehensibility to large masses of people and fulfillment of an educational mission, political and social.

I decided therefore to follow Shostakovitch's career as closely as possible in order to discover whether his music and his career would bear out my apprehension.

Now, in 1942, most of the cards are on the table. Shostakovitch, barely thirty-six years old, has become recognized as the prime composer of the Soviet Union, has been given a semi-official position among the political and ideological leaders of his country, has lately gained the admiration and love of his countrymen for his heroic life and work during the siege of Leningrad, and is well on the way to becoming the artistic hero of those nations whose destinies are at present closely tied up with that of the Soviet Union.

He can look back at a career full of dramatic episodes, in which utter misery, almost total eclipse from the public eye, and then sudden soaring fame followed each other within the space of a few years. He has worked incessantly with an exemplary perseverance and courage and has built up for one of his age an unusually long catalogue of works of all kinds—piano music, operas, ballets, symphonies, and music for the cinema. Since he finished his studies at the Leningrad Conservatory in 1926 he has been a steady teacher of composition there. As a man he has gained the friendship and respect of almost everyone who has ever come into contact with him.

His prestige in the United States at the present time is illustrated by the single fact that his Seventh ("Leningrad") Symphony, despite its cumbersome length, has received more performances here than any other piece of contemporary music in the same length of time. Sometimes these performances have even been simultaneously broadcast from different corners of the country. His First, Fifth, and Sixth symphonies have been recorded by the finest orchestras and some of the scores have been reprinted here. And he has received all this attention while most of the contemporary musical production of American composers and resident foreigners remains unrecorded, unpublished, and unplayed. Shostakovitch is at the present moment the undisputed idol of all "maestros," blond, bald, or gray, who in homage to Russia serve his seven symphonies at regular intervals to their local audiences on the same plate with Brahms, Beethoven, Wagner, and (until recently) Sibelius.

In speeches, public statements, newspaper and magazine articles he is referred to as "the new Beethoven" or "the new Berlioz"; he is discussed more than any other contemporary American or alien composer of the past twenty years; and as the fire-fighting hero-composer whose great symphony circled the world in bombers and transport planes, he has become a familiar figure to every American citizen who sees the newspapers.

Seldom in all the history of music has a composer received fame like this, and seldom has there been a career so rapid and so spectacular.

It seems to me that the time has come for a thorough and objective investigation into this most amazing success story. The music of Shostakovitch should be carefully scrutinized, brought into proper focus, and related to the general artistic production of our time so that we may determine to what extent it deserves this tremendous success, and to what extent the success is the result of a propitious political constellation. As yet there have been only scattered evaluations of Shostakovitch, generally connected with some particular episode in his career (like the first performance of his opera "Lady Macbeth from the District of Mzensk" in New York, or the first performance of his Seventh Symphony). Newspaper reporters and critics would describe and denounce or acclaim the single work in question. Lately the articles about Shostakovitch have been on the level of "human interest" stories. Except for a few articles in musical magazines—mostly informational—nothing more complete has been attempted.

First let us have a brief glance at the man's biography. It is commonly known that Shostakovitch was born in St. Petersburg, September 25, 1906; what is perhaps less commonly known is that the family of the future proletarian composer had no affinities with either the worker class or peasant class of old Russia. His father, an engineer by education, was, according to official biographers, an employee of the Department of Weights and Measures—a civil servant of the imperial regime, whose position in the community might be compared with that of a modest middle-class American business man. However, his professional training and the cultural background and artistic aspirations of his wife provided the family with a more intellectual atmosphere than that of the average bourgeois family of either Russia or America. In Russian terms the Shostakovitch family typified that admirable element in Russian society—the intelligentsia—which comprised in its ranks all that was vital, imaginative, and creative in the nation. Particularly in those dark and dreary years of decay of the imperial regime, the intelligentsia carried a double burden: first, the complex tradition of the cultural past of the people, and second, the responsibility for Russia's future regeneration when liberated from the ossified forms of tzarism.

Of his early days Shostakovitch says: "I became a musician by pure accident. If it had not been for my mother, I should probably never have become one. I had no particular inclination for music. I cannot recall a single instance when I evinced any interest in, or listened to, music when someone was playing at home. My mother was quite anxious that her children . . . at the age of nine should each start studying the piano. . . . After a few months of study I practiced Haydn and Mozart." From other sources we hear that the child showed "extraordinary and perfect memory" and at an early age "knew how to read fairly difficult pieces of music at sight." (Both of Shostakovitch's sisters likewise received a thorough musical training as a result of their mother's enthusiasm and determination, and the elder of the two is now a teacher at the Conservatory.) Clearly the boy's unusual natural musical gift was at first inactive and dormant and needed the in-

sistent encouragement of his mother to bring it to the fore.

Otherwise Shostakovitch's childhood was probably very much like that of any other child of his milieu. He went to school through the milky fogs and drizzly rains of St. Petersburg; he was a pale, frail boy coddled and adored by his parents, and surrounded at home by a studious and serious atmosphere. In the summer, as was customary among the Russian bourgeoisie and intelligentsia, the Shostakovitch family would probably go to a suburban villa, the Russian *datcha,* and there the same industrious and happy life would continue amid the lovely pine forests and quiet lakes surrounding the city of St. Petersburg.

Meanwhile the Russian scene was rapidly changing. First came the war, then the March Revolution of 1917, and its logical outcome (in October, 1917), the assumption of power by Lenin and the establishment of the Soviet government in Russia. It is said that young Dmitri Shostakovitch witnessed the storming of the Winter Palace by the Red Guards on October 23rd—an event which must have made an ineffaceable mark on a youthful, sensitive mind. No one who spent those days in Petrograd can forget them; and they must have played an enormous part in shaping Shostakovitch's convictions and his career.

In 1919 he entered the Petrograd Conservatory. The St. Petersburg-Petrograd-Leningrad Conservatory (founded in 1867 by Anton Rubinstein) has produced a phenomenal crop of great instrumentalists and great composers. It is an exemplary school where excellent technical traditions do not impede the individual development of the student, but supply him with a solid and manifold technical training—a fact which makes most modern Russian music look better "written" than the contemporary music of other countries.

At the Conservatory, under its best teachers, Shostakovitch received a well-balanced training in theory (harmony, composition, counterpoint, fugue, history, orchestration) and piano. When he graduated in 1926 he was already known in the musical circles of Leningrad as *the* promising young composer, and the composition he presented for his graduation was the First Symphony. By this time his political and artistic opinions were well formed, but already he had presumably gone through a series of influences, attractions, and enthusiasms. Like most music-loving Russian youths, he had probably started with a great attachment to the Mozart and Haydn sonatas which he practiced with his mother on the piano; at some point he probably was swept by an ardent passion for the esoteric music of Scriabin (some tendencies in the direction of Scriabin are still detectable in his music, particularly certain inflections of his melodic outline). He began early to love Tchaikovsky with a love often inexplicable to foreigners but natural to every Russian. With approaching maturity he began to understand the great "polyphonic miracle" of Bach and at the same time rejected as evil the Teutonic Wagnerian brew. But the great, the most powerful discovery he made, one which became a deep unshakable devotion with him, was that of Beethoven— Beethoven the revolutionary, the apostle of humanism, the prophet of "things to come."

The developments in the music of "bourgeois" Europe during this period of time were little known to the citizens of the U.S.S.R., but whatever news came from abroad, whatever score or bit of information could be obtained, was avidly read. Shostakovitch's friends and colleagues testify that the works of such men as Stravinsky, Ravel, Hindemith, Bartok, and Milhaud were fairly well known to him, and that he greedily absorbed all musical news arriving from the West. Several years later, speaking at a meeting of the Leningrad association of composers, he urged a closer acquaintance with the scores of contemporary western European composers, whose achievements, he said, "might be very useful to the music of Soviet Russia."

As for his convictions about the nature of his art, the mission of the creative musician, and his relation to politics and the state, these seem to have crystallized around 1927, not without a preceding period of doubt and a kind of creative prostration.

In an autobiographical statement given in 1936 to the *Revue Musicale,* Shostakovitch wrote: "At the Conservatory I absorbed with enthusiasm but without critical judgment all the knowledge and all the kinds of refinement which I was being taught. . . ." But somewhat later, "I understood that music is not only a combination of sounds arranged in this or that order [an idea quite fashionable at that time among several western European composers; see Stravinsky's autobiography] but an art which is *capable of expressing* by its means, *ideas* or sentiments of a most diverse kind. . . . I did not, however, acquire this conviction without pains. It suffices to say that during the whole year 1926 [the year of his graduation from the Conservatory] I did not write a single note, but from 1927 on I have never ceased to compose."

Thus, at the beginning of his career,

the question which has troubled many creative musicians—is music a language capable of expressing *only emotions and feelings* or is it also a vehicle for the expression of *ideas?*—was answered for him. From then on he had unshakable conviction that it could express ideas. From this point it was only a short step to the belief that the composer, like any other intellectual worker, has an educational obligation to fulfill and a political responsibility to bear.

Shostakovitch states it very clearly. "Working without interruption to acquire control over my art," he says, "I applied myself in order to create my own musical style which I sought to render simple and expressive. . . . I cannot conceive of my future creative program outside of our socialist enterprise (*construction socialiste*), and the aim which I assign to my work is that of helping in every way to enlighten our remarkable country." Near the end of this autobiographical statement he completes this idea of the composer's mission in the new socialist state by saying: "There cannot be greater joy for a composer than to be conscious that through his work he contributes to the great impetus of the Soviet musical culture, which is called upon to play a role of the first importance in remolding the human conscience."

From 1927 on and until now, all through the turbulent years of the middle thirties and through the agony of this war, this conviction has grown, become more rooted in him. The repudiation which his work received from the political leaders of his country in 1937, and which seemed for a time to eclipse his career, actually only spurred him on to work harder in order that he might redeem himself in the eyes of these leaders and regain his people's esteem. Any

doubt as to the sincerity of this devotion, any suspicion as to the honesty of his intentions, should be definitely put aside.

Thus the little bourgeois boy, Mitya Shostakovitch, has gone through the tough school of the revolution and emerged completely transformed. He has become an "intellectual worker" of the Proletarian Republic, one hundred per cent Stalinist-Communist, whose chief apostolate is to serve his government (and through it his people) according to this government's wishes and advices. He is honored when they praise him; he tries to see his errors when he is rebuffed. Individual, personal feelings matter only in so far as they are part of the people's fortune, their aspirations and their tragedies. "Music," he contends, "cannot help having a political basis, an idea that the bourgeoisie are slow to comprehend. . . . There can be no music without ideology . . ." (meaning of course political ideology). "The old composers whether they knew it or not were upholding a political theory." He goes on to explain that most of the old masters "were bolstering the rule of the upper classes," that Beethoven was "the forerunner of the revolutionary movement," and that Wagner, "the renegade," was "a revolutionary turned reactionary, to whom we listen in the same spirit as when we visit a museum to study the forms of the old regime." All art thus becomes classified according to a Marxian theory of values in which the intrinsic quality of a work of art depends upon its importance to the revolutionary progress of mankind.

The language of music becomes a vehicle for the statement of political ideologies; musical techniques are relegated to a subservient position; they are important only in so far as they render those ideologies intelligible. Concern with "personal" emotions, "individual" style or technique becomes irrelevant and unacceptable. Even to consider the proposition that transformation of musical techniques or an expression of individualistic emotions could be an end in itself becomes completely heretical. Shostakovitch condemns all such "foolishness" emphatically in his profoundly moving statement published on the eve of the first anniversary of the Russo-German War. "My energies," he writes, "are wholly engaged in the service of my country. Like everything and everyone to-day, my ideas are closely bound up with the emotions born of this war. They must serve with all the power at my command in the cause of *art for victory* over savage Hitlerism, that fiercest and bitterest enemy of human civilization. This is the aim to which I have dedicated my creative work since the morning of June 22, 1941."

Such complete devotion to the just cause of his country and its people necessarily commands respect and admiration. The philosophy upon which it is based is morally far more solid than many other contemporary theories. True enough, the Soviet artistic theory does not leave much room for the independent development of the individual musician; but on the other hand it is free from that pernicious and amoral ego-centricism from which so much music of the late nineteenth and twentieth centuries suffers. It is strangely akin to the noble morality of the artisan-musician of the Middle Ages, who, like Shostakovitch, worked with zeal and self-sacrifice as a servant of a cause he considered higher than himself and his art. The intention is the same and so is the fervor

of the devotion, the difference in this case being that where the medieval musician read the words "glory of God" and "service of His church," Shostakovitch reads "glory of the state" and "service of the people."

Yet as a permanent principle it has its dangers for the artist, as the case of Dmitri Shostakovitch demonstrates.

The musical production of Dmitri Shostakovitch can be conveniently divided into two periods. The first began in 1927, following his graduation from the Conservatory, and lasted until 1936 or, more precisely, January 28, 1936, when the now famous incident concerning his opera, "Lady Macbeth from the District of Mzensk," occurred. Then came a lapse of almost two years when Shostakovitch disappeared from the horizon of Russian artistic life. During these two years he wrote two new symphonies, his Fourth and Fifth, and the latter opened the door back to public favor, and marked the beginning of the second period, when, "reformed" and "rehabilitated," he gradually climbed to his present pinnacle of leadership.

The incident of "Lady Macbeth" has therefore a considerable significance and, although it has already been mentioned in the American press, it cannot be avoided here. Briefly this is what happened. During the years 1930-1932 Shostakovitch wrote an opera on a story by a Russian writer of the nineteenth century, Lesskov, called "Lady Macbeth from the District of Mzensk." It is a naturalistic and lurid story about a provincial, middle-class woman whose lust and boredom drive her to a series of cold-blooded murders and finally land her and her unfaithful lover in Siberia. Shostakovitch tried to give the story a Marxian twist by making the "heroine" a victim of the "decadent and foul bourgeois milieu."

The music of the opera is neither daring nor particularly new. It sounds very much like many naturalistic Russian operas written in the eighties and now happily forgotten. True enough, it is more lively; it has some (not too successful) attempts at bitter "class satire" and "class tragedy"; it has also a few attractively lyrical melodies both in the choruses and in the arias; but on the whole it is old-fashioned, provincial, and unimaginative. The musical language in which it is written is simple enough, but somehow not quite coherent and totally lacking in unity. Pieces of various styles are strung together rather loosely, and the whole opera gives the impression of hasty and somewhat careless workmanship. Thus, for instance, the satirical passages and some of the polyphonic developments are full of the most obnoxious tricks of the *style moderne* of the twenties (dissonant superimposition of chords, "dislocated joints" in the melodic line, and "rhythmical paranoia," or senseless repetition of a metrical figure—all unhappy products of the "modern" musical mind), while the lyrical arias and choruses reflect either Tchaikovsky or Mussorgsky. The realism or naturalism of the piece goes too far and at times it is plainly vulgar and pornographic. Most of the "class satire" is as unconvincing as the "Wooden Soldiers" of the late "Chauve-Souris."

The opera was duly produced in both Russian capitals in 1934 and was hailed as a "great masterpiece," the "work of a genius," "the first monumental work of Soviet musical culture." As such it was exported abroad and produced in the United States under Artur Rodzinski in Cleveland and New York. In New York it created a minor scandal and stirred up a great deal of discussion (chiefly because of the excessive musical realism of a bedroom love scene) which, coupled with the previous success of the First Symphony, "made" Shostakovitch.

For a time it looked as if the gods were favorably inclined to the young composer. But suddenly the storm broke loose. Messrs. Stalin and Molotov visited a performance of "Lady Macbeth" in Moscow in the middle of January, 1937. As a result of this visit a vitriolic article appeared in the *Pravda* on January 28, 1937, condemning Shostakovitch's opera as "disorder instead of music" and arguing that "mad rhythms" and a "confused flow of sound" competed to produce a baffling effect upon the innocent audience. Shostakovitch was said to be "misled by decadent bourgeois tendencies," and although a "gifted composer," was accused of "intentionally turning everything upside down" and writing "neurotic, hysterical, epileptic music influenced by American jazz." This first attack on Shostakovitch was followed by a second one, which appeared in the same paper a few days later and in which his new ballet, "The Limpid Brook," was taken to task in the same way.

In terms of Russian life all this sounded like an artistic death warrant; and such it was taken to be by the obliging critics and gentlemen of the Soviet press (often the same ones who had previously praised Shostakovitch as the great Russian genius). The slander of Shostakovitch in the press actually became so thick that the same official powers which had ordered the condemnation of his opera had to give a "hands off Shostakovitch" order. Shostakovitch was declared to have been "misled," "corrupted by Western bourgeois tendencies," but to be "gifted enough" to rehabilitate himself in the future and thus "not past hope." Two years later the "reformed" composer was returned to the Russian public as an officially changed man, one who had seen his faults and corrected them.

The whole story seems quite unreal now, particularly in view of the present circumstances. Yet it throws an interesting light upon the birth pangs of Soviet Russian art, and is especially significant for the development of Shostakovitch as a musician. These two painful years of banishment from public life were years of "inner self-criticism" (as the Soviet press calls it) during which he simplified his art still farther and *all* of his original musical thinking was definitely swallowed up by the "service to the cause."

It is as difficult to describe the music of Shostakovitch as to describe the form and color of an oyster, not because this music is by an means complicated or "inscrutable in its profundity" (as Soviet Russian criticism puts it) but simply because it is shapeless in style and form and impersonal in color. Yet the oyster has a very individual taste of its own which Shostakovitch unfortunately lacks. For one of his chief weaknesses is absolute eclectic impersonality. Even during his first period, when he still felt himself relatively free to choose or invent his own technique, his music was impersonal.

He still borrows other people's technical and stylistic inventions as if they were communal belongings. He still imitates indiscriminately (and I believe quite unconsciously) here Tchaikovsky and Beethoven, there Berlioz and Rimsky-Korsakov; here again he tries out some device he learned from a score of Stravinsky, or Ravel, or Hindemith, or

from some minor composer of the twenties. During his first period he wrote a greater variety of kinds of music than later, using tricks, devices, and techniques taken from such different sources that they could not possibly lead to a unified style, and jumping from Tchaikovsky to jazzy rhythms of the *"Mitteleuropa"* variety. His operas are so different from his symphonies, his chamber music from his ballets, that one has a hard time recognizing that the same man wrote them; and it is the defects of the music, rather than its qualities, that are recognizable as his own. Thus, for instance, he writes few melodies in which the augmented fourth does not appear; yet this interval is essentially unmelodic and by association reminds us of very stale "melodies" of the late nineteenth century. His exaggerated liking of march rhythms of 4/4 and 2/4 time leads to a kind of wooden squareness in the fast movements of his music. His long melodic *cantilenas,* in generally not more than two parts, are shapeless and awkwardly built. His "tunes" are often from very ordinary sources (in Soviet Russia they were called "marshy" during the years of his eclipse), imitating very common and uninteresting factory or army songs. One would probably not object to them if they had been treated originally; for Haydn, Beethoven, Stravinsky often used tunes coming from the gutter; but how they ennobled them!

The two positive qualities I find in the music of Shostakovitch are of a rather ambiguous order. The first one is his great versatility and efficiency in Conservatory training, which enables him to solve technical problems of a broad variety in a highly skillful manner. Shostakovitch is undoubtedly an excellent craftsman and most of his inventiveness goes into such branches of musical craft as orchestration and efficient part writing (what the Germans call *"guter tonsatz"*). It is not infrequent among contemporary composers that such technical strength conceals a paucity of original musical ideas.

The second quality of Shostakovitch, to foreigners so surprising, is the inherent optimism of his music. As everybody knows, the common view of Russian music and the Russian character is that they are by nature easily depressed and melancholy or just the reverse, boisterously and wildly gay—without any visible reason. This view, erroneous as it is, is well entrenched in people's minds. Thus when a composer from Russia is neither desperately melancholic nor in a state of frenzy, as in a Ballet-Russe-de-Monte-Carlo finale (with its inherent disorder), the foreigner thinks that something new has happened. No one will deny that a completely new life has been built in Russia, yet this has little to do with the national character of the people and their art, which at times in the past has been just as gay and happy and optimistic as the music of Shostakovitch. Glinka, the father of modern Russian music, Borodin, Mussorgsky, and Tchaikovsky himself have numberless pages of the happiest, lightest, gayest music the nineteenth century produced.

Thus to a Russian there would not be anything particularly surprising in the optimism of Shostakovitch. But it takes a redundant, blatant, and unconvincing form. One always feels a kind of compelling force behind it, a force of an extramusical order. It appears to be based on the official syllogistic formula: before the revolution life was desperate, therefore art was gloomy; now the revolution is victorious, therefore art must

be optimistic. It is obvious that this *must* rings like a command of the gods rather than a logical conclusion of a syllogism. The result is that it often forces the composer into a great effort unnatural to his temperament and therefore unsuccessful.

What this *must* tends to do to Russian music in general and to Shostakovitch's music in particular is lamentable. It drives the young composer to naïve and dated formulae such as an excessive and very conventional use of major triads, tunes and cadences in major keys, all of them describing the glorious and victorious events of the present in the most emphatic and banal musical language. (Minor modes are used to describe the dark and gloomy days of the past.) It steers the whole music into a verbose and brassy style which soon becomes dreary and monotonous. It produces that wooden 2/4 or 4/4 rhythm to which I have already referred, and which I suppose is considered "manlier" and "more virile" than the "effeminate" 3/4 or 6/8, and fills the thematic material with such commonplace metrical patterns as one eighth note followed by two sixteenth notes (or vice versa), which most good composers use very sparingly.

In Shostakovitch's second period all these unfortunate characteristics come to full bloom. The substance of Shostakovitch's composition now tends to be of such obvious understandability that his music ceases to be an artistic language in which the adventurous human mind discovers new laws and new problems which it endeavors to solve in a new way. Every technique, every melodic line, every development, polyphonic or monophonic, every rhythm, every formal device is reminiscent of either contemporary or nineteenth-century composers, and is used in such an obvious fashion that after a while one begins to wonder if even the most uneducated masses will not soon tire of it. (I often ask myself if this *a priori* decision, so frequent among intellectuals and politicians, that the masses have a naturally low taste for the arts, is not a proof of their own lack of discrimination.)

Simplification of music is in itself a salutary thing, but there is a moment when simplification becomes too obvious and absurd. Eclecticism is often the sturdy backbone of healthy tradition (was not Johann Sebastian Bach an eclectic to a degree?), but when it pervades a man's music or stands in the way of the invention of a personal style it becomes deplorable. Objectivity should not be confused with impersonality, just as romanticism should not necessarily involve grandiloquent sentimentality and formlessness.

Fortunately Shostakovitch possesses the saving graces of excellent craftsmanship, profound honesty, and a fervent belief in the usefulness of what he is doing. Furthermore, at times there is a graceful lyricism in his music when he forgets himself (particularly in his chamber music, which by its very nature is freer from those moral obligations that govern his long descriptive symphonies), and this natural lyricism shows us that somewhere deep behind the screen of impersonality and moral obligation there still lives an individual, a free artist, a man by the name of Dmitri Shostakovitch.

The actual significance of the case of Shostakovitch can be brought home by restating the crucial question that I asked myself in 1929 in Poland: are we going to see the rise of an eclectic collectivistic art which will put the individual at least temporarily in a completely subservient position to the state and society? Are we going to see the birth of an impersonal art written exclusively for the masses and in the fallacious belief that the masses have to be "talked down to"? For the present the music of Shostakovitch seems to answer this question in the affirmative—at any rate in so far as the music of Soviet Russia is concerned.

Is his art great? Is it unique and incomparably better than most modern music? Certainly not. There are many composers who both write better and have more to say than Shostakovitch. American and alien composers in this country have composed music which sees the concert hall less, but says infinitely more than his celebrated Seventh Symphony. Consider the scores of Piston, Copland, William Schuman, compositions by Stravinsky, Hindemith, Milhaud, Rieti—some of which are never played, because our maestros and their managers ordain otherwise.

It is these maestros and managers who are chiefly responsible for all the uproar in this country over one or two composers for one or two seasons. They have learned too well how to exploit a propitious political situation (what has become now of the "beloved" Finn, Sibelius?) and create a bubble reputation to relieve the stagnation of the concert repertory (always the same pieces of the same composers!); and they are now doing Shostakovitch immense disservice by placing him in a position in which he does not belong.

I sincerely hope that Shostakovitch has the power to undergo another complete regeneration and emerge a truly significant composer. But it is a gross misunderstanding of "collectivist" art to accept the popularity of his music now as evidence that he has found a universal formula. Soon his eclipse may come as swiftly as his leap to fame; this would be just as unfair and would indicate the same disbalance we see at present. Shostakovitch is a young man; he should develop as a solid and respected musician of the great New Russia. He does not now merit the injudicious ac-

claim he is receiving here; neither will he deserve the inevitable repudiation which will come in its wake. Both extremes are shameful evidence that contemporary music is judged indiscriminately and contemporary composers are used irresponsibly.

1943

THOMAS CRAVEN

Modernism

From MEN OF ART

THE WORLD has paid a heavy penalty for Cézanne's genius. The peasants of Aix had hardly sealed the grave of the unloved and misunderstood Master when there appeared in Paris the first of a succession of movements which, under the collective name of Modernism, have mocked the complacency of the orthodox for a quarter of a century. Practically all these movements, or more precisely, cults, have originated, directly or indirectly, from the difficulties and imperfections of the Provençal solitary. In 1906, the year of Cézanne's death, Matisse, Friesz, Braque, Van Dongen, Dufy and Vlaminck, advocating lyrical deformations of nature and the crude rhythms of savages, founded the first Modernist schism in art. They were called, in the spirit of derision, *Fauves,* or wild beasts.

In 1909, Picasso performed his first experiments with congested fractions of geometrical forms, and in the same year, his rival Braque exhibited the first ab-

stract picture. Matisse, with a sneer for his former comrade in crime, tagged the abstract notations with a word of contempt—*Cubism*—and another school was born. Two Americans resident in Paris, Russell and Wright, developing the color-form procedure of Cézanne into an art purporting to combine the properties of architecture and symphonic music, celebrated their day of glory under the banner of Synchronism. Then came Futurism, Orphism, Expressionism, Vorticism, Purism, and a dozen others equally sonorous and Latin. The rivalry was absurdly acrimonious; the distinctions between the sects immaterial. And finally, as a fitting climax to all this school-founding and sciolism, a group of cynical renegades with nothing better to do, contrived, by a campaign of ingenious parody, to burlesque Modernism to death. This flurry which Maurice Raynal wittily described as "sticking a moustache on the smile of Mona Lisa," was called Dada-ism.

During the winter of 1913, the new, or Modernist art, was officially introduced to the American public. The exhibition was adroitly advertised, and a unique furore arose. One picture, a typical specimen of French Cubism provocatively labelled *Nude Descending a Staircase,* sped the issue from aesthetic circles into the field of popular ridicule, and for a moment the new, or immigrant art, loomed on our eastern coast-line as a national menace, a Bolshevik spectre threatening our sacred insularity. Most of us remember those vociferous and ill-mannered times: the orgies of indignation, the bravado of nondescript painters intoxicated with publicity, the protests of dealers and antiquarians, and the piteous bleat of academic retainers trembling for the security of their little jobs. But to some of us it seemed that a new era was beginning. The spirit of art was alive again, and under the stress of French ideas an exhilarating burst of vitality began to sparkle in our musty showrooms. Galleries dedicated to the children of Cézanne were subsidized; French libraries interpreting the Modernist gospel of St. Luke were imported; an exclusively American exhibition, the pictures of which were certified by five experts, added authority to the surging scandal; eccentric magazines containing ferocious manifestoes and infantile illustrations sprang up overnight; and Greenwich Village emerged as the American Bohemia of the new order.

It was easy in those days to be hopeful, to prophesy, if not a renaissance, at least an efflorescence of native genius such as had never before occurred in the Western Hemisphere. But since that memorable uprising of 1913 something has happened. The sensational issues are dead and buried; the lust for battle has dwindled into an ignoble truce with the Academy; the creative stream has run dry; and Modernists, at home and abroad, are wearily sifting and resifting its barren deposits. Let us look into the matter.

First, let us keep in mind the source of the new and militant cults. With the single exception of Futurism, every one of them came out of Paris where art, like professionalized vice, flourishes parasitically in a segregated quarter; where painting is a proliferation of styles and techniques; where any clever schemer with a new bag of tricks may get a following among the café-philosophers. There was some charlatanism in the movements but not a great deal: the majority of painters were sincere men consumed with the desire to be original at any price. Had they been impostors they could never have grown hysterical and blood-thirsty over such childish things. At this point I must correct the common impression that the Modernists had never learned to draw, that is, to draw according to the precepts of the Academy, and that they resorted to subterfuges and preposterous distortions to conceal organic deficiencies in draughtsmanship. Some were prize-winners at the art schools; others respectable teachers; almost all of them had passed through what was known as the "sound training of the best French tradition." It was because of this meaningless training that they repudiated the Academy. They were sick of Impressionism, sick of salon frivolity—of naturalism in all its forms. Painting was either a spiritual force, or it was nothing. They found their redeemer in Cézanne, directly or through his missionaries Van Gogh and Gauguin, and the new movement was on.

Van Gogh is one of the tragic figures of modern art. His fanatic enthusiasms, his ungovernable debauches of the spirit and the flesh alike, and his abnormal sensitivity drove him to violent insanity and in the end to suicide. Seven times he tried to save himself—by religion, love, and art—and in each trial his excesses, often repulsive and always pathetic, would have destroyed a man of lesser faith. It would be difficult to name an artist whose life exhibits a more complete and impassioned surrender to the torments of the spirit. Others—Leonardo da Vinci, Rembrandt and Cézanne—have yielded as intensely to the creative impulse and have produced a far more profound and influential art; but for the parallel of this mad Dutchman in religious ecstasy and self-sacrifice we must turn back to the audacious convictions of St. Francis. His faith in humanity was simply incredible. Alone among Modernists he believed in the indivisible union of art and religion, and in his fierce internal conflicts sought to reconcile his visions with the hard realities of life, and to find in painting a universal language for the regeneration of mankind. We may say that he was only a lunatic reaching for the unattainable, but let us not forget that he was, despite his obvious and deplorable limitations, extraordinarily open-minded, generous and consistent; that he had the courage to face the world honestly; and that his ideas, when put into practice, brought forth canvases of alarming vitality and convincing spiritual truth.

Van Gogh studied Delacroix, Millet, Monticelli, and Japanese prints; his twisted serpentine brush-strokes were derived from Impressionism; but it was from Cézanne that he learned to press nature into the service of his own agitated feelings. While he was essentially a religious painter, he did not make the mistake of trying to paint ecclesiastical subjects. His convictions were not of that sort, and with the best of critical sense he pointed out the falseness of Gauguin's absurd *Crucifixion*. He desired, like Rembrandt, to approach the common things of life with complete spiritual freedom. But his intellectual powers were short-lived and he was incapable of self-discipline. His contacts with nature, indeed with such ordinary things as a postman, a cluster of sunflowers, or a row of cypresses, threw him into a state of frenzy amounting almost to hallucinations. To convey the dramatic force of those terrible contacts he used a symbolical language of his own invention—smiting colors, accentuated contours, forms flattened into violent silhouettes, distorted forms writhing in pain, the pain of his own soul. If his conception of nature and humanity is that of a disordered mind, it is, nevertheless, the most vivid and trenchant conception in Modernist painting. But his art, I fear, is more singular than enduring. It is too remote from normal experiences to influence the world and too dependent upon the excitement of curious sensations to be useful to students. So far, it has proved to be most useful to the dealers. During his lifetime Van Gogh sold four pictures, one for 400 francs, the highest price. Recently one of his canvases went for the record-breaking sum of $85,000.

Gauguin brought the exotic element into Modernist painting. He was an odd compound of the artist and charlatan, of the gypsy and the Parisian *épateur*. Beneath his cruel cynicism lay a vein of brackish sentimentality which, congealing into a savage loathing of humanity, made him sinister and detestable wherever he wandered. A successful stock-broker, he renounced business for painting, took French leave of his wife and children, sailed to Martinique and later to Tahiti where he married a Negress. Though he made a grand show of his hatred of "the disease of civilization," his reversion to primitive nakedness was only half-genuine. He was always grumbling for money, always thinking of the effect of his calculated savagery on the effete society of Paris. Returning to Paris for an exhibition of his painting and failing to take the town by storm, he sailed off to the South Seas again and died in the Marquesas in circumstances of unspeakable wretchedness. It is significant that his last painting was a snow scene of the country he had forsaken but could not forget.

He was a man of diversified talents—boxer, fencer, sailor, painter, sculptor, and poet. But it was his sensational subject-matter that won him notoriety. Cunningly he adapted the surface characteristics of Cézanne's art—the planes and distortions—to tropical settings and figures where they seemed to be peculiarly appropriate. The planes expanded into areas of brilliant color, the distortions appeared to be the natural shapes of negroid figures. Thus his pictures, resembling the flat textile patterns of primitive craftsmen, were received as the genuine expression of the barbaric soul, and not the sophisticated borrowings of a malcontent. Cézanne, however, was not taken in. "Gauguin," he said, "has only turned out fantastic figures. He has stolen my little sensation and carted it round in every tramp steamer." Gauguin's exotic magnetism has about run its course. He attracts only the lazy-minded who are tired of life and turn to art for soothing relief, or defeated painters who wander to strange places because there is nothing at home worth painting.

Matisse, the old chief of the Wild Beasts, entered Modernism through the influences of Cézanne and Van Gogh. To these influences he added his own phenomenal sense of color and his gleanings from the study of Negro sculpture and the Asiatic decorators. His aim was a decorative style comparable to that of the orientals, clean flat design in which he carried the means of expression to the irreducible minimum, throwing aside the representational baggage which he believed had stifled the creative impulse in European art. His early pictures, at first glance, seem to be only spontaneous sketches; actually, they are built on the premises of logic. For example, he would destroy the proportions of any one of his forms, say the human figure, for the sake of the linear balance of the whole picture, distorting the contour of the hip or limbs into an enormous curve to offset the opposing curve of another form. This process, while unquestionably producing a balanced ensemble, was not without its ridiculous aspects, and eventually he abandoned it for a more seemly approximation of natural contours.

Everything that Matisse touches bears the imprint of ease and joy, the enthusiasm which springs from health and conviction, the direct contact with the living model and the greatest fluency in expressing that contact. By transferring the ingredients of genre-painting to the field of decoration, he has created an original style of art, a style in which the relations of the parts are determined by the artist's sense of free rhythm as distinguished from the geometrical symmetry of conventional arabesques. He converts the charm of fruits, flowers and buoyant nudes into silhouettes which, adhering to the everyday character of the model, suggest the liveliness and simplicity of ancient book illuminations. Design of this sort is not the result of the analysis and organization of planes, as in the case of Cézanne, but of the ready shifting of the proportions of silhouettes—of rendering nature in terms of flat pattern. The bulge of a woman's back or hips is expanded or shortened to meet the exigencies of a given space; the natural aspect of a scene—landscape or interior—is not materially altered but skilfully distributed in the interest of a balanced whole. By this method the spontaneity of direct experience is preserved. There is no grim transformation of nature to serve an ideal purpose, no depth of imagination, nothing dramatic—only the joyous responses to nature arranged with exquisite taste. In brief, *le monde visible* of Gautier presented in decorative style.

Matisse's reputation has suffered from his own errors in scale and from the exaggerated claims of his admirers. Having only a faint imagination, he is most impressive in small canvases, but fancying himself a mural designer, he magnifies his still-life patterns and his leaping nudes into large things which dissipate his charm and expose the poverty of his invention as well as the fragility of his bodiless forms. Like Whistler he deals in minor harmonies and subtle arrangements where taste and tact take the place of creative vigor and knowledge. With him Modernism begins to turn back from the strength and substance of Cézanne into the old French tradition of boudoir hangings. He is essentially a light talent, an ornamentalist whose designs are more applicable to silks, cretonnes and ceramics than to pictorial space. His nimble figures are closer to the sprightly nudes of *La Vie Parisienne* than his infatuated followers have ever suspected.

The most famous of the Modernists is that astonishing Spaniard, Picasso, the mainspring, if not the actual founder, of Cubism. Picasso's prominence, however, rests upon his influence, not upon his artistic achievements. If, at any step in his career, he has painted a picture that is more than an experiment, more than an exercise in technical ingenuity, I do not know where he has hidden it. For cleverness alone art has reared no workman more prodigious, but his inventiveness, I submit, would have been more useful in the field of mechanics. By his early contrivances in blue and rose, by his Cubism, his sculpturesque nudes, and his late super-realistic horrors, he has demonstrated that a picture may be perfectly composed, in the narrow or mechanical sense, and yet contain no meaning, and contain no emotional stimulus beyond the temporary shock of surprise or deprecation. He has proved that one cannot create an art by subjecting facts to the tyranny of processes; that true composition is not an extrinsic equation evolved from the styles of others but the final form, the personal tone and order assumed by materials experienced at first-hand. He has attempted to make art out of other art—an academic business; his work is a series of abstractions from the art of his rivals and predecessors. His eclectic searchings are endless: he has imitated Steinlen, Toulouse-Lautrec, Negro sculpture, Cézanne, Van Gogh, Gauguin, the archaic Greeks, El Greco, Ingres and Corot. His paintings are detached studio inventions, laboratory performances destitute of human relationships and all relationships save those pertaining to the sources he has plundered. Picasso is generally credited with having a mighty intellect. I find no evidence to support this opinion. Mighty intellects do not exhaust themselves playing with trifles.

There is nothing mysterious in a cube or a cone; nor is there anything mysterious in Cubism if taken for what it is—an experiment in structure. All artists, the classic especially, have considered the geometrical formation of objects—that is part of their equipment—and in the studies of Uccello and Dürer, we may discover analyses of structure antedating by centuries the Modernist examples. But Cubism, as a distinct school of painting, owes its origin to Cézanne whose forms were composed of colored planes, one defined against the other. Picasso, in his first phase, enlarged upon the planes and changed the contrasting colors into simple areas of light and dark. This process, carried further, abstracted an object into its nearest geometrical equivalent; that is, a human head, though still recognizable as a head, was reduced to an assemblage of geometrical fractions. In his second phase, Picasso split the head into sections and then arbitrarily shuffled the sections together again so as to bring into a single focus aspects observed from several points of view. Or, as his satellites glibly put it, "moving round an object, he seized several successive appearances which, when fused into a single image, reconstituted it in time." The head is now only an eye, a nose and an ear scattered among a splintered wreckage. In its last phase Cubism paradoxically went flat. The three visible planes of the cube, by a gradual process of extension, were projected beyond the limits of vision—to the frame of the canvas—ceasing to function as indications of solidity and becoming automatically three flat tones. The head, needless to say, disappeared. Representation was annihilated. Art at last was pure, perfect, abstract, absolute—and intolerable.

There is nothing unreasonable in Cubism, and there would have been nothing sensational in it had painters kept their experiments in their studios instead of offering them to the world as the loftiest manifestations of the human soul in a state of ecstasy. The contagion spread for several reasons. It was the strongest possible reaction against the stupidities of Impressionism, the diametrical opposite of imitation; it attacked conventional painting in the most combative terms, and its radicalism, being non-representational, was a tonic to young minds surfeited with the Academy; it was a legitimate effort to increase the reality of objects by emphasizing structure and excluding sentimental attachments. But here the good in the movement ends. It was a transitional measure; like Pragmatism, a method and not a philosophy. To argue that it was an independent growth, an art complete in itself, is frankly absurd; and Picasso's defense of his cubes on this ground is obvious rationalization.

Cubism erroneously presupposes that design is an end and not a means, and that all human attributes are irrelevant. It limits the meaning of art to the perception of the abstract relations of the various parts, and shrouds simple processes in an element of mystery by using such awful terminology as "plastic dynamism," "the integration of the plastic consciousness," "the quality of the form is the incommensurable sum of the affinities perceived between the visible manifestations and the tendency of the mind." It postulates the idea that geometrical parts of design—a cube or a triangle—can be identified with specific factors in our psychic life—an idea that has no foundation in experience. Cubism is the apotheosis of structure. It strips objects of all the features and characteristics with which the emotional life is inseparably connected, leaving only the denuded concepts of the physicist and mathematician.

All art, to be sure, implies a certain amount of selection—one cannot include everything—but normally the purpose of selection is to set down one's experiences in forms objectively valuable. Such is its biological function—a means to an end. Why then should the Cubists carry the process to its second stage, to abstract the primary selection until nothing remains but dry bones? The answer is that they have no experiences worth communicating, or in plainer speech, nothing to say. Without a teleological basis, art, if sufficiently pursued, leads to insanity. When the means, let us say, of sexual gratification are withdrawn from actual experience, the victim wanders in a world of fantasies and ineffectual visions; when art is removed from experience and intelligible meaning, the deluded painter begins to read arbitrary and subjective values into his work, denies objective achievement, and in the end suffers a complete drying-up of creative energy.

The last of the shockers was Futurism, a cult manufactured in Italy and launched into Paris amid the beating of drums and the dodging of vegetables. On its practical side it borrowed from Cubism the idea of trying to illustrate simultaneous aspects of movement; theoretically it was a derivative of Croce's *Expressionism*. It had propaganda to offer and was bent on driving it home in the most sensational modern style. The argument of its manifesto was as follows. "The language of the old art is dead. We have a new and more exciting idiom, a set of personal symbols composed of anything and everything.

We will translate into graphic form live states of the soul; we will jerk your sensibilities into the most acute responses. Without shocking emblems of brilliant color and free line we will make you feel art against your will." The argument captivated beginners and defeated professionals: to break with the past, to abolish tradition, to step out like a child into a world of freedom, to invest life with fresh symbols, to feel and to express—thus to create art. Everything was art so long as it was inspired by true feeling.

The influence of Futurism has been of a cryptic nature. As a school it is extinct, having been absorbed by *Expressionism,* a movement which has played havoc among all the arts. Like the other sects, *Expressionism* has flaunted a far-fetched aesthetic, but at bottom it professes a fairly simple creed: "Our contacts with nature—the facts of the visible world—for creative purposes are more important than any amount of learning or traditional knowledge. Given a genuine insight into the world of everyday experience, it is possible for the artist to dispense with all old forms and to create directly, trusting to the pull of such impulses as follow his sensations. Working thus, new forms are inevitable. The burden of dead learning which stultifies academic production is overthrown by an earnest and truthful expression of experience." Again we have "the purity of direct sensation" —the happy notion that "true feeling makes true art"—the Expressionist slogan which has become the painter's panacea and his silencing answer to the inquiring laymen. This notion lends authority to that brand of self-satisfaction which parades as genius; it allows for every imaginable kind of stupidity, and lack of knowledge; and raises the scratches of freaks and incompetents into the ranks of the masters. Hence its popularity. But, like many of the ideas of faith-healers, it holds a grain of truth. It states positively that the artist must have a natural and not a forced interest in his subjects, and rules out of court all virtuosity and academic precedent.

Expressionist theory ignores the fact that individuality develops through convention and the heritage of accumulated knowledge, and that unless we pass our lives totally isolated from a social milieu —which would result in savage ignorance—we are obliged to see, feel, and act on the basis of established conduct. Our mental habits, on the whole, are conventional, and we are permitted to see and construct only through and by the corpus of these conventions. What is called originality is but a slight addition to the mass of accepted and habitual opinions composing the ego. Hear Havelock Ellis on this point: "The self that he thus expresses is a bundle of inherited tendencies that came the man himself can never entirely know whence."

Such, in brief, are the principal divisions of the Modernist revolt. In retrospect, the movement does not seem to be so revolutionary after all, and now that the excitement has subsided, we may wonder what it was that caused so much controversy. It appears that the good in the movement is no different from the good in the schools of the past, a fact witnessed by virtually all Modernist painters who have never missed an opportunity to link their work with the most ancient traditions and to establish their affinity with the Old Masters. The controversy arose from the pretentious claims of the artists and their backers and from the sensational methods of exploitation.

The Modernists were men of the strongest anti-social propensities. They took pride in their aloofness and gloried in their refusal to traffic in bourgeois sentiments and vulgar emotions. "To hell with the public!" they cried. "There is no such thing as popular art! The public has always demanded trash and we will leave that to the academicians!" But these aristocrats of art, these aesthetic thoroughbreds, were not wholly above commerce with the rabble: they employed the most extraordinary tactics in order to persuade, cajole, and bully the public into buying their pictures. In such an atmosphere art turns inward, feeds upon itself, takes refuge in abstractions. It was only natural that men living in a little world of metaphysical disputations should have produced an art divorced from its human context; it was to be expected that the defence of this art should be the hopeless effort to separate social, moral and sentimental activities from what was snobbishly labelled "pure aesthetics." This critical attitude, propped up by the tenets of an unstable psychology, sprang from two bases, the scientific and the emotional, but the machinery involved was identical.

It consisted in restricting the significant factors in the production and appreciation of art to those whose understanding rested upon special training or unusual experience. Thus technique, essentially a matter for painters and a few specialists, became the whole of art, a field completely isolated from vulgar understanding. Into this exclusive field the thoroughbreds dragged the values belonging to the profoundest art and annexed them to minor technical issues.

Furthermore, by describing technical problems in the terms of physiological mechanics and psychology, painters made the simplest processes enormously impressive. The "purification of painting" was the fine name given to this dehumanizing tendency, and to be looked upon as in the know, one was forced to subscribe to the high-sounding chatter about abstraction, empathy, significant form, dynamic relationships, and so forth.

The purification of painting! An enchanting fallacy indeed! "Pure beauty," as Winckelmann said long ago, "is like pure water—it has no taste." Yet this tasteless art multiplied by leaps and bounds. The various purity cults founded on the technique of line and color organization raised mediocrity to a glorious eminence and provided the initiate with the regalia for personal distinction. Poor old Cézanne's little sensation was father to a thousand perversions. To be "highly sensitive" in the esoteric fashion was the supreme honor, and any painter ingenious enough to erect a precious mythology round a few lines, or daubs of color, was assured of enviable notoriety. A tangle of lines, a swirl of tones, and he had produced a subjective cryptogram entitled *Psychic Portrait, Symphony in Blue-Green,* or *Centripetal Force.* Every little technical operation, every shade and detail, was magnified to epochal proportions. He was willing to die to make a table cloth pictorially interesting, willing to sacrifice his life to a pattern of spots and curves, the sole value of which lay in its "abstract beauty"—a theme for the humorist. He was so self-contained that he esteemed man as less valuable than a bowl of fruit or a congestion of cubes. The growth of humanity did not concern him—he was painting the growth of abstractions or the soul of pots and pans. Eventually he talked more about himself and his strange soul-states than about his art, and consulted the Freudian doctors to ascertain the full import of the psychic orgasms aroused within him by a piece of still-life.

Increasing in purity, painting shrank proportionately in human values until, at last, it appealed to a few souls divinely endowed with the "aesthetic emotion." This emotion by means of which one responds purely to art, that is, to its abstract harmonics, has been regarded with suspicion by eminent investigators unable to separate it from other emotions and unable to admit that man, being what he is, a gross bundle of appetites, memories and experiences all bound together into a single receiving system, can react purely to any stimulus. But the suspicion, I believe, is ill-founded. The aesthetic emotion is the unique property of those who love only art and not life; whose receptive apparatus, through disuse, has so shrivelled that it is no longer capable of responding to anything but abstractions. Painters possessing this peculiar emotion are really convinced that they have symbolized the grace of the human body, and the dynamic power and movement of modern machines, by abstract combinations of lines and masses bearing no discoverable relation to the objects in question. They maintain that an abstract art is the reflex of a machine age, and that its technique is the organic expression of the scientific trend of the times, a theory echoed by many writers. It happens, however, that the Modernists, by their own confession, are aggressively hostile to our machine age, and that they live as far from it as possible, preferably in the more romantic quarters of Paris. In the ways of contemporary civilization, they are poorly educated, and their pseudo-scientific technique is an arbitrary method deduced from Cézanne, a Provençal recluse for whom the machine age never existed.

Yet, making allowances for all that is excrescential in Modernism, I find the movement vastly more interesting than its sworn enemy, the official art of France. Even in its slightest activities —the child's play of the customs-house officer Rousseau, the consumptive art of Modigliani and the smartness of Dufy— there are evidences of creative ability— of a personality moulding materials into new and arresting forms instead of faithfully recording the dimensions and visual appearances of nature. On certain departments of the crafts—costume-designing, weaving, print-cloths, pottery and kitchen wares—the influence of Modernism has been gay and beneficial; on the wholesale decoration of interiors its effect has been abominable, largely because the Cubist designers, ignoring the animal and spiritual needs of man, have imposed an eccentric pictorial formula upon utilitarian objects. What the movement will lead to I do not know. In France the more intelligent men, following the example of Lhote, are gradually returning to representational art; the others, professing to symbolize sub-conscious nightmares by indecipherable diagrams which they call *Super-Realism,* are beyond redemption. Matisse, growing old, turns out pretty sentiments for the American trade; and Picasso, to judge by his prize-winning exhibit at the Carnegie Institute, is a candidate for the Academy. The present condition of French painting is not one to make the heart rejoice. There is more hope in North America.

1934

VI. . .

REVIEW

EDWARD M. BRECHER

The Book America Wrote

"WHEN we Americans get through with the English language," remarked the celebrated stove-league philosopher Mr. Dooley, "it'll look like it was run over by a musical comedy."

Mr. Dooley was mistaken. We Americans have been manhandling the King's English for more than three centuries, yet it now looks better than ever. American ingenuity and disrespect for hidebound tradition have immeasurably enriched our common tongue. If you doubt it, look at the evidence for yourself.

You'll find all the evidence you want, laid out in alphabetical order, from *abalone* and *absquatulate* through *guyasticutus* and *pixilated* to *wunk* and *Zu-zu,* in a mammoth new work formally titled "A Dictionary of American English on Historical Principles" *—but promptly nicknamed, in good American fashion, the D. A. E. Designed to prove that our American language has beauty, dignity, and precision as well as the musical-comedy touch Mr. Dooley noted, the D. A. E. refutes all charges that American English is a corrupt jargon.

Scholars at the University of Chicago and elsewhere have been at work on the D. A. E. since 1925. So far they have published ten of a proposed twenty parts, surveying the American language from *A* through *Honk*. They expect to reach the end of the alphabet late in 1942.

The D. A. E. is almost wholly unlike the book you use to check pronunciations, definitions, and spellings. You'll find few pronunciation marks in the D. A. E., and some stumblers which the editors frankly confess they do not know how to define. As for spellings, you'll find so many variations you will conclude that the editors, like Mark Twain, have no use for a man who only knows one way to spell a word.

In place of the usual dictionary contents, you will find quotations—thick gobs of quotations illustrating the part each word has played in American life. Instead, for example, of merely defining *democratic* as meaning "of or pertaining to democracy," the D. A. E. quotes the earliest recorded use of the word in this country, from the Rhode Island *Colonial Record* for the year 1647:

It is agreed . . . that the forme of Government established in Providence Plantations is *Democraticall;* that is to say, a Government held by ye free and voluntarie consent of all, or the greater parte of the free Inhabitants.

By amassing more than 1,000,000 quotations like these from every conceivable American source, and selecting the best of them for publication, the editors of the D. A. E. have made it possible to reconstruct the life history of American words, and of the things to which the words refer. Under *Conestoga wagon,*

Reprinted from the *Saturday Review of Literature,* November 23, 1940, by permission of the author.
* *Compiled at the University of Chicago under the editorship of Sir William A. Craigie and James R. Hulbert.*

for example, you will find quotations describing how those broad-wheeled *prairie schooners* were built in the Conestoga Valley of Pennsylvania; how they first hauled farm produce to Philadelphia and later ventured far into the West; how in later years they became peddlers' wagons from which Conestoga cigars, now called *stogies,* were hawked.

Like a good novel, the D. A. E. starts off with a bang. Here is the very first quotation, illustrating the letter *A* and taken from the Maine *Province and Court Record* for the year 1651:

It is ordered that Miss Batcheller for her adultery shall . . . be branded with the letter *A.*

Clearly New England was no place to commit adultery. Actual branding passed, but in 1837 Nathaniel Hawthorne was writing in the Salem (Mass.) *Gazette* how astonished he was to find "a young woman . . . whose doom it was to wear the letter A on the breast of her gown . . . so that the capital A might have been thought to mean Admirable, or any thing rather than Adultress." The theme haunted Hawthorne for many years, until in 1850 he published his best-selling novel *The Scarlet Letter.*

Creation of an American language, the D. A. E. discloses, began as soon as the Mayflower reached Plymouth. Among the first problems which the Pilgrims faced was the parcelling out of land in the first American subdivision. They decided to cast lots for the choice pieces of ground. Thus a man's ground became his *lot.* Most Englishmen will still look puzzled if you say: "I've just bought a couple of lots on Main Street." But Miles Standish or William Bradford would have had a pretty clear notion of what you meant.

Each part of the country similarly added to our common store of words. Pioneers picked up Indian words like wigwam, moccasin, and papoose from a hundred tribes, French words along the Canadian border and in Louisiana, Spanish words in Florida and the Southwest. By degrees these words were carried throughout the land, so that today you can hear in Maine or Minnesota many words which have migrated all the way from Mexico—*bonanza, ranch, siesta, tornado,* and *vigilante,* to name a few. Others journeyed still further—*barbecue* and *hammock* from Haiti, *chinchilla* and *tapioca* from South America. Still other words got into the American language from nowhere; like Topsy, they just grew. Witness *guyasticutus.*

The guyasticutus was—or is, for all we know—the most ferocious, rambunctious, man-eating wild animal ever exhibited under canvas to gullible Americans. For only ten cents, ladeez and gentlemen, a tenth part of a dollar, you can come into the tent and see with your own eyes this horrendous beast which consumes forty-eleven men, women, and tender babes-in-arms at a gulp, then bellows for forty-eleven more.

No one except its proprietor, alas, has ever actually seen the guyasticutus. For just when the crowd around the entrance has bought the last ticket, the proprietor rushes out of the tent and roars, "Run for your lives, ladeez and gentlemen! Escape before you are swallowed alive! *The guyasticutus has busted loose!*"

The late Professor George Philip Krapp of Columbia University collected many such animals, not found in any zoo. A sort of lexicographical Frank

Buck, Professor Krapp penetrated the densest jungles of American prose and brought back, though not alive, rare specimens of the *kickle-snifter,* which lives in old men's beards and circular lakes; the snowshoe-hooved *swamp gahoon;* the *joint snake,* which separates itself into many segments when you chase it, and reassembles itself after the danger is past; and the *prock,* or *side-winder,* or *side-hill badger,* whose legs are shorter on one side than on the other, enabling it to browse comfortably on the steepest mountain-sides. The *prock* is captured by driving it down-hill to a level spot, where its peculiar anatomy causes it to run around in circles until lassoed. Professor Krapp even succeeded in corraling the elusive *wunk,* a mole-like creature which baffles pursuers by pulling its hole in after it. Some of these beasts, now as extinct as the passenger pigeon, are preserved in the D. A. E. to show that when it comes to concocting animals, Americans are as ingenious as Nature herself.

Each episode in American history gave us an opportunity to show our verbal resourcefulness. The discovery of gold in California, for example, produced the phrases *gold rush* and *things panned out swell. Forty-niners* has been traced back as far as 1856.

Collecting quotations has kept a large staff busy for 15 years. In charge of the work is Sir William Alexander Craigie, a short, bearded Scotsman with gold-rimmed spectacles and an Ascot cravat, as scholarly in appearance as in reputation. Sir William won his academic spurs by editing a "Dictionary of the Older Scottish Tongue from the Twelfth Century to the End of the Seventeenth." He was knighted for bringing to successful completion the monumental "Oxford English Dictionary," by far the greatest dictionary of all time in any language.

Many Americans had suggested an American dictionary of the historical type, but it was the Scotch scholar who aroused sufficient enthusiasm to get the project launched, under the auspices of the University of Chicago, and with financial aid from the Rockefeller-endowed General Education Board.

The appointment of a foreigner to edit an American dictionary was not too well received by those who did not know Sir William. The Chicago *Tribune* greeted him with a headline which puzzled even the learned Oxonian:

MIDWAY SIGNS
LIMEY PROF TO
DOPE YANK TALK

Sir William's colleagues explained to him that Little Egypt had danced on Chicago's Midway during the World's Fair of 1893; thereafter amusement areas elsewhere were called midways. In Chicago, however, Midway became Chicagoese for the University which grew up on the site.

From the beginning Sir William and his American colleagues agreed that the D. A. E. was not to be a dictionary of American slang. Slang words are included only if they became established before 1875. A phrase like *holding the bag* qualifies easily; Thomas Jefferson used it in 1801.

The D. A. E. editors place major emphasis on "those features by which the English of the American colonies and the United States is distinguished from that of England and the rest of the English-speaking world." However, they have included not merely words of American origin but also "every word which has a real connection with the development of the country and the history of its people."

Preparing such a dictionary is a Herculean labor. Scores of readers must scan tens of thousands of American books, magazines, newspapers, and official records. Promising quotations are copied out on slips of paper, together with the source, page, and date. Slips are sent in from all over the country. They are checked for accuracy, sorted in alphabetical order under their keywords, and filed in cubby-holes. A careful count of slips so far collected would take at least a year—but the editors are confident that they have long since passed the million mark. When he launched the project, Sir William had estimated that 100,000 would be sufficient.

Since Sir William's return to England in 1936, Prof. James R. Hulbert has carried on, but transatlantic clippers carry final proof to the learned Scotsman for review and revision.

Amateur researchers everywhere have aided the regular D. A. E. staff by reading rare American works. Professors at many universities have set their graduate students to work, and have pitched in themselves. A New York civil engineer whose hobby is Americanisms kept himself and his office staff busy throughout the depression spotting rare quotations. The National Youth Administration helped.

A Boston amateur, the late Charles W. Ernst, made important contributions. Ernst had a phenomenal photographic memory which enabled him to call back to mind a visual image of any page he had ever read. If you asked him about such a word as *pixilated*—a word most Americans now believe was coined by a Hollywood gag-writer in 1936 to describe Gary Cooper in "Mr.

Deeds Goes to Town"—Ernst would be likely to reply:

"That word has long been used among the fishermen of Marblehead, Mass., I believe. I seem to recall having seen it in print not so many years ago. You might look on page 56 of the 1887 edition of a novel called "Agnes Surriage"—about the middle of the next-to-the-last line of the left-hand page, if my memory doesn't fail me."

Sure enough, that's where you'll find *pixilated*.

Ernst died in 1925; his bulging notebooks now rest in Harvard's Widener Library. Their contents have been repeatedly consulted in preparing the D. A. E.

"The Congressional Record" is one of the most fertile sources of Americanisms. Novels, especially those written in dialect, yield many gems. Frontier newspapers are a happy hunting ground for pioneer material. Among the lushest sources are the books by Mark Twain.

Two scholars who have counted the Americanisms in Twain's voluminous works state that there are more than 12,000 of them, and that Twain was the earliest user of 4342. He used *whoopee* half a century before Walter Winchell re-introduced it, and gave currency to such poker-game phrases as *passing the buck, four-flushing, sitting pretty,* and *new deal.* General Sherman wrote in 1863: "Charleston is not taken, the war is prolonged, and but little chance of its ending until we have a *new deal.*"

For many of Mark Twain's Americanisms his wife deserves part of the credit. Mrs. Clemens permitted no swearing in her home or in her husband's books, so that Sam was reduced from cursing to cussing. Among the Americanisms engendered by Mrs.

Clemens's taboos were *all-fired, Caesar's ghost, Great Guns, Hail Columbia, dad-blame it, dog-gone it, suffering Moses,* and a host of others. The prudery of a still earlier generation of American females gave us *light meat* and *dark meat* to get around mentioning the *breast* of a chicken; and *first and second joints* are so called, to the bafflement of English visitors, because for many years *legs,* even chicken legs, could not be mentioned in polite society.

When writers explain the words they use, dictionary compilers have an easy time. Often, however, words are used in a way which gives no clue to their meaning; the result is a headache for the D. A. E. editors. Witness *none-so-pretties.*

An advertisement in the Newport (R. I.) *Mercury* for March 17, 1759, announced that Jacob Richardson was having a sale at his store on certain articles called none-so-pretties. Half a century later the journal of the Lewis and Clark expedition recorded that those doughty explorers were taking with them ten none-so-pretties for trading with the Indians. But no one bothered to jot down just what a none-so-pretty was. The D. A. E. editors first guessed that none-so-pretties were "an article of haberdashery," now define them tentatively as "a kind of tape." Readers with more precise information on none-so-pretties are invited to write in. The same goes for those who can identify the *Nicholites,* a group of Southern Baptists. Just who were the Nicholites, what did they believe, and how did they come by their name?

The problem of *ash-gum* has been solved.

Dr. Mitford Mathews, brought up in a district of Alabama where many pioneer customs and folkways still survive, ended a lively debate among D. A. E. scholars. Professor Mathews's aunt, like many others, stored her ashes for soap-making in the hollowed-out trunk of a gum tree, and called it her *ash-gum.* That is how you will find *ash-gum* defined in the D. A. E.

The D. A. E. has many uses. When Metro-Goldwyn-Mayer was filming "Gone with the Wind," the question arose: Did youngsters shoot craps in New Orleans before the Civil War? In 1843, according to the D. A. E., a man named Green had written:

The Game of Craps . . . is a game lately introduced into New Orleans, and is fully equal to faro in its . . . ruinous effects.

Impressed, M-G-M purchased a D. A. E. of its own. So typically American a word as *baseball,* however, was not invented here at all; Jane Austen used it in "Northanger Abbey" half a century before its first American appearance.

By the time the D. A. E. is completed late in 1942, it will be almost time to start over again. For while the lexicographers have been surveying our language, we ordinary Americans have been busy concocting more of it. Prohibition, the boom, the depression, and now the European war have been steadily enlarging American English; the dictionary compilers will be hard pressed to catch up. A Spanish general invented *fifth column.* Nazi Germany has given us *totalitarian* and *Blitzkrieg.* Attempts have been made to popularize a new name for traitors, *quislings,* and a new verb for treachery, *to quisle,* derived from the name of Vidkun Quisling, Norway's Benedict Arnold.

Grand-daddy among words for spy or traitor, however, is *cowboy.* This was not originally a Western word;

before the days of dude ranches most cattle-herders thought of themselves as *cow-punchers,* or *cowhands,* or *buck-aroos* (from the Spanish *vaqueros*). The word *cowboy* was in fact an Eastern word, used to describe George III's fifth column in the American colonies. The cowboys of those days were Tory sympathizers who wandered through the woods at night ringing cowbells. Unsuspecting American patriots, hearing the tinkle, sallied forth with lanterns in search of the straying Bossies and Bessies supposedly attached to the bells, and were promptly Blitzkrieged by enemy blunderbusses.

Words, like hats, readily succumb to changes in style. They become obsolete through the invention of newer and more stylish successors. Take the many words our ancestors used to describe a hurried departure. Our great-grandfathers *absquatulated,* as in the sentence: "I absquatulated away from that vicinity in a hurry, you can bet your bottom dollar." Our grandfathers *skedaddled* or *skidooed*. Many of us in our younger days *vamoosed*. Youngsters today simply *scram*.

Absquatulate, incidentally, illustrates our American ability to spell a word in more ways than one. With comparatively solemn faces, the D. A. E. editors list *absquatilate, absquatelate, absquotulate, absquatilize,* and *absquattle,* as in this sentence dated 1848: "Let's likker one more round and then absquattle."

Such obscure words, however, do not constitute the bulk of the D. A. E.'s contents. Many of our commonest words are also Americanisms. As Dr. Mathews has pointed out, when you get up from your *rocking chair,* button your *vest,* put on your *rubbers,* dash for the *elevator,* reach the *sidewalk,* and make a *bee-line* for the automobile which you carelessly *parked* in front of a *hydrant* when you came *downtown,* you are using words of American origin all along the way.

1940

MORTON DAUWEN ZABEL

Sandburg's Testament

A review of *The People, Yes* by Carl Sandburg

THE HARDEST part of being a pioneer comes in remaining a contemporary. This is particularly true in modern poetry, where the average life of a "generation" is five years and where the trail-blazing novelty of the pioneers of twenty-five years ago was so exaggerated by public clamor that within a short time they became as much victimized by critical suspicion and boredom as they had once been by the swollen claims of admiring patriots. To pick up any history or anthology of contemporary verse is to be depressed by the high rate of mortality among poetic reputations. No aid is lacking—from

Reprinted from *Poetry* for October, 1936, by permission of *Poetry* and the author.

group politics and cut-throat rivalries to high-pressure salesmanship and journalistic inflation—in speeding the declines already promised by the ephemeral nature of the average literary beliefs and styles. It would hardly have needed the further discouragement of rapidly shifting critical standards or headlong changes in social and political life to turn the optimism of the American revivalists of 1912 into the despair or silence which many of them found to be the only answer to the contempt directed against them by the rising talents of the post-War years.

We know how few poets of the pre-War revival survived this state of affairs. Several did it in spite of persisting in their original aims; more did it by agile changes of face through the rise and fall of new tastes or styles. The first of these forms of survival carries one risk and the second another. One poet becomes more and more personal in his ways, skeptical in his view of the tumult and disorder around him, and so retreats into his own sphere of private irony or eccentricity; this accounts for the predicament of Robinson or Frost. The other remains young at whatever cost of sober judgment or certain craft, mixes in movements and experiments, and becomes more and more difficult to connect with any kind of esthetic or philosophic stability. He keeps his freshness alive, but becomes too mercurial for believers in real values; his energy keeps him on the stretch but exhausts the confidence of his followers; and so he arrives at the ambiguous authority of Ezra Pound. In this age of high-pressure literary promotion and easy public credulity, nothing seems easier for an author than to win a hearing—and nothing harder than to keep it.

Carl Sandburg's new book, *The Peo-*

ple, Yes (Harcourt, Brace & Co.), is impressive at first sight because in it he speaks with exactly the same voice he used in the *Chicago Poems* of 1914 and yet succeeds in making it as eloquent as any American poem of 1936. He risks two extreme hazards of the contemporary writer. He writes on the social problem, and he writes in popular language. It will be suggested immediately that he has simplified them primarily by stopping short of his full responsibilities as a poet. To this one must agree at once that hardly a fifth of this volume is classifiable by any definition as poetry, although any definition of poetry must include the purpose and imagination that run through its pages, even when they contain nothing but inventories of popular speech or long lists of trades and slogans. But no American poet now living could publish with the same authority and completeness a survey of the specifically American issue in twentieth century poetry—how it has emerged and developed, how it diverges from foreign influence and contacts, and what it may expect, in extension or solution, from the coming talents of the humanitarian front. This long document of 286 pages is not only a guidebook on American themes; it is a manual of words and phrases, episodes and characters, conflicts and forces, and in addition it contains a demonstration of how the social idealism of American poetry may be successfully domesticated in the immediate future.

But its first interest comes from the fact that here Sandburg has summarized his purposes of a quarter-century and handed them as a testament to his inheritors. The book forms a remarkable unity with its predecessors. It is true that such consistency has deprived his work of exact points of interest or decision. His poems as they have appeared in his five volumes have progressively cancelled their predecessors, repeating their themes and dulling their emphasis. Yet Sandburg is one of the few native poets of whom it may be said, with all respect to the priority of Whitman, that he has written no verse, good or bad, but his own. He has sacrificed to his own single-voiced personality—as candidly as Frost or Robinson, but without their irony or close-lipped pessimism —whatever variety or progress might have made him a more forceful character among post-War writers and readers. In this first book since *Good Morning America* eight years ago he shows a purpose not only more serious than it has ever been before, but a talent tuned to uses and broken to duties which many members of the present generation of humanitarian poets, whatever their superior sophistication or craftsmanship, have hardly begun to understand.

In poetry or prose dealing with human causes it is usually a rule that there are no substitutes for thorough practical acquaintance with the matter in hand. Here brilliant technical advantages may display what they are intended to disguise—the writer's failure in immediate knowledge of his materials, or his substitution of journalism or second-hand study for it. Dos Passos' recent novels have given a new weight to the name and labor of Dreiser, and the younger proletarian poets who far outstrip Sandburg in metrical skill or formal rigor— in other words, as artists—throw into fresh relief the ruggedness of his achievement. They show him, by the glibness of their arguments or the abstract condition of their beliefs, to be deeply bred and matured in a cause of which they usually have a keen but merely juvenile understanding, or more often only an academic acquaintance. In other words, Sandburg triumphs on all the scores in which experience counts: in his use of speech and lingoes, in the range and authenticity of his folklore, in the scope of his social familiarity, in the reach of his memory, and in the size and variety of the history he has made of the whole age of industrial labor in America during the past half-century. Compared with these resources the younger talents offer a meagre fare. Their phrases are thin and their colloquialisms synthetic, their data specialized and experiences green, their references as often warped as enriched by literary derivation, and the structure of their poems is held up by rhetoric or the false props of borrowed arguments.

On these grounds *The People, Yes* escapes criticism, even when it does so by casting esthetic claims to the winds. It is a vast retrospect of life and labor in America that suggests an obvious comparison—*Leaves of Grass*. It is prefaced by a poem that announces the casual and miscellaneous nature of its scheme:

Being several stories and psalms nobody
would want to laugh at

interspersed with memoranda variations
worth a second look

along with sayings and yarns traveling on
grief and laughter. . . .

It opens with a spectacle of the "How-deehow powwow," which is the American nation in its immense dimensions and disorder—a "Tower of Babel job" which now stands

                    as a skull and a ghost
a memorandum hardly begun,
swaying and sagging in tall hostile winds,
held up by slow friendly winds—

and so proceeds through 107 sections that alternate, on no apparent principle of contrast or structure, between personal episodes and mass movements, local anecdotes and epic generalities, lists of scenes, trades, occupations, and causes, passages of vague symbolic imagery, long catalogues of popular phrases, catch-words, clichés, and proverbs, and intervals of gnomic lyricism. Nothing has apparently been left out, but everything that Sandburg has put into his earlier poems is here again, particularly from previous surveys like *Many Hats* and *Good Morning America*. The prevailing quality of style is "tough and mystical." It derives from the dogged patience of common humanity in being outwitted by keener brains and criminal exploiters, the pathetic endurance of the underdog who waits grimly for the reprisals of time. This style derives from Whitman only in structure. It has as little to do with his rhetorical strain or oracular grandiloquence as it has with Whitman's final lyric and choral mastery. It has even little of the belabored hardboiledness of Hemingway, Dos Passos, or Phelps Putnam. It comes with the laconic ease of talk on streets and farms, from section-gangs, night shifts, pick-and-shovel outfits, and hobo camp-fires, Union Square soapboxes and grocery-store rag-chewing. From these sources Sandburg has compiled a catalogue of American lore that must astonish anyone. Where he gets it all is beyond telling. Whether all of it is equally authentic or not is beyond present calculation. But it rings true to the American ear far beyond the language of the average "regional" novel or proletarian poem, and one has only to compare any random sample of it with the slang parts of Pound's *Cantos* or Mac-Leish's *Frescoes* to realize that one is the

pure article and the other something like a parody heard from the stage of the London Colosseum.

In other words, Sandburg looks after his facts first, and waits for argument to follow from them. He is empirical in the rough native tradition. If he hears the jeer that "the people is a myth, an abstraction," he asks "What myth would you put in place of the people? And what abstraction would you exchange for this one?" If the cause of social justice has any validity for reformers or poets it must come not from the mind but from "the bowels of that mystic behemoth, the people." The difference between Whitman and Sandburg is primarily a difference between a visionary imagination and a realistic one, between a prophet who deals in the racial and social aspects of humanitarianism and a historian who handles the specific facts of industrial life and labor. Whitman, given his sympathies and cause and with his greater imaginative vision, might have written his book without any immediate contact with its materials, whereas Sandburg, so denied, could have written none of his. The two poets join only at the point which is their common weakness: in the rhapsodic cries and flights that are the diffused and prevalent bane of the one and the merely incidental weakness of the other. Sandburg is saved from this pretension by his plain verbal sanity. He does not discard the lyric imagination; it filters through his pages and produces many short passages of characteristic fancy:

Alive yet the spillover of last night's moon-
    rise
        brought returns of peculiar cash
        a cash of thin air alive yet.

But it is seldom allowed to develop into vague apostrophe or inflated allegory, any more than his language is allowed to use the pompous phrases, French or Latin counterfeit, and hollow pedantry of Whitman's style. In the same way his general tendency is to avoid those vague spectres of human ordeal that make up the panoramic symbolism of Perse's *Anabase,* Aragon's *Front Rouge,* or MacLeish's *Conquistador,* and when such effects do appear they immediately strike the eye with their uneasy falseness, as in parts 29 and 107, to select two examples from opposite ends of the poem. Three lines are enough to show how Sandburg on occasion veers into a pompous phraseology from which his cruder humors must rescue him:

While the rootholds of the earth nourish
    the majestic people
And the new generations with names never
    heard of
Plow deep in broken drums and shoot
    craps for old crowns,

but one also runs into longer passages that come with particular inconclusiveness in the book's last pages, when something more than immortal truisms is wanted for force of thought or art, however such temporizations may agree with the skepticism of history:

    The people will live on.
The learning and blundering people will
    live on.
    They will be tricked and sold and
        again sold
And go back to the nourishing earth for
    rootholds,
    The people so peculiar in renewal and
        comeback,
    You can't laugh off their capacity to
        take it.
The mammoth rests between his cyclonic
    dramas.

This kind of writing, coming on top of the most brisk and vivid realism,

rings with a special shallowness; another poet, stronger in rhetorical powers or symbolic skill, might make poetry of it, but where the general spirit of the poem casts suspicion on matter or ideas untested by hard fact, these references to dreams and mammoths, "cyclonic dramas," "the strength of the winds" and the "constellations of universal law," or to the people as

                    a polychrome,
    a spectrum and a prism
    held in a moving monolith,
    a console organ of changing themes,
    a clavilux of color poems
    wherein the sea offers fog
    and the fog moves off in rain
    and the labrador sunset shortens
    to a nocturne of clear stars
    serene over the shot spray
    of northern lights—

show up as evasions of what either social necessity or poetic strength requires.

In other words, Sandburg, taken in the mass and for the general effect of his detail, is a master without rivals, a poetic realist of great range and authority, a folklorist in the best tradition, and easily the finest reporter of contemporary life that the modern poetic revival has produced, as comparison with Masters, Lindsay, Frost, or their younger successors will show. But taken in the specific poem or argument he offers as unsatisfactory a case to social critics as to literary. He eludes argument and dependability; he seems in the end evasive of responsibility; and his loyal purposes and honesty come to much less than they should. His immense knowledge of human ills and fortunes is too immense; it immerses and engulfs him; he is pulled by so many claims on sympathy and forbearance that nothing survives the prodigious outlay of tolerance and compassion but his inexhaustible supply of pure human nature. His feeling for the masses marching in the darkness with their great bundle of grief is tempered by ironic pathos for the millionaire suicide of Rochester or Marshall Field who left $25,000 for the upkeep of his grave. The farcical delusions of the rich are balanced against the tragic palliatives by which the poor are duped; the meat of privilege and the poison of oppression become mixed up because both destroy their eaters; moral platitudes are cancelled by a wise-crack; and finally the only conclusion permitted him is a tough confidence in the abstract will of the people to save themselves. The answer to the whole urgent problem of human salvation is thrown back on "the folded and quiet yesterdays, put down in the book of the past," or thrown forward by the unanswered question, "Where do we go from here? Where to? What next?" or allowed to hang between unresolved opposites: "The people, yes, out of what is their change from chaos to order and chaos again?"

Obviously these are among the most difficult questions in the world to answer, but neither a poet nor a reformer would ask them if he had no answer to offer. As its title indicates, *The People, Yes* is written as a great affirmation of man's strength and value, but the practical regeneration of the human lot promised throughout the record finally hangs suspended in the void of love and patience. We knew it all before, even if not in this vivid and familiar language, and we are left wanting to know more. No doubt the avoidance of formulated solutions is dictated as much by common sense as by the plain facts of history, but one expects more than common sense or plain facts from a poet or a philosopher. It soon follows that

if Sandburg had worked harder at his social or moral philosophy, he would have been a greater poet. In a book of this kind the test of poetic form is almost beside the point; it would apply in so small a fraction of the content. Yet as soon as one understands what it takes to achieve real form in the construction of language, one sees what it takes to arrive at that form through the structure and integration of thought. If one's thought remains undecided among the evidence at hand, inconclusively empirical or superior to proof, it is likely that the force and authority of the verse will remain scattered and confused among its details, words, and phrases, however abundant and authentic these may be. Sandburg's poetic instrument is exactly fitted to his purposes; it simply happens that those purposes are too vaguely poetic to make the instrument become anything more than the loose, amorphous, copious, semi-prose medium that it still remains after twenty-five years of use. And one may suppose that if he had exerted more labor on the task of filing and concentrating his verse, giving one phrase or anecdote the pith now thinned out over twenty, he would have arrived at something more fixed and specific in his social beliefs. The beliefs might be arbitrary in form; they might not conclude in what communist critics will logically demand and fail to get in the last ten pages of this book; but they would give a coherence and structure to his faith in mankind that would count for more than that faith in its present all-inclusive and unresolved condition. Sandburg himself implies that facts of this kind are beyond such arbitrary mastery:

these lead to no easy pleasant conversation
they fall into a dusty disordered poetry.

And his practical conclusions suggest a similar contempt for the formulations of economic socialism. "Always the storm of propaganda blows"; "yet the sleepers toss in sleep and an end comes of sleep and the sleepers wake." But between these prophecies we get the skepticism of an ironic intelligence which knows so much that it no longer trusts itself: "Who knows the answers, the cold inviolable truth?" "What does justice say?" "Where to? What next?" The potentialities of an epic judgment lie in Sandburg's materials, but he has not realized them. It is doubtful if any poet writing on the premises of Whitman could, since that tradition represents an immense exploration and discovery of poetic resources, but not their proof and mastery as poetry. Hart Crane wrote himself down as a disciple of Whitman, but his verse shows how great a poetic rigor he exerted over his materials, and how far he advanced the cause of American poetry by bringing it to terms with the moral and intellectual conflicts inherent in a genuinely poetic vision. The model of *The Bridge* now appears to be a difficult and confusing one for present poets to follow; the formal structure is too derivative and intricate, the style too complex, and the whole poem strives toward those evils of rhetoric and allegory which seem to be the surest way of producing artificial and didactic verse at the present moment. But if Crane's formal vision were combined with Sandburg's exact realism and thorough mastery of detail, it would be hard to find a more profitable combination for study by the rising poet of humanitarian ambitions. Something of that same merging of talents would have produced in these two poets themselves a richer and firmer art. Sandburg's book lacks exactly what makes Crane's a distinguished achievement, including its failure in a major purpose. Where it succeeds it does so in a way that is Sandburg's personal triumph, and gives him a distinction great enough among the men of his time to ensure him a high place among his fellows in oppression and hope.

1936

HENRY JAMES

The Limitations of Dickens

A review of *Our Mutual Friend* by Charles Dickens

OUR MUTUAL FRIEND is, to our perception, the poorest of Mr. Dickens's works. And it is poor with the poverty not of momentary embarrassment but of permanent exhaustion. For the last ten years it has seemed to us that Mr. Dickens has been unmistakably forcing himself. *Bleak House* was forced; *Little Dorritt* was labored; the present work is dug out as with a spade and pickax. Of course—to anticipate the usual argument—who but Dickens could have written it? Who, indeed? Who else would have established a lady in business in a novel on the admirably solid basis of her always putting on gloves and tying a handkerchief round her head in moments of grief, and of her habitually addressing her family with "Peace! hold!" It is needless to say that Mrs. Reginald Wilfer is first and last the occasion of considerable true humor. When, after conducting her daughter to Mrs. Boffin's carriage, in sight of all the envious neighbors, she is described as enjoying her triumph during the next quarter of an hour by airing herself on the doorstep "in a kind of splendidly serene trance," we laugh with as uncritical a laugh as could be desired of us. We pay the same tribute to her assertions, as she narrates the glories of the society she enjoyed at her father's table, that she has known as many as three copper-plate engravers exchanging the most exquisite sallies and retorts there at one time. But when to these we have added a dozen more happy examples of the humor which was exhaled from every line of Mr. Dickens's earlier writings, we shall have closed the list of the merits of the work before us. To say that the conduct of the story, with all its complications, betrays a long-practiced hand, is to pay no compliment worthy of the author. If this were, indeed, a compliment, we should be inclined to carry it further, and congratulate him on his success in what we should call the manufacture of fiction; for in so doing we should express a feeling that has attended us throughout the book. Seldom, we reflected, had we read a book so intensely *written,* so little seen, known, or felt.

In all Mr. Dickens's works the fantastic has been his great resource; and while his fancy was live and vigorous it accomplished great things. But the fantastic, when the fancy is dead, is a very poor business. The movement of Mr. Dickens's fancy in Mrs. Wilfer and Mr. Boffin and Lady Tippins, and the Lammles and Miss Wren, and even in Eugene Wrayburn, is, to our mind, a movement lifeless, forced, mechanical. It is the letter of his old humor without the spirit. It is hardly too much to say that every character here put before us is a mere bundle of eccentricities, animated by no principle of nature whatever. In former days there reigned in Mr. Dickens's extravagances a comparative consistency; they were exaggerated statements of types that really existed. We had, perhaps, never known a Newman Noggs, nor a Pecksniff, nor a Micawber; but we had known persons of whom these figures were but the strictly logical consummation. But among the grotesque creatures who occupy the pages before us, there is not one whom we can refer to as an existing type. In all Mr. Dickens's satires, indeed, the reader has been called upon, and has willingly consented, to accept a certain number of figures or creatures of pure fancy, for this was the author's poetry. He was, moreover, always repaid for his concession by a peculiar beauty or power in these exceptional characters. But he is now expected to make the same concession with a very inadequate reward. What do we get in return for accepting Miss Jenny Wren as a possible person? This young lady is a type of a certain class of characters of which Mr. Dickens has made a speciality, and with which he has been accustomed to draw alternate smiles and tears, according as he pressed one spring or another. But this is very cheap merriment and very cheap pathos. Miss Jenny Wren is a poor little dwarf, afflicted, as she constantly reiterates, with a "bad back," and "queer legs," who makes doll's dresses, and is for ever pricking at those with whom she converses, in the air, with her needle, and assuring them that she knows their "tricks and their manners." Like all Dickens's pathetic characters, she is a little monster; she is deformed, unhealthy, unnatural; she belongs to the troop of hunchbacks, imbeciles, and precocious children who have carried on the sentimental business in all Mr. Dickens's novels: the little Nells, the Smikes, the Paul Dombeys.

Mr. Dickens goes as far out of the way for his wicked people as he does for his good ones. Rogue Riderhood, indeed, in the present story, is villainous with a sufficient natural villainy; he belongs to that quarter of society in which the author is most at his ease. But was there ever such wickedness as that of the Lammles and Mr. Fledgeby? Not that people have not been as mischievous as they; but was anyone ever mischievous in that singular fashion? Did a couple of elegant swindlers ever take such particular pains to be aggressively inhuman?—for we can find no other word for the gratuitous distortions to which they are subjected. The word "humanity" strikes us as strangely discordant, in the midst of these pages; for, let us boldly declare it, there is no humanity here. Humanity is nearer home than the Boffins, and the Lammles, and the Wilfers, and the Veneerings. It is in what men have in common with each other, and not what they have in distinction. The people just named have nothing in common with mankind at large. What a world were this world if the world of *Our Mutual Friend* were an honest reflection of it! But a community of eccentrics is impossible. Rules alone are consistent with each other; exceptions are inconsistent. Society is maintained by natural sense and

natural feeling. We cannot conceive a society in which these principles are not in some manner represented. Where in these pages are the depositaries of that intelligence without which the movement of life would cease? Who represents nature? Accepting half of Mr. Dickens's persons as intentionally grotesque, where are those exemplars who should afford us the proper measure of their companions' variations? We ought not, in justice to the author, to seek them among his weaker—that is, his mere conventional—characters: in John Harmon, Lizzie Hexam, or Mortimer Lightwood; but we assuredly cannot find them among his stronger—that is, his artificial—creations.

Suppose we take Eugene Wrayburn and Bradley Headstone. They occupy a halfway position between the probable of nature and the habitually impossible of Mr. Dickens. A large portion of the story rests upon the enmity borne by Headstone to Wrayburn, both being in love with the same woman. Wrayburn is a gentleman, and Headstone is one of the people. Wrayburn is well-bred, careless, elegant, skeptical, and idle: Headstone is a high-tempered, hardworking, ambitious young schoolmaster. There lay in the opposition of these two characters a very good story. But the prime requisite was that they should *be* characters: Mr. Dickens, according to his usual plan, has made them simply figures, and between them the story that was to be, the story that should have been, has evaporated. Wrayburn lounges about with his hands in his pockets, smoking a cigar and talking nonsense. Headstone strides about, clenching his fists and biting his lips and grasping his stick. There is one scene in which Wrayburn chaffs the schoolmaster with easy insolence, while the latter writhes impotently under his well-bred sarcasm. This scene is very clever, but it is very insufficient. If the majority of readers were not so very timid in the use of words we should call it vulgar. By this we do not mean to indicate the conventional impropriety of two gentlemen exchanging lively personalities; we mean to emphasize the essentially small character of these personalities. In other words, the moment, dramatically, is great, while the author's conception is weak. The friction of two *men,* of two characters, of two passions, produces stronger sparks than Wrayburn's boyish repartees and Headstone's melodramatic commonplaces.

Such scenes as this are useful in fixing the limits of Mr. Dickens's insight. Insight is, perhaps, too strong a word; for we are convinced that it is one of the chief conditions of his genius not to see beneath the surface of things. If we might hazard a definition of his literary character, we should, accordingly, call him the greatest of the superficial novelists. We are aware that this definition confines him to an inferior rank in the department of letters which he adorns; but we accept this consequence of our proposition. It were, in our opinion, an offense against humanity to place Mr. Dickens among the greatest novelists. For, to repeat what we have already intimated, he has created nothing but figure. He has added nothing to our understanding of human character. He is master of but two alternatives: he reconciles us to what is commonplace, and he reconciles us to what is odd. The value of the former service is questionable; and the manner in which Mr. Dickens performs it sometimes conveys a certain impression of charlatanism. The value of the latter service is incontestable, and here Mr. Dickens is an honest, an admirable artist. But what is the condition of the truly great novelist? For him there are no alternatives, for him there are no oddities, for him there is nothing outside of humanity. He cannot shirk it; it imposes itself upon him. For him alone, therefore, there is a true and a false; for him alone it is possible to be right, because it is possible to be wrong. Mr. Dickens is a great observer and a great humorist, but he is nothing of a philosopher. Some people may hereupon say, so much the better; we say, so much the worse. For a novelist very soon has need of a little philosophy. In treating of Micawber, and Boffin, and Pickwick, *et hoc genus omne,* he can, indeed, dispense with it, for this—we say it with all deference—is not serious writing. But when he comes to tell the story of a passion, a story like that of Headstone and Wrayburn, he becomes a moralist as well as an artist. He must know *man* as well as *men,* and to know man is to be a philosopher. The writer who knows men alone, if he have Mr. Dickens's humor and fancy, will give us figures and pictures for which we cannot be too grateful, for he will enlarge our knowledge of the world, but when he introduces men and women whose interest is preconceived to lie not in the poverty, the weakness, the drollery of their natures, but in their complete and unconscious subjection to ordinary and healthy human emotions, all his humor, all his fancy, will avail him nothing if, out of the fulness of his sympathy, he is unable to prosecute those generalizations in which alone consists the real greatness of a work of art. This may sound like very subtle talk about a very simple matter; it is rather very simple talk about a very subtle matter. A story based upon these elementary passions in which alone we seek the true and final manifestation of character must be told in a spirit of intellectual superiority to those passions. That is, the author must understand what he is talking about. The perusal of a story so told is one of the most elevating experiences within the reach of the human mind. The perusal of a story which is not so told is infinitely depressing and unprofitable.

1865

MARGARET MARSHALL

"Othello"

A review of Margaret Webster's production of *Othello*

Othello, in print, is as careless of the house rules of dramaturgy as it is prolific in bursts of poetry that move like ground swells through the emotions and the mind. Its several characters are believable because they speak with the irresistible energy and authority of the poetry; their relations to one another seem contrived, and the play as play would be stopped at almost any point by one sensible remark, for which the cue is always presenting itself.

Margaret Webster's *Othello* is not only believable; by a *tour de force* of direction she has caused the faulty motivation not to disappear but to seem irrelevant. And only at one point, as I remember, does the unseized cue stand out.

The key to Miss Webster's particular and distinctive solution of a difficult problem lies in her bold use of Iago both as character and as instrument. The hero of this production is not Othello but Iago; the tragedy of the Moor, while it is quite effectively set forth, is, in a sense, the play within the play. Miss Webster might deny this. The audience bears me out. That fact may tell us more about a prevailing attitude toward the clever, sardonic, agile character who has the ruthlessness of his cynicism than about Miss Webster's intentions, but here is, at the very least, an interesting coincidence. (A friend to whom I mentioned this wondered if the sympathy for Iago was an expression of prejudice against a Negro Othello. The answer is no. It was rather the expression of a secret admiration for the man who exercises power—of which every human being secretly feels himself capable—and this admiration includes a kind of contempt for anyone, white or black, yellow or brown, over whom that power is successfully exercised. The ovation given to Paul Robeson at the end of the performance was certainly not simulated. It was just as certainly sentimental in part, and far more self-conscious than the wry sympathy accorded to Iago scene by scene. But cynicism and sentimentality are, after all, two sides of the same coin.)

It happens also that the most accomplished actor in the company is José

Reprinted from *The Nation*, October 13, 1943, by permission of the author.

Ferrer, who plays the role of Iago. Where his acting ends and Miss Webster's direction begins it is impossible to tell—their collaboration is complete. I can only record that he plays the role with passion and joy, as if he were creating it. The ostensible and inadequate motivation—Iago's desire to usurp Cassio's place—turns under one's eyes and ears into the far more sinister and exciting desire to play the part of the villain for the part's sake. Yet he remains understandable in human terms.

And what of Othello? Paul Robeson has an imposing figure and a powerful voice. But he performs rather than acts. Under Miss Webster's direction he performs passably well, but he creates no illusion. He speaks—often sings—Othello's lines, but he is not Othello in the sense that Mr. Ferrer is Iago. And Robeson and Miss Webster have tried to prove that Othello is a Negro; they have attempted also to prove that *Othello* is a play about race. Both theories seem to me false and foolish. Fortunately Miss Webster's artistic sense is superior to her ideology, which has been confined to the public prints and does not appear in the play.

In Shakespeare's conception the essential quality of the Moor is his foreignness. He is the exotic character—so exotic as to bewitch, for all his denials, the innocent English—not Venetian—Desdemona. The stress upon his blackness points up his alien, not his racial, character. There is no particular reason why a Negro should not play Othello or, for that matter, why a Negro should. Color aside, Robeson is simply not the type. The exotic quality is missing. Moreover, Shakespeare's Moor was surely a man of movement, as agile in his way as Iago. Robeson is monumental and inert. He makes no use

whatever of his body, which becomes a dead weight. His voice does move, and it is fit to declaim such wonderful lines as ". . . when I love not thee, Chaos is come again." But even his voice gets out of character; it is too often reminiscent of Paul Robeson, singer of spirituals. Also its great volume is too often unstopped—some of Othello's "Oh's" are simply rushes of vast and shapeless sound.

Miss Webster's Emilia is interesting and right. The physical attraction which binds this knowing, unromantic woman to Iago is played up. The sense of their frank pleasure in each other provides an irrational yet unchallengeable explanation for Emilia's blindness to her husband's machinations. And this characterization adds greatly to the dramatic power of the last scene, in which it falls to Emilia to express and release the play's emotional impact. Uta Hagen's Desdemona is less enchanted than one's memory of the part, but hers too is a very accomplished performance. The physical appearance of James Monks, who plays the part of Cassio, makes him not quite believable as the second in command. However, he improves upon acquaintance and he acts well. Roderigo, in this production, is almost a caricature of the Dupe, and Jack Manning plays that characterization to the hilt.

The settings are unobtrusive, as they should be. And both the settings and Miss Webster's use of a stage limited in depth point up the character of Iago as the manipulator who takes the audience into his confidence.

The play, as it is here projected, is of course not a tragedy, since Iago runs the show. Only in the case of Emilia, interestingly enough, do we feel that she is the dupe not so much of Iago as of her own mixed passions. In the last scene she does arouse pity and terror—but mainly for Emilia. Every other character is essentially a puppet dangling on Iago's strings. There is there-fore no clash of wills, we do not hate the villain, and virtue is only technically triumphant.

1943

EDITORS OF TIME

Disney's Cinesymphony

A review of *Fantasia* by Walt Disney

STRANGE and wonderful are the premières (pronounced "premeers") of Hollywood: the trappings of publicity; the lights and decorations painting the gaudy lily of the Carthay Circle Theatre (where the big premières are held); the pushing, star-gazing crowds; the troops of real live stars ("I seen him! Didja see her?"). This week Manhattan sees a première stranger and more wonderful than any of Hollywood's. The celebrities present, the publicity, the lights on the marquee, may be lost in the blare and blaze of Broadway. But strangeness and wonder belong to the show itself. It is Walt Disney's latest, called *Fantasia*.

As the audience enters and the theatre fills with the sweet confusion of an orchestra tuning up, there are no musicians in the pit. As the curtains part, a huge symphony orchestra appears hazily, on the screen. Before it steps a thin, grinning, bald-headed man. He introduces himself as Deems Taylor, welcomes the audience, on behalf of Leopold Stokowski and Walt Disney, to "an entirely new form of entertainment." When he finishes, Leopold Sto-

kowski himself, his back to the audience, steps into the picture, raises his arms, and the great orchestra swirls into Bach's *D Minor Toccata and Fugue*.

The music comes not simply from the screen, but from everywhere; it is as if a hearer were in the midst of the music. As the music sweeps to a climax, it froths over the proscenium arch, boils into the rear of the theatre, all but prances up & down the aisles. The hazy orchestra begins to dissolve, and weird, abstract ripples and filaments begin an unearthly ballet in Technicolor.

This is the beginning of a symphony concert—but what a concert! Illustrated by Walt Disney; written by Bach, Beethoven, Stravinsky, Dukas, Tchaikovsky, Mussorgsky, Schubert; conducted by Stokowski; master-of-ceremonied by Deems Taylor; played by the Philadelphia Orchestra. Mickey and Stokowski together put on a brand-new act.

When Stokowski's orchestra swings into Tchaikovsky's *Nutcracker Suite*, the ballet on the screen turns into flowers, fairies, fish, falling leaves, mushrooms. Mickey Mouse appears in the

From *Time*, November 18, 1940. Courtesy of *Time*. Copyright Time, Inc., 1940.

title role of Paul Dukas' *Sorcerer's Apprentice,* with silent gusto steals the bearded sorcerer's magic cap, commands the broom to fetch water, forgets how to stop it, nearly drowns in the deluge that follows. To Igor Stravinsky's rip-roaring *Rite of Spring,* a primeval world, complete with dinosaurs, bubbles up, parades by, dies down. To Mussorgsky's spooky *Night on Bald Mountain,* hobgoblins and beldams ride their brooms. To Beethoven's *Pastoral Symphony,* centaurs and centaurettes, Pegasus, Mrs. Pegasus and a nestful of little Pegasi gambol and fly; Bacchus and his crew get a good drenching when the storm comes up. The whole cinesymphony concert lasts two hours and a half (intermission included).

Containing everything from the Pierian well water of Johann Sebastian Bach to the violet-bordered stream of Schubert's *Ave Maria, Fantasia* is a long succession of very large orders. Some of these orders (the flower, fish and mushroom dances of the *Nutcracker Suite,* the hulking, saurian epic of Stravinsky's *Rite,* the eerie, fantastic *Night on Bald Mountain*) are so beautifully filled that they may leave callous critics whispering incredulously to themselves. Others (Micky's *Sorcerer's Apprentice,* the hilarious ostrich and hippopotamus ballets) set a new high in Disney animal muggery. Others (the wave and cloud sequences of Bach's *Fugue,* and a queer series of explosive music visualizations performed by a worried and disembodied sound track, posing diffidently on the screen like a reluctant wire) recall the abstract cinemovies made about five years ago by New Zealand-born Len Lye, show how musical sensation may be transferred to visual images.

It would have taken a Gustave Doré to do justice to the big beauty of Beethoven's *Pastoral Symphony.* No Doré, Disney peoples his classical Olympus with smirking "centaurettes," smirkingly brassiered, with calf-eyed centaurs and kewpie-doll cupids, makes Bacchus' bacchanale look like a nursery lemonade party, leaves his audience wondering whether he is serious, or merely trying to be cute by putting diapers on Olympus.

But, though Disney's toddling cannot keep pace with the giant strides of Ludwig van Beethoven, *Fantasia* as a whole leaves its audience gasping. Critics may deplore Disney's lapses of taste, but he trips, Mickey-like, into an art form that immortals from Aeschylus to Richard Wagner have always dreamed of.

Mickey Began It. The idea for *Fantasia* had been germinating in Disney's mild-looking head for several years. Even before he did *Snow White* he had a vague notion of some day doing a serious opera in animovie style. As early as 1929 he raided the highbrow symphonic repertory to make Saint-Saëns' bone rattling *Danse Macabre* into a Silly Symphony. But the idea did not really sprout until early in 1938, when Leopold Stokowski, on a visit to Hollywood, begged Disney to let him conduct the music for *The Sorcerer's Apprentice,* a Mickey Mouse short. Disney didn't know what he was letting himself in for.

By the time Stokowski's recordings were done, and the animation half finished, the *Apprentice* began to look too good for a short, too expensive for anything but a feature. Before it was finished, white-haired Maestro Stokowski had come out with so many other bright ideas for symphonic animovies that Disney's ambition near went past itself. Calling ace Musi-commentator Deems Taylor from Manhattan to help with advice, Stoky and Disney decided to build around Mickey Mouse's sorcery act a whole program of cinesymphonies.

Keeping his 1,200 artists, animators, sound engineers and helpers mum, Walt Disney started work, soon got the machinery of his new $3,000,000 Burbank, Calif., studio rolling on *Fantasia*. Deciding to go the whole artistic hog, they picked the highest of high-brow classical music. To do right by this music, the old mouse opera comedy was not enough. The Disney studio went high-brow wholesale, and Disney technicians racked their brains for stuff that would startle and awe rather than tickle the audience.

Dinosaurs and Sound Tracks. Conductor Stokowski went to work in Philadelphia's mellow and acoustically perfect old Academy of Music, recording his symphonic accompaniments on sound tracks. This time he worked, not with the Hollywood pickup band that had recorded Mickey's *Sorcerer's Apprentice,* but with his own famed, seasoned Philadelphia Orchestra. For this recording job, no ordinary cinema sound equipment would do. So Disney's ace sound engineer, rangy, Brooklyn-born Bill Garity, developed a whole new system of gadgets capable of catching each section of the Philadelphia Orchestra on a separate sound track. By braiding and patching these sound tracks onto a four-ply master track, he could control the faintest breath of every last bassoon. In their recording operations Garity and Stokowski used 430,000 feet of sound track, cut and patched it eventually into 11,953 feet. When the recordings were played back in a specially equipped studio in Hollywood, brother engineers were astounded to hear Soundman Garity's sound follow characters across the screen, roar down

from the ceiling, whisper behind their backs. RCA and Disney engineers, having built his equipment at a cost of $85,000, called it "Fantasound," and crowed that it would revolutionize cinema production like nothing since the invention of Technicolor.

Meanwhile the Disney lot rang with the sound of classical music. Patient engineers who had never been to a concert in their lives listened to 35 to 710 performances of each composition, ended up whistling Bach, Beethoven and even Stravinsky at breakfast. Idea men, working on the dulcet strains of Beethoven's *Sixth Symphony,* winced at the bedlam of Stravinsky's *Rite* which other technicians were playing next door. (The *Rite* finally had to be quarantined in a special corner of the lot, where its boom-lay-booms could be studied without disturbing the whole studio.)

Stravinsky's *Rite,* which has caused high-brow audiences to rise, shout and pound on their neighbors' skulls in ecstasy, offered a serious problem. To match its cosmic hullabaloo, nothing less than a planetary cataclysm would do. So Disney men began studying nebulae and comets at California's Mount Wilson Observatory, mugged up on theories of protozoic life, earthquakes and other geologic upheavals, did portraits of every prehistoric monster in Manhattan's American Museum of Natural History.

One of them, studying lightning flashes by reclining on a Los Angeles curbstone in a pouring rain, was rushed to headquarters by suspicious police. Famed paleontologists like Barnum Brown of Manhattan's American Museum of Natural History and Chester Stock of California Institute of Technology were called in for advice. A herd of pet iguanas and a baby alligator wriggled over the Burbank lot, while animators studied their lizardy movements. By the time a complete cast had been rounded up for the *Rite,* the Disney zoo contained eusthenopterons, brachiosaurs, brontosaurs, plesiosaurs, mesosaurs, diplodocuses, triceratopses, pterodactyls, trachodons, struthiomimuses, stegosaurs, archaeopteryxes, pteranodons, tyrannosaurs and enough plain run-of-the-Jurassic dinosaurs to people a planet. Studio cameras groaned under the burden of the whole story of evolution.

For Mussorgsky's halloweenish *Night on Bald Mountain,* Disney went outside his own studio for talent, got famed Fairy-Tale Illustrator Kay Nielson (*East of the Sun and West of the Moon*) to design graveyards and ghosts, ended with a Walpurgis nightmare calculated to turn little children's hair white. But Illustrator Nielson's jagged scenes, plus a new high in animation technique, made it by far *Fantasia's* best act. As *Fantasia* took shape, a whole new troupe of Disney comic characters appeared: Hop Low, the self-thwarting little mushroom, who tries to do the Chinese Dance from Tchaikovsky's *Nutcracker Suite,* but can't keep up with the big mushrooms; Ben Ali Gator, premier danseur of an ostrich ballet set to Ponchielli's corny *Dance of the Hours;* Susan, the hippopotamus ballerina whose blimp-like cavortings in a *pas de deux* with Ben Ali Gator literally bring down the house in a wreck of flying plaster; Bacchus and his donkey Jacchus, who trip and roll through the Grant Woodland scape of Beethoven's *Pastoral Symphony.*

Long before *Fantasia* was finished, expenses began to mount, and fellow Hollywoodians began to whisper again about "Disney's Folly." With $200,000

spent on Stokowski's fancy recordings, and a technical bill that overtops *Snow White's,* the total figure for the production amounted to $2,250,000. Because Engineer Garity's new sound mechanism is so complicated and expensive, only twelve theatres at a time will be equipped to show *Fantasia,* and RCA sound-equipment manufacturers figure that it will take several years before small-town cinema houses can get the gadgets to perform it. For the present, *Fantasia* will not be distributed like ordinary films, but will tour the U. S. like twelve road-show companies. But Walt Disney expects *Fantasia* to run for years, "perhaps even after I am gone."

An imposing list of top-flight contemporary composers (Paul Hindemith, Serge Prokofieff, William Grant Still, Deems Taylor, *et al.*) have vowed that they would spend their lives working for Disney if he would give them the chance. Composer Igor Stravinsky himself has signed a contract to do more music with Disney, has blandly averred that Disney's paleontological cataclysm was what he had had in mind all along in his *Rite of Spring.* Musicians and sound engineers who came to hear Soundman Garity's gadgets perform found that such recording had never before been even approached. Music lovers crowed that more ears would be saved for Beethoven by *Fantasia* than by all the symphonic lecture-recitalists in the U. S. The New York Academy of Sciences asked for a private showing of the *Rite of Spring* because they thought its dinosaurs better science than whole museum-loads of fossils and taxidermy.

Meanwhile sharp-faced Cinemartist Disney just crossed his fingers. Said he: "Art is never conscious. Things that have lived were seldom planned that way. If you follow that line, you're on the wrong track. We don't even let the word 'art' be used around the studio. If anyone begins to get arty, we knock them down. What we strive for is entertainment."

1940

<hr/>

WALTER LIPPMANN

H. L. *Mencken*

A review of *Notes on Democracy* by H. L. Mencken

HERE IN TWO hundred pages is Mr. Mencken's philosophy. Here are the premises of that gargantuan attack upon the habits of the American nation which has made Mr. Mencken the most powerful personal influence on this whole generation of educated people. I say personal influence, for one thing this book makes clear, and that is that the man is bigger than his ideas.

If you subtract from this book the personality of H. L. Mencken, if you attempt to restate his ideas in simple unexcited prose, there remains only a collection of trite and somewhat confused ideas. To discuss it as one might discuss the ideas of first rate thinkers like Russell, Dewey, Whitehead, or Santayana would be to destroy the book and to miss its importance. Though it purports to be the outline of a social philosophy, it is really the highly rhetorical expression of a mood which has often in the past and may again in the future be translated into thought. In the best sense of the word the book is sub-rational: it is addressed to those vital preferences which lie deeper than coherent thinking.

The most important political books are often of this sort. Rousseau's "So-cial Contract" and Tom Paine's "Rights of Man" were far inferior as works of the mind to the best thought of the eighteenth century, but they exerted an incalculably great influence because they altered men's prejudices. Mr. Mencken's book is of the same sort. The democratic phase which began in the eighteenth century has about run its course. Its assumptions no longer explain the facts of the modern world and its ideals are no longer congenial to modern men. There is now taking place a radical change of attitude not merely towards parliamentary government but towards the whole conception of popular sovereignty and majority rule. This change is as radical in its way as that which took place, say between 1776 and 1848.

In the United States Mr. Mencken is the most powerful voice announcing the change. The effect of his tremendous polemic is to destroy, by rendering it ridiculous and unfashionable, the democratic tradition of the American pioneers. This attack on the divine right of demos is an almost exact equivalent of the earlier attacks on the kings, the nobles, and the priests. He strikes at the sovereign power, which in Amer-

From Walter Lippmann, *Men of Destiny*. By permission of The Macmillan Company, publishers.

ica today consists of the evangelical churches in the small communities, the proletarian masses in the cities, and the organized smaller business men everywhere. The Baptist and Methodist sects, the city mobs, and the Chamber of Commerce are in power. They are the villains of the piece. Mr. Mencken does not argue with them. He lays violent hands upon them in the conviction, probably correct, that you accomplish results quicker by making your opponent's back teeth rattle than by laboriously addressing his reason. Mr. Mencken, moreover, being an old newspaper man, has rather strong notions about the capacity of mankind to reason. He knows that the established scheme is not supported by reason but by prejudice, prestige, and reverence, and that a good joke is more devastating than a sound argument. He is an eminently practical journalist, and so he devotes himself to dogmatic and explosive vituperation. The effect is a massacre of sacred cows, a holocaust of idols, and the poor boobs are no longer on their knees.

Mr. Mencken is so effective just because his appeal is not from mind to mind but from viscera to viscera. If you analyze his arguments you destroy their effect. You cannot take them in detail and examine their implications. You have to judge him totally, roughly, approximately, without definition, as you would a barrage of artillery, for the general destruction rather than for the accuracy of the individual shots. He presents an experience, and if he gets you, he gets you not by reasoned conviction, but by a conversion which you may or may not be able to dress up later as a philosophy. If he succeeds with you, he implants in you a sense of sin, and then he revives you with grace, and

disposes you to a new pride in excellence and in a non-gregarious excellence.

One example will show what happens if you pause to analyze his ideas. The thesis of this whole book is that we must cease to be governed by "the inferior four-fifths of mankind." Here surely is a concept which a thinker would have paused to define. Mr. Mencken never does define it, and what is more, he quite evidently has no clear idea of what he means. Sometimes he seems to think that the difference between the inferior four-fifths and the superior one-fifth is the difference between the "haves" and the "have nots." At other times he seems to think it is the difference between the swells and the nobodies, between the wellborn and those who come "out of the gutter." At other times he abandons these worldly distinctions and talks and thinks about "free spirits," a spiritual élite, who have no relation either to income or to a family tree. This vagueness as to whether the superior one-fifth are the Prussian Junkers or the Pittsburgh millionaires, or the people who can appreciate Bach and Beethoven, persists throughout the book.

This confusion is due, I think, to the fact that he is an outraged sentimentalist. Fate and his own curiosity have made him a connoisseur of human ignorance. Most educated men are so preoccupied with what they conceive to be the best thought in the field of their interest, that they ignore the follies of uneducated men. A Jacques Loeb would spend very little of his time on biology as taught in an Oklahoma High School. Even William James, who was more interested in the common man than any great philosopher of our time, was looking always for grains of wisdom in the heaps of folly. But Mr. Mencken is

overwhelmingly preoccupied with popular culture. He collects examples of it.
He goes into a rage about it. He cares
so much about it that he cannot detach
himself from it. And he measures it
not by relative standards, but by the
standards which most educated men reserve for a culture of the first order. He
succeeds, of course, in establishing a
reductio ad absurdum of the shibboleths
of liberals. That is worth doing. But
it is well to know what you are doing,
and when Mr. Mencken measures the
culture of the mass by the cultural standards of the élite, he is not throwing any
real light on the modern problem. He
is merely smashing a delusion by means
of an effective rhetorical device.

I doubt, however, if he is aware that
he is using a rhetorical device. When
he measures the popular culture by the
standards of the élite, the humor is all on
the surface. The undertone is earnest
and intensely sincere. One feels that
Mr. Mencken is deeply outraged because
he does not live in a world where all
men love truth and excellence and
honor. I feel it because I detect in this
book many signs of yearning for the
good old days. When Mr. Mencken
refers to feudalism, to kings, to the Prussian aristocracy, to any ordered society
of the ancient régime, he adopts a different tone of voice. I don't mean to
say that he talks like an *émigré* or like
a writer for the *Action Française,* but it
is evident to me that his revolt against
modern democratic society exhausts his
realism, and that the historic alternatives
are touched for him with a romantic
glamour. The older aristocratic societies exist only in his imagination; they
are idealized sufficiently to inhibit that
drastic plainness of perception which
he applies to the democratic society all
about him.

The chief weakness of the book, as a
book of ideas, arises out of this naïve contrast in Mr. Mencken's mind between
the sordid reality he knows and the
splendid society he imagines. He never
seems to have grasped the truth that the
thing he hates is the direct result of the
thing he most admires. This modern
democracy meddling in great affairs
could not be what it is but for that freedom of thought which Mr. Mencken to
his everlasting credit cares more about
than about anything else. It is freedom
of speech and freedom of thought which
have made all questions popular questions. What sense is there then in
shouting on one page for a party of
"liberty," and on another bewailing the
hideous consequences? The old aristoc-
racies which Mr. Mencken admires did
not delude themselves with any nonsense about liberty. They reserved
what liberty there was for a privileged
élite, knowing perfectly well that if you
granted liberty to everyone you would
have sooner or later everything that Mr.
Mencken deplores. But he seems to
think that you can have a privileged,
ordered, aristocratic society with complete liberty of speech. That is as thor-
ough-going a piece of Utopian senti-
mentalism as anything could be. You
might as well proclaim yourself a Roman Catholic and then ask that excerpts
from the *American Mercury* and the
works of Charles Darwin be read from
the altar on the first Sunday of each
month. If Mr. Mencken really wishes
an aristocracy he will have to give up
liberty as he understands it; and if he
wishes liberty he will have to resign
himself to hearing *homo boobiens* speak
his mind.

What Mr. Mencken desires is in substance the distinction, the sense of honor,
the chivalry, and the competence of an

ideal aristocracy combined with the liberty of an ideal democracy. This is an excellent wish, but like most attempts to make the best of both worlds, it results in an evasion of the problem. The main difficulty in democratic society arises out of the increasing practice of liberty. The destruction of authority, of moral values, of cultural standards is the result of using the liberty which has been won during the last three or four centuries. Mr. Mencken is foremost among those who cry for more liberty, and who use that liberty to destroy what is left of the older tradition. I do not quarrel with him for that. But I am amazed that he does not see how fundamentally the spiritual disorder he fights against is the effect of that régime of liberty he fights for. Because he fails to see that, I think he claims too much when he says that he is engaged in a diagnosis of the democratic disease. He has merely described with great emphasis the awful pain it gives him.

In the net result these confusions of thought are a small matter. It is no crime not to be a philosopher. What Mr. Mencken has created is a personal force in American life which has an extraordinarily cleansing and vitalizing effect. How else can you explain the paradox of his popularity, and the certainty that before he dies he will find himself, like Bernard Shaw today, one of the grand old men, one of the beloved patriarchs of his time? How in this land where all politicians, pedagogues, peasants, etc., etc., are preposterous, has Henry L. Mencken, not yet aged fifty, become the pope of popes? The answer is that he has the gift of life. His humor is so full of animal well-being that he acts upon his public like an elixir. The wounds he inflicts heal quickly. His blows have the clean brutality of

a natural phenomenon. They are directed by a warm and violent but an unusually healthy mind which is not divided, as most minds are, by envy and fear and ambition and anxiety. When you can explain the heightening effect of a spirited horse, of a swift athlete, of a dancer really in control of his own body, when you can explain why watching them you feel more alive yourself, you can explain the quality of his influence.

For this reason the Mencken manner can be parodied, but the effect is ludicrous when it is imitated. The same prejudices and the same tricks of phrase employed by others are usually cheap and often nasty. I never feel that in Mr. Mencken himself even when he calls quite harmless people cockroaches and lice. I do not care greatly for phrases like that. They seem to me like spitting on the carpet to emphasize an argument. They are signs that Mr. Mencken writes too much and has occasionally to reach for the effect without working for it. I think he is sometimes lazy, and when he is lazy he is often unfair, not in the grand manner but in the small manner. And yet his wounds are clean wounds and they do not fester. I know, because I have fragments of his shellfire in my own skin. The man is admirable. He writes terribly unjust tirades, and yet I know of nobody who writes for his living who will stay up so late or get up so early to untangle an injustice. He often violates not merely good taste according to the genteel tradition, but that superior kind of good taste according to which a man refuses to hurt those who cannot defend themselves.

Nevertheless I feel certain that insofar as he has influenced the tone of public controversy he has elevated it. The

Mencken attack is always a frontal attack. It is always explicit. The charge is all there. He does not leave the worst unsaid. He says it. And when you have encountered him, you do not have to wonder whether you are going to be stabbed in the back when you start to leave and are thinking of something else.

I have not written this as a eulogy, but as an explanation which to me at least answers the question why Henry

L. Mencken is as popular as he is in a country in which he professes to dislike most of the population. I lay it to the subtle but none the less sure sense of those who read him that here is nothing sinister that smells of decay, but that on the contrary this Holy Terror from Baltimore is splendidly and exultantly and contagiously alive. He calls you a swine, and an imbecile, and he increases your will to live.

1926

DANA B. DURAND

Magic and Experimental Science

A review of *A History of Magic and Experimental Science* by Lynn Thorndike

THE COMPLETION by an American scholar of a monument in a field of European history is, even today, a rather exceptional event. It is true that American-born historians are turning out an ever-increasing flow of articles, monographs, and books which compare favorably with the best that the Old World is producing. We have learned how to comb through archives and manuscript collections with fine professional virtuosity, and our leading scholars make no more mistakes in footnotes than most Europeans. Yet, for the most part, the achievement of the individual American historian has rarely proved sufficiently original to be hailed as "bahnbrechend," nor sufficiently exhaus-

tive to be honored as "magistral." Both of these praises are due, I believe, to the work of LYNN THORNDIKE. The publication of the fifth and sixth volumes of *A History of Magic and Experimental Science* calls for at least a provisional appraisal of his massive achievement.

Even by the test of quantity THORNDIKE's work has few competitors. According to my count, which may not be complete, he has published in book form well over 7000 pages.[1] These include two excellent textbooks, one of which has passed through several editions.[2] I have found references to more than 100 articles—exclusive of reviews—totalling at least 1000 pages. Some of these have been incorporated into chapters of

Reprinted from *Isis*, XXXIII (June, 1942), 691-712, by permission of the author and the History of Science Society.

[1] Cf. "Bibliography of Lynn Thorndike," in *A Bibliography of the Faculty of Political Science, Columbia University, 1830-1930* (New York, 1931), pp. 285-89.

[2] *The History of Medieval Europe*, revised edition (Boston, 1928). *A Short History of Civilization*, second edition (New York, 1929); "When the world war broke out in 1914, I determined to do what little I could to keep civilization alive. This volume is a contribution in that direction" (Preface).

Magic and Experimental Science, but others constitute supplements to material already published in Volumes I to IV. At least one by-product of THORN-DIKE's main activity—his Catalogue of Incipits,[3] prepared in collaboration with PEARL KIBRE—itself takes rank as a monument, an indispensable tool for future research.[4] Another by-product, THORNDIKE's seminar at Columbia University, has also begun to yield its fruit.[5] Finally, lest anyone should suppose that the happy termination of Magic and Experimental Science marks the end of scholarly activity, it should be pointed out that THORNDIKE has promised a number of attractive items for future publication.[6] All of these past and future enterprises, even without Magic and Experimental Science, would be sufficient to win a reputation for unusual productivity.

A History of Magic and Experimental Science originated—its author tells us—in a suggestion made by JAMES HARVEY ROBINSON in 1902-03. ROBINSON proposed, as the subject for a Master's thesis, the study of magic in medieval universities. The resulting dissertation, which appeared in 1905 under the title The Place of Magic in the Intellectual History of Europe,[7] might be described as a prospectus of THORNDIKE's life work. It is noteworthy that at this stage the term "science" did not appear in the title, and indeed it scarcely figured in the book itself. Chronologically The Place of Magic was restricted almost entirely to the period of the Roman Empire. Although he was aware that antecedents of magic-in-science might be found in Greek writers (even in ARISTOTLE), THORNDIKE turned his attention immediately to Roman and Greco-Roman authors, and to a large extent, it is the Latin tradition which has continued to monopolize his interest. Greek and Arabic works have been used in his treatment only insofar as they were known to the West in Latin translation.

After completing this preliminary survey of the classical background—which like so many dissertations had turned out to be only a long running start toward the topic originally proposed—THORNDIKE turned to the Middle Ages. Shortly before the outbreak of the last war, he prepared an account of magic and science during the twelfth and thirteenth centuries. He decided not to publish this work, since it was based only on printed material available in this country. The next ten years, apart from the war period, marked the beginning of that series of Studienreisen which have made LYNN THORNDIKE one of the best known American names in European manuscript rooms. During

---

[3] Full title, A Catalogue of Incipits of Mediaeval Scientific Writings in Latin (The Mediaeval Academy of America, Publication No. 29: Cambridge, Mass., 1937). This has been supplemented by "Additional Incipits of Mediaeval Scientific Writings in Latin," Speculum, XIV (1939), 93-105.

[4] THORNDIKE also drew up a "Prospectus for a Corpus of Medieval Scientific Literature in Latin," Isis, XIV (1930), 363-84, which includes as desiderata 164 items from the general field of medieval science and 85 from medicine.

[5] Published works by THORNDIKE's students include: CARL B. BOYER, The Concepts of the Calculus; A Critical and Historical Discussion of the Derivative and the Integral (New York, 1939); MARSHALL CLAGETT, Giovanni Marliani and Late Medieval Physics (New York, 1941). In preparation is an edition of the Theorica Planetarum of CAMPANUS OF NOVARA, based on six MSS.

[6] Notably an edition of the botanical writings of RUFINUS, one of THORNDIKE's most important "finds"; cf. "Rufinus: a Forgotten Botanist of the Thirteenth Century," Isis, XVIII (1932), 63-76.

[7] (Studies in History, Economics and Public Law, Columbia University, XXIV, 1: New York, 1905).

these years he published a number of articles, from which it was possible to see that a major scholarly project was taking shape.

The first two volumes of *Magic and Experimental Science* appeared in 1923.[8] About half of the first volume consists of an amplification of THORNDIKE's dissertation, *The Place of Magic*. The rest of Volume I carries the story through the Dark Ages to the end of the eleventh century. Volume II covers the twelfth and thirteenth centuries. It was not indicated at the end of these volumes that a sequel might be expected, and it seems possible that THORNDIKE himself did not foresee at the time the magnitude of what lay ahead. At any rate the next installment was eleven years in the making. During this period the only major publication was a volume entitled *Science and Thought in the Fifteenth Century*.[9] Despite the broad title, this work consisted largely of special studies, illustrating several important aspects of fifteenth-century intellectual history, but presenting only a limited *vue d'ensemble*.

Volumes III and IV of *Magic and Experimental Science,* covering the fourteenth and fifteenth centuries, were published in 1934.[10] The steady increase in scale, which had been apparent as the earlier volumes progressed, was enhanced by the inclusion of extensive Latin quotations in the footnotes, and of a veritable forest of Appendices—62 in all. Reflecting and continuing this increased momentum of THORNDIKE's scholarship, the interval between vol-

umes decreased to seven years, and at the same time the scale of treatment expanded still further. Volumes V and VI, appearing in 1941,[11] devote 1287 pages (exclusive of indexes) to the period from 1500 to 1630. This compares with the 707 pages which had been devoted to the fifteenth century, 771 to the fourteenth, 663 to the thirteenth, 302 to the twelfth, and 743 to the preceding ten centuries.

Since the publication of the sixteenth-century volumes is the occasion of the present article, I shall describe them somewhat more fully than the preceding volumes. Roughly speaking Volume V treats the first half of the sixteenth century, Volume VI the second half, with occasional sallies into the first three decades of the seventeenth century. As in the earlier volumes the organization is not rigorously systematic; some chapters are devoted to individual writers, others to groups, still others to special topics. The first chapter, "Intellectual Characteristics," sets forth a number of generalizations about the background of the period. The most noteworthy of these may be given in the author's own words:

New facts were appended to outworn systems, with the result for a time of more confusion than enlightenment (V, 10).
Scientific controversy seldom followed religious lines. . . . Natural and occult science, medicine and mathematics, were like the classics in offering a neutral territory and in affording a common meeting ground where religious and political differ-

[8] (New York: Macmillan Co., 1923; second printing with corrections, 1929).

[9] Subtitle: *Studies in the History of Medicine and Surgery, Natural and Mathematical Science, Philosophy and Politics* (New York: Columbia University Press, 1929).

[10] (*History of Science Society Publications,* New Series, IV; New York: Columbia University Press, 1934).

[11] Also published by the Columbia University Press with the sponsorship of the History of Science Society: Vol. V, xxii+695 pp.; Vol. VI, xviii+766 pp.; price $10.00 per set.

ences could be ignored and temporarily forgotten (V, 11).

As for nationalist separatism, the sixteenth century had still gone only a little way from medieval Latin unity to the idea-tight compartments of modern national languages, where linguistic barriers are even more formidable than tariff walls (V, 12).

It is a surprising and paradoxical fact that, although in the sixteenth century the persecution of witches reached greater proportions than before, and the literature against witchcraft became much more vehement and voluminous, there was less objection to the word magic, and more approving use of it than in the preceding centuries (V, 13).

As the [sixteenth] century wore on, the turning away from ARISTOTLE's natural philosophy and the rise of Paracelsanism encouraged the development of occult philosophy, and a favoring attitude toward natural magic. This tendency continued briskly into the seventeenth century until by its excesses it exhausted and killed itself and was replaced by the sceptical rationalism and enlightenment of the eighteenth century (V, 14).

At the end of Volume VI stands a chapter entitled "Summary and By-Products." In substance this chapter is a sort of semi-statistical autopsy performed by the author on the indexes of all six volumes. An analysis of place and person names brings out, among other points, the continuing frequency in the sixteenth century of citations from Arabic writers in medicine and astrology, despite the humanistic outcry against medieval barbarism; the partial shift of the cultural center of gravity from southern to northern Europe (with the exception of the British Isles which lagged until the end of the century); the continuing importance of Paris as a center of printing and of learning; the wide diffusion of learned

medical practice; the beginnings of scientific correspondence and exchange on an international basis; the absolute pre-eminence of Venice as a center of scientific publication.

A topical analysis of the indexes suggests to THORNDIKE that the sixteenth century, with its "close combing of classical books and sources, [was] a sort of catch-all for the previous history of thought" (VI, 585). Although the index of Volumes V and VI contains many terms which had not appeared in any of the earlier volumes, this fact would not seem to indicate that the sixteenth century surpassed the preceding periods in quantity of innovation. THORNDIKE, indeed, gives the palm for originality and richness of intellectual life to the fourteenth century—an interesting and important conclusion which I shall examine in more detail below.

Between these two summaries at the beginning and the end of the sixteenth-century volumes, THORNDIKE has strung a chain of forty-six highly variegated chapters. Nearly every page is based in some measure on new material. Although many familiar figures make their appearance, the reader will find that even these take on the strange aspect which is common to the scores of obscure philosophasters, occultists, doctors, poets, encyclopedists, dabblers, charlatans and honest men of science who are presented to his attention for the first time. A transcription of the chapter headings will give an impression of the wealth of material:

Volume V: 1, Intellectual Conditions and Characteristics of the Sixteenth Century; 2, LEONARDO DA VINCI: "The Magician of the Renaissance"; 3, ACHILLINI, Aristotelian and Anatomist; 4, COCLES and Chiromancy; 5, NIFO and Demons; 6,

Pomponazzi on Incantations; 7, SYMPHO-
RIEN CHAMPIER; 8, AGRIPPA and Occult
Philosophy; 9, Varied Approaches to Nat-
ural Philosophy; 10, Astrology of the Early
Century; 11, The Conjunction of 1524; 12,
Astrology at Bologna; 13, The Court of
PAUL III (1543-1549); 14, Astronomy and
Astrology at Paris; 15, Astrology Else-
where; 16, The Aftermath of REGIOMON-
TANUS; 17, The Circle of MELANCHTHON;
18, The Copernican Theory; 19, German
Medicine; 20, BRASAVOLA and Pharmacy;
21, Poisons, Fascination, and Hydrophobia;
22, FRACASTORO (1478-1533); 23, Anatomy
from CARPI TO VESALIUS; 24, Alchemy dur-
ing the First Half of the Sixteenth Century;
25, Elements and Occult Virtue; 26, CAR-
DAN; 27, Three Technologists, TAISNIER,
BESSON, and PALISSY; 28, GRATOROLO; 29,
The Paracelsan Revival; 30, THOMAS ERAS-
TUS.

Volume VI: 31, Post-Copernican Astronomy; 32, The New Stars; 33, Astrology
after 1550; 34, The Catholic Reaction:
Index, Inquisition and Papal Bulls; 35,
Adversaries of Astrology; 36, Medicine after 1550; 37, LIBAVIUS and Chemical Controversy; 38, The Sixteenth Century Naturalists; 39, The Lore of Gems; 40, CESAL-
PINO's View of Nature; 41, Efforts toward
a Christian Philosophy of Nature; 42, For
and against ARISTOTLE; 43, Natural Philosophy and Natural Magic; 44, Mystic
Philosophy: Words and Numbers; 45, Divination; 46, The Literature of Magic and
Witchcraft after WIER; 47, The Sceptic and
the Atheist: FRANCESCO SANCHEZ and LU-
CILIO VANINI; 48, Summary and By-Products.

Among the general characteristics
which impress the reader of these volumes easily the first is their erudition.
As a compendium of biographical and
bibliographical information they stand
almost alone in their field. THORNDIKE
threads his way through the maze of
authentic and pirated editions, abridg-
ments and translations with complete

assurance. His comprehensive knowledge of earlier writers makes it easy for
him to spot the repetitions of threadbare
arguments, the adaptations and downright plagiarisms which sprout like
weeds in the fertile sixteenth-century
soil. And throughout the reader has
the comfortable feeling that everything
is quite accurate; there is no temptation
to waste one's energies trying to catch
the author on a misspelled German title
or a defective Latin ending.

The formal presentation of the sixteenth, and to some extent of the fourteenth and fifteenth-century volumes,
unlike their learning, is not impeccable.
It is true that THORNDIKE can, and frequently does write a clean, precise expository prose. Nevertheless the general impression created by these volumes
is one of a certain stylelessness, a string-
ing together of thousands of notes taken
down rapidly and accurately, but without formal polish. Indeed it is sometimes difficult to determine—this was
particularly true in Volumes III and IV
—what criterion was followed in assigning a given item to footnote, appendix
or text. Possibly this defect has resulted
solely from the magnitude of the undertaking and from the diversity of the material, rather than from any inherent
lack of architectonic sense.

In appraising the essential, as opposed
to the accidental qualities of *Magic and
Experimental Science*—I speak now of
the entire work—the natural starting
point is the lengthy review of Volumes
I and II, which was written by GEORGE
SARTON in 1924 (*Isis*, VI, 74-89). Since
this criticism remains the most comprehensive which has been directed against
Magic and Experimental Science, it may
be worth while to summarize it at some
length.

After conceding that *Magic and Experimental Science* must be recognized as a work of major importance, SARTON proceeds directly to his principal point: the title of the book, he charges, is fundamentally misleading. This is not a history of experimental science. It was conceived originally as a history of magic, and science was added (the author himself confesses it) as an afterthought. Moreover, throughout the work, whenever THORNDIKE talks about the experiments which were actually carried out in ancient or medieval times, he fails to tell us what we most want to know: how was each experiment conceived and executed, and what did it prove? Instead of emphasizing the really important experiments—such as PTOLEMY's studies of refraction or PIERRE DE MARICOURT's work on the magnet—THORNDIKE lingers over the "experimenta" and the "secreta" of the medieval physicians, which were little more than semi-magical collections of remedies and recipes, ostensibly tried by experience. THORNDIKE is, of course, aware of this naive use of the term "experimentum" in antiquity and the Middle Ages, but he has insensibly been beguiled into accepting all references to experiment as valid in the modern sense.

Of magic, SARTON concedes, the author has given an adequate definition, but of true science he has displayed only an imperfect and uncritical notion. The main characteristics of science, SARTON asserts, are "its rationality, its scepticism, its progressiveness, its unlimitedness" (80). It is clear from his development of this contrast that, for SARTON, any work which calls itself a history of experimental science should be the record of a "cumulative, a progressive activity." The history of science is for him, as his whole work shows, identical with the chronicle of human progress. In that progress magic is not, as THORNDIKE claims, a causal influence, a creative contributor. It is rather an impediment, a weed which threatens to choke the flowers in the garden of thought. Magic is to science as vice is to virtue. The coexistence of magic and true science—often in the same mind—cannot be denied, but that is simply evidence of the basic duality of the human spirit. The progressive elimination of this flaw is a chronicle of emancipation, a "tale of conquest, of hope, of joy" (88). THORNDIKE by centering his approach in magic, has given us the "depressing recital of unprogressive and hopeless activities."

SARTON justifies the severity of this indictment by the contention that *Magic and Experimental Science* will actually mislead many of those who read it. Scientifically trained readers without historical knowledge, finding in it nothing but a tale of human aberration, will be confirmed in their erroneous preconception that medieval science was nothing but a waste of time. Non-scientific readers will lack both the technical knowledge to check the author's statements, and the perspective to see that he has not been talking about science at all:

After reading this elaborate parody of the history of medieval science, they will imagine that they know something of the subject—yet they will know precious little of it, and their understanding of science will be worse than ever. Truly such a prospect makes one shudder (83).

This is strong language, and in a sense I hesitate to recall it. It is well to do so, however, for the acerbity which it—and indeed the whole review—conveys should not be allowed to persist. Even in his original review, SARTON softened the impact of his criticism by admitting that it was primarily the title which was at fault. In his review of Volumes III and IV (*Isis*, XXIII, 471-75) the tone is distinctly more generous, and I am sure that if SARTON were reviewing the present volumes, he would ungrudgingly acclaim the completion of the only monument of this generation in the history of science worthy to stand with his own *Introduction*.

Any comprehensive judgment must start with the recognition that *Magic and Experimental Science* is not a complete work. THORNDIKE himself says so explicitly. The magnitude of his task imposed a principle of economy, the deliberate avoidance of repeating work satisfactorily accomplished by other scholars. This is particularly true in the case of DUHEM; THORNDIKE rarely cites him except to amplify a point or to correct an error. Though this principle of economy has undoubtedly saved effort to the author, and has cut down the already considerable bulk of the work itself, it is also one of the chief reasons why *Magic and Experimental Science* fails to achieve a rounded synthesis.

But admitting that the avowed partiality of THORNDIKE's aim disarms some of SARTON's criticism, there remains the charge that the title is misleading. This charge also is tacitly admitted by the author, who states that the work might more properly have been called "a history of the relations between magic and experimental science" (III, 22). Perhaps the realization that this was the true subject of the book came too late, or perhaps the title was too cumbersome for the publisher. I find it hard to share SARTON's dismay over this matter. I can hardly believe that many persons would approach *Magic and Experimental Science* under a misapprehension, and come away from it badly disappointed or misled.

Both of these criticisms, then, would seem to be of minor significance. There remains the fundamental question: has THORNDIKE succeeded in demonstrating his central thesis? In his review of 1924 SARTON flatly states that THORNDIKE has failed to prove it in a single instance; he has failed signally to demonstrate a positive, a constructive relation between the history of magic and the history of science. My own examination of the entire work leads me to believe that this judgment calls for modification.

The premises underlying SARTON's contention may be stated as follows: THORNDIKE may understand magic, but he does not understand science. Without an understanding of science, it is *eo ipso* impossible to establish any conclusions as to its relations with magic.

We may agree with SARTON that *Magic and Experimental Science* does present a valid, and perhaps a novel concept of magic. In THORNDIKE's earliest statement, clearly written under the influence of FRAZER's *Golden Bough*, magic is characterized as

primitive man's philosophy . . . his attitude toward nature. . . . It is any change with characteristics and results which we do not expect nor usually see in changes.

In THORNDIKE's latest statement magic is described as

a systematized and ordered marvel-believing and marvel-working, a consistent body of error, attained through sense perception, introspection, reflection, and dreaming, influenced by faith, emotion, appetite, and pleasure, marked by unwarranted association of ideas, without adequate means of correcting error and without proper standards of measurement (V, 13).

In its concrete manifestations magic takes innumerable forms. THORNDIKE is not concerned with the whole of magic, but only with those parts which touch on, or edge toward, science. But even these self-imposed limits still embrace an enormous area, extending from the crudest superstitious folk practices to those disciplines now regarded as pseudo-science, but once regarded as consistent bodies of rational natural knowledge, such as alchemy and astrology. Between these poles lie the areas of black and white magic, of divination with its innumerable weird and often revolting forms of manticism, of fantastic natural philosophies embodying aesthetic, occult, mystical and religious principles.

The conception of science, like that of magic, undergoes clarification as the work proceeds. In the original statement of the thesis, and in the earlier volumes of *Magic and Experimental Science,* science is taken for granted and is not rigorously defined. In Volume V, however, acting perhaps under the sting of SARTON's criticism, THORNDIKE does set forth a positive conception of science which is contrasted, point by point, with the characterization of magic quoted above:

Science is systematized and ordered knowledge, a consistent body of truth, attained through sense perception, introspection, and reflection, aided by mechanical and mathematical instruments, independently of faith, emotion, prejudice, appetite, pleasure, and the like. . . . In magic the desire to attain ends and satisfy human cravings not primarily intellectual was dominant; in science the urge is to measure and know (V, 12 f.).

Of the authentic sciences (as against the pseudo-sciences of astrology and alchemy) which come within THORNDIKE's scope, the most important is medicine. The persistence of occultism and sympathetic magic in learned, as well as

in empirical, medicine can easily be demonstrated throughout the centuries, even into our own day. THORNDIKE's volumes abound in contributions to the history of this strange but fruitful marriage, though they by no means present a complete and justly shaded picture of medical history. Botany is another true science which, through its use in the concoction of remedies is inextricably tangled up with magic. In the penumbra of medicine lie the supposedly empirical study of the properties of poisons, and the lore of amulets and gems. In the field of the physical sciences geological questions, such as the distribution of land and water masses on the earth's surface, or the origins of mountains and fossils, figure prominently in late medieval texts from ALBERTUS MAGNUS to LEONARDO DA VINCI and PALISSY. This subject, indeed, had been opened by PIERRE DUHEM, but THORNDIKE's explorations have extended the field. The mathematical and mechanical disciplines, on the whole, play the least important role in THORNDIKE's discussion, partly because they are least susceptible to magical deformation, partly, again, because they have been so extensively pioneered by DUHEM. Optics, in some respects, the experimental science *par excellence* of the Middle Ages, is not given the attention which it would deserve in a full synthetic account.

Although the treatment of these various fields is somewhat uneven, in nearly every case our understanding of the medieval achievement is sensibly enriched. We see the elaboration of science and pseudo-science, inspired and directed by widely divergent motives, by paranoid megalomania or thaumaturgic ambition, by religious utilitarianism, by curiosity or sheer playfulness, by hunches, by cupidity and lust for power.

It is true that the inner process by which scientific substance is created sometimes eludes us. We see the external juxta-position of something which is obviously magic and something which looks like, or calls itself, or actually is science, while the internal nexus remains obscure. And yet I cannot agree with SARTON when he implies that what emerges from magic is never science, but is anti-science.

On the other hand, it may well be true that, despite the accumulation of instances in the later volumes of *Magic and Experimental Science,* "experiment" itself never fully achieves that concep-tual clarity which SARTON found want-ing in the earlier volumes. The nature of the experimental method is indeed difficult to define, and the most modern discussions prove that it is by no means perfectly grasped, even today. It is not surprising, therefore, that the con-cept should remain somewhat blurred in *Magic and Experimental Science.* There seems to be no clear distinction between such terms as "experience" "empiricism" and "experiment." And within the concept of "experiment" THORNDIKE has not systematically distin-guished the quantitative from the quali-tative approach, a distinction which has been fundamental from antiquity to our own day. There is also no clear separa-tion between unique, casual, passive noting of phenomena, and repeated, planned, active attempts to reproduce them (the *experientia quaesita* of FRAN-CIS BACON). Finally it would seem that THORNDIKE has not sufficiently discrimi-nated between the practical or produc-tive and the speculative or theoretical faculties in scientific operation.

The failure to define the term "experi-ment" may account for another point of uncertainty which occurs to the reader who has reached the end of Volume VI. Is there, or is there not, a radical difference in kind between the experi-ment of antiquity and the Middle Ages, and its counterpart of the seven-teenth century and the modern world? THORNDIKE cannot, of course, be ex-pected to give the answer to this ques-tion, since he does not make a serious entry into the latter period. What he has done—and this is also true of Du-HEM—has been to extend a standing invitation to the historians of seven-teenth-century science to turn their steps backward, instead of restlessly pressing forward along the lines of modern "progress."

This backward march of the histo-rians of modern science has already be-gun independently on a small scale, and the time may come when they will have joined ranks with the slowly advancing body of medievalists. Separate studies have already made it clear that most, if not all of the great seventeenth-century scientists retained the impress of medi-eval habits of thought. The tabular scheme of experimentation devised by FRANCIS BACON is qualitative and par-tially Aristotelian; it bears the stamp of medieval as well as Renaissance pan-sophistic yearnings. KEPLER was an ani-mist; his three laws of planetary motion were the unexpected pot of gold at the end of a Pythagorean rainbow. GALI-LEO was nurtured as a student on the *impetus* physics of the fourteenth-cen-tury Paris School.[12] DESCARTES, as a re-sult of his Jesuit training, never fully emancipated himself from the scholastic

---

[12] Cf. A. KOYRÉ, *Études Galiléennes:* I, *À l'aube de la science classique* (Paris, 1939). KOYRÉ points out that this was only the first stage of GALILEO's development; the crucial stage was precipitated by an intensive study of ARCHIMEDES.

Aristotelian yoke.[13] BOYLE was an occultist.[14] LEIBNIZ proposed to edit the *Calculationes* of that subtlest of fourteenth-century speculators, RICHARD SUISETH.

Instances of medieval survivals of this sort could be multiplied indefinitely. THORNDIKE's method of distilling the residues of magic, applied to the great figures of the "Age of Genius," would undoubtedly yield interesting results. I can hardly believe, however, that such an effort would be fully profitable. For fundamentally the seventeenth century marks an epochal change, a full mutation[15] in the intellectual germ plasm of our culture, beyond the genetic stages traversed in the preceding centuries. THORNDIKE himself seems to recognize that fact in a somewhat cryptic valedictory at the beginning of the sixteenth-century volumes:

. . . it appears that as the Thirty Years War and Treaty of Westphalia make a convenient terminal point for the first political period in modern history since the close of the Middle Ages and the beginning of the Reformation, so we may carry on our account to the verge of the days of GALILEO and KEPLER and DESCARTES, to the writings of VANINI and CAMPANELLA. Then investigations based upon telescope and microscope ushered in a new age of science, at whose portal the present volumes stop. Like MOSES we have brought the reader through the wilderness to within sight of the promised land of modern science. It remains to be seen whether we shall enter in or whether we shall content ourselves with viewing the prospect o'er from the other—magical—side of Jordan (V, 15).

The terminus of *Magic and Experimental Science* is well placed at the threshold of the seventeenth century. For prior to that century the history of science is history; subsequent to that century it is science.

Like most really great works of scholarship, *Magic and Experimental Science* displays a certain "ruling passion" in the personality of its author. In the case of THORNDIKE this might be described as a deep antipathy to established but questionable generalizations. Insofar as he has ever permitted himself to generalize about the nature of the historian's task, THORNDIKE has defended the ideal of strict scientific presentation. As far back as 1910 he wrote:

The scientific historian will see not only that his theme must be developed systematically, but also that every concept which may be implicated in his investigation must be sharply defined and henceforth consistently treated from that one point of view. . . . The historian who has denied the existence of 'facts' will be inclined to look askance also at periods, movements and institutions. He will shake himself free from unjustifiable historical conglomerates as well as from false historical units.[16]

---

[13] Instances of medieval notions in DESCARTES are adduced by THORNDIKE in "The Survival of Mediaeval Intellectual Interests into Early Modern Times," *Speculum*, II (1927), 147-59. Cf. two recent important studies on DESCARTES: JOHN WILD, "The Cartesian Deformation of the Structure of Change and Its Influence on Modern Thought," *Philosophical Review*, L (1941), 36-51; and ALAN GEWIRTZ, "Experience and the Non-mathematical in the Cartesian Method," *Journal of the History of Ideas*, II (1941), 183-210, which attacks the prevalent notion that DESCARTES did not resort to experience to verify deduced conclusions.

[14] Cf. LOUIS TRENCHARD MORE, "Boyle as Alchemist," *Journal of the History of Ideas*, II (1940), 61-76.

[15] The phrase is used by KOYRÉ to characterize the passage from the Parisian *impetus* physics of the late Middle Ages to the Archimedean physics of the seventeenth century; *supra*, note 12.

[16] "The Scientific Presentation of History," *The Popular Science Monthly*, LXXVI (1910), p. 178.

At the time he wrote these lines, THORNDIKE seems to have had great confidence in the future progress of history as a scientific discipline. Perhaps that confidence reflected the youthful ardor which had been fanned by the inspiration of JAMES HARVEY ROBINSON. THORNDIKE suggested, for instance, that "extensive past literatures teeming with human prejudices, motives and ideas are waiting for accurate measurement and estimation." [17] The content of history will be made up of scientific propositions, and its form of presentation, borrowing from mathematics, will consist of "historical symbols, curves, charts and other graphic means of presenting briefly and accurately what prose could compass only in many pages or fail to express with requisite precision and discrimination." [18] THORNDIKE conceded regretfully that "fewer persons would study the reformed presentation than read histories at present." But, he added, "they would learn more truth of value, gain a deeper insight into the true nature of history and have a greater respect for it."

This was the young scholar's program of 1910, and one would search in vain, I believe, for any methodological statements of comparable sweep in THORNDIKE's later writings. I should not have thought it worth while to dwell on this profession of faith—the author himself may no longer accept it to the letter—were it not for the fact that it helps us to understand the origins of the "ruling passion" which I mentioned above.

Originally THORNDIKE's distrust of generalizations seems to have sprung from a rather abstract and impersonal scientific idealism. As his work progressed, however, this distrust seems to have taken on a more personal cast. A certain animus crept in which was hardly to be detected in the statement of 1910. Gradually a concern developed, not merely to avoid making unfounded generalizations, but to uproot those which were already implanted in the popular mind. This concern has expressed itself throughout THORNDIKE's later work in what might be called a "reverse of the medal approach," a zeal to "parcere subiectis et debellare superbos."

The first notable examples of this approach are to be found in his treatment of certain thirteenth-century figures, especially ROGER BACON, whom THORNDIKE quite properly puts in his place as a man *of* his age, not *ahead* of it. The fifteenth century provided further opportunity for deflationary activities. In *Science and Thought* (1929) two chapters are devoted to a critical scrutiny of the great reputations which have attached themselves to the names of NICHOLAS OF CUSA, GEORGE PEURBACH and REGIOMONTANUS. [19] THORNDIKE asserted that the fame of these men had been unduly magnified by their contemporaries and followers, and that modern historians have been taken in by the "piffle" [20]

---

[17] *Ibid.*, p. 179; I do not know whether THORNDIKE ever attempted to carry out such a program. The only suggestion of such an attempt is an article—which I have not been able to consult—entitled: "Measuring Euripides," in *Chapter Alpha of Ohio, Phi Beta Kappa, College for Women Section* (Cleveland, 1916).

[18] "Scientific Presentation," p. 181.

[19] Ch. VII, "Nicholas of Cusa and the Triple Motion of the Earth"; Ch. VIII, "Peurbach and Regiomontanus: Their Great Reputation Re-Examined."

[20] The word does not appear in the chapter in *Science in Thought*, but in chapter XVI, Vol. V of *Magic and Experimental Science*, p. 335. This chapter, "The Aftermath of Regiomontanus," together with chapter XXXI, "Post-Copernican Astronomy," constitute the most important recent contribution to the history of sixteenth-century astronomy.

of Renaissance printers and hack encomiasts. The lines of THORNDIKE's attack may be simply stated: most of the scientific work of these men was unoriginal; where it was original, it was either unsatisfactory as science or unimportant. Thus the famous Latin version of PTOLEMY's *Almagest* which PEURBACH began and REGIOMONTANUS completed "was not a complete and exact translation of the Greek text, but an epitome of it, the sort of work that has commonly been held a reproach of the early Middle Ages, but which we here find the classical Renaissance glorying in." REGIOMONTANUS' work in trigonometry, like that of PEURBACH, was far from original, and the praises which it received merely indicated that its medieval forerunners had been forgotten.[21] In the case of NICHOLAS OF CUSA, the rather fantastic anticipations of COPERNICUS which have been read into his cosmological speculations originate, not in astronomical observation, but in pious scepticism and "docta ignorantia." Having effectively demolished some of the extravagant claims made on behalf of the fifteenth-century cardinal by some of his nineteenth-century admirers, THORNDIKE lets himself go for a page and a half of diatribe against that type of scholarship which selects "as the great names in the history of philosophy and science men whose time was largely occupied by other interests, and whose

fame should and does depend upon something else. . . . When," he asks, "are we ever going to come out of it?"[22]

The critique of these three fifteenth-century thinkers reveals another insistent animus which has increased steadily as THORNDIKE's work has proceeded—a profound distaste for the movement known as humanism and for the period when it flourished, the Renaissance. It might be possible to account for this antipathy as the bias of a professional medievalist. But its roots seem to lie even deeper, embedded in a personal aversion to the whole humanistic discipline and habit of thought, and indeed to any discipline or convention which places the primary emphasis on *form*.

Combining this distaste with his equally firm opposition to historical generalizations about *Zeitgeist*, THORNDIKE frequently indulges in what can only be described as "cracks" against the period "formerly known as the Renaissance" (V, 53); against "'the spirit of the Renaissance,' that rare gas which the historical laboratory has never yet succeeded in holding in solution." Renaissance humanism placed its "emphasis on style rather than science, and show rather than substance" (V, 5). Its "amateurish literary interest" was in large measure responsible for the lack of scientific specialization in the sixteenth century, for the popularity of superficial epitomes and compendiums instead of the solid if

[21] THORNDIKE's attempt to deflate Regiomontanus has met with some opposition. The definitive biography by ERNST ZINNER, *Leben und Wirken des Johannes Müller von Königsberg, genannt Regiomontanus* (Munich, 1938), certainly forces us to agree with GEORGE SARTON that REGIOMONTANUS was an admirable man (review of *Science and Thought* in *Isis*, XIV [1930], 238). At the same time it is true that ZINNER's biography provides considerable evidence to support THORNDIKE's charge that REGIOMONTANUS was heavily indebted to medieval predecessors.

[22] My own studies in the history of fifteenth-century cartography confirm THORNDIKE's charge that the solid achievements of obscure scientists have often been unfairly transferred to better known figures. This is particularly true in the case of the so-called Nicholas of Cusa Map which has been mistakenly regarded as the first modern map of Central Europe; cf. D. B. DURAND, *The Vienna-Klosterneuburg Map Corpus of the Fifteenth Century*, 2 Vols. (Leiden, 1940?), I, 252-64. (N. B. Publication of this work appears to have been interrupted in May, 1940. A bound copy of the corrected proof has been deposited in the Harvard College Library where it may be consulted by those who are interested.)

bulky pabulum which the scholastics manfully swallowed; for the flourishing of scientific quacks and charlatans and plagiarists at the expense of a gullible public, for the prevalence of mudslinging controversy, of "one-sided advocacy of a certain theory or point of view," of "unutterably coarse billingsgate and bluster," in contrast with the dispassionate and impersonal "poise" of the schoolmen (V, 9).

This threefold antipathy—against unfounded generalizations, overmagnification of great names, and exaggerated emphasis on Renaissance humanism—receives full expression in THORNDIKE's treatment of the sixteenth century, and especially of its three mightiest geniuses, LEONARDO DA VINCI, COPERNICUS and VESALIUS. These giants, whom our schoolbooks have taught us to venerate as founders of modern science, emerge from the pages of Magic and Experimental Science with a notable diminution of stature.

The romantic myth of LEONARDO as a transcendental genius, an intellectual Nova, was exploded more than a quarter century ago by PIERRE DUHEM.[23] DUHEM proved conclusively that the great Florentine was no mysterious cosmic happening, flaring up out of nothing and dying away without influence. DUHEM's Études did nothing to diminish our admiration of LEONARDO's amazing genius, and did much to increase our understanding of his creative power. THORNDIKE, unlike DUHEM, seems rather to begrudge the praise that has been lavished on LEONARDO. Of the famous studies and sketches of animal and human anatomy, THORNDIKE notes that

they are "excellent," without further specification, and passes immediately to the residues of magical lore and false science which permeate the Notebooks. Of LEONARDO's work in the field of technology, he notes only that it continued the tradition of preceding centuries. He fails to credit LEONARDO with his true influence on the later tradition of technology, especially on the Theatre des Instruments of JACQUES BESSON, to which a few pages are devoted elsewhere in Volume V.[24] THORNDIKE praises LEONARDO's observation of fossil shells, and quotes without dissent DUHEM's assertion that this fragment in the Notebooks "created Palaeontology" (V. 27). But he hastens to remind us that LEONARDO's notions about the earth were vitiated by a curious belief that it was an organism like the human body with a system of respiration and circulation. THORNDIKE upholds the title of his chapter, "The Magician of the Renaissance," by citing LEONARDO's cry "Voglio far miraculi" (V, 32 f.). He admits that LEONARDO was no necromancer, yet contends that his manuscripts continue the medieval tradition of "experiments" and "secrets" which aimed at the performance of natural magic.

In his chapter on the "Copernican Theory," (V, xviii) THORNDIKE's first concern is to remind us that the De Revolutionibus Orbium Coelestium was not totally without antecedents. From the time of CAMPANUS OF NOVARA in the thirteenth century a number of medieval cosmologists and astronomers had sought to overthrow or at least to simplify the Ptolemaic system. Most of these simplifications, however, seem to

---

[23] Études sur Léonard de Vinci, 3 séries (Paris, 1906-1913).

[24] Magic and Experimental Science, V, 34 f.; V, 593-96. For the LEONARDO tradition of technological drawings in the later sixteenth century, see, among others, A. WOLF, History of Science, Technology, and Philosophy in the 16th and 17th Centuries (London, 1935), pp. 536-40.

have been of a speculative rather than a mathematical order. But even aside from partial medieval anticipations, there were other circumstances which, THORNDIKE feels, should qualify our praise of *De Revolutionibus*. The work was announced under an astrological accompaniment.[25] It reflects a "rather excessive classicism" on the part of its author. It frequently drifts into lyrical, mystical and theosophical rhapsodies, inappropriate to a scientific work.[26] Technically, it failed in its professed aim of eliminating defects in the Ptolemaic calculations. It introduced a new and unnecessary irregularity to account for a non-existent slowing down in the precession of the equinoxes. It was unable to do away entirely with the complex and cumbersome system of eccentrics and epicycles. Indeed, strictly speaking, the Copernican system did not postulate that full heliocentricity which is popularly associated with it today; it placed the center of reference for the planetary motions not in the sun, but in the center of the earth's orbit. It was thus, like the system of PTOLEMY itself, still fundamentally eccentric. Moreover, COPERNICUS himself made very few observations, and these were distinctly inferior to those which underlay such medieval revisions of Ptolemaic calculations as the *Alphonsine Tables*. Finally, the Copernician system involved, a "somewhat incongruous" modification of the traditional Aristotelian arrangement of the elementary spheres.[27]

In the case of VESALIUS, to whom only part of a chapter is devoted,[28] the treatment is again primarily negative. THORNDIKE reminds us that for at least two centuries before the publication of *De Humani Corporis Fabrica* there had been active study of anatomy in the Universities, leading to a wide diffusion of skilled and learned surgical practice. Public dissection of human corpses was common in the Middle Ages. Some of VESALIUS' immediate predecessors, notably BERENGARIO DA CARPI and NICOLAUS MASSA, were sound anatomists, but VESALIUS passes over them in jealous silence. And it was VESALIUS himself who, through his caustic preface, did more than anyone else to establish the myth that all operations in the Middle Ages had been performed by barbers and vulgar uninstructed surgeons—a calumny which has been uncritically accepted by most modern writers. VESALIUS, far from being the demolisher of GALEN which he has usually been painted, "was concerned to restore the text of GALEN to its original form" (V, 525). Although he sneers at scholastic theologians for their controversies as to the nature of the blood and water which flowed from the side of the Crucified, he himself retains many of the occult notions which were current in his age. The entire positive achievement

---

[25] V, 414; but elsewhere THORNDIKE admits that COPERNICUS published nothing which would support belief in astrology (V, 419).

[26] COPERNICUS' well-known passage in praise of the Sun and of the symmetry and harmony in the divine arrangement of the universe is, THORNDIKE declares, "not only not scientific and seems out of place in *De Revolutionibus* but is shallow and fallacious, not to say a trifle insincere" (V, 424). In the next paragraph, however, THORNDIKE excuses this as a "rhapsodical lapse" and admits that the work is "for the most part solidly mathematical both in tone and content."

[27] V, 428; but THORNDIKE ends the chapter by admitting that "it is to be put to the credit of COPERNICUS that he suggested that the same considerations of gravity and of heavy and light applied to the other planets as spherical bodies as to the earth" (V, 429).

[28] V, 522-29.

on which his great fame is supposed to rest is dismissed with the following sentence:

The work of VESALIUS of course contains indications, or at least assertions, of discovery of anatomical details unknown to previous writers on and students of the subject, and denials on the basis of personal dissection and observation of previous beliefs and statements which he rejects as figments (V, 525).

THORNDIKE goes so far as to imply that the only really epoch-making feature of *De Humani Corporis Fabrica* lay in its accompaniment of numerous and elaborate plates (V, 519 f.).

This, I think, is a fair summary of the impression which emerges from THORNDIKE's treatment of what are ordinarily regarded as three of the greatest names in the history of scientific genius. "Debunking" may not be the word to apply to this treatment; perhaps "hagiographophobia" might be coined for the purpose.

But the medal has two sides. The systematic presentation of the reverse of the big names is matched by the frequent presentation of the obverse in the case of obscure men. Naturally, not every one of the hundreds of minor writers drawn in by THORNDIKE's farflung net turns out to be a rare or unique specimen. Yet a surprising proportion of the scientific innovations which THORNDIKE singles out for particular comment are connected with names that the casual reader would not recognize. This is especially the case in his treatment of the fourteenth century which, as we have noted, is credited with the highest degree of originality.

Among the scientific contributions of that fruitful century, one of the most important is the introduction of an ideal of precision in the use and manufacture of various instruments. THORNDIKE, following the lead of DUHEM, emphasizes the fact that astronomers of the later Middle Ages used large, well-constructed instruments, surpassing in some instances those even of the sixteenth century. Thus JEAN DE MURS, while still a student at Paris in 1318, employed a solidly mounted *kardaja* of fifteen-foot radius as contrasted with TYCHO BRAHE's "much vaunted" wall-quadrant of only six feet nine inches radius.[29] It is not uncommon, moreover, to find in fourteenth-century manuscripts observations and calculations carried out in fractions as small as minutes and seconds of time or angle, and occasionally these fractions were fantastically extended even to fifths and sixths. It is well to remember, however, as THORNDIKE admits, that these were "paper" refinements, manifestations of an ideal of precision which far outstripped the practically possible.

Precision, in the fourteenth century, was sought in other fields besides astronomy. The design of mechanical clocks, which, as THORNDIKE has recently shown, goes back at least on paper to the third quarter of the thirteenth century,[30] was translated through the painstaking craftsmanship of medieval metal workers into a manufacturing technique. And that technique was the direct ancestor of the infinite ramifications of modern precision machinery. THORNDIKE also reminds us that systematic recording of weather observations began in the fourteenth century with WILLIAM MERLE of Oxford and EVNO of

---

[29] III, 294 ff.; it seems a little strong, however, to say "apparently it was only in TYCHO BRAHE's day that such large instruments became a rarity."

[30] "Invention of the Mechanical Clock about 1271 A.D.," *Speculum,* XVI (1941), 242-43.

Würzburg.[31] Meteorology, for a long time to come, was to be little more than a frontier province in the great kingdom of magic, yet the introduction of a rudimentary scientific empiricism in the Middle Ages cannot be denied. THORNDIKE notes other instances of quantitative specification in medicine and alchemy,[32] but these are of a crude order; and usually they must be regarded as affectations or fantasies, totally without the possibility of experimental verification. Nevertheless, the evidence provided in the fourteenth-century volume of *Magic and Experimental Science* does support THORNDIKE's contention that "careful measurement of the phenomena" can be credited to some late medieval scientists (IV, 614).

These innovations of an empirical order which THORNDIKE ferrets out in the murky recesses of the fourteenth century are paralleled by advances in speculative thought. Here again the pioneer was PIERRE DUHEM, but THORNDIKE has made important discoveries of his own. To be sure it is difficult to escape the impression that THORNDIKE, *like* DUHEM, has occasionally strained his texts through a porcelain filter to extract a minute residue of modernity. As a rather extreme example of THORNDIKE's method we may cite the chapter (III, xxviii) on the late fourteenth-century scholastic HENRICUS LANGENSTEIN, known as HENRY OF HESSE. Although HENRY is described by THORNDIKE as inferior in originality to his brilliant contemporary, NICOLE ORESME, he nevertheless emerges from the pages of *Magic and Experimental Science* as the precursor of an astounding number of modern scientific discoveries. Among these are the development of a principle of "common nature" (which, however, had been prefigured by ADELARD OF BATH in the twelfth century and ROGER BACON in the thirteenth) vaguely anticipatory of modern notions of universal force or continuity (III, 476 ff.). In common with his predecessor RICHARD SUISETH, the "Calculator," and with his colleague ORESME, HENRY is credited with "an important first step towards the development of modern mathematical method and its application to scientific questions" (III, 492). THORNDIKE speaks of his improvement "at least in some respects" on the theory of the rainbow, of his "fourteenth century variety of relativity" (III, 492), of his "experiments in surface tension" (IV, 614, and III, Appendix 32) and of his anticipation of DARWIN on the evolution of new species (III, 483).

Our immediate response is naturally to enquire whether all these ideas are really there in the words of the cited texts, and, if they are there, whether they constitute full and valid anticipations. As a test case I select a passage of ten lines in which THORNDIKE adduces three "specimens of HENRY OF HESSE's scientific caliber," all of which apparently he regards as of an "advanced" character:

We have sometimes been given the impression that the conception of gaseous substances other than air, as well as the word *Geist* or gas, originated in VAN HELMONT's time. But HENRY offers a good illustration of its medieval currency when he states that the exhalations from water are aqueous, those from earth are nothing but earth reduced to a state of vapor, and those from putrefying corpses are merely flesh in a

---

[31] Vol. III, ch. viii.

[32] Note especially the curious theory of "degrees" in proportion of the elements in mixtures, which was devised by WALTER OF ODINGTON; III, 130 ff.

gaseous condition—*caro subtiliata.* He also, as we have seen, was acquainted with the variation of the magnetic needle near the north pole. He observes that regions become rejuvenated or grow arid and old with climatic change (III, 501).

Fortunately, with the footnote references it is easy to trace these three points to the original text in a modern edition.[33] Concerning the first point the text reads as follows:

Item non solum elevantur ex calefactione inferiorum resolutiones ex terra et aqua, sed eciam ex omnibus corporibus mixtis bone vel male complexionis. Et secundum opinionem probabiliorem exalationes sunt eiusdem speciei cum rebus, a quibus exalant, quia exalatio terre non est nisi terra subtiliata et levificata calefactione, et vapor nisi aqua levificata, et exalatio de carne caro subtiliata.[34]

I leave it to others more expert in seventeenth-century science to determine whether the "levificated" and "subtiliated" "resolutions" of earth, water and flesh are analogous to the different kinds of "Gas" described by VAN HELMONT. It does seem apparent, however, that this interesting and curious passage, when set in its full context, must be regarded as a direct outgrowth of current scholastic discussions of "exhalations" as set forth by ARISTOTLE. THORNDIKE is doubtless right in implying a continuous linkage between this type of discussion and the notions of VAN HELMONT.

The second "advanced" point which THORNDIKE attributes to HENRY OF

HESSE is the reference to the "variation" of the magnetic needle "near the north pole." Two pages earlier what is presumably the same point is put somewhat differently:

. . . the planets may act more potently when in certain ratios of proportion or musical consonance or may lose the virtue in one position which they possess in another, like the magnet in some parts of Norway . . . (III, 499).

HENRY OF HESSE's text is as follows:

Ita videtur in proposito, quod planeta in uno situ influat, et in alio non. Item in partibus Norwigie magnes in uno situ trahit ferrum et in alio propinquo non.[35]

It is plain that this passage refers solely to the attraction of iron by the magnet, and not to the declination of the compass needle, albeit the latter was undoubtedly known at this period.

The third of the "advanced" notions—the "rejuvenation" of regions—is derived from the following passage:

Regiones enim quandoque umificantur iuvenescentes ex caliditatis et humiditatis affluencia. Dehinc ad statum veniunt sue virtutis in aquoso permanentes. Deinde autem exsiccantur et senescunt frigiditate et siccitate et inhabitabiles fiunt.[36]

The proper •context of this passage is stated explicitly in the opening lines of the chapter in which it occurs:

Regionum eciam varie sunt dispositiones radicales et accidentales, unde ARISTOTELES in fine primi metheororum. . . .[37]

---

[33] HUBERT PRUCKNER, *Studien zu den astrologischen Schriften des Heinrich von Langenstein* (*Studien der Bibliothek Warburg,* XIV: Leipzig, 1933). All of the three points in question come from HENRY OF HESSE's *Tractatus contra Astrologos Coniunctionistas de Eventibus Futurorum.*

[34] *Ibid.,* p. 198.

[35] *Ibid.,* p. 163.

[36] *Ibid.,* p. 174.

[37] *Ibid.,* p. 173; the passage of HENRY OF HESSE is substantially an abridgment of *Meteorologica,* I, 14, lines 351a, 19-351b, 4. The originality of this chapter in the *Contra Astrologos* seems to lie in its application of ARISTOTLE's notion of climatological variation to the critique of astrology.

It may not be going too far to state that the first and third of these instances of HENRY's "scientific caliber" prove an important point which, so far as I am aware, THORNDIKE has not brought out explicitly and which, perhaps, he would not accept. A very considerable portion of the "advanced" notions of HENRY OF HESSE, and for that matter of ORESME and others of this group, are the direct outgrowth of subtle speculative elaboration of the Aristotelian text. A detailed and systematic investigation of the way in which ARISTOTLE was creatively interpreted and transformed by these highly ingenious theorists of the later Middle Ages is one of the major historical projects whose desirability is implied by the work of both THORNDIKE and DUHEM.[38]

THORNDIKE has disclaimed any interest in collecting "precursorships" for their own sake. It would seem, however, that his concern for the "reverse of the medal" has frequently led him to linger with obvious satisfaction over those which have been turned up by his excavations. The problem of the "precursor" is by no means simple. One type of scholar is inclined to dismiss the "precursor" as insignificant and without explicit influence in the cumulative statistical roll of human progress; another type, to credit him with an implicit influence which cannot be traced. The soundest approach for the historian of thought is to commit himself to neither of these extremes, but to report the achievement of the "precursor" for what it actually was, an eddy of individual creativeness in the sluggish drift of tradition, which may have affected the course of the waters far below the point where its own stirring disappeared.

But the problem of the "precursor" resolves itself into the broader theory of the historical process of intellectual change. Naturally we are impelled to ask, has THORNDIKE contributed significantly to our understanding of this process? To this question, I think, we must give an affirmative answer.

We may safely say that few historians today are equipped with a sound theory of intellectual innovation.[39] Whether philosophers and psychologists have achieved such a theory I do not know, but if they have, it is to be hoped that they will show how it can be applied to the study of history. THORNDIKE, sensibly enough, refrains from formulating general theories concerning the operations of the human mind. He does, however, express the hope that his volumes may have "supplied data that may prove of value to philosophers and psychologists in determining the laws of thought and our intellectual processes" (II, 982).

This hope is not extravagant. THORNDIKE's positive achievement—it is an important one—may be stated somewhat as follows: he has accumulated a massive body of material which other writers of different temperament and insight

---

[38] For a case study in the creative reinterpretation of ARISTOTLE by a fourteenth-century scientist, see my article "Nicole Oresme and the Mediaeval Origins of Modern Science," *Speculum*, XVI (1941), 167-85. This article also contains remarks on both THORNDIKE and DUHEM which I have avoided repeating here, together with some reflections on the problem of the "precursor" which is treated in the following paragraph. Another, and more detailed case study, is the important monograph of CLAGETT on GIOVANNI MARLIANI, cited above, note 5.

[39] Among the more thoughtful historical students of this problem, I would single out Professor A. P. USHER of Harvard University. Apart from a few general remarks in his *History of Mechanical Inventions* (New York, 1929), *passim*, Professor USHER has so far published little on this subject. I am indebted to him for suggestions which helped in formulating these reflections on the problem of the "precursor" and on the nature of historical process.

can use for a great variety of purposes. Moreover, even apart from success or failure in demonstrating his own thesis, THORNDIKE, by the sheer magnitude of his accumulation, and by the principle of selection which he has followed, has given inferential support to a number of major generalizations concerning historical process. The study of nature, it seems hard to deny, springs from a dual, rather than a single principle of the human spirit. This duality may be considered under a number of aspects: knowledge and power, speculation and operation, magic and science. Because of the multiplicity of these inner dualities and of the permutations which they engender, no unitary approach to the history of human thought is feasible. Various non-converging approaches must be followed, and all must take account of the basic fact that the unit of real innovation is always small, when contrasted at any point or in any individual with the persistence of tradition. I am not sure that THORNDIKE would acknowledge all these methodological considerations as his own; some of them, however, he does state explicitly:

We have seen the same old ideas continually recurring, new ideas appearing with exceeding slowness, men of the same given period holding a common stock of notions and being for the most part in remarkable agreement. Even the most intellectual men seem to have a limited number of ideas, just as humanity has a limited number of domesticated animals. Not only is man unable by taking thought to add one cubit to his stature, he usually equally fails to add one new idea to humanity's small collection. Often men seem to be repeating ideas like parrots. And this is not merely patristic, or scholastic; it is everlastingly human. Yet it has been evident that some of our authors were more original, resourceful, ingenious, inquisitive than others. There is curiosity, occasionally a new question is asked, an old thought put in a novel way, or a new experiment tried (II, 983).

Our final judgment must be that THORNDIKE's primary achievement is not so much the demonstration of a thesis as the illustration of a facet of human activity. But from this vast mass of information certain positive statements and conclusions also emerge and force at least partial assent. THORNDIKE has undoubtedly shown that magic and science co-exist; that co-existence in certain stages of historical development is more than casual, though perhaps less than fully causal in the march of human progress. As a judgment on one aspect of man's complex nature, *Magic and Experimental Science* cannot be denied a measure of finality. That judgment will not please everyone. It may not please the scientifically trained reader, although THORNDIKE has craved his sympathetic attention.[40] It certainly has not pleased SARTON, whose humanistic positivism venerates the creator of a viable truth, the enricher of man's permanent stock of knowledge, as the only true hero. The most sympathetic reader of *Magic and Experimental Science* will be the pure historian, the man who wants to know "wie es eigentlich gewesen." To the historian, the reverse of the medal, even though it may be unattractive, should also be exposed in the museum. It was perhaps with the stric-

[40] Cf. the paper delivered in 1922 before a joint meeting of the History of Science group from the Am. Histor. Association and of Section L, American Association for the Advancement of Science, and published as "The Historical Background of Modern Science," *Scientific Monthly*, XVI (1923), 488-97. THORNDIKE appeals to scientists to study their own past, both in its scientific and its magical aspects, and not to scorn early crude experimentation; pp. 496 f.

tures of SARTON's original review in mind that THORNDIKE wrote the concluding paragraph of his volumes on the fourteenth and fifteenth centuries:

Frankly, it is not for this contribution towards modernity that we most prize these writings of two remote centuries which we have been at some pains to decipher and to set forth. We have taken them as we found them and we esteem them for what they are in their totality, their fourteenth and their fifteenth century *complexio*—a chapter in the history of human thought. Read it and smile or read it and weep, as you please. We would not credit it with the least particle of modern science that does not belong to it, nor would we deprive it of any of that magic which constitutes in no small measure its peculiar charm. Perhaps it would be well to read it and think of what the future historian may say of the mentality and scholasticism of the present era and with what sympathy or antipathy he would be justified in regarding us (IV, 615).

I see no reason why anyone who has read *Magic and Experimental Science* should weep over the spectacle of human error. The moral and spiritual weakness of man is far more distressing than his intellectual debility.

1942

Part 2

Narrative, Poetry, and Drama

VII. . .

ANECDOTE AND REMINISCENCE

WILLIAM HAZLITT

The Young Coleridge

From My First Acquaintance with Poets

My father was a Dissenting Minister at W——m in Shropshire; and in the year 1798 (the figures that compose that date are to me like the "dreaded name of Demogorgon") Mr. Coleridge came to Shrewsbury, to succeed Mr. Rowe in the spiritual charge of a Unitarian congregation there. He did not come till late on the Saturday afternoon before he was to preach; and Mr. Rowe, who himself went down to the coach in a state of anxiety and expectation, to look for the arrival of his successor, could find no one at all answering the description but a round-faced man in a short black coat (like a shooting-jacket) which hardly seemed to have been made for him, but who seemed to be talking at a great rate to his fellow-passengers. Mr. Rowe had scarce returned to give an account of his disappointment, when the round-faced man in black entered, and dissipated all doubts on the subject, by beginning to talk. He did not cease while he staid; nor has he since, that I know of. He held the good town of Shrewsbury in delightful suspense for three weeks that he remained there, "fluttering the *proud Salopians* like an eagle in a dove-cote"; and the Welsh mountains that skirt the horizon with their tempestuous confusion, agree to have heard no such mystic sounds since the days of

High-born Hoel's harp or soft Llewellyn's lay!

As we passed along between W——m and Shrewsbury, and I eyed their blue tops seen through the wintry branches, or the red rustling leaves of the sturdy oak-trees by the roadside, a sound was in my ears as of a Siren's song; I was stunned, startled with it, as from deep sleep; but I had no notion then that I should ever be able to express my admiration to others in motley imagery or quaint allusion, till the light of his genius shone into my soul, like the sun's rays glittering in the puddles of the road. I was at that time dumb, inarticulate, helpless, like a worm by the wayside, crushed, bleeding, lifeless; but now, bursting from the deadly bands that bound them,

With Styx nine times round them,

my ideas float on winged words, and as they expand their plumes, catch the golden light of other years. My soul has indeed remained in its original bondage, dark, obscure, with longings infinite and unsatisfied; my heart, shut up in the prison-house of this rude clay, has never found, nor will it ever find, a heart to speak to; but that my understanding also did not remain dumb and brutish, or at length found a language to express itself, I owe to Coleridge. But this is not to my purpose.

My father lived ten miles from Shrewsbury, and was in the habit of exchanging visits with Mr. Rowe, and with Mr. Jenkins of Whitchurch (nine miles farther on) according to the custom of Dissenting Ministers in each other's neighbourhood. A line of communication is thus established, by which the flame of civil and religious liberty is kept alive, and nourishes its smouldering fire unquenchable, like the fires in the *Agamemnon* of Æschylus, placed at different stations, that waited for ten long years to announce with their blazing pyramids the destruction of Troy. Coleridge had agreed to come over and see my father, according to the courtesy of the country, as Mr. Rowe's probable successor; but in the mean time I had gone to hear him preach the Sunday after his arrival. A poet and a philosopher getting up into a Unitarian pulpit to preach the Gospel, was a romance in these degenerate days, a sort of revival of the primitive spirit of Christianity, which was not to be resisted.

It was in January, 1798, that I rose one morning before daylight, to walk ten miles in the mud, and went to hear this celebrated person preach. Never, the longest day I have to live, shall I have such another walk as this cold, raw, comfortless one, in the winter of the year 1798. *Il y a des impressions que ni le temps ni les circonstances peuvent effacer. Dussé-je vivre des siècles entiers, le doux tems de ma jeunesse ne peut renaître pour moi, ni s'effacer jamais dans ma mémoire.* When I got there, the organ was playing the 100th psalm, and, when it was done, Mr. Coleridge rose and gave out his text, "And he went up into the mountain to pray, HIMSELF, ALONE." As he gave out this text, his voice "rose like a steam of rich distilled perfumes," and when he came to the two last words, which he pronounced loud, deep, and distinct, it seemed to me, who was then young, as

if the sounds had echoed from the bottom of the human heart, and as if that prayer might have floated in solemn silence through the universe. The idea of St. John came into mind, "of one crying in the wilderness, who had his loins girt about, and whose food was locusts and wild honey." The preacher then launched into his subject, like an eagle dallying with the wind. The sermon was upon peace and war; upon church and state—not their alliance, but their separation—on the spirit of the world and the spirit of Christianity, not as the same, but as opposed to one another. He talked of those who had "inscribed the cross of Christ on banners dripping with human gore." He made a poetical and pastoral excursion,—and to shew the fatal effects of war, drew a striking contrast between the simple shepherd boy, driving his team afield, or sitting under the hawthorn, piping to his flock, "as though he should never be old," and the same poor country-lad, crimped, kidnapped, brought into town, made drunk at an alehouse, turned into a wretched drummerboy, with his hair sticking on end with powder and pomatum, a long cue at his back, and tricked out in the loathsome finery of the profession of blood.

Such were the notes our once-lov'd poet sung.

And for myself, I could not have been more delighted if I had heard the music of the spheres. Poetry and Philosophy had met together, Truth and Genius had embraced, under the eye and with the sanction of Religion. This was even beyond my hopes. I returned home well satisfied. The sun that was still labouring pale and wan through the sky, obscured by thick mists, seemed an emblem of the *good cause;* and the cold dank drops of dew that hung half melted on the beard of the thistle, had something genial and refreshing in them; for there was a spirit of hope and youth in all nature, that turned everything into good. The face of nature had not then the brand of JUS DIVINUM on it:

Like to that sanguine flower inscrib'd with woe.

On the Tuesday following, the half-inspired speaker came, I was called down into the room where he was, and went half-hoping, half-afraid. He received me very graciously, and I listened for a long time without uttering a word. I did not suffer in his opinion by my silence. "For those two hours," he afterwards was pleased to say, "he was conversing with W. H.'s forehead!" His appearance was different from what I had anticipated from seeing him before. At a distance, and in the dim light of the chapel, there was to me a strange wildness in his aspect, a dusky obscurity, and I thought him pitted with the small-pox. His complexion was at that time clear, and even bright—

As are the children of yon azure sheen.

His forehead was broad and high, light as if built of ivory, with large projecting eyebrows, and his eyes rolling beneath them like a sea with darkened lustre. "A certain tender bloom his face o'erspread," a purple tinge as we see it in the pale thoughtful complexions of the Spanish portrait-painters, Murillo and Velasquez. His mouth was gross, voluptuous, open, eloquent; his chin good-humoured and round; but his nose, the rudder of the face, the index of the will, was small, feeble, nothing—like what he has done. It might seem that the genius of his face as from a height surveyed and projected him (with sufficient capacity and huge aspiration) into the world unknown of thought and imagination, with nothing to support or guide his veering purpose, as if Columbus had launched his adventurous course for the New World in a shallop, without oars or compass. So at least I comment on it after the event. Coleridge in his person was rather above the common size, inclining to the corpulent, or like Lord Hamlet, "somewhat fat and pursy." His hair (now, alas! grey) was then black and glossy as the raven's, and fell in smooth masses over his forehead. This long, pendulous hair is peculiar to enthusiasts, to those whose minds tend heavenward; and is traditionally inseparable (though of a different colour) from the pictures of Christ. It ought to belong, as a character, to all who preach *Christ crucified,* and Coleridge was at that time one of those!

It was curious to observe the contrast between him and my father, who was a veteran in the cause, and then declining into the vale of years. He had been a poor Irish lad, carefully brought up by his parents, and sent to the University of Glasgow (where he studied under Adam Smith) to prepare him for his future destination. It was his mother's proudest wish to see her son a Dissenting Minister. So if we look back to past generations (as far as eye can reach) we see the same hopes, fears, wishes, followed by the same disappointments, throbbing in the human heart; and so we may see them (if we look forward) rising up for ever, and disappearing, like vapourish bubbles, in the human breast! After being tossed about from congregation to congregation in the heats of the Unitarian controversy, and squabbles about the American war, he had been relegated to an obscure village, where he was to spend the last thirty years of his life, far from the only converse that he loved, the talk about disputed texts of Scripture and the cause of civil and religious liberty. Here he passed his days, repining but resigned, in the study of the Bible, and the perusal of the Commentators,— huge folios, not easily got through, one of which would outlast a winter! Why did he pore on these from morn to night (with the exception of a walk in the fields or a turn in the garden to gather broccoli-plants or kidney-beans of his own rearing, with no small degree of pride and pleasure)? Here were "no figures nor no fantasies,"—neither poetry nor philosophy—nothing to dazzle, nothing to excite modern curiosity; but to his lack-lustre eyes there appeared, within the pages of the ponderous, unwieldy, neglected tomes, the sacred name of JEHOVAH in Hebrew Capitals: pressed down by the weight of the style, worn to the last fading thinness of the understanding; there were glimpses, glimmering notions of the patriarchal wanderings, with palm-trees hovering in the horizon, and processions of camels at the distance of three thousand years; there was Moses with the Burning Bush, the number of the Twelve Tribes, types, shadows, glosses on the law and the prophets; there were discussions (dull enough) on the age of Methuselah, a mighty speculation! there were outlines, rude guesses at the shape of Noah's Ark and of the riches of Solomon's Temple; questions as to the date of the creation, predictions of the end of all things; the great lapses of time, the strange mutations of the globe were unfolded with the voluminous leaf, as it turned over; and though the soul might slumber with an hieroglyphic veil of inscrutable mysteries drawn over it; yet it was a slumber ill-exchanged for all the sharpened realities of sense, wit, fancy, or reason. My father's life was comparatively a dream; but it was a dream of infinity and eternity, of death, the resurrection, and a judgment to come!

No two individuals were ever more unlike than were the host and his guest. A poet was to my father a sort of nondescript: yet whatever added grace to the Unitarian cause was to him welcome. He could hardly have been more surprised or pleased, if our visitor had worn wings. Indeed, his thoughts had wings; and as the silken sounds rustled round our little wainscoted parlour, my father threw back his spectacles over his forehead, his white hairs mixing with its sanguine hue; and a smile of delight beamed across his rugged cordial face, to think that Truth had found a new ally in Fancy! [1] Besides, Coleridge seemed to take considerable notice of me, and that of itself was enough. He talked very familiarly, but agreeably, and glanced over a variety of subjects. At dinner-time he grew more animated, and dilated in a very edifying manner on Mary Wolstonecraft and Mackintosh. The last, he said, he considered (on my father's speaking of his *Vindiciæ Gallicæ* as a capital performance) as a clever, scholastic man—a master of the topics,—or as the ready warehouseman of letters, who knew exactly where to lay his hand on what he wanted, though the goods were not his own. He

---

[1] My father was one of those who mistook his talent after all. He used to be very much dissatisfied that I preferred his Letters to his Sermons. The last were forced and dry; the first came naturally from him. For ease, half-plays on words, and a supine, monkish, indolent pleasantry, I have never seen them equalled. [Hazlitt's note.]

thought him no match for Burke, either in style or matter. Burke was a metaphysician, Mackintosh a mere logician. Burke was an orator (almost a poet) who reasoned in figures, because he had an eye for nature: Mackintosh, on the other hand, was a rhetorician, who had only an eye to commonplaces. On this I ventured to say that I had always entertained a great opinion of Burke, and that (as far as I could find) the speaking of him with contempt might be made the test of a vulgar, democratical mind. This was the first observation I ever made to Coleridge, and he said it was a very just and striking one. I remember the leg of Welsh mutton and the turnips on the table that day had the finest flavour imaginable. Coleridge added that Mackintosh and Tom Wedgwood (of whom, however, he spoke highly) had expressed a very indifferent opinion of his friend Mr. Wordsworth, on which he remarked to them—"He strides on so far before you, that he dwindles in the distance!" Godwin had once boasted to him of having carried on an argument with Mackintosh for three hours with dubious success; Coleridge told him—"If there had been a man of genius in the room, he would have settled the question in five minutes." He asked me if I had ever seen Mary Wolstonecraft, and I said, I had once for a few moments, and that she seemed to me to turn off Godwin's objections to something she advanced with quite a playful, easy air. He replied, that "this was only one instance of the ascendancy which people of imagination exercised over those of mere intellect." He did not rate Godwin very high[2] (this was caprice or prejudice, real or affected)

but he had a great idea of Mrs. Wolstonecraft's powers of conversation, none at all of her talent for book-making. We talked a little about Holcroft. He had been asked if he was not much struck *with* him, and he said, he thought himself in more danger of being struck *by* him. I complained that he would not let me get on at all, for he required a definition of even the commonest word, exclaiming, "What do you mean by a *sensation*, Sir? What do you mean by an *idea*?" This, Coleridge said, was barricadoing the road to truth:—it was setting up a turnpike-gate at every step we took. I forget a great number of things, many more than I remember; but the day passed off pleasantly, and the next morning Mr. Coleridge was to return to Shrewsbury. When I came down to breakfast, I found that he had just received a letter from his friend, T. Wedgwood, making him an offer of £150 a-year if he chose to waive his present pursuit, and devote himself entirely to the study of poetry and philosophy. Coleridge seemed to make up his mind to close with this proposal in the act of tying on one of his shoes. It threw an additional damp on his departure. It took the wayward enthusiast quite from us to cast him into Deva's winding vales, or by the shores of old romance. Instead of living at ten miles distance, of being the pastor of a Dissenting congregation at Shrewsbury, he was henceforth to inhabit the Hill of Parnassus, to be a Shepherd on the Delectable Mountains. Alas! I knew not the way thither, and felt very little gratitude for Mr. Wedgwood's bounty. I was pleasantly relieved from this dilemma; for Mr. Coleridge, asking

[2] He complained in particular of the presumption of his attempting to establish the future immortality of man, "without" (as he said) "knowing what Death was or what Life was"—and the tone in which he pronounced these two words seemed to convey a complete image of both. [Hazlitt's note.]

for a pen and ink, and going to a table to write something on a bit of card, advanced towards me with undulating step, and giving me the precious document, said that that was his address, *Mr. Coleridge, Nether Stowey, Somersetshire;* and that he should be glad to see me there in a few weeks' time, and, if I chose, would come half-way to meet me. I was not less surprised than the shepherd-boy (this simile is to be found in Cassandra) when he sees a thunder-bolt fall close at his feet. I stammered out my acknowledgments and acceptance of this offer (I thought Mr. Wedgwood's annuity a trifle to it) as well as I could; and this mighty business being settled, the poet-preacher took leave, and I accompanied him six miles on the road. It was a fine morning in the middle of winter, and he talked the whole way. The scholar in Chaucer is described as going

———sounding on his way.

So Coleridge went on his. In digressing, in dilating, in passing from subject to subject, he appeared to me to float in air, to slide on ice. He told me in confidence (going along) that he should have preached two sermons before he accepted the situation at Shrewsbury, one on Infant Baptism, the other on the Lord's Supper, shewing that he could not administer either, which would have effectually disqualified him for the object in view. I observed that he continually crossed me on the way by shifting from one side of the foot-path to the other. This struck me as an odd movement; but I did not at that time connect it with any instability of purpose or involuntary change of principle, as I have done since. He seemed unable to keep on in a straight line. He spoke slightingly of Hume (whose *Essays on Mira-*

cles he said was stolen from an objection started in one of South's Sermons —*Credat Judæus Appella!*) I was not very much pleased at this account of Hume, for I had just been reading, with infinite relish, that completest of all metaphysical *choke-pears,* his *Treatise on Human Nature,* to which the *Essays,* in point of scholastic subtlety and close reasoning, are mere elegant trifling, light summer-reading. Coleridge even denied the excellence of Hume's general style, which I think betrayed a want of taste or candour. He, however, made me amends by the manner in which he spoke of Berkeley. He dwelt particularly on his *Essay on Vision* as a masterpiece of analytical reasoning. So it undoubtedly is. He was exceedingly angry with Dr. Johnson for striking the stone with his foot, in allusion to this author's *Theory of Matter and Spirit,* and saying, "Thus I confute him, Sir." Coleridge drew a parallel (I don't know how he brought about the connection) between Bishop Berkeley and Tom Paine. He said the one was an instance of a subtle, the other of an acute mind, than which no two things could be more distinct. The one was a shop-boy's quality, the other the characteristic of a philosopher. He considered Bishop Butler as a true philosopher, a profound and conscientious thinker, a genuine reader of nature and his own mind. He did not speak of his *Analogy,* but of his *Sermons at the Rolls' Chapel,* of which I had never heard. Coleridge somehow always contrived to prefer the *unknown* to the *known.* In this instance he was right. The *Analogy* is a tissue of sophistry, of wire-drawn, theological special-pleading; the *Sermons* (with the Preface to them) are in a fine vein of deep, matured reflection, a candid appeal to our observation of human nature, without pedantry and without bias. I told Coleridge I had written a few remarks, and was sometimes foolish enough to believe that I had made a discovery on the same subject (the *Natural Disinterestedness of the Human Mind*)—and I tried to explain my view of it to Coleridge, who listened with great willingness, but I did not succeed in making myself understood. I sat down to the task shortly afterwards for the twentieth time, got new pens and paper, determined to make clear work of it, wrote a few meagre sentences in the skeleton-style of a mathematical demonstration, stopped half-way down the second page; and, after trying in vain to pump up any words, images, notions, apprehensions, facts, or observations, from that gulf of abstraction in which I had plunged myself for four or five years preceding, gave up the attempt as labour in vain, and shed tears of helpless despondency on the blank, unfinished paper. I can write fast enough now. Am I better than I was then? Oh, no! One truth discovered, one pang of regret at not being able to express it, is better than all the fluency and flippancy in the world. Would that I could go back to what I then was! Why can we not revive past times as we can revisit old places? If I had the quaint Muse of Sir Philip Sidney to assist me, I would write a *Sonnet to the Road between W——m and Shrewsbury,* and immortalise every step of it by some fond enigmatical conceit. I would swear that the very milestones had ears, and that Harmer-hill stooped with all its pines, to listen to a poet, as he passed! I remember but one other topic of discourse in this walk. He mentioned Paley, praised the naturalness and clearness of his style, but condemned his sentiments,

thought him a mere time-serving casuist, and said that "the fact of his work on *Moral and Political Philosophy* being made a text-book in our universities was a disgrace to the national character." We parted at the six-mile stone; and I returned homeward, pensive but much pleased. I had met with unexpected notice from a person whom I believed to have been prejudiced against me. "Kind and affable to me had been his condescension, and should be honoured ever with suitable regard." He was the first poet I had known, and he certainly answered to that inspired name. I had heard a great deal of his powers of conversation, and was not disappointed. In fact, I never met with anything at all like them, either before or since. I could easily credit the accounts which were circulated of his holding forth to a large party of ladies and gentlemen, an evening or two before, on the Berkeleian Theory, when he made the whole material universe look like a transparency of fine words; and another story (which I believe he has somewhere told himself) of his being asked to a party at Birmingham, of his smoking tobacco and going to sleep after dinner on a sofa, where the company found him to their no small surprise, which was increased to wonder when he started up of a sudden, and rubbing his eyes, looked about him, and launched into a three-hours' description of the third heaven, of which he had had a dream, very different from Mr. Southey's *Vision of Judgment,* and also from that other Vision of Judgment, which Mr. Murray, the Secretary of the Bridge-street Junto, has taken into his especial keeping!

On my way back, I had a sound in my ears, it was the voice of Fancy: I had a light before me, it was the face of Poetry. The one still lingers there, the other has not quitted my side! Coleridge in truth met me half-way on the ground of philosophy, or I should not have been won over to his imaginative creed. I had an uneasy, pleasurable sensation all the time, till I was to visit him. During those months the chill breath of winter gave me a welcoming; the vernal air was balm and inspiration to me. The golden sunsets, the silver star of evening, lighted me on my way to new hopes and prospects. *I was to visit Coleridge in the Spring.* This circumstance was never absent from my thoughts, and mingled with all my feelings. I wrote to him at the time proposed, and received an answer postpon-

ing my intended visit for a week or two, but very cordially urging me to complete my promise then. This delay did not damp, but rather increased my ardour. In the mean time I went to Llangollen Vale, by way of initiating myself in the mysteries of natural scenery; and I must say I was enchanted with it. I had been reading Coleridge's description of England, in his fine *Ode on the Departing Year,* and I applied it, *con amore,* to the objects before me. That valley was to me (in a manner) the cradle of a new existence: in the river that winds through it, my spirit was baptised in the waters of Helicon! . . .

1823

THOMAS CARLYLE

Coleridge: Last Phase

From The Life of John Sterling

COLERIDGE sat on the brow of Highgate Hill, in those years, looking down on London and its smoke-tumult, like a sage escaped from the inanity of life's battle; attracting towards him the thoughts of innumerable brave souls still engaged there. His express contributions to poetry, philosophy, or any specific province of human literature or enlightenment, had been small and sadly intermittent; but he had, especially among young inquiring men, a higher than literary, a kind of prophetic or magician character. He was thought to hold, he alone in England, the key of German and other Transcendentalisms; knew the sublime secret of

believing by 'the reason' what 'the understanding' had been obliged to fling out as incredible; and could still, after Hume and Voltaire had done their best and worst with him, profess himself an orthodox Christian, and say and print to the Church of England, with its singular old rubrics and surplices at Allhallowtide, *Esto perpetua.* A sublime man; who, alone in those dark days had saved his crown of spiritual manhood; escaping from the black materialisms, and revolutionary deluges, with 'God, Freedom, Immortality' still his: a king of men. The practical intellects of the world did not much heed him, or carelessly reckoned him a metaphysical dreamer: but to the rising spirits of the young generation he had this dusky sublime character; and sat there as a kind of *Magus,* girt in mystery and enigma; his Dodona oak-grove (Mr. Gilman's house at Highgate) whispering strange things, uncertain whether oracles or jargon.

The Gilmans did not encourage much company, or excitation of any sort, round their sage; nevertheless access to him, if a youth did reverently wish it, was not difficult. He would stroll about the pleasant garden with you, sit in the pleasant rooms of the place,—perhaps take you to his own peculiar room, high up, with a rearward view, which was the chief view of all. A really charming outlook, in fine weather. Close at hand, wide sweep of flowery leafy gardens, their few houses mostly hidden, the very chimney-pots veiled under blossomy umbrage, flowed gloriously down hill; gloriously issuing in wide-tufted undulating plain-country, rich in all charms of field and town. Waving blooming country of the brightest green; dotted all over with handsome villas, handsome groves; crossed by roads and human traffic, here inaudible or heard only as a musical hum: and behind all swam, under olive-tinted haze, the illimitable limitary ocean of London, with its domes and steeples definite in the sun, big Paul's and the many memories attached to it hanging high over all. Nowhere, of its kind, could you see a grander prospect on a bright summer day, with the set of the air going southward,—southward, and so draping with the city-smoke not *you* but the city. Here for hours would Coleridge talk concerning all conceivable things; and liked nothing better than to have an intelligent, or failing that, even a silent and patient human

listener. He distinguished himself to all that ever heard him as at least the most surprising talker extant in this world,—and to some small minority, by no means to all, as the most excellent.

The good man, he was now getting old, towards sixty perhaps; and gave you the idea of a life that had been full of sufferings; a life heavy-laden, half-vanquished, still swimming painfully in seas of manifold physical and other bewilderment. Brow and head were round, and of massive weight, but the face was flabby and irresolute. The deep eyes, of a light hazel, were as full of sorrow as of inspiration; confused pain looked mildly from them, as in a kind of mild astonishment. The whole figure and air, good and amiable otherwise, might be called flabby and irresolute; expressive of weakness under possibility of strength. He hung loosely on his limbs, with knees bent, and stooping attitude; in walking, he rather shuffled than decisively stept; and a lady once remarked, he never could fix which side of the garden-walk would suit him best, but continually shifted, in corkscrew fashion, and kept trying both. A heavy-laden, high-aspiring and surely much-suffering man. His voice, naturally soft and good, had contracted itself into a plaintive snuffle and singsong; he spoke as if preaching,—you would have said, preaching earnestly and also hopelessly the weightiest things. I still recollect his 'object' and 'subject,' terms of continual recurrence in the Kantean province; and how he sung and snuffled them into 'om-m-mject' and 'sum-m-mject,' with a kind of solemn shake or quaver, as he rolled along. No talk, in his century or in any other, could be more surprising.

Sterling, who assiduously attended him, with profound reverence, and was often with him by himself, for a good many months, gives a record of their first colloquy. Their colloquies were numerous, and he had taken note of many; but they are all gone to the fire, except this first, which Mr. Hare has printed,—unluckily without date. It contains a number of ingenious, true and half-true observations, and is of course a faithful epitome of the things said; but it gives small idea of Coleridge's way of talking;—this one feature is perhaps the most recognizable, 'Our interview lasted for three hours, during which he talked two hours and three quarters.' Nothing could be more copious than his talk; and furthermore it was always, virtually or literally, of the nature of a monologue; suffering no interruption, however reverent; hastily putting aside all foreign additions, annotations, or most ingenuous desires for elucidation, as well-meant superfluities which would never do. Besides, it was talk not flowing anywhither like a river, but spreading everywhither in inextricable currents and regurgitations like a lake or sea; terribly deficient in definite goal or aim, nay often in logical intelligibility; *what* you were to believe or do, on any earthly or heavenly thing, obstinately refusing to appear from it. So that, most times, you felt logically lost; swamped near to drowning in this tide of ingenious vocables, spreading out boundless as if to submerge the world.

To sit as a passive bucket and be pumped into, whether you consent or not, can in the long-run be exhilarating to no creature; how eloquent soever the flood of utterance that is descending. But if it be withal a confused unintelligible flood of utterance, threatening to submerge all known landmarks of thought and drown the world and you!

—I have heard Coleridge talk, with eager musical energy, two stricken hours, his face radiant and moist, and communicate no meaning whatsoever to any individual of his hearers,—certain of whom, I for one, still kept eagerly listening in hope; the most had long before given up, and formed (if the room were large enough) secondary humming groups of their own. He began anywhere: you put some question to him, made some suggestive observation: instead of answering this, or decidedly setting out towards answer of it, he would accumulate formidable apparatus, logical swim-bladders, transcendental life-preservers and other precautionary and vehiculatory gear, for setting out; perhaps did at last get under way,—but was swiftly solicited, turned aside by the glance of some radiant new game on this hand or that, into new courses; and ever into new; and before long into all the Universe, where it was uncertain what game you would catch, or whether any.

His talk, alas, was distinguished, like himself, by irresolution: it disliked to be troubled with conditions, abstinences, definite fulfilments;—loved to wander at its own sweet will, and make its auditor and his claims and humble wishes a mere passive bucket for itself! He had knowledge about many things and topics, much curious reading; but generally all topics led him, after a pass or two, into the high seas of theosophic philosophy, the hazy infinitude of Kantean transcendentalism, with its 'sum-m-mjects' and 'om-m-mjects.' Sad enough; for with such indolent impatience of the claims and ignorances of others, he had not the least talent for explaining this or anything unknown to them; and you swam and fluttered in the mistiest wide unintelligible deluge of things, for the most part in a rather profitless uncomfortable manner.

Glorious islets, too, I have seen rise out of the haze; but they were few, and soon swallowed in the general element again. Balmy sunny islets, islets of the blest and the intelligible:—on which occasions those secondary humming groups would all cease humming, and hang breathless upon the eloquent words; till once your islet got wrapt in the mist again, and they could recommence humming. Eloquent artistically expressive words you always had; piercing radiances of a most subtle insight came at intervals; tones of noble pious sympathy, recognizable as pious though strangely coloured, were never wanting long: but in general you could not call this aimless, cloudcapt, cloudbased, lawlessly meandering human discourse of reason by the name of 'excellent talk,' but only of 'surprising'; and were reminded bitterly of Hazlitt's account of it: 'Excellent talker, very,—if you let him start from no premises and come to no conclusion.' Coleridge was not without what talkers call wit, and there were touches of prickly sarcasm in him, contemptuous enough of the world and its idols and popular dignitaries; he had traits even of poetic humour: but in general he seemed deficient in laughter; or indeed in sympathy for concrete human things either on the sunny or on the stormy side. One right peal of concrete laughter at some convicted flesh-and-blood absurdity, one burst of noble indignation at some injustice or depravity, rubbing elbows with us on this solid Earth, how strange would it have been in that Kantean haze-world, and how infinitely cheering amid its vacant air-castles and dim-melting ghosts and shadows! None such ever came. His life had been an abstract thinking and dreaming, idealistic, passed amid the ghosts of defunct bodies and of unborn ones. The moaning singsong of that theosophico-metaphysical monotony left on you, at last, a very dreary feeling.

In close colloquy, flowing within narrower banks, I suppose he was more definite and apprehensive; Sterling in aftertimes did not complain of his unintelligibility, or imputed it only to the abstruse high nature of the topics handled. Let us hope so, let us try to believe so! There is no doubt but Coleridge could speak plain words on things plain: his observations and responses on trivial matters that occurred were as simple as the commonest man's, or were even distinguished by superior simplicity as well as pertinency. 'Ah, your tea is too cold, Mr. Coleridge!' mourned the good Mrs. Gilman once, in her kind, reverential and yet protective manner, handing him a very tolerable though belated cup.—'It's better than I deserve!' snuffled he, in a low hoarse murmur, partly courteous, chiefly pious, the tone of which still abides with me: 'It's better than I deserve!'

But indeed, to the young ardent mind, instinct with pious nobleness, yet driven to the grim deserts of Radicalism for a faith, his speculations had a charm much more than literary, a charm almost religious and prophetic. The constant gist of his discourse was lamentation over the sunk condition of the world; which he recognized to be given up to Atheism and Materialism, full of mere sordid misbeliefs, mispursuits and misresults. All Science had become mechanical; the science not of men, but of a kind of human beavers. Churches themselves had died away into a godless mechanical condition; and stood there as mere Cases of Articles, mere Forms of Churches; like the dried carcasses of once swift camels, which you find left withering in the thirst of the universal desert,—ghastly portents for the present, beneficent ships of the desert no more. Men's souls were blinded, hebetated; sunk under the influence of Atheism and Materialism, and Hume and Voltaire: the world for the present was as an extinct world, deserted of God, and incapable of welldoing till it changed its heart and spirit. This, expressed I think with less of indignation and with more of long-drawn querulousness, was always recognizable as the ground-tone:—in which truly a pious young heart, driven into Radicalism and the opposition party, could not but recognize a too sorrowful truth; and ask of the Oracle, with all earnestness, What remedy, then?

The remedy, though Coleridge himself professed to see it as in sunbeams, could not, except by processes unspeakably difficult, be described to you at all. On the whole, those dead Churches, this dead English Church especially, must be brought to life again. Why not? It was not dead; the soul of it, in this parchedup body, was tragically asleep only. Atheistic Philosophy was true on its side, and Hume and Voltaire could on their own ground speak irrefragably for themselves against any Church: but lift the Church and them into a higher sphere of argument, *they* died into inanition, the Church revivified itself into pristine florid vigour,—became once more a living ship of the desert, and invincibly bore you over stock and stone. But how, but how! By attending to the 'reason' of man, said Coleridge, and duly chaining up the 'understanding' of man: the *Vernunft* (Reason) and *Verstand* (Understanding) of the Germans, it all turned upon these, if you could well understand them,—which

you couldn't. For the rest, Mr. Coleridge had on the anvil various Books, especially was about to write one grand Book *On the Logos,* which would help to bridge the chasm for us. So much appeared, however: Churches, though proved false (as you had imagined), were still true (as you were to imagine): here was an Artist who could burn you up an old Church, root and branch; and then as the Alchymists professed to do with organic substances in general, distil you an 'Astral Spirit' from the ashes, which was the very image of the old burnt article, its airdrawn counterpart,—this you still had, or might get, and draw uses from, if you could. Wait till the Book on the Logos were done;—alas, till your own terrene eyes, blind with conceit and the dust of logic, were purged, subtilized and spiritualized into the sharpness of vision requisite for discerning such an 'om-m-mject.'—The ingenuous young English head, of those days, stood strangely puzzled by such revelations; uncertain whether it were getting inspired, or getting infatuated into flat imbecility; and strange effulgence, of new day or else of deeper meteoric night, coloured the horizon of the future for it.

Let me not be unjust to this memorable man. Surely there was here, in his pious, ever-labouring, subtle mind, a precious truth, or prefigurement of truth; and yet a fatal delusion withal. Prefigurement that, in spite of beaver sciences and temporary spiritual hebetude and cecity, man and his Universe were eternally divine; and that no past nobleness, or revelation of the divine, could or would ever be lost to him. Most true, surely, and worthy of all acceptance. Good also to do what you can with old Churches and practical Symbols of the Noble; nay quit not the burnt ruins of them while you find there is still gold to be dug there. But, on the whole, do not think you can, by logical alchymy, distil astral spirits from them; or if you could, that said astral spirits, or defunct logical phantasms, could serve you in anything. What the light of your mind, which is the direct inspiration of the Almighty, pronounces incredible,—that, in God's name, leave uncredited; at your peril do not try believing that. No subtlest hocus-pocus of 'reason' versus 'understanding' will avail for that feat;—and it is terribly perilous to try it in these provinces!

The truth is, I now see, Coleridge's talk and speculation was the emblem of himself: in it as in him, a ray of heavenly inspiration struggled, in a tragically ineffectual degree, with the weakness of flesh and blood. He says once, he 'had skirted the howling deserts of Infidelity'; this was evident enough: but he had not had the courage, in defiance of pain and terror, to press resolutely across said deserts to the new firm lands of Faith beyond; he preferred to create logical fatamorganas for himself on this hither side, and laboriously solace himself with these.

To the man himself Nature had given, in high measure, the seeds of a noble endowment; and to unfold it had been forbidden him. A subtle lynx-eyed intellect, tremulous pious sensibility to all good and all beautiful; truly a ray of empyrean light;—but imbedded in such weak laxity of character, in such indolences and esuriences as had made strange work with it. Once more, the tragic story of a high endowment with an insufficient will. An eye to discern the divineness of the Heaven's splendours and lightnings, the insatiable wish to revel in their godlike radiances and brilliancies; but no heart to front the scathing terrors of them, which is the first condition of your conquering an abiding-place there. The courage necessary for him, above all things, had been denied this man. His life, with such ray of the empyrean in it, was great and terrible to him; and he had not valiantly grappled with it, he had fled from it; sought refuge in vague daydreams, hollow compromises, in opium, in theosophic metaphysics. Harsh pain, danger, necessity, slavish harnessed toil, were of all things abhorrent to him. And so the empyrean element, lying smothered under the terrene, and yet inextinguishable there, made sad writhings. For pain, danger, difficulty, steady slaving toil, and other highly disagreeable behests of destiny, shall in no wise be shirked by any brightest mortal that will approve himself loyal to his mission in this world; nay, precisely the higher he is, the deeper will be the disagreeableness, and the detestability to flesh and blood, of the tasks laid on him; and the heavier too, and more tragic, his penalties if he neglect them.

For the old Eternal Powers do live forever; nor do their laws know any change, however we in our poor wigs and church-tippets may attempt to read their laws. To *steal* into Heaven,—by the modern method, of sticking ostrich-like your head into fallacies on Earth, equally as by the ancient and by all conceivable methods,—is forever forbidden. High-treason is the name of that attempt; and it continues to be punished as such. Strange enough: here once more was a kind of Heaven-scaling Ixion; and to him, as to the old one, the just gods were very stern! The ever-revolving, never-advancing Wheel (of a kind) was his, through life; and from his Cloud-Juno did not he too procreate strange Centaurs, spectral Puseyisms, monstrous illusory Hybrids, and ecclesiastical Chimeras,—which now roam the earth in a very lamentable manner!

1851

GEORGE MOORE

Taste in Books

From CONFESSIONS OF A YOUNG MAN

IT is said that young men of genius come to London with great poems and dramas in their pockets and find every door closed against them. Chatterton's death perpetuated this legend. But when I, Edward Dayne, came to London in search of literary adventure, I found a ready welcome. Possibly I should not have been accorded any welcome had I been anything but an ordinary person. Let this be waived. I was as covered with "fads" as a distinguished foreigner with stars. Naturalism I wore round my neck, Romanticism was pinned over the heart, Symbolism I carried like a toy revolver in my waistcoat pocket, to be used on an emergency. I do not judge whether I was charlatan or genius, I merely state that I found all—actors, managers, editors, publishers, docile and ready to listen to me. The world may be wicked, cruel, and stupid, but it is patient; on this point I will not be gainsaid, it is patient; I know what I am talking about; I maintain that the world is patient. If it were not, what would have happened? I should have been murdered by the editors of (I will suppress names), torn in pieces by the sub-editors, and devoured by the office boys. There was no wild theory which I did not assail them with, there was no strange plan for the in-

stant extermination of the Philistine, which I did not press upon them, and (here I must whisper), with a fair amount of success, not complete success I am glad to say—that would have meant for the editors a change from their arm-chairs to the benches of the Union and the plank beds of Holloway. The actress when she returned home from the theatre, suggested I had an enemy, a vindictive enemy, who dogged my steps; but her stage experience led her astray. I had no enemy except myself; or to put it scientifically, no enemy except the logical consequences of my past life and education, and these caused me a great and real inconvenience. French wit was in my brain, French sentiment was in my heart; of the English soul I knew nothing, and I could not remember old sympathies, it was like seeking forgotten words; and if I were writing a short story, I had to return in thought to Montmartre or the Champs Elysées for my characters. That I should have forgotten so much in ten years seems incredible, and it will be deemed impossible by many, but that is because few are aware of how little they know of the details of life, even of their own, and are incapable of appreciating the influence of their past upon their present. The visible world is visible only to a few, the moral world is a closed book to nearly all. I was full of France, and France had to be got rid of, or pushed out of sight before I could understand England; I was like a snake striving to slough its skin.

Handicapped as I was with dangerous ideas, and an impossible style, defeat was inevitable. My English was rotten with French idiom; it was like an ill-built wall overpowered by huge masses of ivy; the weak foundations had given way beneath the weight of the parasite; and the ideas I sought to give expression to were green, sour, and immature as apples in August.

Therefore before long the leading journal that had printed two poems and some seven or eight critical articles, ceased to send me books for review, and I fell back upon obscure society papers. Fortunately it was not incumbent on me to live by my pen; so I talked, and watched, and waited till I grew akin to those around me, and my thoughts blended with, and took root in my environment. I wrote a play or two, I translated a French opera, which had a run of six nights, I dramatized a novel, I wrote short stories, and I read a good deal of contemporary fiction.

The first book that came under my hand was "A Portrait of a Lady," by Henry James. Each scene is developed with complete foresight and certainty of touch. What Mr. James wants to do he does. I will admit that an artist may be great and limited; by one word he may light up an abyss of soul; but there must be this one magical and unique word. Shakespeare gives us the word, Balzac, sometimes, after pages of vain striving, gives us the word, Tourgueneff gives it with miraculous certainty; but Henry James, no; a hundred times he flutters about it; his whole book is one long flutter near to the one magical and unique word, but the word is not spoken; and for want of the word his characters are never resolved out of the haze of nebulæ. You are on a bowing acquaintance with them; they pass you in the street, they stop and speak to you, you know how they are dressed, you watch the colour of their eyes. When I think of "A Portrait of a Lady," with its marvellous crowd of well-dressed people, it comes back to me precisely as an accurate memory of a fashionable soirée—the staircase with its ascending figures, the hostess smiling, the host at a little distance with his back turned; some one calls him. He turns; I can see his white kid gloves; the air is as sugar with the odour of the gardenias; there is brilliant light here; there is shadow in the further rooms; the women's feet pass to and fro beneath the stiff skirts; I call for my hat and coat; I light a cigar; I stroll up Piccadilly . . . a very pleasant evening; I have seen a good many people I knew; I have observed an attitude, and an earnestness of manner that proved that a heart was beating.

Mr. James might say, "If I have done this, I have done a great deal," and I would answer, "No doubt you are a man of great talent, great cultivation and not at all of the common herd; I place you in the very front rank, not only of novelists but of men of letters."

I have read nothing of Henry James's that did suggest the manner of a scholar; but why should a scholar limit himself to empty and endless sentimentalities? I will not taunt him with any of the old taunts—why does he not write complicated stories? Why does he not complete his stories? Let all this be waived. I will ask him only why he always avoids decisive action? Why does a woman never say "I will"? Why does a woman never leave the house with her lover? Why does a man never kill a man? Why does a man never kill himself? Why is nothing ever accomplished? In real life murder, adultery, and suicide are of common occurrence; but Mr. James's people live in a calm, sad, and very polite twilight of volition. Suicide or adultery has happened before the story begins, suicide or adultery happens some years hence, when the characters have left the stage, but bang in front of the reader nothing happens. The suppression or maintenance of story in a novel is a matter of personal taste; some prefer character-drawing to adventures, some adventures to character-drawing; that you cannot have both at once I take to be a self-evident proposition; so when Mr. Lang says, "I like adventures," I say, "Oh, do you?" as I might to a man who says "I like sherry," and no doubt when I say I like character-drawing, Mr. Lang says, "Oh, do you?" as he might to a man who says, "I like port." But Mr. James and I are agreed on essentials, we prefer character-drawing to adventures. One, two, or even three determining actions are not antagonistic to character-drawing, the practice of Balzac, and Flaubert, and Thackeray prove that. Is Mr. James of the same mind as the poet Verlaine—

La nuance, pas la couleur,
Seulement la nuance,

. . . .

Tout le reste est littérature.

In connection with Henry James I had often heard the name of W. D. Howells. I bought some three or four of his novels. I found them pretty, very pretty, but nothing more,—a sort of Ashby Sterry done into very neat prose.

He is vulgar, is refined as Henry James; he is more domestic; girls with white dresses and virginal looks, languid mammas, mild witticisms, here, there, and everywhere; a couple of young men, one a little cynical, the other a little over-shadowed by his love, a strong, bearded man of fifty in the background; in a word, a Tom Robertson comedy faintly spiced with American. Henry James went to France and read Tourgueneff. W. D. Howells stayed at home and read Henry James. Henry James's mind is of a higher cast and temper; I have no doubt at one time of his life Henry James said, I will write the moral history of America, as Tourgueneff wrote the moral history of Russia—he borrowed at first hand, understanding what he was borrowing. W. D. Howells borrowed at second hand, and without understanding what he was borrowing. Altogether Mr. James's instincts are more scholarly. Although his reserve irritates me, and I often regret his concessions to the prudery of the age,—no, not of the age but of librarians,—I cannot but feel that his concessions, for I suppose I must call them concessions, are to a certain extent self-imposed, regretfully, perhaps . . . somewhat in this fashion—"True, that I live in an age not very favourable to artistic production, but the art of an age is the spirit of that age; if I violate the prejudices of the age I shall miss its spirit, and an art that is not redolent of the spirit of its age is an artificial flower, perfumeless, or perfumed with the scent of flowers that bloomed three hundred years ago." Plausible, ingenious, quite in the spirit of Mr. James's mind; I can almost hear him reason so; nor does the argument displease me, for it is conceived in a scholarly spirit. Now my conception of W. D. Howells is quite different—I see him the happy father of a numerous family; the sun is shining, the girls and boys are playing on the lawn, they come trooping in to a high tea, and there is dancing in the evening.

My fat landlady lent me a novel by George Meredith,—"Tragic Comedians"; I was glad to receive it, for my admiration of his poetry, with which I was slightly acquainted, was very genuine indeed. "Love in a Valley" is a beautiful poem, and the "Nuptials of Attila," I read it in the *New Quarterly Review* years ago, is very present in my mind, and it is a pleasure to recall its chanting rhythm, and lordly and sombre refrain—"Make the bed for Attila." I expected, therefore, one of my old passionate delights from his novels. I was disappointed, painfully disappointed. But before I say more concerning Mr. Meredith, I will admit at once frankly and fearlessly, that I am not a competent critic, because emotionally I do not understand him, and all except an emotional understanding is worthless in art. I do not make this admission because I am intimidated by the weight and height of the critical authority with which I am overshadowed, but from a certain sense, of which I am as distinctly conscious, viz., that the author is, how shall I put it? the French would say "quelqu'un," that expresses what I would say in English. I remember, too, that although a man may be able to understand anything, that there must be some modes of thoughts and attitudes of mind which we are so naturally antagonistic to, so entirely out of sympathy with, that we are in no true sense critics of them. Such are the thoughts that come to me when I read Mr. George Meredith. I try to console myself with such reflections, and then I break forth, and crying passionately:—jerks, wire, splintered wood. In Balzac, which I know by heart, in Shakespeare, which I have just begun to love, I find words deeply impregnated with the savour of life; but in George Meredith there is nothing but crackjaw sentences, empty and unpleasant in the mouth as sterile nuts. I could select hundreds of phrases which Mr. Meredith would probably call epigrams, and I would defy anyone to say they were wise, graceful or witty. I do not know any book more tedious than "Tragic Comedians," more pretentious, more blatant; it struts and screams, stupid in all its gaud and absurdity as a cockatoo. More than fifty pages I could not read.

How, I asked myself, could the man who wrote the "Nuptials of Attila" write this? but my soul returned no answer, and I listened as one in a hollow mountainside. My opinion of George Meredith never ceases to puzzle me. He is of the north, I am of the south. Carlyle, Mr. Robert Browning, and George Meredith are the three essentially northern writers; in them there is nothing of Latin sensuality and subtlety.

I took up "Rhoda Fleming." I found some exquisite bits of description in it, but I heartily wished them in verse, they were motives for poems; and there was some wit. I remember a passage very racy indeed, of middle-class England. Antony, I think is the man's name, describes how he is interrupted at his tea; a paragraph of seven or ten lines with "I am having my tea, I am at my tea," running through it for refrain. Then a description of a lodging-house dinner: "a block of bread on a lonely plate, and potatoes that looked as if they had committed suicide in their own steam." A little ponderous and stilted, but undoubtedly witty. I read on until I came to a young man who fell from his horse, or had been thrown from his horse, I never knew which, nor did I feel enough interest in the matter to make research; the young man was put to bed by his mother, and once in bed he began to talk! . . . four, five, six, ten pages of talk, and such talk! I can offer no opinion why Mr. George Meredith committed them to paper; it is not narrative, it is not witty, nor is it sentimental, nor is it profound. I read it once; my mind astonished at receiving no sensation cried out like a child at a milkless breast. I read the pages again . . . did I understand? Yes, I understood every sentence, but they conveyed no idea, they awoke no emotion in me; it was like sand, arid and uncomfortable. The story is surprisingly commonplace—the people in it are as lacking in subtlety as those of a Drury Lane melodrama.

"Diana of the Crossways" I liked better, and had I had absolutely nothing to do I might have read it to the end. I remember a scene with a rustic—a rustic who could eat hog a solid hour—that amused me. I remember the sloppy road in the Weald, and the vague outlines of the South Downs seen in starlight and mist. But to come to the great question, the test by which Time will judge us all—the creation of a human being, of a live thing that we have met with in life before, and meet for the first time in print, and who abides with us ever after. Into what shadow has not Diana floated? Where are the magical glimpses of the soul? Do you remember in "Pères et Enfants," when Tourgueneff is unveiling the woman's, shall I say, affection, for Bazaroff, or the interest she feels in him? and exposing at the same time the reasons why she

will never marry him. . . . I wish I had the book by me, I have not seen it for ten years.

After striving through many pages to put Lucien, whom you would have loved, whom I would have loved, that divine representation of all that is young and desirable in man, before the reader, Balzac puts these words in his mouth in reply to an impatient question by Vautrin, who asks him what he wants, what he is sighing for, *"D'être célèbre et d'être aimé,"*—these are soul-waking words, these are Shakespeare words.

Where in "Diana of the Crossways" do we find soul-evoking words like these? With tiresome repetition we are told that she is beautiful, divine; but I see her not at all, I don't know if she is dark, tall, or fair; with tiresome reiteration we are told that she is brilliant, that her conversation is like a display of fireworks, that the company is dazzled and overcome; but when she speaks the utterances are grotesque, and I say that if any one spoke to me in real life as she does in the novel, I should not doubt for an instant that I was in the company of a lunatic. The epigrams are never good, they never come within measurable distance of La Rochefoucauld, Balzac, or even Goncourt. The admirers of Mr. Meredith constantly deplore their existence, admitting that they destroy all illusion of life. "When we have translated half of Mr. Meredith's utterances into possible human speech, then we can enjoy him," says the *Pall Mall Gazette*. We take our pleasures differently; mine are spontaneous, and I know nothing about translating the rank smell of a nettle into the fragrance of a rose, and then enjoying it.

Mr. Meredith's conception of life is crooked, ill-balanced, and out of tune.

What remains?—a certain lustiness. You have seen a big man with square shoulders and a small head, pushing about in a crowd, he shouts and works his arms, he seems to be doing a great deal, in reality he is doing nothing; so Mr. Meredith appears to me, and yet I can only think of him as an artist; his habit is not slatternly, like those of such literary hodmen as Mr. David Christie Murray, Mr. Besant, Mr. Buchanan. There is no trace of the crowd about him. I do not question his right of place, I am out of sympathy with him, that is all; and I regret that it should be so, for he is one whose love of art is pure and untainted with commercialism, and if I may praise it for nought else, I can praise it for this.

I have noticed that if I buy a book because I am advised, or because I think I ought, my reading is sure to prove sterile. *Il faut que cela vient de moi,* as a woman once said to me, speaking of her caprices; a quotation, a chance word heard in an unexpected quarter. Mr. Hardy and Mr. Blackmore I read because I had heard that they were distinguished novelists; neither touched me, I might just as well have bought a daily paper; neither like nor dislike, a shrug of the shoulders—that is all. Hardy seems to me to bear about the same relation to George Eliot as Jules Breton does to Millet—a vulgarisation never offensive, and executed with ability. The story of an art is always the same, . . . a succession of abortive but ever strengthening efforts, a moment of supreme concentration, a succession of efforts weakening the final extinction. George Eliot gathered up all previous attempts, and created the English peasant; and following her peasants there came an endless crowd from Devon, Yorkshire, and the Midland

Counties, and, as they came, they faded into the palest shadows until at last they appeared in red stockings, high heels and were lost in the chorus of opera. Mr. Hardy was the first step down. His work is what dramatic critics would call good, honest, straightforward work. It is unillumined by a ray of genius, it is slow and somewhat sodden. It reminds me of an excellent family coach—one of the old sort hung on C springs—a fat coachman on the box and a footman whose livery was made for his predecessor. In criticising Mr. Meredith I was out of sympathy with my author, ill at ease, angry, puzzled; but with Mr. Hardy I am on quite different terms, I am as familiar with him as with the old pair of trousers I put on when I sit down to write; I know all about his aims, his methods; I know what has been done in that line, and what can be done.

I have heard that Mr. Hardy is country bred, but I should not have discovered this from his writings. They read to me more like a report, yes, a report, —a conscientious, well-done report, executed by a thoroughly efficient writer sent down by one of the daily papers. Nowhere do I find selection, everything is reported, dialogues and descriptions. Take for instance the long evening talk between the farm people when Oak is seeking employment. It is not the absolute and literal transcript from nature after the manner of Henri Monier; for that it is a little too diluted with Mr. Hardy's brains, the edges are a little sharpened and pointed, I can see where the author has been at work filing; on the other hand, it is not synthesized —the magical word which reveals the past, and through which we divine the future—is not seized and set triumphantly as it is in "Silas Marner." The descriptions do not flow out of and form part of the narrative, but are wedged in, and often awkwardly. We are invited to assist at a sheepshearing scene, or at a harvest supper, because these scenes are not to be found in the works of George Eliot, because the reader is supposed to be interested in such things, because Mr. Hardy is anxious to show how jolly country he is.

Collegians, when they attempt character-drawing, create monstrosities, but a practised writer should be able to create men and women capable of moving through a certain series of situations without shocking in any violent way the most generally applicable principles of common sense. I say that a practised writer should be able to do this; that they sometimes do not is a matter which I will not now go into, suffice it for my purpose if I admit that Mr. Hardy can do this. In farmer Oak there is nothing to object to; the conception is logical, the execution is trustworthy; he has legs, arms, and a heart; but the vital spark that should make him of our flesh and of our soul is wanting, it is dead water that the sunlight never touches. The heroine is still more dim, she is stuffy, she is like tow; the rich farmer is a figure out of any melodrama, Sergeant Troy nearly quickens to life; now and then the clouds are liquescent, but a real ray of light never falls.

The story-tellers are no doubt right when they insist on the difficulty of telling a story. A sequence of events—it does not matter how simple or how complicated—working up to a logical close, or, shall I say, a close in which there is a sense of rhythm and inevitableness is always indicative of genius. Shakespeare affords some magnificent examples, likewise Balzac, likewise George Eliot, likewise Tourgueneff; the "Œdipus" is, of course, the crowning and final achievement in the music of sequence and the massy harmonies of fate. But in contemporary English fiction I marvel, and I am repeatedly struck by the inability of writers, even of the first-class, to make an organic whole of their stories. Here, I say, the course is clear, the way is obvious, but no sooner do we enter on the last chapters than the story begins to show incipient shiftiness, and soon it doubles back and turns, growing with every turn weaker like a hare before the hounds. From a certain directness of construction, from the simple means by which Oak's ruin is accomplished in the opening chapters, I did not expect that the story would run hare-hearted in its close, but the moment Troy told his wife that he never cared for her, I suspected something was wrong; when he went down to bathe and was carried out by the current I knew the game was up, and was prepared for anything, even for the final shooting by the rich farmer, and the marriage with Oak, a conclusion which of course does not come within the range of literary criticism.

"Lorna Doone" struck me as childishly garrulous, stupidly prolix, swollen with comments not interesting in themselves and leading to nothing. Mr. Hardy possesses the power of being able to shape events; he can mould them to a certain form; that he cannot breathe into them the spirit of life I have already said, but "Lorna Doone" reminds me of a third-rate Italian opera, *La Fille du Régiment,* or *Ernani;* it is corrupt with all the vices of the school, and it does not contain a single passage of real fervour or force to make us forget the inherent defects of the art of which it is a poor specimen. Wagner made the discovery, not a very wonderful one after all when we think, that an opera had much better be melody from end to end. The realistic school following on Wagner's footsteps discovered that a novel had much better be all narrative—an uninterrupted flow of narrative. Description is narrative, analysis of character is narrative, dialogue is narrative; the form is ceaselessly changing, but the melody of narration is never interrupted.

But the reading of "Lorna Doone" calls to my mind, and very vividly, an original artistic principle of which English romance writers are either strangely ignorant or neglectful, viz., that the sublimation of the *dramatis personæ* and the deeds in which they are involved must correspond, and their relationship should remain unimpaired. Turner's "Carthage" is nature transposed and wonderfully modified. Some of the passages of light and shade there—those of the balustrade—are fugues, and there his art is allied to Bach in sonority and beautiful combination. Turner knew that a branch hung across the sun looked at separately was black, but he painted it light to maintain the equipoise of atmosphere. In the novel the characters are the voice, the deeds are the orchestra. But the English novelist takes 'Arry and 'Arriet, and without question allows them to achieve deeds; nor does he hesitate to pass them into the realms of the supernatural. Such violation of the first principles of narration is never to be met with in the elder writers. Achilles stands as tall as Troy, Merlin is as old and as wise as the world. Rhythm and poetical expression are essential attributes of dramatic genius, but the original sign of race and mission is an instinctive modulation of man with the deeds he attempts or achieves. The man and the deed must be cognate and equal, and the melodic balance and blending are what first separate Homer and Hugo from the fabricators of singular adventures. In Scott leather jerkins, swords, horses, mountains, and castles harmonise completely and fully with food, fighting, words, and vision of life; the chords are simple as Handel's, but they are as perfect. Lytton's work, although as vulgar as Verdi's, is, in much the same fashion, sustained by a natural sense of formal harmony; but all that follows is decadent,—an admixture of romance and realism, the exaggerations of Hugo and the homeliness of Trollope; a litter of ancient elements in a state of decomposition.

The spiritual analysis of Balzac equals the triumphant imagination of Shakespeare, and by different roads they reach the same height of tragic awe, but when improbability, which in these days does duty for imagination, is mixed with the familiar aspects of life, the result is inchoate and rhythmless folly, I mean the regular and inevitable alternation and combination of pa and ma, and dear Annie who lives at Clapham, with the Mountains of the Moon, and the secret of eternal life; this violation of the first principles of art—that is to say, of the rhythm of feeling and proportion, is not possible in France. I ask the reader to recall what was said on the subject of the Club, Tavern, and Villa. We have a surplus population of more than two million women, the tradition that chastity is woman's only virtue still survives, the Tavern and its adjunct Bohemianism have been suppressed, and the Villa is omnipotent and omnipresent; tennis-playing, church on Sundays, and suburban hops engender a craving for excitement for the far away, for the unknown; but the Villa with its tennis-playing, church on Sundays, and suburban hops will not surrender its own existence, it must take a part in the heroic deeds that happen in the Mountains of the Moon; it will have heroism in its own pint pot. Achilles and Merlin must be replaced by Uncle Jim and an undergraduate; and so the Villa is the author of "Rider Haggard," "Hugh Conway," "Robert Buchanan," and the author of "The House on the Marsh."

* * *

The mechanical construction of M. Scribe I had learnt from M. Duval; the naturalistic school had taught me to scorn tricks, and to rely on the action of the sentiments rather than on extraneous aid for the bringing about of a *dénouement;* and I thought of all this as I read "Disenchantment" by Miss Mabel Robinson, and it occurred to me that my knowledge would prove valuable when my turn came to write a novel, for the *mise en place,* the setting forth of this story, seemed to me so loose, that much of its strength had dribbled away before it had rightly begun. But the figure of the Irish politician I accept without reserve. It seems to me grand and mighty in its sorrowfulness. The tall, dark-eyed, beautiful Celt, attainted in blood and brain by generations of famine and drink, alternating with the fervid sensuousness of the girl, her Saxon sense of right alternating with the Celt's hereditary sense of revenge, his dreamy patriotism, his facile platitudes, his acceptance of literature as a sort of bread basket, his knowledge that he is not great nor strong, and can do nothing in the world but love his country; and as he passes his thirtieth year the waxing strong of the disease, nervous disease complex and torturous; to him drink is at once life and death; an article is bread, and to calm him and collect what remains of weak, scattered thought, he must drink. The woman cannot understand that caste and race separate them; and the damp air of spent desire, and the grey and falling leaves of her illusions fill her life's sky. Nor is there any hope for her until the husband unties the awful knot by suicide.

I will state frankly that Mr. R. L. Stevenson never wrote a line that failed to delight me; but he never wrote a book. You arrive at a strangely just estimate of a writer's worth by the mere question: "What is he the author of?" for every writer whose work is destined to live is the author of one book that outshines the other, and, in popular imagination, epitomises his talent and position. What is Shakespeare the author of? What is Milton the author of? What is Fielding the author of? What is Byron the author of? What is Carlyle the author of? What is Thackeray the author of? What is Zola the author of? What is Mr. Swinburne the author of? Mr. Stevenson is the author of shall I say, "Treasure Island," or what?

I think of Mr. Stevenson as a consumptive youth weaving garlands of sad flowers with pale, weak hands, or leaning to a large plate-glass window, and scratching thereon exquisite profiles with a diamond pencil.

I do not care to speak of great ideas, for I am unable to see how an idea can exist, at all events can be great out of language; an allusion to Mr. Stevenson's verbal expression will perhaps make my meaning clear. His periods are fresh and bright, rhythmical in sound, and perfect realizations of their sense; in reading you often think that never before was such definiteness united to such poetry of expression; every page and every sentence rings of its individuality. Mr. Stevenson's style is over smart, well-dressed, shall I say, like a young man walking in the Burlington Arcade? Yes, I will say so, but, I will add, the most gentlemanly young man that ever walked in the Burlington. Mr. Stevenson is competent to understand any thought that might be presented to him, but if he were to use it, it would instantly become neat, sharp, ornamental, light, and graceful; and it would lose all its original richness and harmony. It is not Mr. Stevenson's brain that prevents him from being a thinker, but his style.

Another thing that strikes me in thinking of Stevenson (I pass over his direct indebtedness to Edgar Poe, and his constant appropriation of his methods), is the unsuitableness of the special characteristics of his talent to the age he lives in. He wastes in his limitations, and his talent is vented in prettinesses of style. In speaking of Mr. Henry James, I said that, although he had conceded much to the foolish, false, and hypocritical taste of the time, the concessions he made had in little or nothing impaired his talent. The very opposite seems to me the case with Mr. Stevenson. For if any man living in this end of the century needed freedom of expression for the distinct development of his genius, that man is R. L. Stevenson. He who runs may read, and he with any knowledge of literature will, before I have written the words, have imagined Mr. Stevenson writing in the age of Elizabeth or Anne.

Turn your platitudes prettily, but write no word that could offend the chaste mind of the young girl who has spent her morning reading the Colin Campbell divorce case; so says the age

we live in. The penny paper that may be bought everywhere, that is allowed to lie on every table, prints seven or eight columns of filth, for no reason except that the public likes to read filth; the poet and novelist must emasculate and destroy their work because. . . . Who shall come forward and make answer? Oh, vile, filthy, and hypocritical century, I at least scorn you.

But this is not a course of literature but the story of the artistic development of me, Edward Dayne; so I will tarry no longer with mere criticism, but go direct to the book to which I owe the last temple in my soul—"Marius the Epicurean." Well I remember when I read the opening lines, and how they came upon me sweetly as the flowing breath of a bright spring. I knew that I was awakened a fourth time, that a fourth vision of life was to be given to me. Shelley had revealed to me the unimagined skies where the spirit sings of light and grace; Gautier had shown me how extravagantly beautiful is the visible world and how divine is the rage of the flesh; and with Balzac I had descended circle by circle into the nether world of the soul, and watched its afflictions. Then there were minor awakenings. Zola had enchanted me with decoration and inebriated me with theory; Flaubert had astonished with the wonderful delicacy and subtlety of his workmanship; Goncourt's brilliant adjectival effects had captivated me for a time, but all these impulses were crumbling into dust, these aspirations were etiolated, sickly as faces grown old in gaslight.

I had not thought of the simple and unaffected joy of the heart of natural things; the colour of the open air, the many forms of the country, the birds flying,—that one making for the sea;

the abandoned boat, the dwarf roses and the wild lavender; nor had I thought of the beauty of mildness in life, and how by a certain avoidance of the wilfully passionate, and the surely ugly, we may secure an aspect of temporal life which is abiding and soul-sufficing. A new dawn was in my brain, fresh and fair, full of wide temples and studious hours, and the lurking fragrance of incense; that such a vision of life was possible I had no suspicion, and it came upon me almost with the same strength, almost as intensely, as that divine song of the flesh,—Mademoiselle de Maupin.

Certainly, in my mind, these books will be always intimately associated; and when a few adventitious points of difference be forgotten, it is interesting to note how firm is the alliance, and how cognate and co-equal the sympathies on which it is based; the same glad worship of the visible world, and the same incurable belief that the beauty of material things is sufficient for all the needs of life. Mr. Pater can join hands with Gautier in saying—*je trouve la terre aussi belle que le ciel, et je pense que la correction de la forme est la vertu.* And I too join issue; I too love the great pagan world, its bloodshed, its slaves, its injustice, its loathing of all that is feeble.

But "Marius the Epicurean" was more to me than a mere emotional influence, precious and rare though that may be, for this book was the first in English prose I had come across that procured for me any genuine pleasure in the language itself, in the combination of words for silver or gold chime, and unconventional cadence, and for all those lurking half-meanings, and that evanescent suggestion, like the odour of dead roses, that words retain to the last of other times and elder usage. Until I read "Marius" the English language (English prose) was to me what French must be to the majority of English readers. I read for the sense and that was all; the language itself seemed to me coarse and plain, and awoke in me neither æsthetic emotion nor even interest. "Marius" was the stepping-stone that carried me across the channel into the genius of my own tongue. The translation was not too abrupt; I found a constant and careful invocation of meaning that was a little aside of the common comprehension, and also a sweet depravity of ear for unexpected falls of phrase, and of eye for the less observed depths of colours, which although new was a sort of sequel to the education I had chosen, and a continuance of it in foreign, but not wholly unfamiliar medium, and having saturated myself with Pater, the passage to De Quincey was easy. He, too, was a Latin in manner and in temper of mind; but he was truly English, and through him I passed to the study of the Elizabethan dramatists, the real literature of my race, and washed myself clean.

1888

BENNETT CERF

Hurrah for Capt. Spalding and the Other Marx Brothers

From TRY AND STOP ME

WHAT THIS country needs is a new show for the Marx Brothers. It's all very well to recall their patter of years gone by, and chuckle reminiscently over it, but something fresh along the lines of *The Coconuts* or *Animal Crackers* would give Broadway an unbelievable fillip. The funniest lines usually fell to Groucho. He revived on the radio the other night his "I never forget a face—but I'm willing to make an exception in your case."

One of his funniest routines concerned his African hunting trip which began with "Did I ever tell you how I shot a wild elephant in my pajamas? How he got into my pajamas I'll never know. Getting his tusks off was quite a problem. In Alabama the Tuscaloosa." He came home in a rickshaw. The meter registered $11.40. "Confound it," he roared to the driver. "Didn't I *tell* you not to go through India?"

Then there was the skit where Groucho and Chico served as opposing lawyers. Chico became tongue-tied when it was his turn to question the witness. The judge thundered, "Well, ask your witness some questions." "All-a-right," said Chico. "What's a big-a da animal wid four legs an' a trunk in da front?" "That's irrelevant," screamed Groucho. "Dat's a right," agreed Chico. Groucho crossed the stage, planted his portfolio on the judge's bench, and declared, "I rest my case."

And the time when Groucho proposed to that wonderful foil, Mrs. Rittenhouse. "Your eyes shine," he told her, "like the seat of my blue serge pants." "But you'll have to get out of that house you're living in," he added. "I don't like Junior crossing the tracks. In fact, come to think of it, I don't like Junior."

The weak sister of the Four Marx Brothers on the stage was Zeppo, but when he quit the greasepaint and became an agent, he ended with more pelf than the other three put together. Harpo, who never says a word on the stage, is the wittiest conversationalist in private life, and was one of Alexander Woollcott's favorite companions. Harpo once flew all the way from Hollywood to Bomoseen, Vermont, for a week-end to surprise Woollcott. He painted himself from head to foot with hideous hues, paddled to the Island, and howled like a banshee. Nobody was frightened, however. In fact, nobody was on the Island. Another time, Harpo appeared in a broken-down Model-T Ford. "What on earth do you call that?" scoffed Woollcott. "This is my town car," said Harpo grandly.

"Yes," answered Woollcott, "and the town is Pompeii."

Chico's wife invited an elderly relative to spend a few weeks at his house one time. The visitor was very charming, but her English was on the sketchy side. When Irving Thalberg and his wife, Norma Shearer, were coming for dinner, Chico took the old lady aside. "When Mr. Thalberg says 'pleased to meet you,'" he instructed her, "all you have to do is answer with one word: 'likewise.'" The old lady repeated the word several times, and swore that she would uphold her end without mishap. The Thalbergs arrived. "Pleased to meet you," said Thalberg as expected. The old lady beamed at him. "Wise guy," she said.

The Marx Brothers once became the managers of a prize-fighter. He was a lumbering giant named Cohen, and richly earned the nickname of "Canvasback" by an invariable custom of getting himself knocked cold in Round One of every fight. The boys had a great time with Canvasback Cohen until one day, according to legend, Groucho knocked him out in a gymnasium workout. That was too much. Harpo claims that Canvasback started as a lightweight, but was hit so many times that he swelled out into a heavy.

As long as I have rambled on this far about the Marx Brothers, I'd better quote a few other of their more famous lines, if only to avoid the wrath of thousands of enthusiasts who remember their dialogues almost word for word and are ready to fight at the drop of a wisecrack. In *Horse Feathers,*

Groucho informed his son, "I'd horse-whip you—if I had a horse."

His secretary interrupted him to announce, "Jennings has been waiting to see you for hours, and he is waxing wroth." Groucho's reply to this was, "Tell Roth to wax Jennings for a change."

When Chico entered the scene, Groucho commented, "Hey, you look a lot like a guy I know by the name of Barelli." "I am Barelli," declared Chico. "Aha," said Groucho, "that accounts for the resemblance."

In *Monkey Business,* Groucho discovered a large automatic pistol and near it a few small pearl-handled revolvers. "This gat," announced Groucho, "had gittens." Almost immediately after that deduction, the ship's captain hove into view. "I've got a complaint," roared Groucho. "What is it?" said the captain testily. "Last night when I was in bed in my cabin, who do you think came tiptoeing along the corridor and tapped on my door?" The captain said he didn't know. "Nobody did," declared Groucho, "and that's my complaint."

Marx Brothers addicts will never forget their burlesque of Madame Du Barry. Groucho, essaying the role of high minister, was feverishly embracing Du Barry when Chico came charging into the scene. "Who are you?" snarled Groucho. "King of France," averred Chico. "What?" said Groucho. "You the king? And I the prime minister? France is certainly in one hell of a fix!"

1944

WALT WHITMAN

My Passion for Ferries

From SPECIMEN DAYS

Living in Brooklyn or New York city from this time forward, my life, then, and still more the following years, was curiously identified with Fulton ferry, already becoming the greatest of its sort in the world for general importance, volume, variety, rapidity, and picturesqueness. Almost daily, later, ('50 to '60) I cross'd on the boats, often up in the pilot-houses where I could get a full sweep, absorbing shows, accompaniments, surroundings. What oceanic currents, eddies, underneath—the great tides of humanity also, with ever-shifting movements. Indeed, I have always had a passion for ferries; to me they afford inimitable, streaming, never-failing, living poems. The river and bay scenery, all about New York island, any time of a fine day—the hurrying, splashing sea-tides—the changing panorama of steamers, all sizes, often a string of big ones outward bound to distant ports —the myriads of white-sail'd schooners, sloops, skiffs, and the marvelously beautiful yachts—the majestic Sound boats as they rounded the Battery and came along towards five, afternoon, eastward bound—the prospect off towards Staten Island, or down the Narrows, or the other way up the Hudson—what refreshment of spirit such sights and experiences gave me years ago (and many a time since). My old pilot friends, the Balsirs, Johnny Cole, Ira Smith, William White, and my young ferry friend, Tom Gere—how well I remember them all.

1883

Broadway Sights

From SPECIMEN DAYS

Besides Fulton ferry, off and on for years, I knew and frequented Broadway—that noted avenue of New York's crowded and mixed humanity, and of so many notables. Here I saw, during those times, Andrew Jackson, Webster, Clay, Seward, Martin Van Buren, filibuster Walker, Kossuth, Fitz Greene Halleck, Bryant, the Prince of Wales, Charles Dickens, the first Japanese ambassadors, and lots of other celebrities of the time. Always something novel or inspiriting; yet mostly to me the hurrying and vast amplitude of those never-ending human currents. I remember seeing James Fenimore Cooper in a court-room in Chambers street, back of the city hall, where he was carrying on a law case—I think it was a charge of libel he had brought against someone. I also remember seeing Edgar A. Poe, and having a short interview with him, (it must have been in 1845 or '6,) in his office, second story of a corner building, (Duane or Pearl street.) He was editor and owner or part owner of "The Broadway Journal." The visit was about a piece of mine he had publish'd. Poe was very cordial, in a quiet way, appear'd well in person, dress, &c. I have a distinct and pleasing remembrance of his looks, voice, manner, and matter; very kindly and human, but subdued, perhaps a little jaded. For another of my reminiscences, here on the West Side, just below Houston street, I once saw (it must have been about 1832, of a sharp, bright, January day) a bent, feeble, but stout-built very old man, bearded, swathed in rich furs, with a great ermine cap on his head, led and assisted, almost carried, down the steps of his high front stoop (a dozen friends and servants, emulous, carefully holding, guiding him) and then lifted and tuck'd in a gorgeous sleigh, envel-op'd in other furs, for a ride. The sleigh was drawn by as fine a team of horses as I ever saw. (You needn't think all the best animals are brought up nowadays; never was such horseflesh as fifty years ago on Long Island, or South, or in New York city; folks look'd for spirit and mettle in a nag, not tame speed merely.) Well, I, a boy of perhaps thirteen or fourteen, stopp'd and gazed long at the spectacle of that fur-swathed old man, surrounded by friends and servants, and the careful seating of him in the sleigh. I remember the spirited, champing horses, the driver with his whip, and a fellow-driver by his side, for extra prudence. The old man, the subject of so much attention, I can almost see now. It was John Jacob Astor. . . .

1883

Omnibus Jaunts and Drivers

From Specimen Days

ONE PHASE of those days must by no means go unrecorded—namely, the Broadway omnibuses, with their drivers. The vehicles still (I write this paragraph in 1881) give a portion of the character of Broadway—the Fifth avenue, Madison avenue, and Twenty-third street lines yet running. But the flush days of the old Broadway stages, characteristic and copious, are over. The Yellow-birds, the Red-birds, the original Broadway, the Fourth avenue, the Knickerbocker, and a dozen others of twenty or thirty years ago, are all gone. And the men specially identified with them, and giving vitality and meaning to them—the drivers—a strange, natural, quick-eyed and wondrous race—(not only Rabelais and Cervantes would have gloated over them, but Homer and Shakspere would)—how well I remember them, and must here give a word about them. How many hours, forenoons and afternoons —how many exhilarating night-times I have had—perhaps June or July, in cooler air—riding the whole length of Broadway, listening to some yarn, (and the most vivid yarns ever spun, and the rarest mimicry)—or perhaps I declaiming some stormy passage from Julius Caesar or Richard, (you could roar as loudly as you chose in that heavy, dense, uninterrupted street-bass.) Yes, I knew all the drivers then, Broadway Jack, Dressmaker, Balky Bill, George Storms, Old Elephant, his brother Young Elephant (who came afterward,) Tippy, Pop Rice, Big Frank, Yellow Joe, Pete Callahan, Patsy Dee, and dozens more; for there were hundreds. They had immense qualities, largely animal—eating, drinking, women—great personal pride, in their way—perhaps a few slouches here and there, but I should have trusted the general run of them, in their simple goodwill and honor, under all circumstances. Not only for their comradeship, and sometimes affection—great studies I found them also. (I suppose the critics will laugh heartily, but the influence of those Broadway omnibus jaunts and drivers and declamations and escapades undoubtedly enter'd into the gestation of "Leaves of Grass.")

1883

Plays and Operas Too

From Specimen Days

And certain actors and singers had a good deal to do with the business. All through these years, off and on, I frequented the old Park, the Bowery, Broadway, and Chatham-square theatres, and the Italian operas at Chambers-street, Astor-place or the Battery—many seasons was on the free list, writing for papers even as quite a youth. The old Park theatre—what names, reminiscenses, the words bring back! Placide, Clarke, Mrs. Vernon, Fisher, Clara F., Mrs. Wood, Mrs. Seguin, Ellen Tree, Hackett, the younger Kean, Macready, Mrs. Richardson, Rice—singers, tragedians, comedians. What perfect acting! Henry Placide in "Napoleon's Old Guard" or "Grandfather Whitehead,"— or "the Provoked Husband" of Cibber, with Fanny Kemble as Lady Townley —or Sheridan Knowles in his own "Virginius"—or inimitable Power in "Born to Good Luck." These, and many more, the years of youth onward. Fanny Kemble—name to conjure up great mimic scenes withal—perhaps the greatest. I remember well her rendering of Bianca in "Fazio," and Marianna in "the Wife." Nothing finer did ever stage exhibit—the veterans of all nations said so, and my boyish heart and head felt it in every minute cell. The lady was just matured, strong, better than merely beautiful, born from the footlights, and had three years' practice in London and through the British towns, and then she came to give America that young maturity and roseate power in all their noon, or rather afternoon flush. It was my good luck to see her nearly every night she play'd at the old Park—certainly in all her principal characters.

I heard, these years, well render'd, all the Italian and other operas in vogue, "Sonnambula," "the Puritans," "Der Freischütz," "Huguenots," "Fille d'Regiment," "Faust," "Etoile du Nord," "Poliuto," and others. Verdi's "Ernani," "Rigoletto," and "Trovatore," with Donizetti's "Lucia," or "Favorita" or "Lucrezia," and Auber's "Massaniello," or Rossini's "William Tell" and "Gazza Ladra," were among my special enjoyments. I heard Alboni every time she sang in New York or vicinity—also Grisi, the tenor Mario, and the baritone Badiali, the finest in the world.

This musical passion follow'd my theatrical one. As a boy or young man I had seen, (reading them carefully the day beforehand,) quite all of Shakspere's acting dramas, play'd wonderfully well. Even yet I cannot conceive anything finer than old Booth in "Richard Third," or "Lear," (I don't know yet which was best,) or Iago, (or Pescara, or Sir Giles Overreach, to go outside of Shakspere)—or Tom Hamblin in "Macbeth"—or old Clarke, either as the ghost in "Hamlet," or as Prospero in "the Tempest," with Mrs. Austin as Ariel, and Peter Richings as Caliban. Then other dramas, and fine players in them, Forrest as Metamora or Damon or Brutus—John R. Scott as Tom Cringle or Rolla—or Charlotte Cushman's Lady Gay Spanker in "London Assurance." Then, of some years later, at Castle Garden, Battery, I yet recall the splendid seasons of the Havana musical troupe under Maretzek—the fine band, the cool sea-breezes, the unsurpass'd vocalism—Steffanone, Bosio, Truffi, Marrini in "Marino Faliero," "Don Pasquale," or "Favorita." No better playing or singing ever in New York. It was here, too, I afterward heard Jenny Lind. (The Battery—its past associations—what tales those old trees and walks and sea-walls could tell!)

1883

Hospital Scenes and Persons

From Specimen Days

Letter Writing.——When eligible, I encourage the men to write, and myself, when called upon, write all sorts of letters for them, (including love letters, very tender ones.) Almost as I reel off these memoranda, I write for a new patient to his wife. M. de F., of the 17th Connecticut, company H, has just come up (February 17th) from Windmill point, and is received in ward H, Armory-square. He is an intelligent looking man, has a foreign accent, black-eyed and hair'd, a Hebraic appearance. Wants a telegraph message sent to his wife, New Canaan, Conn. I agree to send the message—but to make things sure I also sit down and write the wife a letter, and dispatch it to the post-office immediately, as he fears she will come on, and he does not wish her to, as he will surely get well.

Saturday, January 30th.——Afternoon, visited Campbell hospital. Scene of cleaning up the ward, and giving the men all clean clothes—through the ward (6) the patients dressing or being dress'd—the naked upper half of the bodies—the good humor and fun—the shirts, drawers, sheets of beds, &c., and the general fixing up for Sunday. Gave J. L. 50 cents.

Wednesday, February 4th.——Visited

Armory-square hospital, went pretty thoroughly through wards E and D. Supplied paper and envelopes to all who wish'd—as usual, found plenty of men who needed those articles. Wrote letters. Saw and talk'd with two or three members of the Brooklyn 14th regt. A poor fellow in ward D, with a fearful wound in a fearful condition, was having some loose splinters of bone taken from the neighborhood of the wound. The operation was long, and one of great pain—yet, after it was well commenced, the soldier bore it in silence. He sat up, propp'd—was much wasted —had lain a long time quiet in one position (not for days only but weeks,) a bloodless, brown-skinn'd face, with eyes full of determination—belong'd to a New York regiment. There was the usual cluster of surgeons, medical cadets, nurses, &c., around his bed—I thought the whole thing was done with tenderness, and done well. In one case, the wife sat by the side of her husband, his sickness typhoid fever, pretty bad. In another, by the side of her son, a mother—she told me she had seven children, and this was the youngest. (A fine, kind, healthy, gentle mother, good-looking, not very old, with a cap on her head, and dress'd like home—what a charm it gave to the whole ward.) I liked the woman nurse in ward E—I noticed how she sat a long time by a poor fellow who had just had, that morning, in addition to his other sicknesses, bad hemorrhage—she gently assisted him, reliev'd him of the blood, holding a cloth to his mouth as he coughed it up—he was so weak he could only just turn his head over on the pillow.

One New York man, with a bright, handsome face, had been lying several months from a most disagreeable wound, receiv'd at Bull Run. A bullet had shot him right through the bladder, hitting him in front, low in the belly, and coming out back. He suffer'd much—the water came out of the wound, by slow but steady quantities, for many weeks—so that he lay almost constantly in a sort of puddle—and there were other disagreeable circumstances. He was of good heart, however. At present comparatively comfortable, had a bad throat, was delighted with a stick of hoarhound candy I gave him, with one or two other trifles.

1883

WILFRID SCAWEN BLUNT

I Have Saved Egypt

From My Diaries

"13th Oct., 1889. Paris.—I have left home once more for the winter, and with a lighter heart than I have lately had. My last act before leaving England was to write two letters severing the last links which bound me to political life. One was to the Kidderminster electors telling them that they must not depend on me to stand again for Parliament, the other to T. P. O'Connor resigning my directorship of the Star. I have intended this for more than a year, but have taken time to reflect, and am sure now that the step is a wise one. As a matter of principle I cannot go on pretending to believe in the Liberal Party, with which I have not an idea in common, beyond Irish Home Rule. As a matter of personal ambition, politics have nothing more to give me. I will not be a parliamentary drudge, and I cannot aspire to lead a party.

"Of doing good in the world in any public way I also despair. I do not see clearly in what direction good lies. I do not love civilised humanity; and poor savage human nature seems a lost cause. I have done what I could for it. I have, I think, saved Egypt from absorption by Europe, and I have certainly, by stopping the Soudan war in 1885, put back the clock of African conquest for a generation, perhaps for a century. But the march of 'Progress' is irresistible in the end; and every year the old-fashioned idea of the rights of uncivilised man dies more completely out. Even in Ireland, the National cause is putting itself in line with nineteenth century thought. The moonlighters and cattle-houghers and rebels of all kinds are disappearing; and, instead, we see Parnell manœuvring and deceiving in Parliament neither more nor less than Gladstone himself, and declaring with Rosebery for Imperial Federation! In all this I have no real lot or part. Ireland will doubtless get something of what she wants, and she has all my good wishes still. But Imperial Federation is not worth going to prison for a second time nor even standing another contested election. I have done enough—possibly too much—and am sick and weary of the machinery of English public life.

"On the other hand stands the world of art and poetry. In this I can still hope to accomplish something, and with an advantage of experience not every poet has. I have a great deal to accomplish before old age takes me and little time. My poems, my memoirs, my book of maxims (the "Wisdom of Merlyn"), my book of the Arab horse. These are work enough for all my remaining strength. Then, how delightful life is in perfect liberty! Never have I felt more capable of enjoyment, of the pleasures of friendship, of the casual incidents of romance, of the continuous happiness of life at home. These harmonize with a literary, not with a political ambition, and so it is best it should be. Am I not right?"

The three weeks that I spent at Paris on this occasion were delightful ones passed all in this mood. I found Lytton at the Embassy, and our old intimate intercourse was renewed. He, older than me by nine years, was already entering that valley of the shadow of old age from which he was never to emerge, and which ended in his death two years later. It was that in which his last volume of verse was written, and he made me the confidant of his sorrows, but this is not the place in which to give them more publicity than the volume itself gave them when it was published after his death. They served to accentuate my own mood of aversion from public affairs, and I spent most of my time with him at the Embassy, the same well-known house and garden where I had spent so much of my early youth officially as a member of it in the days of Lord Cowley and the Second Empire. I paid a visit, too, to the Wagrams at Gros Bois, where I mixed again in French society. The château was at that time undergoing repair of a substantial kind, an experience it had not had since 1830, and my hosts were living in the *dépendance*, an interesting suite of little rooms once the abode of Marshal Berthier's aides-de-camp, and possessed of a certain historic charm, with their Empire furniture and decorations. We shot each day in the great woods.

"Gros Bois, Wagram tells me, has been an oak wood ever since the time of the Druids. It was a royal domain, and had been given over and over again to different favourites of the kings of France. The last instance was when it was bestowed by Napoleon on the Prince's grandfather, as the inscription over the door records, his 'companion in arms.' The estate is of about 4,000 hectares, of which fully half are woodlands, 1,200 being inside the park wall, an ancient enclosure dating from 1650. I never saw so completely isolated a place, nor one quite so enjoyable. The woods are laid out formally (as French woods are) with straight rides or rather drives of grass cut through them, and though there is no old timber, all having been levelled with the ground in 1814, the oak trees grown up again from the stub are very beautiful, and the place is full of woodpeckers, jays, and magpies, besides game. There is a stone recording the death of the late Prince's first roebuck: *Ici mon fils a tué son premier chevreuil*, with the date 1826. This was Wagram's father, who went on till 1888, killing something every day in season and out of season, partridges on their nests if he could find no other, dogs, and sometimes beaters. All is recorded in a book; and he might have been the original of Carlyle's Baron: *qui centum mille perdices plumbo confecit et statim in stercore convertit*. (I am not sure of the Latinity.) He died at the beginning of last year, being about eighty years old, but shooting on to the last week of his life.

"I have received a nice letter from Kidderminster in answer to mine, and the 'Pall Mall Gazette' announces my retirement publicly from political life. The Princess is triumphant at this retirement, as she was always opposed to my politics."

All this was very demoralizing from a public point of view. On the 25th I was joined by my family at Paris, and on the 2nd November we moved on to Rome and Egypt. At Rome, where we spent a month, I found myself once more within the sphere of the serious life of two years before, having many friends among the Irish clergy, who formed so strong an element at the Vatican, and I find many entries in my diary connected with Irish politics, some of which are worth transcribing here.

1919-20

Yankees, the Coming Race

From My Diaries

"31st March.—'The Chronicle' has a sensational but probably true account of an ultimatum sent by the American President to Spain on account of Cuba. It seems likely to lead to war. If so I hope that Spain may be able to hold her own, not that Cuban independence lacks my sympathy, but because between Spain and the United States I am obliged to be on the side of the older and more barbarous country. The Yankees as the coming race of the world would be worse even than ourselves.

1919-20

Death of Queen Victoria, 1901

From My Diaries

"23 Jan., 1901. Sheykh Obeyd.

The Queen is dead of an apoplectic stroke and the great Victorian age is at an end."

Such is almost the first entry in my diary of the new year and the new century. I was in Egypt when the tidings reached me. It was the second day of the Bairam festival, and all our country folk at Sheykh Obeyd were keeping holiday, a glorious morning of sunshine, and I had been watching the foxes in the garden at play among the beans which were coming into flower. It was thus the news reached me. The entry goes on:

"This is notable news. It will mean great changes in the world, for the long understanding amongst the Emperors that England is not to be quarrelled with during the Queen's lifetime will now give place to freer action. The Emperor William does not love his uncle, our new king. On the other hand, it may possibly lead to a less bloody régime in South Africa; not that the Prince of Wales very likely is any more humane than his mother, who had a craze for painting the map Imperial red, but because he knows European opinion better and the limitations of England's power and the necessity of moderating English arrogance. The Queen it was easy to flatter and mislead, the only paper she read was the 'Morning Post,' and the people about her did not dare tell her the real truth of things, but the Prince of Wales hears and knows everything that goes on abroad far more than does Lord Salisbury. All this is to the good. I suppose there must be a new dissolution of Parliament—this also is for the good. As to Her Majesty personally, one does not like to say all one thinks even in one's journal. By all I have ever heard of her she was in her old age a dignified but rather common-place good soul, like how many of our dowagers, narrow-minded in her view of things, without taste in art or literature, fond of money, having a certain industry and business capacity in politics, but easily flattered and expecting to be flattered, quite convinced of her own providential position in the world and always ready to do anything to extend and augment it. She has been so long accustomed to success that she seems to have imagined that everything she did was wise and right, and I should not be surprised if the discreditable failure in South Africa had hastened her end. I see that Roberts went down to Osborne just before the seizure took place, and perhaps she may have insisted upon hearing the whole truth from him and, realizing it for the first time, have had the stroke of which she died. We shall probably be kept in the dark about this for a long while, for the public has got to look upon the old lady as a kind of fetish or idol, and nobody, even now she is dead, will dare print a word not to her glorification."

1919-20

H. G. WELLS

A President and a Dictator

From Experiment in Autobiography

I HAVE BEEN four times to the White House, and twice to the Kremlin, to see the man in occupation. But I have never been, and I am never likely to go, inside the gates of Buckingham Palace. Very early impressions may have something to do with that; I have told of my resistance to my mother's obsession about the dear Queen and my jealousy of the royal offspring; but the main reason for my obstinately republican life, as I see it in my own mind, is my conviction that here in England something has been held on to too long, and that nothing is doing here. A constitutional monarchy substitutes a figure-head for a head and distributes leadership elusively throughout the community. This gives the British system the resisting power of an acephalous invertebrate, and renders it equally incapable of concentrated forward action. In war-time the Crown resumes, or attempts to resume, a centralized author-

Reprinted from *Experiment in Autobiography* (Macmillan, 1934) by permission of Mrs. G. P. Wells.

ity—with such results as I have already glanced at in my account of my war experiences. Quite in accord with the tenacity of an acephalous invertebrate, the empire can be cut to pieces legally, have its South Ireland amputated, see half its shipping laid up and its heavy industries ruined, reconcile itself to the chronic unemployment and demoralization of half its young people, and still, on the strength of a faked budget and a burst of sunny summer weather, believe itself to be essentially successful and invulnerable. So it came about that, almost without thinking it over, as the various League of Nations documents I have quoted bear witness, I had become accustomed to looking westward for the definitive leadership of the English speaking community—and anywhere but in London for the leadership of mankind.

I have told already of my visit to Theodore Roosevelt. It was like visiting any large comfortable, leisurely, free-talking country house. Seeing President Harding had been like attending a politicians' reception in an official building, all loud geniality and handshaking, and the protean White House had taken on the decoration and furniture of a popular club. My call upon President Hoover was a sort of intrusion upon a sickly overworked and overwhelmed man, a month behind in all his engagements and hopeless of ever overtaking them, and the White House, in sympathy, had made itself into a queer ramshackle place like a nest of waiting-rooms with hatstands everywhere, and unexpected doors, never perceptible before or since, through which hurrying distraught officials appeared and vanished. President Hoover did not talk with me at all; he delivered a discourse upon the possible economic self-sufficiency of America that was, I imagine, intended for M. Laval from Paris, who had left Washington a week or so before. I did not find it interesting. After the Harding days there had been a foolish development of etiquette in Washington and instead of going to the President as man to man, the foreign visitor during the Coolidge and Hoover régimes was led—after due enquiries—down to the White House by his ambassador. Henceforth America and the English, it had been decided, were to talk only through a diplomatic pipette. Sir Ronald Lindsay took me down, apologetically, and sat beside me during the encounter, rather like a gentleman who takes a strange dog out to a tea-party, and is not quite sure how it will behave. But I respected the trappings of government and nothing diplomatically serious occurred. I just listened and contained myself. Diplomatic usage, will I suppose, prevent Sir Ronald from ever producing his memories of Men I have Chaperoned to the White House.

All this had been swept away again in 1934. I had had some slight correspondence with the President already; I went to him on my own credentials, and found that this magic White House had changed back again to a large leisurely comfortable private home. All the Hoover untidiness had vanished. Everything was large, cool, orderly and unhurried. Besides Mr. and Mrs. Roosevelt, his daughter Mrs. Dall, Miss Le Hand his personal secretary, and another lady, dined with us and afterwards I sat and talked to him and Mrs. Roosevelt and Miss Le Hand until nearly midnight, easily and pleasantly—as though the world crisis focused anywhere rather than upon the White House.

As everyone knows, the President is a crippled man. He reminded me of William Ernest Henley. He has the same big torso linked to almost useless legs, and he lacked even Henley's practised nimbleness with stick and crutch. But when we sat at dinner and when he was in his study chair, his physical disablement vanished from the picture. Mrs. Roosevelt I found a very pleasant, well-read lady; I had been warned she was a terrible "school marm," but the only trait of the schoolmistress about her was a certain care for precision of statement. There was no pose about either of them. They were not concerned about being what was expected of them, or with the sort of impression they were making; they were just interested in a curious keen detached way about the state of the world. They talked about that, in the manner of independent people who had really not so very much to do with it. We were all in it and we had to play our parts, but there was no reason because one was in a responsible position that one should be mystical or pompous or darkly omniscient about it.

Even if my memory would serve for the task, I would not report the drift and shifting substance of our talk. Only one thing need be recorded, the President's manifest perplexity at some recent turns of British diplomacy, and the wonder that peeped out—a wonder we all share—over the question as to what Sir John Simon imagines he is up to, whether he represents any obscure realities of British thought and, if not, why on earth, in the far east and elsewhere, the two big English-speaking communities seem perpetually discordant and unexpected to each other. My own fixed idea about world peace came naturally enough to the fore. If it were not, I said, for questions of mere polit-ical mechanism, stale traditions, the mental childishness of our British Foreign Office and what not, it would be perfectly possible even now for the English-speaking masses and the Russian mass, with France as our temperamental associate, to be made to say effectively that Peace shall prevail throughout the earth. And it would prevail. Whatever dreams of conquest and dominion might be in a few militant and patriotic brains outside such a combination, would burn but weakly in the cold discouragement of so great a unison. And what was it—prevented that unison?

But that was only one of the topics we touched upon. What concerns me here is not what was said, but the manner in which it was thought about and advanced. I am not thinking primarily of policies and governmental actions here, but of an encounter with a new type of mind. My own ideas about the coming socialist world-state are fixed and explicit. But they are, I am persuaded, implicit in every mind that has been opened to the possibility of unrestricted change. I do not say that the President has these revolutionary ideas in so elaborated and comprehensive a form as they have come to me; I do not think he has. I do not think he is consciously what I have called an Open Conspirator and it is quite clear his formulæ are necessarily limited by the limitations of the popular understanding with which he has to come to terms. But these ideas are sitting all round him now, and unless I misjudge him, they will presently possess him altogether. Events are reinforcing them and carrying him on to action. My impression of both him and of Mrs. Roosevelt is that they are *unlimited* people, entirely modern in the openness of their minds and the

logic of their actions. I have been using the word "blinkered" rather freely
in this section. Here in the White
House, the unblinkered mind was in
possession.

The Roosevelts are something more
than open-minded. Arthur Balfour
was greatly open-minded, but he lacked
the slightest determination to realize
the novel ideas he entertained so freely.
He was set in the habitual acceptance of
the thing that is, church, court, society,
empire, and he did not really believe in
the new thoughts that played about in
his mind. President Roosevelt does.
He has a brain that is certainly as receptive and understanding as Balfour's but,
with that, he has an uncanny disposition for action and realization that Balfour lacked altogether. This man who
can sit and talk so frankly and freely is
also an astute politician and a subtle
manager of masses and men. As the
President thinks and conceives, so forthwith, he acts. Both he and his wife
have the simplicity that says, "But if it is
right we ought to do it." They set
about what they suppose has to be done
without exaltation, without apology or
any sense of the strangeness of such conduct. Such unification of unconventional thought and practical will is
something new in history, and I will
not speculate here about the peculiar
personal and the peculiar American
conditions that may account for it.
But as the vast problems about them
expose and play themselves into their
minds, the goal of the Open Conspiracy
becomes plainer ahead. Franklin Roosevelt does not embody and represent
that goal, but he represents the way
thither. He is being the most effective
transmitting instrument possible for
the coming of the new world order.
He is eminently "reasonable" and fun-

damentally implacable. He demonstrates that comprehensive new ideas
can be taken up, tried out and made
operative in general affairs without rigidity or dogma. He is continuously
revolutionary in the new way without
ever provoking a stark revolutionary
crisis.

Before I visited Washington, I was
inclined to the belief that the forces
against such a replanning of the American social and political system as will
arrest the present slant towards disaster,
the individualistic tradition, the individual lawlessness, the intricate brutal
disingenuousness of political and legal
methods, were so great that President
Franklin Roosevelt was doomed to an
inevitable defeat. I wrote an article
*The Place of Franklin Roosevelt in His-
tory* (Liberty Magazine, October, 1933)
in which I made my bet for his overthrow. But I thought then he was a
man with a definite set of ideas, fixed
and final, in his head, just as I am a man
with a system of conclusions fixed and
definite in my head. But I perceive he
is something much more flexible and
powerful than that. He is bold and unlimited in his objectives because his
mental arms are long and his courage
great, but his peculiar equipment as an
amateur of the first rank in politics,
keeps him in constant touch with political realities and possibilities. He never
lets go of them and they never subdue
him. He never seems to go so far beyond the crowd as to risk his working
leadership, and he never loses sight of
pioneer thought. He can understand
and weigh contemporary speculative
economics, financial specialism and international political psychology, and he
can talk on the radio—over the heads of
the party managers and newspaper proprietors and so forth—quite plainly and

very convincingly to the ordinary voting man.

He is, as it were, a ganglion for reception, expression, transmission, combination and realization, which I take it, is exactly what a modern government ought to be. And if perhaps after all he is, humanly, not quite all that I am saying of him here, he is at any rate enough of what I am saying of him here, for me to make him a chief collateral exhibit in this psycho-political autobiography.

On July the 21st I started from London for Moscow in the company of my eldest son, who wished to meet some Russian biologists with whose work he was acquainted, and to see their laboratories. We left Croydon in the afternoon, spent the night in Berlin and flew on by way of Danzig, Kovno and Welilikje Luki, reaching Moscow before dark on the evening of the 22nd. We flew in clear weather as far as Amsterdam, then through a couple of thunderstorms to Berlin. We were late in reaching the glitter of illuminated Berlin; the raining darkness was flickering with lightning flashes and our plane came down to make its landing with flares burning under its wings along a lane of windy yellow flame against the still red and white lights of the aerodrome. The flight next day from Welilikje Luki to Moscow, flying low and eastward in afternoon sunshine, was particularly golden and lovely.

In 1900, when I wrote *Anticipations,* this would have been as incredible a journey as a trip on Aladdin's carpet; in 1934 it was arranged in the most matter of fact way through a travel agency; it was a little excursion that anyone might make; and the fare was less than the railway fare would have been a third of

a century before. In a little time such a visit will seem as small a matter as a taxi-cab call does now. It is our antiquated political organization and our retrograde imaginations that still hold back such a final abolition of distance.

Moscow I found greatly changed—even from the air this was visible; not set and picturesque, a black-and-gold barbaric walled city-camp about a great fortress, as I had seen it first in 1914; nor definitely shabby, shattered and apprehensive as it had been in the time of Lenin, but untidily and hopefully renascent. There was new building going on in every direction, workers' dwellings, big groups of factories and, amidst the woods, new *datchas* and country clubs. No particular plan was apparent from the air; it looked like a vigorous, natural expansion such as one might see in the most individualistic of cities. We came down over a patchwork of aerodromes and saw many hundreds of planes parked outside the hangars. Russian aviation may be concentrated about Moscow, but this display of air force was certainly impressive. Twenty-two years ago, in my *War in the Air,* I had imagined such wide fields of air fleet, but never then in my boldest cerebrations did I think I should live to see them.

I confess that I approached Stalin with a certain amount of suspicion and prejudice. A picture had been built up in my mind of a very reserved and self-centred fanatic, a despot without vices, a jealous monopolizer of power. I had been inclined to take the part of Trotsky against him. I had formed a very high opinion, perhaps an excessive opinion, of Trotsky's military and administrative abilities, and it seemed to me that Russia, which is in such urgent need of directive capacity at every turn, could not afford to send them into exile. Trotsky's Autobiography, and more particularly the second volume, had modified this judgment but I still expected to meet a ruthless, hard—possibly doctrinaire—and self-sufficient man at Moscow; a Georgian highlander whose spirit had never completely emerged from its native mountain glen.

Yet I had had to recognize that under him Russia was not being merely tyrannized over and held down; it was being governed and it was getting on. Everything I had heard in favour of the First Five Year Plan I had put through a severely sceptical sieve, and yet there remained a growing effect of successful enterprise. I had listened more and more greedily to any first-hand gossip I could hear about both these contrasted men. I had already put a query against my grim anticipation of a sort of Bluebeard at the centre of Russian affairs. Indeed if I had not been in reaction against these first preconceptions and wanting to get nearer the truth of the matter, I should never have gone again to Moscow.

This lonely overbearing man, I thought, may be damned disagreeable, but anyhow he must have an intelligence far beyond dogmatism. And if I am not all wrong about the world, and if he is as able as I am beginning to think him, then he must be seeing many things much as I am seeing them.

I wanted to tell him that I had talked to Franklin Roosevelt of the new prospect of world co-operation that was opening before mankind. I wanted to stress the fact upon which I had dwelt in the White House, that in the English-speaking and Russian-speaking populations, and in the populations geographically associated with them round the temperate zone, there is a major mass of human beings ripe for a common understanding and common co-operation in the preparation of an organised world-state. Quite parallel with that double basis for a world plan, I wanted to say, there is a third great system of possible co-operation in the Spanish-speaking community. These masses, together with the Chinese, constitute an overwhelming majority of mankind, anxious—in spite of their so-called governments—for peace, industry and an organized well-being. Such things as Japanese imperialism, the national egotism of the Quai d'Orsay and of Mussolini, the childish disingenuousness of the British Foreign Office, and German political delirium, would become quite minor obstacles to human unity, if these common dispositions could be marshalled into a common understanding and a common method of expression. The militancy of Japan was not so much a threat to mankind as a useful reminder for us to sink formal differences and spread one explicit will for peace throughout the world. Japan, with a possible but very improbable German alliance, was the only efficient reactionary menace left for civilization to deal with. France was inaggressive in spirit; Great Britain incurably indeterminate. I wanted to find out how far Stalin saw international matters in this shape and, if he proved to be in general agreement, to try and see how far he would go with me in my idea that the present relative impotence of the wider masses of mankind to restrain the smaller fiercer threats of aggressive patriotism, is really due not to anything fundamental in human nature but to old inharmonious traditions, bad education and bad explanations; to our failure, thus far, to get our populations clearly told the true common history of our race and the common objective now before mankind. That objective was the highly organized world community in which service was to take the place of profit. The political dialects and phrases which were directed towards that end were needlessly and wastefully different. Creative impulses were being hampered to the pitch of ineffectiveness by pedantries and misunderstandings.

Was it impossible to bring general political statements up to date, so that the real creative purpose in the Russian will should no longer be made alien and repulsive to the quickened intelligence of the Western World, by an obstinate insistence upon the antiquated political jargon, the class-war cant, of fifty years ago? All things serve their purpose and die, and it was time that even the passing of Karl Marx, intellectually as well as physically, was recognised. It was as absurd now to cling to those old expressions as it would be to try to electrify Russia with the frictional electric machines or the zinc and copper batteries of 1864. Marxist class-war insurrectionism had become a real obstacle to the onward planning of a new world order. This was particularly evident in our English-speaking community.

This ancient doctrine that the proletariat or the politician temporarily representing him, can do no wrong, estranged the competent technologist, who was vitally essential to the new task, and inculcated a spirit of mystical mass enthusiasm opposed to all disciplined cooperation. I wanted to bring it plainly into our talk that Russia was now paying only lip service to human unity and solidarity; that she was in actual fact drifting along a way of her own to a socialism of her own, which was getting out of touch with world socialism, and

training her teeming multitudes to misinterpret and antagonize the greater informal forces in the West making for world socialization and consolidation. Was it not possible, before opportunity slipped away from us, to form a general line of creative propaganda throughout the earth? . . .

It was typical of the way in which mental interchanges lag behind the swift achievements of material progress, that Stalin and I had to talk through an interpreter. He speaks a Georgian language and Russian and he does not even smatter any Western idiom. So we had to carry on our conversation in the presence of a foreign-office representative, Mr. Umansky. Mr. Umansky produced a book in which he made a rapid note in Russian of what each of us said, read out my speeches in Russian to Stalin and his, almost as readily, to me in English, and then sat alert-eyed over his glasses ready for the response. Necessarily a certain amount of my phraseology was lost in the process and a certain amount of Mr. Umansky's replaced it. And our talk went all the slowlier because I was doing my best to check back, by what Stalin said, that he was getting the substance at least, if not the full implications, of what I was saying.

All lingering anticipations of a dour sinister Highlander vanished at the sight of him. He is one of those people who in a photograph or painting become someone entirely different. He is not easy to describe, and many descriptions exaggerate his darkness and stillness. His limited sociability and a simplicity that makes him inexplicable to the more consciously disingenuous, has subjected him to the strangest inventions of whispering scandal. His harmless, orderly, private life is kept rather more private than his immense public importance warrants, and when, a year or so ago, his wife died suddenly of some brain lesion, the imaginative spun a legend of suicide which a more deliberate publicity would have made impossible. All such shadowy undertow, all suspicion of hidden emotional tensions, ceased for ever, after I had talked to him for a few minutes.

My first impression was of a rather commonplace-looking man dressed in an embroidered white shirt, dark trousers and boots, staring out of the window of a large, generally empty, room. He turned rather shyly and shook hands in a friendly manner. His face also was commonplace, friendly and commonplace, not very well modelled, not in any way "fine." He looked past me rather than at me but not evasively; it was simply that he had none of the abundant curiosity which had kept Lenin watching me closely from behind the hand he held over his defective eye, all the time he talked to me.

I began by saying that Lenin at the end of our conversation had said "Come back and see us in ten years." I had let it run to fourteen, but now that I had seen Franklin Roosevelt in Washington I wanted to meet the ruling brain of the Kremlin while my Washington impressions were still fresh, because I thought that the two of them between them indicated the human future as no other two men could do. He said with a quite ordinary false modesty that he was only doing little things—just little things.

The conversation hung on a phase of shyness. We both felt friendly, and we wanted to be at our ease with each other, and we were not at our ease. He had evidently a dread of self-importance in the encounter; he posed not at all,

but he knew we were going to talk of very great matters. He sat down at a table and Mr. Umansky sat down beside us, produced his note book and patted it open in a competent, expectant manner.

I felt there was heavy going before me but Stalin was so ready and willing to explain his position that in a little while the pause for interpretation was almost forgotten in the preparation of new phrases for the argument. I had supposed there was about forty minutes before me, but when at that period I made a reluctant suggestion of breaking off, he declared his firm intention of going on for three hours. And we did. We were both keenly interested in each other's point of view. What I said was the gist of what I had intended to say and that I have told already; the only matter of interest here is how Stalin reacted to these ideas.

I do not know whether it illuminated Stalin or myself most penetratingly, but what impressed me most in that discussion was his refusal to see any sort of parallelism with the processes and methods and aims of Washington and Moscow. When I talked of the planned world to him, I talked in a language he did not understand. He looked at the proposition before him and made nothing of it. He has little of the quick uptake of President Roosevelt and none of the subtlety and tenacity of Lenin. Lenin was indeed saturated with Marxist phraseology, but he had a complete control of this phraseology. He could pour it into new meanings and use it for his own purposes. But Stalin was almost as much a trained mind, trained in the doctrines of Lenin and Marx, as those governess-trained minds of the British Foreign Office and diplomatic service, of which I have already written

so unkindly. He was as little adapt-
able. The furnishing of his mind had
stopped at the point reached by Lenin
when he reconditioned Marxism. His
was not a free impulsive brain nor a
scientifically organized brain; it was a
trained Leninist-Marxist brain. Sometimes I seemed to get him moving as I
wanted him to move, but directly he felt
he was having his feet shifted, he would
clutch at some time-honoured phrase
and struggle back to orthodoxy.

I have never met a man more candid,
fair and honest, and to these qualities
it is, and to nothing occult and sinister,
that he owes his tremendous undisputed ascendency in Russia. I had
thought before I saw him that he might
be where he was because men were
afraid of him, but I realize that he owes
his position to the fact that no one is
afraid of him and everybody trusts him.
The Russians are a people at once childish and subtle, and they have a justifiable fear of subtlety in themselves and
others. Stalin is an exceptionally un-
subtle Georgian. His unaffected orthodoxy is an assurance to his associates
that whatever he does would be done
without fundamental complications
and in the best possible spirit. They
had been fascinated by Lenin, and they
feared new departures from his talis-
manic directions. And Stalin's trained
obduracy to the facts of to-day in our
talk simply reflected, without the slightest originality, the trained and self-pro-
tective obduracy of his associates.

I not only attacked him with the assertion that large scale planning by the
community, and a considerable socialization of transport and staple industries, was dictated by the mechanical
developments of our time, and was going on quite as extensively outside the
boundaries of Sovietdom as within

them, but also I made a long criticism
of the old-fashioned class-war propaganda, in which a macédoine of types
and callings is jumbled up under the
term bourgeoisie. That is one of the
most fatal of the false simplifications
in this collective human brain-storm
which is the Russian Revolution. I said
that great sections in that mixture, the
technicians, scientific workers, medical
men, skilled foremen, skilled producers,
aviators, operating engineers, for instance, would and should supply the
best material for constructive revolution in the West, but that the current
communist propaganda, with its insistence upon a mystical mass directorate,
estranged and antagonised just these
most valuable elements. Skilled workers and directors know that Jack is not
as good as his master. Stalin saw my
reasoning, but he was held back by his
habitual reference to the proletarian
mass—which is really nothing more
than the "sovereign Peepul" of old fashioned democracy, renamed. That is to
say it is nothing but a politician's figment. It was amusing to shoot at him,
with a lively knowledge of the facts of
the October Revolution, an assertion
equally obvious and unorthodox, that
"All revolutions are made by minorities." His honesty compelled him to
admit that "at first" this might be so.
I tried to get back to my idea of the possible convergence of West and East
upon the socialist world state objective,
by quoting Lenin as saying, after the
Revolution, "Communism has now to
learn Business," and adding that in the
West that had to be put the other way
round. Business had now to learn the
socialization of capital—which indeed
is all that this Russian Communism
now amounts to. It is a state-capitalism
with a certain tradition of cosmopoli-

tanism. West and East starting from entirely different levels of material achievement, had each now what the other lacked, and I was all for a planetary rounding off of the revolutionary process. But Stalin, now quite at his ease and interested, sucked thoughtfully at the pipe he had most politely asked my permission to smoke, shook his head and said "Nyet" reflectively. He was evidently very suspicious of this suggestion of complemental co-operation. It might be the thin end of a widening wedge. He lifted his hand rather like a schoolboy who is prepared to recite, and dictated a reply in party formulae. The movement of socialization in America was not a genuine proletarian revolution; the "capitalist" was just saving himself, pretending to divest himself of power and hiding round the corner to come back. That settled that. The one true faith was in Russia; there could be no other. America must have her October Revolution and follow her Russian leaders.

Later on we discussed liberty of expression. He admitted the necessity and excellence of criticism, but preferred that it should be home-made by the party within the party organisation. There, he declared, criticism was extraordinarily painstaking and free. Outside criticism might be biased. . . .

I wound up according to my original intention by insisting upon the outstanding positions of himself and Roosevelt, and their ability to talk to the world in unison. But that came lamely because my hope for some recognition, however qualified, on the part of the man in control of Russia, of the present convergence towards a collective capitalism in the East and West alike, was badly damaged. He had said his piece to all my initiatives and he stayed put. I wished I could have talked good Russian or had an interpreter after my own heart. I could have got nearer to him then. Normal interpreters gravitate inevitably towards stereotyped phrases. Nothing suffers so much in translation as the freshness of an unfamiliar idea . . .

1934

WILLIAM ROPER

The Last Days of Sir Thomas More

From The Mirrour of Vertue in Worldly Greatnes

. . . Came there to him the Lord Chancellor, the Dukes of Norfolk and Suffolk, with Mr Secretary, and certain others of the Privy Council at two separate times, by all policies possible procuring him either precisely to confess the supremacy, or precisely to deny it. Whereunto (as appeareth by his examination in the said great book) they could never bring him. Shortly hereupon Mr Rich (afterwards Lord Rich) then newly the King's Solicitor, Sir Richard Southwell, and Mr Palmer, servant to the Secretary, were sent to Sir Thomas

More into the Tower, to fetch away his books from him. And while Sir Richard Southwell and Mr Palmer were busy in trussing up of his books, Mr Rich, pretending friendly talk with him, among other things of a set course, as it seemed, said thus unto him: "Forasmuch as it is well known (Mr More) that you are a man both wise and well learned, as well in the laws of the Realm, as otherwise, I pray you therefore, Sir, let me be so bold as of good will to put unto you this case. Admit there were, Sir," quoth he, "an Act of Parliament, that all the Realm should take me for the King, would not you (Mr More) take me for the King?" "Yes, Sir," quoth Sir Thomas More, "that would I." "I put the case further" (quoth Mr Rich) "that there were an Act of Parliament that all the Realm should take me for the Pope; would then not you, Mr More, take me for the Pope?" "For answer," quoth Sir Thomas More, "to your first case, the Parliament may well (Mr Rich) meddle with the state of temporal princes; but to make answer to your second case, I will put you this case, Suppose the Parliament would make a law, that God should not be God, would you then, Mr Rich, say God were not God?" "No, Sir," quoth he, "that would I not, since no Parliament may make any such law." "No more" (said Sir Thomas More, as Mr Rich reported of him) "could the Parliament make the King supreme head of the Church." Upon whose only report was Sir Thomas More indicted of treason upon the Statute in which it was made treason to deny the King to be supreme head of the Church, into which indictment were put these words, *maliciously, traitorously, and diabolically.* When Sir Thomas More was brought from the Tower to Westminster Hall to answer the indictment, and at the King's Bench bar before the judges thereupon arraigned, he openly told them that he would upon that indictment have abiden in law, but he thereby should have been driven to confess of himself the matter indeed, which was the denial of the King's supremacy, which he protested was untrue, wherefore thereto he pleaded not guilty, and so reserved unto himself advantage to be taken of the body of the matter after verdict, to avoid that indictment. And moreover added, "if those only odious terms, *maliciously, traitorously, and diabolically* were put out of the indictment, he saw nothing therein justly to charge him." And for proof to the jury that Sir Thomas More was guilty to this treason, Mr Rich was called by them to give evidence unto them, as he did; against whom Sir Thomas More began in this wise to say: "If I were a man (my Lords) that did not regard an oath, I need not (as it is well known) in this place, at this time, nor in this case to stand as an accused person. And if this oath of yours (Mr Rich) be true, then pray I that I may never see God in the face, which I would not say, were it otherwise, to win the whole world." Then recited he unto the discourse of all their communication in the Tower according to the truth, and said, "In faith, Mr Rich, I am sorrier for your perjury than for mine own peril, and you shall understand that neither I, nor no man else to my knowledge ever took you to be a man of such credit as in any matter of importance I, or any other would at any time vouchsafe to communicate with you. And (as you know) of no small while I have been acquainted with you and your conversation, who have known you from your youth hitherto.

For we long dwelled both in one parish together, where, as yourself can tell (I am sorry you compel me so to say) you were esteemed very light of your tongue, a great dicer, and of not commendable fame. And so in your house at the Temple (where hath been your chief bringing up) were you likewise accounted. Can it therefore seem likely unto your honourable Lordships, that I would, in so weighty a cause, so far overshoot myself, as to trust Mr Rich (a man of me always reputed for one of so little truth, as your Lordships have heard) so far above my sovereign Lord the King, or any of his noble councillors, that I would unto him utter the secrets of my conscience touching the King's supremacy, the special point and only mark at my hands so long sought for? A thing which I never did, nor never would, after the Statute thereof made, reveal it, either to the King's Highness himself or to any of his honourable councillors, as it is not unknown unto your house, at sundry times, and several, sent from his Grace's own person unto the Tower to me for none other purpose. Can this in your judgments (my Lords) seem likely to be true? And if I had so done indeed, my Lords, as Mr Rich hath sworn, seeing it was spoke but in familiar secret talk, nothing affirming, and only in putting of cases, without other displeasant circumstances, it cannot justly be taken to be spoken maliciously. And where there is no malice there can be no offence. And over this I can never think (my Lords) that so many worthy bishops, so many honourable personages, and many other worshipful, virtuous, wise, and well-learned men, as at the making of that law were in the Parliament assembled, ever meant to have any man punished by death, in whom there could be found no malice, taking *malitia pro malevolentia.* For if *malitia* be generally taken for sin, no man is there then that can thereof excuse himself. *Quia si dixerimus quod peccatum non habemus, nosmetipsos seducimus, et veritas in nobis non est.* And only this word *maliciously* is in the Statute material, as this term *forcible* is in the statute of forcible entries; by which statute if a man enter peaceably, and put not his adversary out forcibly, it is no offence, but if he put him out forcibly, then by that statute it is an offence. And so shall he be punished by this term *forcible.* Besides this, the manifold goodness of my sovereign Lord the King's Highness himself, that hath been so many ways my singular good Lord and Gracious Sovereign, that hath so dearly loved me, and trusted me even at my first coming into his noble service with the dignity of his honourable Privy Council, vouchsafing to admit me to offices of great credit, and worship most liberally advanced me, and finally with that weighty room of his Grace's high Chancellorship (the like whereof he never did to temporal man before) next to his own royal person the highest officer in this noble realm, so far above my merits or qualities able and meet therefore, of his incomparable benignity honoured and exalted me by the space of twenty years and more, showing his continual favour towards me; and (until, at mine own poor suit, it pleased his Highness, giving me licence, with his Majesty's favour, to bestow the residue of my life wholly for the provision of my soul in the service of God, of his special goodness thereof to discharge and unburden me) most benignly heaped honours more and more upon me; all this his Highness' goodness, I say, so long continued towards me, were, in my mind (my Lords), matter sufficient to convince this slanderous surmise (by this) man so wrongfully imagined against me." Mr Rich seeing himself so disproved, and his credit so foully defaced, caused Sir Richard Southwell and Mr Palmer, that at that time of their communication were in the chamber, to be sworn what words had passed betwixt them. Whereupon Mr Palmer on his deposition said, that he was so busy about the trussing up Sir Thomas More's books in a sack, that he took no heed to their talk. Sir Richard Southwell likewise upon his deposition said, that because he was appointed only to look to the conveyance of his books, he gave no ear unto them. After this, were there many other reasons (not now in my remembrance) by Sir Thomas More in his own defence aleged, to the discredit of Mr Rich his foresaid evidence, and proof of the clearness of his own conscience. All which notwithstanding the jury found him guilty, and incontinent upon the verdict the Lord Chancellor (for that matter chief commissioner) beginning in judgment against him, Sir Thomas More said to him, "My Lord, when I was towards the law, the manner in such case was to ask the prisoner before judgment, why judgment should not be given against him?" Whereupon the Lord Chancellor staying his judgment, wherein he had partly proceeded, demanded of him what he was able to say to the contrary? Who then in this sort mildly made answer: "Forasmuch as, my Lord" (quoth he), "this indictment is grounded upon an Act of Parliament, directly oppugnant to the laws of God and his holy Church, the supreme government of which, or of any part thereof, may no temporal prince presume by any law to take upon him as rightfully belonging to the See of Rome, a spiritual pre-eminence by the mouth of our Saviour himself, personally present upon the earth, to St Peter and his successors, bishops of the same see, by special prerogative, granted, it is therefore in law amongst Christian men insufficient to charge any Christian." And for proof thereof like as amongst divers other reasons and authorities he declared That this Realm, being but one member and small part of the Church, might not make a particular law dischargeable with the general law of Christ's holy Catholic Church, no more than the City of London, being but one poor member in respect of the whole Realm, might make a law against an Act of Parliament to bind the whole Realm unto: so further showed he, that it was contrary both to the laws and statutes of this land, yet unrepealed, as they might evidently perceive in *Magna charta, Quod Ecclesia Anglicana libera sit et habeat omnia jura sua integra, et libertates suas illæsas,* and contrary to that sacred oath which the King's Highness himself, and every other Christian prince always at their coronations received, alleging moreover, that no more might this Realm of England refuse obedience to the See of Rome, than might the child refuse obedience to his natural father. For as St Paul said of the Corinthians, "I have regenerated you my children in Christ," so might St Gregory Pope of Rome (of whom by St Augustine his messenger we first received the Christian faith) of us English men truly say, "You are my children, because I have given to you everlasting salvation, a far better inheritance than any carnal father can leave unto his child, and by spiritual generation have made you my spiritual children in Christ." Then was it thereunto by the

Lord Chancellor answered, that seeing all the bishops, universities, and best learned men of the Realm had to this Act agreed, it was much marvelled that he alone against them all would so stiffly stick and vehemently argue there against. To that Sir Thomas More replied saying, "If the number of bishops and universities be so material, as your Lordships seemeth to take it, then see I little cause (my Lords) why that thing in my conscience should make any change. For I nothing doubt, but that though not in this Realm, yet in Christendom about they be not the least part, that be of my mind therein. But if I should speak of those that be already dead (of whom many be now saints in heaven) I am very sure it is the far greater part of them, that all the while they lived, thought in this case that way that I think now. And therefore am I not bound (my Lords) to conform my conscience to the council of one realm against the General Council of Christendom." Now when Sir Thomas More, for the avoiding of the indictment, had taken as many exceptions as he thought meet and more reasons than I can now remember alleged, the Lord Chancellor, loath to have the burden of the judgment wholly to depend upon himself, then openly asked the advice of the Lord Fitz-James, then the Lord Chief Justice of the King's Bench, and joined in commission with him, whether this indictment were sufficient or not? Who like a wise man answered, "My Lords all, by St Julian" (that was ever his oath) "I must needs confess, that if the Act of Parliament be not unlawful, then is not the indictment in my conscience insufficient." Whereupon the Lord Chancellor said to the rest of the Lords, "Lo, my Lords, lo, you

hear what my Lord Chief Justice saith," and so immediately gave the judgment against him. After which ended, the commissioners yet courteously offered him, if he had anything else to allege for his defence to grant him favourable audience, who answered, "More have I not to say (my Lords) but like as the blessed Apostle St Paul, as we read in the Acts of the Apostles, was present, and consented to the death of St Stephen, and kept their clothes that stoned him to death, and yet be they now both twain holy saints in heaven, and shall continue there friends for ever, so I verily trust and shall therefore right heartily pray, that though your Lordships have now in earth been judges to my condemnation, we may yet hereafter in heaven merrily all meet together to our everlasting salvation." Thus much touching Sir Thomas More's arraignment, being not thereat present myself, have I by the credible report of Sir Anthony Sumtleger Knight, and partly of Sir Richard Heywood, and John Webb Gentleman, with others of good credit, at the hearing thereof present themselves, as far forth as my poor wit and memory would serve me, here truly rehearsed unto you. Now after this arraignment departed he from the bar to the Tower again, led by Sir William Kingston, a tall, strong, and comely knight, Constable of the Tower, his very dear friend, who when he had brought him from Westminster to the Old Swan towards the Tower, there with a heavy heart, the tears running down his cheeks, bade him farewell. Sir Thomas More seeing him so sorrowful, comforted him with as good words as he could, saying, "Good Mr Kingston, trouble not yourself, but be of good cheer. For I will pray for you, and my good Lady your wife, that we may meet in heaven together, where we shall be merry for ever and ever." Soon after Sir William Kingston talking with me of Sir Thomas More, said, "In faith Mr Roper I was ashamed of myself, that at my departure from your father, I found my heart so feeble, and his so strong, that he was fain to comfort me which should rather have comforted him." When Sir Thomas More came from Westminster to the Towerward again, his daughter my wife, desirous to see her father, whom she thought she should never see in this world after, and also to have his final blessing, gave attendance about the Tower wharf, where she knew he should pass by, ere he could enter into the Tower. There tarrying for his coming home, as soon as she saw him, after his blessings on her knees reverently received, she, hasting towards, without consideration of care of herself, pressing in amongst the midst of the throng and the Company of the Guard, that with halbards and bills were round about him, hastily ran to him, and there openly in the sight of all them embraced and took him about the neck and kissed him, who well liking her most daughterly love and affection towards him, gave her his fatherly blessing, and many godly words of comfort besides, from whom after she was departed, she not satisfied with the former sight of her dear father, having respect neither to herself, nor to the press of the people and multitude that were about him, suddenly turned back again, and ran to him as before, took him about the neck, and divers times together most lovingly kissed him, and at last with a full heavy heart was fain to depart from him; the beholding whereof was to many of them that were present thereat so lamentable, that it made them for very sorrow to mourn and weep. So remained Sir Thomas More in the Tower more than a seven-night after his judgment. From whence the day before he suffered he sent his shirt of hair, not willing to have it seen, to my wife, his dearly beloved daughter, and a letter, written with a coal, contained in the foresaid book of his works, plainly expressing the fervent desire he had to suffer on the morrow in these words: "I cumber you, good Margaret, much, but I would be sorry if it should be any longer than to-morrow. For to-morrow is St Thomas' even, and the Octave of St Peter, and therefore to-morrow long I to go to God, that were a day very meet and convenient for me. And I never liked your manners better, than when you kissed me last. For I like when daughterly love, and dear charity hath no leisure to look to worldly courtesy." And so upon the next morning, being Tuesday, St Thomas' even, and the Octave of St Peter in the year of our Lord God 1537, according as he in his letter the day before had wished, early in the morning came to him Sir Thomas Pope, his singular friend, on message from the King and his Council, that he should before nine of the clock in the same morning suffer death, and that therefore forthwith he should prepare himself thereto. "Mr Pope," saith he, "for your good tidings I most heartily thank you. I have been always bounden much to the King's Highness for the benefits and honours which he hath still from time to time most bountifully heaped upon me, and yet more bounded I am to his Grace for putting me into this place, where I have had convenient time and space to have remembrance of my end, and so help me God most of all, Mr Pope, am I bound to his Highness, that it pleased him so shortly to rid me of the miseries of this wretched world. And therefore will I not fail most earnestly to pray for his Grace both here, and also in another world." "The King's pleasure is further," quoth Mr Pope, "that at your execution you shall not use many words." "Mr Pope" (quoth he), "you do well that you give me warning of his Grace's pleasure. For otherwise had I purposed at that time somewhat to have spoken, but of no matter wherewith his Grace, or any other should have had cause to be offended. Nevertheless whatsoever I intend I am ready obediently to conform myself to his Grace's commandment. And I beseech you, good Mr Pope, to be a mean unto his Highness, that my daughter Margaret may be present at my burial." "The King is well contented already" (quoth Mr Pope) "that your wife, children, and other friends shall have free liberty to be present thereat." "O how much beholden," then said Sir Thomas More, "am I to his Grace, that unto my poor burial vouchsafeth to have so gracious consideration." Wherewithal Mr Pope taking his leave of him could not refrain from weeping, which Sir Thomas More perceiving, comforted him in this wise, "Quiet yourself, good Mr Pope, and be not discomforted. For I trust that we shall once in heaven see each other full merrily, where we shall be sure to live and love together in joyful bliss eternally." Upon whose departure Sir Thomas More, as one that had been invited to a solemn feast, changed himself into his best apparel; which Mr Lieutenant espying, advised him to put it off, saying, That he that should have it was but a worthless fellow. "What Mr Lieutenant" (quoth he), "shall I account him a worthless fellow, that will do me this day so singular a benefit? Nay, I assure you, were it cloth of gold I would account it well bestowed on him, as St Cyprian did, who gave his executioner thirty pieces of gold." And albeit at length, through Mr Lieutenant's persuasions, he altered his apparel, yet, after the example of that holy martyr St Cyprian, did he of that little money that was left him, send one angel of gold to his executioner. And so was he brought by Mr Lieutenant out of the Tower, and from thence led towards the place of execution, where going up the scaffold, which was so weak that it was ready to fall, he said to Mr Lieutenant, "I pray you, I pray you, Mr Lieutenant, see me safe up, and for my coming down let me shift for myself." Then desired he all the people thereabouts to pray for him, and to bear witness with him, that he should then suffer death in and for the faith of the holy Catholic Church, which done he kneeled down, and after his prayers said, he turned to the executioner, and with a cheerful countenance spake unto him, "Pluck up thy spirits, man, and be not afraid to do thine office, my neck is very short. Take heed therefore thou shoot not awry for saving thine honesty." So passed Sir Thomas More out of this world to God upon the very same day in which himself had most desired. Soon after whose death came intelligence thereof to the Emperor Charles, whereupon he sent for Sir Thomas Eliott, our English Ambassador, and said unto him, "My Lord Ambassador, we understand that the King your master hath put his faithful servant and grave wise councillor Sir Thomas More to death." Whereunto Sir Thomas Eliott answered, that he understood nothing thereof. "Well," said the Emperor, "it is very true, and this will we say, that if we had been master of such a servant, of whose doings ourselves have had these many years no small experience, we would rather have lost the best city of our dominions, than have lost such a worthy councillor." Which matter was by Sir Thomas Eliott to myself, to my wife, to Mr Clement and his wife, to Mr John Haywood and his wife, and divers others of his friends accordingly reported.

1626

VIII. . .

SIMPLE
NARRATIVE

YOUNGHILL KANG

The Journey of One Thousand Lis

From THE GRASS ROOF

But is there for the night a resting place?
A roof for when the slow, dark hours begin.
Uphill: CHRISTINA GEORGINA ROSSETTI.

THE FIRST day I walked about thirty lis, and I did not stop for lunch, because I was so excited and wanted to walk far. Of course I did not dare take any food from home, for Little Aunt always knew exactly how much left-over food was put downstairs in the backyard, along with *kim-chi* to keep cool, and I did not want anybody to discover I was gone, until the night. But I had in my pocket a large piece of black candy, Ok-Dong-Ya had given me, so about four o'clock when the sun just skated above the Western peaks, I broke my black candy between two smooth stones, and ate some. Nothing was unfamiliar yet. Since boyhood I had known these mountains of tall outline, these trees old and yet always young, now half-clothed in green and renewing their life, this road of natural mud along which I had wandered many times on the way to the village where my crazy-poet commuted in the old days before getting sent to jail by the Japanese detectives. I planned to spend the night in this same village with one of the crazy-poet's rich pupils, a boy of my age. He was just an ordinary boy, although he was so rich, and I knew that he did not think of himself as a big man in the way I thought of myself. So, stopping there, I pretended I was on my way home from visiting the crazy-poet's mother-in-law, that rich widow whose child the fat aunt was. Since he would not be able to understand the mysteries of a big man, I said nothing about going to Seoul and just acted like a little boy, not as one with great plans measuring the clouds. I was treated very well here. The trouble was, I had to be very polite and goody-goody, and I could not get an early start on my journey. As soon as I could, though, I set out again, always going South: direction was all I needed to worry about, because the proverb says, "All roads lead to Seoul."

I figured out as I went along that what I must do was to find out schools in different villages that respected scholarship, hoping they would take me in, for if I stayed in an inn every night, my money would be wasted before I reached Seoul. I walked until late that night, looking for a promising school. By this time my feet were very tired, and again I had had no lunch but the black candy, because I wanted to save all my money for Seoul. At last I found a large good-looking school, with many flowers behind the wall, and the teacher was willing to take me in, but reluctantly. He kept looking at my Western hat and my short hair. He himself was a genteel person, with a quiet well-behaved face that had no radical look. As soon as I went in, I wrote a poem praising the village, its school and the teacher. Then he was much pleased and wrote a poem for me. We became on good terms.

"But how could a young promising poet be so bad as to have his hair cut?" he asked me.

"I was forced to cut my hair because I was with a radical Western group who persecuted me," I told him, "but I am hoping to get it long soon."

This was only what Mark Twain calls a "common lie," not a "damned" one; I had to tell him something in order to get lodging for the night. He was very sympathetic because, as he said, my otherwise good-looking appearance was completely spoiled, but he consoled me by saying I was young yet and my hair would surely grow out again. I then told him about using the hair-tonics which my family had bought, but said hair-tonics did not seem to do much good. So he sympathized and ordered a boy to go out and make dinner ready, and until late, we discussed nothing but ancient classical literature. I gave no sign of the Western learning, because I saw that he was a conservative. He was amazed at my knowledge of the classics. The next morning a good breakfast was brought in to me, and after I had told him my home was Song-Dune-Chi and I was on my way there he also ordered the boy to put me up a good lunch. He said Song-Dune-Chi was the home of several poets, and asked me if I knew a certain poet who was no other than my senior uncle. I did not disclose the fact that this was my uncle, for I knew the less said about my family the better, if I did not want to get stopped by an elder and sent home. The last thing the genteel conservative said to me was:

"Poor boy! Best wishes for your hair! I hope it grows long soon."

The third day I had not walked far when I seemed to be stepping on knives. My feet were hurting badly. But I kept on. They kept aching, aching. My straw sandals, which my father had made, were beginning to wear out and my feet were blistered. I had to stop early that day, and as I could not find a school, I tried to sell my poetry in the home of a private scholar. For him I wrote a very nice poem about my tired feet.

The sun is high in the sky,
  The spirit is willing, but the flesh is
    weak,

was the idea. He was amazed. He at once told his friends and all the village elders lined up to inspect me.

"Here is this little kid," they exclaimed, "with a wise poet inside of him."

I wrote other poems for them. All the time I wanted to cry about my feet, and I finally did. Then they brought salt and hot water and washed my feet and soothed them. But I was not discouraged, although I cried. They feasted me. The fourth day I limped on again and as soon as I had spent some of my money for new shoes, I was all right. I had been fairly fat when I started from home, so I needed only an occasional meal. After my black candy was gone, I chewed the paper it was wrapped in, and then I went without lunch, or only bought more candies from some old Korean woman who sold candy by the wayside for very small amounts, as candy was the cheapest diet I could buy.

My first rainy afternoon I was going through sparsely settled mountain country. Rather early I passed a village which did not smell like having any scholarship, so I went on and on, hoping to get to another village before nightfall. But now rain grew heavier and it was windy. The road was high in a mountain. My feet went into the muddy ruts two or three inches deep until it was very hard to move them at all. Still I went on. The road led up, up. It rained, rained, rained. It grew dark. There was no moon in the sky and no stars. I thought I heard people following me, but when I looked quickly around, there was nobody; only I myself made those steps. I feared this mountain was full of ghosts. Oh, how I was frightened by the trees and rocks! I thought of tigers. And that poem:

After the evening sunset,
Mountain air is good;
When the colors darken,
Yellow Dusk has come.
A tiger is very frightful . . .
Child!
Roam not far from home.

Tigers crossed on ice from China by way of the Yalu River. They were very fierce and sometimes ran away with Korean children, who were thus exhorted to be on their guard by many poems and legends of parents. There was no light around me anywhere, only heavy gloom of sky, darkness of muddy road. Rain, rain, rain. I was baptized to my skin. The wind cried, wailing down between tall rocks. I almost lost myself. Finally I saw a light gleaming over the mountainside, and I headed toward it. It was a small hut of the poorest class, roofed roughly with grass, more like a cow's house than a man's. The old country-woman who opened the door a crack refused to take me in, saying there was an inn three miles on, and shut the door. At first glance, I knew I could not sell my poetry to her, though I had been composing a very good poem as I went along all about the rain. I was so tired that one foot of the ground looked ten miles, and so how could I reach an inn? I sat down on a rock near-by and began to cry from exhaustion and starvation. I was wet and shivering, even the poetry anthology in next my skin was cold to touch and I had only a jack-knife with which to fight the tigers. Again the door opened just a crack. The old woman thrust her head out and asked:

"Have you been Japanizing?"

"No, oh, no," I said, wiping the tears.

The old woman watched me a while, then said:

"Well, well, you can come in here and sleep until morning."

I was grateful. Her floor was warm. I had no supper, and I was hungry, yes, but my hunger was overcome by the fear that she might kick me out in that dark night again. I lay down and became very quiet. I thought of my grandmother and Ok-Dong-Ya, Eul-Choon, and the fat baby.

When morning came, I was given no breakfast, for the old woman suspected me for my short hair and Western hat, but there was the sun, very bright and wonderful, and I was happy to set out upon my way, my head full of dreams and big plans.

During this part of the journey, I was tramping over a thousand mountains. I did not mind the hard work, though all day I walked and did not seem to pass much, but I was always very much afraid of tigers and of ghosts. I was troubled by neither however but by something else. On a dark gloomy misty day, when I was going along through a mountain ravine, a very tall big man, with a turban, a high nose and a black beard all over his face, stepped out from behind some rocks. He was followed by a short man, who was carrying sticks and a rope. The man with the black beard said in a rough frightening voice:

"Have you got any money?"

I took out the few pennies I carried in my pocket and very reluctantly showed them to him, beginning to cry. This was my only way to adapt to the situation: of course I said nothing about the bills I carried in my stocking—a way of hiding money not original with American girls. It is a very good way too. They searched in my clothes, but not under the straw tongue of my sandals where all my money was. Then the short man said:

"No, he hasn't any money! Let him keep his pennies to buy candies. He is small and looks very hungry."

So I was allowed to go on, but always after that, before going high on a mountain by myself, I waited until a monk or a farmer came by, and I went behind him. After passing the mountains, I could have made on an average of thirty miles a day, except for the Japanese police stations. These were little wooden houses about every fifteen miles apart; they had a funny angular look, which I now knew to be Western. They sat behind iron fences and were kept by a new kind of Japanese soldier in khaki uniform. These soldiers had the right to do anything they pleased to the passers-by. If I had not known their Japanese language or had made a bad impression, they would have beaten me, but I adapted to the situation. When they searched me, all they could find were poetry anthologies. They laughed about that; I saw they were very ignorant and could see no value in poetry. Still, sometimes it amused them to detain me, and once I lost more than five hours off my walking-day because they were whimsical. After that I became wiser and whenever I saw a police station, I did not pass it directly, but walked through some man's farm by a roundabout way, concealing myself in the millet and tall grain.

All along I did not ask for food and lodging like a beggar, for I was too proud, but wherever there was a village with scholarly smell, I went to the school and by selling my poems to the school-master, procured a good feed. Once I came to a school that absolutely would not take me in, so then I had to tell about my uncle *pak-sa* and the crazy-poet. With that the village scholars came out to see me and to bow before me. All, it seemed, knew about my uncle *pak-sa* and the crazy-poet, and how the latter was unjustly in jail serving sentence on suspicion. One said he had known my uncle *pak-sa* personally at the capital in the old days, for my uncle had written a petition to the government for him. These old-fashioned scholars appeared to regard my uncle *pak-sa* even more greatly than my own village people, and I found that some of his essays were used in that school as compositional models. Yes, always I found that if I referred to my uncle *pak-sa* or to my crazy-poet uncle, I was treated like a prince. But I was afraid to do that much, for fear my people might be following to bring me back, and besides, it did not seem heroic, nor like giving me much of a kick. I wanted always to be independent.

As I moved farther from my childhood home on this long journey, I seemed more to miss my mother whom

I had never seen. I felt my heart did not ache to be back with my grandmother and Ok-Dong-Ya, but to see my mother, yet her I never knew.

It was from my friend, Sur-Choon, that I first learned the meaning of the word, mother. He was very fond of his mother, and once when I visited him, before my uncle and his grandfather quarrelled, their relationship made me almost to cry out for pain. She thought of nothing all the day long, but giving him pleasure, finding his pens and his playthings, hugging him to console him when he got in trouble. I thought of my own mother whom I could never remember having seen. Surely she would be the most beautiful and unselfish woman.

"O mother, dear, mother dearest!" I would cry to myself in Sur-Choon's tree-house, where we two often slept during the night.

She became my ideal. I knew her best for never having seen her, just as we learn a character better sometimes for a single glance, a few minutes' conversation, than by a whole lifetime of familiarity. Thus my mother lived in the framework of my longing love, more vividly perhaps than if I had been familiar with every line in her face, and I became always lonesome for her.

Now I thought of her when I was very hungry or cold.

"O mother, some day your son will come back to you, bringing fruits of unknown days."

When I had gone a hundred and fifty miles on foot, I saw my first Western train. I was just coming over the mountain into Won-san, when the train cried out below me. I had heard about trains, so I was prepared, but I did not believe that they were really as fierce as lions and tigers, although this was what I had been told. But when that train whizzed on, spitting fire and smoke, hissing, "Whak! Whak!" I jumped very much, and almost fell down. It stopped and many people got on to go to Seoul. I was thrilled to think in how many hours it could do what it took me many days to accomplish, and I stood, struck motionless. When it started I waved. How I longed to be riding upon it in the Western way! All it said was "Whak! Whak!" again, as if it thought nothing of me, so I just shook my fist at its back, and cried: "I too will ride you soon!"

I had come only half-way and I was very tired of walking so much and eating so little, but I had one letter of introduction. This was the address of a radical rich friend of the crazy-poet, who used to visit him and had told me once if I ever came to Seoul, to be sure to stop and see him at the address he gave me. I spent many hungry hours thinking of the rich feast I would get at his house, and when I was tired, I comforted myself by thinking that I might stay with him two or three days to break the journey. He probably would insist on my taking some money too, I thought, which he would let me pay back later. Park Soo-San's idea was that private citizens should help poor students in search of Western education.

He lived beyond Won-san, according to the address given. To reach his village, I had to go about twelve miles out of my way, along an uninviting stony path, little travelled. Since this was not in direct line to Seoul, I was constantly losing direction and making false starts; I did not reach his village until nightfall, though I had been trying to locate it from early dawn, but I persevered. The farther I came from home, the harder it was to find good schools.

Lately I had saved my appetite and my pennies with Mr. Kim in mind. The March evening was gray, bleak, when I entered the village of my crazy-poet uncle's friend and began inquiring for Mr. Kim, but my breast was light with anticipation, and I remember thinking, "Turkey or duck, turkey or duck." My Western hat and my haircut were not greeted with enthusiasm. At last when I had almost had a fight with the villagers to find out where Mr. Kim really lived, on being directed to his house, which was under sighing pine trees, I could only rouse an old woman who was deaf, and I saw no signs of the prosperity I had expected. I finally made out from what she told me, that Mr. Kim was no more, having committed suicide the night that Korea had been annexed by Japan. She alone was brave enough to live in that house because of his wailing ghost.

I had nothing to say. My hunger had all jumped out. I did not feel any aching feet, I did not fear any ghost. I turned about and walked away from the village. Here was the same rock I had passed a short time earlier, the very same, but the mood, how different! The sun had been shining on it then. Now it was bathed in shadow. My tears began flowing and flowing. When I had left all houses behind, I cried out loud. My cry vibrated through the darkness and the night. Oh, ghost that was kind to me!

My tired feet drifted on and they came at last to the next inn. When the innkeeper, a bent old man with patient eyes and a lined face, saw the tears over my face, he invited me to come in and sleep without cost on his kitchen floor. . . .

Then half-way between Won-san and Seoul I suddenly came on a village that appreciated my poetry so much that I stayed there for two days in order to get fat. In this village was a man who had spent many years in Seoul trying to be a *pak-sa* in the days before the Japanese had invaded the country. But he was disappointed in the end, and concerning this, he recited to me a poem:

The will that ate up my bosom was not at
    all fulfilled.
I was the laughing stock over half this
    world of red dust.
Think naught of it—luck is luck:
Why should I grieve?

That was how he felt about everything. He deeply regretted the passing of the old days, but it was no use grieving about them. He said he intended to send his son to the new school and give him his way in everything and even let him cut his hair if he preferred —not because he felt that the way of the younger generation was wiser than that of the older, but "Times are times, just as luck is luck," he said.

He was a fine, wise-looking man, and I could not help wishing my father could have been more tolerant like him. This scholar and the village clubbed together and gave me five dollars for my studies in Seoul. They looked at me with approval and said: "Behold the angelic child!" Then they all bowed low to me because my uncle was a *pak-sa*.

After that I had no more feasts with scholars, for none of the villages just outside of Seoul possessed any scholarship to speak of. Appreciation of poetry became rarer and rarer. Since I could not bear to use the money in my stocking which was my emergency fund to be spent on education, I often went hungry. It was for this reason that I was so bitterly disappointed outside the West gate of Seoul. It was a cold forenoon and a man by the wayside was selling hot beef stew for three pennies. This was exactly what I had left in my pocket without touching my emergency fund. I had had no dinner the night before, except a cake or two, but I had not minded, because I had heard that Seoul was only a few miles farther on. Even with Seoul in sight I was ravenously hungry, and my stomach leaped up to my eyes. For a time I could think of nothing but the aroma of the beef stew. Many peasants were gathered around the peddler, for the road to Seoul began to be thronged and everybody was cold and hungry after walking since early in the morning. Each man paid his three pennies, picked up his wooden bowl and held it out to the man with the dipper. Clutching my wooden bowl, I squeezed my way to the front to a point where I could look down directly into the tureen of beef stew. It was like a thick soup where not much beef was in sight. But I saw one large piece and another smaller piece floating around. Oh, how I aspired to get that large piece! It was all a chance. Each man paid the same amount, but one lucky fellow would get the large piece in his stew. I prayed hard that I might be the lucky man. Hypnotized, my eyes followed the dipper, as Dalksali's eyes used to follow my swinging meat; I tried to calculate the exact moment at which to thrust forward my wooden bowl. Many times I held it out in front of another, only to snatch it back when I saw that the meat was not in the dipper. No one minded me because I was so young and small, and no one else in fact seemed to see that piece of beef. As I danced around this way and that, the peddler not knowing my suspense, quickly caught up that piece of beef in his dipper and poured it into the bowl of a very fat man who had come up late and was having a conversation with a friend all the time while he kept his bowl outstretched. Almost I cried out and let my bowl drop, but the fat man went on talking without noticing that he was the lucky man. Then in haste I thrust up my bowl, for the smaller piece was still there, and oh, it must fall to me! Yes, it wobbled on the edge of the dipper, then fell back again into the beef stew, not into my bowl. There was nothing to do but to eat my soup, although I wanted to throw it out on the ground and roll over and over in disappointment and rage.

It had taken me sixteen days to reach Seoul, a journey of 300 miles or 1,000 lis. I entered by one of the large gates, of which there were eight, East, West, South, and five others with pagodas on top. The Japanese were already engaged in tearing down parts of the wall of Seoul. Seoul had been chief city since 1392, and it is said that 190,000 men labored for two months in the Spring, and 90,000 more worked two months in the Fall to complete this wall.

Inside the gate were such multitudes of people that there was hardly room to push up and I wondered where they were put during the night. There were ginrickashas and automobiles and ponies and wagons all jostling each other. The automobiles were a marvellous sight. They looked to me like some queer kind of animal and I thought, was it possible that this—this creature alone had no ghost? The Koreans think that all things have ghosts. But I knew that for an automobile it could not be. I saw the Electric tramway and longed to take a ride at once on Western machinery, but an old man told me it cost three cents and that seemed high and again I postponed my ride. Then I asked the way to the Students' quarter.

On my way to the Students' quarter, I passed down crooked streets and straight streets, thin streets and thick streets, streets short and streets long, some paved, some of dirt worn hard by many feet. High up in the sky I could not fail to notice the towers of the Roman Catholic Cathedral, so tall and out of proportion to the rest of the architecture that it seemed like a Western giant with a high nose, all on stilts. Members of the old official class had fled from Seoul and many of the nobles' houses, native Korean buildings of stone and mud with thick eaves, were being destroyed by workingmen under the order of the Japanese Government. But the royal audience halls of former emperors were still standing with their high curved roofs of an antique form. How blank they looked, how sorrowful! You knew that inside their ghosts were just crying and wringing their hands over the mad confusion of that ancient city, its scholars all in jail or fled to China, and the Japanese everywhere. The great stone turtle which I passed, of old Korean carving, large as two rooms and built to symbolize longevity, looked to have outlived his days.

I made out that Seoul was laid out around mountain hollows and each section of the city had a separate mountain hollow. There was the Korean Student Hollow and the Chinese Hollow, and the Missionary Hollow, etc. From each of these hollows came a stream which ran through Seoul in the form of a ditch, with bridges here and there where crossing was necessary. I followed one of these streams to the students' hollow. In one of the inns I found a student of Park Soo-San's whom I recognized, a tall thin boy with spectacles. From him I learned the bad news. The Five-Star School, that Korean institution where Park Soo-San had gone and the one I had come up to attend, was just about to go out of existence, owing to persecutions of the Japanese Government. Many other private Korean academies were suffering the same fate. The government wished no competition. My acquaintance advised me, as a practical measurement, to try to get admitted to the Japanese Government School, though he warned me that almost 4,000 eager for the Western learning and deprived of private Korean institutions were trying to get in, and only 200 would be chosen. The examinations for the Spring term were to take place in two weeks.

I waited around for two weeks. The examinations were to be in Arithmetic, History, Japanese Grammar, Japanese Writing, and Oral Japanese, as well as elementary Chinese: it would all be easy for me. I remember little about the examination, except that it was held in the big wooden building of two stories, flying the Japanese flag. Each boy wrote with his photograph on the desk beside him and handed it in with his examination answers. This was so that no rich boy might send a substitute. As I had expected, the examinations were very simple, nor was I surprised when I found that my name was given second place among the 200 successful candidates posted in the school yard. The boy who made first place was the examiner's own son.

1931

IRWIN EDMAN

An Irishman Among the Brahmins

From PHILOSOPHER'S HOLIDAY

ONE MEETS originals among the students every year at a university; some years one of them stands out so that years later that year seems academically to be memorable, or to be earmarked as his. The first I heard of young George O'Connor was a telephone call from the Dean of the College. He was, the Dean said, either a lunatic or a genius, perhaps a little of both. In any case, he thought I had an appreciation of both categories and would find O'Connor interesting. He had had a scrambled education, partly abroad, and had a disordered but vivid mind. Perhaps I could advise him a little. The Dean added that he thought that O'Connor and I would have much in common.

I had hardly put down the telephone when there was a vigorous knock on my door and there entered a young man, powerfully built, with a fresh, rosy face and a head of wild, wavy brown hair. He waved a college catalogue at me.

"My name's O'Connor," he said. "The Dean said you could help me, maybe. I can't find my way through this catalogue, and I don't know what in it to believe, or what half the time it means. Now, this course of yours—Philosophy 72—what on earth is that supposed to be?"

"It's quite clear," I said, rather primly, "in the catalogue. It's a course in the

Philosophy of Religion in which we try to examine the typical forms of religion and the religious experience, the relation of theology to the religious experience, the social implications of religion; it's all there."

"Is it worth taking?" he asked, looking at me with his lively blue eyes. There was not a trace of impertinence in his question; he asked simply for information.

"That's a little hard for me to say," I said. "I believe it is, of course, but you would have to be the judge. The subject is unquestionably interesting and important . . ."

"I know," he said, studying the catalogue carefully. "But these catalogue descriptions aren't worth very much. I've found that out. They all sound so grand. It depends a lot on the man. Students here speak well of it, but students speak well of courses for such accidental reasons. Everyone says it's bright and entertaining. But, well, you know what I mean. Is it worth *taking?* Does it really give you new ideas, or do something to your old ones? Does it make you over, or give you a new world?"

"You want a religious revelation," I said. "This is a course—a course in the philosophy of religion; it is not a religion, or a revelation; it is not intended to be."

"But that's the trouble. I want to know if it's just another course."

"You might try it," I said. "You can always drop it after a week."

George did try it, and tried a seminar besides. In the course, since it was a lecture course, he could not say very much, but he would break in, in the afternoon, with a blazingly new—or what seemed to him a blazingly new—idea he had come upon, in Eddington, in Whitehead, in himself; or sometimes one that he alleged he had got from me. In the seminar, on Plato, he would say things that he had picked up from Heaven knows where. They were not always to the point, but they never failed to have one of their own. I came to know something about him. His father had made a fortune in the lumber business in the West, and had taken his whole family to Europe, much as Henry James, Sr., had taken his family, on the ground that there were no satisfactory schools in America. And, apparently, his father had not been satisfied with those in Europe either. For the family had gone from place to place for several years; George had been in a progressive school in Germany (it was before the days of Hitler), to a strict Calvinist school in Geneva, to another progressive school in England; at the age of sixteen he had become the junior friend of the group of expatriate writers in Paris. He spoke familiarly, justly so, of Ernest Hemingway, and had, I think, been to Spain with him.

He found the chains of a regular academic routine galling. The whole apparatus of examinations, of books to be read at given times, of classes at regular hours—all seemed to him inordinately silly. When he read, he read with perspicacity and accuracy, but he could not be trusted to read a book when assigned. I tried to win him to a sense of the necessary discipline of the intellectual life, especially for a young man who wished to be a writer. "You must know something to write about," I said, "and you must be clear. You can learn a lot here and a lot about handling what you learn."

George seemed to agree. For a few weeks there would be work and there would be a diminution of protest. But one day, along about the middle of November, George appeared looking very grave.

"I am leaving college," he said. "I can't stand it any more. I don't see how you can."

"What's the matter," I asked, "now?"

"Just the same as always," he said, intensely; "the place is too confoundedly intellectual. All the intellectual words, but no ideas with life in them. Ghosts of the mind walking around the campus. I often wonder how you can stand it, but I caught sight of you crossing the campus the other day, and I began to understand why. You're absorbed and you're near-sighted. You don't see that it's there."

He took out a typewritten manuscript, single-spaced, and apparently long. "Would you look at this?" he said. "It's a resignation I am sending, with explanations, to the Dean."

It was indeed a resignation with explanations! With citations from everybody from Rousseau to Dewey, George explained to the Dean that, despite the many kindnesses of the latter, and all the concessions he had made him, he must leave college. Education, George explained, was in a bad way, and it was doing everything it could to kill the souls of its students and paralyse their minds. It gave all the vocabulary of ideas, but few ideas, and those ideas were dead. It substituted method for substance; it was the shell and husk of intellectual training and imaginative life. George could put up with it no longer. He was leaving. That, with all the rhetoric—or most of it—boiled away, was what George had to say to the Dean. It was a sort of manifesto; George felt that by leaving college he had nothing to lose but his chains, the irons that were constricting his spirit.

"Shall I send it?" he said.

"I think not," I said. "It's pretty theatrical, a little impolite and unappreciative, and it's unjust. Half the things you say here you learned here. You have built up a monster simply for the sake of destroying it. If you'd spent more time on your courses and less on your sensitive soul, you'd get further and be wiser. May I tear up the letter? You've got it out of your system."

George smiled amused, half-reluctant agreement. I tore the letter into pieces and threw them into the waste-basket. I wish now I hadn't done so. Some of it would be worth quoting now, for it was, for all its bravura, far from silly. George was, it is true, ingeniously finding reasons for not doing the work he was supposed to be doing for his courses. He would have read Malinowski's work on primitive religion if he had found it on his own; but it became a tyranny of the academy when it was prescribed, as it was, for the course he was taking with me. But I knew many of the things he said were sound, and what was more, he knew that I knew it. He was an incarnation, not unengaging, of the eternal malcontent on a campus, the perpetual, surprised discoverer of the way in which the machinery of a university, like the machinery of many other enterprises, defeats its purposes by

swallowing them. So had many a mystic in the Church of which George was still a communicant rebelled against the ecclesiastical organization. Thus had many a pietist in eighteenth-century Germany rebelled against the intellectualism of those who spent their lives proving and defining the God whose being they no longer felt and whose presence they had long forgotten. There must be many, among both students and teachers, who have come to feel as George now felt. But among the teachers the machinery had itself often become engrossing, and there were students to whom the machinery and the formulas were all education meant, or could mean. I had seen two or three of the liveliest minds and most imaginative tempers among students who had fled from, or been exiled from, the academy because they had felt as George now felt, and adapted themselves less than he. And I had also seen what had in time become of some of them. It requires a very strong character, tenacity of purpose, and singleness of aim to work in isolation, especially when one is young. Liveliness of mind and acuteness of feeling often disintegrate into nothingness without the discipline of a period of orientation in principles, in intellectual handling of facts; the discovery of the manner in which facts themselves are distinguished from fancies, the way in which facts themselves are discovered. I tried to explain some of this to George, and to point out that the thirst for experience is slaked but not satisfied if one has not the equipment through which experience becomes enriched with meaning. That was, on the whole, what an intellectual training could do for a poet or a mind. It could do it despite the mechanization of a university, the routine of the classroom, the formal habit of mind inevitable among those who repeatedly deal with the same materials which they expound year after year to the uninformed and, for the most part, uncritical young.

"You sound fair enough," George said. "I'll be good; I'll try again, and I promise not to come in with a manifesto or a resignation for a couple of months, anyway."

"Good," I said.

"Yes, I know," he continued, "people in this university are too busy to be bothered by the raising of fundamental issues."

"Not only in universities, George."

"I'll be good," said George. "I see you have quiz books to read."

He was "good," too, for quite a long period. He did remarkably well on the examinations at mid-term, including those in courses that he did not like or value very highly. I was rather pleased with the conversion I had made. I looked forward to a sobered George who should combine the vitality and freshness of a poet's temper with the discipline of a scientist's method and a philosopher's analysis. Something would come of that youth yet. There was a lot to be said for the collegiate apparatus when tinctured with sympathy and understanding; so I congratulated myself.

I was a little premature. It was April. The sunlight played softly over streets that made one long to be where there were no streets at all. George was not the only one in that afternoon class whose mind and eyes seemed to be elsewhere. I had a hard time myself keeping to the theme of the relation between religion and science. I returned to my office and sat wondering. "Great God! I'd rather be a pagan suckled in a creed outworn." I wondered why the solar system was so arranged, or the Gregorian calendar, that Easter vacation came so late this year. It would be pleasant to stand on a lea and have glimpses that might make one less forlorn.

There was a knock on the door; George appeared and began decisively and without preliminary:

"I haven't come this time to ask you whether you think I *ought* to leave college. I am leaving. That is settled. I'm going to Bermuda and I don't know how long I shall stay. But I know I am not coming back to the university. It's no go. Perhaps it's my fault, but there's something wrong with this college. It isn't all my fault. I'm not the only one. Oh, I know: you'll tell me I'd stay if I had to; that I'm a spoilt child of the rich; that I'm self-indulgent and romantic; that I lack discipline. You've told me all that before . . . Some of it is true. But this time I've made up my mind. And I've made up my mind about something else, too. I think you ought to come along . . ."

"But the term isn't over, George. I can't just pack up and leave and go to Bermuda, even if I wanted to. As a matter of fact, I do."

"But why not?" said George. "You will have to leave some time. April is as good a time as any to quit this death in life. I've been thinking about you. It's rather remarkable that you've kept alive at all; it really is. Committee meetings, papers, quizzes, professional meetings, the same courses year after year. I've come to tell you, if you will permit the impertinence, that it is still possible to save your soul. If you don't come now, once and for all, you probably never will. I'm sailing on Friday; that gives you three days. I shall come in tomorrow to ask you what you've decided."

George was quite impatient with me the next day when he returned and found me still unprepared to go out into the Indian wilderness, first stop Bermuda, and abandon the educational market-place. He almost pleaded with me not to commit myself irrevocably to the sterility of the society of teachers and scholars. He went to Bermuda and I received a note from him. He was bicycling and reading Wordsworth's Prelude.

I haven't heard from George save indirectly since. He's given me, as well as the university, up as a job. That was ten years ago. But the fact that, so far as I can gather, in point of fame or worldly success George has not amounted to very much, does not prove that he was altogether wrong or that morally or spiritually he is a failure. Oxford and Shelley had a difficult time with each other, too. I do not think the university would have destroyed George; it might have made him. But I have seen spirits destroyed; youthful lovers of literature turned into pedants, some of them now quite respected in academic circles; lovers of wisdom petrified into classroom exponents of doctrine; passionate revolutionaries turned into reactionaries, or, perhaps even more sadly, passionless liberals. I have seen the word become deadened by the flesh, and the letter kill the spirit. And on April days sometimes still I feel a trip to Bermuda or somewhere, and for ever, might be good for some of us in the academy and for the academy itself. The mystics and the heretics are important events in the history of the Church of a living God. Saints have flourished in solitude and visions have been seen there.

But George was mistaken in thinking the greatest stultification comes in the academy; one sees it worse outside. The students I knew best at college are shocking to meet sometimes ten years after. They were awakened at and by college, by ideas and imagination. The world, not the academy, killed them, and George by this time must be complaining about the world on the same grounds upon which he used to cavil at the college. For the greatest regimentations come not from ideas, nor from the machinery of academic life, but from the machinery of living. Or George may have found out, on the other hand, how empty freedom can be.

1938

NATHANIEL SOUTHGATE SHALER

A Lesson from Agassiz

From The Autobiography of Nathaniel Southgate Shaler

Agassiz's laboratory was then in a rather small two-storied building looking much like a square dwelling house, which stood where the College Gymnasium now stands. . . . Agassiz had recently moved into it from a shed on the marsh near Brighton Bridge, the original tenants, the engineers, having come to riches in the shape of the brick structure now known as the Lawrence Building. In this primitive establishment Agassiz's laboratory, as distinguished from the storerooms where the collections were crammed, occupied one room about thirty feet long and fifteen feet wide—what is now the west room on the lower floor of the edifice. In this place, already packed, I had assigned to me a small pine table with a rusty tin pan upon it. . . .

When I sat me down before my tin pan, Agassiz brought me a small fish, placing it before me with the rather stern requirement that I should study it, but should on no account talk to any one concerning it, nor read anything relating to fishes, until I had his permission to do so. To my inquiry, "What shall I do?" he said in effect: "Find out what you can without damaging the specimen: when I think that you have done the work, I will question you." In the course of an hour I thought I had compassed that fish; it was rather an unsavory object, giving forth the stench of old alcohol, then loathsome to me,

though in time I came to like it. Many of the scales were loosened so that they fell off. It appeared to me to be a case for a summary report, which I was anxious to make and get on to the next stage of the business. But Agassiz, though always within call, concerned himself no further with me that day, nor the next, nor for a week. At first, this neglect was distressing; but I saw that it was a game, for he was, as I discerned rather than saw, covertly watching me. So I set my wits to work upon the thing, and in the course of a hundred hours or so thought I had done much—a hundred times as much as seemed possible at the start. I got interested in finding out how the scales went in series, their shape, the form and placement of the teeth, etc. Finally, I felt full of the subject, and probably expressed it in my bearing; as for words about it, then, there were none from my master except his cheery "Good morning." At length, on the seventh day, came the question, "Well?" and my disgorge of learning to him as he sat on the edge of my table, puffing his cigar. At the end of the hour's telling, he swung off and away, saying: "That is not right." Here I began to think that, after all, perhaps the rules for scanning Latin verse were not the worst infliction in the world. Moreover, it was clear that he was playing a game with me to find if I were capable of doing hard, continuous work without the support of a teacher, and this stimulated me to labor. I went at the task anew, discarded my first notes, and in another week of ten hours a day labor I had results which astonished myself, and satisfied him. Still there was no trace of praise in word or manner. He signified that it would do by placing before me about a half a peck of bones, telling me to see what I could make of them, with no further directions to guide me. I soon found that they were the skeletons of half a dozen fishes of different species—the jaws told me so much at a first inspection. The task evidently was to fit the separate bones together in their proper order. Two months or more went to this task, with no other help than an occasional looking over my grouping, with the stereotyped remark: "That is not right." Finally, the task was done, and I was again set upon alcoholic specimens—this time a remarkable lot of specimens, representing perhaps twenty species of the side-swimmers or *Pleuronectidæ*.

I shall never forget the sense of power in dealing with things which I felt in beginning the more extended work on a group of animals. I had learned the art of comparing objects, which is the basis of the naturalist's work. At this stage I was allowed to read and to discuss my work with others about me. I did both eagerly, and acquired a considerable knowledge of the literature of ichthyology, becoming especially interested in the system of classification, then most imperfect. I tried to follow Agassiz's scheme of division into the order of ctenoids and ganoids, with the result that I found one of my species of side-swimmers had cycloid scales on one side and ctenoid on the other. This not only shocked my sense of the value of classification in a way that permitted of no full recovery of my original respect for the process, but for a time shook my confidence in my master's knowledge. At the same time I had a malicious pleasure in exhibiting my *find* to him, expecting to repay in part the humiliation which he had evidently tried to inflict on my conceit. To my question as to how the nondescript should be classified, he said: "My boy, there are now two of us who know that."

This incident of the fish made an end of my novitiate. After that, with a suddenness of transition which puzzled me, Agassiz became very communicative; we passed, indeed, into the relation of friends of like age and purpose, and he actually consulted me as to what I should like to take up as a field of study. Finding that I wished to devote myself to geology, he set me to work on the *Brachiopoda* as the best group of fossils to serve as data in determining the Palæozoic horizons. So far as his rather limited knowledge of the matter went, he guided me in the field about Cambridge, in my reading, and to acquaintances of his who were concerned with earth structures.

1909

OLIVER WENDELL HOLMES

My Hunt After "The Captain"

IN THE dead of the night which closed upon the bloody field of Antietam, my household was startled from its slumbers by the loud summons of a telegraphic messenger. The air had been heavy all day with rumors of battle, and thousands and tens of thousands had walked the streets with throbbing hearts, in dread anticipation of the tidings any hour might bring.

We rose hastily, and presently the messenger was admitted. I took the envelope from his hand, opened it, and read:—

HAGERSTOWN, 17th

To —— —— H——

Capt H—— wounded shot through the neck thought not mortal at Keedysville

WILLIAM G LEDUC

Through the neck—no bullet left in wound. Windpipe, food pipe, carotid, jugular, half a dozen smaller, but still formidable, vessels, a great braid of nerves, each as big as a lamp wick, spinal cord—ought to kill at once, if at all. *Thought not* mortal, or *not thought* mortal—which was it? The first; that is better than the second would be.— "Keedysville, a post office, Washington County, Maryland." Leduc? Leduc? Don't remember that name.—The boy is waiting for his money. A dollar and thirteen cents. Has nobody got thirteen cents? Don't keep that boy waiting—how do we know what messages he has got to carry?

The boy *had* another message to carry. It was to the father of Lieutenant Colonel Wilder Dwight, informing him that his son was grievously wounded in the same battle, and was lying at Boonsborough, a town a few miles this side of Keedysville. This I learned the next morning from the civil and attentive officials at the Central Telegraph Office.

Calling upon this gentleman, I found that he meant to leave in the quarter past two o'clock train, taking with him Dr. George H. Gay, an accomplished and energetic surgeon, equal to any difficult question or pressing emergency. I agreed to accompany them, and we met in the cars. I felt myself peculiarly fortunate in having companions whose society would be a pleasure, whose feelings would harmonize with my own, and whose assistance I might, in case of need, be glad to claim.

It is of the journey which we began together, and which I finished apart, that I mean to give my *Atlantic* readers an account. They must let me tell my story in my own way, speaking of many little matters that interested or amused me, and which a certain leisurely class of elderly persons, who sit at their firesides and never travel, will, I hope, follow with a kind of interest. For, besides the main object of my excursion, I could not help being excited by the incidental sights and occurrences of a trip which to a commercial traveler or a newspaper reporter would seem quite commonplace and undeserving of record. There are periods in which all places and people seem to be in a conspiracy to impress us with their individuality—in which every ordinary locality seems to assume a special significance and to claim a particular notice—in which every person we meet is either an old acquaintance or a character; days in which the strangest coincidences are continually happening, so that they get to be the rule, and not the exception. Some might naturally think that anxiety and the weariness of a prolonged search after a near relative would have prevented my taking any interest in or paying any regard to the little matters around me. Perhaps it had just the contrary effect, and acted like a diffused stimulus upon the attention. When all the faculties are wide-awake in pursuit of a single object, or fixed in the spasm of an absorbing emotion, they are oftentimes clairvoyant in a marvelous degree in respect to many collateral things, as Wordsworth has so forcibly illustrated in his sonnet on the Boy of Windermere, and as Hawthorne has developed with such metaphysical accuracy in that chapter of his wondrous story where Hester walks forth to meet her punishment.

Be that as it may—though I set out with a full and heavy heart, though many times my blood chilled with what were perhaps needless and unwise fears, though I broke through all my habits without thinking about them, which is almost as hard in certain circumstances as for one of our young fellows to leave his sweetheart and go into a Peninsular campaign, though I did not always know when I was hungry nor discover that I was thirsting, though I had a worrying ache and inward tremor underlying all the outward play of the senses and the mind, yet it is the simple truth that I did look out of the car windows with an eye for all that passed, that I did take cognizance of strange sights and singular people, that I did act much as persons act from the ordinary prompt-

ings of curiosity, and from time to time even laugh very nearly as those do who are attacked with a convulsive sense of the ridiculous, the epilepsy of the diaphragm.

By a mutual compact, we talked little in the cars. A communicative friend is the greatest nuisance to have at one's side during a railroad journey, especially if his conversation is stimulating and in itself agreeable. "A fast train and a 'slow' neighbor" is my motto. Many times, when I have got upon the cars, expecting to be magnetized into an hour or two of blissful reverie, my thoughts shaken up by the vibrations into all sorts of new and pleasing patterns, arranging themselves in curves and nodal points, like the grains of sand in Chladni's famous experiment,—fresh ideas coming up to the surface, as the kernels do when a measure of corn is jolted in a farmer's wagon,—all this without volition, the mechanical impulse alone keeping the thoughts in motion, as the mere act of carrying certain watches in the pocket keeps them wound up—many times, I say, just as my brain was beginning to creep and hum with this delicious locomotive intoxication, some dear detestable friend, cordial, intelligent, social, radiant, has come up and sat down by me and opened a conversation which has broken my daydream, unharnessed the flying horses that were whirling along my fancies, and hitched on the old weary omnibus team of everyday associations, fatigued my hearing and attention, exhausted my voice, and milked the breasts of my thought dry during the hour when they should have been filling themselves full of fresh juices. My friends spared me this trial.

My companions proposed to stay at one of the best-known and longest-established of the New York caravansaries, and I accompanied them. We were particularly well lodged, and not uncivilly treated. The traveler who supposes that he is to repeat the melancholy experience of Shenstone, and have to sigh over the reflection that he has found "his warmest welcome at an inn," has something to learn at the offices of the great city hotels. The unheralded guest who is honored by mere indifference may think himself blest with singular good fortune. If the despot of the Patent Annunciator is only mildly contemptuous in his manner, let the victim look upon it as a personal favor. The coldest welcome that a threadbare curate ever got at the door of a bishop's palace, the most icy reception that a country cousin ever received at the city mansion of a mushroom millionaire, is agreeably tepid compared to that which the Rhadamanthus who dooms you to the more or less elevated circle of his inverted Inferno vouchsafes, as you step up to enter your name on his dog's-eared register. I have less hesitation in unburdening myself of this uncomfortable statement, as on this particular trip I met with more than one exception to the rule. Officials become brutalized, I suppose, as a matter of course. One cannot expect an office clerk to embrace tenderly every stranger who comes in with a carpetbag, or a telegraph operator to burst into tears over every unpleasant message he receives for transmission. Still, humanity is not always totally extinguished in these persons. I discovered a youth in the telegraph office of the Continental Hotel, in Philadelphia, who was as pleasant in conversation, and as graciously responsive to inoffensive questions, as if I had been his childless opulent uncle, and my will not made.

The boys cry the "N' York *Heddle*," instead of *"Herald"*; I remember that years ago in Philadelphia; we must be getting near the farther end of the dumbbell suburb. A bridge has been swept away by a rise of the waters, so we must approach Philadelphia by the river. Her physiognomy is not distinguished—*nez camus,* as a Frenchman would say; no illustrious steeple, no imposing tower, the water edge of the town looking bedraggled, like the flounce of a vulgar rich woman's dress that trails on the sidewalk. The *New Ironsides* lies at one of the wharves, elephantine in bulk and color, her sides narrowing as they rise, like the walls of a hock glass.

I went straight to the house in Walnut Street where the Captain would be heard of, if anywhere in this region. His lieutenant colonel was there, gravely wounded; his college friend and comrade in arms, a son of the house, was there, injured in a similar way; another soldier, brother of the last, was there, prostrate with fever. A fourth bed was waiting ready for the Captain, but not one word had been heard of him, though inquiries had been made in the towns from and through which the father had brought his two sons and the lieutenant colonel. And so my search is, like a *Ledger* story, to be continued.

I rejoined my companions in time to take the noon train for Baltimore. Our company was gaining in number as it moved onwards. We had found upon the train from New York a lovely, lonely lady, the wife of one of our most spirited Massachusetts officers, the brave Colonel of the ——th Regiment, going to seek her wounded husband at Middletown, a place lying directly in our track. She was the light of our party while we were together on our pilgrimage, a fair, gracious woman, gentle, but courageous.

Not long after leaving Philadelphia, we passed a solitary sentry keeping guard over a short railroad bridge. It was the first evidence that we were approaching the perilous borders, the marches where the North and the South mingle their angry hosts, where the extremes of our so-called civilization meet in conflict, and the fierce slave driver of the Lower Mississippi stares into the stern eyes of the forest feller from the banks of the Aroostook. All the way along, the bridges were guarded more or less strongly. In a vast country like ours, communications play a far more complex part than in Europe, where the whole territory available for strategic purposes is so comparatively limited. Belgium, for instance, has long been the bowling alley where kings roll cannon balls at each other's armies; but here we are playing the game of live ninepins *without any alley*.

We left Baltimore and the Eutaw House, to take the cars for Frederick. As we stood waiting on the platform, a telegraphic message was handed in silence to my companion. Sad news: the lifeless body of the son he was hastening to see was even now on its way to him in Baltimore. It was no time for empty words of consolation: I knew what he had lost, and that now was not the time to intrude upon a grief borne as men bear it, felt as women feel it.

Colonel Wilder Dwight was first made known to me as the friend of a beloved relative of my own, who was with him during a severe illness in Switzerland, and for whom while living, and for whose memory when dead, he retained the warmest affection. Since that, the story of his noble deeds of daring, of his capture and escape, and a brief visit home before he was able to rejoin his regiment, had made his name familiar to many among us, myself among the number. His memory has been honored by those who had the largest opportunity of knowing his rare promise, as a man of talents and energy of nature. His abounding vitality must have produced its impression on all who met him; there was a still fire about him which anyone could see would blaze up to melt all difficulties and recast obstacles into implements in the mould of an heroic will. These elements of his character many had the chance of knowing; but I shall always associate him with the memory of that pure and noble friendship which made me feel that I knew him before I looked upon his face, and added a personal tenderness to the sense of loss which I share with the whole community.

Here, then, I parted, sorrowfully, from the companions with whom I set out on my journey.

There was a great confusion of carriages and wagons at the stopping place of the train, so that it was a long time before I could get anything that would carry us. At last I was lucky enough to light on a sturdy wagon, drawn by a pair of serviceable bays, and driven by James Grayden, with whom I was destined to have a somewhat continued acquaintance. We took up a little girl who had been in Baltimore during the late Rebel inroad. It made me think of the time when my own mother, at that time six years old, was hurried off from Boston, then occupied by the British soldiers, to Newburyport, and heard the people saying that "the redcoats were coming, killing and murdering everybody as they went along." Frederick looked cheerful for a place that had so recently been in an enemy's hands.

Here and there a house or shop was shut up, but the national colors were waving in all directions, and the general aspect was peaceful and contented. I saw no bullet marks or other sign of the fighting which had gone on in the streets.

At the United States Hotel, where many were lying, I heard mention of an officer in an upper chamber, and, going there, found Lieutenant Abbott, of the Twentieth Massachusetts Volunteers, lying ill with what looked like typhoid fever. While there, who should come in but the ubiquitous Lieutenant Wilkins, of the same Twentieth, often confounded with his namesake who visited the Flying Island, and with some reason, for he must have a pair of wings under his military upper garment, or he could never be in so many places at once. He was going to Boston in charge of the lamented Dr. Revere's body. From his lips I learned something of the mishaps of the regiment. My Captain's wound he spoke of as less grave than at first thought; but he mentioned incidentally having heard a story recently that he was *killed,*—a fiction, doubtless,—a mistake,—a palpable absurdity,—not to be remembered or made any account of. Oh, no! but what dull ache is this in that obscurely sensitive region, somewhere below the heart, where the nervous centre called the *semilunar ganglion* lies unconscious of itself until a great grief or a mastering anxiety reaches it through all the nonconductors which isolate it from ordinary impressions? I talked awhile with Lieutenant Abbott, who lay prostrate, feeble, but soldier-like and uncomplaining, carefully waited upon by a most excellent lady, a captain's wife, New England born, loyal as the Liberty on a golden ten-dollar piece, and of lofty bearing enough to have sat for that goddess's portrait. She had stayed in Frederick through the Rebel inroad, and kept the star-spangled banner where it would be safe, to unroll it as the last Rebel hoofs clattered off from the pavement of the town.

Near by Lieutenant Abbott was an unhappy gentleman, occupying a small chamber, and filling it with his troubles. When he gets well and plump, I know he will forgive me if I confess that I could not help smiling in the midst of my sympathy for him. He had been a well-favored man, he said, sweeping his hand in a semicircle, which implied that his acute-angled countenance had once filled the goodly curve he described. He was now a perfect Don Quixote to look upon. Weakness had made him querulous, as it does all of us, and he piped his grievances to me in a thin voice with that finish of detail which chronic invalidism alone can command. He was starving—he could not get what he wanted to eat. He was in need of stimulants, and he held up a pitiful two-ounce phial containing three thimblefuls of brandy—his whole stock of that encouraging article. Him I consoled to the best of my ability, and afterwards, in some slight measure, supplied his wants. Feed this poor gentleman up, as these good people soon will, and I should not know him, nor he himself. We are all egotists in sickness and debility. An animal has been defined as "a stomach ministered to by organs"; and the greatest man comes very near this simple formula after a month or two of fever and starvation.

James Grayden and his team pleased me well enough, and so I made a bargain with him to take us, the lady and myself, on our further journey as far as Middletown. As we were about starting from the front of the United States Hotel, two gentlemen presented themselves and expressed a wish to be allowed to share our conveyance. I looked at them and convinced myself that they were neither Rebels in disguise, nor deserters, nor camp followers, nor miscreants, but plain, honest men on a proper errand. The first of them I will pass over briefly. He was a young man, of mild and modest demeanor, chaplain to a Pennsylvania regiment, which he was going to rejoin. He belonged to the Moravian Church, of which I had the misfortune to know little more than what I had learned from Southey's *Life of Wesley,* and from the exquisite hymns we have borrowed from its rhapsodists. The other stranger was a New Englander of respectable appearance, with a grave, hard, honest, hay-bearded face, who had come to serve the sick and wounded on the battlefield and in its immediate neighborhood. There is no reason why I should not mention his name, but I shall content myself with calling him the Philanthropist.

So we set forth, the sturdy wagon, the serviceable bays, with James Grayden their driver, the gentle lady, whose serene patience bore up through all delays and discomforts, the Chaplain, the Philanthropist, and myself, the teller of this story.

And now, as we emerged from Frederick, we struck at once upon the trail from the great battlefield. The road was filled with straggling and wounded soldiers. All who could travel on foot —multitudes with slight wounds of the upper limbs, the head or face—were told to take up their beds—a light burden, or none at all—and walk. Just as the battlefield sucks everything into its red vortex for the conflict, so does it drive everything off in long, diverging rays

after the fierce centripetal forces have met and neutralized each other. For more than a week there had been sharp fighting all along this road. Through the streets of Frederick, through Crampton's Gap, over South Mountain, sweeping at last the hills and the woods that skirt the windings of the Antietam, the long battle had traveled, like one of those tornadoes which tear their path through our fields and villages. The slain of higher condition, "embalmed" and iron-cased, were sliding off on the railways to their far homes; the dead of the rank and file were being gathered up and committed hastily to the earth; the gravely wounded were cared for hard by the scene of conflict, or pushed a little way along to the neighboring villages; while those who could walk were meeting us, as I have said, at every step in the road. It was a pitiable sight, truly pitiable, yet so vast, so far beyond the possibility of relief, that many single sorrows of small dimensions have wrought upon my feelings more than the sight of this great caravan of maimed pilgrims. The companionship of so many seemed to make a joint stock of their suffering; it was next to impossible to individualize it, and so bring it home as one can do with a single broken limb or aching wound. Then they were all of the male sex, and in the freshness or the prime of their strength. Though they tramped so wearily along, yet there was rest and kind nursing in store for them. These wounds they bore would be the medals they would show their children and grandchildren by and by. Who would not rather wear his decorations beneath his uniform than on it?

Yet among them were figures which arrested our attention and sympathy. Delicate boys, with more spirit than strength, flushed with fever or pale with exhaustion or haggard with suffering, dragged their weary limbs along as if each step would exhaust their slender store of strength. At the roadside sat or lay others, quite spent with their journey. Here and there was a house at which the wayfarers would stop, in the hope, I fear often vain, of getting refreshment; and in one place was a clear cool spring, where the little bands of the long procession halted for a few moments, as the trains that traverse the desert rest by its fountains. My companions had brought a few peaches along with them, which the Philanthropist bestowed upon the tired and thirsty soldiers with a satisfaction which we all shared. I had with me a small flask of strong waters, to be used as a medicine in case of inward grief. From this, also, he dispensed relief, without hesitation, to a poor fellow who looked as if he needed it. I rather admired the simplicity with which he applied my limited means of solace to the first comer who wanted it more than I; a genuine benevolent impulse does not stand on ceremony, and had I perished of colic for want of a stimulus that night, I should not have reproached my friend the Philanthropist any more than I grudged my other ardent friend the two dollars and more which it cost me to send the charitable message he left in my hands.

It was a lovely country through which we were riding. The hillsides rolled away into the distance. The men of this region seemed to ride in the saddle very generally, rather than drive. They looked sober and stern, less curious and lively than Yankees, and I fancied that a type of features familiar to us in the countenance of the late John Tyler, our accidental President, was fre-

quently met with. The women were still more distinguishable from our New England pattern. Soft, sallow, succulent, delicately finished about the mouth and firmly shaped about the chin, dark-eyed, full-throated, they looked as if they had been grown in a land of olives. There was a little toss in their movement, full of muliebrity. I fancied there was something more of the duck and less of the chicken about them, as compared with the daughters of our leaner soil; but these are mere impressions caught from stray glances, and if there is any offense in them, my fair readers may consider them all retracted.

Full in the middle of the road, caring little for whom or what they met, came long strings of army wagons, returning empty from the front after supplies. James Grayden stated it as his conviction that they had a little rather run into a fellow than not. I liked the looks of these equipages and their drivers; they meant business. Drawn by mules mostly, six, I think, to a wagon, powdered well with dust, wagon, beast, and driver, they came jogging along the road, turning neither to right nor left —some driven by bearded, solemn white men, some by careless, saucy-looking Negroes, of a blackness like that of anthracite or obsidian. There seemed to be nothing about them, dead or alive, that was not serviceable. Sometimes a mule would give out on the road; then he was left where he lay, until by and by he would think better of it, and get up, when the first public wagon that came along would hitch him on, and restore him to the sphere of duty.

It was evening when we got to Middletown. The gentle lady who had graced our homely conveyance with her company here left us. She found her husband, the gallant Colonel, in very comfortable quarters, well cared for, very weak from the effects of the fearful operation he had been compelled to undergo, but showing the same calm courage to endure as he had shown manly energy to act. It was a meeting full of heroism and tenderness, of which I heard more than there is need to tell. Health to the brave soldier, and peace to the household over which so fair a spirit presides!

Dr. Thompson, the very active and intelligent surgical director of the hospitals of the place, took me in charge. He carried me to the house of a worthy and benevolent clergyman of the German Reformed Church, where I was to take tea and pass the night. What became of the Moravian chaplain I did not know; but my friend the Philanthropist had evidently made up his mind to adhere to my fortunes. He followed me, therefore, to the house of the "Dominie," as a newspaper correspondent calls my kind host, and partook of the fare there furnished me. He withdrew with me to the apartment assigned for my slumbers, and slept sweetly on the same pillow where I waked and tossed. Nay, I do affirm that he did, unconsciously, I believe, encroach on that moiety of the couch which I had flattered myself was to be my own through the watches of the night, and that I was in serious doubt at one time whether I should not be gradually, but irresistibly, expelled from the bed which I had supposed destined for my sole possession. As Ruth clave unto Naomi, so my friend the Philanthropist clave unto me. "Whither thou goest, I will go; and where thou lodgest, I will lodge." A really kind, good man, full of zeal, determined to help somebody, and absorbed in his one thought, he doubted

nobody's willingness to serve him, going, as he was, on a purely benevolent errand. When he reads this, as I hope he will, let him be assured of my esteem and respect; and if he gained any accommodation from being in my company, let me tell him that I learned a lesson from his active benevolence. I could, however, have wished to hear him laugh once before we parted, perhaps forever. He did not, to the best of my recollection, even smile during the whole period that we were in company. I am afraid that a lightsome disposition and a relish for humor are not so common in those whose benevolence takes an active turn as in people of sentiment who are always ready with their tears and abounding in passionate expressions of sympathy.

My benevolent companion having already made a preliminary exploration of the hospitals of the place, before sharing my bed with him, as above mentioned, I joined him in a second tour through them. The authorities of Middletown are evidently leagued with the surgeons of that place, for such a breakneck succession of pitfalls and chasms I have never seen in the streets of a civilized town. It was getting late in the evening when we began our rounds. The principal collections of the wounded were in the churches. Boards were laid over the tops of the pews, on these some straw was spread, and on this the wounded lay, with little or no covering other than such scanty clothes as they had on. There were wounds of all degrees of severity, but I heard no groans or murmurs. Most of the sufferers were hurt in the limbs, some had undergone amputation, and all had, I presume, received such attention as was required. Still, it was but a rough and dreary kind of comfort that the extemporized hospitals suggested. I could not help thinking the patients must be cold; but they were used to camp life, ánd did not complain. The men who watched were not of the soft-handed variety of the race. One of them was smoking his pipe as he went from bed to bed. I saw one poor fellow who had been shot through the breast; his breathing was labored, and he was tossing, anxious and restless. The men were debating about the opiate he was to take, and I was thankful that I happened there at the right moment to see that he was well narcotized for the night. Was it possible thàt my Captain could be lying on the straw in one of these places? Certainly *possible,* but not probable; but as the lantern was held over each bed, it was with a kind of thrill that I looked upon the features it illuminated. Many times, as I went from hospital to hospital in my wanderings, I started as some faint resemblance —the shade of a young man's hair, the outline of his half-turned face—recalled the presence I was in search of. The face would turn towards me and the momentary illusion would pass away, but still the fancy clung to me. There was no figure huddled up on its rude couch, none stretched at the roadside, none toiling languidly along the dusty pike, none passing in car or in ambulance, that I did not scrutinize, as if it might be that for which I was making my pilgrimage to the battlefield.

"There are two wounded Secesh," said my companion. I walked to the bedside of the first, who was an officer, a lieutenant, if I remember right, from North Carolina. He was of good family, son of a judge in one of the higher courts of his state, educated, pleasant, gentle, intelligent. One moment's intercourse with such an enemy, lying helpless and wounded among strangers, takes away all personal bitterness towards those with whom we or our children have been but a few hours before in deadly strife. The basest lie which the murderous contrivers of this Rebellion have told is that which tries to make out a difference of race in the men of the North and South. It would be worth a year of battleś to abolish this delusion, though the great sponge of war that wiped it out were moistened with the best blood of the land. My Rebel was of slight, scholastic habit, and spoke as one accustomed to tread carefully among the parts of speech. It made my heart ache to see him, a man finished in the humanities and Christian culture, whom the sin of his forefathers and the crime of his rulers had set in barbarous conflict against others of like training with his own—a man who, but for the curse that it is laid on our generation to expiate, would have been a fellow worker with them in the beneficent task of shaping the intelligence and lifting the moral standard of a peaceful and united people.

On Sunday morning, the twenty-first, having engaged James Grayden and his team, I set out with the Chaplain and the Philanthropist for Keedysville. Our track lay through the South Mountain Gap and led us first to the town of Boonsborough, where, it will be remembered, Colonel Dwight had been brought after the battle. We saw the positions occupied in the Battle of South Mountain, and many traces of the conflict. In one situation a group of young trees was marked with shot, hardly one having escaped. As we walked by the side of the wagon, the Philanthropist left us for a while and climbed a hill, where along the line of a fence he found traces of the most desperate fighting. A ride of some three hours brought us to Boonsborough, where I roused the unfortunate army surgeon who had charge of the hospitals, and who was trying to get a little sleep after his fatigues and watchings. He bore this cross very creditably, and helped me to explore all places where my soldier might be lying among the crowds of wounded. After the useless search, I resumed my journey, fortified with a note of introduction to Dr. Letterman, also with a bale of oakum which I was to carry to that gentleman, this substance being employed as a substitute for lint. We were obliged also to procure a pass to Keedysville from the Provost Marshal of Boonsborough. As we came near the place, we learned that General McClellan's headquarters had been removed from this village some miles farther to the front.

On entering the small settlement of Keedysville, a familiar face and figure blocked the way, like one of Bunyan's giants. The tall form and benevolent countenance, set off by long, flowing hair, belonged to the excellent Mayor Frank B. Fay, of Chelsea, who, like my Philanthropist, only still more promptly, had come to succor the wounded of the great battle. It was wonderful to see how his single personality pervaded this torpid little village; he seemed to be the centre of all its activities. All my questions he answered clearly and decisively, as one who knew everything that was going on in the place. But the one question I had come five hundred miles to ask,—*Where is Captain H.?*—he could not answer. There were some thousands of wounded in the place, he told me, scattered about everywhere. It would be a long job to hunt up my Captain; the

only way would be to go to every house and ask for him. Just then, a medical officer came up.

"Do you know anything of Captain H., of the Massachusetts Twentieth?"

"Oh, yes; he is staying in that house. I saw him there, doing very well."

A chorus of hallelujahs arose in my soul, but I kept them to myself. Now, then, for our twice-wounded volunteer, our young centurion whose double-barred shoulder straps we have never yet looked upon. Let us observe the proprieties, however; no swelling upward of the mother,—no *hysterica passio,*—we do not like scenes. A calm salutation—then swallow and hold hard. That is about the programme.

A cottage of squared logs, filled in with plaster, and whitewashed. A little yard before it, with a gate swinging. The door of the cottage ajar—no one visible as yet. I push open the door and enter. An old woman, Margaret Kitzmuller her name proves to be, is the first person I see.

"Captain H. here?"

"Oh, no, sir—left yesterday morning for Hagerstown—in a milk cart."

The Kitzmuller is a beady-eyed, cheery-looking ancient woman, answers questions with a rising inflection, and gives a good account of the Captain, who got into the vehicle without assistance, and was in excellent spirits.—Of course he had struck for Hagerstown as the terminus of the Cumberland Valley Railroad, and was on his way to Philadelphia via Chambersburg and Harrisburg, if he were not already in the hospitable home of Walnut Street, where his friends were expecting him.

I might follow on his track or return upon my own; the distance was the same to Philadelphia through Harrisburg as through Baltimore. But it was very difficult, Mr. Fay told me, to procure any kind of conveyance to Hagerstown, and on the other hand I had James Grayden and his wagon to carry me back to Frederick. It was not likely that I should overtake the object of my pursuit with nearly thirty-six hours start, even if I could procure a conveyance that day. In the meantime James was getting impatient to be on his return, according to the direction of his employers. So I decided to go back with him.

But there was the great battlefield only about three miles from Keedysville, and it was impossible to go without seeing that. James Grayden's directions were peremptory, but it was a case for the higher law. I must make a good offer for an extra couple of hours, such as would satisfy the owners of the wagon, and enforce it by a personal motive. I did this handsomely, and succeeded without difficulty. To add brilliancy to my enterprise, I invited the Chaplain and the Philanthropist to take a free passage with me.

We followed the road through the village for a space, then turned off to the right and wandered somewhat vaguely, for want of precise directions, over the hills. Inquiring as we went, we forded a wide creek in which soldiers were washing their clothes, the name of which we did not then know, but which must have been the Antietam.

On coming near the brow of the hill, we met a party carrying picks and spades. "How many?" "Only one." The dead were nearly all buried, then, in this region of the field of strife. We stopped the wagon, and, getting out, began to look around us. Hard by was a large pile of muskets, scores, if not hundreds, which had been picked up

and were guarded for the Government. A long ridge of fresh gravel rose before us. A board stuck up in front of it bore this inscription, the first part of which was, I believe, not correct: "The Rebel General Anderson and 80 Rebels are buried in this hole." Other smaller ridges were marked with the number of dead lying under them. The whole ground was strewed with fragments of clothing, haversacks, canteens, cap boxes, bullets, cartridge boxes, cartridges, scraps of paper, portions of bread and meat. I saw two soldiers' caps that looked as though their owners had been shot through the head. In several places I noticed dark red patches where a pool of blood had curdled and caked, as some poor fellow poured his life out on the sod.

I then wandered about in the cornfield. It surprised me to notice that, though there was every mark of hard fighting having taken place here, the Indian corn was not generally trodden down. One of our cornfields is a kind of forest, and, even when fighting, men avoid the tall stalks as if they were trees. At the edge of this cornfield lay a gray horse, said to have belonged to a Rebel colonel, who was killed near the same place. Not far off were two dead artillery horses in their harness. Another had been attended to by a burying party, who had thrown some earth over him; but his last bedclothes were too short, and his legs stuck out stark and stiff from beneath the gravel coverlet. It was a great pity that we had no intelligent guide to explain to us the position of that portion of the two armies which fought over this ground. There was a shallow trench before we came to the cornfield, too narrow for a road, as I should think, too elevated for a watercourse, and which seemed to have been used as a rifle pit; at any rate, there had been hard fighting in and about it. This and the cornfield may serve to identify the part of the ground we visited, if any who fought there should ever look over this paper. The opposing tides of battle must have blended their waves at this point, for portions of gray uniform were mingled with the "garments rolled in blood" torn from our own dead and wounded soldiers. I picked up a Rebel canteen, and one of our own—but there was something repulsive about the trodden and stained relics of the stale battlefield. It was like the table of some hideous orgy left uncleared, and one turned away disgusted from its broken fragments and muddy heeltaps. A bullet or two, a button, a brass plate from a soldier's belt, served well enough for mementos of my visit, with a letter which I picked up, directed to Richmond, Virginia, its seal unbroken. "N. C. Cleaveland County. E. Wright to J. Wright." On the other side, "A few lines from W. L. Vaughn," who has just been writing for the wife to her husband, and continues on his own account. The postscript, "tell John that nancy's folks are all well and has a verry good Little Crop of corn a growing." I wonder if, by one of those strange chances of which I have seen so many, this number or leaf of the *Atlantic* will not sooner or later find its way to Cleveland County, North Carolina, and E. Wright, widow of James Wright, and Nancy's folks get from these sentences the last glimpse of husband and friend as he threw up his arms and fell in the bloody cornfield at Antietam? I will keep this stained letter for them until peace comes back, if it comes in my time, and my pleasant North Carolina Rebel of the Middletown Hospital will, perhaps, look these

poor people up, and tell them where to send for it.

On the battlefield I parted with my two companions, the Chaplain and the Philanthropist. They were going to the front, the one to find his regiment, the other to look for those who needed his assistance. We exchanged cards and farewells, I mounted the wagon, the horses' heads were turned homewards, my two companions went their way, and I saw them no more. On my way back, I fell into talk with James Grayden. Born in England, Lancashire; in this country since he was four years old. Had nothing to care for but an old mother; didn't know what he should do if he lost her. Though so long in this country, he had all the simplicity and childlike light-heartedness which belong to the Old World's people. He laughed at the smallest pleasantry, and showed his great white English teeth; he took a joke without retorting by an impertinence; he had a very limited curiosity about all that was going on; he had small store of information; he lived chiefly in his horses, it seemed to me. His quiet animal nature acted as a pleasing anodyne to my recurring fits of anxiety, and I liked his frequent, " 'Deed I don' know, sir," better than I have sometimes relished the large discourse of professors and other very wise men.

I have not much to say of the road which we were traveling for the second time. Reaching Middletown, my first call was on the wounded Colonel and his lady. She gave me a most touching account of all the suffering he had gone through with his shattered limb before he succeeded in finding a shelter, showing the terrible want of proper means of transportation of the wounded after the battle. It occurred to me, while at this house, that I was more or less famished, and for the first time in my life I begged for a meal, which the kind family with whom the Colonel was staying most graciously furnished me.

After tea, there came in a stout army surgeon, a Highlander by birth, educated in Edinburgh, with whom I had pleasant, not unstimulating talk. He had been brought very close to that immane and nefandous Burke and Hare business which made the blood of civilization run cold in the year 1828, and told me, in a very calm way, with an occasional pinch from the mull to refresh his memory, some of the details of those frightful murders, never rivaled in horror until the wretch Dumollard, who kept a private cemetery for his victims, was dragged into the light of day. He had a good deal to say, too, about the Royal College of Surgeons in Edinburgh, and the famous preparations, mercurial and the rest, which I remember well having seen there,—the *"sudabit multum,"* and others,—also of our New York Professor Carnochan's handiwork, a specimen of which I once admired at the New York College. But the Doctor was not in a happy frame of mind, and seemed willing to forget the present in the past: things went wrong, somehow, and the time was out of joint with him.

Dr. Thompson, kind, cheerful, companionable, offered me half his own wide bed, in the house of Dr. Baer, for my second night in Middletown. Here I lay awake again another night. Close to the house stood an ambulance in which was a wounded Rebel officer, attended by one of their own surgeons. He was calling out in a loud voice, all night long, as it seemed to me, "Doctor! Doctor! Driver! Water!" in loud, complaining tones, I have no doubt of real suffering, but in strange contrast with the silent patience which was the almost universal rule.

The courteous Dr. Thompson will let me tell here an odd coincidence, trivial, but having its interest as one of a series. The Doctor and myself lay in the bed, and a lieutenant, a friend of his, slept on the sofa. At night, I placed my match box, a Scotch one, of the Macpherson-plaid pattern, which I bought years ago, on the bureau, just where I could put my hand upon it. I was the last of the three to rise in the morning, and on looking for my pretty match box I found it was gone. This was rather awkward—not on account of the loss, but of the unavoidable fact that one of my fellow lodgers must have taken it. I must try to find out what it meant.

"By the way, Doctor, have you seen anything of a little plaid-pattern match box?"

The Doctor put his hand to his pocket, and, to his own huge surprise and my great gratification, pulled out *two* match boxes exactly alike, both printed with the Macpherson plaid. One was his, the other mine, which he had seen lying round and naturally took for his own, thrusting it into his pocket, where it found its twin brother from the same workshop. In memory of which event we exchanged boxes, like two Homeric heroes.

This curious coincidence illustrates well enough some supposed cases of plagiarism, of which I will mention one where my name figured. When a little poem called "The Two Streams" was first printed, a writer in the New York *Evening Post* virtually accused the author of it of borrowing the thought from a baccalaureate sermon of President Hopkins, of Williamstown, and printed a quotation from that discourse, which, as I thought, a thief or catchpoll might well consider as establishing a fair presumption that it was so borrowed. I was at the same time wholly unconscious of ever having met with the discourse or the sentence which the verses were most like, nor do I believe I ever had seen or heard either. Some time after this, happening to meet my eloquent cousin, Wendell Phillips, I mentioned the fact to him, and he told me that *he* had once used the special image said to be borrowed, in a discourse delivered at Williamstown. The spores of a great many ideas are floating about in the atmosphere. We no more know where all the growths of our mind came from than where the lichens which eat the names off from the gravestones borrowed the germs that gave them birth. The two match boxes were just alike, but neither was a plagiarism.

In the morning I took to the same wagon once more, but, instead of James Grayden, I was to have for my driver a young man who spelt his name "Phillip Ottenheimer," and whose features at once showed him to be an Israelite. I found him agreeable enough, and disposed to talk. So I asked him many questions about his religion, and got some answers that sound strangely in Christian ears. He was from Wittenberg, and had been educated in strict Jewish fashion. From his childhood he had read Hebrew, but was not much of a scholar otherwise. A young person of his race lost caste utterly by marrying a Christian. The Founder of our religion was considered by the Israelites to have been "a right smart man, and a great doctor." But the horror with which the reading of the New Testament by any young person of their faith would be regarded was as great, I

judged by his language, as that of one of our straitest sectaries would be if he found his son or daughter perusing the *Age of Reason*.

In approaching Frederick, the singular beauty of its clustered spires struck me very much, so that I was not surprised to find "Fair-View" laid down about this point on a railroad map. I wish some wandering photographer would take a picture of the place, a stereoscopic one, if possible, to show how gracefully, how charmingly, its group of steeples nestles among the Maryland hills. The town had a poetical look from a distance, as if seers and dreamers might dwell there. The first sign I read, on entering its long street, might perhaps be considered as confirming my remote impression. It bore these words: "Miss Ogle, Past, Present, and Future." On arriving, I visited Lieutenant Abbott, and the attenuated unhappy gentleman, his neighbor, sharing between them as my parting gift what I had left of the balsam known to the pharmacopœia as *spiritus vini gallici*. I took advantage of General Shriver's always open door to write a letter home, but had not time to partake of his offered hospitality. The railroad bridge over the Monocacy had been rebuilt since I passed through Frederick, and we trundled along over the track toward Baltimore.

It was a disappointment, on reaching the Eutaw House, where I had ordered all communications to be addressed, to find no telegraphic message from Philadelphia or Boston, stating that Captain H. had arrived at the former place, "wound doing well in good spirits expects to leave soon for Boston." After all, it was no great matter; the Captain was, no doubt, snugly lodged before this in the house called Beautiful, at— Walnut Street, where that "grave and beautiful damsel named Discretion" had already welcomed him, smiling, though "the water stood in her eyes," and had "called out Prudence, Piety, and Charity, who, after a little more discourse with him, had him into the family."

The friends I had met at the Eutaw House had all gone but one, the lady of an officer from Boston, who was most amiable and agreeable, and whose benevolence, as I afterwards learned, soon reached the invalids I had left suffering at Frederick. General Wool still walked the corridors, inexpansive, with Fort McHenry on his shoulders, and Baltimore in his breeches pocket, and his courteous aid again pressed upon me his kind offices. About the doors of the hotel the newsboys cried the papers in plaintive, wailing tones, as different from the sharp accents of their Boston counterparts as a sigh from the southwest is from a northeastern breeze. To understand what they said was, of course, impossible to any but an educated ear, and if I made out "Stŏarr" and "Clipp'rr," it was because I knew beforehand what must be the burden of their advertising coranach.

I set out for Philadelphia on the morrow, Tuesday the twenty-third, there beyond question to meet my Captain, once more united to his brave wounded companions under that roof which covers a household of as noble hearts as ever throbbed with human sympathies. Back River, Bush River, Gunpowder Creek—lives there the man with soul so dead that his memory has cerements to wrap up these senseless names in the same envelopes with their meaningless localities? But the Susquehanna,—the broad, the beautiful, the historical, the poetical Susquehanna,—the river of Wyoming and of Gertrude, dividing the shores where

aye those sunny mountains half-way down
Would echo flageolet from some romantic town,

did not my heart renew its allegiance to the poet who has made it lovely to the imagination as well as to the eye, and so identified his fame with the noble stream that it "rolls mingling with his name forever"? The prosaic traveler perhaps remembers it better from the fact that a great sea monster, in the shape of a steamboat, takes him, sitting in the car, on its back, and swims across with him like Arion's dolphin—also that mercenary men on board offer him canvasbacks in the season, and ducks of lower degree at other periods.

At Philadelphia again at last! Drive fast, O colored man and brother, to the house called Beautiful, where my Captain lies sore wounded, waiting for the sound of the chariot wheels which bring to his bedside the face and the voice nearer than any save one to his heart in his hour of pain and weakness! Up a long street with white shutters and white steps to all the houses. Off at right angles into another long street with white shutters and white steps to all the houses. Off again at another right angle into still another long street with white shutters and white steps to all the houses. The natives of this city pretend to know one street from another by some individual differences of aspect; but the best way for a stranger to distinguish the streets he has been in from others is to make a cross or other mark on the white shutters.

This corner house is the one. Ring softly—for the Lieutenant Colonel lies there with a dreadfully wounded arm, and two sons of the family, one wounded like the Colonel, one fighting with death in the fog of a typhoid fever, will start with fresh pangs at the least sound you can make. I entered the house, but no cheerful smile met me. The sufferers were each of them thought to be in a critical condition. The fourth bed, waiting its tenant day after day, was still empty. *Not a word from my Captain.*

Then, foolish, fond body that I was, my heart sank within me. Had he been taken ill on the road, perhaps been attacked with those formidable symptoms which sometimes come on suddenly after wounds that seemed to be doing well enough, and was his life ebbing away in some lonely cottage, nay, in some cold barn or shed, or at the wayside, unknown, uncared for? Somewhere between Philadelphia and Hagerstown, if not at the latter town, he must be, at any rate. I must sweep the hundred and eighty miles between these places as one would sweep a chamber where a precious pearl had been dropped. I must have a companion in my search, partly to help me look about, and partly because I was getting nervous and felt lonely. Charley said he would go with me—Charley, my Captain's beloved friend, gentle, but full of spirit and liveliness, cultivated, social, affectionate, a good talker, a most agreeable letter writer, observing, with large relish of life, and keen sense of humor. He was not well enough to go, some of the timid ones said; but he answered by packing his carpetbag, and in an hour or two we were on the Pennsylvania Central Railroad in full blast for Harrisburg.

I should have been a forlorn creature but for the presence of my companion. In his delightful company I half forgot my anxieties, which, exaggerated as they may seem now, were not unnatural after what I had seen of the confusion and distress that had followed the great battle, nay, which seem almost justified by the recent statement that "high officers" were buried after that battle whose names were never ascertained. I noticed little matters, as usual. The road was filled in between the rails with cracked stones, such as are used for macadamizing streets. They keep the dust down, I suppose, for I could not think of any other use for them. By and by the glorious valley which stretches along through Chester and Lancaster counties opened upon us. Much as I had heard of the fertile regions of Pennsylvania, the vast scale and the uniform luxuriance of this region astonished me. The grazing pastures were so green, the fields were under such perfect culture, the cattle looked so sleek, the houses were so comfortable, the barns so ample, the fences so well kept, that I did not wonder when I was told that this region was called the England of Pennsylvania. The people whom we saw were, like the cattle, well nourished; the young women looked round and wholesome.

"Grass makes girls," I said to my companion, and left him to work out my Orphic saying, thinking to myself that, as guano makes grass, it was a legitimate conclusion that Ichaboe must be a nursery of female loveliness.

As the train stopped at the different stations, I inquired at each if they had any wounded officers. None as yet; the red rays of the battlefield had not streamed off so far as this. Evening found us in the cars; they lighted candles in spring candlesticks; odd enough I thought it in the land of oil wells and unmeasured floods of kerosene. Some fellows turned up the back of a seat so as to make it horizontal, and began gambling or pretending to gamble; it looked as if they were trying to pluck a young countryman; but appearances are deceptive, and no deeper stake than "drinks for the crowd" seemed at last to be involved. But remembering that murder has tried of late years to establish itself as an institution in the cars, I was less tolerant of the doings of these "sportsmen" who tried to turn our public conveyance into a traveling Frascati. They acted as if they were used to it, and nobody seemed to pay much attention to their manœuvres.

We arrived at Harrisburg in the course of the evening, and attempted to find our way to the Jones House, to which we had been commended. By some mistake, intentional on the part of somebody, as it may have been, or purely accidental, we went to the Herr House instead. I entered my name in the book, with that of my companion. A plain, middle-aged man stepped up, read it to himself in low tones, and coupled to it a literary title by which I have been sometimes known. He proved to be a graduate of Brown University, and had heard a certain Phi Beta Kappa poem delivered there a good many years ago. I remembered it, too; Professor Goddard, whose sudden and singular death left such lasting regret, was the Orator. I recollect that while I was speaking a drum went by the church, and how I was disgusted to see all the heads near the windows thrust out of them, as if the building were on fire. *Cedat armis toga.* The clerk in the office, a mild, pensive, unassuming young man, was very polite in his manners, and did all he could to make us comfortable. He was of a literary turn, and knew one of his guests in his character of author. At tea, a mild old gentleman, with white hair and beard, sat next us. He, too, had come hunting after his son, a lieutenant in a Pennsylvania regiment. Of these, father and son, more presently.

After tea we went to look up Dr. Wilson, chief medical officer of the hospitals in the place, who was staying at the Brady House. A magnificent old toddy mixer, Bardolphian in hue and stern of aspect, as all grog dispensers must be, accustomed as they are to dive through the features of men to the bottom of their souls and pockets to see whether they are solvent to the amount of sixpence, answered my question by a wave of one hand, the other being engaged in carrying a dram to his lips. His superb indifference gratified my artistic feeling more than it wounded my personal sensibilities. Anything really superior in its line claims my homage, and this man was the ideal bartender, above all vulgar passions, untouched by commonplace sympathies, himself a lover of the liquid happiness he dispenses, and filled with a fine scorn of all those lesser felicities conferred by love or fame or wealth or any of the round-about agencies for which his fiery elixir is the cheap, all-powerful substitute.

Dr. Wilson was in bed, though it was early in the evening, not having slept for I don't know how many nights.

"Take my card up to him, if you please."

"This way, sir."

A man who has not slept for a fortnight or so is not expected to be as affable, when attacked in his bed, as a French princess of old time at her morning receptions. Dr. Wilson turned toward me, as I entered, without effusion, but without rudeness. His thick, dark moustache was chopped off square at the lower edge of the upper lip, which implied a decisive, if not a peremptory, style of character.

I am Doctor So-and-So, of Hubtown, looking after my wounded son. (I gave my name and said *Boston,* of course, in reality.)

Dr. Wilson leaned on his elbow and looked up in my face, his features growing cordial. Then he put out his hand, and good-humoredly excused his reception of me. The day before, as he told me, he had dismissed from the service a medical man hailing from ——, Pennsylvania, bearing my last name, preceded by the same two initials; and he supposed, when my card came up, it was this individual who was disturbing his slumbers. The coincidence was so unlikely *a priori,* unless some forlorn parent without antecedents had named a child after me, that I could not help cross-questioning the Doctor, who assured me deliberately that the fact was just as he had said, even to the somewhat unusual initials. Dr. Wilson very kindly furnished me all the information in his power, gave me directions for telegraphing to Chambersburg, and showed every disposition to serve me.

On returning to the Herr House, we found the mild, white-haired old gentleman in a very happy state. He had just discovered his son, in a comfortable condition, at the United States Hotel. He thought that he could probably give us some information which would prove interesting. To the United States Hotel we repaired, then, in company with our kind-hearted old friend, who evidently wanted to see me as happy as himself. He went upstairs to his son's chamber, and presently came down to conduct us there.

Lieutenant P——, of the Pennsylvania ——th, was a very fresh, bright-looking young man, lying in bed from the effects of a recent injury received in action. A grape shot, after passing through a post

and a board, had struck him in the hip, bruising, but not penetrating or breaking. He had good news for me.

That very afternoon, a party of wounded officers had passed through Harrisburg, going east. He had conversed in the barroom of this hotel with one of them, who was wounded about the shoulder (it might be the lower part of the neck) and had his arm in a sling. He belonged to the Twentieth Massachusetts; the Lieutenant saw that he was a Captain, by the two bars on his shoulder strap. His name was my family name; he was tall and youthful, like my Captain. At four o'clock he left in the train for Philadelphia. Closely questioned, the Lieutenant's evidence was as round, complete, and lucid as a Japanese sphere of rock crystal.

Te Deum laudamus! The Lord's name be praised! The dead pain in the semilunar ganglion (which I must remind my reader is a kind of stupid, unreasoning brain, beneath the pit of the stomach, common to man and beast, which aches in the supreme moments of life, as when the dam loses her young ones, or the wild horse is lassoed) stopped short. There was a feeling as if I had slipped off a tight boot, or cut a strangling garter—only it was all over my system. What more could I ask to assure me of the Captain's safety? As soon as the telegraph office opens tomorrow morning, we will send a message to our friends in Philadelphia, and get a reply, doubtless, which will settle the whole matter.

The hopeful morrow dawned at last, and the message was sent accordingly. In due time, the following reply was received:—

Phil Sept 24 I think the report you have heard that W [the Captain] has gone east must be an error we have not seen or heard of him here M L H

DE PROFUNDIS CLAMAVI! He *could* not have passed through Philadelphia without visiting the house called Beautiful, where he had been so tenderly cared for after his wound at Ball's Bluff, and where those whom he loved were lying in grave peril of life or limb. Yet he *did* pass through Harrisburg, going east, going to Philadelphia, on his way home. Ah, this is it! He must have taken the late night train from Philadelphia for New York, in his impatience to reach home. There is such a train, not down in the guidebook, but we were assured of the fact at the Harrisburg depot. By and by came the reply from Dr. Wilson's telegraphic message: nothing had been heard of the Captain at Chambersburg. Still later, another message came from our Philadelphia friend, saying that he was seen on *Friday* last at the house of Mrs. K——, a well-known Union lady, in Hagerstown. Now this could not be true, for he did not leave Keedysville until *Saturday;* but the name of the lady furnished a clue by which we could probably track him. A telegram was at once sent to Mrs. K——, asking information. It was transmitted immediately, but when the answer would be received was uncertain, as the Government almost monopolized the line. I was, on the whole, so well satisfied that the Captain had gone east that, unless something were heard to the contrary, I proposed following him in the late train, leaving a little after midnight for Philadelphia.

This same morning we visited several of the temporary hospitals, churches and schoolhouses, where the wounded were lying. In one of these, after looking round as usual, I asked aloud, "Any Massachusetts men here?" Two bright faces lifted themselves from their pillows and welcomed me by name. The one nearest me was Private John B. Noyes, of Company B, Massachusetts Thirteenth, son of my old college class tutor, now the reverend and learned Professor of Hebrew, and so forth, in Harvard University. His neighbor was Corporal Armstrong, of the same company. Both were slightly wounded, doing well. I learned then and since from Mr. Noyes that they and their comrades were completely overwhelmed by the attentions of the good people of Harrisburg,—that the ladies brought them fruits and flowers, and smiles, better than either,—and that the little boys of the place were almost fighting for the privilege of doing their errands. I am afraid there will be a good many hearts pierced in this war that will have no bullet mark to show.

There were some heavy hours to get rid of, and we thought a visit to Camp Curtin might lighten some of them. A rickety wagon carried us to the camp, in company with a young woman from Troy, who had a basket of good things with her for a sick brother. "Poor boy! he will be sure to die," she said. The rustic sentries uncrossed their muskets and let us in. The camp was on a fair plain, girdled with hills, spacious, well kept apparently, but did not present any peculiar attraction for us. The visit would have been a dull one had we not happened to get sight of a singular-looking set of human beings in the distance. They were clad in stuff of different hues, gray and brown being the leading shades, but both subdued by a neutral tint, such as is wont to harmonize the variegated apparel of travel-stained vagabonds. They looked slouchy, listless, torpid—an ill-conditioned crew, at first sight, made up of such fellows as an old woman would drive away from her hen roost with a broomstick. Yet these were estrays from the fiery army which has given our generals so much trouble —"Secesh prisoners," as a bystander told us. A talk with them might be profitable and entertaining. But they were tabooed to the common visitor, and it was necessary to get inside of the line which separated us from them.

A solid, square captain was standing near by, to whom we were referred. Look a man calmly through the very centre of his pupils and ask him for anything with a tone implying entire conviction that he will grant it, and he will very commonly consent to the thing asked, were it to commit hari-kari. The captain acceded to my postulate, and accepted my friend as a corollary. As one string of my own ancestors was of Batavian origin, I may be permitted to say that my new friend was of the Dutch type, like the Amsterdam galiots, broad in the beam, capacious in the hold, and calculated to carry a heavy cargo rather than to make fast time. He must have been in politics at some time or other, for he made orations to all the "Secesh," in which he explained to them that the United States considered and treated them like children, and enforced upon them the ridiculous impossibility of the Rebels' attempting to do anything against such a power as that of the National Government.

Much as his discourse edified them and enlightened me, it interfered somewhat with my little plans of entering into frank and friendly talk with some of these poor fellows, for whom I could not help feeling a kind of human sympathy, though I am as venomous a hater of the Rebellion as one is like to find under the Stars and Stripes. It is fair to take a man prisoner. It is fair to make speeches to a man. But to take a man prisoner and then make speeches to him while in durance is *not* fair.

I began a few pleasant conversations, which would have come to something but for the reason assigned.

One old fellow had a long beard, a drooping eyelid, and a black clay pipe in his mouth. He was a Scotchman from Ayr, dour enough, and little disposed to be communicative, though I tried him with the "Twa Briggs," and, like all Scotchmen, he was a reader of "Burrns." He professed to feel no interest in the cause for which he was fighting, and was in the army, I judged, only from compulsion. There was a wild-haired, unsoaped boy, with pretty, foolish features enough, who looked as if he might be about seventeen, as he said he was. I give my questions and his answers literally.

"What state do you come from?"

"Georgy."

"What part of Georgia?"

"Midway."

(How odd that is! My father was settled for seven years as pastor over the church at Midway, Georgia, and this youth is very probably a grandson or great-grandson of one of his parishioners.)

"Where did you go to church, when you were at home?"

"Never went inside 'f a church b't once in m' life."

"What did you do before you became a soldier?"

"Nothin'."

"What do you mean to do when you get back?"

"Nothin'."

Who could have any other feeling than pity for this poor human weed, this dwarfed and etiolated soul, doomed by neglect to an existence but one degree above that of the idiot?

With the group was a lieutenant, buttoned close in his gray coat—one button gone, perhaps to make a breastpin for some fair traitorous bosom. A short, stocky man, undistinguishable from one of the "subject race" by any obvious meanderings of the *sangre azul* on his exposed surfaces. He did not say much, possibly because he was convinced by the statements and arguments of the Dutch captain. He had on strong, iron-heeled shoes, of English make, which he said cost him seventeen dollars in Richmond.

I put the question, in a quiet, friendly way, to several of the prisoners, what they were fighting for. One answered, "For our homes." Two or three others said they did not know, and manifested great indifference to the whole matter, at which another of their number, a sturdy fellow, took offense, and muttered opinions strongly derogatory to those who would not stand up for the cause they had been fighting for. A feeble, attenuated old man, who wore the Rebel uniform, if such it could be called, stood by without showing any sign of intelligence. It was cutting very close to the bone to carve such a shred of humanity from the body politic to make a soldier of.

We were just leaving when a face attracted me, and I stopped the party. "That is the true Southern type," I said to my companion. A young fellow, a little over twenty, rather tall, slight, with a perfectly smooth, boyish cheek, delicate, somewhat high features, and a fine, almost feminine mouth, stood at the opening of his tent, and as we turned toward him fidgeted a little nervously with one hand at the loose canvas, while he seemed at the same time not unwilling to talk. He was from Mississippi, he said, had been at Georgetown College, and was so far imbued with letters that even the name of the literary humility before him was not new to his ears. Of course I found it easy to come into magnetic relation with him, and to ask him without incivility what *he* was fighting for. "Because I like the excitement of it," he answered. I know those fighters with women's mouths and boys' cheeks; one such from the circle of my own friends, sixteen years old, slipped away from his nursery and dashed in under an assumed name among the red-legged Zouaves, in whose company he got an ornamental bullet mark in one of the earliest conflicts of the war.

"Did you ever see a genuine Yankee?" said my Philadelphia friend to the young Mississippian.

"I have shot at a good many of them," he replied modestly, his woman's mouth stirring a little, with a pleasant, dangerous smile.

The Dutch captain here put his foot into the conversation, as his ancestors used to put theirs into the scale when they were buying furs of the Indians by weight—so much for the weight of a hand, so much for the weight of a foot. It deranged the balance of our intercourse; there was no use in throwing a fly where a paving stone had just splashed into the water, and I nodded a good-bye to the boy fighter, thinking how much pleasanter it was for my friend the captain to address him with unanswerable arguments and crushing statements in his own tent than it would be to meet him on some remote picket and offer his fair proportions to the quick eye of a youngster who would draw a bead on him before he had time to say *dunder and blixum*.

We drove back to the town. No message. After dinner still no message. Dr. Cuyler, Chief Army Hospital Inspector, is in town, they say. Let us hunt him up—perhaps he can help us.

We found him at the Jones House. A gentleman of large proportions, but of lively temperament, his frame knit in the North, I think, but ripened in Georgia, incisive, prompt, but good-humored, wearing his broad-brimmed, steeple-crowned felt hat with the least possible tilt on one side,—a sure sign of exuberant vitality in a mature and dignified person like him,—businesslike in his ways, and not to be interrupted while occupied with another, but giving himself up heartily to the claimant who held him for the time. He was so genial, so cordial, so encouraging, that it seemed as if the clouds, which had been thick all the morning, broke away as we came into his presence, and the sunshine of his large nature filled the air all around us. He took the matter in hand at once, as if it were his own private affair. In ten minutes he had a second telegraphic message on its way to Mrs. K—— at Hagerstown, sent through the Government channel from the State Capitol—one so direct and urgent that I should be sure of an answer to it, whatever became of the one I had sent in the morning.

While this was going on, we hired a dilapidated barouche, driven by an odd young native, neither boy nor man, "as a codling when 't is almost an apple," who said "wery" for "very," simple and sincere, who smiled faintly at our pleasantries, always with a certain reserve of suspicion, and a gleam of the shrewdness that all men get who live in the atmosphere of horses. He drove us round by the Capitol grounds, white with tents, which were disgraced in my eyes by unsoldierly scrawls in huge letters, thus: THE SEVEN BLOOMSBURY BROTHERS, DEVIL'S HOLE, and similar inscriptions. Then to the Beacon Street of Harrisburg, which looks upon the Susquehanna instead of the Common, and shows a long front of handsome houses with fair gardens. The river is pretty nearly a mile across here, but very shallow now. The codling told us that a Rebel spy had been caught trying its fords a little while ago, and was now at Camp Curtin with a heavy ball chained to his leg—a popular story, but a lie, Dr. Wilson said. A little farther along we came to the barkless stump of the tree to which Mr. Harris, the Cecrops of the city named after him, was tied by the Indians for some unpleasant operation of scalping or roasting, when he was rescued by friendly savages, who paddled across the stream to save him. Our youngling pointed out a very respectable-looking stone house as having been "built by the Indians" about those times. Guides have queer notions occasionally.

I was at Niagara just when Dr. Rae arrived there with his companions and dogs and things from his Arctic search after the lost navigator.

"Who are those?" I said to my conductor.

"Them?" he answered. "Them's the men that's been out West, out to Michig'n, aft' *Sir Ben Franklin.*"

Ten o'clock in the evening was approaching. The telegraph office would presently close, and as yet there were no tidings from Hagerstown. Let us step over and see for ourselves. A message! A message!

Captain H still here leaves seven tomorrow for Harrisburg Penna Is doing well

Mrs H K——

A note from Dr. Cuyler to the same effect came soon afterwards to the hotel.

We shall sleep well to-night; but let us sit awhile with nubiferous, or, if we may coin a word, nepheligenous accompaniment, such as shall gently narcotize the over-wearied brain and fold its convolutions for slumber like the leaves of a lily at nightfall. For now the over-tense nerves are all unstraining themselves, and a buzz, like that which comes over one who stops after being long jolted upon an uneasy pavement, makes the whole frame alive with a luxurious languid sense of all its inmost fibres. Our cheerfulness ran over, and the mild, pensive clerk was so magnetized by it that he came and sat down with us. He presently confided to me, with infinite naïveté and ingenuousness, that, judging from my personal appearance, he should not have thought me the writer that he in his generosity reckoned me to be. His conception, so far as I could reach it, involved a huge, uplifted forehead, embossed with protuberant organs of the intellectual faculties, such as all writers are supposed to possess in abounding measure. While I fell short of his ideal in this respect, he was pleased to say that he found me by no means the remote and inaccessible personage he had imagined, and that I had nothing of the dandy about me, which last compliment I had a modest consciousness of most abundantly deserving.

Sweet slumbers brought us to the morning of Thursday. The train from Hagerstown was due at 11.15 A. M. We took another ride behind the codling, who showed us the sights of yesterday over again. Being in a gracious mood of mind, I enlarged on the varying aspects of the town pumps and other striking objects which we had once inspected, as seen by the different lights of evening and morning. After this, we visited the schoolhouse hospital. A fine young fellow, whose arm had been shattered, was just falling into the spasms of lockjaw. The beads of sweat stood large and round on his flushed and contracted features. He was under the effect of opiates—why not (if his case was desperate, as it seemed to be considered) stop his sufferings with chloroform? It was suggested that it might *shorten life*. "What then?" I said. "Are a dozen additional spasms worth living for?"

The time approached for the train to arrive from Hagerstown, and we went to the station. I was struck, while waiting there, with what seemed to me a great want of care for the safety of the people standing round. Just after my companion and myself had stepped off the track, I noticed a car coming quietly along at a walk, as one may say, without engine, without visible conductor, without any person heralding its approach, so silently, so insidiously, that I could not help thinking how very near it came to flattening out me and my match box worse than the Ravel pantomimist and his snuffbox were flattened out in the play. The train was late,—fifteen minutes, half an hour late,—and I began to get nervous, lest something had happened. While I was looking for it, out started a freight train, as if on purpose to meet the cars I was expecting, for a grand smash-up. I shivered at the thought, and asked an employé of the road, with whom I had formed an acquaintance a few minutes old, why there should not be a collision of the expected train with this which was just going out. He smiled an official smile, and answered that they arranged to prevent that, or words to that effect.

Twenty-four hours had not passed from that moment when a collision *did* occur, just out of the city, where I feared it, by which at least eleven persons were killed and from forty to sixty more were maimed and crippled!

To-day there was the delay spoken of, but nothing worse. The expected train came in so quietly that I was almost startled to see it on the track. Let us walk calmly through the cars, and look around us.

In the first car, on the fourth seat to the right, I saw my Captain; there saw I him, even my first-born, whom I had sought through many cities.

"How are you, Boy?"

"How are you, Dad?"

Such are the proprieties of life, as they are observed among us Anglo-Saxons of the nineteenth century, decently disguising those natural impulses that made Joseph, the Prime Minister of Egypt, weep aloud so that the Egyptians and the house of Pharaoh heard—nay, which had once overcome his shaggy old uncle Esau so entirely that he fell on his brother's neck and cried like a baby in the presence of all the women. But the hidden cisterns of the soul may be filling fast with sweet tears, while the windows through which it looks are undimmed by a drop or a film of moisture.

These are times in which we cannot live solely for selfish joys or griefs. I had not let fall the hand I held, when a sad, calm voice addressed me by name. I fear that at the moment I was too much absorbed in my own feelings; for certainly at any other time I should have yielded myself without stint to the sympathy which this meeting might well call forth.

"You remember my son, Cortland Saunders, whom I brought to see you once in Boston?"

"I do remember him well."

"He was killed on Monday, at Shepherdstown. I am carrying his body back with me on this train. He was my only child. If you could come to my house,—I can hardly call it my home now,—it would be a pleasure to me."

This young man, belonging in Philadelphia, was the author of a *New System of Latin Paradigms,* a work showing extraordinary scholarship and capacity. It was this book which first made me acquainted with him, and I kept him in my memory, for there was genius in the youth. Some time afterwards he came to me with a modest request to be introduced to President Felton, and one or two others, who would aid him in a course of independent study he was proposing to himself. I was most happy to smooth the way for him, and he came repeatedly after this to see me and express his satisfaction in the opportunities for study he enjoyed at Cambridge. He was a dark, still, slender person, always with a trance-like remoteness, a mystic dreaminess of manner, such as I never saw in any other youth. Whether he heard with difficulty, or whether his mind reacted slowly on an alien thought, I could not say; but his answer would often be behind time, and then a vague, sweet smile, or a few words spoken under his breath, as if he had been trained in sick men's chambers. For such a youth, seemingly destined for the inner life of contemplation, to be a soldier seemed almost unnatural. Yet he spoke to me of his intention to offer himself to his country, and his blood must now be reckoned among the precious sacrifices which will make her soil sacred forever. Had he lived, I doubt not that he would have redeemed the rare promise of his earlier years. He has done better, for he has died that unborn generations may attain the hopes held out to our nation and to mankind.

So, then, I had been within ten miles of the place where my wounded soldier was lying, and then calmly turned my back upon him to come once more round by a journey of three or four hundred miles to the same region I had left! No mysterious attraction warned me that the heart warm with the same blood as mine was throbbing so near my own. I thought of that lovely, tender passage where Gabriel glides unconsciously by Evangeline upon the great river. Ah, me! if that railroad crash had been a few hours earlier, we two should never have met again, after coming so close to each other!

The source of my repeated disappointments was soon made clear enough. The Captain had gone to Hagerstown, intending to take the cars at once for Philadelphia, as his three friends actually did do, and as I took it for granted he certainly would. But as he walked languidly along, some ladies saw him across the street, and, seeing, were moved with pity, and, pitying, spoke such soft words that he was tempted to accept their invitation and rest awhile beneath their hospitable roof. The mansion was old, as the dwellings of gentlefolks should be; the ladies were some of them young, and all were full of kindness; there were gentle cares, and unasked luxuries, and pleasant talk, and music sprinklings from the piano, with a sweet voice to keep them company —and all this after the swamps of the Chickahominy, the mud and flies of Harrison's Landing, the dragging marches, the desperate battles, the fretting wound, the jolting ambulance, the log house, and the rickety milk cart! Thanks, uncounted thanks to the angelic ladies whose charming attentions detained him from Saturday to Thursday, to his great advantage and my infinite bewilderment! As for his wound, how could it do otherwise than well under such hands? The bullet had gone smoothly through, dodging everything but a few nervous branches, which would come right in time and leave him as well as ever.

Fling open the window blinds of the chamber that looks out on the waters and towards the western sun! Let the joyous light shine in upon the pictures that hang upon its walls and the shelves thick-set with the names of poets and philosophers and sacred teachers, in whose pages our boys learn that life is noble only when it is held cheap by the side of honor and of duty. Lay him in his own bed, and let him sleep off his aches and weariness. So comes down another night over this household, unbroken by any messenger of evil tidings —a night of peaceful rest and grateful thoughts; for this our son and brother was dead and is alive again, and was lost and is found.

1862

SAINT LUKE

Paul and the Silversmiths

From THE KING JAMES TRANSLATION OF THE BIBLE, ACTS, 19:*21*—20:*1*

AFTER these things were ended, Paul purposed in the spirit, when he had passed through Macedonia and Achaia, to go to Jerusalem, saying, "After I have been there, I must also see Rome." So he sent into Macedonia two of them that ministered unto him, Timotheus and Erastus; but he himself stayed in Asia for a season. And the same time there arose no small stir about that way. For a certain man named Demetrius, a silversmith, which made silver shrines for Diana, brought no small gain unto the craftsmen, whom he called together with the workmen of like occupation, and said,

"Sirs, ye know that by this craft we have our wealth. Moreover, ye see and hear that not alone at Ephesus, but almost throughout all Asia this Paul hath persuaded and turned away much people, saying that they be no gods, which are made with hands. So that not only this our craft is in danger to be set at naught, but also that the temple of the great goddess Diana should be despised, and her magnificence should be destroyed, whom all Asia and the world worshippeth."

And when they heard these sayings, they were full of wrath, and cried out, saying, "Great is Diana of the Ephesians."

And the whole city was filled with confusion; and having caught Gaius and Aristarchus, men of Macedonia, Paul's companions in travel, they rushed with one accord into the theatre. And when Paul would have entered in unto the people, the disciples suffered him not. And certain of the chief of Asia, which were his friends, sent unto him, desiring him that he would not adventure himself into the theatre. Some therefore cried one thing and some another, for the assembly was confused, and the more part knew not wherefore they were come together. And they drew Alexander out of the multitude, the Jews putting him forward. And Alexander beckoned with the hand, and would have made his defense unto the people. But when they knew that he was a Jew, all with one voice about the space of two hours cried out, "Great is Diana of the Ephesians." And when the town clerk had appeased the people, he said,

"Ye men of Ephesus, what man is there that knoweth not how the city of the Ephesians is a worshipper of the great goddess Diana, and of the image which fell down from Jupiter? Seeing then that these things cannot be spoken against, ye ought to be quiet, and to do nothing rashly. For ye have brought hither these men, which are neither robbers of churches, nor yet blasphemers of your goddess. Wherefore if Demetrius, and the craftsmen which are with him, have a matter against any man, the law is open, and there are deputies; let them implead one another. But if ye inquire any thing concerning other matters, it shall be determined in a lawful assembly. For we are in danger to be called in question for this day's uproar, there being no cause whereby we may give an account of this concourse."

And when he had thus spoken, he dismissed the assembly.

And after the uproar was ceased, Paul called unto him the disciples, and embraced them, and departed for to go into Macedonia.

c.80A.D.

LUDWIG BEMELMANS

Prison Visit

From The Donkey Inside

ATOP ONE of the foothills of Pichincha, high above the city of Quito, bathed in sunlight, stands a white building with a cupola. It is the Panóptico, and it has an evil name. Don Juan Palacios in Guayaquil had recited its horrors to me, and wherever I asked permission to visit the prison I was told with politeness and much regret that this one wish could not be granted. Diplomats in cautious conversation told me again that its cells were subterranean and wet, that the prisoners were chained to the walls, underfed, without proper clothing. Bony, feverish victims of political miscalculation, who died slowly, without consolation, and stank to high heaven. Lucky were they who were sent to exile in the Galápagos Islands or marched into the jungles of the Oriente; there death was quick and in the daylight.

The magnificent name of the prison and its story drew me up the hill, which I climbed in short stages of thirty paces at a time. For a while, when you return from the low lands, it is difficult to breathe in Quito, and you proceed by resting on a streetcorner, advancing thirty paces, leaning against a house and then a tree. Thus I arrived at the Panóptico.

Outside, propped against the building, were two sentries in khaki uniforms, with legs crossed, resting their hands on the barrels of their guns. They were talking and laughing; one turned, when the other pointed at me, and raised his eyebrows.

"I would like to see the Director of the prison."

Ah, he said, but that was not so easy; there had to be arrangements made for this ahead of time, a letter, an introduction, a pass, or else one had to arrive in the company of an official of the Government, or at least of a policeman.

I told him that I knew all that, but that my visit was an exception, that I was a prison official myself, from the United States of North America, that I was the secretary of the warden of a prison.

The soldier's eyes grew respectful and obedient, he leaned away from the building, saluted, and dragging his gun behind him he almost ran up the portico to the door, where he told the story to the man who sat on guard there. The guard stood up and said, "But certainly, come in, come in, the Director will be happy to see you."

Door after door opened. By the time I arrived in the reception room of the Director's apartment I had shaken hands with several officials and rapidly answered questions.

What prison?

A prison in the State of New York.

Ahhh!

A man motioned to a red leather couch in the comfortably furnished room. There were white curtains, a few cages with birds singing in them, and under my feet a green carpet. Much light came in at a high window.

A small man entered. He wore a long, tightly buttoned black coat. One of his hands was in a black glove; he held this hand in back of him. He had a small white spade beard, a distinguished face. He stood away about ten feet from me, and bowed. I got up.

He said, "Sing Sing?" I answered, "Sing Sing." The door opened again and a young man was shown in. The little old man turned to him and said with raised eyebrows, "Warden Lawes, Sing Sing."

The Director bowed deeply. He was followed by a retinue of secretaries and assistants and guards. As he sat down on the couch beside me and pumped my hand, he repeated "Sing Sing" as if it were the name of his first love. He picked a stray hair off the collar of my coat, and then, standing up, I was introduced to the staff, and someone was quickly sent for something to drink. An order was given for luncheon, and then from a drawer of his desk the Director slipped a worn Colt .25 into his pocket and said, "Permit me," and went ahead.

"I will go ahead," he said. "You do not know the way."

He was athletic, of good bearing; I think partly Indian. His clothes were simple; he used his chest and lips at times as Mussolini does, the body swaying with both hands at the hips, the lower lip rolled out as in pouting.

We passed two heavy gates, went through a long tunnel, turned to the right, and entered one of the cellblocks in the star-shaped building.

"Our population in this prison is five hundred and five men, and twenty-four women. Most of them are here for crimes of passion. The population of Ecuador is about three million."

"Where does the music come from?"

"From the political prisoners. We have three of them. They are not forced to work, so they sing and play guitars; here they are."

Without stopping their song, the three young men nodded to the Warden. They were in a cell with flowers at the window and a small parrot in a cage; two sat on the bed, the third on a three-legged stool.

"Now we go to the shops." We crossed a wide square and entered a house filled with the noises of hammering, sawing, the smell of wood and leather, and above that the smell of lilies from the prison yard. The prisoners sang here also; the windows were high and without bars. They stood up as the Warden came in; their faces remained at ease. Shoes were made here and some furniture, small trunks lined with paper on which flower designs were printed. In another part of the room men were carving small skulls out of ivory nuts, and one was arranging a miniature of the Crucifixion scene inside a small bottle. Some of the men smoked, some rested, all smiled as the Warden spoke to them. They all very proudly showed their work. The

Warden told them all, "Warden Lawes —Sing Sing," and in a few words described my famous prison to them. He stopped and spoke to several men and told me what crimes they had committed. Some of the men asked him questions, and he answered with interest, thinking awhile before he spoke. He usually touched the men or held them by the arm; he bowed and smiled when he had finished with them, and he told his assistant to note several things the men requested.

From this room we climbed the stone steps up to the roof of the prison. Lilies were blooming in the gardens below; on the south side there was a swimming pool into which a stream of water poured from the mouth of a stone lion. A sentry lay on the roof. He got up and kicked the magazine under his pill-box and reached for the rifle which lay on the blanket on which he had been reading; he pulled down his coat and started pacing up and down, the gun over his shoulder.

"Does anyone ever escape from here?"

"Yes, sometimes," said the Warden. "Here, right here, is where they escape." He pointed to the roof of the cellblock that was nearest to the mountain. To clear a wall that is eighteen feet high, a man had to run and then jump out and down a distance of some thirty-four feet; he landed in a thicket of candelabra cacti on the other side of the fence. I asked the Warden how they punished the men when they caught them. "If he jumps well," said the Warden, "he's gone. It's not easy; he must want to be free very badly, and I would not like to risk it, would you? His friends will hide him and we have one less prisoner. If he jumps badly, he falls down into the yard here and is perhaps dead—at least

he will break both his legs. He will never jump again; the pain, that is enough punishment. And you, Señor; in Sing Sing, what you do?"

"Oh, we lock them up in a dungeon, with bread and water and no light, for a week, two weeks, a month."

"I do not believe in that," he said with the Mussolini gesture. "I do not believe in vengeance. Look here, down over the edge; this man is a bad fellow, I had to do something. I have put him alone by himself on half-rations. But I gave him the dog and cats and I come to see him and talk to him. I am troubled with his stupidity."

I crept to the edge of the roof and looked down. In a court by himself sat a young, wild-haired fellow. His half-ration consisted of a big bowl of soup, a small pail half full of rice, and a loaf of black bread. The dog and cats were sitting close to him waiting for the remnants of his meal.

"You know," continued the Warden, "he is my only problem prisoner; before, it was full of them. The military ran this institution; the military mind is stupid—boom, huuuump, march, one, two, three, four, eyes right—shouting, marching is all they know. I am an advocate; I try to be humanitarian; not soft, please do not mistake me, I mean economic with life; that is my idea. I look at my prisoner when he comes in, I have studied the science of criminology, I have a knowledge of the system Bertillon. I am sorry when a man is brought in and I can see by his nose, his eyes, his jaw, and his skull, that he is a bad fellow for whom I can do nothing. That one I send away, to the Galápagos. It's not bad for them there; they can sleep and fish. Here he would do terrible damage.

"Here I keep the men and women

who have perhaps even killed somebody, who have done something in one moment of their life that was wrong; they know it, I know it, we're both sorry; let us make the best of it. First of all I tell them to forget it and work. I know each man here. I hope they all like me as much as I like them.

"We have no death penalty here in Ecuador. The maximum sentence is for sixteen years; that is for cold murder.

"All prisoners receive wages, the current wages that would be paid if the man worked outside. The wages are divided in three parts. One-third goes to the prison, and by this the institution supports itself; one-third goes to the man for pocket money; and one-third is saved for him, with interest, for the day when he is freed. If he has a family, the pocket money and the savings account are split according to the needs of his wife and children, but he must receive some money for himself and a small sum for his freedom; he may not want to go back to his family. Any of them can go out, if I say yes. A prisoner's wife can visit him; she can go out into the garden with him, and bring his children. He can sometimes go home with her. And I like it when they paint. Here, look into this cell."

We had come down from the roof. Almost every cell had pictures in watercolors or crayons—simple pictures of landscapes, saints, animals, in flat poster effects; some in brilliant colors, some uncertain and shaky. They were painted on the walls of the cells and sometimes along the corridors.

The Warden knew all the rare ones. He showed them to me with pride, and particular pride at the absence of pornographic ones.

"I would let them alone if there were any," he said. "A man's cell is his private room here. He can do what he wants. I am just glad I have never found any.

"Now let us go to the women."

The twenty-four women live in a prison within the prison. Here there are more flowers, three tangerine trees, and clouds of linen hanging over them.

These women have stabbed cheating lovers; one of them did away with her baby. They spend their days washing and ironing the drawers, undershirts, and socks of the cadets at the military academy. Their children are with them. Little boys and girls run and sing in the yard. They go out to school and come back to eat with Mama. The little houses, of one room each, are orderly, and all the women were smiling. One was nursing her baby.

"Born here," said the Warden with pride, and pinched its cheeks.

We said our good-bys and walked back to the reception room. While we waited for luncheon he pouted again in the Mussolini manner, crossed his legs, and looked out of the window over Quito. He turned abruptly to pose a question which apparently had difficulty in forming itself into words.

"Señor Lawes," he blurted, "I have heard so much of you. I have read so much in magazines. Your stories are published in our Spanish journals very often. I have seen a moving picture that you have written. You are such an intelligent man and so—what is the word?—efficient, and also—what is it? —versatile. How you do it? Here I have a little prison with five hundred people. I am busy all day and half the night and every Sunday—I have not had a vacation for a year. How can you do it? I think it's wonderful."

1941

IX. . .

SHORT STORY

JACK LONDON

To Build a Fire

DAY HAD broken cold and gray, exceedingly cold and gray, when the man turned aside from the main Yukon trail and climbed the high earth-bank, where a dim and little-travelled trail led eastward through the fat spruce timberland. It was a steep bank, and he paused for breath at the top, excusing the act to himself by looking at his watch. It was nine o'clock. There was no sun nor hint of sun, though there was not a cloud in the sky. It was a clear day, and yet there seemed an intangible pall over the face of things, a subtle gloom that made the day dark, and that was due to the absence of sun. This fact did not worry the man. He was used to the lack of sun. It had been days since he had seen the sun, and he knew that a few more days must pass before that cheerful orb, due south, would just peep above the sky-line and dip immediately from view.

The man flung a look back along the way he had come. The Yukon lay a mile wide and hidden under three feet of ice. On top of this ice were as many feet of snow. It was all pure white, rolling in gentle undulations where the ice-jams of the freeze-up had formed. North and south, as far as his eye could see, it was unbroken white, save for a dark hair-line that curved and twisted from around the spruce-covered island to the south, and that curved and twisted away into the north, where it disappeared behind another spruce-covered island. This dark hair-line was the trail —the main trail—that led south five hundred miles to the Chilcoot Pass, Dyea, and salt water; and that led north seventy miles to Dawson, and still on to the north a thousand miles to Nulato, and finally to St. Michael on Bering Sea, a thousand miles and half a thousand more.

But all this—the mysterious, far-reaching hair-line trail, the absence of the sun from the sky, the tremendous cold, and the strangeness and weirdness of it all —made no impression on the man. It was not because he was long used to it. He was a newcomer in the land, a *chechaquo,* and this was his first winter. The trouble with him was that he was without imagination. He was quick and alert in the things of life, but only in the things, and not in the significances. Fifty degrees below zero meant eighty-odd degrees of frost. Such fact impressed him as being cold and uncomfortable, and that was all. It did not lead him to meditate upon his frailty as a creature of temperature, and upon man's frailty in general, able only to live within certain narrow limits of heat and cold; and from there on it did not lead him to the conjectural field of immortality and man's place in the universe. Fifty degrees below zero stood for a bite of frost that hurt and that must be guarded against by the use of mittens, ear-flaps, warm moccasins, and thick socks. Fifty degrees below zero was to

Reprinted from *The Call of the Wild and Other Stories* (Macmillan, 1931) by permission of Irving Shepard, manager, Jack London Ranch.

him just precisely fifty degrees below zero. That there should be anything more to it than that was a thought that never entered his head.

As he turned to go on, he spat speculatively. There was a sharp, explosive crackle that startled him. He spat again. And again, in the air, before it could fall to the snow, the spittle crackled. He knew that at fifty below spittle crackled on the snow, but this spittle had crackled in the air. Undoubtedly it was colder than fifty below—how much colder he did not know. But the temperature did not matter. He was bound for the old claim on the left fork of Henderson Creek, where the boys were already. They had come over across the divide from the Indian Creek country, while he had come the roundabout way to take a look at the possibilities of getting out logs in the spring from the islands in the Yukon. He would be into camp by six o'clock; a bit after dark, it was true, but the boys would be there, a fire would be going, and a hot supper would be ready. As for lunch, he pressed his hand against the protruding bundle under his jacket. It was also under his shirt, wrapped up in a handkerchief and lying against the naked skin. It was the only way to keep the biscuits from freezing. He smiled agreeably to himself as he thought of those biscuits, each cut open and sopped in bacon grease, and each enclosing a generous slice of fried bacon.

He plunged in among the big spruce trees. The trail was faint. A foot of snow had fallen since the last sled had passed over, and he was glad he was without a sled, travelling light. In fact he carried nothing but the lunch wrapped in the handkerchief. He was surprised, however, at the cold. It certainly was cold, he concluded, as he rubbed his numb nose and cheek-bones with his mittened hand. He was a warm-whiskered man, but the hair on his face did not protect the high cheek-bones and the eager nose that thrust itself aggressively into the frosty air.

At the man's heels trotted a dog, a big native husky, the proper wolf-dog, gray-coated and without any visible or temperamental difference from its brother, the wild wolf. The animal was depressed by the tremendous cold. It knew that it was no time for travelling. Its instinct told it a truer tale than was told to the man by the man's judgment. In reality, it was not merely colder than fifty below zero; it was colder than sixty below, than seventy below. It was seventy-five below zero. Since the freezing-point is thirty-two above zero, it meant that one hundred and seven degrees of frost obtained. The dog did not know anything about thermometers. Possibly in its brain there was no sharp consciousness of a condition of very cold such as was in the man's brain. But the brute had its instinct. It experienced a vague but menacing apprehension that subdued it and made it slink along at the man's heels, and that made it question eagerly every unwonted movement of the man as if expecting him to go into camp or to seek shelter somewhere and build a fire. The dog had learned fire, and it wanted fire, or else to burrow under the snow and cuddle its warmth away from the air.

The frozen moisture of its breathing had settled on its fur in a fine powder of frost, and especially were its jowls, muzzle, and eyelashes whitened by its crystalled breath. The man's red beard and mustache were likewise frosted, but more solidly, the deposit taking the form of ice and increasing with every warm, moist breath he exhaled. Also, the man was chewing tobacco, and the muzzle of ice held his lips so rigidly that he was unable to clear his chin when he expelled the juice. The result was that a crystal beard of the color and solidity of amber was increasing its length on his chin. If he fell down it would shatter itself, like glass, into brittle fragments. But he did not mind the appendage. It was the penalty all tobacco-chewers paid in that country, and he had been out before in two cold snaps. They had not been so cold as this, he knew, but by the spirit thermometer at Sixty Mile he knew they had been registered at fifty below and at fifty-five.

He held on through the level stretch of woods for several miles, crossed a wide flat of niggerheads, and dropped down a bank to the frozen bed of a small stream. This was Henderson Creek, and he knew he was ten miles from the forks. He looked at his watch. It was ten o'clock. He was making four miles an hour, and he calculated that he would arrive at the forks at half-past twelve. He decided to celebrate that event by eating his lunch there.

The dog dropped in again at his heels, with a tail drooping discouragement, as the man swung along the creek-bed. The furrow of the old sled-trail was plainly visible, but a dozen inches of snow covered the marks of the last runners. In a month no man had come up or down that silent creek. The man held steadily on. He was not much given to thinking, and just then particularly he had nothing to think about save that he would eat lunch at the forks and that at six o'clock he would be in camp with the boys. There was nobody to talk to; and, had there been, speech would have been impossible because of the ice-muzzle on his mouth. So he continued monotonously to chew to-

bacco and to increase the length of his amber beard.

Once in a while the thought reiterated itself that it was very cold and that he had never experienced such cold. As he walked along he rubbed his cheek-bones and nose with the back of his mittened hand. He did this automatically, now and again changing hands. But rub as he would, the instant he stopped, his cheek-bones went numb, and the following instant the end of his nose went numb. He was sure to frost his cheeks; he knew that, and experienced a pang of regret that he had not devised a nose-strap of the sort Bud wore in cold snaps. Such a strap passed across the cheeks, as well, and saved them. But it didn't matter much, after all. What were frosted cheeks? A bit painful, that was all; they were never serious.

Empty as the man's mind was of thoughts, he was keenly observant, and he noticed the changes in the creek, the curves and bends and timber-jams, and always he sharply noted where he placed his feet. Once, coming around a bend, he shied abruptly, like a startled horse, curved away from the place where he had been walking, and retreated several paces back along the trail. The creek he knew was frozen clear to the bottom, —no creek could contain water in that arctic winter,—but he knew also that there were springs that bubbled out from the hillsides and ran along under the snow and on top the ice of the creek. He knew that the coldest snaps never froze these springs, and he knew likewise their danger. They were traps. They hid pools of water under the snow that might be three inches deep, or three feet. Sometimes a skin of ice half an inch thick covered them, and in turn was covered by the snow. Sometimes there were alternate layers of water and ice-skin, so that when one broke through he kept on breaking through for a while, sometimes wetting himself to the waist.

That was why he had shied in such panic. He had felt the give under his feet and heard the crackle of a snow-hidden ice-skin. And to get his feet wet in such a temperature meant trouble and danger. At the very least it meant delay, for he would be forced to stop and build a fire, and under its protection to bare his feet while he dried his socks and moccasins. He stood and studied the creek-bed and its banks, and decided that the flow of water came from the right. He reflected awhile, rubbing his nose and cheeks, then skirted to the left, stepping gingerly and testing the footing for each step. Once clear of the danger, he took a fresh chew of tobacco and swung along at his four-mile gait.

In the course of the next two hours he came upon several similar traps. Usually the snow above the hidden pools had a sunken, candied appearance that advertised the danger. Once, again, however, he had a close call; and once, suspecting danger, he compelled the dog to go on in front. The dog did not want to go. It hung back until the man shoved it forward, and then it went quickly across the white, unbroken surface. Suddenly it broke through, floundered to one side, and got away to firmer footing. It had wet its forefeet and legs, and almost immediately, the water that clung to it turned to ice. It made quick efforts to lick the ice off its legs, then dropped down in the snow and began to bite out the ice that had formed between the toes. This was a matter of instinct. To permit the ice to remain would mean sore feet. It did not know this. It merely obeyed the mysterious prompting that arose from the deep crypts of its being. But the

man knew, having achieved a judgment on the subject, and he removed the mitten from his right hand and helped tear out the ice-particles. He did not expose his fingers more than a minute, and was astonished at the swift numbness that smote them. It certainly was cold. He pulled on the mitten hastily, and beat the hand savagely across his chest.

At twelve o'clock the day was at its brightest. Yet the sun was too far south on its winter journey to clear the horizon. The bulge of the earth intervened between it and Henderson Creek, where the man walked under a clear sky at noon and cast no shadow. At half-past twelve, to the minute, he arrived at the forks of the creek. He was pleased at the speed he had made. If he kept it up, he would certainly be with the boys by six. He unbuttoned his jacket and shirt and drew forth his lunch. The action consumed no more than a quarter of a minute, yet in that brief moment the numbness laid hold of the exposed fingers. He did not put the mitten on, but, instead, struck the fingers a dozen sharp smashes against his leg. Then he sat down on a snow-covered log to eat. The sting that followed upon the striking of his fingers against his leg ceased so quickly that he was startled. He had no chance to take a bite of biscuit. He struck the fingers repeatedly and returned them to the mitten, baring the other hand for the purpose of eating. He tried to take a mouthful, but the ice-muzzle prevented. He had forgotten to build a fire and thaw out. He chuckled at his foolishness, and as he chuckled he noted the numbness creeping into the exposed fingers. Also, he noted that the stinging which had first come to his toes when he sat down was already passing away. He wondered whether the toes were warm or numb. He moved them inside the moccasins and decided that they were numb.

He pulled the mitten on hurriedly and stood up. He was a bit frightened. He stamped up and down until the stinging returned into the feet. It certainly was cold, was his thought. That man from Sulphur Creek had spoken the truth when telling how cold it sometimes got in the country. And he had laughed at him at the time! That showed one must not be too sure of things. There was no mistake about it, it *was* cold. He strode up and down, stamping his feet and threshing his arms, until reassured by the returning warmth. Then he got out matches and proceeded to make a fire. From the undergrowth where high water of the previous spring had lodged a supply of seasoned twigs, he got his fire-wood. Working carefully from a small beginning, he soon had a roaring fire, over which he thawed the ice from his face and in the protection of which he ate his biscuits. For the moment the cold of space was outwitted. The dog took satisfaction in the fire stretching out close enough for warmth and far enough away to escape being singed.

When the man had finished, he filled his pipe and took his comfortable time over a smoke. Then he pulled on his mittens, settled the ear-flaps of his cap firmly about his ears, and took the creek trail up the left fork. The dog was disappointed and yearned back toward the fire. This man did not know cold. Possibly all the generations of his ancestry had been ignorant of cold, of real cold, of cold one hundred and seven degrees below freezing-point. But the dog knew; all its ancestry knew, and it had inherited the knowledge. And it knew that it was not good to walk abroad in such fearful cold. It was the time to lie snug in a hole in the snow and wait for a curtain of cloud to be drawn across the face of outer space whence this cold came. On the other hand, there was no keen intimacy between the dog and the man. The one was the toil-slave of the other, and the only caresses it had ever received were the caresses of the whip-lash and of harsh and menacing throat-sounds that threatened the whip-lash. So the dog made no effort to communicate its apprehension to the man. It was not concerned in the welfare of the man; it was for its own sake that it yearned back toward the fire. But the man whistled, and spoke to it with the sound of whip-lashes, and the dog swung in at the man's heels and followed after.

The man took a chew of tobacco and proceeded to start a new amber beard. Also, his moist breath quickly powdered with white his mustache, eyebrows, and lashes. There did not seem to be so many springs on the left fork of the Henderson, and for half an hour the man saw no signs of any. And then it happened. At a place where there were no signs, where the soft, unbroken snow seemed to advertise solidity beneath, the man broke through. It was not deep. He wet himself halfway to the knees before he floundered out to the firm crust.

He was angry, and cursed his luck aloud. He had hoped to get into camp with the boys at six o'clock, and this would delay him an hour, for he would have to build a fire and dry out his foot-gear. This was imperative at that low temperature—he knew that much; and he turned aside to the bank, which he climbed. On top, tangled in the underbrush about the trunks of several small spruce trees, was a high-water deposit of dry fire-wood—sticks and twigs, principally, but also larger portions of seasoned branches and fine, dry, last-year's grasses. He threw down several large pieces on top of the snow. This served for a foundation and prevented the young flame from drowning itself in the snow it otherwise would melt. The flame he got by touching a match to a small shred of birch-bark that he took from his pocket. This burned even more readily than paper. Placing it on the foundation, he fed the young flame with wisps of dry grass and with the tiniest dry twigs.

He worked slowly and carefully, keenly aware of his danger. Gradually, as the flame grew stronger, he increased the size of the twigs with which he fed it. He squatted in the snow, pulling the twigs out from their entanglement in the brush and feeding directly to the flame. He knew there must be no failure. When it is seventy-five below zero, a man must not fail in his first attempt to build a fire—that is, if his feet are wet. If his feet are dry, and he fails, he can run along the trail for half a mile and restore his circulation. But the circulation of wet and freezing feet cannot be restored by running when it is seventy-five below. No matter how fast he runs, the wet feet will freeze the harder.

All this the man knew. The old-timer on Sulphur Creek had told him about it the previous fall, and now he was appreciating the advice. Already all sensation had gone out of his feet. To build the fire he had been forced to remove his mittens, and the fingers had quickly gone numb. His pace of four miles an hour had kept his heart pumping blood to the surface of his body and to all the extremities. But the instant he stopped, the action of the pump eased down. The cold of space smote the unprotected tip of the planet, and he, being

on that unprotected tip, received the full force of the blow. The blood of his body recoiled before it. The blood was alive, like the dog, and like the dog it wanted to hide away and cover itself up from the fearful cold. So long as he walked four miles an hour, he pumped that blood, willy-nilly, to the surface; but now it ebbed away and sank down into the recesses of his body. The extremities were the first to feel its absence. His wet feet froze the faster, and his exposed fingers numbed the faster, though they had not yet begun to freeze. Nose and cheeks were already freezing, while the skin of all his body chilled as it lost its blood.

But he was safe. Toes and nose and cheeks would be only touched by the frost, for the fire was beginning to burn with strength. He was feeding it with twigs the size of his finger. In another minute he would be able to feed it with branches the size of his wrist, and then he could remove his wet foot-gear and, while it dried, he could keep his naked feet warm by the fire, rubbing them at first, of course, with snow. The fire was a success. He was safe. He remembered the advice of the old-timer on Sulphur Creek, and smiled. The old-timer had been very serious in laying down the law that no man must travel alone in the Klondike after fifty below. Well, here he was; he had had the accident; he was alone; and he had saved himself. Those old-timers were rather womanish, some of them, he thought. All a man had to do was to keep his head, and he was all right. Any man who was a man could travel alone. But it was surprising, the rapidity with which his cheeks and nose were freezing. And he had not thought his fingers could go lifeless in so short a time. Lifeless they were, for he could scarcely make them move together to grip a twig, and they seemed remote from his body and from him. When he touched a twig, he had to look and see whether or not he had hold of it. The wires were pretty well down between him and his finger-ends.

All of which counted for little. There was the fire, snapping and crackling and promising life with every dancing flame. He started to untie his moccasins. They were coated with ice; the thick German socks were like sheaths of iron halfway to the knees; and the moccasin strings were like rods of steel all twisted and knotted as by some conflagration. For a moment he tugged with his numb fingers, then, realizing the folly of it, he drew his sheath-knife.

But before he could cut the strings, it happened. It was his own fault, or, rather, his mistake. He should not have built the fire under the spruce tree. He should have built it in the open. But it had been easier to pull the twigs from the brush and drop them directly on the fire. Now the tree under which he had done this carried a weight of snow on its boughs. No wind had blown for weeks, and each bough was fully freighted. Each time he had pulled a twig he had communicated a slight agitation to the tree—an imperceptible agitation, so far as he was concerned, but an agitation sufficient to bring about the disaster. High up in the tree one bough capsized its load of snow. This fell on the boughs beneath, capsizing them. This process continued spreading out and involving the whole tree. It grew like an avalanche, and it descended without warning upon the man and the fire, and the fire was blotted out! Where it had burned was a mantle of fresh and disordered snow.

The man was shocked. It was as though he had just heard his own sentence of death. For a moment he sat and stared at the spot where the fire had been. Then he grew very calm. Perhaps the old-timer on Sulphur Creek was right. If he had only a trail-mate he would have been in no danger now. The trail-mate could have built the fire. Well, it was up to him to build the fire over again, and this second time there must be no failure. Even if he succeeded, he would most likely lose some toes. His feet must be badly frozen by now, and there would be some time before the second fire was ready.

Such were his thoughts, but he did not sit and think them. He was busy all the time they were passing through his mind. He made a new foundation for a fire, this time in the open, where no treacherous tree could blot it out. Next, he gathered dry grasses and tiny twigs from the high-water flotsam. He could not bring his fingers together to pull them out, but he was able to gather them by the handful. In this way he got many rotten twigs and bits of green moss that were undesirable, but it was the best he could do. He worked methodically, even collecting an armful of the larger branches to be used later when the fire gathered strength. And all the while the dog sat and watched him, a certain yearning wistfulness in its eyes, for it looked upon him as the fire-provider, and the fire was slow in coming.

When all was ready, the man reached in his pocket for a second piece of birch-bark. He knew the bark was there, and, though he could not feel it with his fingers, he could hear its crisp rustling as he fumbled for it. Try as he would, he could not clutch hold of it. And all the time, in his consciousness, was the knowledge that each instant his feet were freezing. This thought tended to put him in a panic, but he fought against it and kept calm. He pulled on his mittens with his teeth, and threshed his arms back and forth, beating his hands with all his might against his sides. He did this sitting down, and he stood up to do it; and all the while the dog sat in the snow, its wolf-brush of a tail curled around warmly over its fore-feet, its sharp wolf-ears pricked forward intently as it watched the man. And the man, as he beat and threshed with his arms and hands felt a great surge of envy as he regarded the creature that was warm and secure in its natural covering.

After a time he was aware of the first far away signals of sensation in his beaten fingers. The faint tingling grew stronger till it evolved into a stinging ache that was excruciating, but which the man hailed with satisfaction. He stripped the mitten from his right hand and fetched forth the birch-bark. The exposed fingers were quickly going numb again. Next he brought out his bunch of sulphur matches. But the tremendous cold had already driven the life out of his fingers. In his effort to separate one match from the others, the whole bunch fell in the snow. He tried to pick it out of the snow, but failed. The dead fingers could neither touch nor clutch. He was very careful. He drove the thought of his freezing feet, and nose, and cheeks out of his mind, devoting his whole soul to the matches. He watched, using the sense of vision in place of that of touch, and when he saw his fingers on each side the bunch, he closed them—that is, he willed to close them, for the wires were down, and the fingers did not obey. He pulled the mitten on the right hand, and beat it fiercely against his knee. Then, with both mittened hands, he scooped the bunch of matches, along with much snow, into his lap. Yet he was no better off.

After some manipulation he managed to get the bunch between the heels of his mittened hands. In this fashion he carried it to his mouth. The ice crackled and snapped when by a violent effort he opened his mouth. He drew the lower jaw in, curled the upper lip out of the way, and scraped the bunch with his upper teeth in order to separate a match. He succeeded in getting one, which he dropped on his lap. He was no better off. He could not pick it up. Then he devised a way. He picked it up in his teeth and scratched it on his leg. Twenty times he scratched before he succeeded in lighting it. As it flamed he held it with his teeth to the birch-bark. But the burning brimstone went up his nostrils and into his lungs, causing him to cough spasmodically. The match fell into the snow and went out.

The old-timer on Sulphur Creek was right, he thought in the moment of controlled despair that ensued: after fifty below, a man should travel with a partner. He beat his hands, but failed in exciting any sensation. Suddenly he bared both hands, removing the mittens with his teeth. He caught the whole bunch between the heels of his hands. His arm-muscles not being frozen enabled him to press the hand-heels tightly against the matches. Then he scratched the bunch along his leg. It flared into flame, seventy sulphur matches at once! There was no wind to blow them out. He kept his head to one side to escape the strangling fumes, and held the blazing bunch to the birch-bark. As he so held it, he became aware of sensation in his hand. His flesh was burning. He could smell it. Deep down below the surface he could feel it. The sensation developed into pain that grew acute. And still he endured it, holding the flame of the matches clumsily to the bark that would not light readily because his own burning hands were in the way, absorbing most of the flame.

At last, when he could endure no more, he jerked his hands apart. The blazing matches fell sizzling into the snow, but the birch-bark was alight. He began laying dry grasses and the tiniest twigs on the flame. He could not pick and choose, for he had to lift the fuel between the heels of his hands. Small pieces of rotten wood and green moss clung to the twigs, and he bit them off as well as he could with his teeth. He cherished the flame carefully and awkwardly. It meant life, and it must not perish. The withdrawal of blood from the surface of his body now made him begin to shiver, and he grew more awkward. A large piece of green moss fell squarely on the little fire. He tried to poke it out with his fingers, but his shivering frame made him poke too far, and he disrupted the nucleus of the little fire, the burning grasses and tiny twigs separating and scattering. He tried to poke them together again, but in spite of the tenseness of the effort, his shivering got away with him, and the twigs were hopelessly scattered. Each twig gushed a puff of smoke and went out. The fire-provider had failed. As he looked apathetically about him, his eyes chanced on the dog, sitting across the ruins of the fire from him, in the snow, making restless, hunching movements, slightly lifting one forefoot and then the other, shifting its weight back and forth on them with wistful eagerness.

The sight of the dog put a wild idea into his head. He remembered the tale of the man, caught in a blizzard, who killed a steer and crawled inside the carcass, and so was saved. He would kill the dog and bury his hands in the warm body until the numbness went out of them. Then he could build another fire. He spoke to the dog, calling it to him; but in his voice was a strange note of fear that frightened the animal, who had never known the man to speak in such way before. Something was the matter, and its suspicious nature sensed danger—it knew not what danger, but somewhere, somehow, in its brain arose an apprehension of the man. It flattened its ears down at the sound of the man's voice, and its restless, hunching movements and the liftings and shiftings of its forefeet became more pronounced; but it would not come to the man. He got on his hands and knees and crawled toward the dog. This unusual posture again excited suspicion, and the animal sidled mincingly away.

The man sat up in the snow for a moment and struggled for calmness. Then he pulled on his mittens, by means of his teeth, and got upon his feet. He glanced down at first in order to assure himself that he was really standing up, for the absence of sensation in his feet left him unrelated to the earth. His erect position in itself started to drive the webs of suspicion from the dog's mind; and when he spoke peremptorily, with the sound of whip-lashes in his voice, the dog rendered its customary allegiance and came to him. As it came within reaching distance, the man lost his control. His arms flashed out to the dog, and he experienced genuine surprise when he discovered that his hands could not clutch, that there was neither bend nor feeling in the fingers. He had forgotten for the moment that they were frozen and that they were freezing more and more. All this happened quickly, and before the animal could get away, he encircled its body with his arms. He sat down in the snow, and in this fashion held the dog, while it snarled and whined and struggled.

But it was all he could do, hold its body encircled in his arms and sit there. He realized that he could not kill the dog. There was no way to do it. With his helpless hands he could neither draw nor hold his sheath-knife nor throttle the animal. He released it, and it plunged wildly away, with tail between its legs, and still snarling. It halted forty feet away and surveyed him curiously, with ears sharply pricked forward. The man looked down at his hands in order to locate them, and found them hanging on the ends of his arms. It struck him as curious that one should have to use his eyes in order to find out where his hands were. He began threshing his arms back and forth, beating the mittened hands against his sides. He did this for five minutes, violently, and his heart pumped enough blood up to the surface to put a stop to his shivering. But no sensation was aroused in the hands. He had an impression that they hung like weights on the ends of his arms, but when he tried to run the impression down, he could not find it.

A certain fear of death, dull and oppressive, came to him. This fear quickly became poignant as he realized that it was no longer a mere matter of freezing his fingers and toes, or of losing his hands and feet, but that it was a matter of life and death with the chances against him. This threw him into a panic, and he turned and ran up the creek-bed along the old, dim trail. The dog joined in behind and kept up with him. He ran blindly, without inten-tion, in fear such as he had never known in his life. Slowly, as he ploughed and floundered through the snow, he began to see things again,—the banks of the creek, the old timber-jams, the leafless aspens, and the sky. The running made him feel better. He did not shiver. Maybe, if he ran on, his feet would thaw out; and, anyway, if he ran far enough, he would reach camp and the boys. Without doubt he would lose some fingers and toes and some of his face; but the boys would take care of him, and save the rest of him when he got there. And at the same time there was another thought in his mind that said he would never get to the camp and the boys; that it was too many miles away, that the freezing had too great a start on him, and that he would soon be stiff and dead. This thought he kept in the background and refused to consider. Sometimes it pushed itself forward and demanded to be heard, but he thrust it back and strove to think of other things.

It struck him as curious that he could run at all on feet so frozen that he could not feel them when they struck the earth and took the weight of his body. He seemed to himself to skim along above the surface, and to have no connection with the earth. Somewhere he had once seen a winged Mercury, and he wondered if Mercury felt as he felt when skimming over the earth.

His theory of running until he reached camp and the boys had one flaw in it: he lacked the endurance. Several times he stumbled, and finally he tottered, crumpled up, and fell. When he tried to rise, he failed. He must sit and rest, he decided, and next time he would merely walk and keep on going. As he sat and regained his breath, he noted that he was feeling quite warm and comfortable. He was not shivering, and it even seemed that a warm glow had come to his chest and trunk. And yet, when he touched his nose or cheeks, there was no sensation. Running would not thaw them out. Nor would it thaw out his hands and feet. Then the thought came to him that the frozen portions of his body must be extending. He tried to keep this thought down, to forget it, to think of something else; he was aware of the panicky feeling that it caused, and he was afraid of the panic. But the thought asserted itself, and persisted, until it produced a vision of his body totally frozen. This was too much, and he made another wild run along the trail. Once he slowed down to a walk, but the thought of the freezing extending itself made him run again.

And all the time the dog ran with him, at his heels. When he fell down a second time, it curled its tail over its forefeet and sat in front of him, facing him, curiously eager and intent. The warmth and security of the animal angered him, and he cursed it till it flattened down its ears appeasingly. This time the shivering came more quickly upon the man. He was losing in his battle with the frost. It was creeping into his body from all sides. The thought of it drove him on, but he ran no more than a hundred feet, when he staggered and pitched headlong. It was his last panic. When he had recovered his breath and control, he sat up and entertained in his mind the conception of meeting death with dignity. However, the conception did not come to him in such terms. His idea of it was that he had been making a fool of himself, running around like a chicken with its head cut off—such was the simile that occurred to him. Well, he was bound to freeze anyway, and he might as well take it decently. With this new-found peace of mind came the first glimmerings of drowsiness. A good idea, he thought, to sleep off to death. It was like taking an anæsthetic. Freezing was not so bad as people thought. There were lots worse ways to die.

He pictured the boys finding his body next day. Suddenly he found himself with them, coming along the trail and looking for himself. And, still with them, he came around a turn in the trail and found himself lying in the snow. He did not belong with himself any more, for even then he was out of himself, standing with the boys and looking at himself in the snow. It certainly was cold, was his thought. When he got back to the States he could tell the folks what real cold was. He drifted on from this to a vision of the old-timer on Sulphur Creek. He could see him quite clearly, warm and comfortable, and smoking a pipe.

"You were right, old hoss; you were right," the man mumbled to the old-timer of Sulphur Creek.

Then the man drowsed off into what seemed to him the most comfortable and satisfying sleep he had ever known. The dog sat facing him and waiting. The brief day drew to a close in a long, slow twilight. There were no signs of a fire to be made, and, besides, never in the dog's experience had it known a man to sit like that in the snow and make no fire. As the twilight drew on, its eager yearning for the fire mastered it, and with a great lifting and shifting of forefeet, it whined softly, then flattened its ears down in anticipation of being chidden by the man. But the man remained silent. Later, the dog whined loudly. And still later it crept close to the man and caught the scent of death. This made the animal bristle and back away. A little longer it delayed, howling under the stars that leaped and danced and shone brightly in the cold sky. Then it turned and trotted up the trail in the direction of the camp it knew, where were the other food-providers and fire-providers.

1908

RING LARDNER

Champion

MIDGE KELLY scored his first knockout when he was seventeen. The knockee was his brother Connie, three years his junior and a cripple. The purse was a half dollar given to the younger Kelly by a lady whose electric had just missed bumping his soul from his frail little body.

Connie did not know Midge was in the house, else he never would have risked laying the prize on the arm of the least comfortable chair in the room, the better to observe its shining beauty. As Midge entered from the kitchen, the crippled boy covered the coin with his hand, but the movement lacked the speed requisite to escape his brother's quick eye.

"Watcha got there?" demanded Midge.

"Nothin'," said Connie.

"You're a one-legged liar!" said Midge.

He strode over to his brother's chair and grasped the hand that concealed the coin.

"Let loose!" he ordered.

Connie began to cry.

"Let loose and shut up your noise," said the elder, and jerked his brother's hand from the chair arm.

The coin fell onto the bare floor. Midge pounced on it. His weak mouth widened in a triumphant smile.

"Nothin', huh?" he said. "All right, if it's nothin' you don't want it."

"Give that back," sobbed the younger.

"I'll give you a red nose, you little sneak! Where'd you steal it?"

"I didn't steal it. It's mine. A lady give it to me after she pretty near hit me with a car."

"It's a crime she missed you," said Midge.

Midge started for the front door. The cripple picked up his crutch, rose from his chair with difficulty, and, still sobbing, came toward Midge. The latter heard him and stopped.

"You better stay where you're at," he said.

"I want my money," cried the boy.

"I know what you want," said Midge.

Doubling up the fist that held the half dollar, he landed with all his strength on his brother's mouth. Connie fell to the floor with a thud, the crutch tumbling on top of him. Midge stood beside the prostrate form.

"Is that enough?" he said. "Or do you want this, too?"

And he kicked him in the crippled leg.

"I guess that'll hold you," he said.

There was no response from the boy on the floor. Midge looked at him a moment, then at the coin in his hand, and then went out into the street, whistling.

An hour later, when Mrs. Kelly came home from her day's work at Faulkner's Steam Laundry, she found Connie on the floor, moaning. Dropping on her knees beside him, she called him by name a score of times. Then she got up and, pale as a ghost, dashed from the house. Dr. Ryan left the Kelly abode about dusk and walked toward Halsted Street. Mrs. Dorgan spied him as he passed her gate.

"Who's sick, Doctor?" she called.

"Poor little Connie," he replied. "He had a bad fall."

"How did it happen?"

"I can't say for sure, Margaret, but I'd almost bet he was knocked down."

"Knocked down!" exclaimed Mrs. Dorgan. "Why, who—?"

"Have you seen the other one lately?"

"Michael? No, not since mornin'. You can't be thinkin'—"

"I wouldn't put it past him, Margaret," said the doctor gravely. "The lad's mouth is swollen and cut, and his poor, skinny little leg is bruised. He surely didn't do it to himself and I think Helen suspects the other one."

"Lord save us!" said Mrs. Dorgan. "I'll run over and see if I can help."

"That's a good woman," said Dr. Ryan, and went on down the street.

Near midnight, when Midge came home, his mother was sitting at Connie's bedside. She did not look up.

"Well," said Midge, "what's the matter?"

She remained silent. Midge repeated his question.

"Michael, you know what's the matter," she said at length.

"I don't know nothin'," said Midge.

"Don't lie to me, Michael. What did you do to your brother?"

"Nothin'."

"You hit him."

"Well, then, I hit him. What of it? It ain't the first time."

Her lips pressed tightly together, her face like chalk, Ellen Kelly rose from her chair and made straight for him. Midge backed against the door.

"Lay off'n me, Ma. I don't want to fight no woman."

Still she came on, breathing heavily.

"Stop where you're at, Ma," he warned.

There was a brief struggle and Midge's mother lay on the floor before him.

"You ain't hurt, Ma. You're lucky I didn't land good. And I told you to lay off'n me."

"God forgive you, Michael!"

Midge found Hap Collins in the showdown game at the Royal.

"Come on out a minute," he said.

Hap followed him out on the walk.

"I'm leavin' town for a w'ile," said Midge.

"What for?"

"Well, we had a little run-in up to the house. The kid stole a half buck off'n me, and when I went after it he cracked me with his crutch. So I nailed him. And the old lady came at me with a chair and I took it off'n her and she fell down."

"How is Connie hurt?"

"Not bad."

"What are you runnin' away for?"

"Who the hell said I was runnin' away? I'm sick and tired o' gettin' picked on; that's all. So I'm leavin' for a w'ile and I want a piece o' money."

"I ain't only got six bits," said Happy.

"You're in bad shape, ain't you? Well, come through with it." Happy came through.

"You oughtn't to hit the kid," he said.

"I ain't astin' you who can I hit," snarled Midge. "You try to put somethin' over on me and you'll get the same dose. I'm goin' now."

"Go as far as you like," said Happy, but not until he was sure that Kelly was out of hearing.

Early the following morning, Midge boarded a train for Milwaukee. He had no ticket, but no one knew the difference. The conductor remained in the caboose.

On a night six months later, Midge hurried out of the "stage door" of the Star Boxing Club and made for Duane's saloon, two blocks away. In his pocket were twelve dollars, his reward for having battered up one Demon Dempsey through the six rounds of the first preliminary.

It was Midge's first professional engagement in the manly art. Also it was the first time in weeks that he had earned twelve dollars.

On the way to Duane's he had to pass Niemann's. He pulled his cap over his eyes and increased his pace until he had gone by. Inside Niemann's stood a trusting bartender, who for ten days had staked Midge to drinks and allowed him to ravage the lunch on a promise to come in and settle the moment he was paid for the "prelim."

Midge strode into Duane's and aroused the napping bartender by slapping a silver dollar on the festive board.

"Gimme a shot," said Midge.

The shooting continued until the wind-up at the Star was over and part of the fight crowd joined Midge in front of Duane's bar. A youth in the early twenties, standing next to young Kelly, finally summoned sufficient courage to address him.

"Wasn't you in the first bout?" he ventured.

"Yeh," Midge replied.

"My name's Hersch," said the other. Midge received the startling information in silence.

"I don't want to butt in," continued Mr. Hersch, "but I'd like to buy you a drink."

"All right," said Midge, "but don't overstrain yourself."

Mr. Hersch laughed uproariously and beckoned to the bartender.

"You certainly gave that wop a trimmin' tonight," said the buyer of the drink, when they had been served. "I thought you'd kill him."

"I would if I hadn't let up," Midge replied. "I'll kill 'em all."

"You got the wallop all right," the other said admiringly.

"Have I got the wallop?" said Midge. "Say, I can kick like a mule. Did you notice them muscles in my shoulders?"

"Notice 'em? I couldn't help from noticin' 'em," said Hersch. "I says to the fella settin' alongside o' me, I says: 'Look at them shoulders! No wonder he can hit,' I says to him."

"Just let me land and it's good-by, baby," said Midge. "I'll kill 'em all."

The oral manslaughter continued until Duane's closed for the night. At parting, Midge and his new friend shook hands and arranged for a meeting the following evening.

For nearly a week the two were together almost constantly. It was Hersch's pleasant rôle to listen to Midge's modest revelations concerning himself, and to buy every time Midge's glass was empty. But there came an evening when Hersch regretfully announced that he must go home to supper.

"I got a date for eight bells," he confided. "I could stick till then, only I must clean up and put on the Sunday clo'es, 'cause she's the prettiest little thing in Milwaukee."

"Can't you fix it for two?" asked Midge.

"I don't know who to get," Hersch replied. "Wait, though. I got a sister and if she ain't busy, it'll be O. K. She's no bum for looks herself."

So it came about that Midge and Emma Hersch and Emma's brother and the prettiest little thing in Milwaukee foregathered at Wall's and danced half the night away. And Midge and Emma danced every dance together, for though every little onestep seemed to induce a new thirst of its own, Lou Hersch stayed too sober to dance with his own sister.

The next day, penniless at last in spite of his phenomenal ability to make someone else settle, Midge Kelly sought out Doc Hammond, matchmaker for the Star, and asked to be booked for the next show.

"I could put you on with Tracy for the next bout," said Doc.

"What's they in it?" asked Midge.

"Twenty if you cop," Doc told him.

"Have a heart," protested Midge. "Didn't I look good the other night?"

"You looked all right. But you aren't Freddie Welsh yet by a consid'able margin."

"I ain't scared of Freddie Welsh or none of 'em," said Midge.

"Well, we don't pay our boxers by the size of their chests," Doc said. "I'm offerin' you this Tracy bout. Take it or leave it."

"All right; I'm on," said Midge, and

he passed a pleasant afternoon at Duane's on the strength of his booking.

Young Tracy's manager came to Midge the night before the show.

"How do you feel about this go?" he asked.

"Me?" said Midge. "I feel all right. What do you mean, how do I feel?"

"I mean," said Tracy's manager, "that we're mighty anxious to win, 'cause the boy's got a chanct in Philly if he cops this one."

"What's your proposition?" asked Midge.

"Fifty bucks," said Tracy's manager.

"What do you think I am, a crook? Me lay down for fifty bucks. Not me!"

"Seventy-five, then," said Tracy's manager.

The market closed on eighty and the details were agreed on in short order. And the next night Midge was stopped in the second round by a terrific slap on the forearm.

This time Midge passed up both Niemann's and Duane's, having a sizable account at each place, and sought his refreshment at Stein's farther down the street.

When the profits of his deal with Tracy were gone, he learned, by first-hand information from Doc Hammond and the matchmakers at the other "clubs," that he was no longer desired for even the cheapest of preliminaries. There was no danger of his starving or dying of thirst while Emma and Lou Hersch lived. But he made up his mind, four months after his defeat by Young Tracy, that Milwaukee was not the ideal place for him to live.

"I can lick the best of 'em," he reasoned, "but there ain't no more chanct for me here. I can maybe go east and get on somewheres. And besides—"

But just after Midge had purchased a

ticket to Chicago with the money he had "borrowed" from Emma Hersch "to buy shoes," a heavy hand was laid on his shoulders and he turned to face two strangers.

"Where are you goin', Kelly?" inquired the owner of the heavy hand.

"Nowheres," said Midge. "What the hell do you care?"

The other stranger spoke:

"Kelly, I'm employed by Emma Hersch's mother to see that you do right by her. And we want you to stay here till you've done it."

"You won't get nothin' but the worst of it, monkeying with me," said Midge.

Nevertheless, he did not depart for Chicago that night. Two days later, Emma Hersch became Mrs. Kelly, and the gift of the groom, when once they were alone, was a crushing blow on the bride's pale cheek.

Next morning, Midge left Milwaukee as he had entered it—by fast freight.

"They's no use kiddin' ourself any more," said Tommy Haley. "He might get down to thirty-seven in a pinch, but if he done below that a mouse could stop him. He's a welter; that's what he is and he knows it as well as I do. He's growed like a weed in the last six mont's. I told him, I says, 'If you don't quit growin' they won't be nobody for you to box, only Willard and them.' He says, 'Well, I wouldn't run away from Willard if I weighed twenty pounds more.'"

"He must hate himself," said Tommy's brother.

"I never seen a good one that didn't," said Tommy. "And Midge is a good one; don't make no mistake about that. I wisht we could of got Welsh before the kid growed so big. But it's too late now. I won't make no holler, though,

if we can match him up with the Dutchman."

"Who do you mean?"

"Young Goetz, the welter champ. We mightn't not get so much dough for the bout itself, but it'd roll in afterward. What a drawin' card we'd be, 'cause the people pays their money to see the fella with the wallop, and that's Midge. And we'd keep the title just as long as Midge could make the weight."

"Can't you land no match with Goetz?"

"Sure, 'cause he needs the money. But I've went careful with the kid so far and look at the results I got! So what's the use of takin' a chanct? The kid's comin' every minute and Goetz is goin' back faster'n big Johnson did. I think we could lick him now; I'd bet my life on it. But six mont's from now they won't be no risk. He'll of licked hisself before that time. Then all as we'll have to do is sign up with him and wait for the referee to stop it. But Midge is so crazy to get at him now that I can't hardly hold him back."

The brothers Haley were lunching in a Boston hotel. Dan had come down from Holyoke to visit with Tommy and to watch the latter's protégé go twelve rounds, or less, with Bud Cross. The bout promised little in the way of a contest, for Midge had twice stopped the Baltimore youth and Bud's reputation for gameness was all that had earned him the date. The fans were willing to pay the price to see Midge's hay-making left, but they wanted to see it used on an opponent who would not jump out of the ring the first time he felt its crushing force. But Cross was such an opponent, and his willingness to stop boxing-gloves with his eyes, ears, nose and throat had long enabled him to escape the horrors of honest labor. A game boy was Bud, and he showed it in his battered, swollen, discolored face.

"I should think," said Dan Haley, "that the kid'd do whatever you tell him after all you done for him."

"Well," said Tommy, "he's took my dope pretty straight so far, but he's so sure of hisself that he can't see no reason for waitin'. He'll do what I say, though; he'd be a sucker not to."

"You got a contrac' with him?"

"No, I don't need no contrac'. He knows it was me that drug him out o' the gutter and he ain't goin' to turn me down now, when he's got the dough and bound to get more. Where'd he of been at if I hadn't listened to him when he first come to me? That's pretty near two years ago now, but it seems like last week. I was settin' in the s'loon acrost from the Pleasant Club in Philly, waitin' for McCann to count the dough and come over, when this little bum blowed in and tried to stand the house off for a drink. They told him nothin' doin' and to beat it out o' there, and then he seen me and come over to where I was settin' and ast me wasn't I a boxin' man and I told him who I was. Then he ast me for money to buy a shot and I told him to set down and I'd buy it for him.

"Then we got talkin' things over and he told me his name and told me about fightn' a couple o' prelims out to Milwaukee. So I says, 'Well, boy, I don't know how good or how rotten you are, but you won't never get nowheres trainin' on that stuff.' So he says he'd cut it out if he could get on in a bout and I says I would give him a chanct if he played square with me and didn't touch no more to drink. So we shook hands and I took him up to the hotel with me and give him a bath and the next day I bought him some clo'es. And I staked him to eats and sleeps for

over six weeks. He had a hard time breakin' away from the polish, but finally I thought he was fit and I give him his chanct. He went on with Smiley Sayer and stopped him so quick that Smiley thought sure he was poisoned.

"Well, you know what he's did since. The only beatin' in his record was by Tracy in Milwaukee before I got hold of him, and he's licked Tracy three times in the last year.

"I've gave him all the best of it in a money way and he's got seven thousand bucks in cold storage. How's that for a kid that was in the gutter two years ago? And he'd have still more yet if he wasn't so nuts over clo'es and got to stop at the good hotels and so forth."

"Where's his home at?"

"Well, he ain't really got no home. He came from Chicago and his mother canned him out o' the house for bein' no good. She give him a raw deal, I guess, and he says he won't have nothin' to do with her unlest she comes to him first. She's got a pile o' money, he says, so he ain't worryin' about her."

The gentleman under discussion entered the café and swaggered to Tommy's table, while the whole room turned to look.

Midge was the picture of health despite a slightly colored eye and an ear that seemed to have no opening. But perhaps it was not his healthiness that drew all eyes. His diamond horse-shoe tie pin, his purple cross-striped shirt, his orange shoes and his light blue suit fairly screamed for attention.

"Where you been?" he asked Tommy. "I been lookin' all over for you."

"Set down," said his manager.

"No time," said Midge. "I'm goin' down to the w'arf and see 'em unload the fish."

"Shake hands with my brother Dan," said Tommy.

Midge shook with the Holyoke Haley.

"If you're Tommy's brother, you're O. K. with me," said Midge, and the brothers beamed with pleasure.

Dan moistened his lips and murmured an embarrassed reply, but it was lost on the young gladiator.

"Leave me take twenty," Midge was saying. "I prob'ly won't need it, but I don't like to be caught short."

Tommy parted with a twenty dollar bill and recorded the transaction in a small black book the insurance company had given him for Christmas.

"But," he said, "it won't cost you no twenty to look at them fish. Want me to go along?"

"No," said Midge hastily. "You and your brother here prob'ly got a lot to say to each other."

"Well," said Tommy, "don't take no bad money and don't get lost. And you better be back at four o'clock and lay down a w'ile."

"I don't need no rest to beat this guy," said Midge. "He'll do enough layin' down for the both of us."

And laughing even more than the jest called for, he strode out through the fire of admiring and startled glances.

The corner of Boylston and Tremont was the nearest Midge got to the wharf, but the lady awaiting him was doubtless a more dazzling sight than the catch of the luckiest Massachusetts fisherman. She could talk, too—probably better than the fish.

"O you Kid!" she said, flashing a few silver teeth among the gold. "O you fighting man!"

Midge smiled up at her.

"We'll go somewheres and get a drink," he said. "One won't hurt."

In New Orleans, five months after he had rearranged the map of Bud Cross for the third time, Midge finished training for his championship bout with the Dutchman.

Back in his hotel after the final workout, Midge stopped to chat with some of the boys from up north, who had made the long trip to see a champion dethroned, for the result of this bout was so nearly a foregone conclusion that even the experts had guessed it.

Tommy Haley secured the key and the mail and ascended to the Kelly suite. He was bathing when Midge came in, half an hour later.

"Any mail?" asked Midge.

"There on the bed," replied Tommy from the tub.

Midge picked up the stack of letters and postcards and glanced them over. From the pile he sorted out three letters and laid them on the table. The rest he tossed into the waste-basket. Then he picked up the three and sat for a few moments holding them, while his eyes gazed off into space. At length he looked again at the three unopened letters in his hand; then he put one in his pocket and tossed the other two at the basket. They missed their target and fell on the floor.

"Hell!" said Midge, and stooping over picked them up.

He opened one postmarked Milwaukee and read:

Dear Husband:

I have wrote to you so manny times and got no anser and I dont know if you ever got them, so I am writeing again in the hopes you will get this letter and anser. I dont like to bother you with my trubles and I would not only for the baby and I am not asking you should write to me but only send a little money and I am not asking for myself but the baby has not been well a day sence last Aug. and the dr. told me she cant live much longer unless I give her better food and thats impossible the way things are. Lou has not been working for a year and what I make dont hardley pay for the rent. I am not asking for you to give me any money, but only you should send what I loaned when convenient and I think it amts. to about $36.00. Please try and send that amt. and it will help me, but if you cant send the whole amt. try and send me something.

Your wife,
Emma.

Midge tore the letter into a hundred pieces and scattered them over the floor.

"Money, money, money!" he said. "They must think I'm made o' money. I s'pose the old woman's after it too."

He opened his mother's letter:

dear Michael Connie wonted me to rite and say you must beet the dutchman and he is sur you will and wonted me to say we wont you to rite and tell us about it, but I gess you havent no time to rite or we herd from you long beffore this but I wish you would rite jest a line or 2 boy becaus it wuld be better for Connie then a barl of medisin. It wuld help me to keep things going if you send me money now and then when you can spair it but if you cant send no money try and fine time to rite a letter onley a few lines and it will please Connie, jest think boy he hasent got out of bed in over 3 yrs. Connie says good luck.

Your Mother,
Ellen F. Kelly.

"I thought so," said Midge. "They're all alike."

The third letter was from New York. It read:

Hon:—This is the last letter you will get from me before your champ, but I will send you a telegram Saturday, but I can't say as much in a telegram as in a letter and I am writeing this to let you know I am thinking of you and praying for good luck.

Lick him good hon and don't wait no longer than you have to and don't forget to wire me as soon as its over. Give him that little old left of yours on the nose hon and don't be afraid of spoiling his good looks because he couldn't be no homlier than he is. But don't let him spoil my baby's pretty face. You won't will you hon.

Well hon I would give anything to be there and see it, but I guess you love Haley better than me or you wouldn't let him keep me away. But when your champ hon we can do as we please and tell Haley to go to the devil.

Well hon I will send you a telegram Saturday and I almost forgot to tell you I will need some more money, a couple hundred say and you will have to wire it to me as soon as you get this. You will won't you hon.

I will send you a telegram Saturday and remember hon I am pulling for you.

Well good-by sweetheart and good luck.

Grace.

"They're all alike," said Midge. "Money, money, money."

Tommy Haley, shining from his ablutions, came in from the adjoining room.

"Thought you'd be layin' down," he said.

"I'm goin' to," said Midge, unbuttoning his orange shoes.

"I'll call you at six and you can eat up here without no bugs to pester you. I got to go down and give them birds their tickets."

"Did you hear from Goldberg?" asked Midge.

"Didn't I tell you? Sure; fifteen weeks at five hundred, if we win. And we can get a guarantee o' twelve thousand, with privileges either in New York or Milwaukee."

"Who with?"

"Anybody that'll stand up in front of you. You don't care who it is, do you?"

"Not me. I'll make 'em all look like a monkey."

"Well you better lay down aw'ile."

"Oh, say, wire two hundred to Grace for me, will you? Right away; the New York address."

"Two hundred! You just sent her three hundred last Sunday."

"Well, what the hell do you care?"

"All right, all right. Don't get sore about it. Anything else?"

"That's all," said Midge, and dropped onto the bed.

"And I want the deed done before I come back," said Grace as she rose from the table. "You won't fall down on me, will you, hon?"

"Leave it to me," said Midge. "And don't spend no more than you have to."

Grace smiled a farewell and left the café. Midge continued to sip his coffee and read his paper.

They were in Chicago and they were in the middle of Midge's first week in vaudeville. He had come straight north to reap the rewards of his glorious victory over the broken down Dutchman. A fortnight had been spent in learning his act, which consisted of a gymnastic exhibition and a ten minutes' monologue on the various excellences of Midge Kelly. And now he was twice daily turning 'em away from the Madison Theater.

His breakfast over and his paper read, Midge sauntered into the lobby and asked for his key. He then beckoned to a bell-boy, who had been hoping for that very honor.

"Find Haley, Tommy Haley," said Midge. "Tell him to come up to my room."

"Yes, sir, Mr. Kelly," said the boy, and proceeded to break all his former records for diligence.

Midge was looking out of his seventh-story window when Tommy answered the summons.

"What'll it be?" inquired his manager.

There was a pause before Midge replied.

"Haley," he said, "twenty-five per cent's a whole lot o' money."

"I guess I got it comin', ain't I?" said Tommy.

"I don't see how you figger it. I don't see where you're worth it to me."

"Well," said Tommy, "I didn't expect nothin' like this. I thought you was satisfied with the bargain. I don't want to beat nobody out o' nothin', but I don't see where you could have got anybody else that would of did all I done for you."

"Sure, that's all right," said the champion. "You done a lot for me in Philly. And you got good money for it, didn't you?"

"I ain't makin' no holler. Still and all, the big money's still ahead of us yet. And if it hadn't of been for me, you wouldn't of never got within grabbin' distance."

"Oh, I guess I could of went along all right," said Midge. "Who was it that hung that left on the Dutchman's jaw, me or you?"

"Yes, but you wouldn't been in the ring with the Dutchman if it wasn't for how I handled you."

"Well, this won't get us nowheres. The idear is that you ain't worth no twenty-five per cent now and it don't make no diff'rence what come off a year or two ago."

"Don't it?" said Tommy. "I'd say it made a whole lot of difference."

"Well, I say it don't and I guess that settles it."

"Look here, Midge," Tommy said, "I thought I was fair with you, but if you don't think so, I'm willin' to hear what you think is fair. I don't want nobody callin' me a Sherlock. Let's go down to business and sign up a contrac'. What's your figger?"

"I ain't namin' no figger," Midge replied. "I'm sayin' that twenty-five's too much. Now what are you willin' to take?"

"How about twenty?"

"Twenty's too much," said Kelly.

"What ain't too much?" asked Tommy.

"Well, Haley, I might as well give it to you straight. They ain't nothin' that ain't too much."

"You mean you don't want me at no figger?"

"That's the idear."

There was a minute's silence. Then Tommy Haley walked toward the door.

"Midge," he said, in a choking voice, "you're makin' a big mistake, boy. You can't throw down your best friends and get away with it. That damn woman will ruin you."

Midge sprang from his seat.

"You shut your mouth!" he stormed. "Get out o' here before they have to carry you out. You been spongin' off o' me long enough. Say one more word about the girl or about anything else and you'll get what the Dutchman got. Now get out!"

And Tommy Haley, having a very vivid memory of the Dutchman's face as he fell, got out.

Grace came in later, dropped her numerous bundles on the lounge and perched herself on the arm of Midge's chair.

"Well?" she said.

"Well," said Midge, "I got rid of him."

"Good boy!" said Grace. "And now I think you might give me that twenty-five per cent."

"Besides the seventy-five you're already gettin'?" said Midge.

"Don't be no grouch, hon. You don't look pretty when you're grouchy."

"It ain't my business to look pretty," Midge replied.

"Wait till you see how I look with the stuff I bought this mornin'!"

Midge glanced at the bundles on the lounge.

"There's Haley's twenty-five per cent," he said, "and then some."

The champion did not remain long without a manager. Haley's successor was none other than Jerome Harris, who saw in Midge a better meal ticket than his popular-priced musical show had been.

The contract, giving Mr. Harris twenty-five per cent of Midge's earnings, was signed in Detroit the week after Tommy Haley had heard his dismissal read. It had taken Midge just six days to learn that a popular actor cannot get on without the ministrations of a man who thinks, talks and means business. At first Grace objected to the new member of the firm, but when Mr. Harris had demanded and secured from the vaudeville people a one-hundred dollar increase in Midge's weekly stipend, she was convinced that the champion had acted for the best.

"You and my missus will have some great old times," Harris told Grace. "I'd of wired her to join us here, only I seen the Kid's bookin' takes us to Milwaukee next week, and that's where she is."

But when they were introduced in the

Milwaukee hotel, Grace admitted to herself that her feeling for Mrs. Harris could hardly be called love at first sight. Midge, on the contrary, gave his new manager's wife the many times over and seemed loath to end the feast of his eyes.

"Some doll," he said to Grace when they were alone.

"Doll is right," the lady replied, "and sawdust where her brains ought to be."

"I'm li'ble to steal that baby," said Midge, and he smiled as he noted the effect of his words on his audience's face.

On Tuesday of the Milwaukee week the champion successfully defended his title in a bout that the newspapers never reported. Midge was alone in his room that morning when a visitor entered without knocking. The visitor was Lou Hersch.

Midge turned white at sight of him.

"What do you want?" he demanded.

"I guess you know," said Lou Hersch. "Your wife's starvin' to death and your baby's starvin' to death and I'm starvin' to death. And you're dirty with money."

"Listen," said Midge, "if it wasn't for you, I wouldn't never saw your sister. And, if you ain't man enough to hold a job, what's that to me? The best thing you can do is keep away from me."

"You give me a piece o' money and I'll go."

Midge's reply to the ultimatum was a straight right to his brother-in-law's narrow chest.

"Take that home to your sister."

And after Lou Hersch had picked himself up and slunk away, Midge thought: "It's lucky I didn't give him my left or I'd of croaked him. And if I'd hit him in the stomach, I'd of broke his spine."

There was a party after each evening performance during the Milwaukee engagement. The wine flowed freely and Midge had more of it than Tommy Haley ever would have permitted him. Mr. Harris offered no objection, which was possibly just as well for his own physical comfort.

In the dancing between drinks, Midge had his new manager's wife for a partner as often as Grace. The latter's face as she floundered round in the arms of the portly Harris, belied her frequent protestations that she was having the time of her life.

Several times that week, Midge thought Grace was on the point of starting the quarrel he hoped to have. But it was not until Friday night that she accommodated. He and Mrs. Harris had disappeared after the matinee and when Grace saw him again at the close of the night show, she came to the point at once.

"What are you tryin' to pull off?" she demanded.

"It's none o' your business, is it?" said Midge.

"You bet it's my business; mine and Harris's. You cut it short or you'll find out."

"Listen," said Midge, "have you got a mortgage on me or somethin'? You talk like we was married."

"We're goin' to be, too. And to-morrow's as good a time as any."

"Just about," Midge said. "You got as much chanct o' marryin' me to-morrow as the next day or next year and that ain't no chanct at all."

"We'll find out," said Grace.

"You're the one that's got somethin' to find out."

"What do you mean?"

"I mean I'm married already."

"You lie!"

"You think so, do you? Well, s'pose

you go to this here address and get acquainted with my missus."

Midge scrawled a number on a piece of paper and handed it to her. She stared at it unseeingly.

"Well," said Midge, "I ain't kiddin' you. You go there and ask for Mrs. Michael Kelly, and if you don't find her, I'll marry you to-morrow before breakfast."

Still Grace stared at the scrap of paper. To Midge it seemed an age before she spoke again.

"You lied to me all this w'ile."

"You never ast me was I married. What's more, what the hell diff'rence did it make to you? You got a split, didn't you? Better'n fifty-fifty."

He started away.

"Where you goin'?"

"I'm goin' to meet Harris and his wife."

"I'm goin' with you. You're not goin' to shake me now."

"Yes, I am, too," said Midge quietly. "When I leave town to-morrow night, you're going to stay here. And if I see where you're going to make a fuss, I'll put you in a hospital where they'll keep you quiet. You can get your stuff to-morrow mornin' and I'll slip you a hundred bucks. And then I don't want to see no more o' you. And don't try and tag along now or I'll have to add another K.O. to the old record."

When Grace returned to the hotel that night, she discovered that Midge and the Harrises had moved to another. And when Midge left town the following night, he was again without a manager, and Mr. Harris was without a wife.

Three days prior to Midge Kelly's ten-round bout with Young Milton in New York City, the sporting editor of *The News* assigned Joe Morgan to write two or three thousand words about the champion to run with a picture lay-out for Sunday.

Joe Morgan dropped in at Midge's training quarters Friday afternoon. Midge, he learned, was doing road work, but Midge's manager, Wallie Adams, stood ready and willing to supply reams of dope about the greatest fighter of the age.

"Let's hear what you've got," said Joe, "and then I'll try to fix up something."

So Wallie stepped on the accelerator of his imagination and shot away.

"Just a kid; that's all he is; a regular boy. Get what I mean? Don't know the meanin' o' bad habits. Never tasted liquor in his life and would prob'bly get sick if he smelled it. Clean livin' put him up where he's at. Get what I mean? And modest and unassumin' as a school girl. He's so quiet you wouldn't never know he was round. And he'd go to jail before he'd talk about himself.

"No job at all to get him in shape, 'cause he's always that way. The only trouble we have with him is gettin' him to light into these poor bums they match him up with. He's scared he'll hurt somebody. Get what I mean? He's tickled to death over this match with Milton, 'cause everybody says Milton can stand the gaff. Midge'll maybe be able to cut loose a little this time. But the last two bouts he had, the guys hadn't no business in the ring with him, and he was holdin' back all the w'ile for the fear he'd kill somebody. Get what I mean?"

"Is he married?" inquired Joe.

"Say, you'd think he was married to hear him rave about them kiddies he's got. His fam'ly's up in Canada to their summer home and Midge is wild to get

up there with 'em. He thinks more o'
that wife and them kiddies than all the
money in the world. Get what I mean?"

"How many children has he?"

"I don't know, four or five, I guess.
All boys and every one of 'em a dead
ringer for their dad."

"Is his father living?"

"No, the old man died when he was
a kid. But he's got a grand old mother
and a kid brother out in Chi. They're
the first ones he thinks about after a
match, them and his wife and kiddies.
And he don't forget to send the old
woman a thousand bucks after every
bout. He's goin' to buy her a new
home as soon as they pay him off for this
match."

"How about his brother? Is he going
to tackle the game?"

"Sure, and Midge says he'll be a champion before he's twenty years old.
They're a fightin' fam'ly and all of 'em
honest and straight as a die. Get what
I mean? A fella that I can't tell you
his name come to Midge in Milwaukee
onct and wanted him to throw a fight
and Midge give him such a trimmin' in
the street that he couldn't go on that
night. That's the kind he is. Get what
I mean?"

Joe Morgan hung around the camp
until Midge and his trainers returned.

"One o' the boys from *The News*,"
said Wallie by way of introduction. "I
been givin' him your fam'ly hist'ry."

"Did he give you good dope?" he inquired.

"He's some historian," said Joe.

"Don't call me no names," said Wallie
smiling. "Call us up if they's anything
more you want. And keep your eyes on
us Monday night. Get what I mean?"

The story in Sunday's *News* was read
by thousands of lovers of the manly art.
It was well written and full of human
interest. Its slight inaccuracies went
unchallenged, though three readers, besides Wallie Adams and Midge Kelly,
saw and recognized them. The three
were Grace, Tommy Haley and Jerome
Harris and the comments they made
were not for publication.

Neither the Mrs. Kelly in Chicago nor
the Mrs. Kelly in Milwaukee knew that
there was such a paper as the New York
News. And even if they had known of
it and that it contained two columns of
reading matter about Midge, neither
mother nor wife could have bought it.
For *The News* on Sunday is a nickel a
copy.

Joe Morgan could have written more
accurately, no doubt, if instead of Wallie
Adams, he had interviewed Ellen Kelly
and Connie Kelly and Emma Kelly and
Lou Hersch and Grace and Jerome Harris and Tommy Haley and Hap Collins
and two or three Milwaukee bartenders.

But a story built on their evidence
would never have passed the sporting
editor.

"Suppose you can prove it," that gentleman would have said. "It wouldn't
get us anything but abuse to print it.
The people don't want to see him
knocked. He's champion."

1929

WALTER D. EDMONDS

Death of Red Peril

JOHN BROUGHT his off eye to bear on me:—

What do them old coots down to the store do? Why, one of 'em will think up a horse that's been dead forty year and then they'll set around remembering this and that about that horse until they've made a resurrection of him. You'd think he was a regular Grattan Bars, the way they talk, telling one thing and another, when a man knows if that horse hadn't 've had a breeching to keep his tail end off the ground he could hardly have walked from here to Boonville.

A horse race is a handsome thing to watch if a man has his money on a sure proposition. My pa was always a great hand at a horse race. But when he took to a boat and my mother he didn't have no more time for it. So he got interested in another sport.

Did you ever hear of racing caterpillars? No? Well, it used to be a great thing on the canawl. My pa used to have a lot of them insects on hand every fall, and the way he could get them to run would make a man have his eyes examined.

The way we raced caterpillars was to set them in a napkin ring on a table, one facing one way and one the other. Outside the napkin ring was drawed a circle in chalk three feet acrost. Then a man lifted the ring and the handlers was allowed one jab with a darning needle to get their caterpillars started. The one that got outside the chalk circle the first was the one that won the race.

I remember my pa tried out a lot of breeds, and he got hold of some pretty fast steppers. But there wasn't one of them could equal Red Peril. To see him, you wouldn't believe he could run. He was all red and kind of stubby, and he had a sort of a wart behind that you'd think would get in his way. There wasn't anything fancy in his looks. He'd just set still studying the ground and make you think he was dreaming about last year's oats; but when you set him in the starting ring he'd hitch himself up behind like a man lifting on his galluses, and then he'd light out for glory.

Pa come acrost Red Peril down in Westernville. Ma's relatives resided there, and it being Sunday we'd all gone in to church. We was riding back in a hired rig with a dandy trotter, and Pa was pushing her right along and Ma was talking sermon and clothes, and me and my sister was setting on the back seat playing poke your nose, when all of a sudden Pa hollers, "Whoa!" and set the horse right down on the breeching. Ma let out a holler and come to rest on the dashboard with her head under the horse. "My gracious land!" she says. "What's happened?" Pa was out on the other side of the road right down in the mud in his Sunday pants, a-wropping up something in his yeller handkerchief. Ma begun to get riled.

"What you doing, Pa?" she says. "What you got there?" Pa was putting his handkerchief back into his inside pocket. Then he come back over the wheel and got him a chew. "Leeza," he says, "I got the fastest caterpillar in seven counties. It's an act of Providence I seen him, the way he jumped the ruts." "It's an act of God I ain't laying dead under the back end of that horse," says Ma. "I've gone and spoilt my Sunday hat." "Never mind," says Pa; "Red Peril will earn you a new one." Just like that he named him. He was the fastest caterpillar in seven counties.

When we got back onto the boat, while Ma was turning up the supper, Pa set him down to the table under the lamp and pulled out the handkerchief. "You two devils stand there and there," he says to me and my sister, "and if you let him get by I'll leather the soap out of you."

So we stood there and he undid the handkerchief, and out walked one of them red, long-haired caterpillars. He walked right to the middle of the table, and then he took a short turn and put his nose in his tail and went to sleep.

"Who'd think that insect could make such a break for freedom as I seen him make?" says Pa, and he got out a empty Brandreth box and filled it up with some towel and put the caterpillar inside. "He needs a rest," says Pa. "He needs to get used to his stall. When he limbers up I'll commence training him. Now then," he says, putting the box on the shelf back of the stove, "don't none of you say a word about him."

He got out a pipe and set there smoking and figuring, and we could see he was studying out just how he'd make a world-beater out of that bug. "What you going to feed him?" asks Ma. "If I wasn't afraid of constipating him," Pa says, "I'd try him out with milkweed."

Next day we hauled up the Lansing Kill Gorge. Ned Kilbourne, Pa's driver, come aboard in the morning, and he took a look at that caterpillar. He took him out of the box and felt his legs and laid him down on the table and went clean over him. "Well," he says, "he don't look like a great lot, but I've knowed some of that red variety could chug along pretty smart." Then he touched him with a pin. It was a sudden sight.

It looked like the rear end of that caterpillar was racing the front end, but it couldn't never quite get by. Afore either Ned or Pa could get a move Red Peril had made a turn around the sugar bowl and run solid aground in the butter dish.

Pa let out a loud swear. "Look out he don't pull a tendon," he says. "Butter's a bad thing. A man has to be careful. Jeepers," he says, picking him up and taking him over to the stove to dry, "I'll handle him myself. I don't want no rum-soaked bezabors dishing my beans."

"I didn't mean harm, Will," says Ned. "I was just curious."

There was something extraordinary about that caterpillar. He was intelligent. It seemed he just couldn't abide the feel of sharp iron. It got so that if Pa reached for the lapel of his coat Red Peril would light out. It must have been he was tender. I said he had a sort of a wart behind, and I guess he liked to find it a place of safety.

We was all terrible proud of that bird. Pa took to timing him on the track. He beat all known time holler. He got to know that as soon as he crossed the chalk he would get back safe in his quarters. Only when we tried sprinting him across the supper table, if he saw a piece of butter he'd pull up short and bolt back where he come from. He had a mortal fear of butter.

Well, Pa trained him three nights. It was a sight to see him there at the table, a big man with a needle in his hand, moving the lamp around and studying out the identical spot that caterpillar wanted most to get out of the needle's way. Pretty soon he found it, and then he says to Ned, "I'll race him agin all comers at all odds." "Well, Will," says Ned, "I guess it's a safe proposition."

II

We hauled up the feeder to Forestport and got us a load of potatoes. We raced him there against Charley Mack, the bank-walker's, Leopard Pillar, one of them tufted breeds with a row of black buttons down the back. The Leopard was well liked and had won several races that season, and there was quite a few boaters around that fancied him. Pa argued for favorable odds, saying he was racing a maiden caterpillar; and there was a lot of money laid out, and Pa and Ned managed to cover the most of it. As for the race, there wasn't anything to it. While we was putting him in the ring—one of them birchbark and sweet grass ones Indians make—Red Peril didn't act very good. I guess the smell and the crowd kind of upset him. He was nervous and kept fidgeting with his front feet; but they hadn't more'n lifted the ring than he lit out under the edge as tight as he could make it, and Pa touched him with the needle just as he lepped the line. Me and my sister was supposed to be in bed, but Ma had gone visiting in Forestport and we'd snuck in and was under the table, which had a red cloth onto it, and I can tell you there was some shouting. There

was some couldn't believe that insect had been inside the ring at all; and there was some said he must be a cross with a dragon fly or a side-hill gouger; but old Charley Mack, that'd worked in the camps, said he guessed Red Peril must be descended from the caterpillars Paul Bunyan used to race. He said you could tell by the bump on his tail, which Paul used to put on all his caterpillars, seeing as how the smallest pointed object he could hold in his hand was a peavy.

Well, Pa raced him a couple of more times and he won just as easy, and Pa cleared up close to a hundred dollars in three races. That caterpillar was a mammoth wonder, and word of him got going and people commenced talking him up everywhere, so it was hard to race him around these parts.

But about that time the lock keeper of Number One on the feeder come across a pretty swift article that the people round Rome thought high of. And as our boat was headed down the gorge, word got ahead about Red Peril, and people began to look out for the race.

We come into Number One about four o'clock, and Pa tied up right there and went on shore with his box in his pocket and Red Peril inside the box. There must have been ten men crowded into the shanty, and as many more again outside looking in the windows and door. The lock tender was a skinny bezabor from Stittville, who thought he knew a lot about racing caterpillars; and, come to think of it, maybe he did. His name was Henry Buscerck, and he had a bad tooth in front he used to suck at a lot.

Well, him and Pa set their caterpillars on the table for the crowd to see, and I must say Buscerck's caterpillar was as handsome a brute as you could wish to look at, bright bay with black points and a short fine coat. He had a way of looking right and left, too, that made him handsome. But Pa didn't bother to look at him. Red Peril was a natural marvel, and he knew it.

Buscerck was a sly, twirpish man, and he must've heard about Red Peril—right from the beginning, as it turned out; for he laid out the course in yeller chalk. They used Pa's ring, a big silver one he'd bought secondhand just for Red Peril. They laid out a lot of money, and Dennison Smith lifted the ring. The way Red Peril histed himself out from under would raise a man's blood pressure twenty notches. I swear you could see the hair lay down on his back. Why, that black-pointed bay was left nowhere! It didn't seem like he moved. But Red Peril was just gathering himself for a fast finish over the line when he seen it was yeller. He reared right up; he must've thought it was butter, by Jeepers, the way he whirled on his hind legs and went the way he'd come. Pa begun to get scared, and he shook his needle behind Red Peril, but that caterpillar was more scared of butter than he ever was of cold steel. He passed the other insect afore he'd got halfway to the line. By Cripus, you'd ought to 've heard the cheering from the Forestport crews. The Rome men was green. But when he got to the line, danged if that caterpillar didn't shy agin and run around the circle twicet, and then it seemed like his heart had gone in on him, and he crept right back to the middle of the circle and lay there hiding his head. It was the pitifullest sight a man ever looked at. You could almost hear him moaning, and he shook all over.

I've never seen a man so riled as Pa was. The water was running right out of his eyes. He picked up Red Peril and he says, "This here's no race." He picked up his money and he says, "The course was illegal, with that yeller chalk." Then he squashed the other caterpillar, which was just getting ready to cross the line, and he looks at Buscerck and says, "What're you going to do about that?"

Buscerck says, "I'm going to collect my money. My caterpillar would have beat."

"If you want to call that a finish you can," says Pa, pointing to the squashed bay one, "but a baby could see he's still got to reach the line. Red Peril got to wire and come back and got to it again afore your hayseed worm got half his feet on the ground. If it was any other man owned him," Pa says, "I'd feel sorry I squashed him."

He stepped out of the house, but Buscerck laid a-hold of his pants and says, "You got to pay, Hemstreet. A man can't get away with no such excuses in the city of Rome."

Pa didn't say nothing. He just hauled off and sunk his fist, and Buscerck come to inside the lock, which was at low level right then. He waded out the lower end and he says, "I'll have you arrested for this." Pa says, "All right; but if I ever catch you around this lock again I'll let you have a feel with your other eye."

Nobody else wanted to collect money from Pa, on account of his build, mostly, so we went back to the boat. Pa put Red Peril to bed for two days. It took him all of that to get over his fright at the yeller circle. Pa even made us go without butter for a spell, thinking Red Peril might know the smell of it. He was such an intelligent, thinking animal, a man couldn't tell nothing about him.

III

But next morning the sheriff comes aboard and arrests Pa with a warrant and takes him afore a justice of the peace. That was old Oscar Snipe. He'd heard all about the race, and I think he was feeling pleasant with Pa, because right off they commenced talking breeds. It would have gone off good only Pa'd been having a round with the sheriff. They come in arm in arm, singing a Hallelujah meeting song; but Pa was polite, and when Oscar says, "What's this?" he only says, "Well, well."

"I hear you've got a good caterpillar," says the judge.

"Well, well," says Pa. It was all he could think of to say.

"What breed is he?" says Oscar, taking a chew.

"Well," says Pa, "well, well."

Ned Kilbourne says he was a red one.

"That's a good breed," says Oscar, folding his hands on his stummick and spitting over his thumbs and between his knees and into the sandbox all in one spit. "I kind of fancy the yeller ones myself. You're a connesewer," he says to Pa, "and so'm I, and between connesewers I'd like to show you one. He's as neat a stepper as there is in this county."

"Well, well," says Pa, kind of cold around the eyes and looking at the lithograph of Mrs. Snipe done in a hair frame over the sink.

Oscar slews around and fetches a box out of his back pocket and shows us a sweet little yeller one.

"There she is," he says, and waits for praise.

"She was a good woman," Pa said after a while, looking at the picture, "if any woman that's four times a widow can be called such."

"Not her," says Oscar. "It's this yeller caterpillar."

Pa slung his eyes on the insect which Oscar was holding, and it seemed like he'd just got an idea.

"Fast?" he says, deep down. "That thing run! Why, a snail with the stringhalt could spit in his eye."

Old Oscar come to a boil quick.

"Evidence. Bring me the evidence."

He spit, and he was that mad he let his whole chew get away from him without noticing. Buscerck says, "Here," and takes his hand off'n his right eye.

Pa never took no notice of nothing after that but the eye. It was the shiniest black onion I ever see on a man. Oscar says, "Forty dollars!" And Pa pays and says, "It's worth it."

But it don't never pay to make an enemy in horse racing or caterpillars, as you will see, after I've got around to telling you.

Well, we raced Red Peril nine times after that, all along the Big Ditch, and you can hear to this day—yes, sir—that there never was a caterpillar alive could run like Red Peril. Pa got rich onto him. He allowed to buy a new team in the spring. If he could only've started a breed from that bug, his fortune would've been made and Henry Ford would've looked like a bent nickel alongside of me to-day. But caterpillars aren't built like Ford cars. We beat all the great caterpillars of the year, and it being a time for a late winter, there was some fast running. We raced the Buffalo Big Blue and Fenwick's Night Mail and Wilson's Joe of Barneveld. There wasn't one could touch Red Peril. It was close into October when a crowd got together and brought up the Black

Arrer of Ava to race us, but Red Peril beat him by an inch. And after that there wasn't a caterpillar in the state would race Pa's.

He was mighty chesty them days and had come to be quite a figger down the canawl. People come aboard to talk with him and admire Red Peril; and Pa got the idea of charging five cents a sight, and that made for more money even if there wasn't no more running for the animile. He commenced to get fat.

And then come the time that comes to all caterpillars. And it goes to show that a man ought to be as careful of his enemies as he is lending money to friends.

IV

We was hauling down the Lansing Kill again and we'd just crossed the aqueduct over Stringer Brook when the lock keeper, that minded it and the lock just below, come out and says there was quite a lot of money being put up on a caterpillar they'd collected down in Rome.

Well, Pa went in and he got out Red Peril and tried him out. He was fat and his stifles acted kind of stiff, but you could see with half an eye he was still fast. His start was a mite slower, but he made great speed once he got going. "He's not in the best shape in the world," Pa says, "and if it was any other bug I wouldn't want to run him. But I'll trust the old brute," and he commenced brushing him up with a toothbrush he'd bought a-purpose.

"Yeah," says Ned. "It may not be right, but we've got to consider the public."

By what happened after, we might have known that we'd meet up with that caterpillar at Number One Lock; but there wasn't no sign of Buscerck, and Pa was so excited at racing Red Peril again that I doubt if he noticed where he was at all. He was all rigged out for the occasion. He had on a black hat and a new red boating waistcoat, and when he busted loose with his horn for the lock you'd have thought he wanted to wake up all the deef-and-dumbers in seven counties. We tied by the upper gates and left the team to graze; and there was quite a crowd on hand. About nine morning boats was tied along the towpath, and all the afternoon boats waited. People was hanging around, and when they heard Pa whanging his horn they let out a great cheer. He took off his hat to some of the ladies, and then he took Red Peril out of his pocket and everybody cheered some more.

"Who owns this here caterpillar I've been hearing about?" Pa asks. "Where is he? Why don't he bring out his pore contraption?"

A feller says he's in the shanty.

"What's his name?" says Pa.

"Martin Henry's running him. He's called the Horned Demon of Rome."

"Dinged if I ever thought to see him at my time of life," says Pa. And he goes in. Inside there was a lot of men talking and smoking and drinking and laying money faster than leghorns can lay eggs, and when Pa comes in they let out a great howdy, and when Pa put down the Brandreth box on the table they crowded round; and you'd ought to 've heard the mammoth shout they give when Red Peril climbed out of his box. And well they might. Yes, sir!

You can tell that caterpillar's a thoroughbred. He's shining right down to the root of each hair. He's round, but he ain't too fat. He don't look as supple as he used to, but the folks can't tell that. He's got the winner's look, and he prances into the centre of the ring with a kind of delicate canter that was as near single footing as I ever see a caterpillar get to. By Jeepers Cripus! I felt proud to be in the same family as him, and I wasn't only a little lad.

Pa waits for the admiration to die down, and he lays out his money, and he says to Martin Henry, "Let's see your ring-boned swivel-hocked imitation of a bug."

Martin answers, "Well, he ain't much to look at, maybe, but you'll be surprised to see how he can push along."

And he lays down the dangedest lump of worm you ever set your eyes on. It's the kind of insect a man might expect to see in France or one of them furrin lands. It's about two and a half inches long and stands only half a thumbnail at the shoulder. It's green and as hairless as a newborn egg, and it crouches down squinting around at Red Peril like a man with sweat in his eye. It ain't natural nor refined to look at such a bug, let alone race it.

When Pa seen it, he let out a shout and laughed. He couldn't talk from laughing.

But the crowd didn't say a lot, having more money on the race than ever was before or since on a similar occasion. It was so much that even Pa commenced to be serious. Well, they put 'em in the ring together and Red Peril kept over on his side with a sort of intelligent dislike. He was the brainiest article in the caterpillar line I ever knowed. The other one just hunkered down with a mean look in his eye.

Millard Thompson held the ring. He counted, "One—two—three—and off." Some folks said it was the highest he knew how to count, but he always got that far anyhow, even if it took quite a while for him to remember what figger to commence with.

The ring come off and Pa and Martin Henry sunk their needles—at least they almost sunk them, for just then them standing close to the course seen that Horned Demon sink his horns into the back end of Red Peril. He was always a sensitive animal, Red Peril was, and if a needle made him start you can think for yourself what them two horns did for him. He cleared twelve inches in one jump—but then he sot right down on his belly, trembling.

"Foul!" bellers Pa. "My 'pillar's fouled."

"It ain't in the rule book," Millard says.

"It's a foul!" yells Pa; and all the Forestport men yell, "Foul! Foul!"

But it wasn't allowed. The Horned Demon commenced walking to the circle—he couldn't move much faster than a barrel can roll uphill, but he was getting there. We all seen two things then. Red Peril was dying, and we was losing the race. Pa stood there kind of foamy in his beard, and the water running right out of both eyes. It's an awful thing to see a big man cry in public. But Ned saved us. He seen Red Peril was dying, the way he wiggled, and he figgered, with the money he had on him, he'd make him win if he could.

He leans over and puts his nose into Red Peril's ear, and he shouts, "My Cripus, you've gone and dropped the butter!"

Something got into that caterpillar's brain, dying as he was, and he let out the smallest squeak of a hollering fright I ever listened to a caterpillar make. There was a convulsion got into him. He looked like a three-dollar mule with the wind colic, and then he gave a bound. My holy! How that caterpillar did rise up. When he come down again, he was stone⋅dead, but he lay with his chin across the line. He'd won the race. The Horned Demon was blowing bad and only halfway to the line. . . .

Well, we won. But I think Pa's heart was busted by the squeal he heard Red Peril make when he died. He couldn't abide Ned's face after that, though he knowed Ned had saved the day for him. But he put Red Peril's carcase in his pocket with the money and walks out.

And there he seen Buscerck standing at the sluices. Pa stood looking at him. The sheriff was alongside Buscerck and Oscar Snipe on the other side, and Buscerck guessed he had the law behind him.

"Who owns that Horned Demon?" says Pa.

"Me," says Buscerck with a sneer. "He may have lost, but he done a good job doing it."

Pa walks right up to him.

"I've got another forty dollars in my pocket," he says, and he connected sizably.

Buscerck's boots showed a minute. Pretty soon they let down the water and pulled him out. They had to roll a couple of gallons out of him afore they got a grunt. It served him right. He'd played foul. But the sheriff was worried, and he says to Oscar, "Had I ought to arrest Will?" (Meaning Pa.)

Oscar was a sporting man. He couldn't abide low dealing. He looks at Buscerck there, shaping his belly over the barrel, and he says, "Water never hurt a man. It keeps his hide from cracking." So they let Pa alone. I guess they didn't think it was safe to have a man in jail that would cry about a caterpillar. But then they hadn't lived alongside of Red Peril like us.

1934

ERNEST HEMINGWAY

My Old Man

I GUESS looking at it, now, my old man was cut out for a fat guy, one of those regular little roly fat guys you see around, but he sure never got that way, except a little toward the last, and then it wasn't his fault, he was riding over the jumps only and he could afford to carry plenty of weight then. I remember the way he'd pull on a rubber shirt over a couple of jerseys and a big sweat shirt over that, and get me to run with him in the forenoon in the hot sun. He'd have, maybe, taken a trial trip with one of Razzo's skins early in the morning after just getting in from Torino at four o'clock in the morning and beating it out to the stables in a cab and then with the dew all over everything and the sun just starting to get going, I'd help him pull off his boots and he'd get into a pair of sneakers and all these sweaters and we'd start out.

"Come on, kid," he'd say, stepping up and down on his toes in front of the jock's dressing room, "let's get moving." Then we'd start off jogging around the infield once, maybe, with him ahead, running nice, and then turn out the gate and along one of those roads with all the trees along both sides of them that run out from San Siro. I'd go ahead of him when we hit the road and I could run pretty good and I'd look around and he'd be jogging easy just behind me and after a little while I'd look around again and he'd begun to sweat. Sweating heavy and he'd just be dogging it along with his eyes on my back, but when he'd catch me looking at him he'd grin and say, "Sweating plenty?" When my old man grinned, nobody could help but grin too. We'd keep right on running out toward the mountains and then my old man would yell, "Hey, Joe!" and I'd look back and he'd be sitting under a tree with a towel he'd had around his waist wrapped around his neck.

I'd come back and sit down beside him and he'd pull a rope out of his pocket and start skipping rope out in the sun with the sweat pouring off his face and him skipping rope out in the white dust with the rope going cloppetty, cloppetty, clop, clop, clop, and the sun hotter, and him working harder up and down a patch of the road. Say, it was a treat to see my old man skip rope, too. He could whirr it fast or lop it slow and fancy. Say, you ought to have seen wops look at us sometimes, when they'd come by, going into town walking along with big white steers hauling the cart. They sure looked as though they thought the old man was nuts. He'd start the rope whirring till they'd stop dead still and watch him, then give the steers a cluck and a poke with the goad and get going again.

When I'd sit watching him working out in the hot sun I sure felt fond of him. He sure was fun and he done his work so hard and he'd finish up with a regular whirring that'd drive the sweat out on his face like water and then sling the rope at the tree and come over and sit down with me and lean back against the tree with the towel and a sweater wrapped around his neck.

"Sure is hell keeping it down, Joe," he'd say and lean back and shut his eyes and breathe long and deep, "it ain't like when you're a kid." Then he'd get up and before he started to cool we'd jog along back to the stables. That's the way it was keeping down to weight. He was worried all the time. Most jocks can just about ride off all they want to. A jock loses about a kilo every time he rides, but my old man was sort of dried out and he couldn't keep down his kilos without all that running.

I remember once at San Siro, Regoli, a little wop, that was riding for Buzoni, came out across the paddock going to the bar for something cool; and flicking his boots with his whip, after he'd just weighed in and my old man had just weighed in too, and came out with the saddle under his arm looking red-faced and tired and too big for his silks and he stood there looking at young Regoli standing up to the outdoors bar, cool and kid-looking, and I said, "What's the matter, Dad?" 'cause I thought maybe Regoli had bumped him or something and he just looked at Regoli and said, "Oh, to hell with it," and went on to the dressing room.

Well, it would have been all right, maybe, if we'd stayed in Milan and ridden at Milan and Torino, 'cause if there ever were any easy courses, it's those two. "Pianola, Joe," my old man said when he dismounted in the winning stall after what the wops thought was a hell of steeplechase. I asked him once. "This course rides itself. It's the pace you're going at, that makes riding the jumps dangerous, Joe. We ain't going any pace here, and they ain't really bad jumps either. But it's the pace always— not the jumps—that makes the trouble."

San Siro was the swellest course I'd ever seen but the old man said it was a dog's life. Going back and forth between Mirafiore and San Siro and riding just about every day in the week with a train ride every other night.

I was nuts about the horses, too. There's something about it, when they come out and go up the track to the post. Sort of dancy and tight looking with the jock keeping a tight hold on them and maybe easing off a little and letting them run a little going up. Then once they were at the barrier it got me worse than anything. Especially at San Siro with that big green infield and the mountains way off and the fat wop starter with his big whip and the jocks fiddling them around and then the barrier snapping up and that bell going off and them all getting off in a bunch and then commencing to string out. You know the way a bunch of skins gets off. If you're up in the stand with a pair of glasses all you see is them plunging off and then that bell goes off and it seems like it rings for a thousand years and then they come sweeping round the turn. There wasn't ever anything like it for me.

But my old man said one day, in the dressing room, when he was getting into his street clothes, "None of these things are horses, Joe. They'd kill that bunch of skates for their hides and hoofs up at Paris." That was the day he'd won the Premio Commercio with Lantorna shooting her out of the field the last hun-

dred meters like pulling a cork out of a bottle.

It was right after the Premio Commercio that we pulled out and left Italy. My old man and Holbrook and a fat wop in a straw hat that kept wiping his face with a handkerchief were having an argument at a table in the Galleria. They were all talking French and the two of them was after my old man about something. Finally he didn't say anything any more but just sat there and looked at Holbrook, and the two of them kept after him, first one talking and then the other, and the fat wop always butting in on Holbrook.

"You go out and buy me a *Sportsman,* will you, Joe?" my old man said, and handed me a couple of soldi without looking away from Holbrook.

So I went out of the Galleria and walked over to in front of the Scala and bought a paper, and came back and stood a little way away because I didn't want to butt in and my old man was sitting back in his chair looking down at his coffee and fooling with a spoon and Holbrook and the big wop were standing and the big wop was wiping his face and shaking his head. And I came up and my old man acted just as though the two of them weren't standing there and said, "Want an ice, Joe?" Holbrook looked down at my old man and said slow and careful, "You son of a bitch," and he and the fat wop went out through the tables.

My old man sat there and sort of smiled at me, but his face was white and he looked sick as hell and I was scared and felt sick inside because I knew something had happened and I didn't see how anybody could call my old man a son of a bitch, and get away with it. My old man opened up the *Sportsman* and studied the handicaps for a while and then he said, "You got to take a lot of things in this world, Joe." And three days later we left Milan for good on the Turin train for Paris, after an auction sale out in front of Turner's stables of everything we couldn't get into a trunk and a suit case.

We got into Paris early in the morning in a long, dirty station the old man told me was the Gare de Lyon. Paris was an awful big town after Milan. Seems like in Milan everybody is going somewhere and all the trams run somewhere and there ain't any sort of a mix-up, but Paris is all balled up and they never do straighten it out. I got to like it, though, part of it, anyway, and say, it's got the best race courses in the world. Seems as though that were the thing that keeps it all going and about the only thing you can figure on is that every day the buses will be going out to whatever track they're running at, going right out through everything to the track. I never really got to know Paris well, because I just came in about once or twice a week with the old man from Maisons and he always sat at the Café de la Paix on the Opera side with the rest of the gang from Maisons and I guess that's one of the busiest parts of the town. But, say, it is funny that a big town like Paris wouldn't have a Galleria, isn't it?

Well, we went out to live at Maisons-Lafitte, where just about everybody lives except the gang at Chantilly, with a Mrs. Meyers that runs a boarding house. Maisons is about the swellest place to live I've ever seen in all my life. The town ain't so much, but there's a lake and a swell forest that we used to go off bumming in all day, a couple of us kids, and my old man made me a sling shot and we got a lot of things with it but the best one was a magpie. Young Dick Atkinson shot a rabbit with it one day and we put it under a tree and were all sitting around and Dick had some cigarettes and all of a sudden the rabbit jumped up and beat it into the brush and we chased it but we couldn't find it. Gee, we had fun at Maisons. Mrs. Meyers used to give me lunch in the morning and I'd be gone all day. I learned to talk French quick. It's an easy language.

As soon as we got to Maisons, my old man wrote to Milan for his license and he was pretty worried till it came. He used to sit around the Café de Paris in Maisons with the gang, there were lots of guys he'd known when he rode up at Paris, before the war, lived at Maisons, and there's a lot of time to sit around because the work around a racing stable, for the jocks, that is, is all cleaned up by nine o'clock in the morning. They take the first bunch of skins out to gallop them at 5.30 in the morning and they work the second lot at 8 o'clock. That means getting up early all right and going to bed early, too. If a jock's riding for somebody too, he can't go boozing around because the trainer always has an eye on him if he's a kid and if he ain't a kid he's always got an eye on himself. So mostly if a jock ain't working he sits around the Café de Paris with the gang and they can all sit around about two or three hours in front of some drink like a vermouth and seltz and they talk and tell stories and shoot pool and it's sort of like a club or the Galleria in Milan. Only it ain't really like the Galleria because there everybody is going by all the time and there's everybody around at the tables.

Well, my old man got his license all right. They sent it through to him without a word and he rode a couple of times. Amiens, up country and that sort of thing, but he didn't seem to get any engagement. Everybody liked him and whenever I'd come into the Café in the forenoon I'd find somebody drinking with him because my old man wasn't tight like most of these jockeys that have got the first dollar they made riding at the World's Fair in St. Louis in nineteen ought four. That's what my old man would say when he'd kid George Burns. But it seemed like everybody steered clear of giving my old man any mounts.

We went out to wherever they were running every day with the car from Maisons and that was the most fun of all. I was glad when the horses came back from Deauville and the summer. Even though it meant no more bumming in the woods, 'cause then we'd ride to Enghien or Tremblay or St. Cloud and watch them from the trainers' and jockeys' stand. I sure learned about racing from going out with that gang and the fun of it was going every day.

I remember once out at St. Cloud. It was a big two hundred thousand franc race with seven entries and Kzar a big favorite. I went around to the paddock to see the horses with my old man and you never saw such horses. This Kzar is a great big yellow horse that looks like just nothing but run. I never saw such a horse. He was being led around the paddocks with his head down and when he went by me I felt all hollow inside he was so beautiful. There never was such a wonderful, lean, running built horse. And he went around the paddock putting his feet just so and quiet and careful and moving easy like he knew just what he had to do and not jerking and standing up on his legs and getting wild eyed like you see these selling platers with a shot of dope in them. The crowd was so thick I couldn't see him again except just his legs going by

and some yellow and my old man started out through the crowd and I followed him over to the jocks' dressing room back in the trees and there was a big crowd around there, too, but the man at the door in a derby nodded to my old man and we got in and everybody was sitting around and getting dressed and pulling shirts over their heads and pulling boots on and it all smelled hot and sweaty and liniment and outside was the crowd looking in.

The old man went over and sat down beside George Gardner that was getting into his pants and said, "What's the dope, George?" just in an ordinary tone of voice 'cause there ain't any use him feeling around because George either can tell him or he can't tell him.

"He won't win," George says very low, leaning over and buttoning the bottoms of his breeches.

"Who will?" my old man says, leaning over close so nobody can hear.

"Kircubbin," George says, "and if he does, save me a couple of tickets."

My old man says something in a regular voice to George and George says, "Don't ever bet on anything I tell you," kidding like, and we beat it out and through all the crowd that was looking in, over to the 100 franc mutuel machine. But I knew something big was up because George is Kzar's jockey. On the way he gets one of the yellow odds-sheets with the starting prices on and Kzar is only paying 5 for 10, Cefisidote is next at 3 to 1 and fifth down the list this Kircubbin at 8 to 1. My old man bets five thousand on Kircubbin to win and puts on a thousand to place and we went around back of the grandstand to go up the stairs and get a place to watch the race.

We were jammed in tight and first a man in a long coat with a gray tall hat and a whip folded up in his hand came out and then one after another the horses, with the jocks up and a stable boy holding the bridle on each side and walking along, followed the old guy. That big yellow horse Kzar came first. He didn't look so big when you first looked at him until you saw the length of his legs and the whole way he's built and the way he moves. Gosh, I never saw such a horse. George Gardner was riding him and they moved along slow, back of the old guy in the gray tall hat that walked along like he was a ring master in a circus. Back of Kzar, moving along smooth and yellow in the sun, was a good looking black with a nice head with Tommy Archibald riding him; and after the black was a string of five more horses all moving along slow in a procession past the grandstand and the pesage. My old man said the black was Kircubbin and I took a good look at him and he was a nice-looking horse, all right, but nothing like Kzar.

Everybody cheered Kzar when he went by and he sure was one swell-looking horse. The procession of them went around on the other side past the pelouse and then back up to the near end of the course and the circus master had the stable boys turn them loose one after another so they could gallop by the stands on their way up to the post and let everybody have a good look at them. They weren't at the post hardly any time at all when the gong started and you could see them way off across the infield all in a bunch starting on the first swing like a lot of little toy horses. I was watching them through the glasses and Kzar was running well back, with one of the bays making the pace. They swept down and around and came pounding past and Kzar was way back when they passed us and this Kircubbin horse in front and going smooth. Gee, it's awful when they go by you and then you have to watch them go farther away and get smaller and smaller and then all bunched up on the turns and then come around towards into the stretch and you feel like swearing and goddamning worse and worse. Finally they made the last turn and came into the straightaway with this Kircubbin horse way out in front. Everybody was looking funny and saying "Kzar" in sort of a sick way and them pounding nearer down the stretch, and then something came out of the pack right into my glasses like a horse-headed yellow streak and everybody began to yell "Kzar" as though they were crazy. Kzar came on faster than I'd ever seen anything in my life and pulled up on Kircubbin that was going fast as any black horse could go with the jock flogging hell out of him with the gad and they were right dead neck and neck for a second but Kzar seemed going about twice as fast with those great jumps and that head out— but it was while they were neck and neck that they passed the winning post and when the numbers went up in the slots the first one was 2 and that meant that Kircubbin had won.

I felt all trembly and funny inside, and then we were all jammed in with the people going downstairs to stand in front of the board where they'd post what Kircubbin paid. Honest, watching the race I'd forgot how much my old man had bet on Kircubbin. I'd wanted Kzar to win so damned bad. But now it was all over it was swell to know we had the winner.

"Wasn't it a swell race, Dad?" I said to him.

He looked at me sort of funny with his derby on the back of his head. "George Gardner's a swell jockey, all right," he said. "It sure took a great jock to keep that Kzar horse from winning."

Of course I knew it was funny all the time. But my old man saying that right out like that sure took the kick all out of it for me and I didn't get the real kick back again ever, even when they posted the numbers upon the board and the bell rang to pay off and we saw that Kircubbin paid 67.50 for 10. All round people were saying, "Poor Kzar! Poor Kzar!" And I thought, I wish I were a jockey and could have rode him instead of that son of a bitch. And that was funny, thinking of George Gardner as a son of a bitch because I'd always liked him and besides he'd given us the winner, but I guess that's what he is, all right.

My old man had a big lot of money after that race and he took to coming into Paris oftener. If they raced at Tremblay he'd have them drop him in town on their way back to Maisons and he and I'd sit out in front of the Café de la Paix and watch the people go by. It's funny sitting there. There's streams of people going by and all sorts of guys come up and want to sell you things, and I loved to sit there with my old man. That was when we'd have the most fun. Guys would come by selling funny rabbits that jumped if you squeezed a bulb and they'd come up to us and my old man would kid with them. He could talk French just like English and all those kind of guys knew him 'cause you can always tell a jockey —and then we always sat at the same table and they got used to seeing us there. There were guys selling matrimonial papers and girls selling rubber eggs that when you squeezed them a rooster came out of them and one old wormy-looking guy that went by with post-cards of Paris, showing them to everybody, and, of course, nobody ever bought any, and then he would come back and show the under side of the pack and they would all be smutty post-cards and lots of people would dig down and buy them.

Gee, I remember the funny people that used to go by. Girls around supper time looking for somebody to take them out to eat and they'd speak to my old man and he'd make some joke at them in French and they'd pat me on the head and go on. Once there was an American woman sitting with her kid daughter at the next table to us and they were both eating ices and I kept looking at the girl and she was awfully good looking and I smiled at her and she smiled at me but that was all that ever came of it because I looked for her mother and her every day and I made up ways that I was going to speak to her and I wondered if I got to know her if her mother would let me take her out to Auteuil or Tremblay but I never saw either of them again. Anyway, I guess it wouldn't have been any good, anyway, because looking back on it I remember the way I thought out would be best to speak to her was to say, "Pardon me, but perhaps I can give you a winner at Enghien today?" and, after all, maybe she would have thought I was a tout instead of really trying to give her a winner.

We'd sit at the Café de la Paix, my old man and me, and we had a big drag with the waiter because my old man drank whisky and it cost five francs, and that meant a good tip when the saucers were counted up. My old man was drinking more than I'd ever seen him, but he wasn't riding at all now and besides he said that whisky kept his weight down. But I noticed he was putting it on, all right, just the same.

He'd busted away from his old gang out at Maisons and seemed to like just sitting around on the boulevard with me. But he was dropping money every day at the track. He'd feel sort of doleful after the last race, if he'd lost on the day, until we'd get to our table and he'd have his first whisky and then he'd be fine.

He'd be reading the *Paris-Sport* and he'd look over at me and say, "Where's your girl, Joe?" to kid me on account I had told him about the girl that day at the next table. And I'd get red, but I liked being kidded about her. It gave me a good feeling. "Keep your eye peeled for her, Joe," he'd say, "she'll be back."

He'd ask me questions about things and some of the things I'd say he'd laugh. And then he'd get started talking about things. About riding down in Egypt, or at St. Moritz on the ice before my mother died, and about during the war when they had regular races down in the south of France without any purses, or betting or crowd or anything just to keep the breed up. Regular races with the jocks riding hell out of the horses. Gee, I could listen to my old man talk by the hour, especially when he'd had a couple or so of drinks. He'd tell me about when he was a boy in Kentucky and going coon hunting, and the old days in the States before everything went on the bum there. And he'd say, "Joe, when we've got a decent stake, you're going back there to the States and go to school."

"What've I got to go back there to go to school for when everything's on the bum there?" I'd ask him.

"That's different," he'd say and get the waiter over and pay the pile of saucers and we'd get a taxi to the Gare St. Lazare and get on the train out to Maisons.

One day at Auteuil, after a selling steeplechase, my old man bought in the winner for 30,000 francs. He had to bid a little to get him but the stable let the horse go finally and my old man had his permit and his colors in a week. Gee, I felt proud when my old man was an owner. He fixed it up for stable space with Charles Drake and cut out coming in to Paris, and started his running and sweating out again, and him and I were the whole stable gang. Our horse's name was Gilford, he was Irish bred and a nice, sweet jumper. My old man figured that training him and riding him, himself, he was a good investment. I was proud of everything and I thought Gilford was as good a horse as Kzar. He was a good, solid jumper, a bay, with plenty of speed on the flat, if you asked him for it, and he was a nice-looking horse, too.

Gee, I was fond of him. The first time he started with my old man up, he finished third in a 2500 meter hurdle race and when my old man got off him, all sweating and happy in the place stall, and went in to weigh, I felt as proud of him as though it was the first race he'd ever placed in. You see, when a guy ain't been riding for a long time, you can't make yourself really believe that he has ever rode. The whole thing was different now, 'cause down in Milan, even big races never seemed to make any difference to my old man, if he won he wasn't ever excited or anything, and now it was so I couldn't hardly sleep the night before a race and I knew my old man was excited, too, even if he didn't show it. Riding for yourself makes an awful difference.

Second time Gilford and my old man started, was a rainy Sunday at Auteuil, in the Prix du Marat, a 4500 meter steeplechase. As soon as he'd gone out I beat it up in the stand with the new glasses my old man had bought for me to watch them. They started way over at the far end of the course and there was some trouble at the barrier. Something with goggle blinders on was making a great fuss and rearing around and busted the barrier once, but I could see my old man in our black jacket, with a white cross and a black cap, sitting up on Gilford, and patting him with his hand. Then they were off in a jump and out of sight behind the trees and the gong going for dear life and the pari-mutuel wickets rattling down. Gosh, I was so excited, I was afraid to look at them, but I fixed the glasses on the place where they would come out back of the trees and then out they came with the old black jacket going third and they all sailing over the jump like birds. Then they went out of sight again and then they came pounding out and down the hill and all going nice and sweet and easy and taking the fence smooth in a bunch, and moving away from us all solid. Looked as though you could walk across on their backs they were all so bunched and going so smooth. Then they bellied over the big double Bull-finch and something came down. I couldn't see who it was, but in a minute the horse was up and galloping free and the field, all bunched still, sweeping around the long left turn into the straightaway. They jumped the stone wall and came jammed down the stretch toward the big water-jump right in front of the stands. I saw them coming and hollered at my old man as he went by, and he was leading by about a length and riding way out, and light as a monkey, and they were racing for the water-jump. They took off over the big hedge of the water-jump in a pack and then there was a crash, and two horses pulled sideways out of it, and kept on going, and three others were piled up. I couldn't see my old man anywhere. One horse kneed himself up and the jock had hold of the bridle and mounted and went slamming on after the place money. The other horse was up and away by himself, jerking his head and galloping with the bridle rein hanging and the jock staggered over to one side of the track against the fence. Then Gilford rolled over to one side off my old man and got up and started to run on three legs with his front off hoof dangling and there was my old man laying there on the grass flat out with his face up and blood all over the side of his head. I ran down the stand and bumped into a jam of people and got to the rail and a cop grabbed me and held me and two big stretcher-bearers were going out after my old man and around on the other side of the course I saw three horses, strung way out, coming out of the trees and taking the jump.

My old man was dead when they brought him in and while a doctor was listening to his heart with a thing plugged in his ears, I heard a shot up the track that meant they'd killed Gilford. I lay down beside my old man, when they carried the stretcher into the hospital room, and hung onto the stretcher and cried and cried, and he looked so white and gone and so awfully dead, and I couldn't help feeling that if my old man was dead maybe they didn't need to have shot Gilford. His hoof might have got well. I don't know. I loved my old man so much.

Then a couple of guys came in and one of them patted me on the back and then went over and looked at my old man and then pulled a sheet off the cot and spread it over him; and the other was telephoning in French for them to send the ambulance to take him out to Maisons. And I couldn't stop crying, crying and choking, sort of, and George Gardner came in and sat down beside me on the floor and put his arm around me and says, "Come on, Joe, old boy. Get up and we'll go out and wait for the ambulance."

George and I went out to the gate and I was trying to stop bawling and George wiped off my face with his handkerchief and we were standing back a little ways while the crowd was going out of the gate and a couple of guys stopped near us while we were waiting for the crowd to get through the gate and one of them was counting a bunch of mutuel tickets and he said, "Well, Butler got his, all right."

The other guy said, "I don't give a goddam if he did, the crook. He had it coming to him on the stuff he's pulled."

"I'll say he had," said the other guy, and tore the bunch of tickets in two.

And George Gardner looked at me to see if I'd heard and I had all right and he said, "Don't you listen to what those bums said, Joe. Your old man was one swell guy."

But I don't know. Seems like when they get started they don't leave a guy nothing.

1923

———————————————————————————————

BEN HUR LAMPMAN

When the Old Man Got Misplaced

THE OLD woman, she was pretty well blowed that time, for a fact. She was all out of wind and as mad as one of them bald-faced hornets. Way it happened, she seen six or seven of Peterson's prize Cotswolds in the clover—they gotten in through a gap in the fence somewheres—and she couldn't find the old man right away for to chivvy them sheep off the place. And when the old woman taken the notion for to do it herself, why, sir, that there Cotswold ram, big and ugly, he chased her clean through the bob-wire, a-scratching her some.

Whilst on her way back to the farmyard, for to find the old man and give him a piece of her mind, dagnab me if she didn't diskiver that Lulubelle gotten into the corn. Lulubelle, she was as good-natured a critter as ever you see —but the old woman just naturally couldn't get that there cow out'n the corn patch. The old woman was fitten to tie, time she come through the last gate.

A man knows how they are, even the best of them—they save it all up and then blame it on you. Way they tell it, a man is never around when he should be, and then when he shouldn't be, why, a man is practically underfoot. And him and her, a-living alone away up there on the river, all them years, they was forever a-jowering and a-jawing, one at t'other, anyhow. Seemed like it

From *The Wild Swan*, published by Thomas Y. Crowell, 1947. Copyright 1947 by Ben Hur Lampman; reprinted by permission of the publisher.

kept them two from being so lonely most of the while, though he set a heap of store by her, and she by him. But a man knows how they are.

So the old woman come into the farmyard, and she looked all around, but there wasn't hide nor hair of the old fool, as she says to herself. She was plumb tuckered out, but that didn't lessen her spunk none, and time the old woman had her second wind, she began for to call and to call. "Yoo-hoo!" But there wasn't no manner of answer. The echo come back from the hillside, and sad-like, and the old woman, she began for to fret and to worry. It p'intedly wasn't like the old man not to be somewheres around. The old fool! And she began for to look and to look, a-keeping right on hollering, until after a bit the old woman fairly was on the dead gallop. Her heart was a-thumping like a cock grouse on a log, and her nubbin of hair come undid, and one of her stockings come down to her heel. "Yoo-hoo!" And that there echo a-mocking her, as though it was a-going for to bust into tears.

Well, sir, as a man heerd that story many the time, the old woman she leant over the curbing and she looked far into the well, just in case. And away down there in the water was only her own puckered face a-looking up at her. But one bucket was down and one bucket was up, and the rope was all right, and she figgered that maybe the old man hadn't come to his death by drownding. And she taken a good look all through the barn, and into the haymow, and a wood rat run out'n the hay, and the old woman begun for to shake and to tremble. And she looked into the mangers, and she looked into the tool shed and the feed bin, and then she run and looked under the house. When she got

to her feet, the old woman looked all around again, but her glasses was blurred and she couldn't see very well —on account of the cobwebs.

Happened there hadn't ary cross word passed between him and her that morning, so she knowed that the old man wasn't a-sulking somewheres, and she knowed that he wouldn't of left the place without a-telling her. That there was some comfort to her. "Dear Lord," the old woman whispered, a-standing there in the farmyard, "if so be there's no harm come to the old fool, I'll never call him a old fool again. Amen." That's the way it is with them, as a man knows, and right then the old woman meant it. But far back in her mind, fearful-like, the old woman already was a-planning the funeral. All them years they been together, him and her, seemed mighty short to her then; mighty dear.

But after a bit the old woman taken holt of herself, like a sensible person, and tried for to figger it out. She wasn't mad no more; she wasn't a-shaking. "Lemme see," she says to herself, "he's got Blinker with him, wherever he is, and no matter what has happened to him, the old dog wouldn't leave him. Yes, wherever he is, this very moment, he's got Blinker with him." So she seen that the thing for to do was to hunt all over the farm, and into the wood lot, and call Blinker whilst she hunted. The old woman had come to her senses, though her heart was cold with what she feared, and she tucked in her hair again, and made it snug with the hairpins, and yanked up her stocking, and she began for to walk, and whilst she walked she called Blinker. She'd nary a thought for Cotswold nor cow.

Turned out that was what she ought to of done in the first place, but first she was too mad, and then she was too frightened, for to think of it. "Blinker! Here, Blinker! Here, Blinker!" She never had thought to be a-calling Blinker like that, with a lump in her throat whilst she called. Lord, she never would call the old man a old fool again. So help her, Lord, she wouldn't. "Here, Blinker! Here, Blinker!"

The old woman's heart, it give a great leap, for of a sudden she seen Blinker far off as he jumped up from the mowing, to stand and look towards her. But he took nary step to come to her. "He's a-standing guard," the old woman says to herself. "Blinker is a-standing guard." She scratched herself some more a-climbing through the bob-wire, and then she began for to run again. Running wouldn't do no good, she knowed right well, but she had for to run.

And as she drawed nigh to the hay-cock she seen that Blinker was a-wagging his tail and a-grinning. But the idea she had, it was so fixed in the old woman's mind that she didn't realize what he meant. She run up to that hay-cock and looked over it—and there was the old man, full length, with his hat over his eyes. She like to gone down in a heap when she seen him. But the old man's whiskers was a-rising and a-falling, and a-rising and a-falling, regular-like. And she distinctly heerd him snore.

The old woman was minded for to drop down on her knees, there in the mowing, and thank the good Lord for His goodness—but something flashed through her mind, bright as a bird when the clouds roll by, and she tried for to catch it. "Let's see," says she to herself. "There's Peterson's Cotswolds in the clover, and there's Lulubelle in the corn —and here he is, the old fool, a-laying there a-snoring his head off, in his blue overalls and his blue cotton shirt." It come to the old woman then, from away back in her childhood, whilst she smiled down on the old man—she had half a mind for to kiss him, whiskers and all— and she said that there poem out loud:—

"Little Boy Blue, come blow your horn,
  The sheep's in the medder, the cow's
    in the corn;
Where's the boy that looks arter the sheep?
  He's under the haystack, fast asleep."

The old man, he never stopped a-snoring. Then she taken a timothy stalk and, a-giggling like a girl, she leant over and tickled one of them fur-bearing ears of his'n. Well, sir, he woke up with a snort, and he jerked the old hat from his eyes, and he jumped to his feet, and he began for to jower and to jaw. He might just as well have fetched her a cuff. Matter of fact, the old man might just as well have cuffed a she-bobcat. "You old fool!" she says. And then them two was at it again.

1945

KATHARINE BRUSH

Night Club

Promptly at quarter of ten P.M. Mrs. Brady descended the steps of the Elevated. She purchased from the newsdealer in the cubbyhole beneath them a next month's magazine and a to-morrow morning's paper and, with these tucked under one plump arm, she walked. She walked two blocks north on Sixth Avenue; turned and went west. But not far west. Westward half a block only, to the place where the gay green awning marked *Club Français* paints a stripe of shade across the glimmering sidewalk. Under this awning Mrs. Brady halted briefly, to remark to the six-foot doorman that it looked like rain and to await his performance of his professional duty. When the small green door yawned open she sighed deeply and plodded in.

The foyer was a blackness, an airless velvet blackness like the inside of a jeweler's box. Four drum-shaped lamps of golden silk suspended from the ceiling gave it light (a very little) and formed the jewels: gold signets, those, or cufflinks for a giant. At the far end of the foyer there were black stairs, faintly dusty, rippling upward toward an amber radiance. Mrs. Brady approached and ponderously mounted the stairs, clinging with one fist to the mangy velvet rope that railed their edge.

From the top, Miss Lena Levin observed the ascent. Miss Levin was the checkroom girl. She had dark-at-the-roots blonde hair and slender hips upon which, in moments of leisure she wore her hands, like buckles of ivory loosely attached. This was a moment of leisure. Miss Levin waited behind her counter. Row upon row of hooks, empty as yet, and seeming to beckon— wee curved fingers of iron—waited behind her.

"Late," said Miss Levin, "again."

"Go wan!" said Mrs. Brady. "It's only ten to ten. *Whew!* Them *stairs!*"

She leaned heavily, sideways, against Miss Levin's counter and, applying one palm to the region of her heart, appeared at once to listen and to count. "Feel!" she cried then in a pleased voice.

Miss Levin obediently felt.

"Them stairs," continued Mrs. Brady darkly, "with my bad heart, will be the death of me. Whew! Well, dearie! What's the news?"

"You got a paper," Miss Levin languidly reminded her.

"Yeah!" agreed Mrs. Brady with sudden vehemence. "I got a paper!" She slapped it upon the counter. "An' a lot of time I'll get to *read* my paper, won't I now? On a Saturday night!" she moaned. "Other nights is bad enough, dear knows—but *Saturday* nights! How I dread 'em! Every Saturday night I say to my daughter, I say, 'Geraldine, I can't,' I say, 'I can't go through it again, an' that's all there is to it,' I say. 'I'll *quit*,' I say, An' I *will*, too!" added Mrs. Brady firmly, if indefinitely.

Miss Levin, in defense of Saturday nights, mumbled some vague something about tips.

"Tips!" Mrs. Brady hissed it. She almost spat it. Plainly money was nothing, nothing at all, to this lady. "I just wish," said Mrs. Brady and glared at Miss Levin, "I just wish *you* had to spend one Saturday night, just one, in that dressing room! Bein' pushed an' stepped on and near knocked down by that gang of hussies, an' them orderin' an' bossin' you 'round like you was *black,* an' usin' your things an' then sayin' they're sorry, they got no change, they'll be back. Yah! They *never* come back!"

"There's Mr. Costello," whispered Miss Levin through lips that, like a ventriloquist's, scarcely stirred.

"An' as I was sayin'," Mrs. Brady said at once brightly, "I got to leave you. Ten to ten, time I was on the job."

She smirked at Miss Levin, nodded, and right-about-faced. There, indeed, Mr. Costello was. Mr. Billy Costello, manager, proprietor, monarch of all he surveyed. From the doorway of the big room, where the little tables herded in a ring around the waxen floor, he surveyed Mrs. Brady, and in such a way that Mrs. Brady, momentarily forgetting her bad heart, walked fast, scurried faster, almost ran.

The door of her domain was set politely in an alcove, beyond silken curtains looped up at the sides. Mrs. Brady reached it breathless, shouldered it open, and groped for the electric switch. Lights sprang up, a bright white blaze, intolerable for an instant to the eyes, like sun on snow. Blinking, Mrs. Brady shut the door.

The room was a spotless, white-tiled place, half beauty shop, half dressing room. Along one wall stood washstands, sturdy triplets in a row, with pale-green liquid soap in glass balloons afloat above them. Against the opposite wall there was a couch. A third wall backed an elongated glass-topped dressing table; and over the dressing table and over the washstands long rectangular sheets of mirror reflected lights, doors, glossy tiles, lights multiplied. . . .

Mrs. Brady moved across this glitter like a thick dark cloud in a hurry. At the dressing table she came to a halt, and upon it she laid her newspaper, her magazine, and her purse—a black purse worn gray with much clutching. She divested herself of a rusty black coat and a hat of the mushroom persuasion, and hung both up in a corner cupboard which she opened by means of one of a quite preposterous bunch of keys. From a nook in the cupboard she took down a lace-edged handkerchief with long streamers. She untied the streamers and tied them again around her chunky black alpaca waist. The handkerchief became an apron's baby cousin.

Mrs. Brady relocked the cupboard door, fumbled her keyring over, and unlocked a capacious drawer of the dressing table. She spread a fresh towel on the plate-glass top, in the geometrical center, and upon the towel she arranged with care a procession of things fished from the drawer. Things for the hair. Things for the complexion. Things for the eyes, the lashes, the brows, the lips, and the finger nails. Things in boxes and things in jars and things in tubes and tins. Also, an ash tray, matches, pins, a tiny sewing kit, a pair of scissors. Last of all, a hand-printed sign, a nudging sort of sign:

NOTICE!

These articles, placed here for your convenience, are the property of the *maid*.

And directly beneath the sign, propping it up against the looking-glass, a china saucer, in which Mrs. Brady now slyly laid decoy money: two quarters and two dimes, in four-leaf-clover formation.

Another drawer of the dressing table yielded a bottle of bromo seltzer, a bottle of aromatic spirits of ammonia, a tin of sodium bicarbonate, and a teaspoon. These were lined up on a shelf above the couch.

Mrs. Brady was now ready for anything. And (from the grim, thin pucker of her mouth) expecting it.

Music came to her ears. Rather, the beat of music, muffled, rhythmic, remote. *Umpa-um, umpa-um, umpa-um-mm——* Mr. "Fiddle" Baer and his band, hard at work on the first fox-trot of the night. It was teasing, foot-tapping music; but the large solemn feet of Mrs. Brady were still. She sat on the couch and opened her newspaper; and for some moments she read uninterruptedly, with special attention to the murders, the divorces, the breaches of promise, the funnies.

Then the door swung inward, admitting a blast of Mr. "Fiddle" Baer's best, a whiff of perfume, and a girl.

Mrs. Brady put her paper away.

The girl was *petite* and darkly beautiful; wrapped in fur and mounted on tall jeweled heels. She entered humming the ragtime song the orchestra was playing, and while she stood near the dressing table, stripping off her gloves, she continued to hum it softly to herself:

"Oh, I know my baby loves me,
I can tell my baby loves me."

Here the dark little girl got the left glove off, and Mrs. Brady glimpsed a platinum wedding ring.

"Cause there ain't no maybe
In my baby's
Eyes."

The right glove came off. The dark little girl sat down in one of the chairs that faced the dressing table. She doffed her wrap, casting it carelessly over the chair-back. It had a cloth-of-gold lining, and "Paris" was embroidered in curlicues on the label. Mrs. Brady hovered solicitously near.

The dark little girl, still humming, looked over the articles "placed here for your convenience," and picked up the scissors. Having cut off a very small hangnail with the air of one performing a perilous major operation, she seized and used the manicure buffer, and after that the eyebrow pencil. Mrs. Brady's mind, hopefully calculating the tip, jumped and jumped again like a taximeter.

"Oh, I know my baby loves me. . . ."

The dark little girl applied powder and lipstick belonging to herself. She examined the result searchingly in the mirror and sat back, satisfied. She cast some silver *Klink! Klink!* into Mrs. Brady's saucer, and half rose. Then, remembering something, she settled down again.

The ensuing thirty seconds were spent by her in pulling off her platinum wedding ring, tying it in a corner of a lace handkerchief, and tucking the handkerchief down the bodice of her tight white-velvet gown.

"There!" she said.

She swooped up her wrap and trotted toward the door, jeweled heels merrily twinkling.

"Cause there ain't no maybe——"

The door fell shut.

Almost instantly it opened again, and another girl came in. A blonde, this. She was pretty in a round-eyed babyish way; but Mrs. Brady, regarding her, mentally grabbed the spirits of ammonia bottle. For she looked terribly ill. The round eyes were dull, the pretty, silly little face was drawn. The thin hands, picking at the fastenings of a spacious bag, trembled and twitched.

Mrs. Brady cleared her throat. "Can I do something for you, Miss?"

Evidently the blonde girl had believed herself alone in the dressing room. Panic, and something else. Something very like murderous hate—but for an instant only, so that Mrs. Brady, whose perceptions were never quick, missed it altogether.

"A glass of water?" suggested Mrs. Brady.

"No," said the girl, "no." She had one hand in the beaded bag now. Mrs. Brady could see it moving, causing the bag to squirm like a live thing, and the fringe to shiver. "Yes!" she cried abruptly. "A glass of water—please—you get it for me."

She dropped onto the couch. Mrs. Brady scurried to the water cooler in the corner, pressed the spigot with a determined thumb. Water trickled out thinly. Mrs. Brady pressed harder, and scowled, and thought, "Something's wrong with this thing. I mustn't forget, next time I see Mr. Costello——"

When again she faced her patient, the patient was sitting erect. She was thrusting her clenched hand back into the beaded bag again.

She took only a sip of the water, but it seemed to help her quite miraculously. Almost at once color came to her cheeks, life to her eyes. She grew young again —as young as she was. She smiled up at Mrs. Brady.

"Well!" she exclaimed. "What do you know about that!" She shook her honey-colored head. "I can't imagine what came over me."

"Are you better now?" inquired Mrs. Brady.

"Yes. Oh, yes, I'm better now. You see," said the blonde girl confidentially, "we were at the theater, my boy friend and I, and it was hot and stuffy—I guess that must have been the trouble." She paused, and the ghost of her recent distress crossed her face. "God! I thought that last act *never* would end!" she said.

While she attended to her hair and complexion she chattered gayly to Mrs. Brady, chattered on with scarcely a stop for breath, and laughed much. She said, among other things, that she and her "boy friend" had not known one another very long, but that she was "ga-ga" about him. "He is about me, too," she confessed. "He thinks I'm grand."

She fell silent then, and in the looking-glass her eyes were shadowed, haunted. But Mrs. Brady, from where she stood, could not see the looking-glass; and half a minute later the blonde girl laughed and began again. When she went out she seemed to dance out on little winged feet; and Mrs. Brady, sighing, thought it must be nice to be young . . . and happy like that.

The next arrivals were two. A tall, extremely smart young woman in black chiffon entered first, and held the door open for her companion; and the instant the door was shut, she said, as though it had been on the tip of her tongue for hours, "Amy, what under the sun *happened?*"

Amy, who was brown-eyed, brown-bobbed-haired, and patently annoyed with something, crossed to the dressing table and flopped into a chair before she made reply.

"Nothing," she said wearily then.

"That's nonsense!" snorted the other. "Tell me. Was it something she said?

She's a tactless ass, of course. Always was."

"No, not anything she said. It was ——" Amy bit her lip. "All right! I'll tell you. Before we left your apartment I just happened to notice that Tom had disappeared. So I went to look for him —I wanted to ask him if he'd remembered to tell the maid where we were going—Skippy's subject to croup, you know, and we always leave word. Well, so I went into the kitchen, thinking Tom might be there mixing cocktails— and there he was—and there *she* was!"

The full red mouth of the other young woman pursed itself slightly. Her arched brows lifted. "Well?"

Her matter-of-factness appeared to infuriate Amy. "He was *kissing* her!" she flung out.

"Well?" said the other again. She chuckled softly and patted Amy's shoulder, as if it were the shoulder of a child. "You're surely not going to let *that* spoil your whole evening? Amy *dear!* Kissing may once have been serious and significant—but it isn't nowadays. Nowadays, it's like shaking hands. It means nothing."

But Amy was not consoled. "I hate her!" she cried desperately. "Redheaded *thing!* Calling me 'darling' and 'honey,' and s-sending me handkerchiefs for C-Christmas—and then sneaking off behind closed doors and k-kissing my h-h-husband. . . ."

At this point Amy quite broke down, but she recovered herself sufficiently to add with venom, "I'd like to slap her!"

"Oh, oh, oh," smiled the tall young woman, "I wouldn't do that!"

Amy wiped her eyes with what might well have been one of the Christmas handkerchiefs, and confronted her friend. "Well, what *would* you do, Claire? If you were I?"

"I'd forget it," said Claire, "and have a good time. I'd kiss somebody myself. You've no idea how much better you'd feel!"

"I don't do——" Amy began indignantly; but as the door behind her opened and a third young woman—redheaded, earringed, exquisite—lilted in, she changed her tone. "Oh, hello!" she called sweetly, beaming at the newcomer via the mirror. "We were wondering what had become of you!"

The red-headed girl, smiling easily back, dropped her cigarette on the floor and crushed it out with a silver-shod toe. "Tom and I were talking to 'Fiddle' Baer," she explained. "He's going to play 'Clap Yo' Hands' next, because it's my favorite. Lend me a comb, will you, somebody?"

"There's a comb there," said Claire, indicating Mrs. Brady's business comb.

"But imagine using it!" murmured the red-headed girl. "Amy darling, haven't you one?"

Amy produced a tiny comb from her rhinestone purse. "Don't forget to bring it when you come," she said, and stood up. "I'm going on out; I want to tell Tom something."

She went.

The red-headed young woman and the tall black-chiffon one were alone, except for Mrs. Brady. The red-headed one beaded her incredible lashes. The tall one, the one called Claire, sat watching her. Presently she said, "Sylvia, look here." And Sylvia looked. Anybody, addressed in that tone, would have.

"There is one thing," Claire went on quietly, holding the other's eyes, "that I want understood. And that is, '*Hands off!*' Do you hear me?"

"I don't know what you mean."

"You do know what I mean!"

The red-headed girl shrugged her shoulders. "Amy told you she saw us, I suppose."

"Precisely. And," went on Claire, gathering up her possessions and rising, "as I said before, you're to keep away." Her eyes blazed sudden white-hot rage. "Because, as you very well know, he belongs to me," she said and departed, slamming the door.

Between eleven o'clock and one Mrs. Brady was very busy indeed. Never for more than a moment during those two hours was the dressing room empty. Often it was jammed, full to overflowing with curled cropped heads, with ivory arms and shoulders, with silk and lace and chiffon, with legs. The door flapped in and back, in and back. The mirrors caught and held—and lost —a hundred different faces. Powder veiled the dressing table with a thin white dust; cigarette stubs, scarlet at the tips, choked the ash-receiver. Dimes and quarters clattered into Mrs. Brady's saucer—and were transferred to Mrs. Brady's purse. The original seventy cents remained. That much, and no more, would Mrs. Brady gamble on the integrity of womankind.

She earned her money. She threaded needles and took stitches. She powdered the backs of necks. She supplied towels for soapy, dripping hands. She removed a speck from a teary blue eye and pounded the heel on a slipper. She curled the straggling ends of a black bob and a gray bob, pinned a velvet flower on a lithe round waist, mixed three doses of bicarbonate of soda, took charge of a shed pink-satin girdle, collected, on hands and knees, several dozen fake pearls that had wept from a broken string.

She served chorus girls and school

girls, gay young matrons and gayer young mistresses, a lady who had divorced four husbands, and a lady who had poisoned one, the secret (more or less) sweetheart of a Most Distinguished Name, and the Brains of a bootleg gang —She saw things. She saw a yellow check, with the ink hardly dry. She saw four tiny bruises, such as fingers might make, on an arm. She saw a girl strike another girl, not playfully. She saw a bundle of letters some man wished he had not written, safe and deep in a brocaded handbag.

About midnight the door flew open and at once was pushed shut, and a gray-eyed, lovely child stood backed against it, her palms flattened on the panels at her sides, the draperies of her white chiffon gown settling lightly to rest around her.

There were already five damsels of varying ages in the dressing room. The latest arrival marked their presence with a flick of her eyes, and, standing just where she was, she called peremptorily, "Maid!"

Mrs. Brady, standing just where *she* was, said, "Yes, Miss?"

"Please come here," said the girl.

Mrs. Brady, as slowly as she dared, did so.

The girl lowered her voice to a tense half-whisper. "Listen! Is there any way I can get out of here except through this door I came in?"

Mrs. Brady stared at her stupidly.

"Any window?" persisted the girl. "Or anything?"

Here they were interrupted by the exodus of two of the damsels-of-varying ages. Mrs. Brady opened the door for them—and in so doing caught a glimpse of a man who waited in the hall outside, a debonair, old-young man with a girl's furry wrap hung over his arm, and his hat in his hand.

The door clicked. The gray-eyed girl moved out from the wall, against which she had flattened herself—for all the world like one eluding pursuit in a cinema.

"What about that window?" she demanded, pointing.

"That's all the farther it opens," said Mrs. Brady.

"Oh! And it's the only one—isn't it?"

"It is."

"Damn," said the girl. "Then there's *no* way out?"

"No way but the door," said Mrs. Brady testily.

The girl looked at the door. She seemed to look *through* the door, and to despise and to fear what she saw. Then she looked at Mrs. Brady. "Well," she said, "then I s'pose the only thing to do is to stay in here."

She stayed. Minutes ticked by. Jazz crooned distantly, stopped, struck up again. Other girls came and went. Still the gray-eyed girl sat on the couch, with her back to the wall and her shapely legs crossed, smoking cigarettes, one from the stub of another.

After a long while she said, "Maid!"

"Yes, Miss?"

"Peek out that door, will you, and see if there's anyone standing there."

Mrs. Brady peeked, and reported that there was. There was a gentleman with a little bit of a black mustache standing there. The same gentleman, in fact, who was standing there "just after you come in."

"Oh, Lord," sighed the gray-eyed girl. "Well . . . I can't stay here all *night,* that's one sure thing."

She slid off the couch, and went listlessly to the dressing table. There she occupied herself for a minute or two. Suddenly, without a word, she darted out.

Thirty seconds later Mrs. Brady was elated to find two crumpled one-dollar bills lying in her saucer. Her joy, however, died a premature death. For she made an almost simultaneous second discovery. A saddening one. Above all, a puzzling one.

"Now what for," marveled Mrs. Brady, "did she want to walk off with them *scissors?*"

This at twelve-twenty-five.

At twelve-thirty a quartette of excited young things burst in, babbling madly. All of them had their evening wraps with them; all talked at once. One of them, a Dresden-china girl with a heart-shaped face, was the center of attention. Around her the rest fluttered like monstrous butterflies; to her they addressed their shrill exclamatory cries. "Babe," they called her.

Mrs. Brady heard snatches: "Not in this state unless. . . ." "Well, you can in Maryland, Jimmy says." "Oh, there must be some place nearer than. . . ." "Isn't this *marvelous?*" "When did it happen, Baby? When did you decide?"

"Just now," the girl with the heart-shaped face sang softly, "when we were dancing."

The babble resumed. "But listen, Babe, what'll your mother and father? . . ." "Oh, never mind, let's hurry." "Shall we be warm enough with just these thin wraps, do you think? Babe, will you be warm enough? Sure?"

Powder flew and little pocket combs marched through bright marcels. Flushed cheeks were painted pinker still.

"My pearls," said Babe, "are *old.* And my dress and my slippers are *new.*

Now let's see—what can I *borrow?*"

A lace handkerchief, a diamond bar-pin, a pair of earrings were proffered. She chose the bar-pin, and its owner un-pinned it proudly, gladly.

"I've got blue garters!" exclaimed an-other girl.

"Give me one, then," directed Babe. "I'll trade with you. . . . There! That fixes that."

More babbling, "Hurry! Hurry up!" . . . "Listen, are you *sure* we'll be warm enough? Because we can stop at my house, there's nobody home." "Give me that puff, Babe, I'll powder your back." "And just to think a week ago you'd never even met each other!" "Oh, hurry *up, let's get started!*" "I'm ready." "So'm I." "Ready, Babe? You look adorable." "Come on, every-body."

They were gone again, and the dress-ing room seemed twice as still and vacant as before.

A minute of grace, during which Mrs. Brady wiped the spilled powder away with a damp gray rag. Then the door jumped open again. Two evening gowns appeared and made for the dress-ing table in a bee line. Slim tubular gowns they were, one silver, one palest yellow. Yellow hair went with the sil-ver gown, brown hair with the yellow. The silver-gowned, yellow-haired girl wore orchids on her shoulder, three of them, and a flashing bracelet on each fragile wrist. The other girl looked less prosperous; still, you would rather have looked at her.

Both ignored Mrs. Brady's cosmetic display as utterly as they ignored Mrs. Brady, producing full filled equipment of their own.

"Well," said the girl with the orchids, rouging energetically, "how do you like him?"

"Oh-h—all right."

"Meaning, 'Not any,' hmm? I sus-pected as much!" The girl with the orchids turned in her chair and scanned her companion's profile with disap-proval. "See here, Marilee," she drawled, "are you going to be a damn fool *all* your life?"

"He's fat," said Marilee dreamily. "Fat, and—greasy, sort of. I mean, greasy in his mind. Don't you know what I mean?"

"I know one thing," declared the girl with orchids. "I know Who He Is! And if I were you, that's all I'd need to know. *Under the circumstances.*"

The last three words, stressed mean-ingly, affected the girl called Marilee curiously. She grew grave. Her lips and lashes drooped. For some seconds she sat frowning a little, breaking a black-sheathed lipstick in two and fit-ting it together again.

"She's worse," she said finally, low.

"Worse?"

Marilee nodded.

"Well," said the girl with orchids, "there you are. It's the climate. She'll never be anything *but* worse, if she doesn't get away. Out West, or some-where."

"I know," murmured Marilee.

The other girl opened a tin of eye shadow. "Of course," she said dryly, "suit yourself. She's not *my* sister."

Marilee said nothing. Quiet she sat, breaking the lipstick, mending it, break-ing it.

"Oh, well," she breathed finally, wea-rily, and straightened up. She propped her elbows on the plate-glass dressing-table top and leaned toward the mirror, and with the lipstick she began to make her coral-pink mouth very red and gay and reckless and alluring.

Nightly at one o'clock Vane and Moreno dance for the *Club Français*. They dance a tango, they dance a waltz; then, by way of encore, they do a Black Bottom, and a trick of their own called the Wheel. They dance for twenty, thirty minutes. And while they dance you do not leave your table—for this is what you came to see. Vane and Moreno. The new New York thrill. The sole justification for the five-dollar couvert extorted by Billy Costello.

From one until half past, then, was Mrs. Brady's recess. She had been looking forward to it all the evening long. When it began—when the opening chords of the tango music sounded stirringly from the room outside—Mrs.

Brady brightened. With a right good will she sped the parting guests.

Alone, she unlocked her cupboard and took out her magazine—the magazine she had bought three hours before. Heaving a great breath of relief and satisfaction, she plumped herself on the couch and fingered the pages. Immediately she was absorbed, her eyes drinking up printed lines, her lips moving soundlessly.

The magazine was Mrs. Brady's favorite. Its stories were true stories, taken from life (so the Editor said); and to Mrs. Brady they were live, vivid threads in the dull, drab pattern of her night.

1927

GEORGE H. COREY

$595 F.O.B.

"Know what this is?" asked the Police Lieutenant.

"Sure, it's a metal rasp," replied Slim.

"Ever see one like it before?" queried the officer.

"Certainly, we use them all the time out at the auto plant," Slim answered.

"Ever see this particular file before?"

The Lieutenant pushed the rasp over the edge of the desk close to the faces of the two men standing before him. Slim, young and straight, turned to the bent figure of Monahan at his side. The old man's eyes were intent upon the file. The Lieutenant raised his voice and repeated:

"I asked you if you'd ever seen this particular file before?"

Light, ochreous and feeble, from a lamp on the police desk fell across the two men's puzzled faces. Their eyes were fixed upon the smooth, sweat-stained handle of the rasp held in the policeman's outstretched arm. On its blackened, circular end they read the letters, T I N Y, crudely scratched into the greasy wood. The old man twisted his head and stared at the bare, green wall behind the desk. Slim lifted his eyes to the level of the officer's tense face.

"Recognize it, now?" asked the Lieutenant.

"It's Tiny's, I guess," Slim said.

Monahan nodded his spotty, bald head slowly up and down. The policeman relaxed and leaned back into his

Reprinted from the magazine *Story*. Copyright, 1935, by Story Magazine, Inc.

chair. He dropped the heavy file onto the top of the desk and picked up two pieces of typewritten paper.

"I want you to sign these papers," he said. "All it says on them is that you have identified this file as one used by this fellow Tiny Cady at the auto plant."

He handed each of the men a paper and continued:

"Sign them and go home to bed. If you want to think it over, we've got a couple of cells downstairs for thinking."

Slim looked dumbly at Monahan as the old man shrugged his shoulders and said:

"There's no out on that. Give us a pen."

"Seems like a hell of a lot of rumpus over a guy stealin' a lousy fifty-cent file," murmured Slim.

The Lieutenant blotted the signatures and rose from his chair. He stepped down from the dais, walked around in front of the desk and stood beside the two men.

"You've got nothing to worry about, boys. Go on home now."

Obediently Slim and Monahan moved off toward the door to the street.

Monahan and Slim walked along in silence until they reached the corner of Canal and Royal Streets. The hands on a big clock in front of a jewelry store pointed to 6:30. It was light now and the street cars rattling down toward the river were crowded with factory workers. Monahan looked at the clock and said:

"Crise, Slim, we can just about make it to the factory."

Slim didn't answer him.

"C'mon, Slim, we got to step on it," repeated Monahan.

"I'm not going back to the factory,

Monahan. If they ask you about me tell 'em I'm through. Tell 'em I've quit," replied Slim.

Slim turned quickly and crossed the street. He continued down Canal Street and turned off at Tehopatoulas. A few doors from the corner he entered a saloon crowded with longshoremen. They were gathered round a small bar and seated at tables drinking sugar mash whiskey. Slim slid into a chair at a table in a corner and ordered a double shot. The first swallow tasted like all the evil-smelling sweet things his nose had ever encountered. The whiskey's sickening, sweet smell was dissipated by the knife-like burn it set up in his throat. The next drink went easier.

Quick warmth and a loosening of tension followed the next glass. The jumbled happenings of the past twelve hours became fused with the events of the last year.

Tiny's friendly, grinning face was a haven of refuge on that first day in the auto factory. Slim tagged along behind the big Texan as he showed the newcomer where to stow his clothes and where to get his tools. Clad in makeshift work clothes worn shabby by his bulging knees and elbows, Tiny pointed out Slim's locker and gave him the key. The Texan's head, which towered a foot above Slim's, was topped with the battered crown of a soft hat that had once been gray. The brim had been carefully cut away and its original color was lost under heavy smudges of grease and dirt. Other workmen passed through the locker room while Slim got into his overalls. Tiny's face, red and alive, seemed ever set to break into a great roar of laughter. Slim looked at the faces of other workmen. In the colorless light coming through the frosted glass windows they were grim, the color of green slate.

"Ever done this kind of work before?" asked Tiny.

"Never in my life," said Slim. "I was a sailor last thing I did."

"You're goin' to be a metal finisher now, kid," continued Tiny. "You've got to learn to sling a file, see? It's a hell of a job, but you'll get onto it."

"I hope so," Slim smiled.

"You'll get wise to everything in quick order," added Tiny.

"I'm kind of light to swing a file and do much good, ain't I?" added Slim.

"That's all right. There ain't room enough on that damned line for many guys as big as me."

"Okay, I'm all set. Where do we go?" said Slim, buttoning his pants.

"Wait a minute, kid, or what do they call you?"

"My name's Slim. Slim Ewell."

"Okay then, Slim, but wait a second. These here lockers, see them? Well, never put nothin' in them you don't want the superintendent to see. The bastards go through 'em every once in a while lookin' for Union Cards, Wobbly tickets, and booze. They'll fire you cold for findin' any of 'em. Watch your step on that stuff."

"Who's our boss?" asked Slim.

"I'm head of the crew you'll work in, but a big Polack named Krakowski's foreman of the whole line. He ain't a bad guy, but he's gettin' old and cranky. Raises hell sometimes, but don't pay no attention to him."

"I'm scared I'll bugger things up there at first," said Slim.

"Don't worry 'bout that. There's lots of new guys turnin' to on the line, these days."

"Who else's in your crew, Tiny?"

"I got four good guys that's been here quite a while. A young guy named Joey, an Irishman 'bout your size named Monahan, a German called Gus, and a big Greek. That makes six of us now. We get a dime apiece for every unit that comes over the line. Did they explain that part to you?"

"A dime apiece for each car?" asked Slim.

Tiny burst into a deep belly-laugh.

"Crise, no. Not a dime apiece. The six of us splits a dime."

"That don't seem like much money, does it?"

"It ain't, Slim, but we bats off a hell of a lot of dimes. Right now the line ain't goin' so fast on account they got a lot of green men startin' in. We're runnin' 'bout fifty bodies an hour just now, but I hear they're goin' to step it up today yet."

"Step it up to more than fifty?"

"Wait'll you see the line when that Polack turns that ol' switch so's she's rollin' seventy and eighty jobs an hour along her back. It's a bitch-kitty, then, I'll tell ya."

Tiny opened the door leading to the factory and a wave of sounds enveloped them. They walked through a maze of machinery clustered thick with men. Tiny raised an arm in a friendly salute as he passed each group. The workmen lifted their faces from their tasks to return the greeting. Slim followed carefully behind the big Texan until they drew up to a long steel track that ran from one end of the factory to the other. Tiny put his hands to his mouth and shouted into Slim's ear:

"That's the line, Kid. Half a mile long."

Slim stepped back a few feet to look at the other end. Directly in front of him he saw two steel tracks, several feet apart, across which were suspended steel rollers. In a narrow fissure down the center and parallel with the tracks an endless chain moved slowly forward. On both sides of the "line" as far as he could see hundreds of men were working on the gray metal shells which crudely resembled the bodies of automobiles.

"This is the sedan line," Slim roared. "The bodies roll off the other end all finished, painted and everything."

Slim's eyes fell upon a thick white mark painted on the floor at right angles to the line. Twenty feet farther down he noticed a similar line. He nudged Tiny and pointed to the white marking nearest him. Tiny glanced at his pointing finger and yelled:

"Got to finish your job this side of that mark. Other side of it the bodies belong to the grinders. Let's go now! Watch me for a minute and then you can start."

Tiny picked up a huge file and walked to the end of the line where four other men, files in hand, stood waiting. No one noticed Slim as he stepped back to watch Tiny. A body had just moved over the white marking leaving the line vacant directly in front of Tiny's men. The crew stood rigid, looking upward toward the welding-room.

The deafening noise of thousands of men under a single roof, beating, scraping and grinding raw metal was suddenly augmented by the piercing screech of an overhead crane which slung the next body onto the line. The body was hardly free of the crane before the five men, led by Tiny, attacked it with their files. Slim watched the big Texan maneuver for a position behind the moving steel shell. This crew's job was to smooth the rough, welded seams on the rear panel of the bodies. Tiny was first to swing into action. Legs apart, the file held in his two massive hands, he lunged upon the narrow strip of crinkly steel. A deep rasping sound rose over the factory's unending rumble as his file bit into the raw, blue metal. Tiny hurled himself against the welt of steel again and another sliver of metal peeled off. His face became tense; globules of sweat dropped from his forehead onto his dirt-caked arms. The lunging movement fell into a rhythm. One, two—lunge. Quickly the huge rasp under Tiny's mighty arms sliced the rough weld into a sleek glistening seam. As the body moved over the white marking on the floor, Tiny, followed by the other four men, withdrew from it and ran to cast themselves upon the next unit already in place behind them. As the crew backed away from the finished body another gang crowded in to take their places. This crew carried electric grinders that filled the air with showers of white sparks as their whirling emery stones slid across the metal.

Tiny shoved a file into Slim's hands and pushed him into position behind the waiting body. He shouted to him:

"You got the idea, now. Eat 'em up."

The big file mocked at Slim. It slipped over the brittle surface of the metal, hardly making a scratch. The arms of the other men in the crew were in his way and the body moved out of reach before he could swing his file across the weld. Desperately he beat his file against the seam, but the metal remained rough and blue. Gently, Tiny swept him to one side just as the body approached the white marking and with quick, powerful strokes of his file ground the weld even and shiny.

Krakowski, the pig-eyed Polish foreman, stood alongside the line watching the new man. Now and then he barked a command that was drowned in the thunder of thousands of tools beating against metal.

Slim's confused nervousness became a paralyzing fright at the sight of the Polish foreman, Krakowski. The chunky figure of the boss of the line leaned heavily against a packing crate abreast the metal finisher's sector. In quick glances stolen between strokes of his file, Slim's eyes took in the Pole's bald, pumpkin-shaped head set upon a massive, beef-red neck. Two small, misshapen ears broke its symmetry. His eyes, shoe-button shaped and set wide apart, were fixed upon the moving forms of the metal finishers.

The fright that had seized Slim fled as he noted that the foreman's attention was directed toward Tiny and not upon himself. The Pole's squatty head and bulbous eyes followed the rhythmic motions of the giant metal finisher's body. His heavy lips, rolled inward tight against his teeth.

The superintendent of the plant, a cat-faced man wearing thick, sweat-smeared glasses, tapped Krakowski's shoulder. The foreman turned quickly, bowed stiffly and smiled. The superintendent's attention was riveted upon the big metal finisher. The two men stood beside each other watching Tiny's arms move machine-like over a rough seam. They saw the crude blue weld become smooth and bright beneath the powerful strokes of his rasp. The superintendent cupped his hands to his mouth and shouted in a voice loud enough for Slim, at the end of the line, to hear.

"Keep an eye on him, Krakowski. He's got the makings of a foreman."

Tiny, aware now that he was being watched, expanded his effort with savage attacks upon the brittle metal.

When Slim looked up from his task next, the two bosses had moved down the assembly line to the next operation.

The metal finishing crew sat eating their lunches in the material storage yard outside the plant. In grease-smudged work clothes they lolled over wooden packing cases, stuffing lumps of bread and meat into their mouths. Slim emptied his mouth enough to talk, and said to the group:

"Honest to Crise, Tiny, I heard him. The boss said it loud enough for me to hear, 'Keep an eye on him, Krakowski. He's got the makin's of a foreman.' I heard him say it to the foreman."

"Dot's no more tan right," said the diabetic German, Gus.

"Eferyone knows Tiny's the bes' goddamned man on the line."

A slice of bread crust between the big metal finisher's lips swerved upward as his mouth tightened into a grin. He made an awkward gesture with his free hand to protest his embarrassment. Steve, the taciturn Greek, another member of the crew, nodded his head in agreement; Joey, a youngster whose face was ancient with dissipation and hard work, emptied his mouth with a hurried swallow and said:

"I wouldn't want to be in your shoes, Tiny. Not with that bastard Krakowski for a foreman. He's goin' to ride your tail till you're plain nuts. You just watch."

Gus nodded his head up and down and added:

"The kid's right, Tiny. I'fe been in dis place a lonk time and I know dot Polack. I know how he figures tinks."

"He can't hurt me any," laughed Tiny.

"Don't kit yourself, poy," replied Gus. "I vas here ten years ago ven dot bastard started on de lines. Efery time I sees Krakowski lookin' at you I tinks of ven he vas a metal finisher. Dot ain't so long ago. He vas like a bull, so strong. Jost de same like dis boss looks at you vorkin' so fine now, da bosses used to look at Krakowski. In tree years dey made from him a foreman."

Tiny listened to Gus and answered slowly.

"He ain't got no reason to ride me. I ain't goin' to get his job. He's been here for years."

"Dot's chust de trouble, Tiny. Vot you tink dis damned Polack tink vhen de boss says you make a goot foreman?"

Tiny shrugged his shoulders and answered lazily.

"I don't know what the hell he's liable to think."

"Youse younk mans don't know vot old man tink. Krakowski's gettin' old. Maybe he's forty already. Dot's old for de line. How many foremans hass ve got? It's de same always. Seven foremans. For ten years ve haff always seven foremans. *Now* you know vot dot guy tinks?" asked Gus.

"Gus is right," interrupted Joey, "the Polack's figurin' you're after his job from now on. Who wouldn't? There ain't no signs of their needin' an extra foreman."

"Dot's right, Choey," replied Gus. "Krakowski's old and soft now. Vot you tink happen to him if de boss say 'back on de line you go, Krakowski'? Dot vould kill him. You know vhere is Svenson, now, vot vas foreman on number six? Ven dey put dat collich poy in Svenson's chob and pushed de Svede back on de line he chumped in de river. Vot else could he do?"

The crew sat silent over their crumpled sandwich wrappings. The German's words ended the conversation.

The five minute warning whistle sent them scurrying into the factory.

The feud between Krakowski and Tiny became a subject of guarded conversation among the men. Each day's gossip brought fresh evidence of bitter combat. Only yesterday Tiny had retaliated to the Pole's constant heckling with a barbed gesture. As the power was shut off for the noon hour and Krakowski walked away from the metal-finishing sector, Tiny broke into a loud whistle to the tune of "The Old Gray Mare, She Ain't What She Used to Be." The workmen on the opposite side took up the tune. The infuriated Pole flushed crimson and shuffled his feet clumsily in an attempt to fall out of step with the beat of the refrain. The whistling pursued him along the assembly line for a hundred yards.

Krakowski stood beside Tiny's crew scrutinizing its work for flaws. The crew was working smoothly and he found nothing with which to torment Tiny. Slim watched the big Texan cast quick glances at the Pole. The boss metal finisher knew the foreman had his eyes on him and he swung into an exhibition demonstration. The back-breaking task of pulling a huge file across a rough seam kept the other five men in the crew tense and hurried. The giant Tiny made it seem like an effortless, almost playful task. His sinewy arms dragged the big rasp over the steel with uncanny ease, the sound of his file above the others, and beat a steady rhythm. One, two—one, two, the crisp metal seemed to turn soft under Tiny's great arms.

The serpentine procession of steel-gray hulls moved along the assembly line at a rate of fifty units an hour. At this speed the metal finishers were hard pressed for time to complete their tasks. Krakowski left their sector and moved to a place beneath the overhead crane. He shouted up to the man in the control box above him. As the man poked his head through a little window in the box, the foreman raised two fingers on his right hand. The crane operator returned the signal and rolled the screeching hoist back to the welding-room. Slim saw the Pole give the signal. He nudged Tiny with his elbow and said:

"He's pushing her up to seventy an hour."

Tiny passed the word through the crew. They cursed the foreman with vicious grunts that were lost in the deafening noise. The raw steel shells moved faster, the noise grew louder.

Krakowski walked back along the line and surveyed the chaos in the metal finishing crew. Seventy units an hour called for an inhuman expenditure of effort. Slim, a competent workman now, wallowed in sweat and confusion. Furiously he swung his rasps over the seam as he battled to clip a few seconds from each unit of work. One, two— one, two—a stroke of the file every two seconds; twenty strokes for every unit, seventy bodies an hour; a cent and a half for Slim, a cent and a half for Tiny; one, two—one, two—thirty strokes every minute, one, two—one, two; fourteen hundred strokes every hour. Economical transportation at $595, F.O.B. the factory.

The noon whistle blew and the men dropped their tools before the machinery stopped. Exhausted from the murderous pace of the past hour they flopped onto the material cases flanking the line. Tiny and Slim, the last to leave the job, looked about the place to rest. Slim found a big, unopened box and raised himself wearily onto it. As the big metal finisher heaved his tired frame over the crate Krakowski appeared alongside of him.

"I'm goin' to have to put two more men in your crew, Cady," said the Pole.

"What's wrong with our gang?" asked Tiny.

"Can't keep up. You see for yourself," replied Krakowski.

"Give us a while to get used to the new speed," pleaded Tiny.

"Adding two men will cut hell out of our pay," added Slim.

"Not while we're running at seventy an hour it won't," said Krakowski.

"You know damned well we won't hold that rate long," argued Tiny. "We'll be back at fifty in no time. You know that."

"That's not my fault. Two new men will report to you after lunch. You break them in." Krakowski turned and walked away leaving the two metal finishers sullen with futility and anger.

Warm weather came and the metal-finishing crew sat about the material yard eating lunch. With the late spring came the end of the peak production period and work on the line lagged. There were still eight men in the crew, though the amount of work had dwindled. Slim lay on a bale of cushion padding and stuffed the remainder of a sandwich into his mouth. He mopped his moist head and body with a blackened towel wrapped around one hand. With eight men in the crew instead of six and production down, the lunch hour had become a surly lull in the day's labor. The two new men tried vainly to overcome the unfriendliness with which the rest of the crew had accepted them. Tiny defended them but his arguments angered the rest of the crew.

Two extra men cut the old crew's pay one-quarter.

The two new men finished their lunches and invented an excuse to move off from the old-timers. As they passed out of sight Tiny spoke up:

"I feel sorry for those poor bastards. They can't help being shoved into our crew."

No one answered the crew boss. Slim and the others knew it was true, but that didn't help their pay checks. Gus, the German, daubed his dirty towel over the endless stream of sweat pouring from his face and said:

"It's dot goddamned Krakowski's fault. Dis business can't go on, Tiny. Efery day it's gettin' worser. Last veek ve draw how much?"

"A lousy nineteen bucks, that's all," answered Slim.

The German continued: "Und for you, Tiny, it is vorser dan for us. How much did dey dock you for dose files vot was missing?"

"Eight smackers!" said Tiny bitterly.

"Eight dollars! Crise, that's half your pay," exclaimed Joey.

Joey and the Greek rose and started off toward the tobacco shop across the street.

"Where you goin'?" asked Slim.

"Healey, that Union organizer's givin' a speech today across the street in the lunch room. We're goin' to listen to him," said Joey.

Tiny sat across from Gus and Slim and watched Joey and the Greek pass through the factory gate. When they had disappeared from sight Tiny leaned over close to the other two men and said:

"Gus, I'm worried about the crew. Krakowski keeps them so cussed mad all the time that they're gettin' sloppy."

"I've seen it comin'," said Gus.

"What in hell can I do? I can't fire these two extra men. And even with the line runnin' slow, I can't do everyone's work. It's gettin' so sloppy the inspectors had me on the carpet this mornin'."

"Dot's dangerous, Tiny," warned the German. "Ven de vork gets sloppy den Krakowski can do anythink to you and it's all right mit de boss. Vonce he shows de boss quality is missink in de vork den he can make from you a sveeper, a 'privy man'; or maybe shoff you into de paint boot."

"What would you do, Gus?" asked Slim.

"Dot I couldn't tell you. Dere is nottink to do mit a guy like Krakowski. I'm old und I know sometink vot goes on in de Polack's head. Only an olt man can 'furshay' dis tink. De Polack is olt. He's got no money, vot mit eight kits to raise. All his life he vorked hard for de bosses. Vun day he hears de boss say you make a goot foreman. In dot tick head he tinks—'Vot becomes of Krakowski if dey makes dis Tiny a foreman?' Beck to de line, he tinks and den—out on de street—or de river, like Svenson."

"Maybe Choey and de Greek got de right idea," continued Gus, rising from his box. "Maybe Healey and his Union beesiness is vot ve haf to get first. I don't know. Anyvay, vy don't you and Slim come to his meetink tonight? De rest of de crew iss goink."

Slim and Tiny sat without talking. The German walked away toward the assembly building.

"Maybe that's an idea," said Slim.

"Won't do no harm findin' out what it's all about," agreed Tiny.

"I'll find out from Joey where Healey's holdin' tonight's meetin'," said Slim as he rose to his feet. The warning whistle blew and the two men joined the stream of workers returning to the assembly lines.

Tiny and Slim took their seats in the dirty meeting hall and looked around for the familiar faces of their crew. About fifty men were gathered in the room when Healey rose to the platform and called for silence. He surveyed his audience for a moment and then began to talk. Piece by piece he built the background of labor's struggle against capital. Then he launched into his immediate cause.

"And how long are you sniveling idiots going to slave for the pittance your bloated bosses toss you each week? How much longer are you going to let them treat you like animals? No, not even animals suffer the abuses heaped upon you.

"What animal do you know of that must pull a 'privy cord' so that some other slave will take his place on the line while he rushes to the toilet? Does any animal live by a system of work so inhuman that it allows not even time for a man to perform a fundamental act of nature? Name me any other animal than your poor selves who is so mistrusted, so driven and persecuted that his master must make him perform these acts of nature on a stage set in the center of the factory, on a stage so that his hirelings may count the seconds he is away from his work?"

Short, angry laughs told Healey he was on the right track. He continued:

"In the yard where you eat lunch are piles of raw material, men. Close your eyes and think of it for a moment. It's covered carefully with tarpaulins and guarded day and night. The wood stacked in the timber yard is covered and watched. Even the great piles of coal are protected from the wind and rain. These raw materials are valuable; the company paid out money for them and they're cared for.

"But you—you laborers, what care or protection do you get? When that pile of sheet metal can't be used it is soaked in grease and guarded. But, you, when the factory is through with you, at the end of the season, what happens? Out you go. Onto the street. Like a mangy dog, an unwanted whore. Out you go to starve, steal or die until you are wanted again.

"We don't ask for much, men. We're not asking for their riches. We ask for as much care as they give the raw materials; the sheet metal, the steel or the wood they use in the cars we build. Is that too much to ask for? To be treated as well as a piece of steel?"

A roar of approval went up from Healey's audience.

"What ill-begotten swine are you that your bosses must spy on you like thieves? That you should let them steal into your lockers and search your clothes? That you should squirm before them and pray not to be fired for their findings on these marauding, illegal entries into your personal effects?

"You call yourselves men and yet you consent to these slave-driving bosses' denying you the rights your forefathers fought and died to get. The right to unite for protection from starvation and death. The right to work like human beings and not beasts."

The little Irishman darted back and forth across the platform. The dull, thirsty minds of his listeners soaked up his words. Tiny, seated next to Slim, shifted uneasily on his chair.

Indignation spread slowly through the crowd. Healey halted for an instant and drank a glass of water. While he paused, the smoke of discontentment burst into flames in scattered sections of the room.

"That means the foreman, too," one of the men yelled.

"That's right, Krakowski, and the others. They're worse than the bosses," yelled another workman.

Healey held his hands above his head, begging for silence. Desperately he pounded a table with a water glass and shouted for order. The men could not be silenced. The Union organizer let the outburst run its course.

In a few minutes it subsided. There was no one with whom to argue. Quiet established, Healey took a short cut to his goal. He stepped out to the edge of the platform and called out:

"Who's going to be the first to join, then? Who's going to get card number one and fire the first shot in the battle against the slave-drivers?"

This challenge threw the assemblage into an angry demonstration. The clumsy workmen pushed and shoved one another to reach the platform first. In the disorder of the movement, Tiny and Slim slipped out of the hall unnoticed.

They walked along the cool, dark street in silence for more than a block. Under the flickering glare of a street lamp Slim looked up at the big metal finisher and said:

"Healey's right, Tiny. We're gettin' rooked."

"Sure we are, but we'd lose what little we're not gettin' rooked out of if we signed up with the Union."

"How do you figure that, Tiny?"

"Krakowski and the bosses knew about that meetin'."

"What can they do? Ain't no law against goin' to a meetin'," Slim argued.

"No, but there is against joinin' the Union. The company had half a dozen stools in that crowd. The poor saps who sign up will be out on their tails before the ink's dry on their Union Cards."

"What the hell's the difference, Tiny? We're not gettin' anywhere workin'."

"No, but we're eatin' and that's somethin'. No sir, they don't get my job, now! Not with a thousand guys waitin' at that factory gate every mornin'. Waitin' for someone to get fired."

"Healey told us yesterday not to be so scared of that gang waiting at the gate every morning. He says they ain't workmen at all. Just a bunch of bums hired by the company to keep us scared of our jobs," continued Slim.

"Maybe they are bums. What's the difference? It don't take a hell of a lot of brains to sling a file does it? That's the trouble with the Union. I know we're gettin' a rooking, same as I know the Polack's trying to get my job, but what's the sense of fightin'?" added Tiny.

"But Healey says if we all get together we've got a chance."

"Healey's talkin' through his hat, Slim. What chance have we got? In any other business maybe he's right, but in the auto business we've got no chance. The company's got the jobs broken down so simple that they can take the dumbest cluck in the world, shove a tool in his hand, throw him on the line and in two days they've got an auto worker."

"But if we all struck at the same time, we might tie them up."

"That's more of the Irishman's pipe dreams. The bosses ain't sleepin'. Look at the green men they're pourin' into the factory every day. Where are they comin' from? Down here in New Orleans? Not on your life! Georgia

Crackers, Hill-billys from up North, poor bastards that never seen more'n a dollar in their lives. Think Healey can get those guys to strike?"

"Not right away, maybe," argued Slim.

"Damned right. And when they get wise to themselves there'll be more mountain boys to shove into their jobs."

"The way you see it then, there ain't nothin' we can do?"

"Not while the company's holdin' all the aces, Slim. Only thing to do is to play their game for all you can get out of it, then get out. I've missed more than one meal tryin' to beat the bosses. Twice I've been busted higher 'an a kite fightin' for Unions. Once in Galveston in the dock strike and once in the mine war in Georgia. Besides, Slim, maybe I'll get a break at the plant. Joinin' the Union won't help my chances of gettin' one."

The two men arrived in front of Tiny's tottering, two-storied shack and turned up the cinder path to the porch stairs. As Tiny slipped the key into the lock Slim lowered his voice to a whisper and said:

"I hope you get a break from the bastards, Tiny. You got it comin' to you."

The Union organizer's work took its toll along the line. In the weeks that followed Healey's first appearance outside the factory gates, dozens of men lost their jobs. Mysteriously, but quickly the names on the Union roster had found their way into the company's office. Swiftly these names were sliced from the payroll.

The crew leaders and foremen sweated and raged to break in the army of green men hired to fill the vacant places. Most of them had never had tools in their hands before. Yesterday they were farmers, banjo players, race track touts, or vacuum-cleaner salesmen. Tomorrow they would be skilled auto workers.

In crews such as Tiny's, where some degree of skill was needed, the green men brought chaos and confusion. The experienced Greek and Gus had been fired. A flabby-armed piano tuner and a pot-bellied bartender struggled in their places. Tiny pleaded for replacements. Krakowski shook his head understandingly, shrugged his shoulders and did nothing.

The great snake of blue-gray steel slid stealthily onward. Tiny tore off his workshirt and pitched into the work with a fiendish burst of effort. Slim and Monahan, too, battled to cover the green men's work. It was futile. Farther and farther they lagged, holding the succeeding crews from their work. This kept up all day. Every half hour the metal finishers fell so far behind that the line had to be halted. During one of the long halts in the afternoon the superintendent stopped beside the metal finishers and surveyed the confusion. Krakowski close at his side, explained it to him.

Half an hour after the plant had closed down Tiny's crew was still hard at it. Groggy with fatigue, they completed the last unit of the schedule. Tiny and Slim dropped onto a bench to rest before washing up. They were alone but a few seconds before Krakowski appeared from the other side of the factory.

"Finally finished up, eh?" said the Pole.

"Yeh! Finally!" grunted Tiny.

"Bad business, this holding up the line, Cady," continued the foreman. "Costs the company a lot of money."

"Why the hell don't you give me some men who can work?" said Tiny.

"Those two birds will never make finishers," added Slim.

"Wot can I do, Cady? That's all they hire; green men. Other crews get along with green men," the Pole countered.

"You better get us better men tomorrow, Krakowski," threatened Tiny.

"That's what I came to tell you about," the foreman replied. "The superintendent gave me orders to transfer you and Slim to the paint booth tomorrow. Both of you start there in the morning."

Tiny jumped to his feet.

"The paint booth? Why you son —
— —." He was shouting.

"I've checked you off this operation. In the morning you'll get new cards from the boss of the paint booth."

The Pole wheeled about and walked away.

Muffled beneath grotesque equipment suggestive of deep sea divers, Slim and Tiny walked heavily toward the paint spraying booth. The thickly padded, paint-stiffened clothes made their movements robot-like. Slim followed Tiny into the long enclosure where the finished bodies received the widely advertised *"Gorgeous New Colors."* They stopped before a huge, mirrored, incandescent bulb that flooded the line with hot, sharp light. Before them, on the inert line, stood a body heavily impregnated with a dull gray priming coat. The atmosphere was still and hot. A dozen men, clad in the same thick uniforms, passed silently along the line. Tiny and Slim greeted them with stiff, upward movements of their arms.

A warning bell rang and the two men set up their equipment ready for work. Slim flicked on three more powerful flood lamps and watched Tiny test his spray gun. The big Texan wore a bulky pair of coveralls the legs of which were tucked into the tops of heavy overshoes. Stout cords bound the open ends of his sleeves tight around his wrists. The coarse coveralls encircled his neck snugly, making the costume airtight. Over Tiny's forehead was drawn a piece of rough toweling that extended back over his head and neck in the manner of a hood. Its ends were tucked under his close-fitting collar. Only that part of his face between chin and eyes was exposed to the murderous irritation of the paint-laden atmosphere.

As the line began to move Tiny slipped a breathing-mask over his mouth, leaving only his eyes and patches of his face exposed. Over these areas he rubbed a thick layer of vaseline. Slim adjusted his breathing mask, signaling Tiny the equipment was ready and stepped back from the glare of the floodlamps.

The Texan grasped the spray gun in his gloved hands and pressed the control trigger.

A hissing explosion burst from the nozzle and a fine spray of paint rained upon the smooth body panels. Some of the paint hit its goal, covering the sleek, gray sheets of metal with a layer of bright green pigment. Much of it, however, missed its mark and shot out into the still air. This same operation was taking place at half a dozen places down the line. Across from Tiny, on the other side of the line another sprayer was covering the other half of the body. In a few minutes the booth was choked with a dense precipitation of multicolored paint. Overhead a whining exhaust fan whisked bits of the contaminated air out of the shed. Most of the pigment that missed its goal settled upon the dust in the air and hung suspended in the atmosphere.

In the dazzling light the pupils of Tiny's eyes contracted into narrow slits and floating particles of pigment settled on his vaseline-coated face mottling it with the colors of the spectrum. Beneath the thickly padded worksuit his body pumped a flood of hot sweat that sought escape from the airtight uniform in thick streams that ran down his back and legs. Slim saw brown circular stains appear at his crotch and knees.

Outside on the line Krakowski was having trouble. Tiny and Slim knew it was serious as they stood idly by the motionless conveyor waiting for the line to move. Delays grew more frequent. During the precious noon periods when, for an hour, they were free of the booth, workers on the line outside told them of Krakowski's problems. One day it was the metal finishing crew. Then it was the grinders, or the door hangers whose work lagged until the line had to be halted. The delays were costly and the management hounded the befuddled Pole. Hour after hour Krakowski rushed up and down the line shouting orders, goading the men to greater effort, wrestling tools from their hands.

Frantically he struggled to instill order and speed. Tiny and Slim knew his effort was futile. The experienced men were disgruntled and shirked deliberately; the green men, confused and frightened, accomplished little. Patiently the two men waited for the superintendent to return them to the metal finishing section.

Tiny and Slim were back slinging their files again. For three weeks the big metal finisher had been laboring to keep his crew abreast the mounting

work. Tiny's return to the line as boss metal finisher became a personal victory to each of the old-timers on the line—a victory of the men over the bosses. They speeded up their work and helped the green men. Delays became infrequent and the line approached its normal swift pace.

They were in production on a new model car. *"Amazingly New,"* Slim read in the newspaper advertisements. *"The Car that Has Revolutionized Motoring"* at $595 F.O.B. the factory. The finishers' jobs hadn't changed, though. The welded seams on the rear panels were a little wider and took longer to trim smooth.

Slim pulled the privy cord and waited for a relief man to take his place at the line. In a few minutes he appeared and Slim handed him his file. Then he started off in the direction of the toilet in the center of the plant. He wanted to smoke a cigarette and there was only one safe place to do it. Halfway to the overhead toilet Slim doubled back on his trail, cut across two assembly lines and headed toward the superintendent's office. When the superintendent's office had been built a narrow space had been left between it and the end of the factory. Slim looked carefully to see that no one was watching and slipped into the open end of the hiding place. Stealthily he opened a fresh pack and lit up. He inhaled a thick mouthful of smoke and felt it flood his lungs. As he exhaled he watched the blue spirals of smoke curl upward toward the roof. The place was doubly safe because the superintendent's office was roofless and he smoked continuously. Flat on his back, Slim lay on the concrete floor, cigarette in his hand. He listened to the noise of voices in the superintendent's office. From the other side of the open-topped office Slim heard a strange voice say:

"We can't have another series of delays again. Detroit's raising hell with me already."

Slim held his cigarette motionless as he listened to the voice of the superintendent reply:

"No need to worry, Chief. I think I've got it licked."

"What was it?" asked the Chief.

"One of my foremen fell down on the job. He's getting old and I guess I've got to ease him out," continued the superintendent.

Slim stabbed the lighted end of his butt onto the concrete and listened eagerly.

"I hope that solves it. Are you going to have to send to Detroit for a new foreman?"

"I don't think so, Chief. I've got a big metal finisher here who's a demon for work. I'm checking up on him now. If he's clear of the Union I'm going to give him a try at the job."

Swiftly and noiselessly Slim rose and slipped out of the fissure between the office and the factory wall. He sought the shortest route back to the line. He could still hear the bosses talking as he approached the open space in front of the offices. His eyes swept the clearing as he prepared to step out into the open space. Suddenly he stopped short and stepped back. Leaning against a pillar, a few feet in front of the boss's office Slim saw Krakowski. His thick neck was rigid and his hands shuffled a batch of time cards clumsily.

The conversation inside ended and the Pole walked hurriedly toward the opposite end of the factory. Slim waited until he was out of sight, then he started back to the crew.

For an hour the line had been moving at a stiff pace. The metal finishing crew was working feverishly. Tiny held his hot file between handfuls of cotton waste. A warning nudge in his ribs from a workman in the next crew told him the boss was coming. Silent elbows prodded into ribs telegraphed the news from one end of the plant to the other. Tiny nudged Slim and he in turn put the man next to him on guard.

Slim looked up and saw Krakowski's chunky form weaving through clumps of workmen a hundred feet ahead of him. Deftly the foreman slipped through the knots of men. A few feet ahead of the metal finishers he stopped and tapped a stubby finger on the shoulder of a man in the next crew. The lazy Georgian grinder looked up at the foreman and smiled. He was a well known character in the auto plant whose defiance of the company's stringent rules against loafing had won him a reputation for bravery. At least twice a day he was to be found seated on the debris-littered floor of the half-exposed toilet, the sport sheet of the *Times-Picayune* on his knee and his back resting against the cool, circular tile of the water closet.

The big grinder looked up at Krakowski and raised his ear to the Pole's moving lips. The foreman turned away as the grinder dropped his rasp and reached for a piece of cotton waste.

Tiny had just completed the seam in front of him as Krakowski's hand touched his wrist. The big metal finisher looked up and the foreman leaned over and spoke to him. Slim's elbow, pressed quickly into the ribs of a man in the next crew, started the telegraphic nudge toward the other end of the line. Krakowski moved off in the direction of the superintendent's office. Tiny and the grinder followed close behind him. Two relief men answered the signal on the privy cord. They took the two vacated places.

It was almost time to knock off for the day and Tiny hadn't returned. Anxiously the metal finishers watched for him. Slim tried to dissipate his concern by thinking of a lot of good things that might have happened. Maybe they had made Tiny an inspector or a foreman. The peculiarly fixed squint in the Pole's eyes when he led Tiny away an hour before made these pleasantries hard to believe. A grinder in the crew ahead pressed his flexed arm into Slim's back. He raised his eyes, but could not see Tiny. Between strokes of his file he darted quick glances in the direction of the other end of the factory. At last the familiar hulk came into sight.

Tiny moved rapidly toward his crew. Abreast them he reached out, grabbed the relief man's arm and snatched the file from the surprised worker's hands. Tiny's eyes seemed to be focused on some far-off object. His smile was gone and the lean muscles of his face were drawn uncomfortably snug over their framework. Lips pressed tight against teeth and strangely expressionless eyes forbade questioning. Slim tried to catch his eye. The crew went on with its work.

Tiny snatched up a piece of cord and broke it in two. He tied one piece around the wooden handle of his file, placed it on the edge of a bench at his side and then slipped out of his overalls. Slim looked at the clock on the wall, but it was still a half hour before quitting time. The big metal finisher picked up the file again, took a deep breath and dropped the rasp between his pants and his belly. Then he tied the loose end of string on the file handle to his pants belt. The heavy end of the rasp slid down his right trouser leg.

With the other piece of string he fastened the dangling end of the file tight against his leg. The rest of the crew looked at one another with bewilderment. Tiny shook his leg, made certain the file was secure, and strode off toward the locker room.

A few minutes before quitting time the Georgian grinder from the next crew returned and took off his overalls. Slowly he rolled them into a bundle. The five o'clock whistle blew and Slim hastened over to him.

"What happened?"

"Got fired," drawled the grinder.

"Not Tiny, too?"

"Sure, canned both of us."

"I don't believe it. What happened?" continued Slim.

"Honest to Crise, Slim, we got fired."

"What for?"

"Union cards. Both of us."

"You're nuts. Tiny didn't belong to the Union."

"I know it. They framed the poor bastard."

"Who framed him?" asked Slim.

"Krakowski," replied the grinder. "He knew they were goin' through the lockers this mornin' an' he planted a green card in Tiny's coat pocket. Tiny's name was signed on it and it was stamped paid with the Union seal. I seen it up in front, just now."

"But Tiny could prove he didn't belong. We all know he didn't."

"Not a chance. Krakowski had Healey up there and he swore Tiny was a member."

"The dirty bastard," mumbled Slim. "What did Tiny say?"

"After Healey spoke up, he didn't say nothin'. He just stood there kind of dumb-like."

A sudden kick against the leg of

Slim's chair bolted the parade of scenes from his mind. He looked up and saw a dirty apron drawn tight around a bartender's distended belly.

"Whatcha goin' to have, kid? Can't sit here all day on a coupl'a shots."

"Nothin' more, thanks," Slim answered. "I'm leaving now."

He rose and walked quietly over the sawdust-covered floor to the street. Aimlessly he drifted toward Canal Street. At the corner of Tehoupatoulas, a kid selling newspapers yelled and waved a bundle of papers. Absently, Slim fished a nickel out of his pants pocket and dropped it into the outstretched black hand.

Across the street the benches in front of the station were empty. Slim crossed the street, chose a dry seat and slid onto it. Listlessly he opened the damp newspaper on his lap, flipped it right-side-up and started to read. In huge letters sprawled across the sheet's eight columns he spelled out:

LABOR RED SLAYS AUTO FOREMAN

A three-column picture of Tiny filled the center of the page. Under the picture was a single word caption— *WANTED.* A two-column bulletin at the right of the page was headed with:

DISGRUNTLED RED LABOR AGITATOR SLAYS BOSS ON EVE OF DISMISSAL
POLICE COMB CITY FOR AUTO WORKER

Special—The body of Otto Krakowski, a foreman in the River Auto Plant, was found early this morning in a passageway at the side of his home at 2348 Ponce de Leon Avenue. Almost simultaneously a police net was thrown over New Orleans and surrounding parishes to apprehend the man believed to be his assailant, Tiny Cady, 30, discharged worker formerly employed in the River Auto Plant. Krakowski's body was discovered just before dawn this morning by Joseph Kline, a milkman. The victim's head had been brutally battered with a huge file which has already been identified by two of Cady's fellow employees as one used by the former worker at the auto plant. A careful check-up by the police of the Eighth Precinct Station revealed that Cady had stolen the file following his discharge late yesterday.

Factory officials name Cady as a dangerous Red labor agitator who has been responsible for much of the Union trouble experienced recently at the River plant. Police were told by factory officials of Cady's discharge yesterday, following their discovery of a quantity of Communistic literature in his possession. The missing labor Red was also prominent in the illicitly organized labor union discovered a short time ago at the auto plant. Chief of Police Davis is confident he will have the man suspected of Krakowski's murder in custody before nightfall. A police cordon has been thrown around all exits from the city and a careful guard is being kept at the suspected man's home at 212½ Bottom Street. Chief Davis believes Cady's arrest will solve one of the most brutal murders this city has experienced in many years.

Factory officials are lending every aid to the police in their effort to locate Cady who is described as a powerful man, six feet, three inches in height. According to information furnished the police this morning, Cady harbored a grudge against his former foreman, Krakowski, for the latter's having brought to light the Communistic labor activities which resulted in his discharge from the factory.

1935

WILLIAM FAULKNER

That Evening Sun Go Down

Monday is no different from any other week day in Jefferson now. The streets are paved now, and the telephone and electric companies are cutting down more and more of the shade trees —the water oaks, the maples and locusts and elms—to make room for iron poles bearing clusters of bloated and ghostly and bloodless grapes, and we have a city laundry which makes the rounds on Monday morning, gathering the bundles of clothes into bright-colored, specially-made motor cars: the soiled wearing of a whole week now flees apparitionlike behind alert and irritable electric horns, with a long diminishing noise of rubber and asphalt like tearing silk, and even the Negro women who still take in white people's washing after the old custom, fetch and deliver it in automobiles.

But fifteen years ago, on Monday morning the quiet, dusty, shady streets would be full of Negro women with, balanced on their steady, turbaned heads, bundles of clothes tied up in sheets, almost as large as cotton bales, carried so without touch of hand between the kitchen door of the white house and the blackened washpot beside a cabin door in Negro Hollow.

Nancy would set her bundle on the top of her head, then upon the bundle in turn she would set the black straw sailor hat which she wore winter and summer. She was tall, with a high, sad face sunken a little where her teeth were missing. Sometimes we would go a part of the way down the lane and across the pasture with her, to watch the balanced bundle and the hat that never bobbed nor wavered, even when she walked down into the ditch and up the other side and stooped through the fence. She would go down on her hands and knees and crawl through the gap, her head rigid, uptilted, the bundle steady as a rock or a balloon and rise to her feet again and go on.

Sometimes the husbands of the washing women would fetch and deliver the clothes, but Jesus never did that for Nancy, even before father told him to stay away from our house, even when Dilsey was sick and Nancy would come to cook for us.

And then about half the time we'd have to go down the lane to Nancy's cabin and tell her to come on and cook breakfast. We would stop at the ditch, because father told us to not have anything to do with Jesus—he was a short black man, with a razor scar down his face—and we would throw rocks at Nancy's house until she came to the door, leaning her head around it without any clothes on.

'What yawl mean, chunking my house?' Nancy said. 'What you little devils mean?'

'Father says for you to come on and get breakfast,' Caddy said. 'Father says it's over a half an hour now, and you've got to come this minute.'

'I aint studying no breakfast,' Nancy said. 'I going to get my sleep out.'

'I bet you're drunk,' Jason said. 'Father says you're drunk. Are you drunk, Nancy?'

'Who says I is?' Nancy said. 'I got to get my sleep out. I aint studying no breakfast.'

So after a while we quit chunking the cabin and went back home. When she finally came, it was too late for me to go to school. So we thought it was whisky until that day they arrested her again and they were taking her to jail and they passed Mr. Stovall. He was the cashier in the bank and a deacon in the Baptist church, and Nancy began to say:

'When you going to pay me, white man? When you going to pay me, white man? It's been three times now since you paid me a cent——' Mr. Stovall knocked her down, but she kept on saying, 'When you going to pay me, white man? It's been three times now since——' until Mr. Stovall kicked her in the mouth with his heel and the marshal caught Mr. Stovall back, and Nancy lying in the street, laughing. She turned her head and spat out some blood and teeth and said, 'It's been three times now since he paid me a cent.'

That was how she lost her teeth, and all that day they told about Nancy and Mr. Stovall, and all that night the ones that passed the jail could hear Nancy singing and yelling. They could see her hands holding to the window bars, and a lot of them stopped along the fence, listening to her and to the jailer trying to make her stop. She didn't shut up until almost daylight, when the jailer began to hear a bumping and scraping upstairs and he went up there and found Nancy hanging from the window bar. He said that it was cocaine and not whisky, because no nigger would try to commit suicide unless he was full of cocaine, because a nigger full of cocaine wasn't a nigger any longer.

The jailer cut her down and revived her; then he beat her, whipped her. She had hung herself with her dress. She had fixed it all right, but when they arrested her she didn't have on anything except a dress and so she didn't have anything to tie her hands with and she couldn't make her hands let go of the window ledge. So the jailer heard the noise and ran up there and found Nancy hanging from the window, stark naked, her belly already swelling out a little, like a little balloon.

When Dilsey was sick in her cabin and Nancy was cooking for us, we could see her apron swelling out; that was before father told Jesus to stay away from the house. Jesus was in the kitchen, sitting behind the stove, with his razor scar on his black face like a piece of dirty string. He said it was a watermelon that Nancy had under her dress.

'It never come off of your vine, though,' Nancy said.

'Off of what vine?' Caddy said.

'I can cut down the vine it did come off of,' Jesus said.

'What makes you want to talk like that before these chillen?' Nancy said. 'Whyn't you go on to work? You done et. You want Mr. Jason to catch you hanging around his kitchen, talking that way before these chillen?'

'Talking what way?' Caddy said. 'What vine?'

'I cant hang around white man's kitchen,' Jesus said. 'But white man can hang around mine. White man can come in my house, but I cant stop him. When white man want to come in my house, I aint got no house. I cant stop him, but he cant kick me outen it. He cant do that.'

Dilsey was still sick in her cabin. Father told Jesus to stay off our place. Dilsey was still sick. It was a long time. We were in the library after supper.

'Isn't Nancy through in the kitchen yet?' mother said. 'It seems to me that she has had plenty of time to have finished the dishes.'

'Let Quentin go and see,' father said. 'Go and see if Nancy is through, Quentin. Tell her she can go on home.'

I went to the kitchen. Nancy was through. The dishes were put away and the fire was out. Nancy was sitting in a chair, close to the cold stove. She looked at me.

'Mother wants to know if you are through,' I said.

'Yes,' Nancy said. She looked at me. 'I done finished.' She looked at me.

'What is it?' I said. 'What is it?'

'I aint nothing but a nigger,' Nancy said. 'It aint none of my fault.'

She looked at me, sitting in the chair before the cold stove, the sailor hat on her head. I went back to the library. It was the cold stove and all, when you think of a kitchen being warm and busy and cheerful. And with a cold stove and the dishes all put away, and nobody wanting to eat at that hour.

'Is she through?' mother said.

'Yessum,' I said.

'What is she doing?' mother said.

'She's not doing anything. She's through.'

'I'll go and see,' father said.

'Maybe she's waiting for Jesus to come and take her home,' Caddy said.

'Jesus is gone,' I said. Nancy told us how one morning she woke up and Jesus was gone.

'He quit me,' Nancy said. 'Done gone to Memphis, I reckon. Dodging them city po-lice for a while, I reckon.'

'And a good riddance,' father said. 'I hope he stays there.'

'Nancy's scaired of the dark,' Jason said.

'So are you,' Caddy said.

'I'm not,' Jason said.

'Scairy cat,' Caddy said.

'I'm not,' Jason said.

'You, Candace!' mother said. Father came back.

'I am going to walk down the lane with Nancy,' he said. 'She says that Jesus is back.'

'Has she seen him?' mother said.

'No. Some Negro sent her word that he was back in town. I wont be long.'

'You'll leave me alone, to take Nancy home?' mother said. 'Is her safety more precious to you than mine?'

'I wont be long,' father said.

'You'll leave these children unprotected with that Negro about?'

'I'm going too,' Caddy said. 'Let me go, Father.'

'What would he do with them, if he were unfortunate enough to have them?' father said.

'I want to go, too,' Jason said.

'Jason!' mother said. She was speaking to father. You could tell that by the way she said the name. Like she believed that all day father had been trying to think of doing the thing she wouldn't like the most, and that she knew all the time that after a while he would think of it. I stayed quiet, because father and I both knew that mother would want him to make me stay with her if she just thought of it in time. So father didn't look at me. I was the oldest. I was nine and Caddy was seven and Jason was five.

'Nonsense,' father said. 'We wont be long.'

Nancy had her hat on. We came to the lane. 'Jesus always been good to me,' Nancy said. 'Whenever he had two dollars, one of them was mine.'

We walked in the lane. 'If I can just get through the lane,' Nancy said, 'I be all right then.'

The lane was always dark. 'This is where Jason got scared on Hallowe'en,' Caddy said.

'I didn't,' Jason said.

'Cant Aunt Rachel do anything with him?' father said. Aunt Rachel was old. She lived in a cabin beyond Nancy's, by herself. She had white hair and she smoked a pipe in the door, all day long; she didn't work any more. They said she was Jesus' mother. Sometimes she said she was and sometimes she said she wasn't any kin to Jesus.

'Yes you did,' Caddy said. 'You were scairder than Frony. You were scairder than T. P. even. Scairder than niggers.'

'Cant nobody do nothing with him,' Nancy said. 'He say I done woke up the devil in him and aint but one thing going to lay it down again.'

'Well, he's gone now,' father said. 'There's nothing for you to be afraid of now. And if you'd just let white men alone.'

'Let what white men alone?' Caddy said. 'How let them alone?'

'He aint gone nowhere,' Nancy said. 'I can feel him. I can feel him now, in this lane. He hearing us talk, every word, hid somewhere, waiting. I aint seen him, and I aint going to see him again but once more, with that razor in his mouth. That razor on that string down his back, inside his shirt. And then I aint going to be even surprised.'

'I wasn't scaired,' Jason said.

'If you'd behave yourself, you'd have kept out of this,' father said. 'But it's all right now. He's probably in St. Louis now. Probably got another wife by now and forgot all about you.'

'If he has, I better not find out about it,' Nancy said. 'I'd stand there right over them, and every time he wropped her, I'd cut that arm off. I'd cut his head off and I'd slit her belly and I'd shove——'

'Hush,' father said.

'Slit whose belly, Nancy?' Caddy said.

'I wasn't scaired,' Jason said. 'I'd walk right down this lane by myself.'

'Yah,' Caddy said. 'You wouldn't dare to put your foot down in it if we were not here too.'

Dilsey was still sick, so we took Nancy home every night until mother said, 'How much longer is this going on? I to be left alone in this big house while you take home a frightened Negro?'

We fixed a pallet in the kitchen for Nancy. One night we waked up, hearing the sound. It was not singing and it was not crying, coming up the dark stairs. There was a light in mother's room and we heard father going down the hall, down the back stairs, and Caddy and I went into the hall. The floor was cold. Our toes curled away from it while we listened to the sound. It was like singing and it wasn't like singing, like the sounds that Negroes make.

Then it stopped and we heard father going down the back stairs, and we went to the head of the stairs. Then the sound began again, in the stairway, not loud, and we could see Nancy's eyes halfway up the stairs, against the wall. They looked like cat's eyes do, like a big cat against the wall, watching us. When we came down the steps to where she was, she quit making the sound again, and we stood there until father came back up from the kitchen, with his pistol in his hand. He went back down with Nancy and they came back with Nancy's pallet.

We spread the pallet in our room. After the light in mother's room went off, we could see Nancy's eyes again. 'Nancy,' Caddy whispered, 'are you asleep, Nancy?'

Nancy whispered something. It was oh or no, I dont know which. Like nobody had made it, like it came from nowhere and went nowhere, until it was like Nancy was not there at all; that I had looked so hard at her eyes on the stairs that they had got printed on my eyeballs, like the sun does when you have closed your eyes and there is no sun. 'Jesus,' Nancy whispered. 'Jesus.'

'Was it Jesus?' Caddy said. 'Did he try to come into the kitchen?'

'Jesus,' Nancy said. Like this: Jeeee-eeeeeeeeeeeesus, until the sound went out, like a match or a candle does.

'It's the other Jesus she means,' I said.

'Can you see us, Nancy?' Caddy whispered. 'Can you see our eyes too?'

'I aint nothing but a nigger,' Nancy said. 'God knows. God knows.'

'What did you see down there in the kitchen?' Caddy whispered. 'What tried to get in?'

'God knows,' Nancy said. We could see her eyes. 'God knows.'

Dilsey got well. She cooked dinner. 'You'd better stay in bed a day or two longer,' father said.

'What for?' Dilsey said. 'If I had been a day later, this place would be to rack and ruin. Get on out of here now, and let me get my kitchen straight again.'

Dilsey cooked supper too. And that night, just before dark, Nancy came into the kitchen.

'How do you know he's back?' Dilsey said. 'You aint seen him.'

'Jesus is a nigger,' Jason said.

'I can feel him,' Nancy said. 'I can feel him laying yonder in the ditch.'

'Tonight?' Dilsey said. 'Is he there tonight?'

'Dilsey's a nigger too,' Jason said.

'You try to eat something,' Dilsey said.

'I dont want nothing,' Nancy said.

'I aint a nigger,' Jason said.

'Drink some coffee,' Dilsey said. She poured a cup of coffee for Nancy. 'Do you know he's out there tonight? How come you know it's tonight?'

'I know,' Nancy said. 'He's there, waiting. I know. I done lived with him too long. I know what he is fixing to do fore he know it himself.'

'Drink some coffee,' Dilsey said. Nancy held the cup to her mouth and blew into the cup. Her mouth pursed out like a spreading adder's, like a rubber mouth, like she had blown all the color out of her lips with blowing the coffee.

'I aint a nigger,' Jason said. 'Are you a nigger, Nancy?'

'I hellborn, child,' Nancy said. 'I wont be nothing soon. I going back where I come from soon.'

She began to drink the coffee. While she was drinking, holding the cup in both hands, she began to make the sound again. She made the sound into the cup and the coffee sploshed out onto her hands and her dress. Her eyes looked at us and she sat there, her elbows on her knees, holding the cup in both hands, looking at us across the wet cup, making the sound.

'Look at Nancy,' Jason said. 'Nancy cant cook for us now. Dilsey's got well now.'

'You hush up,' Dilsey said. Nancy held the cup in both hands, looking at us, making the sound, like there were two of them: one looking at us and the other making the sound. 'Whyn't you let Mr. Jason telefoam the marshal?' Dilsey said. Nancy stopped then, holding the cup in her long brown hands. She tried to drink some coffee again, but it sploshed out of the cup, onto her hands and her dress, and she put the cup down. Jason watched her.

'I cant swallow it,' Nancy said. 'I swallows but it wont go down me.'

'You go down to the cabin,' Dilsey said. 'Frony will fix you a pallet and I'll be there soon.'

'Wont no nigger stop him,' Nancy said.

'I aint a nigger,' Jason said. 'Am I, Dilsey?'

'I reckon not,' Dilsey said. She looked at Nancy. 'I dont reckon so. What you going to do, then?'

Nancy looked at us. Her eyes went fast, like she was afraid there wasn't time to look, without hardly moving at all. She looked at us, at all three of us at one time. 'You member that night I stayed in yawls' room?' she said. She told about how we waked up early the next morning, and played. We had to play quiet, on her pallet, until father woke up and it was time to get breakfast. 'Go and ask your maw to let me stay here tonight,' Nancy said. 'I wont need no pallet. We can play some more.'

Caddy asked mother. Jason went too. 'I cant have Negroes sleeping in the bedrooms,' mother said. Jason cried. He cried until mother said he couldn't have any dessert for three days if he didn't stop. Then Jason said he would stop if Dilsey would make a chocolate cake. Father was there.

'Why dont you do something about it?' mother said. 'What do we have officers for?'

'Why is Nancy afraid of Jesus?' Caddy said. 'Are you afraid of father, Mother?'

'What could the officers do?' father said. 'If Nancy hasn't seen him, how could the officers find him?'

'Then why is she afraid?' mother said.

'She says he is there. She says she knows he is there tonight.'

'Yet we pay taxes,' mother said. 'I must wait here alone in this big house while you take a Negro woman home.'

'You know that I am not lying outside with a razor,' father said.

'I'll stop if Dilsey will make a chocolate cake,' Jason said. Mother told us to go out and father said he didn't know if Jason would get a chocolate cake or not, but he knew what Jason was going to get in about a minute. We went back to the kitchen and told Nancy.

'Father said for you to go home and lock the door, and you'll be all right,' Caddy said. 'All right from what, Nancy? Is Jesus mad at you?' Nancy was holding the coffee cup in her hands again, her elbows on her knees and her hands holding the cup between her knees. She was looking into the cup. 'What have you done that made Jesus mad?' Caddy said. Nancy let the cup go. It didn't break on the floor, but the coffee spilled out, and Nancy sat there with her hands still making the shape of the cup. She began to make the sound again, not loud. Not singing and not unsinging. We watched her.

'Here,' Dilsey said. 'You quit that, now. You get aholt of yourself. You wait here. I going to get Versh to walk home with you.' Dilsey went out.

We looked at Nancy. Her shoulders kept shaking, but she quit making the sound. We watched her. 'What's Jesus going to do to you?' Caddy said. 'He went away.'

Nancy looked at us. 'We had fun that night I stayed in yawls' room, didn't we?'

'I didn't,' Jason said. 'I didn't have any fun.'

'You were asleep in mother's room,' Caddy said. 'You were not there.'

'Let's go down to my house and have some more fun,' Nancy said.

'Mother wont let us,' I said. 'It's too late now.'

'Dont bother her,' Nancy said. 'We can tell her in the morning. She wont mind.'

'She wouldn't let us,' I said.

'Dont ask her now,' Nancy said. 'Dont bother her now.'

'She didn't say we couldn't go,' Caddy said.

'We didn't ask,' I said.

'If you go, I'll tell,' Jason said.

'We'll have fun,' Nancy said. 'They wont mind, just to my house. I been working for yawl a long time. They wont mind.'

'I'm not afraid to go,' Caddy said. 'Jason is the one that's afraid. He'll tell.'

'I'm not,' Jason said.

'Yes, you are,' Caddy said. 'You'll tell.'

'I wont tell,' Jason said. 'I'm not afraid.'

'Jason aint afraid to go with me,' Nancy said. 'Is you, Jason?'

'Jason is going to tell,' Caddy said. The lane was dark. We passed the pasture gate. 'I bet if something was to jump out from behind that gate, Jason would holler.'

'I wouldn't,' Jason said. We walked down the lane. Nancy was talking loud.

'What are you talking so loud for, Nancy?' Caddy said.

'Who; me?' Nancy said. 'Listen at Quentin and Caddy and Jason saying I'm talking loud.'

'You talk like there was five of us here,' Caddy said. 'You talk like father was here too.'

'Who; me talking loud, Mr. Jason?' Nancy said.

'Nancy called Jason "Mister,"' Caddy said.

'Listen how Caddy and Quentin and Jason talk,' Nancy said.

'We're not talking loud,' Caddy said. 'You're the one that's talking like father——'

'Hush,' Nancy said; 'hush, Mr. Jason.'

'Nancy called Jason "Mister" aguh——'

'Hush,' Nancy said. She was talking loud when we crossed the ditch and stooped through the fence where she used to stoop through with the clothes on her head. Then we came to her house. We were going fast then. She opened the door. The smell of the house was like the lamp and the smell of Nancy was like the wick, like they were waiting for one another to begin to smell. She lit the lamp and closed the door and put the bar up. Then she quit talking loud, looking at us.

'What're we going to do?' Caddy said.

'What do yawl want to do?' Nancy said.

'You said we would have some fun,' Caddy said.

There was something about Nancy's house; something you could smell besides Nancy and the house. Jason smelled it, even. 'I dont want to stay here,' he said. 'I want to go home.'

'Go home, then,' Caddy said.

'I dont want to go by myself,' Jason said.

'We're going to have some fun,' Nancy said.

'How?' Caddy said.

Nancy stood by the door. She was looking at us, only it was like she had emptied her eyes, like she had quit using them. 'What do you want to do?' she said.

'Tell us a story,' Caddy said. 'Can you tell a story?'

'Yes,' Nancy said.

'Tell it,' Caddy said. We looked at Nancy. 'You dont know any stories.'

'Yes,' Nancy said. 'Yes I do.'

She came and sat in a chair before the hearth. There was a little fire there. Nancy built it up, when it was already hot inside. She built a good blaze. She told a story. She talked like her eyes looked, like her eyes watching us and her voice talking to us did not belong to her. Like she was living somewhere else, waiting somewhere else. She was outside the cabin. Her voice was inside and the shape of her, the Nancy that could stoop under a barbed wire fence with a bundle of clothes balanced on her head as though without weight, like a balloon, was there. But that was all. 'And so this here queen come walking up to the ditch, where that bad man was hiding. She was walking up to the ditch, and she say, "If I can just get past this here ditch," was what she say . . .'

'What ditch?' Caddy said. 'A ditch like that one out there? Why did a queen want to go into a ditch?'

'To get to her house,' Nancy said. She looked at us. 'She had to cross the ditch to get into her house quick and bar the door.'

'Why did she want to go home and bar the door?' Caddy said.

Nancy looked at us. She quit talking. She looked at us. Jason's legs stuck straight out of his pants where he sat on Nancy's lap. 'I dont think that's a good story,' he said. 'I want to go home.'

'Maybe we had better,' Caddy said.

She got up from the floor. 'I bet they are looking for us right now.' She went toward the door.

'No,' Nancy said. 'Dont open it.' She got up quick and passed Caddy. She didn't touch the door, the wooden bar.

'Why not?' Caddy said.

'Come back to the lamp,' Nancy said. 'We'll have fun. You dont have to go.'

'We ought to go,' Caddy said. 'Unless we have a lot of fun.' She and Nancy came back to the fire, the lamp.

'I want to go home,' Jason said. 'I'm going to tell.'

'I know another story,' Nancy said. She stood close to the lamp. She looked at Caddy, like when your eyes look up at a stick balanced on your nose. She had to look down to see Caddy, but her eyes looked like that, like when you are balancing a stick.

'I wont listen to it,' Jason said. 'I'll bang on the floor.'

'It's a good one,' Nancy said. 'It's better than the other one.'

'What's it about?' Caddy said. Nancy was standing by the lamp. Her hand was on the lamp, against the light, long and brown.

'Your hand is on that hot globe,' Caddy said. 'Dont it feel hot to your hand?'

Nancy looked at her hand on the lamp chimney. She took her hand away, slow. She stood there, looking at Caddy, wringing her long hand as though it were tied to her wrist with a string.

'Let's do something else,' Caddy said.

'I want to go home,' Jason said.

'I got some popcorn,' Nancy said. She looked at Caddy and then at Jason and then at me and then at Caddy again. 'I got some popcorn.'

'I dont iike popcorn,' Jason said. 'I'd rather have candy.'

Nancy looked at Jason. 'You can hold the popper.' She was still wringing her hand; it was long and limp and brown.

'All right,' Jason said. 'I'll stay a while if I can do that. Caddy cant hold it. I'll want to go home again if Caddy holds the popper.'

Nancy built up the fire. 'Look at Nancy putting her hands in the fire,' Caddy said. 'What's the matter with you, Nancy?'

'I got popcorn,' Nancy said. 'I got some.' She took the popper from under the bed. It was broken. Jason began to cry.

'Now we cant have any popcorn,' he said.

'We ought to go home, anyway,' Caddy said. 'Come on, Quentin.'

'Wait,' Nancy said; 'wait. I can fix it. Dont you want to help me fix it?'

'I dont think I want any,' Caddy said. 'It's too late now.'

'You help me, Jason,' Nancy said. 'Dont you want to help me?'

'No,' Jason said. 'I want to go home.'

'Hush,' Nancy said; 'hush. Watch. Watch me. I can fix it so Jason can hold it and pop the corn.' She got a piece of wire and fixed the popper.

'It wont hold good,' Caddy said.

'Yes it will,' Nancy said. 'Yawl watch. Yawl help me shell some corn.'

The popcorn was under the bed too. We shelled it into the popper and Nancy helped Jason hold the popper over the fire.

'It's not popping,' Jason said. 'I want to go home.'

'You wait,' Nancy said. 'It'll begin to pop. We'll have fun then.' She was sitting close to the fire. The lamp was turned up so high it was beginning to smoke.

'Why dont you turn it down some?' I said.

'It's all right,' Nancy said. 'I'll clean it. Yawl wait. The popcorn will start in a minute.'

'I dont believe it's going to start,' Caddy said. 'We ought to start home, anyway. They'll be worried.'

'No,' Nancy said. 'It's going to pop. Dilsey will tell um yawl with me. I been working for yawl long time. They wont mind if yawl at my house. You wait, now. It'll start popping any minute now.'

Then Jason got some smoke in his eyes and he began to cry. He dropped the popper into the fire. Nancy got a wet rag and wiped Jason's face, but he didn't stop crying.

'Hush,' she said. 'Hush.' But he didn't hush. Caddy took the popper out of the fire.

'It's burned up,' she said. 'You'll have to get some more popcorn, Nancy.'

'Did you put all of it in?' Nancy said.

'Yes,' Caddy said. Nancy looked at Caddy. Then she took the popper and opened it and poured the cinders into her apron and began to sort the grains, her hands long and brown, and we watching her.

'Haven't you got any more?' Caddy said.

'Yes,' Nancy said; 'yes. Look. This here aint burnt. All we need to do is——'

'I want to go home,' Jason said. 'I'm going to tell.'

'Hush,' Caddy said. We all listened. Nancy's head was already turned toward the barred door, her eyes filled with red lamplight. 'Somebody is coming,' Caddy said.

Then Nancy began to make that

sound again, not loud, sitting there above the fire, her long hands dangling between her knees; all of a sudden water began to come out on her face in big drops, running down her face, carrying in each one a little turning ball of firelight like a spark until it dropped off her chin. 'She's not crying,' I said.

'I aint crying,' Nancy said. Her eyes were closed. 'I aint crying. Who is it?'

'I dont know,' Caddy said. She went to the door and looked out. 'We've got to go now,' she said. 'Here comes father.'

'I'm going to tell,' Jason said. 'Yawl made me come.'

The water still ran down Nancy's face. She turned in her chair. 'Listen. Tell him. Tell him we going to have fun. Tell him I take good care of yawl until in the morning. Tell him to let me come home with yawl and sleep on the floor. Tell him I wont need no pallet. We'll have fun. You member last time how we had so much fun?'

'I didn't have fun,' Jason said. 'You hurt me. You put smoke in my eyes. I'm going to tell.'

Father came in. He looked at us. Nancy did not get up.

'Tell him,' she said.

'Caddy made us come down here,' Jason said. 'I didn't want to.'

Father came to the fire. Nancy looked up at him. 'Cant you go to Aunt Rachel's and stay?' he said. Nancy looked up at father, her hands between her knees. 'He's not here,' father said. 'I would have seen him. There's not a soul in sight.'

'He in the ditch,' Nancy said. 'He waiting in the ditch yonder.'

'Nonsense,' father said. He looked at Nancy. 'Do you know he's there?'

'I got the sign,' Nancy said.

'What sign?'

'I got it. It was on the table when I come in. It was a hogbone, with blood meat still on it, laying by the lamp. He's out there. When yawl walk out that door, I gone.'

'Gone where, Nancy?' Caddy said.

'I'm not a tattletale,' Jason said.

'Nonsense,' father said.

'He out there,' Nancy said. 'He looking through that window this minute, waiting for yawl to go. Then I gone.'

'Nonsense,' father said. 'Lock up your house and we'll take you on to Aunt Rachel's.'

' 'Twont do no good,' Nancy said. She didn't look at father now, but he looked down at her, at her long, limp, moving hands. 'Putting it off wont do no good.'

'Then what do you want to do?' father said.

'I dont know,' Nancy said. 'I cant do nothing. Just put it off. And that dont do no good. I reckon it belong to me. I reckon what I going to get aint no more than mine.'

'Get what?' Caddy said. 'What's yours?'

'Nothing,' father said. 'You all must get to bed.'

'Caddy made me come,' Jason said.

'Go on to Aunt Rachel's,' father said.

'It wont do no good,' Nancy said. She sat before the fire, her elbows on her knees, her long hands between her knees. 'When even your own kitchen wouldn't do no good. When even if I was sleeping on the floor in the room with your chillen, and the next morning there I am, and blood—'

'Hush,' father said. 'Lock the door and put out the lamp and go to bed.'

'I scared of the dark,' Nancy said. 'I scared for it to happen in the dark.'

'You mean you're going to sit right here with the lamp lighted?' father said. Then Nancy began to make the sound again, sitting before the fire, her long hands between her knees. 'Ah, damnation,' father said. 'Come along, chillen. It's past bedtime.'

'When yawl go home, I gone,' Nancy said. She talked quieter now, and her face looked quiet, like her hands. 'Anyway, I got my coffin money saved up with Mr. Lovelady.' Mr. Lovelady was a short, dirty man who collected the Negro insurance, coming around to the cabins or the kitchens every Saturday morning, to collect fifteen cents. He and his wife lived at the hotel. One morning his wife committed suicide. They had a child, a little girl. He and the child went away. After a week or two he came back alone. We would see him going along the lanes and the back streets on Saturday mornings.

'Nonsense,' father said. 'You'll be the first thing I'll see in the kitchen tomorrow morning.'

'You'll see what you'll see, I reckon,' Nancy said. 'But it will take the Lord to say what that will be.'

We left her sitting before the fire.

'Come and put the bar up,' father said. But she didn't move. She didn't look at us again, sitting quietly there between the lamp and the fire. From some distance down the lane we could look back and see her through the open door.

'What, Father?' Caddy said. 'What's going to happen?'

'Nothing,' father said. Jason was on father's back, so Jason was the tallest of all of us. We went down into the ditch. I looked at it, quiet. I couldn't see much where the moonlight and the shadows tangled.

'If Jesus is hid here, he can see us, cant he?' Caddy said.

'He's not there,' father said. 'He went away a long time ago.'

'You made me come,' Jason said, high; against the sky it looked like father had two heads, a little one and a big one. 'I didn't want to.'

We went up out of the ditch. We could still see Nancy's house and the open door, but we couldn't see Nancy now, sitting before the fire with the door open, because she was tired. 'I just done got tired,' she said. 'I just a nigger. It aint no fault of mine.'

But we could hear her, because she began just after we came up out of the ditch, the sound that was not singing and not unsinging. 'Who will do our washing now, Father?' I said.

'I'm not a nigger,' Jason said, high and close above father's head.

'You're worse,' Caddy said, 'you are a tattletale. If something was to jump out, you'd be scairder than a nigger.'

'I wouldn't,' Jason said.

'You'd cry,' Caddy said.

'Caddy,' father said.

'I wouldn't!' Jason said.

'Scairy cat,' Caddy said.

'Candace!' father said.

1931

JESSE STUART

Nest Egg

"SHAN, I don't want to tell you the second time to break that hen from sittin' on a nest egg," Mom said. "I don't have enough hens to spare to let one sit on a nest egg."

"Why don't you put more eggs under her, Mom?" I asked. "I never saw a hen that wants to sit on a nest like she does."

"It's too late in summer," Mom said. "She'd hatch off a gang of little chickens in dog-days and they'd die. Now you go take that nest egg from her nest."

"All right, Mom," I said.

The wilted grass was hot beneath my bare feet as I walked across the carpet of wilted crab-grass to a patch of paw-paw sprouts. I followed a little path into the pawpaw sprouts where the white agate sun had wilted the pawpaw leaves until they hung in wilted clusters. When I approached the nest, the old Sebright hen raised her wings and clucked. I thought she was tryin' to tell me to stay away. And when I started to put my hand back under her to get the egg, she pecked my arm in three places faster than I could wink my eyes. Each place she pecked me, my arm bled.

I don't blame her for sittin' in this cool place, I thought. I don't blame her for fightin' over the egg. She laid the egg.

Since Mom had asked me to take the nest egg from the nest, I ran my hand under her and got the egg and put it beside the nest. And when she started rollin' it back under her with her long hooked bill, I left the pawpaw patch.

"Did you take the egg outten that nest?" Mom asked me soon as I reached the house.

"I took it out this time, Mom," I said. "Look at my arm!"

"That hen's a mean old hussy," Mom said.

That week hadn't passed when Mom called her chickens around the corncrib and fed them shelled corn. Since we lived in the woods and our closest neighbor lived a mile away, hawks, hoot owls, and varmints often caught our chickens. Once a week Mom called them to the corncrib to feed and count them.

"Shan, the old Sebright hen's not here," Mom said. Mom knew her chickens since we had such a variety of mixed chickens there were hardly any two with the same color of feathers.

"I guess something's caught 'er," I said.

"With her bright feathers she's a flowerpot for a hoot owl," Mom said.

Twenty-one days had passed when I saw this old Sebright hen goin' up the hill toward the woods with one little chicken. The nest egg had hatched. I didn't tell Mom what I had seen. I'd let her find out for herself. The old Sebright never came to the corncrib when Mom called our chickens to the house to feed and count them. She lived alone in the woods with her one chicken.

August passed and September came. The leaves had started to turn brown on the trees. I was out huntin' for a hen's nest when I heard a hen cackle, and I

From *Tales From The Plum Grove Hills* by Jesse Stuart, published and copyrighted 1946 by E. P. Dutton & Co., Inc.

looked in time to see our old Sebright hen and her one chicken that was growin' tall and well-feathered disappear into the brush. I was glad to know that they were still alive and I wondered when they would come to the house. And this was a secret I kept from Mom and Pa.

It was in early October that Pa had finished cuttin' our late corn. He had come across the ridge and followed the path down the point to our house. When he reached the house, Mom was callin' our chickens to the corncrib to feed and count them.

"Sall, this reminds me of something," Pa said. "It must've been two miles back on the ridge, I either saw a Sebright hen with a young chicken with her 'r I saw a pheasant and a young one. They flew through the brush like wild quails before I could get close!"

"Did you take that egg from under that old hen that day?" Mom turned around and asked me.

"I did, Mom," I said.

"I don't want you to lie to me," Mom said.

"I'm tellin' you the truth," I said.

"I guess I saw a couple of pheasants," Pa said.

It was in late November, when the worms and bugs had gone into the ground for the winter, that the old Sebright hen came to the corncrib when Mom called the chickens. Hunger had forced her to come down from the high hills with her young rooster. She was very proud of him; though he was nearly as tall as she was, she clucked to him as if he were still a tiny chicken that had just come from the egg. When one of the hens came close to him, she flogged the hen.

Mom looked at Pa and Pa looked at Mom. They didn't say anything at first,

but each stood there lookin' at the old hen and young rooster and then they looked at me.

"But, Mom, I did take the egg from her nest," I said.

"Where did you put the egg?" Mom asked.

"Over in the grass beside the nest."

"Didn't you know an old sittin' hen will roll an egg ten feet to get it back in the nest?"

"No," I said.

"There'll be bad luck among our chickens," Pa said.

"We're havin' enough bad luck already," Mom said. "I can't raise chickens as fast as something catches 'em. I missed eight in September and eleven in October. Since the trees lost their leaves so the hoot owls could see the chickens, I've lost seventeen this month."

"We'll lose more now," Pa said. "I'd put that young gentleman in the skillet and fry 'im if he wasn't sich a fine-lookin' young rooster."

"Don't do it, Pa," I said. "She's had a hard time raisin' 'im."

"Pap had this same thing to happen when I was a little boy," Pa said. "Before the year was over he lost every chicken he had with the cholera. They died in piles."

I didn't want to say anything to Pa, but I didn't see why a hen's sittin' on a nest egg and hatchin' it and raisin' her chicken had anything to do with the cholera. I wanted to beg him to keep this young rooster that I called Nest Egg. Pa must've forgot about killin' 'im and fryin' 'im, for November and December came and passed and Nest Egg still ran with his mother.

Nest Egg wasn't six months old when he started crowin'. Now he was much larger than his mother. He was tall and he had big legs and little straight spurs that looked like long locust thorns. His mother still ran with him and clucked to him, but he didn't pay his mother much attention. He would often stand lookin' at the spring sun and never bat his eyes. He had a mean-lookin' eye and a long crooked bill that looked like a chicken hawk's bill. He didn't look like his mother. Pa said that he was a cross between a Sebright and a black game. He had almost every variety of colors. I thought he was a mongrel rooster—a mixture of many breeds.

We had five roosters at our house; all five of them ran Nest Egg. They'd run him and flog him. Once our black game rooster, War Hawk, just missed Nest Egg's hawk-shaped head with his long, straight spur that had killed four of our roosters. But Nest Egg outran War Hawk. He took to the brush cacklin'.

"He won't always be a-runnin' you, Nest Egg," I said while War Hawk boasted to the big flock of hens around 'im.

Durin' the spring months we seldom saw Nest Egg. He kept a safe distance away from the house. He stayed away from the five old roosters who fought him every time he got near one's flock of hens. But once Mom was huntin' a hen's nest in the woods and she saw a chicken hawk swoop low to catch a hen. She saw Nest Egg hit the hawk with all the power he had. Mom said he tore a small wind-puff of feathers from the hawk. Mom told Pa about Nest Egg's fight with the hawk.

"He's a-goin' to make a powerful fightin' rooster," Pa said. "Any rooster that's game enough to hit a hawk has good metal."

And Pa was right in his prediction about Nest Egg. In early June we saw him a-runnin' Big Bill, our gray game rooster. In late June he whipped Red Ranger, our red game rooster. In July he whipped Lightnin', our black Minorca rooster. Three days later, he whipped our "scrub" rooster that was mixed with many breeds of chickens. We called him Mongrel. He had whipped all the roosters but War Hawk.

"If Nest Egg can stay outten the way of War Hawk's spurs," Pa said, "he'll whip old War Hawk. He's a young rooster that's run over the hills and scratched for a livin' and he's got better wind."

It was in the middle of August when Nest Egg came down to the barn. He tiptoed, flapped his wings, and crowed in the barn lot. This was War Hawk's territory. It was the choice territory War Hawk had taken for his flocks of hens. Not one of our roosters had dared to venture on War Hawk's territory. Maybe, Nest Egg had come down from the hills to challenge War Hawk's supremacy. Since he had whipped Big Bill, Red Ranger, Lightnin', and Mongrel he wouldn't be chased by War Hawk. He was a year old now and he felt his youth. He was ready to fight. And when War Hawk heard another rooster crowin' on his territory, he came runnin' with a flock of hens following 'im. He challenged young Nest Egg for a fight.

At first War Hawk and Nest Egg sparred at each other. War Hawk had fought many fights and maybe he was feelin' out his young opponent. They stuck their heads out at each other and pecked; then they came together with all their might and the feathers flew. Nest Egg hit War Hawk so hard that he knocked him backwards.

Again they struck and again, again,

again. Each time the feathers flew lazily away with the August wind. Then War Hawk leaped high into the air and spurred at Nest Egg's head. His spur cut a place in Nest Egg's red comb. That seemed to make Nest Egg madder than ever. He rushed in and grabbed War Hawk by the comb and pushed his head against the ground while he flogged him with wings and feet. When Nest Egg's bill-hold gave away, he left a gap in War Hawk's battered comb.

War Hawk was gettin' weaker. But he leaped high into the air and spurred at Nest Egg's head; Nest Egg dodged and the spur missed his head. That must have given Nest Egg an idea, for he leaped high in the air and War Hawk leaped high to meet him. War Hawk caught Nest Egg's spur in his craw, which ripped it open. War Hawk fell on the barn lot where he had seen others fall. As War Hawk lay dyin', Nest Egg stood above him on his tiptoes and crowed. He was the new king of our barn lot.

Nest Egg's victory over War Hawk spread among our neighbors and many of them asked to bring their roosters to fight Nest Egg.

"He's not the fightin' stock," Pa told them. "He's only a scrub rooster. I don't like to fight chickens, but if it's a pleasure to you, bring your roosters around."

In September he killed Warfield Flaughtery's great Hercules game rooster that had never lost once in fight in fifty-three fights. Hercules had whipped War Hawk. Two weeks later he killed Warfield Flaughtery's young game rooster, Napoleon. In early October he killed Eif Nippert's red game rooster, Red Devil; two days later

he spurred Ennis Sneed's gray game rooster, Big Bee Martin, blind in both eyes. Later that month he pecked a hole in a hoot owl's head that had caught one of our hens. Before January he had killed nineteen roosters and one hoot owl.

"He's some rooster," Pa said. "But he's sure to bring us bad luck."

Pa was offered fifty dollars for Nest Egg by a man from a showboat on the Ohio River. He watched Nest Egg kill his twenty-fifth rooster before he offered Pa the money.

"He's bad among my other roosters here," Pa said. "They used to make him live in the woods; now he makes them live in the woods. But I don't want to sell him."

"That's a big price, Mick," Mom said. "You'd better take it."

But Pa wouldn't sell him. Finally, the man from the showboat offered Pa seventy-five dollars. Then he said he wouldn't offer him another dime. He started back toward town, turned around, and came back and offered Pa a hundred-dollar bill, the first hundred-dollar bill that any of us had ever seen.

"I still won't sell 'im," Pa said.

Then the man went away and Mom was mad.

"Hundred dollars is a lot of money, Mick."

"I like that rooster," Pa said. "I'm not a-sellin' 'im."

Anybody would like Nest Egg if he could've seen him strut about the barn lot with fifty hens around him. He had nearly half the flock followin' him. When Nest Egg wanted one of our other roosters' hens, he just said something to her in his language and she followed 'im. And now when Mom called our chickens to the corncrib to feed and count them, she found that our flock was gradually growin'. This was the first time since we had had chickens that our flock had increased without our raisin' chickens or buyin' them. Mom couldn't understand how the number had grown. She saw several different-colored hens among our flock.

In February our flock increased seven; in March it increased twelve; in April it increased twenty-seven; in May it had increased thirty-two. In the meantime, Nest Egg had fought seven more fights and had killed six of the roosters; the seventh finally recovered.

In May, Warfield Flaughtery came to our house with his mule and express wagon.

"Mick, have you got some extra hens in your flock?" he asked Pa.

"Think we have, Warfield," Pa said. "How many did you lose?"

"About sixty," he told Pa.

"Would you know your hens?" Pa asked.

"Shore would," he said. "Call your hens to the corncrib."

"You're not right sure the hawks, hoot owls, and varmints didn't take some of them?" Pa asked.

"I'm sure they didn't," he said. "A two-legged varmint got 'em."

"Do you mean I stole your chickens?" Pa said.

"Not exactly," he grunted.

"They must've come to my rooster," Pa said.

"They didn't do that," Warfield said as Pa called the chickens and they came runnin'. "They wouldn't follow that scrub rooster."

Warfield and Pa were mad. Mom heard them talkin' and hurried to the corncrib.

"Then take your hens," Pa said. "Here's a coop. Catch 'em and put 'em in it."

Mom stood by and didn't say anything until Warfield got Nest Egg's mother. Mom made him put her down.

"You're a-takin' hens that I've raised," Mom said.

But Warfield insisted that he wasn't and kept takin' our hens until he had sixty. Then he hauled them away on his express wagon. He must have told others about our havin' his chickens. Jake Hix came and claimed thirty of our hens. And Pa let 'im have 'em. And then Cy Pennix came and wanted fourteen. We knew that Cy didn't even raise chickens and Pa wouldn't let 'im have 'em. Pa and Cy almost had a fight, but Pa told 'im to climb on his express-wagon seat and get outten the hollow fast as his mule could take him. Wiley Blevins, Ott Jarvis, and Jot Seagraves came and claimed our chickens. "Who do you think I am?" Pa asked them. "A chicken thief?" Pa showed them the way back down the hollow and they told Pa that he would be sorry.

"That rooster's a-bringin' us bad luck," Pa said. "These men live from one to three miles from us. Nest Egg is goin' back into the hills now since worms are scarce here. And he meets with other roosters and their flocks and he steals the hens. God knows I'm not a chicken thief. It's that good-lookin' rooster Nest Egg that the hens all take to. He tolls the hens here."

In June the four neighbors that Pa had chased away had indicted Pa for stealin' their chickens. Pa was branded as a chicken thief, for it was printed in the *Greenwood County News* about his bein' indicted by four men. And before the trial was called in August, Warfield Flaughtery came back with his express wagon and hauled away forty-six more hens; Jake Hix came and claimed seventy. He said all his hens had left, and Mom said our flock had increased more than a hundred. Warfield Flaughtery and Jake Hix had always been good neighbors to us, but Warfield's roosters had always killed our roosters before, and now Nest Egg had killed two of his best games and he was sore at us over it. Pa asked him if he'd been summoned for a witness in the trial, and he told Pa that he and Jake both had.

Pa was tried on the indictment made by Cy Pennix. The courthouse was filled with people to see how the trial ended since there'd been much chicken stealin' in our county. We proved that Cy Pennix didn't even have any chickens—that he had just claimed our chickens but did not get them. And Pa came clear. Then Wiley Blevins's indictment was next to be tried. And when Wiley said that he would swear to his chickens' feathers, Judge Whittlecomb threw the case out of court. Since Warfield Flaughtery and Jake Hix had claimed and had taken their hens, saying they knew them by the colors, they got scared at the decision made by Judge Whittlecomb and they hauled the chickens they had taken from us back before sunset.

"That Nest Egg's a wonder," Pa said. "Our flock has doubled and he's killed fifty-one roosters. He's just a little past two years old."

But boys threatened me when I went to the store. They threatened me because Nest Egg had killed their roosters. And neighborhood men threatened Pa over our rooster. Once Pa got a letter that didn't have a name signed to it and in it was a threat to burn our barn. He got another letter and the man said he was a little man, that he would meet Pa sometime in the dark. He said a bullet would sink into a chicken thief in the dark same as it would in the daytime.

"I didn't know as little a thing as a rooster could get people riled like that," Pa said. "I didn't know a rooster could turn a whole community of people against a man."

Cy Pennix shook his fist at Pa and dared him to step across the line fence onto his land. And Warfield Flaughtery wouldn't speak to Pa. Tim Flaughtery hit me with a rock and ran. And often Pa would get up in the night and put on his clothes and walk over to our barn. He was afraid somebody would slip in to burn it.

"I feel something's a-goin' to happen soon," Pa told me one day in September. "This can't go on. Our flock is increasin' day by day. Look at the chickens about this place!"

There were chickens every place. Even our old roosters had increased their flocks with hens that Nest Egg had tolled to our house—hens that could not join Nest Egg's ever increasin' flock. When we gathered eggs, two of us took bushel baskets. We found hens' nests under the ferns, under the rock cliffs, under the smokehouse corncrib,—in hollow logs and stumps,—and once I found a hen's nest with twenty-two eggs in it on top of our kitchen behind the flue. An egg rolled off and smashed on Pa's hat is how come us to find the nest. We had to haul eggs to town four times a week now.

One early October mornin' when Mom called our chickens to the corncrib to feed them, Nest Egg didn't come steppin' proudly on his tiptoes. And that mornin' he hadn't awakened Pa at four o'clock by his six lusty crows. I missed my first day of school to help Pa hunt for Nest Egg. We looked around the barn. We scoured the steep hill slopes, lookin' under each greenbrier cluster and in each sprout thicket. We looked every place in Nest Egg's territory and were about to give up the hunt when we walked under the white-oak chicken roost between the barn and house. We found Nest Egg sprawled on the ground beneath the roost with several hens gathered around him cacklin'. A tiny screech owl was sittin' on Nest Egg's back, peckin' a small hole in his head.

"Think of that," Pa said. "A rooster game and powerful as Nest Egg would be killed by a damned little screech owl no bigger than my fist. A hundred-dollar rooster killed in his prime by a worthless screech owl."

Pa reached down and grabbed the owl by the head and wrung its neck. "I can't stand to see it take another bite from Nest Egg's head," he said.

I stood over Nest Egg and cried.

"No ust to cry, Shan," Pa said. "Nest Egg's dead. That damned owl fouled 'im. It flew into the chicken roost and lit on his back when he was asleep. It pecked his head until it finished 'im."

"But I haf to cry," I said, watchin' Pa take his bandanna from his pocket to wipe the tears from his eyes.

1944

THOMAS HARDY

The Three Strangers

AMONG THE few features of agricultural England which retain an appearance but little modified by the lapse of centuries, may be reckoned the high, grassy, and furzy downs, coombs, or ewe-leases, as they are indifferently called, that fill a large area of certain counties in the south and south-west. If any mark of human occupation is met with hereon it usually takes the form of the solitary cottage of some shepherd.

Fifty years ago such a lonely cottage stood on such a down, and may possibly be standing there now. In spite of its loneliness, however, the spot, by actual measurement, was not more than five miles from a county-town. Yet that affected it little. Five miles of irregular upland, during the long inimical seasons, with their sleets, snows, rains, and mists, afford withdrawing space enough to isolate a Timon or a Nebuchadnezzar; much less, in fair weather, to please that less repellent tribe, the poets, philosophers, artists, and others who "conceive and meditate of pleasing things."

Some old earthen camp or barrow, some clump of trees, at least some starved fragment of ancient hedge, is usually taken advantage of in the erection of these forlorn dwellings. But, in the present case, such a kind of shelter had been disregarded. Higher Crowstairs, as the house was called, stood quite detached and undefended. The only reason for its precise situation seemed to be the crossing of two footpaths at right angles hard by, which may have crossed there and thus for a good five hundred years. Hence the house was exposed to the elements on all sides. But, though the wind up here blew unmistakably when it did blow, and the rain hit hard whenever it fell, the various weathers of the winter season were not quite so formidable on the coomb as they were imagined to be by dwellers on low ground. The raw rimes were not so pernicious as in the hollows, and the frosts were scarcely so severe. When the shepherd and his family who tenanted the house were pitied for their sufferings from the exposure, they said that upon the whole they were less inconvenienced by "wuzzes and flames" (hoarses and phlegms) than when they had lived by the stream of a snug neighboring valley.

The night of March 28, 182—, was precisely one of the nights that were wont to call forth these expressions of commiseration. The level rain-storm smote walls, slopes, and hedges like the clothyard shafts of Senlac and Crecy. Such sheep and out-door animals as had no shelter stood with their buttocks to the wind; while the tails of little birds trying to roost on some scraggy thorn were blown inside out like umbrellas. The gable end of the cottage was stained with wet, and the eavesdropping flapped against the wall. Yet never was commiseration for the shepherd more misplaced, for that cheerful rustic was entertaining a large party in glorification of the christening of his second girl.

The guests had arrived before the rain began to fall, and they were all now assembled in the chief, or living, room of the dwelling. A glance into the apartment at eight o'clock on this eventful evening would have resulted in the opinion that it was as cosey and comfortable a nook as could be wished for in boisterous weather. The calling of its inhabitant was proclaimed by a number of highly polished sheep-crooks without stems that were hung ornamentally over the fireplace, the curl of each shining crook varying from the antiquated type engraved in the patriarchal pictures of old family Bibles to the most approved fashion of the last local sheep-fair. The room was lighted by half a dozen candles, having wicks only a trifle smaller than the grease which enveloped them, in candlesticks that were never used but at high-days, holy-days, and family feasts. The lights were scattered about the room, two of them standing on the chimney-piece. This position of candles was in itself significant. Candles on the chimney-piece always meant a party.

On the hearth, in front of a back-brand to give substance, blazed a fire of thorns, that crackled "like the laughter of the fool."

Nineteen persons were gathered here. Of these, five women, wearing gowns of various bright hues, sat in chairs along the wall; girls shy and not shy filled the window-bench; four men, including Charley Jake, the hedge-carpenter, Elijah New, the parish-clerk, and John Pitcher, a neighboring dairy-man, the shepherd's father-in-law, lolled in the settle; a young man and maid, who were blushing over tentative *pourparlers* on a life-companionship, sat beneath the corner cupboard; and an elderly engaged man of fifty or upwards moved restlessly about from spots where his betrothed was not to the spot where she was. Enjoyment was pretty general, and so much the more prevailed in being unhampered by conventional restrictions. Absolute confidence in one another's good opinion begot perfect ease, while the finishing stroke of manner, amounting to a truly princely serenity, was lent to the majority by the absence of any expression or trait denoting that they wished to get on in the world, enlarge their minds, or do any eclipsing thing whatever—which now-adays so generally nips the bloom and *bonhomie* of all except the two extremes of the social scale.

Shepherd Fennel had married well, his wife being a dairy-man's daughter from the valley below, who brought fifty guineas in her pocket—and kept them there till they should be required for ministering to the needs of a coming family. This frugal woman had been somewhat exercised as to the character that should be given to the gathering. A sit-still party had its advantages; but an undisturbed position of ease in chairs and settles was apt to lead on the men to such an unconscionable deal of toping that they would sometimes fairly drink the house dry. A dancing-party was the alternative; but this, while avoiding the foregoing objection on the score of good drink, had a counter-balancing disadvantage in the matter of good victuals, the ravenous appetites engendered by the exercise causing immense havoc in the buttery. Shepherdess Fennel fell back upon the intermediate plan of mingling short dances with short periods of talk and singing, so as to hinder any ungovernable rage in either. But this scheme was entirely confined to her own gentle mind; the shepherd himself was in the mood to exhibit the most reckless phases of hospitality.

The fiddler was a boy of those parts, about twelve years of age, who had a wonderful dexterity in jigs and reels, though his fingers were so small and short as to necessitate a constant shifting for the high notes, from which he scrambled back to the first position with sounds not of unmixed purity of tone. At seven the shrill tweedle-dee of this youngster had begun, accompanied by a booming ground-bass from Elijah New, the parish-clerk, who had thought-fully brought with him his favorite musical instrument, the serpent. Dancing was instantaneous, Mrs. Fennel privately enjoining the players on no account to let the dance exceed the length of a quarter of an hour.

But Elijah and the boy, in the excitement of their position, quite forgot the injunction. Moreover, Oliver Giles, a man of seventeen, one of the dancers, who was enamoured of his partner, a fair girl of thirty-three rolling years, had recklessly handed a new crown-piece to the musicians, as a bribe to keep going as long as they had muscle and wind. Mrs. Fennel, seeing the steam begin to generate on the countenances of her guests, crossed over and touched the fiddler's elbow and put her hand on the serpent's mouth. But they took no notice, and fearing she might lose her character of genial hostess if she were to interfere too markedly, she retired and sat down helplessly. And so the dance whizzed on with cumulative fury, the performers moving in their planet-like courses, direct and retrograde, from apogee to perigee, till the hand of the well-kicked clock at the bottom of the room had travelled over the circumference of an hour.

While these cheerful events were in course of enactment within Fennel's pastoral dwelling, an incident having considerable bearing on the party had occurred in the gloomy night without. Mrs. Fennel's concern about the growing fierceness of the dance corresponded in point of time with the ascent of a human figure to the solitary hill of Higher Crowstairs from the direction of the distant town. This personage strode on through the rain without a pause, following the little-worn path which, farther on in its course, skirted the shepherd's cottage.

It was nearly the time of full moon, and on this account, though the sky was lined with a uniform sheet of dripping cloud, ordinary objects out-of-doors were readily visible. The sad, wan light revealed the lonely pedestrian to be a man of supple frame; his gait suggested that he had somewhat passed the period of perfect and instinctive agility, though not so far as to be otherwise than rapid of motion when occasion required. In point of fact, he might have been about forty years of age. He appeared tall, but a recruiting sergeant, or other person accustomed to the judging of men's heights by the eye, would have discerned that this was chiefly owing to his gauntness, and that he was not more than five feet eight or nine.

Notwithstanding the regularity of his tread there was caution in it, as in that of one who mentally feels his way; and despite the fact that it was not a black coat nor a dark garment of any sort that he wore, there was something about him which suggested that he naturally belonged to the black-coated tribes of men. His clothes were of fustian, and his boots hobnailed, yet in his progress he showed not the mud-accustomed bearing of hobnailed and fustianed peasantry.

By the time that he had arrived abreast of the shepherd's premises the rain came down, or rather came along, with yet more determined violence. The outskirts of the little settlement partially broke the force of wind and rain, and this induced him to stand still. The most salient of the shepherd's domestic erections was an empty sty at the forward corner of his hedgeless garden, for in these latitudes the principle of masking the homelier features of your establishment by a conventional frontage was unknown. The traveller's eye was attracted to this small building by the pallid shine of the wet slates that covered it. He turned aside, and, finding it empty, stood under the pent-roof for shelter.

While he stood, the boom of the serpent within the adjacent houses, and the lesser strains of the fiddler, reached the spot as an accompaniment to the surging hiss of the flying rain on the sod, its louder beating on the cabbage-leaves of the garden, on the eight or ten beehives just discernible by the path, and its dripping from the eaves into a row of buckets and pans that had been placed under the walls of the cottage. For at Higher Crowstairs, as at all such elevated domiciles, the grand difficulty of house-keeping was an insufficiency of water; and a casual rainfall was utilized by turning out, as catchers, every utensil that the house contained. Some queer stories might be told of the contrivances for economy in suds and dishwaters that are absolutely necessitated in upland habitations during the droughts of summer. But at this season there were no such exigencies; a mere acceptance of what the skies bestowed was sufficient for an abundant store.

At last the notes of the serpent ceased, and the house was silent. This cessation of activity aroused the solitary pedestrian from the reverie into which he had lapsed, and, emerging from the shed, with an apparently new intention, he walked up the path to the house door. Arrived here, his first act was to kneel down on a large stone beside the row of vessels, and to drink a copious draught from one of them. Having quenched his thirst he rose and lifted his hand to knock, but paused with his eye upon the panel. Since the dark surface of the wood revealed absolutely nothing, it was evident that he must be mentally looking through the door, as if he wished to measure thereby all the possibilities that a house of this sort might include, and how they might bear upon the question of his entry.

In his indecision he turned and surveyed the scene around. Not a soul was anywhere visible. The garden path stretched downward from his feet, gleaming like the track of a snail; the roof of the little well (mostly dry), the well-cover, the top rail of the garden gate, were varnished with the same dull liquid glaze; while, far away in the vale, a faint whiteness of more than usual extent showed that the rivers were high in the meads. Beyond all this winked a few bleared lamp-lights through the beating drops, lights that denoted the situation of the county-town from which he had appeared to come. The absence of all notes of life in that direction seemed to clinch his intentions, and he knocked at the door.

Within, a desultory chat had taken the place of movement and musical sound. The hedge-carpenter was suggesting a song to the company, which nobody just then was inclined to undertake, so that the knock afforded a not unwelcome diversion.

"Walk in," said the shepherd, promptly.

The latch clicked upward, and out of the night our pedestrian appeared upon the door-mat. The shepherd arose, snuffed two of the nearest candles, and turned to look at him.

Their light disclosed that the stranger was dark in complexion and not unprepossessing as to feature. His hat, which for a moment he did not remove, hung low over his eyes, without concealing that they were large, open, and determined, moving with a flash rather than a glance round the room. He seemed pleased with the survey, and, baring his shaggy head, said, in a rich deep voice, "The rain is so heavy, friends, that I ask leave to come in and rest a while."

"To be sure, stranger," said the shepherd. "And faith, you've been lucky in choosing your time, for we are having a bit of a fling for a glad cause—though, to be sure, a man could hardly wish that glad cause to happen more than once a year."

"Nor less," spoke up a woman. "For 'tis best to get your family over and done with, as soon as you can, so as to be all the earlier out of the fag o't."

"And what may be this glad cause?" asked the stranger.

"A birth and christening," said the shepherd.

The stranger hoped his host might not be made unhappy either by too many or too few of such episodes, and being invited by a gesture to a pull at the mug, he readily acquiesced. His manner, which, before entering, had been so dubious, was now altogether that of a careless and candid man.

"Late to be traipsing athwart this coomb—hey?" said the engaged man of fifty.

"Late it is, master, as you say. I'll take a seat in the chimney-corner, if you have nothing to urge against it, ma'am, for I am a little moist on the side that was next the rain."

Mrs. Shepherd Fennel assented, and made room for the self-invited comer, who having got completely inside the chimney-corner, stretched out his legs and his arms with the expansiveness of a person quite at home.

"Yes, I am rather thin in the vamp," he said, freely, seeing that the eye of the shepherd's wife fell upon his boots, "and I am not well fitted, either. I have had some rough times lately, and have been forced to pick up what I can get in the way of wearing, but I must find a suit better fit for working-days when I reach home."

"One of hereabouts?" she inquired.

"Not quite that—farther up the country."

"I thought so. And so am I; and by your tongue you come from my neighborhood."

"But you would hardly have heard of me," he said, quickly. "My time would be long before yours, ma'am, you see."

This testimony to the youthfulness of his hostess had the effect of stopping her cross-examination.

"There is only one thing more wanted to make me happy," continued the newcomer, "and that is a little baccy, which I am sorry to say I am out of."

"I'll fill your pipe," said the shepherd.

"I must ask you to lend me a pipe likewise."

"A smoker, and no pipe about ye?"

"I have dropped it somewhere on the road."

The shepherd filled and handed him a new clay pipe, saying, as he did so, "Hand me your baccy-box—I'll fill that, too, now I am about it."

The man went through the movement of searching his pockets.

"Lost that, too?" said his entertainer, with some surprise.

"I am afraid so," said the man, with some confusion. "Give it to me in a screw of paper." Lighting his pipe at the candle with a suction that drew the whole flame into the bowl, he resettled himself in the corner, and bent his looks upon the faint steam from his damp legs, as if he wished to say no more.

Meanwhile the general body of guests had been taking little notice of this visitor by reason of an absorbing discussion in which they were engaged with the band about a tune for the next dance. The matter being settled, they were about to stand up, when an interruption came in the shape of another knock at the door.

At sound of the same the man in the chimney-corner took up the poker and began stirring the fire as if doing it thoroughly were the one aim of his existence; and a second time the shepherd said "Walk in!" In a moment another man stood upon the straw-woven door-mat. He, too, was a stranger.

This individual was one of a type radically different from the first. There was more of the commonplace in his manner, and a certain jovial cosmopolitanism sat upon his features. He was several years older than the first arrival, his hair being slightly frosted, his eyebrows bristly, and his whiskers cut back from his cheeks. His face was rather full and flabby, and yet it was not altogether a face without power. A few grog-blossoms marked the neighborhood of his nose. He flung back his long drab great-coat, revealing that beneath it he wore a suit of cinder-gray shade throughout; large, heavy seals of some metal or other that would take a polish, dangling from his fob, as his only personal ornament. Shaking the water-drops from his low-crowned glazed hat, he said, "I must ask for a few minutes' shelter, comrades, or I shall be wetted to my skin before I get to Casterbridge."

"Make yourself at home, master," said the shepherd, perhaps a trifle less heartily than on the first occasion. Not that Fennel had the least tinge of niggardliness in his composition; but the room was far from large, spare chairs were not numerous, and damp companions were not altogether desirable at close quarters for the women and girls in their bright-colored gowns.

However, the second comer, after taking off his great-coat, and hanging his hat on a nail in one of the ceiling-beams as if he had been specially invited to put it there, advanced and sat down at the table. This had been pushed so closely into the chimney-corner, to give all available room to the dancers, that its inner edge grazed the elbow of the man who had ensconced himself by the fire; and thus the two strangers were brought into close companionship. They nodded to each other by way of breaking the ice of unacquaintance, and the first stranger handed his neighbor the family mug—a huge vessel of brown ware, having its upper edge worn away like a threshold by the rub of whole generations of thirsty lips that had gone the way of all flesh, and bearing the following inscription burned upon its rotund side in yellow letters:

THERE is NO FUN
UNTiL i CUM

The other man, nothing loath, raised the mug to his lips, and drank on, and on, and on—till a curious blueness overspread the countenance of the shepherd's wife, who had regarded with no little surprise the first stranger's free offer to the second of what did not belong to him to dispense.

"I knew it!" said the toper to the shepherd, with much satisfaction. "When I walked up your garden before coming in, and saw the hives all of a row, I said to myself, 'Where there's bees there's honey, and where there's honey there's mead.' But mead of such a truly comfortable sort as this I really didn't expect to meet in my older days." He took yet another pull at the mug, till it assumed an ominous elevation.

"Glad you enjoy it!" said the shepherd, warmly.

"It is goodish mead," assented Mrs. Fennel, with an absence of enthusiasm which seemed to say that it was possible to buy praise for one's cellar at too heavy a price. "It is trouble enough to make, and really I hardly think we shall make any more. For honey sells well, and we ourselves can make shift with a drop o' small mead and metheglin for common use from the comb-washings."

"Oh, but you'll never have the heart!" reproachfully cried the stranger in cinder-gray, after taking up the mug a third time and setting it down empty. "I love mead when 'tis old like this, as I love to go to church o' Sundays, or to relieve the needy any day of the week."

"Ha, ha, ha!" said the man in the chimney-corner, who, in spite of the taciturnity induced by the pipe of tobacco, could not or would not refrain from this slight testimony to his comrade's humor.

Now, the old mead of those days, brewed of the purest first-year or maiden honey—four pounds to the gallon, with its due complement of white of eggs, cinnamon, ginger, cloves, mace, rosemary, yeast, and processes of working, bottling, and cellaring—tasted remarkably strong; but it did not taste so strong as it actually was. Hence, presently the stranger in cinder-gray at the table, moved by its creeping influence unbuttoned his waistcoat, threw himself back in his chair, spread his legs, and made his presence felt in various ways.

"Well, well, as I say," he resumed, "I am going to Casterbridge, and to Casterbridge I must go. I should have been almost there by this time; but the rain drove me into your dwelling, and I'm not sorry for it."

"You don't live in Casterbridge?" said the shepherd.

"Not as yet, though I shortly mean to move there."

"Going to set up in trade, perhaps?"

"No, no," said the shepherd's wife. "It is easy to see that the gentleman is rich, and don't want to work at anything."

The cinder-gray stranger paused, as if to consider whether he would accept that definition of himself. He presently rejected it by answering, "Rich is not quite the word for me, dame. I do work, and I must work. And even if I only get to Casterbridge by midnight I must begin work there at eight to-morrow morning. Yes, het or wet, blow or snow, famine or sword, my day's work to-morrow must be done."

"Poor man! Then, in spite o' seeming, you be worse off than we," replied the shepherd's wife.

" 'Tis the nature of my trade, men and maidens. 'Tis the nature of my trade more than my poverty. . . . But really and truly I must be up and off, or I shan't get a lodging in the town." However, the speaker did not move, and directly added, "There's time for one more draught of friendship before I go, and I'd perform it at once if the mug were not dry."

"Here's a mug o' small," said Mrs. Fennel. "Small, we call it, though to be sure 'tis only the first wash o' the combs."

"No," said the stranger disdainfully. "I won't spoil your first kindness by partaking o' your second."

"Certainly not," broke in Fennel. "We don't increase and multiply every day, and I'll fill the mug again." He went away to the dark place under the stairs where the barrel stood. The shepherdess followed him.

"Why should you do this?" she said, reproachfully, as soon as they were alone. "He's emptied it once, though it held enough for ten people; and now he's not contented wi' the small, but must needs call for more o' the strong! And a stranger unbeknown to any of us. For my part, I don't like the look o' the man at all."

"But he's in the house, my honey; and 'tis a wet night, and a christening. Daze it, what's a cup of mead or less? there'll be plenty more next bee-burning."

"Very well—this time, then," she answered, looking wistfully at the barrel. "But what is the man's calling, and where is he one of, that he should come in and join us like this?"

"I don't know. I'll ask him again."

The catastrophe of having the mug drained dry at one pull by the stranger in cinder-gray was effectually guarded against this time by Mrs. Fennel. She poured out his allowance in a small cup, keeping the large one at a discreet distance from him. When he had tossed off his portion the shepherd renewed his inquiry about the stranger's occupation.

The latter did not immediately reply, and the man in the chimney-corner, with sudden demonstrativeness, said, "Anybody may know my trade—I'm a wheelwright."

"A very good trade for these parts," said the shepherd.

"And anybody may know mine—if they've the sense to find it out," said the stranger in cinder-gray.

"You may generally tell what a man is by his claws," observed the hedge-carpenter, looking at his own hands. "My fingers be as full of thorns as an old pincushion is of pins."

The hands of the man in the chimney-corner instinctively sought the shade, and he gazed into the fire as he resumed his pipe. The man at the table took up the hedge-carpenter's remark, and added, smartly, "True; but the oddity of my trade is that, instead of setting a mark upon me it sets a mark upon my customers."

No observation being offered by anybody in elucidation of this enigma, the shepherd's wife once more called for a song. The same obstacles presented themselves as at the former time—one had no voice, another had forgotten the first verse. The stranger at the table, whose soul had now risen to a good working temperature, relieved the difficulty by exclaiming that, to start the company, he would sing himself. Thrusting one thumb into the armhole of his waistcoat, he waved the other hand in the air, and, with an extemporizing gaze at the shining sheep-crooks above the mantlepiece, began:

"Oh, my trade it is the rarest one,
　　　　Simple shepherds all—
My trade is a sight to see;
For my customers I tie, and take them up
　　on high,
And waft 'em to a far countree."

The room was silent when he had finished the verse—with one exception, that of the man in the chimney-corner, who, at the singer's word, "Chorus!" joined him in a deep bass voice of musical relish—

"And waft 'em to a far countree!"

Oliver Giles, John Pitcher the dairyman, the parish-clerk, the engaged man of fifty, the row of young women against the wall, seemed lost in thought not of the gayest kind. The shepherd looked meditatively on the ground, the shepherdess gazed keenly at the singer, and with some suspicion; she was doubting whether this stranger were merely singing an old song from recollection, or was composing one there and then for the occasion. All were as perplexed

at the obscure revelation as the guests at Belshazzar's Feast, except the man in the chimney-corner, who quietly said, "Second verse, stranger," and smoked on.

The singer thoroughly moistened himself from his lips inward, and went on with the next stanza as requested:

"My tools are but common ones,
　　　　Simple shepherds all—
My tools are no sight to see;
A little hempen string, and a post whereon
　　to swing,
Are implements enough for me!"

Shepherd Fennel glanced around. There was no longer any doubt that the stranger was answering his question rhythmically. The guests one and all started back with suppressed exclamations. The young woman engaged to the man of fifty fainted half-way, and would have proceeded, but finding him wanting in alacrity for catching her, she sat down trembling.

"Oh, he's the ——!" whispered the people in the background, mentioning the name of an ominous officer. "He's come to do it. 'Tis to be at Casterbridge jail to-morrow—the man for sheep-stealing—the poor clockmaker we heard of, who used to live away at Shottsford and had no work to do—Timothy Sommers, whose family were a-starving, and so he went out of Shottsford by the high-road, and took a sheep in open daylight, defying the farmer and the farmer's wife and the farmer's lad, and every man jack among 'em. He" (and they nodded towards the stranger of the deadly trade) "is come from up the country to do it because there's not enough to do in his own county-town, and he's got the place here now our own county-man's dead; he's going to live in the same cottage under the prison wall."

The stranger in cinder-gray took no notice of this whispered string of observation, but again wetted his lips. Seeing that his friend in the chimney-corner was the only one who reciprocated his joviality in any way, he held out his cup towards that appreciative comrade, who also held out his own. They clinked together, the eyes of the rest of the room hanging upon the singer's actions. He parted his lips for the third verse, but at that moment another knock was audible upon the door. This time the knock was faint and hesitating.

The company seemed scared; the shepherd looked with consternation towards the entrance, and it was with some effort that he resisted his alarmed wife's deprecatory glance and uttered for the third time the welcoming words, "Walk in!"

The door was gently opened, and another man stood upon the mat. He, like those who had preceded him, was a stranger. This time it was a short, small personage, of fair complexion, and dressed in a decent suit of dark clothes.

"Can you tell me the way to—?" he began; when, gazing round the room to observe the nature of the company among whom he had fallen, his eyes lighted on the stranger in cinder-gray. It was just at the instant when the latter, who had thrown his mind into his song with such a will that he scarcely heeded the interruption, silenced all whispers and inquiries by bursting into his third verse:

"Tomorrow is my working day,
          Simple shepherds all—
Tomorrow is a working day for me:
For the farmer's sheep is slain, and the lad
     who did it ta'en,
And on his soul may God ha' merc-y!"

The stranger in the chimney-corner, waving cups with the singer so heartily that his mead splashed over on the hearth, repeated in his bass voice as before:

"And on his soul may God ha' merc-y!"

All this time the third stranger had been standing in the door-way. Finding now that he did not come forward or go on speaking, the guests particularly regarded him. They noticed, to their surprise, that he stood before them the picture of abject terror—his knees trembling, his hand shaking so violently that the door-latch by which he supported himself rattled audibly; his white lips were parted, and his eyes fixed on the merry officer of justice in the middle of the room. A moment more and he had turned, closed the door, and fled.

"What a man can it be?" said the shepherd.

The rest, between the awfulness of their late discovery and the odd conduct of this third visitor, looked as if they knew not what to think, and said nothing. Instinctively they withdrew farther and farther from the grim gentleman in their midst, whom some of them seemed to take for the Prince of Darkness himself, till they formed a remote circle, an empty space of floor being left between them and him—

". . . circulus, cujus centrum diabolus."

The room was so silent—though there were more than twenty people in it— that nothing could be heard but the patter of the rain against the window-shutters, accompanied by the occasional hiss of a straw drop that fell down the chimney into the fire, and the steady puffing of the man in the corner, who had now resumed his pipe of long clay.

The stillness was unexpectedly broken. The distant sound of a gun reverberated through the air—apparently from the direction of the county-town.

"Be jiggered!" cried the stranger who had sung the song, jumping up.

"What does that mean?" asked several.

"A prisoner escaped from the jail—that's what it means."

All listened. The sound was repeated, and none of them spoke but the man in the chimney-corner, who said, quietly, "I've often been told that in this county they fire a gun at such times; but I never heard it till now."

"I wonder if it is *my* man?" murmured the personage in cinder-gray.

"Surely it is!" said the shepherd, involuntarily. "And surely we've seen him! That little man who looked in at the door by now, and quivered like a leaf when he seed ye and heard your song."

"His teeth chattered, and the breath went out of his body," said the dairyman.

"And his heart seemed to sink within him like a stone," said Oliver Giles.

"And he bolted as if he'd been shot at," said the hedge-carpenter.

"True—his teeth chattered, and his heart seemed to sink; and he bolted as if he'd been shot at," slowly summed up the man in the chimney-corner.

"I didn't notice it," remarked the hangman.

"We were all a-wondering what made him run off in such a fright," faltered one of the women against the wall, "and now 'tis explained."

The firing of the alarm-gun went on at intervals, low and sullenly, and their suspicions became a certainty. The sinister gentleman in cinder-gray roused himself. "Is there a constable here?" he asked, in thick tones. "If so, let him step forward?"

The engaged man of fifty stepped quavering out of the corner, his betrothed beginning to sob on the back of the chair.

"You are a sworn constable?"

"I be, sir."

"Then pursue the criminal at once, with assistance, and bring him back here. He can't have gone far."

"I will, sir, I will—when I've got my staff. I'll go home and get it, and come sharp here, and start in a body."

"Staff!—never mind your staff; the man'll be gone!"

"But I can't do nothing without my staff—can I, William, and John, and Charles Jake? No; for there's the King's royal crown a-painted on en in yaller and gold, and the lion and the unicorn, so as when I raise en up and hit my prisoner, 'tis made a lawful blow thereby. I wouldn't 'tempt to take a man without my staff—no, not I. If I hadn't the law to gie me courage, why, instead o' my taking up him he might take up me!"

"Now, I'm a King's man myself, and can give you authority enough for this," said the formidable officer in gray. "Now then, all of ye, be ready. Have ye any lanterns?"

"Yes—have ye any lanterns?—I demand it!" said the constable.

"And the rest of you able-bodied—"

"Able-bodied men—yes—the rest of ye!" said the constable.

"Have you some good stout staves and pitchforks—"

"Staves and pitchforks—in the name o' the law! And take 'em in yer hands and go in quest, and do as we in authority tell ye!"

Thus aroused, the men prepared to give chase. The evidence was, indeed, though circumstantial, so convincing that but little argument was needed to show the shepherd's guests that after what they had seen it would look very much like connivance if they did not instantly pursue the unhappy third stranger, who could not as yet have gone more than a few hundred yards over such uneven country.

A shepherd is always well provided with lanterns; and, lighting these hastily, and with hurdle staves in their hands, they poured out of the door, taking a direction along the crest of the hill, away from the town, the rain having fortunately a little abated.

Disturbed by the noise, or possibly by unpleasant dreams of her baptism, the child who had been christened began to cry heart-brokenly in the room overhead. These notes of grief came down through the chinks of the floor to the ears of the women below, who jumped up one by one, and seemed glad of the excuse to ascend and comfort the baby, for the incidents of the last half-hour greatly oppressed them. Thus in the space of two or three minutes the room on the ground-floor was deserted quite.

But it was not for long. Hardly had the sound of footsteps died away when a man returned round the corner of the house from the direction the pursuers had taken. Peeping in at the door, and seeing nobody there, he entered leisurely. It was the stranger of the chimney-corner, who had gone out with the rest. The motive of his return was shown by his helping himself to a cut piece of skimmer-cake that lay on a ledge beside where he had sat, and which he had apparently forgotten to take with him. He also poured out half a cup more mead from the quantity that remained, ravenously eating and drinking these as he stood. He had not finished when another figure came in just as quietly—his friend in cinder-gray.

"Oh—you here?" said the latter, smiling. "I thought you had gone to help in the capture." And this speaker also revealed the object of his return by looking solicitously round for the fascinating mug of old mead.

"And I thought you had gone," said the other, continuing his skimmer-cake with some effort.

"Well, on second thoughts, I felt there were enough without me," said the first, confidentially, "and such a night as it is, too. Besides, 'tis the business o' the Government to take care of its criminals —not mine."

"True; so it is. And I felt as you did, that there were enough without me."

"I don't want to break my limbs running over the humps and hollows of this wild country."

"Nor I neither, between you and me."

"These shepherd people are used to it—simple-minded souls, you know, stirred up to anything in a moment. They'll have him ready for me before the morning, and no trouble to me at all."

"They'll have him and we shall have saved ourselves all labor in the matter."

"True, true. Well, my way is to Casterbridge; and 'tis as much as my legs will do to take me that far. Going the same way?"

"No, I am sorry to say! I have to get home over there" (he nodded indefinitely to the right) "and I feel as you do, that it is quite enough for my legs to do before bedtime."

The other had by this time finished the mead in the mug, after which, shaking hands heartily at the door, and wishing each other well, they went their several ways.

In the meantime the company of pursuers had reached the end of the hog's-back elevation which dominated this part of the coomb. They had decided on no particular plan of action; and, finding that the man of the baleful trade was no longer in their company, they seemed quite unable to form any such plan now. They descended in all directions down the hill, and straightway several of the party fell into the snare set by Nature for all misguided midnight ramblers over this part of the cretaceous formation. The "lynches," or flint slopes, which belted the escarpment at intervals of a dozen yards, took the less cautious ones unawares, and losing their footing on the rubbly steep, they slid sharply downward, the lanterns rolling from their hands to the bottom, and there lying on their sides till the horn was scorched through.

When they had again gathered themselves together, the shepherd, as the man who knew the country best, took the lead, and guided them round these treacherous inclines. The lanterns, which seemed rather to dazzle their eyes and warn the fugitive, than to assist them in the explorations, were extinguished, due silence was observed; and in this more rational order they plunged into the vale. It was a grassy, briery, moist defile, affording some shelter to any person who had sought it; but the party perambulated it in vain, and ascended on the other side. Here they wandered apart, and after an interval closed together again to report progress. At the second time of closing in they found themselves near a lonely ash, the single tree on this part of the upland, probably sown there by a passing bird some fifty years before. And here, standing a little to one side of the trunk as motionless as the trunk itself, appeared the man they were in quest of, his outline being well defined against the sky beyond. The band noiselessly drew up and faced him.

"Your money or your life!" said the constable, sternly to the still figure.

"No, no," whispered John Pitcher. "'Tisn't our side ought to say that. That's the doctrine of vagabonds like him, and we be on the side of the law."

"Well, well," replied the constable, impatiently; "I must say something, mustn't I? and if you had all the weight o' this undertaking upon your mind, perhaps you'd say the wrong thing, too! Prisoner at the bar, surrender, in the name of the Father—the Crown, I mane!"

The man under the tree seemed now to notice them for the first time, and giving them no opportunity whatever for exhibiting their courage, he strolled slowly towards them. He was, indeed, the little man, the third stranger; but his trepidation had in a great measure gone.

"Well, travellers," he said; "did I hear ye speak to me?"

"You did; you've got to come and be our prisoner at once," said the constable. "We arrest ye on the charge of not biding in Casterbridge jail in a decent proper manner to be hung to-morrow morning. Neighbors, do your duty, and seize the culpet!"

On hearing the charge, the man seemed enlightened, and, saying not another word, resigned himself with preternatural civility to the search party, who, with their staves in their hands, surrounded him on all sides, and marched him back towards the shepherd's cottage.

It was eleven o'clock by the time they arrived. The light shining from the open door, a sound of men's voices within, proclaimed to them as they approached the house that some new events had arisen in their absence. On entering they discovered the shepherd's living-room to be invaded by two officers from Casterbridge jail, and a well-known magistrate who lived at the nearest county-seat, intelligence of the escape having become generally circulated.

"Gentlemen," said the constable, "I have brought back your man—not without risk and danger; but every one must do his duty! He is inside this circle of able-bodied persons, who have lent me useful aid, considering their ignorance of Crown work. Men, bring forward your prisoner!" And the third stranger was led to the light.

"Who is this?" said one of the officials.

"The man," said the constable.

"Certainly not," said the turnkey; and the first corroborated his statement.

"But how can it be otherwise?" asked the constable. "Or why was he so terrified at sight o' the singing instrument of the law who sat there?" Here he related the strange behavior of the third stranger on entering the house during the hangman's song.

"Can't understand it," said the officer, coolly. "All I know is that it is not the condemned man. He's quite a different character from this one; a gauntish fellow, with dark hair and eyes, rather good-looking, and with a musical bass voice that if you heard it once you'd never mistake as long as you lived."

"Why, souls—'twas the man in the chimney-corner!"

"Hey—what?" said the magistrate, coming forward after inquiring particulars from the shepherd in the background. "Haven't you got the man after all?"

"Well, sir," said the constable, "he's the man we were in search of, that's true; and yet he's not the man we were in search of. For the man we were in search of was not the man we wanted, sir, if you understand my everyday way;

for 'twas the man in the chimney-corner!"

"A pretty kettle of fish altogether!" said the magistrate. "You had better start for the other man at once."

The prisoner now spoke for the first time. The mention of the man in the chimney-corner seemed to have moved him as nothing else could do. "Sir," he said, stepping forward to the magistrate, "take no more trouble about me. The time is come when I may as well speak. I have done nothing; my crime is that the condemned man is my brother. Early this afternoon I left home at Shottsford to tramp it all the way to Casterbridge jail to bid him farewell. I was benighted and called here to rest and ask the way. When I opened the door I saw before me the very man, my brother, that I thought to see in the condemned cell at Casterbridge. He was in this chimney-corner; and jammed close to him, so that he could not have got out if he had tried, was the executioner who'd come to take his life, singing a song about it, and not knowing that it was his victim who was close by, joining in to save appearances. My brother looked a glance of agony at me, and I knew he meant, 'Don't reveal what you see; my life depends on it.' I was so terror-struck that I could hardly stand, and, not knowing what I did, I turned and hurried away."

The narrator's manner and tone had the stamp of truth, and his story made a great impression on all around. "And do you know where your brother is at the present time?" asked the magistrate.

"I do not. I have never seen him since I closed this door."

"I can testify to that, for we've been between ye ever since," said the constable.

"Where does he think to fly to?—what is his occupation?"

"He's a watch and clock maker, sir."

"A said a was a wheelwright—a wicked rogue," said the constable.

"The wheels of clocks and watches he meant, no doubt," said Shepherd Fennel. "I thought his hands was palish for 's trade."

"Well, it appears to me that nothing can be gained by retaining this poor man in custody," said the magistrate. "Your business lies with the other, unquestionably."

And so the little man was released offhand; but he looked nothing the less sad on that account, it being beyond the power of magistrate or constable to raze out the written troubles in his brain, for they concerned another whom he regarded with more solicitude than himself. When this was done, and the man had gone his way, the night was found to be so far advanced that it was deemed useless to renew the search before the next morning.

Next day, accordingly, the quest for the clever sheep-stealer became general and keen, to all appearance at least. But the intended punishment was cruelly disproportioned to the transgression, and the sympathy of a great many country folk in that district was strongly on the side of the fugitive. Moreover, his marvellous coolness and daring in hob-and-nobbing with the hangman under the unprecedented circumstances of the shepherd's party, won their admiration. So that it may be questioned if all those who ostensibly made themselves so busy in exploring woods and fields and lanes were quite so thorough when it came to the private examination of their own lofts and out-houses. Stories were afloat of a mysterious figure being occasionally seen in some old overgrown track-way or other, remote from turnpike-roads; but when a search was instituted in any of these suspected quarters nobody was found. Thus the days and weeks passed without tidings.

In brief, the bass-voiced man of the chimney-corner was never recaptured. Some said that he went across the sea, others that he did not, but buried himself in the depths of a populous city. At any rate, the gentleman in cinder-gray never did his morning's work at Casterbridge, nor met anywhere at all, for business purposes, the genial comrade with whom he had passed an hour of relaxation in the lonely house on the coomb.

The grass has long been green on the graves of Shepherd Fennel and his frugal wife; the guests who made up the christening-party have mainly followed their entertainers to the tomb; the baby in whose honor they all had met is a matron in the sear and yellow leaf. But the arrival of the three strangers at the shepherd's that night, and the details connected therewith, is a story as well known as ever in the country about Higher Crowstairs.

1883

LORD DUNSANY

The Highwayman

Tom o' the Roads had ridden his last ride, and was now alone in the night. From where he was, a man might see the white, recumbent sheep and the black outline of lonely downs, and the grey line of the farther and lonelier downs beyond them; or in the hollows far below him, out of the pitiless wind, he might see the grey smoke of hamlets arising from black valleys. But all alike was black to the eyes of Tom, and all the sounds were silence in his ears; only his soul struggled to slip from the iron chains and to pass southwards into Paradise. And the wind blew and blew.

For Tom to-night had nought but the wind to ride; they had taken his true black horse on the day when they took from him the green fields and the sky, men's voices and the laughter of women, and had left him alone with chains about his neck to swing in the wind for ever. And the wind blew and blew.

But the soul of Tom o' the Roads was nipped by the cruel chains, and whenever it struggled to escape it was beaten backwards into the iron collar by the wind that blows from Paradise from the south. And swinging there by the neck, there fell away old sneers from off his lips, and scoffs that he had long since scoffed at God fell from his tongue, and there rotted old bad lusts out of his heart, and from his fingers the stains of deeds that were evil; and they all fell to the ground and grew there in pallid rings and clusters. And when these ill

things had all fallen away, Tom's soul was clean again, as his early love had found it, a long while since in spring; and it swung up there in the wind with the bones of Tom, and with his old torn coat and rusty chains.

And the wind blew and blew.

And ever anon the soul of the sepulchred, coming from consecrated acres, would go by beating up the wind to Paradise past the Gallows Tree and past the soul of Tom, that might not go free.

Night after night Tom watched the sheep upon the downs with empty hollow sockets, till his dead hair grew and covered his poor dead face, and hid the shame of it from the sheep. And the wind blew and blew.

Sometimes on gusts of the wind came some one's tears, and beat and beat against the iron chains, but could not rust them through. And the wind blew and blew.

And every evening all the thoughts that Tom had ever uttered came flocking in from doing their work in the world, the work that may not cease, and sat along the gallows branches and chirruped to the soul of Tom, the soul that might not go free. All the thoughts that he had ever uttered! And the evil thoughts rebuked the soul that bore them because they might not die. And all those he had uttered the most furtively, chirruped the loudest and the shrillest in the branches all the night.

And all the thoughts that Tom had ever thought about himself now pointed

"The Highwayman" by Lord Dunsany, from *Sword of Welleran and Other Stories* published by John W. Luce & Company.

at the wet bones and mocked at the old torn coat. But the thoughts that he had had of others were the only companions that his soul had to soothe it in the night as it swung to and fro. And they twittered to the soul and cheered the poor dumb thing that could have dreams no more, till there came a murderous thought and drove them all away.

And the wind blew and blew.

Paul, Archbishop of Alois and Vayence, lay in his white sepulchre of marble, facing full to the southwards towards Paradise. And over his tomb was sculptured the Cross of Christ that his soul might have repose. No wind howled here as it howled in the lonely tree-tops up upon the downs, but came with gentle breezes, orchard scented, over the low lands from Paradise from the southwards, and played about forget-me-nots and grasses in the consecrated land where lay the Reposeful round the sepulchre of Paul, Archbishop of Alois and Vayence. Easy it was for a man's soul to pass from such a sepulchre, and, flitting low over remembered fields, to come upon the garden lands of Paradise and find eternal ease.

And the wind blew and blew.

In a tavern of foul repute three men were lapping gin. Their names were Joe and Will and the gypsy Puglioni; no other names had they, for of whom their fathers were they had no knowledge, but only dark suspicions.

Sin had caressed and stroked their faces often with its paws, but the face of Puglioni Sin had kissed all over the mouth and chin. Their food was robbery and their pastime murder. All of them had incurred the sorrow of God and the enmity of man. They sat at a table with a pack of cards before them, all greasy with the marks of cheating thumbs. And they whispered to one another over their gin, but so low that the landlord of the tavern at the other end of the room could hear only muffled oaths, and knew not by Whom they swore or what they said.

These three were the staunchest friends that ever God had given unto man. And he to whom their friendship had been given had nothing else besides, saving some bones that swung in the wind and rain, and an old torn coat and iron chains, and a soul that might not go free.

But as the night wore on, the three friends left their gin and stole away, and crept down to that graveyard where rested in his sepulchre Paul, Archbishop of Alois and Vayence. At the edge of the graveyard, but outside the consecrated ground, they dug a hasty grave, two digging while one watched in the wind and rain. And the worms that crept in the unhallowed ground wondered and waited.

And the terrible hour of midnight came upon them with its fears, and found them still beside the place of tombs. And the three friends trembled at the horror of such an hour in such a place, and shivered in the wind and drenching rain, but still worked on. And the wind blew and blew.

Soon they had finished. And at once they left the hungry grave with all its worms unfed, and went away over the wet fields stealthily but in haste, leaving the place of tombs behind them in the midnight. And as they went they shivered, and each man as he shivered cursed the rain aloud. And so they came to the spot where they had hidden a ladder and a lantern. There they held a long debate whether they should light the lantern, or whether they should go without it for fear of the King's men. But in the end it seemed better to them that they should have the light of the lantern, and risk being taken by the King's men and hanged, than that they should come suddenly face to face in the darkness with whatever one might come face to face with a little after midnight about the Gallows Tree.

On three roads in England whereon it was not the wont of folks to go their ways in safety, travellers to-night went unmolested. But the three friends walking several paces wide of the King's highway, approached the Gallows Tree, and Will carried the lantern and Joe the ladder, but Puglioni carried a great sword wherewith to do the work which must be done. When they came close, they saw how bad was the case with Tom, for little remained of that fine figure of a man and nothing at all of his great resolute spirit, only as they came they thought they heard a whimpering cry like the sound of a thing that was caged and unfree.

To and fro, to and fro in the wind swung the bones and soul of Tom, for the sins he had sinned on the King's highway against the laws of the King; and with shadows and a lantern through the darkness, at the peril of their lives, came the three friends that his soul had won before it swung in chains. Thus the seeds of Tom's own soul that he had sown all his life had grown into a Gallows Tree that bore in season iron chains in clusters; while the careless seeds that he had strewn here and there, a kindly jest and a few merry words, had grown into the triple friendship that would not desert his bones.

Then the three set the ladder against the tree, and Puglioni went up with his sword in his right hand, and at the top of it he reached up and began to hack at the neck below the iron collar. Pres-

ently, the bones and the old coat and the soul of Tom fell down with a rattle, and a moment afterwards his head that had watched so long alone swung clear from the swinging chain. These things Will and Joe gathered up, and Puglioni came running down his ladder, and they heaped upon its rungs the terrible remains of their friend, and hastened away wet through with the rain, with the fear of phantoms in their hearts and horror lying before them on the ladder. By two o'clock they were down again in the valley out of the bitter wind, but they went on past the open grave into the graveyard all among the tombs, with their lantern and their ladder and the terrible thing upon it, which kept their friendship still. Then these three, that had robbed the Law of its due and proper victim, still sinned on for what was still their friend, and levered out the marble slabs from the sacred sepulchre of Paul, Archbishop of Alois and Vayence. And from it they took the very bones of the Archbishop, himself, and carried them away to the eager grave that they had left, and put them in and shoveled back the earth. But all that lay upon the ladder they placed, with a few tears, within the great white sepulchre under the Cross of Christ, and put back the marble slabs.

Thence the soul of Tom, arising hallowed out of sacred ground, went at dawn down the valley, and, lingering a little about his mother's cottage and old haunts of childhood, passed on and came to the wide lands beyond the clustered homesteads. There, there met with it all the kindly thoughts that the soul of Tom had ever had, and they flew and sang beside it all the way southwards, until at last, with singing all about it, it came to Paradise.

But Will and Joe and the gypsy Puglioni went back to their gin, and robbed and cheated again in the tavern of foul repute, and knew not in their sinful lives they had sinned one sin at which the Angels smiled.

1916

SIR ARTHUR CONAN DOYLE

The Adventure of the Blue Carbuncle

I HAD called upon my friend Sherlock Holmes upon the second morning after Christmas, with the intention of wishing him the compliments of the season. He was lounging upon the sofa in a purple dressing-gown, a pipe-rack within his reach upon the right, and a pile of crumpled morning papers, evidently newly studied, near at hand. Beside the couch was a wooden chair, and on the angle of the back hung a very seedy and disreputable hard-felt hat, much the worse for wear, and cracked in several places. A lens and a forceps lying upon the seat of the chair suggested that the hat had been suspended in this manner for the purpose of examination.

"You are engaged," said I; "perhaps I interrupt you."

"Not at all. I am glad to have a friend with whom I can discuss my results. The matter is a perfectly trivial one" (he jerked his thumb in the direction of the old hat), "but there are points in connection with it which are not entirely devoid of interest and even of instruction."

I seated myself in his arm-chair and warmed my hands before his crackling fire, for a sharp frost had set in, and the windows were thick with the ice crystals. "I suppose," I remarked, "that, homely as it looks, this thing has some deadly story linked on to it—that it is the clue which will guide you in the solution of some mystery and the punishment of some crime."

"No, no. No crime," said Sherlock Holmes, laughing. "Only one of those whimsical little incidents which will happen when you have four million human beings all jostling each other within the space of a few square miles. Amid the action and reaction of so dense a swarm of humanity, every possible combination of events may be expected to take place, and many a little problem will be presented which may be striking and bizarre without being criminal. We have already had experience of such."

"So much so," I remarked, "that of the last six cases which I have added to my notes, three have been entirely free of any legal crime."

"Precisely. You allude to my attempt to recover the Irene Adler papers, to the singular case of Miss Mary Sutherland, and to the adventure of the man with the twisted lip. Well, I have no doubt that this small matter will fall into the same innocent category. You know Peterson, the commissionaire?"

"Yes."

"It is to him that this trophy belongs."

"It is his hat."

"No, no; he found it. Its owner is unknown. I beg that you will look upon it, not as a battered billycock, but as an intellectual problem. And, first, as to how it came here. It arrived upon Christmas morning, in company with a good fat goose, which is, I have no doubt, roasting at this moment in front of Peterson's fire. The facts are these: about four o'clock on Christmas morning, Peterson, who, as you know, is a very honest fellow, was returning from some small jollification, and was making his way homeward down Tottenham Court Road. In front of him he saw, in the gaslight, a tallish man, walking with a slight stagger, and carrying a white goose slung over his shoulder. As he reached the corner of Goodge Street, a row broke out between this stranger and a little knot of roughs. One of the latter knocked off the man's hat, on which he raised his stick to defend himself, and, swinging it over his head, smashed the shop window behind him. Peterson had rushed forward to protect the stranger from his assailants; but the man, shocked at having broken the window, and seeing an official-looking person in uniform rushing toward him, dropped his goose, took to his heels, and vanished amid the labyrinth of small streets which lie at the back of Tottenham Court Road. The roughs had also fled at the appearance of Peterson, so that he was left in possession of the field of battle, and also of the spoils of victory in the shape of this battered hat and a most unimpeachable Christmas goose."

"Which surely he restored to their owner?"

"My dear fellow, there lies the problem. It is true that 'For Mrs. Henry Baker' was printed upon a small card which was tied to the bird's left leg, and it is also true that the initials 'H. B.' are legible upon the lining of this hat; but as there are some thousands of Bakers, and some hundreds of Henry Bakers in this city of ours, it is not easy to restore lost property to any one of them."

"What, then, did Peterson do?"

"He brought round both hat and goose to me on Christmas morning, knowing that even the smallest problems are of interest to me. The goose we retained until this morning, when there were signs that, in spite of the slight frost, it would be well that it should be eaten without unnecessary delay. Its finder has carried it off, therefore, to fulfil the ultimate destiny of a goose, while I continue to retain the hat of the unknown gentleman who lost his Christmas dinner."

"Did he not advertise?"

"No."

"Then, what clue could you have as to his identity?"

"Only as much as we can deduce."

"From his hat?"

"Precisely."

"But you are joking. What can you gather from this old battered felt?"

"Here is my lens. You know my methods. What can you gather yourself as to the individuality of the man who has worn this article?"

I took the tattered object in my hands and turned it over rather ruefully. It was a very ordinary black hat of the usual round shape, hard, and much the worse for wear. The lining had been of red silk, but was a good deal discolored. There was no maker's name; but, as Holmes had remarked, the initials "H. B." were scrawled upon one side. It was pierced in the brim for a hat-securer, but the elastic was missing. For the rest, it was cracked, exceedingly dusty, and spotted in several places, although there seemed to have been some attempt to hide the discolored patches by smearing them with ink.

"I can see nothing," said I, handing it back to my friend.

"On the contrary, Watson, you can see everything. You fail, however, to reason from what you see. You are too timid in drawing your inferences."

"Then, pray tell me what it is that you can infer from this hat?"

He picked it up and gazed at it in the peculiar introspective fashion which was characteristic of him. "It is perhaps less suggestive than it might have been," he remarked, "and yet there are a few inferences which are very distinct, and a few others which represent at least a strong balance of probability. That the man was highly intellectual is of course obvious upon the face of it, and also that he was fairly well-to-do within the last three years, although he has now fallen upon evil days. He had foresight, but has less now than formerly, pointing to a moral retrogression, which, when taken with the decline of his fortunes, seems to indicate some evil influence, probably drink, at work upon him. This may account also for the obvious fact that his wife has ceased to love him."

"My dear Holmes!"

"He has, however, retained some degree of self-respect," he continued, disregarding my remonstrance. "He is a man who leads a sedentary life, goes out little, is out of training entirely, is middle-aged, has grizzled hair which he has had cut within the last few days, and which he anoints with lime-cream. These are the more potent facts which are to be deduced from his hat. Also, by-the-way, that it is extremely improbable that he has gas laid on in his house."

"You are certainly joking, Holmes."

"Not in the least. Is it possible that even now, when I give you these results, you are unable to see how they are attained?"

"I have no doubt that I am very stupid; but I must confess that I am unable to follow you. For example, how did you deduce that this man was intellectual?"

For answer Holmes clapped the hat upon his head. It came right over the forehead and settled upon the bridge of his nose. "It is a question of cubic capacity," said he; "a man with so large a brain must have something in it."

"The decline of his fortunes, then?"

"This hat is three years old. These flat brims curled at the edge came in then. It is a hat of the very best quality. Look at the band of ribbed silk and the excellent lining. If this man could afford to buy so expensive a hat three years ago, and has had no hat since, then he has assuredly gone down in the world."

"Well, that is clear enough, certainly. But how about the foresight and the moral retrogression?"

Sherlock Holmes laughed. "Here is the foresight," said he, putting his finger upon the little disk and loop of the hat-securer. "They are never sold upon hats. If this man ordered one, it is a sign of a certain amount of foresight, since he went out of his way to take this precaution against the wind. But since we see that he has broken the elastic, and has not troubled to replace it, it is obvious that he has less foresight now than formerly, which is a distinct proof of a weakening nature. On the other hand, he has endeavored to conceal some of these stains upon the felt by daubing them with ink, which is a sign that he has not entirely lost his self-respect."

"Your reasoning is certainly plausible."

"The further points, that he is middle-aged, that his hair is grizzled, that it has been recently cut, and that he uses lime-cream, are all to be gathered from a close examination of the lower part of the lining. The lens discloses a large number of hair-ends, clean cut by the scissors of the barber. They all appear to be adhesive, and there is a distinct odor of lime-cream. This dust, you will observe, is not the gritty, gray dust of the street, but the fluffy brown dust of the house, showing that it has been hung up indoors most of the time; while the marks of moisture upon the inside are proof positive that the wearer perspired very freely, and could, therefore, hardly be in the best of training."

"But his wife—you said that she had ceased to love him."

"This hat has not been brushed for weeks. When I see you, my dear Watson, with a week's accumulation of dust upon your hat, and when your wife allows you to go out in such a state, I shall fear that you also have been unfortunate enough to lose your wife's affection."

"But he might be a bachelor."

"Nay, he was bringing home the goose as a peace-offering to his wife. Remember the card upon the bird's leg."

"You have an answer to everything. But how on earth do you deduce that the gas is not laid on in his house?"

"One tallow stain, or even two, might come by chance; but when I see no less than five, I think that there can be little doubt that the individual must be brought into frequent contact with burning tallow—walks upstairs at night probably with his hat in one hand and a guttering candle in the other. Anyhow, he never got tallow-stains from a gas-jet. Are you satisfied?"

"Well, it is very ingenious," said I, laughing; "but since, as you said just now, there has been no crime committed, and no harm done, save the loss of the goose, all this seems to be rather a waste of energy."

Sherlock Holmes had opened his mouth to reply, when the door flew open, and Peterson, the commissionaire, rushed into the apartment with flushed cheeks and the face of a man who is dazed with astonishment.

"The goose, Mr. Holmes! The goose, sir!" he gasped.

"Eh? What of it, then? Has it returned to life and flapped off through the kitchen window?" Holmes twisted himself round upon the sofa to get a fairer view of the man's excited face.

"See here, sir! See what my wife found in its crop!" He held out his hand and displayed upon the center of the palm a brilliantly scintillating blue stone, rather smaller than a bean in size, but of such purity and radiance that it twinkled like an electric point in the dark hollow of his hand.

Sherlock Holmes sat up with a whistle. "By Jove, Peterson!" said he, "this is treasure trove indeed. I suppose you know what you have got?"

"A diamond, sir? A precious stone. It cuts into glass as though it were putty."

"It's more than a precious stone. It is *the* precious stone."

"Not the Countess of Morcar's blue carbuncle!" I ejaculated.

"Precisely so. I ought to know its size and shape, seeing that I have read the advertisement about it in *The Times* every day lately. It is absolutely unique, and its value can only be conjectured, but the reward offered of £1000 is certainly not within a twentieth part of the market price.

"A thousand pounds! Great Lord of mercy!" The commissionaire plumped down into a chair, and stared from one to the other of us.

"That is the reward, and I have reason to know that there are sentimental considerations in the background which would induce the countess to part with half her fortune if she could but recover the gem."

"It was lost, if I remember aright, at the 'Hotel Cosmopolitan,'" I remarked.

"Precisely so, on December 22d, just five days ago. John Horner, a plumber, was accused of having abstracted it from the lady's jewel-case. The evidence against him was so strong that the case has been referred to the Assizes. I have some account of the matter here, I believe." He rummaged amid his newspapers, glancing over the dates, until at last he smoothed one out, doubled it over, and read the following paragraph:

"'Hotel Cosmopolitan Jewel Robbery. John Horner, 26, plumber, was brought up upon the charge of having upon the 22d inst. abstracted from the jewel-case of the Countess of Morcar the valuable gem know as the blue carbuncle. James Ryder, upper-attendant at the hotel, gave his evidence to the effect that he had shown Horner up to the dressing-room of the Countess of Morcar upon the day of the robbery, in order that he might solder the second bar of the grate, which was loose. He had remained with Horner some little time, but had finally been called away. On returning, he found that Horner had disappeared, that the bureau had been forced open, and that the small morocco casket in which, as it afterwards transpired, the countess was accustomed to keep her jewel, was lying empty upon the dressing table. Ryder instantly gave the alarm, and Horner was arrested the same evening; but the stone could not be found either upon his person or in his rooms. Catherine Cusack, maid to the countess, deposed to having heard Ryder's cry of dismay on discovering the robbery, and to having rushed into the room, where she found matters as described by the last witness. Inspector Bradstreet, B division, gave evidence as to the arrest of Horner, who struggled frantically, and protested his innocence in the strongest terms. Evidence of a previous conviction for robbery having been given against the prisoner, the magistrate refused to deal summarily with the offense, but referred it to the Assizes. Horner, who had shown signs of intense emotion during the proceedings, fainted away at the conclusion, and was carried out of court.'

"Hum! So much for the police court," said Holmes, thoughtfully, tossing aside the paper. "The question for us now to solve is the sequence of events leading from a rifled jewel-case at one end to the crop of a goose in Tottenham Court Road at the other. You see, Watson, our little deductions have suddenly assumed a much more important and less innocent aspect. Here is the stone; the stone came from the goose, and the goose came from Mr. Henry Baker, the gentleman with the bad hat and all the other characteristics with which I have bored you. So now we must set ourselves very seriously to finding this gentleman, and ascertaining what part he has played in this little mystery. To do this, we must try the simplest means first, and these lie undoubtedly in an advertisement in all the evening papers. If this fail, I shall have recourse to other methods."

"What will you say?"

"Give me a pencil and that slip of paper. Now, then: 'Found at the corner of Goodge Street, a goose and a black felt hat. Mr. Henry Baker can have the same by applying at 6:30 this evening at 221B, Baker Street.' That is clear and concise."

"Very. But will he see it?"

"Well, he is sure to keep an eye on the papers, since, to a poor man, the loss was a heavy one. He was clearly so scared by his mischance in breaking the window and by the approach of Peterson, that he thought of nothing but flight; but since then he must have bitterly regretted the impulse which caused him to drop his bird. Then, again, the introduction of his name will cause him to see it, for everyone who knows him will direct his attention to it. Here you are, Peterson, run down to the advertising agency, and have this put in the evening papers."

"In which, sir?"

"Oh, in the *Globe, Star, Pall Mall, St. James's, Evening News, Standard, Echo,* and any others that occur to you."

"Very well, sir. And this stone?"

"Ah, yes, I shall keep the stone. Thank you. And, I say, Peterson, just buy a goose on your way back, and leave it here with me, for we must have one to give to this gentleman in place of the one which your family is now devouring."

When the commissionaire had gone, Holmes took up the stone and held it against the light. "It's a bonny thing," said he. "Just see how it glints and sparkles. Of course it is a nucleus and focus of crime. Every good stone is. They are the devil's pet baits. In the larger and older jewels every facet may stand for a bloody deed. This stone is not yet twenty years old. It was found in the banks of the Amoy River in Southern China, and is remarkable in having every characteristic of the carbuncle, save that it is blue in shade, instead of ruby red. In spite of its youth, it has already a sinister history. There have been two murders, a vitriol-throwing, a suicide, and several robberies brought about for the sake of this forty-grain weight of crystallized charcoal. Who would think that so pretty a toy would be a purveyor to the gallows and the prison? I'll lock it up in my strong box now, and drop a line to the countess to say that we have it."

"Do you think that this man Horner is innocent?"

"I cannot tell."

"Well, then, do you imagine that this other one, Henry Baker, had anything to do with the matter?"

"It is, I think, much more likely that Henry Baker is an absolutely innocent man, who had no idea that the bird which he was carrying was of considerably more value than if it were made of solid gold. That, however, I shall determine by a very simple test, if we have an answer to our advertisement."

"And you can do nothing until then?"

"Nothing."

"In that case I shall continue my professional round. But I shall come back in the evening at the hour you have mentioned, for I should like to see the solution of so tangled a business."

"Very glad to see you. I dine at seven. There is a wood-cock, I believe. By the way, in view of recent occurrences, perhaps I ought to ask Mrs. Hudson to examine its crop."

I had been delayed at a case, and it was a little after half-past six when I found myself in Baker Street once more. As I approached the house I saw a tall man in a Scotch bonnet with a coat which was buttoned up to his chin, waiting outside in the bright semicircle which was thrown from the fanlight. Just as I arrived, the door was opened, and we were shown up together to Holmes's room.

"Mr. Henry Baker, I believe," said he, rising from his arm-chair, and greeting his visitor with the easy air of geniality which he could so readily assume. "Pray take this chair by the fire, Mr. Baker. It is a cold night, and I observe that your circulation is more adapted for summer than for winter. Ah, Watson, you have just come at the right time. Is that your hat, Mr. Baker?"

"Yes, sir, that is undoubtedly my hat."

He was a large man, with rounded shoulders, a massive head, and a broad, intelligent face, sloping down to a pointed beard of grizzled brown. A touch of red in nose and cheeks, with a slight tremor of his extended hand, recalled Holmes's surmise as to his habits. His rusty black frock-coat was buttoned right up in front, with the collar turned up, and his lank wrists protruded from his sleeves without a sign of cuff or shirt. He spoke in a slow staccato fashion, choosing his words with care, and gave the impression generally of a man of learning and letters who had had ill-usage at the hands of fortune.

"We have retained these things for some days," said Holmes, "because we expected to see an advertisement from you giving your address. I am at a loss to know now why you did not advertise."

Our visitor gave a rather shamefaced laugh. "Shillings have not been so plentiful with me as they once were," he remarked. "I had no doubt the gang of roughs who assaulted me carried off both my hat and the bird. I did not

care to spend more money in a hopeless attempt at recovering them."

"Very naturally. By-the-way, about the bird, we were compelled to eat it."

"To eat it!" Our visitor half rose from his chair in his excitement.

"Yes, it would have been of no use to anyone had we not done so. But I presume that this other goose upon the sideboard, which is about the same weight and perfectly fresh, will answer your purpose equally as well?"

"Oh, certainly, certainly"; answered Mr. Baker, with a sign of relief.

"Of course, we still have the feathers, legs, crop, and so on of your own bird, so if you wish—"

The man burst into a hearty laugh. "They might be useful to me as relics of my adventure," said he, "but beyond that I can hardly see what use the *disjecta membra* of my late acquaintance are going to be to me. No, sir, I think that, with your permission, I will confine my attentions to the excellent bird which I perceive upon the sideboard."

Sherlock Holmes glanced sharply across at me with a slight shrug of his shoulders.

"There is your hat, then, and there your bird," said he. "By-the-way, would it bore you to tell me where you got the other one from? I am somewhat of a fowl fancier, and I have seldom seen a better grown goose."

"Certainly, sir," said Baker, who had risen and tucked his newly gained property under his arm. "There are a few of us who frequent the 'Alpha Inn,' near the Museum—we are to be found in the Museum itself during the day, you understand. This year our good host, Windigate by name, instituted a goose club, by which, on consideration of some few pence every week, we were each to receive a bird at Christmas. My pence were duly paid, and the rest is familiar to you. I am much indebted to you, sir, for a Scotch bonnet is fitted neither to my years nor my gravity." With a comical pomposity of manner he bowed solemnly to both of us and strode off upon his way.

"So much for Mr. Henry Baker," said Holmes, when he had closed the door behind him. "It is quite certain that he knows nothing whatever about the matter. Are you hungry, Watson?"

"Not particularly."

"Then I suggest that we turn our dinner into a supper, and follow up this clue while it is still hot."

"By all means."

It was a bitter night, so we drew on our ulsters and wrapped cravats about our throats. Outside, the stars were shining coldly in a cloudless sky, and the breath of the passers-by blew out into smoke like so many pistol shots. Our footfalls rang out crisply and loudly as we swung through the Doctors' quarter. Wimpole Street, Harley Street, and so through Wigmore Street into Oxford Street. In a quarter of an hour we were in Bloomsbury at the "Alpha Inn," which is a small public-house at the corner of one of the streets which runs down into Holborn. Holmes pushed open the door of the private bar, and ordered two glasses of beer from the ruddy-faced, white-aproned landlord.

"Your beer should be excellent if it is as good as your geese," said he.

"My geese!" The man seemed surprised.

"Yes. I was speaking only half an hour ago to Mr. Henry Baker, who was a member of your goose club."

"Ah! yes, I see. But you see, sir, them's not *our* geese."

"Indeed! Whose, then?"

"Well, I got the two dozen from a salesman in Covent Garden."

"Indeed? I know some of them. Which was it?"

"Breckinridge is his name."

"Ah! I don't know him. Well, here's your good health, landlord, and prosperity to your house. Goodnight."

"Now for Mr. Breckinridge," he continued, buttoning up his coat, as we came out into the frosty air. "Remember, Watson, that though we have so homely a thing as a goose at one end of this chain, we have at the other a man who will certainly get seven years penal servitude unless we can establish his innocence. It is possible that our inquiry may not confirm his guilt; but, in any case, we have a line of investigation which has been missed by the police, and which a singular chance has placed in our hands. Let us follow it out to the bitter end. Faces to the south, then, and quick march!"

We passed across Holborn, down Endell Street, and so through a zigzag of slums to Covent Garden Market. One of the largest stalls bore the name Breckinridge upon it, and the proprietor, a horsey-looking man, with a sharp face and trim side-whiskers was helping a boy to put up the shutters.

"Good evening. It's a cold night," said Holmes.

The salesman nodded, and shot a questioning glance at my companion.

"Sold out of geese, I see," continued Holmes, pointing at the bare slabs of marble.

"Let you have 500 tomorrow morning."

"That's no good."

"Well, there are some on the stall with the gas-flare."

"Ah, but I was recommended to you."

"Who by?"

"The landlord of the 'Alpha.'"

"Oh, yes; I sent him a couple of dozen."

"Fine birds they were, too. Now where did you get them from?"

To my surprise the question provoked a burst of anger from the salesman.

"Now, then, mister," said he, with his head cocked and his arms akimbo, "what are you driving at? Let's have it straight, now."

"It is straight enough. I should like to know who sold you the geese which you supplied to the 'Alpha.'"

"Well, then, I sha'n't tell you. So now!"

"Oh, it is a matter of no importance; but I don't know why you should be so warm over such a trifle."

"Warm! You'd be as warm, maybe, if you were as pestered as I am. When I pay good money for a good article there should be an end of the business; but it's 'Where are the geese?' and 'Who did you sell the geese to?' and 'What will you take for the geese?' One would think they were the only geese in the world, to hear the fuss that is made over them."

"Well, I have no connection with any other people who have been making inquiries," said Holmes, carelessly. "If you won't tell us the bet is off, that is all. But I'm always ready to back my opinion on a matter of fowls, and I have a fiver on it that the bird I ate is country bred."

"Well, then, you've lost your fiver, for it's town bred," snapped the salesman.

"It's nothing of the kind."

"I say it is."

"I don't believe it."

"D'you think you know more about fowls than I, who have handled them ever since I was a nipper? I tell you, all those birds that went to the 'Alpha' were town bred."

"You'll never persuade me to believe that."

"Will you bet, then?"

"It's merely taking your money, for I know that I am right. But I'll have a sovereign on with you, just to teach you not to be obstinate."

The salesman chuckled grimly. "Bring me the books, Bill," said he.

The small boy brought round a small thin volume and a great greasy-backed one, laying them out together beneath the hanging lamp.

"Now then, Mr. Cocksure," said the salesman, "I thought that I was out of geese, but before I finish you'll find that there is still one left in my shop. You see this little book?"

"Well?"

"That's the list of the folk from whom I buy. D'you see? Well, then, here on this page are the country folk, and the numbers and their names are where their accounts are in the big ledger. Now, then! You see this other page in red ink? Well, that is a list of my town suppliers. Now, look at that third name. Just read it out to me."

"Mrs. Oakshott, 117, Brixton Road— 249," read Holmes.

"Quite so. Now turn that up in the ledger."

Holmes turned to the page indicated. "Here you are, 'Mrs. Oakshott, 117, Brixton Road, egg and poultry supplier.'"

"Now, then, what's the last entry?"

"'December 22. Twenty-four geese at 7s. 6d.'"

"Quite so. There you are. And underneath?"

"'Sold to Mr. Windigate of the 'Alpha,' at 12s.'"

"What have you to say now?"

Sherlock Holmes looked deeply cha-grined. He drew a sovereign from his pocket and threw it down upon the slab, turning away with the air of a man whose disgust is too deep for words. A few yards off he stopped under a lamp-post, and laughed in the hearty, noiseless fashion which was peculiar to him.

"When you see a man with whiskers of that cut and the 'pink 'un' protruding out of his pocket, you can always draw him by a bet," said he. "I dare say that if I had put £100 down in front of him, that man would not have given me such complete information as was drawn from him by the idea that he was doing me on a wager. Well, Watson, we are, I fancy, nearing the end of our quest, and the only point which remains to be determined is whether we should go on to this Mrs. Oakshott tonight, or whether we should reserve it for tomor-row. It is clear from what that surly fellow said that there are others besides ourselves who are anxious about the matter, and I should—"

His remarks were suddenly cut short by a loud hubbub which broke out from the stall which we had just left. Turn-ing round we saw a little rat-faced fel-low standing in the center of the circle of yellow light which was thrown by the swinging lamp, while Breckinridge, the salesman, framed in the door of his stall, was shaking his fists fiercely at the cringing figure.

"I've had enough of you and your geese," he shouted. "I wish you were all at the devil together. If you come pes-tering me any more with your silly talk I'll set the dog at you. You bring Mrs. Oakshott here and I'll answer her, but what have you to do with it? Did I buy the geese off you?"

"No; but one of them was mine all the same," whined the little man.

"Well, then, ask Mrs. Oakshott for it."
"She told me to ask you."

"Well, you can ask the King of Proo-sia, for all I care. I've had enough of it. Get out of this!" He rushed fiercely forward, and the inquirer flitted away into the darkness.

"Ha! this may save us a visit to Brix-ton Road," whispered Holmes. "Come with me, and we will see what is to be made of this fellow." Striding through the scattered knots of people who lounged round the flaring stalls, my companion speedily overtook the little man and touched him upon the shoul-der. He sprang round, and I could see in the gaslight that every vestige of color had been driven from his face.

"Who are you, then? What do you want?" he asked, in a quavering voice.

"You will excuse me," said Holmes, blandly, "but I could not help overhear-ing the questions which you put to the salesman just now. I think that I could be of assistance to you."

"You? Who are you? How could you know anything of the matter?"

"My name is Sherlock Holmes. It is my business to know what other people don't know."

"But you can know nothing of this?"

"Excuse me, I know everything of it. You are endeavoring to trace some geese which were sold by Mrs. Oakshott, of Brixton Road, to a salesman named Breckinridge, by him in turn to Mr. Windigate, of the 'Alpha,' and by him to his club, of which Mr. Henry Baker is a member."

"Oh, sir, you are the very man whom I have longed to meet," cried the little fellow, with outstretched hands and quivering fingers. "I can hardly ex-plain to you how interested I am in this matter."

Sherlock Holmes hailed a four-wheeler which was passing. "In that case we had better discuss it in a cosy room rather than in this windswept market-place," said he. "But pray tell me, before we go farther, who it is that I have the pleasure of assisting."

The man hesitated for an instant. "My name is John Robinson," he answered, with a side-long glance.

"No, no; the real name," said Holmes, sweetly. "It is always awkward doing business with an *alias.*"

A flush sprang to the white cheeks of the stranger. "Well, then," said he, "my real name is James Ryder."

"Precisely so. Head attendant at the 'Hotel Cosmopolitan.' Pray step into the cab, and I shall soon be able to tell you everything which you would wish to know."

The little man stood glancing from one to the other of us with half-frightened, half-hopeful eyes, as one who is not sure whether he is on the verge of a windfall or of a catastrophe. Then he stepped into the cab, and in half an hour we were back in the sitting-room at Baker Street. Nothing had been said during our drive, but the high, thin breathing of our new companion, and the claspings and unclaspings of his hands, spoke of the nervous tension within him.

"Here we are!" said Holmes, cheerily, as we filed into the room. "The fire looks very seasonable in this weather. You look cold, Mr. Ryder. Pray take the basket-chair. I will just put on my slippers before we settle this little matter of yours. Now, then! You want to know what became of those geese?"

"Yes, sir."

"Or rather, I fancy, of that goose. It was one bird, I imagine, in which you were interested—white, with a black bar across the tail."

Ryder quivered with emotion. "Oh, sir," he cried, "can you tell me where it went to?"

"It came here."

"Here?"

"Yes, and a most remarkable bird it proved. I don't wonder that you should take an interest in it. It laid an egg after it was dead—the bonniest, brightest little blue egg that ever was seen. I have it here in my museum."

Our visitor staggered to his feet and clutched the mantelpiece with his right hand. Holmes unlocked his strongbox, and held up the blue carbuncle, which shone out like a star, with a cold, brilliant, many-pointed radiance. Ryder stood glaring with a drawn face, uncertain whether to claim or to disown it.

"The game's up, Ryder," said Holmes, quietly. "Hold up, man, or you'll be into the fire! Give him an arm back into his chair, Watson. He's not got blood enough to go in for felony with impunity. Give him a dash of brandy. So! Now he looks a little more human. What a shrimp it is, to be sure!"

For a moment he had staggered and nearly fallen, but the brandy brought a tinge of color into his cheeks, and he sat staring with frightened eyes at his accuser.

"I have almost every link in my hands, and all the proofs which I could possibly need, so there is little which you need tell me. Still, that little may as well be cleaned up to make the case complete. You had heard, Ryder, of this blue stone of the Countess of Morcar's?"

"It was Catherine Cusack who told me of it," said he, in a crackling voice.

"I see—her ladyship's waiting-maid. Well, the temptation of sudden wealth so easily acquired was too much for you, as it has been for better men before you;

but you were not very scrupulous in the means you used. It seems to me, Ryder, that there is the making of a very pretty villain in you. You knew that this man Horner, the plumber, had been concerned in some such matter before, and that suspicion would rest the more readily upon him. What did you do, then? You made some small job in my lady's room—you and your confederate Cusack —and you managed that he should be the man sent for. Then, when he had left, you rifled the jewel-case, raised the alarm, and had this unfortunate man arrested. You then—"

Ryder threw himself down suddenly upon the rug and clutched at my companion's knees. "For God's sake, have mercy!" he shrieked. "Think of my father! of my mother! It would break their hearts. I never went wrong before! I never will again. I swear it. I'll swear it on a Bible. Oh, don't bring it into court! For Christ's sake, don't!"

"Get back into your chair!" said Holmes, sternly. "It is very well to cringe and crawl now, but you thought little enough of this poor Horner in the dock for a crime of which he knew nothing."

"I will fly, Mr. Holmes. I will leave the country, sir. Then the charge against him will break down."

"Hum! We will talk about that. And now let us hear a true account of the next act. How came the stone into the goose, and how came the goose into the open market? Tell us the truth, for there lies your only hope of safety."

Ryder passed his tongue over his parched lips. "I will tell you it just as it happened, sir," said he. "When Horner had been arrested, it seemed to me that it would be best for me to get away with the stone at once, for I did not know at what moment the police might

not take it into their heards to search me and my room. There was no place about the hotel where it would be safe. I went out, as if on some commission, and I made for my sister's house. She had married a man named Oakshott, and lived in Brixton Road, where she fattened fowls for the market. All the way there every man I met seemed to me to be a policeman or a detective; and, for all that it was a cold night, the sweat was pouring down my face before I came to the Brixton Road. My sister asked me what was the matter, and why I was so pale; but I told her that I had been upset by the jewel robbery at the hotel. Then I went into the back yard and smoked a pipe, and wondered what it would be best to do.

"I had a friend once called Maudsley, who went to the bad, and has just been serving his time in Pentonville. One day he had met me, and fell into talk about the ways of thieves, and how they could get rid of what they stole. I knew that he would be true to me, for I knew one or two things about him; so I made up my mind to go right on to Kilburn, where he lived, and take him into my confidence. He would show me how to turn the stone into money. But how to get to him in safety? I thought of the agonies I had gone through in coming from the hotel. I might at any moment be seized and searched, and there would be the stone in my waistcoat pocket. I was leaning against the wall at the time, and looking at the geese which were waddling about round my feet, and suddenly an idea came into my head which showed me how I could beat the best detective that ever lived.

"My sister had told me some weeks before that I might have the pick of her geese for a Christmas present, and I knew that she was always as good as her word. I would take my goose now, and in it I would carry my stone to Kilburn. There was a little shed in the yard, and behind this I drove one of the birds—a fine big one, white, with a barred tail. I caught it, and, prying its bill open, I thrust the stone down its throat as far as my finger could reach. The bird gave a gulp, and I felt the stone pass along its gullet and down into its crop. But the creature flapped and struggled, and out came my sister to know what was the matter. As I turned to speak to her the brute broke loose and fluttered off among the others.

" 'Whatever were you doing with that bird, Jem?' says she.

" 'Well,' said I, 'you said you'd give me one for Christmas, and I was feeling which was the fattest.'

" 'Oh,' says she, 'we've set yours aside for you—Jem's bird, we call it. It's the big white one over yonder. There's twenty-six of them, which makes one for you, and one for us, and two dozen for the market.'

" 'Thank you, Maggie,' says I; 'but if it is all the same to you, I'd rather have that one I was handling just now.'

" 'The other is a good three pound heavier,' said she, 'and we fattened it expressly for you.'

" 'Never mind. I'll have the other, and I'll take it now,' said I.

" 'Oh, just as you like,' said she, a little huffed. 'Which is it you want, then?'

" 'That white one with the barred tail, right in the middle of the flock.'

" 'Oh, very well. Kill it and take it with you.'

"Well, I did what she said, Mr. Holmes, and I carried the bird all the way to Kilburn. I told my pal what I had done, for he was a man that it was easy to tell a thing like that to. He laughed until he choked, and we got a knife and opened the goose. My heart turned to water, for there was no sign of the stone, and I knew that some terrible mistake had occurred. I left the bird, rushed back to my sister's, and hurried into the back yard. There was not a bird to be seen there.

" 'Where are they all, Maggie?' I cried.

" 'Gone to the dealer's, Jem.'

" 'Which dealer's?'

" 'Breckinridge, of Covent Garden.'

" 'But was there another with a barred tail?' I asked, 'the same as the one I chose?'

" 'Yes, Jem; here were two barred-tailed ones, and I could never tell them apart.'

"Well, then, of course I saw it all, and I ran off as hard as my feet would carry me to this man Breckinridge; but he had sold the lot at once, and not one word would he tell me as to where they had gone. You heard him yourselves to-night. Well, he has always answered me like that. My sister thinks that I am going mad. Sometimes I think that I am myself. And now—and now I am myself a branded thief, without ever having touched the wealth for which I sold my character. God help me! God help me!" He burst into convulsive sobbing, with his face buried in his hands.

There was a long silence, broken only by his heavy breathing, and by the measured tapping of Sherlock Holmes's finger-tips upon the edge of the table. Then my friend rose and threw open the door.

"Get out!" said he.

"What, sir! Oh, heaven bless you!"

"No more words. Get out!"

And no more words were needed.

There was a rush, a clatter upon the stairs, the bang of a door, and the crisp rattle of running footfalls from the street.

"After all, Watson," said Holmes, reaching up his hand for his clay pipe, "I am not retained by the police to supply their deficiencies. If Horner were in danger it would be another thing; but this fellow will not appear against him, and the case must collapse. I suppose that I am commuting a felony, but it is just possible that I am saving a soul. This fellow will not go wrong again; he is too terribly frightened. Send him to jail now, and you make him a jail-bird for life. Besides, it is the season of forgiveness. Chance has put in our way a most singular and whimsical problem, and its solution is its own reward. If you will have the goodness to touch the bell, doctor, we will begin another investigation, in which, also, a bird will be the chief feature."

1891

SAKI

(H. H. Munro)

The Stalled Ox

THEOPHIL ESHLEY was an artist by profession, a cattle painter by force of environment. It is not to be supposed that he lived on a ranch or a dairy farm, in an atmosphere pervaded with horn and hoof, milking-stool, and branding-iron. His home was in a park-like, villa-dotted district that only just escaped the reproach of being suburban. On one side of his garden there abutted a small, picturesque meadow, in which an enterprising neighbour pastured some small picturesque cows of the Channel Island persuasion. At noonday in summertime the cows stood knee-deep in tall meadow-grass under the shade of a group of walnut trees, with the sunlight falling in dappled patches on their mouse-sleek coats. Eshley had conceived and executed a dainty picture of two reposeful milch-cows in a setting of walnut tree and meadow-grass and filtered sunbeam, and the Royal Academy had duly exposed the same on the walls of its Summer Exhibition. The Royal Academy encourages orderly, methodical habits in its children. Eshley had painted a successful and acceptable picture of cattle-drowsing picturesquely under walnut trees, and as he had begun, so, of necessity, he went on. His "Noontide Peace," a study of two dun cows under a walnut tree, was followed by "A Midday Sanctuary," a study of a walnut tree, with two dun cows under it. In due succession, there came "Where the Gad-Flies Cease from Troubling," "The Haven of the Herd," and "A Dream in Dairyland," studies of walnut trees and

From *The Short Stories of Saki* by H. H. Munro.   Copyright 1930 by The Viking Press, Inc., N. Y.

dun cows. His two attempts to break away from his own tradition were signal failures: "Turtle Doves Alarmed by Sparrow-hawk" and "Wolves on the Roman Campagna" came back to his studio in the guise of abominable heresies, and Eshley climbed back into grace and the public gaze with "A Shaded Nook Where Drowsy Milkers Dream."

On a fine afternoon in late autumn he was putting some finishing touches to a study of meadow weeds when his neighbour, Adela Pingsford, assailed the outer door of his studio with loud peremptory knockings.

"There is an ox in my garden," she announced, in explanation of the tempestuous intrusion.

"An ox," said Eshley blankly, and rather fatuously; "what kind of ox?"

"Oh, I don't know what kind," snapped the lady. "A common or garden ox, to use the slang expression. It is the garden part of it that I object to. My garden has just been put straight for the winter, and an ox roaming about in it won't improve matters. Besides, there are the chrysanthemums just coming into flower."

"How did it get into the garden?" asked Eshley.

"I imagine it came in by the gate," said the lady impatiently; "it couldn't have climbed the walls, and I don't suppose any one dropped it from an aeroplane as a Bovril advertisement. The immediately important question is not how it got in, but how to get it out."

"Won't it go?" said Eshley.

"If it was anxious to go," said Adela Pingsford rather angrily, "I should not have come here to chat with you about it. I'm practically all alone; the housemaid is having her afternoon out and the cook is lying down with an attack of neuralgia. Anything that I may have learned at school or in after life about how to remove a large ox from a small garden seems to have escaped from my memory now. All I could think of was that you were a near neighbour and a cattle painter, presumably more or less familiar with the subjects that you painted, and that you might be of some slight assistance. Possibly I was mistaken."

"I paint dairy cows, certainly," admitted Eshley, "but I cannot claim to have had any experience in rounding up stray oxen. I've seen it done on a cinema film, of course, but there were always horses and lots of other accessories; besides, one never knows how much of those pictures are faked."

Adela Pingsford said nothing, but led the way to her garden. It was normally a fair-sized garden, but it looked small in comparison with the ox, a huge mottled brute, dull red about the head and shoulders, passing to dirty white on the flanks and hind-quarters, with shaggy ears and large blood-shot eyes. It bore about as much resemblance to the dainty paddock heifers that Eshley was accustomed to paint as the chief of a Kurdish nomad clan would to a Japanese teashop girl. Eshley stood very near the gate while he studied the animal's appearance and demeanour. Adela Pingsford continued to say nothing.

"It's eating a chrysanthemum," said Eshley at last, when the silence had become unbearable.

"How observant you are," said Adela bitterly. "You seem to notice everything. As a matter of fact, it has got six chrysanthemums in its mouth at the present moment."

The necessity for doing something was becoming imperative. Eshley took a step or two in the direction of the animal, clapped his hands, and made noises of the "Hish" and "Shoo" variety. If the ox heard them it gave no outward indication of the fact.

"If any hens should ever stray into my garden," said Adela, "I should certainly send for you to frighten them out. You 'shoo' beautifully. Meanwhile, do you mind trying to drive that ox away? That is a *Mademoiselle Louise Bichot* that he's begun on now," she added in icy calm, as a glowing orange head was crushed into the huge munching mouth.

"Since you have been so frank about the variety of the chrysanthemum," said Eshley, "I don't mind telling you that this is an Ayrshire ox."

The icy calm broke down; Adela Pingsford used language that sent the artist instinctively a few feet nearer to the ox. He picked up a pea-stick and flung it with some determination against the animal's mottled flanks. The operation of mashing *Mademoiselle Louise Bichot* into a petal salad was suspended for a long moment, while the ox gazed with concentrated inquiry at the stick-thrower. Adela gazed with equal concentration and more obvious hostility at the same focus. As the beast neither lowered its head nor stamped its feet Eshley ventured on another javelin exercise with another pea-stick. The ox seemed to realize at once that it was to go; it gave a hurried final pluck at the bed where the chrysanthemums had been, and strode swiftly up the garden. Eshley ran to head it towards the gate, but only succeeded in quickening its pace from a walk to a lumbering trot. With an air of inquiry, but with no real hesitation, it crossed the tiny strip of turf that the charitable called the croquet lawn, and pushed its way through the open French window into the morning-room. Some chrysanthemums and

other autumn herbage stood about the room in vases, and the animal resumed its browsing operations; all the same, Eshley fancied that the beginnings of a hunted look had come into its eyes, a look that counselled respect. He discontinued his attempt to interfere with its choice of surroundings.

"Mr. Eshley," said Adela in a shaking voice, "I asked you to drive that beast out of my garden, but I did not ask you to drive it into my house. If I must have it anywhere on the premises I prefer the garden to the morning-room."

"Cattle drives are not in my line," said Eshley; "if I remember I told you so at the outset."

"I quite agree," retorted the lady, "painting pretty pictures of pretty little cows is what you're suited for. Perhaps you'd like to do a nice sketch of that ox making itself at home in my morning-room?"

This time it seemed as if the worm had turned; Eshley began striding away.

"Where are you going?" screamed Adela.

"To fetch implements," was the answer.

"Implements? I won't have you use a lasso. The room will be wrecked if there's a struggle."

But the artist marched out of the garden. In a couple of minutes he returned, laden with easel, sketching-stool, and painting materials.

"Do you mean to say that you're going to sit quietly down and paint that brute while it's destroying my morning-room?" gasped Adela.

"It was your suggestion," said Eshley, setting his canvas in position.

"I forbid it; I absolutely forbid it!" stormed Adela.

"I don't see what standing you have in the matter," said the artist; "you can hardly pretend that it's your ox, even by adoption."

"You seem to forget that it's in my morning-room, eating my flowers," came the raging retort.

"You seem to forget that the cook has neuralgia," said Eshley; "she may be just dozing off into a merciful sleep and your outcry will awaken her. Consideration for others should be the guiding principle of people in our station of life."

"The man is mad!" exclaimed Adela tragically. A moment later it was Adela herself who appeared to go mad. The ox had finished the vase-flowers and the cover of *Israel Kalisch,* and appeared to be thinking of leaving its rather restricted quarters. Eshley noticed its restlessness and promptly flung it some bunches of Virginia creeper leaves as an inducement to continue the sitting.

"I forget how the proverb runs," he observed; "something about 'better a dinner of herbs than a stalled ox where hate is.' We seem to have all the ingredients for the proverb ready to hand."

"I shall go to the Public Library and get them to telephone for the police," announced Adela, and, raging audibly, she departed.

Some minutes later the ox, awakening probably to the suspicion that oil cake and chopped mangold was waiting for it in some appointed byre, stepped with much precaution out of the morning-room, stared with grave inquiry at the no longer obtrusive and pea-stick-throwing human, and then lumbered heavily but swiftly out of the garden. Eshley packed up his tools and followed the animal's example and "Larkdene" was left to neuralgia and the cook.

The episode was the turning-point in Eshley's artistic career. His remarkable picture, "Ox in a Morning-room, Late Autumn," was one of the sensations and successes of the next Paris Salon, and when it was subsequently exhibited at Munich it was bought by the Bavarian Government, in the teeth of the spirited bidding of three meat-extract firms. From that moment his success was continuous and assured, and the Royal Academy was thankful, two years later, to give a conspicuous position on its walls to his large canvas "Barbary Apes Wrecking a Boudoir."

Eshley presented Adela Pingsford with a new copy of *Israel Kalisch,* and a couple of finely flowering plants of *Madame André Blusset,* but nothing in the nature of a real reconciliation has taken place between them.

1928

THOMAS WOLFE

Only the Dead Know Brooklyn

Dere's no guy livin' dat knows Brooklyn t'roo an' t'roo, because it'd take a guy a lifetime just to find his way aroun' duh f—— town.

So like I say, I'm waitin' for my train t' come when I sees dis big guy standin' deh—dis is duh foist I eveh see of him. Well, he's lookin' wild, y'know, an' I can see dat he's had plenty, but still he's holdin' it; he talks good an' is walkin' straight enough. So den, dis big guy steps up to a little guy dat's standin' deh, an' says, "How d'yuh get t' Eighteent' Avenoo an' Sixty-sevent' Street?" he says.

"Jesus! Yuh got me, chief," duh little guy says to him. "I ain't been heah long myself. Where is duh place?" he says. "Out in duh Flatbush section somewhere?"

"Nah," duh big guy says. "It's out in Bensonhoist. But I was neveh deh befoeh. How d'yuh get deh?"

"Jesus," duh little guy says, scratchin' his head, y'know—yuh could see duh little guy didn't know his way about— "yuh got me, chief. I neveh hoid of it. Do any of youse guys know where it is?" he says to me.

"Sure," I says. "It's out in Bensonhoist. Yuh take duh Fourt' Avenoo express, get off at Fifty-nint' Street, change to a Sea Beach local deh, get off at Eighteent' Avenoo an' Sixty-toid, an' den walk down foeh blocks. Dat's all yuh got to do," I says.

"G'wan!" some wise guy dat I neveh seen befoeh pipes up. "Whatcha talkin' about?" he says—oh, he was wise, y'know. "Duh guy is crazy! I tell yuh what yuh do," he says to duh big guy. "Yuh change to duh West End line at Toity-sixt'," he tells him. "Get off at Noo Utrecht an' Sixteent' Avenoo," he says. "Walk two blocks oveh, foeh blocks up," he says, "an' you'll be right deh." Oh, a *wise* guy, y'know.

"Oh, yeah?" I says. "Who told *you* so much?" He got me sore because he was so wise about it. "How long you been livin' heah?" I says.

"All my life," he says. "I was bawn in Williamsboig," he says. "An' I can tell you t'ings about dis town you neveh hoid of," he says.

"Yeah?" I says.

"Yeah," he says.

"Well, den, you can tell me t'ings about dis town dat nobody else has eveh hoid of, either. Maybe you make it all up yoehself at night," I says, "befoeh you go to sleep—like cuttin' out papeh dolls, or somp'n."

"Oh, yeah?" he says. "You're pretty wise, ain't yuh?"

"Oh, I don't know," I says. "Duh boids ain't usin' my head for Lincoln's statue yet," I says. "But I'm wise enough to know a phony when I see one."

"Yeah?" he says. "A wise guy, huh? Well, you're so wise dat some one's goin' t'bust yuh one right on duh snoot some day," he says. "Dat's how wise *you* are."

Well, my train was comin', or I'da smacked him den and dere, but when I seen duh train was comin', all I said was, "All right, mugg! I'm sorry I can't stay to take keh of you, but I'll be seein' yuh sometime, I hope, out in duh cemetery." So den I says to duh big guy, who'd been standin' deh all duh time, "You come wit me," I says. So when we gets onto duh train I says to him, "Where yuh goin' out in Bensonhoist?" I says. "What numbeh are yuh lookin' for?" I says. *You* know—I t'ought if he told me duh address I might be able to help him out.

"Oh," he says, "I'm not lookin' for no one. I don't know no one out deh."

"Then whatcha goin' out deh for?" I says.

"Oh," duh guy says, "I'm just goin' out to see duh place," he says. "I like duh sound of duh name—Bensonhoist, y'know—so I t'ought I'd go out an' have a look at it."

"Whatcha tryin' t'hand me?" I says. "Whatcha tryin' t'do—kid me?" *You* know, I t'ought duh guy was bein' wise wit me.

"No," he says, "I'm tellin' yuh duh troot. I like to go out an' take a look at places wit nice names like dat. I like to go out an' look at all kinds of places," he says.

"How'd yuh know deh was such a place," I says, "if yuh neveh been deh befoeh?"

"Oh," he says, "I got a map."

"A *map?*" I says.

"Sure," he says, "I got a map dat tells me about all dese places. I take it wit me every time I come out heah," he says.

And Jesus? Wit dat, he pulls it out of his 'pocket, an' so help me, but he's *got* it—he's tellin' duh troot—a big map of duh whole f—— place with all duh different pahts mahked out. You know

—Canarsie an' East Noo Yawk an' Flatbush, Bensonhoist, Sout' Brooklyn, duh Heights, Bay Ridge, Greenpernt—duh whole goddam layout, he's got it right deh on duh map.

"You been to any of dose places?" I says.

"Sure," he says, "I been to most of 'em. I was down in Red Hook just last night," he says.

"Jesus! Red Hook!" I says. "Whatcha do down deh?"

"Oh," he says, "nuttin' much. I just walked aroun'. I went into a coupla places an' had a drink," he says, "but most of the time I just walked aroun'."

"Just walked aroun'?" I says.

"Sure," he says, "just lookin' at t'ings, y'know."

"Where'd yuh go?" I asts him.

"Oh," he says, "I don't know duh name of duh place, but I could find it on my map," he says. "One time I was walkin' across some big fields where deh ain't no houses," he says, "but I could see ships oveh deh all lighted up. Dey was loadin'. So I walks across duh fields," he says, "to where duh ships are."

"Sure," I says, "I know where you was. You was down to duh Erie Basin."

"Yeah," he says, "I guess dat was it. Dey had some of dose big elevators an' cranes an' dey was loadin' ships, an' I could see some ships in drydock all lighted up, so I walks across duh fields to where dey are," he says.

"Den what did yuh do?" I says.

"Oh," he says, "nuttin' much. I came on back across duh fields after a while an' went into a coupla places an' had a drink."

"Didn't nuttin' happen while yuh was in dere?" I says.

"No," he says. "Nuttin' much. A coupla guys was drunk in one of duh places an' started a fight, but dey bounced 'em out," he says, "an' den one of duh guys stahted to come back again, but duh bartender gets his baseball bat out from under duh counteh, so duh guy goes on."

"Jesus!" I said. "Red Hook!"

"Sure," he says. "Dat's where it was, all right."

"Well, you keep outa deh," I says. "You stay away from deh."

"Why?" he says. "What's wrong wit it?"

"Oh," I says, "it's a good place to stay away from, dat's all. It's a good place to keep out of."

"Why?" he says. "Why is it?"

Jesus! Whatcha gonna do wit a guy as dumb as dat? I saw it wasn't no use to try to tell him nuttin', he wouldn't know what I was talkin' about, so I just says to him, "Oh, nuttin'. Yuh might get lost down deh, dat's all."

"Lost?" he says. "No, I wouldn't get lost. I got a map," he says.

A map! Red Hook! Jesus!

So den duh guy begins to ast me all kinds of nutty questions: how big was Brooklyn an' could I find my way aroun' in it, an' how long would it take a guy to know duh place.

"Listen!" I says. "You get dat idea outa yoeh head right now," I says. "You ain't neveh gonna get to know Brooklyn," I says. "Not in a hunderd yeahs. I been livin' heah all my life," I says, "an' I don't even know all deh is to know about it, so how do you expect to know duh town," I says, "when you don't even live heah?"

"Yes," he says, "but I got a map to help me find my way about."

"Map or no map," I says, "yuh ain't gonna get to know Brooklyn wit no map," I says.

"Can you swim?" he says, just like dat. Jesus! By dat time, y'know, I begun to see dat duh guy was some kind of nut. He'd had plenty to drink, of course, but he had dat crazy look in his eye I didn't like. "Can you swim?" he says.

"Sure," I says. "Can't you?"

"No," he says. "Not more'n a stroke or two. I neveh loined good."

"Well, it's easy," I says. "All yuh need is a little confidence. Duh way I loined, me older bruddeh pitched me off duh dock one day when I was eight yeahs old, cloes an' all. 'You'll swim,' he says. 'You'll swim all right—or drown.' An', believe me, I swam! When yuh know yuh got to, you'll do it. Duh only t'ing yuh need is confidence. An' once you've loined," I says, "you've got nuttin' else to worry about. You'll neveh forget it. It's somp'n dat stays wit yuh as long as yuh live."

"Can yuh swim good?" he says.

"Like a fish," I tells him. "I'm a regulah fish in duh wateh," I says. "I loined to swim right off duh docks wit all duh oddeh kids," I says.

"What would you do if yuh saw a man drownin'?" duh guy says.

"Do? Why, I'd jump in an' pull him out," I says. "Dat's what I'd do."

"Did yuh eveh see a man drown?" he says.

"Sure," I says. "I see two guys—bot' times at Coney Island. Dey got out too far, an' neider one could swim. Dey drowned befoeh any one could get to 'em."

"What becomes of people after dey've drowned out heah?" he says.

"Drowned out where?" I says.

"Out heah in Brooklyn."

"I don't know whatcha mean," I says. "Neveh hoid of no one drownin' heah in Brooklyn, unless you mean a swimmin' pool. Yuh can't drown in Brooklyn," I says. "Yuh gotta drown somewhere else—in duh ocean, where dere's wateh."

"Drownin'," duh guy says, lookin' at his map. "Drownin'." Jesus! I could see by den he was some kind of nut, he had dat crazy expression in his eyes when he looked at you, an' I didn't know what he might do. So we was comin' to a station, an' it wasn't my stop, but I got off anyway, an' waited for duh next train.

"Well, so long, chief," I says. "Take it easy, now."

"Drownin'," duh guy says, lookin' at his map. "Drownin'."

Jesus! I've t'ought about dat guy a t'ousand times since den an' wondered what eveh happened to 'm goin' out to look at Bensonhoist because he liked duh name! Walkin' aroun' t'roo Red Hook by himself at night an' lookin' at his map! How many people did I see get drowned out heah in Brooklyn! How long would it take a guy wit a good map to know all deh was to know about Brooklyn!

Jesus! What a nut *he* was! I wondeh what eveh happened to 'im, anyway! I wondeh if some one knocked him on duh head, or if he's still wanderin' aroun' in duh subway in duh middle of duh night wit his little map! Duh poor guy! Say, I've got to laugh, at dat, when I t'ink about him! Maybe he's found out by now dat he'll neveh live long enough to know duh whole of Brooklyn. It'd take a guy a lifetime to know Brooklyn t'roo an' t'roo. An' even den, yuh wouldn't know it all.

1935

AUSTIN STRONG

"She Shall Have Music"

I HEARD with an inward ping of pleasure the whistle of the paddle-wheel steamer warning us that she was swinging her enormous bustle around Brant Point.

The clock in the Unitarian Church began striking the hour.

"The boat's late," I said.

My companion said nothing, but sat beside me upright as an exclamation point, remote as a portrait.

Though we saw him here every morning in his accustomed chair in the Captains' Room, we knew little about him save that he had traveled widely and that he had a native eloquence if he could be induced to talk. Now he had "rounded Brant Point" for good, to end his days in peace on Nantucket Island where he was born.

I smiled as I listened to the deep-toned bell booming circles of sound over the huddled roofs of the gray town. This bronze beauty is not only a Portuguese but a papist, blessed by no less a dignitary than the patriarch of Lisbon. It was bought in that city at the beginning of the last century by a public-spirited sea captain and set up in the gold-capped tower of the South Church, where for over a hundred years this good Catholic has called the freethinking and tolerant Protestants to their nonconforming meetings.

"Yes, sir, she's half an hour late," I said again, but Mr. Bolling had inherited from his Quaker forebears the gift of silence. His thin face was aquiline and his aristocratic nose discouraged familiarity. His hands rested neatly folded upon his gold-headed Malacca cane through which ran a tasseled cord; his gold-rimmed eyeglasses hung from a black silk ribbon; his linen was immaculate, always freshly laundered, creaking with starch.

Hoping to lure him into conversation I said facetiously: "There's a star-face for you, Mr. Bolling!"

I pointed my pipe at a flaming thing in a skirt cut high above her knees, who teetered past our windows on high heels, her hair bobbed boy-fashion, a cigarette between her lips.

Mr. Bolling began banging on the floor with his cane. He turned and held me with a blazing eye, then spoke in a slow, cultivated voice, each word delivered with precision as if he enjoyed the taste of every syllable.

"What's the fun of being a woman if one can't be feminine. These be-bottomed strutters aren't women—they're newts!"

I sat up with interest.

"Tell me, Mr. Bolling, did you ever see a really beautiful woman?"

By a lucky chance I struck a gusher. He gave his panama a tilt, leaned far back, placed a neatly shod foot on the railing, and became someone entirely different: someone warm, expansive, eloquent. He came out from his cell of silence like an escaping Trappist as he stared through the windows at the sunlit square.

"It happened right here on Main Street, up there in front of Ashley's Store, 'Parker's Corner' in my day. You won't believe this when I tell you that right now my heart skips a beat as I recall when I first saw her rounding the head of the square like a brand-new frigate with all sails drawing, flags and pennants flying! My, my, it was a picture! You just couldn't keep your mind where it ought to be when she went by. I don't know how to put it, but even in broad daylight her skin seemed luminous, as if she carried a lamp within her. She came from some enchanted land to dwell among us sober folk who lived in Nantucket under the drab Quaker discipline.

"Though I was a boy of twelve and she a grown woman, I fell in love with her, and don't you believe a boy can't fall in love at twelve. It was very real with me—so real in fact that I would race ahead of her to wait on the corners just to watch her go by, refreshing the whole street with her beauty. There was something magical about her, for when you caught a look from her eyes something inside of you melted away. Never was there a kinder glance. It came to you slowly from under long eyelashes, just for you, for your very own, finding its way to your heart's core, and there it would lie for the rest of the day curled up and warm like some secret good news. I was not alone in my adoration, for the whole town loved her—men, women, children, dogs, off-Islanders, and all hands round!

"Her hair was reddish gold that flashed back the sunlight like a ship's binnacle. I tell you it was so golden you could lose a twenty-dollar gold piece in it and have a hard time finding it. And there was nothing sexless about her like these slab-sided pullets you see on Main Street. No, sir, there was no mistaking that she was a woman. She had a small waist, little feet, and a shapely bosom, round and firm, from which rose a lovely neck. She wore earrings, sir, the like of which I've never seen before nor since: tiny sprays of wheat exquisitely fashioned out of pure gold to curve up and around the lobes of her ears. My, my, they were just joy and rapture to behold, and did the things to you they were designed to do. Now you won't believe this, but they were the first earrings I ever saw on a woman, for only the sailors wore them in our Quaker town where most of the women were forced to imprison their beauty within muslin caps or those hideous gray poke bonnets.

"She lived opposite us with a sick father, a retired widower, who had left Nantucket in his youth and established a business in Montevideo where he spent most of his life. After his wife's death he returned with his daughter to end his days like most of us on this precious 'elbow of sand.' Our houses were opposite each other on the same street near the edge of the town where the moors begin. I would get up early on Sunday mornings just to watch her come out of the house to go to church. Occasionally a priest would come from the mainland by the packet to celebrate Mass for the few Catholics who lived here in those days. It was a sight to see her come out of her front door carrying a thick brass-bound prayerbook and a rosary of gold beads twisted around her wrist. She wore black lace mittens and a soft mantilla over her hair. I would listen for the crisp rustle of her ruffled black silk dress which stood stiffly around her like a bell.

"We heard that her mother was Spanish and a gold-head like her daughter. I can testify that a fair-haired Castilian makes for a loveliness indescribable. I only saw it once again, and that was in Paris when I watched the Empress Eugénie driving by in the Bois de Boulogne.

"We never saw her father, for his illness kept him a prisoner in the house, but we knew that he was difficult and that she was having a sad time nursing him, though you would never guess from seeing her that there was a thing on her mind but laughter from the joy of living.

"Yes, sir, it's a glorious thing to be a beautiful woman, but you've got to know how to be one and she did, full and bye, you know what I mean—she carried it! Though she was naturally lovely she had something extra, an inward grace I suppose you'd call it. Well, whatever it was, it captured and enraptured the Islanders, bringing color and brightness into their lonely lives. And let me tell you it was lonely around here in those days. Imagine three-quarters of the menfolk scattered all over the seven oceans for years at a time. It was hard on the women left behind and she knew it. But she wasn't soft, for that wouldn't have gone down with our shrewd people. She had a straight back, tough as hickory, which her Nantucket forebears had given her, and a whiplash humor which acted like a strong tonic on the lonely and the anxious. That's why no woman was ever known to be jealous of her.

"Yes, it's a funny thing, come to think of it, that though the Quakers on our island were very strict and frowned on color and beauty in any form, they somehow never frowned on her—nobody could. She was accepted by the people like one of those strange, beautiful birds the sailors brought back from the tropics, and they let her go free and unhindered. Life was dull as fog for most of us—no theaters, games, or parties, and lights out at curfew. She sensed the dreariness of our lives and unconsciously took it upon herself to cheer us; and, believe me, she did it in the most enchanting way.

"The gods, in an expansive mood, gave her a voice. Each note had a life of its own and rose from her throat full, clear, and round. I knew instinctively it was something rare, for whenever she sang she stole your thoughts away—far away to uncharted places. Naturally we children went plumb crazy about her and would waylay her after school, surrounding and pressing her close in a giggling, squirming circle, holding her prisoner until she sang herself free.

"She sang us South American love songs and gay ballads while dignified ship captains with tall hats and reefer coats stopped to lean on whalebone canes, and drivers in low-slung wagons loaded with barrels of whale oil fresh from wild sea battles eased their horses to the curb and listened; doors opened a crack on Petticoat Row; windows were pushed up in houses opposite; the street sweeper rested on his broom, while even the Quakers in their mouse-colored clothes slowed their pace as they walked discreetly by with downcast eyes.

"Then one day we were stunned by the news which exploded in our faces. She was going to marry a Nantucket Quaker! Everyone groaned and there was much talk on Main Street. Somehow it seemed all wrong and wicked that such beauty was condemned to the prison of a disciplined life.

"Our bird of paradise was trapped in a cage. As for me, it was my first meeting with jealousy. Such hatred filled me against that inoffensive, placid young Quaker that it still frightens me to recall its intensity. I cannot remember much about him, for my fury kept him out of focus, but I know that I would have gladly done away with him if I had known how. No one on the Island understood what she had in common with him, for it seemed like the union of ice and fire, but there was no doubt that she loved him with all the splendor of her heart.

"After her father's death her Quaker took her to the Meeting House on First Day, where she sat in a gay flowered dress among the dove-gray women, while he joined the menfolk across the aisle. After an hour's silence she was brought before the elders and other weighty members and instructed for her Certificate of Membership into the Society of Friends. It must have been a wrench for her to forswear her allegiance to her own church, with all her love of color and beauty, and surrender herself to the plain life where loveliness was anathema. But she did it. Yes, sir, she went over to them hook, line, and sinker.

"She stood up there among them like a Jacqueminot rose in a cabbage patch and was solemnly warned against 'vain and frothy conversation,' of the snares and vanities of adornment and the wearing of 'Babylonian garments.' She was instructed to speak the plain Scripture language of *thee* and *thou* and to learn all the Queries and Advices, and told that vocal music was forbidden as 'it articulates ideas which may convey poison to the mind and tends to seduce the thoughts of youth which makes no selection, but learns all that falls in their way.' She was gravely warned that her singing must cease forever and through the discipline of silence she must 'keep down the willings and the runnings.'

"Well, sir, the poor girl promised them everything and she was duly signed up and delivered to a life as dull as stale porridge. Lord, I shall never forget the night before her wedding. I couldn't sleep for heartache, and sat like a silly coof at the open window of my attic room staring at the stars which hung close down over the Island. I remember everything about that night: the sound of the heavy surf on the South Shore, the faint gaggle of a skein of wild geese high overhead on their long, strong flight to the Carolinas, a moon that was trying to turn night into day. Have you ever noticed how the moonlight changes the gold on the South Church into a misty silver? I remember how still everything was; the whole world held its breath as if aware something ominous was going to happen.

"A dog barked over 'Egypt' way and was promptly silenced. I knew the night was a weather-breeder, for I could just hear, faint as conscience, the foreboding sound of the bell buoy occasionally tolling outside the Eastern jetty.

"I heard the click of a latch. Then a hooded figure slipped out of the back door of the house opposite and headed straight for the open moors. I knew it was she. In an instant I was down the stairs and out of the house, fast after her. But I found she was hard to keep up with, for she was young and strong and swift, while I was a short-legged youngster. I followed her until my breath hurt me and my feet were full of pain. Then to my dismay I lost sight of her.

"I began to walk vaguely towards the center of the moors, hoping against hope to find her. I must have gone some distance, for a blister fastened on my heel like a wasp and forced me to limp. Tired, sore, and frightened by the loneliness, I turned to go home, when I heard singing coming in faint wisps, high over the distant booming of the surf. I followed the sound for a long way until I came to a sunken bowl in the moors, and there I saw her at the bottom standing straight and still as a statue with her pale face to the moon.

"I sat down on the edge of the bowl fascinated. She had thrown off her cloak, which made a pool of black at her feet, and stood dressed in scarlet brocade covered with bright leaves of gold; a high tortoise-shell comb held a mantilla above her head, and there was fresh arbutus at her waist and in her hair. As I had never seen jewels in my life before, I fancied I saw a magic ring of light around her neck and a star at each ear.

"She sang as I never hope to hear a mortal sing again. I lay curled up in a tight ball against the cold and listened as she sang and sang through the night, while I floated in and out of sleep until finally the cold roused me and made me flap my arms to keep warm. Still she sang and still I listened, until the first hint of dawn came to warn her.

"At the end she became inspired and sang like someone possessed. It's funny how children sense things. I knew I was looking at something I should not be seeing. It was her farewell forever to her singing and to her freedom. I've heard of a swan song, but I guess I'm one of the few who ever heard it from a human being. When I tried to rise to go away and leave her to herself I slipped on the edge and rolled ignominiously down the bowl to her feet.

My sudden appearance struck her off her guard. She knelt, held me tight in her strong arms, gave a great dry gasp, then rose, and gripping my hand hard she led me off over the moors for home.

"To ease my limping she put her arm about me, helping me over the rough places. I forgot the pain, for it was pure bliss to feel her so close. I can still recall the good scent of her—of sandalwood, fresh linen, and young health. When we reached the edge of the town she knelt, wiped my eyes, and after straightening my clothes she kissed me tenderly, and for no reason at all we both wept. She turned and ran into her house—the most beautiful woman that ever was made.

"I never saw her again. I saw the dead thing they made of her, for I went to her wedding the next day at the Friends' Meeting House. It was awful to sit there for over an hour trying to guess by the backs of the bonnets which one was hers. I tell you it was solemn. We all sat in stillness in a plain wooden house painted white, with the sun pouring in at the many-paned windows; the only sound was the faint twittering of birds outside and it made you realize that the Quakers don't need cathedrals, high altars, or lofty rose windows; their silence creates something august and awe-inspiring.

"Presently two men chosen as the groomsmen came forward and the young Quaker stood up pink and clean, and I must admit he looked very handsome as he stood there in quiet dignity, dressed in a new gray suit with a fresh linen stock at his throat. I craned my neck to look at the bride. To my dismay I did not recognize her. Her golden crown was gone, hidden behind a gray poke bonnet, her lithe young figure made clumsy by heavy clothes.

They had made her just another gray counterpart of their drab and monotonous selves. I caught a fleeting glimpse under her bonnet of a waxen cheek as she rose to join hands with her young bridegroom. Then, according to the custom of the Friends, they married themselves to each other.

"He spoke in such a low voice I could not catch his words, but presently her voice rang out and I heard it for the last time; she spoke and the place was filled with the magic and warmth of her.

"'In the presence of the Lord and this Assembly,' she said, 'I take thee to be my husband, promising with divine assistance to be unto thee a loving and faithful wife until death shall separate us.'

"I did not wait as the two groomsmen brought the marriage certificate on the table to be signed, but slipped out and went behind the Meeting House where, like a puppy, I was sick upon the grass."

Mr. Bolling removed his foot from the railing, fell silent, and showed signs of retiring within his cell.

"What happened then?" I asked, tapping the ashes from my pipe.

"Oh, she disappeared right here in our midst. The Friends lived so close among themselves they seemed to shut unseen doors on the life around them. It was nothing you could put your finger on; we'd pass them in the street, buy things in their shops, go to school to them; they were good, kind, and gentle and yet they were away from us and seemed to live behind a glass wall.

"Boylike, I soon forgot all about her. I went to Boston, married, seldom came to Nantucket. Life changed, many people left the Island, and she and her husband drifted off with many of the Friends who migrated to 'America.' Years afterwards I met an old Quaker lady in Philadelphia who was a distinguished Greek professor in a girls' college. Tiny, round, and pink, she was the spit and image of Benjamin Franklin. She fooled you on first sight, for you thought 'Here's a dear little charmer' until you met her penetrating gaze head-on. It was something of a shock when you realized you stood completely unmasked as two quiet gray eyes examined you with interest and dry humor.

"She became quite animated, however, when she heard I came originally from the Island of Nantucket, and fairly melted when she found that I had known the Quakeress from South America. She sat for some time in silence and then told me the end of the story with a depth of feeling surprising in a Friend.

"'She came to our town in Pennsylvania,' she said, 'with her tall young husband, and I can bear witness that she came to us like the clear-eyed daughter of Zeus, Athene herself. None of us had imagined that human beauty could reach such inspired perfection; truly "a girl beautiful as an immortal in nature and form." They lived in a fine house, for her husband prospered and they had a few precious years together, filled with happiness, when tragedy came out of a sky without menace and struck her down: her only son, their high hope, was born dead. Her husband soon followed, carried off by an epidemic, and she was left completely bereft of human ties.

"'She lived on in our town and clung to our faith. She came to all our meetings, but was never moved by the Spirit to rise and speak; but drifted in and out of our lives remote and alone. She was still radiant to look upon, but she was a puzzle and a heartache to us. The Quakers are a wise people, with knowledge of human suffering, but she baffled us; we could not understand how so strong a character could break, and it was some time before we realized that she was not altogether with us. We were moved by the sight of her, for it was like looking at an exquisite crystal goblet with a crack in it.

"'Then a very strange and beautiful thing happened. It was at a Quarterly Meeting when many Friends came from far and near with important elders and visiting overseers. Our Meeting House was filled to overflowing and we had a particularly long silence that morning, deep and centered down, when to the surprise of us all, the poor lovely thing rose in our midst and removed her bonnet. A pin caught in the ribbon, freeing her hair, spilling gold over her shoulder, and we saw that she was even more beautiful than we had thought. She turned, and smiled on us one by one; then lifting up her voice she began to sing.

"'There was no consternation. No one moved. We sat in deep meditation while she filled the Meeting House with celestial music. She sang and she sang, a glorious Latin hymn of praise which lifted us plain, humble Quakers to the very gates of Heaven itself. After the meeting she was gently brought before the overseers and asked why she had thus disobeyed the Friends' advice against music in any form, and she replied like an honest child: "I had a concern."

"'The elders withdrew to wrestle with the problem and they pondered for many hours. Finally, to their everlasting credit, they brought in their verdict:—

"'WHEREAS, *It being the decision of this Quarterly Meeting of the Religious Society of Friends, and whereas she was*

moved by a concern beyond human ju-
risdiction; therefore, be it Resolved,
That she be allowed whenever and
wherever the Spirit doth move her, to
lift up her voice and sing to the ever-
lasting glory of God.'"

The good Catholic bell in the tower
of the Unitarian Church began booming
the noon hour. We both slowly rose
and left the Captains' Room in silence.

1942

X. . .

HISTORY

FRED LANDON

Old Huronia: Cradle of Martyrs

From Lake Huron

The Huron country was roughly the territory at the southern end of Georgian Bay, lying between Lake Simcoe and the Severn River on the east and Nottawasaga Bay on the west. It formed the upper two-thirds of the present county of Simcoe and the traveler who goes north from Toronto to Midland passes directly through the former habitat of the Huron tribes. For a century and more farmers have been coming upon old burial pits, ash heaps and other indications of the once numerous Indian villages. Great numbers of tomahawks and arrowheads have been found at the scenes of ancient battles. Historians with their documents and archaeologists with their spades have been studying the country for a long period, yet much remains to be learned and some of the most interesting discoveries have come only within the last decade.

Samuel de Champlain, the "Father of New France," was also the father of the missions to the Huron Indians. His deeply religious nature was stirred by the thought that this heathen people might be Christianized and to this end he brought members of the Récollet order to Quebec in 1615. When their resources proved inadequate to the undertaking he gave his support to the Jesuits who succeeded them. The task was challenging. The tribes living to the south of Georgian Bay were as yet almost untouched by white influence and while almost constantly at war were settled in villages and had a primitive agriculture. The Jesuit mind quickly pictured an Indian nation Christianized, set apart from white men and governed by the Church. The dream was never realized but the effort toward its accomplishment forms one of the most dramatic stories of American history.

Jean de Brébeuf was the first Jesuit to enter the Huron country and he was still there and died for his faith when the enterprise came to disaster. Today he is invariably the central figure in any pictorial representation of the North American martyrs and this pre-eminence seems to have been conceded to him from a time soon after his death. He was born in 1593 in Normandy, that province of northern France which contributed so much to the racial stock of French Canada. Father Charles Lalemant described him as "a pious and prudent man, and of robust constitution," and all that we know of him indicates that he possessed in large measure a practical common sense derived from his Norman ancestry. He entered the Jesuit novitiate at Rouen in 1617, but five years later his health had become impaired. Perhaps because of this, his courses of study were shortened and it is said that he never studied dogmatic theology at all. "Still," says one of his biographers, "he knew enough to solve the difficulties of the sorcerers and the sachems who sat around him at the council fires near Lake Huron."

Brébeuf's nature, "like a furnace white hot," would have welcomed martyrdom at any time. When persecution was at its height in 1637 and death seemed imminent, he wrote in farewell to his superior, Le Jeune: "We are perhaps about to give our blood and our lives in the cause of our Master, Jesus Christ. . . . Blessed be His Name forever, that He has chosen us, among so many better than we, to aid Him to bear His cross in this land!"

He frequently claimed to have seen visions of angels and devils and of the glories of the other world. One such vision, which came to him in the winter of 1640, was of a great cross approaching from the direction of the Iroquois country.

"How large was it?" his companions asked.

"Large enough to crucify us all," was the grim response.

There are many references to Brébeuf's bodily strength and he himself on occasion made play with his name, saying that he was an ox, fit only to bear burdens. The record of his journeys and of the privations which he endured are proof of his great vigor yet, strangely, when the final testing came he succumbed to the torture of the Iroquois in less than four hours while the frail and weak Lalemant lasted for nearly seventeen. Possibly it was the titanic power of will with which he resisted his tormentors' efforts to break him down which finally snapped the life cord.

Brébeuf first went to the Huron country in 1625, accompanied by a fellow Jesuit, Anne de Noüe, and the Récollet priest, La Roche Dallion. But these companions soon withdrew and until 1629, when the English seized Quebec and expelled the French, he toiled alone. No record remains of his experiences during those four years but the knowledge which he acquired of the language and customs of the Huron must have been of inestimable value when, following the restoration of Quebec to France in 1634, he resumed his labors.

This second attack upon the stronghold of heathen superstition was to be on a larger scale, Brébeuf being accompanied by Fathers Ambrose Davost and Antoine Daniel. The journey to the Huron country was accomplished in the face of difficulties which few men would have surmounted. It was reckoned to be nine hundred miles from Quebec to Huronia and even Brébeuf, with his giant strength and his past experience of such journeying, nearly despaired of arriving at the destination. Davost was robbed of his baggage and his precious writing materials and abandoned by his Huron companions among the Algonquin of Allumette Island. Daniel was likewise deserted and left to shift for himself. Yet both men, making their way through a wilderness of which they were almost entirely ignorant, managed to arrive safely at their goal.

Brébeuf has left us an unforgettable picture of the hardships of such a journey. The missionaries were not mere passengers in the canoes but were themselves required to toil hour after hour, day after day, with the paddle, work for which they were unfitted and in which they had little experience. Thirty-five times in this journey the canoe and its contents had to be lifted from the water and carried over rough portages. Even more often missionary and Indians alike had to wade waist-deep in the rushing current of rivers, hauling their craft where it was impossible to paddle. When the long day of toil closed, their bed was a bare rock and their food the thin porridge prepared from some crushed Indian corn. And always there was the stench of tired-out savages and the stings of an infinite number of mosquitoes and gnats. To men of culture and refinement the strain of such surroundings was severe, but Brébeuf adds yet one more item: "the long and wearisome silence to which one is reduced, I mean in the case of newcomers, who have, for the time, no person in their company who speaks their own tongue and who do not understand that of the Savages."

In contrast to the streamlined Indian, with his breechclout, moccasins and some daubs of paint, no costume would seem less suited to wilderness travel than the long black robe of the Jesuit. With this handicap the missionaries had to make their way through mud and water and tangled forest trails, at the same time carrying their share of the common burdens. It is characteristic of the thoroughness with which the Jesuit order regulated its affairs that not long after this journey of 1634 Brébeuf was commissioned to prepare instructions for those who might be called upon to journey with the Indians.

"You must be prompt in embarking and disembarking," was one of Brébeuf's very practical admonitions. "Tuck up your gowns so that they will not get wet, and so that you will not carry either water or sand into the canoe. To be properly dressed you must have your feet and legs bare; while crossing the rapids you can wear your shoes, and, in the long portages, even your leggings. Be careful not to annoy anyone in the canoe with your hat; it would be better to take your nightcap."

And there was also the important warning that the savages had no sense of propriety. Brébeuf's Jesuit brethren would be forced to witness, as he also had been forced to witness, gross obscenities and indecencies. "Leaving a highly civilized community," Brébeuf wrote to his associates, "you fall into the hands of barbarous people who care but little for your Philosophy or your Theology. All the fine qualities which might make you loved and respected in France are like pearls trampled under the feet of swine."

But he was able to offer a compensation for such trials of their faith. "Jesus Christ is our true greatness," he wrote, "and having found Jesus Christ in his cross, you have found the roses in the thorns, sweetness in bitterness, all in nothing."

There was need of consolation and inspiration for the men who were to live among the Huron. On the walls of their mission chapels were pictures showing in vivid colors the torments of Hell, pictures which fascinated their savage charges, yet on more than one occasion the only comparison they could make for the scenes about them was that it was Hell itself on earth. Iroquoian cruelty to captives is everywhere recorded with horror and detestation but the Huron also were no amateurs in this barbaric practice. No amusement was more enjoyed than the torture of an enemy, Iroquois preferred. The Jesuits at first questioned the propriety of being present at such horrible festivities but decided that as they could not prevent the practices they might possibly ameliorate the captive's sufferings and even find opportunity to baptize him. Thus we have authentic accounts in their narratives of the ghastly types of torture which were later inflicted upon some of the missionaries themselves.

The frequent necessity of living with the Indians in their rude dwellings, whether through lack of other shelter or during missionary journeys, produced a severe mental strain. "Now that we have Christians in every village," wrote Brébeuf in 1636, "you shall have to tramp for miles along unbeaten trails to reach them, carrying on your back whatever luggage you wish to bring along. There you shall have to stay two or three weeks and share an Indian family's cabin with its inconceivable wretchedness and inconvenience."

The smoke and overpowering stench, the indecencies and lack of all privacy in the rude dwellings must have been cruelly revolting to sensitive minds. The vessels in which the wretched food was prepared were never cleaned. Sick and diseased savages were in close and constant contact with those that were well and with the white men. Though the Huron were more advanced than the Montagnais tribe, to whom the Jesuits also went, and had much more inventiveness, they never achieved adequate provision for their comfort in the wintertime. The Jesuits refer frequently to the torture which they suffered from the smoke in Indian dwellings. The fumes when stirred up by a winter wind would become so dense and biting that throats, nostrils and eyes were in a continual state of inflammation.

"One would prefer the blow of a tomahawk," wrote one of the fathers, "to living during whole years the life one must lead here every day while working for the conversion of these barbarians. If you go to visit them in their cabins you will find there a miniature picture of Hell, seeing nothing ordinarily but fire and smoke, and on every side naked bodies, black and half roasted, mingling pellmell with the dogs which are held as dear as the children of the house, and share the beds, plates and food of their masters. Everything is in a cloud of dust and, if you must go in, you will not reach the end of the cabin before you are completely befouled with soot, filth and dirt."

But life in Huronia was not all grim and horrible. However intent these men might be on the task before them, they were not unmindful of the human comedy being enacted about them and in their writings we find many pleasant little pictures of Indian life. Nor was it a forbidding land in which they dwelt. It was for most of the year a smiling country, fertile lands intersected by pleasant little rivers. The winters were severe but there was also the smiling spring, the warm months of summer and the mild autumn days of harvest with all their splendor of color.

There must have been many evenings when, at the close of a day of toil, the fathers sat together, watching the setting sun, talking perhaps of days gone by and of friends far away, days in Paris or Rouen or other ancient French cities. What a contrast between Paris or Rouen and the life of an Indian village near the shore of Georgian Bay!

When the Jesuits first came to the Huron country they estimated the population at thirty thousand, scattered in a score or more of villages. From time to time these villages were moved to new locations as the fields about them became exhausted or when the accumulation of filth was beyond what even an Indian could stand. Brébeuf, upon his return to Huronia in 1634, chose a small settlement known as Ihonatiria as the place of residence for himself and his two associates. Three years later two villages known as Ossossané and Tean-austayae became the missionary centers. A further change was made after 1638 when Father Jerome Lalemant succeeded Brébeuf in the office of superior. One of his first acts was to provide for a census of the Huron nation. The population was found to be about twenty thousand in all, divided among thirty-two villages and hamlets, adults numbering about twelve thousand. After careful study Lalemant decided that instead of scattering his forces throughout the several villages it would be well to have a central residence from which the fathers could go out to their charges and to which they would at intervals return for rest and refreshment. "It was our thought," he wrote, "that while building a house remote from the neighborhood of the villages, it would serve among other things as a retreat and a place of recollection for our Gospel laborers who, after their combats, would find in this solitude a place of delight."

The site chosen was on the bank of the River Wye, a little stream emptying into one of the indentations of Georgian Bay. Though it was less than a mile to the bay and several of the Huron villages were at no great distance, the place was somewhat isolated. The first structure erected was but an ordinary Indian long house, covered with bark and no more pretentious than those in use elsewhere. One end was partitioned off to provide a chapel. In the next few years more permanent buildings were added, of wooden construction but placed upon stone foundations—a residence, a chapel and storehouses for grain and roots. At a date not earlier than 1646 and probably not before 1648 protecting walls and

bastions were added. The place was known as Sainte Marie.

More than a score of Jesuits are recorded as having lived within this center and even a greater number of soldiers, artisans and lay helpers were to be found there. Six men who resided at Sainte Marie were among the eight martyrs who were canonized in 1930. Five who lost their lives in Huronia have already been mentioned—the sixth was Isaac Jogues whose death took place in the Iroquois country to which he had been sent on a special mission in 1646.

One of those in residence during the last days was Joseph Bressani, Italian by birth, who had come to Canada in 1642. He fell into the hands of the Iroquois two years later and was cruelly tortured over a period of more than two months. During one week he was brought out nightly to provide a spectacle for young and old. At times details of Indian torture were so horrible that the Jesuits, candid as they were in such matters, did no more than allude to them. This, it would appear, was true of Bressani. His captors, in the end, seem to have reached their capacity for cruelty and let him pass into the hands of Dutch traders who sent him off to France. Writing at this time to the General of the Jesuits at Rome, he said of his condition:

"I do not know if your Paternity will recognize the handwriting of one whom you once knew very well. The letter is soiled and ill-written; because the writer has only one finger of his right hand left entire, and cannot prevent the blood from his wounds, which are still open, from staining the paper. His ink is gunpowder mixed with water, and his table is the earth."

Bressani arrived in France in the autumn of 1644, but in the following spring he was again at Quebec, horribly disfigured yet eager to resume his duties. He was sent at once to the Huron country, arriving there in the autumn of 1645. Fate did not bring to him the martyr's crown but in heroism and self-sacrifice he falls not a whit below those so distinguished.

The Jesuit writings tell us much concerning the activities of the period during which Sainte Marie was headquarters of the mission work. Long years of patient sacrifice seemed at last to be bringing fruit. There had been a time when the fathers thought themselves fortunate if by some subterfuge they might secretly place a drop of water on the head of a dying infant and so rescue it from perdition. But now there were some real converts, drawn by Christian teaching from their heathen practices. In half a dozen Indian villages, bearing new and Christian names, St. Ignace and St. Joseph, St. Louis and St. Michel, were rude little chapels in which the converts assembled at the sound of the bell to receive instruction from one of the fathers.

The cause was gaining but it was far from triumphing. Indifference, if not actual hostility, was still shown by the greater number of the braves. Converts were loath to abandon the feasts, the dances and the games which formed so important a part of the social life. The medicine men, with their incantations and charms, were the sworn enemies of the priests and embraced every opportunity to vilify and slander them. When misfortune fell upon the villages, pestilence, famine, fire or war, it was at once attributed to the "black robes." "It is the priest that kills us," was the oft-repeated cry. "Before he came we were happy and prosperous. He has bewitched the country."

Indeed, it did seem that an evil influence had fallen upon the Huron nation. Pestilence and battle had decreased their numbers and their spirits were low. From a time before white men ever entered the country there had been conflict with the Iroquois and the menace was now becoming greater each year. In 1645 the Huron sought an alliance with the Andastes who dwelt on the banks of the Susquehanna, but without success. Two years later there was no communication between Huronia and Quebec—the way was barred by lurking Iroquois. Broken in spirit, dejected and fearful, the nation seemed incapable of taking even the most obvious measures for its defense.

In 1648 a Huron party succeeded in making its way as far as Three Rivers on the St. Lawrence, and when attacked at that place routed its assailants, the warriors proudly bearing the scalps back to their own country. It was a hollow triumph, however, for in their absence another Iroquois war party had entered Huronia and on the fourth day of July made a sudden attack on the mission village of St. Joseph, the Teanaustayae of former days, once Brébeuf's headquarters.

As always, there was no warning. Father Daniel was on the point of dismissing his converts at the close of Mass when the savage war whoop was heard. In a moment the invaders were within the walls, killing young and old alike. Daniel fell pierced by a score of arrows and bullets. His body, hacked and torn, was cast into the flames of his burning church. He was the first of the Huronia martyrs and had served his order for twenty-eight years. He was a native of Dieppe.

The final blow came in March of 1649.

Through the preceding winter an Iroquois party, numbering at least a thousand warriors, had moved stealthily through the forests, arriving in the very heart of the Huron country without discovery. On March 16, before daylight, the palisaded mission station of St. Ignace was attacked and within a few minutes was in complete possession of the invaders. Fugitives carried warning to the near-by village of St. Louis, most of whose inhabitants at once fled, but the warriors, numbering less than one hundred, decided to fight it out. The two Jesuit missionaries who were present, Brébeuf and Gabriel Lalemant, elected to remain with them.

The defense of St. Louis was almost the last gesture of defiance of the Huron. Three times the enemy was beaten back from the wooden palisades which surrounded the town and when breaches were made in the walls a hand-to-hand struggle continued. But in the end the fighting rear guard was struck down and those who survived were made prisoners, the two Jesuits with them. The town was in flames as the victorious Iroquois returned to St. Ignace. There at the end of tortures so devilish as almost to bar description and too revolting to be dwelt upon, died the second and third of the martyrs of Huronia. Lalemant had been in the country less than eight months, Brébeuf more than eighteen years.

News of the Iroquois attack came quickly to Sainte Marie. At nine o'clock thick smoke and the reflection of flames were seen in the direction of St. Louis. A few minutes later two Huron, breathless and shaking with fear, brought word of its capture. The day that followed was filled with suspense for Father Ragueneau and for his fellow Jesuits. Fugitives came in, many of them wounded or burned, seeking refuge and help. While attention was being given to these suffering people thoughts constantly turned to the brethren elsewhere. Where was Brébeuf? Where was Lalemant? The day passed with the question unanswered, nor was it fully answered until four days had passed. But in the meantime there was much to do. At any moment Sainte Marie itself might hear the dreaded war whoop. Prayers were said without ceasing. Vows were made to Saint Joseph, patron saint of the colony. Iroquois scouts appeared on the edge of the clearing but none approached the fort. Elsewhere, however, there was ferocious fighting and even a seeming change of fortune. But by this time the Iroquois raiders had satisfied their blood lust and had turned homeward, dragging numerous prisoners with them, many of whom they tomahawked as they journeyed. But before they left they bound numbers of helpless captives to stakes within the bark houses of St. Ignace and then set the place afire.

On the morning of March 20 an armed party set out from Sainte Marie to search for the bodies of the missing brethren. The snow of mid-March still lay deep in the forests and along the trails, here and there dyed deep red where some unfortunate prisoner had been tomahawked. No doubt existed as to the fate that had befallen the two missing priests. Huron who as prisoners had witnessed their torture and had later escaped had told of the horror attending those last hours. All that they told was confirmed by the condition of the bodies found in the ashes of St. Ignace. Fire and the knife, red-hot stones and boiling water had all been used to satisfy Iroquois vengeance.

"We saw no part of his [Brébeuf's]

body," wrote Ragueneau, "from head to foot, which was not burned, even to his eyes, in the sockets of which these wretches had placed live coals."

"I saw and touched all the wounds," wrote Christophe Regnaut, a lay brother who was present with the party. "We buried these precious Relics on Sunday, the 21st of March, 1649, with much Consolation." The place of burial was within the walls of Sainte Marie on the little River Wye.

When the mission buildings were abandoned in the next few weeks the bodies were exhumed, the flesh removed from the bones and reburied. But the bones themselves were regarded as precious relics and Regnaut has recorded for us the reverence which was given to them.

"All the bones were well scraped," he writes, "and the care of drying them was given to me. I put them every day into a little oven which we had, made of clay, after having heated it slightly, and when in a state to be packed, they were separately enveloped in silk stuff. Then they were put into two small chests, and we brought them to Quebec, where they are held in great veneration."

In later years Brébeuf's family in France sent to Quebec a silver bust, the base of which was made to contain his skull. It was for a long time in the custody of the Jesuits at Quebec but in the late eighteenth century was given into the care of the Hospital Sisters of the Hôtel-Dieu, in whose venerable institution it may still be seen.

Gabriel Lalemant, who perished with Brébeuf at St. Ignace, came of a good Parisian family belonging to the curious hereditary *gens de robe* (practitioners of the law). The emphasis which has always been placed upon the vigor and strength of Brébeuf has its contrast in the frequent references to the weakness of Lalemant. Both Ragueneau and Bressani mention it, and Marie de l'Incarnation expressed her astonishment at finding one so delicate in such surroundings as New France afforded. There were, in all, three Lalemants sent from France to the Indian missions. Charles Lalemant, who arrived in 1625, was an uncle of the martyred Gabriel. Jerome, a younger brother of Charles, went to Huronia as superior in 1638 but was superior at Quebec in 1648 when the Iroquois holocaust began. He died at Quebec in 1673 and his brother Charles survived him but one year.

Two more names were yet to be added to the roll of Huronia's martyrs. In the Petun country, lying along the south shore of Nottawasaga Bay, were two missionaries who remained at their post even after the tragedy of March 1649, though they were distant but two days' journey and knew that at any time the Iroquois might search them out. The blow came some months later. The mission station of St. Jean was attacked in December and there Father Charles Garnier fell before the bullets of the invaders. Wounded and dying, he dragged himself from one to another of his Indian converts, giving them absolution, until a blow from a tomahawk ended his own life.

His co-worker at St. Jean, Noël Chabanel, who had left two days before in company with some Indians, was deserted by all save one when the Iroquois war cries were heard. His companion, an apostate Huron, in the end turned upon the missionary, killed him and threw his body into the Nottawasaga River. The roster of Huronia's martyrs was completed.

1944

CARL VAN DOREN

The Treachery of General Charles Lee

From THE SECRET HISTORY OF THE AMERICAN REVOLUTION

ON DECEMBER 13, 1776 a party of British dragoons at Basking Ridge, New Jersey, captured Major General Charles Lee, who was second in command in the American army and had no doubt he should be first. Only that morning he had written to General Gates that Washington was "most damnably deficient." Lee, after Magaw's loss of Fort Washington a month before, had been ordered to join the main army, but had delayingly preferred to harass the flank of Howe who was pursuing Washington in his retreat from New York towards Philadelphia. American troops, Lee insisted, could not face the British in pitched battles and should stick to guerrilla fighting. In his separate command he had, he apparently thought, a chance to make himself conspicuous by some dramatic stroke for which he would get all the credit. Instead he was humiliatingly taken prisoner at a tavern four miles from his lines, and was carried, tied on a horse, bareheaded and without a greatcoat, to Brunswick, where the more hilarious among his captors are said to have celebrated by making his horse drunk.

Lee's whole career had been spectacular. Born in England, no relation to the patriotic Virginia Lees, he had come to America with Braddock, survived the defeat, and later been adopted by the Mohawk and briefly married to a Seneca woman. Returning to Europe, he served under Burgoyne in Portugal, was put on a colonel's half pay at the end of that war, and went as a soldier of fortune to Poland and southeastern Europe. In England he wrote violently against the Tories till 1773. After that he wrote violently against them in America, which on May 6, 1774 he called liberty's "last and only asylum"—nearly two years before Paine said almost the same thing in *Common Sense*. From New York to Virginia Lee consorted with the patriot leaders, hoping to command the American army which he urged them to raise. In May he was buying an estate in Berkeley county, Virginia (West Virginia), with the specific motive of recommending himself, as a landowner, to the Continental Congress. On June 7 he wrote from Philadelphia to Burgoyne in Boston, abusing the king and the ministry. "Of all courts I am persuaded that ours is the most corrupt and hostile to the rights of humanity." Congress was pleased by such thoroughgoing language, and Washington valued Lee as a professional soldier. Self-confident and articulate, he impressed, and continued to impress, many Americans.

At the same time, he looked out for himself. When on June 17 he was appointed one of the four major generals he did not accept till Congress on the 19th resolved to indemnify him "for any loss of property he might sustain." Not till the 22nd did he write to denounce his half pay as a British colonel, now that he was an American general. Though he resented being less than commander-in-chief, he caused little trouble in New England or New York, or in the south during the summer of 1776. On his return in October he so represented his private affairs to Congress that they advanced him $30,000 to repay the money he had borrowed to buy his plantation. Encouraged by this substantial tribute, and by agreeable praise for his defence of South Carolina, Lee felt more sure of himself than ever, and more dissatisfied with Washington, whose recent "manœuvre of Fort Washington," Lee said in his letter to Gates of December 13, "has completely unhinged the goodly fabric we have been building."

For a month after his capture Lee was held in New Jersey while Washington, joined by Lee's army, crossed and recrossed the Delaware, captured a whole command of Hessians, broke the British line at Princeton, and forced Howe to draw back to Brunswick. In New York, Lee found himself regarded not as a prisoner of war subject to exchange but as a deserter from the British army. Yet though he was confined in the City Hall, with a sentry at his door, he had one of the largest and best rooms, had his table "very handsomely kept by the General," and was allowed to entertain guests every day at dinner. One of his early callers was Henry Strachey, secretary to the Howe brothers' peace commission, who called at least twice before February 9. Whether at Strachey's suggestion or of his own accord, Lee on the 9th wrote a letter to Washington enclosing a letter to Congress. He had, he informed Congress, important proposals to make. Would they send a committee to him, on General Howe's guarantee they would be safe?

Congress thought Lee insolent, for supposing they might meet such a demand, and unlikely to be of any use, now he had carelessly let himself be captured and lost to the American army. What he then had in mind is not clear. He later said he had discovered Howe's plan of campaign for the year 1777 and would have revealed it to the committee, even though this meant violating the confidence Howe had hospitably placed in him. Having received no answer from Congress, Lee on March 19 wrote again to Washington. This brought an answer, dated April 1, saying that Congress could not send a committee but would try to arrange for Lee's exchange. Lee had before that, on March 29, drawn up a plan to be followed by the Howes if they desired an early triumph.

He felt sure, he said, that Great Britain must win. But since this could be only after heavy losses on both sides, "I think myself not only justifiable but bound in conscience to furnish all the lights I can to enable 'em [the Howes] to bring matters to a conclusion." In his opinion nothing was to be gained by taking Philadelphia. Congress, expecting this, had arranged to continue the rebel government elsewhere. It would be better to send a British expedition to Alexandria and Annapolis and there proclaim a general pardon to all rebels who would surrender on a given day. This would reduce Maryland and intimidate Virginia and Pennsylvania. "I am so confident of the event that I will venture to assert with the penalty of my life, if the plan is fully carried out and no accidents (such as a rupture betwixt the powers of Europe) intervenes, that in less than two months from the date of the proclamation not a spark of this desolating war remains unextinguished in any part of the continent."

"Mr. Lee's Plan 29th March 1777," endorsed in Strachey's handwriting, presumably reached the Howes, but they made small use of it, if they made any. While they did send an expedition to and up the Chesapeake, it was only as a route to Philadelphia, which Lee had advised them not to bother with. The Howes had more influential American advisers than Lee.

Joseph Galloway, member of the First Continental Congress, ablest of all the Pennsylvania loyalists, arrived in New York before Lee, and was introduced to Lord Howe on January 21. Galloway believed that "the power of the rebellion is pretty well broken, and that, though 'tis probable that the colonies may make some further efforts, those efforts will be only feeble and ineffectual. . . . Pennsylvania itself (which certainly could subsist better alone than any other province) was in extreme distress for clothing, salt, dry goods, and all other importable necessities; and . . . if the fleet constantly blocked up the ports during the next summer the business might be concluded, almost without the intervention of the army." By February 18 Galloway was laying plans to raise a loyalist militia in Pennsylvania, seize Congress, and destroy the bridge of boats which Washington had thrown across the Schuylkill for a possible retreat from Philadelphia. On March 17 Galloway said 100 loyalists were sworn together in the scheme for taking Congress. On April 4 he was worried because a spy he had sent to Philadelphia, to find pilots who might assist the British in getting past the American defences in the Delaware, had been captured and might be hanged—as

James Molesworth had been. The move against Philadelphia was already settled upon by the Howes, possibly with some reference to Galloway's advice, certainly against Lee's.

Lee emerges from the record as a busybody, willing to side with either party as the chance offered, in the arrogant assumption that if only he were given a free hand he could bring about a reasonable, conclusive peace. Having failed in his application—almost an order—to Congress, he fraternized in New York with British officers who were his old friends but none of whom, it appears, took him very seriously. In June he was confined for a time on the *Centurion*. The British government ruled against holding him as a deserter, and on December 27 he was given his liberty on parole, though not to go outside the city limits. He informed Washington, who in January sent Elias Boudinot, American commissary general of prisoners, under a flag to New York to see if Lee could be exchanged. Lee had a new proposal for the Americans. Since they could not, he still insisted, hope to stand up to British soldiers, they should build a great fortress at Pittsburgh, send their money, old men, women, and children to it, and prepare an escape for Congress down the Mississippi to Spanish territory. Boudinot, who had given the British his word not to carry messages out of New York, was shocked at Lee's willingness to deceive Howe, who knew nothing, Lee said, of this proposal. And Boudinot wondered how Lee could be so reckless—or so unregarded?—as to carry the scheme written out in his pocket.

Washington, who according to Lee "was not fit to command a sergeant's guard," still thought he needed Lee in the American army. There were delays in the exchange. Lee hated the sea, and persuaded the British not to send him to Philadelphia by ship but to let him travel through New Jersey. On April 5 he was "enlarged" on parole, acknowledging himself a prisoner of the king's army and pledging his "faith and sacred honour that I will not directly or indirectly do anything contrary to the interest of his Majesty or his government." Yet he went promptly to Congress at York, where he told President Laurens that Washington, "considering how he is surrounded, cannot do without me"; and on the 13th wrote to Washington, at Valley Forge, sending him a plan for the complete reorganization of the American army. At York it was arranged that the Americans would give up General Prescott, captured in Rhode Island, for Lee.

About the end of the month he arrived at Valley Forge, to be welcomed like a hero. Washington rode out four miles to meet him, dismounted, and greeted Lee "as if it had been his brother." The general officers waited for them two miles from camp. Lines of soldiers were drawn up all the way to Headquarters. There was an "elegant dinner," with music. "A room was assigned to him back of Mrs. Washington's sitting room, and all his baggage was stored in it. The next morning he lay very late, and breakfast was detained for him."

At once Lee was again a busybody, and a double-dealer. At his last meeting with Howe, Lee told Boudinot, Howe thought independence a crazy idea, Lee thought it a shrewd one. Since America had nothing but the independence it claimed, it could at least offer to yield that in a treaty with the British government, and might get something in exchange. Howe granted

that independence might have value as a strategic pretext. On May 3—or perhaps a few days before—Lee wrote a letter to General James Robertson, of the British army, who turned it over to Clinton, Howe's recent successor as commander-in-chief. (The letter survives among the Clinton papers.) If more confidence had been placed in Lee the past year, he said, he might have ended the war. He supposed he had been denied the opportunity on the ground that he was in danger of being tried for desertion, and so may have offered his services to avoid punishment. In his present safe situation he might be listened to. His advice was that Great Britain should pass an act of indemnity without exceptions and renounce any right to tax the colonies. America should forget independence and promise to obey the navigation acts. All that remained was to give Lee authority to take the first step with these proposals, and he would "at the risk of my popularity divulge them."

And on June 4, after Lee had been for two weeks with the American army, he sent friendly communications to both Lord Howe and Clinton. The first was through a British officer whom Lee met at an exchange of prisoners on that day. He took him "aside for a moment and told him that he was very unhappy in and very adverse to the present course of affairs, and that he might assure Lord Howe that he had acted entirely as he had promised him and wished for nothing so much as to promote every idea of peace." The second was a letter which Lee wrote that day to Clinton, to congratulate him on his promotion to succeed Howe. "General Lee presents his most sincere and humble respects to Sir Henry Clinton. He wishes him all possible happiness and health and begs, whatever may be the event of the present unfortunate contest, that he will believe General Lee to be his most respectful and obliged humble servant." This was twenty-four days before the battle of Monmouth.

Lee, who had sat on the board that tried Benjamin Church, knew perfectly well that correspondence like this with Howe and Clinton was forbidden by army regulations and would be impossible to explain away if found out. He swore on June 9 that he acknowledged the independence of the United States and would to the utmost of his power support, maintain, and defend it against the king and his successors, abetters, assistants, and adherents. Yet Lee certainly did not let himself think of his secret correspondences as treason. He persisted in seeing the conflict as essentially a political one, between two parties who had taken to arms. A compromise peace would be good for both of them, and good for the Empire. He was the man to engineer the compromise. Men have been hanged for slighter misjudgments than Lee's. Vanity, envy, and frustration had brought him to a point where all his thoughts and words were violent. He scolded Congress for promoting other generals while he was a prisoner. He wrote with almost intolerable arrogance to Washington, who tolerated it.

When Lee resumed his military duties on May 20 the Americans were sure the British would soon evacuate Philadelphia, and Washington at Valley Forge was making ready to follow them, attacking from the flank or rear. If they set out for New York, Washington's left would encounter them first. Lee was assigned to that post of honour, but declined. The British, he thought as late as June 15, would go in the other

direction, to Delaware or Maryland. If he actually knew the British intentions, and hoped to keep Washington from strengthening his left, this was of course plain treason. But it is not at all likely that Lee, whom the British never valued or trusted, had been told what the British meant to do; and it is very likely that he was positive they would go south because he had himself advised it the year before. On the 18th they started north across New Jersey, and the Americans followed. Lafayette led the advance corps in the pursuit. When he was ordered to attack at Monmouth, Lee jealously asserted his right to take command. Lafayette, who though a major general was not yet twenty-one, gracefully yielded to the experienced soldier. In the battle on the 28th Lee retreated with the main body of his forces, and the army was in a headless confusion when Washington came up and took command himself. This again might look more like treason in Lee if his retreat had not been in keeping with his fixed theory that American troops were no match for British except in guerrilla skirmishes. But an American general so anxious as Lee to please British generals was bound to lack spontaneity and fire in attacking British soldiers. Lee's fraternizing had made him indecisive, and his indecision at Monmouth was, in effect, treachery.

Denying any guilt, he demanded a court martial. The court on August 12 after a long and complicated trial found him guilty of disobedience to orders, misbehaviour before the enemy, and disrespect to the commander-in-chief, and suspended him from the army for twelve months. He never returned to it, and had no further dangerous opportunity for his overbearing, underhanded mischief. 1941

VERNON LOUIS PARRINGTON

The Great Barbecue

From The Beginnings of Critical Realism

Horace Greeley and Henry Carey were only straws in the wind that during the Gilded Age was blowing the doctrine of paternalism about the land. A Colonel Sellers was to be found at every fireside talking the same blowsy doctrine. Infectious in their optimism, naïve in their faith that something would be turned up for them by the government if they made known their wants, they were hoping for dollars to be put in their pockets by a generous administration at Washington. Congress had rich gifts to bestow—in lands, tariffs, subsidies, favors of all sorts; and when influential citizens made their wishes known to the reigning statesmen, the sympathetic politicians were quick to turn the government into the fairy godmother the voters wanted it to be. A huge barbecue was spread to which all presumably were invited. Not quite all, to be sure; inconspicuous persons, those who were at home on the farm or at work in the mills and offices, were overlooked; a good many indeed out of the total number of the American people. But all the important persons, leading bankers and promoters and business men, received invitations. There wasn't room for everybody and these were presumed to represent the whole. It was a splendid feast. If the waiters saw to it that the choicest portions were served to favored guests, they were not unmindful of their numerous home-spun constituency and they loudly proclaimed the fine democratic principle that what belongs to the people should be enjoyed by the people—not with petty bureaucratic restrictions, not as a social body, but as individuals, each free citizen using what came to hand for his own private ends, with no questions asked.

It was sound Gilded Age doctrine. To a frontier people what was more democratic than a barbecue, and to a paternalistic age what was more fitting than that the state should provide the beeves for roasting. Let all come and help themselves. As a result the feast was Gargantuan in its rough plenty. The abundance was what was to be expected of a generous people. More food, to be sure, was spoiled than was eaten, and the revelry was a bit unseemly; but it was a fine spree in the name of the people, and the invitations had been written years before by Henry Clay. But unfortunately what was intended to be jovially democratic was marred by displays of plebeian temper. Suspicious commoners with better eyes than manners discovered the favoritism of the waiters and drew attention to the difference between their own meager helpings and the heaped-up plates of more favored guests. It appeared indeed that there was gross discrimination in the service; that the farmers' pickings from the Homestead Act were scanty in com-

From *The Beginnings of Critical Realism in America* by Vernon L. Parrington, copyright, 1930, by Harcourt, Brace and Company, Inc.   Reprinted by permission.

parison with the speculators' pickings from the railway land grants. The *Crédit Mobilier* scandal and the Whisky Ring scandal and divers other scandals came near to breaking up the feast, and the genial host—who was no other than the hero of Appomattox—came in for some sharp criticism. But after the more careless ones who were caught with their fingers where they didn't belong, had been thrust from the table, the eating and drinking went on again till only the great carcasses were left. Then at last came the reckoning. When the bill was sent in to the American people the farmers discovered that they had been put off with the giblets while the capitalists were consuming the turkey. They learned that they were no match at a barbecue for more voracious guests, and as they went home unsatisfied, a sullen anger burned in their hearts that was to express itself later in fierce agrarian revolts.

What reason there was for such anger, how differently rich and poor fared at the democratic feast, is suggested by the contrast between the Homestead Act and the Union Pacific land-grant. Both were war-time measures and both had emerged from the agitations of earlier decades. By the terms of the former the homesteader got his hundred and sixty acres at the price of $1.25 an acre; by the terms of the latter the promoters got a vast empire for nothing. It was absurd, of course, but what would you have? The people wanted the railway built and Collis P. Huntington was willing to build it on his own terms. The government was too generous to haggle with public-spirited citizens, and too Whiggish to want to discourage individual enterprise. Ever since the cession of California there had been much talk of a continental railway to tie the country

together. In the first years the talk in Congress had all been of a great national venture; the road must be built by the nation to serve the common interests of the American people. But unfortunately sectional jealousies prevented any agreement as to the route the survey lines were to run, and the rising capitalism was becoming powerful enough to bring into disfavor any engagement of the government in a work that promised great rewards. Under its guidance political opinion was skillfully turned into the channel of private enterprise. The public domain backed by the public credit, it was agreed, must pay for the road, but the government must not seek to control the enterprise or look to profit from it directly; the national reward would come indirectly from the opening-up of vast new territories.

The definite shift in policy came about the year 1855. In 1837 Stephen A. Douglas had been the driving force behind the state enterprise of building the Illinois Central Railway. In 1853 he proposed that the Pacific Railroad should be built by private enterprise. With the change promptly came a request for a patriotic land-grant. The government was expected to provide the road, it appeared, but private enterprise was to own it and manage it in the interest of speculators rather than the public. For old-fashioned souls like Thomas A. Benton, who still remembered the Jeffersonian concern for the common well-being, it was a bitter mess to swallow.

I would have preferred [he said] that Congress should have made the road, as a national work, on a scale commensurate with its grandeur and let out the use of it to companies, who would fetch and carry on the best terms for the people and the government. But that hope has vanished . . . a private company has become the resource and the preference. I embrace it as such, utterly scouting all plans for making private roads at national expense, of paying for the use of roads built with our land and money, of bargaining with corporations or individuals for the use of what we give them.

With this speech the old Jeffersonianism pulled down its flag and the new Whiggery ran up its black banner. The Gilded Age had begun and Old Bullion Benton had outlived his time. In the tumultuous decades that followed there was to be no bargaining with corporations for the use of what the public gave; they took what they wanted and no impertinent questions were asked. The hungriest will get the most at the barbecue. A careless wastefulness when the supply is unlimited is perhaps natural enough. There were hardheaded men in the world of Beriah Sellers who knew how easy it was to overreach the simple, and it was they who got most from the common pot. We may call them buccaneers if we choose, and speak of the great barbecue as a democratic debauch. But why single out a few, when all were drunk? Whisky was plentiful at barbecues, and if too liberal potations brought the Gilded Age to the grossest extravagancies, if when it cast up accounts it found its patrimony gone, it was only repeating the experience of a certain man who went down to Jericho. To create a social civilization requires sober heads, and in this carousal of economic romanticism sober heads were few—the good Samaritan was busy elsewhere.

The doctrine of preëmption and exploitation was reaping its harvest. The frontier spirit was having its splurge, and progress was already turning its face in another direction. Within the next half-century this picturesque America with its heritage of crude energy— greedy, lawless, capable—was to be transformed into a vast uniform middle-class land, dedicated to capitalism and creating the greatest machine-order known to history. A scattered agricultural people, steeped in particularistic jealousies and suspicious of centralization, was to be transformed into an urbanized factory people, rootless, migratory, drawn to the job as by a magnet. It was to come about the more easily because the American farmer had never been a land-loving peasant, rooted to the soil and thriving only in daily contact with familiar acres. He had long been half middle-class, accounting unearned increment the most profitable crop, and buying and selling land as if it were calico. And in consequence the vigorous individualism that had sprung from frontier conditions decayed with the passing of the frontier, and those who had lost in the gamble of preëmption and exploitation were added to the growing multitude of the proletariat. It was from such materials, supplemented by a vast influx of immigrants, that was fashioned the America we know today with its standardized life, its machine culture, its mass psychology —an America to which Jefferson and Jackson and Lincoln would be strangers.

                                                                1930

General Grant

From The Beginnings of Critical Realism

GREATEST of all the heroes of the age was the victor of Appomattox. His fame was in all men's mouths, and his reputation was substantial enough to withstand the attacks of enemies and the gross shortcomings of his own character. It was not for any singular or remarkable qualities of mind or personality that General Grant was taken to the heart of his generation, but rather because he was so completely a product of the times, so strikingly an embodiment of its virtues and weaknesses. In his spectacular career were the sharp contrasts that appealed to a plebeian people wanting in fine and discriminating standards of appraisal. He had come up from the people and the marks of his origins—the slovenly manners and uncritical force of frontier folk-ways—were stamped on him as indelibly as they were stamped on his fellow soldiers who proclaimed his greatness. To a later generation he seems an odd and unaccountable figure for the high rôle of national hero, yet he was as native and homespun as Lincoln, like him sprung from the common stock and learning his lessons from harsh experience, a figure blown to huge dimensions by the passions of civil war. A generation that discovered something praiseworthy in the "smartness" of Jim Fisk, in the burly acquisitiveness of Commodore Vanderbilt, or in the clever humbuggery of Barnum the Showman, certainly would judge with no very critical eyes the claims to greatness of a grim leader of armies who succeeded where so many before had failed.

General Grant was no conventional military hero. It was not the gold stars on his epaulets that dazzled his generation. The people of the North had seen too many gold stars rise and set on the military horizon, they had been stricken too sorely by the bitter struggle, to be caught by military popinjays. They had gone through the fire and any hero of theirs must himself have passed through the fire. It was something veracious in the man, something solid and unyielding in the soldier, something plain as an old shoe in the field marshal of bloody battles, that caught the imagination of the North and made Grant a hero—this together with a certain gift of pungent phrase, befitting the leader of democratic hosts, that served to spread his fame amongst the common people. Vicksburg did much for his reputation, but the demand for "unconditional surrender," sent to a Confederate leader, did far more. The words fixed his character in the popular mind. Here at last was a fighting man who instead of planning how to fall back, as other generals did, thought only of going ahead; so the popular judgment shut its eyes to his dull plebeian character and set a wreath on his brows. It rested there somewhat grotesquely. In spite of a deep unconscious integrity and a stubborn will that drove him forward along whatever path his feet were set on, he was the least imposing of military

From *The Beginnings of Critical Realism in America* by Vernon L. Parrington, copyright, 1930, by Harcourt, Brace and Company, Inc. Reprinted by permission.

heroes. Short, stooped, lumpish in mind and body, unintellectual and unimaginative, devoid of ideas and with no tongue to express the incoherent emotions that surged dully in his heart, he was a commonplace fellow that no gold braid could set off. He hated war and disliked soldiering, yet accepting life with a stolid fatalism he fought his bloody way to ultimate victory.

Graduated from West Point after four sterile years of drill, quite uneducated and unread even in his profession, he served for a time at different army posts, went through the Mexican War—which he looked upon as a stupid imperialistic debauch—as quartermaster without gaining distinction, and eventually, oppressed by the eventless routine of garrison life, he fell into the habit of solitary drinking and was dismissed from the service. Misfortune that it seemed, it was his making. Only as a volunteer could he have risen so quickly to high command; as a captain or major in the regular army he would have been detailed as drill-master to the raw troops and have had no chance. Nevertheless hard times came with his dismissal. Indolent by nature and inclined to drift, he was as incompetent a man in practical affairs as one could find in a frontier township. But with a wife and children to support he must turn his hand to something, so he tried his luck at farming, selling real estate, and various odd jobs, yet all the time growing poorer and seedier, till the war came and picking him up flung him to mountain heights of popularity and reputation. Thereafter till his death he was accounted the greatest American of his generation. No accumulating evidence of his well-meaning but witless incapacity in civic and political affairs could

pluck from his brows the wreath that had been thrust upon him.

In his spectacular career Grant was an embodiment of the dreams of all the Beriah Sellerses of the Gilded Age. He was a materialistic hero of a materialistic generation. He was dazzled by wealth and power, and after years of bitter poverty he sat down in the lap of luxury with huge content. He took what the gods sent, and if houses and fast horses and wines and cigars were showered upon him he accepted them as a child would accept gifts from a fairy godmother. He had had enough of skimping meanness; with his generation he wanted to slough off the drabness of the frontier; he wanted the good things of life that had so long been denied him, and he was not scrupulous about looking a gift horse in the mouth. He sought out the company of rich men. He was never happier than when enjoying the luxury of Jay Cooke's mansion in Philadelphia or riding with A. T. Stewart in Central Park. As he grew fat and stodgy the vulgar side of his plebeian nature was thrown into sharper relief. He accepted gifts with both hands, and he seems never to have suspected the price that would be exacted of the President for the presents to the General. He never realized how great a bill was sent to the American people for the wine he drank or the cigars he smoked with his wealthy hosts; yet if the wine had been molten gold and the cigars platinum they would have been far cheaper. In return for a few boxes of choice Havanas, Jay Cooke laid his hands on millions of western lands for the Northern Pacific Railway. It was the way of the Gilded Age, and Grant was only doing what all his friends and associates were doing. If he accepted a fifty-thousand-dollar house in Philadelphia, his comrade General Sherman accepted a hundred-thousand-dollar house at Washington. Such gifts were not bribes; they were open and aboveboard; it was the free and easy way of the times. What the age was careless about is the fact that it is hard to refuse a reasonable request from one's fairy godmother, and what the General never understood is that if one is President such a godmother is certain to be a very dangerous member of the family.

There was far too much of that sort of thing all about him for Grant to serve as President with credit to himself or profit to the country. Honest himself, he was the source of more dishonesty in others than any other American President. His eight years in the White House marked the lowest depths—in domestic affairs at least—to which any American administration has fallen. They were little better than a national disgrace. All the festering evils of post-war times came to a head and pock-marked the body politic from head to foot. Scandal and corruption whispered all about him, the hands of his closest advisers were dirty; yet he stubbornly refused to hear the whispers or see the dirt. In judging men and policies he was no more than a child. He could never distinguish between an honest man and a rascal. He was loyal to his friends and open-handedness he regarded as a mark of friendship. In the end it turned out that like the thieves of Jericho his blatant followers despoiled him of pretty nearly everything.

In what must pass for his political views Grant was as naïvely uninformed as a Wyoming cowboy. Utterly wanting in knowledge of political principles, he was a fit leader for the organized mob that called itself the Republican party, whose chief objective was the raiding of the treasure-box of which it was the responsible guardian. He had been nominally a Democrat and the first vote he cast for President he cast for Buchanan. After Lincoln's death he turned naturally to President Johnson and was one of his supporters till the wily Radical group got his ear and carried him over to the rival camp. They wanted his reputation to hide under, and they took possession of it with no great credit to the General's reputation. Thereafter he was a Republican of the Whig wing. It was where he belonged. He was swayed politically by his emotional reactions and it was natural for him to drift into the opulent camp of money and power. His frontier democracy sloughed away and with his generation he went over easily to a buccaneer capitalism. No social conscience obtruded itself to give him trouble. His millionaire friends were Whig Republicans and with his respect for rich men, his admiration for material success, he found himself in congenial company amongst the Whig group. About the only political policy he ever interested himself in was the policy of a protective tariff, and his Whig associates took care that his interest did not wane. Yet so completely did the naïve General reflect the spirit of the Gilded Age that his noisy followers, conspiring to confuse in the public mind southern reconstruction and capitalistic expansion, and hiding a precious set of rascals in the folds of the bloody flag, came near to making him President for a third term. The General was bitterly disappointed at their failure, and the General's wife, who liked to live in the White House, was even more disappointed. To millions of Americans Grant was an authentic hero, to Mark Twain he was a very great man, and to Jay Cooke he was a pawn to be used in the noble strategy of fortune-seeking. What a comedy it all seems now—yet one that leaves an unpleasant taste in the mouth.

Yet to dismiss the stolid General thus is scarcely to do justice to the substantial core of the man. There remains the work written in pain during his last days, the two volumes of *Memoirs* that in their plain directness—as uninspired, says a late biographer, as "a bale of hay"

—laid bare his honest simplicity and rugged meagerness. No blackguard and no charlatan could have written such pages. If General Grant was not the great man so many thought, he was a native growth from American soil, endowed like his age with a dogged will and a plodding energy, and he gave his country what he had. Though the branches of the tree were ungainly and offered too hospitable shelter to unseemly birds of the night, the gnarly trunk was sound at the heart.

1930

FREDERICK LEWIS ALLEN

CRASH!

From ONLY YESTERDAY

EARLY in September the stock market broke. It quickly recovered, however; indeed, on September 19th the averages as compiled by the *New York Times* reached an even higher level than that of September 3rd. Once more it slipped, farther and faster, until by October 4th the prices of a good many stocks had coasted to what seemed first-class bargain levels. Steel, for example, after having touched 261¾ a few weeks earlier, had dropped as low as 204; American Can, at the closing on October 4th, was nearly twenty points below its high for the year; General Electric was over fifty points below its high; Radio had gone down from 114¾ to 82½.

A bad break, to be sure, but there had been other bad breaks, and the speculators who escaped unscathed proceeded

to take advantage of the lesson they had learned in June and December of 1928 and March and May of 1929: when there was a break it was a good time to buy. In the face of all this tremendous liquidation, brokers' loans as compiled by the Federal Reserve Bank of New York mounted to a new high record on October 2nd, reaching $6,804,000,000—a sure sign that margin buyers were not deserting the market but coming into it in numbers at least undiminished. (Part of the increase in the loan figure was probably due to the piling up of unsold securities in dealers' hands, as the spawning of investment trusts and the issue of new common stock by every manner of business concern continued unabated.) History, it seemed, was about to repeat itself, and those who

From *Only Yesterday* by Frederick Lewis Allen. Published by Harper & Brothers. Copyright, 1931, by Frederick Lewis Allen.

picked up Anaconda at 109¾ or American Telephone at 281 would count themselves wise investors. And sure enough, prices once more began to climb. They had already turned upward before that Sunday in early October when Ramsay MacDonald sat on a log with Herbert Hoover at the Rapidan camp and talked over the prospects for naval limitation and peace.

Something was wrong, however. The decline began once more. The wiseacres of Wall Street, looking about for causes, fixed upon the collapse of the Hatry financial group in England (which had led to much forced selling among foreign investors and speculators), and upon the bold refusal of the Massachusetts Department of Public Utilities to allow the Edison Company of Boston to split up its stock. They pointed, too, to the fact that the steel industry was undoubtedly slipping, and to the accumulation of "undigested" securities. But there was little real alarm until the week of October 21st. The consensus of opinion, in the meantime, was merely that the equinoctial storm of September had not quite blown over. The market was readjusting itself into a "more secure technical position."

In view of what was about to happen, it is enlightening to recall how things looked at this juncture to the financial prophets, those gentlemen whose wizardly reputations were based upon their supposed ability to examine a set of graphs brought to them by a statistician and discover, from the relation of curve to curve and index to index, whether things were going to get better or worse. Their opinions differed, of course; there never has been a moment when the best financial opinion was unanimous. In examining these opinions, and the out-

givings of eminent bankers, it must furthermore be acknowledged that a bullish statement cannot always be taken at its face value: few men like to assume the responsibility of spreading alarm by making dire predictions, nor is a banker with unsold securities on his hands likely to say anything which will make it more difficult to dispose of them, unquiet as his private mind may be. Finally, one must admit that prophecy is at best the most hazardous of occupations. Nevertheless, the general state of financial opinion in October, 1929, makes an instructive contrast with that in February and March, 1928, when, as we have seen, the skies had not appeared any too bright.

Some forecasters, to be sure, were so unconventional as to counsel caution. Roger W. Babson, an investment adviser who had not always been highly regarded in the inner circles of Wall Street, especially since he had for a long time been warning his clients of future trouble, predicted early in September a decline of sixty or eighty points in the averages. On October 7th the Standard Trade and Securities Service of the Standard Statistics Company advised its clients to pursue an "ultra-conservative policy," and ventured this prediction: "We remain of the opinion that, over the next few months, the trend of common-stock prices will be toward lower levels." Poor's *Weekly Business and Investment Letter* spoke its mind on the "great common-stock delusion" and predicted "further liquidation in stocks." Among the big bankers, Paul M. Warburg had shown months before this that he was alive to the dangers of the situation. These commentators—along with others such as the editor of the *Commercial and Financial Chronicle* and the financial editor of the *New*

York Times—would appear to deserve the 1929 gold medals for foresight.

But if ever such medals were actually awarded, a goodly number of leather ones would have to be distributed at the same time. Not necessarily to the Harvard Economic Society, although on October 19th, after having explained that business was "facing another period of readjustment," it predicted that "if recession should threaten serious consequences for business (as is not indicated at present) there is little doubt that the Reserve System would take steps to ease the money market and so check the movement." The Harvard soothsayers proved themselves quite fallible: as late as October 26th, after the first wide-open crack in the stock market, they delivered the cheerful judgment that "despite its severity, we believe that the slump in stock prices will prove an intermediate movement and not the precursor of a business depression such as would entail prolonged further liquidation." This judgment turned out, of course, to be ludicrously wrong; but on the other hand the Harvard Economic Society was far from being really bullish. Nor would Colonel Leonard P. Ayres of the Cleveland Trust Company get one of the leather medals. He almost qualified when, on October 15th, he delivered himself of the judgment that "there does not seem to be as yet much real evidence that the decline in stock prices is likely to forecast a serious recession in general business. Despite the slowing down in iron and steel production, in automobile output, and in building, the conditions which result in serious business depressions are not present." But the skies, as Colonel Ayres saw them, were at least partly cloudy. "It seems probable," he said, "that stocks have been passing not

so much from the strong to the weak as from the smart to the dumb."

Professor Irving Fisher, however, was more optimistic. In the newspapers of October 17th he was reported as telling the Purchasing Agents Association that stock prices had reached "what looks like a permanently high plateau." He expected to see the stock market, within a few months, "a good deal higher than it is today." On the very eve of the panic of October 24th he was further quoted as expecting a recovery in prices. Only two days before the panic, the *Boston News Bureau* quoted R. W. McNeel, director of McNeel's Financial Service, as suspecting "that some pretty intelligent people are now buying stocks." "Unless we are to have a panic—which no one seriously believes—stocks have hit bottom," said Mr. McNeel. And as for Charles E. Mitchell, chairman of the great National City Bank of New York, he continuously and enthusiastically radiated sunshine. Early in October Mr. Mitchell was positive that, despite the stock-market break, "The industrial situation of the United States is absolutely sound and our credit situation is in no way critical. . . . The interest given by the public to brokers' loans is always exaggerated," he added. "Altogether too much attention is paid to it." A few days later Mr. Mitchell spoke again: "Although in some cases speculation has gone too far in the United States, the markets generally are now in a healthy condition. The last six weeks have done an immense amount of good by shaking down prices. . . . The market values have a sound basis in the general prosperity of our country." Finally, on October 22nd, two days before the panic, he arrived in the United States from a short trip to Europe with these reassuring words: "I know of nothing fundamentally wrong with the stock market or with the underlying business and credit structure. . . . The public is suffering from 'brokers' loanitis.'"

Nor was Mr. Mitchell by any means alone in his opinions. To tell the truth, the chief difference between him and the rest of the financial community was that he made more noise. One of the most distinguished bankers in the United States, in closing a deal in the early autumn of 1929, said privately that he saw not a cloud in the sky. Habitual bulls like Arthur Cutten were, of course, insisting that they were "still bullish." And the general run of traders presumably endorsed the view attributed to "one large house" in mid-October in the *Boston News Bureau's* "Broad Street Gossip," that "the recent break makes a firm foundation for a big bull market in the last quarter of the year." There is no doubt that a great many speculators who had looked upon the midsummer prices as too high were now deciding that deflation had been effected and were buying again. Presumably most financial opinion agreed also with the further statement which appeared in the "Broad Street Gossip" column on October 16th, that "business is now too big and diversified, and the country too rich, to be influenced by stock-market fluctuations"; and with the editorial opinion of the *News Bureau,* on October 19th, that "whatever recessions (in business) are noted, are those of the runner catching his breath. . . . The general condition is satisfactory and fundamentally sound."

The disaster which was impending was destined to be as bewildering and frightening to the rich and the powerful and the customarily sagacious as to the foolish and unwary holder of fifty shares of margin stock.

The expected recovery in the stock market did not come. It seemed to be beginning on Tuesday, October 22nd, but the gains made during the day were largely lost during the last hour. And on Wednesday, the 23rd, there was a perfect Niagara of liquidation. The volume of trading was over six million shares, the tape was 104 minutes late when the three-o'clock gong ended trading for the day, and the *New York Times* averages for fifty leading railroad and industrial stocks lost 18.24 points— a loss which made the most abrupt declines in previous breaks look small. Everybody realized that an unprecedented number of margin calls must be on their way to insecurely margined traders, and that the situation at last was getting serious. But perhaps the turn would come tomorrow. Already the break had carried prices down a good deal farther than the previous breaks of the past two years. Surely it could not go on much longer.

The next day was Thursday, October 24th.

On that momentous day stocks opened moderately steady in price, but in enormous volume. Kennecott appeared on the tape in a block of 20,000 shares, General Motors in another of the same amount. Almost at once the ticker tape began to lag behind the trading on the floor. The pressure of selling orders was disconcertingly heavy. Prices were going down. . . . Presently they were going down with some rapidity. . . . Before the first hour of trading was over, it was already apparent that they were going down with an altogether unprecedented and amazing violence. In brokers' offices all over the country, tape-watchers looked at one another in astonishment and perplexity. Where on earth was this torrent of selling orders coming from?

The exact answer to this question will probably never be known. But it seems probable that the principal cause of the break in prices during that first hour on October 24th was not fear. Nor was it short selling. It was forced selling. It was the dumping on the market of hundreds of thousands of shares of stock held in the name of miserable traders whose margins were exhausted or about to be exhausted. The gigantic edifice of prices was honeycombed with speculative credit and was now breaking under its own weight.

Fear, however, did not long delay its coming. As the price structure crumbled there was a sudden stampede to get out from under. By eleven o'clock traders on the floor of the Stock Exchange were in a wild scramble to "sell at the market." Long before the lagging ticker could tell what was happening, word had gone out by telephone and telegraph that the bottom was dropping out of things, and the selling orders redoubled in volume. The leading stocks were going down two, three, and even five points between sales. Down, down, down. . . . Where were the bargain-hunters who were supposed to come to the rescue at times like this? Where were the investment trusts, which were expected to provide a cushion for the market by making new purchases at low prices? Where were the big operators who had declared that they were still bullish? Where were the powerful bankers who were supposed to be able at any moment to support prices? There seemed to be no support whatever. Down, down, down. The roar

of voices which rose from the floor of the Exchange had become a roar of panic.

United States Steel had opened at 205½. It crashed through 200 and presently was at 193½. General Electric, which only a few weeks before had been selling above 400, had opened this morning at 315—now it had slid to 283. Things were even worse with Radio: opening at 68¾, it had gone dismally down through the sixties and the fifties and forties to the abysmal price of 44½. And as for Montgomery Ward, vehicle of the hopes of thousands who saw the chain store as the harbinger of the new economic era, it had dropped headlong from 83 to 50. In the space of two short hours, dozens of stocks lost ground which it had required many months of the bull market to gain.

Even this sudden decline in values might not have been utterly terrifying if people could have known precisely what was happening at any moment. It is the unknown which causes real panic.

Suppose a man walked into a broker's branch office between twelve and one o'clock on October 24th to see how things were faring. First he glanced at the big board, covering one wall of the room, on which the day's prices for the leading stocks were supposed to be recorded. The LOW and LAST figures written there took his breath away, but soon he was aware that they were unreliable: even with the wildest scrambling, the boys who slapped into place the cards which recorded the last prices shown on the ticker could not keep up with the changes: they were too numerous and abrupt. He turned to the shining screen across which ran an uninterrupted procession of figures from the ticker. Ordinarily the practiced tape-watcher could tell from a moment's glance at the screen how things were faring, even though the Exchange now omitted all but the final digit of each quotation. A glance at the board, if not his own memory, supplied the missing digits. But today, when he saw a run of symbols and figures like

R   WX
6.5½.5.4.   9.8⅞¾½¼.8.7½.7.

he could not be sure whether the price of "6" shown for Radio meant 66 or 56 or 46; whether Westinghouse was sliding from 189 to 187 or from 179 to 177. And presently he heard that the ticker was an hour and a half late; at one o'clock it was recording the prices of half-past eleven! All this that he saw was ancient history. What was happening on the floor now?

At ten-minute intervals the bond ticker over in the corner would hammer off a list of selected prices direct from the floor, and a broker's clerk would grab the uncoiling sheet of paper and shear it off with a pair of scissors and read the figures aloud in a mumbling expressionless monotone to the white-faced men who occupied every seat on the floor and stood packed at the rear of the room. The prices which he read out were *ten or a dozen or more points below those recorded on the ticker.* What about the stocks not included in that select list? There was no way of finding out. The telephone lines were clogged as inquiries and orders from all over the country converged upon the Stock Exchange. Once in a while a voice would come barking out of the broker's rear office where a frantic clerk was struggling for a telephone connection: "Steel at ninety-six!" Small comfort, however, to know what Steel was doing; the men outside were des-

perately involved in many another stock than Steel; they were almost completely in the dark, and their imaginations had free play. If they put in an order to buy or to sell, it was impossible to find out what became of it. The Exchange's whole system for the recording of current prices and for communicating orders was hopelessly unable to cope with the emergency, and the sequel was an epidemic of fright.

In that broker's office, as in hundreds of other offices from one end of the land to the other, one saw men looking defeat in the face. One of them was slowly walking up and down, mechanically tearing a piece of paper into tiny and still tinier fragments. Another was grinning shamefacedly, as a small boy giggles at a funeral. Another was abjectly beseeching a clerk for the latest news of American & Foreign Power. And still another was sitting motionless, as if stunned, his eyes fixed blindly upon the moving figures on the screen, those innocent-looking figures that meant the smash-up of the hopes of years. . . .

GL.   AWW. JMP.
8.7.5.2.1.90.89.7.6.   3.2½.2.   6.5.3.2½.

A few minutes after noon, some of the more alert members of a crowd which had collected on the street outside the Stock Exchange, expecting they knew not what, recognized Charles E. Mitchell, erstwhile defender of the bull market, slipping quietly into the offices of J. P. Morgan & Company on the opposite corner. It was scarcely more than nine years since the House of Morgan had been pitted with the shrapnel-fire of the Wall Street explosion; now its occupants faced a different sort of calamity equally near at hand. Mr. Mitchell was followed shortly by Albert H. Wiggin, head of the Chase National Bank; William Potter, head of the Guaranty Trust Company; and Seward Prosser, head of the Bankers Trust Company. They had come to confer with Thomas W. Lamont of the Morgan firm. In the space of a few minutes these five men, with George F. Baker, Jr., of the First National Bank, agreed in behalf of their respective institutions to put up forty millions apiece to shore up the stock market. The object of the two-hundred-and-forty-million-dollar pool thus formed, as explained subsequently by Mr. Lamont, was not to hold prices at any given level, but simply to make such purchases as were necessary to keep trading on an orderly basis. Their first action, they decided, would be to try to steady the prices of the leading securities which served as bell wethers for the list as a whole. It was a dangerous plan, for with hysteria spreading there was no telling what sort of *débâcle* might be impending. But this was no time for any action but the boldest.

The bankers separated. Mr. Lamont faced a gathering of reporters in the Morgan offices. His face was grave, but his words were soothing. His first sentence alone was one of the most remarkable understatements of all time. "There has been a little distress selling on the Stock Exchange," said he, "and we have held a meeting of the heads of several financial institutions to discuss the situation. We have found that there are no houses in difficulty and reports from brokers indicate that margins are being maintained satisfactorily." He went on to explain that what had happened was due to a "technical condition of the market" rather than to any fundamental cause.

As the news that the bankers were meeting circulated on the floor of the Exchange, prices began to steady. Soon a brisk rally set in. Steel jumped back to the level at which it had opened that morning. But the bankers had more to offer the dying bull market than a Morgan partner's best bedside manner.

At about half-past one o'clock Richard Whitney, vice-president of the Exchange, who usually acted as floor broker for the Morgan interests, went into the "Steel crowd" and put in a bid of 205 —the price of the last previous sale—for 10,000 shares of Steel. He bought only 200 shares and left the remainder of the order with the specialist. Mr. Whitney then went to various other points on the floor, and offered the price of the last previous sale for 10,000 shares of each of fifteen or twenty other stocks, reporting what was sold to him at that price and leaving the remainder of the order with the specialist. In short, within the space of a few minutes Mr. Whitney offered to purchase something in the neighborhood of twenty or thirty million dollars' worth of stock. Purchases of this magnitude are not undertaken by Tom, Dick, and Harry; it was clear that Mr. Whitney represented the bankers' pool.

The desperate remedy worked. The semblance of confidence returned. Prices held steady for a while; and though many of them slid off once more in the final hour, the net results for the day might well have been worse. Steel actually closed two points higher than on Wednesday, and the net losses of most of the other leading securities amounted to less than ten points apiece for the whole day's trading.

All the same, it had been a frightful day. At seven o'clock that night the tickers in a thousand brokers' offices were still chattering; not till after 7:08 did they finally record the last sale made on the floor at three o'clock. The volume of trading had set a new record—

12,894,650 shares. ("The time may come when we shall see a five-million-share day," the wise men of the Street had been saying twenty months before!) Incredible rumors had spread wildly during the early afternoon—that eleven speculators had committed suicide, that the Buffalo and Chicago exchanges had been closed, that troops were guarding the New York Stock Exchange against an angry mob. The country had known the bitter taste of panic. And although the bankers' pool had prevented for the moment an utter collapse, there was no gainsaying the fact that the economic structure had cracked wide open.

Things looked somewhat better on Friday and Saturday. Trading was still on an enormous scale, but prices for the most part held. At the very moment when the bankers' pool was cautiously disposing of as much as possible of the stock which it had accumulated on Thursday and was thus preparing for future emergencies, traders who had sold out higher up were coming back into the market again with new purchases, in the hope that the bottom had been reached. (Hadn't they often been told that "the time to buy is when things look blackest"?) The newspapers carried a very pretty series of reassuring statements from the occupants of the seats of the mighty; Herbert Hoover himself, in a White House statement, pointed out that "the fundamental business of the country, that is, production and distribution of commodities, is on a sound and prosperous basis." But toward the close of Saturday's session prices began to slip again. And on Monday the rout was under way once more.

The losses registered on Monday were terrific—17½ points for Steel, 47½ for General Electric, 36 for Allied Chemical, 34½ for Westinghouse, and so on down a long and dismal list. All Saturday afternoon and Saturday night and Sunday the brokers had been struggling to post their records and go over their customers' accounts and send out calls for further margin, and another avalanche of forced selling resulted. The prices at which Mr. Whitney's purchases had steadied the leading stocks on Thursday were so readily broken through that it was immediately clear that the bankers' pool had made a strategic retreat. As a matter of fact, the brokers who represented the pool were having their hands full plugging up the "air-holes" in the list—in other words, buying stocks which were offered for sale without any bids at all in sight. Nothing more than this could have been accomplished, even if it could have been wisely attempted. Even six great banks could hardly stem the flow of liquidation from the entire United States. They could only guide it a little, check it momentarily here and there.

Once more the ticker dropped ridiculously far behind, the lights in the brokers' offices and the banks burned till dawn, and the telegraph companies distributed thousands of margin calls and requests for more collateral to back up loans at the banks. Bankers, brokers, clerks, messengers were almost at the end of their strength; for days and nights they had been driving themselves to keep pace with the most terrific volume of business that had ever descended upon them. It did not seem as if they could stand it much longer. But the worst was still ahead. It came the next day, Tuesday, October 29th.

The big gong had hardly sounded in the great hall of the Exchange at ten o'clock Tuesday morning before the storm broke in full force. Huge blocks of stock were thrown upon the market for what they would bring. Five thousand shares, ten thousand shares appeared at a time on the laboring ticker at fearful recessions in price. Not only were innumerable small traders being sold out, but big ones, too, protagonists of the new economic era who a few weeks before had counted themselves millionaires. Again and again the specialist in a stock would find himself surrounded by brokers fighting to sell—and nobody at all even thinking of buying. To give one single example: during the bull market the common stock of the White Sewing Machine Company had gone as high as 48; on Monday, October 28th, it had closed at 11⅛. On that black Tuesday, somebody—a clever messenger boy for the Exchange, it was rumored—had the bright idea of putting in an order to buy at 1—and in the temporarily complete absence of other bids he actually got his stock for a dollar a share! The scene on the floor was chaotic. Despite the jamming of the communication system, orders to buy and sell—mostly to sell—came in faster than human beings could possibly handle them; it was on that day that an exhausted broker, at the close of the session, found a large waste-basket which he had stuffed with orders to be executed and had carefully set aside for safe-keeping—and then had completely forgotten. Within half an hour of the opening the volume of trading had passed three million shares, by twelve o'clock it had passed eight million, by half-past one it had passed twelve million, and when the closing gong brought the day's madness to an end the gigantic record of 16,410,030 shares had been set.

Toward the close there was a rally, but by that time the average prices of fifty leading stocks, as compiled by the *New York Times,* had fallen nearly forty points. Meanwhile there was a near-panic in other markets—the foreign stock exchanges, the lesser American exchanges, the grain market.

So complete was the demoralization of the stock market and so exhausted were the brokers and their staffs and the Stock Exchange employees, that at noon that day, when the panic was at its worst, the Governing Committee met quietly to decide whether or not to close the Exchange. To quote from an address made some months later by Richard Whitney: "In order not to give occasion for alarming rumors, this meeting was not held in the Governing Committee Room, but in the office of the president of the Stock Clearing Corporation directly beneath the Stock Exchange floor. . . . The forty governors came to the meeting in groups of two and three as unobtrusively as possible. The office they met in was never designed for large meetings of this sort, with the result that most of the governors were compelled to stand, or to sit on tables. As the meeting progressed, panic was raging overhead on the floor. . . . The feeling of those present was revealed by their habit of continually lighting cigarettes, taking a puff or two, putting them out and lighting new ones —a practice which soon made the narrow room blue with smoke. . . ." Two of the Morgan partners were invited to the meeting and, attempting to slip into the building unnoticed so as not to start a new flock of rumors, were refused admittance by one of the guards and had to remain outside until rescued by a member of the Governing Committee.

After some deliberation, the governors finally decided not to close the Exchange.

It was a critical day for the banks, that Tuesday the 29th. Many of the corporations which had so cheerfully loaned money to brokers through the banks in order to obtain interest at 8 or 9 per cent were now clamoring to have these loans called—and the banks were faced with a choice between taking over the loans themselves and running the risk of precipitating further ruin. It was no laughing matter to assume the responsibility of millions of dollars' worth of loans secured by collateral which by the end of the day might prove to have dropped to a fraction of its former value. That the call money rate never rose above 6 per cent that day, that a money panic was not added to the stock panic, and that several Wall Street institutions did not go down into immediate bankruptcy, was due largely to the nerve shown by a few bankers in stepping into the breach. The story is told of one banker who went grimly on authorizing the taking over of loan after loan until one of his subordinate officers came in with a white face and told him that the bank was insolvent. "I dare say," said the banker, and went ahead unmoved. He knew that if he did not, more than one concern would face insolvency.

The next day—Wednesday, October 30th—the outlook suddenly and providentially brightened. The directors of the Steel Corporation had declared an extra dividend; the directors of the American Can Company had not only declared an extra dividend, but had raised the regular dividend. There was another flood of reassuring statements—though by this time a cheerful statement from a financier fell upon somewhat

skeptical ears. Julius Klein, Mr. Hoover's Assistant Secretary of Commerce, composed a rhapsody on continued prosperity. John J. Raskob declared that stocks were at bargain prices and that he and his friends were buying. John D. Rockefeller poured Standard Oil upon the waters: "Believing that fundamental conditions of the country are sound and that there is nothing in the business situation to warrant the destruction of values that has taken place on the exchanges during the past week, my son and I have for some days been purchasing sound common stocks." Better still, prices rose—steadily and buoyantly. Now at last the time had come when the strain on the Exchange could be relieved without causing undue alarm. At 1:40 o'clock Vice-President Whitney announced from the rostrum that the Exchange would not open until noon the following day and would remain closed all day Friday and Saturday—and to his immense relief the announcement was greeted, not with renewed panic, but with a cheer.

Throughout Thursday's short session the recovery continued. Prices gyrated wildly—for who could arrive at a reasonable idea of what a given stock was worth, now that all settled standards of value had been upset?—but the worst of the storm seemed to have blown over. The financial community breathed more easily; now they could have a chance to set their houses in order.

It was true that the worst of the panic was past. But not the worst prices. There was too much forced liquidation still to come as brokers' accounts were gradually straightened out, as banks called for more collateral, and terror was renewed. The next week, in a series of short sessions, the tide of prices receded once more—until at last on November 13th the bottom prices for the year 1929 were reached. Beside the figures hung up in the sunny days of September they made a tragic showing:

	High price Sept. 3, 1929	Low price Nov. 13, 1929
American Can	181⅞	86
American Telephone & Telegraph	304	197¼
Anaconda Copper	131½	70
General Electric	396¼	168⅛
General Motors	72¾	36
Montgomery Ward	137⅞	49¼
New York Central	256⅜	160
Radio	101	28
Union Carbide & Carbon	137⅞	59
United States Steel	261¾	150
Westinghouse E. & M.	289⅞	102⅝
Woolworth	100⅜	52¼
Electric Bond & Share	186¾	50¼

The *New York Times* averages for fifty leading stocks had been almost cut in half, falling from a high of 311.90 in September to a low of 164.43 on November 13th; and the *Times* averages for twenty-five leading industrials had fared still worse, diving from 469.49 to 220.95.

The Big Bull Market was dead. Billions of dollars' worth of profits—and paper profits—had disappeared. The grocer, the window-cleaner, and the seamstress had lost their capital. In every town there were families which had suddenly dropped from showy affluence into debt. Investors who had dreamed of retiring to live on their fortunes now found themselves back once more at the very beginning of the long road to riches. Day by day the newspapers printed the grim reports of suicides.

Coolidge-Hoover Prosperity was not yet dead, but it was dying. Under the impact of the shock of panic, a multitude of ills which hitherto had passed unnoticed or had been offset by stock-market optimism began to beset the body economic, as poisons seep through the human system when a vital organ has ceased to function normally. Although the liquidation of nearly three billion dollars of brokers' loans contracted credit, and the Reserve Banks lowered the rediscount rate, and the way in which the larger banks and corporations of the country had survived the emergency without a single failure of large proportions offered real encouragement, nevertheless the poisons were there: overproduction of capital; over-ambitious expansion of business concerns; overproduction of commodities under the stimulus of installment buying and buying with stock-market profits; the maintenance of an artificial price level for many commodities; the depressed condition of European trade. No matter how many soothsayers of high finance proclaimed that all was well, no matter how earnestly the President set to work to repair the damage with soft words and White House conferences, a major depression was inevitably under way.

Nor was that all. Prosperity is more than an economic condition; it is a state of mind. The Big Bull Market had been more than the climax of a business cycle; it had been the climax of a cycle in American mass thinking and mass emotion. There was hardly a man or woman in the country whose attitude toward life had not been affected by it in some degree and was not now affected by the sudden and brutal shattering of hope. With the Big Bull Market gone and prosperity going, Americans were soon to find themselves living in an altered world which called for new adjustments, new ideas, new habits of thought, and a new order of values. The psychological climate was changing; the ever-shifting currents of American life were turning into new channels.

The Post-war Decade had come to its close. An era had ended.

1931

ARTHUR D. DIVINE

Miracle at Dunkirk

I AM STILL amazed about the whole Dunkirk affair. There was from first to last a queer, medieval sense of miracle about it. You remember the old quotation about the miracle that crushed the Spanish Armada, "God sent a wind." This time "God withheld the wind." Had we had one onshore breeze of any strength at all, in the first days, we would have lost a hundred thousand men.

The pier at Dunkirk was the unceasing target of bombs and shellfire throughout, yet it never was hit. Two hundred and fifty thousand men embarked from that pier. Had it been blasted . . .

The whole thing from first to last was covered with that same strange feeling of something supernatural. We muddled, we quarreled, everybody swore and was bad-tempered and made the wildest accusations of inefficiency and worse in high places. Boats were badly handled and broke down, arrangements went wrong.

And yet out of all that mess we beat the experts, we defied the law and the prophets, and where the Government and the Board of Admiralty had hoped to bring away 30,000 men, we brought away 335,000. If that was not a miracle, there are no miracles left.

When I heard that small boats of all sorts were to be used at Dunkirk, I volunteered at once, having no vast opinion of the navy as small-boat handlers. I had been playing with the navy off and on since the beginning of the year, mine sweeping and submarine hunting, convoying, and so on. So friends of mine at the Admiralty passed me through without formalities, and within two hours of my first telephone call I was on my way to Sheerness. From Sheerness I acted as navigator for a party of small boats round to Ramsgate, and at Ramsgate we started work. The evacuation went on for something over a week, but to me the most exciting time was the night before the last.

I was given a motorboat about as long as my drawing room at home, 30 feet. She had one cabin forward and the rest was open, but she had twin engines and was fairly fast. For crew we had one sub-lieutenant, one stoker and one gunner. For armament we had two Bren guns—one my own particular pet which I had stolen—and rifles. In command of our boat we had a real live Admiral

Reprinted from *The Reader's Digest,* December, 1940, by permission of the author and the publishers.

—Taylor, Admiral in charge of small boats.

We first went out to French fishing boats gathered off Ramsgate, boats from Caen and Le Havre, bright little vessels with lovely names—*Ciel de France, Ave Maria, Gratia Plena, Jeanne Antoine.* They had helped at Calais and Boulogne and in the preceding days at Dunkirk, and the men were very tired, but when we passed them new orders they set out again for Dunkirk.

They went as the leaders of the procession, for they were slow. With them went a handful of Dutch *schouts,* stumpy little coasting vessels commandeered at the collapse of Holland, each flying the white ensign of the Royal Navy, sparkling new, and each fitted out with a Lewis gun. Next went coasters, colliers, paddle steamers that in time of peace had taken trippers around the harbor for a shilling, tugs towing mud scows with brave names like *Galleon's Reach* and *Queen's Channel.*

There was a car ferry, surely on its first trip in the open sea. There were yachts; one the *Skylark*—what a name for such a mission! There were dock-yard tugs, towing barges. There were sloops, mine sweepers, trawlers, destroyers. There were Thames fire floats, Belgian drifters, lifeboats from all around the coast, lifeboats from sunken ships. I saw the boats of the old *Dunbar Castle,* sunk eight months before. Rolling and pitching in a cloud of spray were open speedboats, wholly unsuited for the Channel chop.

There was the old *Brighton Belle* that carried holiday crowds in the days before the Boer War. She swept mines in the Great War, and she swept mines in this war through all the fury of last winter. I know; I sailed with her then. Coming back from her second trip to Dunkirk, she struck the wreck of a ship sunk by a magnetic mine and slowly sank. Her captain, a Conservative party agent in civil life, got 400 men safely off and at the last even saved his dog.

There was never such a fleet went to war before, I think. As I went round the western arm of the harbor near sunset, passing out orders, it brought my heart into my throat to watch them leave. They were so small! Little boats like those you see in the bight of Sandy Hook fishing on a fine afternoon. Some were frowsy, with old motorcar tires for fenders, and some of them were bright with paint and chromium—little white boats that were soon lost to view across the ruffled water. And as they went there came round from the foreland a line of fishing boats—shrimp catchers and what not, from the east coast—to join the parade.

When this armada of oddments was under way, we followed with the faster boats—Royal Air Force rescue launches, picket boats and the like—and with us went an X-lighter, a flatboat, kerosene-powered built for landing troops at Gallipoli and a veteran of *that* evacuation more than 20 years ago.

It was the queerest, most nondescript flotilla that ever was, and it was manned by every kind of Englishman, never more than two men, often only one, to each small boat. There were bankers and dentists, taxi drivers and yachtsmen, longshoremen, boys, engineers, fishermen and civil servants. There were bright-faced Sea Scouts and old men whose skins looked fiery red against their white hair. Many were poor; they had no coats, but made out with old jerseys and sweaters. They wore cracked rubber boots. They were wet, chilled to the bone, hungry; they were unarmed and unprotected, and they sailed toward the pillars of smoke and fire and the thunder of the guns, into waters already slick with the oil of sunken boats, knowing perfectly well the special kind of hell ahead. Still, they went, plugging gamely along.

I had a feeling, then and after, that this was something bigger than organization, something bigger than the mere requisitioning of boats. In a sense it was the naval spirit that has always been the foundation of England's greatness, flowering again and flowering superbly. I believe 887 was the official figure for the total of boats that took part over the ten days of the evacuation. But I think there were more than a thousand craft in all. I myself know of fishermen who never registered, waited for no orders, but, all unofficial, went and brought back soldiers. Quietly, like that.

It was dark before we were well clear of the English coast. It wasn't rough, but there was a little chop on, sufficient to make it very wet, and we soaked the Admiral to the skin. Soon, in the dark, the big boats began to overtake us. We were in a sort of dark traffic lane, full of strange ghosts and weird, unaccountable waves from the wash of the larger vessels. When destroyers went by, full tilt, the wash was a serious matter to us little fellows. We could only spin the wheel to try to head into the waves, hang on, and hope for the best.

Mere navigation was dangerous in the dark. Clouds hung low and blotted out the stars. We carried no lights, we had no signals, no means of recognition of friend or foe. Before we were half-way across we began to meet the first of the returning stream. We dodged white, glimmering bow waves of vessels that had passed astern, only to fall into the way of half-seen shapes ahead.

There were shouts in the darkness, but only occasionally the indignant stutter of a horn. We went "by guess and by God."

From the halfway mark, too, there were destroyers on patrol crossing our line of passage, weaving a fantastic warp of foam through the web of our progress. There were collisions, of course. Dover for days was full of destroyers with bows stove in, coasting vessels with great gashes amidships, ships battered, scraped and scarred. The miracle is that there were not ten for every one that happened.

Even before it was fully dark we had picked up the glow of the Dunkirk flames, and now as we drew nearer the sailing got better, for we could steer by them and see silhouetted the shapes of other ships, of boats coming home already loaded, and of low dark shadows that might be the enemy motor torpedo boats.

Then aircraft started dropping parachute flares. We saw them hanging all about us in the night, like young moons. The sound of the firing and the bombing was with us always, growing steadily louder as we got nearer and nearer. The flames grew, too. From a glow they rose up to enormous plumes of fire that roared high into the everlasting pall of smoke. As we approached Dunkirk there was an air attack on the destroyers and for a little the night was brilliant with bursting bombs and the fountain sprays of tracer bullets.

The beach, black with men, illumined by the fires, seemed a perfect target, but no doubt the thick clouds of smoke were a useful screen.

When we got to the neighborhood of the mole there was a lull. The aircraft had dispersed and apparently had done no damage, for there was nothing sinking. They had been there before, however, and the place was a shambles of old wrecks, British and French, and all kinds of odds and ends. The breakwaters and lighthouse were magnificently silhouetted against the flames of burning oil tanks—enormous flames that licked high above the town. Further inshore and to the east of the docks the town itself was burning furiously, but down near the beach where we were going there was no fire and we could see rows of houses standing silent and apparently empty.

We had just got to the eastward of the pier when shelling started up. There was one battery of 5.9's down between La Panne and Nieuport that our people simply could not find and its shooting was uncannily accurate. Our place was in the corner of the beach at the mole and as they were shelling the mole, the firing was right over our heads. Nothing, however, came near us in the first spell.

The picture will always remain sharp-etched in my memory—the lines of men wearily and sleepily staggering across the beach from the dunes to the shallows, falling into little boats, great columns of men thrust out into the water among bomb and shell splashes. The foremost ranks were shoulder deep, moving forward under the command of young subalterns, themselves with their heads just above the little waves that rode in to the sand. As the front ranks were dragged aboard the boats, the rear ranks moved up, from ankle deep to knee deep, from knee deep to waist deep, until they, too, came to shoulder depth and their turn.

Some of the big boats pushed in until they were almost aground, taking appalling risks with the falling tide. The men scrambled up the sides on rope nets, or climbed hundreds of ladders, made God knows where out of new, raw wood and hurried aboard the ships in England.

The little boats that ferried from the beach to the big ships in deep water listed drunkenly with the weight of men. The big ships slowly took on lists of their own with the enormous numbers crowded aboard. And always down the dunes and across the beach came new hordes of men, new columns, new lines.

On the beach was a destroyer, bombed and burned. At the water's edge were ambulances, abandoned when their last load had been discharged.

There was always the red background, the red of Dunkirk burning. There was no water to check the fires and there were no men to be spared to fight them. Red, too, were the shell bursts, the flash of guns, the fountains of tracer bullets.

The din was infernal. The 5.9 batteries shelled ceaselessly and brilliantly. To the whistle of shells overhead was added the scream of falling bombs. Even the sky was full of noise—anti-aircraft shells, machine-gun fire, the snarl of falling planes, the angry hornet noise of dive bombers. One could not speak normally at any time against the roar of it and the noise of our own engines. We all developed "Dunkirk throat," a sore hoarseness that was the hallmark of those who had been there.

Yet through all the noise I will always remember the voices of the young subalterns as they sent their men aboard, and I will remember, too, the astonishing discipline of the men. They had fought through three weeks of retreat, always falling back, often without orders, often without support. Transport had failed. They had gone sleepless. They had been without food and water.

Yet they kept ranks as they came down the beaches, and they obeyed commands.

Veterans of Gallipoli and of Mons agreed this was the hottest spot they had ever been in, yet morale held. I was told stories of French troops that rushed the boats at first so that stern measures had to be taken, but I saw nothing like that. The Frenchmen I brought off were of the rear guard, fine soldiers, still fighting fit.

Having the Admiral on board, we were not actually working the beaches but were in control of operations. We moved about as necessary, and after we had spent some time putting small boats in touch with their towing boats, the 5.9 battery off Nieuport way began to drop shells on us. It seemed pure spite. The nearest salvo was about 20 yards astern, which was close enough.

We stayed there until everybody else had been sent back, and then went pottering about looking for stragglers. While we were doing that, a salvo of shells got one of our troopships alongside the mole. She was hit clean in the boilers and exploded in one terrific crash. There were then, I suppose, about 1000 Frenchmen on the mole. We had seen them crowding along its narrow crest, outlined against the flames. They had gone out under shellfire to board the boat, and now they had to go back again, still being shelled. It was quite the most tragic thing I ever have seen in my life. We could do nothing with our little park dinghy.

While they were still filing back to the beach and the dawn was breaking with uncomfortable brilliance, we found one of our stragglers—a navy whaler. We told her people to come aboard, but they said that there was a motorboat aground and they would have to fetch off her crew. They went in, and we waited.

It was my longest wait, ever. For various reasons they were terribly slow. When they found the captain of the motorboat, they stood and argued with him and he wouldn't come off anyway. Damned plucky chap. He and his men lay quiet until the tide floated them later in the day. Then they made a dash for it, and got away.

We waited for them until the sun was up before we got clear of the mole. By then, the fighting was heavy inshore, on the outskirts of the town, and actually in some of the streets.

Going home, the Jerry dive bombers came over us five times, but somehow left us alone though three times they took up an attacking position. A little down the coast, towards Gravelines, we picked up a boatload of Frenchmen rowing off. We took them aboard. They were very much bothered as to where our "ship" was, said quite flatly that it was impossible to go to England in a thing like ours. Too, too horribly dangerous!

One of the rare touches of comedy at Dunkirk was the fear of the sea among French poilus from inland towns. They were desperately afraid to forfeit solid land for the unknown perils of a little boat. When, on the last nights of the evacuation, the little boats got to the mole many refused to jump in, despite the hell of shells and bombs behind them. I saw young sub-lieutenants grab poilus by the collar and the seat of the pants and rush them overside into waiting launches.

There was comedy of a sort, too, in the misadventures of the boats. The yachting season hadn't begun and most of the pleasure boats had been at their winter moorings when the call came; their engines had not been serviced and they broke down in the awkwardest places. The water supply at Dunkirk had been bombed out of use in the first days, and the navy ferried water across to keep the troops alive. Some of the water went in proper water cans, but most of it was put into two-gallon gasoline tins. *Of course* some of these tins got into the gasoline dumps, with lamentable results. I ran out of gasoline myself in the angle between Dunkirk mole and the beach, with heavy shelling going on and an Admiral on board. He never even said "damn." But we were lucky. A *schout* with spare fuel was lying a mile or so from the beach, near a buoy. I got to her with my last drop of reserve.

Then, for grim humor, there is the tale of the young sub-lieutenant, no more than a boy, whom I saw from time to time on one side of the Channel or the other. He was sent in the early days of the show to the beach east of Gravelines, where he was told there was a pocket of English troops cut off. He landed at the beach with only a revolver and walked off into the sand dunes to hunt for them. In the darkness he suddenly saw two faint shapes moving, and called out, "Here we are, boys, come to take you off."

There was silence, and then a guttural, *"Lieber Gott!"*

"So," the boy told me, "I shot them and came away."

He had walked right into the German army.

One of the greatest surprises of the whole operation was the failure of the German E-boats—motor torpedo boats. We crossed by a path that was well lit by light buoys, spread clean across from Goodwins to Dunkirk Roads. Well-handled E-boats could have got among us in the dark and played havoc—either in the Channel or in Dunkirk Roads.

I had stopped once off one of the light buoys when a division of destroyers passed me. They could see me only as a small dark shape on the water, if at all, and had I had torpedoes I could have picked off the leaders. I might have been a German motorboat, and if the German navy had any real fighting spirit I ought to have been a German motorboat. They did send a few boats in, and I believe they claimed one of our destroyers somewhere off La Panne, but they never pressed the attack home, never came in force against our motley armada off the beaches. The German navy lost a great chance.

Germany, in fact, failed in three ways at Dunkirk. Against a routed army she failed on land to drive home her advantage, though she had strategic and numerical superiority. She failed in the air, though with half a million men narrowed into one small semi-circle, she should have been able—if air power ever could be decisive—to secure decisive victory. And at sea, her motorboats were so lamentably handled that we almost disregarded them. For long hours on end we were sheep for the slaughtering, but we got back to Ramsgate safely each time. There we watched the debarkations, two and three hundred men from each of the larger boats marching in an endless brown stream down the narrow curve of the east harbor wall. Among each load would be five or six wounded. The hospital ships went in to Dover; at Ramsgate we saw mainly the pitiful survivors of ships bombed on the way over —men with their skin flayed by oil burns, torn by bomb splinters, or wounded by machine-gun fire from the air. Most of them were unbandaged and almost untended. They were put ashore just as they were pulled from the water, the most pitiful wrecks of men. Yet they were surprisingly few.

Well, that's the story of Dunkirk, as I saw the show. Just afterward, I volunteered for a new picnic farther down the coast. Our 51st Division had got cut off with a portion of the French army in the new battle which had developed from the Somme downward, and our job was to try to get it away.

I was given a Brighton Beach boat as warship this time, one of those things that takes trippers for a cruise around the bay. We left before dawn on a Wednesday morning and made the first half of the crossing in fog. We headed for Dieppe at first, but Dieppe had already fallen, and we veered toward St. Valery-en-Caux, a little down the coast. I knew the place well, having been there two or three days before war broke out. We sighted the French coast in the early afternoon and closed to within about five miles of it. Our destroyer escort never turned up, though we heard it having a bright little scrap on its own just below the horizon to the southwest.

About the middle of the afternoon, we sighted two boats rowing toward us and picked them up. They were full of French seamen who said that they were the last survivors of St. Valery. They had fought the Germans from their ship with machine guns until she sank under them, and then had rowed out of the harbor. They were very badly shot about, many of them dead and a large number wounded. I was called onto the tug to give first aid. We stowed them on two of our faster boats and sent the wounded off.

The German planes were buzzing around most of the time, but high up. Just as I got back to my own boat we got the signal to scatter. Three Heinkels had come over to deal with us.

My engine wouldn't start, as I had not been on board to see that it was warmed up, and the boat ahead of me was out of action with a fouled propeller. Neither of us could move, so we had to sit and watch the attack. The bombing was pretty good, but not good enough. For a long time it looked as if bombs from the first Heinkel were falling absolutely straight at us, tiny black specks that grew most horribly. They fell about 15 or 20 yards clear, and though they blew us sideways over the water they did us no harm.

Then the second bomber dived and dropped eight bombs, and again they fell just clear. While the third was maneuvering, my engineer got the engine going. I threw a towline to the other fellow, and we got under way. I had the flight of the bombs pretty well judged by then, and we worked clear of the third attack.

We started out for England. The bombers, having used up all their bombs, left us and we had a spell of quiet. However, big fighters came out to have another smack. We were far from the rest of the fleet and going along lamely. They attacked the others from a height, but when they came to us—thinking we were helpless, I suppose—they dived low and machine-gunned us heavily.

I was standing at the tiller, steering, and there was no sort of cover. One of the bullets got me through the middle. It felt like the kick of a mule, and knocked me away from the tiller to the bottom boards. However, there was not much real pain then, and I got up and examined myself. From the looks of the hole, I didn't think I had much of a chance. I told them to put me on the bottom boards, forward, and gave my gunner the course for the English coast. The tug picked us up after a time, and we were towed to New Haven, arriving about six next morning.

I was weak from loss of blood and wasn't betting too heavily on my chances of survival. However, I was operated on within an hour of landing, and it was found that I had been amazingly lucky. The bullet had done no serious damage.

I went to a hospital at Brighton. After three weeks the Admiralty moved me to a country hospital so that I could have a quiet rest. I didn't. We had 28 siren warnings in 20 days, and were bombed one night.

I am now back in town. The Admiralty offers me a commission, as a reward of virtue, I suppose, but the medical examiners say that I cannot go to sea. I don't want a shore job, so I have turned down the offer. I shall be a good boy and sit in an office awhile until the wound is better. Then I shall wangle my way to sea. I think I know how.

Meanwhile we are all right here. Germany is not starving us out; she is not going to invade us out; and she isn't going to air-raid us out. If I can't quite see yet how we are going to win—the method and so on—I certainly can't see how we are going to be defeated.

Twenty miles of sea is still twenty miles of sea, and the Straits of Dover are the best tank trap the world has ever devised.

1940

XI. . .

POETRY

ROBINSON JEFFERS
Point Joe

Point Joe has teeth and has torn ships; it
    has fierce and solitary beauty;
Walk there all day you shall see nothing
    that will not make part of a poem.

I saw the spars and planks of shipwreck on
    the rocks, and beyond the desolate
Sea-meadows rose the warped wind-bitten
    van of the pines, a fog-bank vaulted

Forest and all, the flat sea-meadows at that
    time of the year were plated
Golden with the low flower called footsteps
    of the spring, millions of flowerets,

Whose light suffused upward into the fog
    flooded its vault, we wandered
Through a weird country where the light
    beat up from earthward, and was
    golden.

One other moved there, an old Chinaman
    gathering seaweed from the searocks,
He brought it in his basket and spread it
    flat to dry on the edge of the meadow.

Permanent things are what is needful in a
    poem, things temporally
Of great dimension, things continually re-
    newed or always present.

Grass that is made each year equals the
    mountains in her past and future;
Fashionable and momentary things we
    need not speak of.

Man gleaning food between the solemn
    presences of land and ocean,
On shores where better men have ship-
    wrecked, under fog and among flow-
    ers,

Equals the mountains in his past and fu-
    ture; that glow from the earth was
    only
A trick of nature's, one must forgive nature
    a thousand graceful subtleties.

                           1924

ARCHIBALD MACLEISH
You, Andrew Marvell

And here face down beneath the sun
And here upon earth's noonward height
To feel the always coming on
The always rising of the night

To feel creep up the curving east
The earthy chill of dusk and slow
Upon those under lands the vast
And ever climbing shadow grow

And strange at Ecbatan the trees
Take leaf by leaf the evening strange
The flooding dark about their knees
The mountains over Persia change

And now at Kermanshah the gate
Dark empty and the withered grass
And through the twilight now the late
Few travelers in the westward pass

And Baghdad darken and the bridge
Across the silent river gone
And through Arabia the edge
Of evening widen and steal on

And deepen on Palmyra's street
The wheel rut in the ruined stone
And Lebanon fade out and Crete
High through the clouds and overblown

And over Sicily the air
Still flashing with the landward gulls
And loom and slowly disappear
The sails above the shadowy hulls

And Spain go under and the shore
Of Africa the gilded sand
And evening vanish and no more
The low pale light across that land

Nor now the long light on the sea

And here face downward in the sun
To feel how swift how secretly
The shadow of the night comes on . . .

1930

HENRY WADSWORTH LONGFELLOW

The Tide Rises, the Tide Falls

The tide rises, the tide falls,
The twilight darkens, the curlew calls;
Along the sea-sands damp and brown
The traveller hastens toward the town,
    And the tide rises, the tide falls.

Darkness settles on roofs and walls,
But the sea, the sea in darkness calls;
The little waves, with their soft, white
    hands,
Efface the footprints in the sands,
    And the tide rises, the tide falls.

The morning breaks; the steeds in their
    stalls
Stamp and neigh, as the hostler calls;
The day returns, but nevermore
Returns the traveller to the shore,
    And the tide rises, the tide falls.

1880

THOMAS HARDY

In a Wood

Pale beech and pine so blue,
    Set in one clay,
Bough to bough cannot you
    Live out your day?
When the rains skim and skip,
Why mar sweet comradeship,
Blighting with poison-drip
    Neighborly spray?

Heart-halt and spirit-lame,
    City-opprest,
Unto this wood I came
    As to a nest;
Dreaming that sylvan peace
Offered the harrowed ease—
Nature a soft release
    From men's unrest.

But, having entered in,
    Great growths and small
Show them to men akin—
    Combatants all!
Sycamore shoulders oak,
Bines the slim sapling yoke,
Ivy-spun halters choke
    Elms stout and tall.

Touches from ash, O wych,
    Sting you like scorn!
You, too, brave hollies, twitch
    Sidelong from thorn.
Even the rank poplars bear
Lothly a rival's air,
Cankering in black despair
    If overborne.

Since, then, no grace I find
    Taught me of trees,
Turn I back to my kind,
    Worthy as these.
There at least smiles abound,
There discourse trills around,
There, now and then, are found
    Life-loyalties.

1887

MATTHEW ARNOLD

In Harmony with Nature

To a Preacher

"In Harmony with Nature?" Restless
    fool,
Who with such heat dost preach what were
    to thee,
When true, the last impossibility—
To be like Nature strong, like Nature cool!
Know, man hath all which Nature hath,
    but more,
And in that *more* lie all his hopes of good.
Nature is cruel, man is sick of blood;
Nature is stubborn, man would fain adore;
Nature is fickle, man hath need of rest;
Nature forgives no debt, and fears no
    grave;
Man would be mild, and with safe con-
    science blest.
Man must begin, know this, where Nature
    ends;
Nature and man can never be fast friends.
Fool, if thou canst not pass her, rest her
    slave!

                   1849

ALFRED, LORD TENNYSON

Are God and Nature Then at Strife?

From In Memoriam

LIV.

O, yet we trust that somehow good
Will be the final goal of ill,
To pangs of nature, sins of will,
Defects of doubt, and taints of blood;

That nothing walks with aimless feet;
That not one life shall be destroyed,
Or cast as rubbish to the void,
When God hath made the pile complete;

That not a worm is cloven in vain;
That not a moth with vain desire
Is shriveled in a fruitless fire,
Or but subserves another's gain.

Behold, we know not anything;
I can but trust that good shall fall
At last—far off—at last, to all,
And every winter change to spring.

So runs my dream; but what am I?
An infant crying in the night;
An infant crying for the light,
And with no language but a cry.

LV.

The wish, that of the living whole
No life may fail beyond the grave,
Derives it not from what we have
The likest God within the soul?

Are God and Nature then at strife,
That Nature lends such evil dreams?
So careful of the type she seems,
So careless of the single life,

That I, considering everywhere
Her secret meaning in her deeds,
And finding that of fifty seeds
She often brings but one to bear,

I falter where I firmly trod,
And falling with my weight of cares
Upon the great world's altar-stairs
That slope through darkness up to God,

I stretch lame hands of faith, and grope,
And gather dust and chaff, and call
To what I feel is Lord of all,
And faintly trust the larger hope.

LVI.

"So careful of the type?" but no.
From scarpèd cliff and quarried stone
She cries, "A thousand types are gone;
I care for nothing, all shall go.

"Thou makest thine appeal to me:
I bring to life, I bring to death;
The spirit does but mean the breath:
I know no more." And he, shall he,

Man, her last work, who seemed so fair,
Such splendid purpose in his eyes,
Who rolled the psalm to wintry skies,
Who built him fanes of fruitless prayer,

Who trusted God was love indeed
And love Creation's final law—
Though Nature, red in tooth and claw
With ravine, shrieked against his creed—

Who loved, who suffered countless ills,
Who battled for the True, the Just,
Be blown about the desert dust,
Or sealed within the iron hills?

No more? A monster then, a dream,
A discord. Dragons of the prime,
That tare each other in their slime,
Were mellow music matched with him.

O life as futile, then, as frail!
O for thy voice to soothe and bless!
What hope of answer, or redress?
Behind the veil, behind the veil.

LVII.

Peace; come away: the song of woe
Is after all an earthly song.
Peace; come away: we do him wrong
To sing so wildly: let us go.

Come; let us go: your cheeks are pale;
But half my life I leave behind.
Methinks my friend is richly shrined;
But I shall pass, my work will fail.

Yet in these ears, till hearing dies,
One set slow bell will seem to toll
The passing of the sweetest soul
That ever looked with human eyes.

I hear it now, and o'er and o'er,
Eternal greetings to the dead;

And "Ave, Ave, Ave," said,
"Adieu, adieu," for evermore.

1850

The Higher Pantheism

The sun, the moon, the stars, the seas, the
hills and the plains,—
Are not these, O Soul, the Vision of Him
who reigns?

Is not the Vision He, though He be not
that which He seems?
Dreams are true while they last, and do we
not live in dreams?

Earth, these solid stars, this weight of body
and limb,
Are they not sign and symbol of thy division from Him?

Dark is the world to thee; thyself art the
reason why,
For is He not all but thou, that hast power
to feel "I am I"?

Glory about thee, without thee; and thou
fulfillest thy doom,
Making Him broken gleams and a stifled
splendor and gloom.

Speak to Him, thou, for He hears, and
Spirit with Spirit can meet—
Closer is He than breathing, and nearer
than hands and feet.

God is law, say the wise; O Soul, and let us
rejoice,
For if He thunder by law the thunder is yet
His voice.

Law is God, say some; no God at all, says
the fool,
For all we have power to see is a straight
staff bent in a pool;

And the ear of man cannot hear, and the
eye of man cannot see;

But if we could see and hear, this Vision—
    were it not He?

             1869

ALGERNON CHARLES SWINBURNE

The Higher Pantheism in a Nutshell

One, who is not, we see; but one, whom
    we see not, is.
Surely this is not that; but that is assuredly
    this.

What, and wherefore, and whence? for
    under is over and under;
If thunder could be without lightning,
    lightning could be without thunder.

Doubt is faith, in the main; but faith, on
    the whole, is doubt.
We cannot believe by proof; but could we
    believe without?

Why, and whither, and how? for barley
    and rye are not clover;
Neither are straight lines curves—yet over
    is under and over.

Two and two may be four, but four and
    four are not eight;
Fate and God may be twain, but God is
    the same thing as fate.

Ask a man what he thinks, and get from
    a man what he feels;
God, once caught in the fact, shows you
    a fair pair of heels.

Body and spirit are twins; God only knows
    which is which—
The soul squats down in the flesh, like a
    tinker drunk in a ditch.

More is the whole than a part, but half is
    more than the whole;

Clearly, the soul is the body—but is not the
    body the soul?

One and two are not one, but one and noth-
    ing is two;
Truth can hardly be false, if falsehood can-
    not be true.

Once the mastodon was; pterodactyls were
    common as cocks.
Then the mammoth was God; now is He a
    prize ox.

Parallels all things are—yet many of these
    are askew;
You are certainly I, but certainly I am not
    you.

Springs the rock from the plain, shoots the
    stream from the rock;
Cocks exist for the hen, but hens exist for
    the cock.

God, whom we see not, is; and God, who
    is not, we see.
Fiddle, we know, is diddle; and diddle, we
    take it, is dee.

             1880

GEORGE MEREDITH

Meditation Under Stars

What links are ours with orbs that are
    So resolutely far?—
The solitary asks, and they
Give radiance as from a shield:
    Still at the death of day,
    The seen, the unrevealed.
    Implacable they shine
To us who would of Life obtain
An answer for the life we strain,
    To nourish with one sign.
Nor can imagination throw
The penetrative shaft: we pass
The breath of thought, who would divine
    If haply they may grow

As Earth; have our desire to know;
If life comes there to grain from grass,
And flowers like ours of toil and pain;
  Has passion to beat bar,
  Win space from cleaving brain;
  The mystic link attain,
Whereby star holds on star.

Those visible immortals beam
  Allurement to the dream:
Ireful at human hungers brook
  No question in the look.
  Forever virgin to our sense,
  Remote they wane to gaze intense:
Prolong it, and in ruthlessness they smite
The beating heart behind the ball of sight:
  Till we conceive their heavens hoar,
  Those lights they raise but sparkles frore,
And Earth, our blood-warm Earth, a shud-
    dering prey
To that frigidity of brainless ray.
Yet space is given for breath of thought
Beyond our bounds when musing: more
When to that musing love is brought,
And love is asked of love's wherefore.
'Tis Earth's, her gift; else have we naught:
Her gift, her secret, here our tie.
And not with her and yonder sky?
Bethink you: were it Earth alone
Breeds love, would not her region be
  The sole delight and throne
  Of generous Deity?

  To deeper than this ball of sight
Appeal the lustrous people of the night.
Fronting yon shoreless, sown with fiery
    sails,
  It is our ravenous that quails,
Flesh by its craven thirsts and fears dis-
    traught.
  The spirit leaps alight,
  Doubts not in them is he,
The binder of his sheaves, the same, the
    right:
Of magnitude to magnitude is wrought,
To feel it large of the great life they hold:
In them to come, or vaster intervolved,
The issues known in us, our unsolved
    solved:

That there with toil Life climbs the self-
    same Tree,
Whose roots enrichment have from ripe-
    ness dropped.

So may we read and little find them cold:
Let it but be the lord of Mind to guide
Our eyes; no branch of Reason's growing
    lopped;
Nor dreaming on a dream; but fortified
By day to penetrate black midnight; see,
Hear, feel, outside the senses; even that we,
The specks of dust upon a mound of mold,
We who reflect those rays, though low our
    place,
  To them are lastingly allied.

So may we read, and little find them cold:
Not frosty lamps illuming dead space,
Not distant aliens, not senseless Powers.
The fire is in them whereof we are born;
The music of their motion may be ours.
Spirit shall deem them beckoning Earth
    and voiced
Sisterly to her, in her beams rejoiced.
Of love, the grand impulsion, we behold
  The love that lends her grace
  Among the starry fold.
Then at new flood of customary morn,
  Look at her through her showers,
  Her mists, her streaming gold,
A wonder edges the familiar face:
She wears no more that robe of printed
    hours;
Half strange seems Earth, and sweeter than
    her flowers.

                                    1888

JAMES RUSSELL LOWELL
Credidimus Jovem Regnare

O days endeared to every Muse,
When nobody had any Views,
Nor, while the cloudscape of his mind
By every breeze was new designed,
Insisted all the world should see

Camels or whales where none there be!
O happy days, when men received
From sire to son what all believed,
And left the other world in bliss,
Too busy with bedevilling this!

Beset by doubts of every breed
In the last bastion of my creed,
With shot and shell for Sabbath-chime,
I watch the storming-party climb,
Panting (their prey in easy reach),
To pour triumphant through the breach
In walls that shed like snowflakes tons
Of missiles from old-fashioned guns,
But crumble 'neath the storm that pours
All day and night from bigger bores.
There, as I hopeless watch and wait
The last life-crushing coil of Fate,
Despair finds solace in the praise
Of those serene dawn-rosy days
Ere microscopes had made us heirs
To large estates of doubts and snares,
By proving that the title-deeds,
Once all-sufficient for men's needs,
Are palimpsests that scarce disguise
The tracings of still earlier lies,
Themselves as surely written o'er
An older fib erased before.

So from these days I fly to those
That in the landlocked Past repose,
Where no rude wind of doctrine shakes
From bloom-flushed boughs untimely
    flakes;
Where morning's eyes see nothing strange,
No crude perplexity of change,
And morrows trip along their ways
Secure as happy yesterdays.
Then there were rulers who could trace
Through heroes up to gods their race,
Pledged to fair fame and noble use
By veins from Odin filled or Zeus,
And under bonds to keep divine
The praise of a celestial line.
Then priests could pile the altar's sods,
With whom gods spake as they with gods,
And everywhere from haunted earth
Broke springs of wonder, that had birth
In depths divine beyond the ken
And fatal scrutiny of men;

Then hills and groves and streams and seas
Thrilled with immortal presences,
Not too ethereal for the scope
Of human passion's dream or hope.

Now Pan at last is surely dead,
And King No-Credit reigns instead,
Whose officers, morosely strict,
Poor Fancy's tenantry evict,
Chase the last Genius from the door,
And nothing dances any more.
Nothing?   Ah, yes, our tables do,
Drumming the Old One's own tattoo,
And, if the oracles are dumb,
Have we not mediums?   Why be glum?

Fly thither?   Why, the very air
Is full of hindrance and despair!
Fly thither?   But I cannot fly;
My doubts enmesh me if I try,—
Each lilliputian, but, combined,
Potent a giant's limbs to bind.
This world and that are growing dark;
A huge interrogation mark,
The Devil's crook episcopal,
Still borne before him since the Fall,
Blackens with its ill-omened sign
The old blue heaven of faith benign.
Whence?   Whither?   Wherefore?   How?
    Which?   Why?
All ask at once, all wait reply.
Men feel old systems cracking under 'em;
Life saddens to a mere conundrum
Which once Religion solved, but she
Has lost—has Science found?—the key.

What was snow-bearded Odin, trow,
The mighty hunter long ago,
Whose horn and hounds the peasant hears
Still when the Northlights shake their
    spears?
Science hath answers twain, I 've heard;
Choose which you will, nor hope a third;
Whichever box the truth be stowed in,
There's not a sliver left of Odin.
Either he was a pinchbrowed thing,
With scarcely wit a stone to fling,
A creature both in size and shape
Nearer than we are to the ape,
Who hung sublime with brat and spouse

By tail prehensile from the boughs,
And, happier than his maimed descend-
        ants,
The culture-curtailed *in*dependents,
Could pluck his cherries with both paws,
And stuff with both his big-boned jaws;
Or else the core his name enveloped
Was from a solar myth developed,
Which, hunted to its primal shoot,
Takes refuge in a Sanskrit root,
Thereby to instant death explaining
The little poetry remaining.
Try it with Zeus, 'tis just the same;
The thing evades, we hug a name;
Nay, scarcely that,—perhaps a vapor
Born of some atmospheric caper.
All Lempriere's fables blur together
In cloudy symbols of the weather,
And Aphrodite rose from frothy seas
But to illustrate such hypotheses.
With years enough behind his back,
Lincoln will take the selfsame track,
And prove, hulled fairly to the cob,
A mere vagary of Old Prob.
Give the right man a solar myth,
And he'll confute the sun therewith.

They make things admirably plain,
But one hard question *will* remain:
If one hypothesis you lose,
Another in its place you choose,
But, your faith gone, O man and brother,
Whose shop shall furnish you another?
One that will wash, I mean, and wear,
And wrap us warmly from despair?
While they are clearing up our puzzles,
And clapping prophylactic muzzles
On the Actæon's hounds that sniff
Our devious track through But and If,
Would they'd explain away the Devil
And other facts that won't keep level,
But rise beneath our feet or fail,
A reeling ship's deck in a gale!
God vanished long ago, iwis,
A mere subjective synthesis;
A doll, stuffed out with hopes and fears,
Too homely for us pretty dears,
Who want one that conviction carries,
Last make of London or of Paris.
He gone, I felt a moment's spasm,

But calmed myself with Protoplasm,
A finer name, and, what is more,
As enigmatic as before;
Greek, too, and sure to fill with ease
Minds caught in the Symplègades
Of soul and sense, life's two conditions,
Each baffled with its own omniscience.
The men who labor to revise
Our Bibles will, I hope, be wise,
And print it without foolish qualms
Instead of God in David's psalms:
Noll had been more effective far
Could he have shouted at Dunbar,
"Rise, Protoplasm!" No dourest Scot
Had waited for another shot.

And yet I frankly must confess
A secret unforgivingness,
And shudder at the saving chrism
Whose best New Birth is Pessimism;
My soul—I mean the bit of phosphorus,
That fills the place of what that was for
        us—
Can't bid its inward bores defiance
With the new nursery-tales of science.
What profits me, though doubt by doubt,
As nail by nail, be driven out,
When every new one, like the last,
Still holds my coffin-lid as fast?
Would I find thought a moment's truce,
Give me the young world's Mother Goose
With life and joy in every limb,
The chimney-corner tales of Grimm!

Our dear and admirable Huxley
Cannot explain to me why ducks lay,
Or, rather, how into their eggs
Blunder potential wings and legs
With will to move them and decide
Whether in air or lymph to glide.
Who gets a hair's-breadth on by showing
That Something Else set all agoing?
Farther and farther back we push
From Moses and his burning bush;
Cry, "Art Thou there?" Above, below,
All Nature mutters *yes* and *no!*
'Tis the old answer: we're agreed
Being from Being must proceed,
Life be Life's source. I might as well
Obey the meeting-house's bell,

And listen while Old Hundred pours
Forth through the summer-opened doors,
From old and young.   I hear it yet,
Swelled by bass-viol and clarinet,
While the gray minister, with face
Radiant, let loose his noble bass.
If Heaven it reached not, yet its roll
Waked all the echoes of the soul,
And in it many a life found wings
To soar away from sordid things.
Church gone and singers too, the song
Sings to me voiceless all night long,
Till my soul beckons me afar,
Glowing and trembling like a star.
Will any scientific touch
With my worn strings achieve as much?

I don't object, not I, to know
My sires were monkeys, if 'twas so;
I touch my ear's collusive tip
And own the poor-relationship.
That apes of various shapes and sizes
Contained their germs that all the prizes
Of senate, pulpit, camp, and bar win
May give us hopes that sweeten Darwin.
Who knows but from our loins may spring
(Long hence) some winged sweet-throated
        thing
As much superior to us
As we to Cynocephalus?

This is consoling, but, alas,
It wipes no dimness from the glass
Where I am flattening my poor nose,
In hope to see beyond my toes.
Though I accept my pedigree,
Yet where, pray tell me, is the key
That should unlock a private door
To the Great Mystery, such no more?
Each offers his, but one nor all
Are much persuasive with the wall
That rises now, as long ago,
Between I wonder and I know,
Nor will vouchsafe a pin-hole peep
At the veiled Isis in its keep.
Where is no door, I but produce
My key to find it of no use.
Yet better keep it, after all,
Since Nature's economical,
And who can tell but some fine day

(If it occur to her) she may,
In her good-will to you and me,
Make door and lock to match the key?
                              1887

ALFRED EDWARD HOUSMAN
In My Own Shire

In my own shire, if I was sad,
Homely comforters I had:
The earth, because my heart was sore,
Sorrowed for the son she bore;
And standing hills, long to remain,
Shared their short-lived comrade's pain.
And bound for the same bourn as I,
On every road I wandered by,
Trod beside me, close and dear,
The beautiful and death-struck year:
Whether in the woodland brown
I heard the beechnut rustle down,
And saw the purple crocus pale
Flower about the autumn dale;
Or littering far the fields of May
Lady-smocks a-bleaching lay,
And like a skylit water stood
The bluebells in the azured wood.

Yonder, lightening other loads,
The seasons range the country roads,
But here in London streets I ken
No such helpmates, only men;
And these are not in plight to bear,
If they would, another's care.
They have enough as 'tis: I see
In many an eye that measures me
The mortal sickness of a mind
Too unhappy to be kind.
Undone with misery, all they can
Is to hate their fellow man;
And till they drop they needs must still
Look at you and wish you ill.
                              1896

ARTHUR HUGH CLOUGH

In the Great Metropolis

Each for himself is still the rule;
We learn it when we go to school—
   The devil take the hindmost, O!

And when the schoolboys grow to men,
In life they learn it o'er again—
   The devil take the hindmost, O!

For in the church and at the bar,
On 'Change, at court, wher'er they are,
   The devil take the hindmost, O!

Husband for husband, wife for wife,
And careful that in married life
   The devil takes the hindmost, O!

From youth to age, what'er the game,
The unvarying practice is the same—
   The devil takes the hindmost, O!

And after death, we do not know,
But scarce can doubt, wher'er we go,
   The devil takes the hindmost, O!

Ti rol de rol, ti rol de ro,
The devil takes the hindmost, O!

                                    1862

WALT WHITMAN

Give Me the Splendid Silent Sun

1

Give me the splendid silent sun with his
   beams full-dazzling,
Give me juicy autumnal fruit ripe and red
   from the orchard,
Give me a field where the unmow'd grass
   grows,
Give me an arbor, give me the trellis'd
   grape,

Give me fresh corn and wheat, give me
   serene-moving animals teaching content,
Give me nights perfectly quiet as on high
   plateaus west of the Mississippi, and
   I looking up at the stars,
Give me odorous at sunrise a garden of
   beautiful flowers where I can walk
   undisturb'd,
Give me for marriage a sweet-breath'd
   woman of whom I should never tire,
Give me a perfect child, give me away aside
   from the noise of the world a rural
   domestic life,
Give me to warble spontaneous songs recluse by myself, for my own ears
   only,
Give me solitude, give me Nature, give me
   again O Nature your primal sanities!

These demanding to have them, (tired
   with ceaseless excitement, and rack'd
   by the war-strife,)
These to procure incessantly asking, rising
   in cries from my heart,
While yet incessantly asking still I adhere
   to my city,
Day upon day and year upon year O city,
   walking your streets,
Where you hold me enchain'd a certain
   time refusing to give me up,
Yet giving to make me glutted, enrich'd of
   soul, you give me forever faces;
(O I see what I sought to escape, confronting, reversing my cries,
I see my own soul trampling down what it
   ask'd for.)

2

Keep your splendid silent sun,
Keep your woods O Nature, and the quiet
   places by the woods,
Keep your fields of clover and timothy,
   and your corn-fields and orchards,
Keep the blossoming buckwheat fields
   where the Ninth-month bees hum;
Give me faces and streets—give me these
   phantoms incessant and endless along
   the trottoirs!
Give me interminable eyes—give me

women—give me comrades and lovers by the thousand!

Let me see new ones every day—let me hold new ones by the hand every day!

Give me such shows—give me the streets of Manhattan!

Give me Broadway, with the soldiers marching—give me the sound of the trumpets and drums!

(The soldiers in companies or regiments— some starting away, flush'd and reck- less,

Some, their time up, returning with thinn'd ranks, young, yet very old, worn, marching, noticing nothing;)

Give me the shores and wharves heavy- fringed with black ships!

O such for me! O an intense life, full to repletion and varied!

The life of the theater, bar-room, huge hotel, for me!

The saloon of the steamer! the crowded excursion for me! the torchlight pro- cession!

The dense brigade bound for the war, with high piled military wagons follow- ing;

People, endless, streaming, with strong voices, passions, pageants,

Manhattan streets with their powerful throbs, with beating drums as now,

The endless and noisy chorus, the rustle and clank of muskets, (even the sight of the wounded),

Manhattan crowds, with their turbulent musical chorus!

Manhattan faces and eyes forever for me.
                                        1865

CARL SANDBURG
Four Preludes on Playthings of the Wind

'The past is a bucket of ashes.'

I

The woman named To-morrow
sits with a hairpin in her teeth
and takes her time
and does her hair the way she wants it
and fastens at last the last braid and coil
and puts the hairpin where it belongs
and turns and drawls: Well, what of it?
My grandmother, Yesterday, is gone.
What of it?   Let the dead be dead.

II

The doors were cedar
and the panels strips of gold
and the girls were golden girls
and the panels read and the girls chanted:
    We are the greatest city,
    the greatest nation:
    nothing like us ever was.
The doors are twisted on broken hinges.
Sheets of rain swish through on the wind
    where the golden girls ran and the panels
    read:
    We are the greatest city,
    the greatest nation:
    nothing like us ever was.

III

It has happened before.
Strong men put up a city and got a nation
    together,
And paid singers to sing and women to
    warble: We are the greatest city,
    the greatest nation:
    nothing like us ever was.

And while the singers sang
and the strong men listened
and paid the singers well
and felt good about it all,

From *Smoke and Steel* by Carl Sandburg, copyright, 1920, by Harcourt, Brace and Company, Inc. Reprinted by permission.

there were rats and lizards who listened
. . . and the only listeners left now
. . . are . . . the rats . . . and the lizards.

And there are black crows
crying, 'Caw, caw,'
bringing mud and sticks
building a nest
over the words carved
on the doors where the panels were cedar
and the strips on the panels were gold
and the golden girls came singing:
   We are the greatest city,
   the greatest nation:
   nothing like us ever was.

The only singers now are crows crying,
   'Caw, caw,'
And the sheets of rain whine in the wind
   and doorways.
And the only listeners now are . . . the
   rats . . . and the lizards.

                    IV
The feet of the rats
scribble on the door sills;
the hieroglyphs of the rat footprints
chatter the pedigrees of the rats
and babble of the blood
and gabble of the breed
of the grandfathers and the great-grandfathers
of the rats

And the wind shifts
and the dust on a door sill shifts
and even the writing of the rat footprints
tells us nothing, nothing at all
about the greatest city, the greatest nation
where the strong men listened
and the women warbled: Nothing like us
   ever was.
                                1920

WYSTAN HUGH AUDEN

Sharp and Silent in the Clear October Lighting[1]

Sharp and silent in the
Clear October lighting
Of a Sunday morning
   The great city lies;
And I at a window
Looking over water
At the world of Business
   With a lover's eyes.

All mankind, I fancy,
When anticipating
Anything exciting
   Like a rendez-vous,
Occupy the time in
Purely random thinking,
For when love is waiting
   Logic will not do.

Much as he would like to
Concentrate completely
On the precious Object,
   Love has not the power:
Goethe put it neatly;
No one cares to watch the
Loveliest sunset after
   Quarter of an hour.

So I pass the time, dear,
Till I see you, writing
Down whatever nonsense
   Comes into my head;
Let the life that has been
Lightly buried in my
Personal Unconscious
   Rise up from the dead.

Why association
Should see fit to set a
Bull-dog by a trombone
   On a grassy plain
Littered with old letters,
Leaves me simply guessing,

I suppose it's La Con-
-dition Humaine.

As at lantern lectures
Image follows image;
Here comes a steam-roller
  Through an orange grove,
Driven by a nursemaid
As she sadly mutters:
"Zola, poor old Zola
  Murdered by a stove."

Now I hear Saint Francis
Telling me in breezy
Tones as we are walking
  Near a power-house:
"Loving birds is easy,
Any fool can do it,
But I must admit it's
  Hard to love the louse."

Malinowski, Rivers,
Benedict and others
Show how common culture
  Shapes the separate lives:
Matrilineal races
Kill their mothers' brothers
In their dreams and turn their
  Sisters into wives.

As an intellectual
Member of the Middle
Classes or what-have-you
  So I have to dream:
Essence without Form is
Free but ineffectual,
Birth and education
  Guide the living stream.

Who when looking over
Faces in the subway,
Each with its uniqueness,
  Would not, did he dare,
Ask what forms exactly
Suited to their weakness
Love and desperation
  Take to govern there.

Would not like to know what
Influence occupation

Has on human vision
  Of the human fate:
Do all clerks for instance
Pigeon-hole creation,
Brokers see the Ding-an-
  -sich as Real Estate?

When a politician
Dreams about his sweetheart,
Does he multiply her
  Face into a crowd,
Are her fond responses
All-or-none reactions,
Does he try to buy her,
  Is the kissing loud?

Strange are love's mutations:
Thus, the early poem
Of the flesh sub rosa
  Has been known to grow
Now and then into the
Amor intellectu-
-alis of Spinoza;
  How we do not know.

Slowly we are learning,
We at least know this much,
That we have to unlearn
  Much that we were taught,
And are growing chary
Of emphatic dogmas;
Love like Matter is much
  Odder than we thought.

Love requires an Object,
But this varies so much,
Almost, I imagine,
  Anything will do:
When I was a child, I
Loved a pumping-engine,
Thought it every bit as
  Beautiful as you.

Love has no position,
Love's a way of living,
One kind of relation
  Possible between
Any things or persons
Given one condition,
The one sine qua non
  Being mutual need.

Through it we discover
An essential secret
Called by some Salvation
  And by some Success;
Crying for the moon is
Naughtiness and envy,
We can only love what-
  -ever we possess.

I believed for years that
Love was the conjunction
Of two oppositions;
  That was all untrue;
Every young man fears that
He is not worth loving:
Bless you, darling, I have
  Found myself in you.

I should love to go on
Telling how I love you,
Thanking you for happy
  Changes in my life,
But it would be silly
Seeing that you know it
And that any moment
  Now you may arrive.

When two lovers meet, then
There's an end of writing
Thought and Analytics:
  Lovers, like the dead,
In their loves are equal;
Sophomores and peasants,
Poets and their critics
  Are the same in bed.

1940

JOHN MILTON

When the Assault Was Intended for the City

Captain or Colonel, or Knight in Arms,
Whose chance on these defenseless doors
  may seize,
If deed of honor did thee ever please,

Guard them, and him within protect from
  harms:
He can requite thee, for he knows the
  charms
That call fame on such gentle acts as these;
And he can spread thy name o'er lands and
  seas,
Whatever clime the sun's bright circle
  warms.
Lift not thy spear against the Muses'
  bower:
The great Emathian conqueror bid spare
The house of Pindarus, when temple and
  tower
Went to the ground; and the repeated air
Of sad Electra's poet had the power
To save the Athenian walls from ruin bare.

1645

STEPHEN SPENDER

Thoughts During an Air Raid[1]

Of course, the entire effort is to put myself
Outside the ordinary range
Of what are called statistics. A hundred
  are killed
In the outer suburbs. Well, well, I carry
  on.
So long as the great 'I' is propped upon
This girdered bed which seems more like
  a hearse,
In the hotel bedroom with flowering wall-
  paper
Which rings in wreathes above, I can ig-
  nore
The pressure of those names under my
  fingers
Heavy and black as I rustle the paper,
The wireless wail in the lounge margin.
Yet supposing that a bomb should dive
Its nose right through this bed, with me
  upon it?
The thought is obscene. Still, there are
  many

[1] From *Ruins and Visions,* published by Random House, Inc., 1942. Reprinted by permission of Random House, Inc.

To whom my death would only be a name,
One figure in a column. The essential is
That all the 'I's should remain separate
Propped up under flowers, and no one
  suffer
For his neighbour. Then horror is post-
  poned
For everyone until it settles on him
And drags him to that incommunicable
  grief
Which is all mystery or nothing.

1942

HENRY NEWBOLT
Drake's Drum

Drake he's in his hammock an' a thousand
  mile away,
  (Capten, art tha sleepin' there below?)
Slung atween the round shot in Nombre
  Dios Bay,
  An' dreamin' arl the time o' Plymouth
  Hoe.
Yarnder lumes the island, yarnder lie the
  ships,
  Wi' sailor lads a-dancin' heel-an'-toe,
An' the shore-lights flashin', an' the night-
  tide dashin'
  He sees et arl so plainly as he saw et long
  ago.

Drake he was a Devon man, an' ruled the
  Devon seas,
  (Capten, art tha sleepin' there below?),
Rovin' tho' his death fell, he went wi' heart
  at ease,
  An' dreamin' arl the time o' Plymouth
  Hoe,
"Take my drum to England, hang et by
  the shore,
  Strike et when your powder's runnin'
  low;

If the Dons sight Devon, I'll quit the port
  o' Heaven,
  An' drum them up the Channel as we
  drummed them long ago."

Drake he's in his hammock till the great
  Armadas come,
  (Capten, art tha sleepin' there below?),
Slung atween the round shot, listenin' for
  the drum,
  An' dreamin' arl the time o' Plymouth
  Hoe.
Call him on the deep sea, call him up the
  Sound,
  Call him when ye sail to meet the foe;
Where the old trade's plyin' an' the old
  flag's flyin',
  They shal find him, ware an' wakin', as
  they found him long ago.

1897

RUPERT BROOKE
The Soldier

If I should die, think only this of me:
That there's some corner of a foreign field
That is for ever England. There shall be
In that rich earth a richer dust concealed;
A dust whom England bore, shaped, made
  aware,
Gave, once, her flowers to love, her ways
  to roam,
A body of England's, breathing English
  air,
Washed by the rivers, blest by suns of
  home.

And think, this heart, all evil shed away,
A pulse in the eternal mind, no less
Gives somewhere back the thoughts by
  England given;

Her sights and sounds; dreams happy as
    her day;
And laughter, learnt of friends; and gentle-
    ness,
In hearts at peace, under an English
    heaven.

                                            1915

ARCHIBALD MACLEISH

Lines for an Interment

Now it is fifteen years you have lain in the
    meadow:
The boards at your face have gone through:
    the earth is
Packed down and the sound of the rain is
    fainter:
The roots of the first grass are dead:

It's a long time to lie in the earth with your
    honor:
The world Soldier the world has been mov-
    ing on:

The girls wouldn't look at you twice in the
    cloth cap:
Six years old they were when it happened:

It bores them even in books: 'Soissons be-
    sieged!'
As for the gents they have joined the
    American Legion:

Belts and a brass band and the ladies'
    auxiliaries:
The Californians march in the OD silk:

We are all acting again like civilized be-
    ings:
People mention it at tea . . .

The Facts of Life we have learned are
    Economic:
You were deceived by the detonations of
    bombs:

You thought of courage and death when
    you thought of warfare:
Hadn't they taught you the fine words
    were unfortunate?

Now that we understand we judge without
    bias:
We feel of course for those who had to die:

Women have written us novels of great
    passion
Proving the useless death of the dead was
    a tragedy:

Nevertheless it is foolish to chew gall:
The foremost writers on both sides have
    apologized:

The Germans are back in the Midi with
    cropped hair:
The English are drinking the better beer
    in Bavaria:

You can rest now in the rain in the Belgian
    meadow—
Now that it's all explained away and for-
    gotten:
Now that the earth is hard and the wood
    rots:

Now you are dead . . .

                                            1933

ARTHUR HUGH CLOUGH

Say Not the Struggle Naught Availeth

Say not the struggle naught availeth,
    The labor and the wounds are vain,
The enemy faints not, nor faileth,
    And as things have been they remain.

If hopes were dupes, fears may be liars;
    It may be, in yon smoke concealed,
Your comrades chase e'en now the fliers,
    And, but for you, possess the field.

The selection from Archibald MacLeish, *Poems,* is used by permission of the publishers, Houghton
Mifflin Company.

For while the tired waves, vainly breaking,
  Seem here no painful inch to gain,
Far back, through creeks and inlets mak-
  ing,
Comes silent, flooding in, the main.

And not by eastern windows only,
  When daylight comes, comes in the
    light,
In front, the sun climbs slow, how slowly,
  But westward, look, the land is bright.
                        1862

STEPHEN SPENDER

Ultima Ratio Regum[1]

The guns spell money's ultimate reason
In letters of lead on the spring hillside.
But the boy lying dead under the olive
  trees
Was too young and too silly
To have been notable to their important
  eye.
He was a better target for a kiss.

When he lived, tall factory hooters never
  summoned him.
Nor did restaurant plate-glass doors revolve
  to wave him in.
His name never appeared in the papers.
The world maintained its traditional wall
Round the dead with their gold sunk deep
  as a well,
Whilst his life, intangible as a Stock Ex-
  change rumour, drifted outside.

O too lightly he threw down his cap
One day when the breeze threw petals
  from the trees.
The unflowering wall sprouted with guns,
Machine-gun anger quickly scythed the
  grasses;

Flags and leaves fell from hands and
  branches;
The tweed cap rotted in the nettles.

Consider his life which was valueless
In terms of employment, hotel ledgers,
  news files.
Consider. One bullet in ten thousand kills
  a man.
Ask. Was so much expenditure justified
On the death of one so young and so silly
Lying under the olive trees, O world, O
  death?
                        1942

WILFRID GIBSON

The Conscript[2]

Indifferent, flippant, earnest, but all bored,
The doctors sit in the glare of electric light
Watching the endless stream of naked
  white
Bodies of men for whom their hasty award
Means life or death maybe of the living
  death
Of mangled limbs, blind eyes or a dark-
  ened brain:
And the chairman as his monocle falls
  again
Pronounces each doom with easy indiffer-
  ent breath.
Then suddenly I shudder as I see
A young man move before them wearily,
Cadaverous as one already dead:
But still they stare untroubled as he stands
With arms outstretched and drooping
  thorn-crowned head,
The nail-marks glowing in his feet and
  hands.
                        1920

[1] From *Ruins and Visions*, published by Random House, Inc., 1942. Reprinted by permission of Random House, Inc.

[2] From Wilfrid Gibson, *Neighbors*. By permission of The Macmillan Company, publishers.

SIEGFRIED SASSOON

At the Cenotaph[1]

I saw the Prince of Darkness, with his
    Staff,
Standing bare-headed by the Cenotaph:
Unostentatious and respectful, there
He stood, and offered up the following
    prayer:
"Make them to forget, O Lord, what this
    Memorial
    Means; their discredited ideas revive;
Breed new belief that War is purgatorial
    Proof of the pride and power of being
    alive;
Men's biologic urge to readjust
    The map of Europe, Lord of Hosts,
    increase;
Lift up their hearts in large destructive
    lust;
    And crown their heads with blind vin-
    dictive Peace."
The Prince of Darkness to the Cenotaph
Bowed. As he walked away I heard him
    laugh.

                                   1933

On Reading the War Diary of a Defunct Ambassador[2]

So that's your Diary—that's your private
    mind
Translated into shirt-sleeved History.
    That
Is what diplomacy has left behind
For after-ages to peruse, and find
What passed beneath your elegant silk-hat.

You were a fine old gentleman; compact
Of shrewdness, charm, refinement and
    finesse.
Impeccable in breeding, taste and dress,

No diplomatic quality you lacked—
No tittle of ambassadorial tact.

I can imagine you among "the guns,"
Urbanely peppering partridge, grouse, or
    pheasant—
Guest of those infinitely privileged ones
Whose lives are padded, petrified, and
    pleasant.
I visualise you feeding off gold plate
And gossiping on grave affairs of State.

Now you're defunct; your gossip's gravely
    printed;
The world discovers where you lunched
    and dined
On such and such a day; and what was
    hinted
By ministers and generals far behind
The all-important conflict, carnage-tinted.

The world can read the rumours that you
    gleaned
From various Fronts; the well-known
    Names you met;
Each conference you attended and con-
    vened;
And (at appropriate moments) what you
    ate.
Thus (if the world's acute) it can derive
Your self, exact, uncensored and alive.

The world will find no pity in your pages;
No exercise of spirit worthy of mention;
Only a public-funeral grief-convention;
And all the circumspection of the ages.
But I, for one, am grateful, overjoyed,
And unindignant that your punctual pen
Should have been so constructively em-
    ployed
In manifesting to unprivileged men
The visionless officialized fatuity
That once kept Europe safe for Perpetuity.

                                   1926

---

[1] From *The Road to Ruin*, Faber & Faber, 1933. Reprinted by permission of the author.
[2] From *Satirical Poems* by Siegfried Sassoon. By permission of The Viking Press, Inc., N. Y.

HENRY WADSWORTH LONGFELLOW

The Arsenal at Springfield

This is the Arsenal. From floor to ceiling,
  Like a huge organ, rise the burnished
    arms;
But from their silent pipes no anthem peal-
    ing
  Startles the villages with strange alarms.

Ah! what a sound will rise, how wild and
    dreary,
  When the death-angel touches those
    swift keys!
What loud lament and dismal Miserere
  Will mingle with their awful sympho-
    nies!

I hear even now the infinite fierce chorus,
  The cries of agony, the endless groan,
Which, through the ages that have gone
    before us,
  In long reverberations reach our own.

On helm and harness rings the Saxon
    hammer,
  Through Cimbric forest roars the Norse-
    man's song,
And loud, amid the universal clamor,
  O'er distant deserts sounds the Tartar
    gong.

I hear the Florentine, who from his palace
  Wheels out his battle-bell with dreadful
    din,
And Aztec priests upon their teocallis
  Beat the wild war-drum made of ser-
    pent's skin;

The tumult of each sacked and burning
    village;
  The shout that every prayer for mercy
    drowns;
The soldiers' revels in the midst of pillage;

The wail of famine in beleaguered
    towns;
The bursting shell, the gateway wrenched
    asunder,
  The rattling musketry, the clashing
    blade;
And ever and anon, in tones of thunder,
  The diapason of the cannonade.

Is it, O man, with such discordant noises,
  With such accursed instruments as these,
Thou drownest Nature's sweet and kindly
    voices,
  And jarrest the celestial harmonies?

Were half the power that fills the world
    with terror,
  Were half the wealth bestowed on camps
    and courts,
Given to redeem the human mind from
    error,
  There were no need of arsenals nor forts:

The warrior's name would be a name ab-
    horrèd!
  And every nation, that should lift again
Its hand against a brother, on its forehead
  Would wear forevermore the curse of
    Cain!

Down the dark future, through long gener-
    ations,
  The echoing sounds grow fainter and
    then cease;
And like a bell, with solemn, sweet vi-
    brations,
  I hear once more the voice of Christ say,
    "Peace!"

Peace! and no longer from its brazen
    portals
  The blast of War's great organ shakes
    the skies!
But beautiful as songs of the immortals,
  The holy melodies of love arise.

                   1844

ALFRED, LORD TENNYSON

Vision of the Parliament of Man

From LOCKSLEY HALL

I had been content to perish, falling on the
    foeman's ground,
When the ranks are rolled in vapour, and
    the winds are laid with sound.

But the jingling of the guinea helps the
    hurt that Honour feels,
And the nations do but murmur, snarling
    at each other's heels.

Can I but relive in sadness? I will turn
    that earlier page.
Hide me from my deep emotion, O thou
    wondrous Mother-Age!

Make me feel the wild pulsation that I
    felt before the strife,
When I heard my days before me, and
    the tumult of my life;

Yearning for the large excitement that the
    coming years would yield,
Eager-hearted as a boy when first he leaves
    his father's field,

And at night along the dusky highway
    near and nearer drawn,
Sees in heaven the light of London flaring
    like a dreary dawn;

And his spirit leaps within him to be gone
    before him then,
Underneath the light he looks at, in among
    the throngs of men:

Men, my brothers, men the workers, ever
    reaping something new:
That which they have done but earnest of
    the things that they shall do:

For I dipt into the future, far as human eye
    could see,
Saw the Vision of the world, and all the
    wonder that would be;

Saw the heavens fill with commerce, ar-
    gosies of magic sails,
Pilots of the purple twilight, dropping
    down with costly bales;

Heard the heavens fill with shouting, and
    there rained a ghastly dew
From the nations' airy navies grappling in
    the central blue;

Far along the world-wide whisper of the
    south-wind rushing warm,
With the standards of the peoples plung-
    ing through the thunder-storm;

Till the war-drum throbbed no longer, and
    the battle-flags were furled
In the Parliament of man, the Federation
    of the world.

There the common sense of most shall
    hold a fretful realm in awe,
And the kindly earth shall slumber, lapt in
    universal law.

So I triumphed ere my passion sweeping
    through me left me dry,
Left me with the palsied heart, and left
    me with the jaundiced eye;

Eye, to which all order festers, all things
    here are out of joint:
Science moves, but slowly, slowly, creeping
    on from point to point:

Slowly comes a hungry people, as a lion
    creeping nigher,
Glares at one that nods and winks behind
    a slowly-dying fire.

Yet I doubt not through the ages one in-
    creasing purpose runs.
And the thoughts of men are widened with
    the process of the suns.

What is that to him that reaps not harvest
    of his youthful joys,
Though the deep heart of existence beat
    for ever like a boy's?

Knowledge comes, but wisdom lingers,
and I linger on the shore,
And the individual withers, and the world
is more and more.

Knowledge comes, but wisdom lingers, and
he bears a laden breast,
Full of sad experience, moving toward the
stillness of his rest.

Hark, my merry comrades call me, sounding on the bugle-horn,
They to whom my foolish passion were a
target for their scorn:

Shall it not be scorn to me to harp on such
a mouldered string?
I am shamed through all my nature to have
loved so slight a thing.

Weakness to be wroth with weakness!
woman's pleasure, woman's pain—
Nature made them blinder motions
bounded in a shallower brain:

Woman is the lesser man, and all thy
passions, matched with mine,
Are as moonlight unto sunlight, and as
water unto wine—

Here at least, where nature sickens, nothing. Ah, for some retreat
Deep in yonder shining Orient, where my
life began to beat;

Where in wild Mahratta-battle fell my father evil-starred;—
I was left a trampled orphan, and a selfish
uncle's ward.

Or to burst all links of habit—there to
wander far away,
On from island unto island at the gateways
of the day.

Larger constellations burning, mellow
moons and happy skies,
Breadths of tropic shade and palms in
cluster, knots of Paradise.

Never comes the trader, never floats an
European flag,
Slides the bird o'er lustrous woodland,
swings the trailer from the crag;

Droops the heavy-blossomed bower, hangs
the heavy-fruited tree—
Summer isles of Eden lying in dark-purple
spheres of sea.

There methinks would be enjoyment more
than in this march of mind,
In the steamship, in the railway, in the
thoughts that shake mankind.

There the passions cramped no longer shall
have scope and breathing space:
I will take some savage woman, she shall
rear my dusky race.

Iron-jointed, supple-sinewed, they shall
dive, and they shall run,
Catch the wild goat by the hair, and hurl
their lances in the sun;

Whistle back the parrot's call, and leap the
rainbows of the brooks,
Not with blinded eyesight poring over
miserable books—

Fool, again the dream, the fancy! but I
know my words are wild,
But I count the gray barbarian lower than
the Christian child.

I, to herd with narrow foreheads, vacant of
our glorious gains,
Like a beast with lower pleasures, like a
beast with lower pains!

Mated with a squalid savage—what to me
were sun or clime?
I the heir of all the ages, in the foremost
files of time—

I that rather held it better men should
perish one by one,
Than that earth should stand at gaze like
Joshua's moon in Ajalon!

Not in vain the distance beacons. Forward, forward let us range,
Let the great world spin for ever down the
  ringing grooves of change.

Through the shadow of the globe we
  sweep into the younger day:
Better fifty years of Europe than a cycle
  of Cathay.

Mother-Age (for mine I knew not) help
  me as when life begun:
Rift the hills, and roll the waters, flash the
  lightnings, weigh the Sun. . . .

1842

THOMAS HOOD

The Song of the Shirt

With fingers weary and worn,
  With eyelids heavy and red,
A woman sat, in unwomanly rags,
  Plying her needle and thread—
Stitch! stitch! stitch!
  In poverty, hunger, and dirt,
And still with a voice of dolorous pitch
  She sang the "Song of the Shirt."

"Work! work! work!
  While the cock is crowing aloof!
And work—work—work,
  Till the stars shine through the roof!
It's Oh! to be a slave
  Along with the barbarous Turk,
Where woman has never a soul to save,
  If this is Christian work.

"Work—work—work,
  Till the brain begins to swim;
Work—work—work,
  Till the eyes are heavy and dim!
Seam, and gusset, and band,
  Band, and gusset, and seam,
Till over the buttons I fall asleep,
  And sew them on in a dream!

"Oh, men, with sisters dear!
  Oh, men, with mothers and wives!
It is not linen you're wearing out
  But human creatures' lives!
Stitch—stitch—stitch,
  In poverty, hunger, and dirt,
Sewing at once, with a double thread,
  A Shroud as well as a Shirt.

"But why do I talk of Death?
  That phantom of grisly bone,
I hardly fear its terrible shape,
  It seems so like my own—
It seems so like my own,
  Because of the fasts I keep;
Oh, God! that bread should be so dear,
  And flesh and blood so cheap!

"Work—work—work!
  My labor never flags;
And what are its wages? A bed of straw,
  A crust of bread—and rags.
That shattered roof—this naked floor—
  A table—a broken chair—
And a wall so blank, my shadow I thank
  For sometimes falling there!

"Work—work—work!
  From weary chime to chime,
Work—work—work,
  As prisoners work for crime!
Band, and gusset, and seam,
  Seam, and gusset, and band,
Till the heart is sick, and the brain be-
    numbed,
  As well as the weary hand.

"Work—work—work,
  In the dull December light,
And work—work—work,
  When the weather is warm and bright—
While underneath the eaves
  The brooding swallows cling
As if to show me their sunny backs
  And twit me with the spring.

"Oh! but to breathe the breath
  Of the cowslip and primrose sweet—
With the sky above my head,
  And the grass beneath my feet;

For only one short hour
  To feel as I used to feel,
Before I knew the woes of want
  And the walk that costs a meal.

"Oh! but for one short hour!
  A respite however brief!
No bléssed leisure for love or hope,
  But only time for grief!
A little weeping would ease my heart,
  But in their briny bed
My tears must stop, for every drop
  Hinders needle and thread!"

Seam, and gusset, and band,
  Band, and gusset, and seam,
Work—work—work,
  Like the engine that works by steam!
A mere machine of iron and wood
  That toils for Mammon's sake,
Without a brain to ponder and craze
  Or a heart to feel—and break!

With fingers weary and worn,
  With eyelids heavy and red,
A woman sat, in unwomanly rags,
  Plying her needle and thread—
Stitch! stitch! stitch!
  In poverty, hunger, and dirt,
And still with a voice of dolorous pitch—
Would that its tone could reach the rich!—
  She sang this "Song of the Shirt!"
                                  1843

SIDNEY LANIER

The Symphony

"O Trade! O Trade! would thou wert
    dead!
The Time needs heart—'tis tired of head:
We're all for love," the violins said.
"Of what avail the rigorous tale
Of bill for coin and box for bale?
Grant thee, O Trade! thine uttermost hope:
Level red gold with blue sky-slope,
And base it deep as devils grope:

When all's done, what hast thou won
Of the only sweet that's under the sun?
Ay, canst thou buy a single sigh
Of true love's least, least ecstasy?"
Then, with a bridegroom's heart-beats
    trembling,
All the mightier strings assembling
Ranged them on the violins' side
As when the bridegroom leads the bride,
And, heart in voice, together cried:
"Yea, what avail the endless tale
Of gain by cunning and plus by sale?
Look up the land, look down the land,
The poor, the poor, the poor, they stand
Wedged by the pressing of Trade's hand
Against an inward-opening door
That pressure tightens evermore:
They sigh a monstrous foul-air sigh
For the outside leagues of liberty,
Where Art, sweet lark, translates the sky
Into a heavenly melody.
'Each day, all day' (these poor folks say),
'In the same old year-long, drear-long way,
We weave in the mills and heave in the
    kilns,
We sieve mine-meshes under the hills,
And thieve much gold from the Devil's
    bank tills,
To relieve, O God, what manner of ills?—
The beasts, they hunger, and eat, and die;
And so do we, and the world's a sty;
Hush, fellow-swine: why nuzzle and cry?
Swinehood hath no remedy
Say many men, and hasten by,
Clamping the nose and blinking the eye.
But who said once, in the lordly tone,
Man shall not live by bread alone
But all that cometh from the Throne?
  Hath God said so?
  But Trade saith *No:*
And the kilns and the curt-tongued mills
    say *Go!*
There's plenty that can, if you can't: we
  know.
Move out, if you think you're underpaid.
The poor are prolific; we're not afraid;
Trade is trade.'"
Thereat this passionate protesting
Meekly changed, and softened till
It sank to sad requesting

And suggesting sadder still:
"And oh, if men might sometime see
How piteous-false the poor decree
That trade no more than trade must be!
Does business mean, *Die, you—live, I?*
Then 'Trade is trade' but sings a lie:
'Tis only war grown miserly.
If business is battle, name it so:
War-crimes less will shame it so,
And widows less will blame it so.
Alas, for the poor to have some part
In yon sweet living lands of Art,
Makes problem not for head, but heart.
Vainly might Plato's brain revolve it:
Plainly the heart of a child could solve it."
And then, as when from words that seem
    but rude
We pass to silent pain that sits abroad
Back in our heart's great dark and solitude,
So sank the strings to gentle throbbing
Of long chords change-marked with sob-
    bing—
Motherly sobbing, not distinctlier heard
Than half wing-openings of the sleeping
    bird,
Some dream of danger to her young hath
    stirred.
Then stirring and demurring ceased, and
    lo!
Every least ripple of the strings' song-flow
Died to a level with each level bow
And made a great chord tranquil-surfaced
    so,
As a brook beneath his curving bank doth
    go
To linger in the sacred dark and green
Where many boughs the still pool overlean
And many leaves make shadow with their
    sheen.
  But presently
A velvet flute-note fell down pleasantly
Upon the bosom of that harmony,
And sailed and sailed incessantly,
As if a petal from a wild-rose blown
Had fluttered down upon that pool of tone
And boatwise dropped o' the convex side
And floated down the glassy tide
And clarified and glorified
The solemn spaces where the shadows bide.
From the warm concave of that fluted note

Somewhat, half song, half odor, forth did
    float,
As if a rose might somehow be a throat:
"When Nature from her far-off glen
Flutes her soft messages to men,
  The flute can say them o'er again;
  Yea, Nature, singing sweet and lone,
Breathes through life's strident polyphone
The flute-voice in the world of tone.
  Sweet friends,
   Man's love ascends
To finer and diviner ends
Than man's mere thought e'er compre-
    hends:
For I, e'en I,
  As here I lie,
A petal on a harmony,
Demand of Science whence and why
Man's tender pain, man's inward cry,
When he doth gaze on earth and sky?
I am not overbold:
  I hold
Full powers from Nature manifold.
I speak for each no-tonguèd tree
That, spring by spring, doth nobler be,
And dumbly and most wistfully,
His mighty prayerful arms outspreads
Above men's oft-unheeding heads,
And his big blessing downward sheds.
I speak for all-shaped blooms and leaves,
Lichens on stones and moss on eaves,
Grasses and grains in ranks and sheaves;
Broad-fronded ferns and keen-leaved canes,
And briery mazes bounding lanes,
And marsh-plants, thirsty-cupped for rains,
And milky stems and sugary veins;
For every long-armed woman-vine
That round a piteous tree doth twine;
For passionate odors, and divine
Pistils, and petals crystalline;
All purities of shady springs,
All shynesses of film-winged things
That fly from tree-trunks and bark-rings;
All modesties of mountain-fawns
That leap to covert from wild lawns,
And tremble if the day but dawns;
All sparklings of small beady eyes
Of birds, and sidelong glances wise
Wherewith the jay hints tragedies;
All piquancies of prickly burs,

And smoothnesses of downs and furs,
Of eiders and of minevers;
All limpid honeys that do lie
At stamen-bases, nor deny
The humming-birds' fine roguery,
Bee-thighs, nor any butterfly;
All gracious curves of slender wings,
Bark-mottlings, fibre-spiralings,
Fern-wavings and leaf-flickerings;
Each dial-marked leaf and flower-bell
Wherewith in every lonesome dell
Time to himself his hours doth tell;
All tree-sounds, rustlings of pine-cones,
Wind-sighings, doves' melodious moans,
And night's unearthly under-tones;
All placid lakes and waveless deeps,
All cool reposing mountain-steeps,
Vale-calms and tranquil lotos-sleeps;—
Yea, all fair forms, and sounds, and lights,
And warmths, and mysteries, and mights,
Of Nature's utmost depths and heights,
—These doth my timid tongue present,
Their mouthpiece and leal instrument
And servant, all love-eloquent.
I heard, when 'All for love' the violins
  cried:
So, Nature calls through all her system
  wide,
Give me thy love, O man, so long denied.
Much time is run, and man hath changed
  his ways,
Since Nature, in the antique fable-days,
Was hid from man's true love by proxy
  fays,
False fauns and rascal gods that stole her
  praise.
The nymphs, cold creatures of man's
  colder brain,
Chilled Nature's streams till man's warm
  heart was fain
Never to lave its love in them again.
Later, a sweet Voice Love thy neighbor
  said,
Then first the bounds of neighborhood
  outspread
Beyond all confines of old ethnic dread.
Vainly the Jew might wag his covenant
  head:
'All men are neighbors,' so the sweet Voice
  said.

So, when man's arms had circled all man's
  race,
The liberal compass of his warm embrace
Stretched bigger yet in the dark bounds of
  space;
With hands a-grope he felt smooth Na-
  ture's grace,
Drew her to breast and kissed her sweet-
  heart face:
Yea, man found neighbors in great hills
  and trees
And streams and clouds and suns and
  birds and bees,
And throbbed with neighbor-loves in lov-
  ing these.
But oh, the poor! the poor! the poor!
That stand by the inward-opening door
Trade's hand doth tighten ever more,
And sigh their monstrous foul-air sigh
For the outside hills of liberty,
Where Nature spreads her wild blue sky
For Art to make into melody!
Thou Trade! thou king of the modern
  days!
  Change thy ways,
  Change thy ways;
Let the sweaty laborers file
  A little while,
  A little while,
Where Art and Nature sing and smile.
Trade! is thy heart all dead, all dead?
And hast thou nothing but a head?
I'm all for heart," the flute-voice said,
And into sudden silence fled,
Like as a blush that while 'tis red
Dies to a still, still white instead.

  Thereto a thrilling calm succeeds,
Till presently the silence breeds
A little breeze among the reeds
That seems to blow by sea-marsh weeds:
Then from the gentle stir and fret
Sings out the melting clarionet,
Like as a lady sings while yet
Her eyes with salty tears are wet.
"O Trade! O Trade!" the Lady said,
"I too will wish thee utterly dead
If all thy heart is in thy head.
For O my God! and O my God!
What shameful ways have women trod

At beckoning of Trade's golden rod!
Alas when sighs are traders' lies,
And heart's-ease eyes and violet eyes
  Are merchandise!
O purchased lips that kiss with pain!
O cheeks coin-spotted with smirch and
  stain!
O trafficked hearts that break in twain!
  And yet what wonder at my sisters'
    crime?
So hath Trade withered up Love's sinewy
  prime,
Men love not women as in olden time.
Ah, not in these cold merchantable days
Deem men their life an opal gray, where
  plays
The one red Sweet of gracious ladies'-
  praise.
Now, comes a suitor with sharp prying
  eye—
Says, *Here, you Lady, if you'll sell, I'll buy:*
Come, heart for heart—a trade? What!
  weeping? why?
Shame on such wooers' dapper mercery!
I would my lover kneeling at my feet
In humble manliness should cry, *O Sweet!*
I know not if thy heart my heart will greet:
I ask not if thy love my love can meet:
Whate'er thy worshipful soft tongue shall
  say,
I'll kiss thine answer, be it yea or nay:
I do but know I love thee, and I pray
To be thy knight until my dying day.
Woe him that cunning trades in hearts con-
  trives!
Base love good women to base loving
  drives
If men loved larger, larger were our lives;
And wooed they nobler, won they nobler
  wives."

There thrust the bold straightforward horn
To battle for that lady lorn,
With heartsome voice of mellow scorn,
Like any knight in knighthood's morn.
  "Now comfort thee," said he,
    "Fair Lady.
For God shall right thy grievous wrong,
And man shall sing thee a true-love
  song,

Voiced in act his whole life long,
  Yea, all thy sweet life long,
    Fair Lady.
Where's he that craftily hath said,
The day of chivalry is dead?
I'll prove that lie upon his head,
  Or I will die instead,
    Fair Lady.
Is Honor gone into his grave?
Hath Faith become a caitiff knave,
And Selfhood turned into a slave
  To work in Mammon's cave,
    Fair Lady?
Will Truth's long blade ne'er gleam again?
Hath Giant Trade in dungeons slain
All great contempts of mean-got gain
  And hates of inward stain,
    Fair Lady?
For aye shall name and fame be sold,
And place be hugged for the sake of gold,
And smirch-robed Justice feebly scold
  At Crime all money-bold,
    Fair Lady?
Shall self-wrapt husbands aye forget
Kiss-pardons for the daily fret
Wherewith sweet wifely eyes are wet—
  Blind to lips kiss-wise set—
    Fair Lady?
Shall lovers higgle, heart for heart,
Till wooing grows a trading mart
Where much for little, and all for part,
  Make love a cheapening art,
    Fair Lady?
Shall woman scorch for a single sin
That her betrayer may revel in,
And she be burnt, and he but grin
  When that the flames begin,
    Fair Lady?
Shall ne'er prevail the woman's plea,
We maids would far, far whiter be
If that our eyes might sometimes see
  Men maids in purity,
    Fair Lady?
Shall Trade aye salve his conscience-aches
With jibes at Chivalry's old mistakes—
The wars that o'erhot knighthood makes
  For Christ's and ladies' sake,
    Fair Lady?
Now by each knight that e'er hath prayed
To fight like a man and love like a maid,

Since Pembroke's life, as Pembroke's blade,
  I' the scabbard, death, was laid,
     Fair Lady,
I dare avouch my faith is bright
That God doth right and God hath might.
Nor time hath changed His hair to white,
  Nor His dear love to spite,
     Fair Lady.
I doubt no doubts: I strive, and shrive my
  clay,
And fight my fight in the patient modern
  way
For true love and for thee—ah me! and
  pray
  To be thy knight until my dying day,
     Fair Lady."
Made end that knightly horn, and spurred
  away
Into the thick of the melodious fray.
And then the hautboy played and smiled,
And sang like any large-eyed child,
Cool-hearted and all undefiled.
  "Huge Trade!" he said,
"Would thou wouldst lift me on thy head
And run wher'er my finger led!
Once said a Man—and wise was He—
Never shalt thou the heavens see,
Save as a little child thou be."
Then o'er sea-lashings of commingling
  tunes
The ancient wise bassoons,
  Like weird
  Gray-beard
Old harpers sitting on the high sea-dunes,
  Chanted runes:
"Bright-waved gain, gray-waved loss,
The sea of all doth lash and toss,
One wave forward and one across:
But now 'twas trough, now 'tis crest,
And worst doth foam and flash to best,
  And curst to blest.

"Life! Life! thou sea-fugue, writ from
  east to west,
  Love, Love alone can pore
  On thy dissolving score
  Of harsh half-phrasings,
    Blotted ere writ,
  And double erasings
    Of chords most fit.

Yea, Love, sole music-master blest,
May read thy weltering palimpsest.
To follow Time's dying melodies through,
And never to lose the old in the new,
And ever to solve the discords true—
  · Love alone can do.
And ever Love hears the poor-folks' crying,
And ever Love hears the women's sighing,
And ever sweet knighthood's death-defy-
  ing,
And ever wise childhood's deep implying,
But never a trader's glozing and lying.

"And yet shall Love himself be heard,
Though long deferred, though long de-
  ferred:
O'er the modern waste a dove hath
  whirred:
Music is Love in search of a word."
                1875

ALGERNON CHARLES SWINBURNE
To Walt Whitman in America

Send but a song oversea for us,
  Heart of their hearts who are free,
Heart of their singer, to be for us
  More than our singing can be;
Ours, in the tempest at error,
With no light but the twilight of terror;
  Send us a song oversea!

Sweet-smelling of pine-leaves and grasses,
  And blown as a tree through and
    through
With the winds of the keen mountain-
  passes,
  And tender as sun-smitten dew;
Sharp-tongued as the winter that shakes
The wastes of your limitless lakes,
  Wide-eyed as the sea-line's blue.

O strong-winged soul with prophetic
  Lips hot with the bloodbeats of song,

With tremor of heartstrings magnetic,
  With thoughts as thunders in throng,
With consonant ardors of chords
That pierce men's souls as with swords
  And hale them hearing along,

Make us too music, to be with us
  As a word from a world's heart warm,
To sail the dark as a sea with us,
  Full-sailed, outsinging the storm,
A song to put fire in our ears
Whose burning shall burn up tears,
  Whose sign bid battle reform;

A note in the ranks of a clarion,
  A word in the wind of cheer,
To consume as with lightning the carrion
  That makes time foul for us here;
In the air that our dead things infest
A blast of the breath of the west,
  Till east way as west way is clear.

Out of the sun beyond sunset,
  From the evening whence morning shall
  be,
With the rollers in measureless onset,
  With the van of the storming sea,
With the world-wide wind, with the breath
That breaks ships driven upon death,
  With the passion of all things free,

With the sea-steeds footless and frantic,
  White myriads for death to bestride
In the charge of the ruining Atlantic
  Where deaths by regiments ride,
With clouds and clamors of waters,
With a long note shriller than slaughter's
  On the furrowless fields world-wide.

With terror, with ardor and wonder,
  With the soul of the season that wakes
When the weight of a whole year's thunder
  In the tidestream of autumn breaks,
Let the flight of the wide-winged word
Come over, come in and be heard,
  Take form and fire for our sakes.

For a continent bloodless with travail
  Here toils and brawls as it can,
And the web of it who shall unravel
  Of all that peer on the plan;

Would fain grow men, but they grow not,
And fain be free, but they know not
  One name for freedom and man?

One name, not twain for division;
  One thing, not twain, from the birth;
Spirit and substance and vision,
  Worth more than worship is worth;
Unbeheld, unadored, undivined,
The cause, the center, the mind,
  The secret and sense of the earth.

Here as a weakling in irons,
  Here as a weanling in bands,
As a prey that the stake-net environs,
  Our life that we looked for stands;
And the man-child naked and dear,
Democracy, turns on us here
  Eyes trembling with tremulous hands.

It sees not what season shall bring to it
  Sweet fruit of its bitter desire;
Few voices it hears yet sing to it,
  Few pulses of hearts reaspire;
Foresees not time, nor forehears
The noises of imminent years,
  Earthquake, and thunder, and fire:

When crowned and weaponed and curb-
  less
  It shall walk without helm or shield
The bare burnt furrows and herbless
  Of war's last flame-stricken field,
Till godlike, equal with time,
It stand in the sun sublime,
  In the godhead of man revealed.

Round your people and over them
  Light like raiment is drawn,
Close as a garment to cover them
  Wrought not of mail nor of lawn;
Here, with hope hardly to wear,
Naked nations and bare
  Swim, sink, strike out for the dawn.

Chains are here, and a prison,
  Kings, and subjects, and shame,
If the God upon you be arisen,
  How should our songs be the same?

How, in confusion of change,
How shall we sing, in a strange
   Land, songs praising his name?

God is buried and dead to us,
   Even the spirit of earth,
Freedom; so have they said to us,
   Some with mocking and mirth,
Some with heartbreak and tears;
And a God without eyes, without ears,
   Who shall sing of him, dead in the
     birth?

The earth-god Freedom, the lonely
   Face lightening, the footprint unshod,
Not as one man crucified only
   Nor scourged with but one life's rod;
The soul that is substance of nations,
Reincarnate with fresh generations;
   The great god Man, which is God.

But in weariest of years and obscurest
   Doth it live not at heart of all things,
The one God and one spirit, a purest
   Life, fed from unstanchable springs?
Within love, within hatred it is,
And its seed in the stripe as the kiss,
   And in slaves is the germ, and in kings.

Freedom we call it, for holier
   Name of the soul's there is none;
Surelier it labors, if slowlier,
   Than the meters of star or of sun;
Slowlier than life into breath,
Surelier than time into death,
   It moves till its labor be done.

Till the motion be done and the measure
   Circling through season and clime,
Slumber and sorrow and pleasure,
   Vision of virtue and crime;
Till consummate with conquering eyes,
A soul disembodied, it rise
   From the body transfigured of time.

Till it rise and remain and take station
   With the stars of the worlds that rejoice;
Till the voice of its heart's exultation
   Be as theirs an invariable voice;
By no discord of evil estranged,

By no pause, by no breach in it changed,
   By no clash in the chord of its choice.

It is one with the world's generations,
   With the spirit, the star, and the sod;
With the kingless and king-stricken na-
     tions,
   With the cross, and the chain, and the
     rod;
The most high, the most secret, most
     lonely,
The earth-soul Freedom, that only
   Lives, and that only is God.

                  1871

WALT WHITMAN

Hang Your Whole Weight Upon Me

From SONG OF MYSELF

Earth! you seem to look for something at
   my hands,
Say, old top-knot, what do you want?

Man or woman, I might tell how I like
   you, but cannot,
And might tell what it is in me and what it
   is in you, but cannot,
And might tell that pining I have, that
   pulse of my nights and days.

Behold, I do not give lectures or a little
   charity,
When I give I give myself.

You there, impotent, loose in the knees,
Open your scarf'd chops till I blow grit
   within you,
Spread your palms and lift the flaps of your
   pockets,
I am not to be denied, I compel, I have
   stores plenty and to spare,
And any thing I have I bestow.

I do not ask who you are, that is not important to me,

You can do nothing and be nothing but
    what I will infold you.

To cotton-field drudge or cleaner of privies
    I lean,
On his right cheek I put the family kiss,
And in my soul I swear I never will deny
    him. . . .

I seize the descending man and raise him
    with resistless will,
O despairer, here is my neck,
By God, you shall not go down! hang your
    whole weight upon me.

I dilate you with tremendous breath, I
    buoy you up,
Every room of the house do I fill with an
    arm'd force,
Lovers of me, bafflers of graves.

                     1855

WILLIAM MORRIS

The Day Is Coming

Come hither, lads, and harken, for a tale
    there is to tell,
Of the wonderful days a-coming, when all
    shall be better than well.

And the tale shall be told of a country, a
    land in the midst of the sea,
And folk shall call it England in the days
    that are going to be.

There more than one in a thousand in the
    days that are yet to come,
Shall have some hope of the morrow, some
    joy of the ancient home.

For then—laugh not, but listen to this
    strange tale of mine—
All folk that are in England shall be better
    lodged than swine.

Then a man shall work and bethink him,
    and rejoice in the deeds of his hand,
Nor yet come home in the even too faint
    and weary to stand.

Men in that time a-coming shall work and
    have no fear
For tomorrow's lack of earning and the
    hunger-wolf anear.

I tell you this for a wonder, that no man
    then shall be glad
Of his fellow's fall and mishap to snatch at
    the work he had,

For that which the worker winneth shall
    then be his indeed,
Nor shall half be reaped for nothing by
    him that sowed no seed.

O strange new wonderful justice! But for
    whom shall we gather the gain?
For ourselves and for each of our fellows,
    and no hand shall labor in vain.

Then all Mine and all Thine shall be Ours,
    and no more shall any man crave
For riches that serve for nothing but to
    fetter a friend for a slave.

And what wealth then shall be left us
    when none shall gather gold
To buy his friend in the market, and pinch
    and pine the sold?

Nay, what save the lovely city, and the
    little house on the hill,
And the wastes and the woodland beauty,
    and the happy fields we till;

And the homes of ancient stories, the
    tombs of the mighty dead;
And the wise men seeking out marvels,
    and the poet's teeming head;

And the painter's hand of wonder; and
    the marvelous fiddle-bow,
And the banded choirs of music—all those
    that do and know.

For all these shall be ours and all men's;
  nor shall any lack a share
Of the toil and the gain of living in the
  days when the world grows fair.

Ah! such are the days that shall be! But
  what are the deeds of today,
In the days of the years we dwell in, that
  wear our lives away?

Why, then, and for what are we waiting?
  There are three words to speak—
WE WILL IT—and what is the foeman but
  the dream-strong wakened and weak?

O why and for what are we waiting?
  while our brothers droop and die,
And on every wind of the heavens a wasted
  life goes by.

How long shall they reproach us where
  crowd on crowd they dwell,
Poor ghosts of the wicked city, the gold-
  crushed, hungry hell?

Through squalid life they labored, in sordid grief they died,
Those sons of a mighty mother, those props
  of England's pride.

They are gone; there is none can undo it,
  nor save our souls from the curse;
But many a million cometh, and shall they
  be better or worse?

It is we must answer and hasten, and open
  wide the door
For the rich man's hurrying terror, and
  the slow-foot hope of the poor.

Yea, the voiceless wrath of the wretched,
  and their unlearned discontent,
We must give it voice and wisdom till the
  waiting-tide be spent.

Come, then, since all things call us, the
  living and the dead,
And o'er the weltering tangle a glimmering light is shed.

Come, then, let us cast off fooling, and put
  by ease and rest,
For the Cause alone is worthy till the good
  days bring the best.

Come, join in the only battle wherein no
  man can fail,
Where whoso fadeth and dieth, yet his
  deed shall still prevail.

Ah! come, cast off all fooling, for this, at
  least, we know:
That the Dawn and the Day is coming,
  and forth the Banners go.

                                    1884

RALPH WALDO EMERSON

Hamatreya

Bulkeley, Hunt, Willard, Hosmer, Mer-
  iam, Flint,
Possessed the land which rendered to their
  toil
Hay, corn, roots, hemp, flax, apples, wool
  and wood.
Each of these landlords walked amidst his
  farm,
Saying, ' 'Tis mine, my children's and my
  name's.
How sweet the west wind sounds in my
  own trees!
How graceful climb those shadows on my
  hill!
I fancy these pure waters and the flags
Know me, as does my dog: we sympathize;
And, I affirm, my actions smack of the soil.'

Where are these men? Asleep beneath
  their grounds:
And strangers, fond as they, their furrows
  plough.
Earth laughs in flowers, to see her boastful
  boys

Earth-proud, proud of the earth which is
  not theirs;
Who steer the plough, but cannot steer
  their feet
Clear of the grave.
They added ridge to valley, brook to pond,
And sighed for all that bounded their
  domain;
'This suits me for a pasture; that's my
  park;
We must have clay, lime, gravel, granite-
  ledge,
And misty lowland, where to go for peat.
The land is well,—lies fairly to the south.
'Tis good, when you have crossed the sea
  and back,
To find the sitfast acres where you left
  them.'
Ah! the hot owner sees not Death, who
  adds
Him to his land, a lump of mould the
  more.
Hear what the Earth says:—

EARTH-SONG

'Mine and yours;
Mine, not yours.
Earth endures;
Stars abide—
Shine down in the old sea;
Old are the shores;
But where are old men?
I who have seen much,
Such have I never seen.

'The lawyer's deed
Ran sure,
In tail,
To them, and to their heirs
Who shall succeed,
Without fail,
Forevermore.

'Here is the land,
Shaggy with wood,
With its old valley,
Mound and flood.
But the heritors?—

Fled like the flood's foam.
The lawyer, and the laws,
And the kingdom,
Clean swept herefrom.

'They called me theirs,
Who so controlled me;
Yet every one
Wished to stay, and is gone,
How am I theirs,
If they cannot hold me,
But I hold them?'

When I heard the Earth-song
I was no longer brave;
My avarice cooled
Like lust in the chill of the grave.

1847

ARTHUR HUGH CLOUGH

The Latest Decalogue

Thou shalt have one God only; who
Would be at the expense of two?
No graven images may be
Worshiped, except the currency:
Swear not at all; for, for thy curse
Thine enemy is none the worse:
At church on Sunday to attend
Will serve to keep the world thy friend:
Honor thy parents; that is, all
From whom advancement may befall;
Thou shalt not kill; but need'st not strive
Officiously to keep alive:
Do not adultery commit;
Advantage rarely comes of it:
Thou shalt not steal; an empty feat,
When it's so lucrative to cheat:
Bear not false witness; let the lie
Have time on its own wings to fly:
Thou shalt not covet, but tradition
Approves all forms of competition.

1862

KENNETH FEARING

Dirge

1-2-3 was the number he played but today
   the number came 3-2-1;
Bought his Carbide at 30 and it went to 29;
   had the favorite at Bowie but the
   track was slow—

O executive type, would you like to drive
   a floating-power, knee-action, silk-
   upholstered six? Wed a Hollywood
   star? Shoot the course in 58?
   Draw to the ace, king, jack?
O fellow with a will who won't take no,
   watch out for three cigarettes on the
   same, single match; O democratic
   voter born in August under Mars,
   beware of liquidated rails—

Denouement to denouement, he took a personal pride in the certain, certain
   way he lived his own, private life,
But nevertheless, they shut off his gas; nevertheless, the bank foreclosed; nevertheless, the landlord called; nevothe-
   less, the radio broke,

And twelve o'clock arrived just once too
   often,
Just the same he wore one gray tweed suit,
   bought one straw hat, drank one
   straight Scotch, walked one short
   step, took one long look, drew one
   deep breath,
Just one too many,

And wow he died as wow he lived,
Going whop to the office and blooie home
   to sleep and biff got married and
   bam had children and oof got fired,
Zowie did he live and zowie did he die,

With who the hell are you at the corner of
   his casket, and where the hell're we
   going on the right-hand silver knob,

and who the hell cares walking second from the end with an American
   Beauty wreath from why the hell not,

Very much missed by the circulation staff
   of the New York Evening Post;
   deeply, deeply mourned by the
   B.M.T.,

Wham, Mr. Roosevelt; pow, Sears Roebuck; awk, big dipper; bop, summer
   rain;
Bong, Mr., bong, Mr., bong, Mr., bong.
                                    c. 1930-1935.

▼▼▼▼▼▼▼▼▼▼▼▼▼▼▼▼▼▼▼▼▼

WILLIAM ROSE BENÉT

Men on Strike

You say the President should not step in,
Sacrosanct Management not be touched at
   all. . . .
If they refuse to bargain, won't play ball,
And just sit tight because they're sure to
   win,
Because they have the money and the
   power
And to the labor argument present
Merely their boot-soles, reading, with evi-
   dent
Obliviousness, the comics, hour by hour—

If they say merely, "This is what we'll pay.
If you don't like it, strike!" (that's what
   they say
In substance) you grow purple and deplore
Not *their* contumacy, but Labor's nerve.
"They got the bargaining that they de-
   serve!"
But is that all Labor is fighting for?

The real rock-bottom issue is as plain
As the plain people: a job at decent wage,

Without paternalism or patronage,
That meets the cost of living and can sustain
A family's self-respect; a decent place
To hang your hat; have children; under God
Make yourself more than a robot or a clod;
Be a real member of the human race.
Is that so much to ask, when corporations
Bulge with their profits and their bonds and stocks?
What is it in the human mind that mocks
Fair play, till foul disaster shakes the nations?
What is it that will not reason, will not plan,
Will not respect the dignity of Man?

It costs so much to live; it costs so much
To raise a family. Above your head
Hangs still the old disabling human dread
Of age and illness. Others keep their clutch
On the employed because the unemployed,
Many and needy, persist on every hand.
Supply thus beautifully meets Demand—
The perfect balance that must not be destroyed!
Cheap labor and big profits, that's prosperity!
Let the rest perish or rot! Have no dubiety,
That's the old jungle law of our society—
Substantially, an eternal verity!
No ceiling on our prices, or the enjoyment
Of what we make—ignore all unemployment.

Sometimes, America, you seem to me
Typified by the gambler and the sport
Of the Mississippi steamboat, with a quart
In his hip-pocket, and a fancy-free
Skin-'em-alive and wolfish gaiety—
The poker-player of that famed resort,
The old Last Chance saloon, still glad to thwart
Any approach to rationality.
You live in legend, you rejoice in myth.

Our highly-colored chimeras, how we love them,
Though a world starve! But can we rise above them
Even to recognize as kin and kith
The homeless veteran, the mere man who bids
For a decent job to keep his wife and kids?

Or will our manufacturers remain
Forever in the sport and gambler class
Trusting to luck on what they may amass,
Reeling like drunkards in a golden rain,
Repulsing, with cries of agonizing pain,
Demands from workers whom the system pinches—
System? What system? Do we grow by inches
Through endless years dwarf stature to attain?
Pontifically our journals of "good will"
Anoint and crown free private enterprise
And *laissez faire*. Has God in Heaven not eyes
To oversee and save his children still
No matter what they do, how deaf and dumb
They choose to be, till Atom's kingdom come!

Drone on, drone on, great editorial We!
Shout, huge advertisements, in all the papers!
Make monkeys of the strikers cutting capers.
They love to strike, enjoy to disagree!
They'd seize the plants, and don't know ABC
About the business. Of course they're always wrong!
They'd better get back and stay where they belong.
Say, isn't this the Country of the Free?
The Country of the Free! I saw the sun
Light endless fields of grain. I saw the bread
Of life destroyed while millions went unfed,
Unhoused, ill-clothed. I saw injustice done

Negro and Jew; heard apes in Congress
    rant
Age-old pernicious blather and stale cant.

The Country of the Free! Yes, a great
    land.
Thank God that I have known it East to
    West
And North to South, and still I love it best
Of all the various world the seas command.
I have known Americans of finest grain,
Honest and fearless, humorous and keen.
Beauty beyond all purchase I have seen
In the human spirit's eminent domain.
And shoulder to shoulder now I know they
    stand:
Our valiant dead and all our valiant living
To vivify with giving and forgiving
This Country of the Free, the impartial
    land
That it might be; with heart and mind and
    nerve
Its many-in-one to strengthen and preserve.

I will not see it a pen for bleating sheep
Watched by sly wolves; or, in the new dark
    ages,
Industrial feudal lords dispensing wages
Each from his fief and his baronial keep,
While small stockholders pull their caps
    and scrape
Their little crumbs of dividends together,
And are told they are the Owners, and
    wonder whether
They are caught in some strange night-
    mare past escape.
I will not think enormous trusts—and
    what
A word is Trust!—can rack this land
    asunder
To disunited states, and harrow under
Plain human rights, all benefits forgot
Of human toil, of the great heart and hand
That bound the continent they call Their
    Land.

Land of huge fortunes and stupendous
    luck,

Landgraves, manorial lords, the privateers
(A golden sound in Israel Thorndike's
    ears!),
Railroads and banks and trusts that ran
    amuck,
Seizure of public earth, monopoly,
Titanic names like Vanderbilt and Gould,
Astor and Morgan, and other great, who
    ruled
For many a year the Country of the Free—
With all your passion for the picturesque,
With all your freedom for the Ragged
    Dicks
To climb, by industry or politics,
To wealth or fame, the picture grows
    grotesque
Now, in this age, when, whatsoe'er the
    weather,
We must fairly live together or die to-
    gether.

Labor is a new giant? Yes, it's true.
And, "What did you expect?" seems a
    fair question;
And even if it gives you indigestion,
Are giants in this land so strange to you?
"Captains of Industry" made quite a few;
The Oil King and the Banker and the
    Scot.
Giants must Have; The Others must Have
    Not.
How feels the foot inside the other shoe?
Well, Gamblers, will you gamble? Will
    you say,
"Let's really get together; join our
    strength;
Not waste in civil war! The world at
    length
Is due for a big new housecleaning day.
For human rights—come on—let's stake
    our pride!
World, we are moving—all tin-horns
    stand aside!"

                                  1946

RUDYARD KIPLING

The "Mary Gloster"

I've paid for your sickest fancies; I've
   humoured your crackedest whim—
Dick, it's your daddy, dying; you've got to
   listen to him!
Good for a fortnight, am I? The doctor
   told you? He lied.
I shall go under by morning, and— Put
   that nurse outside.
'Never seen death yet, Dickie? Well,
   now is your time to learn,
And you'll wish you held my record before
   it comes to your turn.
Not counting the Line and the Foundry,
   the Yards and the village, too,
I've made myself and a million; but I'm
   damned if I made you.
Master at two-and-twenty, and married at
   twenty-three—
Ten thousand men on the pay-roll, and
   forty freighters at sea!
Fifty years between 'em, and every year of
   it fight,
And now I'm Sir Anthony Gloster, dying,
   a baronite:
For I lunched with his Royal 'Ighness—
   what was it the papers had?
"Not least of our merchant-princes."
   Dickie, that's me, your dad!
I didn't begin with askings. I took my
   job and I stuck;
I took the chances they wouldn't, an' now
   they're calling it luck.
Lord, what boats I've handled—rotten and
   leaky and old!
Ran 'em, or—opened the bilge-cock, pre-
   cisely as I was told.
Grub that 'ud bind you crazy, and crews
   that 'ud turn you grey,
And a big fat lump of insurance to cover
   the risk on the way.
The others they dursn't do it; they said
   they valued their life

(They've served me since as skippers). I
   went, and I took my wife.
Over the world I drove 'em, married at
   twenty-three,
And your mother saving the money and
   making a man of me.
I was content to be master, but she said
   there was better behind;
She took the chances I wouldn't, and I fol-
   lowed your mother blind.
She egged me to borrow the money, an'
   she helped me to clear the loan,
When we bought half-shares in a cheap
   'un and hoisted a flag of our own.
Patching and coaling on credit, and living
   the Lord knew how,
We started the Red Ox freighters—we've
   eight-and-thirty now.
And those were the days of clippers, and
   the freights were clipper-freights,
And we knew we were making our for-
   tune, but she died in Macassar
   Straits—
By the Little Paternosters, as you come to
   the Union Bank—
And we dropped her in fourteen fathom; I
   pricked it off where she sank.
Owners we were, full owners, and the boat
   was christened for her,
And she died in the *Mary Gloster*. My
   heart, how young we were!
So I went on a spree round Java and well-
   nigh ran her ashore,
But your mother came and warned me
   and I wouldn't liquor no more:
Strict I stuck to my business, afraid to stop
   or I'd think,
Saving the money (she warned me), and
   letting the other men drink.
And I met M'Cullough in London (I'd
   saved five 'undred then),
And 'tween us we started the Foundry—
   three forges and twenty men:
Cheap repairs for the cheap 'uns. It paid,
   and the business grew,
For I bought me a steam-lathe patent, and
   that was a gold mine too.

"Cheaper to build 'em than buy 'em," I said, but M'Cullough he shied,

And we wasted a year in talking before we moved to the Clyde.

And the Lines were all beginning, and we all of us started fair,

Building our engines like houses and staying the boilers square.

But M'Cullough 'e wanted cabins with marble and maple and all,

And Brussels an' Utrecht velvet, and baths and a Social Hall,

And pipes for closets all over, and cutting the frames too light,

But M'Cullough he died in the Sixties, and— Well, I'm dying tonight. . . .

I knew—*I* knew what was coming, when we bid on the *Byfleet's* keel—

They piddled and piffled with iron. I'd given my orders for steel!

Steel and the first expansions. It paid, I tell you, it paid,

When we came with our nine-knot freighters and collared the long-run trade!

And they asked me how I did it, and I gave 'em the Scripture text,

"You keep your light so shining a little in front o' the next!"

They copied all they could follow, but they couldn't copy my mind,

And I left 'em sweating and stealing a year and a half behind.

Then came the armour-contracts, but that was M'Cullough's side;

He was always best in the Foundry, but better, perhaps, he died.

I went through his private papers; the notes was plainer than print;

And I'm no fool to finish if a man'll give me a hint.

(I remember his widow was angry.) So I saw what his drawings meant,

And I started the six-inch rollers, and it paid me sixty per cent.

Sixty per cent *with* failures, and more than twice we could do,

And a quarter-million to credit, and I saved it all for you!

I thought—it doesn't matter—you seemed to favour your ma,

But you're nearer forty than thirty, and I know the kind you are.

Harrer an' Trinity College! I ought to ha' sent you to sea—

But I stood you an education, an' what have you done for me?

The things I knew was proper you wouldn't thank me to give,

And the things I knew was rotten you said was the way to live.

For you muddled with books and pictures, an' china an' etchin's an' fans,

And your rooms at college was beastly—more like a whore's than a man's;

Till you married that thin-flanked woman, as white and as stale as a bone,

An' she gave you your social nonsense; but where's that kid o' your own?

I've seen your carriages blocking the half o' the Cromwell Road,

But never the doctor's brougham to help the missus unload.

(So there isn't even a grandchild, an' the Gloster family's done.)

Not like your mother, she isn't. *She* carried her freight each run.

But they died, the pore little beggars! At sea she had 'em—they died.

Only you, an' you stood it. You haven't stood much beside.

Weak, a liar, and idle, and mean as a collier's whelp

Nosing for scraps in the galley. No help —my son was no help!

So he gets three 'undred thousand, in trust and the interest paid.

I wouldn't give it you, Dickie—you see, I made it in trade.

You're saved from soiling your fingers, and if you have no child,

It all comes back to the business. 'Gad, won't your wife be wild!

'Calls and calls in her carriage, her 'andkerchief up to 'er eye:

"Daddy! dear daddy's dyin'!" and doing her best to cry.

Grateful?   Oh, yes, I'm grateful, but keep
    her away from here.
Your mother 'ud never ha' stood 'er, and,
    anyhow, women are queer. . . .
There's women will say I've married a
    second time. Not quite!
But give pore Aggie a hundred, and tell
    her your lawyers'll fight.
She was the best o' the boiling—you'll
    meet her before it ends.
I'm in for a row with the mother—I'll
    leave you settle my friends.
For a man he must go with a woman,
    which women don't understand—
Or the sort that say they can see it they
    aren't the marrying brand.
But I wanted to speak o' your mother
    that's Lady Gloster still;
I'm going to up and see her, without its
    hurting the will.
Here! Take your hand off the bell-pull.
    Five thousand's waiting for you,
If you'll only listen a minute, and do as I
    bid you do.
They'll try to prove me crazy, and, if you
    bungle, they can;
And I've only you to trust to! (O God,
    why ain't it a man?)
There's some waste money on marbles, the
    same as M'Cullough tried—
Marbles and mausoleums—but I call that
    sinful pride.
There's some ship bodies for burial—we've
    carried 'em, soldered and packed;
Down in their wills they wrote it, and no-
    body called *them* cracked.
But me—I've too much money, and people
    might . . .   All my fault:
It come o' hoping for grandsons and buy-
    ing that Wokin' vault. . . .
I'm sick o' the 'ole dam' business. I'm
    going back where I came.
Dick, you're the son o' my body, and you'll
    take charge o' the same!
I want to lie by your mother, ten thousand
    mile away,
And they'll want to send me to Woking;
    and that's where you'll earn your pay.
I've thought it out on the quiet, the same
    as it ought to be done—

Quiet, and decent, and proper—an' here's
    your orders, my son.
You know the Line?   You don't, though.
    You write to the Board, and tell
Your father's death has upset you an'
    you're goin' to cruise for a spell,
An' you'd like the *Mary Gloster*—I've held
    her ready for this—
They'll put her in working order and
    you'll take her out as she is.
Yes, it was money idle when I patched her
    and laid her aside
(Thank God, I can pay for my fancies!)
    —the boat where your mother died,
By the Little Paternosters, as you come to
    the Union Bank,
We dropped her—I think I told you—and
    I pricked it off where she sank.
['Tiny she looked on the grating—that
    oily, treacly sea—]
'Hundred and Eighteen East, remember,
    and South just Three.
Easy bearings to carry—Three South—
    Three to the dot;
But I gave McAndrew a copy in case of
    dying—or not.
And so you'll write to McAndrew, he's
    Chief of the Maori Line;
They'll give him leave, if you ask 'em and
    say it's business o' mine.
I built three boats for the Maoris, an' very
    well pleased they were,
An' I've known Mac since the Fifties, and
    Mac knew me—and her.
After the first stroke warned me I sent
    him the money to keep
Against the time you'd claim it, com-
    mittin' your dad to the deep;
For you are the son o' my body, and Mac
    was my oldest friend,
I've never asked 'im to dinner, but he'll
    see it out to the end.
Stiff-necked Glasgow beggar! I've heard
    he's prayed for my soul,
But he couldn't lie if you paid him, and
    he'd starve before he stole.
He'll take the *Mary* in ballast—you'll find
    her a lively ship;
And you'll take Sir Anthony Gloster, that
    goes on 'is wedding-trip,

Lashed in our old deck-cabin with all
    three port-holes wide,
The kick o' the screw beneath him and
    the round blue seas outside!
Sir Anthony Gloster's carriage—our 'ouse-
    flag flyin' free—
Ten thousand men on the pay-roll and
    forty freighters at sea!
He made himself and a million, but this
    world is a fleetin' show,
And he'll go to the wife of 'is bosom the
    same as he ought to go—
By the heel of the Paternosters—there isn't
    a chance to mistake—
And Mac'll pay you the money as soon as
    the bubbles break!
Five thousand for six weeks' cruising, the
    staunchest freighter afloat,
And Mac he'll give you your bonus the
    minute I'm out o' the boat!
He'll take you round to Macassar, and
    you'll come back alone;
He knows what I want o' the *Mary*. . . .
    I'll do what I please with my own.
Your mother 'ud call it wasteful, but I've
    seven-and-thirty more;
I'll come in my private carriage and bid it
    wait at the door. . . .
For my son 'e was never a credit: 'e
    muddled with books and art,
And 'e lived on Sir Anthony's money and
    'e broke Sir Anthony's heart.
There isn't even a grandchild, and the
    Gloster family's done—
The only one you left me, O mother, the
    only one!
Harrer and Trinity College—me slavin'
    early an' late—
An' he thinks I'm dying crazy, and you're
    in Macassar Strait!
Flesh o' my flesh, my dearie, for ever an'
    ever amen,
That first stroke come for a warning. I
    ought to ha' gone to you then.
But—cheap repairs for a cheap 'un—the
    doctors said I'd do.

Mary, why didn't *you* warn me? I've
    allus heeded to you,
Excep'—I know—about women; but you
    are a spirit now;
An', wife, they was only women, and
    I was a man. That's how.
An' a man 'e must go with a woman, as
    you *could* not understand;
But I never talked 'em secrets. I paid
    'em out o' hand.
Thank Gawd, I can pay for my fancies!
    Now what's five thousand to me,
For a berth off the Paternosters in the
    haven where I would be?
I believe in the Resurrection, if I read my
    Bible plain,
But I wouldn't trust 'em at Wokin'; we're
    safer at sea again.
For the heart it shall go with the treasure
    —go down to the sea in ships.
I'm sick of the hired women. I'll kiss
    my girl on her lips!
I'll be content with my fountain. I'll
    drink from my own well,
And the wife of my youth shall charm
    me—an' the rest can go to Hell!
(Dickie, *he* will, that's certain.) I'll lie
    in our standin'-bed,
An' Mac'll take her in ballast—an' she
    trims best by the head. . . .
Down by the head an' sinkin', her fires
    are drawn and cold,
And the water's splashin' hollow on the
    skin of the empty hold—
Churning an' choking and chuckling,
    quiet and scummy and dark—
Full to her lower hatches and risin' steady.
    Hark!
That was the after-bulkhead. . . . She's
    flooded from stem to stern. . . .
'Never seen death yet, Dickie? . . .
    Well, now is your time to learn!
                     1896

PERCY BYSSHE SHELLEY

Ozymandias

I met a traveller from an antique land
Who said: Two vast and trunkless legs of
stone
Stand in the desert. Near them, on the
sand,
Half sunk, a shattered visage lies, whose
frown,
And wrinkled lip, and sneer of cold com-
mand,
Tell that its sculptor well those passions
read
Which yet survive, (stamped on these
lifeless things,)
The hand that mocked them and the
heart that fed:
And on the pedestal these words appear:
"My name is Ozymandias, king of kings:
Look on my works, ye Mighty, and de-
spair!"
Nothing beside remains. Round the
decay
Of that colossal wreck, boundless and bare
The lone and level sands stretch far away.
1818

STEPHEN VINCENT BENET

Litany for Dictatorships

For all those beaten, for the broken heads,
The fosterless, the simple, the oppressed,
The ghosts in the burning city of our
time . . .

For those taken in rapid cars to the house
and beaten
By the skilful boys, the boys with the rubber fists,
—Held down and beaten, the table cutting their loins,

Or kicked in the groin and left, with the
muscles jerking
Like a headless hen's on the floor of the
slaughter-house
While they brought the next man in with
his white eyes staring.
For those who still said "Red Front!" or
"God Save the Crown!"
And for those who were not courageous
But were beaten nevertheless.
For those who spit out the bloody stumps
of their teeth
Quietly in the hall,
Sleep well on stone or iron, watch for
the time
And kill the guard in the privy before they
die,
Those with the deep-socketed eyes and
the lamp burning.

For those who carry the scars, who walk
lame—for those
Whose nameless graves are made in the
prison-yard
And the earth smoothed back before
morning and the lime scattered.

For those slain at once. For those living
through months and years
Enduring, watching, hoping, going each
day
To the work or the queue for meat or the
secret club,
Living meanwhile, begetting children,
smuggling guns,
And found and killed at the end like rats
in a drain.

For those escaping
Incredibly into exile and wandering there.
For those who live in the small rooms of
foreign cities
And who yet think of the country, the
long green grass,
The childhood voices, the language, the
way wind smelt then,
The shape of rooms, the coffee drunk at
the table,

The talk with friends, the loved city, the
    waiter's face,
The gravestones, with the name, where
    they will not lie
Nor in any of that earth. Their children
    are strangers.

For those who planned and were leaders
    and were beaten
And for those, humble and stupid, who
    had no plan
But were denounced, but grew angry, but
    told a joke,
But could not explain, but were sent
    away to the camp,
But had their bodies shipped back in the
    sealed coffins,
"Died of pneumonia." "Died trying to
    escape."

For those growers of wheat who were shot
    by their own wheat-stacks,
For those growers of bread who were sent
    to the ice-locked wastes,
And their flesh remembers their fields.

For those denounced by their smug, hor-
    rible children
For a peppermint-star and the praise of
    the Perfect State,
For all those strangled or gelded or merely
    starved
To make perfect states; for the priest
    hanged in his cassock,
The Jew with his chest crushed in and
    his eyes dying,
The revolutionist lynched by the private
    guards
To make perfect states, in the names of
    the perfect states.

For those betrayed by the neighbors they
    shook hands with
And for the traitors, sitting in the hard
    chair
With the loose sweat crawling their hair
    and their fingers restless
As they tell the street and the house and
    the man's name.

And for those sitting at table in the house
With the lamp lit and the plates and the
    smell of food,
Talking so quietly; when they hear the
    cars
And the knock at the door, and they look
    at each other quickly
And the woman goes to the door with a
    stiff face,
Smoothing her dress.
        "We are all good citizens here.
We believe in the Perfect State."
            And that was the last
Time Tony or Karl or Shorty came to the
    house
And the family was liquidated later.
It was the last time.
        We heard the shots in the night
But nobody knew next day what the
    trouble was
And a man must go to his work. So I
    didn't see him
For three days, then, and me near out of
    my mind
And all the patrols on the streets with their
    dirty guns
And when he came back, he looked
    drunk, and the blood was on him.

For the women who mourn their dead in
    the secret night,
For the children taught to keep quiet, the
    old children,
The children spat-on at school.
        For the wrecked laboratory,
The gutted house, the dunged picture, the
    pissed-in well,
The naked corpse of Knowledge flung in
    the square
And no man lifting a hand and no man
    speaking.

For the cold of the pistol-butt and the
    bullet's heat,
For the rope that chokes, the manacles
    that bind,
The huge voice, metal, that lies from a
    thousand tubes
And the stuttering machine-gun that
    answers all.

For the man crucified on the crossed machine-guns
Without name, without resurrection, without stars,
His dark head heavy with death and his flesh long sour
With the smell of his many prisons— John Smith, John Doe,
John Nobody—oh, crack your mind for his name!
Faceless as water, naked as the dust,
Dishonored as the earth the gas-shells poison
And barbarous with portent.
                                        This is he.
This is the man they ate at the green table
Putting their gloves on ere they touched the meat.
This is the fruit of war, the fruit of peace,
The ripeness of invention, the new lamb,
The answer to the wisdom of the wise.
And still he hangs, and still he will not die,
And still, on the steel city of our years
The light fails and the terrible blood streams down.
We thought we were done with these things but we were wrong.
We thought, because we had power, we had wisdom.
We thought the long train would run to the end of Time.
We thought the light would increase.
Now the long train stands derailed and the bandits loot it.
Now the boar and the asp have power in our time.
Now the night rolls back on the West and the night is solid.
Our fathers and ourselves sowed dragon's teeth.
Our children know and suffer the armed men.

                                        1936

ARCHIBALD MACLEISH
Speech to a Crowd

Tell me my patient friends: awaiters of messages:
From what other shore—from what stranger—
Whence was the word to come? Who was to lesson you?

Listeners under a child's crib in a manger:
Listeners once by oracles: now by the transoms:
Whom are you waiting for? Who do you think will explain?

Listeners thousands of years and still no answer:
Writers at night to Miss Lonely-Hearts: awkward spellers:
Open your eyes! There is only earth and the man!

There is only you in the world: you on the telephone!
No one else is on the air to whisper:
No one else but you will push the bell.

No one knows if you don't: neither ships
Nor landing-fields decode the dark between:
You have your eyes and what your eyes see IS.

The earth you see is really the earth you are seeing:
The sun is truly excellent: truly warm:
Women are beautiful as you have seen them—

Their breasts (believe it) like cooing of doves in a portico:
They bear at their breasts tenderness softly. Look at them!
Look at yourselves. You are strong. You are well formed.

Look at the world—the world you never
took!
It is really true you may live in the world
heedlessly:
Why do you wait to read it in a book
then?

Write it yourselves! Write to yourselves
if you need to!
Tell yourselves there is sun and the sun
will rise:
Tell yourselves the earth has food to feed
you—

Let the dead men say that men must die.
Who better than you can know what death
is?
How can a bone or a broken body surmise
it?

Let the dead weep with their whistling
breath:
Laugh at them! Say that murdered gods
may wake
But we who work have end of work together!

Tell yourselves the earth is yours to take.
Waiting for messages out of the dark you
were poor.
The world was always there: you would
not take it.

1936

JOHN KEATS

Ode on a Grecian Urn

Thou still unravished bride of quietness,
Thou foster-child of silence and slow
time,
Sylvan historian, who canst thus express
A flowery tale more sweetly than our
rhyme:
What leaf-fringed legend haunts about thy
shape

Of deities or mortals, or of both,
In Tempe or the dales of Arcady?
What men or gods are these? What
maidens loth?
What mad pursuit? What struggle to
escape?
What pipes and timbrels? What
wild ecstasy?

Heard melodies are sweet, but those un-
heard
Are sweeter; therefore, ye soft pipes,
play on;
Not to the sensual ear, but, more endeared,
Pipe to the spirit ditties of no tone:
Fair youth, beneath the trees, thou canst
not leave
Thy song, nor ever can those trees be
bare;
Bold Lover, never, never canst thou
kiss,
Though winning near the goal—yet, do
not grieve;
She cannot fade, though thou hast not
thy bliss,
Forever wilt thou love, and she be
fair!

Ah, happy, happy boughs! that cannot
shed
Your leaves, nor ever bid the Spring
adieu:
And, happy melodist, unwearièd,
Forever piping songs forever new;
More happy love! more happy, happy
love!
Forever warm and still to be enjoyed,
Forever panting, and forever young;
All breathing human passion far above,
That leaves a heart high-sorrowful and
cloyed,
A burning forehead, and a parching
tongue.

Who are these coming to the sacrifice?
To what green altar, O mysterious
priest,
Lead'st thou that heifer lowing at the
skies,

And all her silken flanks with garlands
dressed?
What little town by river or sea shore,
Or mountain-built with peaceful citadel,
Is emptied of this folk, this pious
morn?
And, little town, thy streets for evermore
Will silent be; and not a soul to tell
Why thou art desolate, can e'er re-
turn.

O Attic shape! Fair attitude! with brede
Of marble men and maidens over-
wrought,
With forest branches and the trodden
weed;
Thou, silent form, dost tease us out of
thought
As doth eternity: Cold Pastoral!
When old age shall this generation
waste,
Thou shalt remain, in midst of other
woe
Than ours, a friend to man, to whom thou
say'st,
"Beauty is truth, truth beauty,"—that
is all
Ye know on earth, and all ye need to
know.

1819

PERCY BYSSHE SHELLEY

Hymn to Intellectual Beauty

The awful shadow of some unseen Power
Floats though unseen among us, visiting
This various world with as inconstant
wing
As summer winds that creep from flower
to flower;
Like moonbeams that behind some piny
mountain shower,
It visits with inconstant glance
Each human heart and countenance;

Like hues and harmonies of evening,
Like clouds in starlight widely spread,
Like memory of music fled,
Like aught that for its grace may be
Dear, and yet dearer for its mystery.

Spirit of BEAUTY, that dost consecrate
With thine own hues all thou dost shine
upon
Of human thought or form, where art
thou gone?
Why dost thou pass away, and leave our
state,
This dim vast vale of tears, vacant and
desolate?
Ask why the sunlight not forever
Weaves rainbows o'er yon mountain
river;
Why aught should fail and fade that once
is shown;
Why fear and dream and death and
birth
Cast on the daylight of this earth
Such gloom; why man has such a scope
For love and hate, despondency and hope.

No voice from some sublimer world hath
ever
To sage or poet these responses given;
Therefore the names of Demon, Ghost,
and Heaven,
Remain the records of their vain endeavor,
Frail spells, whose uttered charm might
not avail to sever,
From all we hear and all we see,
Doubt, chance, and mutability.
Thy light alone, like mist o'er mountains
driven,
Or music by the night wind sent
Through strings of some still instru-
ment,
Or moonlight on a midnight stream,
Gives grace and truth to life's unquiet
dream.

Love, Hope, and Self-esteem, like clouds,
depart
And come, for some uncertain moments
lent.
Man' were immortal and omnipotent,

Didst thou, unknown and awful as thou
    art,
Keep with thy glorious train firm state
    within his heart.
  Thou messenger of sympathies
  That wax and wane in lovers' eyes!
Thou, that to human thought art nourish-
    ment,
  Like darkness to a dying flame,
  Depart not as thy shadow came,
  Depart not, lest the grave should be,
Like life and fear, a dark reality!

While yet a boy I sought for ghosts, and
    sped
  Through many a listening chamber,
    cave and ruin,
  And starlight wood, with fearful steps
    pursuing
Hopes of high talk with the departed
    dead;
I called on poisonous names with which
    our youth is fed.
  I was not heard—I saw them not—
  When, musing deeply on the lot
Of life, at that sweet time when winds are
    wooing
  All vital things that wake to bring
  News of birds and blossoming,—
  Sudden, thy shadow fell on me;
I shrieked, and clasped my hands in ec-
    stasy!

I vowed that I would dedicate my powers
  To thee and thine—have I not kept the
    vow?
  With beating heart and streaming eyes,
    even now
I call the phantoms of a thousand hours
Each from his voiceless grave: they have in
    visioned bowers
  Of studious zeal or love's delight
  Outwatched with me the envious
    night—
They know that never joy illumed my
    brow
  Unlinked with hope that thou wouldst
    free

This world from its dark slavery,
  That thou, O awful LOVELINESS,
Wouldst give whate'er these words can-
    not express.

The day becomes more solemn and serene
  When noon is past; there is a harmony
  In autumn, and a luster in its sky,
Which through the summer is not heard
    or seen,
As if it could not be, as if it had not been!
  Thus let thy power, which like the truth
  Of nature on my passive youth
Descended, to my onward life supply
  Its calm,—to one who worships thee,
  And every form containing thee,
Whom, SPIRIT fair, thy spells did bind
To fear himself, and love all humankind.
                                    1816

EDNA ST. VINCENT MILLAY

Euclid Alone Has Looked on Beauty Bare

Euclid alone has looked on Beauty bare.
Let all who prate of Beauty hold their
    peace,
And lay them prone upon the earth and
    cease
To ponder on themselves, the while they
    stare
At nothing, intricately drawn nowhere
In shapes of shifting lineage; let geese
Gabble and hiss, but heroes seek release
From dusty bondage into luminous air.
O blinding hour, O holy, terrible day,
When first the shaft into his vision shone
Of light anatomized! Euclid alone
Has looked on Beauty bare. Fortunate
    they

From: *The Harp Weaver and Other Poems*, published by Harper & Brothers. Copyright, 1920, by Edna St. Vincent Millay.

Who, though only once and then but far
    away,
Have heard her massive sandal set on
    stone.
                         1923

WILLIAM SCHWENCK GILBERT

The Aesthete

If you're anxious for to shine in the high
    aesthetic line as a man of culture
    rare,
You must get up all the germs of the tran-
    scendental terms, and plant them
    everywhere.
You must lie upon the daisies, and dis-
    course in novel phrases of your com-
    plicated state of mind,
The meaning doesn't matter if it's only
    idle chatter of a transcendental kind.
    And everyone will say,
    As you walk your mystic way,
"If this young man expresses himself in
    terms too deep for *me*,
Why, what a very singularly deep young
    man this deep young man must be!"

Be eloquent in praise of the very dull old
    ways which have long since passed
    away,
And convince 'em, if you can, that the
    reign of good Queen Anne was
    Culture's palmiest day.
Of course you will pooh-pooh whatever's
    fresh and new, and declare it's crude
    and mean,
For Art stopped short in the cultivated
    court of the Empress Josephine.
    And everyone will say,
    As you walk your mystic way,
"If that's not good enough for him which
    is good enough for *me*,

Why, what a very cultivated kind of youth
    this kind of youth must be!"

Then a sentimental passion of a vegetable
    fashion must excite your languid
    spleen,
An attachment *à la* Plato for a bashful
    young potato, or a not-too-French
    French bean!
Though the Philistines may jostle, you will
    rank as an apostle in the high aes-
    thetic band,
If you walk down Piccadilly with a poppy
    or a lily in your medieval hand.
    And everyone will say,
    As you walk your flowery way,
"If he's content with a vegetable love,
    which would certainly not suit *me*,
Why, what a most particularly pure young
    man this pure young man must be!"
                         1881

KARL SHAPIRO

General and Personal Idiom

FROM ESSAY ON RIME

In one of the most widely circulated
Anthologies of current rime, a speech,
The actual peroration of a man
Fated to die, is set within the text
Beside the most exemplary and abstruse
Of modern poems. Vanzetti's broken
    English
Seen in the context of self-conscious art
In company with the works of gifted minds
At perfect ease, argues a new confusion.
By what philosophy the editor
Attempts to hold this tragic martyred thing
A hostage to the literary cause
Is, in a sense, our present argument.
For much of modern rime denotes this
    bent
To cancel out the distance and the line

From *Essay on Rime* by Karl Shapiro, Reynal & Hitchcock, N.Y.

Between the language of spontaneous na-
  ture
And that of formal artifice. So basic
A solecism cries out for explanation.

Compare the plea for innocence in a play,
Bassanio's for instance with the words
Vanzetti used before the New England
  court.
One lives and dies in the imagination;
Its reference to existence is oblique
And only by suggestion can impinge
Upon the behavior of the audience.
The other is what the audience knows as
  real,
A fact of the statistical world, as like
An actor's agonizing as true blood
To a splash of crimson paint upon a dress.
Our editor pursues the rule of thumb
Allowed by poets themselves in his collec-
  tion.
Some can no longer verify the news
Except by dramatization; they report
Events as symbols of events, and speech
As poetry. Lacking the prime restraint
Of artists who process experience
Before using it raw, they yield to haste,
Lay out the poem with scissors and with
  paste
Like so much copy for the linotype.

The question is one of language. In the
  past
Prose had a separate rhetoric, rime had
  caste;
The stage was not the agora and vice versa.
Not even the rustic at the play would think
A tragedy history, and though an embit-
  tered ode
Might cost the author's head, it was a thing
That held to its linguistic mode. Satire
Was not the pistol of straight accusation,
And hate itself was filtered through the
  skin
Of grammar. So much the worse for us
Whose poets converge on every medium
Of linguistic expression and swarm across
The Rubicon from art to actuality,
Not stinting to bear off the documents
Of the new trivium, Sociology,

Psychoanalysis and Economics. To quote
Is an accepted practice of our rime,
As if poetry needs the authority
Of laboratories and the latest news
Of battle and the rights of the majority.

I speak of those innumerable epics, large
And small, which crowd into the latest row
Of poetry books upon the wall; of wild
Auricular prophecies of the idea-mad,
The humorless hymns to government in
  particular,
The bread-and-butter verses of the poor
In talent; of those who speak in deference
To dialectics, to whom a billboard ad
Has multiple reference, and who find in
  Alice
An allegory and not an innocent child.

Suspect the novelist the title of whose book
Is lifted from a sermon or a play:
His backbone bends in an apology.
Suspect the poet who wallows in symbol-
  ogy
And reinforces what he has to say
With "indigestible portions"; who takes
  phrases,
Sentences, paragraphs and passages
Into the soft gray matter of his brain
And over them secretes his nacreous pearl.
The prominent symbol of our verse is
  "bone."
How few successes lead our failures on.

The broad use of the raw untreated data
Of science and of whole experience
Expresses a more serious confusion
In rime than the chaos of prosody.
To redefine the general idiom
And separate it from the personal
In poetry seems imperative in our day.
We cannot justify our own excesses
By citing connoisseurs of bric-a-brac;
What they have rescued from the drift and
  wrack
Of all the past or the immediate present
Is their own property; nor does their need
Imply ours necessarily. Even to those
Who thought they saw, like Whitman, the
  Just City

We owe no public debt.   His oratory
On democratic vistas and geography
Is as particular to his character
As vocatives and the wind-blown beard.
     The pity
Of *Leaves of Grass* is that the straw is
     eaten
And the good wheat left over by our poets.
The wide style of the dry Americana,
Appealing as it is to messengers
Of the official muse, really encloses
A special doctrine of philosophy
As scholarly as Emerson's.   But who
Except Hart Crane has tasted the pure
     manna
Of *Song of Myself,* the naked seed of rime?
When Whitman had the nation on his
     brain
He served us ill, in my opinion; his leap
Into the personal infinite, however,
Saved him from drowning in his Susque-
     hanna.

There is a general idiom to all rime,
A special idiom to one generation,
And, thirdly, the idiom of the single pen.
The poet who does not know by sure in-
     stinct
The first, is headed for the rocks of prose.
How many a gallant prelude or frail lyric
Is overturned for ignorance of the sea
Of language.   The poet who neither feels
     nor knows
The flow and current of the second kind
Falls to mere manners and nostalgia.
But he who cannot use the first and second
To personal advantage shows no mind
For poetry as the function of one heart.
If anonymity is indeed a failing,
And so we think today, the greater part
Of our anthology is left unsigned;
Its poems appear as nameless synonyms
In the faint collective effort of our art.

I do not here attempt the definition
Of rime, which is the province of esthetics,
But to point out its ratio to language.

In the mathematical sense, rime is a power,
Prose raised to the numerical exponent
Of three or six or even *n,* depending
Upon the propensity of the literature
At a particular time and on the bent
Of the particular poet.   It is therefore
A heightening and a measure of intensity.
In the physical sense, rime is the nuclear
And vital element of speech and prose,
The very protoplasm of the tongue,
Or that organic substance which survives
The structures it creates.   Words are as
     lives,
Deaths and mutations, and the poet learns
Through search for life, the biology of
     rime.
In the theological sense, rime is the ghost
And prose the flesh of language.   Poets
     may boast
That they have known the mystic rose of
     good,
The blessed face of truth, the host of
     beauty;
They press the oil and elevate the wine,
For poetry like philosophy is divine
And wells up from the uncreated will. . . .
                                        1946

▼▼▼▼▼▼▼▼▼▼▼▼▼▼▼▼▼▼▼▼▼▼▼▼▼

WYSTAN HUGH AUDEN

Voltaire at Ferney[1]

Perfectly happy now, he looked at his es-
     tate.
An exile making watches glanced up as he
     passed,
And went on working; where a hospital
     was rising fast
A joiner touched his cap; an agent came
     to tell
Some of the trees he'd planted were pro-
     gressing well.
The white alps glittered.   It was summer.
     He was very great.

[1] From *Another Time,* published by Random House, Inc., 1940.   Copyright, 1945, by W. H. Auden.
Reprinted by permission of Random House, Inc.

Far off in Paris, where his enemies
Whispered that he was wicked, in an up-
  right chair
A blind old woman longed for death and
  letters. He would write
"Nothing is better than life." But was
  it? Yes, the fight
Against the false and the unfair
Was always worth it. So was gardening.
  Civilise.

Cajoling, scolding, scheming, cleverest of
  them all,
He'd led the other children in a holy war
Against the infamous grown-ups; and, like
  a child, been sly
And humble when there was occasion for
The two-faced answer or the plain pro-
  tective lie,
But patient like a peasant waited for their
  fall.

And never doubted, like D'Alembert, he
  would win:
Only Pascal was a great enemy, the rest
Were rats already poisoned; there was
  much, though, to be done,
And only himself to count upon.
Dear Diderot was dull but did his best;
Rousseau, he'd always known, would blub-
  ber and give in.

Night fell and made him think of women:
  Lust
Was one of the great teachers; Pascal was
  a fool.
How Emilie had loved astronomy and bed;
Pimpette had loved him too like scandal;
  he was glad.
He'd done his share of weeping for Jeru-
  salem: As a rule
It was the pleasure-haters who became un-
  just.

Yet, like a sentinel, he could not sleep.
  The night was full of wrong,
Earthquakes and executions. Soon he
  would be dead,
And still all over Europe stood the horrible
  nurses

Itching to boil their children. Only his
  verses
Perhaps could stop them: He must go on
  working. Overhead
The uncomplaining stars composed their
  lucid song.

                                              1940

MATTHEW ARNOLD

Dover Beach

The sea is calm to-night.
The tide is full, the moon lies fair
Upon the straits;—on the French coast the
  light
Gleams and is gone; the cliffs of England
  stand,
Glimmering and vast, out in the tranquil
  bay.
Come to the window, sweet is the night-
  air!
Only, from the long line of spray
Where the sea meets the moon-blanched
  land,
Listen! you hear the grating roar
Of pebbles which the waves draw back,
  and fling,
At their return, up the high strand,
Begin, and cease, and then again begin,
With tremulous cadence slow, and bring
The eternal note of sadness in.

Sophocles long ago
Heard it on the Ægean, and it brought
Into his mind the turbid ebb and flow
Of human misery; we
Find also in the sound a thought,
Hearing it by this distant northern sea.
The Sea of Faith
Was once, too, at the full, and round
  earth's shore
Lay like the folds of a bright girdle furled.
But now I only hear
Its melancholy, long, withdrawing roar,
Retreating, to the breath

Of the night-wind, down the vast edges
　　drear
And naked shingles of the world.

Ah, love, let us be true
To one another! for the world, which
　　seems
To lie before us like a land of dreams,
So various, so beautiful, so new,
Hath really neither joy, nor love, nor light,
Nor certitude, nor peace, nor help for pain;
And we are here as on a darkling plain
Swept with confused alarms of struggle
　　and flight,
Where ignorant armies clash by night.

1867

ARCHIBALD MACLEISH

"Dover Beach"—A Note to That Poem

　　　　　　　　　　The wave withdrawing
Withers with seaward rustle of flimsy
　　water
Sucking the sand down: dragging at
　　empty shells:
The roil after it settling: too smooth:
　　smothered. . . .

After forty a man's a fool to wait in the
Sea's face for the full force and the roar-
　　ing of
Surf to come over him: droves of careen-
　　ing water.
After forty the tug's out and the salt and
　　the
Sea follow it: less sound and violence:
Nevertheless the ebb has its own beauty—
Shells sand and all and the whispering
　　rustle.
There's earth in it and the bubbles of foam
　　gone.

Moreover—and this too has its lovely
　　uses—

It's the outward wave that spills the in-
　　ward forward
Tripping the proud piled mute virginal
Mountain of water in wallowing welter of
　　light and
Sound enough—thunder for miles back:
　　it's a fine and a
Wild smother to vanish in: pulling down—
Tripping with outward ebb the urgent
　　inward.

Speaking alone for myself it's the steep
　　hill and the
Toppling lift of the young men I am to-
　　ward now—
Waiting for that as the wave for the next
　　wave.
Let them go over us all I say with the
　　thunder of
What's to be next in the world. It's we
　　will be under it!

1936

RALPH WALDO EMERSON

The Problem

I like a church; I like a cowl;
I love a prophet of the soul;
And on my heart monastic aisles
Fall like sweet strains, or pensive smiles;
Yet not for all his faith can see
Would I that cowlèd churchman be.
Why should the vest on him allure,
Which I could not on me endure?

Not from a vain or shallow thought
His awful Jove young Phidias brought;
Never from lips of cunning fell
The thrilling Delphic oracle;
Out from the heart of nature rolled
The burdens of the Bible old;
The litanies of nations came,

Like the volcano's tongue of flame,
Up from the burning core below,—
The canticles of love and woe:
The hand that rounded Peter's dome
And groined the aisles of Christian Rome
Wrought in a sad sincerity;
Himself from God he could not free;
He builded better than he knew;—
The conscious stone to beauty grew.

Know'st thou what wove yon woodbird's
      nest
Of leaves, and feathers from her breast?
Or how the fish outbuilt her shell,
Painting with morn each annual cell?
Or how the sacred pine-tree adds
To her old leaves new myriads?
Such and so grew these holy piles,
Whilst love and terror laid the tiles.
Earth proudly wears the Parthenon,
As the best gem upon her zone,
And Morning opes with haste her lids
To gaze upon the Pyramids;
O'er England's abbeys bends the sky,
As on its friends, with kindred eye;
For out of Thought's interior sphere
These wonders rose to upper air;
And Nature gladly gave them place,
Adopted them into her race,
And granted them an equal date
With Andes and with Ararat.

These temples grew as grows the grass;
Art might obey, but not surpass.
The passive Master lent his hand
To the vast soul that o'er him planned;
And the same power that reared the shrine
Bestrode the tribes that knelt within.
Ever the fiery Pentecost
Girds with one flame the countless host,
Trances the heart through chanting choirs,
And through the priest the mind inspires.
The word upon the prophet spoken
Was writ on tables yet unbroken;
The word by seers or sibyls told,
In groves of oak, or fanes of gold,
Still floats upon the morning wind,

Still whispers to the willing mind.
One accent of the Holy Ghost
The heedless world hath never lost.
I know what say the fathers wise,—
The Book itself before me lies,
Old *Chrysostom,* best Augustine,
And he who blent both in his line,
The younger *Golden Lips* or mines,
Taylor, the Shakspere of divines,
His words are music in my ear,
I see his cowlèd portrait dear;
And yet, for all his faith could see,
I would not the good bishop be.

                                    1840

HENRY ADAMS
Prayer to the Virgin of Chartres

Gracious Lady:—

Simple as when I asked your aid before;
Humble as when I prayed for grace in
      vain
Seven hundred years ago; weak, weary,
      sore
In heart and hope, I ask your help again.

You, who remembered all, remember me;
An English scholar of a Norman name,
I was a thousand who then crossed the sea
To wrangle in the Paris schools for fame.

When your Byzantine portal was still
      young
I prayed there with my master Abailard;
When *Ave Maris Stella* was first sung,
I helped to sing it here with Saint Bernard.

When Blanche set up your gorgeous Rose
      of France
I stood among the servants of the Queen;
And when Saint Louis made his penitence,
I followed barefoot where the King had
      been.

The selection from Henry Adams, *Letters to a Niece,* is used by permission of the publishers, Houghton Mifflin Company.

For centuries I brought you all my cares,
And vexed you with the murmur of a
    child;
You heard the tedious burden of my pray-
    ers;
You could not grant them, but at least you
    smiled.

If then I left you, it was not my crime,
Or if a crime, it was not mine alone.
All children wander with the truant Time.
Pardon me too! You pardoned once your
    Son!

For He said to you:—"Wist ye not that I
Must be about my Father's business?"
    So,
Seeking his Father he pursued his way
Straight to the Cross towards which we all
    must go.

So I too wandered off among the host
That racked the earth to find the Father's
    clue.
I did not find the Father, but I lost
What now I value more, the Mother,—
    You!

I thought the fault was yours that foiled
    my search;
I turned and broke your image on its
    throne,
Cast down my idol, and resumed my
    march
To claim the Father's empire for my own.

Crossing the hostile sea, our greedy band
Saw rising hills and forests in the blue;
Our Father's kingdom in the promised
    land!
—We seized it, and dethroned the Father
    too.

And now we are the Father, with our
    brood,
Ruling the Infinite, not Three but One;
We made our world and saw that it was
    good;
Ourselves we worship, and we have no
    Son.

Yet we have Gods, for even our strong
    nerve
Falters before the Energy we own.
Which shall be master? Which of us
    shall serve?
Which wears the fetters? which shall bear
    the crown?

Brave though we be, we dread to face
    the Sphinx,
Or answer the old riddle she still asks.
Strong as we are, our reckless courage
    shrinks
To look beyond the piece-work of our
    tasks.

But when we must, we pray, as in the
    past
Before the Cross on which your Son was
    nailed.
Listen, dear lady! You shall hear the
    last
Of the strange prayers Humanity has
    wailed:

Prayer to the Dynamo

Mysterious Power! Gentle Friend!
Despotic Master! Tireless Force!
You and We are near the End.
Either You or We must bend
To bear the martyrs' Cross.

We know ourselves, what we can bear
As men; our strength and weakness too;
Down to the fraction of a hair;
And know that we, with all our care
And knowledge, know not you.

You come in silence, Primal Force,
We know not whence, or when, or why;
You stay a moment in your course
To play; and, lo! you leap across
To Alpha Centauri!

We know not whether you are kind,
Or cruel in your fiercer mood;
But be you Matter, be you Mind,
We think we know that you are blind,
And we alone are good.

We know that prayer is thrown away,
For you are only force and light;
A shifting current; night and day;
We know this well, and yet we pray,
For prayer is infinite,

Like you! Within the finite sphere
That bounds the impotence of thought,
We search an outlet everywhere
But only find that we are here
And that you are—are not!

What are we then? the lords of space?
The master-mind whose tasks you do?
Jockey who rides you in the race?
Or are we atoms whirled apace,
Shaped and controlled by you?

Still silence! Still no end in sight!
No sound in answer to our cry!
Then, by the God we now hold tight,
Though we destroy soul, life and light,
Answer you shall—or die!

We are no beggars! What care we
For hopes or terrors, love or hate?
What for the universe? We see
Only our certain destiny
And the last word of Fate.

Seize, then, the Atom! rack his joints!
Tear out of him his secret spring!
Grind him to nothing!—though he points
To us, and his life-blood anoints
Me—the dead Atom-King!

———

A curious prayer, dear lady! is it not?
Strangely unlike the prayers I prayed to
    you!
Stranger because you find me at this spot,
Here, at your feet, asking your help anew.

Strangest of all, that I have ceased to strive,
Ceased even care what new coin fate
    shall strike.
In truth it does not matter. Fate will give
Some answer; and all answers are alike.

So, while we slowly rack and torture
    death

And wait for what the final void will
    show,
Waiting I feel the energy of faith
Not in the future science, but in you!

The man who solves the Infinite, and
    needs
The force of solar systems for his play,
Will not need me, nor greatly care what
    deeds
Made me illustrious in the dawn of day.

He will send me, dethroned, to claim my
    rights,
Fossil survival of an age of stone,
Among the cave-men and the troglodytes
Who carved the mammoth on the mam-
    moth's bone.

He will forget my thought, my acts, my
    fame,
As we forget the shadows of the dusk,
Or catalogue the echo of a name
As we the scratches on the mammoth's
    tusk.

But when, like me, he too has trod the
    track
Which leads him up to power above con-
    trol,
He too will have no choice but wander
    back
And sink in helpless hopelessness of soul,

Before your majesty of grace and love,
The purity, the beauty and the faith;
The depth of tenderness beneath; above,
The glory of the life and of the death.

When your Byzantine portal still was
    young,
I came here with my master Abailard;
When *Ave Maris Stella* was first sung,
I joined to sing it here with Saint Ber-
    nard.

When Blanche set up your glorious Rose
    of France,
In scholar's robes I waited on the Queen;
When good Saint Louis did his penitence,

My prayer was deep like his: my faith as
    keen.

What loftier prize seven hundred years
    shall bring,
What deadlier struggles for a larger air,
What immortality our strength shall wring
From Time and Space, we may—or may
    not—care;

But years, or ages, or eternity,
Will find me still in thought before your
    throne,
Pondering the mystery of Maternity,
Soul within Soul,—Mother and Child in
    One!

Help me to see! not with my mimic
    sight—
With yours! which carried radiance, like
    the sun,
Giving the rays you saw with—light in
    light—
Tying all suns and stars and worlds in
    one.

Help me to know! not with my mock-
    ing art—
With you, you knew yourself unbound by
    laws;
Gave God your strength, your life, your
    sight, your heart,
And took from him the Thought that Is
    —the Cause.

Help me to feel! not with my insect
    sense,—
With yours that felt all life alive in you;
Infinite heart beating at your expense;
Infinite passion breathing the breath you
    drew!

Help me to bear! not my own baby load,
But yours; who bore the failure of the
    light,
The strength, the knowledge and the
    thought of God,—
The futile folly of the Infinite!
                          1920

WILLIAM BLAKE

"Mock on, Mock on, Voltaire, Rousseau"

Mock on, mock on, Voltaire, Rousseau;
Mock on, mock on; 'tis all in vain!
You throw the sand against the wind,
And the wind blows it back again.

And every sand becomes a gem
Reflected in the beams divine;
Blown back they blind the mocking eye,
But still in Israel's paths they shine.

The Atoms of Democritus
And Newton's Particles of Light
Are sands upon the Red Sea shore,
Where Israel's tents do shine so bright.
                        c. 1800-1810.

FRANCIS THOMPSON

The Hound of Heaven

I fled Him, down the nights and down
    the days;
  I fled Him, down the arches of the
    years;
I fled Him, down the labyrinthine ways
  Of my own mind; and in the mist of
    tears
I hid from Him, and under running
    laughter.
    Up vistaed hopes, I sped;
    And shot, precipitated,
  Adown Titanic glooms of chasmèd
    fears,
From those strong Feet that followed, fol-
    lowed after.
    But with unhurrying chase,
    And unperturbèd pace,
Deliberate speed, majestic instancy,
    They beat—and a Voice beat
    More instant than the Feet:
"All things betray thee, who betrayest
    Me."

I pleaded, outlaw-wise,
By many a hearted casement, curtained
    red,
  Trellised with intertwining charities;
(For, though I knew His love Who fol-
    lowèd,
    Yet was I sore adread
Lest, having Him, I must have naught
    beside).
But, if one little casement parted wide,
  The gust of His approach would crash
    it to.
  Fear wist not to evade, as Love wist to
    pursue.
Across the margent of the world I fled,
  And troubled the gold gateways of the
    stars,
  Smiting for shelter on their clangèd bars;
    Fretted to dulcet jars
And silvern chatter the pale ports o' the
    moon.
I said to Dawn, Be sudden—to Eve, Be
    soon:
  With thy young skyey blossoms heap
    me over
    From this tremendous Lover—
Float thy vague veil about me, lest He see!
  I tempted all His servitors, but to find
My own betrayal in their constancy,
In faith to Him their fickleness to me,
  Their traitorous trueness, and their loyal
    deceit.
To all swift things for swiftness did I sue;
  Clung to the whistling mane of every
    wind.
    But whether they swept, smoothly
    fleet,
    The long savannahs of the blue;
    Or whether, thunder-driven,
    They clanged His chariot 'thwart a
    heaven
  Plashy with flying lightnings round the
    spurn o' their feet:
    Fear wist not to evade as Love wist to
    pursue.
    Still with unhurrying chase,
    And unperturbèd pace,
  Deliberate speed, majestic instancy,
    Came on the following Feet,
    And a Voice above their beat:

"Naught shelters thee, who wilt not
    shelter Me."

I sought no more that after which I
    strayed
    In face of man or maid;
But still within the little children's eyes
    Seems something, something that re-
    plies,
They at least are for me, surely for me!
I turned me to them very wistfully;
But just as their young eyes grew sudden
    fair
    With dawning answers there,
Their angel plucked them from me by the
    hair.
"Come then, ye other children, Nature's,—
    share
With me" (said I) "your delicate fellow-
    ship;
    Let me greet you lip to lip,
    Let me twine with you caresses,
    Wantoning
    With our Lady-Mother's vagrant
    tresses;
    Banqueting
    With her in her wind-walled palace,
    Underneath her azured daïs;
Quaffing, as your taintless way is,
    From a chalice
Lucent-weeping out of the dayspring."
    So it was done:
I in their delicate fellowship was one—
Drew the bolt of Nature's secrecies.
    I knew all the swift importings
    On the willful face of skies;
    I knew how the clouds arise
    Spumèd of the wild sea-snortings—
    All that's born or dies,
    Rose and drooped with; made them
    shapers
Of mine own moods, or wailful or divine;
    With them joyed and was bereaven.
    I was heavy with the even,
    When she lit her glimmering tapers
    Round the day's dead sanctities;
    I laughed in the morning's eyes.
I triumphed and I saddened with all
    weather:
    Heaven and I wept together,

And its sweet tears were salt with mortal
    mine;
Against the red throb of its sunset-heart
    I laid my own to beat,
    And share commingling heat.
But not by that, by that, was eased my
    human smart;
In vain my tears were wet on Heaven's
    gray cheek.
For ah! we know not what each other
    says,
    These things and I: in sound *I* speak—
Their sound is but their stir, they speak by
    silences.
Nature, poor stepdame, cannot slake my
    drouth;
    Let her, if she would owe me,
Drop yon blue bosom-veil of sky, and
    show me
The breasts o' her tenderness:
Never did any milk of hers once bless
    My thirsting mouth.
    Nigh and nigh draws the chase,
    With unperturbèd pace,
Deliberate speed, majestic instancy,
    And past those noisèd Feet
    A Voice comes yet more fleet—
"Lo! naught contents thee, who content'st
    not Me."

Naked I wait Thy love's uplifted stroke!
My harness piece by piece Thou hast
    hewn from me,
    And smitten me to my knee:
    I am defenseless utterly.
    I slept, methinks, and woke,
And, slowly gazing, find me stripped in
    sleep.
In the rash lustihead of my young powers,
    I shook the pillaring hours
And pulled my life upon me; grimed with
    smears,
I stand amid the dust o' the mounded
    years—
My mangled youth lies dead beneath the
    heap.
My days have crackled and gone up in
    smoke,
Have puffed and burst as sun-starts on a
    stream.

    Yea, faileth now even dream
The dreamer, and the lute the lutanist;
Even the linked fantasies, in whose blos-
    somy twist
I swung the earth a trinket at my wrist,
Are yielding—cords of all too weak ac-
    count
For earth, with heavy griefs so overplussed.
    Ah! is Thy love indeed
A weed, albeit an amaranthine weed,
Suffering no flowers except its own to
    mount?
    Ah! must—
    Designer infinite!—
Ah! must Thou char the wood ere Thou
    canst limn with it?
My freshness spent its wavering shower i'
    the dust;
And now my heart is as a broken fount,
Wherein tear-drippings stagnate, spilt
    down ever
    From the dank thoughts that shiver
Upon the sighful branches of my mind.
    Such is: what is to be?
The pulp so bitter, how shall taste the
    rind?
I dimly guess what Time in mist con-
    founds;
Yet ever and anon a trumpet sounds
From the hid battlements of Eternity:
Those shaken mists a space unsettle, then
Round the half-glimpsèd turrets slowly
    wash again.
    But not ere him who summoneth
    I first have seen, enwound
With glooming robes purpureal, cypress-
    crowned:
His name I know, and what his trumpet
    saith.
Whether man's heart or life it be which
    yields
    Thee harvest, must Thy harvest fields
    Be dunged with rotten death?

    Now of that long pursuit
    Comes on at hand the bruit;
That Voice is round me like a bursting
    sea:
    "And is thy earth so marred,
    Shattered in shard on shard?

Lo, all things fly thee, for thou fliest Me!
  Strange, piteous, futile thing!
Wherefore should any set thee love apart?
Seeing none but I makes much of naught"
  (He said),
"And human love needs human meriting:
  How hast thou merited—
Of all man's clotted clay the dingiest clot?
  Alack, thou knowest not
How little worthy of any love thou art!
Whom wilt thou find to love ignoble thee,
  Save Me, save only Me?
All which I took from thee I did but take,
  Not for thy harms,
But just that thou might'st seek it in My
  arms.
  All which thy child's mistake
Fancies as lost, I have stored for thee at
  . home:
  Rise, clasp My hand, and come!"

Halts by me that footfall:
  Is my gloom, after all,
Shade of His hand, outstretched caress-
  ingly?—
  "Ah, fondest, blindest, weakest,
I am He Whom thou seekest!
Thou dravest love from thee, who dravest
  Me."
                                    1893

Shall these bones live? shall these
Bones live? And that which had been
  contained
In the bones (which were already dry)
  said chirping:
Because of the goodness of this Lady
And because of her loveliness, and because
She honours the Virgin in meditation,
We shine with brightness. And I who
  am here dissembled
Proffer my deeds to oblivion, and my love
To the posterity of the desert and the fruit
  of the gourd.
It is this which recovers
My guts the strings of my eyes and the in-
  digestible portions
Which the leopards reject. The Lady is
  withdrawn
In a white gown, to contemplation, in a
  white gown.
Let the whiteness of bones atone to for-
  getfulness.
There is no life in them. As I am for-
  gotten
And would be forgotten, so I would forget
Thus devoted, concentrated in purpose. And God said
Prophesy to the wind, to the wind only
  for only
The wind will listen. And the bones
  sang chirping
With the burden of the grasshopper, say-
  ing

T. S. ELIOT

The Goodness of This Lady

From Ash-Wednesday

Lady, three white leopards sat under a
  juniper-tree
In the cool of the day, having fed to
  satiety
On my legs my heart my liver and that
  which had been contained
In the hollow round of my skull. And
  God said

Lady of silences
Calm and distressed
Torn and most whole
Rose of memory
Rose of forgetfulness
Exhausted and life-giving
Worried reposeful
In the single Rose
Is now the Garden
Where all loves end
Terminate torment
Of love unsatisfied
The greater torment
Of love satisfied

End of the endless
Journey to no end
Conclusion of all that
Is inconclusible
Speech without word and
Word of no speech
Grace to the Mother
For the Garden
Where all love ends.

Under a juniper-tree the bones sang, scattered and shining
We are glad to be scattered, we did little good to each other,
Under a tree in the cool of the day, with the blessing of sand,
Forgetting themselves and each other, united
In the quiet of the desert. This is the land which ye
Shall divide by lot. And neither division nor unity
Matters. This is the land. We have our inheritance.

1930

BEN JONSON

It Is Not Growing Like a Tree

It is not growing like a tree
In bulk, doth make men better be;
Or standing long an oak, three hundred year,
To fall a log at last, dry, bald, and sear:
A lily of a day
Is fairer far in May;
Although it fall and die that night,
It was the plant and flower of light.
In small proportions we just beauties see,
And in short measures life may perfect be.

1616

SIR EDWARD DYER

My Mind to Me a Kingdom Is

My mind to me a kingdom is;
Such present joys therein I find
That it excels all other bliss
That earth affords or grows by kind.
Though much I want which most would have,
Yet still my mind forbids to crave.

No princely pomp, no wealthy store,
No force to win the victory,
No wily wit to salve a sore,
No shape to feed a loving eye;
To none of these I yield as thrall—
For why? My mind doth serve for all.

I see how plenty surfeits oft,
And hasty climbers soon do fall;
I see that those which are aloft
Mishap doth threaten most of all;
They get with toil, they keep with fear—
Such cares my mind could never bear.

Content to live, this is my stay;
I seek no more than may suffice;
I press to bear no haughty sway;
Look, what I lack my mind supplies.
Lo, thus I triumph like a king,
Content with that my mind doth bring.

Some have too much, yet still do crave;
I little have, and seek no more.
They are but poor, though much they have,
And I am rich with little store.
They poor, I rich; they beg, I give;
They lack, I leave; they pine, I live.

I laugh not at another's loss;
I grudge not at another's pain;
No worldly waves my mind can toss;
My state at one doth still remain.
I fear no foe, I fawn no friend;
I loathe not life, nor dread my end.

Some weigh their pleasure by their lust,
  Their wisdom by their rage of will;
Their treasure is their only trust;
  A cloakéd craft their store of skill.
But all the pleasure that I find
Is to maintain a quiet mind.

My wealth is health and perfect ease;
  My conscience clear my chief defense;
I neither seek by bribes to please,
  Nor by deceit to breed offense,
Thus do I live; thus will I die;
Would all did so as well as I!

1588

ROBERT GREENE
Sweet Are the Thoughts That Savor of Content

Sweet are the thoughts that savor of content;
  The quiet mind is richer than a crown;
Sweet are the nights in careless slumber spent;
  The poor estate scorns fortune's angry frown.
Such sweet content, such minds, such sleep, such bliss,
Beggars enjoy, when princes oft do miss.

The homely house that harbors quiet rest;
  The cottage that affords no pride nor care;
The mean that 'grees with country music best;
  The sweet consort of mirth and music's fare;
Obscuréd life sets down a type of bliss:
A mind content both crown and kingdom is.

1591

THOMAS CAMPION
The Man of Life Upright

The man of life upright,
  Whose guiltless heart is free
From all dishonest deeds,
  Or thought of vanity,

The man whose silent days
  In harmless joys are spent,
Whom hopes cannot delude,
  Nor sorrow discontent;

That man needs neither towers
  Nor armor for defence,
Nor secret vaults to fly
  From thunder's violence.

He only can behold
  With unaffrighted eyes
The horrors of the deep
  And terrors of the skies.

Thus, scorning all the cares
  That fate or fortune brings,
He makes the heaven his book,
  His wisdom heavenly things,

Good thoughts his only friends,
  His wealth a well-spent age,
The earth his sober inn
  And quiet pilgrimage.

1601

SIR HENRY WOTTON
The Character of a Happy Life

How happy is he born and taught
That serveth not another's will;
Whose armor is his honest thought,
And simple truth his utmost skill!

Whose passions not his masters are;
Whose soul is still prepared for death,

Untied unto the world by care
Of public fame or private breath;

Who envies none that chance doth raise,
Nor vice; who never understood
How deepest wounds are given by praise;
Nor rules of state, but rules of good;

Who hath his life from rumors freed;
Whose conscience is his strong retreat;
Whose state can neither flatterers feed,
Nor ruin make oppressors great;

Who God doth late and early pray
More of His grace than gifts to lend;
And entertains the harmless day
With a religious book or friend;

—This man is freed from servile bands
Of hope to rise or fear to fall:
Lord of himself, though not of lands,
And having nothing, yet hath all.

                                                    1651

JOHN HEYWOOD
The Tale of the Pardoner

FROM THE PLAY CALLED
THE FOUR PP.

Pard. Well, sir, then mark what I can say!
  I have been a pardoner many a day,
  And done greater cures ghostly
  Than ever he did bodily;
  Namely, this one which ye shall hear,
  Of one departed within this seven year,
  A friend of mine, and likewise I
  To her again was as friendly—
  Who fell so sick so suddenly
  That dead she was even by-and-by,
  And never spake with priest nor clark,
  Nor had no whit of this holy wark,
  For I was thence, it could not be;
  Yet heard, I say, she asked for me.
  But when I bethought me how this
      chanced,

And that I have to heaven advanced
So many souls to me but strangers
And could not keep my friend from
    dangers,
But she to die so dangerously
For her soul's health especially,
That was the thing that grieved me
    so
That nothing could release my woe
Till I had tried even out of hand
In what estate her soul did stand.
For which trial, short tale to make,
I took this journey for her sake.
Give ear, for here beginneth the story!
From hence I went to purgatory,
And took with me this gear in my fist,
Whereby I may do there what I list.
I knocked, and was let in quickly;
But, Lord, how low the souls made
    curtsy!
And I to every soul again
Did give a beck them to retain,
And axed them this question than:
If that the soul of such a woman
Did late among them there appear.
Whereto they said she came not here.
Then feared I much it was not well.
Alas! thought I, she is in hell!
For with her life I was so acquainted
That sure I thought she was not sainted.
With this it chanced me to sneeze;
'Christ help!' quoth a soul that lay for
    his fees.
'Those words,' quoth I, 'thou shalt not
    lees!'
Then with these pardons of all degrees
I paid his toll, and set him so quite
That straight to heaven he took his
    flight.
And I from thence to hell that night,
To help this woman, if I might,
Not as who saith by authority,
But by the way of entreaty.
And first to the devil that kept the gate
I came, and spake after this rate:
'All hail, sir devil!' and made low curtsy.
'Welcome!' quoth he, this smilingly:
He knew me well, and I at last
Remembered him since long time past,
For, as good hap would have it chance,

This devil and I were of old acquaint-
  ance,
For oft in the play of Corpus Christi
He hath played the devil at Coventry.
By his acquaintance and my behaviour
He showed to me right friendly favour.
And—to make my return the shorter—
I said to this devil: 'Good master porter,
For all old love, if it lie in your power,
Help me to speak with my lord and
  your.'
'Be sure,' quoth he, 'no tongue can tell
What time thou couldest have come so
  well,
For this day Lucifer fell,
Which is our festival in hell.
Nothing unreasonable craved this day
That shall in hell have any nay.
But yet beware thou come not in
Till time thou may thy passport win.
Wherefore stand still, and I will wit
If I can get thy safe-conduit.'
He tarried not, but shortly gat it,
Under seal, and the devil's hand at it,
In ample wise, as ye shall hear.
Thus it began: 'Lucifer,
By the power of God chief devil of
  hell,
To all the devils that there do dwell,
And every of them, we send greeting,
Under straight charge and command-
  ing,
That they aiding and assistant be
To such a pardoner'—and named me—
'So that he may at liberty
Pass safe without his jeopardy
Till that he be from us extinct
And clearly out of hell's precinct.
And, his pardons to keep safeguard,
We will they lie in the porter's ward.
Given in the furnace of our palace,
In our high court of matters of malice,
Such a day and year of our reign.'
'God save the devil!' quoth I, 'for plain,
I trust this writing to be sure.'
'Then put thy trust,' quoth he, 'in ure,
Since thou art sure to take no harm.'
This devil and I walked arm in arm,
So far till he had brought me thither
Where all the devils of hell togither

Stood in array in such apparel
As for that day there meetly fell:
Their horns well gilt, their claws full
  clean,
Their tails well kempt, and, as I ween,
With sothery butter their bodies
  anointed—
I never saw devils so well appointed.
The master devil sat in his jacket,
And all the souls were playing at racket.
None other rackets they had in hand
Save every soul a good firebrand;
Wherewith they played so prettily
That Lucifer laughed merrily,
And all the residue of the fiends
Did laugh full well together like friends.
But of my friend I saw no whit,
Nor durst not axe for her as yet.
Anon all this rout was brought in si-
  lence,
And I by an usher brought in presence.
Then to Lucifer low as I could
I knelt. Which he so well allowed
That thus he becked; and, by Saint An-
  thony,
He smiled on me well-favouredly,
Bending his brows, as broad as barn-
  durs,
Shaking his ears, as rugged as burs,
Rolling his eyes, as round as two bushels,
Flashing the fire out of his nose-thrills,
Gnashing his teeth so vaingloriously
That methought time to fall to flattery.
Wherewith I told, as I shall tell:
'O pleasant picture! O prince of hell!
Featured in fashion abominable!
And since that it is inestimable
For me to praise thee worthily,
I leave off praise, unworthy
To give thee praise, beseeching thee
To hear my suit, and then to be
So good to grant the thing I crave.
And, to be short, this would I have—
The soul of one which hither is flitted
Delivered hence, and to me remitted.
And in this doing, though all be not
  quit,
Yet some part I shall deserve it,
As thus: I am a pardoner,
And over souls, as a controller,

Throughout the earth my power doth
    stand,
Where many a soul lieth on my hand,
That speed in matters as I use them,
As I receive them or refuse them;
Whereby, what time thy pleasure is
Ye shall require any part of this,
The least devil here that can come
    thither
Shall choose a soul and bring him
    hither.'
'Now,' quoth the devil, 'we are well
    pleased!
What is his name thou wouldest have
    eased?'
'Nay,' quoth I, 'be it good or evil,
My coming is for a she devil.'
'What callest her?' quoth he, 'thou
    whoreson!'
'Forsooth,' quoth I, 'Margery Coorson.'
'Now, by our honour,' said Lucifer,
'No devil in hell shall withhold her!
And if thou wouldest have twenty mo,
Were not for justice, they should go.
For all we devils within this den
Have more to do with two women
Than with all the charge we have be-
    side.
Wherefore, if thou our friend will be
    tried,
Apply thy pardons to women so
That unto us there come no mo.'
To do my best I promised by oath.
Which I have kept; for, as the faith
    go'th,
At these days to heaven I do procure
Ten women to one man, be sure.
Then of Lucifer my leave I took,
And straight unto the master cook.
I was had into the kitchen,
For Margery's office was therein.
All things handled there discreetly,
For every soul beareth office meetly,
Which might be seen to see her sit
So busily turning of the spit;
For many a spit here hath she turned,
And many a good spit hath she burned,
And many a spit full hot hath toasted
Before the meat could be half roasted.

And, ere the meat were half roasted in-
    deed,
I took her then from the spit for speed.
But when she saw this brought to pass,
To tell the joy wherein she was,
And of all the devils, for joy how they
Did roar at her delivery,
And how the chains in hell did ring,
And how all the souls therein did sing,
And how we were brought to the gate,
And how we took our leave thereat—
Be sure lack of time suffereth nat
To rehearse the twentieth part of that!
Wherefore, this tale to conclude briefly,
This woman thanked me chiefly
That she was rid of this endless death;
And so we departed on Newmarket
    Heath.
And if that any man do mind her,
Who list to seek her, there shall he find
    her!

                                    c. 1569

ALFRED EDWARD HOUSMAN

To an Athlete Dying Young

The time you won your town the race
We chaired you through the market-place;
Man and boy stood cheering by,
And home we brought you shoulder-high.

Today, the road all runners come,
Shoulder-high we bring you home,
And set you at your threshold down,
Townsman of a stiller town.

Smart lad, to slip betimes away
From fields where glory does not stay,
And early though the laurel grows
It withers quicker than the rose.

Eyes the shady night has shut
Cannot see the record cut,

And silence sounds no worse than cheers
After earth has stopped the ears.

Now you will not swell the rout
Of lads that wore their honors out,
Runners whom renown outran
And the name died before the man.

So set, before its echoes fade,
The fleet foot on the sill of shade,
And hold to the low lintel up
The still-defended challenge cup.

And round that early-laurelled head
Will flock to gaze the strengthless dead,
And find unwithered on its curls
The garland briefer than a girl's.

1896

EDGAR ALLAN POE

To One in Paradise

Thou wast that all to me, love,
  For which my soul did pine—
A green isle in the sea, love,
  A fountain and a shrine,
All wreathed with fairy fruits and flowers,
  And all the flowers were mine.

Ah, dream too bright to last!
  Ah, starry Hope! that didst arise
But to be overcast!
  A voice from out the Future cries,
"On! on!"—but o'er the Past
  (Dim gulf!) my spirit hovering lies
Mute, motionless, aghast!

For, alas! alas! with me
  The light of Life is o'er!
  No more—no more—no more—
(Such language holds the solemn sea
  To the sands upon the shore)
Shall bloom the thunder-blasted tree,
  Or the stricken eagle soar!

And all my days are trances,
  And all my nightly dreams
Are where thy gray eye glances,
  And where thy footstep gleams—
In what ethereal dances,
  By what eternal streams.

1834

MATTHEW ARNOLD

Requiescat

Strew on her roses, roses,
  And never a spray of yew!
In quiet she reposes:
  Ah, would that I did too!

Her mirth the world required;
  She bathed it in smiles of glee.
But her heart was tired, tired,
  And now they let her be.

Her life was turning, turning,
  In mazes of heat and sound.
But for peace her soul was yearning,
  And now peace laps her round.

Her cabined, ample spirit,
  It fluttered and failed for breath.
To-night it doth inherit
  The vasty hall of death.

1853

WILLIAM SHAKESPEARE

Full Fathom Five

Full fathom five thy father lies:
  Of his bones are coral made;
Those are pearls that were his eyes;
  Nothing of him that doth fade
But doth suffer a sea-change
Into something rich and strange.

Sea-nymphs hourly ring his knell:
Ding-dong!
Hark! now I hear them,—Ding-dong,
bell!
1611

WILLIAM E. HENLEY

Invictus

Out of the night that covers me,
Black as the Pit from pole to pole,
I thank whatever gods may be
For my unconquerable soul.

In the fell clutch of circumstance
I have not winced nor cried aloud.
Under the bludgeonings of chance
My head is bloody, but unbowed.

Beyond this place of wrath and tears
Looms but the Horror of the shade,
And yet the menace of the years
Finds, and shall find, me unafraid.

It matters not how strait the gate,
How charged with punishments the scroll,
I am the master of my fate:
I am the captain of my soul.
1875

ROBERT BROWNING

Prospice

Fear death?—to feel the fog in my throat,
The mist in my face,
When the snows begin, and the blasts de-
note
I am nearing the place,
The power of the night, the press of the
storm,
The post of the foe;

Where he stands, the Arch Fear in a vis-
ible form,
Yet the strong man must go:
For the journey is done and the summit
attained,
And the barriers fall,
Though a battle's to fight ere the guerdon
be gained,
The reward of it all.
I was ever a fighter, so—one fight more,
The best and the last!
I would hate that death bandaged my
eyes, and forebore,
And bade me creep past.
No! let me taste the whole of it, fare like
my peers
The heroes of old,
Bear the brunt, in a minute pay glad life's
arrears
Of pain, darkness and cold.
For sudden the worst turns the best to the
brave,
The black minute's at end,
And the elements' rage, the fiend-voices
that rave,
Shall dwindle, shall blend,
Shall change, shall become first a peace
out of pain,
Then a light, then thy breast,
O thou soul of my soul! I shall clasp
thee again,
And with God be the rest!
1864

JOHN KEATS

When I Have Fears That I May Cease to Be

When I have fears that I may cease to be
Before my pen has gleaned my teeming
brain,
Before high pilèd books, in charact'ry,
Hold like rich garners the full-ripened
grain;

When I behold, upon the night's starred
    face,
Huge cloudy symbols of a high romance,
And think that I may never live to trace
Their shadows, with the magic hand of
    chance;
And when I feel, fair creature of an hour!
That I shall never look upon thee more,
Never have relish in the faery power
Of unreflecting love!—then on the shore
Of the wide world I stand alone, and
    think
Till love and fame to nothingness do
    sink.

1818

ROBERT LOUIS STEVENSON

Requiem

Under the wide and starry sky,
Dig the grave and let me lie.
Glad did I live and gladly die,
    And I laid me down with a will.

This be the verse you grave for me:
Here he lies where he longed to be;
Home is the sailor, home from the sea,
And the hunter home from the hill.

1887

WALT WHITMAN

Come Lovely and Soothing Death

From WHEN LILACS LAST IN THE DOORYARD BLOOMED

Come lovely and soothing death,
Undulate round the world, serenely arriv-
    ing, arriving,
In the day, in the night, to all, to each,
Sooner or later delicate death.

Prais'd be the fathomless universe,
For life and joy, and for objects and knowl-
    edge curious,
And for love, sweet love—but praise!
    praise! praise!
For the sure-enwinding arms of cool-en-
    folding death.

Dark mother always gliding near with
    soft feet,
Have none chanted for thee a chant of
    fullest welcome?
Then I chant it for thee, I glorify thee
    above all,
I bring thee a song that when thou must
    indeed come, come unfalteringly.

Approach strong deliveress,
When it is so, when thou hast taken them,
    I joyously sing the dead,
Lost in the loving floating ocean of thee,
Laved in the flood of thy bliss O death.

From me to thee glad serenades,
Dances for thee I propose saluting thee,
    adornments and feastings for thee,
And the sights of the open landscape and
    the high-spread sky are fitting,
And life and the fields, and the huge and
    thoughtful night.

The night in silence under many a star,
The ocean shore and the husky whispering
    wave whose voice I know,
And the soul turning to thee O vast and
    well-veil'd death,
And the body gratefully nestling close to
    thee.

Over the tree-tops I float thee a song,
Over the rising and sinking waves, over
    the myriad fields and the prairies
    wide,
Over the dense-pack'd cities all and the
    teeming wharves and ways,
I float this carol with joy, with joy to thee
    O death.

1865

XII. . .

DRAMA

NORMAN CORWIN

Radio Primer

SOLOIST. This is a Radio Primer.

QUARTET. Fa la, fa la, fa la.

SOLOIST. The most elementary show
you've heard

QUARTET. By far, by far, by far.

SOLOIST. An alphabetical primer.

QUARTET. A, B; C, D; F, E;

SOLOIST. Degree by degree,
From A to Z,
Our Primer will prim
The radio industry!

QUARTET. The ra-di-o in-dust-ry!

NARRATOR. A. A stands for announcers.
What are announcers?

Music: Orchestra. A bright tune behind:

DEFINER (*singing*).
Announcers are men who announce;
They have pep, they have zip,
they have bounce;
They win friends and influence
masses
By diction which simply sur-
passes
The fanciest talk on Parnassus;
They never coax, wheedle, or
flounce.
They stress only what really
counts.
And no matter what the time of
day or the circumstances or
their personal or public
opinions or the state of the
nation or the weather or
their last quarterly earnings, their soul is in their
work up to the last *ounce!*

QUARTET (*singing*). *Good* to the last
ounce!

DEFINER. There are all kinds of announcers. This is well. Some announcers
are very commanding:

COMMANDING ANNOUNCERS.[1] Go now!
Tear out! Don't fail! Remember
the name! Don't be fooled! Insist
on! Send in! Try once!

DEFINER. Others are more appealing:

PLEADING ANNOUNCERS. Why not try?
Have you ever wondered? Won't
you ask?

DEFINER. And some are very friendly:

FRIENDLY ANNOUNCERS. Friends, I want to
tell you about an easy way . . . Did
you ever wake up in the morning
feeling . . .

DEFINER. Now there are many verbs and
adjectives in the vocabulary of announcers, but only three conjunctions.

ANNOUNCERS. And now . . . But first
. . . And next we hear . . .

NARRATOR. So much for announcing.

QUARTET (*singing*). So much for announcing.

NARRATOR. B. B stands for breakfast food.
What is breakfast food?

DEFINER. Breakfast food is what you have
to eat before you can be a hero. Anthropologists tell us . . .

ANTHROPOLOGIST. The ancient Aztecs, at
the height of their culture, used to eat
three square breakfasts a day.

DEFINER. Historians testify . . .

HISTORIAN. Inscriptions at the time of the
destruction of the temple by Samson
show that on the day of his fateful
act, Samson ate a heaping dish of
Whammies.

DEFINER. But that's not all. Astronomers
report . . .

ASTRONOMER. The composition of the sun,
which is the entire source of the
earth's energy, is as follows: eighteen per cent hydrogen, thirty-one per
cent carbon, six per cent helium, and

forty-five per cent breakfast food.

NARRATOR. So much for breakfast food.

QUARTET (*singing*). So much for breakfast food.

NARRATOR. C. C stands for Crossley. What is Crossley?[2]

DEFINER. Crossley is a system of measuring radio audiences. If a program is rated at thirty points, that is very good because it means about twenty-five million people are listening. Twenty-five million is very good.

NARRATOR. If only seven million listeners are listening, that is not so good, you tried your best, we know how you feel, too bad, maybe some other time.

DEFINER. If only one million hear you, you are talking to yourself.

NARRATOR. Radio people take Crossley ratings very seriously. This may be seen by consulting Figure 1, which consists of a scene in the office of an advertising agency handling a big radio account.

R.M. J.B.?

J.B. Yes, R.M.?

R.M. What's our Crossley this week?

J.B. Twenty-six and two-tenths.

R.M. What was it in the last report?

J.B. Twenty-six and three-tenths.

R.M. You mean to say we've dropped a tenth of a point?

J.B. Yes, R.M.

R.M. And in the report before that we also dropped a tenth?

J.B. Two-tenths.

R.M. I can't stand it.
Desk drawer opening; a gun being removed.

J.B. What are you doing, R.M.?

R.M. What does it look like, J.B.?

J.B. Like suicide. But don't be hasty. Next week we may go up a point.
Shot.

J.B. He done it! I didn't think he would do it, but he done it.
Phone receiver off.

J.B. Give me Stickney's office, quick. . . . H.S., this is J.B. . . . I'm in R.M.'s office—I mean the *late* R.M.'s office.

. . . Well, he just shot himself. . . . Too bad because of the *publicity?* . . . Don't be silly; it'll boost our Crossley five points!

NARRATOR. So much for Crossley.

QUARTET (*singing*). So much for Crossley.

NARRATOR. D. D stands for deadline.

DEFINER. A deadline is the time something has to be done by or ready at. Authors and directors hate deadlines. Often an author will be overheard to say:

AUTHOR. But I ain't finished with the script.

DEFINER. To which a producer often will be heard to reply:

PRODUCER. Well, you should of been. Next time, don't wait till the last day before starting on it.

DEFINER. If a program is not ready on schedule, it cannot be postponed a couple of hours or days. This is why radio directors sing the Deadline Song when they are deep in trouble with vexed spirits, and ten minutes of script to cut with only forty seconds left to cut it in before going on the air. The Deadline Song is a radio folksong, the author of which is unknown, and it goes as follows:

DIRECTOR. (*singing, plaintively and naïvely*).

A deadline is the one thing I abhor.
Go away, deadline, and don't come back no more.
Go away, and stay away, because you are a pest.
There ought to be a law to put you under arrest.
A deadline is hungry, a deadline must be fed.
Some day I'm gonna get so mad I'll kill a deadline dead.

NARRATOR. E. E stands for experts.

DEFINER. An expert is a man who knows all the answers to questions he asks himself. He makes predictions which, if they turn out wrong he forgets about, but if they turn out right he reminds you of. Experts know everything except how each other got to be expert.

NARRATOR. Experts are busy men. It is not easy to be an expert on foreign affairs. The toll charges are very high. *Phone ringing.*

SECRETARY. The News Behind the News Behind the News, good afternoon. Who? Collect call from King Michael?[3] Put him on. (*To Boss.*) Rumania on the Number 4 wire.

BOSS. (*picking up phone; very straightaway, as though answering a routine interoffice call*). Hello, Mike. Say, I got a call from Stefanovich this afternoon asking me to say in my broadcast tonight that . . . What? . . . I know, but he claims that . . . I see . . . Yup. Well, now . . . uh-uh . . . No, I checked that last night. Got it right from headquarters. Hm? . . . Not according to my information. Certainly not . . . Well, that may be; I'm just telling you what he told me, for what it's worth.

(*Phone rings.*)

SECRETARY. The News Behind the News Behind the News . . . I can't understand you. *Who?* . . . Does he know you? . . . What's it in relation to, Mr. Check? Japan? . . . Well, just a minute. (*Up, to Boss.*) Can you speak to a Mr. Check relating to the Japanese situation on the Number 2 phone?

. . . Huh? I can't hear you. Mike — hold on for a second, will you?

BOSS. (*Sotto, to Secretary:*) Keep your hand over the phone here; I don't want Mike to overhear this. (*Takes up other phone.*) Hello? . . . How are you, Chiang? (*Sotto, to Secretary:*) For future reference, it's Chiang Kai-shek, not Mr. Check. (*Back to phone.*) Hello? Well, what's new along the Yangtze, Chiangtze? I mean, what's new along the Yiang, Chiang?

Phone rings.

SECRETARY. The News Behind the News Behind the News, good afternoon!

QUARTET (*singing*). That will be all for experts.

NARRATOR. F. F stands for filter.

DEFINER. A filter is a gadget which makes you sound dead, or, if alive, on the other end of a telephone. You are an honorary filter user if you are a ghost or a conscience. Nobody ever thinks thoughts to himself in radio withouten he does it on a filter.

FILTER VOICE. Do you suppose anybody is listening to us?

FULL VOICE. Well, gosh, the Workshop[4] has always had a pretty good audience.

FILTER VOICE. It has, eh? Do you think you can hold that audience?

FULL VOICE. Why, er—we had been hoping—er . . .

FILTER VOICE. (*A mean, dirty laugh.*)

NARRATOR. Filter voices are usually mean. Some directors can't get along without a filter. Others hate filters and never use them. That will be all for filters.

QUARTET (*singing*). That will be all for filters.

NARRATOR. G. G stands for grief.

DEFINER. Grief is an emotion without which actresses would not be happy. Actresses learn how to cry before anything else. This is fortunate for programs which experience a lot of grief. There are three main types of crying. First is the wait-until-the-door-closes-before-breaking-down kind. Figure 3.

GIRL (*keeping a stiff upper lip*). Goodbye, John.

JOHN. Good-bye. . . . It's better this way, isn't it?

GIRL. Yes. It's better this way.

JOHN. Well . . . I guess that's all.

GIRL. Yes . . . I guess that's all.
Door closes.

GIRL. (*Breaks down in great sobs.*)

DEFINER. Next is the hard-to-tell-from-a-laugh kind.
Demonstration.[5]

DEFINER. Next is the rippling-rhythm kind.
Demonstration.[6]

NARRATOR. Thank you, that will be all for grief.

QUARTET (*singing*). Thank you very much indeed.

NARRATOR. H. H stands for Heterodyne.

DEFINER. What did you say?

NARRATOR. Heterodyne.

CAST. (*Ad-lib conference, whispered but audible, on the question of how "heterodyne" got into this primer. Nobody seems to think it belongs. At length the Narrator comes out of it to say:*)

NARRATOR. That will be all for Heterodyne.

QUARTET (*singing*). That will be all for Heterodyne.

NARRATOR. I. I stands for inspiration. What is inspiration?

DEFINER. Inspiration is a peachy thing which listeners get from cheerful and optimistic programs. It is not the kind of inspiration which moves one to write a poem or a symphony or paint a great painting, but rather the kind which makes you feel better about your troubles. This is well. Inspirational programs are based on the ancient Syrian definition of trouble, which is:

SYRIAN. Trouble is a bubble.

DEFINER. Poetry inspires people more than prose. One of the greatest radio poets of inspiration is an anonymous man named Elwood Prue, who says he intends to be buried in a Time Capsule along with a copy of his verse just brought out by the Muses Press, named *Wings over Everything,* to be unearthed in 2941 A.D. For a specimen of the art of Mr. Prue, see Figure 6.

PRUE. If you broke a leg this morning, do not mind;
You could have broken two or gone stone blind.
If your skull was badly fractured, do not fret—
There will be a silver lining in it yet,
For the gloom is always blackest ere the storm—
Just wait awhile, and you'll be back in form.

If you lost your job this morning, do not worry;
Somebody is sure to find it in a hurry.
If your girl rejected you, do not lose hope;
She may turn out to be a fearful dope.
For the black is always gloomest ere the storm.
Just stick along, and you'll be back to norm.

If you have but one shirt left, do not despair.
That's better than being absolutely bare.
If you're sentenced to be hanged 'most any day,
Cheer up; we all die sometime, anyway. . . .
For the black is always stormest ere the gloom,
No matter where you are, or what, or whom.

NARRATOR. That will be enough for inspiration.

QUARTET (*singing*). That will be enough for inspiration.

NARRATOR. J. J stands for Jupiter. What is Jupiter?

DEFINER. Jupiter is an outpost of the enemy in children's programs. It is inhabited by wicked Jupes, whose skin is green and whose eyes are on stalks, like lobsters'. Jupes bear no resemblance to earth men except in their lust for power and the fact that they speak English, which is the universal language of the universe.

NARRATOR. Though one of the most powerful planets in the cosmos, Jupiter has a tough fight on its hands, because mankind happens to be represented by Tex, Millicent, and the Professor. This is illustrated in Figure 8.
Fade in sound of whirring.

PROFESSOR. Turn on the death ray, Tex, and let 'em have it.

TEX. I can't, Professor. The atomic-integrator-exhalator-condenser coil is busted!

PROFESSOR. Zounds! Jumping gyroscopes! What'll we do now?

MILLICENT. The Jupiter fleet is bearing down on us at six thousand miles per second!

TEX. Gosh! Looks like we're done for.

MILLICENT. Wait, Professor—I think I can fix it!

PROFESSOR. Only seconds are left.

MILLICENT. There!
Sound of switch.

MILLICENT. How's that?

PROFESSOR. Ah! Fixed!

TEX. Great, Millicent! You have saved civilization! This means peace in our time! Just wait till I spray 'em with this death ray.

PROFESSOR. Get set, Tex.

TEX. I await your order, Professor.

PROFESSOR. Ready! Aim! Fire!
Sound of death ray in action.

NARRATOR. That will be all for Jupiter.

QUARTET (*singing*). That will be all for Jupiter.

NARRATOR. K. K stands for killer.

DEFINER. A killer is a man with a gun, because if he didn't have a gun nobody could hear him kill. He has bad manners and is uneducated.

KILLER. Don't gimme none o' dat lip.

DEFINER. This is well, for otherwise he would neither terrify nor intimidate.

REFINED KILLER. Please do not give me any of that lip, please.

QUARTET (*singing*). That will be all—for killers!

NARRATOR. L. L stands for laughter.

DEFINER. Laughter is something without which a comedy program could not be comic. Thousands and thousands of dollars are spent to get a good laugh on the air. This is well. Figure 9 demonstrates how it is possible to get a good laugh on the air for next to nothing.
A very hearty laugh.

NARRATOR. M. M stands for mother.

DEFINER. To be a mother one must not only have children but philosophy. All mothers are wise, and most of them speak with a sectional accent.

MOTHER. If y'ask me, I think yer bein' made a fool of, Jed. There comes a time in a man's life when he either gits up and gits or he shrugs his shoulders and figgers he's about done fer. An' it's a heap better, my son, to go gittin' up an' gittin', 'stead o' quittin'.

NARRATOR. We will proceed now with N.

QUARTET (*singing*). We will proceed with N.

NARRATOR. N stands for narrators.

DEFINER. Narrators are deep-voiced men full of information, who keep track of characters in plays or tell you dates in history.

NARRATOR. Everything that happens is ominous to some narrators, mostly on account of it's an ominous world.
Music: Orchestra, agitato. Hold under:

NARRATOR (*gravely*). On busy Fifth Avenue, in mid-Manhattan today, two women in their early thirties, pert, prosperous, but nearsighted, collided as they were stepping off a curbstone.

FIRST WOMAN. Oh, I beg your pardon!

SECOND WOMAN. That's quite all right.

NARRATOR. And so the world goes!
Music: Orchestra. Big fanfare of ominous character.

NARRATOR. That much for narrators.

QUARTET. *That* for narrators!

NARRATOR. O. O stands for Orson.

*Music: Orchestra, introductory meas-
ures of "Who Is Sylvia?"*

SOLOIST. Who is Orson? What is he,
    That all the critics hail him?
    Holy terror of the Mercury,
    Publicity doth trail him.
    En-fant terr-*i*ble, dum, da-da-da-
        da dee dee,
    He is all he's cracked up to
        be.

    Who is Orson, Orson Welles,
    That he is so terrific? [7]
    East and west his fortune swells,
    Atlantic to Pacific.
    Every undertaking eventually
        jells;
    All is well that ends with Welles.

NARRATOR. P. P stands for press.

DEFINER. Press means newspapers. There
    are all kinds of newspapers. This is
    well. Most of the press believes radio
    is here to stay, and likewise most of
    radio believes the press is here to stay.
    This is well. Some papers have their
    doubts about radio drama, however,
    as may be seen in Figure 11.

FIRST RADIO MAN. Well, chief, the show's
    all lined up and the announcements
    have gone out.

SECOND RADIO MAN. Fine. Did you stress
    the angle of the bigness of the produc-
    tion setup?

FIRST RADIO MAN. Yes, sir, I listed every-
    thing: script by Ernest Hemingway,
    music by Sibelius, orchestra of seventy-
    five men under Stokowski, Deems
    Taylor announcing, cast of sixty-two
    including eight stars, a choir of
    twenty voices, a sound-effects crew of
    seven, and four hundred extras.

SECOND RADIO MAN. Good. I see the
    Chronicle gave it an excellent advance
    notice. How did the *Evening Clar-
    ion-Call* list it?

FIRST RADIO MAN. "Ten-thirty to eleven
    P.M., sketch." [8]

NARRATOR. We will go on to other things.

QUARTET (*singing*). We will go on.

NARRATOR. Q. Q stands for quiz pro-
    grams.

DEFINER. Quiz programs are programs
    which make you feel good if you
    know the answers which the guy at
    the microphone doesn't, but if he does
    know the answers and you don't—
    well, then you figure he's spent all his
    life reading encyclopedias, and who
    wants to do that? Life's too short,
    anyway.

NARRATOR. Quiz fans have a national an-
    them which was written last July
    Fourth by Francis Scott Shapiro, and
    which follows without further intro-
    duction.

*Music: Orchestra. A rapid, dizzy
little tune.*

CHORUS. Who did it? Who done it?
    The derby, who won it?
    Who said it? Who wrote it?
    How far can you quote it?
    What is a cantata?
    Who sang *Traviata*?

SOLOIST. And when is the mating season of
    the microscopic rhizopod commonly
    known as the amoeba?

CHORUS. Who was the inventor?
    What shade is magenta?
    How often? How many?
    Where are they, if any?
    From Brooklyn, how far is
    The ghat of Benares?

SOLOIST. And is a mollusk a temple of
    prayer in Arabia or a farmers' co-op-
    erative in Russia or a South American
    melon?

CHORUS. Where are the Antilles?
    How dread are the willies?
    Who started the custom?
    Whose father was Rustum?
    How good is an army
    That's fed on pastrami?

SOLOIST. And if a train traveling eighty
    miles an hour overtakes another train
    traveling sixty miles an hour on the
    same track, is that, I ask you, any
    kind of a way to run a railroad?

CHORUS. No, no, no, no, the answer is no!

NARRATOR. R. R stands for remote control.

DEFINER. Remote control is a dandy way of picking up broadcasts from outside a studio; in fact, it is the only way. Engineers are wizards, bless their hearts, and when they get to fooling around with the wires and coils and all like that, almost anything can happen, and often does.

NARRATOR. Listeners will not soon forget the first pickup of the transmission of sound through electrical energy generated in the brain of the North Dakota chinch bug. This sound, which occurs at a frequency too high for the human ear to hear, was picked up by means of microphonic megamplification. This is well. The result may be heard by consulting Figure 12-A, which follows. (*Silence.*) That was a sound beyond the reach of the human ear, amplified sixteen thousand, two hundred forty-nine times.

QUARTET (*singing*). Sixteen thousand, two hundred forty-nine.

NARRATOR. S. S stands for soporific.

DEFINER. A soporific is what you need after a hard day's work in the office, or in the kitchen, or both, when your nerves are on edge and Junior-has-been-such-an-aggravation-all-day-you-have-no-idea. Soporifics put you to sleep, and in radio the best soporifics have voices deeper even than narrators, mainly because they feel the world more keenly, and besides it is getting late at night.

NARRATOR. Some soporifics have been known to put listeners to sleep for periods ranging up to four days. The organ, either hand or electric, is indispensable to soporification, as indicated clearly in Figure 14.

Music: Organ. A lush, even overripe accompaniment behind:

SOPORIFIC. When Phoebe doth her grummons gather up

And in the trancid night forsoonly sup

Of myrrh and the smerds of Arcady,

When chumblers in the dim-lit aspenade

Bestrew the glamorantine of the glade,

Then come, love, cast thy wampts and cherybdibs

And frolls and fulsome friptures on the air,

For hearts that beat in wambeldon garoome

Can ne'er the druid fluid flume the frume.

QUARTET (*singing, with organ*). Can ne'er the druid fluid flume the frume.

NARRATOR. T. T stands for temperament.[9]

DEFINER. Temperament is when somebody with talent makes a mistake and wishes to take it out on somebody else, or when somebody without talent wishes to conduct himself in a manner as if he did have.

NARRATOR. Stars are supposed to be temperamental, and when they are not, they are regarded with wonder and amazement by people who work with them, as may be seen in Figure 15.

FIRST ACTOR. I was on a show with Harriet Hartburn the other night.

SECOND ACTOR. Zat so? How's she to work with?

FIRST ACTOR. Just wonderful. She dropped her script once, and when I picked it up for her, she looked straight at me and smiled and said, "Thank you."

SECOND ACTOR. No kidding? She said that?

FIRST ACTOR. Absolutely. "Thank you"— just like that.

SECOND ACTOR. There's a swell girl for ya!

FIRST ACTOR. Gosh, yes. Democratic.

SECOND ACTOR. Gosh.

FIRST ACTOR. Yeah. Gee.

NARRATOR. That will be all for temperament.

QUARTET (*singing*). Temperament, that will be all for.

NARRATOR. U. U stands for understatement.

DEFINER. Understatement is when a character has so much character that nothing affects him as much as it would affect a character with less character. The British are famous understaters, as may be gathered from the typical case of Sir Ronald Brindsley-Brettingham, who was captured by cannibals in southwest Borneo and boiled for dinner one night. As the chef was adding chives and thyme to the pot, Sir Ronald quipped:

SIR RONALD (*brightly*). I say, gentlemen. I'm really in a frightful stew . . . ha, ha, ha!

NARRATOR. This is very good understatement, for actually, as you can well imagine, it was no laughing matter.

DEFINER. In radio there is sometimes understatement in sound, such as when a person enters a room withouten you hear a door open or any footsteps. He just suddenly appears and starts talking, just like that.

NARRATOR. He just floats in.

DEFINER. Yes, that's right. This is known as productional understatement, or sound man's night off.

NARRATOR. That will be all for understatement.

QUARTET (*singing*). That will be all.

NARRATOR. V. V stands for *Variety*. What is *Variety*?

SOLOIST.   CHORUS.

Oh, pity on him

                    O pity on him

Who knows not what
    Variety is!

A man in the show
    game has *no* biz

Not to know what
    Variety is.

                    A man in the show
                        game has *no*
                        biz.

No biz

                    No biz

Not to know the *main*
    mag of the *show*
    biz.

It's the mag

                    It's the mag

It's the *main* mag of the
    show biz.

CHORUS.   *Variety, Variety,*
    All radio society
    Deems it an impropriety
    Not to read *Variety*.
    Sing, sing *Variety*.

SOLOIST. But wheresoever *Variety* is sung,
    It must be in a strange and different tongue:
        A hundred is a C,
        A thousand is a G,
        A snowstorm is a bliz,
        A rainstorm is a driz,
    An independent station is an indie,
    Chicago's either Chi or it is
        windy:

CHORUS. C, G, bliz, driz, indie, windy.

SOLOIST.   The cinema is Pix,
        The hinterland is Stix,
        The people there are Hix,
        And critics all are Crix.
    A good week's biz is perky or it's
        glossy;
    Australia is a continent called
        Aussie.

CHORUS. C, G, bliz, driz, indie, windy;
    Pix, stix, hix, crix, glossy, Aussie.

SOLOIST.   A première is preem,
        Good business is steam,
        The stage is the legit,
        And sex appeal is *it!*

CHORUS. What better jargon combo could
        a Mencken wish
    Than wow, biff, baddie, duo,
        nabe, and opposish?

SOLOIST. To work on the staff of *Variety*
    Your name must have only *four*
        letters,
    Although if one just wants to *buy*
        it, he
    Can of course spell his name with
        more letters.
    Each name has a four-letter par

Such as Ibee, Wood, Scho, Flin,
and Char.
Full many a turkey's been panned
By a four-letter man named Land,
And many a show sent below
deck
By the critic who calls himself
Odec,
And if a script's awful, then woe
be
If caught and reviewed by Hobe.[10]

CHORUS. *Variety, Variety,*
All radio society
Deems it an impropriety
Not to read *Variety.*
Sing, sing *Variety!*

NARRATOR. W. W stands for wisdom.

DEFINER. Wisdom is a rare quality which
only a few people have in sufficient
quantity to make a radio program out
of. It is very nice to be full of it,
because then you can live your life
wisely and advise people in trouble
how to get out of trouble so's they
can go home from the studio feeling
better until they get into some more
trouble. This is well. One of the
wisest men known to man is Judge
Solomon A. Trumbull, whose philosophy of life is based on the ancient
Swedish legend:

SWEDE. Trouble is a bubble.

NARRATOR. Judge Trumbull is justly famed
for his brilliant radio analysis of personal problems, such as typified in
the case of Mr. B.—see Figure 16
—who came to Judge Trumbull
weighted down by vexations of the
most vexing sort.

MR. B. Judge Trumbull, your Honor, I'm
a poor man. All my life I woiked
hard to make a living, woiking hard.
Even I took in boarders. My wife,
she halped me. Judge Trumbull,
your Honor, I'm in such a trouble . . .

JUDGE. Go on, Mr. B, just tell me everything.

MR. B. Well, it began like this: Where I
woik, in the same plant, only in the
molding department, woiks a man, a
middle-aged man about my age, who
I felt very sorry for.

JUDGE. I see. Now why did you feel sorry
for him?

MR. B. Well, in the foist place, he lost two
fingers in the last war, and besides
which he's got a cross-eye, and on top
of it all, he's an orphan.

JUDGE. An orphan, you say?

MR. B. Yes. Nobody left in the woild but
him.

JUDGE. I see. Go on.

MR. B. So I feel so sorry for him, I take
him into my house as a boarder. I
treat him like a brudder. I let him
wear my shoits and smoke my pipe
and listen to my radio. Every Sunday night he listens to the Columbus
Woikshop, and that's okay by me,
because I'm feeling sorry for the man.
Judge Trumbull, it's such a trouble,
it's such a trouble I'm in!

JUDGE. Now go right on, Mr. B.!

MR. B. Well, after I treat this man like a
brudder for six months, I come home
from a lodge meeting one night, and
I find him and my wife coming down
the front stairs, with suitcases in their
hand. So I says, "Where are you
going all of a sudden like this?" So
he says to me, he says, "Your wife is
running away with me, that's where
we're going! Now get out of the
way or we'll be late for the train."
So I'm so dumbfondled I just stand
there spitchless. So he gets mad and
angry, and raises his voice so even
the neighbors could hear him, and he
says to me, he says, "YOU BETTER GET
OUT OF MY WAY OR I'LL MAKE *trouble*
FOR YOU!" And my wife, she also
hollers on me; she says to me, she
says, "BEAT IT NOW, OR WE'LL *both*
MAKE TROUBLE FOR YOU!"

JUDGE. I see. Now what is your particular problem, Mr. B.?

MR. B. Well, Judge Trumbull, your Honor,
what I want to know is this: CAN
they make trouble for me?

QUARTET (*singing*). That will be all for wisdom!

NARRATOR. X. X stands for experiment.

DEFINER. An experiment in radio is something nobody ever tries except strange people with a funny look. Good businessmen know better than to try experiments, which they figure ought to be done only by scientific-looking artists or artistic-looking scientists.

NARRATOR. The experimental stage lasts a long time on account of you can't play too safe when it comes to trying out new things; and after all, Rome wasn't built in a day, and one swallow doesn't make a summer. In fact, the incubation period for an experimental program idea can sometimes last indefinitely. See Figure 17.

L.J. Well, what do you think of the idea, G.W.?

G.W. Has it been done before?

L.J. Yes. Eight shows had a similar idea last year.

G.W. Mm. Hasn't caught on much, has it?

L.J. Still, eight shows is eight shows, G.W.

G.W. Yes, I know, L.J., but still and all . . . I don't want to *experiment* . . .

L.J. Well, then, how about putting on a quiz show or an amateur program?

G.W. Now that's more like it. Risky, I grant you, but I'll take a chance! I'm not afraid to gamble!

QUARTET (*singing*). He's not afraid to gamble.

NARRATOR. Y. Y stands for nothing in particular. It *could* stand for yes-men.

DEFINER. A yes-man is a man whose great ambition in life is to rise so high that he can say No and have yes-men of his own.

NARRATOR. Or Y could stand for Yacht.

DEFINER. A yacht is what you get to own if you're a successful yes-man who finally gets to say no and whose Crossley is thirty-five.

NARRATOR. Or Y could stand for "you."

DEFINER. "You" is an indispensable pronoun in song lyrics, rhyming as it does with Sky So Blue, I'll Be True, What'll I Do, Are We Through, and Who.

NARRATOR. Very well then, as stated above, Y stands for nothing in particular.

QUARTET (*singing*). Nothing in partic-,
No, nothing in par-
tic-,
Particuli,
Particula,
Y stands for nothing
in particular.

NARRATOR. Z. Z stands for ze end of ze program.

DEFINER. Zat is well.

QUARTET (*singing*). ZAT——IS——WELL!

Music: Orchestra vamps into:

SOLOIST. This was a Radio Primer,

QUARTET. Fa la, fa la, fa la,

SOLOIST. The most elementary show you've heard,

QUARTET. By far, by far, by far.

SOLOIST. An alphabetical primer,

QUARTET. A, B; C, D; F, E.

SOLOIST. Having thus come
From A to Z,
Our Primer has prum
The Radio Indust-ry!

QUARTET. The Ra-di-o In-dust-ry!

RADIO PRIMER

[NOTES]

Of all scripts in this collection, this is least likely to be often performed. Not many radio stations will allow their most sacred policies and practices to be kidded in this fashion, especially when the kidding is done by a sustaining program.

But an even more practical reason why the Primer will seldom be heard is that no production can get far without the music Lyn Murray composed to my lyrics; and music runs into money. This is a fairly expensive sustainer to sustain, requiring as it does a large orchestra, five singers, and a big cast.

Casting. Unless one has access to unlimited budget and acting resources, the cast had better consist of the most expert doublers in the area.

Acting. The models for most of these characters are legion and everywhere. A quick whirl of the dial will exhibit friendly, pleading, and commanding announcers, and a lot I didn't have time to mention: the driving, the emphasized-adjective, the smile-in-the-voice, the listen-to-the-sound-of-his-own-voice announcer.

The anthropologist, the historian and the astronomer should be uncolored and honest; the secretary to the expert on foreign affairs should be Beatrice Kaye or reasonably like her; the expert himself should be extremely high pressure and modeled somewhat in age and pitch and mannerism after Wythe ("According to My Information") Williams, who apparently has a correspondent in every bunker of every main fortification in Europe.

Elwood Prue should be not far removed from Ted Malone in his delivery; that is, happy in the belief that this is a wonderful country, a wonderful age, and a wonderful world. Fate is a cute thing to Prue, and adversity is a sweet old dear.

Tex, Millicent and the Professor are, of course, comic-strip characters—aggressive, forthright, and quick to make decisions in any emergency. Ted Di Corsia played the Professor with a Slavic accent; Tex was an American with big biceps, and Millicent was the epitome of the modern funny-page heroine, a ravishing blonde with a figure and an affinity for trouble in a troubled universe. How do newspapers get away with their comic-strip sweater girls, by the way? If radio one day decided to exhibit as much sex for Junior as the ordinary newspaper page of comic strips, there would be a pincers movement against the networks by the F.C.C. the very next morning.

For an idea of the mother, tune in to any program on any station any day except Sunday, from eight in the morning to seven-thirty at night, and possibly beyond those hours.

The narrator who is demonstrated under the N's is based mainly on the *March of Time's* Van Voorhees, who cups his ear and makes Judgment Day seem close at hand in every announcement.

Sound. No special problems. Ray Kremer's idea for the death ray used by Tex and the Professor in the Jupiter sequence was a spark-plug device. It worked.

Music. Arrangements for the use of Lyn Murray's score have to be made with Mr. Murray directly.

The song "Who Is Orson?"—a parody on Schubert's "Who Is Sylvia?"—was arranged under the supervision of Beatrice Kaye herself. There is no describing the Kaye technique. It is, to most listeners, what Miss Kaye sang of Orson—terrific.

Rehearsal Routine. Not an easy show to rehearse. The scene between the foreign expert and his secretary is especially difficult, since it involves two perspectives which change and overlap. Theoretically the mike stays on the Number 1 wire, which is the secretary's. But the Number 2 is close to the Number 1, and we stay there when the girl crosses to hold the Number 4 wire so that King Michael won't overhear the conversation with Chiang Kai-shek, while the expert crosses the room to come on mike. This is getting complicated, right here. Better draw yourself a diagram.

Additional Notes. 1. Two actors in alternation.

2. A pain in the neck to most sustaining programs. Because of variables in the checking of sustaining programs as against commercials, the sustainer is always represented as having a smaller rating than it has actually achieved. The mathematical basis for this is too complicated to discuss here, but there is a growing school in radio which pays less attention to ratings than to the business of producing the best programs one knows how, within the requirements of taste and personal and corporate integrity. Adherents to this school feel that too much emphasis has been placed upon ratings by radio and advertising executives, arguing that Major Bowes will always have a rating far superior to the NBC Symphony or the New York Philharmonic, and so what? The Major's rating, they say, should in no way reflect on symphony programs to their detriment.

3. This was before the Germans began editing the Balkans. Change it to any current figure.

4. Or your particular program.

5. Simple hysteria.

6. Adults sometimes sob in rhythm, the way infants do. Only for better reasons, of course.

7. The exploitation motif of the advertising campaign for Welles's picture *Citizen Kane,* then running, was "It's terrific." Hence the allusion was topical.

8. This comment on listings applies far more widely than one might suspect. Some newspaper publishers, resenting the fact that radio is here to stay as a competitive advertising medium and a disseminator of news, refuse to print more than the barest listings. This policy works against the interests of only one group, the subscribers to the paper. What is unquestionably the best system of listings yet devised in any daily periodical is the one John Mc-Manus created for the New York tabloid, *PM.*

9. Cut out of the original production in its entirety, because of time. It is included here in order to give the producer wider option for over-all cutting, according to whatever sections play best in his particular company.

10. The broadcast *was* caught and reviewed by Hobe (Morrison), and he didn't like it very much.

1941

LADY AUGUSTA GREGORY

Spreading the News

PERSONS

Bartley Fallon.	James Ryan.
Mrs. Fallon.	Mrs. Tarpey.
Jack Smith.	Mrs. Tully.
Shawn Early.	A Policeman (JO MULDOON).
Tim Casey.	A Removable Magistrate.

SCENE: The outskirts of a Fair. An Apple Stall. Mrs. Tarpey sitting at it. Magistrate and Policeman enter.

MAGISTRATE. So that is the Fair Green. Cattle and sheep and mud. No system. What a repulsive sight!

POLICEMAN. That is so, indeed.

MAGISTRATE. I suppose there is a good deal of disorder in this place?

POLICEMAN. There is.

MAGISTRATE. Common assault?

POLICEMAN. It's common enough.

MAGISTRATE. Agrarian crime, no doubt?

POLICEMAN. That is so.

MAGISTRATE. Boycotting? Maiming of cattle? Firing into houses?

POLICEMAN. There was one time, and there might be again.

MAGISTRATE. That is bad. Does it go any farther than that?

POLICEMAN. Far enough, indeed.

MAGISTRATE. Homicide, then! This district has been shamefully neglected! I will change all that. When I was in the Andaman Islands, my system never failed. Yes, yes, I will change all that. What has that woman on her stall?

POLICEMAN. Apples mostly—and sweets.

MAGISTRATE. Just see if there are any unlicensed goods underneath—spirits or the like. We had evasions of the salt tax in the Andaman Islands.

POLICEMAN. (Sniffing cautiously and upsetting a heap of apples.) I see no spirits here—or salt.

MAGISTRATE. (To Mrs. Tarpey.) Do you know this town well, my good woman?

MRS. TARPEY. (Holding out some apples.) A penny the half-dozen, your honour.

POLICEMAN. (Shouting.) The gentleman is asking do you know the town! He's the new magistrate!

MRS. TARPEY. (Rising and ducking.) Do I know the town? I do, to be sure.

MAGISTRATE. (Shouting.) What is its chief business?

MRS. TARPEY. Business, is it? What business would the people here have but to be minding one another's business?

MAGISTRATE. I mean what trade have they?

MRS. TARPEY. Not a trade. No trade at all but to be talking.

MAGISTRATE. I shall learn nothing here.

(James Ryan comes in, pipe in mouth. Seeing Magistrate he retreats quickly, taking pipe from mouth.)

MAGISTRATE. The smoke from that man's

From Seven Short Plays by Lady Augusta Gregory. Courtesy of G. P. Putnam's Sons.

pipe had a greenish look; he may be growing unlicensed tobacco at home. I wish I had brought my telescope to this district. Come to the post-office, I will telegraph for it. I found it very useful in the Andaman Islands.

(*Magistrate and Policeman go out left.*)

MRS. TARPEY. Bad luck to Jo Muldoon, knocking my apples this way and that way. (*Begins arranging them.*) Showing off he was to the new magistrate.

(*Enter Bartley Fallon and Mrs. Fallon.*)

BARTLEY. Indeed it's a poor country and a scarce country to be living in. But I'm thinking if I went to America it's long ago the day I'd be dead!

MRS. FALLON. So you might, indeed.

(*She puts her basket on a barrel and begins putting parcels in it, taking them from under her cloak.*)

BARTLEY. And it's a great expense for a poor man to be buried in America.

MRS. FALLON. Never fear, Bartley Fallon, but I'll give you a good burying the day you'll die.

BARTLEY. Maybe it's yourself will be buried in the graveyard of Cloonmara before me, Mary Fallon, and I myself that will be dying unbeknownst some night, and no one a-near me. And the cat itself may be gone straying through the country, and the mice squealing over the quilt.

MRS. FALLON. Leave off talking of dying. It might be twenty years you'll be living yet.

BARTLEY. (*With a deep sigh.*) I'm thinking if I'll be living at the end of twenty years, it's a very old man I'll be then!

MRS. TARPEY. (*Turns and sees them.*) Good morrow, Bartley Fallon; good morrow, Mrs. Fallon. Well, Bartley, you'll find no cause for complaining to-day; they are all saying it was a good fair.

BARTLEY. (*Raising his voice.*) It was not a good fair, Mrs. Tarpey. It was a scattered sort of a fair. If we didn't expect more, we got less. That's the way with me always; whatever I have to sell goes down and whatever I have to buy goes up. If there's ever any misfortune coming to this world, it's on myself it pitches, like a flock of crows on seed potatoes.

MRS. FALLON. Leave off talking of misfortunes, and listen to Jack Smith that is coming the way, and he singing.

(*Voice of Jack Smith heard singing:*)

I thought, my first love,
    There'd be but one house between
        you and me,
And I thought I would find
    Yourself coaxing my child on your
        knee.
Over the tide
    I would leap with the leap of a
        swan,
Till I came to the side
    Of the wife of the Red-haired man!

(*Jack Smith comes in; he is a red-haired man, and is carrying a hayfork.*)

MRS. TARPEY. That should be a good song if I had my hearing.

MRS. FALLON. (*Shouting.*) It's "The Red-haired Man's Wife."

MRS. TARPEY. I know it well. That's the song that has a skin on it!

(*She turns her back to them and goes on arranging her apples.*)

MRS. FALLON. Where's herself, Jack Smith?

JACK SMITH. She was delayed with her washing; bleaching the clothes on the hedge she is, and she daren't leave them, with all the tinkers that do be passing to the fair. It isn't to the fair I came myself, but up to the Five Acre Meadow I'm going, where I have a contract for the hay. We'll get a share of it into tramps to-day. (*He lays down hayfork and lights his pipe.*)

BARTLEY. You will not get it into tramps to-day. The rain will be down on it by evening, and on myself too. It's seldom I ever started on a journey but the rain would come down on me before I'd find any place of shelter.

JACK SMITH. If it didn't itself, Bartley, it is my belief you would carry a leaky pail on your head in place of a hat, the way you'd not be without some cause of complaining.

(*A voice heard, "Go on, now, go on out o' that. Go on I say."*)

JACK SMITH. Look at that young mare of Pat Ryan's that is backing into Shaughnessy's bullocks with the dint of the crowd! Don't be daunted, Pat, I'll give you a hand with her.

(*He goes out, leaving his hayfork.*)

MRS. FALLON. It's time for ourselves to be going home. I have all I bought put in the basket. Look at there, Jack Smith's hayfork he left after him! He'll be wanting it. (*Calls.*) Jack Smith! Jack Smith!—He's gone through the crowd—hurry after him, Bartley, he'll be wanting it.

BARTLEY. I'll do that. This is no safe place to be leaving it. (*He takes up fork awkwardly and upsets the basket.*) Look at that now! If there is any basket in the fair upset, it must be our own basket! (*He goes out to right.*)

MRS. FALLON. Get out of that! It is your own fault, it is. Talk of misfortunes and misfortunes will come. Glory be! Look at my new egg-cups rolling in every part—and my two pound of sugar with the paper broke——

MRS. TARPEY. (*Turning from stall.*) God help us, Mrs. Fallon, what happened your basket?

MRS. FALLON. It's himself that knocked it down, bad manners to him. (*Putting things up.*) My grand sugar that's destroyed, and he'll not drink his tea without it. I had best go back to the shop for more, much good may it do him!

(*Enter Tim Casey.*)

TIM CASEY. Where is Bartley Fallon, Mrs. Fallon? I want a word with him before he'll leave the fair. I was afraid he might have gone home by this, for he's a temperate man.

MRS. FALLON. I wish he did go home! It'd be best for me if he went home straight from the fair green, or if he never came with me at all! Where is he, is it? He's gone up the road (*jerks elbow*) following Jack Smith with a hayfork.

(*She goes out to left.*)

TIM CASEY. Following Jack Smith with a hayfork! Did ever any one hear the like of that. (*Shouts.*) Did you hear that news, Mrs. Tarpey?

MRS. TARPEY. I heard no news at all.

TIM CASEY. Some dispute I suppose it was that rose between Jack Smith and Bartley Fallon, and it seems Jack made off, and Bartley is following him with a hayfork!

MRS. TARPEY. Is he now? Well, that was quick work! It's not ten minutes since the two of them were here, Bartley going home and Jack going to the Five Acre Meadow; and I had my apples to settle up, that Jo Muldoon of the police had scattered, and when I looked round again Jack Smith was gone, and Bartley Fallon was gone, and Mrs. Fallon's basket upset, and all in it strewed upon the ground— the tea here—the two pound of sugar there—the egg-cups there—Look, now, what a great hardship the deafness puts upon me, that I didn't hear the commincement of the fight! Wait till I tell James Ryan that I see below; he is a neighbour of Bartley's, it would be a pity if he wouldn't hear the news!

(*She goes out. Enter Shawn Early and Mrs. Tully.*)

TIM CASEY. Listen, Shawn Early! Listen, Mrs. Tully, to the news! Jack Smith and Bartley Fallon had a falling out, and Jack knocked Mrs. Fallon's basket into the road, and Bartley made an attack on him with a hayfork, and away with Jack, and Bartley after him. Look at the sugar here yet on the road!

SHAWN EARLY. Do you tell me so? Well, that's a queer thing, and Bartley Fallon so quiet a man!

MRS. TULLY. I wouldn't wonder at all. I would never think well of a man that would have that sort of a mouldering look. It's likely he has overtaken Jack by this.

(Enter James Ryan and Mrs. Tarpey.)

JAMES RYAN. That is great news Mrs. Tarpey was telling me! I suppose that's what brought the police and the magistrate up this way. I was wondering to see them in it a while ago.

SHAWN EARLY. The police after them? Bartley Fallon must have injured Jack so. They wouldn't meddle in a fight that was only for show!

MRS. TULLY. Why wouldn't he injure him? There was many a man killed with no more of a weapon than a hayfork.

JAMES RYAN. Wait till I run north as far as Kelly's bar to spread the news! (He goes out.)

TIM CASEY. I'll go tell Jack Smith's first cousin that is standing there south of the church after selling his lambs. (Goes out.)

MRS. TULLY. I'll go telling a few of the neighbours I see beyond to the west. (Goes out.)

SHAWN EARLY. I'll give word of it beyond at the east of the green.

(Is going out when Mrs. Tarpey seizes hold of him.)

MRS. TARPEY. Stop a minute, Shawn Early, and tell me did you see red Jack Smith's wife, Kitty Keary, in any place?

SHAWN EARLY. I did. At her own house she was, drying clothes on the hedge as I passed.

MRS. TARPEY. What did you say she was doing?

SHAWN EARLY. (Breaking away.) Laying out a sheet on the hedge. (He goes.)

MRS. TARPEY. Laying out a sheet for the dead! The Lord have mercy on us! Jack Smith dead, and his wife laying out a sheet for his burying! (Calls out.) Why didn't you tell me that before, Shawn Early? Isn't the deafness the great hardship? Half the world might be dead without me knowing of it or getting word of it at all! (She sits down and rocks herself.) O my poor Jack Smith! To be going to his work so nice and so hearty, and to be left stretched on the ground in the full light of the day! (Enter Tim Casey.)

TIM CASEY. What is it, Mrs. Tarpey? What happened since?

MRS. TARPEY. O my poor Jack Smith!

TIM CASEY. Did Bartley overtake him?

MRS. TARPEY. O the poor man!

TIM CASEY. Is it killed he is?

MRS. TARPEY. Stretched in the Five Acre Meadow!

TIM CASEY. The Lord have mercy on us! Is that a fact?

MRS. TARPEY. Without the rites of the Church or a ha'porth!

TIM CASEY. Who was telling you?

MRS. TARPEY. And the wife laying out a sheet for his corpse. (Sits up and wipes her eyes.) I suppose they'll wake him the same as another? (Enter Mrs. Tully, Shawn Early, and James Ryan.)

MRS. TULLY. There is great talk about this work in every quarter of the fair.

MRS. TARPEY. Ochone! cold and dead. And myself maybe the last he was speaking to!

JAMES RYAN. The Lord save us! Is it dead he is?

TIM CASEY. Dead surely, and the wife getting provision for the wake.

SHAWN EARLY. Well, now, hadn't Bartley Fallon great venom in him?

MRS. TULLY. You may be sure he had some cause. Why would he have made an end of him if he had not? (To Mrs. Tarpey, raising her voice.) What was it rose the dispute at all, Mrs. Tarpey?

MRS. TARPEY. Not a one of me knows. The last I saw of them, Jack Smith was standing there, and Bartley Fallon was standing there, quiet and easy, and he listening to "The Red-haired Man's Wife."

MRS. TULLY. Do you hear that, Tim Casey? Do you hear that, Shawn Early and James Ryan? Bartley Fallon was here this morning listening to red Jack Smith's wife, Kitty Keary that was! Listening to her and whispering with her! It was she started the fight so!

SHAWN EARLY. She must have followed him from her own house. It is likely some person roused him.

TIM CASEY. I never knew, before, Bartley Fallon was great with Jack Smith's wife.

MRS. TULLY. How would you know it? Sure it's not in the streets they would be calling it. If Mrs. Fallon didn't know of it, and if I that have the next house to them didn't know of it, and if Jack Smith himself didn't know of it, it is not likely you would know of it, Tim Casey.

SHAWN EARLY. Let Bartley Fallon take charge of her from this out so, and let him provide for her. It is little pity she will get from any person in this parish.

TIM CASEY. How can he take charge of her? Sure he has a wife of his own. Sure you don't think he'd turn souper and marry her in a Protestant church?

JAMES RYAN. It would be easy for him to marry her if he brought her to America.

SHAWN EARLY. With or without Kitty Keary, believe me it is for America he's making at this minute. I saw the new magistrate and Jo Muldoon of the police going into the post-office as I came up—there was hurry on them—you may be sure it was to telegraph they went, the way he'll

be stopped in the docks at Queenstown!

MRS. TULLY. It's likely Kitty Keary is gone with him, and not minding a sheet or a wake at all. The poor man, to be deserted by his own wife, and the breath hardly gone out yet from his body that is lying bloody in the field! (*Enter Mrs. Fallon.*)

MRS. FALLON. What is it the whole of the town is talking about? And what is it you yourselves are talking about? Is it about my man Bartley Fallon you are talking? Is it lies about him you are telling, saying that he went killing Jack Smith? My grief that ever he came into this place at all!

JAMES RYAN. Be easy now, Mrs. Fallon. Sure there is no one at all in the whole fair but is sorry for you!

MRS. FALLON. Sorry for me, is it? Why would any one be sorry for me? Let you be sorry for yourselves, and that there may be shame on you for ever and at the day of judgment, for the words you are saying and the lies you are telling to take away the character of my poor man, and to take the good name off of him, and to drive him to destruction! That is what you are doing!

SHAWN EARLY. Take comfort now, Mrs. Fallon. The police are not so smart as they think. Sure he might give them the slip yet, the same as Lynchehaun.

MRS. TULLY. If they do get him, and if they do put a rope around his neck, there is no one can say he does not deserve it!

MRS. FALLON. Is that what you are saying, Bridget Tully, and is that what you think? I tell you it's too much talk you have, making yourself out to be such a great one, and to be running down every respectable person! A rope, is it? It isn't much of a rope was needed to tie up your own furniture the day you came into Martin Tully's house, and you never bringing as much as a blanket, or a penny, or a suit of clothes with you and I myself bringing seventy pounds and two feather beds. And now you are stiffer than a woman would have a hundred pounds! It is too much talk the whole of you have. A rope is it? I tell you the whole of this town is full of liars and schemers that would hang you up for half a glass of whiskey. (*Turning to go.*) People they are you wouldn't believe as much as daylight from without you'd get up to have a look at it yourself. Killing Jack Smith indeed! Where are you at all, Bartley, till I bring you out of this? My nice quiet little man! My decent comrade! He that is as kind and as harmless as an innocent beast of the field! He'll be doing no harm at all if he'll shed the blood of some of you after this day's work! That much would be no harm at all. (*Calls out.*) Bartley! Bartley Fallon! Where are you? (*Going out.*) Did any one see Bartley Fallon? (*All turn to look after her.*)

JAMES RYAN. It is hard for her to believe any such a thing, God help her!
(*Enter Bartley Fallon from right, carrying hayfork.*)

BARTLEY. It is what I often said to myself, if there is ever any misfortune coming to this world it is on myself it is sure to come!
(*All turn round and face him.*)

BARTLEY. To be going about with this fork and to find no one to take it, and no place to leave it down, and I wanting to be gone out of this— Is that you, Shawn Early? (*Holds out fork.*) It's well I met you. You have no call to be leaving the fair for a while the way I have, and how can I go till I'm rid of this fork? Will you take it and keep it until such time as Jack Smith——

SHAWN EARLY. (*Backing.*) I will not take it, Bartley Fallon, I'm very thankful to you!

BARTLEY. (*Turning to apple stall.*) Look at it now, Mrs. Tarpey, it was here I got it; let me thrust it in under the stall. It will lie there safe enough, and no one will take notice of it until such time as Jack Smith——

MRS. TARPEY. Take your fork out of that! Is it to put trouble on me and to destroy me you want? putting it there for the police to be rooting it out maybe. (*Thrusts him back.*)

BARTLEY. That is a very unneighbourly thing for you to do, Mrs. Tarpey. Hadn't I enough care on me with that fork before this, running up and down with it like the swinging of a clock, and afeard to lay it down in any place! I wish I never touched it or meddled with it at all!

JAMES RYAN. It is a pity, indeed, you ever did.

BARTLEY. Will you yourself take it, James Ryan? You were always a neighbourly man.

JAMES RYAN. (*Backing.*) There is many a thing I would do for you, Bartley Fallon, but I won't do that!

SHAWN EARLY. I tell you there is no man will give you any help or any encouragement for this day's work. If it was something agrarian now——

BARTLEY. If no one at all will take it, maybe it's best to give it up to the police.

TIM CASEY. There'd be a welcome for it with them surely! (*Laughter.*)

MRS. TULLY. And it is to the police Kitty Keary herself will be brought.

MRS. TARPEY. (*Rocking to and fro.*) I wonder now who will take the expense of the wake for poor Jack Smith?

BARTLEY. The wake for Jack Smith!

TIM CASEY. Why wouldn't he get a wake as well as another? Would you begrudge him that much?

BARTLEY. Red Jack Smith dead! Who was telling you?

SHAWN EARLY. The whole town knows of it by this.

BARTLEY. Do they say what way did he die?

JAMES RYAN. You don't know that yourself, I suppose, Bartley Fallon? You don't know he was followed and that he was laid dead with the stab of a hayfork?

BARTLEY. The stab of a hayfork!

SHAWN EARLY. You don't know, I suppose, that the body was found in the Five Acre Meadow?

BARTLEY. The Five Acre Meadow!

TIM CASEY. It is likely you don't know that the police are after the man that did it?·

BARTLEY. The man that did it!

MRS. TULLY. You don't know, maybe, that he was made away with for the sake of Kitty Keary, his wife?

BARTLEY. Kitty Keary, his wife! (*Sits down bewildered.*)

MRS. TULLY. And what have you to say now, Bartley Fallon?

BARTLEY. (*Crossing himself.*) I to bring that fork here, and to find that news before me! It is much if I can ever stir from this place at all, or reach as far as the road!

TIM CASEY. Look, boys, at the new magistrate, and Jo Muldoon along with him! It's best for us to quit this.

SHAWN EARLY. That is so. It is best not to be mixed in this business at all.

JAMES RYAN. Bad as he is, I wouldn't like to be an informer against any man. (*All hurry away except Mrs. Tarpey, who remains behind her stall. Enter magistrate and policeman.*)

MAGISTRATE. I knew the district was in a bad state, but I did not expect to be confronted with a murder at the first fair I came to.

POLICEMAN. I am sure you did not, indeed.

MAGISTRATE. It was well I had not gone home. I caught a few words here and there that roused my suspicions.

POLICEMAN. So they would, too.

MAGISTRATE. You heard the same story from everyone you asked?

POLICEMAN. The same story or if it was not altogether the same, anyway it was no less than the first story.

MAGISTRATE. What is that man doing? He is sitting alone with a hayfork. He has a guilty look. The murder was done with a hayfork!

POLICEMAN. (*In a whisper.*) That's the very man they say did the act; Bartley Fallon himself!

MAGISTRATE. He must have found escape difficult—he is trying to brazen it out. A convict in the Andaman Islands tried the same game, but he could not escape my system! Stand aside— Don't go far—have the handcuffs ready. (*He walks up to Bartley, folds his arms, and stands before him.*) Here, my man, do you know anything of John Smith?

BARTLEY. Of John Smith! Who is he, now?

POLICEMAN. Jack Smith, sir——Red Jack Smith!

MAGISTRATE. (*Coming a step nearer and tapping him on the shoulder.*) Where is Jack Smith?

BARTLEY. (*With a deep sigh, and shaking his head slowly.*) Where is he, indeed?

MAGISTRATE. What have you to tell?

BARTLEY. It is where he was this morning, standing in this spot, singing his share of songs—no, but lighting his pipe— scraping a match on the sole of his shoe——

MAGISTRATE. I ask you, for the third time, where is he?

BARTLEY. I wouldn't like to say that. It is a great mystery, and it is hard to say of any man, did he earn hatred or love. ·

MAGISTRATE. Tell me all you know.

BARTLEY. All that I know— Well, there are the three estates; there is Limbo, and there is Purgatory, and there is——

MAGISTRATE. Nonsense! This is trifling! Get to the point.

BARTLEY. Maybe you don't hold with the clergy so? That is the teaching of the clergy. Maybe you hold with the old people. It is what they do be saying, that the shadow goes wandering, and the soul is tired, and the body is taking a rest— The shadow! (*Starts up.*) I was nearly sure I saw Jack Smith not ten minutes ago at the corner of the forge, and I lost him again— Was it his ghost I saw, do you think?

MAGISTRATE. (*To policeman.*) Conscience-struck! He will confess all now!

BARTLEY. His ghost to come before me! It is likely it was on account of the fork! I to have it and he to have no way to defend himself the time he met with his death!

MAGISTRATE. (*To policeman.*) I must note down his words. (*Takes out notebook.*) (*To Bartley:*) I warn you that your words are being noted.

BARTLEY. If I had ha' run faster in the beginning, this terror would not be on me at the latter end! Maybe he will cast it up against me at the day of judgment— I wouldn't wonder at all at that.

MAGISTRATE. (*Writing.*) At the day of judgment——

BARTLEY. It was soon for his ghost to appear to me—is it coming after me always by day it will be, and stripping the clothes off in the night time?— I wouldn't wonder at all at that, being as I am an unfortunate man!

MAGISTRATE. (*Sternly.*) Tell me this truly. What was the motive of this crime?

BARTLEY. The motive, is it?

MAGISTRATE. Yes; the motive; the cause.

BARTLEY. I'd sooner not say that.

MAGISTRATE. You had better tell me truly. Was it money?

BARTLEY. Not at all! What did poor Jack Smith ever have in his pockets unless it might be his hands that would be in them?

MAGISTRATE. Any dispute about land?

BARTLEY. (*Indignantly.*) Not at all! He never was a grabber or grabbed from any one!

MAGISTRATE. You will find it better for you if you tell me at once.

BARTLEY. I tell you I wouldn't for the whole world wish to say what it was —it is a thing I would not like to be talking about.

MAGISTRATE. There is no use in hiding it. It will be discovered in the end.

BARTLEY. Well, I suppose it will, seeing that mostly everybody knows it before. Whisper here now. I will tell no lie; where would be the use? (*Puts his hand to his mouth, and Magistrate stoops.*) Don't be putting the blame on the parish, for such a thing was never done in the parish before—it was done for the sake of Kitty Keary, Jack Smith's wife.

MAGISTRATE. (*To policeman.*) Put on the handcuffs. We have been saved some trouble. I knew he would confess if taken in the right way.

(*Policeman puts on handcuffs.*)

BARTLEY. Handcuffs now! Glory be! I always said, if there was ever any misfortune coming to this place it was on myself it would fall. I to be in handcuffs! There's no wonder at all in that.

(*Enter Mrs. Fallon, followed by the rest. She is looking back at them as she speaks.*)

MRS. FALLON. Telling lies the whole of the people of this town are; telling lies, telling lies as fast as a dog will trot! Speaking against my poor respectable man! Saying he made an end of Jack Smith! My decent comrade! There is no better man and no kinder man in the whole of the five parishes! It's little annoyance he ever gave to any one! (*Turns and sees him.*) What in the earthly world do I see before me? Bartley Fallon in charge of the police! Handcuffs on him! O Bartley, what did you do at all at all?

BARTLEY. O Mary, there has a great misfortune come upon me! It is what I always said, that if there is ever any misfortune——

MRS. FALLON. What did he do at all, or is it bewitched I am?

MAGISTRATE. This man has been arrested on a charge of murder.

MRS. FALLON. Whose charge is that? Don't believe them! They are all liars in this place! Give me back my man!

MAGISTRATE. It is natural you should take his part, but you have no cause of complaint against your neighbours. He has been arrested for the murder of John Smith, on his own confession.

MRS. FALLON. The saints of heaven protect us! And what did he want killing Jack Smith?

MAGISTRATE. It is best you should know all. He did it on account of a love affair with the murdered man's wife.

MRS. FALLON. (Sitting down.) With Jack Smith's wife! With Kitty Keary!— Ochone, the traitor!

THE CROWD. A great shame, indeed. He is a traitor, indeed.

MRS. TULLY. To America he was bringing her, Mrs. Fallon.

BARTLEY. What are you saying, Mary? I tell you——

MRS. FALLON. Don't say a word! I won't listen to any word you'll say! (Stops her ears.) O, isn't he the treacherous villain? Ochone go deo!

BARTLEY. Be quiet till I speak! Listen to what I say!

MRS. FALLON. Sitting beside me on the ass car coming to the town, so quiet and so respectable, and treachery like that in his heart!

BARTLEY. Is it your wits you have lost or is it I myself that have lost my wits?

MRS. FALLON. And it's hard I earned you, slaving, slaving—and you grumbling, and sighing, and coughing, and discontented, and the priest wore out anointing you, with all the times you threatened to die!

BARTLEY. Let you be quiet till I tell you!

MRS. FALLON. You to bring such a disgrace into the parish. A thing that was never heard of before!

BARTLEY. Will you shut your mouth and hear me speaking?

MRS. FALLON. And if it was for any sort of a fine handsome woman, but for a little fistful of a woman like Kitty Keary, that's not four feet high hardly, and not three teeth in her head unless she got new ones! May God reward you, Bartley Fallon, for the black treachery in your heart and the wickedness in your mind, and the red blood of poor Jack Smith that is wet upon your hand!

(Voice of Jack Smith heard singing.)

The sea shall be dry,
The earth under mourning and ban!
Then loud shall he cry
For the wife of the red-haired man!

BARTLEY. It's Jack Smith's voice—I never knew a ghost to sing before—. It is after myself and the fork he is coming! (Goes back. Enter Jack Smith.) Let one of you give him the fork and I will be clear of him now and for eternity!

MRS. TARPEY. The Lord have mercy on us! Red Jack Smith! The man that was going to be waked!

JAMES RYAN. Is it back from the grave you are come?

SHAWN EARLY. Is it alive you are, or is it dead you are?

TIM CASEY. Is it yourself at all that's in it?

MRS. TULLY. Is it letting on you were to be dead?

MRS. FALLON. Dead or alive, let you stop Kitty Keary, your wife, from bringing my man away with her to America!

JACK SMITH. It is what I think, the wits are gone astray on the whole of you. What would my wife want bringing Bartley Fallon to America?

MRS. FALLON. To leave yourself, and to get quit of you she wants, Jack Smith, and to bring him away from myself.

That's what the two of them had settled together.

JACK SMITH. I'll break the head of any man that says that! Who is it says it? (*To Tim Casey:*) Was it you said it? (*To Shawn Early:*) Was it you?

ALL TOGETHER. (*Backing and shaking their heads.*) It wasn't I said it!

JACK SMITH. Tell me the name of any man that said it!

ALL TOGETHER. (*Pointing to Bartley.*) It was *him* that said it!

JACK SMITH. Let me at him till I break his head!

(*Bartley backs in terror. Neighbours hold Jack Smith back.*)

JACK SMITH. (*Trying to free himself.*) Let me at him! Isn't he the pleasant sort of a scarecrow for any woman to be crossing the ocean with! It's back from the docks of New York he'd be turned (*trying to rush at him again*), with a lie in his mouth and treachery in his heart, and another man's wife by his side, and he passing her off as his own! Let me at him can't you.

(*Makes another rush, but is held back.*)

MAGISTRATE. (*Pointing to Jack Smith.*) Policeman, put the handcuffs on this man. I see it all now. A case of false impersonation, a conspiracy to defeat the ends of justice. There was a case in the Andaman Islands, a murderer of the Mopsa tribe, a religious enthusiast——

POLICEMAN. So he might be, too.

MAGISTRATE. We must take both these men to the scene of the murder. We must confront them with the body of the real Jack Smith.

JACK SMITH. I'll break the head of any man that will find my dead body!

MAGISTRATE. I'll call more help from the barracks. (*Blows Policeman's whistle.*)

BARTLEY. It is what I am thinking, if myself and Jack Smith are put together in the one cell for the night, the handcuffs will be taken off him, and his hands will be free, and murder will be done that time surely!

MAGISTRATE. Come on! (*They turn to the right.*)

1906

S. N. BEHRMAN

End of Summer

CHARACTERS

WILL DEXTER
MRS. WYLER
PAULA FROTHINGHAM
ROBERT
LEONIE FROTHINGHAM

SAM FROTHINGHAM
DR. KENNETH RICE
DENNIS MCCARTHY
DR. DEXTER
BORIS, COUNT MIRSKY

SCENE: The action of the play takes place in the living room of Bay Cottage, the Frothinghams' summer place in Northern Maine.

TIME: The present.

ACT ONE

.SCENE. *The verandah-living room of the Frothingham estate. Bay Cottage in Northern Maine. It is a charmingly furnished room with beautiful old distinguished pieces. A chintz couch and chairs give the room an air of informality. Beyond the door back you see a spacious, more formal room. Through the series of glass windows over the curving window seat on the right wall you see the early budding lilac and sumach. Woodbine and Virginia creeper are sprawling over the fence of native stone. Silver birch and maple are beginning to put out their leaves. The tops of red pine and cedar are visible over the rocks which fall away to the sea.*

TIME. *The present. A lovely afternoon in May.*

AT RISE: MRS. WYLER, *a very old lady and* WILL DEXTER, *an attractive, serious boy, are engaged in conversation.* MRS. WYLER *is knitting.*

WILL. When you were a young girl in Cleveland, did you see much of Mr. Rockefeller?

MRS. WYLER. Not much. Of course my husband saw him every day at the office. But he never came to our house. We were young and worldly. He was strict and religious.

WILL. Did you suspect, in those days, how rich you were going to be?

MRS. WYLER. Mercy no! We debated a long time before we moved up to Cleveland from Oil City. My mother thought Oil City was no place to bring up a young girl. She finally persuaded my father to let us move up to Cleveland. But there was a lot of talk about the expense.

WILL. Was Oil City lively?

MRS. WYLER. (*Demurely.*) It was pretty rough! I remember the celebration when they ran the first pipe-line through to Pittsburgh. That was a celebration!

WILL. The oil just poured, didn't it? Gushed out of the ground in great jets, and the people swarmed from everywhere to scoop it up.

MRS. WYLER. I remember we had a gusher in our backyard. We put a fence around it to keep the cows from lapping up the oil.

WILL. Were you excited?

MRS. WYLER. Not by the oil.

WILL. I should think you would have been!

MRS. WYLER. (*Dryly.*) We weren't. Oil was smelly. We wanted to get away from it. We discovered bath-salts.

WILL. You didn't know it was the true fountain of your—dynasty?

MRS. WYLER. We left it to the men—as I look back over my life the principal excitement came from houses—buying and building houses. The shack in Oil City to the mansion on Fifth Avenue. We had houses everywhere —houses in London, houses in Paris, Newport and this—and yet, it seemed to me, we were always checking in and out of hotels.

WILL. It seems strange to think—

MRS. WYLER. What?

WILL. This golden stream — that you stumbled on so accidentally—it's flowing still—quenchless—and you on it— all you dynastic families—floating along in it—in luxurious barges!

MRS. WYLER. When I read these books about the early days of oil—these debunking books, you call them—they make me smile.

WILL. Do they? Why? I'd like to know that.

MRS. WYLER. They're so far from the truth.

WILL. Are they?

MRS. WYLER. Of course they are!

WILL. Why?

MRS. WYLER. Because they're written from a foreign point of view—not *our* point of view. We did as well as anybody could have done according to our lights.

WILL. Yes, but what sort of lights were they?

MRS. WYLER. (*Tolerantly.*) There you are!

WILL. How lucky you were!

MRS. WYLER. (*Teasing him.*) Our young men didn't moon about. They made opportunities for themselves!

WILL. Or did the opportunities make them? All you had to do was pack your week-end bag and pioneer.

MRS. WYLER. Is the world quite exhausted then?

WILL. Possibly not, but our pioneering might take a form you would find— unpalatable.

MRS. WYLER. Yes, yes. (*Benevolently.*) I suppose you're one of those young radicals our colleges are said to be full of nowadays. Tell me, what do you young radicals stand for?

WILL. I haven't decided exactly what I'm for, but I'm pretty certain what I'm against.

MRS. WYLER. (*Pumping him.*) Most young people are bored by the past. You're full of curiosity. Why is that?

WILL. (*Not committing himself.*) I'm interested.

MRS. WYLER. At my age to be permitted to talk of one's youth is an indulgence. Ask me anything you like. At my age also one has no reason for restraint. I have had the bad judgment to survive most of my contemporaries.

WILL. I love talking to you, Mrs. Wyler. I think you're very wise.

MRS. WYLER. (*With a sigh.*) Go on thinking so—I'll try not to disillusion you! (*A moment's pause.*) Are you staying on here at Bay Cottage?

WILL. Oh, no, I have to go back to Amherst to get my degree.

MRS. WYLER. And after that?

WILL. (*Humorously.*) The dole! (*The old lady laughs.*)

MRS. WYLER. My daughter tells me she's invited your father here.

WILL. Yes.

MRS. WYLER. I shall be so glad to meet him. He's an inventor, isn't he?

WILL. He's a physicist. Specializes in—

MRS. WYLER. Don't tell me—in spite of my great wisdom I can't keep up with science. Whenever anybody makes a scientific explanation to me I find there are two things I don't know instead of just one.

WILL. (*Cheerfully.*) Anyway, Dad's been fired.

MRS. WYLER. I am very sorry to hear that.

WILL. He's been working on a method for improving high-speed steel.

MRS. WYLER. Did he fail?

WILL. He succeeded. (MRS. WYLER *is surprised.*) They decided that his discovery, if perfected and marketed, might increase the technological unemployment. They have decided therefore to call a halt on scientific discovery—especially in those branches where it might have practical results. That is one of the differences, Mrs. Wyler, between my day—and yours—in your day, you put a premium on invention—we declare a moratorium on it. (*The old lady gives him a shrewd look.*)

MRS. WYLER. Yes, yes. I am perfectly sure that you're in for a hard time, Will.

WILL. (*Lightly, shrugging his shoulders.*) As I have been elected by my class as the one most likely to succeed, I am not worrying, Mrs. Wyler. All I have to do is bide my time.

MRS. WYLER. (*Amused.*) I am perfectly certain you'll come out! Paula tells me you and your friend, Dennis McCarthy, want to start some kind of magazine.

WILL. Yes. A national magazine for undergraduate America. You see, Mrs. Wyler, before the rift in our so-called system, college men were supposed to live exclusively in a world of ukuleles, football slogans, and petting-parties— *College Humor* sort of thing. But it was never entirely true. Now it is less true than ever. This magazine —if we can get it going—would be a forum for intercollegiate thought. It would be the organ of critical youth as opposed—to the other.

MRS. WYLER. What other?

WILL. The R.O.T.C., the Vigilantes and the Fascists—the Youth Movement of guns and sabres—

MRS. WYLER. I see. Well, I wish you luck, Will.

WILL. Thank you. (PAULA FROTHINGHAM *comes in, a lovely young girl in gay summer slacks.*)

PAULA. (*To* WILL.) Aren't you swimming? Hello, Granny.

WILL. Your grandmother and I have been discussing life.

PAULA. With a capital L, I suppose?

WILL. Enormous! I've been getting data on the pioneer age. Your grandmother thinks the reason we're in the condition we're in is because we're lazy.

MRS. WYLER. (*Mildly.*) Lazy? Did I say that?

WILL. In a way.

MRS. WYLER. If I said it, it must be so. Everybody over seventy is infallible!

PAULA. (*Nestling to her.*) Darling.

MRS. WYLER. Survival is quite a knack. You children don't realize it.

WILL. Oh, don't we though! It's getting harder every day.

MRS. WYLER. Nonsense! At your age you can't help it.

WILL. In your stately opulence that's what you think, Mrs. Wyler. You just don't know!

MRS. WYLER. Nonsense! Do you think your generation has a monopoly on hard times?

WILL. Now please don't tell me we've had depressions before?

MRS. WYLER. (*Rising to go.*) Paula, your young man is impertinent. Don't have anything to do with him. (*She goes out.*)

PAULA. What a conquest you've made of Granny! Way and ahead of all my beaus!

WILL. That undistinguished mob! Who couldn't?

PAULA. As long as you admit there is a mob . . .

WILL. Why wouldn't there be? Everybody loves you for your money!

PAULA. (*Confidently.*) I know it! And of all the fortune-hunters I've had dangling after me you're easily the most . . .

WILL. Blatant!

PAULA. That's it! Blatant! Like my new slacks?

WILL. Love 'em.

PAULA. Love me?

WILL. Loathe you.

PAULA. Good! Kiss? (*They kiss quickly.*)

WILL. Funny thing about your grandmother . . .

PAULA. Now I won't have you criticising Granny . . .

WILL. I'm crazy about her. You feel she's been through everything and that she understands everything. Not this though. Not the essential difference between her times and ours.

PAULA. Oh dear! Is it the end of the world then?

WILL. The end of this world.

PAULA. (*Goes to window seat right, with a sigh.*) Such a pretty world. (*She points through windows at the garden and sea beyond.*) Look at it! Too bad it has to go! Meantime before it quite dissolves let's go for a swim. (*She starts for door.*)

WILL. (*Abstracted.*) All right . . . (*Following her to window seat*).

PAULA. (*She turns back.*) What's on your mind?

WILL. Wanted to speak to you about something. . . .

PAULA. What?

WILL. (*Embarrassed slightly.*) Er—your mother. . . .

PAULA. What's Mother gone and done now? Out with it. Or is it you? My boyfriends are always in love with Mother. I've had to contend with that all my life. So if it's that you needn't even mention it . . . come on.

WILL. No, but really, Paula. . . .

PAULA. Well then, out with it! What is it!

WILL. This. (*He gives her note.*) Found it on my breakfast tray this morning in a sealed envelope marked "Confidential."

PAULA. (*Reading note aloud, rather bewildered.*) "To give my little girl a good time with. Leonie Frothingham."

WILL. And this! (*He hands her check. PAULA takes it and looks at it.*)

PAULA. A hundred dollars. Does Mother think her little girl can have a good time with *that?* She doesn't know her little girl!

WILL. But what'll I do with it? How'll I get it back to her?

PAULA. Over my dead body you'll get it back to her! You'll spend it on Mother's little girl. Now come on swimming!

WILL. Does your mother put one of these on every breakfast tray?

PAULA. Argue it out with her.

WILL. I can't. It would seem ungracious. You must give it back to her for me.

PAULA. Catch me! Don't take it too seriously. She slips all the kids something every once in a while. She knows my friends are all stony. You overestimate the importance of money, Will—it's a convenience, that's all. You've got a complex on it.

WILL. I have! I've got to have. It's all right to be dainty about money when you've lots of it as you have. . . .

PAULA. Rotten with it is the expression, I believe. . . .

WILL. I repudiate that expression. It is genteel and moralistic. You can't be rotten with money—you can only be *alive* with it.

PAULA. You and the rest of our crowd make me feel it's bad taste to be rich. But what can I do? I didn't ask for it!

WILL. I know. But look here . . . I've got

a brother out of college two years who's worked six weeks in that time and is broke and here I am in an atmosphere with hundred-dollar bills floating around!

PAULA. (*With check.*) Send him that!

WILL. Misapplication of funds!

PAULA. (*Warmly.*) Mother would be only too . . .

WILL. I know she would—but that isn't the point. . . . You know, Paula—

PAULA. What?

WILL. Sometimes I think if we weren't in love with each other we should be irreconcilable enemies—

PAULA. Nothing but sex, eh?

WILL. That's all.

PAULA. In that case—(*They kiss.*)

WILL. That's forgiving. But seriously, Paula—

PAULA. Seriously what?

WILL. I can't help feeling I'm here on false pretenses. What am I doing with a millionaire family—with you? If your mother knew what I think, and what I've let you in for in college—she wouldn't touch me with a ten-foot pole. And you too—I'm troubled about the superficiality of your new opinions. Isn't your radicalism—acquired coloring?

PAULA. I hope not. But—so is all education.

WILL. I know but—!

PAULA. What are you bleating about? Didn't I join you on that expedition to Kentucky to be treated by that sovereign state as an offensive foreigner? My back aches yet when I remember that terrible bus ride. Didn't I get my name in the papers picketing? Didn't I give up my holiday to go with you to the Chicago Peace Congress? Didn't I?

WILL. (*Doubtfully.*) Yes, you did.

PAULA. But you're not convinced. Will darling, don't you realize that since knowing you and your friends, since I've, as you say, acquired your point of view about things, my life has had an excitement and a sense of reality it's never had before. I've simply come alive—that's all! Before then I was bored—terribly bored without knowing why. I wanted something more—fundamental—without knowing what. You've made me see. I'm terribly grateful to you, Will darling. I always shall be.

WILL. You are a dear, Paula, and I adore you—but—

PAULA. Still unconvinced?

WILL. This money of yours. What'll it do to us?

PAULA. I'll turn it over to you. Then you can give me an allowance—and save your pride.

WILL. I warn you, Paula—

PAULA. What?

WILL. If you turn it over to me, I'll use it in every way I can to make it impossible for anyone to have so much again.

PAULA. That's all right with me, Will.

WILL. Sometimes you make me feel I'm taking candy from babies.

PAULA. The candy is no good for the baby, anyway. Besides, let's cross that bridge when we come to it. (ROBERT, *the butler, enters.*)

ROBERT. I beg your pardon, Miss Frothingham.

PAULA. Yes, Robert?

ROBERT. Telephone for you.

PAULA. Thank you, Robert. (*She crosses to table back of sofa for telephone.*) (*At phone.*) Yes—this is Paula—Dad!—Darling!—Where are you? . . . but how wonderful . . . I thought you were in New York . . . well, come right over this minute. . . . Will you stay the night? . . . Oh, too bad! . . . I'll wait right here for you. Hurry, darling! Bye! (*She hangs up.*) Imagine, dad! He's motoring up to Selena Bryant's at Murray Bay—I'm dying to have you meet him. He's the lamb of the world.

WILL. Not staying long, is he?

PAULA. No. He wants to see Mother he says. I wonder . . . oh, dear!

WILL. What?

PAULA. I was so excited I forgot to tell him. . . .

WILL. What?

PAULA. That a new friend of Mother's is coming.

WILL. The Russian?

PAULA. The Russian's here. He dates from last winter. You're behind the times, Will.

WILL. Who's the new friend?

PAULA. I'm not sure about it all yet. Maybe Mother isn't either. But I've had some experience in watching them come and go and my instinct tells me Dr. Rice is elected.

WILL. Who is Dr. Rice?

PAULA. Psychoanalyst from New York. (*Burlesquing slightly.*) The last word, my dear—(*At this point the object of* PAULA's *maternal impulse comes in, running a little and breathless, like a young girl.* LEONIE FROTHINGHAM, *as she has a daughter of nearly twenty, must be herself forty, but, at this moment, she might be sixteen. She is slim, girlish, in a young and quivering ecstasy of living and anticipation. For* LEONIE, *her daughter is an agreeable phenomenon whom she does not specially relate to herself biologically—a lovely apparition who hovers intermittently, in the wild garden of her life. There is something, for all her gaiety, heartbreaking about* LEONIE, *something childish and child-like—an acceptance of people instantly and uncritically at the best of their own valuation. She is impulsive and warm-hearted and generous to a fault. Her own fragile and exquisite loveliness she offers to the world half shyly, tentatively, bearing it like a cup containing a precious liquid of which not a drop must be spilled. A spirituelle amoureuse, she is repelled by the gross or the voluptuary; this is not hypocrisy—it is, in* LEONIE, *a more serious defect than that. In the world in which she moves hypocrisy is merely a social lubricant but this myopia—alas for* LEONIE!—*springs from a congenital and temperamental inability to face anything but the pleasantest and the most immediately appealing and the most flattering aspects of things—in life and in her own nature. At this moment, though, she is the loveliest fabrication of Nature, happy in the summer sun and loving all the world.*)

LEONIE. My darlings, did you ever know such a day?

WILL. (*He is a shy boy with her.*) It's nice!

LEONIE. Nice! It's . . . (*Her gesture conveys her utter inadequacy to express the beauties of the day.*) It's—radiant! It knows it's radiant! The world is pleased with herself today. Is the world a woman? Today she is—a lovely young girl in blue and white.

WILL. In green and white.

LEONIE. (*Agreeing—warmly.*) In green and white!—It depends where you look, doesn't it? I'm just off to the station to meet Dr. Rice. Will, you'll be fascinated by him.

PAULA. (*Cutting in—crisply.*) Sam telephoned.

LEONIE. Sam!

PAULA. Your husband. My father. Think back, Leonie.

LEONIE. Darling! Where is he?

PAULA. He's on his way here. He telephoned from Miller's Point.

LEONIE. Is he staying?

PAULA. No.

LEONIE. Why not?

PAULA. He's going on to Selena Bryant's.

LEONIE. What is this deep friendship between Sam and Selena Bryant?

PAULA. Now, Leonie, don't be prudish!

LEONIE. (*Appealing for protection to* WILL.) She's always teasing me. She's always teasing everybody about everything. Developed quite a vein.

I must warn you, Paula—sarcasm isn't feminine. In their hearts men don't like it. Do you like it, Will? Do you really like it?

WILL. I hate it!

LEONIE. (*In triumph to* PAULA.) There you see! He hates it!

PAULA. (*Tersely.*) He doesn't always hate it!

LEONIE. (*Her most winning smile on* WILL.) Does she bully you, Will? Don't let her bully you. The sad thing is, Paula, you're so charming. Why aren't you content to be charming? Are you as serious as Paula, Will? I hope not.

WILL. Much more.

LEONIE. I'm sorry to hear that. Still, for a man, it's all right, I suppose. But why are the girls nowadays so determined not to be feminine? Why? It's coming back you know—I'm sure of it—femininity is due for a revival.

PAULA. So are Herbert Hoover and painting on china.

LEONIE. Well I read that even in Russia . . . the women . . . (*She turns again to* WILL *whom she feels sympathetic.*) It isn't as if women had done such marvels with their—masculinity! Have they? Are things better because women vote? Not that I can see. They're worse. As far as I can see the women simply reinforce the men in their—mistakes.

WILL. (*To* PAULA.) She has you there!

LEONIE. (*With this encouragement warming to her theme.*) When I was a girl the calamities of the world were on a much smaller scale. It's because the women, who, after all, are half of the human race, stayed at home and didn't bother. Now they do bother—and look at us!

PAULA. Well, that's as Victorian as anything I ever—

LEONIE. I'd love to have been a Victorian. They were much happier than we are, weren't they? Of course they were.

PAULA. (*Defending herself to* WILL.) It's

only Mother that brings out the crusader in me—(*To* LEONIE.) When you're not around I'm not like that at all. Am I, Will? (*But* WILL *is given no chance to answer because* LEONIE *is holding a sprig of lilac to his nostrils.*)

LEONIE. Smell. (WILL *smells.*) Isn't it delicious?

WILL. It's lovely.

LEONIE. Here. . . . (*She breaks off a sprig and pins it into his lapel. While she is doing it she broaches a delicate subject quite casually to* PAULA.) Oh, by the way, Paula . . .

PAULA. Yes, Mother?

LEONIE. Did you mention to Sam that— that Boris—

PAULA. I didn't, no. It slipped my mind.

LEONIE. It doesn't matter in the least.

PAULA. Father isn't staying anyway . . .

LEONIE. Well, why shouldn't he? You must make him. I want him to meet Dr. Rice. He's really a most extraordinary man.

PAULA. Where'd you *find* him?

LEONIE. I met him at a party at Sissy Drake's. He *saved* Sissy.

PAULA. From what?

LEONIE. From that awful eye-condition.

PAULA. Is he an oculist too?

LEONIE. (*To* WILL.) She went to every oculist in the world—she went to Baltimore and she went to Vienna. Nobody could do a thing for her—her eyes kept blinking—twitching really in the most unaccountable way. It was an ordeal to talk to her—and of course she must have undergone agonies of embarrassment. But Dr. Rice psychoanalyzed her and completely cured her. How do you suppose? Well, he found that the seat of the trouble lay in her unconscious. It was too simple. She blinked in that awful way because actually she couldn't bear to look at her husband. So she divorced Drake and since she's married to Bill Wilmerding she's as normal as you or me. Now I'll take you into a little secret. I'm having Dr. Rice up to see Boris. Of course Boris mustn't know it's for him.

PAULA. What's the matter with Boris?

LEONIE. I'm not sure. I think he's working too hard.

WILL. What's he working at?

LEONIE. Don't you know? Didn't you tell him, Paula? His father's memoirs. He's the son, you know, of the great Count Mirsky!

WILL. I know.

LEONIE. I must show you the photographs of his father—wonderful old man with a great white beard like a snowstorm—looks like Moses—a Russian Moses—and Boris is sitting on his knees—couldn't be over ten years old and wearing a fur cap and boots—boots!—and they drank tea out of tall glasses with raspberry jelly in—people came from all over the world, you know, to see his father . . . !

WILL. Isn't it strange that Count Mirsky's son should find himself in this strange house on this odd headland of Maine—Maine of all places!—writing his father's life? It's fantastic!

PAULA. (With some malice.) Is Dr. Rice going to help you acclimate him?

LEONIE. I hope so. You and Paula will have to entertain him—you young intellectuals. Isn't it a pity I have no mind? (She rises and crosses to table right to arrange lily-of-the-valley sprigs in a vase.)

PAULA. (To WILL.) She knows it's her greatest asset. Besides she's a fake.

WILL. (Gallantly.) I'm sure she is.

LEONIE. Thank you, my dears. It's gallant of you. (She crosses to PAULA—embraces her from behind.) But I'm not deceived. I know what Paula thinks of me—she looks down on me because I won't get interested in sociology. There never were any such things about when I was a girl. The trouble is one generation never has any perspective about another generation.

WILL. That's what your mother was say-

ing to me just a little while ago.

LEONIE. Was she? (She sits left of WILL.) I'm sure though Mother and I are much closer—that is, we understand each other better than Paula and I. Don't you think so, Paula?

PAULA. (Considering it.) Yes. I do think so.

LEONIE. I knew you'd agree. Something's happened between my generation and Paula's. New concepts. I don't know what they are exactly but I'm very proud that Paula's got them.

PAULA. (Laughing helplessly.) Oh, Mother! You reduce everything to absurdity!

LEONIE. (Innocently.) Do I? I don't mean to. At any rate it's a heavenly day and I adore you and I don't care about anything so long as you're happy. I want you to be happy.

PAULA. (Helplessly.) Oh dear!

LEONIE. What's the matter?

PAULA. You're saying that!

LEONIE. Is that wrong? Will—did I say something wrong?

PAULA. You want me to be happy. It's like saying you want me to be eight feet tall and to sing like Lily Pons.

LEONIE. Is it like that? Why? Will . . .

WILL. (Gravely feeling he must stand up for PAULA, but hating to.) Paula means . . . (Pause.)

LEONIE. Yes . . . ?

WILL. (Miserable.) She means—suppose there isn't any happiness to be had? Suppose the supply's run out?

LEONIE. But, Will, really . . . ! On a day like this! Why don't you go swimming? (Rises.) Nothing like seawater for—morbidity! Run out indeed! And today of all days! Really! (Gets gloves.) I'm disappointed in you, Will. I counted on you especially . . .

WILL. (Abjectly.) I was only fooling!

LEONIE. Of course he was. (Sits on arm of sofa beside WILL.) Will, I rely on you. Don't let Paula brood. Can't she drop the sociology in the summer?

I think in the fall you're much better
—braced—for things like that. Keep
her happy, Will.

WILL. I'll do my best now that—thanks to
you—I have the means.

LEONIE. Oh . . . (*Remembering.*) Oh,
you didn't mind, did you? I hope
you didn't mind.

WILL. (*Embarrassed.*) Very generous of
you.

LEONIE. Generous! Please don't say that.
After all—we who are in the embar-
rassing position nowadays of being
rich must do something with our
money, mustn't we? That's why I'm
helping Boris to write this book.
Noblesse oblige. Don't you think so,
Will? Boris tells me that the Russians—the *present* Russians—

WILL. You mean the Bolsheviks?

LEONIE. Yes, I suppose I do. He says they
don't like his father at all any more
and won't read his works because in
his novels he occasionally went on the
assumption that rich people had souls
and spirits too. You don't think like
that too, do you, Will—that because
I'm rich I'm just not worth bothering
about at all— No, you couldn't!
(*The appeal is tremulous.* WILL *suc-
cumbs entirely.*)

WILL. (*Bluntly.*) Mrs. Frothingham, I
love you!

LEONIE. (*Rises from arm of sofa and sits
in sofa beside* WILL. *To* PAULA.)
Isn't he sweet? (*To* WILL.) And I
love you, Will. Please call me Leonie.
Do you know how Mother happened
to name me Leonie? I was born in
Paris, you know, and I was to be
called Ruhama after my father's sister.
But Mother said no. No child of
mine, she said, shall be called Ruhama. She shall have a French name.
And where do you think she got
Leonie?

WILL. From the French version of one of
those Gideon Bibles.

LEONIE. (*As breathless as if it happened
yesterday.*) Not at all. From a
novel the nurse was reading. She
asked the nurse what she was reading
and the nurse gave her the paper book
and Mother opened it and found
Leonie!

WILL. What was the book?

LEONIE. Everyone wants to know that . . .
But I don't know. Mother didn't
know. She kept the book to give to
me when I grew up. But one day
she met M. Jusserand on a train—he
was the French Ambassador to Washington, you know—and he picked up
the book in Mother's compartment
and he read a page of it and threw it
out of the window because it was
trash! You see what I've had to live
down.

WILL. Heroic!

LEONIE. I hope you stay all summer, Will.
I won't hear of your going anywhere
else.

WILL. Don't worry. I have nowhere else
to go!

LEONIE. Tell me—that magazine you and
Dennis want to start—will it be gay?

WILL. Not exactly.

LEONIE. Oh, dear! I know. Columns
and columns of reading matter and no
pictures. Tell me—your father is
coming to dine, isn't he? I am so
looking forward to meeting him. I
love scientific men. They're usually
so nice and understanding. Now,
I've really got to go. (*Rises and starts
out.*)

PAULA. Dennis will be on that train.

LEONIE. Oh, good! I like Dennis. He
makes me laugh and I like people
around who make me laugh, but I
do wish he'd dress better. Why can't
radicals be chic? I saw a picture of
Karl Marx the other day and he looks
like one of those advertisements before you take something. I'll look
after Dennis, Will—save you going
to the station— (*To* PAULA.) And
Paula, tell Sam—

PAULA. Yes?

LEONIE. (*Forgetting the message to* SAM.)

You know, I asked Dr. Rice if he would treat me professionally and he said I was uninteresting to him because I was quite normal. Isn't that discouraging? Really, I must cultivate something. Good-bye, darlings. (*She runs out.*)

WILL. But what was the message to Sam? (*He sits.*)

PAULA. (*Helplessly.*) I'll never know. Neither will she. (WILL *laughs.*) What can you do with her? She makes me feel like an opinionated old woman. And I worry about her.

WILL. Do you?

PAULA. Yes. She arouses my maternal impulse.

WILL. (*Who feels he can be casual about* LEONIE *now that she is gone.*) She relies rather too much on charm!

PAULA. (*Turning on him bitterly.*) Oh, she does, does she! (*Goes over to sofa and sits right of* WILL.) You renegade. You ruin all my discipline with Mother. You're like a blushing schoolboy in front of her . . .

WILL. (*Protesting sheepishly.*) Now, Paula, don't exaggerate!

PAULA. You are! I thought in another minute you were going to ask her to the frat dance. And where was all that wonderful indignation about her leaving you the check? Where was the insult to your pride? Where was your starving brother in Seattle? Where? Where?

WILL. I don't know but somehow you can't face your mother with things like that. It seems cruel to face her with realities. She seems outside of all that.

PAULA. (*Conceding that.*) Well, you're going to be no help to me in handling Mother, I can see that!

WILL. (*Changing subject—a bit sensitive about having yielded so flagrantly to* LEONIE.) This Russian—

PAULA. What about him?

WILL. (*Gauche.*) Platonic, do you suppose?

PAULA. Don't be naïve! (*Enter* SAM FROTHINGHAM, PAULA's *father, a very pleasant-faced, attractive man between forty-five and fifty.*)

SAM. Oh, hello. (WILL *rises.*)

PAULA. (*Flying to him.*) Darling!—

SAM. (*They meet center and embrace.*) Hello, Paula. Delighted to see you.

PAULA. This is Will Dexter.

SAM. (*Shaking hands with* WILL.) How do you do?

WILL. I'm delighted to meet you.

PAULA. (*To* WILL.) Wait for me at the beach, will you, Will?

WILL. No, I'll run down to the station and ride back with the others.

PAULA. Okay. (SAM *nods to him.* WILL *goes out.*)

SAM. (*Crosses to front of sofa.*) Nice boy. (*Follows her.*)

PAULA. Like him?

SAM. Do you?

PAULA. I think so.

SAM. Special?

PAULA. Sort of.

SAM. Very special?

PAULA. (*Sits right end of sofa.*) Well—not sure.

SAM. Wait till you are. You've lots of time.

PAULA. Oh, he's not exactly impulsive.

SAM. Then he's just a fool.

PAULA. How are you, darling?

SAM. Uneasy.

PAULA. With me!

SAM. Especially.

PAULA. Darling, why?

SAM. I'll tell you. That's why I've come.

PAULA. Everything all right?

SAM. Oh, fine.

PAULA. (*Mystified.*) Then . . . ?

SAM. (*Switching off.*) How's Leonie?

PAULA. Fine. Delighted you were coming.

SAM. Was she?

PAULA. She really was. She's off to Ellsworth to meet a doctor.

SAM. Doctor?

PAULA. Psychoanalyst she's having up to massage her Russian's complexes.

SAM. (*Laughing.*) Oh— (*With a sigh.*) What's going to happen to Leonie?

PAULA. Why? She's on the crest!

SAM. She needs that elevation. Otherwise she sinks.

PAULA. Well—you know Mother . . .

SAM. Yes. (*A moment's pause.*) Paula?

PAULA. Yes, dad.

SAM. The fact is—it's ridiculous I should feel so nervous about telling you—but the fact is . . .

PAULA. What?

SAM. I've fallen in love. I want to get married. There! Well, thank God that's out! (*He wipes his forehead, quite an ordeal.*) Romance at my age. It's absurd, isn't it?

PAULA. Selena Bryant?

SAM. Yes.

PAULA. She has a grown son.

SAM. (*Smiling at her.*) So have I—a grown daughter.

PAULA. You'll have to divorce Mother.

SAM. Yes.

PAULA. Poor Leonie!

SAM. Well, after all—Leonie—you know how we've lived for years.

PAULA. Has Leonie hurt you?

SAM. Not for a long time. If this with Selena hadn't happened we'd have gone on forever, I suppose. But it has.

PAULA. You know, I have a feeling that, in spite of everything, this is going to be a shock to Leonie.

SAM. Paula?

PAULA. Yes.

SAM. Do you feel I'm deserting you? (*She turns her head away. She is very moved.*)

PAULA. No—you know how fond I am of you—I want you to be . . .

SAM. (*Deeply affected.*) Paula . . . !

PAULA. Happy. (*A silence. She is on the verge of tears.*)

SAM. I must make you see my side, Paula.

PAULA. (*Vehemently.*) I do!

SAM. It isn't only that—you're so young—but somehow—we decided very soon after you were born, Leonie and I,

that our marriage could only continue on this sort of basis. For your sake we've kept it up. I thought I was content to be an—appendage—to Leonie's entourage. But I'm not—do you know what Selena—being with Selena and planning with Selena for ourselves has made me see—that I've never had a home. Does that sound mawkish?

PAULA. I thought you loved Bay Cottage.

SAM. Of our various menages this is my favorite—it's the simplest. And I've had fun here with you—watching you grow up. But very soon after I married Leonie I found this out—that when you marry a very rich woman it's always *her* house you live in. (*A moment's pause.*)

PAULA. I'm awfully happy for you, Sam, really I am. You deserve everything but I can't help it I . . .

SAM. I know. (*A pause.*) Paula . . .

PAULA. Yes, dad?

SAM. You and I get on so well together—always have—Selena adores you and really—when you get to know her . . .

PAULA. I like Selena enormously. She's a dear. Couldn't be nicer.

SAM. I'm sure you and she would get on wonderfully together. Of course, Leonie will marry again. She's bound to. Why don't you come to live with us? When you want to . . .

PAULA. Want to!

SAM. All the time then. Leonie has such a busy life.

PAULA. It's awfully sweet of you.

SAM. Sweet of me! Paula!

PAULA. Where are you going to live?

SAM. New York. Selena has her job to do.

PAULA. She's terribly clever, isn't she?

SAM. She's good at her job.

PAULA. It must be wonderful to be independent. I hope I shall be. I hope I can make myself.

SAM. No reason you can't.

PAULA. It seems to take so much—

SAM. What sort of independence?

PAULA. Leonie's independent, but that independence doesn't mean anything somehow. She's always been able to do what she likes.

SAM. So will you be.

PAULA. That doesn't count somehow. It's independence in a vacuum. No, it doesn't count.

SAM. Maybe it isn't independence you want then?

PAULA. Yes, it is. I want to be able to stand on my own feet. I want to be —justified.

SAM. (*Understandingly.*) Ah! That's something else. (*A little amused.*) That's harder!

PAULA. I mean it, really I do—(*Pause.*) It's curious—how—adrift—this makes me feel. As if something vital, something fundamental had smashed. I wonder how Mother'll take it. I think —unconsciously—she depends on you much more than she realizes. You were a stabilizing force, Sam, in spite of everything and now . . .

SAM. (*Seriously.*) *You* are the stabilizing force, if you ask me, Paula . . .

PAULA. I don't know.

SAM. What's worrying you, Paula? Is it this Russian?

PAULA. Oh, I think he's harmless really.

SAM. What then?

PAULA. That one of these days—

SAM. What?

PAULA. That one of these days—now that you're going—somebody will come along—who won't be harmless.— You know, I really love Leonie. (LEONIE *comes running in just ahead of* DR. KENNETH RICE, DENNIS *and* WILL. LEONIE *is in the gayest spirits.* DR. RICE *is handsome, dark, magnetic, quiet, masterful. He is conscious of authority and gives one the sense of a strange, genius-like intuition.* DENNIS *is a flamboyant Irishman, a little older than* WILL, *gawky, black-haired, slovenly, infinitely brash.*

SAM *and* PAULA *rise.* LEONIE *comes down to center with* KENNETH *at her left.* WILL *remains back of sofa.* DENNIS *follows down to right center.*)

LEONIE. Oh, Sam, how perfectly . . . This is Dr. Rice—my husband Sam Frothingham—and my daughter Paula! Sam, Dennis McCarthy.

DENNIS. How do you do? (*No one pays any attention to him.* DR. RICE *shakes hands with* SAM *and* PAULA. LEONIE *keeps bubbling, her little laugh tinkling through her chatter.*)

LEONIE. It's courageous of me, don't you think, Dr. Rice, to display such a daughter? Does she look like me? I'll be very pleased if you tell me that she does. Sit down, sit down, everybody.

DENNIS. (*Holding up his pipe.*) You don't mind if I—?

LEONIE. No, no, not at all—(*She sits center chair,* PAULA *sits on right end sofa,* DENNIS *sinks into chair, right, by table.*) Sam! How well you're looking! Are you staying at Selena's? How is Selena?

SAM. She's very well.

LEONIE. Dr. Rice knows Selena.

KENNETH. Yes, indeed!

LEONIE. I envy Selena, you know, above all women. So brilliant, so attractive and so self-sufficient. That is what I envy in her most of all. I have no resources—I depend so much on other people. (*Turns to* RICE.) Do you think, Dr. Rice, you could make me self-sufficient?

KENNETH. I think I could.

LEONIE. How perfectly marvelous!

KENNETH. But I shouldn't dream of doing it!

LEONIE. But if I beg you to?

KENNETH. Not even if you beg me to.

LEONIE. But why?

KENNETH. It would deprive your friends of their most delightful avocation.

LEONIE. Now that's very graceful. You see, Sam, there are men who still pay me compliments.

SAM. I can't believe it!

LEONIE. You must keep it up, Dr. Rice, please. So good for my morale. (*To* PAULA.) Oh, my dear, we've been having the most wonderful argument—(*To* DENNIS.) Haven't we?

DENNIS. Yes.

LEONIE. All the way in from Ellsworth— (*To* RICE.) Really, Doctor, it's given me new courage . . .

PAULA. New courage for what?

LEONIE. I've always been afraid to say it for fear of being old-fashioned—but Dr. Rice isn't afraid.

KENNETH. (*Explaining to* SAM.) It takes great courage, Mr. Frothingham, to disagree with the younger generation.

SAM. It does indeed.

PAULA. Well, what is it about?

LEONIE. Yes—what *was* it about, Dennis?

DENNIS. Statistics and theology. Some metaphysics thrown in.

SAM. Good heavens! (*Sits.*)

DENNIS. Statistics as a symbol.

WILL. Dr. Rice still believes in the individual career.

KENNETH. I hang my head in shame!

DENNIS. He doesn't know that as a high officer of the National Student Federation, I have at my fingers' ends the statistics which rule our future, the statistics which constitute our horizon. Not your future, Paula, because you are living parasitically on the stored pioneerism of your ancestors.

PAULA. Forgive me, Reverend Father!

DENNIS. I represent, Doctor, the Unattached Youth of America—

KENNETH. Well, that's a career in itself! (*They laugh.*)

DENNIS. (*Imperturbable.*) When we presently commit the folly of graduating from a benevolent institution at Amherst, Massachusetts, there will be in this Republic two million like us. Two million helots. (*Leaning over* LEONIE.) But Dr. Rice pooh-poohs statistics.

LEONIE. (*Arranging his tie.*) Does he, Dennis?

DENNIS. He says the individual can surmount statistics, violate the graphs. Superman!

WILL. Evidently Dr. Rice got in just under the wire.

KENNETH. I'd never submit to statistics, Mr. Dexter—I'd submit to many things but not to statistics.

LEONIE. Such dull things to submit to—

DENNIS. You must be an atheist, Dr. Rice.

KENNETH. Because I don't believe in statistics?—the new God?

LEONIE. Well, *I'm* a Protestant and I don't believe in them either.

DENNIS. Well, Protestant is a loose synonym for atheist—and I, as an Irishman—and a—

KENNETH. Young man—

DENNIS. Yes?

KENNETH. Have you ever heard Bismarck's solution of the Irish problem?

DENNIS. No. What?

KENNETH. Oh, it's entirely irrelevant.

LEONIE. Please tell us. I adore irrelevancies.

KENNETH. Well, he thought the Irish and the Dutch should exchange countries. The Dutch, he thought, would very soon make a garden out of Ireland, and the Irish would forget to mend the dikes. (*They laugh.*)

LEONIE. That's not irrelevant—

DENNIS. It is an irrelevance, but pardonable in an adversary losing an argument.

KENNETH. (*To* PAULA.) Miss Frothingham, you seem very gracious. Will you get me out of this?

PAULA. No, I'm enjoying it.

LEONIE. Whatever you may say, Dennis, it's an exciting time to be alive.

DENNIS. That is because your abnormal situation renders you free of its major excitement—

LEONIE. And what's that, Dennis?

DENNIS. The race with malnutrition.

KENNETH. But that race, Mr.—?

DENNIS. McCarthy.

KENNETH. Is the eternal condition of mankind. Perhaps mankind won't survive the solution of that problem.

WILL. (*With heat.*) It's easy to sit in this living room—and be smug about the survival of the fittest—especially when you're convinced you're one of the fittest. But there are millions who won't concede you that superiority, Dr. Rice. There are millions who are so outrageously demanding that they actually insist on the right to live! They may demand it one day at the cost of your complacency.

LEONIE. Will! We were just chatting.

WILL. I'm sorry! The next thing Dr. Rice'll be telling us is that war is necessary also—to keep us stimulated—blood-letting for the other fellow.

KENNETH. Well, as a matter of fact, there's something to be said for that too. If you haven't settled on a career yet, Mr. Dexter, may I suggest evangelism?

DENNIS. But Dr. Rice—!

KENNETH. And now, Mrs. Frothingham, before these young people heckle me too effectively, may I escape to my room?

LEONIE. (*Rising.*) Of course. Though I don't think you need be afraid of their heckling, Doctor. You say things which I've always believed but never dared say.

KENNETH. (*As they walk out.*) Why not?

LEONIE. I don't know — somehow — I lacked the — the authority. I want to show you your rooms myself. (*Leaving the room, followed by* RICE.) I'll be right back, Sam—(RICE *nods to them and follows her out. As they go out she keeps talking to him.*) I am giving you my father's rooms— he built the wing especially so that when he wanted to work he'd be away from the rest of the house—you have the sea and the garden—(*They are off. A moment's pause.*)

PAULA. Well, that's a new type for Leonie!

DENNIS. There's something Rasputinish about him. What's he doing in Maine?

WILL. What, for the matter of that, are you and I doing in Maine? We should be in New York, jockeying for position on the bread-line. Let's go to the beach, Dennis. Pep us up for the struggle.

DENNIS. In that surf? It looks angry. I can't face life today.

PAULA. Swim'll do you good.

DENNIS. (*Starting for garden.*) It's not a swim I want exactly but a float—a vigorous float. Lead me to the pool, Adonais—

WILL. All right. (*As he starts to follow,* DENNIS, DR. DEXTER, WILL'S *father, comes in ushered by* ROBERT. *He is a dusty little man with a bleached yellow Panama hat. He keeps wiping his perspiring face with an old handkerchief. He doesn't hear very well.*)

DENNIS. Ah, the enemy—! (PAULA *and* SAM *rise.*)

WILL. Hello, dad. You remember Paula.

DEXTER. Yes . . . yes, I do.

WILL. (*Introducing* SAM.) My father— Mr. Frothingham.

SAM. Very glad to see you.

DEXTER. (*Shaking hands.*) Thank you.

DENNIS. (*Pointing dramatically at* DEXTER.) Nevertheless I repeat—the enemy!

PAULA. Dennis!

WILL. Oh, he's used to Dennis!

DEXTER. (*Wipes his forehead.*) Yes, and besides it was very dusty on the road.

PAULA. Won't you sit down? (DEXTER *does so, in center chair. The others remain standing.*)

WILL. How long did it take you to drive over, dad?

DEXTER. Let's see—left New Brunswick at two. . . .

WILL. (*Looks at watch.*) Three and one half hours—pretty good—the old tin Lizzie's got life in her yet.

DEXTER. You young folks having a good time, I suppose? (*He looks around him absent-mindedly.*)

PAULA. Dennis has been bullying us.

DEXTER. He still talking? (*Mildly.*) It's the Irish in him.

DENNIS. (*Nettled.*) You forgot to say shanty!

DEXTER. (*Surprised.*) Eh? Why should I say that?

WILL. Dennis is a snob. Wants all his titles.

DENNIS. You misguided children don't realize it—but here—in the guise of this dusty, innocent-seeming man—sits the enemy.

DEXTER. (*Turning as if stung by a fly—cupping his hand to his ear.*) What? What did he say?

DENNIS. The ultimate enemy, the true begetter of the fatal statistics—Science. You betray us, Paula, by having him in the house; *you* betray us, Will, by acknowledging him as a father.

DEXTER. (*Wiping his forehead.*) Gosh, it's hot!

SAM. (*Sensing a fight and urging it on—solemnly.*) Can all this be true, Dr. Dexter?

DEXTER. What be true?

SAM. Dennis's accusation.

DEXTER. I am slightly deaf and McCarthy's presence always fills me with gratitude for that affliction.

DENNIS. It's perfectly obvious. You've heard of technological unemployment. Well, here it sits, embodied in Will's father. Day and night with diabolical ingenuity and cunning he works out devices to unemploy us. All over the world, millions of us are being starved and broken on the altar of Science. We Catholics understand that. We Catholics repudiate the new Moloch that has us by the throat.

WILL. Do you want us to sit in mediaeval taverns with Chesterton and drink beer? (*DEXTER turns to DENNIS; as if emerging suddenly from an absent-minded daze, he speaks with great authority, casually but with clarity and precision.*)

DEXTER. The fact is, my voluble young friend, I am not the Moloch who is destroying you but that you and the hordes of the imprecise and the vaguely trained—are destroying me! I have, you will probably be pleased to learn, just lost my job. I have been interrupted in my work. And why? Because I am successful. Because I have found what, with infinite patience and concentration, I have been seeking to discover. From the elusive and the indeterminate and the invisible, I have crystallized a principle which is visible and tangible and —predictable. From the illimitable icebergs of the unknown I have chipped off a fragment of knowledge, a truth which so-called practical men may put to a use which will make some of your numbers unnecessary in the workaday world. Well—what of it, I say?—who decrees that you shall be supported? Of what importance are your lives and futures and your meandering aspirations compared to the firmness and the beauty and the cohesion of the principles I seek, the truth I seek? None—none whatever! Whether you prattle on an empty stomach or whether you prattle on a full stomach can make no difference to anybody that I can see. (*To* PAULA *abruptly, rising.*) And now, young woman, as I have been invited here to spend the night, I'd like to see my room!

PAULA. (*Crossing to him.*) Certainly! Come with me. I'll have Robert show you your room. (*They go to door back. She calls.*) Robert! (ROBERT *enters.*) Will you take Dr. Dexter to his room? (DEXTER *follows* ROBERT *out.*)

SAM. Gosh! I thought he was deaf!

WILL. He can hear when he wants to! (*To* DENNIS.) Now will you be good!

DENNIS. I'm sorry—I didn't know he'd lost his job or I wouldn't have . . .

WILL. Oh, that's all right. Well, Dennis, how does it feel to be superfluous?

DENNIS. (*Sourly.*) The man's childish! (*He goes out, door right through garden.*)

PAULA. Isn't he marvelous? Don't you love Will's father?

SAM. Crazy about him. He's swell.

WILL. He's a pretty good feller. He seems absent-minded but actually he's extremely present-minded. If you'll excuse me, I'm going out to soothe Dennis. (*He follows* DENNIS *out.*) (*A pause.*)

SAM. That young man appears to have sound antecedents.

PAULA. Oh, yes—Will's all right, but—oh, Sam—!

SAM. What?

PAULA. With you gone—I'm terrified for Leonie. I really am! When I think of the foolish marriages Leonie would have made if not for you!

SAM. It's a useful function, but I'm afraid I'll have to give it up!

PAULA. (*With new determination.*) Sam . . .

SAM. Yes, Paula.

PAULA. If Leonie goes Russian—

SAM. Well?

PAULA. Or if she goes Freudian—?

SAM. In any case you and this boy'll probably be getting married.

PAULA. That's far from settled yet.

SAM. Why?

PAULA. Will's scared.

SAM. Is he?

PAULA. Of getting caught in Leonie's silken web.

SAM. That's sensible of him. (LEONIE *comes back, half running, breathless.*)

LEONIE. Well! Isn't Dr. Rice attractive?

SAM. (*Rising.*) Very.

PAULA. (*Rising.*) And so depressed about himself! (*She goes out—door right.*)

LEONIE. Isn't it extraordinary, Dr. Rice having achieved the position he has—at his age? He's amazing. And think of it, Sam—not yet forty.

SAM. Anybody under forty is young to me!

LEONIE. How old are you, Sam?

SAM. Forbidden ground, Leonie.

LEONIE. I should know, shouldn't I, but I don't. I know your birthday—I always remember your birthday . . .

SAM. You do indeed!

LEONIE. It's June 14. But I don't know how old you are.

SAM. Knowledge in the right place—ignorance in the right place!

LEONIE. (*Meaning it.*) You're more attractive and charming than ever.

SAM. You're a great comfort.

LEONIE. It's so nice to see you!

SAM. And you too! (*He is not entirely comfortable—not as unself-conscious and natural as she is.*)

LEONIE. Sometimes I think Paula should see more of you. I think it would be very good for her. What do you think of her new friends?

SAM. They seem nice.

LEONIE. They're all poor and they're very radical. They look on me—my dear, they have the most extraordinary opinion of me . . .

SAM. What is that?

LEONIE. I'm fascinated by them. They think of me as a hopeless kind of spoiled Bourbon living away in a never-never land—a kind of Marie Antoinette . . . (*She laughs.*) It's delicious!

SAM. Is Paula radical too?

LEONIE. I think she's trying to be. She's a strange child.

SAM. How do you mean?

LEONIE. Well, when I was a child I was brought up to care only if people were charming or attractive or . . .

SAM. Well-connected . . .

LEONIE. Yes . . . These kids don't care a hoot about that.

SAM. I think the difference between their generation and ours is that we were romantic and they're realistic.

LEONIE. Is that it?

SAM. I think so.

LEONIE. What makes that?

SAM. Changes in the world—the war—the depression. . . .

LEONIE. What did people blame things on before—the war?

SAM. (*Smiling.*) Oh, on the tariff and on the Republicans—and on the Democrats! Leonie—

LEONIE. Yes, Sam.

SAM. I—I really have something to tell you.

LEONIE. (*Looks up at him curiously.*) What? (*Pause.*)

SAM. I am in love with Selena Bryant. We want to get married.

LEONIE. (*Pause—after a moment.*) Human nature is funny! Mine is!

SAM. Why?

LEONIE. I know I ought to be delighted to release you. Probably I should have spoken to you about it myself before long — separating. And yet — when you tell me—I feel—a pang . . .

SAM. That's very sweet of you.

LEONIE. One's so possessive—one doesn't want to give up anything.

SAM. For so many years our marriage has been at its best—a friendship. Need that end?

LEONIE. No, Sam. It needn't. I hope truly that it won't.

SAM. What about Paula?

LEONIE. Did you tell Paula?

SAM. Yes. . . .

LEONIE. Did she . . . ?

SAM. (*Rising.*) Leonie . . .

LEONIE. (*Pauses.*) Yes, Sam.

SAM. A little while ago you said—you thought Paula ought to see more of me.

LEONIE. Yes . . . I did. . . . (*She is quite agitated suddenly. The thought has crossed her mind that perhaps PAULA has told SAM that she would prefer to go with him. This hurts her deeply, not only for the loss of PAULA but because, from the bottom of her being, she cannot bear not to be loved.*)

SAM. Don't you think then . . . for a time at least . . .

LEONIE. (*Defeatist in a crisis.*) Paula doesn't like me! (*It is sudden and completely accepted conviction.*)

SAM. Leonie!

LEONIE. She'd rather go with you!

SAM. Not at all—it's only that . . .

LEONIE. I know what Paula thinks of me. . . .

SAM. Paula adores you. It's only that . . .

LEONIE. It's only that what—

SAM. Well, for instance—if you should get married—

LEONIE. What if I did?

SAM. (*Coming to stand close to her left.*) It would mean a considerable readjustment for Paula—wouldn't it? You can see that.

LEONIE. (*Rising.*) But it would too with you and Selena.

SAM. (*Taking step toward her.*) She knows Selena. She admires Selena.

LEONIE. (*Rising and walking down to front of sofa.*) What makes you think she wouldn't admire—whomever I married?

SAM. (*After a moment, completely serious now.*) There's another aspect of it which I think for Paula's sake you should consider most carefully.

LEONIE. What aspect?

SAM. (*Coming down to her.*) Paula's serious. You know that yourself. She's interested in things. She's not content to be a Sunday-supplement heiress—floating along—she wants to do things. Selena's a working woman. Selena can help her.

LEONIE. I know. I'm useless.

SAM. I think you ought to be unselfish about this.

LEONIE. Paula can do what she likes, of course. If she doesn't love me . . .

SAM. Of course she loves you.

LEONIE. If she prefers to live with you and Selena I shan't stand in her way. (*Her martyrish resignation irritates SAM profoundly. He feels that really LEONIE should not be allowed to get away with it.*)

SAM. You're so vain, Leonie.

LEONIE. (*Refusing to argue.*) I'm sorry. (*This makes it worse. SAM goes deeper.*)

SAM. After all, you're Paula's mother. Can't you look at her problem—objectively?

LEONIE. Where my emotions are involved I'm afraid I never know what words like that mean. (*He blunders in worse, farther than he really means to go.*)

SAM. (*Flatly.*) Well, this sort of thing isn't good for Paula.

LEONIE. (*Very cold, very hurt.*) What sort of thing? (*A moment's pause. He is annoyed with himself at the ineptitude of his approach.*) Be perfectly frank. You can be with me. What sort of thing?

SAM. Well—Leonie—(*With a kind of desperate bluntness.*) You've made a career of flirtation. Obviously Paula isn't going to. You know you and Paula belong to different worlds. (*With some heat.*) And the reason Paula is the way she is is because she lives in an atmosphere of perpetual conflict.

LEONIE. Conflict? Paula?

SAM. With herself. About you.

LEONIE. (*Rising.*) That's too subtle for me, I'm afraid.

SAM. Paula's unaware of it herself.

LEONIE. Where did you acquire this amazing psychological insight? You never used to have it. Of course! From Selena. Of course!

SAM. I've never discussed this with Selena.

LEONIE. No?

SAM. She's told me she'd be happy to have Paula but . . .

LEONIE. That's extremely generous of her —to offer without discussion. . . .

SAM. (*She has him there; he loses his temper.*) It's impossible for you to consider anything without being personal.

LEONIE. I am afraid it is. I don't live on this wonderful rarefied, intellectual plane inhabited by Selena and yourself—and where you want to take Paula. I'm sorry if I've made Paula serious, I'm sorry she's in a perpetual conflict about me. I'm sorry I've let her in for—this sort of thing! I'm

sorry! (*She is on the verge of tears. She runs out.*)

SAM. Leonie . . . ! (*He follows her to door back, calling.*) Leonie! (*But it is too late. She is gone. He turns back into room.*) Damn! (PAULA *comes in—from beach, door right.*)

PAULA. Where's Leonie?

SAM. She just went upstairs.

PAULA. I've been showing Dr. Rice our rock-bound coast.

SAM. What's he like?

PAULA. Hard to say. He's almost too sympathetic. At the same time—

SAM. What?

PAULA. At the same time—he is inscrutable! I can't tell whether I like him or dislike him. You say Selena knows him. What does she say about him?

SAM. Selena isn't crazy about him.

PAULA. Why not?

SAM. Brilliant charlatan, she says—also a charmer.

PAULA. I gather that, and I resent him. How'd you come out with Leonie?

SAM. I've made a mess of it. I'm a fool!

PAULA. My going with you, you mean?

SAM. Yes.

PAULA. Sam . . .

SAM. Yes?

PAULA. Will you mind very much . . .

SAM. What?

PAULA. If I don't go with Selena and you?

SAM. But I thought you said—and especially if she marries somebody—

PAULA. (*Slowly.*) That's just what I'm thinking of—

SAM. What's happened?

PAULA. There's no way out of it, Sam— I've got to stay.

SAM. But why?

PAULA. (*Simply, looking up at him.*) Somebody's got to look after Leonie. . . . (KENNETH *enters.*)

KENNETH. My first glimpse of Maine. A masculine Riviera.

PAULA. It's mild now. If you want to see it really virile—come in the late fall.

KENNETH. You've only to crook your little finger. I'll be glad to look at more of Maine whenever you have the time. (*Sits, facing her.*)

PAULA. Of course. Tomorrow?

KENNETH. Yes. Tomorrow. (*To* SAM.) You know, from Mrs. Frothingham's description—(*Looking back at* PAULA, *intently.*) I never could have imagined her. Not remotely. (ROBERT *enters.*)

SAM. What is it, Robert?

ROBERT. Mrs. Frothingham would like to see Dr. Rice in her study.

KENNETH. (*Rising.*) Oh, thank you. (*He walks to door back.*) Excuse me. (*He goes upstairs.* PAULA *and* SAM *have continued looking front. As* KENNETH *starts upstairs they slowly turn and look at one another. The same thought has crossed both their minds—they both find themselves looking suddenly into a new and dubious vista.*)

Curtain

ACT TWO

SCENE I

SCENE: *The same.*

TIME: *Midsummer—late afternoon.*

AT RISE: KENNETH *is at a bridge table working out a chess problem. He hears voices and footsteps approaching. Gets up, unhurried, and looks off into garden. Sees* BORIS *and* LEONIE *approaching. As they come in he strolls off—they do not see him.* LEONIE's *arms are full of flowers. She is looking for* KENNETH. COUNT MIRSKY *follows her in.*

COUNT MIRSKY, *a Russian, is very good-looking, mongoloid about the eyes. His English is beautiful, with a slight and attractive accent. He is tense, jittery—a mass of jangled nerves—his fingers tremble as he lights one cigarette after another. He is very pale—his pallor accentuated by a dark scarf he wears around his neck.*

BORIS. (*Stopping center.*) It appears he is not here either.

LEONIE. He? Who? (*Crossing to table behind sofa to put some flowers in vase.*)

BORIS. When you're in the garden with me you think—perhaps he is in the house. When you are in the house you think perhaps he is in the garden.

LEONIE. Boris, darling, you have the odd habit of referring to mysterious characters without giving me any hint who they are. Is that Russian symbolism? There will be a long silence; then you will say: He would not approve, or they can't hear us. It's a bit mystifying.

BORIS. (*Crossing to stand near her.*) You know who I mean.

LEONIE. (*Going to table right to put flowers in vase.*) Really, you flatter me. I'm not a mystic, you know, Boris. I'm a simple extrovert. When you say "he," why can't it refer to someone definite—and if possible to someone I know.

BORIS. (*Crossing to back of table, facing her across it.*) You know him, all right.

LEONIE. There you go again! *Really,* Boris!

BORIS. (*Moving closer to her around table.*) You've been divorced now for several weeks. You're free. We were only waiting for you to be free—

LEONIE. (*Moving away, sitting in chair, right.*) Now that I am free you want to coerce me. It's a bit unreasonable, don't you think? (BORIS *walks to end of window-seat and sits.*) (*Enter* KENNETH, *door back.*)

KENNETH. (*Strolling across stage toward* LEONIE.) Hello, Leonie. Count Mirsky—

LEONIE. Kenneth—I haven't seen you all day.

KENNETH. I've been in my room slaving away at a scientific paper.

LEONIE. My house hums with creative activity. I love it. It gives me a sense of vicarious importance. What's your paper on?

KENNETH. Shadow-neurosis.

LEONIE. Shadow-neurosis. How marvelous! What does it mean?

KENNETH. (*Looking at* BORIS.) It is a sensation of non-existence.

LEONIE. Is it common?

KENNETH. Quite. The victim knows that he exists and yet he feels that he does not!

LEONIE. In a curious way I can imagine a sensation like that—do you know I actually can. Isn't it amusing?

BORIS. The doctor is so eloquent. Once he describes a sensation it becomes very easy to feel it.

LEONIE. That's an entrancing gift. Why are you so antagonistic to Kenneth? He wants to help you but you won't let him. I asked him here to help you.

KENNETH. (*To* BORIS.) Your skepticism about this particular disease is interesting, Count Mirsky, because, as it happens, you suffer from it.

BORIS. (*Bearing down on* KENNETH.) Has it ever occurred to you that you are a wasted novelist?

KENNETH. Though I have not mentioned you in my article I have described you.

LEONIE. (*Rising and crossing left to table behind sofa.*) You should be flattered, Boris.

BORIS. I am!

LEONIE. Another case history! I've been reading some of Kenneth's scientific textbooks. Most fascinating form of biography. Who was that wonderful fellow who did such odd things—Mr. X.? You'd never think you could get so interested in anonymous people. I'd have given anything to meet Mr. X.—though I must say I'd feel a bit nervous about having him in the house.

KENNETH. How is your book getting along, Count Mirsky?

BORIS. Very well. Oh—so—

KENNETH. Far along in it?

BORIS. Quite.

LEONIE. I'm crazy to see it. He's dedicating it to me but he hasn't let me see a word of it!

KENNETH. For a very good reason.

LEONIE. What do you mean?

KENNETH. Because there is no book. There never has been a book.

LEONIE. (*She lets flowers drop.*) Kenneth!

KENNETH. Isn't that true, Count Mirsky?

BORIS. It is not!

KENNETH. Then why don't you let us see a bit of it?

LEONIE. Oh, do! At least the dedication page.

KENNETH. A chapter—

BORIS. Because it isn't finished yet.

LEONIE. Well, it doesn't have to be finished. We know the end, don't we? The end belongs to the world.

KENNETH. Let us see it, Count.

BORIS. I can't.

KENNETH. What are you calling the book?

BORIS. I haven't decided yet.

KENNETH. May I suggest a title to you—?

LEONIE. Oh, do! What shall we call it, Kenneth?

KENNETH. "The Memoirs of a Boy Who Wanted to Murder His Father."

LEONIE. What!

BORIS. (*Gripping arms of chair.*) I am not a hysterical woman, Doctor—and I'm not your patient!

LEONIE. But Kenneth—Boris worshipped his father.

KENNETH. No, he hated him. He hated

him when he was alive and he hates him still. He grew up under the overwhelming shadow of this world-genius whom, in spite of an immense desire to emulate and even surpass—he felt he could never emulate and never surpass—nor even equal— Did you worship your father, Count Mirsky?

BORIS. It's true! I hated him!

LEONIE. Boris!

BORIS. I hated him!

KENNETH. Now you can let us see the book, can't you—now that we know the point of view—just a bit of it?

LEONIE. I'm more crazy than ever to see it now. I can tell you a little secret now, Boris. I was afraid—I was rather afraid—that your book would be a little like one of those statues of an ancestor in a frock-coat. Now it sounds really exciting. You hated him. But how perfectly marvelous! I can't wait to see it now. Do run up to your study and bring it down, Boris—do!

BORIS. No.

LEONIE. That's very unpleasant of you.

BORIS. You might as well know it then. There isn't any book. There never will be. Not by me.

LEONIE. But I don't understand—every day—in your room working—all these months!

BORIS. (*Facing her.*) One wants privacy! Possibly you can't realize that. You who always have to have a house full of people.

LEONIE. (*Goes back to flowers at table.*) Boris!

KENNETH. (*Rising.*) Why don't you write the book anyway, Count Mirsky? There is a vogue these days for vituperative biography.

BORIS. I am not interested in the vogue.

KENNETH. We are quite used nowadays to children who dislike their fathers. The public—

BORIS. To titillate the public would not compensate me for forcing myself to recall the atmosphere of saintly sadism in which my childhood was spent—I can still smell that living room, I can still smell those stinking, sexless pilgrims who used to come from all over the world to get my saintly father's blessing. I used to sit with my mother in a room no bigger than a closet to get away from the odor of that nauseating humanitarianism. There was no privacy in the Villa Mirskovitch. Oh, no—it was a Mecca—do you understand—a Mecca!

KENNETH. Yes, I think I understand.

BORIS. Well, I have been paying the haloed one back. I have been getting privacy at his expense at last.

LEONIE. Why have you never told me before that you felt this way about your father?

BORIS. I never said anything about him. It was you who did the talking. You always raved about the great man with that characteristic American enthusiasm for what you don't know.

LEONIE. Nevertheless, the world recognizes your father as a great man. The books are there to prove it. There they are. You can't write books like that without greatness—no matter what you say. You are a petulant child. Your father was a great man.

BORIS. It makes no difference how great he was — those pilgrims stank! (LEONIE *turns away.*)

KENNETH. I suggest that to write that book, even if no one ever sees the manuscript but you, might amuse you —kind of revenge which, when you were a boy, you were in no position to take.

BORIS. Are you trying to cure me, Doctor? Please don't trouble. I don't need your particular species of professionalism. I do not need any help from you. (*He goes to door back, turns to* LEONIE. LEONIE *looks bewilderedly at* KENNETH. BORIS *goes out.*)

LEONIE. How did you know? You're uncanny!

KENNETH. All in the day's work.

LEONIE. Why is it I always get myself involved with men weaker than myself? I certainly am no tower of strength.

KENNETH. Possibly not—but you are generous and impulsive. You have a tendency to accept people at the best of their own valuation.

LEONIE. I want to help them. I do help them. After they get used to my help, after they get to count on my help, I get impatient with them. Why, I ask myself, can't people help themselves?

KENNETH. And very natural.

LEONIE. I seem to attract people like that!

KENNETH. Leonie—you are the last woman on earth Count Mirsky should marry. He would only transfer his hatred of his father to you.

LEONIE. I don't think I understand you, Kenneth—really I don't—and I do so want to understand things.

KENNETH. Well—your charm, your gaiety, your position, your wealth, your beauty—these would oppress him. Again, he cannot be himself.—Or, if he is himself, it is to reveal his nonentity, his inferiority—again the secondary rôle—Leonie Frothingham's husband—the son of Count Mirsky—the husband of Leonie Frothingham. Again the shadow—again, eternally and always—non-existence. Poor fellow. (*Pause.*)

LEONIE. I'm so grateful to you, Kenneth.

KENNETH. Nonsense. You mustn't be grateful to me because I—exercise my profession.

LEONIE. I want to express my gratitude—in some tangible form. I've been thinking of nothing else lately. I can't sleep for thinking of it.

KENNETH. Well, if it gives you insomnia, you'd better tell me about it.

LEONIE. I want to make it possible for you to realize your ambition.

KENNETH. Ambition? What ambition?

LEONIE. Ah! You've forgotten, haven't you? But you let it slip out one day —you pump me professionally—but I do the same to you—non-professionally.

KENNETH. You terrify me!

LEONIE. That night last winter when we went to dinner in that little restaurant where you go with your doctor friends . . . you told me your dream.

KENNETH. My censor must have been napping.

LEONIE. He was. Or she was. What sex is your censor?

KENNETH. That's none of your business.

LEONIE. I'm sorry.

KENNETH. Which of my dreams was I so reckless as to reveal to you?

LEONIE. To have a sanatorium of your own one day—so you can carry out your own ideas of curing patients.

KENNETH. Oh, that! Out of the question.

LEONIE. Why?

KENNETH. To do it on the scale I visualize, would cost more than I'm ever likely to save out of my practice.

LEONIE. I'll give you the sanatorium. I've never given anyone anything like that before. What fun!

KENNETH. Will I find it all wrapped up in silver foil on Christmas morning?

LEONIE. Yes. You will! You will! We'll have a suite in it for Mr. X.—for all your anonymous friends—we'll entertain the whole alphabet!

KENNETH. You see, Leonie!

LEONIE. What do you mean? I thought you'd be—

KENNETH. Of course, it's terribly generous of you. I'm deeply touched. But . . .

LEONIE. But . . . ?

KENNETH. I'm a stranger to you.

LEONIE. Kenneth!

KENNETH. Outside of my professional relation—such as I have with scores of patients—little more than that.

LEONIE. I thought—

KENNETH. And yet you are willing to back me in a venture that would cost a sizeable fortune—just on that. Leonie! Leonie!

LEONIE. It would be the best investment I've ever made. Paula's always telling me I have no social consciousness. Well, this would be.—It would keep me from feeling so useless. I do feel useless, Kenneth. Please!

KENNETH. I'm sorry. I couldn't hear of it. Of course, it's out of the question.

LEONIE. It isn't. I can afford it. Why shouldn't I? It would be helping so many people—you have no right to refuse. It's selfish of you to refuse.

KENNETH. I distrust impulsive altruism. You will forgive me, Leonie, but it may often do harm.

LEONIE. How do you mean, Kenneth?

KENNETH. I gather you are about to endow a radical magazine for the *boys*—

LEONIE. Will and Dennis! I thought it would be nice to give them something to do!

KENNETH. Yes. You are prepared to back them in a publication which, if it attained any influence, would undermine the system which makes you and your people like you possible.

LEONIE. But it never occurred to me anyone would read it.

KENNETH. There is a deplorably high literacy in this country. Unfortunately it is much easier to learn to read than it is to learn to think.

LEONIE. Well, if you don't think it's a good idea, Kenneth, I won't do it. But this sanatorium is different.

KENNETH. Why?

LEONIE. Because, if you must know it, it would be helping you—and that means everything in the world to me. There, I've said it. It's true! Kenneth—are you terrified?

KENNETH. You adorable child!

LEONIE. It's extraordinary, Kenneth—but you are the first strong man who's ever come into my life—(*Enter* PAULA, DENNIS, WILL, *door back*.) Oh, I'm very glad to see you! Will! Hullo, Dennis. You all know Dr. Rice.

Mr. Dexter, Mr. McCarthy. Sit down, everybody. Well, children, how is New York? (DENNIS *crosses down front of them to chair left by sofa and sits.*)

WILL. Stifling, thank you.

LEONIE. Any luck yet?

WILL. I am available, but New York is dead to its chief opportunity.

LEONIE. Then you can stay here for a bit. You can both stay here.

DENNIS. That was all right when we were in college, Mrs. Frothingham. Can't do it now.

LEONIE. Oh, you're working. I'm so glad!

DENNIS. I beg your pardon. Did you say working?

LEONIE. Well, then! I don't see why you can't stay here and take a holiday.

WILL. From what?

LEONIE. Since none of you are doing anything in town, you might as well stay here and do nothing and be comfortable.

DENNIS. Yes, but it's an ethical question. When we're in New York doing nothing, we belong to the most respectable vested group going! The unemployed. As such we have a status, position, authority. But if we stay here doing nothing—what are we? Low-down parasites.

KENNETH. No jobs about anywhere, eh?

WILL. Extinct commodity.

DENNIS. I did pretty well last week.

LEONIE. Really?

DENNIS. I was rejected by seven newspapers—including the *Bronx Home News* and the *Yonkers Herald*—six magazines and trade papers—a total of twenty-eight rejections in all, representing a net gain over the previous week of seven solid rejections. I submit to you, gentlemen, that's progress—pass the cigars, Will.

LEONIE. Couldn't you stay here and be rejected by mail?

DENNIS. Doesn't give you that same feeling somehow—that good, rich, dark-brown sensation of not being wanted!

LEONIE. You know, Kenneth, in a curious way, Dennis reminds me a bit of Mr. X.

DENNIS. And who's X.?

LEONIE. A sporting acquaintance.

DENNIS. There's one thing I'd like to ask Dr. Rice. . . . Do you mind?

KENNETH. At your service.

DENNIS. (*Turning chair and facing* KENNETH *upstage.*) In the psychoanalytic hierarchy Freud is the god, isn't he?

KENNETH. Of one sect, yes.

DENNIS. Well, the original sect—

KENNETH. Yes. . . .

DENNIS. Now, every psychoanalyst has to have himself analyzed. That's true, isn't it, Doctor?

KENNETH. Generally speaking—yes.

DENNIS. As I understand it, the highest prices go to those nearest the Master himself.

KENNETH. This boy is irreverent . . .

DENNIS. I know whereof I speak. I prepared an article on the subject for *Fortune.*

WILL. Rejection number three hundred.

DENNIS. I am afraid, Will, that you are a success worshipper!

LEONIE. Dennis is an *enfant terrible,* and he exhausts himself keeping it up!

DENNIS. I have examined the racket with a microscopic patience and this I find to be true: at the top of the hierarchy is the Great Pan Sexualist of Vienna. To be an orthodox and accepted Freudian, you must have been analyzed by another of the same. Now what I am burning to know is this: Who analyzed Sig Freud himself? Whom does he tell his repressions to? Why, the poor guy must be lonely as hell!

LEONIE. What would you do with him, Kenneth? He has no repressions whatever!

KENNETH. He needs some badly.

LEONIE. I wonder what Dennis would confess to his psychoanalyst that he isn't always shouting to the world?

DENNIS. I'd make the psychoanalyst talk. (*To* KENNETH. *Beckoning.*) Tell me, Doctor, what did you dream last night?

KENNETH. (*Behind his cupped hand.*) Not in public.

DENNIS. (*Rises and crosses straight right.*) You see—he's repressed! I tell you these psychoanalysts are repressed. They've got nobody to talk to! I'm going swimming. It's pathetic! (*He goes out.*)

LEONIE. I'm going too. He makes me laugh. How about you, Kenneth?

KENNETH. Oh, I'll watch.

LEONIE. (*To others.*) Come along with us. There's plenty of time for a swim before dinner. (KENNETH *starts out with* LEONIE . . . *stops on the way.*)

KENNETH. I suppose you and your Irish friend edited the comic paper at college?

WILL. No, we edited the serious paper.

KENNETH. Just the same it must have been very funny. (*He goes out after* LEONIE.)

WILL. Don't think that feller likes me much.

PAULA. You're psychic.

WILL. Well, for the matter of that I'm not crazy about him either.

PAULA. Don't bother about him. Concentrate on me!

WILL. How are you, darling?

PAULA. Missed you.

WILL. (*Pulls her to sofa and sits with her.* PAULA *left end sofa.*) And I you. Pretty lousy in town without you.

PAULA. Oh, poor darling!

WILL. Although my star is rising. I did some book-reviews for the New York *Times* and the *New Masses.*

PAULA. What a gamut!

WILL. I made, in fact, a total of eleven dollars. The student most likely to succeed in the first four months since graduation has made eleven dollars.

PAULA. Wonderful!

WILL. My classmates were certainly clairvoyant. As a matter of fact, I shouldn't have told you. Now I'll be tortured thinking you're after me for my money.

PAULA. You'll never know!

WILL. (*Putting arm around her shoulders and drawing her to him.*) What've you been doing?

PAULA. Lying in the sun mostly.

WILL. Poor little Ritz girl.

PAULA. Wondering what you do every night.

WILL. Forty-second Street Library mostly. Great fun! Voluptuary atmosphere!

PAULA. Is your life altogether so austere?

WILL. Well, frankly, no. Not altogether.

PAULA. Cad!

WILL. What do you expect?

PAULA. Loyalty.

WILL. I am loyal. But you go around all day job-hunting. You find you're not wanted. It's reassuring after that to find a shoulder to lean on, sort of haven where you *are* wanted. Even the public library closes at ten. You have to go somewhere. If I'm ever Mayor of New York, I'll have the public libraries kept open all night . . . the flop-houses of the intellectuals!

PAULA. Is it anyone special . . . ?

WILL. Just a generalized shoulder.

PAULA. Well, you're going to have a special one from now on—mine! You know, the way you're avoiding the issue is all nonsense.

WILL. You mean my gallant fight against you?

PAULA. I've decided that you are conventional and bourgeois. You're money-ridden.

WILL. Eleven dollars. They say a big income makes you conservative.

PAULA. I don't mean your money. I mean —my money. It's childish to let an artificial barrier like that stand between us. It's also childish to ignore it.

WILL. (*Rising.*) I don't ignore it. That's what worries me. I count on it. Already I find myself counting on it. I can't help it. Sitting and waiting in an office for some bigwig who won't see me or for some underling who won't see me I think: "Why the Hell should I wait all day for this stuffed shirt?" I don't wait. Is it because of you I feel in a special category? Do I count on your money? Is that why I don't wait as long as the other fellow? There's one consolation: the other fellow doesn't get the job either. But the point is disquieting!

PAULA. What a Puritan you are!

WILL. (*Sitting beside her again.*) Will I become an appendage to you—like your mother's men?

PAULA. You're bound to—money or no money.

WILL. (*Taking her into his arms.*) I suppose I might as well go on the larger dole—

PAULA. What?

WILL. Once you are paid merely for existing—you are on the dole. I rather hoped, you know—

PAULA. What?

WILL. It's extraordinary the difference in one's thinking when you're in college and when you're out—

PAULA. How do you mean?

WILL. Well, when I was in college, my interest in the—"movement"—was really impersonal. I imagined myself giving my energies to the poor and the downtrodden in my spare time. I didn't really believe I'd be one of the poor and downtrodden myself. In my heart of hearts I was sure I'd break through the iron law of Dennis's statistics and land a job somewhere. But I can't—and it's given a tremendous jolt to my self-esteem.

PAULA. But you'll come through. I'm sure of it. I wish you could learn to look at my money as a means rather than an end.

WILL. I'd rather use my own.

PAULA. You're proud.

WILL. I am.

PAULA. It's humiliating but I'm afraid I've got to ask you to marry me, Will.

WILL. It's humiliating but considering my feelings I see no way out of accepting you.

PAULA. You submit?

WILL. (*Kissing her hand.*) I submit.

PAULA. After a hard campaign—victory!

WILL. You *are* a darling.

PAULA. (*Getting up and crossing to center.*) I can't tell you what a relief it'll be to get away from this house.

WILL. Why?

PAULA. I don't know. It's getting very complicated.

WILL. Leonie?

PAULA. *And* Boris. *And* Dr. Rice. Funny thing how that man . . .

WILL. What?

PAULA. Makes you insecure somehow.

WILL. Supposed to do just the opposite.

PAULA. He answers every question—and yet he's secretive. I've never met a man who—who—

WILL. Who what?

PAULA. Really, I can't stand Dr. Rice.

WILL. I believe he fascinates you.

PAULA. He does. I don't deny that. And I can't tell you how I resent it. Isn't it silly? (*The old lady* WYLER *in a wheel chair is propelled in by a nurse. The old lady is much wasted since the preceding summer; she is touched with mortality.*) Granny!

MRS. WYLER. Paula! How are you, my dear?

PAULA. I came up to see you before, but you were asleep.

MRS. WYLER. Nurse told me. (*Exit* NURSE, *door left.*)

PAULA. You remember Will?

WILL. How do you do, Mrs. Wyler?

MRS. WYLER. Of course. How do you do, young man?

PAULA. Well, this is quite an adventure for you, isn't it, Granny?

MRS. WYLER. You're the boy who was always so curious about my youth.

WILL. Yes.

MRS. WYLER. I've forgotten most of it. Now I just live from day to day. The past is just this morning. (*A moment's pause.*) And I don't always remember that very well. Aren't there insects who live only one day? The morning is their youth and the afternoon their middle age. . . .

PAULA. You don't seem yourself today. Not as cheerful as usual.

MRS. WYLER. Can't I have my moods, Paula? I am pleased to be reflective today. People are always sending me funny books to read. I've been reading one and it depressed me.

PAULA. Well, I'll tell you something to cheer you up, Granny—Will and I are going to be married.

MRS. WYLER. Have you told your mother?

PAULA. Not yet. It's a secret. (*Enter* KENNETH.)

KENNETH. Well, Mrs. Wyler! Wanderlust today?

MRS. WYLER. Yes! Wanderlust!

KENNETH. Paula, if you're not swimming, what about our walk, and our daily argument?

MRS. WYLER. What argument?

KENNETH. Paula is interested in my subject. She hovers between skepticism and fascination.

PAULA. No chance to hover today, Kenneth. Will's improving his tennis. Sorry.

KENNETH. So am I.

MRS. WYLER. I've a surprise for you, Paula.

PAULA. What?

MRS. WYLER. Your father's coming.

PAULA. No!

MRS. WYLER. Yes.

PAULA. But how—! How do you know?

MRS. WYLER. Because I've sent for him, and he wired me he's coming. He's driving from Blue Hill. He should be here now.

PAULA. That's too—! Oh, Granny, that's marvelous! Will, let's drive out to meet him, shall we? Does Mother know?

MRS. WYLER. I only had Sam's wire an hour ago.

PAULA. Granny, you're an angel.

MRS. WYLER. Not quite yet. Don't hurry me, child.

PAULA. Come on, Will. (*Exit* PAULA *and* WILL.)

MRS. WYLER. I can see you are interested in Paula. You are, aren't you, Dr. Rice?

KENNETH. Yes. She's an extraordinary child. Adores her father, doesn't she?

MRS. WYLER. How would you cure that, Doctor?

KENNETH. It's quite healthy.

MRS. WYLER. Really? I was hoping for something juicy in the way of interpretation.

KENNETH. Sorry!

MRS. WYLER. What an interesting profession yours is, Dr. Rice.

KENNETH. Why particularly?

MRS. WYLER. Your province is the soul. Strange region.

KENNETH. People's souls, I find are, on the whole, infinitely more interesting than their bodies. I have been a general practitioner and I know.

MRS. WYLER. These young people—don't they frighten you?

KENNETH. Frighten!

MRS. WYLER. They are so radical—prepared to throw everything overboard —every tradition—

KENNETH. Paula's friends have nothing to lose, any change would be—in the nature of velvet for them.

MRS. WYLER. What do you think of Will?

KENNETH. I'm afraid I've formed no strongly defined opinion on Will.

MRS. WYLER. Oh, I see—That is a comment in itself.

KENNETH. He's nondescript.

MRS. WYLER. Do you mean to point that out to Paula?

KENNETH. I don't think so. That won't be necessary.

MRS. WYLER. Why not?

KENNETH. Blood will tell.

MRS. WYLER. That's very gracious of you, Doctor. (*Pause.*) And what do you think of Leonie?

KENNETH. Very endearing—and very impulsive.

MRS. WYLER. For example—I mean of the latter—

KENNETH. She offered to build me a sanatorium—a fully equipped modern sanatorium.

MRS. WYLER. Did she? Convenient for you.

KENNETH. Except that I refused.

MRS. WYLER. Wasn't that quixotic?

KENNETH. Not necessarily. (PAULA *and* SAM *enter, door back.*)

PAULA. Here he is!

MRS. WYLER. Sam!

SAM. Louise!

PAULA. He wouldn't come if I'd ask him. He said so shamelessly. You know Dr. Rice?

SAM. Of course.

KENNETH. Excuse me. (KENNETH *goes out.*)

SAM. Well, Louise!

MRS. WYLER. Hello, Sam. (SAM *kisses her.*)

SAM. How's she behaving?

PAULA. Incorrigible. Dr. Prentiss tells her to rest in her room. You see how she obeys him. She'll obey you though.

SAM. Well, I'll sneak her away from Dr. Prentiss and take her abroad.

MRS. WYLER. I want to go to Ethiopia. Run along, dear. I want to talk to Sam.

PAULA. Keep him here, Granny. Pretend you're not feeling well.

MRS. WYLER. I'll try. (*Exit* PAULA *door back.*) Well, Sam—

SAM. I got your wire last night. Here I am.

MRS. WYLER. It's nice of you.

SAM. Oh, now, Louise. You know you're the love of my life.

MRS. WYLER. Yes, Sam, I know—but how is Selena?

SAM. Flourishing.

MRS. WYLER. You're all right then?

SAM. Unbelievably.

MRS. WYLER. I knew you would be.

SAM. And you?

MRS. WYLER. I'm dying, Sam.

SAM. Not you—

MRS. WYLER. Don't contradict me. Besides, I'm rather looking forward to it.

SAM. Is Dr. Prentiss—?

MRS. WYLER. Dr. Prentiss soft-soaps me. I let him. It relieves his mind. But that's why I've sent for you.

SAM. You know, my dear—

MRS. WYLER. Yes, Sam. I know I can count on you. I'm dying. And I'm dying alone. I have to talk to somebody. You're the only one.

SAM. Is anything worrying you?

MRS. WYLER. Plenty.

SAM. What, dear?

MRS. WYLER. The future. Not my own. That's fixed or soon will be. But Leonie's—Paula's—

SAM. Aren't they all right?

MRS. WYLER. I am surrounded by aliens. The house is full of strangers. That Russian upstairs; this doctor.

SAM. Rice? Are you worried about him?

MRS. WYLER. What is he after? What does he want? He told me Leonie offered to build him a sanatorium—

SAM. Did he accept it?

MRS. WYLER. No. He refused. But something tells me he will allow himself to be persuaded.

SAM. I don't think Rice is a bad feller really. Seems pretty sensible. Are you worried about this boy—Dexter, and Paula?

MRS. WYLER. Not in the same way. I like the boy. But Paula—I'm worried about what the money'll do to her. We know what it's done to Leonie. You know, Sam, in spite of all her romantic dreams Leonie has a kind of integrity. But I often wonder if she's ever been really happy.

SAM. Oh, now, Louise, this pessimism's unlike you—

MRS. WYLER. This money we've built our lives on—it used to symbolize security —but there's no security in it any more.

SAM. Paula'll be all right. I count on Paula.

MRS. WYLER. In the long run. But that may be too late. One can't let go of everything, Sam. It isn't in nature. That's why I've asked you to come. I want you to remain as executor under my will.

SAM. Well, I only resigned because— since I'm no longer married to Leonie—

MRS. WYLER. What has that got to do with it?

SAM. All right.

MRS. WYLER. Promise?

SAM. Certainly.

MRS. WYLER. I feel something dark ahead, a terror—

SAM. Now, now, you've been brooding.

MRS. WYLER. Outside of you—Will is the soundest person I'll leave behind me, the healthiest—but in him too I feel a recklessness that's just kept in—I see a vista of the unknown—to us the unknown was the West, land—physical hardship—but he's hard and bitter underneath his jocularity—he isn't sure, he says, what he is— Once he is sure, what will he do?—I want you to watch him, Sam, for Paula's sake.

SAM. I will.

MRS. WYLER. They're all strange and dark . . . And this doctor. A soul doctor. We didn't have such things—I am sure that behind all this is a profound and healing truth. But sometimes truths may be perverted, and this particular doctor—how are we to know where his knowledge ends and his pretension begins? Now that I am dying, for the first time in my life I know fear. Death seems easy and simple, Sam—a self-indulgence—but can I afford it? (*She smiles up at him. He squeezes her hand.*)

SAM. Everything will be all right. Trust me.

MRS. WYLER. I do. (*A pause.*) You'll stay the night?

SAM. Of course.

MRS. WYLER. Now I feel better.

SAM. That's right. (*Pause.*)

MRS. WYLER. I'd like to live till autumn.

SAM. Of course you will. Many autumns.

MRS. WYLER. Heaven forbid. But this autumn. The color—the leaves turn. (*Looking out window.* SAM *looks too.*) The expression seems strange. What do they turn to?

SAM. (*Softly, helping her mood.*) Their mother. The earth.

MRS. WYLER. I'm happy now. I'm at peace.

SAM. (*Puts arm around her and draws her to him.*) That's better.

MRS. WYLER. (*Smiling up at him.*) It's very clever of me to have sent for you, Sam. I'm pleased with myself. Now, Sam, let 'em do their worst—

SAM. (*Smiling back at her and patting her hand.*) Just let 'em . . . !

Curtain

SCENE II

SCENE: *The same.*

TIME: *A few hours later—before dinner.* LEONIE *is standing in doorway looking out.* BORIS *center; he is fatalistically quiet at first.*

BORIS. What it comes to is this then! You're through with me. You want me to go!

LEONIE. I'm no good to you! I can no longer help you.

BORIS. Frustrated altruist!

LEONIE. You hate me!

BORIS. That would be encouraging!

LEONIE. We have nothing more for each other.

BORIS. Less than we had in the beginning!

LEONIE. Less than I thought we had.

BORIS. (*Walking toward her.*) And the man of science?

LEONIE. What?

BORIS. (*Still bearing down on her.*) This intricate man of science. You fluctuate so, Leonie. (*Facing her.*)

LEONIE. Please, Boris. I've failed. Can't we part—beautifully?

BORIS. What do you want to do? Go out on the bay and say farewell before the villagers in a barge drawn by a flock of swans? Shall we have a little orchestra to play—with the strings sobbing—and the bassoon off key?

LEONIE. You are bitter and cruel. Why? I've tried to help you. Why are you bitter?

BORIS. (*Moving close to her.*) At least I'm honest. Can you say the same?

LEONIE. (*Breaking away from him.*) I don't know what you mean by that.

BORIS. (*Getting in front of her.*) Yes, you do.

LEONIE. You're eating yourself up. You're killing yourself. There's the great lovely world outside and you sit in your room hating—

BORIS. What do you recommend? Cold showers and Swedish massage? What does the man of science prescribe for me?

LEONIE. Why do you hate Kenneth so?

BORIS. I'm jealous, my dear!

LEONIE. Poor Boris. You're beyond a simple emotion like that, aren't you?

BORIS. I envy you, Leonie. All like you.

LEONIE. Do you?

BORIS. I envy all sentimental liars who gratify their desires on high principle. It makes all your diversions an exercise in piety. You're sick of me and want to sleep with the man of science. (LEONIE *turns away. He seizes her arms and turns her to him.*) Does this suffice for you? No. It must be that you can no longer help me. (*Little silent laugh.*) My sainted father was like that! God!

LEONIE. This is the end, Boris.

BORIS. Of course it is. I tell you this

though: Beware of him, Leonie. Beware of him.

LEONIE. Your hatred of Kenneth—like all your hatreds — they're unnatural, frightening. I'm frightened of you. (*Turning from him.*)

BORIS. (*Crossing before her, closing door so she can't escape.*) Much better to be frightened of him. You know what I think. What does he think? Does he tell you? Do you know?

LEONIE. Yes, I know.

BORIS. You know what he tells you. This clairvoyant who gets rich profoundly analyzing the transparent. (*Enter* KENNETH, *door back.*)

KENNETH. Your mother would like to see you, Leonie.

LEONIE. Is she all right? (BORIS *goes upstage to small table. Gets cigarette.*)

KENNETH. Oh, very chipper. Mr. Frothingham is with her.

LEONIE. She sent for Sam, didn't she? I wonder why.

BORIS. Perhaps she felt the situation too complicated—even for *you,* Dr. Rice.

KENNETH. I don't think so.

BORIS. You are so Olympian, Dr. Rice. Would it be possible to anger you?

KENNETH. Symptoms, my dear Count, never anger me. I study them.

BORIS. Really, you are in a superb position. I quite envy you. One might cut oneself open in front of you—and it would be a symptom. Wouldn't it?

LEONIE. Boris, please—what's the good?

BORIS. (*Crossing slowly to* LEONIE.) You are quite right, my dear, no good— no good in the world. Give your mother this message for me. Tell her that under the circumstances I shall simplify the situation by withdrawing.

LEONIE. You make me very unhappy, Boris.

BORIS. How agreeable then that you have Dr. Rice here—to resolve your unhappiness. (*Crosses quickly to table behind sofa and puts out cigarette.*)

LEONIE. (*Following him.*) Where will you be in case I—in case you— Boris?

BORIS. Don't worry about me. A magazine syndicate has offered me a great deal for *sentimental* reminiscences of my father. Imagine that, sentimental! They have offered me — charming Americanism — a ghostwriter. It will be quaint—one ghost collaborating with another ghost. (*Raising hand like Greek priest.*) My blessings, Leonie. (*Kisses her hand.*) You have been charming. Dr. Rice— (*He bows formally. Exit* BORIS.)

LEONIE. Poor Boris— (*She sinks into a chair, overcome.*)

KENNETH. He's part of the past. You must forget him.

LEONIE. Poor Boris!

KENNETH. You will forget him.

LEONIE. I'll try.

KENNETH. Exorcised!

LEONIE. You know, Kenneth, I feel you are the only one in the world I can count on.

KENNETH. Not me.

LEONIE. Whom else?

KENNETH. Yourself!

LEONIE. Light reed! Fragile! Fragile!

KENNETH. Pliant but unbreakable.

LEONIE. No. Don't think much of myself, Kenneth. Really I don't. My judgment seems to be at fault somehow. Paula thinks so too. She's always lecturing me. (*Sits right end of sofa.*)

KENNETH. Paula can't abide me.

LEONIE. It's not true!

KENNETH. You know, Leonie, I have an instinct in these matters—so, also, has your daughter.

LEONIE. Don't you like Paula?

KENNETH. I love her. Everyone connected with you.

LEONIE. Kenneth! How dear of you! Of course Paula and I are poles apart. Look at her friends!

KENNETH. Raffish!

LEONIE. (*A little taken aback by this.*)

Oh, do you think so? All of them? Don't you like Will?

KENNETH. Nice enough. Clever in his way. With an eye to the main chance.

LEONIE. Really?

KENNETH. Naturally—penniless boy.

LEONIE. I've always encouraged Paula to be independent. I've never tried to impose my ideals or my standards on her. Have I done wrong to give her her own head this way? She's such a darling, really. She's killing, you know. So superior, so knowing. The other day—the other day, Kenneth . . . I took her to lunch in town and she criticized me—now what do you think about?

KENNETH. (*Sitting on arm of chair.*) For once my intuition fails me.

LEONIE. About my technique with men. She said it was lousy. Isn't it delicious?

KENNETH. Not more specific than simply lousy?

LEONIE. She said I threw myself at men instead of reversing the process.

KENNETH. But I should think she would have approved of that. She makes such a fetish of being candid!

LEONIE. That's just what I said—exactly. I said I couldn't pretend—that I couldn't descend to—technique. I said that when my feelings were involved I saw no point in not letting the other person see it. I reproached her for deviousness. Strange ideas that child has—strange!

KENNETH. I'm afraid her generation is theory-ridden! (*Pause.*)

LEONIE. Kenneth?

KENNETH. Yes, Leonie?

LEONIE. It's true of course.

KENNETH. What?

LEONIE. Paula's—criticism. I can't conceal my feelings. Least of all—from you. (*Slight pause.*)

KENNETH. Why should you?

LEONIE. Oh, Kenneth, I'm so useless! You know how useless I am!

KENNETH. I know only that you are gracious and lovely—and that you have the gift of innocence.

LEONIE. I hate my life. It's been so scattered—emotionally.

KENNETH. Whose isn't?

LEONIE. You are such a comfort. Really it's too much now to expect me to do without you. Kenneth?

KENNETH. Yes . . . Leonie.

LEONIE. Will you be a darling—and marry me?

KENNETH. Leonie?

LEONIE. (*Returning his gaze.*) Yes, Kenneth.

KENNETH. Have you thought this over?

LEONIE. It's the first time—the very first time—that I've ever been sure.

KENNETH. You are so impulsive, Leonie.

LEONIE. Kenneth, don't you think we'd have a chance—you and I—don't you think? (*Enter PAULA, door back.*)

PAULA. (*Realizes she has interrupted a tête-à-tête.*) Oh, sorry—!

LEONIE. Paula dear, have you been with Mother?

PAULA. Yes. Granny wants to see you, as a matter of fact.

LEONIE. Oh, I forgot! Is she all right? Cheerful?

PAULA. Oh, very.

LEONIE. I'll be right there. Stay and talk to Kenneth, Paula. He thinks you don't like him. Prove to him it isn't true. Do you think you could be gracious, Paula? Or is that too old-fashioned? (*Exit LEONIE door back. In the following scene PAULA determines to get rid of the tantalizing and irritating mixed feelings she has about KENNETH, her sense of distrusting, disliking and simultaneously being fascinated by him—she feels he has something up his sleeve; she is playing a game to discover what it is and yet she becomes increasingly conscious that game is not unpleasant to her because of her interest in her victim.*)

PAULA. Leonie's all a-flutter. What is it?

KENNETH. She was just telling me—she envies you your poise.

PAULA. Your intentions are honorable, I hope.

KENNETH. Old hat, Paula.

PAULA. I beg your pardon.

KENNETH. Undergraduate audacity. Scott Fitzgerald. Old hat.

PAULA. We don't like each other much, do we?

KENNETH. That's regrettable.

PAULA. And yet—I'm very curious about you.

KENNETH. What would you like to know?

PAULA. Your motive.

KENNETH. Ah!

PAULA. And yet even if you told me—

KENNETH. You wouldn't believe it?

PAULA. (*Facing him.*) No. Now why is that? Even when you are perfectly frank, your frankness seems to me—a device. Now why is that?

KENNETH. I'll tell you.

PAULA. Why?

KENNETH. Because you yourself are confused, muddled, unsure, contradictory. I am simple and co-ordinated. You resent that. You dislike it. You envy it. You would like such simplicity for yourself. But, as you are unlikely to achieve it, you soothe yourself by distrusting me.

PAULA. You say I'm muddled. Why am I muddled?

KENNETH. You've accepted a set of premises without examining them or thinking about them. You keep them like jewels in a box and dangle them. Then you put them back in the box, confident that they belong to you. But as they don't you feel an occasional twinge of insecurity—

PAULA. Do you mind dropping the parables—?

KENNETH. Not at all—

PAULA. Why am I muddled? For example—

KENNETH. You're a walking contradiction in terms—

PAULA. For example?

KENNETH. For example—for example—your radicalism. Your friends. Your point of view. Borrowed. Unexamined. Insincere.

PAULA. Go on.

KENNETH. You are rich and you are exquisite. Why are you rich and exquisite? (*Walking back to face her.*) Because your forbears were not moralistic but ruthless. Had they been moralistic, had they been concerned, as you pretend to be, with the "predatory system"—this awful terminology—you'd be working in a store somewhere wrapping packages or waiting on querulous housewives with bad skins or teaching school. Your own origins won't bear a moralistic investigation. You must know that. Your sociology and economics must teach you that.

PAULA. Suppose I repudiate my origins?

KENNETH. That takes more courage than you have.

PAULA. Don't be so sure.

KENNETH. But why should you? If you had a special talent or were a crusader there might be some sense in it. But you have no special talent and you are not a crusader. Much better to be decorative. Much better for a world starving for beauty. Instead of repudiating your origins you should exult in them and in that same predatory system that made you possible. (*Crossing to table behind sofa for cigarette.*) (*Pause.*)

PAULA. What were your origins?

KENNETH. (*Lighting cigarette.*) Anonymous.

PAULA. What do you mean?

KENNETH. I was discovered on a doorstep.

PAULA. Really?

KENNETH. Like Moses.

PAULA. Where were you brought up?

KENNETH. In a foundling asylum in New England. The place lacked charm. This sounds like an unpromising beginning but actually it was more stimulating than you might imagine. I remember as a kid of twelve going to the library in Springfield and getting down the *Dictionary of National Biography* and hunting out the bastards. Surprising how many distinguished ones there were and are. I allied myself early with the brilliant and variegated company of the illegitimate.

PAULA. You don't know who your parents were?

KENNETH. No.

PAULA. Did you get yourself through college?

KENNETH. *And* medical school.

PAULA. Did you practice medicine?

KENNETH. For a bit. I devoted myself—when the victims would let me—to their noses and throats. It was a startling occupation. But I gave up tonsilectomy for the soul. The poor have tonsils but only the rich have souls. My instinct was justified—as you see.

PAULA. You've gone pretty far.

KENNETH. Incredible journey!

PAULA. Having come from—from—

KENNETH. The mud—?

PAULA. Well—I should think you'd be more sympathetic to the underdogs.

KENNETH. No, why should I? The herd bores me. It interests me only as an indication of the distance I've travelled.

PAULA. Will would say that you are a lucky individual who—

KENNETH. Yes, that is what Will would say. It always satisfies the mediocrity to call the exceptional individual lucky.

PAULA. You don't like Will?

KENNETH. I despise him.

PAULA. Why?

KENNETH. I detest these young firebrands whose incandescence will be extinguished by the first job! I detest radicals who lounge about in country-houses.

PAULA. You're unfair to Will.

KENNETH. I have no interest in being fair to him. We were discussing you.

PAULA. You are too persuasive. I don't believe you.

KENNETH. My advice to you is to find out what you want before you commit yourself to young Mr. Dexter.

PAULA. But I have committed myself.

KENNETH. Too bad.

PAULA. For him or for me?

KENNETH. For both of you; but for him particularly.

PAULA. Why?

KENNETH. I see precisely the effect your money will have on him. He will take it and the feeling will grow in him that in having given it you have destroyed what he calls his integrity. He will even come to believe that if not for this quenching of initiative he might have become a flaming leader of the people. At the same time he will be aware that both these comforting alibis are delusions—because he has no integrity to speak of nor any initiative to speak of. Knowing they are lies he will only proclaim them the louder, cling to them the harder. He will hate you as the thief of his character—petty larceny, I must say.

PAULA. (*Jumping up, taking several steps away from him.*) That's a lie.

KENNETH. Will is an American Puritan. A foreigner—Boris, for example—marries money, feeling that he gives value received. Very often he does. But young Dexter will never feel that —and maybe he'll be right.

PAULA. You hate Will.

KENNETH. You flatter him.

PAULA. How did you get to know so much about people? About what they feel and what they will do?

KENNETH. I began by knowing myself—but not lying to myself. (*A silence. He looks at her. He takes in her loveliness. He speaks her name, in a new voice, softly.*) Paula—

PAULA. (*She looks at him fixedly.*) What?

KENNETH. Paula—

PAULA. What?

KENNETH. Do you know me any better now? Do you trust me any better now?

PAULA. I don't know. (*Enter* WILL.)

KENNETH. Paula, Paula, Paula— (PAULA *starts toward door back.*) Don't go, Paula!

WILL. Oughtn't you to be changing for dinner? (PAULA *stops upstage.*) Hello, Doctor. What's the matter?

KENNETH. May I congratulate him?

WILL. What's he been saying?

KENNETH. Paula told me she is going to marry you.

PAULA. The doctor is a cynic.

KENNETH. We were discussing the European and American points of view toward money marriages—There's a great difference. The European fortune-hunter, once he has landed the bag, has no more twinge of conscience than a big-game hunter when he has made his kill. The American—

WILL. Is that what you think I am, Doctor?

KENNETH. (*To* PAULA *amiably.*) You see. He resents the mere phrase. But my dear boy, that is no disgrace. We are all fortune-hunters—

PAULA. (*Pointedly.*) Not all, Kenneth—!

KENNETH. But I see no difference at all between the man who makes a profession of being charming to rich ladies—or any other—specialist. The former is more arduous.

PAULA. Are you defending Will or yourself?

KENNETH. I am generalizing. (*To* WILL.) Congratulations! I admit that to scatter congratulations in this way is glib, but we live in a convention of glibness. Good God, we congratulate people when they marry and when they produce children—we skim lightly over these tremendous hazards— Excuse me. (*Exit* KENNETH.)

WILL. God damn that man!

PAULA. Will!

WILL. I can't stand him—not from the moment I saw him—because he's incapable of disinterestedness himself, he can't imagine it in others. He's the kind of cynical, sneering— He's a marauder. The adventurer with the cure-all. This is just the moment for him. And this is just the place!

PAULA. I've never seen you lose your temper before, Will.

WILL. You know why, don't you?

PAULA. Why?

WILL. Because he's right! While he was talking I felt like hitting him. At the same time a voice inside me said: Can you deny it? When I came in here he was saying your name. He was looking at you—it seems he hasn't quite decided, has he?

PAULA. I'm worried about him and Leonie—

WILL. He's got Leonie hook, line and sinker. That's obvious.

PAULA. She mustn't! Will, she mustn't!

WILL. You can't stop it—you can't do anything for Leonie. Nobody can do anything for anybody. Nobody should try.

PAULA. Will—you mustn't go back to New York. You must stay and help me.

WILL. Sorry. Nothing doing.

PAULA. Will!

WILL. I have a feeling you'll rather enjoy saving Leonie from the doctor.

PAULA. Will! That's not fair, Will!

WILL. It may not be fair but it is obvious. Also, it is obvious that the doctor won't mind being saved.

PAULA. It's lucky for both of us that one of us has some self-control.

WILL. No, I won't stay here. I hate the place, I hate Dr. Rice, I hate myself for being here!

PAULA. Don't let me down, Will—I need you terribly just now—

WILL. (*At white heat.*) I haven't quite the technique of fortune hunting yet —in the European manner. Which of the two is he after—you or Leonie? Will he flip a coin?

PAULA. I hate you! I hate you!

WILL. Well, we know where we are at any rate.

PAULA. Yes. We do! (LEONIE *comes running in. She wears an exquisite summer evening frock. She is breathless with happiness.*)

LEONIE. Paula! Why aren't you dressed? I want you to wear something especially lovely tonight! Do you like this? It's new. I haven't worn it before. (*She twirls for them.*) I've a surprise for you, Will. You'll know what it is in a minute. I was thinking of you and it popped into my mind. You know, Will, I'm very, very fond of you. And I think you are equally fond of me. I can't help liking people who like me. I suppose you think I'm horribly vain. But then, everybody's vain about something. (BUTLER *comes in with cocktails and sandwiches, to table right of fireplace.*) If they're not, they're vain about their lack of vanity. I believe that's a mot! Pretty good for a brainless— Here, Will, have a cocktail— (WILL *takes cocktail.*) Paula—what's your pet vanity? She thinks mine's my looks but it's not. If I had my way I shouldn't look at all the way I look. (*Enter* DR. DEXTER, *door back. He wears a sea-green baggy dinner-suit; he looks as "hicky" and uncertain as ever.*)

DEXTER. Good evening, Mrs. Frothingham.

LEONIE. Dr. Dexter—how good of you to come. Delighted to see you.

DEXTER. Good evening. Hello, Will.

WILL. Dad!

DEXTER. Mrs. Frothingham invited me. Didn't you know?

LEONIE. (*Takes* DEXTER'S *arm and goes to* WILL.) You told me you had to leave tomorrow to visit your father in Brunswick so I just called him up in Brunswick—

DEXTER. She sent the car all the way for me. Nice car. Great springs.

LEONIE. (*To* WILL.) Now you won't have to leave tomorrow. You can both spend the week-end here.

WILL. (*Walking away a little right.*) Awfully nice of you, Leonie.

LEONIE. (*Following him.*) (DEXTER *sits on sofa.*) You see, Will, I leave the big issues to the professional altruists. I just do what I can toward making those around me happy. And that's *my* vanity! (*Enter* DENNIS, *door back.*)

DENNIS. Well! Well! Fancy that now, Hedda!

LEONIE. Oh, hello, Dennis, just in time for a cocktail. (LEONIE *leads him over to sofa.* WILL *is isolated down right center.*)

DENNIS. (*To* DEXTER.) How are you?

DEXTER. (*Not friendly.*) I'm all right.

DENNIS. Complicated week-end! You and the Healer! Faraday and Cagliostro. That'll be something.

LEONIE. (*Takes* DENNIS'S *arm.*) Everybody tells me to like you, Dennis. I'm in such a mood that I'm going to make the effort.

DENNIS. I've been waiting for this. I'm thrilled!

LEONIE. (*Strolling with him across stage front.*) Something tells me you could be very charming if you wanted to. Tell me, Dennis, have you ever tried being lovable and sweet?

DENNIS. For you, Mrs. Frothingham, I would willingly revive the age of chivalry!

LEONIE. But there's no need of that. I just want you to be nice. Here, have a cocktail. Give you courage.

DENNIS. Just watch me from now on, Mrs. Frothingham.

LEONIE. I will. Passionately. (*Hands him cocktail.*) I'll be doing nothing else. (BUTLER *crosses back of sofa, offers* DEXTER *and* PAULA *cocktails.* DR. RICE *comes in.*)

DENNIS. (*Stage sigh.*) A-h-h! The doctor! Just in time to look at my tongue, Doctor.

KENNETH. That won't be necessary, young

man. I can tell—It's excessive.

LEONIE. (*Crossing to* KENNETH.) Kenneth—you remember Will's father—Dr. Dexter.

KENNETH. How do you do? (*They shake hands. A second* BUTLER *has come in and he and* ROBERT *are passing cocktails and hors d'oeuvres.* LEONIE *keeps circulating among her guests.* KENNETH *and* DEXTER *are in the center—*DENNIS, *obeying a malicious impulse, presides over them. Announces a theme on which he eggs them on to utter variations.*)

DENNIS. A significant moment, ladies and gentlemen—the magician of Science meets the magician of Sex—The floating libido bumps the absolute! What happens?

DEXTER. (*Cupping his hand to his ear.*) What? (WILL *crosses to door and looks out moodily.*)

DENNIS. The absolute hasn't got a chance. Isn't that right, Dr. Rice?

KENNETH. I shouldn't venture to contradict a young intellectual. Especially a very young intellectual.

LEONIE. (*Crosses front of* KENNETH, *to* DENNIS.) There, you see, I'm afraid, after all, I'll have to give you up, Dennis. You can't be lovable. You can't be sweet.

DENNIS. But I didn't promise to be winsome to everybody, only to you.

LEONIE. You really must treat him, Kenneth. He has no censor at all.

DENNIS. My censor is the Catholic tradition. We Catholics anticipated both Marx and Freud by a little matter of nineteen centuries. Spiritually, we have a Communion in the Holy Ghost—Communion. As for Dr. Rice, he offers confession without absolution. He is inadequate. (LEONIE *returns with tray of canapes.*)

LEONIE. It seems such bad taste to discuss religion at cocktail time. Try a stuffed olive.

DEXTER. By the time you got your beautiful new world, true science will have perished.

LEONIE. Aren't you too pessimistic, Dr. Dexter? Too much science has made you gloomy. Kenneth, the depression hasn't stopped your work, has it? Depression or no depression— (WILL *springs up.*)

WILL. (*Tensely.*) That's right, Leonie. (*Everyone faces* WILL.) Depression or no depression—war or peace—revolution or reaction—Kenneth will reign supreme! (KENNETH *stares at him.* WILL *confronts him.*)

LEONIE. Will!

WILL. Yes, Leonie. His is the power and the glory!

LEONIE. Dennis, this is your influence—

WILL. I admire you unreservedly, Doctor. Of your kind you are the best. You are the essence.

KENNETH. You embarrass me.

WILL. Some men are born ahead of their time, some behind, but you are made pat for the instant. Now is the time for you—when people are unemployed and distrust their own capacities—when people suffer and may be tempted—when integrity yields to despair—now is the moment for you!

KENNETH. (*Strolling closer to him so they are face to face.*) When, may I ask, is the moment for you—when if ever?

WILL. After your victory. When you are stuffed and inert with everything you want, then will be the time for me. (*He goes out.*)

PAULA. (*Running after* WILL.) Will . . . Will . . . Will . . . (*She follows him out.*)

LEONIE. (*Devastated by this strange behavior.*) What is it? I don't like it when people stand in the middle of the floor and make speeches. What's the matter with him? Dennis, do you know?

DENNIS. (*With a look at* KENNETH.) I can guess.

LEONIE. Has he quarreled with Paula?

Paula is so inept. She doesn't know how to . . . At the same time, if he had a grievance, why couldn't he have kept it until after dinner? (*Enter* ROBERT.)

ROBERT. Dinner is served. (*Exit* ROBERT.)

LEONIE. Well, we'll do what we can. Sam is dining with Mother in her room, Boris has a headache. Dennis, you and Dr. Dexter—

DENNIS. You've picked me, Dr. Dexter. I congratulate you.

DEXTER. Thank God, I can't hear a word you say. (*Exit* DEXTER, *door back.*)

DENNIS. (*Sadistically.*) Oh, yes, he can. And we'll fight it out on these lines if it takes all dinner. (*He follows* DEXTER *out.*)

LEONIE. What extraordinary behavior! What do you suppose, Kenneth— shall I go after them?

KENNETH. I wouldn't. It's their problem. Give them time.

LEONIE. (*Reassured.*) You are so wise, Kenneth. How did I ever get on without you? I have that secure feeling that you are going to be my last indiscretion. When I think how neatly I've captured you—I feel quite proud. I guess my technique isn't so lousy after all. (*She takes his arm and swings along beside him as they waltz in to dinner.*)

Curtain

ACT THREE

SCENE: *The same.*

TIME: *Late that fall. The trees have turned. The sumach have put out the brilliant red flowers of autumn.*

AT RISE: WILL *and* DENNIS *have just arrived, and are standing at fireplace, back.* LEONIE *comes in to greet them.* SAM *strolls in with her.*

LEONIE. I'm so glad to see you! (*She shakes hands with each of them warmly.*) Will! How are you? (*To* DENNIS.) It's so good of you to come.

SAM. (*Shaking hands with* WILL.) Very glad to see you.

WILL. Thanks. (SAM *shakes hands with* DENNIS.)

LEONIE. Sam drove over for a few hours from Blue Hill to talk business to me. He hasn't had much luck so far. It's simply wonderful having you boys here—it's like old times. I didn't tell Paula. (*To* SAM.) I did all this on my own. It's a surprise for Paula.

DENNIS. She'll be overcome when she sees me. Maybe you should prepare her.

WILL. Where is Paula?

LEONIE. Isn't it provoking! She and Kenneth went for a walk. They should have been back long before this. (*Turning back to them.*) Paula hasn't been at all herself, Will. I thought you would cheer her up.

DENNIS. I will be glad to do what I can, of course. Several very stubborn cases have yielded to my charm.

LEONIE. I'm sure! Do sit down. (*She sits.*)

DENNIS. (*Taking out his pipe.*) Do you mind? (WILL *sits.*)

LEONIE. Oh, please—I can't tell you how I appreciate your coming—

DENNIS. (*The harassed business man.*) Well, as a matter of fact, Leonie, it wasn't easy to get away from the office—

LEONIE. Are you in an office?

DENNIS. Sometimes as many as fifteen in a day. (LEONIE *laughs.*) But when I got your appealing letter — *and* the return tickets — I'm chivalrous at heart, you know, Leonie—

LEONIE. I know you are!

SAM. How's town?

WILL. Very hot.

SAM. I'm just on my way down. Stopped by to go over several things with Leonie—

LEONIE. Poor Sam's been having an awful time with me. He keeps putting things in escrow. Where is escrow?

DENNIS. It's where squirrels put nuts in the winter-time.

LEONIE. I see! Dennis is much more lucid than you, Sam.

DENNIS. I have a knack for making the abstruse translucent. Especially in economics. Now, would you like to know why England went off gold?

LEONIE. No, I wouldn't.

DENNIS. I shall yield to your subconscious demand and tell you.

LEONIE. (*To others.*) Help!

DENNIS. I see that there is no audience for my peculiar gift.

LEONIE. You know, Will, I've thought perhaps you were angry with us.

WILL. Why?

LEONIE. You haven't been here for so long. (*To* SAM.) Since Granny died—none of them have been here. Did Paula write you about Granny's funeral?

WILL. No. She didn't.

LEONIE. Of course I hate funerals—I can't bear them—but this was so—natural. Mother wanted to live till the fall and she did. It was a dreaming blue sky and there was that poignant haze over the hills and over the bay, and the smell of burning wood from some-where. Burning wood never smells at any other time the way it does in Indian summer. And the colors that day! Did you ever, Sam, see such a day?

SAM. It was beautiful.

LEONIE. They say the colors of autumn are the colors of death, but I don't be-lieve that. They were in such strength that day. I cried—but not on account of Mother—that kind of day always makes me cry a little bit anyway. You couldn't cry over con-signing anyone you loved to an earth

like that—on a day like that. I put some blazing leaves over her, but when I passed there the other day, they were withered and brown—

SAM. (*Chiding her.*) Now Leonie—

LEONIE. Sam thinks I shouldn't talk about Mother. But I don't see why. She doesn't depress me. I think of her with joy. She had a wonderful life.

SAM. She was a wonderful woman.

LEONIE. (*To* WILL.) Imagine, Will— when Sam was here last time—you were here that week-end—she *knew*. She asked Sam to be executor of her will.

SAM. (*Very annoyed at her for bringing this up.*) Leonie—

LEONIE. Why didn't you tell me, Sam, then?

SAM. Seemed no point.

LEONIE. She didn't want me to know, did she?

SAM. No. She didn't want to distress you. (*A moment's pause.*)

LEONIE. What can be keeping Paula? (*She glances out of the window.*) Sam, do you want to talk business to me some more?

SAM. I'd like to talk to Will a minute.

LEONIE. Oh—yes. Well, Dennis, wouldn't you like me to show you to your room? (*She rises, goes to door into hallway.* DENNIS *follows.*)

DENNIS. Thanks. I've got to answer a chain letter.

LEONIE. I've given you a room you've never had. The tower room.

DENNIS. Is it ivory? I won't be comfort-able if it isn't ivory.

LEONIE. Well just this once you're going to be uncomfortable — and like it! (*She goes out.*)

DENNIS. (*Tragically.*) And for this I gave up a superb view of the gas-house on 149th Street. (*He goes out.*)

SAM. (*Rises and goes up toward fireplace.*) Will—

WILL. Yes, Mr. Frothingham.

SAM. Oh—call me Sam.

WILL. All right.

SAM. I'll have to be pushing off in an hour or so. I rather wanted to talk to you.

WILL. Yes—

SAM. (*Wipes his forehead.*) Gosh, Leonie's a difficult woman to talk business to. (*Sits.*)

WILL. I can imagine that. She's not interested in business.

SAM. *She—is—not!!!*

WILL. What do you want to speak to me about?

SAM. Paula.

WILL. What about Paula?

SAM. As I'm her father—I hope you won't think me—

WILL. Of course not—

SAM. It's not altogether easy—

WILL. Do you want me to help you?

SAM. Yes. I wish you would!

WILL. You're worried about Paula and me, aren't you? So was her grandmother. You think me irresponsible. Less responsible for example—(*As if making a random comparison*) than Dr. Rice?

SAM. Well, as a matter of fact, I've rather gotten to know Dr. Rice, and in many respects, he's a pretty sound feller. (*Rising and going to stand above* WILL.) Hang it all, Will, I like you, and I don't like to preach to you, you know.

WILL. Go on.

SAM. Well, there are—from my point of view at least—a lot of nonsensical ideas knocking about. I'd like to point out just one thing to you. Your radicalism and all that— Well, the point is this—if you marry Paula—and I hope you do, because I like you—and, what is more important, Paula likes you—you'll have responsibilities. Paula will be rich. Very rich. Money means responsibility. Now, I shouldn't, for example, like you to start radical magazines with it. I shouldn't like you to let money drift through your fingers in all sorts of aimless, millennial directions that won't get anywhere.

WILL. Who told you that was my intention?

SAM. A little bird.

WILL. With a black moustache?

SAM. Does that matter?

WILL. No.

SAM. (*Putting hand on* WILL's *shoulder.*) As a matter of fact, I'm not worried about you at all. Money, I expect, will do to you what getting power does to radical opposition, once it gets office—

WILL. Emasculate me, you mean?

SAM. Well, hardly. Mature you. Once you're rich yourself, I have no doubt you'll be—

WILL. Sound.

SAM. Yes. Sound. But your friends— this McCarthy boy—

WILL. Well, I can easily cut Dennis—all my poor and unsound friends—

SAM. (*Quietly.*) I'm sorry you're taking this tone with me, Will. I'm the last person in the world to ask you to drop anybody. I'd be ashamed of you if you did. Only—

WILL. Only?

SAM. I must tell you that I am in position —by virtue of the will left by Mrs. Wyler—to keep Paula's money from being used for any purpose that might be construed as—subversive.

WILL. From whose point of view?

SAM. (*Quietly.*) From mine.

WILL. I see.

SAM. Possibly you may not believe this— but I trust you, Will. Mrs. Wyler trusted you.

WILL. You needn't worry. Paula seems to have other interests apparently.

SAM. What do you mean?

WILL. Sounder interests— (DENNIS *enters, through door back.*)

DENNIS. The tower room lets in light on four sides, but nothing to look at. Just the sea and the landscape.

SAM. What did you do with Leonie?

DENNIS. She's gone to her mother's room to potter around.

SAM. Maybe I can get her attention while

she's pottering. Excuse me. (SAM *goes out.*)

DENNIS. Poor Leonie—she's the last of the lovely ladies. The inheritance taxes'll get 'em soon. You know we were by way of getting our magazine from Leonie when Dr. Rice spiked our guns. So I'm leaving. My time is too valuable. But the Healer won't last forever, and when he goes, I shall return. Take heart, my good man. I know you feel a little tender about this, but remember, my lad, it's the Cause that counts. Remember what Shaw says: "There is no money but the devil's money. It is all tainted and it might as well be used in the service of God." (*A moment —*WILL *is obviously thinking of something else.*) What's the matter?

WILL. Nothing.

DENNIS. (*Bringing down chair to sit left of* WILL *he imitates* RICE's *manner.*) Now you must speak, young man— how can I sublimate your subconscious troubles, if you won't speak? Are you unhappy about Paula, my lad? (*No answer.*) Tell me what's happened between you—relieve your soul, and, as a reward, I may make you co-editor of our magazine. (*No response. He rises and walks to opposite side of table.*) No? Assistant editor you remain. I may even fire you. Yes, I think I will fire you. (*Crossing in front of* WILL *to fireplace.*) Dexter—you're through. Go upstairs and get your check. (*Rubs his hands together in glee.*) God, it gives me a sense of power to fire a man—especially an old friend! (PAULA *and* KENNETH *come in door right from the garden.*)

PAULA. (*Amazed to see them.*) Will! But how—! Dennis!

WILL. (*Rather coolly.*) Hello, Paula.

DENNIS. We came to surprise you. Now that we have surprised you, we can go home.

WILL. Leonie asked me to come.

PAULA. Oh. Well, it's very nice to see you.

WILL. Thanks.

PAULA. When I wired you to come a few weeks ago, you were too busy. It takes Leonie, doesn't it?

DENNIS. You should have tried me, Paula. Hello, Dr. Rice. How's business? Any suppressions today?

KENNETH. (*Significantly.*) Apparently not.

DENNIS. Well, come on up to my room, Doctor, and we'll play Twenty Questions. (*He goes out.*)

WILL. Hello, Dr. Rice.

KENNETH. How are you?

PAULA. Will—I'm awfully glad to see you. I was just going to write you to thank you for the sweet letter you sent me after Granny died.

KENNETH. I'm afraid it's my fault, Dexter. I do my best to keep Paula so busy that she finds no time to write letters.

WILL. I was sure I could count on you, Doctor. (WILL *goes out.*)

PAULA. You enjoy hurting Will, don't you?

KENNETH. When there is an obstacle in my path, I do my best to remove it.

PAULA. What makes you think it is only Will that stands between us— That if left to myself I—

KENNETH. Because it is true. Were it not for the squids of idealistic drivel spouted around you by Will and his friends, there would be no issue at all between us. I resent even an imputed rivalry with someone I despise.

PAULA. Rivalry?

KENNETH. Paula— There's no reason any longer why I shouldn't tell you the truth.

PAULA. What is it, Kenneth?

KENNETH. (*After a moment — slowly.*) Do you know what I feel like? I feel like a man on a great height, irresistibly tempted to jump over. Do you want the truth really? (*She says nothing. Somehow his words, his voice, his attitude make her feel that really now he may reveal something which before he wouldn't have revealed. He is in a trance-like state almost; she feels it; she is rather horribly fascinated—somehow, though she distrusts him utterly, some instinct tells her that, at this moment actually he is tempted by a force, disruptive to himself, to tell her the truth.)* Don't you know it? Don't you feel it? (*Pause.*) Haven't you known it? Haven't you felt it? (*A moment's pause.*) I love you.

PAULA. What?

KENNETH. I love you. (*A pause. She is too stupefied to speak. She too is under a spell. She is fascinated by him—by the enormity of this. She rises, walks away from him to stand by sofa.*)

PAULA. I suppose I should be afraid of you. I'm not afraid of you.

KENNETH. I am afraid of you. You tempt me to venture the impossible. That is impractical. And I have always been eminently practical.

PAULA. I'm sure you have. (*She feels herself talking automatically, as if out of a hypnotic state—at the same time some vanity and shrewdness keeps pounding inside her: "See how far he will go—see how far he will go!"*)

KENNETH. I have lived by a plan. The plan has matured. But I have yearned for a face that would give me joy, for the voice that would soothe me. It is your face. It is your voice. (PAULA *is fighting not to scream; at the same time she is caught in a nightmarish fascination.*)

PAULA. (*Very faintly.*) Don't you love Mother?

KENNETH. No. (*A moment's pause.*) You are the youth I have never had, the security I have never had—you are the home I have hungered for. (*Moves toward her—stands over her and a little back.*) That I am standing near you now, that I have achieved a share in your life, that you

are listening to me, that you are thinking of me and of what I am, to the exclusion of everything else in the whirling universe—this is a miracle so devastating, that it makes any future possible—Paula—

PAULA. What?

KENNETH. Paula?

PAULA. What *is* it!

KENNETH. (*Bending over her.*) Paula . . . (*It is as if he got a sexual joy from saying her name.*) I love your name. I love to say your name.

PAULA. I *am* afraid of you. I'm sorry for you.

KENNETH. Do you think me insane?

PAULA. Yes.

KENNETH. Because I am ambitious, because I am forthright, because I deal scientifically with the human stuff around me—you think me insane. Because I am ruthless and romantic, you think me insane. This boy you think you love—who spends his time sniveling about a system he is not strong enough to dominate—is he sane?

PAULA. I don't expect you to—

KENNETH. When I hear the chatter of your friends, it makes me sick. While they and their kind prate of co-operative commonwealths, the strong man takes power, and rides over their backs—which is all their backs are fit for. Never has the opportunity for the individual career been so exalted, so infinite in its scope, so horizontal. House-painters and minor journalists become dictators of great nations. (*With puckish humor—leaning on arm of her chair.*) Imagine what a really clever man could do! See what he has done! (*He smiles, makes a gesture of modest self-assertion, indicating the room as part of his conquest. She laughs, rather choked and embarrassed. He goes on.*) And this I have done alone. From an impossible distance—I have come to you, so that when I speak, you can hear. What might we not do together, Paula—you and I—(*To her surprise,* PAULA *finds herself arguing an inconceivable point. She loathes the strange fascination she feels in this man, and yet is aware that it might turn to her advantage.*)

PAULA. We don't want the same things.

KENNETH. You want what everyone wants who has vitality and imagination—new forms of power—new domains of knowledge—the ultimate sensations.

PAULA. You *are* romantic, aren't you?

KENNETH. Endlessly. And endlessly—realistic. (*Staring at her.*) What are you thinking?

PAULA. (*Shrewd against him—against herself.*) I keep thinking—what you want now—what you're after now?

KENNETH. (*Moving toward her.*) You don't believe then—that I love you?

PAULA. (*Leaning back in chair—not looking at him.*) You are a very strange man.

KENNETH. I am simple really. I want everything. That's all!

PAULA. And you don't care how you get it.

KENNETH. Don't be moralistic, Paula—I beg you. I am directly in the tradition of your own marauding ancestors. They pass now for pioneers—actually they fell on the true pioneers, and wrested what they had found away from them, by sheer brutal strength. I am doing the same thing—but more adroitly.

PAULA. Why are you so honest with me?

KENNETH. (*With his most charming smile.*) Perhaps because I feel that, in your heart, you too are an adventurer. (*A pause. During these half-spell-bound instants a thought has been forming slowly in* PAULA's *mind that crystallizes now. This man is the enemy. This man is infinitely cunning, infinitely resourceful. Perhaps—just the possibility—he really feels this passion for her. If so, why*

not use this weakness in an antagonist so ruthless? She will try.)

PAULA. I shouldn't listen to you—(*A moment. He senses her cunning. He looks at her.*)

KENNETH. You don't trust me?

PAULA. Have I reason to trust you?

KENNETH. What reason would you like? What proof would you like?

PAULA. Aren't you going to marry Mother?

KENNETH. Only as an alternative.

PAULA. Will you—tell her so? Will you give up the alternative?

KENNETH. And if I do?

PAULA. What shall I promise you?

KENNETH. Yourself.

PAULA. (*Looks at him—speaks.*) And if I do?

KENNETH. Then . . .

PAULA. (*Taking fire.*) You say you love me! If you feel it—really feel it—You haven't been very adventurous for all your talk! Taking in Mother and Sam! Give up those conquests. Tell her! Tell Mother! Then perhaps I will believe you.

KENNETH. And then?

PAULA. Take your chances!

KENNETH. (*Quietly.*) Very well.

PAULA. You will?

KENNETH. I will.

PAULA. You'll tell Mother—you love me?

KENNETH. Yes.

PAULA. (*Going to the foot of the stairs, calls:*) Mother! Mother!

LEONIE. (*Offstage.*) Yes, Paula. I'm coming right down! I've the most marvelous surprise for you! Wait and see! (PAULA *walks to end of sofa—looking at* KENNETH. LEONIE *comes in. She is wearing an exquisite old-fashioned silk wedding-dress which billows around her in an immense shimmering circle. She is a vision of enchantment.*)

LEONIE. (*In a great flurry of excitement.*) Children, look what I found! It's Mother's. It's the dress she was married in. I was poking around in

Granny's room while Sam was talking to me about bonds, and I came upon it. Do you like it, Kenneth? Isn't it adorable? Have you ever . . . What's the matter? Don't you like it?

PAULA. It's very pretty.

LEONIE. (*Overwhelmed by the inadequacy of this word.*) Pretty! Pretty! (*She hopes for more from* KENNETH.) Kenneth . . . ?

KENNETH. It's exquisite.

LEONIE. Isn't it? (*She whirls around in the dress.*) Isn't it? Yes. Exquisite. Can you imagine the scene? Can you imagine Granny walking down the aisle—and all the august spectators in mutton-chop whiskers and Prince Alberts? We've lost something these days—a good deal— oh, I don't miss the mutton-chops— but in ceremony, I mean—in punctilio and grace. . . .

PAULA. (*Cutting ruthlessly through the nostalgia.*) Mother!

LEONIE. What is it, Paula?

PAULA. Kenneth has something to tell you.

LEONIE. Kenneth?

PAULA. Yes. He has something to tell you.

LEONIE. Have you, Kenneth?

KENNETH. Yes.

LEONIE. What is it?

KENNETH. (*Quietly.*) I love Paula. I want to marry Paula. (*A pause. Granny's wedding dress droops.*)

LEONIE. Do you mean that, Kenneth?

KENNETH. Yes.

LEONIE. (*Piteously.*) This isn't very nice of you, Paula.

PAULA. I had nothing to do with it. I loathe Kenneth. But I wanted you to know him. Now you see him, Mother, your precious Lothario— there he is! Look at him!

LEONIE. These clothes are picturesque, but I think our modern ones are more comfortable. I think—I feel quite faint—isn't it ridiculous? (*She sways.*)

PAULA. I'm sorry, Mother. I had to. But I love you. I really do.

LEONIE. (*Very faint.*) Thank you, Paula.

PAULA. You'd better go up and lie down. I'll come to you in a moment.

LEONIE. Yes. I think I'd better. Yes. (*She begins to sob; she goes out, hiding her face in the lace folds of her dress.* PAULA, *having gone with her to the door, rings bell for* ROBERT, *turns to* KENNETH.)

PAULA. I suppose you're going to tell me this isn't cricket. Well, don't, because it will only make me laugh. To live up to a code with people like you is only to be weak and absurd.

KENNETH. (*His voice is low and even but tense with hate.*) You, Miss Frothingham, are my *last* miscalculation. I might even say my first. Fortunately, not irreparable! (ROBERT *enters.*)

PAULA. Robert.

ROBERT. Yes, Miss Frothingham.

PAULA. (*Still staring fixedly at* KENNETH.) Dr. Rice is leaving. Will you see that his bags are packed, please?

ROBERT. Yes, Miss. (*He goes out.*)

KENNETH. Forgive me—for having overestimated you. (*He goes out door right.* PAULA *comes slowly down and sits on sofa. She gets a reaction herself now from all she has been through; this game hasn't been natural to her; she is trembling physically; she is on the verge of tears.* WILL *comes in.*)

PAULA. Will—Will darling— (*She clings to* WILL.)

WILL. (*Worried.*) Paula!

PAULA. Put your arms around me, Will— hold me close— (WILL *obeys.*)

WILL. What's happened?

PAULA. I've tricked him. I made him say in front of Mother that he loved me, that he wanted to marry me. Poor Leonie! But it had to be done! And do you know, Will—at the end I felt—gosh, one has so many selves, Will. I must tell you—for the—

well, for the completeness of the record—

WILL. (*Curious.*) What?

PAULA. At the end I felt I had to do it—not only to save Leonie—but to save myself. Can you understand that? I felt horribly drawn to him, and by the sordid thing I was doing— But it's over. Thank God it's over. Will, darling, these six weeks have been hell without you. When I got your letter about Granny, I sat down and cried. I wanted to go right to New York to be with you. And yet I couldn't. How could I? But now, Will—I don't want to wait for you any longer. I've done what I can. It's cost me almost—Will—I need you terribly—

WILL. And I you, Paula. But listen, darling—I've decided during the weeks I've been away from you— I can't marry you now— I can't face what I'd become—

PAULA. But Will, I— (*Springing up.*) But Will, I'll give up the money. I'll live with you anywhere.

WILL. I know that, Paula. But I mustn't. You mustn't let me. I've thought it all out. You say you'd live with me anywhere. But what would happen? Supposing I didn't get a job? Would we starve? We'd take fifty dollars a week from your grandmother's estate. It would be foolish not to. Taking fifty, why not seventy-five? Why not two hundred? I can't let myself in for it, Paula. (*A long pause.*) Paula, darling—do you hate me?

PAULA. No.

WILL. Supposing you weren't rich? Is it a world in which, but for this, I'd have to sink? If it is, I'm going to damn well do what I can to change it. I don't have to scrabble for the inheritance of dead men. That's for Kenneth—one robber baron—after the lapse of several generations—succeeding another. I don't want this damn fortune to give me an unfair advantage over people as good as I am who haven't got it. (*Torn with pity for her.*) Paula—my dearest—what can I do?

PAULA. I see that you can't do anything. I quite see. Still—

WILL. I love you, Paula, and I'll be longing for you terribly, but I can't marry you—not till there's somebody for you to marry. When I've struck my stride, I won't care about Sam, or the money, or anything, because I'll be on my own. If you feel the way I do, you'll wait.

PAULA. (*Very still voice.*) Of course, Will. I'll wait.

WILL. (*Overcome with gratitude and emotion—seizes her in his arms passionately.*) Darling—darling— (LEONIE *comes in.* WILL, *overcome with emotion, goes out.*)

LEONIE. It's easy to say "lie down." But what happens then? Thoughts assail you. Thoughts . . .

PAULA. Mother . . .

LEONIE. Kenneth's going. He's leaving. I suppose you're happy. It's the end —the end of summer.

PAULA. (*Herself shaken with emotion.*) Mother— (*She wants to talk to* LEONIE, *to tell her what has happened, but* LEONIE *is lost in her own maze.*)

LEONIE. It's cold here. I hate this place. I'm going to sell it. (*She sits, in chair, right of fireplace.*) I've always wanted things around me to be gay and warm and happy. I've done my best. I must be wrong. Why do I find myself this way? With nothing. With nothing.

PAULA. (*Running to her mother and throwing herself on her knees beside her.*) Mother—Mother darling—

LEONIE. (*Not responding, reflectively.*) I suppose the thing about me that is wrong is that love is really all I care about. (*A moment's pause.*) I suppose I should have been interested in other things. Good works. Do they sustain you? But I couldn't somehow. I think when you're not in love—you're dead. Yes, that must be why I'm . . . (*Her voice trails off rather.* PAULA *drops her head in her mother's lap and begins to cry.*)

LEONIE. (*Surprised.*) Paula—what is it? What's the matter? Are you sorry? It's all right, child.

PAULA. (*Through her tears.*) It's Will—

LEONIE. Will?

PAULA. He's going away.

LEONIE. Why don't you go with him?

PAULA. He doesn't want me.

LEONIE. That's not true. It must be something else.

PAULA. The money.

LEONIE. Oh, the money. Yes, the money. The money won't do anything for you. It'll work against you. It's worked against me. It gives you the illusion of escape—but always you have to come back to yourself. At the end of every journey—you find yourself.

PAULA. What shall I do, Mother?

LEONIE. You and Will want the same things. In the end you will find them. But don't let him find them with someone else. Follow him. Be near him. When he is depressed and discouraged, let it be your hand that he touches, your face that he sees.

PAULA. (*Breathless.*) Mother—you're right—he told me last summer—"you must have a shoulder to lean on"—

LEONIE. Let it be your shoulder, Paula; follow him. Be near him.

PAULA. Thank you, Mother.

LEONIE. (*Ruefully.*) I am telling you what *I* should do. It must be bad advice.

PAULA. (*Gratefully.*) Darling! (DENNIS *and* WILL *come in.*)

DENNIS. Here you are! We're off to the boat! Thirty minutes! Why don't you and Paula come too? What do you say, Leonie?

LEONIE. You know, all these years I've been coming up here, and I've never been on the Bar Harbor boat.

DENNIS. It may be said, Mrs. Frothingham, if you have never been on the Bar Harbor boat, that you have not lived!

LEONIE. Really! I'd always heard it was poky.

DENNIS. Poky! The *Normandie* of the Kennebec poky! Mrs. Frothingham!

LEONIE. It's fun, is it? But doesn't it get into New York at some impossible hour?

DENNIS. At seven A.M.

LEONIE. Seven! (*She shudders.*)

DENNIS. (*The brisk executive.*) Seven! Yes, sir! At my desk at nine! All refreshed and co-ordinated and ready to attack my South American correspondence.

LEONIE. I must learn not to believe him, mustn't I?

DENNIS. I am my own master, Leonie. All day for nine mortal hours I grind out escape fiction for the pulp magazines. But one day I shall become famous and emerge into the slicks and then I doubt very much whether I shall come here.

LEONIE. I shall miss you.

DENNIS. Then I'll come.

LEONIE. I hate to have you go, Dennis. You cheer me up. Why don't you stay?

DENNIS. Impossible, Leonie. I must go to New York to launch the magazine. But for the moment, good-bye, Leonie. As a reward for your hospitality I shall send you the original copy of one of my stories. Would you like to escape from something?

LEONIE. (*Smiling wanly.*) I would indeed!

DENNIS. Think no more about it. You're as good as free. The story is yours, typed personally on my Underwood.

Those misplaced keys—those inaccuracies—how they will bemuse posterity! (*He goes out.*)

WILL. (*Awkwardly.*) Good-bye, Leonie.

LEONIE. Good-bye, Will. (*He goes out without looking at* PAULA. *In pantomime,* LEONIE *urges* PAULA *to go after him.* PAULA *kisses her quickly and runs out after* WILL. *Left alone,* LEONIE *walks to the chair in which her mother sat so often—she looks through the glowing autumn at the darkening sea.* KENNETH *comes in. There is a pause.*)

KENNETH. Leonie—

LEONIE. Yes, Kenneth.

KENNETH. I don't expect you to understand this. I shall not try to make you understand it.

LEONIE. Perhaps I'd better not.

KENNETH. Really I am amused at myself —highly entertained. That I should have almost had to practice on myself what hitherto I have reserved for my patients—that I who have made such a fetish of discipline and restraint so nearly succumbed to an inconsistency. I must revise my notion of myself.

LEONIE. And I too.

KENNETH. Why? Why you?

LEONIE. I seem to be a survival—Paula's directness—and your calculations— they are beyond me.

KENNETH. Nevertheless, it's curious how you and Paula are alike—no wonder that, for a moment at least, you seemed to me—interchangeable.

LEONIE. Did you know it from the beginning—that it was Paula?

KENNETH. I was attracted by her resemblance to you—for exercising this attraction I hated her. She felt it too— from the beginning and she must have hated me from the beginning. Between us there grew up this strange, unnatural antagonism—

LEONIE. What?

KENNETH. This fused emotion of love and hate. It had to be brought out into the open. It's a familiar psychosis—

the unconscious desire of the daughter to triumph over the mother.

LEONIE. But I don't understand—

KENNETH. There is so much in these intricate relationships that the layman can't understand—

LEONIE. You mean that you—felt nothing for Paula?

KENNETH. No, I don't mean that at all. But I saw that what I felt for her was some twisted reflection of what I felt for you. And I saw there was only one way out of it—to let her triumph over you. I told her that I loved her. But this was not enough. I must repeat it in front of you. You must witness her triumph. I made it possible. I gave her her great moment. Well, you see what it's done. It freed her so beautifully that she was able to go to Will. They've gone away together. Perfect cure for her as well as for myself. (*A moment's pause.*)

LEONIE. It all sounds almost too perfect, Kenneth.

KENNETH. I said I didn't expect you to understand it—you have lived always on your emotions. You have never bothered to delve beneath them. You are afraid to, aren't you?

LEONIE. I know this, Kenneth. I heard you say that you loved Paula. I heard your voice. No, I can't accept this, Kenneth! It's not good enough. I've never done that before. I'd only think now that everything you did, everything you said, was to cover what you felt. And I'd end by telling myself that I believed you. I'd end by taking second best from you. No, I must guard myself from that. I felt this a month ago—that's why I sent for Will.

KENNETH. Some day, Leonie, you will learn that feeling is not enough.

LEONIE. But I trust my instinct, Kenneth.

KENNETH. That, Leonie, is your most adorable trait—

LEONIE. What?

KENNETH. That trust—that innocence. If

it weren't for that, you wouldn't be you—and everyone wouldn't love you—

LEONIE. Oh, no, Kenneth— (DENNIS *comes in.*)

DENNIS. Oh, excuse me. But I left my brief-case. Oh, here it is. (*He picks it up.*) Without my brief-case I am a man without a Destiny. With it I am—

KENNETH. A man with a brief-case.

LEONIE. (*Crossing rather desperately to* DENNIS—*this straw in the current.*) What's in it—your stories?

DENNIS. Stories—no, that wouldn't matter. I am fertile; I can spawn stories. But the plans for the magazine are in here—the future of Young America is here—

LEONIE. Will you stay and have a whiskey and soda?

DENNIS. Thanks, but if I do, I shall miss the boat.

LEONIE. Suppose you do?

KENNETH. Leonie—that would delay the millennium one day.

DENNIS. The doctor's right. That would be selfish.

LEONIE. Be selfish. Please stay.

DENNIS. No. Once you are enlisted in a cause, you can't live a personal life. It is a dedication.

LEONIE. Kenneth is leaving. I shall be lonely, Dennis. I can't bear to be alone.

KENNETH. Your need for people is poignant, isn't it, Leonie?

LEONIE. Stay for dinner. After dinner we can talk about your magazine.

DENNIS. Oh, well—that makes it possible for me to stay. Thank you, Kenneth. (*He goes to sofa, sits, busying himself with brief-case.*) (*She goes to console to make highball.*)

KENNETH. Send me your magazine, Dennis. I shall be honored to be the first subscriber.

DENNIS. I'll be glad to. Your patients can read it in the waiting-room instead of the *National Geographic.*

KENNETH. Your first subscriber—and very possibly your last. (*He crosses to door and turns back.*) Good-bye, Leonie. Good luck, Dennis. We who are about to retire—salute you. (*She does not look at him. He bows formally to* DENNIS's *back, makes a gesture of "good luck" and exits.*)

DENNIS. Trouble with that fellow is—he lives for himself. No larger interest. That's what dignifies human beings, Leonie—a dedication to something greater than themselves.

LEONIE. (*Coming down to hand him his highball.*) Yes? Here's your whiskey and soda. I envy you, Dennis. I wish I could dedicate myself to something—something outside myself.

DENNIS. (*Rising to sit beside her.*) Well, here's your opportunity, Leonie—it's providential. You couldn't do better than this magazine. It would give you a new interest—impersonal. It would emancipate you, Leonie. It would be a perpetual dedication to Youth—to the hope of the world. The world is middle-aged and tired. But we—

LEONIE. (*Wistfully.*) Can you refresh us, Dennis?

DENNIS. Refresh you? Leonie, we can rejuvenate you!

LEONIE. (*Grateful there is some one there —another human being she can laugh with.*) That's an awfully amusing idea. You make me laugh.

DENNIS. (*Eagerly selling the idea.*) In the youth of any country, there is an immense potentiality—

LEONIE. You're awfully serious about it, aren't you, Dennis?

DENNIS. Where the magazine is concerned, Leonie, I am a fanatic.

LEONIE. I suppose if it's really successful —it'll result in my losing everything I have—

DENNIS. It'll be taken from you anyway. You'll only be anticipating the inevitable.

LEONIE. Why—how clever of me!

DENNIS. Not only clever but grateful.

LEONIE. Will you leave me just a little to live on—?

DENNIS. Don't worry about that—come the Revolution—you'll have a friend in high office. (LEONIE *accepts grate-fully this earnest of security. They touch glasses in a toast as the curtain falls.*)

1936

JOHN GALSWORTHY

Strife

CHARACTERS

JOHN ANTHONY, *Chairman of the Trenartha Tin Plate Works.*

EDGAR ANTHONY, *his son,*
FREDERIC H. WILDER,　　　*Directors*
WILLIAM SCANTLEBURY,　　*of the same.*
OLIVER WANKLIN,

HENRY TENCH, *Secretary of the same.*

FRANCIS UNDERWOOD, C. E., *Manager of the same.*

SIMON HARNESS, *a Trades Union official.*

DAVID ROBERTS,
JAMES GREEN,
JOHN BULGIN,　　*the workmen's committee.*
HENRY THOMAS,
GEORGE ROUS,

HENRY ROUS,
LEWIS,
JAGO,　　　　　　*workmen at*
EVANS,　　　　　　*the Trenartha*
A BLACKSMITH,　　*Tin Plate*
DAVIES,　　　　　　*Works.*
A RED-HAIRED YOUTH,
BROWN,

FROST, *valet to John Anthony.*

ENID UNDERWOOD, *wife of Francis Underwood, daughter of John Anthony.*

ANNIE ROBERTS, *wife of David Roberts.*

MADGE THOMAS, *daughter of Henry Thomas.*

MRS. ROUS, *mother of George and Henry Rous.*

MRS. BULGIN, *wife of John Bulgin.*

MRS. YEO, *wife of a workman.*

A PARLORMAID *to the Underwoods.*

JAN, *Madge's brother, a boy of ten.*

A CROWD OF MEN ON STRIKE.

The action takes place on February 7th between the hours of noon and six in the afternoon, close to the Trenartha Tin Plate Works, on the borders of England and Wales, where a strike has been in progress throughout the winter.
ACT I. The dining-room of the Manager's house.
ACT II. SCENE I. The kitchen of the Roberts' cottage near the works.
　　SCENE II. A space outside the works.
ACT III. The drawing-room of the Manager's house.

ACT I

It is noon. In the Underwoods' dining-room a bright fire is burning. On one side of the fireplace are double-doors leading to the drawing-room, on the other side a door leading to the hall. In the center of the room a long dining-table without a cloth is set out as a Board table. At the head of it, in the Chairman's seat, sits JOHN ANTHONY, *an old man, big, clean-shaven, and high-colored, with thick white hair, and thick dark eyebrows. His movements are rather slow and feeble, but his eyes are very much alive. There is a glass of water by his side. On his right sits his son* EDGAR, *an earnest-looking man of thirty, reading a newspaper. Next him* WANKLIN, *a man with jutting eye-brows and silver-streaked light hair, is bending over transfer papers.* TENCH, *the Secretary, a short and rather humble, nervous man, with side whiskers, stands helping him. On* WANKLIN'S *right sits* UNDERWOOD, *the Manager, a quiet man, with a long, stiff jaw, and steady eyes. Back to the fire is* SCANTLEBURY, *a very large, pale, sleepy man, with gray hair, rather bald. Between him and the Chairman are two empty chairs.*

WILDER. (*Who is lean, cadaverous, and complaining, with drooping gray mustaches, stands before the fire.*) I say, this fire's the devil! Can I have a screen, Tench?

SCANTLEBURY. A screen, ah!

TENCH. Certainly, Mr. Wilder. (*He looks at* UNDERWOOD.) That is—perhaps the Manager—perhaps Mr. Underwood——

SCANTLEBURY. These fireplaces of yours, Underwood——

UNDERWOOD. (*Roused from studying some papers.*) A screen? Rather! I'm sorry. (*He goes to the door with a little smile.*) We're not accustomed to complaints of too much fire down here just now.

(*He speaks as though he holds a pipe between his teeth, slowly, ironically.*)

WILDER. (*In an injured voice.*) You mean the men. H'm! (UNDERWOOD *goes out.*)

SCANTLEBURY. Poor devils!

WILDER. It's their own fault, Scantlebury.

EDGAR. (*Holding out his paper.*) There's great distress among them, according to the *Trenartha News.*

WILDER. Oh, that rag! Give it to Wanklin. Suit his Radical views. They call us monsters, I suppose. The editor of that rubbish ought to be shot.

EDGAR. (*Reading.*) "If the Board of worthy gentlemen who control the Trenartha Tin Plate Works from their arm-chairs in London would condescend to come and see for

themselves the conditions prevailing amongst their workpeople during this strike——"

WILDER. Well, we *have* come.

EDGAR. (*Continuing.*) "We cannot believe that even their leg-of-mutton hearts would remain untouched."

(WANKLIN *takes the paper from him.*)

WILDER. Ruffian! I remember that fellow when he hadn't a penny to his name; little snivel of a chap that's made his way by blackguarding everybody who takes a different view to himself.

(ANTHONY *says something that is not heard.*)

WILDER. What does your father say?

EDGAR. He says "The kettle and the pot."

WILDER. H'm!

(*He sits down next to* SCANTLEBURY.)

SCANTLEBURY. (*Blowing out his cheeks.*) I shall boil if I don't get that screen.

(UNDERWOOD *and* ENID *enter with a screen, which they place before the fire.* ENID *is tall; she has a small, decided face, and is twenty-eight years old.*)

ENID. Put it closer, Frank. Will that do, Mr. Wilder? It's the highest we've got.

WILDER. Thanks, capitally.

SCANTLEBURY. (*Turning, with a sigh of pleasure.*) Ah! Merci, Madame!

ENID. Is there anything else you want, Father? (ANTHONY *shakes his head.*) Edgar—anything?

EDGAR. You might give me a "J" nib, old girl.

ENID. There are some down there by Mr. Scantlebury.

SCANTLEBURY. (*Handing a little box of nibs.*) Ah! your brother uses "J's." What does the manager use? (*With expansive politeness.*) What does your husband use, Mrs. Underwood?

UNDERWOOD. A quill!

SCANTLEBURY. The homely product of the goose. (*He holds out quills.*)

UNDERWOOD. (*Drily.*) Thanks, if you can spare me one. (*He takes a quill.*) What about lunch, Enid?

ENID. (*Stopping at the double-doors and looking back.*) We're going to have lunch here, in the drawing-room, so you needn't hurry with your meeting.

(WANKLIN *and* WILDER *bow, and she goes out.*)

SCANTLEBURY. (*Rousing himself, suddenly.*) Ah! Lunch! That hotel —— Dreadful! Did you try the white-bait last night? Fried fat!

WILDER. Past twelve! Aren't you going to read the minutes, Tench?

TENCH. (*Looking for the* CHAIRMAN'S *assent, reads in a rapid and monotonous voice.*) "At a Board Meeting held the 31st of January at the Company's Offices, 512 Cannon Street, E. C. Present—Mr. Anthony in the chair, Messrs. F. H. Wilder, William Scantlebury, Oliver Wanklin, and Edgar Anthony. Read letters from the Manager dated January 20th, 23d, 25th, 28th, relative to the strike at the Company's Works. Read letters to the Manager of January 21st, 24th, 26th, 29th. Read letter from Mr. Simon Harness, of the Central Union, asking for an interview with the Board. Read letters from the Men's Committee, signed David Roberts, James Green, John Bulgin, Henry Thomas, George Rous, desiring conference with the Board; and it was resolved that a special Board Meeting be called for February 7th at the house of the Manager, for the purpose of discussing the situation with Mr. Simon Harness and the Men's Committee on the spot. Passed twelve transfers, signed and sealed nine certificates and one balance certificate."

(*He pushes the book over to the* CHAIRMAN.)

ANTHONY. (*With a heavy sigh.*) If it's your pleasure, sign the same.

(*He signs, moving the pen with difficulty.*)

WANKLIN. What's the Union's game, Tench? They haven't made up their split with the men. What does Harness want this interview for?

TENCH. Hoping we shall come to a compromise, I think, sir; he's having a meeting with the men this afternoon.

WILDER. Harness! Ah! He's one of those cold-blooded, cool-headed chaps. I distrust them. I don't know that we didn't make a mistake to come down. What time'll the men be here?

UNDERWOOD. Any time now.

WILDER. Well, if we're not ready, they'll have to wait—won't do them any harm to cool their heels a bit.

SCANTLEBURY. (*Slowly.*) Poor devils! It's snowing. *What* weather!

UNDERWOOD. (*With meaning slowness.*) This house'll be the warmest place they've been in this winter.

WILDER. Well, I hope we're going to settle this business in time for me to catch the 6:30. I've got to take my wife to Spain tomorrow. (*Chattily.*) My old father had a strike at his works in '69; just such a February as this. They wanted to shoot him.

WANKLIN. What! In the close season?

WILDER. By George, there was no close season for employers then! He used to go down to his office with a pistol in his pocket.

SCANTLEBURY. (*Faintly alarmed.*) Not seriously?

WILDER. (*With finality.*) Ended in his shootin' one of 'em in the legs.

SCANTLEBURY. (*Unavoidably feeling his thigh.*) No? Which?

ANTHONY. (*Lifting the agenda paper.*) To consider the policy of the Board in relation to the strike. (*There is a silence.*)

WILDER. It's this infernal three-cornered duel—the Union, the men, and ourselves.

WANKLIN. We needn't consider the Union.

WILDER. It's my experience that you've always got to consider the Union, confound them! If the Union were going to withdraw their support from the men, as they've done, why did they ever allow them to strike at all?

EDGAR. We've had that over a dozen times.

WILDER. Well, I've never understood it! It's beyond me. They talk of the engineers' and furnacemen's demands being excessive—so they are—but that's not enough to make the Union withdraw their support. What's behind it?

UNDERWOOD. Fear of strikes at Harper's and Tinewell's.

WILDER. (*With triumph.*) Afraid of other strikes—now, that's a reason! Why couldn't we have been told that before?

UNDERWOOD. You were.

TENCH. You were absent from the Board that day, sir.

SCANTLEBURY. The men must have seen they had no chance when the Union gave them up. It's madness.

UNDERWOOD. It's Roberts!

WILDER. Just our luck, the men finding a fanatical firebrand like Roberts for leader. (*A pause.*)

WANKLIN. (*Looking at* ANTHONY.) Well?

WILDER. (*Breaking in fussily.*) It's a regular mess. I don't like the position we're in; I don't like it; I've said so for a long time. (*Looking at* WANKLIN.) When Wanklin and I came down here before Christmas it looked as if the men must collapse. You thought so too, Underwood.

UNDERWOOD. Yes.

WILDER. Well, they haven't! Here we are, going from bad to worse—losing our customers—shares going down!

SCANTLEBURY. (*Shaking his head.*) M'm! M'm!

WANKLIN. What loss have we made by this strike, Tench?

TENCH. Over fifty thousand, sir!

SCANTLEBURY. (*Pained.*) You don't say!

WILDER. We shall never get it back.

TENCH. No, sir.

WILDER. Who'd have supposed the men were going to stick out like this—

nobody suggested that. (*Looking angrily at* TENCH.)

SCANTLEBURY. (*Shaking his head.*) I've never liked a fight—never shall.

ANTHONY. No surrender! (*All look at him.*)

WILDER. Who wants to surrender? (ANTHONY *looks at him.*) I—I want to act reasonably. When the men sent Roberts up to the Board in December —then was the time. We ought to have humored him; instead of that the Chairman—(*Dropping his eyes before* ANTHONY's)—er—we snapped his head off. We could have got them in then by a little tact.

ANTHONY. No compromise!

WILDER. There we are! This strike's been going on now since October, and as far as I can see it may last another six months. Pretty mess we shall be in by then. The only comfort is, the men'll be in a worse!

EDGAR. (*To* UNDERWOOD.) What sort of state are they really in, Frank?

UNDERWOOD. (*Without expression.*) Damnable!

WILDER. Well, who on earth would have thought they'd have held on like this without support!

UNDERWOOD. Those who know them.

WILDER. I defy anyone to know them! And what about tin? Price going up daily. When we do get started we shall have to work off our contracts at the top of the market.

WANKLIN. What do you say to that, Chairman?

ANTHONY. Can't be helped!

WILDER. Shan't pay a dividend till goodness knows when!

SCANTLEBURY. (*With emphasis.*) We ought to think of the shareholders. (*Turning heavily.*) Chairman, I say we ought to think of the shareholders. (ANTHONY *mutters.*)

SCANTLEBURY. What's that?

TENCH. The Chairman says he *is* thinking of you, sir.

SCANTLEBURY. (*Sinking back into torpor.*) Cynic!

WILDER. It's past a joke. *I* don't want to go without a dividend for years if the Chairman does. We can't go on playing ducks and drakes with the Company's prosperity.

EDGAR. (*Rather ashamedly.*) I think we ought to consider the men.

(*All but* ANTHONY *fidget in their seats.*)

SCANTLEBURY. (*With a sigh.*) We mustn't think of our private feelings, young man. That'll never do.

EDGAR. (*Ironically.*) I'm not thinking of our feelings. I'm thinking of the men's.

WILDER. As to that—we're men of business.

WANKLIN. That *is* the little trouble.

EDGAR. There's no necessity for pushing things so far in the face of all this suffering—it's—it's cruel.

(*No one speaks, as though* EDGAR *had uncovered something whose existence no man prizing his self-respect could afford to recognize.*)

WANKLIN. (*With an ironical smile.*) I'm afraid we mustn't base our policy on luxuries like sentiment.

EDGAR. I detest this state of things.

ANTHONY. We didn't seek the quarrel.

EDGAR. I know that, sir, but surely we've gone far enough.

ANTHONY. No. (*All look at one another.*)

WANKLIN. Luxuries apart, Chairman, we must look out what we're doing.

ANTHONY. Give way to the men once and there'll be no end to it.

WANKLIN. I quite agree, but——

(ANTHONY *shakes his head.*) You make it a question of bedrock principle? (ANTHONY *nods.*) Luxuries again, Chairman! The shares are below par.

WILDER. Yes, and they'll drop to a half when we pass the next dividend.

SCANTLEBURY. (*With alarm.*) Come, come! Not so bad as that.

WILDER. (*Grimly.*) You'll see! (*Craning forward to catch* ANTHONY's *speech.*) I didn't catch——

TENCH. (*Hesitating.*) The Chairman says, sir, "Fais que—que—devra——"

EDGAR. (*Sharply.*) My father says: "Do what we ought—and let things rip."

WILDER. Tcha!

SCANTLEBURY. (*Throwing up his hands.*) The Chairman's a Stoic—I always said the Chairman was a Stoic.

WILDER. Much good that'll do us.

WANKLIN. (*Suavely.*) Seriously, Chairman, are you going to let the ship sink under you, for the sake of—a principle?

ANTHONY. She won't sink.

SCANTLEBURY. (*With alarm.*) Not while I'm on the Board, I hope.

ANTHONY. (*With a twinkle.*) Better rat, Scantlebury.

SCANTLEBURY. What a man!

ANTHONY. I've always fought them; I've never been beaten yet.

WANKLIN. We're with you in theory, Chairman. But we're not all made of cast-iron.

ANTHONY. We've only to hold on.

WILDER. (*Rising and going to the fire.*) And go to the devil as fast as we can!

ANTHONY. Better go to the devil than give in!

WILDER. (*Fretfully.*) That may suit you, sir, but it doesn't suit me, or anyone else, I should think. (ANTHONY *looks him in the face—a silence.*)

EDGAR. I don't see how we can get over it that to go on like this means starvation to the men's wives and families.

(WILDER *turns abruptly to the fire, and* SCANTLEBURY *puts out a hand to push the idea away.*)

WANKLIN. I'm afraid again that sounds a little sentimental.

EDGAR. Men of business are excused from decency, you think?

WILDER. Nobody's more sorry for the men than I am, but if they (*lashing himself*) choose to be such a pig-headed lot, it's nothing to do with us; we've quite enough on *our* hands to think of ourselves and the shareholders.

EDGAR. (*Irritably.*) It won't kill the shareholders to miss a dividend or two; I don't see that *that's* reason enough for knuckling under.

SCANTLEBURY. (*With grave discomfort.*) You talk very lightly of your dividends, young man; I don't know where we are.

WILDER. There's only one sound way of looking at it. We can't go on ruining *ourselves* with this strike.

ANTHONY. No caving in!

SCANTLEBURY. (*With a gesture of despair.*) Look at him!

(ANTHONY *is leaning back in his chair. They do look at him.*)

WILDER. (*Returning to his seat.*) Well, all I can say is, if that's the Chairman's view, I don't know what we've come down here for.

ANTHONY. To tell the men that we've got nothing for them— (*Grimly.*) They won't believe it till they hear it spoken in plain English.

WILDER. H'm! Shouldn't be a bit surprised if that brute Roberts hadn't got us down here with the very same idea. I hate a man with a grievance.

EDGAR. (*Resentfully.*) We didn't pay him enough for his discovery. I always said that at the time.

WILDER. We paid him five hundred and a bonus of two hundred three years later. If that's not enough! What does he want, for goodness' sake?

TENCH. (*Complainingly.*) Company made a hundred thousand out of his brains, and paid him seven hundred—that's the way he goes on, sir.

WILDER. The man's a rank agitator! Look here, I hate the Unions. But now we've got Harness here let's get him to settle the whole thing.

ANTHONY. No! (*Again they look at him.*)

UNDERWOOD. Roberts won't let the men assent to that.

SCANTLEBURY. Fanatic! Fanatic!

WILDER. (*Looking at* ANTHONY.) And not the only one! (*Frost enters from the hall.*)

FROST. (*To* ANTHONY.) Mr. Harness from the Union, waiting, sir. The men are here too, sir.

(ANTHONY *nods.* UNDERWOOD *goes to the door, returning with* HARNESS, *a pale, clean-shaven man with hollow cheeks, quick eyes, and lantern jaw*—FROST *has retired.*)

UNDERWOOD. (*Pointing to* TENCH's *chair.*) Sit there next to the Chairman, Harness, won't you?

(*At* HARNESS's *appearance, the Board have drawn together, as it were, and turned a little to him, like cattle at a dog.*)

HARNESS. (*With a sharp look around, and a bow.*) Thanks! (*He sits—his accent is slightly nasal.*) Well, gentlemen, we're going to do business at last, I hope.

WILDER. Depends on what you *call* business, Harness. Why don't you make the men come in?

HARNESS. (*Sardonically.*) The men are far more in the right than you are. The question with us is whether we shan't begin to support them again.

(*He ignores them all, except* ANTHONY, *to whom he turns in speaking.*)

ANTHONY. Support them if you like; we'll put in free labor and have done with it.

HARNESS. That won't do, Mr. Anthony. You can't get free labor, and you know it.

ANTHONY. We shall see that.

HARNESS. I'm quite frank with you. We were forced to withhold our support from your men because some of their demands are in excess of current rates. I expect to make them withdraw those demands today: if they do, take it straight from me, gentlemen, we shall back them again at once. Now, I want to see something fixed upon before I go back tonight. Can't we have done with this old-fashioned tug-of-war business? What good's it doing you? Why don't you recognize once for all that these people are men like yourselves, and want what's good for them just as you want what's good for you— (*Bitterly.*) Your motor-cars, and champagne, and eight-course dinners.

ANTHONY. If the men will come in, we'll do something for them.

HARNESS. (*Ironically.*) Is that your opinion too, sir—and yours—and yours? (*The Directors do not answer.*) Well, all I can say is: It's a kind of high and mighty aristocratic tone I thought we'd grown out of—seems I was mistaken.

ANTHONY. It's the tone the men use. Remains to be seen which can hold out longest—they without us, or we without them.

HARNESS. As business men, I wonder you're not ashamed of this waste of force, gentlemen. You know what it'll all end in.

ANTHONY. What?

HARNESS. Compromise—it always does.

SCANTLEBURY. Can't you persuade the men that their interests are the same as ours?

HARNESS. (*Turning, ironically.*) I could persuade them of that, sir, if they were.

WILDER. Come, Harness, you're a clever man, you don't believe all the Socialistic claptrap that's talked nowadays. There's no real difference between their interests and ours.

HARNESS. There's just one very simple question I'd like to put to you. Will you pay your men one penny more than they force you to pay them? (*WILDER is silent.*)

WANKLIN. (*Chiming in.*) I humbly thought that not to pay more than was necessary was the A B C of commerce.

HARNESS. (*With irony.*) Yes, that seems to be the A B C of commerce, sir; and the A B C of commerce is between your interests and the men's.

SCANTLEBURY. (*Whispering.*) We ought to arrange something.

HARNESS. (*Drily.*) Am I to understand then, gentlemen, that your Board is going to make no concessions?

(WANKLIN *and* WILDER *bend forward as if to speak, but stop.*)

ANTHONY. (*Nodding.*) None.

(WANKLIN *and* WILDER *again bend forward, and* SCANTLEBURY *gives an unexpected grunt.*)

HARNESS. You were about to say something, I believe? (*But* SCANTLEBURY *says nothing.*)

EDGAR. (*Looking up suddenly.*) We're sorry for the state of the men.

HARNESS. (*Icily.*) The men have no use for your pity, sir. What they want is justice.

ANTHONY. Then let *them* be just.

HARNESS. For that word "just" read "humble," Mr. Anthony. Why should they be humble? Barring the accident of money, aren't they as good men as you?

ANTHONY. Cant!

HARNESS. Well, I've been five years in America. It colors a man's notions.

SCANTLEBURY. (*Suddenly, as though avenging his uncompleted grunt.*) Let's have the men in and hear what they've got to say!

(ANTHONY *nods, and* UNDERWOOD *goes out by the single door.*)

HARNESS. (*Drily.*) As I'm to have an interview with them this afternoon, gentlemen, I'll ask you to postpone your final decision till that's over.

(*Again* ANTHONY *nods, and taking up his glass drinks.*)

(UNDERWOOD *comes in again, followed by* ROBERTS, GREEN, BULGIN, THOMAS, ROUS. *They file in, hat in hand, and stand silent in a row.* ROBERTS *is lean, of middle height, with a slight stoop. He has a little rat-gnawn, brown-gray beard, mustaches, high cheek-bones, hollow cheeks, small fiery eyes. He wears an old and grease-stained blue serge suit, and carries an old bowler hat. He stands nearest the Chair-*

man. GREEN, *next to him, has a clean, worn face, with a small gray goatee beard and drooping mustaches, iron spectacles, and mild, straightforward eyes. He wears an overcoat, green with age, and a linen collar. Next to him is* BULGIN, *a tall, strong man, with a dark mustache, and fighting jaw, wearing a red muffler, who keeps changing his cap from one hand to the other. Next to him is* THOMAS, *an old man with a gray mustache, full beard, and weatherbeaten, bony face, whose overcoat discloses a lean, plucky-looking neck. On his right,* ROUS, *the youngest of the five, looks like a soldier; he has a glitter in his eyes.*)

UNDERWOOD. (*Pointing.*) There are some chairs there against the wall, Roberts; won't you draw them up and sit down?

ROBERTS. Thank you, Mr. Underwood— we'll stand—in the presence of the Board. (*He speaks in a biting and staccato voice, rolling his r's, pronouncing his a's like an Italian a, and his consonants short and crisp.*) How are you, Mr. Harness? Didn't expect t' have the pleasure of seeing you till this afternoon.

HARNESS. (*Steadily.*) We shall meet again then, Roberts.

ROBERTS. Glad to hear that; we shall have some news for you to take to your people.

ANTHONY. What do the men want?

ROBERTS. (*Acidly.*) Beg pardon, I don't quite catch the Chairman's remark.

TENCH. (*From behind the Chairman's chair.*) The Chairman wishes to know what the men have to say.

ROBERTS. It's what the Board has to say we've come to hear. It's for the Board to speak first.

ANTHONY. The Board has nothing to say.

ROBERTS. (*Looking along the line of men.*) In that case we're wasting the Directors' time. We'll be taking our feet off this pretty carpet.

(*He turns, the men move slowly, as though hypnotically influenced.*)

WANKLIN. (*Suavely.*) Come, Roberts, you didn't give us this long cold journey for the pleasure of saying that.

THOMAS. (*A pure Welshman.*) No, sir, an' what I say iss——

ROBERTS. (*Bitingly.*) Go on, Henry Thomas, go on. You're better able to speak to the—Directors than me. (THOMAS *is silent.*)

TENCH. The Chairman means, Roberts, that it was the men who asked for the conference; the Board wish to hear what they have to say.

ROBERTS. Gad! If I was to begin to tell ye all they have to say, I wouldn't be finished today. And there'd be some that'd wish they'd never left their London palaces.

HARNESS. What's your proposition, man? Be reasonable.

ROBERTS. You want reason, Mr. Harness? Take a look round this afternoon before the meeting. (*He looks at the men; no sound escapes them.*) You'll see some very pretty scenery.

HARNESS. All right, my friend; you won't put me off.

ROBERTS. (*To the men.*) We shan't put Mr. Harness off. Have some champagne with your lunch, Mr. Harness; you'll want it, sir.

HARNESS. Come, get to business, man!

THOMAS. What we're asking, look you, is just simple justice.

ROBERTS. (*Venomously.*) Justice from London? What are you talking about, Henry Thomas? Have you gone silly? (THOMAS *is silent.*) We know very well what we are— discontented dogs—never satisfied. What did the Chairman tell me up in London? That I didn't know what I was talking about. I was a foolish, uneducated man, that knew nothing of the wants of the men I spoke for.

EDGAR. Do please keep to the point.

ANTHONY. (*Holding up his hand.*) There can only be one master, Roberts.

ROBERTS. Then, be Gad, it'll be us.

(*There is a silence;* ANTHONY *and* ROBERTS *stare at one another.*)

UNDERWOOD. If you've nothing to say to the Directors, Roberts, perhaps you'll let Green or Thomas speak for the men.

(GREEN *and* THOMAS *look anxiously at* ROBERTS, *at each other, and the other men.*)

GREEN. (*An Englishman.*) If I'd been listened to, gentlemen——

THOMAS. What I'fe got to say iss what we'fe all got to say——

ROBERTS. Speak for yourself, Henry Thomas.

SCANTLEBURY. (*With a gesture of deep spiritual discomfort.*) Let the poor men call their souls their own!

ROBERTS. Aye, they shall keep their souls, for it's not much body that you've left them, Mr. (*with biting emphasis, as though the word were an offense*) Scantlebury! (*To the men.*) Well, will you speak, or shall I speak for you?

ROUS. (*Suddenly.*) Speak out, Roberts, or leave it to others.

ROBERTS. (*Ironically.*) Thank you, George Rous. (*Addressing himself to* ANTHONY.) The Chairman and Board of Directors have honored us by leaving London and coming all this way to hear what we've got to say; it would not be polite to keep them any longer waiting.

WILDER. Well, thank God for that!

ROBERTS. Ye will not dare to thank Him when I have done, Mr. Wilder, for all your piety. Maybe your God up in London has no time to listen to the working man. I'm told He is a wealthy God; but if He listens to what I tell Him, He will know more than ever He learned in Kensington.

HARNESS. Come, Roberts, you have your own God. Respect the God of other men.

ROBERTS. That's right, sir. We have another God down here; I doubt He is rather different to Mr. Wilder's. Ask Henry Thomas; he will tell you whether his God and Mr. Wilder's are the same.

(THOMAS *lifts his hand, and cranes his head as though to prophesy.*)

WANKLIN. For goodness' sake, let's keep to the point, Roberts.

ROBERTS. I rather think it is the point, Mr. Wanklin. If you can get the God of Capital to walk through the streets of Labor, and pay attention to what he sees, you're a brighter man than I take you for, for all that you're a Radical.

ANTHONY. Attend to me, Roberts! (ROBERTS *is silent.*) You are here to speak for the men, as I am here to speak for the Board. (*He looks slowly round.*)

(WILDER, WANKLIN, *and* SCANTLEBURY *make movements of uneasiness, and* EDGAR *gazes at the floor. A faint smile comes on* HARNESS's *face.*)

Now then, what is it?

ROBERTS. Right, sir!

(*Throughout all that follows, he and* ANTHONY *look fixedly upon each other. Men and Directors show in their various ways suppressed uneasiness, as though listening to words that they themselves would not have spoken.*)

The men can't afford to travel up to London; and they don't trust you to believe what they say in black and white. They know what the post is (*he darts a look at* UNDERWOOD *and* TENCH), and what Directors' meetings are: "Refer it to the manager—let the manager advise us on the men's condition. Can we squeeze them a little more?"

UNDERWOOD. (*In a low voice.*) Don't hit below the belt, Roberts!

ROBERTS. Is it below the belt, Mr. Underwood? The men know. When I came up to London, I told you the position straight. An' what came of it? I was told I didn't know what I was talkin' about. I can't afford to travel up to London to be told that again.

ANTHONY. What have you to say for the men?

ROBERTS. I have this to say—and first as to their condition. Ye shall 'ave no need to go and ask your manager. Ye can't squeeze them any more. Every man of us is well-nigh starving. (*A surprised murmur rises from the men.* ROBERTS *looks round.*) Ye wonder why I tell ye that? Every man of us is going short. We can't be no worse off than we've been these weeks past. Ye needn't think that by waiting ye'll drive us to come in. We'll die first, the whole lot of us. The men have sent for ye to know, once and for all, whether ye are going to grant them their demands. I see the sheet of paper in the Secretary's hand. (TENCH *moves nervously.*) That's it, I think, Mr. Tench. It's not very large.

TENCH. (*Nodding.*) Yes.

ROBERTS. There's not one sentence of writing on that paper that we can do without.

(*A movement amongst the men.* ROBERTS *turns on them sharply.*)

Isn't that so?

(*The men assent reluctantly.* ANTHONY *takes from* TENCH *the paper and peruses it.*)

Not one single sentence. All those demands are fair. We have not asked anything that we are not entitled to ask. What I said up in London, I say again now: there is not anything on that piece of paper that a just man should not ask, and a just man give. (*A pause.*)

ANTHONY. There is not one single demand on this paper that we will grant.

(*In the stir that follows on these words,* ROBERTS *watches the Directors and* ANTHONY *the men.* WILDER *gets up abruptly and goes over to the fire.*)

ROBERTS. D'ye mean that?

ANTHONY. I do.

(WILDER *at the fire makes an emphatic movement of disgust.*)

ROBERTS. (*Noting it, with dry intensity.*) Ye best know whether the condition of the Company is any better than the condition of the men. (*Scanning the Directors' faces.*) Ye best know whether you can afford your tyranny —but this I tell ye: if ye think the men will give way the least part of an inch, ye're making the worst mistake ye ever made. (*He fixes his eyes on* SCANTLEBURY.) Ye think because the Union is not supporting us—more shame to it!—that we'll be coming on our knees to you one fine morning. Ye think because the men have got their wives an' families to think of— that it's just a question of a week or two——

ANTHONY. It would be better if you did not speculate so much on what we think.

ROBERTS. Aye! It's not much profit to us! I will say this for you, Mr. Anthony— ye know your own mind! (*Staring at* ANTHONY.) I can reckon on ye!

ANTHONY. (*Ironically.*) I am obliged to you!

ROBERTS. And I know mine. I tell ye this: The men will send their wives and families where the country will have to keep them; an' they will starve sooner than give way. I advise ye, Mr. Anthony, to prepare yourself for the worst that can happen to your Company. We are not so ignorant as you might suppose. We know the way the cat is jumping. Your position is not all that it might be—not exactly!

ANTHONY. Be good enough to allow us to judge of our position for ourselves. Go back, and reconsider your own.

ROBERTS. (*Stepping forward.*) Mr. Anthony, you are not a young man now; from the time I remember anything ye have been an enemy to every man that has come into your works. I don't say that ye're a mean man, or a cruel man, but ye've grudged them the say of any word in their own fate.

Ye've fought them down four times. I've heard ye say ye love a fight— mark my words—ye're fighting the last fight ye'll ever fight——

(TENCH *touches* ROBERTS's *sleeve.*)

UNDERWOOD. Roberts! Roberts!

ROBERTS. Roberts! Roberts! I mustn't speak my mind to the Chairman, but the Chairman may speak his mind to me!

WILDER. What are things coming to?

ANTHONY. (*With a grim smile at* WILDER.) Go on, Roberts; say what you like!

ROBERTS. (*After a pause.*) I have no more to say.

ANTHONY. The meeting stands adjourned to five o'clock.

WANKLIN. (*In a low voice to* UNDERWOOD.) We shall never settle anything like this.

ROBERTS. (*Bitingly.*) We thank the Chairman and Board of Directors for their gracious hearing.

(*He moves toward the door; the men cluster together stupefied; then* ROUS, *throwing up his head, passes* ROBERTS *and goes out. The others follow.*)

ROBERTS. (*With his hand on the door— maliciously.*) Good day, gentlemen!

(*He goes out.*)

HARNESS. (*Ironically.*) I congratulate you on the conciliatory spirit that's been displayed. With your permission, gentlemen, I'll be with you again at half-past five. Good morning!

(*He bows slightly, rests his eyes on* AN- THONY, *who returns his stare unmoved, and, followed by* UNDERWOOD, *goes out. There is a moment of uneasy silence.* UNDERWOOD *reappears in the doorway.*)

WILDER. (*With emphatic disgust.*) Well!

(*The double-doors are opened.*)

ENID. (*Standing in the doorway.*) Lunch is ready. (EDGAR, *getting up abruptly, walks out past his sister.*)

WILDER. Coming to lunch, Scantlebury?

SCANTLEBURY. (*Rising heavily.*) I sup- pose so, I suppose so. It's the only thing we can do.

(*They go out through the double-doors.*)

WANKLIN. (*In a low voice.*) Do you really mean to fight to a finish, Chair- man? (ANTHONY *nods.*)

WANKLIN. Take care! The essence of things is to know when to stop.

(ANTHONY *does not answer.*)

WANKLIN. (*Very gravely.*) This way dis- aster lies. The ancient Trojans were fools to your father, Mrs. Underwood.

(*He goes out through the double-doors.*)

ENID. I want to speak to Father, Frank.

(UNDERWOOD *follows* WANKLIN *out.* TENCH, *passing round the table, is re- storing order to the scattered pens and papers.*)

ENID. Aren't you coming, Dad?

(ANTHONY *shakes his head.* ENID *looks meaningly at* TENCH.)

ENID. Won't you go and have some lunch, Mr. Tench?

TENCH. (*With papers in his hand.*) Thank you, ma'am, thank you!

(*He goes slowly, looking back.*)

ENID. (*Shutting the doors.*) I do hope it's settled, Father!

ANTHONY. No!

ENID. (*Very disappointed.*) Oh! Haven't you done anything?

(ANTHONY *shakes his head.*)

ENID. Frank says they all want to come to a compromise, really, except that man Roberts.

ANTHONY. *I* don't.

ENID. It's such a horrid position for us. If you were the wife of the manager, and lived down here, and saw it all. You can't realize, Dad!

ANTHONY. Indeed?

ENID. We see *all* the distress. You re- member my maid Annie, who mar- ried Roberts? (ANTHONY *nods.*) It's so wretched, her heart's weak; since the strike began, she hasn't even been getting proper food. I know it for a fact, Father.

ANTHONY. Give her what she wants, poor woman!

ENID. Roberts won't let her take anything from *us.*

ANTHONY. (*Staring before him.*) I can't

be answerable for the men's obstinacy.

ENID. They're all suffering. Father! Do stop it, for my sake!

ANTHONY. (*With a keen look at her.*) You don't understand, my dear.

ENID. If I were on the Board, I'd do something.

ANTHONY. What would you do?

ENID. It's because you can't bear to give way. It's so——

ANTHONY. Well?

ENID. So unnecessary.

ANTHONY. What do *you* know about necessity? Read your novels, play your music, talk your talk, but don't try and tell *me* what's at the bottom of a struggle like this.

ENID. I live down here, and see it.

ANTHONY. What d' you imagine stands between you and your class and these men that you're sorry for?

ENID. (*Coldly.*) I don't know what you mean, Father.

ANTHONY. In a few years you and your children would be down in the condition they're in, but for those who have the eyes to see things as they are and the backbone to stand up for themselves.

ENID. You don't know the state the men are in.

ANTHONY. I know it well enough.

ENID. You don't, Father; if you did, you wouldn't——

ANTHONY. It's you who don't know the simple facts of the position. What sort of mercy do you suppose you'd get if no one stood between you and the continual demands of labor? This sort of mercy— (*He puts his hand up to his throat and squeezes it.*) First would go your sentiments, my dear; then your culture, and your comforts would be going all the time!

ENID. I don't believe in barriers between classes.

ANTHONY. You—don't—believe—in—barriers—between the classes?

ENID. (*Coldly.*) And I don't know what

that has to do with this question.

ANTHONY. It will take a generation or two for you to understand.

ENID. It's only you and Roberts, Father, and you know it! (ANTHONY *thrusts out his lower lip.*) It'll ruin the Company.

ANTHONY. Allow me to judge of that.

ENID. (*Resentfully.*) I won't stand by and let poor Annie Roberts suffer like this! And think of the children, Father! I warn you.

ANTHONY. (*With a grim smile.*) What do you propose to do?

ENID. That's my affair.

(ANTHONY *only looks at her.*)

ENID. (*In a changed voice, stroking his sleeve.*) Father, you *know* you oughtn't to have this strain on you— you know what Dr. Fisher said!

ANTHONY. No old man can afford to listen to old women.

ENID. But you *have* done enough, even if it really is such a matter of principle with you.

ANTHONY. You think so?

ENID. Don't, Dad! (*Her face works.*) You—you might think of *us!*

ANTHONY. I am.

ENID. It'll break you down.

ANTHONY. (*Slowly.*) My dear, I am not going to funk; on that you may rely.

(*Re-enter* TENCH *with papers; he glances at them, then plucking up courage.*)

TENCH. Beg pardon, Madam, I think I'd rather see these papers were disposed of before I get my lunch.

(ENID, *after an impatient glance at him, looks at her father, turns suddenly, and goes into the drawing-room.*)

TENCH. (*Holding the papers and a pen to* ANTHONY, *very nervously.*) Would you sign these for me, please, sir?

(ANTHONY *takes the pen and signs.*)

TENCH. (*Standing with a sheet of blotting paper behind* EDGAR's *chair, begins, speaking nervously.*) I owe my position to you, sir.

ANTHONY. Well?

TENCH. I'm obliged to see everything that's going on, sir; I—I depend upon the Company entirely. If anything were to happen to it, it'd be disastrous for me. (ANTHONY *nods*.) And, of course, my wife's just had another; and so it makes me doubly anxious just now. And the rates are really terrible down our way.

ANTHONY. (*With grim amusement*.) Not more terrible than they are up mine.

TENCH. No, sir? (*Very nervously*.) I know the Company means a great deal to you, sir.

ANTHONY. It does; I founded it.

TENCH. Yes, sir. If the strike goes on, it'll be very serious. I think the Directors are beginning to realize that, sir.

ANTHONY. (*Ironically*.) Indeed?

TENCH. I know you hold very strong views, sir, and it's always your habit to look things in the face; but I don't think the Directors—like it, sir, now they—they see it.

ANTHONY. (*Grimly*.) Nor you, it seems.

TENCH. (*With a ghost of a smile*.) No, sir; of course I've got my children, and my wife's delicate; in my position I *have* to think of these things. (AN-THONY *nods*.) It wasn't *that* I was going to say, sir, if you'll excuse me (*hesitates*)——

ANTHONY. Out with it, then!

TENCH. I know—from my own father, sir, that when you get on in life you do feel things dreadfully——

ANTHONY. (*Almost paternally*.) Come, out with it, Tench!

TENCH. I don't like to say it, sir.

ANTHONY. (*Stonily*.) You must.

TENCH. (*After a pause, desperately bolting it out*.) I think the Directors are going to throw you over, sir.

ANTHONY. (*Sits in silence*.) Ring the bell!

(TENCH *nervously rings the bell and stands by the fire*.)

TENCH. Excuse me for saying such a thing. I was *only* thinking of you, sir.

(FROST *enters from the hall; he comes to the foot of the table, and looks at AN-THONY; TENCH covers his nervousness by arranging papers*.)

ANTHONY. Bring me a whisky and soda.

FROST. Anything to eat, sir?

(ANTHONY *shakes his head. FROST goes to the sideboard, and prepares the drink*.)

TENCH. (*In a low voice, almost supplicating*.) If you *could* see your way, sir, it would be a great relief to my mind, it would indeed. (*He looks up at ANTHONY, who has not moved*.) It does make me so very anxious. I haven't slept properly for weeks, sir, and that's a fact.

(ANTHONY *looks in his face, then slowly shakes his head*.)

TENCH. (*Disheartened*.) No, sir? (*He goes on arranging papers. FROST places the whisky and soda on a salver and puts it down by ANTHONY's right hand. He stands away, looking gravely at ANTHONY*.)

FROST. *Nothing* I can get you, sir?

(ANTHONY *shakes his head*.) You're aware, sir, of what the doctor said, sir?

ANTHONY. I am.

(*A pause. FROST suddenly moves closer to him, and speaks in a low voice*.)

FROST. This strike, sir; puttin' all this strain on you. Excuse me, sir, is it—is it worth it, sir? (ANTHONY *mutters some words that are inaudible*.) Very good, sir!

(*He turns and goes out into the hall. TENCH makes two attempts to speak; but meeting his Chairman's gaze he drops his eyes, and, turning dismally, he too goes out. ANTHONY is left alone. He grips the glass, tilts it, and drinks deeply; then sets it down with a deep and rumbling sigh, and leans back in his chair*.)

The curtain falls.

ACT II

SCENE I

It is half-past three. In the kitchen of Roberts's cottage a meager little fire is burning. The room is clean and tidy, very barely furnished, with a brick floor and whitewashed walls, much stained with smoke. There is a kettle on the fire. A door opposite the fireplace opens inward from a snowy street. On the wooden table are a cup and saucer, a teapot, knife, and plate of bread and cheese. Close to the fireplace in an old arm-chair, wrapped in a rug, sits MRS. ROBERTS, *a thin and dark-haired woman about thirty-five, with patient eyes. Her hair is not done up, but tied back with a piece of ribbon. By the fire, too, is* MRS. YEO, *a red-haired, broad-faced person. Sitting near the table is* MRS. ROUS, *an old lady, ashen-white, with silver hair; by the door, standing, as if about to go, is* MRS. BULGIN, *a little pale, pinched-up woman. In a chair, with her elbows resting on the table, and her face resting in her hands, sits* MADGE THOMAS, *a good-looking girl of twenty-two, with high cheek-bones, deep-set eyes, and dark untidy hair. She is listening to the talk, but she neither speaks nor moves.*

MRS. YEO. So he give me a sixpence, and that's the first bit o' money *I* seen this week. There ain't much 'eat to this fire. Come and warm yerself, Mrs. Rous, you're lookin' as white as the snow, you are.

MRS. ROUS. (*Shivering—placidly.*) Ah! but the winter my old man was took was the proper winter. Seventy-nine that was, when none of you was hardly born—not Madge Thomas, nor Sue Bulgin. (*Looking at them in turn.*) Annie Roberts, 'ow old were you, dear?

MRS. ROBERTS. Seven, Mrs. Rous.

MRS. ROUS. Seven—well, ther'! A tiny little thing!

MRS. YEO. (*Aggressively.*) Well, I was ten myself, I remembers it.

MRS. ROUS. (*Placidly.*) The Company hadn't been started three years. Father was workin' on the acid, that's 'ow he got 'is pisoned leg. I kep' sayin' to 'im, "Father, you've got a pisoned leg." "Well," 'e says, "Mother, pison or no pison, I can't afford to go a-layin' up." An' two days after, he was on 'is back, and never got up again. It was Providence! There wasn't none o' these Compensation Acts then.

MRS. YEO. Ye hadn't no strike that winter. (*With grim humor.*) This winter's 'ard enough for me. Mrs. Roberts, you don't want no 'arder winter, do you? Wouldn't seem natural to 'ave a dinner, would it, Mrs. Bulgin?

MRS. BULGIN. We've had no bread and tea last four days.

MRS. YEO. You got that Friday's laundry job?

MRS. BULGIN. (*Dispiritedly.*) They said they'd give it me, but when I went last Friday, they were full up. I got to go again next week.

MRS. YEO. Ah! There's too many after that. I sent Yeo out on the ice to put on the gentry's skates an' pick up what 'e can. Stops 'im from broodin' about the 'ouse.

MRS. BULGIN. (*In a desolate, matter-of-fact voice.*) Leavin' out the men—it's bad enough with the children. I keep 'em in bed, they don't get so hungry when they're not running about; but they're that restless in bed they worry your life out.

MRS. YEO. You're lucky they're all so small. It's the goin' to school that makes 'em 'ungry. Don't Bulgin give you *anythin'*?

MRS. BULGIN. (*Shakes her head, then, as*

though by afterthought.) Would if he could, I s'pose.

MRS. YEO. (*Sardonically.*) What! 'Aven't 'e got no shares in the Company?

MRS. ROUS. (*Rising with tremulous cheerfulness.*) Well, good-by, Annie Roberts, I'm going along home.

MRS. ROBERTS. Stay an' have a cup of tea, Mrs. Rous?

MRS. ROUS. (*With the faintest smile.*) Roberts'll want 'is tea when he comes in. I'll just go an' get to bed; it's warmer there than anywhere.

(*She moves very shakily toward the door.*)

MRS. YEO. (*Rising and giving her an arm.*) Come on, Mother, take my arm; we're all goin' the same way.

MRS. ROUS. (*Taking the arm.*) Thank you, my dearies!

(*They go out, followed by* MRS. BULGIN.)

MADGE. (*Moving for the first time.*) There, Annie, you see that! I told George Rous, "Don't think to have my company till you've made an end of all this trouble. You ought to be ashamed," I said, "with your own mother looking like a ghost, and not a stick to put on the fire. So long as you're able to fill your pipes, you'll let us starve." "I'll take my oath, Madge," he said, "I've not had smoke nor drink these three weeks!" "Well, then, why do you go on with it?" "I can't go back on Roberts!" . . . That's it! Roberts, always Roberts! They'd all drop it but for him. When *he* talks it's the devil that comes into them.

(*A silence.* MRS. ROBERTS *makes a movement of pain.*) Ah! *You* don't want him beaten! He's your man. With everybody like their own shadows! (*She makes a gesture toward* MRS. ROBERTS.) If Rous wants me, he must give up Roberts. If *he* gave him up—they all would. They're only waiting for a lead. Father's against him—they're all against him in their hearts.

MRS. ROBERTS. You won't beat Roberts! (*They look silently at each other.*)

MADGE. Won't I? The cowards—when their own mothers and their own children don't know where to turn.

MRS. ROBERTS. Madge!

MADGE. (*Looking searchingly at* MRS. ROBERTS.) I wonder he can look *you* in the face. (*She squats before the fire, with her hands out to the flame.*) Harness is here again. They'll have to make up their minds today.

MRS. ROBERTS. (*In a soft, slow voice, with a slight West-country burr.*) Roberts will never give up the furnacemen and engineers. 'Twouldn't be right.

MADGE. You can't deceive me. It's just his pride. (*A tapping at the door is heard; the women turn as* ENID *enters. She wears a round fur cap, and a jacket of squirrel's fur. She closes the door behind her.*)

ENID. Can I come in, Annie?

MRS. ROBERTS. (*Flinching.*) Miss Enid! Give Mrs. Underwood a chair, Madge!

(MADGE *gives* ENID *the chair she has been sitting on.*)

ENID. Thank you! Are you any better?

MRS. ROBERTS. Yes, M'm; thank you, M'm.

ENID. (*Looking at the sullen* MADGE *as though requesting her departure.*) Why did you send back the jelly? I call that really wicked of you!

MRS. ROBERTS. Thank you, M'm, I'd no need for it.

ENID. Of course! It was Roberts' doing, wasn't it? How can he let all this suffering go on amongst you?

MADGE. (*Suddenly.*) What suffering?

ENID. (*Surprised.*) I beg your pardon!

MADGE. Who said there was suffering?

MRS. ROBERTS. Madge!

MADGE. (*Throwing her shawl over her head.*) Please to let us keep ourselves to ourselves. We don't want you coming here and spying on us.

ENID. (*Confronting her, but without rising.*) I didn't speak to *you*.

MADGE. (*In a low, fierce voice.*) Keep

your kind feelings to yourself. You think you can come amongst us, but you're mistaken. Go back and tell the Manager that.

ENID. (*Stonily.*) This is not your house.

MADGE. (*Turning to the door.*) No, it is not my house; keep clear of my house, Mrs. Underwood.

(*She goes out.* ENID *taps her fingers on the table.*)

MRS. ROBERTS. Please to forgive Madge Thomas, M'm; she's a bit upset today.
(*A pause.*)

ENID. (*Looking at her.*) Oh, I think they're so *stupid,* all of them.

MRS. ROBERTS. (*With a faint smile.*) Yes, M'm.

ENID. Is Roberts out?

MRS. ROBERTS. Yes, M'm.

ENID. It is *his doing,* that they don't come to an agreement. Now isn't it, Annie?

MRS. ROBERTS. (*Softly, with her eyes on* ENID, *and moving the fingers of one hand continually on her breast.*) They do say that your father, M'm——

ENID. My father's getting an old man, and you know what old men are.

MRS. ROBERTS. I am sorry, M'm.

ENID. (*More softly.*) I don't expect *you* to feel sorry, Annie. I know it's his fault as well as Roberts's.

MRS. ROBERTS. I'm sorry for anyone that gets old, M'm; it's dreadful to get old, and Mr. Anthony was such a fine old man I always used to think.

ENID. (*Impulsively.*) He always liked you, don't you remember? Look here, Annie, what can I do? I do so want to know. You don't get what you ought to have. (*Going to the fire, she takes the kettle off, and looks for coals.*) And you're so naughty, sending back the soup and things!

MRS. ROBERTS. (*With a faint smile.*) Yes, M'm?

ENID. (*Resentfully.*) Why, you haven't even got coals?

MRS. ROBERTS. If you please, M'm, to put the kettle on again; Roberts won't have long for his tea when he comes

in. He's got to meet the men at four.

ENID. (*Putting the kettle on.*) That means he'll lash them into a fury again. Can't you stop his going, Annie? (MRS. ROBERTS *smiles ironically.*) Have you tried? (*A silence.*) Does he know how ill you are?

MRS. ROBERTS. It's only my weak 'eart, M'm.

ENID. You used to be so well when you were with us.

MRS. ROBERTS. (*Stiffening.*) Roberts is always good to me.

ENID. But you ought to have everything you want, and you have nothing!

MRS. ROBERTS. (*Appealingly.*) They tell me I don't look like a dyin' woman?

ENID. Of course you don't; if you could only have proper— Will you see my doctor if I send him to you? I'm sure he'd do you good.

MRS. ROBERTS. (*With faint questioning.*) Yes, M'm.

ENID. Madge Thomas oughtn't to come here; she only excites you. As if I didn't know what suffering there is amongst the men! I do feel for them dreadfully, but you know they *have* gone too far.

MRS. ROBERTS. (*Continually moving her fingers.*) They say there's no other way to get better wages, M'm.

ENID. (*Earnestly.*) But, Annie, that's why the Union won't help them. My husband's very sympathetic with the men, but he says they're not underpaid.

MRS. ROBERTS. No, M'm?

ENID. They never think how the Company could go on if we paid the wages they want.

MRS. ROBERTS. (*With an effort.*) But the dividends having been so big, M'm.

ENID. (*Taken aback.*) You all seem to think the shareholders are rich men, but they're not—most of them are really no better off than working men. (MRS. ROBERTS *smiles.*) They have to keep up appearances.

MRS. ROBERTS. Yes, M'm?

ENID. You don't have to pay rates and taxes, and a hundred other things that they do. If the men didn't spend such a lot in drink and betting they'd be quite well off!

MRS. ROBERTS. They say, workin' so hard, they must have some pleasure.

ENID. But surely not low pleasure like that.

MRS. ROBERTS. (*A little resentfully.*) Roberts never touches a drop; and he's never had a bet in his life.

ENID. Oh! but he's not a com—— I mean he's an engineer—a superior man.

MRS. ROBERTS. Yes, M'm. Roberts says they've no chance of other pleasures.

ENID. (*Musing.*) Of course, I know it's hard.

MRS. ROBERTS. (*With a spice of malice.*) And they say gentlefolk's just as bad.

ENID. (*With a smile.*) I go as far as most people, Annie, but you know, yourself, that's nonsense.

MRS. ROBERTS. (*With a painful effort.*) A lot o' the men never go near the Public; but even they don't save but very little, and that goes if there's illness.

ENID. But they've got their clubs, haven't they?

MRS. ROBERTS. The clubs only give up to eighteen shillin's a week, M'm, and it's not much amongst a family. Robert says workin' folk have always lived from hand to mouth. Sixpence today is worth more than a shillin' tomorrow, that's what they say.

ENID. But that's the spirit of gambling.

MRS. ROBERTS. (*With a sort of excitement.*) Roberts says a working man's life is all a gamble, from the time 'e's born to the time 'e dies.

(ENID *leans forward, interested.* MRS. ROBERTS *goes on with a growing excitement that culminates in the personal feeling of the last words.*)
He says, M'm, that when a working man's baby is born, it's a toss-up from breath to breath whether it ever draws another, and so on all 'is life; an' when he comes to be old, it's the workhouse or the grave. He says that without a man is very near, and pinches and stints 'imself and 'is children to save, there can't be neither surplus nor security. That's why he wouldn't have no children (*she sinks back*), not though I *wanted* them.

ENID. Yes, yes, I know!

MRS. ROBERTS. No, you don't, M'm. You've got your children, and you'll never need to trouble for them.

ENID. (*Gently.*) You oughtn't to be talking so much, Annie. (*Then, in spite of herself.*) But Roberts was paid a lot of money, wasn't he, for discovering that process?

MRS. ROBERTS. (*On the defensive.*) All Roberts's savin's have gone. He's always looked forward to this strike. He says he's no right to a farthing when the others are suffering. 'Tisn't so with all o' them! Some don't seem to care no more than that —so long as they get their own.

ENID. I don't see how they can be expected to when they're suffering like this. (*In a changed voice.*) But Roberts ought to think of *you!* It's all terrible! The kettle's boiling. Shall I make the tea? (*She takes the teapot and, seeing tea there, pours water into it.*) Won't you have a cup?

MRS. ROBERTS. No, thank you, M'm. (*She is listening, as though for footsteps.*) I'd sooner you didn't see Roberts, M'm, he gets so wild.

ENID. Oh! but I must, Annie; I'll be quite calm, I promise.

MRS. ROBERTS. It's life an' death to him, M'm.

ENID. (*Very gently.*) I'll get him to talk to me outside, we won't excite you.

MRS. ROBERTS. (*Faintly.*) No, M'm.

(*She gives a violent start.* ROBERTS *has come in, unseen.*)

ROBERTS. (*Removing his hat—with subtle mockery.*) Beg pardon for coming in; you're engaged with a lady, I see.

ENID. Can I speak to you, Mr. Roberts?

ROBERTS. Whom have I the pleasure of addressing, Ma'am?

ENID. But surely you know me! I'm Mrs. Underwood.

ROBERTS. (*With a bow of malice.*) The daughter of our Chairman.

ENID. (*Earnestly.*) I've come on purpose to speak to you; will you come outside a minute? (*She looks at* MRS. ROBERTS.)

ROBERTS. (*Hanging up his hat.*) I have nothing to say, Ma'am.

ENID. But I *must* speak to you, please.
(*She moves toward the door.*)

ROBERTS. (*With sudden venom.*) I have not the time to listen!

MRS. ROBERTS. David!

ENID. Mr. Roberts, *please!*

ROBERTS. (*Taking off his overcoat.*) I am sorry to disoblige a lady—Mr. Anthony's daughter.

ENID. (*Wavering, then with sudden decision.*) Mr. Roberts, I know you've another meeting of the men. (ROBERTS *bows.*) I came to appeal to you. Please, try to come to some compromise; give way a little, if it's only for your own sakes!

ROBERTS. (*Speaking to himself.*) The daughter of Mr. Anthony begs me to give way a little, if it's only for our own sakes!

ENID. For everybody's sake; for your wife's sake.

ROBERTS. For my wife's sake, for everybody's sake—for the sake of Mr. Anthony.

ENID. Why are you so bitter against my father? He has never done anything to you.

ROBERTS. Has he not?

ENID. He can't help his views, any more than you can help yours.

ROBERTS. I really didn't know that I had a right to views!

ENID. He's an old man, and you——
(*Seeing his eyes fixed on her, she stops.*)

ROBERTS. (*Without raising his voice.*) If I saw Mr. Anthony going to die, and I could save him by lifting my hand, I would not lift the little finger of it.

ENID. You—you—
(*She stops again, biting her lips.*)

ROBERTS. I would not, and that's flat!

ENID. (*Coldly.*) You don't mean what you say, and you know it!

ROBERTS. I mean every word of it.

ENID. But why?

ROBERTS. (*With a flash.*) Mr. Anthony stands for tyranny! That's why!

ENID. Nonsense!

(MRS. ROBERTS *makes a movement as if to rise, but sinks back in her chair.*)

ENID. (*With an impetuous movement.*) Annie!

ROBERTS. Please not to touch my wife!

ENID. (*Recoiling with a sort of horror.*) I believe—you are mad.

ROBERTS. The house of a madman then is not the fit place for a lady.

ENID. I'm not afraid of you.

ROBERTS. (*Bowing.*) I would not expect the daughter of Mr. Anthony to be afraid. Mr. Anthony is not a coward like the rest of them.

ENID. (*Suddenly.*) I suppose you think it brave, then, to go on with the struggle.

ROBERTS. Does Mr. Anthony think it brave to fight against women and children? Mr. Anthony is a rich man, I believe; does he think it brave to fight against those who haven't a penny? Does he think it brave to set children crying with hunger, an' women shivering with cold?

ENID. (*Putting up her hand, as though warding off a blow.*) My father is acting on his principles, and you know it!

ROBERTS. And so am I!

ENID. You hate us; and you can't bear to be beaten!

ROBERTS. Neither can Mr. Anthony, for all that he may say.

ENID. At any rate you might have pity on your wife.

(MRS. ROBERTS, *who has her hand pressed to her breast, takes it away, and tries to calm her breathing.*)

ROBERTS. Madam, I have no more to say. (*He takes up the loaf. There is a knock at the door, and* UNDERWOOD *comes in. He stands looking at them.* ENID *turns to him, then seems undecided.*)

UNDERWOOD. Enid!

ROBERTS. (*Ironically.*) You were not needing to come for your wife, Mr. Underwood. We are not rowdies.

UNDERWOOD. I know that, Roberts. I hope Mrs. Roberts is better.

(ROBERTS *turns away without answering.*)

Come, Enid!

ENID. I make one more appeal to you, Mr. Roberts, for the sake of your wife.

ROBERTS. (*With polite malice.*) If I might advise ye, Ma'am—make it for the sake of your husband and your father.

(ENID, *suppressing a retort, goes out.* UNDERWOOD *opens the door for her and follows.* ROBERTS, *going to the fire, holds out his hands to the dying glow.*)

ROBERTS. How goes it, my girl? Feeling better, are you?

(MRS. ROBERTS *smiles faintly. He brings his overcoat and wraps it round her.*)

(*Looking at his watch.*) Ten minutes to four! (*As though inspired.*) I've seen their faces; there's no fight in them, except for that one old robber.

MRS. ROBERTS. Won't you stop and eat, David? You've 'ad nothing all day!

ROBERTS. (*Putting his hand to his throat.*) Can't swallow till those old sharks are out o' the town. (*He walks up and down.*) I shall have a bother with the men—there's no heart in them, the cowards. Blind as bats, they are—can't see a day before their noses.

MRS. ROBERTS. It's the women, David.

ROBERTS. Ah! So they say! They can remember the women when their own bellies speak! The women never stop them from the drink; but from a little suffering to themselves in a sacred cause, the women stop them fast enough.

MRS. ROBERTS. But think o' the children, David.

ROBERTS. Ah! If they will go breeding themselves for slaves, without a thought o' the future o' them they breed—

MRS. ROBERTS. (*Gasping.*) That's enough, David; don't begin to talk of that—I won't—I can't——

ROBERTS. (*Staring at her.*) Now, now, my girl!

MRS. ROBERTS. (*Breathlessly.*) No, no, David—I won't!

ROBERTS. There, there! Come, come! That's right! (*Bitterly.*) Not one penny will they put by for a day like this. Not they! Hand to mouth—Gad!—I know them! They've broke my heart. There was no holdin' them at the start, but now the pinch 'as come.

MRS. ROBERTS. How can you expect it, David? They're not made of iron.

ROBERTS. Expect it? Wouldn't I expect what I would do meself? Wouldn't I starve an' rot rather than give in? What one man can do, another can.

MRS. ROBERTS. And the women?

ROBERTS. This is not women's work.

MRS. ROBERTS. (*With a flash of malice.*) No, the women may die for all you care. That's their work.

ROBERTS. (*Averting his eyes.*) Who talks of dying? No one will die till we have beaten these——

(*He meets her eyes again, and again turns his away. Excitedly.*)

This is what I've been waiting for all these months. To get the old robbers down, and send them home again without a farthin's worth o' change. I've seen their faces, I tell you, in the valley of the shadow of defeat.

(*He goes to the peg and takes down his hat.*)

MRS. ROBERTS. (*Following with her eyes—softly.*) Take your overcoat, David; it must be bitter cold.

ROBERTS. (*Coming up to her—his eyes*

are furtive.) No, no! There, there,
stay quiet and warm. I won't be
long, my girl.

MRS. ROBERTS. (*With soft bitterness.*)
You'd better take it.

(*She lifts the coat. But* ROBERTS *puts
it back, and wraps it round her. He tries
to meet her eyes, but cannot.* MRS. ROB-
ERTS *stays huddled in the coat, her eyes,
that follow him about, are half malicious,
half yearning. He looks at his watch
again, and turns to go. In the doorway
he meets* JAN THOMAS, *a boy of ten in
clothes too big for him, carrying a penny
whistle.*)

ROBERTS. Hallo, boy!

(*He goes.* JAN *stops within a yard of*
MRS. ROBERTS, *and stares at her without a
word.*)

MRS. ROBERTS. Well, Jan!

JAN. Father's coming; sister Madge is
coming. (*He sits at the table and
fidgets with his whistle; he blows
three vague notes; then imitates a
cuckoo.*)

(*There is a tap on the door. Old*
THOMAS *comes in.*)

THOMAS. A very coot tay to you, Ma'am.
It is petter that you are.

MRS. ROBERTS. Thank you, Mr. Thomas.

THOMAS. (*Nervously.*) Roberts in?

MRS. ROBERTS. Just gone on to the meeting,
Mr. Thomas.

THOMAS. (*With relief, becoming talkative.*)
This is fery unfortunate, look you!
I came to tell him that we must make
terms with London. It is a fery great
pity he is gone to the meeting. He
will be kicking against the pricks, I
am thinking.

MRS. ROBERTS. (*Half rising.*) He'll never
give in, Mr. Thomas.

THOMAS. You must not be fretting, that
is very pat for you. Look you, there
iss hartly any mans for supporting him
now, but the engineers and George
Rous. (*Solemnly.*) This strike is no
longer coing with Chapel, look you!
I have listened carefully, an' I have
talked with her. (JAN *blows.*) Sst!

I don't care what th' others say, I say
that *Chapel means us* to be stopping
the trouple, that is what I make of
her; and it is my opinion that this is
the fery best thing for all of us. If
it wasn't my opinion, I ton't say—
but it is my opinion, look you.

MRS. ROBERTS. (*Trying to suppress her excitement.*) I don't know what'll come
to Roberts, if you give in.

THOMAS. It is no disgrace whateffer! All
that a mortal man coult do he hass
tone. It iss against Human Nature
he hass gone; fery natural—any man
may do that; but Chapel has spoken
and he must not go against her.
(JAN *imitates the cuckoo.*) Ton't
make that squeaking! (*Going to the
door.*) Here iss my daughter come
to sit with you. A fery goot day,
Ma'am—no fretting—rememper!

(MADGE *comes in and stands at the open
door, watching the street.*)

MADGE. You'll be late, Father; they're beginning. (*She catches him by the
sleeve.*) For the love of God, stand
up to him, Father—this time!

THOMAS. (*Detaching his sleeve with dignity.*) Leave me to do what's proper,
girl!

(*He goes out.* MADGE, *in the center of
the open doorway, slowly moves in, as
though before the approach of someone.*)

ROUS. (*Appearing in the doorway.*)
Madge!

(MADGE *stands with her back to* MRS.
ROBERTS, *staring at him with her head up
and her hands behind her.*)

ROUS. (*Who has a fierce, distracted look.*)
Madge! I'm going to the meeting.

(MADGE, *without moving, smiles con-
temptuously.*)

D'ye hear me?

(*They speak in quick low voices.*)

MADGE. I hear! Go, and kill your own
mother, if you must.

(ROUS *seizes her by both her arms.
She stands rigid, with her head bent back.
He releases her, and he too stands mo-
tionless.*)

ROUS. I swore to stand by Roberts. I swore that! Ye want me to go back on what I've sworn.

MADGE. (*With slow soft mockery.*) You are a pretty lover!

ROUS. Madge!

MADGE. (*Smiling.*) I've heard that lovers do what their girls ask them (JAN *sounds the cuckoo's notes.*)—but that's not true, it seems!

ROUS. You'd make a blackleg of me!

MADGE. (*With her eyes half-closed.*) Do it for me!

ROUS. (*Dashing his hand across his brow.*) Damn! I can't!

MADGE. (*Swiftly.*) Do it for me!

ROUS. (*Through his teeth.*) Don't play the wanton with me!

MADGE. (*With a movement of her hand toward* JAN—*quick and low.*) I would be *that* for the children's sake.

ROUS. (*In a fierce whisper.*) Madge! Oh, Madge!

MADGE. (*With soft mockery.*) But *you* can't break your word for me!

ROUS. (*With a choke.*) Then, Begod, I can! (*He turns and rushes off.*)

(MADGE *stands, with a faint smile on her face, looking after him. She turns to* MRS. ROBERTS.)

MADGE. I have done for Roberts!

MRS. ROBERTS. (*Scornfully.*) Done for my man, with that——! (*She sinks back.*)

MADGE. (*Running to her, and feeling her hands.*) You're as cold as a stone! You want a drop of brandy. Jan, run to the "Lion"; say I sent you for Mrs. Roberts.

MRS. ROBERTS. (*With a feeble movement.*) I'll just sit quiet, Madge. Give Jan —his—tea.

MADGE. (*Giving* JAN *a slice of bread.*) There, ye little rascal. Hold your piping. (*Going to the fire, she kneels.*) It's going out.

MRS. ROBERTS. (*With a faint smile.*) 'Tis all the same! (JAN *begins to blow his whistle.*)

MADGE. Tsht! Tsht!—you—— (JAN *stops.*)

MRS. ROBERTS. (*Smiling.*) Let 'im play, Madge.

MADGE. (*On her knees at the fire, listening.*) Waiting an' waiting. I've no patience with it; waiting an' waiting —that's what a woman has to do! Can you hear them at it—I can!

(JAN *begins again to play his whistle;* MADGE *gets up; half tenderly she ruffles his hair; then, sitting, leans her elbows on the table, and her chin on her hands. Behind her, on* MRS. ROBERTS's *face the smile has changed to horrified surprise. She makes a sudden movement, sitting forward, pressing her hands against her breast. Then slowly she sinks back; slowly her face loses the look of pain, the smile returns. She fixes her eyes again on* JAN, *and moves her lips and finger to the tune.*)

The curtain falls.

SCENE II

It is past four. In a gray, failing light, an open muddy space is crowded with workmen. Beyond, divided from it by a barbed-wire fence, is the raised towing-path of a canal, on which is moored a barge. In the distance are marshes and snow-covered hills. The "Works" high wall runs from the canal across the open space, and in the angle of this wall is a rude platform of barrels and boards. On it, HARNESS is standing. ROBERTS, a little apart from the crowd, leans his back against the wall. On the raised towing-path two bargemen lounge and smoke indifferently.

HARNESS. (*Holding out his hand.*) Well, I've spoken to you straight. If I speak till tomorrow I can't say more.

JAGO. (*A dark, sallow, Spanish-looking man with a short, thin beard.*) Mister, want to ask you! Can they get blacklegs?

BULGIN. (*Menacing.*) Let 'em try.

(*There are savage murmurs from the crowd.*)

BROWN. (*A round-faced man.*) Where could they get 'em then?

EVANS. (*A small, restless, harassed man, with a fighting face.*) There's always blacklegs; it's the nature of 'em. There's always men that'll save their own skins.

(*Another savage murmur. There is a movement, and old* THOMAS, *joining the crowd, takes his stand in front.*)

HARNESS. (*Holding up his hand.*) They can't get them. But that won't help you. Now, men, be reasonable. Your demands would have brought on us the burden of a dozen strikes at a time when we were not prepared for them. The Unions live by Justice, not to one, but all. Any fair man will tell you—you were ill-advised! I don't say you go too far for that which you're entitled to, but you're going too far for the moment; you've dug a pit for yourselves. Are you to stay there, or are you to climb out? Come!

LEWIS. (*A clean-cut Welshman with a dark mustache.*) You've hit it, Mister! Which is it to be? (*Another movement in the crowd, and* ROUS, *coming quickly, takes his stand next* THOMAS.)

HARNESS. Cut your demands to the right pattern, and we'll see you through; refuse, and don't expect me to waste my time coming down here again. I'm not the sort that speaks at random, as you ought to know by this time. If you're the sound men I take you for—no matter who advises you against it—(*he fixes his eyes on* ROBERTS) you'll make up your minds to come in, and trust to us to get your terms. Which is it to be? Hands together, and victory—or—the starvation you've got now?

(*A prolonged murmur from the crowd.*)

JAGO. (*Sullenly.*) Talk about what you know.

HARNESS. (*Lifting his voice above the murmur.*) Know? (*With cold passion.*) All that you've been through, my friend, I've been through—I was through it when I was no bigger than (*pointing to a youth*) that shaver there; the Unions then weren't what they are now. What's made them strong? It's hands together that's made them strong. I've been through it all, I tell you, the brand's on my soul yet. I know what you've suffered—there's nothing you can tell me that I don't know; but the whole is greater than the part, and you are only the part. Stand by us, and we will stand by you.

(*Quartering them with his eyes, he waits. The murmuring swells; the men form little groups.* GREEN, BULGIN, *and* LEWIS *talk together.*)

LEWIS. Speaks very sensible, the Union chap.

GREEN. (*Quietly.*) Ah, if I'd been *listened* to, you'd 'ave 'eard sense these two months past.

(*The bargemen are seen laughing.*)

LEWIS. (*Pointing.*) Look at those two blanks over the fence there!

BULGIN. (*With gloomy violence.*) They'd best stop their cackle, or I'll break their jaws.

JAGO. (*Suddenly.*) You say the furnacemen's paid enough?

HARNESS. I did not say they were paid enough; I said they were paid as much as the furnacemen in similar works elsewhere.

EVANS. That's a lie! (*Hubbub.*) What about Harper's?

HARNESS. (*With cold irony.*) You may look at home for lies, my man. Harper's shifts are longer, the pay works out the same.

HENRY ROUS. (*A dark edition of his brother George.*) Will ye support us in double pay overtime Saturdays?

HARNESS. Yes, we will.

JAGO. What have ye done with our subscriptions?

HARNESS. (*Coldly.*) I have told you what we *will* do with them.

EVANS. Ah! *will*, it's always will! Ye'd have our mates desert us. (*Hubbub.*)

BULGIN. (*Shouting.*) Hold your row.

(EVANS *looks round angrily.*)

HARNESS. (*Lifting his voice.*) Those who know their right hands from their lefts know that the Unions are neither thieves nor traitors. I've said my say. Figure it out, my lads; when you want me, you know where I shall be.

(*He jumps down, the crowd gives way, he passes through them, and goes away. A* BARGEMAN *looks after him, jerking his pipe with a derisive gesture. The men close up in groups, and many looks are cast at* ROBERTS, *who stands alone against the wall.*)

EVANS. He wants you to turn blacklegs, that's what he wants. He wants ye to go back on us. Sooner than turn blackleg—I'd starve, I would.

BULGIN. Who's talkin' o' blacklegs—mind what you're saying, will you?

BLACKSMITH. (*A youth with yellow hair and huge arms.*) What about the women?

EVANS. They can stand what we can stand, I suppose, can't they?

BLACKSMITH. Ye've no wife?

EVANS. An' don't want one.

THOMAS. (*Raising his voice.*) Aye! Give us the power to come to terms with London, lads.

DAVIES. (*A dark, slow-fly, gloomy man.*) Go up the platform, if you got anything to say, go up an' say it.

(*There are cries of "Thomas!" He is pushed toward the platform; he ascends it with difficulty, and bares his head, waiting for silence. A hush.*)

RED-HAIRED YOUTH. (*Suddenly.*) Coot old Thomas!

(*A hoarse laugh; the bargemen exchange remarks; a hush again, and* THOMAS *begins speaking.*)

THOMAS. We are all in the tepth together, and it iss Nature that has put us there.

HENRY ROUS. It's London put us there!

EVANS. It's the Union.

THOMAS. It iss not Lonton; nor it iss not the Union—it iss Nature. It iss no disgrace whateffer to a potty to give in to Nature. For this Nature iss a fery pig thing; it is pigger than what a man is. There iss more years to my hett than to the hett of anyone here. It is fery pat, look you, this coing against Nature. It is pat to make other potties suffer, when there is nothing to pe cot py it.

(*A laugh.* THOMAS *angrily goes on.*) What are ye laughing at? It is pat, I say! We are fighting for principle; there is no potty that shall say I am not a peliever in principle. Putt when Nature says, "No further," then it is no coot snapping your fingers in her face. (*A laugh from* ROBERTS, *and murmurs of approval.*)

This Nature must pe humort. It is a man's pisiness to pe pure, honest, just, and merciful. That's what Chapel tells you. (*To* ROBERTS, *angrily.*) And, look you, David Roberts, Chapel tells you ye·can do that without coing against Nature.

JAGO. What about the Union?

THOMAS. I ton't trust the Union; they haf treated us like tirt. "Do what we tell you," said they. I haf peen captain of the furnacemen twenty years, and I say to the Union—(*excitedly*)—"Can you tell me then, as well as I can tell you, what iss the right wages for the work that these men do?" For fife and twenty years I haf paid my moneys to the Union and —(*with great excitement*)—for nothings! What iss that but roguery, for all that this Mr. Harness says!

(*Murmurs.*)

EVANS. Hear, hear.

HENRY ROUS. Get on with you! Cut on with it then!

THOMAS. Look you, if a man toes not trust me, am I coing to trust him?

JAGO. That's right.

THOMAS. Let them alone for rogues, and act for ourselves. (*Murmurs.*)

BLACKSMITH. That's what we been doin', haven't we?

THOMAS. (*With increased excitement.*) I wass brought up to do for meself. I wass brought up to go without a thing, if I hat not moneys to puy it. There iss too much, look you, of doing things with other people's moneys. We haf fought fair, and if we haf peen peaten, it iss no fault of ours. Gif us the power to make terms with Lonton for ourself; if we ton't succeed, I say it iss petter to take our peating like men, than to tie like togs, or hang on to others' coat-tails to make them do our pisiness for us!

EVANS. (*Muttering.*) Who wants to?

THOMAS. (*Craning.*) What's that? If I stand up to a potty, and he knocks me town, I am not to go hollering to other potties to help me; I am to stand up again; and if he knocks me town properly, I am to stay there, isn't that right? (*Laughter.*)

JAGO. No Union!

HENRY ROUS. Union!

(*Others take up the shout.*)

EVANS. Blacklegs!

(BULGIN *and the* BLACKSMITH *shake their fists at* EVANS.)

THOMAS. (*With a gesture.*) I am an olt man, look you.

(*A sudden silence, then murmurs again.*)

LEWIS. Olt fool, with his "No Union!"

BULGIN. Them furnace chaps! For twopence I'd smash the faces o' the lot of them.

GREEN. If I'd a-been listened to at the first——

THOMAS. (*Wiping his brow.*) I'm comin' now to what I was coing to say——

DAVIES. (*Muttering.*) An' time too!

THOMAS. (*Solemnly.*) Chapel says: Ton't carry on this strife! Put an end to it!

JAGO. That's a lie! Chapel says go on!

THOMAS. (*Scornfully.*) Inteet! I haf ears to my head.

RED-HAIRED YOUTH. Ah! long ones!

(*A laugh.*)

JAGO. Your ears have misbeled you then.

THOMAS. (*Excitedly.*) Ye cannot be right if I am, ye cannot haf it both ways.

RED-HAIRED YOUTH. Chapel can though!

(*"The Shaver" laughs; there are murmurs from the crowd.*)

THOMAS. (*Fixing his eyes on "The Shaver."*) Ah! ye're coing the roat to tamnation. An' so I say to all of you. If ye co against Chapel I will not pe with you, nor will any other Got-fearing man.

(*He steps down from the platform.* JAGO *makes his way toward it. There are cries of "Don't let 'im go up!"*)

JAGO. Don't let him go up? That's free speech, that is. (*He goes up.*) I ain't got much to say to you. Look at the matter plain; ye've come the road this far, and now you want to chuck the journey. We've all been in one boat; and now you want to pull in two. We engineers have stood by you; ye're ready now, are ye, to give us the go-by? If we'd a-known that before, we'd not a-started out with you so early one bright morning! That's all I've got to say. Old man Thomas a'n't got his Bible Lesson right. If you give up to London, or to Harness, now, it's givin' us the chuck—to save your skins—you won't get over that, my boys; it's a dirty thing to do.

(*He gets down; during his little speech, which is ironically spoken, there is a restless discomfort in the crowd.* ROUS, *stepping forward, jumps on the platform. He has an air of fierce distraction. Sullen murmurs of disapproval from the crowd.*)

ROUS. (*Speaking with great excitement.*) I'm no blanky orator, mates, but wot I say is drove from me. What I say is yuman nature. Can a man set an' see 'is mother starve? Can 'e now?

ROBERTS. (*Starting forward.*) Rous!

ROUS. (*Staring at him fiercely.*) Sim

'Arness said fair! I've changed my mind!

ROBERTS. Ah! Turned your coat you mean!

(*The crowd manifests a great surprise*).

LEWIS. (*Apostrophizing* ROUS.) Hallo! What's turned him round?

ROUS. (*Speaking with intense excitement.*) 'E said fair. "Stand by us," 'e said, "and we'll stand by you." That's where we've been makin' our mistake this long time past; and who's to blame for 't? (*He points at* ROBERTS.) That man there! "No," 'e said, "fight the robbers," 'e said, "squeeze the breath out o' them!" But it's not the breath out o' them that's being squeezed; it's the breath out of *us* and *ours,* and that's the book of truth. I'm no orator, mates, it's the flesh and blood in me that's speakin', it's the heart o' me. (*With a menacing, yet half-ashamed movement toward* ROBERTS.) He'll speak to you again, mark my words, but don't ye listen. (*The crowd groans.*) It's hell fire that's on the man's tongue. (ROBERTS *is seen laughing.*) Sim 'Arness is right. What are we without the Union—handful o' parched leaves—a puff o' smoke. I'm no orator, but I say: Chuck it up! Chuck it up! Sooner than go on starving the women and the children.

(*The murmurs of acquiescence almost drown the murmurs of dissent.*)

EVANS. What's turned *you* to blacklegging?

ROUS. (*With a furious look.*) Sim 'Arness knows what he's talking about. Give us power to come to terms with London; I'm no orator, but I say— have done wi' this black misery!

(*He gives his muffler a twist, jerks his head back, and jumps off the platform. The crowd applauds and surges forward. Amid cries of "That's enough!" "Up Union!" "Up Harness!"* ROBERTS *quietly ascends the platform. There is a moment of silence.*)

BLACKSMITH. We don't want to hear you. Shut it!

HENRY ROUS. Get down!

(*Amid such cries they surge toward the platform.*)

EVANS. (*Fiercely.*) Let 'im speak! Roberts! Roberts!

BULGIN. (*Muttering.*) He'd better look out that I don't crack his skull.

(ROBERTS *faces the crowd, probing them with his eyes till they gradually become silent. He begins speaking. One of the bargemen rises and stands.*)

ROBERTS. You don't want to hear me, then? You'll listen to Rous and to that old man, but not to me. You'll listen to Sim Harness of the Union that's treated you *so fair;* maybe you'll listen to those men from London? Ah! you groan! What for? You love their feet on your necks, don't you? (*Then as* BULGIN *elbows his way toward the platform, with calm pathos.*) You'd like to break my jaw, John Bulgin. Let me speak, then do your smashing, if it gives you pleasure. (BULGIN *stands motionless and sullen.*) Am I a liar, a coward, a traitor? If only I were, ye'd listen to me, I'm sure. (*The murmurings cease, and there is now dead silence.*) Is there a man of you here that has less to gain by striking? Is there a man of you that had more to lose? Is there a man of you that has given up *eight hundred* pounds since this trouble here began? Come now, is there? How much has Thomas given up— ten pounds or five, or what? You listen to him, and what had he to say? "None can pretend," he said, "that I'm not a believer in principle (*with biting irony*)—but when Nature says: 'No further, 't es going agenst Nature.'" *I* tell you if a man cannot say to Nature: "Budge me from this if you can!" (*with a sort of exaltation*) —his principles are but his belly. "Oh, but," Thomas says, "a man can be pure and honest, just and merci-

ful, and take off his hat to Nature!"
I tell you Nature's neither pure nor
honest, just nor merciful. You chaps
that live over the hill, an' go home
dead beat in the dark on a snowy
night—don't ye fight your way every
inch of it? Do ye go lyin' down an'
trustin' to the tender mercies of this
merciful Nature? Try it and you'll
soon know with what ye've got to
deal. 'T es only by that (*he strikes
a blow with his clenched fist*)—in Nature's face that a man can be a man.
"Give in," says Thomas, "go down
on your knees; throw up your foolish
fight, an' perhaps," he said, "perhaps
your enemy will chuck you down a
crust."

JAGO. Never!

EVANS. Curse them!

THOMAS. I nefer said that.

ROBERTS. (*Bitingly.*) If ye did not say it,
man, ye meant it. An' what did ye
say about Chapel? "Chapel's against
it," ye said. "She's against it!" Well,
if Chapel and Nature go hand in
hand, it's the first I've ever heard of
it. That young man there (*pointing
to* ROUS) said I 'ad 'ell fire on my
tongue. If I had I would use it all
to scorch and wither this talking of
surrender. Surrendering's the work
of cowards and traitors.

HENRY ROUS. (*As* GEORGE ROUS *moves forward.*) Go for him, George—don't
stand his lip!

ROBERTS. (*Flinging out his finger.*) Stop
there, George Rous, it's no time
this to settle personal matters. (ROUS
stops.) But there was one other
spoke to you—Mr. Simon Harness.
We have not much to thank Mr.
Harness and the Union for. They
said to us, "Desert your mates, or
we'll desert you." An' they did desert us.

EVANS. They did.

ROBERTS. Mr. Simon Harness is a clever
man, but he has come too late. (*With
intense conviction.*) For all that

Mr. Simon Harness says, for all that
Thomas, Rous, for all that any man
present here can say—*We've won the
fight!*

(*The crowd sags nearer, looking eagerly
up. With withering scorn.*)
You've felt the pinch o't in your bellies. You've forgotten what that fight
'as been; many times I have told you;
I will tell you now this once again.
The fight o' the country's body and
blood against a blood-sucker. The
fight of those that spend themselves
with every blow they strike and every
breath they draw, against a thing that
fattens on them, and grows and grows
by the law of *merciful* Nature. That
thing is Capital! A thing that buys
the sweat o' men's brows, and the torture o' their brains, at its own price.
Don't I know that? Wasn't the work
o' *my* brains bought for seven hundred pounds, and hasn't one hundred
thousand pounds been gained them
by that seven hundred without the
stirring of a finger? It is a thing
that will take as much and give you
as little as it can. That's *Capital!*
A thing that will say—"I'm very sorry
for you, poor fellows—you have a
cruel time of it, I know," but will not
give one sixpence of its dividends to
help you have a better time. That's
Capital! Tell me, for all their talk,
is there one of them that will consent to another penny on the Income
Tax to help the poor? That's Capital! A white-faced, stony-hearted monster! Ye have got it on its knees;
are ye to give up at the last minute
to save your miserable bodies pain?
When I went this morning to those
old men from London, I looked into
their very 'earts. One of them was
sitting there—Mr. Scantlebury, a mass
of flesh nourished on us: sittin' there
for all the world like the shareholders in this Company, that sit not moving tongue nor finger, takin' dividends—a great dumb ox that can only

be roused when its food is threatened. I looked into his eyes and I saw *he was afraid*—afraid for himself and his dividends, afraid for his fees, afraid of the very shareholders he stands for; and all but one of them's afraid—like children that go into a wood at night, and start at every rustle of the leaves. I ask you, men (*he pauses, holding out his hand till there is utter silence*) —give me a free hand to tell them: "Go back to London. The men have nothing for you!" (*A murmuring.*) Give me that, an' I swear to you, within a week you shall have from London all you want.

EVANS, JAGO, *and* OTHERS. A free hand! Give him a free hand! Bravo— bravo!

ROBERTS. 'Tis not for this little moment of time we're fighting (*the murmuring dies*), not for ourselves, our own little bodies, and their wants, 'tis for all those that come after throughout all time. (*With intense sadness.*) Oh! men—for the love o' them, don't roll up another stone upon their heads, don't help to blacken the sky, an' let the bitter sea in over them. They're welcome to the worst that can happen to me, to the worst that can happen to us all, aren't they—aren't they? If we can shake (*passionately*) that white-faced monster with the bloody lips, that has sucked the life out of our-selves, our wives, and children, since the world began. (*Dropping the note of passion, but with utmost weight and intensity.*) If we have not the hearts of men to stand up against it breast to breast, and eye to eye, and force it backward till it cry for mercy, it will go on sucking life; and we shall stay forever what we are (*in almost a whisper*), less than the very dogs.

(*An utter stillness, and* ROBERTS *stands rocking his body slightly, with his eyes burning the faces of the crowd.*)

EVANS *and* JAGO. (*Suddenly.*) Roberts! (*The shout is taken up.*)

(*There is a slight movement in the crowd, and* MADGE, *passing below the towing-path, stops by the platform, look-ing up at* ROBERTS. *A sudden doubting silence.*)

ROBERTS. "Nature," says that old man, "give in to Nature." I tell you, strike your blow in Nature's face—an' let it do its worst!

(*He catches sight of* MADGE, *his brows contract, he looks away.*)

MADGE. (*In a low voice—close to the plat-form.*) Your wife's dying!

(ROBERTS *glares at her as if torn from some pinnacle of exaltation.*)

ROBERTS. (*Trying to stammer on.*) I say to you—answer them—answer them——

(*He is drowned by the murmur in the crowd.*)

THOMAS. (*Stepping forward.*) Ton't you hear her, then?

ROBERTS. What is it? (*A dead silence.*)

THOMAS. Your wife, man!

(ROBERTS *hesitates, then with a gesture, he leaps down, and goes away below the towing-path, the men making way for him. The standing bargeman opens and prepares to light a lantern. Daylight is fast failing.*)

MADGE. He needn't have hurried! Annie Roberts is dead.

(*Then in the silence, passionately.*) You pack of blinded hounds! How many more women are you going to let to die?

(*The crowd shrinks back from her, and breaks up in groups, with a confused, uneasy movement.* MADGE *goes quickly away below the towing-path. There is a hush as they look after her.*)

LEWIS. There's a spitfire, for ye!

BULGIN. (*Growling.*) I'll smash 'er jaw.

GREEN. If I'd a-been listened to, that poor woman——

THOMAS. It's a judgment on him for coing against Chapel. I tolt him how 't would be!

EVANS. All the more reason for sticking by 'im. (*A cheer.*) Are you goin' to desert him now 'e's down? Are you going to chuck him over, now 'e's lost 'is wife?

(*The crowd is murmuring and cheering all at once.*)

ROUS. (*Stepping in front of platform.*) Lost his wife! Aye! Can't ye see? Look at home, look at your own wives! What's to save them? Ye'll have the same in all your houses before long!

LEWIS. Aye, aye!

HENRY ROUS. Right! George, right!
          (*There are murmurs of assent.*)

ROUS. It's not us that's blind, it's Roberts. How long will ye put up with 'im!

HENRY ROUS, BULGIN, DAVIES. Give 'im the chuck!   (*The cry is taken up.*)

EVANS. (*Fiercely.*) Kick a man that's down? Down?

HENRY ROUS. Stop his jaw there!

(EVANS *throws up his arm at a threat from* BULGIN. *The bargeman, who has lighted the lantern, holds it high above his head.*)

ROUS. (*Springing on to the platform.*) What brought him down then, but 'is own black obstinacy? Are ye goin' to follow a man that can't see better than that where he's goin'?

EVANS. He's lost 'is wife.

ROUS. An' whose fault's that but his own? 'Ave done with 'im, I say, before he's killed your own wives and mothers.

DAVIES. Down 'im!

HENRY ROUS. He's finished!

BROWN. We've had enough of 'im!

BLACKSMITH. Too much!

(*The crowd takes up these cries, excepting only* EVANS, JAGO, *and* GREEN, *who is seen to argue mildly with the* BLACKSMITH.)

ROUS. (*Above the hubbub.*) We'll make terms with the Union, lads.
                                        (*Cheers.*)

EVANS. (*Fiercely.*) Ye blacklegs!

BULGIN. (*Savagely—squaring up to him.*) Who are ye callin' blacklegs, Rat?

(EVANS *throws up his fists, parries the blow, and returns it. They fight. The bargemen are seen holding up the lantern and enjoying the sight. Old* THOMAS *steps forward and holds out his hands.*)

THOMAS. Shame on your strife!

(*The* BLACKSMITH, BROWN, LEWIS, *and the* RED-HAIRED YOUTH *pull* EVANS *and* BULGIN *apart. The stage is almost dark.*)

The curtain falls.

ACT III

It is five o'clock. In the UNDERWOODS' *drawing-room, which is artistically furnished,* ENID *is sitting on the sofa working at a baby's frock.* EDGAR, *by a little spindle-legged table in the center of the room, is fingering a china-box. His eyes are fixed on the double-doors that lead into the dining-room.*

EDGAR. (*Putting down the china-box, and glancing at his watch.*) Just on five, they're all in there waiting, except Frank. Where's he?

ENID. He's had to go down to Gasgoyne's about a contract. Will you want him?

EDGAR. He can't help us. This is a director's job. (*Motioning toward a single door half hidden by a curtain.*) Father in his room?

ENID. Yes.

EDGAR. I wish he'd stay there, Enid.
          (ENID *looks up at him.*)
This is a beastly business, old girl?

(*He takes up the little box again and turns it over and over.*)

ENID. I went to the Roberts's this afternoon, Ted.

EDGAR. That wasn't very wise.

ENID. He's simply killing his wife.

EDGAR. We are, you mean.

ENID. (*Suddenly.*) Roberts *ought* to give way!

EDGAR. There's a lot to be said on the men's side.

ENID. I don't feel half so sympathetic with them as I did before I went. They just set up class feeling against you. Poor Annie was looking dreadfully bad—fire going out, and nothing fit for her to eat.

(EDGAR *walks to and fro.*) But she would stand up for Roberts. When you see all this wretchedness going on and feel you can do nothing, you have to shut your eyes to the whole thing.

EDGAR. If you can.

ENID. When I went I was all on their side, but as soon as I got there I began to feel quite different at once. People talk about sympathy with the working classes; they don't know what it means to try and put it into practice. It seems hopeless.

EDGAR. Ah! well.

ENID. It's dreadful going on with the men in this state. I do hope the Dad will make concessions.

EDGAR. He won't. (*Gloomily.*) It's a sort of religion with him. Curse it! I know what's coming! He'll be voted down.

ENID. They wouldn't dare!

EDGAR. They will—they're in a funk.

ENID. (*Indignantly.*) He'd never stand it!

EDGAR. (*With a shrug.*) My dear girl, if you're beaten in a vote, you've got to stand it.

ENID. Oh! (*She gets up in alarm.*) But would he resign?

EDGAR. Of course! It goes to the roots of his beliefs.

ENID. But he's so *wrapped up in this company,* Ted! There'd be nothing left for him! It'd be dreadful! (EDGAR *shrugs his shoulders.*) Oh, Ted, he's so old now! You mustn't let them!

EDGAR. (*Hiding his feelings in an outburst.*) My sympathies in this strike are all on the side of the men.

ENID. He's been Chairman for more than thirty years! He made the whole thing! And think of the bad times they've had; it's always been he who pulled them through. Oh, Ted, you must——

EDGAR. What is it you want? You said just now you hoped he'd make concessions. Now you want me to back him in not making them. This isn't a game, Enid!

ENID. (*Hotly.*) It isn't a game to *me* that the Dad's in danger of losing all he cares about in life. If he won't give way, and he's beaten, it'll simply break him down!

EDGAR. Didn't you say it was dreadful going on with the men in this state?

ENID. But you can't see, Ted. Father'll never get over it! You must stop them somehow. The others are afraid of him. If you back him up——

EDGAR. (*Putting his hand to his head.*) Against my convictions—against yours! The moment it begins to pinch one personally——

ENID. It isn't personal, it's the Dad!

EDGAR. Your family or yourself, and over goes the show!

ENID. (*Resentfully.*) If you don't take it seriously, I do.

EDGAR. I am as fond of him as you are; that's nothing to do with it.

ENID. We can't tell about the men; it's all guesswork. But we know the Dad might have a stroke any day. D'you mean to say that he isn't more to you than——

EDGAR. Of course he is.

ENID. I don't understand you then.

EDGAR. H'm!

ENID. If it were for oneself it would be different, but for your own father! You don't seem to realize.

EDGAR. I realize perfectly.

ENID. It's your first duty to save him.

EDGAR. I wonder.

ENID. (*Imploring.*) Oh, Ted! It's the only interest he's got left; it'll be like a death-blow to him!

EDGAR. (*Restraining his emotion.*) I know.

ENID. Promise!

EDGAR. I'll do what I can.

(*He turns to the double-doors.*)

(*The curtained door is opened, and* AN-
THONY *appears.* EDGAR *opens the double-
doors, and passes through.*)

(SCANTLEBURY's *voice is faintly heard:*
"*Past five; we shall never get through
—have to eat another dinner at that hotel!*"
The doors are shut. ANTHONY *walks forward.*)

ANTHONY. You've been seeing Roberts, I
hear.

ENID. Yes.

ANTHONY. Do you know what trying to
bridge such a gulf as this is like?

(ENID *puts her work on the little table,
and faces him.*)

Filling a sieve with sand!

ENID. Don't!

ANTHONY. You think with your gloved
hands you can cure the trouble of the
century.   (*He passes on.*)

ENID. Father! (ANTHONY *stops at the
double-doors.*) I'm only thinking of
you!

ANTHONY. (*More softly.*) I can take care
of myself, my dear.

ENID. Have you thought what'll happen
if you're beaten (*she points*)—in
there?

ANTHONY. I don't mean to be.

ENID. Oh! Father, don't give them a
chance. You're not well; need you
go to the meeting at all?

ANTHONY. (*With a grim smile.*) Cut and
run?

ENID. But they'll out-vote you!

ANTHONY. (*Putting his hand on the doors.*)
We shall see!

ENID. I beg you, Dad!

(ANTHONY *looks at her softly.*)
Won't you?

(ANTHONY *shakes his head. He opens
the doors. A buzz of voices comes in.*)

SCANTLEBURY. Can one get dinner on that
6:30 train up?

TENCH. No, sir, I believe not, sir.

WILDER. Well, I shall speak out; I've had
enough of this.

EDGAR. (*Sharply.*) What?

(*It ceases instantly.* ANTHONY *passes
through, closing the doors behind him.*
ENID *springs to them with a gesture of
dismay. She puts her hand on the knob,
and begins turning it; then goes to the fireplace, and taps her foot on the fender.
Suddenly she rings the bell.* FROST *comes
in by the door that leads into the hall.*)

FROST. Yes, M'm?

ENID. When the men come, Frost, please
show them in here; the hall's cold.

FROST. I could put them in the pantry,
M'm.

ENID. No. I don't want to—to offend
them; they're so touchy.

FROST. Yes, M'm. (*Pause.*) Excuse me,
Mr. Anthony's 'ad nothing to eat all
day.

ENID. I know, Frost.

FROST. Nothin' but two whiskies and
sodas, M'm.

ENID. Oh! you oughtn't to have let him
have those.

FROST. (*Gravely.*) Mr. Anthony is a little
difficult, M'm. It's not as if he were
a younger man, an' knew what was
good for 'im; he will have his own
way.

ENID. I suppose we all want that.

FROST. Yes, M'm. (*Quietly.*) Excuse me
speakin' about the strike. I'm sure if
the other gentlemen were to give up
to Mr. Anthony, and quietly let the
men 'ave what they want, afterwards,
that'd be the best way. I find that
very useful with him at times, M'm.

(ENID *shakes her head.*)
If he's crossed, it makes him violent
(*with an air of discovery*), and I've
noticed in my own case, when I'm violent I'm always sorry for it afterwards.

ENID. (*With a smile.*) Are *you* ever violent, Frost?

FROST. Yes, M'm; oh! sometimes very violent.

ENID. I've never seen you.

FROST. (*Impersonally.*) No, M'm; that is
so.

(ENID *fidgets toward the back of the
door.*)

(*With feeling.*) Bein' with Mr. Anthony, as you know, M'm, ever since
I was fifteen, it worries me to see him
crossed like this at his age. I've taken
the liberty to speak to Mr. Wanklin
(*dropping his voice*)—seems to be the
most sensible of the gentlemen—but
'e said to me: "That's all very well,
Frost, but this strike's a very serious
thing," 'e said. "Serious for all parties, no doubt," I said, "but yumor
'im, sir," I said, "yumor 'im. It's like
this, if a man comes to a stone wall,
'e doesn't drive 'is 'ead against it, 'e
gets over it." "Yes," 'e said, "you'd
better tell your master that." (FROST
looks at his nails.) That's where it
is, M'm. I said to Mr. Anthony this
morning: "Is it worth it, sir?" "Damn
it," he said to me, "Frost! Mind
your own business, or take a month's
notice!" Beg pardon, M'm, for using
such a word.

ENID. (*Moving to the double-doors, and
listening.*) Do you know that man
Roberts, Frost?

FROST. Yes, M'm; that's to say, not to speak
to. But to *look* at 'im you can tell
what *he's* like.

ENID. (*Stopping.*) Yes?

FROST. He's not one of these 'ere ordinary 'armless Socialists. 'E's violent; got a fire inside 'im. What I
call "personal." A man may 'ave
what opinions 'e likes, so long as
'e's not personal; when 'e's that 'e's
not safe.

ENID. I think that's what my father feels
about Roberts.

FROST. No doubt, M'm, Mr. Anthony has
a feeling against him.

(ENID *glances at him sharply, but finding him in perfect earnest, stands biting
her lips, and looking at the double-doors.*)
It's a regular right down struggle
between the two. I've no patience
with this Roberts; from what I 'ear
he's just an ordinary workin' man
like the rest of 'em. If he did invent a thing he's no worse off than

'undreds of others. My brother invented a new kind o' dumb-waiter—
nobody gave *him* anything for it, an'
there it is, bein' used all over the place.
(ENID *moves closer to the double-doors.*)
There's a kind o' man that never forgives the world, because 'e wasn't
born a gentleman. What I say is—
no man that's a gentleman looks
down on another because 'e 'appens
to be a class or two above 'im, no
more than if 'e 'appens to be a class
or two below.

ENID. (*With slight impatience.*) Yes, I
know, Frost, of course. Will you
please go in and ask if they'll have
some tea; say I sent you.

FROST. Yes, M'm.

(*He opens the doors gently and goes in.
There is a momentary sound of earnest,
rather angry talk.*)

WILDER. I don't agree with you.

WANKLIN. We've had this over a dozen
times.

EDGAR. (*Impatiently.*) Well, what's the
proposition?

SCANTLEBURY. Yes, what does your father
say? Tea? Not for me, not for
me!

WANKLIN. What I understand the Chairman to say is this——

(FROST *re-enters, closing the door behind him.*)

ENID. (*Moving from the door.*) Won't
they have any tea, Frost?

(*She goes to the little table, and remains
motionless, looking at the baby's frock.*)
(*A parlormaid enters from the hall.*)

PARLORMAID. A Miss Thomas, M'm.

ENID. (*Raising her head.*) Thomas?
What Miss Thomas—d' you mean
a——?

PARLORMAID. Yes, M'm.

ENID. (*Blankly.*) Oh! Where is she?

PARLORMAID. In the porch.

ENID. I don't want—— (*She hesitates.*)

FROST. Shall I dispose of her, M'm?

ENID. I'll come out. No, show her in
here, Ellen.

(*The* PARLORMAID *and* FROST *go out.*

ENID, *pursing her lips, sits at the little table, taking up the baby's frock. The* PARLORMAID *ushers in* MADGE THOMAS *and goes out;* MADGE *stands by the door.*)

ENID. Come in. What is it? What have you come for, please?

MADGE. Brought a message from Mrs. Roberts.

ENID. A message? Yes.

MADGE. She asks you to look after her mother.

ENID. I don't understand.

MADGE. (*Sullenly.*) That's the message.

ENID. But—what—why?

MADGE. Annie Roberts is dead.

(*There is a silence.*)

ENID. (*Horrified.*) But it's only a little more than an hour since I saw her.

MADGE. Of cold and hunger.

ENID. (*Rising.*) Oh! that's not true! the poor thing's heart— What makes you look at me like that? I tried to help her.

MADGE. (*With suppressed savagery.*) I thought you'd like to know.

ENID. (*Passionately.*) It's so unjust! Can't you see that I want to help you all?

MADGE. I never harmed anyone that hadn't harmed me first.

ENID. (*Coldly.*) What harm have I done you? Why do you speak to me like that?

MADGE. (*With the bitterest intensity.*) You come out of your comfort to spy on us! A week of hunger, that's what *you* want!

ENID. (*Standing her ground.*) Don't talk nonsense!

MADGE. I saw her die; her hands were blue with the cold.

ENID. (*With a movement of grief.*) Oh! why wouldn't she let me help her? It's such senseless pride!

MADGE. Pride's better than nothing to keep your body warm.

ENID. (*Passionately.*) I won't talk to you! How can you tell what I feel? It's not my fault that I was born better off than you.

MADGE. We don't want your money.

ENID. You don't understand, and you don't want to; please to go away!

MADGE. (*Balefully.*) You've killed her, for all your soft words, you and your father——

ENID. (*With rage and emotion.*) That's wicked! My father is suffering himself through this wretched strike.

MADGE. (*With somber triumph.*) Then tell him Mrs. Roberts is dead! That'll make him better.

ENID. Go away!

MADGE. When a person hurts us we get it back on them.

(*She makes a sudden and swift movement toward* ENID, *fixing her eyes on the child's frock lying across the little table.* ENID *snatches the frock up, as though it were the child itself. They stand a yard apart, crossing glances.*)

MADGE. (*Pointing to the frock with a little smile.*) Ah! You felt *that!* Lucky it's her mother—not her children— you've to look after, isn't it? *She* won't trouble you long!

ENID. Go away!

MADGE. I've given you the message.

(*She turns and goes out into the hall.* ENID, *motionless till she has gone; sinks down at the table, bending her head over the frock, which she is still clutching to her. The double-doors are opened, and* ANTHONY *comes slowly in; he passes his daughter, and lowers himself into an armchair. He is very flushed.*)

ENID. (*Hiding her emotion—anxiously.*) What is it, Dad? (ANTHONY *makes a gesture, but does not speak.*) Who was it?

(ANTHONY *does not answer.* ENID *going to the double-doors meets* EDGAR *coming in. They speak together in low tones.*)

What is it, Ted?

EDGAR. That fellow Wilder! Taken to personalities! He was downright insulting.

ENID. What did he say?

EDGAR. Said Father was too old and feeble

to know what he was doing! The Dad's worth six of him!

ENID. Of course he is.

(*They look at* ANTHONY.)

(*The doors open wider;* WANKLIN *appears with* SCANTLEBURY.)

SCANTLEBURY. (*Sotto voce.*) I don't like the look of this!

WANKLIN. (*Going forward.*) Come, Chairman! Wilder sends you his apologies. A man can't do more.

(WILDER, *followed by* TENCH, *comes in, and goes to* ANTHONY.)

WILDER. (*Glumly.*) I withdraw my words, sir. I'm sorry. (ANTHONY *nods to him.*)

ENID. You haven't come to a decision, Mr. Wanklin? (WANKLIN *shakes his head.*)

WANKLIN. We're all here, Chairman; what do you say? Shall we get on with the business, or shall we go back to the other room?

SCANTLEBURY. Yes, yes; let's get on. We must settle something.

(*He turns from a small chair, and settles himself suddenly in the largest chair with a sigh of comfort.*)

(WILDER *and* WANKLIN *also sit; and* TENCH, *drawing up a straight-backed chair close to his Chairman, sits on the edge of it with the minute-book and a stylographic pen.*)

ENID. (*Whispering.*) I want to speak to you a minute, Ted.

(*They go out through the double-doors.*)

WANKLIN. Really, Chairman, it's no use soothing ourselves with a sense of false security. If this strike's not brought to an end before the General Meeting, the shareholders will certainly haul us over the coals.

SCANTLEBURY. (*Stirring.*) What—what's that?

WANKLIN. I know it for a fact.

ANTHONY. Let them!

WILDER. And get turned out?

WANKLIN. (*To* ANTHONY.) I don't mind martyrdom for a policy in which I believe, but I object to being burnt for someone else's principles.

SCANTLEBURY. Very reasonable—you must see that, Chairman.

ANTHONY. We owe it to other employers to stand firm.

WANKLIN. There's a limit to that.

ANTHONY. You were all full of fight at the start.

SCANTLEBURY. (*With a sort of groan.*) We thought the men would give in, but they—haven't!

ANTHONY. They will!

WILDER. (*Rising and pacing up and down.*) I can't have my reputation as a man of business destroyed for the satisfaction of starving the men out. (*Almost in tears.*) I can't have it! How can we meet the shareholders with things in the state they are?

SCANTLEBURY. Hear, hear—hear, hear!

WILDER. (*Lashing himself.*) If anyone expects me to say to them I've lost you fifty thousand pounds and sooner than put my pride in my pocket I'll lose you another. (*Glancing at* ANTHONY.) It's—it's unnatural! *I don't want* to go against you, sir——

WANKLIN. (*Persuasively.*) Come, Chairman, we're *not* free agents. We're part of a machine. Our only business is to see the Company earns as much profit as it safely can. If you blame me for want of principle, I say that we're Trustees. Reason tells us we shall never get back in the saving of wages what we shall lose if we continue this struggle—really, Chairman, we *must* bring it to an end, on the best terms we can make.

ANTHONY. No.

(*There is a pause of general dismay.*)

WILDER. It's a deadlock then. (*Letting his hands drop with a sort of despair.*) Now I shall never get off to Spain!

WANKLIN. (*Retaining a trace of irony.*) You hear the consequences of your victory, Chairman?

WILDER. (*With a burst of feeling.*) My wife's *ill!*

SCANTLEBURY. Dear, dear! You don't say so.

WILDER. If I don't get her out of this cold, I won't answer for the consequences.

(*Through the double-doors* EDGAR *comes in looking very grave.*)

EDGAR. (*To his father.*) Have you heard this, sir? Mrs. Roberts is dead!

(*Everyone stares at him, as if trying to gauge the importance of this news.*)

Enid saw her this afternoon; she had no coals, or food, or anything. It's enough!

(*There is silence, everyone avoiding the other's eyes, except* ANTHONY, *who stares hard at his son.*)

SCANTLEBURY. You don't suggest that we could have helped the poor thing?

WILDER. (*Flustered.*) The woman was in bad health. Nobody can say there's any responsibility on us. At least—not on me.

EDGAR. (*Hotly.*) I say that we *are* responsible.

ANTHONY. War is war!

EDGAR. Not on women!

WANKLIN. It not infrequently happens that women are the greatest sufferers.

EDGAR. If we knew that, all the more responsibility rests on us.

ANTHONY. This is no matter for amateurs.

EDGAR. Call me what you like, sir. It's sickened me. We had no right to carry things to such a length.

WILDER. I don't like this business a bit—that Radical rag will twist it to their own ends; see if they don't! They'll get up some cock-and-bull story about the poor woman's dying from starvation. I wash my hands of it.

EDGAR. You can't. None of us can.

SCANTLEBURY. (*Striking his fist on the arm of his chair.*) But I protest against this——

EDGAR. Protest as you like, Mr. Scantlebury. It won't alter facts.

ANTHONY. That's enough.

EDGAR. (*Facing him angrily.*) No, sir. I tell you exactly what I think. If we pretend the men are not suffering, it's humbug; and if they're suffering, we know enough of human nature to know the women are suffering more, and as to the children—well—it's damnable! (SCANTLEBURY *rises from his chair.*)

I don't say that we meant to be cruel, I don't say anything of the sort; but I do say it's criminal to shut our eyes to the facts. We employ these men, and we can't get out of it. I don't care so much about the men, but I'd sooner resign my position on the Board than go on starving women in this way.

(*All except* ANTHONY *are now upon their feet;* ANTHONY *sits grasping the arms of his chair and staring at his son.*)

SCANTLEBURY. I don't—I don't like the way you're putting it, young sir.

WANKLIN. You're rather overshooting the mark.

WILDER. I should think so indeed!

EDGAR. (*Losing control.*) It's no use blinking things! If *you* want to have the death of women on your hands—*I* don't!

SCANTLEBURY. Now, now, young man!

WILDER. On *our* hands? Not on *mine,* I won't have it!

EDGAR. We are five members of this Board; if we were four against it, why did we let it drift till it came to this? You know perfectly well why—because we hoped we should starve the men out. Well, all we've done is to starve one woman out!

SCANTLEBURY. (*Almost hysterically.*) I protest, I protest! I'm a humane man —we're all humane men!

EDGAR. (*Scornfully.*) There's nothing wrong with our *humanity.* It's our imaginations, Mr. Scantlebury.

WILDER. Nonsense! My imagination's as good as yours.

EDGAR. If so, it isn't good enough.

WILDER. I foresaw this!

EDGAR. Then why didn't you put your foot down?

WILDER. Much good that would have done.
(*He looks at* ANTHONY.)

EDGAR. If you, and I, and each one of us here who say that our imaginations are so good——

SCANTLEBURY. (*Flurried.*) I never said so.

EDGAR. (*Paying no attention.*) —had put our feet down, the thing would have been ended long ago, and this poor woman's life wouldn't have been crushed out of her like this. For all we can tell there may be a dozen other starving women.

SCANTLEBURY. For God's sake, sir, don't use that word at a—at a Board meeting; it's—it's monstrous.

EDGAR. I *will* use it, Mr. Scantlebury.

SCANTLEBURY. Then I shall not listen to you. I shall not listen! It's painful to me. (*He covers his ears.*)

WANKLIN. None of us are opposed to a settlement, except your father.

EDGAR. I'm certain that if the shareholders knew——

WANKLIN. I don't think you'll find their imaginations are any better than ours. Because a woman happens to have a weak heart——

EDGAR. A struggle like this finds out the weak spots in everybody. Any child knows that. If it hadn't been for this cut-throat policy, she needn't have died like this; and there wouldn't be all this misery that anyone who isn't a fool can see is going on.

(*Throughout the foregoing* ANTHONY *has eyed his son; he now moves as though to rise, but stops as* EDGAR *speaks again.*)

I don't defend the men, or myself, or anybody.

WANKLIN. You may have to! A coroner's jury of disinterested sympathizers may say some very nasty things. We mustn't lose sight of our position.

SCANTLEBURY. (*Without uncovering his ears.*) Coroner's jury! No, no, it's not a case for that!

EDGAR. I've had enough of cowardice.

WANKLIN. Cowardice is an unpleasant word, Mr. Edgar Anthony. It will look very like cowardice if we suddenly concede the men's demands when a thing like this happens; we must be careful!

WILDER. Of course we must. We've no knowledge of this matter, except a rumor. The proper course is to put the whole thing into the hands of Harness to settle for us; that's natural, that's what we *should* have come to anyway.

SCANTLEBURY. (*With dignity.*) Exactly! (*Turning to* EDGAR.) And as to you, young sir, I can't sufficiently express my—my distaste for the way you've treated the whole matter. You ought to withdraw! Talking of starvation, talking of cowardice! Considering what our views are! Except your own father—we're all agreed the only policy is—is one of goodwill—it's most irregular, it's most improper, and all I can say is it's—it's given me pain— (*He places his hand over his heart.*)

EDGAR. (*Stubbornly.*) I withdraw nothing.

(*He is about to say more when* SCANTLEBURY *once more covers up his ears.* TENCH *suddenly makes a demonstration with the minute-book. A sense of having been engaged in the unusual comes over all of them, and one by one they resume their seats.* EDGAR *alone remains on his feet.*)

WILDER. (*With an air of trying to wipe something out.*) I pay no attention to what young Mr. Anthony has said. Coroner's jury! The idea's preposterous. I—I move this amendment to the Chairman's motion: That the dispute be placed at once in the hands of Mr. Simon Harness for settlement, on the lines indicated by him this morning. Anyone second that? (*TENCH writes in his book.*)

WANKLIN. I do.

WILDER. Very well, then; I ask the Chairman to put it to the Board.

ANTHONY. (*With a great sigh—slowly.*)

We have been made the subject of an attack. (*Looking round at* WILDER *and* SCANTLEBURY *with ironical contempt.*) I take it on *my* shoulders. I am seventy-six years old. I have been Chairman of this Company since its inception two-and-thirty years ago. I have seen it pass through good and evil report. My connection with it began in the year that this young man was born.

(EDGAR *bows his head.* ANTHONY, *gripping his chair, goes on.*)

I have had to do with "men" for fifty years; I've always stood up to them; I have never been beaten yet. I have fought the men of this Company four times, and four times I have beaten them. It has been said that I am not the man I was. (*He looks at* WILDER.) However that may be, I am man enough to stand to my guns.

(*His voice grows stronger. The double-doors are opened.* ENID *slips in, followed by* UNDERWOOD, *who restrains her.*)

The men have been treated justly, they have had fair wages, we have always been ready to listen to complaints. It has been said that times have changed; if they have, I have not changed with them. Neither will I. It has been said that masters and men are equal! Cant! There can only be one master in a house! Where two men meet, the better man will rule. It has been said that Capital and Labor have the same interests. Cant! Their interests are as wide asunder as the poles. It has been said that the Board is only part of a machine. Cant! We *are* the machine; its brains and sinews; it is for us to lead and to determine what is to be done, and to do it without fear or favor. Fear of the men! Fear of the shareholders! Fear of our own shadows! Before I am like that, I hope to die.

(*He pauses, and meeting his son's eyes, goes on.*)

There is only one way of treating "men"—with *the iron hand*. This half-and-half business, the half-and-half manners of this generation, has brought all this upon us. Sentiment and softness, and what this young man, no doubt, would call his social policy. You can't eat cake and have it! This middle-class sentiment, or socialism, or whatever it may be, is rotten. Masters are masters, men are men! Yield one demand, and they will make it six. They are (*he smiles grimly*) like Oliver Twist, asking for more. If I were in *their* place I should be the same. But I am not in their place. Mark my words: one fine morning, when you have given way here, and given way there—you will find you have parted with the ground beneath your feet, and are deep in the bog of bankruptcy; and with you, floundering in that bog, will be the very men you have given way to. I have been accused of being a domineering tyrant, thinking only of my pride—I am thinking of the future of this country, threatened with the black waters of confusion, threatened with mob government, threatened with what I cannot see. If by any conduct of mine I help to bring this on us, I shall be ashamed to look my fellows in the face.

(ANTHONY *stares before him, at what he cannot see, and there is perfect stillness.* FROST *comes in from the hall, and all but* ANTHONY *look round at him uneasily.*)

FROST. (*To his master.*) The men are here, sir. (ANTHONY *makes a gesture of dismissal.*) Shall I bring them in, sir?

ANTHONY. Wait!

(FROST *goes out,* ANTHONY *turns to face his son.*)

I come to the attack that has been made upon me.

(EDGAR, *with a gesture of deprecation, remains motionless with his head a little bowed.*)

A woman has died. I am told that her blood is on my hands; I am told that on my hands is the starvation and the suffering of other women and of children.

EDGAR. I said "on *our* hands," sir.

ANTHONY. It is the same. (*His voice grows stronger and stronger, his feeling is more and more manifest.*) I am not aware that if my adversary suffer in a fair fight not sought by me, it is *my* fault. If I fall under *his* feet —as fall I may—I shall not complain. That will by *my* lookout—and this is —his. I cannot separate, as I would, these men from their women and children. A fair fight is a fair fight! Let them learn to think before they pick a quarrel!

EDGAR. (*In a low voice.*) But is it a fair fight, Father? Look at them, and look at us! They've only this one weapon!

ANTHONY. (*Grimly.*) And you're weak-kneed enough to teach them how to use it! It seems the fashion nowadays for men to take their enemy's side. I have not learnt that art. Is it my fault that they quarreled with their Union too?

EDGAR. There is such a thing as Mercy.

ANTHONY. And Justice comes before it.

EDGAR. What seems just to one man, sir, is injustice to another.

ANTHONY. (*With suppressed passion.*) You accuse me of injustice—of what amounts to inhumanity—of cruelty—

(EDGAR *makes a gesture of horror—a general frightened movement.*)

WANKLIN. Come, come, Chairman.

ANTHONY. (*In a grim voice.*) These are the words of my own son. They are the words of a generation that I don't understand; the words of a soft breed.

(*A general murmur. With a violent effort* ANTHONY *recovers his control.*)

EDGAR. (*Quietly.*) I said it of *myself*, too, Father.

(*A long look is exchanged between them, and* ANTHONY *puts out his hand with a gesture as if to sweep the personalities away; then places it against his brow, swaying as though from giddiness. There is a movement toward him. He moves them back.*)

ANTHONY. Before I put this amendment to the Board, I have one more word to say. (*He looks from face to face.*) If it is carried, it means that we shall fail in what we set ourselves to do. It means that we shall fail in the duty that we owe to all Capital. It means that we shall fail in the duty that we owe ourselves. It means that we shall be open to constant attack to which we as constantly shall have to yield. Be under no misapprehension—run this time, and you will never make a stand again! You will have to fly like curs before the whips of your own men. If that is the lot you wish for, you will vote for this amendment.

(*He looks again, from face to face, finally resting his gaze on* EDGAR; *all sit with their eyes on the ground.* ANTHONY *makes a gesture, and* TENCH *hands him the book. He reads.*)

"Moved by Mr. Wilder, and seconded by Mr. Wanklin: 'That the men's demands be placed at once in the hands of Mr. Simon Harness for settlement on the lines indicated by him this morning.'" (*With sudden vigor.*) Those in favor: Signify the same in the usual way!

(*For a minute no one moves; then hastily, just as* ANTHONY *is about to speak,* WILDER's *hand and* WANKLIN's *are held up, then* SCANTLEBURY's, *and last* EDGAR's, *who does not lift his head.*)

Contrary? (ANTHONY *lifts his own hand.*) (*In a clear voice.*) The amendment is carried. I resign my position on this Board.

(ENID *gasps, and there is dead silence.*

ANTHONY *sits motionless, his head slowly drooping; suddenly he heaves as though the whole of his life had risen up within him.*)

Fifty years! You have disgraced me, gentlemen. Bring in the men!

(*He sits motionless, staring before him. The Board draws hurriedly together, and forms a group.* TENCH *in a frightened manner speaks into the hall.* UNDERWOOD *almost forces* ENID *from the room.*)

WILDER. (*Hurriedly.*) What's to be said to them? Why isn't Harness here? Ought we to see the men before he comes? I don't——

TENCH. Will you come in, please?

(*Enter* THOMAS, GREEN, BULGIN, *and* ROUS, *who file up in a row past the little table.* TENCH *sits down and writes. All eyes are fixed on* ANTHONY, *who makes no sign.*)

WANKLIN. (*Stepping up to the little table with nervous cordiality.*) Well, Thomas, how's it to be? What's the result of your meeting?

ROUS. Sim Harness has our answer. He'll tell you what it is. We're waiting for him. He'll speak for us.

WANKLIN. Is that so, Thomas?

THOMAS. (*Sullenly.*) Yes. Roberts will not be coming; his wife is dead.

SCANTLEBURY. Yes, yes! Poor woman! Yes! Yes!

FROST. (*Entering from the hall.*) Mr. Harness, sir! (*As* HARNESS *enters, he retires.*)

(HARNESS *has a piece of paper in his hand, he bows to the Directors, nods toward the men, and takes his stand behind the little table in the very center of the room.*)

HARNESS. Good evening, gentlemen.

(TENCH, *with the paper he has been writing, joins him; they speak together in low tones.*)

WILDER. We've been waiting for you, Harness. Hope we shall come to some——

FROST. (*Entering from the hall.*) Roberts! (*He goes.*)

(ROBERTS *comes hastily in, and stands staring at* ANTHONY. *His face is drawn and old.*)

ROBERTS. Mr. Anthony, I am afraid I am a little late; I would have been here in time but for something that—has happened. (*To the men.*) Has anything been said?

THOMAS. No! But, man, what made ye come?

ROBERTS. Ye told us this morning, gentlemen, to go away and consider our position. We have reconsidered it; we are here to bring you the men's answer. (*To* ANTHONY.) Go ye back to London. We have nothing for you. By no jot or tittle do we abate our demands, nor will we until the whole of those demands are yielded.

(ANTHONY *looks at him but does not speak. There is a movement amongst the men as though they were bewildered.*)

HARNESS. Roberts!

ROBERTS. (*Glancing fiercely at him, and back to* ANTHONY.) Is that clear enough for ye? Is it short enough and to the point? Ye made a mistake to think that we would come to heel. Ye may break the body, but ye cannot break the spirit. Get back to London, the men have nothing for ye.

(*Pausing uneasily he takes a step toward the unmoving* ANTHONY.)

EDGAR. We're all sorry for you, Roberts, but——

ROBERTS. Keep your sorrow, young man. Let your father speak!

HARNESS. (*With the sheet of paper in his hand, speaking from behind the little table.*) Roberts!

ROBERTS. (*To* ANTHONY, *with passionate intensity.*) Why don't ye answer?

HARNESS. Roberts!

ROBERTS. (*Turning sharply.*) What is it?

HARNESS. (*Gravely.*) You're talking without the book; things have traveled past you.

(*He makes a sign to* TENCH, *who beck-*

ons the Directors. *They quickly sign his copy of the terms.*)

Look at this, man! (*Holding up his sheet of paper.*) "Demands conceded, *with the exception of those relating to the engineers and furnacemen.* Double wages for Saturday's overtime. Night-shifts as they are." These terms have been agreed. The men go back to work again tomorrow. The strike is at an end.

ROBERTS. (*Reading the paper, and turning on the men. They shrink from him, all but* ROUS, *who stands his ground. With deadly stillness.*) Ye have gone back on me? I stood by ye to the death; ye waited for *that* to throw me over!

(*The men answer, all speaking together.*)

ROUS. It's a lie!

THOMAS. Ye were past endurance, man.

GREEN. If ye'd listen to me——

BULGIN. (*Under his breath.*) Hold your jaw!

ROBERTS. Ye waited for *that!*

HARNESS. (*Taking the Directors' copy of the terms, and handing his own to* TENCH.) That's enough, men. You had better go.

(*The men shuffle slowly, awkwardly away.*)

WILDER. (*In a low, nervous voice.*) There's nothing to stay for now, I suppose. (*He follows to the door.*) I shall have a try for that train! Coming, Scantlebury?

SCANTLEBURY. (*Following with* WANKLIN.) Yes, yes; wait for me.

(*He stops as* ROBERTS *speaks.*)

ROBERTS. (*To* ANTHONY.) But *ye* have not signed them terms! They can't make terms without their Chairman! Ye would never sign them terms!

(ANTHONY *looks at him without speaking.*)

Don't tell me ye have! for the love o' God! (*With passionate appeal.*) I reckoned on ye!

HARNESS. (*Holding out the Directors' copy of the terms.*) *The Board has signed!*

(ROBERTS *looks dully at the signatures—dashes the paper from him, and covers up his eyes.*)

SCANTLEBURY. (*Behind his hand to* TENCH.) Look after the Chairman! He's not well; he's not well—he had no lunch. If there's any fund started for the women and children put me down for—for twenty pounds.

(*He goes out into the hall, in cumbrous haste; and* WANKLIN, *who has been staring at* ROBERTS *and* ANTHONY *with twitchings on his face, follows.* EDGAR *remains seated on the sofa, looking at the ground;* TENCH, *returning to the bureau, writes in his minute-book.* HARNESS *stands by the little table, gravely watching* ROBERTS.)

ROBERTS. Then you're no longer Chairman of this Company! (*Breaking into half-mad laughter.*) Ah! ha—ah, ha, ha! They've thrown ye over—thrown over their Chairman: Ah—ha—ha! (*With a sudden dreadful calm.*) So—they've done us both down, Mr. Anthony?

(ENID, *hurrying through the double-doors, comes quickly to her father.*)

ANTHONY. Both broken men, my friend Roberts!

HARNESS. (*Coming down and laying his hands on* ROBERTS'S *sleeve.*) For shame, Roberts! Go home quietly, man; go home!

ROBERTS. (*Tearing his arm away.*) Home? (*Shrinking together—in a whisper.*) Home!

ENID. (*Quietly to her father.*) Come away, dear! Come to your room!

(ANTHONY *rises with an effort. He turns to* ROBERTS, *who looks at him. They stand several seconds, gazing at each other fixedly;* ANTHONY *lifts his hand, as though to salute, but lets it fall. The expression of* ROBERTS' *face changes from hostility to wonder. They bend their heads in token of respect.* ANTHONY *turns, and slowly walks toward the curtained door. Suddenly he sways as though about*

*to fall, recovers himself, and is assisted out
by* EDGAR *and* ENID; UNDERWOOD *follows,
but stops at the door.* ROBERTS *remains
motionless for several seconds, staring intently after* ANTHONY, *then goes out into
the hall.*)

TENCH. (*Approaching* HARNESS.) It's a
great weight off my mind, Mr. Harness! But what a painful scene, sir!
(*He wipes his brow.*)

(HARNESS, *pale and resolute, regards
with a grim half-smile the quavering*
TENCH.)

It's all been so violent! What did he
mean by: "Done us both down"? If
he has lost his wife, poor fellow, he
oughtn't to have spoken to the Chairman like that!

HARNESS. A woman dead; and the two
best men both broken!

TENCH. (*Staring at him—suddenly excited.*) D'you know, sir — these
terms, they're the *very* same we drew
up together, you and I, and put to
both sides before the fight began?
All this—all this—and—and what
for?

HARNESS. (*In a slow grim voice.*) That's
where the fun comes in!

(UNDERWOOD *without turning from the
door makes a gesture of assent.*)

The curtain falls.

1909

WHO'S WHO IN COLLEGE READER

ADAMS, HENRY (1838-1918)
Preparation for Teaching History, 96. *The Tendency of History*, 98. *Prayer to the Virgin of Chartres*, 791.
Easily the most discussed today of all the Adamses, Henry Adams was for a brief time teacher of history in Harvard College and editor of the *North American Review*. His was the first historical seminar at Harvard, and Henry Cabot Lodge, whom he advised on preparation for the teaching of history, was among his first students. His later works are marked by the pessimistic belief that intellectual energy is the same as physical energy and tends to dissipate itself in the universe. His "Prayer to the Virgin of Chartres" indicates his personal recourse to faith.

ADLER, MORTIMER J. (1902-)
The Reading of "Reading," 230.
Mortimer J. Adler, teacher at the University of Chicago, has won wide attention by his position in education. "The abolition of the elective system," he has written, "goes to the very heart of the problem. Liberal education is developed only when a curriculum can be devised which is the same for all men . . ." His prescriptive program calls also for discipline in methodology, and his "best seller" *How to Read a Book* is a contribution to prescriptive methodology. Our selection is a representative chapter in this book.

ALLEN, FREDERICK LEWIS (1890-)
Crash! 720.
A native of Boston, Frederick Lewis Allen served on the editorial staffs of the *Atlantic* and *Century* before becoming editor of *Harper's*. "Crash!" is the climactic chapter out of Mr. Allen's *Only Yesterday,* which demonstrates that the nearly contemporary scene provides the liveliest sort of history.

ARNOLD, MATTHEW (1822-1888)
In Harmony with Nature, 743. *Dover Beach*, 789. *Requiescat*, 803.
English essayist, educator, critic, and poet, who tried persistently but often despairingly to keep the culture of his time from being eclipsed by the machinery of living. "Dover Beach" (1867) reveals his excellent poetic technique as well as his characteristic pessimism.

AUDEN, WYSTAN HUGH (1907-)
Sharp and Silent in the Clear October Lighting, 752. *Voltaire at Ferney*, 788.
A British writer, recently become an American citizen, who is best known for poetry of wide range in content and technique, but who has experimented also in the fields of drama and essay. He has lectured extensively in America.

BEEBE, WILLIAM (1877-)
Elephants of the Sea, 193.
Born in Brooklyn, William Beebe has wandered far from that borough of New York City, which is supposed to have such a strong hold on its citizens. But his wanderings have been largely on scientific expeditions. He is curator of

ornithology for the New York Zoological Society. "Elephants of the Sea" can be matched for interest many times in his writings, since Mr. Beebe is able to endow all his work with a remarkable zest.

BEHRMAN, S. N. (1893-   )
End of Summer, 831.
Samuel Nathaniel Behrman turned to the stage after practicing journalism in New York City. His sophisticated plays are equally remarkable for their teasing presentation of theme and for their entertainment value. In "End of Summer," Mr. Behrman bites the hand that has sometimes fed him—Freudian psychology.

BEMELMANS, LUDWIG (1898-   )
Prison Visit, 562.
Illustrator and author, Ludwig Bemelmans came to the United States from Bavaria in 1914. Before he was known as a writer, his drawings had appeared in *Vogue, The New Yorker,* and other magazines. "Prison Visit" is from *The Donkey Inside* (1941), a book based on his visit to Ecuador.

BENÉT, STEPHEN VINCENT (1898-1943)
Litany for Dictatorships, 780.
Recipient of a Master's degree from Yale, Stephen Benét's success as a writer diverted him from the teaching career that he had contemplated. Two works from his pen are acclaimed masterpieces, the short story "The Devil and Daniel Webster" and the long poem *John Brown's Body.* An ardent believer in democracy, Benét wrote several poems in defense of our government and society, just before his untimely death. Of these political poems, "Litany for Dictatorships" is the most celebrated.

BENÉT, WILLIAM ROSE (1886-   )
Men on Strike, 773.
A more subtle poet than the bright genius who was his younger brother, William Rose Benét has never attained that brother's popularity. Scattered through his volumes of verse, however, are many poems whose message is explicit enough. The just wrath of "Men on Strike" is not elsewhere matched but suggests a vein the author might well develop.

BENNETT, ARNOLD (1867-1931)
Why a Classic Is a Classic, 239.
Prolific British author of novels, stories, plays, and essays, best known perhaps for *The Old Wives' Tale* (1908), one of the outstanding novels of the twentieth century. His series of essays on literary taste, from which "Why a Classic Is a Classic" has been taken, reveals his persistent interest in the various aspects of writing and reading.

BLAKE, WILLIAM (1757-1827)
"Mock on, Mock on, Voltaire, Rousseau," 794.
A sensitive London mystic who poured his soul with equal genius into engravings and poetry. As an engraver he is best known for his astounding interpretations of the book of *Job* (c. 1825), Dante's *Divine Comedy* (1825-27), and Chaucer's *Canterbury Tales.* His most admired short lyrics are the complementary *Songs of Innocence* (1789) and *Songs of Experience* (1794), in which his poetic images are not as symbolic and cryptic as in some of his later poems.

BLUNT, WILFRID SCAWEN (1840-1922)
I Have Saved Egypt, 498. *Yankees, the Coming Race*, 500. *Death of Queen Victoria, 1901*, 500.
British government servant whose defense of East Indian, Egyptian, and Irish nationalism in numerous prose treatises contrasts sharply with his somewhat conventional poetry.

BOAS, FRANZ (1858-1942)
Racial Prejudices, 165.
Born in Minden, Westphalia, Franz Boas studied at the Universities of Heidelberg, Bonn, and Kiel, before coming to the New World to make investigations in anthropology in Puerto Rico and Mexico. Appointed first at Clark University, he spent the greater part of his teaching career at Columbia. "Racial Prejudices" is the first chapter in *The Mind of Primitive Man*, one of the most important contributions by a scientist to liberalism.

BORLAND, HAL (1900-   )
February Winds, 130. *A Day in March*, 130. *Lilacs*, 132. *Green Hills*, 133. *Live Waters*, 133.
A native of Nebraska, Hal Borland grew up on a Colorado ranch, served in the Navy, turned to engineering and ultimately to writing. This last interest brought him to New York, where he acquired a degree in literature from Columbia in 1923, and subsequently earned a wide reputation as a miscellaneous writer of essays, poetry, fiction, radio and motion picture scripts, and books dealing with American folklore and outdoor life. Readers of the *New York Sunday Times* editorial page have long read and admired his unsigned little essays on the ways of nature in all seasons of the year. It is from these charming vignettes that selections have been made for this anthology. Mr. Borland has a home in the Connecticut hills north of Stamford, but his love of the American countryside everywhere takes him to all points of the compass, and he is constantly on the wing!

BRADFORD, GAMALIEL (1863-1932)
God's Vagabond: Saint Francis of Assisi, 60.
Chief American contributor during the twenties to the "new biography," Gamaliel Bradford claimed Saint-Beuve as a master. Hypochondria kept Bradford a lifelong invalid, but after he discovered his true bent, it did not much handicap his productiveness. "God's Vagabond" is one of nearly a hundred "psychographs" (as he called them) that Bradford made after he was fifty.

BRECHER, EDWARD M. (1911-   )
The Book America Wrote, 417.
Mr. Brecher was educated at Wisconsin, Swarthmore, Minnesota, and Brown. After serving as assistant to the Chairman of the Federal Communications Commission, and Manager of Radio Station WQQW in Washington, D. C., he became assistant editor of Consumers' Union *Reports* in New York City. He has written for *The Atlantic Monthly, Harper's, The Reader's Digest, Nature*, and other magazines.

BROOKE, RUPERT (1887-1915)
The Soldier, 755.
A young English scholar-poet who lost his life early in the First World War but not until he had won enduring fame for sonnets that throb with youthful idealism. Of these the most popular is "The Soldier," reprinted here.

BROOKS, ROBERT R. R. (1905-   )
The N.L.R.B. and Democracy, 304.
Born in Rome, Italy, Robert R. R. Brooks was Rhodes Scholar from Connecticut, 1926-1929, after a notable career as an athlete at Wesleyan. Having overtaxed his heart rowing at Oxford, he was asked to coach the varsity crew there. On his return to America, he did graduate study in economics at Yale, taught at Williams, and became dean of the latter institution. Possibly because he was in England during the general strike, he has taken an especial interest in the relations of capital and labor.

BROUN, HEYWOOD (1888-1939)
The Fifty-First Dragon, 144.
A great-hearted journalist, Heywood Broun twice lost his job as columnist for espousing liberal causes, first during the Sacco-Vanzetti trial and second after attacking the *World* and the *Nation* for suppressing the news. He was one of the founders and the first president of the American Newspaper Guild. "The Fifty-First Dragon" appears as a reminder that Heywood Broun once contributed to the sports page.

BROWNING, ROBERT (1812-1889)
Prospice, 804.
Bracketed with Tennyson as one of the two greatest Victorian poets. He was a genius of extraordinary erudition and range, an experimenter in verse forms, a classical scholar, an acute psychologist, a poet-philosopher. Although his power of sustained creative flight is revealed best in *The Ring and the Book*—a parade of the principals in an Italian murder trial—his most popular poems are the shorter "dramatic monologues," like "My Last Duchess," and such stirring narratives as "How They Brought the Good News From Ghent to Aix." "Prospice," reprinted here, is his courageous view of death.

BRUSH, KATHARINE (1902-   )
Night Club, 612.
Born in Middletown, Conn., and educated at the Centenary Collegiate Institute, Hackettstown, N. J., Mrs. Brush began her writing career as a reporter for the Boston *Traveler* in 1918. Her first fiction was published five years later. "Night Club" reveals the harsh reality of work in the business of entertainment, and the strange blindness of the woman attendant who seeks romance in reading while overlooking it in the life with which she deals nightly.

BUCHANAN, JOSEPH R. (1851-1924)
The Trials of a Labor Editor, 24.
The Story of a Labor Editor, from which "The Trials of a Labor Editor" is taken, is one of the best autobiographical narratives by a labor organizer. It tells how the author, a native of Hannibal, Mo., migrated to Leadville, Colo., as a printer; became a partisan of labor there; then, as a labor journalist and organizer, had a share in some of the fiercest industrial struggles of the nineteenth century. The book terminates with the trial and execution of the leading Chicago anarchists.

BURCH, BRADLEY (1924-   )
Where Is the Humor? 106. *Eve of Battle,* 108. *Don't Leave Me Here,* 109.
Glory Is a Word for Kings, 110.
A young New York idealist whose college career was interrupted by service in the army in Europe, which brought to him a wound in action and to his coura-

geous young wife a series of letters from the front, of which three are here published for the first time.

CAMPION, THOMAS (1567-1620)
The Man of Life Upright, 799.
An Elizabethan physician whose artistic interests led him also into the fields of poetry, music, literary criticism, and philosophy. Many of his fine lyrics he set to music of his own composition. In "The Man of Life Upright," reprinted here, his love of verse and of philosophy blend.

CANFIELD, DOROTHY (1879-   )
Supply and Demand, 317.
Something in the blood took Dorothea Canfield Fisher back to Vermont, a family home since colonial days; but the way was round about, for Mrs. Fisher was born in Kansas, studied at Ohio State University, Columbia, and the Sorbonne before she and her husband chose to live on a Vermont farm. "Supply and Demand" contains as much "horse sense," a native would "allow," as if it had been written by a Yankee.

CARLYLE, THOMAS (1795-1881)
The "Rape" of Alsace-Lorraine, 88. *Coleridge: Last Phase,* 474.
The son of a Scottish stonemason, who became one of the most famous of the Victorian philosophers, social critics, historians, and biographers. He condemned the loss of spiritual values in his time, attacked legislative cure-alls, hated democracy, and praised work and hero worship. His *Sartor Resartus* (1833-34) is a spiritual autobiography; his *French Revolution* (1837), a sulphurous and subjective treatment of his theme. The selections reprinted in this anthology reveal the historical and biographical qualities of his voluminous literary labors.

CERF, BENNETT (1898-   )
Hurrah for Captain Spalding and the Other Marx Brothers, 491.
Publisher of the Modern Library and Random House books, Bennett Cerf became an author when his friends insisted that he put some of his humorous stories (of which he seemed to have an inexhaustible supply) into print. From that he was graduated into anecdotage and then became a columnist for the *Saturday Review of Literature.* "Hurrah for Captain Spalding" belongs to the second stage. Mr. Cerf should be commended especially for his interest in the theater, which has led him into publishing ventures, like *The Complete Greek Drama,* that no other publisher would hazard.

CLEMENS, SAMUEL. *See* MARK TWAIN

CLOUGH, ARTHUR HUGH (1819-1861)
In the Great Metropolis, 750. *Say Not the Struggle Naught Availeth,* 756. *The Latest Decalogue,* 772.
A short-lived scholar-poet and a friend of Matthew Arnold (*q.v.*) whose shorter poems are marked by the melancholy despair that bedevilled his last years. Of these shorter poems, "The Latest Decalogue" is a satire on the Victorian concept of the ten commandments; and the rugged verses beginning "Say not the struggle naught availeth" were effectively quoted by Winston Churchill to bolster the courage of a nation under savage German air assaults in 1940.

COREY, GEORGE H.
$595 F.O.B., 620.
Wanderer, manual laborer, dentist, and teacher of oral surgery in Shantung Chris-

tian University, George Corey had learned to value the amenities of life through a knowledge of the "blood, sweat, and tears" that produced them before he turned to writing for expression. "$595 F.O.B.," his first published short story, has a factualism that comes from Dr. Corey's experiences as an assembler in a Ford factory.

CORWIN, NORMAN (1910-   )
Radio Primer, 809.
Born in Boston, Norman Corwin got a newspaper job, when he was ready to embark on a career, by sending out identical letters to sixty New England newspapers. He transferred to radio and became a director-producer for CBS in 1938. He is the author of three books of plays: *13 by Corwin, More by Corwin,* and *On a Note of Triumph.* "Radio Primer" was first produced on May 4, 1941, as the opening program of *Twenty-Six by Corwin,* under the direction of the author. The musical score was composed and conducted by Lyn Murray.

CRAIG, EDWARD GORDON (1872-   )
Proposals Old and New, 326.
Notable British actor, stage designer, and producer. He was the son of Ellen Terry, the famous actress, and wrote his mother's biography, *Ellen Terry and Her Secret Self,* in 1931. After acting from 1889 to 1897, he devoted himself entirely to stage designing and to the production of plays, including *Hamlet* for the Moscow Art Theatre in 1905. He is the author of *The Art of the Theatre* (1905), *The Theatre Advancing* (1919), and other books and many articles.

CRAVEN, THOMAS (1889-   )
Modernism, 405.
Thomas Craven has only Albert S. Barnes, "the Argyrol man," as a serious competitor as America's first critic of art. Both are men of strong convictions which they do not trammel in expression. "Modernism" probably indicates that they would collide if they met. A native of Kansas and a graduate of Kansas Wesleyan, Mr. Craven had a varied career before he became a free-lance writer in 1914. His best books are *Men of Art* and *Modern Art.*

DEKKER, THOMAS (1572?-1632)
Of Winter, 129.
A miscellaneous free-lance writer of the time of Elizabeth and James I who is best known for such realistic comedies as "The Shoemakers' Holiday" and "The Honest Whore," but who also wrote satires on men and manners, like *The Gull's Hornbook,* exposures of roguery, like *The Bellman of London,* and numerous journalistic pamphlets dealing with London life. That he did not confine his shrewd and accurate observation to mere men and women is revealed in his little essay on winter that is reprinted here.

DEWEY, JOHN (1859-   )
The Influence of Darwin on Philosophy, 186.
The ablest philosopher that America has produced, John Dewey is satisfied to call his thought "experimentalism," and thereby indicate the tentativeness of all his conclusions. In *Experience and Nature,* one of the great books of our time, Dewey destroyed the dichotomy of the world and the self created by the empirical fallacy of sensory ionization. Experience involves, beyond separation, both the world and the self. Less dramatic in effect, "The Influence of Darwin on Philosophy" demonstrates Dewey's ability to see new connections in old concatenations.

DIVINE, ARTHUR D. (1904-   )
Miracle at Dunkirk, 731.
Professional journalist, Arthur Durham Divine has written two minor descriptive masterpieces of heroism in World War II: "Miracle at Dunkirk" and "Firedrake," the story of a destroyer which seemed unsinkable but which finally went down after taking a battering such as no ship had ever endured before.

DOS PASSOS, JOHN (1896-   )
The American Plan, 21.
In adopting the "discontinuous" method of narration in his fictional trilogy, *U.S.A.,* in order to represent the chaos of modern times, John Dos Passos was faced with the problem of "timing" his episodes. This he solved by inventing three devices: the "newsreel," the "camera eye," and the "poetic biography." "The American Plan" is representative of the last device. Chicago-born, a graduate of Harvard College, John Dos Passos drove an ambulance in World War I and acquired from this experience material for his first books, *One Man's Initiation* and *Three Soldiers.* Later he became the historian in fiction of the "lost generation."

DOYLE, SIR ARTHUR CONAN (1859-1930)
The Adventure of the Blue Carbuncle, 671.
Seldom has a fiction writer's name become more closely linked with that of his literary creation than has Doyle's with that of Sherlock Holmes, the master sleuth who first appeared in "A Study in Scarlet" (1887) and then in delightful reincarnations for several decades. In spite of the merit of Dr. Doyle's historical novel, *The White Company* (1891), the Scottish physician will continue to be known primarily as the author of the famous detective stories, of which a typically exciting example is reprinted here.

DREW, ELIZABETH (1887-   )
Saki, 350.
An English-born literary critic who has keen power of analysis, and flavor and charm of expression. She graduated from Lady Margaret Hall, Oxford, with first honors in English Language and Literature, and then lectured at Girton College, Cambridge. For many years she has lived in America, where she has taught at the Bread Loaf School of English and at Smith College, and has lectured extensively elsewhere. She is the author of *Discovering Poetry, Discovering Drama, The Enjoyment of Literature,* and (with John L. Sweeny) *Directions in Modern Poetry.*

DUNSANY, LORD (1878-   )
The Highwayman, 668.
An Irish writer of one-act plays and short stories whose literary work is seasoned with characteristically Celtic romance, mystery, charm, and whimsicality. Perhaps the most popular of his playlets is the creepy "A Night in an Inn" (1916). *A Dreamer's Tales* (1910) and *Tales of Wonder* (1916) are two of the best collections of his stories.

DURAND, DANA B. (1905-   )
Magic and Experimental Science, 442.
Student of medieval history at Harvard and later teacher at Williams College, Dana B. Durand decided, after participating in World War II, "to give up the academic profession and continue in government service." He is at present with the OMGUS in Germany. He writes, "The republication of my article, if it takes

place, would be a gratifying finis to my scholarly career." The editors of this book hope publication herein does not mean "finis" to Mr. Durand's scholarly career.

DYER, SIR EDWARD (d. 1607)
My Mind to Me a Kingdom Is, 798.

An Elizabethan courtier, diplomat, and scholar who is best remembered by the typical poem reprinted in this collection, "My Mind to Me a Kingdom Is."

EDMAN, IRWIN (1896-   )
An Irishman Among the Brahmins, 529.

That "rara avis," a popular teacher of philosophy, Irwin Edman has used his instructional techniques and personal charm to counsel a large public in the ways of urbane living and thinking in *Richard Kane Looks at Life* and *Philosopher's Holiday.* "An Irishman Among the Brahmins" is a chapter in the latter book.

EDMONDS, WALTER D. (1903-   )
Death of Red Peril, 593.

An "upstate" New Yorker by birth, Walter D. Edmonds has made that area almost legendary by his tall tales written in the idiom of the locale. "Death of Red Peril" is certainly one of the tallest of these tales. Edmonds' best known books are *Rome Haul, Erie Water, Mostly Canallers,* and *Drums Along the Mohawk.*

ELIOT, THOMAS STEARNS (1888-   )
The Goodness of This Lady, 797.

The most influential poet in the English-speaking world at the end of the twenties was T. S. Eliot, who, in "Prufrock" and "The Waste Land," wrote of the decline of western culture in a Spenglerian mood. Mr. Eliot found his own stay in religious faith. "The Goodness of This Lady" is a section of "Ash Wednesday."

EMERSON, RALPH WALDO (1803-1882)
Hamatreya, 771. *The Problem,* 790.

"One of your very best poets, in my opinion," James Stephens, the Irish poet, declared of Ralph Waldo Emerson in a public lecture. "Hamatreya" scoffs at subservience to property rights, and "The Problem" questions allegiance to empty forms— favorite themes of the Concord poet. Emerson was not held in very high regard as a poet in his day, but he was acknowledged as the Lyceum's most inspired lecturer. The lectures became essays and the essays a philosophy with contradictions that were never reconciled.

FAULKNER, WILLIAM (1897-   )
That Evening Sun Go Down, 636.

The preëminence of William Faulkner as a writer of fiction was acknowledged abroad before it was conceded in the United States, where readers found his substance morbid and his methods confusing. But appreciation that his substance is authentic and his methods are boldly experimental has shifted the popular attitude towards him. *As I Lay Dying, The Sound and the Fury,* and *The Hamlet* are now regarded as among the most important novels of this generation. The Deep South is the locale for his short stories as well as for his novels; more specifically, the area around Oxford, Miss., as in "That Evening Sun Go Down," is the area for his camera eye. Here Faulkner spent his boyhood and youth; here he returned after World War I, in which he was injured as an airman; and here he has had his home.

FEARING, KENNETH (1902-   )
Dirge, 773.
Born, like Ernest Hemingway, in Oak Park, Ill., but educated at the University of Wisconsin, Kenneth Fearing saw something of the seamy side of life before establishing himself in journalism and settling in New York as a free-lance writer. He has written both fiction and poetry, but his verse is better known than his short stories and novels. In "Dirge" he has utilized the grossness of tabloid statement and of jazz rhythms to secure the effect of metropolitan insensibility to human tragedy.

FISHER, DOROTHY CANFIELD. *See* CANFIELD, DOROTHY

GALSWORTHY, JOHN (1867-1933)
Strife, 879.
British novelist, dramatist, essayist, and social philosopher, winner of the Nobel prize in 1932. His series of seven tales of the Forsyth family began with *The Man of Property* in 1906 and continued through *Swan Song* in 1928; they present the history of a typical clan of upper-middleclass philistines in the decades from 1886 through the chaotic twenties of the following century. His dramas, from "The Silver Box" (1906) through "Escape" (1926), are presentations of social and economic problems of his own time. "Strife" (1909)—the play reprinted in this anthology—is a detached and balanced study of the struggle between capital and labor, with neither side winning.

GIBSON, WILFRID (1878?-   )
The Conscript, 757.
A prolific producer since 1902 of short lyrics and longer dramatic poems, written in simple language and dealing in the main with nature and the experiences and emotions of the working poor in country and town. His *Collected Poems* (1905-25) was published in 1926.

GILBERT, SIR WILLIAM SCHWENCK (1836-1911)
The Aesthete, 786.
Author of the fanciful and lively *Bab Ballads* (1869-73), but famous especially for his satirical lyrics contributed to the comic "Savoy Operas," done in collaboration with the composer Sir Arthur Sullivan. In these immensely popular light operas he thrust, in a mood of airy nonsense, at various British patterns of living and thinking of his own time. "The Aesthete," reprinted here, is part of his spoofing in *Patience* (1881) at the "aesthetic school" of Oscar Wilde and his associates.

GRAVES, ROBERT (1895-   )
Recent Prose—with Alan Hodge, 242.
Poet of the First World War who wrote verse that ranged from the whimsical to the metaphysical. In *A Survey of Modernist Poetry* (1927), written with Laura Riding, he emerged as a literary critic; in *Good-bye to All That* (1929) as a rebellious autobiographer; and in *I, Claudius* (1934) as an historical novelist. *The Reader Over Your Shoulder*, done in 1943 with Alan Hodge, is an extremely provocative comment on English prose style; from this handbook the selection in the present anthology has been reproduced.

GRAY, GEORGE W. (1886-   )
Deeper Into the Atom, 205.
A career may be made out of interpreting the advances of science to the layman. But one needs, like George W. Gray, a scientific training to do a really competent

job. "Deeper Into the Atom," one of the essays in *The Advancing Front of Science,* demonstrates the competence of this Texan to explain both theory and process for lay comprehension.

GREENE, ROBERT (1560?-1592)

Sweet Are the Thoughts That Savor of Content, 799.

A "University Wit" and miscellaneous writer of the late Elizabethan period who turned his hand with equal success to dramas ("Friar Bacon and Friar Bungay," 1589?), artificial romances of euphuistic and arcadian types (*Menaphon,* 1589), pseudo-realistic rogue treatises (Conny-catching pamphlets, 1591-92), and lyrics, most of which appeared as incidental elements in his plays and "novels." Like many of the writing fraternity of his time, he lived furiously and died young.

GREGORY, LADY ISABELLA AUGUSTA PERSSE (1852-1932)

Spreading the News, 821.

A leading and active figure in the Irish Renaissance and an associate of W. B. Yeats in the establishment of the famous Abbey Theater. Besides doing much translating from early Irish romances, she wrote several lively, realistic, one-act comedies of Irish village life, of which "Spreading the News" (1904), reprinted in this anthology, is a typical example.

HARDY, THOMAS (1840-1928)

The Three Strangers, 653. *In a Wood,* 742.

A *"tradition* Victorian" who turned early from architecture to literature and throughout a long life produced a wealth of novels, stories, and poetry. In the field of the novel his work covered a quarter of a century, from *Desperate Remedies* (1871) to *Jude the Obscure* (1896). Then he turned again to poetry and produced several volumes of verse, down to his death. The best of his fiction deals with "character and environment"—to use his own phrase. He is most powerful in his tales of southwestern England, known to his readers as Wessex. His mood, both in prose and poetry, is generally regarded as cynical and pessimistic, and many of his novels raised storms of moral indignation when they first appeared.

HAZLITT, WILLIAM (1778-1830)

Mr. Cobbett, 343. *The Young Coleridge,* 467.

Essayist, critic, and biographer of the romantic period of the early nineteenth century. He wrote vivid and acute comments on the Elizabethan dramatists and particularly on Shakespeare, and criticisms of the stage of his own time. He is known best, however, for his *Table Talk, or Original Essays on Men and Manners* (1821-22), "talking" essays on miscellaneous themes. His interest in the literary labors of his contemporaries, he revealed in *The Spirit of the Age* (1825) and in such biographical bits as those reprinted in the present anthology. His style was vigorous and contentious, and extraordinarily rich, varied, and easy.

HEMINGWAY, ERNEST (1898-   )

My Old Man, 600.

Son of an Illinois physician, Ernest Hemingway comes naturally by his detached interest in injuries to the human frame and viscera. But as a writer, Hemingway is equally successful in depicting human tenderness and human violence. Both are mixed in "My Old Man," as they are in much of his fiction. Since giving up newspaper work, he has written five volumes of short stories and five novels.

HENLEY, WILLIAM ERNEST (1849-1903)
Invictus, 804.
A late nineteenth century British imperialist, friend of Robert Louis Stevenson, and a bold experimenter in verse-making. He is known best for "Invictus," a vigorous challenge to the fate that cost him the loss of a foot from tuberculosis, but he also wrote many more charming but less popular poems, including a verse-description of his friend Stevenson.

HEYWOOD, JOHN (1497?-1580?)
The Tale of the Pardoner, 800.
A Tudor writer of "interludes," or short playlets of an early pre-Elizabethan type, who was a director of entertainments in the court of Henry VIII. Some of these playlets are didactic but most are realistic and designed solely to entertain. This is true of "The Play of the Four PP" (*c.* 1520-22), a contest in telling tall tales, rather than a drama, from which the whopping lie of the Pardoner is here reprinted. All familiar with Chaucer's *Canterbury Tales* will not miss noting Heywood's debt to the earlier poet.

HODGE, ALAN (1915-   )
Recent Prose—with Robert Graves, 242.
Born in Scarborough, on the Yorkshire coast of England, Alan Hodge is the son of a Cunard line captain. Mr. Hodge grew up in Liverpool, attended one of the colleges of Oxford, and then became a journalist. He was in Spain during the Civil War and in Warsaw when the Germans invaded Poland. *The Reader Over Your Shoulder* is the second book he has done with Robert Graves, the first being *The Long Week End,* a social history of Great Britain between two world wars.

HOLMES, OLIVER WENDELL (1809-1894)
My Hunt After "The Captain," 536.
America's most popular occasional poet and wit, Oliver Wendell Holmes was also a distinguished physician. It was the thought that he might save the life of his wounded son that took him to the front in the series of adventures described in "My Hunt After 'The Captain.' " The son, Oliver Wendell Holmes, Jr., four times wounded in the Civil War, became the great dissenting justice of the Supreme Court, winning his appointment from Theodore Roosevelt.

HOOD, THOMAS (1799-1845)
The Song of the Shirt, 762.
A sentimental and prolific editor of a series of London magazines who contributed numerous verses, good, bad, and indifferent, to his own publications. His humorous verse-narratives do not seem particularly funny now, but his social lyrics, such as "The Song of the Shirt" (1843) and "The Bridge of Sighs" (1844) have a universal quality of bitter truth. The popularity of the first of these moving poems, reprinted in the present anthology, is revealed by the inscription on Hood's monument: "He sang the Song of the Shirt."

HOPKINS, GERARD MANLEY (1844-1889)
The Communist Future, 91. *Sprung Rhythm,* 92.
A Roman Catholic professor of Greek at the University of Dublin whose poems, although composed between 1870 and 1890, were not published in an absolutely complete collection until 1930. His experiments with verse, and especially his employment of what he called "sprung rhythm," have given him a wide vogue among young contemporary makers of verse.

HOUSMAN, ALFRED EDWARD (1859-1936)

In My Own Shire, 749. *To an Athlete Dying Young,* 802.

A professor of Latin at University College, London, and later at Cambridge, whose classical learning is reflected in the lean compression of verses that are exquisite in their restrained economy of content and effect. He is best known for *A Shropshire Lad,* published in 1896 and not succeeded by a second volume until 1922. Housman's poetry is as meager in amount as it is high in lyrical quality.

JAMES, HENRY (1843-1916)

The Limitations of Dickens, 428.

The most conscious craftsman that the novel had produced up to his time, Henry James jeopardized his popularity in his native country by long residence abroad and by finally accepting British citizenship. James would be quite astonished at his present vogue in America, but that vogue is the result of much discriminating criticism which has been written since his time. James himself possessed an acute critical faculty, and his review of Dickens not only assesses correctly the merits and defects of that novelist but also reveals his own deep reflection on the art of the fiction writer.

JEFFERS, ROBINSON (1887-   )

Point Joe, 741.

Struck by a sentence in Nietzsche, "The Poets lie too much," Robinson Jeffers decided "not to feign any emotion that I did not feel; . . . . not to say anything because it was popular, or generally accepted, or fashionable in intellectual circles, unless I myself believed it; and not to believe easily." Readers of Mr. Jeffers's verse are readily persuaded that he has adhered to this harsh and austere creed. "Point Joe" gives more positive hints as to what he believes should be the substance of poetry. Point Joe is not far distant from Carmel, California, where, on a cliff above the sea, the poet-recluse has his home and study-tower.

JEFFERSON, THOMAS (1743-1826)

One Generation Hath No Right to Bind Another, 73. *Natural Aristocracy,* 76.

Among the "left-wingers" at the outbreak of the American Revolution, Thomas Jefferson compromised in order to bring together radical and conservative elements when he became President of the United States in 1800. Besides shaping the fundamental democratic philosophy of his country, Jefferson doubled its territory, improved its architecture, and gave it its system of state universities. The two letters chosen to reveal his original views are from a correspondence which was the most voluminous of its time and the most distinguished.

JONSON, BEN (1572-1637)

It Is Not Growing Like a Tree, 798.

The most scholarly and one of the most productive of the Elizabethan and Stuart dramatists. Although he is best known as the author of extraordinary "comedies of humor," like "Every Man in his Humor" (1598), "Volpone" (1605), and "The Alchemist" (1610), he also wrote dramatic satires of other types—some heavy with pedantry—and a couple of fairly successful classical tragedies. In his own time he was widely known also as the creator, with Inigo Jones, scene-painter and designer, of elaborate *masques,* or court entertainments containing music, dancing, and much pageantry. His lyric poems, of which one is reprinted in this anthology, appeared first in his plays and masques.

KANG, YOUNGHILL (1903-)

The Journey of One Thousand Lis, 521.

Born in a Korean village, Younghill Kang saw as a boy the horrors of the Japanese annexation of his homeland; and after eight more years spent in acquiring an education in Seoul and Tokyo, he broke away from the Orient and made his way to America. In the new world his genius and industry helped him to distinction. He has served his adopted country as Assistant Professor of Oriental Culture in New York University, member of the staff of the Division of Far Eastern Art of the Metropolitan Museum of Art, New York City, technical adviser to the United States government on Far Eastern economics, and, after the Second World War, education expert in Korea. He is a poet, essayist, and lecturer, and the author of two notable autobiographical novels, *The Grass Roof* (1931), from which a chapter is reprinted here, and *East Goes West* (1937).

KEATS, JOHN (1795-1821)

Ode on a Grecian Urn, 783. *When I Have Fears That I May Cease to Be,* 804.

One of the most melodious and lyrical of the English poets of the Romantic Period. His first volume, *Poems,* appeared in 1817, and in the four years that followed until his death from tuberculosis in Rome he wrote almost consistently great verses, which reveal the influence upon him especially of Greek and medieval art. The best of his longer poems are "Endymion," "The Eve of St. Agnes," and "Hyperion," all written in 1818. Of his shorter lyrics, his "Ode on a Grecian Urn" and his sonnets—of which the poignant "When I Have Fears That I May Cease to Be" is reprinted here—are his most often quoted. His contemporary, Shelley, immortalized him in the elegiac poem, "Adonais."

KIPLING, RUDYARD (1865-1936)

The "Mary Gloster," 776.

Kipling's birth in Bombay and his early life in India directed much of his writing in fiction and verse to that complex country and helped, certainly, to make him one of the most outstanding of imperialistic writers. His novels, of which *Kim* is the greatest, and his short stories are exciting, rich, and romantic. His poems and ballads are ringing and exotic. His stories for children, *The Jungle Book* (1894), *The Second Jungle Book* (1895), and the *Just So Stories* (1902), still fascinate youngsters. The moving dramatic monologue of "The 'Mary Gloster,'" reprinted here, is an illustration of the sturdy comment on characters and living that strengthened some of his best poetry.

LAMPMAN, BEN HUR (1886-)

When the Old Man Got Misplaced, 609.

Born in Wisconsin, Mr. Lampman drifted first to North Dakota, where he founded and published the Michigan City *Arena* in 1905, and then to Oregon, where he was editor and publisher of the *Gold Hill News* from 1912 to 1916, and successively staff member, editorial writer, and associate editor of the Portland *Oregonian*. He also found time to become the author of *How Could I Be Forgetting* (1929), *The Tramp Printer* (1934), *Here Comes Somebody* (1935), *At the End of the Car Line* (1942), and *The Wild Swan* (1947), from which the present story has been reprinted. His skill in interpreting Oregon life and characters won him an honorary M.A. from the University of Oregon in 1943, and the O. Henry Memorial Short Story Award in 1943 and again in 1945.

LANDON, FRED (1880-   )

Old Huronia: Cradle of Martyrs, 701.

The historians of the United States have no monopoly of distinguished historical writing; Fred Landon, Librarian and Professor of History at the University of Western Ontario, can match them for style and substance. "Old Huronia: Cradle of Martyrs" is an excerpt from *Lake Huron,* the first volume in the American Lakes Series.

LANIER, SIDNEY (1842-1881)

The Symphony, 763.

One of the few southern voices not muted by the Civil War, Sidney Lanier gained fame as a flutist, scholar, and poet in a lamentably short career. He was born in Georgia, attended Oglethorpe College, fought in the Civil War, and lectured in Baltimore on poetry and the novel. "The Symphony" is original in form, but its sensuous detail and its hostility to trade come from the Pre-Raphaelites.

LARDNER, RING (1885-1933)

Champion, 580.

Few readers of Ring Lardner's stories probably ever knew he was a graduate of the Armour Institute of Technology. Lardner found himself when, as a sports writer, he began the "You know me, Al" sketches. Under sentence of death from tuberculosis, he turned out more serious fiction and won the respect of the literary gentry. "Champion" is a study in sadism.

LEACOCK, STEPHEN (1869-1944)

My Fishing Pond, 137.

An English-born Canadian who became head of the Department of Political Economy at McGill University and one of the Dominion's foremost humorists. His forty-odd volumes display a curious division into college texts and scientific treatises and shrewd, if deliberately satirical and absurd, parodies and nonsense books. Of these last, the most humorous are perhaps *Literary Lapses* (1910), *Nonsense Novels* (1911), and *Frenzied Fiction* (1918). "My Fishing Pond," reprinted here, is one of his many fugitive, short essays on human whims and follies.

LINCOLN, ABRAHAM (1809-1865)

You Do Not Work Much, 81. *I Dislike Slavery,* 82. *I Will Risk the Dictatorship,* 84.

The most loved president of the United States was a railroad lawyer of great ability; it is said that he declined to become chief counsel to the New York Central Railroad. A capacity to seize the pertinent thing in a mass of facts and a power to organize a simple but telling argument—traits which developed in his legal career—made him the hardest opponent a man could draw, as Stephen Douglas discovered. Lincoln displayed in his correspondence the same logic which made him irresistible on the platform.

LIPPMANN, WALTER (1889-   )

H. L. Mencken, 438.

One-time assistant in philosophy at Harvard to George Santayana, Walter Lippmann really derived more from the lectures in psychology and political theory of a visiting Englishman, Graham Wallas. In *A Preface to Politics* he is much indebted to Wallas. But Lippmann outgrew the need of a mentor and became one of America's most independent commentators on politics and morals. "H. L. Mencken" is a neat example of the logician operating on the casuist.

LONDON, JACK (1876-1916)

To Build a Fire, 569.

Supposedly the child of an astrologer named William Henry Chaney, Jack London grew up in the family of John London, an Irish policeman whom his mother married. He knocked about the Oakland waterfront and he knocked about the world before he acquired the simplest rudiment of an education and began to write. "To Build a Fire" is a product of his quest for gold in the Yukon.

LONGFELLOW, HENRY W. (1807-1882)

The Tide Rises, the Tide Falls, 742.   *The Arsenal at Springfield,* 759.

A name for all that is mawkish and sentimental in poetry, Henry W. Longfellow wrote some verse of the first order. Associated with figures in the shipping business from his youth on, Longfellow wrote of the sea and of the peace in which commerce could flourish. "The Arsenal at Springfield" was circulated separately as a peace-tract. "The Tide Rises, the Tide Falls" contrasts the immutability of the sea with the mutability of man.

LOWELL, JAMES RUSSELL (1819-1891)

Credidimus Jovem Regnare, 746.

A kindly man and a savage critic, James Russell Lowell epitomized his own limitation—didacticism—in *A Fable for Critics.* It was an ardent faith that made him a good abolitionist and Republican, but that same faith made him vulnerable to the challenge of Darwinism. "I hate it," he confessed in a letter; "I hate it because I fear it will hurt me somehow."

LOWES, JOHN LIVINGSTON (1867-1945)

Originality and the Moulding of Conventions, 253.

A scholar who could write, John Livingston Lowes once taught mathematics at Washington and Jefferson College, but after two years of this discipline he turned to teaching English literature, and at the time of his death was one of the most distinguished literary scholars at Harvard. His best known books are *Convention and Revolt in Poetry* (from which the present selection is taken) and *The Road to Xanadu,* an analysis of the technique of Coleridge.

LUKE (First century A.D.)

Paul and the Silversmiths, 561.

The "beloved physician" and companion of St. Paul in the first century of the Christian Church. He was a Greek convert to Christianity whose zeal for the new faith led him to address to "most excellent Theophilus," a Roman governor whom he sought to convert, both *The Gospel According to St. Luke* and *The Acts of the Apostles,* two of the most indispensable books of the New Testament. It is from the second of these documents that the stirring tale of St. Paul's adventure with the silversmiths of Ephesus has been here reprinted.

MACLEISH, ARCHIBALD (1892-   )

You, Andrew Marvell, 741.   *Lines for an Interment,* 756.   *Speech to a Crowd,* 782. *"Dover Beach"—a Note to That Poem,* 790.

Archibald MacLeish has "made" everything he has wished to "make" all his life. At Hotchkiss and later at Yale he "made" the football and swimming teams as well as the literary magazine. He "made" Phi Beta Kappa and a senior society. At Harvard Law School he was first man in his class; out of World War I he got a captaincy. Taking time out to learn to write poetry, he made the grade and became one of the distinguished poets of his time. Later he worked for *Fortune* and was Librarian of the Library of Congress.

MARSHALL, MARGARET (1900-   )
"Othello," 432.
Margaret Marshall began her career as a reviewer of books and plays on a Missoula newspaper while attending the University of Montana. She joined the staff of the *Nation* in 1924 and became that magazine's literary editor in 1937.

MEREDITH, GEORGE (1828-1909)
Meditation Under Stars, 745.
A sophisticated and highly intellectual poet, novelist, and critic of the late Victorian period. Of his poems, the most sustained is his *Modern Love* (1862), a poetical record, in a sequence of fifty sixteen-line stanzas, of his ten-year struggle to be adjusted to a wife from whom he was ultimately divorced. Of his novels, the best are *The Ordeal of Richard Feverel* (1859), *The Egoist* (1879), and *Diana of the Crossways* (1885). His essay *On the Idea of Comedy and the Uses of the Comic Spirit* (1877) is probably the keenest of all studies of the comic spirit in literature.

MILLAY, EDNA ST. VINCENT (1892-   )
Euclid Alone Has Looked on Beauty Bare, 785.
Product of a Maine seaport and of Greenwich Village, with a little shaping by Vassar in between, Edna St. Vincent Millay has written some of the best lyric poetry of our time, her range extending from "counting-out" rhymes to the sonnet. "Euclid Alone Has Looked on Beauty Bare" reveals her mastery of the latter form.

MILNE, LORUS J. (1910-   )
The Water's Skin, 134.
Dr. Milne was born in Toronto, Ontario. He took his B.A. degree at the University of Toronto in 1933, winning both honors in biology and the gold medal of his class. A fellowship at Harvard was followed by a Harvard M.A. in 1934 and Ph.D. in 1936. He has since taught in New York State, Texas, Virginia, and Pennsylvania. Dr. Milne published over fifty scientific papers in a technical style before he came to realize that there is more fun in writing in a popular style. Since then, his short and fascinating articles on natural history have appeared in numerous high-grade magazines. He and his wife both believe that biology and literature go very well together.

MILTON, JOHN (1608-1674)
When the Assault Was Intended for the City, 754.
Author of *Paradise Lost* (1667), the only important epic of art in the English language. But if Milton had never written this long religious narrative, he would still rank near the top of English writers because of his magnificent dramatic poem *Samson Agonistes* (1671), his elegy "Lycidas" (1638), and his complementary lyrics "L'Allegro" and "Il Penseroso" (1638?). His prose treatises, written during the stormy period of his services to the revolutionary Commonwealth and Protectorate, seem heavy and formal today, with the possible exception of his *Areopagitica* (1644), an argument for the freedom of the press. Of his many fine sonnets, the one reprinted here is an excellent example.

MOORE, GEORGE (1852-1933)
Taste in Books, 480.
An Irish-born novelist whose tales were written largely under the influence of the French naturalists of his own time. Of his novels, *Esther Waters* (1894) is usually considered his best. He lived in Paris, where he studied painting, in London, where he did most of his writing, and in Dublin, where, in the first decade of the

twentieth century, he participated in the Irish Renaissance movement. His auto-biographies, *Confessions of a Young Man* (1888) and *Memoirs of My Dead Life* (1906), contain characteristically satirical reactions against Victorian respectability.

MORLEY, CHRISTOPHER (1890-   )
On Time, 150.
Son of a mathematician, Christopher Morley grew up in Haverford, Pa., and in Baltimore, where his father held, successively, professorships at Haverford College and Johns Hopkins. Morley himself was graduated from the former institution, after which he was a Rhodes Scholar at New College, Oxford. Working first for Doubleday, Page, he was then successively on the staffs of the *Ladies Home Journal,* the Philadelphia *Evening Ledger,* the New York *Evening Post,* and the *Saturday Review of Literature.* The literary flair of his journalism is well illustrated by "On Time."

MORRIS, WILLIAM (1834-1896)
The Day Is Coming, 770.
Late Victorian poet, novelist, painter, publisher, designer, decorator, pamphleteer, politician, socialist, and man of many activities. Although his long narrative poems, like *The Earthly Paradise* (1868-70), a series of twenty-four "twice-told tales" from classical, medieval, and Scandinavian sources, were constructed according to the conception of the poet as a master craftsman rather than an inspired bard, they are almost consistently entertaining and colorful. In spite of the variety of his work in literature, book-designing, and practical arts, his labors have a unity that came from his efforts to bring beauty to a drab Victorian England. The poem reprinted in this anthology reveals his active interest in socialism, a political philosophy that he ultimately rejected.

MORRISON, THEODORE (1901-   )
Dover Beach Revisited, 353.
Director of "English A" at Harvard (which in most places is called "Freshman English") and teacher at the Bread Loaf School of English for many summers, Theodore Morrison can exemplify the excellencies he would have his students seek in writing. Mr. Morrison is the author of two books of verse, *Serpent in the Cloud* and *Notes of Death and Life,* as well as of many scattered essays. Contributed to *Harper's,* "Dover Beach Revisited" urbanely suggests that an author's meaning might be quite as good as a reader's.

MUNRO, H. H. *See* SAKI

MUSSELMAN, M. M. (1899-   )
Wheels in His Head, 13.
M. M. Musselman wrote the book about his father "A. J." after seven and a half years of writing motion-picture scripts at Hollywood, the proper preparation, he avers, for the biographer of as "wacky" a genius as the inventor of the mechanical midnight baby-rocker and the coaster brake. But more than Hollywood prepared the son for his major task. Born in Wichita, Kansas, on a Sunday (Feb. 19, 1899), the event keeping "A. J." away from his golf, "M. M." was graduated from the School of Journalism of the University of Illinois and wrote for newspapers, the "pulps," and radio, before undertaking either Hollywood or his father.

NABOKOV (or NABOKOFF), NICOLAS (1903-   )
The Case of Dmitri Shostakovitch, 393.
A distinguished native of Lubcza, White Russia, who came to America in 1933 with an education obtained in St. Petersburg, Yalta, the Conservatories of Stuttgart

and Berlin, and the University of Paris. Having completed his studies in 1926, he remained in Paris for seven years as an active member of the music, literary, and artistic colony there. His first service in America was as lecturer at the Barnes Foundation, Merion, Pennsylvania. From 1936 to 1941 he was Head of the Department of Music at Wells College, Aurora, New York, and then for four years the Director of Music and Liberal Arts tutor at St. John's College, Annapolis, Maryland. After serving as First Deputy Chief of Music, Theatre, and Film Control for the United States Military Government overseas, he returned to America in 1947 to act as Head of the Russian Unit of the Voice of America. He is now Professor of Counterpoint, Composition, Formal Analysis, and Music History at the Peabody Conservatory in Baltimore. "By training," he wrote to the editors, "I am primarily a musician-composer, secondarily, a teacher of composition and writer on musical and general aesthetic topics."

NEVINS, ALLAN (1890-   )
Ideas in History, 370.
After a career in journalism, highlighted by editorial service on three New York dailies, the *Post,* the *Sun,* and the *World,* Allan Nevins became a professor of history, first at Cornell, then at Columbia. He is the author and editor of many historical studies; his reflections on his profession are found in *The Gateway to History* (1938), from which the present selection has been taken.

NEWBOLT, SIR HENRY JOHN (1862-1938)
Drake's Drum, 755.
Naval historian and poet who sang of the glories of Britain's sea power. "Drake's Drum" (1914), reprinted here, is the most widely known of his various heroic narrative poems and ballads.

NIEBUHR, REINHOLD (1892-   )
Is Religion Counter-Revolutionary? 334.
Professor of Applied Christianity at Union Theological Seminary since 1930, Reinhold Niebuhr had served a long pastorate in Detroit (1915-1928) before assuming his post. For a time, Dr. Niebuhr sided with those theologians who hoped for a common moral and social program with the political radicals. The essay in this anthology, originally contributed to *Radical Religion,* a quarterly founded by Dr. Niebuhr, no longer represents the author's point of view, but is offered here as one exposition of a position on the left.

NYE, BILL (1850-1896)
My Thanks for the Same, 94.
Edgar W. Nye, who was born in Wisconsin but who for a time edited a paper in Wyoming, took his pen name from a poker companion whom Bret Harte had immortalized in "The Heathen Chinee." Comparing Nye with other "Western" humorists, Professor Cairns has written, "He probably had more genius, and certainly more refinement, than either Shaw or Locke, but he had less didactic purpose, and his fame is likely to be even shorter lived than theirs."

O'HIGGINS, HARVEY (1876-1929)
Alias Walt Whitman, 42.
A Canadian-born Irish journalist, Harvey O'Higgins became an American citizen during World War I and served as Associate Chairman of George Creel's Committee for Public Information. O'Higgins became very much a convert to the teachings of Freud and interpreted the behavior of both fictional characters in his

novels and of celebrated personages from the Freudian standpoint. His study of Whitman, though open to some objections, is almost a classic illustration of the Freudian approach.

PARRINGTON, VERNON LOUIS (1871-1929)
The Great Barbecue, 714. *General Grant*, 717.
By abjuring the "belletristic" approach to literary history and by borrowing hints from Taine, from his colleague J. Allen Smith, and from Charles Beard, Professor Vernon L. Parrington, of the University of Washington, introduced students of American literature to a new kind of history with the first volume of *Main Currents in American Thought*. Though he did not live to complete this great project, Mr. Parrington established for himself a secure niche as an interpreter. The selections here are from the fragmentary but spirited third volume.

POE, EDGAR ALLAN (1809-1849)
To One in Paradise, 803.
As a literary innovator, Edgar Allan Poe has few equals. He is regarded not only as the father of the short story but also as sire of that special form, the detective story. In his criticism, he employed a psychological approach and an analytical method when both of these were rare enough in that area. But he was especially inventive as poet, utilizing novel techniques and subject matter. Poe's very inventiveness, however, obscures the subjective quality of the bulk of his verse. "To One in Paradise" is a deeply felt, as well as a perfect, lyric.

READ, HERBERT (1893-   )
The Politics of the Unpolitical, 268.
English poet, critic, and essayist; Director of the Museum of Modern Art, London, Author of *Naked Warriors* (1919); *Eclogues* (1919), *Phases of English Poetry* (1928), *The Meaning of Art* (1931), *Poems, 1914-1934* (1935), *Art and Society* (1936), *Poetry and Anarchism; Collected Essays* (1938), and other books.

RICKETTS, EDWARD F. (1897-   )
The Sea-Cow—with John Steinbeck, 140.
Edward F. Ricketts is Director of the Pacific Biological Laboratories, which supplies marine specimens for college and research laboratories. One of John Steinbeck's oldest friends, he took the novelist with him on a trip to investigate the marine life of the Gulf of California, a trip which resulted also in the book, *The Sea of Cortez*, from which "The Sea-Cow" (hardly a form of marine life) is excerpted.

ROBINSON, JAMES HARVEY (1863-1936)
On Various Kinds of Thinking, 176.
A distinguished historian and teacher who, after resigning from Columbia University in protest against faculty dismissals for pacifist views during World War I, helped to found the New School for Social Research. Robinson later wrote *The Mind in the Making* (1921), portions of which have been more anthologized, perhaps, than any other nonfiction work.

ROOSEVELT, FRANKLIN DELANO (1882-1945)
First Inaugural Address, 287.
Personality *and* president, Franklin Delano Roosevelt could better instruct his generation that "there is nothing to fear but fear itself" than could any other man, for he had conquered the incapacitating fears engendered by infantile paralysis as well as the physical incapacity conferred by the dreadful disease. In fireside chat

and in international conference, he exuded a hope that elevated the hearts of men when their very natures justified depression. He was *Plutarchist* and cosmopolitan. He was so definitely "the New Deal" that with his demise there was little left of that movement.

ROOSEVELT, THEODORE (1858-1919)

The New Nationalism, 276.

Student of naval history and of imperialism, Theodore Roosevelt had some of the characteristics of a "jingo." Certainly his seizure of the Panama Canal and his pronouncement of the "Roosevelt Corollary" to the Monroe Doctrine caused more disquiet among our neighbors on this continent than did the acts of any other man save those of James K. Polk. But it is possible to forgive "T. R." his opportunism in international affairs when one considers how he assailed domestic evils. There was no integration between "trust busting," conservation, and forced arbitration of labor disputes save the conscience of Roosevelt. However, when he had time to read and reflect during the years following his retirement, he was able to offer the country in 1912 an integrated program in "The New Nationalism," in which some see suggestions for "the New Deal."

ROPER, WILLIAM (1496-1578)

The Last Days of Sir Thomas More, 510.

Husband of Margaret Roper, the daughter of Sir Thomas More (1478-1535), the great scholar and statesman who was martyred for refusing to subscribe to the Act of Supremacy that made Henry VIII head of the Church in England and who was canonized in the four-hundredth year of his death. Roper's tribute to his famous father-in-law, *The Mirrour of Vertue in Worldly Greatnes. Or the Life of Syr T. More* (Paris, 1626), is one of the outstanding biographies in English.

RUSKIN, JOHN (1819-1900)

The Nature of Theft by Unjust Profits, 85.

Victorian interpreter of nature, art, and social ethics and economics. His earlier books, *Modern Painters* (1843-1860), *The Seven Lamps of Architecture* (1849), and *The Stones of Venice* (1851-1853), although they deal mainly with painting and allied arts, reveal, nevertheless, that fundamental interest in social philosophy which became his consuming passion in his later writings, *Unto This Last* (1862), *Munera Pulveris* (1862-63), *The Crown of Wild Olive* (1866), and the eccentric and violent *Fors Clavigera* (1871-84). The selection from Ruskin reprinted in this anthology is an expression of the ideas of the later Ruskin, the zealous industrial reformer. It is one of the *Twenty-Five Letters to a Working Man of Sunderland on the Laws of Work,* published in a collection that bears the title *Time and Tide.*

SAINT LUKE. *See* LUKE

SAKI (H. H. MUNRO) (1870-1916)

The Stalled Ox, 684.

The pseudonym which H. H. Munro took from the name of the cupbearer in *The Rubaiyat of Omar Khayyam* and under which he wrote many brilliant short stories, novels, and plays. "Saki" was born in Burma, lived as foreign correspondent and contributor to many London periodicals, and died in action in the First World War. His short stories, collected in 1930, are brilliantly compressed, ingenious, fantastic, and satirical. "The Stalled Ox" reprinted here, is an excellent example of his consistently fine work in story telling.

SANDBURG, CARL (1878-   )

Four Preludes on Playthings of the Wind, 751.

Free-verse poet, Carl Sandburg can produce raucous dissonance or the softest melody, expressions of brute power or of tender regard. He is a true follower of Whitman, yet a good Symbolist poet as well as a Scandinavian mystic. It is the last two that are found in "Four Preludes." Sandburg is also the leading Lincoln biographer and one of the most successful collectors of American folksongs.

SAROYAN, WILLIAM (1908-   )

Love, Death, Sacrifice and So Forth, 159.

The most exuberant of literary beings, William Saroyan, explaining how he began to write at nine, declares, "I didn't think of writing, I did it." Behind his writing, however, is a rough encounter with the world in which neither took the other's measure. Of Armenian descent, deprived of his father when he was very young, Saroyan sold papers at eight, was a telegraph boy at thirteen, and a vineyard laborer at sixteen. The selection in this anthology is really unclassifiable; its author thinks it is a short story; the editors have arbitrarily made it an essay.

SASSOON, SIEGFRIED (1886-   )

At the Cenotaph, 758. *On Reading the War Diary of a Defunct Ambassador,* 758.

A British poet of the First World War whose war poems, collected in 1919, reveal his sense of the horror and bitterness of a conflict in which he took active part. His *Memoirs of a Fox-Hunting Man* (1928) and *Memoirs of an Infantry Officer* (1930) are brilliant autobiographies.

SCHLAUCH, MARGARET (1898-   )

Semantics: Vocabulary in Motion, 216.

Dr. Schlauch, Professor of English, New York University, and specialist in linguistics, Chaucer, and Middle English literature, has been awarded fellowships by the American Association of University Women and the Guggenheim Memorial Foundation, and has traveled extensively in Europe, Central America, and Mexico. Among her books are *Chaucer's Constance and Accused Queens* (1927), *Medieval Narrative* (1928), *Saga of the Volsungs* (1930), *Romance in Iceland* (1933), and *The Gift of Tongues* (1942), from which the selection in this volume has been taken.

SHAKESPEARE, WILLIAM (1564-1616)

Full Fathom Five, 803.

Of the greatest dramatic poet in English literature it is necessary here only to echo the praise of Ben Jonson, a contemporary dramatist: "He was not of an age, but for all time." In a professional lifetime of writing and acting, this poet-actor produced, alone or in collaboration, about forty dramas, a magnificent sonnet sequence of one hundred and fifty-four stanzas, two longer narrative poems, and in the matrix of his plays, a wealth of short songs and lyrics. The quaint but moving dirge reprinted here is Ariel's song to the shipwrecked prince Ferdinand in *The Tempest,* Shakespeare's last comedy.

SHALER, NATHANIEL SOUTHGATE (1841-1906)

A Lesson from Agassiz, 534.

The distinguished pupil of a distinguished scientist, Nathaniel Southgate Shaler was born in Kentucky and educated at Harvard, where for three years he studied geology and zoology under the celebrated Swiss scientist, Louis Agassiz. After two years in the Union Army, he returned to Harvard as assistant to Agassiz. In

1869 he became professor of paleontology (later geology) there. He was also Dean of Lawrence Scientific School and director of the Atlantic Coast Division of the United States Geological Survey. The selection in this anthology is from his *Autobiography*.

SHAPIRO, KARL (1914-   )
General and Personal Idiom, 786.
Karl Shapiro is one of the best of a new generation of American poets. He has written a semisatirical autobiographical poem, entitled "Recapitulations" and printed in *Poetry: A Magazine of Verse* (December, 1946), from which we learn that he was born in Baltimore "under the roof where Poe expired" and that as a youth he learned "to despise all uncles, all Congressmen, all police." The war took Shapiro to the South Pacific; after its termination he held the poetry fellowship in the Library of Congress. "General and Personal Idiom" is a passage from *Essay on Rime,* his third volume of verse.

SHELLEY, PERCY BYSSHE (1792-1822)
Ozymandias, 780.　*Hymn to Intellectual Beauty,* 784.
One of the most brilliant and rebellious of the English romantic poets. Although an excellent prose critic, as attested by "A Defense of Poetry" (1821), he is best known as the author of such poems as "Ode to the West Wind" (1819), "The Cloud" (1820), "Adonais" (1821)—his tribute to his dead brother poet, John Keats—"The Cenci" (1819), a drama; and "Prometheus Unbound" (1820). His "Hymn to Intellectual Beauty" (1816) and his sonnet "Ozymandias" (1818), both reprinted here, are, respectively, a statement of his creative creed and an echo of his rebellious attitude toward human pride and tyranny.

SITWELL, SIR OSBERT (1892-   )
A Letter to My Son, 116.
The second of a talented family of British poets and prose writers—the others are Edith and Sacheverell—who have done much experimenting in verse. In addition to his poetry, Sir Osbert has written several novels and numerous social essays and critical studies.

SPENDER, STEPHEN (1909-   )
Thoughts During an Air Raid, 754.　*Ultima Ratio Regum,* 757.
A member of a remarkable group of contemporary British writers who developed at Oxford in the twenties. He has used his poetry as a vehicle for his political creeds. In "Vienna" (1934) he indicted Nazi Germany, and in "Trial of a Judge" (1938) he contrasted Nazism unfavorably with Communism. *The Destructive Element* (1934) is a volume of criticism, *The Burning Cactus* (1936), a collection of short stories, and *The Backward Son* (1940), a novel.

STEINBECK, JOHN (1902-   )
The Sea-Cow—with Edward F. Ricketts, 140.
Of mixed Irish and German stock, John Ernst Steinbeck was born in Salinas, California, took an irregular college course at Stanford, and knocked about America (even laying bricks at Madison Square Garden), before he wrote his first novel, *A Cup of Gold.* Now with ten novels and several books of short stories to his credit, Steinbeck is known to every well-read American. By common consent, his best novels are *In Dubious Battle* and *The Grapes of Wrath,* both dealing with migrant labor in his native state. "The Sea-Cow" comes from a book of nonfiction, *The Sea of Cortez,* which is the ancient name of the Gulf of California, where

Steinbeck went with his friend, the marine biologist Edward F. Ricketts, to study the sea life of that great body of water.

STEVENSON, ROBERT LOUIS (1850-1894)

Requiem, 805.

A Scottish writer of novels, short stories, essays, criticisms, travelogues, and verse. Driven by natural restlessness and by the tragic need of seeking a climate suited to his poor health, he travelled widely, always with pen in hand. His best known novels are his breath-taking tales of adventure by sea, such as *Treasure Island* (1883) and *Kidnapped* (1888), and his allegory of sin and retribution *Dr. Jekyll and Mr. Hyde* (1886). His familiar essays on life and living have simplicity and charm. *A Child's Garden of Verse* (1885) contains little poems as often quoted as nursery rhymes. His "Requiem" is cut into the stone beneath which the gypsy-footed writer rests in Samoa.

STRONG, AUSTIN (1881-   )

"She Shall Have Music," 691.

Landscape architect, playwright, and story writer. His mother was the step-daughter of Robert Louis Stevenson, and as a boy Mr. Strong lived for a time with the novelist and poet at Vailima, Samoa. He began life as a landscape artist, but dropped this occupation in 1905 to devote himself to writing plays and stories. Among his plays are "The Exile" (1903) and "The Little Father of the Wilderness" (1905), both written in collaboration with his uncle Lloyd Osbourne, Stevenson's stepson. Later plays are "Three Wise Fools" (1918), "Seventh Heaven" (1922), and "A Play Without a Name" (1928). He has also written many short stories and articles.

STUART, JESSE (1907-   )

Nest Egg, 647.

An earnest mountaineer, native of Riverton, Ky., Jesse Stuart first won attention with a book of verse, *The Man With the Bull Tongue Plow.* But his prose is really better than his verse; his unaffected narratives are as close to life as dust to shrubbery along a dirt road in the country in midsummer. "Nest Egg," from *Tales From the Plum Grove Hills,* is an example of his work in this genre.

SWINBURNE, ALGERNON CHARLES (1837-1909)

The Higher Pantheism in a Nutshell, 745. *To Walt Whitman in America,* 767.

Late Victorian poet and critic who rebelled against the social conventions of his period and shocked his more restrained contemporaries by the sensual lushness of much of his early verse. He was influenced by the Pre-Raphaelite Rossetti and by the French Baudelaire; he was fascinated by classical and medieval themes; he was a genius in the skill and melody of his meter. His closet tragedies are less admired than his Greek-spirited "Atalanta in Calydon" (1865) and his medieval narrative poem "Tristram of Lyonesse" (1882). His essays, studies, and critical monographs in the field of Elizabethan drama are often more sentimental than sound.

SYMONDS, JOHN ADDINGTON (1840-1893)

The Death of Sir Philip Sidney, 37.

A British scholar-essayist who spent most of his life in Italy. His most ambitious work is his seven-volume *History of the Renaissance in Italy* (1875-86). He also wrote a notable series of biographies, which includes his *Life of Sir Philip Sidney* (1878); the extract in the present anthology was taken from this study.

TAYLOR, DEEMS (1885-   )
The Monster, 53.

Composer and musical critic, Joseph Deems Taylor has become one of the best known authorities in his field, not merely through his contributions to newspapers and encyclopedias but also through his appearances on the radio and on the motion-picture screen.

TENNYSON, ALFRED LORD (1809-1892)
Are God and Nature Then at Strife? 743. *The Higher Pantheism,* 744. *Vision of the Parliament of Man,* 760.

The most popular of Victorian poets and Poet Laureate from the death of Words-worth in 1850 to his own death. The greatest of his long poems is *In Memoriam* (1850), a tribute to his dead friend, Arthur Henry Hallam; the most popular is his *Idylls of the King* (1859), a Victorian reconstruction of the tales of King Arthur and his knights. Many of his poems, such as "The Princess" (1857), "Locksley Hall" (1842), and "Locksley Hall Sixty Years After" (1886), are metrical comments on Victorian conceptions of living; others, such as "Ulysses," "The Lotus Eaters," and "Oenone," are based on Greek themes. Tennyson's closet dramas were less successful than his lyrics. Of the selections reproduced in this anthology, "Are God and Nature Then at Strife?" is from *In Memoriam;* "Vision of the Parliament of Man," from "Locksley Hall."

THOMPSON, FRANCIS (1859-1907)
The Hound of Heaven, 794.

A devout Roman Catholic, English poet famous for his profoundly moving poetic allegory of God's love for the rebellious Christian, "The Hound of Heaven" (*Poems,* 1893), reprinted in this anthology.

THURBER, JAMES (1894-   )
The Macbeth Murder Mystery, 156.

American cartoonist, philosopher, humorist, journalist, and playwright. He has served on the Columbus *Dispatch,* the Chicago *Tribune* (Paris), and the New York *Evening Post,* and has been a contributor to *The New Yorker* since 1926. With Elliott Nugent he wrote "The Male Animal," a successful comedy. He is also the author of *Is Sex Necessary?* (with E. B. White), *The Owl in the Attic, The Seal in the Bedroom, My Life and Hard Times, The Middle Aged Man on the Flying Trapeze, Let Your Mind Alone, The Last Flower, Fables for Our Time,* and *My World—and Welcome to It.*

Time, EDITORS OF (1923-   )
Average Man, 3. *In Egypt Land,* 56. *Disney's Cinesymphony,* 434.

The newsmagazine *Time,* founded by Henry R. Luce and Briton Hadden in 1923, is distinguished by a pungent, but often eccentric, style of clipped phraseology. Notoriously reactionary on political and economic issues, *Time* is broadly liberal in its defense of racial and religious minorities. It reports diversions, inventions, and distractions with the popeyed excitement of a small boy who has just seen his first giraffe.

TOMLINSON, HENRY MAJOR (1873-   )
Bed-Books and Night-Lights, 153.

A British writer of essays, novels, and travel books of great vividness, originality, and charm. His *London River* (1921) is a collection of essays, his *Gallions Reach* (1927), a story of the sea, his *All Our Yesterdays* (1930), a novel dealing with the period of the First World War, and his *Morning Light* (1947), a magnificent sea-adventure of the nineteenth century.

TUNIS, JOHN R. (1889-   )
First Gentleman of Philadelphia, 7.
Native of Boston but not of Beacon Street, John R. Tunis became a sports writer after graduating from Harvard and serving in World War I. No other sports writer has attacked with such meritorious vigor the sham of "amateurism" as it is revealed in the great spectacles of "top competition" in this country. Tunis has great respect, however, for the man who makes an honest living out of his countrymen's avid interest in athletics.

TWAIN, MARK (SAMUEL CLEMENS) (1835-1910)
How to Lecture Impromptu, 95.
Easily the most successful humorist in our history, Mark Twain desired to be respected as a serious thinker. No one did more to baffle him in that end than his irrepressible self, yet such a book as *Mark Twain in Eruption,* edited by Bernard De Voto out of Twain's manuscripts, shows how seriously he reflected on men and events. And the letter reprinted here shows also that even his humorous effects may have been premeditated.

UREY, HAROLD (1893-   )
Bomb Control Not Impossible, 112.
Discoverer of the hydrogen atom with the atomic weight of two, and specialist in the "structure of atoms and molecules, thermodynamic properties of gases, absorption spectra, Raman spectra, and Isotopes," Harold Urey is one of the most distinguished chemical physicists that America has produced. Drafted from his professorship at Columbia for the "Manhattan Project," he writes about the necessity of atomic control with as full a knowledge as anyone possesses.

VAN DOREN, CARL (1885-   )
The Treachery of General Charles Lee, 709.
Authority on the eighteenth century in both England and America, as well as critic of contemporary letters (the rôle in which he is best known), Carl Van Doren has done impressive lives of Swift and Franklin and a very exciting book on the political intrigues and travail which gave this country birth, *The Secret History of the American Revolution.*

VEBLEN, THORSTEIN (1857-1929)
Summary and Trial Balance, 330.
America's first "institutional" economist is also her most iconoclastic. Roughly treated by academic administrators after due and full provocation, Veblen vented his wrath on our colleges and universities in *The Higher Learning.* No less provocative are *The Theory of the Leisure Class* and *The Engineers and the Price System.* Veblen studied and taught at Carlton, Johns Hopkins, Yale, Cornell, Chicago, Stanford, Missouri, and the New School for Social Research.

WEEKS, EDWARD (1898-   )
Notes on an Old Friend, 142.
Occupant of an editorial chair made famous by James Russell Lowell, William Dean Howells, Thomas Bailey Aldrich, and others, Edward Weeks has brought new life to *The Atlantic Monthly,* one of the best magazines published in America today. One year as a manuscript reader and book salesman, after Harvard and Cambridge University, was Mr. Weeks's preparation for his rôle.

WELLS, HERBERT GEORGE (1866-1946)

A President and a Dictator, 501.

An amazingly productive and miscellaneous British writer of tireless imagination and energy, who wrote on almost every subject that occurred to him and in almost every literary form. His early pseudo-scientific tales are represented by *The Time Machine* (1895) and *The Invisible Man* (1897); his less fantastic novels by *The History of Mr. Polly* (1910) and *Mr. Britling Sees It Through* (1916); his historical interests by the imposing *Outline of History* (1920). His essentially socialistic creeds he expressed in both narrative and expository forms. His *Experiment in Autobiography* (1934) is characteristically frank.

WHITMAN, WALT (1819-1892)

My Passion for Ferries, 493. *Broadway Sights,* 493. *Omnibus Jaunts and Drivers* 494. *Plays and Operas Too,* 495. *Hospital Scenes and Persons,* 496. *Give Me the Splendid Silent Sun,* 750. *Hang Your Whole Weight Upon Me,* 769. *Come Lovely and Soothing Death,* 805.

Whitman asked "recorders ages hence" to publish his name and hang up his picture "as that of the tenderest lover" of all mankind. This is the dominant theme among the many themes of *Leaves of Grass,* which was first published in 1855 and which has been fought over ever since. Whitman's poetry in this anthology was selected from that book, the prose from *Specimen Days,* a volume of autobiographical jottings.

WIENER, NORBERT (1894-   )

A Scientist Rebels, 114.

Son of Leo Wiener, professor of Slavic languages at Harvard, Norbert Wiener, himself a professor of mathematics at Massachusetts Institute of Technology, is counted today among the world's foremost mathematical analysts. He served at the Aberdeen Proving Ground in Maryland in World War I and did work for the National Defense Research Committee during World War II.

WILSON, WOODROW (1856-1924)

The Lawyer and the Community, 290.

The twenty-eighth President of the United States of America was born in Staunton, Virginia, educated at Princeton and Johns Hopkins, and admitted to the bar. He took up college teaching, however, as a profession and taught history, government, economics, and jurisprudence at Bryn Mawr, Wesleyan, and Princeton. His skill in administration brought him to the presidency of Princeton in 1902; he resigned in 1910 to become Governor of New Jersey. From the chief of a state, he became chief of his nation; he was President for two terms, from 1913-1921. President Wilson's two terms in the White House were marked by the passage of the Seventeenth Amendment, providing for the direct popular election of Senators, the Eighteenth, establishing national prohibition, and the Nineteenth, bringing votes to women. With his reëlection in 1916, he became a war president. Outstanding in these years were his Fourteen Points for Peace, his heroic fight for the League of Nations Covenant, and his winning of the Nobel peace prize. Opposed by an isolationist Senate, he toured the country to defend stubbornly his plans for the League of Nations, but suffered a stroke as a result of the strain and was invalided until his death five years later. Woodrow Wilson wrote, with brilliancy and clarity, several books, chief of which are his *Congressional Government: A Study in American Politics* (1885); his five-volume *History of the American People* (1902), and his *Constitutional Government in the United States* (1908).

WOLFE, THOMAS C. (1900-1938)
A Writer's Creation and Vision of Life, 103. *Only the Dead Know Brooklyn,* 688.
One of the most remarkable of contemporary American novelists. He was born in
Ashville, N. C., and educated at the University of North Carolina and at Harvard.
In 1924 he joined the staff of the Department of English at New York University
and taught there until the award of a Guggenheim Fellowship in 1930 made it
possible for him to devote all his time to his overmastering ambition to write.
His earliest novel was *Look Homeward Angel* (1929), an autobiographical narrative that created an immense sensation. It was followed by *Of Time and the River*
(1932), and by several novels, stories, and sketches drawn posthumously from the
accumulation of Wolfe's ceaseless outpourings: *The Web and the Rock* (1939),
You Can't Go Home Again (1940), and *The Hills Beyond* (1941). His *Letters
to His Mother,* edited by John S. Terry, appeared in 1943.

WOOLF, VIRGINIA (1882-1941)
The Art of Biography, 365.
One of the outstanding women novelists, biographers, and critics of modern England. In her novels, from *Jacob's Room* (1922) to *The Years* (1937), she experimented with an impressionistic and intensive style. She wrote many brilliant essays, chiefly in the field of literary criticism. A highly lyrical and sensitive genius,
she killed herself early in the Second World War, apparently to escape the terror
which it had imposed upon her.

WOOLLCOTT, ALEXANDER (1887-1943)
The Town-Crier Begs to Differ, 104.
Immortalized as Sheridan Whiteside in Kaufman and Hart's "The Man Who Came
to Dinner," Alexander Woollcott was the great Pooh-Bah of our times; but he was
also a person of real integrity, as the letter from "The Town Crier," used in this
anthology, indicates. During his lifetime he worked for two Philadelphia and four
New York newspapers; he was also on the staff of *Stars and Stripes* and *The New
Yorker*. On invitation of the authors of the play, he successfully assumed the rôle
of Whiteside himself.

WOTTON, SIR HENRY (1568-1639)
The Character of a Happy Life, 799.
Statesman and poet in the time of Elizabeth and of the first of the Stuart monarchs,
Wotton epitomized in *The Character of a Happy Life* (1614), reprinted here, the
quiet philosophy of living which had guided him through rich, varied, and satisfy-
ing experiences.

WRIGHT, FRANK LLOYD (1869-   )
Organic Architecture, 322.
Leading American exponent of functionalism in architecture, Frank Lloyd Wright
began his career in Chicago in 1893, the year of the famous Columbia Exposition.
Wright has designed both homes and factory buildings, palaces and offices. He
has written extensively on his art.

ZABEL, MORTON DAUWEN (1901-   )
Sandburg's Testament, 422.
Successor to Harriet Munro as editor of *Poetry: A Magazine of Verse,* Morton
Dauwen Zabel has proved discriminating as both an editor and a critic. He has
since edited *Literary Opinion in America* and taught at Loyola (Chicago), where
he is head of the English Department.

Index of Titles